CW00546638

Passenger Ships
of the 20th Century
An illustrated Encyclopedia

David W Latimer

To the two women in my life,
my wife Barbara and my daughter Kim,
both of whom were of such help and
understanding during a long research
period which has culminated in this
publication about seven thousand
other ladies.

The author pictured in the Australian National Maritime
Museum's public research facility, the Vaughan Evans Library.
Andrew Frolows/Australian National Maritime Museum

6 5 4 3 2 1

Design by Colourpoint Books, Newtownards
Printed by W&G Baird Limited

ISBN 1 898392 70 6

About the Author

David Latimer was born and brought up in
Pukekohe, near Auckland, New Zealand. His
enthusiasm for ships stems from his father's love
of yachts and from his own boyhood visits to
Auckland Harbour in the late 1930s.

On leaving school he moved to Sydney,
Australia, to work for QANTAS Airways,
making frequent crossings of the Tasman Sea
between Australia and New Zealand in the
1950s. Later he became an Australian
Immigration officer based in Britain, with
regular visits to Tilbury and Southampton docks.

Eventually returning to Sydney, David became
involved in the manufacture and marketing of
cosmetics and pharmaceuticals until his recent
retirement. He now lives in Sydney, Australia,
and has used his retirement to compile this
encyclopedia.

Colourpoint Books
Unit D5, Ards Business Centre
Jubilee Road
NEWTOWNARDS
County Down
Northern Ireland
BT23 4YH
Tel: 028 9182 0505
Fax: 028 9182 1900
E-mail: info@colourpoint.co.uk
Web-site: www.colourpoint.co.uk

Cover Pictures
Front cover:

Main picture – *Seabourn Sun* (1999 – Seabourn
Cruise Lines)

Bottom pictures (left to right) – *Grand Princess*
(1998 – P&O Princess Cruises); *Color Festival*
(1994 – Color Line); *Gabriella* (1992 – Viking
Line)

Rear cover:

(left to right) – *Otway* (1909 – Orient Line);
Orsova (1954 – Orient Line); *Aurora* (2000 –
P&O Cruises)

Contents

Acknowledgements

The generosity, assistance and guidance of many people have been instrumental in this book going to press.

So many contacts were made over several years that a blanket "thank you" would be almost mandatory to reach them all. For those that I acknowledge by name here, my eternal thanks. For those that I have missed, also my eternal thanks. I am sure that we shall be crossing each other's paths again.

The following individuals rendered their time and shared their knowledge readily: Ross and Denise Blackmore of Cruise About Pty Ltd, Sydney; Geoff Dobbins of Sydney, First Officer, Merchant Navy retired (ex-P&O *Arcadia* and *Coromandel*); Robert Henderson, maritime historian, Sydney; Mike James, Royal Australian Navy publicity officer; Jeffrey Mellefont, Public Affairs Manager of the Australian National Maritime Museum; Jan Harbison, Francis Prentice and Helen Phillips of the Vaughan Evans Library, housed within the Australian National Maritime Museum; Barry Thompson, ships master retired.

Organisations who were also generous with their data and time: Australian National Maritime Museum; State Library of NSW, Sydney; Strathfield Library, Sydney; Turramurra Travel, Sydney.

Photographs

Similarly, the providers of ships' photos cannot be thanked enough, particularly when the number required to meet the criteria of this publication is taken into account. Individual people and major shipping companies have assisted in every possible way when asked to contribute photos/transparencies/CD-ROMs and data sheets – this book is all the better for their major contributions.

Individuals who have helped are Micke Asklander, Sweden; Peter Asklander, Sweden; Marko Stampehl, Sweden; Alison Avery, Read McCarthy Group, Sydney; Susan and Chris Burritt, Chicago; Natalia Dunkley, Sydney; Anders Bergenek, Sweden; David Gillian and Graham Bell, Chief Engineer and Marine Engineering Assistant of the *Doulos* respectively; Robert Henderson, maritime historian, Sydney; Nils Nordenbrink, Sweden; Tommi Rotonen, Sweden; Frank Schoenstedt, Denmark; Marko Stampehl, Sweden; and Laurel Rixon, Sydney.

Corporations who have helped are: Aida Cruises, Neu-Isenburg, Germany (Kerstin Hennig and Heidi Tressner); Airtours, Manchester, UK (Emma Leyland); Alaska Marine Highway System, Juneau, Alaska (Linda S Mickle and the photographers engaged by AMHS – Karin Lew (MV *Columbia*), Duncan Murrell (MV *Kennikott*), David Weintraub (MV *Malaspina*) and a staff member of AMHS (MV *Matanuska*)); American Classic Voyages Co, New Orleans, Louisiana, USA (Robin Terry); American Hawaii Cruises, New Orleans, Louisiana, USA (Robin Terry); BC Ferries, Victoria, British Columbia, Canada (Patricia Stephens); Caledonian MacBrayne (Robert Donaldson and Arlene Hay); Cape Canaveral Cruise Lines (JJ Barnes); Carnival Cruise Lines, Miami, USA (Tim Ho); Captain Cook Cruises, Sydney (Tracy Davies and Danielle Wright); Celebrity Cruises, Weybridge, UK (Kate Selley and Michelle Armstrong); Cie de Iles du Ponant, Nantes (Daniel Nedzela and Monika Marot); Clipper Cruise Line, St Louis, Missouri, USA (Meredith Bussen); Colorline, Oslo (Hege Walderhaug, Mari Winkler Solberg and Helge Otta Mathisen); Columbia Yacht Club, Chicago, USA (Susan and Chris Burritt, and all the members); Costa Cruises, Genoa (Mr Fordred and Ana Torres); Creative Cruising, Sydney (Ernie Skalsky); Crystal Cruises, Los Angeles, California, USA (Tina Bryan); Cunard Line, Miami and Sydney (Julie Davis, Jan Ross, Michelle Warren and Bruce Good); Delta Queen Coastal Voyages, New Orleans, Louisiana, USA (Robin Terry); DFDS Seaways, Copenhagen (Julie Spagna, Tommy Christensen and Henrik Vaupel); Estline, Tallin (Siiri Same); Ferrimaroc, Almeria (Mike Barker and Emilia Vinuesa); Festival Cruises, Greece and Sydney, Australia (Mary Kelly, Sydney); Fred Olsen Lines, UK (Wendy Jeffreys); Freedom Ship International Inc, Palm Harbor, Florida, USA (Roger Gooch); Golden Sun Cruises, Piraeus (Rosalyn Riego de Dios); Great Lakes Cruise Company, Ann Arbor, Michigan, USA (Christopher Conlin); Hapag-Lloyd, Germany (Isolde Susset and Martina Faehnemann); Holland America Line, Seattle, Washington, USA (Courtney McKenzie); Irish Ferries, Dublin (Dermot Mulligan); Islas Galapagos Turismo Y Vapores, Salvador (Margarita Bueno); Isle of Man Steam Packet Co Ltd, Douglas, Isle of Man (Geoff Corkish); Lindblad Expeditions, New York (Colleen Bradley, Med Helal and Martin Millican); Louis Cruises, Nicosia (George Michaelides); Marine Atlantic, St Johns, Newfoundland, Canada (Noreen Martin); Marine Expeditions, Toronto, Canada (Med Halal); Mediterranean Shipping Co Ltd, Naples, Italy, and Sydney, Australia (Giuliana Alvino and Ross McAlpine respectively); Mercy Ships, Garden Valley, Texas, USA (Glenn Price, Sharon Nelson and Jim Paterson); Cie Meridionale de Navigation, Marseille, France (Claudio Cisasaro); MG Media Communications, Sydney, Australia (Andrew Mevissen); Noble-Caledonia (Sally McColgan); Norfolk Line (Chris Riddell); Norwegian Caribbean Line (Alison Avery and Fran Sevcik); NYK, Tokyo (Nobuyoshi Ebihara and the NYK PR team); Operation Mobilisation Ships Ministry, Mosbach, Germany (Carol Anne); Orient Lines, London, UK (the PR staff); P&O Cruises, Sydney, Australia (Gavin Smith); P&O Cruises, UK (Amanda Griffiths and Ray Hankin); P&O Princess Cruises, Los Angeles, California, USA (Denise Seomin & Denise Stanley); Peregrine Adventures, Melbourne, Australia (Andrew Prossin and Carla Santos); Porto Santo Line, Portugal (Maria Joao Clode); Quadrant PR, Cardiff, UK (Sian Thomas); Quark Expeditions, London, UK (Renee Shorter and per courtesy of the original photographers PS Kristensen and BC Alexander for their photos of *Kapitan Khlebnikov*, Per Breiehagen (*Sovetsiky Sojus*) and Brad Stahl (*Kapitan Dranitsyn*)); Radisson Seven Seas Cruises, Fort Lauderdale, Florida, USA (Andrew Poulton); Read McCarthy Group, Sydney, Australia (Alison Avery); Royal Caribbean Cruise Line, Weybridge, UK (Kate Selley and Michelle Armstrong); Royal Olympic Cruises, UK (Bernadette Askouni); Sea Containers Ltd, London, UK (Maureen Elliott); Silja Line (Leila Sahlstedt); Smyril Line, Torshavn, Faroe Islands (Samuel Arnoldson); Society Expeditions, Seattle, Washington, USA (Michael Lomax and Angela Swanson); Special Expeditions (Jan Cooper and Colleen Bradley); Star Cruises, Singapore (Alison Avery and Jansen Chan); Superfast Ferries, Athens, Greece (Yannis Criticos and Ariadne Psimarra); Swan Hellenic, London, UK (Paula Duggin and Liz Curtis); TT-Line, Melbourne, Australia (Fiona Daldy); United States Lines, New Orleans, Louisiana, USA (Robin Terry); Unity Line, Poland (Izabela Koperska); Viking Line, Mariehamn; Windstar Cruises, Seattle, Washington, USA (Sarah Johnson)

Computer Gurus

And last, but never least, my plaudits and love to my three adult children for giving of their time and depth of knowledge of computer equipment to someone trying to grapple with the technology. You were all so supportive: daughter Kim and two sons Lee and Gene. I could not have coped without your presence.

Introduction

Motivation to bury myself in methodical research, then write this book was probably inspired within me as I emerged from primary school into college many, many years ago.

Auckland is New Zealand's premier city with a magnificent harbour setting and, as a young boy, I use to eagerly anticipate the fortnightly bus trip to that city with my Mother from Pukekohe, a land-locked, truly rural town miles from the sea and 31 miles (51 kilometres) from Auckland's Waitemata Harbour. Pukekohe didn't even have a river or lake to call its own. And, on each trip, the bus would commence descending down Anzac Avenue to the terminal while I gazed in awe at the gleaming white superstructures atop the black or white hulls of some wonderful ships of that time. They would either be dockside, or waiting out in the stream for a berth. A minute's stroll from the bus terminal, and I would be standing alongside these majestic vessels . . . and gaping.

Somewhere else in my early days, I was smitten with the Christopher Columbus quotation – "And the sea will grant each man new hope as sleep brings dreams" – and would lay awake at night upon returning to my home from Auckland's wharves and imagine myself on board one of those man-made beautiful creations.

On one memorable day, 29 March 1937, my father drove us in his Chevrolet Tourer into Auckland to be part of the 3,000 people waiting on the shore of Mechanics Bay to welcome the pioneering Captain Edwin C Musick who was piloting his Pan American flying boat *Clipper II* from San Francisco to Auckland to test the viability of opening a Pacific air service. As a child, the consequences of this flight were totally lost on me. Here was I witnessing an event that would harm my beloved passenger ships 25 years later.

For the record, the survey and proving flight to link the USA with New Zealand and to establish 'stepping stones' (for fuel, service, catering supplies, etc) from the Alameda, California flying boat base to Honolulu (18 h 9 m), Honolulu to Kingman Reef near Wake Island (8 h 27 m), Kingman Reef to Pago Pago (7 h 55 m) and Pago Pago to Auckland (12 h 22 m) was accomplished in actual flying time of 46 hours and 53 minutes. Today's route time is 13 hours. The flying boat was a Sikorsky S-42B equipped with 4 x Pratt & Whitney Hornet 55-D1-G engines, each developing 700 hp (522 kW) and capable of delivering a cruising speed of 140 mph (224 kph) with 32 passengers and five crew.

The excitement of that moment stayed with me for years, and when I joined QANTAS Airways in Sydney as a trainee personnel officer, I was unwittingly aiding and abetting the 'enemy' in the sky to eventually conquer sea travel as it was then enjoyed.

My virgin voyage from Auckland to Sydney on the *Aorangi* remains forever locked in my mind: the moment I stepped aboard to put my feet down on the teak deck, which was faintly throbbing with the idling Sulzer diesels deep in the hull; the moment when the hum of the generators mixed with sailing announcements from the PA system; the moment when she commenced a series of siren blasts which roared from the bass baritone depths of the engine room; the moment I caught my first streamer heaved from dockside by a relative, with both of us giving little tugs which tremored up and down the length of the streamer; the moment when the brass band burst into the emotive Maori Farewell; then the moment when, ever so slowly, we realised that the dock was moving away from us and our bonds to the land were released. And we were on our own island about to be surrounded by the world's oceans and seas.

I count myself fortunate to have been able to travel on a number of passenger liners and ferries in my lifetime between New Zealand's islands via the *Tamahine, Hinemoa, Maori, Wahine* and *Rangatira;* between Australia and New Zealand across the Tasman Sea on the *Aorangi, Monowai, Wanganella* and *Oriental Queen;* Sydney to England on the *Fairsky;* Colombo to Singapore on the *Cathay;* Singapore to Auckland on the *Arcadia;* latter day cruises on the *Fairstar;* numbers of

ferry voyages across the English Channel, the Irish Sea, the Scandinavian routes and the Bosphorus area....and familiarisation luncheons on any ship that enters Sydney harbour.

During a period living in London, I came even closer to the death of the passenger liner in the sixties! As an official immigration officer for Australia House in the Strand, one of my duties was to be present at either Southampton or Tilbury Docks to ensure the applicants for immigration to Australia had a smooth introduction to the changes that were about to take place in their lives. Another was to prepare them for shipboard life for their next three-to-five weeks on ships such as the *Oriana, Canberra, Orsova, Oronsay, Himalaya, Iberia, Orcades, Northern Star, Southern Cross, Fairsky, Fairsea, Castel Felice, Arcadia* and others.

Ironically, simultaneously with my appointment to Australia House, my wife landed a position as secretary to the London Managing Director of Firth Brown Ltd, Park Lane. It wasn't until a few days later that she realised that unwittingly she had joined the parent company that owned the world-renowned John Brown & Co Ltd shipyards at Clydebank – so a visit to that great maritime entity was booked mentally for our first visit to Scotland. John Brown had built some of the ships to which I was allocating passages for intending migrants: these were the *Flavia, Fedor Shalyapin, Leonid Sobinov, Rangitiki, Rangitata, Rangitane, Ruahine, Orsova, Oronsay, Arcadia* etc.

One day, the chief immigration officer asked me to alternate between Southampton Dock and London airport departure points. And, suddenly, I was walking through...and under...and around... passenger aircraft! The cost of one immigration passage between the British Isles and Australia by ship was £10; and it was exactly the same for a flight out by Comet, Boeing 707, Britannias and Douglas DC-8s! Quite markedly, Australia House was now being inundated by requests for aircraft seats while filling the passenger ships became harder by the day. The turnaround factor for aircraft was days compared with weeks for a ship. And gradually, the immigrant vessels became fewer. Simultaneously, demand for airline travel overtook sea voyages...and the shipping annihilation was under way, slowly, but ever so surely.

This reference publication was motivated by the constant bombardment of reader's letters to cruise magazines asking after the fate or fortune of ships on which they had travelled, as a passenger, a migrant or a member of the armed forces during the major wars. These included practically every type of vessel from passenger liners, cruise ships, ferries, line-haul ships, emigrant ships, pilgrim ships, Victory ships, Liberty ships and even converted naval ships. The *Cruise Travel* periodical from the USA published regularly letters headed "Whatever Became of ...?" and sought to give answers to its readers. Similarly, the internet 'newsgroups', which bring people of common interests together over cyberspace for chat sessions, are constantly seeking knowledge of the whereabouts of 'such and such a ship'. They would number roughly one hundred enquiries a day, or even more if the very popular emigration sites attached to the subject of genealogy were included!

This quick search encyclopedia should fill a void in maritime reference books and provide answers and information for ex-passengers' queries.

Ship owners and charterers come and go, merge or perish but a ship is oblivious to land-based goings-on and undertakes her duties in a serene world of her own. Certainly, a ship will get caught up in the odd controversy, be sold, be chartered out, have writs attached to her mast and sometimes suffer indignities from the commercial empires involved with them. But a ship will still maintain her seagoing majesty which sailors love and shorebound people envy. And when a ship passes on, it either goes to heaven (the seabed) or to hell (the breaker's yard) . . . much like life itself.

And, sadly, the attritional approach to new buildings is

seeing most of the traditionally-designed classics disappear to be replaced by slab-sided, mega-storey, atrium-pierced, high tonnage, thousand feet plus (330 metres plus) new age vessels which will convey masses of passengers from a base port to an out-and-back itinerary, with the odd long-haul, perhaps global, voyage. But one must go with the times, and I am slowly gaining an admiration for some of the new tonnages being disgorged from the shipbuilders' yards. They are still ships, and they still require water beneath them. I love them all!

Many great passenger liners in the classic mould are falling by the wayside in the face of enormous costs for owners/operators to comply with rigid new rules regarding safety, such as SOLAS regulations. Pollution factors, marine fuel costs and the like are making the classic liners redundant, if not age itself. But several hang in there hoping for one more chance to carry landlubbers into their world of salt air, azure blue seas and blasts of their 'goosebumps' sirens in port. The new regulations have been sorely needed…but at a cost to aging technology.

But shiplovers everywhere should be thankful that there is a resurgence of shipbuilding, spawned by a growing and dynamic cruise ship industry. Millions of guests, which passengers are oft-times referred to these days, are carried out and back from home ports for periods ranging from one day to three weeks or more, with global cruising of 90 days becoming more popular year-by-year. Shipping companies have seen an upward spiral in cruising numbers and their belief in the future is clearly displayed by almost continual press releases of new building contracts being let in the world's shipyards.

And, let's face it, despite some of the modern era designs and internal glitziness, every ship has a beauty which is enhanced by the presence of the sea; so the cruising public will come to accept the futuristic change in ship profiles and interior treatments as the evolution of an all-inclusive cruise programme with the ship as a complete resort…as opposed to driving or flying to a land-based beachside resort somewhere.

Finally, it is important to know that five years' casual research into every vessel carrying passengers, falling within the criteria set for this book, culminated in intensive full-time research for a year leading up to the end result. Every detail has been cross-referenced with libraries, maritime museums, publications, registers, trade journals, owners, operators and virtually anything recorded about each ship appearing within this volume.

Now, ask the question 'Where is she now?' and the answer will be within these pages.

Criteria: Exceptions and Explanations

The majority of maritime books seem to confine their research and inclusions to a minimum of 10,000 grt. As a result, some smaller ships are omitted when they are truly deserving of a place in ship listings and books on maritime history. As you will see below, a minimum gross registered tonnage of 3,000 has been selected for this publication, thereby uncovering some very interesting vessels from obscurity.

As the title indicates, this book deals with the period 1900 to 2000.

If a ship was delivered to her owners prior to 1900, but there was a name change after 1900, for whatever reason, then that ship is included, with the new owner/operator's name and date.

The following criteria have been meticulously adhered to throughout this work:

• Minimum gross registered tonnage is 3,000 grt.
• Minimum passenger number is 50, provided that these are all berthed.
• The hull is to be a mono-hull (single hull). The exception being, for instance, the RADISSON DIAMOND (1992) with catamaran hull (a radical departure from the norm), in view of her being a major cruise ship of some significance and one with conventional power and propulsion systems.
• Each ship to be conventionally propelled (ie screw driven) from the stern. While this precludes stern-wheelers and paddle-steamers, it permits nuclear-powered ships such as the SAVANNAH (1962).
• Where a ship is assisted by windpower, that ship is included if the screw is revolved by a traditional power plant from which emissions are through a conventional funnel, such as with the WIND SURF (1997). This ship would then be included only if it qualifies through other criteria.
• Gross registered tonnages and passenger numbers are shown as the last known configuration. Some older ships' data may have become vague over the years, but every effort has been made by cross-referencing such entries with all known publications. In the rare instance that a GRT cannot be proven, then the appropriate space for GRT is left blank.
• Likewise, the passenger capacity of some vessels has not been recorded in the past, or the number is disputed, in which case the rare blank space will occur. The years after 1918 and 1945 led to frenetic migration voyages and the 'official' numbers carried by all manner of vessels were suspect in many ways. This still applies to those countries who operate a shipping industry, but in almost a clandestine

manner.
• Similarly, the year of a ship's name change (in parenthesis) may be missing on occasion, due to having been taken off Lloyd's Register of Shipping and then having undergone multiple changes of name via a number of owners and operators. The great majority of such changes occurred in Mediterranean and communist countries.

For the most part, ocean-going ships sailing in open water form the basis of the book. But there are exceptions: dedicated river cruise ships plying the Danube river, for instance, are included if they enter the Black Sea as part of their voyage and meet all other criteria. There are some dedicated lake cruise ships (ie on the Great Lakes of North America) that are included, for the reason that they had occasion to enter the St Lawrence river at some stage to the point where ocean-going vessels penetrated from the North Atlantic.

Ferries meeting the criteria are also within this book. As these vessels quite often end up as cruise ships (indeed, many new large ferries are designed as cruise ferries), then that point of reference must be included. To be honest, the modern-day mega-ferry design and silhouette and those of new-buildings of cruise ships follow a similar pattern and, at a distance, can virtually only be recognized by the positioning and vertical nature of the bridges, plus slightly differing designs of the bow and stern structures on ferries. Where a ferry provides cabin accommodation normally, but has been converted to aircraft-style reclining seats after being repositioned to a short-sea service (day boats), it has still been included within this encyclopedia.

Ferries on short runs without cabin accommodation and only providing recliner seats for a voyage are excluded, unless they carry a minimum of 500 passengers. Such vessels are often refered to as day boats, in order to distinguish them from night boats which occasionally provide berths for their passengers.

Some purpose-built train ferries are included. Normally this would not have been the case, but for the commissioning of the English Channel tunnel! As a consequence, English Channel train ferries are being traded and converted to conventional ferries or cruise ships.

Dedicated freight RoRo ferries, despite meeting the criteria of tonnage, berth availability of 50 and over, etc, have been excluded, unless a passenger-freight RoRo is involved.

No double-ended ferries are included, regardless again of meeting all criteria. However, if the funnel/s is/are raked towards the stern, or if there is only one forward bridge, then such a vessel is included.

Passenger-cargo ships are listed only where their passenger figure and berths numbers meet the minimum criteria. The majority of passenger-cargo vessels limit their passenger berths to 12, thereby complying with International Maritime Laws which stipulate that ships carrying in excess of 12 passengers must carry a resident doctor on board. In shipping circles, passenger-cargo vessels with 12-or-less passenger berths are referred to as 'twelves'. There was a waiver issued to some British ships at one time, but that is another story for another time.

Student education ships are included.

Refugee ships gain mention, although in some cases the quality and configuration of the passenger accommodation left a lot to be desired. However, the obligations bestowed upon the masters of such ships in conveying human beings from somewhere to somewhere meets our criteria.

The same applies to 'Victory' ships, 'Liberty' ships and other mass-produced World War Two tonnage, only for the reason that, following their wartime troop-carrying voyages, some were also used as stopgap passenger vessels. This was during the period in which shipping companies, en masse, were trying to resurrect their decimated passenger fleets.

Pilgrim ships, often converted from passenger vessels to convey followers of Islam to and from Mecca in questionable accommodation decks, are included on the basis, referred to above, in respect of obligations thrust upon ships' masters and owners.

Where completion dates follow the name of each ship, this date is the actual year in which the vessel was delivered to her owners. During the course of my research, many publications quote either the year a ship was laid down, or the launch year, in lieu of the correct 'build/delivery' year. Through the years, especially when a ship has changed hands, names, owners, operators, been repositioned to a new route, converted to a different style of vessel, etc, some confusion has crept in.

At first glance, a ship's name may appear several times in this book with a referral to another name. Such entries are purely to record such repetitions as, in most cases, the original owners have chartered the ship out for a period but, once the charter has expired, the ship reverts to her former name.

There are also occasions where a ship may have preserved its original name through living an unblemished life, only to have it changed for a brief period when it goes to the breakers for conversion into scrap. This is where the original ship is sold to a shipbreaking yard on the condition that they give the vessel a new name for delivery to that yard. This then enables the retention and future application of the prime name by the original owner. For example, the RANGITATA became the RANG for the ten-day tow to the breaker's yard at Split, Croatia, in 1962. Seasonal repositioning also leads to a ship's first given name being changed for six months, then reverting to the original name for the following six months, eg BLACK PRINCE and VENUS, CELTIC PRIDE and ROGALIN.

Possibly the most confusing data involving the shipping industry is that applicable to gross registered tonnages (GRT). Prior to 1982 GRT was simply a multiplication by 100 of the cubic capacity within the hull of each vessel. After 1982 the measurement required calculations based clearly on a vessel's total enclosed spaces which had revenue-earning potential, eg enclosed spaces within a hull or upon deck. It is on the basis of GRT rating that ships are levied fees for canal transit, docking, and so on. This has generated some very innovative naval architecture, such as the Italian creation of the 'Magrodome' – a glass/acrylic/aluminium sliding roof which was positioned over a swimming pool on the sundeck of several ocean liners and ultimately some cruise ships. It was only activated to form a roof above the pool in inclement weather, but it did occasion some serious rethinking on the GRT subject. However, GRT now applies to all vessels, and is generally regarded as a compromise between the loose definition that applied before 1982 and the subsequent carefully thought out calculations.

The rationale behind the inclusion of routes (in occasional instances) for some vessels is to indicate the regions in which they operate at the date of publication. However, these can vary from time-to-time. For instance, the trading routes of ferries is a moving feast: ferries are switched from route to route frequently throughout a season, owing to their almost perpetual operation to timetables for the transportation of passengers, cars, trailers, coaches, etc from point-to-point. If a ship breaks down, a 'game of chess', played by the operators, ensues. Switching company-owned vessels is one way out of a predicament, but quite often vessels are placed under short-term charter from another operator, even necessitating a change of name for a short period. Quite often a freight ferry which normally carries trailers only, with accommodation for drivers only, will be switched to a passenger-car ferry route to assist the normal operator. Some such examples are within these pages.

A further problem of servicing traditional routes by the ferry operators has been the rush into high-speed catamarans which give faster turnarounds port-to-port, greater profits for that reason, and enable passengers to extend their holiday or business trip by the hours saved in travelling. But the poor handling in bad weather conditions, along with occasional damage to motor vehicles and injuries to some passengers, has forced some ferry owners to fall back on their conventional ferries for six months of the year – that is, of course, if they retained them. Many did not and are now having to scramble for short-season charters.

Although catamarans often comply with this book's criteria relating to tonnage, passenger capacity and car/trailer capacity, they have been excluded from the listings for the reasons that they are not monohulls, sometimes have a different propulsion system from the norm, and rarely have accommodation berths/cabins.

In view of the extensive interest in shipping books in so many parts of the world, any reference to distance or dimensions is in both imperial and metric units, except where a nautical mile is concerned!. This still remains, in maritime and aeronautical language, a calculation based on the curvature of the earth's surface, and is equal to the length of one minute of time to 6,076.12 ft or 1,852 m. Both ships and aircraft express their through-the-water or through-the-air speed, respectively, in knots, one knot equating to one nautical mile.

Another deviation from the norm occurs in the dimensions of each ship: the general measurement term 'draft' is the predominant term. However, in the past, and particularly in the period 1900–30, some ships were measured for 'depth' – this is the height at a declared deck level (say the main deck) above the floor of a cargo hold or other specific floor from which to measure.

Photographs accompanying a ship's data may not necessarily carry the current name, but be representative of her at some stage during her lifetime.

The data in each case is presented in uniform fashion . The following example and key may serve as a guide:

ALANDSFARJAN[1] **(1987)**[2]
6172 grt[3]; 1500 psrs[4];
250 cars or 220 cars + 22 trailers[5]
343'6 x 62'7 x 15'8 (104 x 18.9 x 4.6 m)[9]
2 x 10-cylinder B+W diesel engines via twin screw.[10]
Ferry owned by Finlandexpressen[11] and operated by the Viking Line[12] on the Sweden-Finland service.[13]
Built by Helsingor Skibsvaerft Og Maskinbyg[14] for Jydsk Faergefart[15] as the KATTEGAT[16](1972).[17] Renamed n.f. TIGER[18] (1978[19], P&O Normandy Ferries) and TIGER (1985, Townsend Car Ferries Ltd).

Key
1. Ship's last or original name
2. Year of build or last change of name
3. Gross Registered Tonnage
4. Passenger capacity
5. Vehicle carrying capacity

6. Length
7. Beam
8. Draft or depth
9. Dimensions in metric units
10. Propulsion equipment
11. Owner
12. Operator
13. Service or route
14. Builder
15. Original owner
16. Original name
17. Original build year
18. Other names
19. Year of name change

During the compilation of this work, one area which presented recurrent difficulties was that of the naming of vessels of Russian and Greek origin. Due to the Russian use of Cyrillic lettering, there have been countless misspellings of Soviet ships in the past and an infinite variety of choices of name for any one vessel. Therefore, Russian ships included in this book show alternative names. Similarly, Greek vessels use language symbols along with English nameboards. Quite often, however, the name on the bow does not correspond to that on the bridge or sundeck or stern. Notations within the data contained in this publication will alert the reader to a naming problem, and will provide alternative spellings

Disclaimer
While every endeavour has been made for this publication to be accurate, and methodical application has been undertaken with intensive research through libraries, maritime museums, shipping companies and the majority of maritime authors, there are occasions when the very complexity of the shipping industry produces differing opinions as to gross tonnages, passenger numbers, etc. In such instances, I have taken a 'majority wins' approach and included the information in a logical manner.
However, as in all things maritime, my final arbiter is Lloyd's Register of Shipping.

Flotsam and Jetsam — Some Interesting Facts

While researching material for this book, some interesting information was revealed about certain ships and aspects of the shipping industry.
As these are related here, it should be noted that no information has been included relating to either World War One or Two, as the destruction and events which transpired during those two horrendous periods of our world's history were abnormal. The following details concern the periods 1900–13, 1919–39 and 1945–2000.

• Ships that were laid down, launched and completed in three different names:
1. FRED C. AINSWORTH (1950) was laid down as the AMERICAN SHIPPER (1942), launched as the PASS CHRISTIAN (1942) and completed as the FRED C. AINSWORTH (T-AP 181) (1943).
2. BAY STATE (1973) was laid down as the AMERICAN BANKER (1941), launched as the BILOXI (1941) and completed as the HENRY GIBBINS (1941).
3. VILLE DE BRUGES (1940) was laid down as the LONE STAR STATE (1922), launched as the PRESIDENT TAFT (1922) and completed as the PRESIDENT HARDING (1922).
4. BAYANO (1918) was laid down as the CAUCA (1917), launched as the ARGUAN (1917) and completed as the BAYANO (1918).
5. QUEEN OF SCANDINAVIA (1990) was laid down as the SKANDIA (1979), launched as the SILVIA REGINA (1980) and completed as the FINLANDIA (1980).

• Ships laid down in one name but sold during construction and renamed by the new owners: the FLAMENCO (1997).

• Ships that were launched but never completed:
1. The PRINCIPESA JOLANDA (1907) broken up for scrap immediately after capsizing during her launching. Settled on the seabed with her starboard side exposed and was broken up for scrap on the spot.
2. The AUSONIA (1915), which was launched as a passenger ship, but only partially completed as an aircraft carrier at the time of the worldwide collapse of the Deutsch Mark. This persuaded her builder, Blohm & Voss, to cut their losses by breaking her up for scrap in 1922.
3. The STOCKHOLM (1938), which was broken up for scrap after being gutted by fire during her fitout seven months after launching.

• Ships that were delayed during construction:
1. The PARIS (1921) was laid down in 1913, but not completed until 1921.
2. The STATENDAM (1929) was laid down in 1921, launched in 1924 and completed in 1929.
3. The STENA GERMANICA (1987) was ordered in 1979 but not completed for delivery until 1987.
4. The ALBANIA was laid down in 1914 but not completed until 1920.
5. The ABKHAZIA (1956) was laid down in 1939 as the MARIENBURG and completed in 1946 as the LENSOVIET.

• Ships laid down and launched in one country, but completed in another:
1. The STATENDAM (1929) was laid down in Belfast in 1921, launched in Belfast, but completed in Rotterdam in 1929.
2. The NORD NEPTUNUS (1991) which, as the STENA TOPPER, was fabricated in Linz, Austria, and completed in Galati, Romania, in 1977.
3. The RIPA (1997) which, as the OXFORDSHIRE, was launched in Schiedam, Holland, and completed in Belfast, Northern Ireland, in 1957.

• A passenger ship that was sunk by a another vessel which was in the process of being launched off her slipway: the passenger liner ISTHMIA (1966) had, as the SUECIA (1929), completed berthing operations when a hawser snapped and she swung on the tide into the path of a brand new tanker which slid into the water and immediately rammed the SUECIA, sinking her. She was refloated and operated successfully for another 29 years.

• Ship which was completed, then sank at her berth just prior to sailing on her maiden voyage: the KRONPRINZESSIN CECILIE (1907), which later became the MOUNT VERNON, USS (1914).

• Ship which sank three times prior to her maiden voyage: the WESTERDAM (1946), which had completed her high hull work on the slips and had been moved to her fitting out berth when the Germans invaded Holland in 1940. The Dutch suspended all work on the ship to prevent the Germans taking her over, but then she was sunk by Allied aircraft. The Germans raised her, only to have the Dutch underground sink her in 1944. The Germans again raised her, but the Dutch repeated the sinking in January 1945. After the war ceased, the Dutch raised her for completion and placement on the lucrative North Atlantic run from 1946 to 1965, at which time she was broken up for scrap.

• Ships that were lost on their maiden voyage: the TITANIC

(1912), the HANS HEDTOFT (1958) and the HIGHLAND HOPE (1930).

• Ships that were lost on their return maiden voyage: the SOBRAON (1900), the GEORGES PHILIPPAR (1932) and the MAGDALENA (1949).

• Ships which met disaster after changing to new owners:
1. The TYRONE (1912), which was wrecked on her delivery voyage to new owners in Dunedin, New Zealand.
2. The PRESIDENT QUEZON (1939), which was wrecked on her delivery voyage.
3. The ISLA DE CABERRA (1973), which was broken up for scrap after catching fire a few weeks after changing owners.

• Ships which were broken up in two different locations:
1. The OLYMPIC (1911), which was scrapped in Jarrow and Inverkeithing.
2. The ATLANTICA (1964), which was scrapped in Piraeus and Barcelona.

• Ships that had previously sunk, were raised and resumed voyages: the PRESIDENT QUEZON (1939) and the ADMIRAL NAKHIMOV (1949).

• Ship that had sunk twice, was raised and resumed service: the CONTE VERDI (1923).

• Ships that have changed hands and had their original names contracted or partially recycled:
1. The CORAL PRINCESS (1993) was CORA PRINCESS (1990).
2. The RANG (1962) was RANGITATA (1929).
3. The MAR JULIA (1997) which was WILLIAM (1992), ex-EARL WILLIAM (1977) and PEARL WILLIAM (1993).
4. The COSTA PLAYA (1995), which was both INNSTAR (1981) and FINNSTAR (1978).
5. The PEARL (1993) was the OCEAN PEARL (1987) and PEARL OF SCANDINAVIA (1982).

• Ships that were not meant to be?:
1. The PIETER CORNELISZOON HOOFT (1926), which was gutted by fire on the slips, caught fire during her fitout, then caught fire 6 years later while at her berth.
2. The SOJUS (1980) which, as the HANSA (1935), sank after hitting a mine off Warnemünde. She was raised by the Russians and rebuilt as a passenger-cargo ship which caught fire and was completely gutted in 1954. She was rebuilt again and operated until she was broken up for scrap in 1981.

• Ship that struck the same outcrop of rocks two days apart, with the second grounding sending her to the bottom: the HIGHLAND PRIDE (1910).

• Ship that was completed in 1952, but had an 11-year old engine fitted was the AUGUSTUS (now the PHILIPPINES). A twin bank of 12-cylinder Fiat diesel engines had been constructed in Italy in 1941, then stored during the war.

• Ship that was designed with the latest technology of her day and scheduled to operate between two specific ports as a passenger ferry. It was only discovered that one of the ports had not altered its existing layout until the WILLIAM CARSON (Canadian National Railways) was conducting her maiden voyage in 1955. Her formal inaugural voyage was delayed for three years.

• Ship that was ordered by a customer who never received it: the MARIENBURG (1939), which was built at Stettin under contract to Ostrreussen Baderdienst, but was delivered up as a World War II prize to the Russian Government to be named LENSOVIET (1946).

• Ship that caught fire and was completely gutted at her dock while her new owners were registering her new name: the SATRUSTEGUI (1953) which, as the EXPLORADOR IRADIER (1948), was being re-registered as the ISLA DE CABRERA (1973). The owner-elect opted out of the contract on the basis of non-delivery on time.

• Ship whose owner issued a specific instruction to the builder, after the ship was launched on 28 April 1965 as the ITALIA, to slow the actual fitting out down. The ship was finally delivered to the customer two and a quarter years later in August 1967.

• Ship bearing two names simultaneously: the NEPTUNE (1972) with POSEIDON on her stern (Greek for God of the sea).

• Ship that sailed over 3,400 miles (5850 km) without a stern or a rudder: the LLANGIBBY CASTLE (1929) which was torpedoed in the South Atlantic on 16 January 1942 with 26 lives lost. She managed to make 6 knots and, unescorted through U-boat-riddled waters, she sailed 700 miles (1,330 km) to Horta in the Azores, then the dangerous leg to Gibraltar for temporary repairs, then on to England.

• Ship which was hidden from the Germans for five years during World War Two: the KRONPRINS FREDERIK which was launched in 1940 at the Helsinor Shipyards in Denmark as the German army was invading the Low Countries of Europe. The Danes hid the ship in a quiet backwater of Copenhagen and dispersed the fitout materials and furnishings throughout Denmark to prevent the Germans from completing the ship. After the war she was hurriedly completed and undertook her maiden voyage for DFDS in May 1946 from Copenhagen to Harwich.

• Ship that has endured numerous changes of owners for over 40 years, but has retained her original name throughout: the MONTEREY (1956).

• Ship with the longest-serving record: MEDINA (1914), which is now the DOULOS (1978) and still sailing after 86 years.

• Last active passenger ship to have been equipped with steam turbines: Sitmar's FAIRSKY (1984), now the PACIFIC SKY (2000).

• First ship to have her lifeboats stowed inboard: the WILLEM RUYS (1947), which became the ACHILLE LAURO (1965).

• First ship to install an a la carte restaurant on board: the AMERIKA (1905), which became the EDMUND B. ALEXANDER, USS (1941).

• First ship to have a squash court on board: THE AZUR (1987).

• First ship to have an ice-skating rink on board: the VOYAGER OF THE SEAS (1999).

• First ship to have a rock-climbing wall installed: VOYAGER OF THE SEAS (1999).

• First, second and third ships to have a golf course on board: the ILE DE FRANCE (1927), the LEGEND OF THE SEAS (1995) and the GRAND PRINCESS (1998) respectively.

• First British passenger ship built with turbo-electric propulsion machinery installed: the VICEROY OF INDIA (1929).

• First passenger liner to be fitted with fin stabilisers: the

CHUSAN (1950), whose Captain reported that the fins had reduced the vessel's roll by 90%. It should be noted here that the CONTE DE SAVOIA (1932) had gyroscopes incorporated into her hull 18 years earlier.

- First trans-Atlantic passenger ship to be equipped with twin screw: the CITY OF NEW YORK (1888).

- First ship to have a quadruple screw fitted: the AUGUSTUS (1928), which became the SPARVIERO (1943).

- First ship to be constructed with an all-welded hull: the AFRICAN COMET (1941), which became the ARTHUR MIDDLETON, USS (1942).

- First passenger ship to be lit electrically: the AMORIGNE (1876).

- First ship to have all cabins and public rooms air-conditioned: the NITTA MARU (1956).

- First ship to exceed 30,000 grt, have four funnels and be propelled by a quadruple screw: the LUSITANIA (1907).

- First ship to have square quadruple funnels: the MASHU MARU (1948).

- First deep sea turbine-equipped ship: the VICTORIAN (1905).

- First turbo-electric powered ship: the NORMANDIE (1935).

- First ship to use radar: the NORMANDIE (1935).

- First large, all-iron, screw-propelled ocean-going ship to cross the Atlantic: the GREAT BRITAIN (1843), which was designed by Brunel and was the world's largest ship at the time.

- First ocean-going twin screw ship: the RUAHINE (1866).

- First ship to have wireless equipment installed: the LUCANIA (1891).

- First major commercial use of morse code by a ship: the REPUBLIC (1903), which summoned help on 23 January 1909 after being rammed in dense fog off the Nantucket Light by the FLORIDA.

- First commercial ship to be nuclear-powered: the passenger-cargo vessel SAVANNAH (1962).

- First-known cruise ship: the IBERIA (1844), when P&O Lines advertised a trip from London to Athens, Smyrna and Constantinople via Vigo, Oporto, Lisbon, Cadiz and Gibraltar.

- First purpose-built ship to be configured to one-class passenger operation: the SOUTHERN CROSS (1955).

- First passenger ship to be designed with engines and funnel aft: the SOUTHERN CROSS (1955).

- First Atlantic liner to be fitted with non-conventional funnels: the ROTTERDAM (1959).

- First known use of 'jumboising': the MARATHON (1904), which was cut in half and had a 50' (15.2 m) section implanted to give her an additional 153 grt to an overall of 7848 grt.

- First recorded accident involving three ships: the TARSUS (1946) was waiting to enter dry dock in 1960 when the tanker PETER ZORANIC collided with the tanker WORLD HARMONY, then smashed out-of-control into the TARSUS. Fire engulfed all three ships, with the TARSUS being declared a total constructive loss.

- First ship to initiate a policy of being a total smoke-free zone (including open decks) was the PARADISE (1998).

- First ship to project compressed air bubbles through slots in the bow to break up ice was the FINNCARRIER (1975).

- First ship to be steam-driven by triple expansion engines: the AUSTRALASIAN (1884).

- First passenger ship to be fully-equipped with diesel propulsion machinery: the ABA (1921).

- First passenger ship on the trans-Atlantic service to be fully equipped with diesel engines was the GRIPSHOLM (1925).

- First British liner to be launched by a reigning British monarch: the SOUTHERN CROSS (1954) by Queen Elizabeth II, one year after her coronation.

- Accident prone ship No 1: the CITY OF ATLANTA (1904), which rammed and sank the schooner FRANK B. WITHERBEE on 3 October 3 1913 near Diamond Shoals off the coast of Virginia. Seven years later, she rammed and sank the concrete freighter CAPE FEAR in Narragansett Bay, Rhode Island on 29 October 1920. Collided with and sank the schooner AZUA off the New Jersey coast on 14 May 1930. She was finally sent to the bottom by a German torpedo off Cape Hatteras on 19 January 19 1942.

- Accident prone ship No 2: the ALEUTIAN (1923), which , as the PANAMA (1905), collided with the troop transport SARATOGA, USS, off Staten Island, New York on 30 July 1917. On 16 December 1921 she rammed the destroyer GRAHAM, USS, off Seagirt, New Jersey. As the ALEUTIAN, she ran aground on Maud Island at the entrance to the Seymour Narrows, British Columbia on 24 February 1929. Finally, she hit a rock in Uyak Bay, Kodiak Island, Alaska on 26 May 1929 and sank in deep water.

- Accident prone ship No 3: the ALEUTIAN (1929) which, as the MEXICO (1906), was rammed by the Old Dominion liner HAMILTON in New York harbour on 14 December 1922. On 27 September 1926 she ran aground on the Madagascar Reef, from which she eventually freed herself. Fourteen months later, on 25 November 1927, she struck the Blanquill, a reef in the Gulf of Cameche near Veracruz, but again survived to live out an accident-free period of 27 years before being scrapped.

- Accident prone ship No 4: the METAPAN (1909), which ran aground on the Salmaneda Reef off the coast of Colombia on 11 June 1912 and freed herself ten days later. On 9 August 1913 she sank alongside her berth in New York. She was then rammed by the freighter IOWAN in New York harbour and sank in shallow water on 15 October 1914. Several years later, on 24 March 1922, she collided with the schooner CHARLES A. DEAN off Barnegat, New Jersey. Finally, she was torpedoed and sank on 1 October 1943 in the eastern Mediterranean Sea.

- Accident prone ship No 5: the MAORI (1907), which must rank as the most accident-prone vessel of them all. Launched on 11 November 1906, her first skirmish was immediate: she slid down the slipway into the water, surged across the River Clyde and slammed into the opposite south bank. She was slipped for damage inspection but was cleared and immediately set out to sea for her offshore trials. Within hours she had run aground again and put back for repairs in dry dock. She then underwent her second attempt at her sea trials, passed, and commenced her positioning voyage to

New Zealand. En route, she ran aground once more without incurring any damage, refloated, and made landfall in New Zealand without any further incidents. Union Steamship Company officials had become so sceptical about their new vessel that the welcome was almost behind closed doors! But she gave the company and her country excellent service until, in 1944, she was laid up for sale and went to China as the HWA LIEN (1946). But she hadn't yet ended her pranks – on the delivery voyage she ran out of food and water, which caused a schedule alteration to call at Darwin for replenishments. On 13 January 1951 she sank at her moorings in Keelung Harbour. Four months later she was raised and broken up for scrap, with the exception of part of her hull which was converted into a harbour barge. She had finally died after so many suicide attempts.

• Accident-prone ship No 6: the MINNEHAHA (1900), which rammed and sank a tug in her first year at sea; bore down on the Admiralty Pier at Dover and narrowly avoided absolute calamity during thick fog in 1901. In 1906 she collided with the Cunard Line's ETRURIA (7700 grt, 500' long, 834 m). In 1910 she stranded herself on the Scilly Isles on 18 April. Despite the Atlantic Transport Line's management mentally writing the vessel off as a total constructive loss, she suddenly refloated. On 7 September 1917 she took a torpedo off Fastnet which finally sank her with the loss of 42 lives.

• Ships currently operating which are more than 40 years of age: DOULOS (1978), PETR VELIKI (1939), POBEDA (1928), RIVIERA STAR (1944) and BRITANIS (1932).

• Most popular alphabetical usage in naming passenger ships and ferries: S (882 times), A (730 times), C (640 times) and M (620 times).

• The only shipping line in the world owned by a post office: the Folkline which is owned and operated by the National Post Office of Finland (one of their ships is the FOLKLINER).

• Most popular name, or word incorporated into a name: PRINCESS (78 times), VIKING (33 times), PRESIDENT (74 times), EMPRESS (27 times) EMPIRE (52 times), ROYAL (26 times), PRINCE (47 times), VICTORIA (22 times), QUEEN (42 times), ORIENTAL (17 times), PRIDE (35 times) and STENA*(64 times).
* Company name prefix to fleet

• Ships featuring the greatest number of name changes: RIVIERA STAR (11), ENCHANTED ISLE (11), STAR OF VENICE (9) and ENCHANTED SEAS (9).

Gazetteer

This gazetteer contains geographical locations mentioned within this book. As such, it only provides a brief mention of location and anything that is concerned with the maritime connections of the city, town, bay, reef, etc.

Aalborg: see under Alborg.

Aberdeen: former shipbuilding port between the mouths of the rivers Dee and Don, Scotland.

Ablasserdam: town located ten miles (17 km) south-east and upstream from Rotterdam, Holland.

Abo: see under Turku.

Abrolhos Island: lying in the Atlantic Ocean off the coast of Brazil.

Admiralty Islands: coral island group forming part of the Bismarck Archipelago linked to Papua and New Guinea.

Aegean Sea: an arm of the Mediterranean Sea, cluttered by numerous islands, and bounded to the west by the Greek peninsula, to the east by Turkey and to the south by Crete and the Sea of Crete.

Akitsu: shipbuilding town 18 miles (30 km) east of Hiroshima, Japan.

Alameda: shipbuilding seaport on an island in San Francisco Bay.

Aland Islands: an island group belonging to Finland and lying in the Gulf of Bothnia.

Alang: shipbreaking town in the Gulf of Cambay on the Arabian Sea, 150 miles (255 km) north of Mumbai, India.

Alaska: northernmost state of the USA and separated from the USA by Canada.

Alborg: a shipbuilding city in northern Jutland, Denmark. Also known as Aalborg.

Alexandria: seaport city on the Mediterranean coast of Egypt.

Algahan Reef: a shipping hazard only five miles (8 km) outside the port of Jeddah, Saudi Arabia.

Algeciras: seaport on Algeciras Bay, Spain, west of Gibraltar.

Alghero: coastal town on the Mediterranean Sea shore of north-western Sardinia.

Aliaga: seaport town specialising in shipbreaking, situated in an inlet of Candarli Bay in Izmir province, Turkey.

Alicante: seaport capital of Alicante province in southern Spain on the Mediterranean Sea.

Almeria: seaport city on the Gulf of Almeria, an inlet of the Mediterranean Sea on the southern coast of Spain.

Amazon River: a 3,869 mile (6,448 km) long river which carries the largest water volume in the world, hosts the world's largest rain forest area and is navigable by ocean-going ships for 2,200 miles

(3,680 km) to Iquitos, Peru from the Atlantic Ocean. The seaport of Belem is at the mouth of the Amazon.

Ambrose Light: clear marker in the main channel approaching New York from the Atlantic Ocean.

Amstel River: flows through central Amsterdam, Holland.

Amsterdam: seaport capital of the Netherlands situated on 96 islands at the junction of the rivers Amstel and Ijzer (also known as the Yser river).

Anapa: coastal town on the Black Sea, south of the Kerchenskij Strait, leading into the Sea of Azov.

Ancona: seaport on the Adriatic Sea on the central east coast of Italy.

Andaman and Nicobar Islands: a large chain of islands forming a union territory of India in the south-eastern part of the Bay of Bengal.

Angola: a republic on the west African coast with a number of natural harbours.

Annaba: seaport city on a natural harbour in the Annaba Gulf near the mouth of the Wadi Seybous in north-eastern Algeria on the Mediterranean Sea. Formerly known as Bone and Bona.

Annaba Gulf: a natural enclosed water basin between Capes Garda and Rosa in north-east Algeria on the Mediterranean Sea.

Annam: a region in central Vietnam extending from the Ma river to the south and Ba Kiem Cape on the South China Sea.

Anser Group: a gathering of hazardous rocky outcrops seven miles (12 km) west of Wilson's Promontory, Victoria, Australia.

Antarctica: plateau continent at the southern extremity of the globe, with a land mass making it the fifth largest continent on earth.

Antwerp: seaport on the Scheldt river, Belgium, 52 miles (88 km) from the North Sea and English Channel.

Aomori: port city on Aomori Bay in northern Honshu leading into Mutsu Bay, Japan.

Apra: a deep water harbour also known as Port Apra on the west coast of Guam in the Mariana Islands of the Pacific Ocean.

Arafura Sea: a relatively calm sea north of Australia, south-west of Papua-New Guinea and east of Timor.

Aran Island: small island in Galway Bay, Republic of Ireland.

Ardrossan: seaport on the Firth of Clyde in south-west Scotland.

Arkhangelsk: shipbuilding port on the Northern Dvina river, Russia, 30 miles (50 km) from the White Sea.

Arm Chair Island: one of numerous islets within the Hong Kong and Kowloon harbour precincts.

Arromanches: small town in Normandy on the English Channel, 15 miles (25 km) north-west of Caen.

Ascension Island: part of the British colony in the South Atlantic Ocean. St Helena lies 730 miles (1,216 km) to the south-east.

Askim: a riverside town accessible from the Oslo Fjord, Norway.

Athens: capital city of Greece and with its port being at Piraeus to the east.

Atlantic City: resort and capital city of New Jersey, USA.

Auckland: largest city in New Zealand and a seaport on an isthmus with a separate harbour either side. It is in the North Island of New Zealand.

Avarua Harbour: although nominated as the port for Rarotonga in the South Pacific Ocean, oceangoing ships are compelled to lie off the Avarua Reef and move passengers and cargo by tender or lighter.

Aviles: a shipbreaking town in the Ria de Aviles, an inlet of the Bay of Biscay, in northern Spain.

Avola Anchorage: a moorings area off Avola, Sicily, in the Calabrian Rise region of the Ionian Sea.

Awashima Island: located in the Inland Sea of Japan.

Ayr: small port on the Firth of Clyde, 30 miles (48 km) south-west of Glasgow.

Azores: group of islands in the mid-Atlantic Ocean, 860 miles (1,440 km) west of Lisbon, Portugal. There are three major seaports: Ponta Delgada, Angra do Heroismo and Horta.

Badcall Bay: on the west coast of Scotland, north of Eddrachillis Bay.

Badcall Islands: a scattered group of small islets south of Badcall Bay and in Eddrachillis Bay, on the west coast of Scotland.

Bagenkop: town on the south-west tip of Langeland Island, 24 miles (40 km) south of Svendborg, Denmark.

Bahamas: independent state within the West Indies, with Nassau as its capital. The nation consists of over 700 coral atolls.

Bahia: a state on the east coast of Brazil, bordering the Atlantic Ocean.

Bahrain: a sandy island which is an independent state in the Persian Gulf and linked to Saudi Arabia by a road causeway.

Baia: shipbuilding village in the Bay of Naples, Italy.

Baie des Anges: near Nice on the French Riviera.

Baja California: (Lower California) arid, desolate peninsula of north-west Mexico, separating the Gulf of California and the Pacific Ocean.

Baku: seaport city in the Caspian Sea and the capital of Azerbaijan.

Balboa: port town on the Pacific coast of the Panama Canal zone.

Balearic Islands: group of islands in the Mediterranean Sea off the east coast of Spain to whom they belong. They include Majorca (Mallorca), Minorca, Ibiza and Formenttera.

Balikpapan: town in Indonesia in the Kalimantan province of Indonesian east Borneo, facing the Makasar Strait.

Ballard: shipbuilding town in Washington state, USA.

Baltic Sea: separated from the North Sea by the Danish Kattegat and Skagerrak: this water mass is touched by the coastlines of Sweden, Finland, Russia, Estonia, Latvia, Lithuania, Poland, Germany and Denmark.

Baltimore: seaport near the head of Chesapeake Bay, Maryland, USA.

Bandar Abbas: deep water seaport tucked away behind the island of Qeshm in south Iran on the Strait of Hormuz which links the Persian Gulf with the Gulf of Oman, Iran.

Bandar-e-Bushehur: seaport in the Arabian Gulf in south-western Iran.

Bangkok: capital city of Thailand and port on the Menam Chao Phraya river, 19 miles (32 km) from the Gulf of Thailand. Also known as Krung Thep.

Banka Island: lying off the south-east coastline of Sumatra, Indonesia, and separated by the Banka Strait.

Banka Strait: water separation between Banka Island and Sumatra, Indonesia, linking the Java Sea with Strait of Malacca at the latter's point of joining the South China Sea.

Banzart: also known as Bizerte or Bizerta, Tunisia. A seaport situated on the channel between Buhayrat (Lake) Banzart and the Mediterranean Sea.

Barcelona: seaport capital of Barcelona province in the Mediterranean Sea on the north-east coastline of Spain.

Bardsey Island: lying in Cardigan Bay, north-west Wales, two miles (3.4 km) south of the mainland and separated from it by Bardsey

Sound, which joins the Irish Sea at its westernmost point.

Bar Harbor: the port of entry for ferries from Yarmouth, Nova Scotia. It is on Mount Desert Island facing Frenchman Bay, Maine, USA.

Bari: seaport in Italy on the Adriatic Sea.

Barkley Sound: an inlet of the Pacific Ocean on the south-west side of Vancouver Island, British Columbia, Canada.

Barnegat Shoals: shallow sandbars off the coast of New Jersey.

Barra Island: at the southern end of the Outer Hebrides, Scotland, bounded by the Minch to the east, the Atlantic Ocean to the west and the Sound of Barra to the north.

Barrett's Reef: a notorious navigation hazard just outside and south-west of Wellington Harbour, New Zealand.

Barrow-in-Furness: former shipbuilding port in Cumbria, England.

Barwon Heads: on the western side of the entrance to Port Phillip Bay, Victoria, Australia.

Bass Strait: dividing the mainland of Australia from the island state of Tasmania. The weather and seas can be appalling to ships of any tonnage.

Bata: seaport town on the Atlantic coastline of equatorial Guinea belonging to Spain.

Batangas: seaport city in south-western Luzon, Philippines.

Bay of Bengal: an arm of the Indian Ocean bordered in the west by India and the east by Myanmar, and receiving the waters of the Rivers Ganges, Krishna, Irrawaddy and Brahmaputra.

Bay of Biscay: one of the most treacherous stretches of water in the world, with mountainous seas, constant storms and gale-force winds. The Bay lies along the western coastline of France and the northern coastline of Spain.

Bay of Cadiz: inlet of the Atlantic Ocean just north of the Strait of Gibraltar. Its major seaport is Cadiz, Spain.

Bay of Fundy: an inlet of the Atlantic Ocean between Nova Scotia and New Brunswick, Canada, with a tidal range of 69 feet (21 m).

Bay of Livorno: an inlet of the Gulf of Genoa and the Ligurian Sea, Italy.

Bay of Lubeck: an arm of the Baltic Sea with the city of Lubeck at its head in north Germany.

Bayonne: port town in New Jersey, USA six miles (10 km) from New York city.

Beachy Head: a chalk headland 578 feet (175 m) above the English Channel and south-west of Eastbourne, east Sussex, England.

Beaumont: second seaport of Texas, USA.

Beirut: largest city and seaport capital of Lebanon, lying along the eastern Mediterranean Sea.

Bejaia: see Bougie.

Belem: Atlantic Ocean seaport city on Guajara Bay at the mouth of the Amazon river, Brazil. Also known as Para.

Belfast: port capital of Northern Ireland and home of Harland and Wolff shipbuilders.

Bella Bella: town on an island cluster lying off the British Columbia, Canada, shoreline on the Queen Charlotte Sound, 270 miles (450 km) north of Vancouver.

Belle Isle Strait: (1) between Newfoundland and Labrador, Canada, on the main shipping route to Canada from Europe; (2) in the Great Lakes close to Detroit, USA.

Bellowes Rocks: positioned at the entrance to Table Bay, South Africa.

Benghazi: seaport (and joint capital of Libya, with Tripoli) on the Gulf of Sirte in the Mediterranean Sea.

Benodet: village between Rochefort and Brest on the Bay of Biscay, France.

Beppu: port town on the island of Kyushu, Japan.

Bergen: seaport city at the head of the By Fjord, western Norway.

Bermuda: British Crown dependency in the North Atlantic Ocean, 670 miles (1,120 km) east of South Carolina, USA. One of the great coral atolls.

Bight of Benin: lying within the Gulf of Guinea, this is a bay of the Atlantic Ocean on the west African coast, extending from Cape St Paul in Ghana to the north to the Nun outlet of the Niger river.

Bilbao: seaport in the Basque province of Viscaya in the Bay of Biscay region of the Atlantic Ocean.

Bill of Portland: see Portland Bill.

Birkenhead: former dock complex and home of Cammell Laird shipbuilders on the River Mersey, opposite Liverpool, UK.

Bishop Rock: an isolated rock in the Scilly Isles, England, upon which a lighthouse has been erected, and it is said that a west–east transatlantic crossing is finished once the lighthouse had been passed.

Bizerta: see Banzart.

Bizerte: see Banzart.

Black Sea: shared by coastlines of Russia, Ukraine, Georgia, Turkey, Bulgaria and Romania.

Blanquilla Reef: in the Gulf of Cameche near Vera Cruz, Mexico.

Block Island: lying nine miles (14 km) between Block Island Sound and the Atlantic Ocean, offshore from the town of New Shoreham in southern Rhode Island, USA.

Bloody Foreland: a promontory jutting into the Atlantic Ocean, 15 miles (24 km) north of Aran Island, Co Donegal, Republic of Ireland.

Bluff: the southernmost town on the South Island of New Zealand and positioned as a port on Foveaux Strait which runs between the Pacific Ocean and the Tasman Sea, and separates the South Island from Stewart Island.

Blunt's Reef: lying off Cape Mendocino, California.

Blyth: small port in Northumberland, England.

Boa Nova Rocks: an outcrop of rocks near Leixoes, Portugal.

Bocas Del-Toro: a seaport town in a cluster of islands on the Atlantic Ocean coastline north of Almirante Bay, Panama.

Bokn Fjord: located in the extreme south-west of Norway, this fjord is 12 miles (20 km) wide at the entry point between Karm Island in the south and Tungenes peninsula. The fjord extends inland a distance of 28 miles (45 km).

Bolnes: shipbuilding town on the Maas river, east of Rotterdam, Holland.

Bombay: see Mumbai, India.

Bona: see Annaba.

Bone: see Annaba.

Bonn: city situated at the confluence of the Rivers Rhine and Sieg, Germany.

Boom: town situated south of Antwerp, with access to the Scheldt river.

Boora Point: north-east promontory at the entrance to Long Bay, Sydney, featuring a sheer cliff face.

Bordeaux: seaport on the mouth of the River Garonne, France.

Bordertown: shipbreaking town in New Jersey, USA.

Borkum Island: an island and town in the Ems river estuary, Germany.

Bornholm: island in the Baltic Sea administered by Denmark.

Bosphorus Sea: linking the Black Sea with the Sea of Marmara, and separating Europe from Asia Minor.

Bosporus Sea: see Bosphorus Sea.

Boston: state capital of Massachusetts, USA, and seaport at the head of Boston Bay on the Gulf of Maine.

Bougie: seaport city in Algeria. Also known as Bejaia.

Boulogne: seaport in northeastern France on the English Channel, referred to as Boulogne-sur-Mer to avoid confusion with the Parisian suburb of the same name.

Bream Head: a promontory outside the heads of Whangarei Harbour, North Island, New Zealand.

Breda: shipbuilding industries area of Venice, Italy.

Bremen: inland seaport on the River Weser, Germany, 40 miles (64 km) from the North Sea where Bremerhaven is located as Bremen's outport.

Bremerhaven: seaport on the North Sea at the mouth of the River Weser, Germany. Formerly Wesermunde.

Brest: seaport with shipbuilding operations in north-western France.

Breton Strait: 20 miles (34 km) east of Cape Ray, Newfoundland, Canada.

Brier Island: situated at the southern end of the Bay of Fundy, Nova Scotia, Canada, with that bay on its western side and St Mary's Bay to the east. The treacherous shipping navigation area of the island is known as the North-West Ledges.

Brindisi: seaport on the Adriatic coast in southern Italy.

Brisbane: capital city of the state of Queensland, with a port on the Brisbane river which meanders from the coast 12 miles (20 km) westwards to the Coral and Tasman Seas.

Bristol Channel: situated between the south coast of Wales and the counties of Somerset and Devon in England.

British Virgin Islands: small group of islands in the Caribbean.

Briton Ferry: port at the mouth of the River Neath, south Wales, and engaged in shipbreaking operations.

Britannia Beach: near Squamish on the east shoreline of Plumper Cove, an inlet of the Strait of St Georgia, British Columbia, Canada.

Brittany: a region of north-west France shaped as a peninsula standing between the English Channel and the Bay of Biscay.

Brownsville: port on the Rio Grande river, Texas, near the Mexican border.

Bruges: see Brugge.

Brugge: capital of West Flanders province, north Belgium. It has access to the port of Zeebrugge by canal.

Buenos Aires: Argentina's chief seaport city situated at the head of the River de la Plata on the Atlantic coast.

Bull Rocks: a craggy rock projection just off Portland Island which is at the northern end of Hawke Bay, New Zealand, in the South Pacific Ocean.

Burcht: riverside suburb of Antwerp, Belgium.

Burgas: seaport city on the Black Sea coast of Bulgaria in the Gulf of Burgaski, 50 miles (83 km) north of the Turkish border.

Burma: see Myanmar.

Burntisland: a small town on the north side of the Firth of Forth opposite the city of Edinburgh.

Bur-Sudan: see Port Sudan.

Busan: industrial city in South Korea.

Bushire: see Bandar-e-Bushehur.

Butt of Lewis: promontory at the northern extremity of the Isle of Lewis in the Outer Hebrides, Scotland.

Buzzards Bay: an inlet of the Atlantic Ocean extending 30 miles (48 km) into the state of Massachusetts, USA.

Cabot Strait: flowing between the Atlantic Ocean and the Gulf of St Lawrence, and separating Newfoundland from Nova Scotia, Canada.

Cadiz: one of Europe's oldest towns with a modern seaport on the Bay of Cadiz.

Cagliari: capital and chief port of Sardinia.

Cairns: seaport city on Trinity Bay, North Queensland, Australia, and a home-port for Great Barrier Reef excursions and cruise ships.

Cairo: capital city of Egypt on the east bank of the River Nile.

Calais: seaport in northeastern France on the English Channel, opposite Dover 20 miles (34 km) away and the shortest point between France and England.

Calumet River: running through south Chicago, USA, where Calumet harbour is located and where a sea channel gives access to the Great Lakes system.

Camalti: town near the Black Sea in the province of Kastamonu, Turkey.

Camden: shipbuilding centre on the Delaware river, New Jersey, USA, opposite Philadelphia.

Campana: town on the tributary of the River Plate, north-west of Montevideo, Uruguay.

Campbeltown: seaport town on the eastern side of the peninsula of Kintyre, Argyll and Bute, Scotland, situated north of the Mull of Kintyre and in the Kilbrannan Sound.

Canaries Current: a cold ocean current flowing south along the north-west coast of Africa from El Dar-el-Beida to Cape Verde.

Canary Islands: a group of Spanish volcanic islands in the Atlantic Ocean, 58 miles (96 km) off the west coast of Africa.

Cannes: seaport resort on the Golfe de la Napoule, French Riviera.

Canton: see Guangzhou.

Canton Island: more commonly known as Rawaki Atoll in the Rawaki Island group, administered as part of Kiribati, Pacific Ocean.

Cape Barra: a headland projecting into the Indian Ocean at the southern extreme of the Mozambique Channel, with Inhambane Bay to its west.

Cape Bojeador: large headland on the Atlantic coast of Morocco.

Cape Bojidoru: situated on the South China Sea coastline of Luzon, Philippines on a main shipping channel.

Cape Bon: a 50-mile (82 km) peninsula running into the Mediterranean Sea in northeastern Tunis.

Cape Bowling Green: the eastern headland projecting into the Coral Sea and protecting Bowling Green Bay. The city of Townsville,

Queensland, is 24 miles (40 km) away on the western shoreline running out to Cape Cleveland.

Cape Canet: headland in southeastren France on the Mediterranean coast.

Cape Caxine: a promontory at the end of the Strait of Gibraltar.

Cape Charles: part of an isthmus 20 miles (34 km) north of Norfolk, Virginia, USA.

Cape Clear: the southernmost tip of the Republic of Ireland located on Clear Island, 12 miles (20 km) from Skibbereen. Fastnet Rock is five miles (8 km) further south.

Cape Cod: a narrow isthmus in Massachusetts Bay with a sandy peninsula practically enclosing Cape Cod Bay, Massachusetts, USA.

Cape Cod Canal: in Buzzard's Bay, USA.

Cape Farewell: the southernmost tip of Greenland in the North Atlantic Ocean.

Cape Finisterre: a promontory jutting out into the Atlantic Ocean on the north-east coast of Portugal.

Cape Flattery: the northwestern-most point of Washington state, USA, situated on the Strait of Juan de Fuca, which connects the Strait of Georgia to the Pacific Ocean opposite Vancouver Island, Canada. The cape is an extension of an extremely rocky part of the area.

Cape Frances: on the south coast of Vuelta Abaja, Cuba, at the extreme south-west of Cortes Bay.

Cape Guardafui: the eastern geographical limit of the Gulf of Aden which links with the Arabian Sea at this point. Located on the Horn of Africa, which is now known as Raas Caseyr.

Cape Hatteras: a sandbar forming a promontory on Hatteras Island, North Carolina, USA, with dangerous shallows extending for 70 miles (113 km) into the Atlantic Ocean.

Cape Jackson: a rocky headland with submerged reefs extending out into Cook Strait, north of the South Island of New Zealand.

Cape Leeuwin: promontory in the south-west of Western Australia, with the Indian Ocean to the west and Flinders Bay to the east.

Capelle: town on the River Meuse lying 27 miles (45 km) south-east of Rotterdam, Holland.

Cape Lookout: located in North Carolina, USA, with a prominent lighthouse standing guard over a particularly treacherous part of a the state's Atlantic coastline.

Cape Lookout: headland jutting into the Pacific Ocean and located 72 miles (120 km) west of Portland, Oregon, and 60 miles (100 km) south of the Columbia river mouth.

Cape Matapan: a long peninsula to the west of the Gulf of Lakonia and is the most southern extremity of the Peloponnesus, Greece.

Cape May: on the northern side of Delaware Bay, on the Atlantic Ocean coastline of the USA.

Cape Mendocino: a promontory 200 miles (330 km) north of San Francisco, California.

Cape Moreton: situated at the extreme northern end of Moreton Island which lies 36 miles (60 km) north-east of Brisbane, Queensland, Australia.

Cape Nomozaki: one of the headlands on Omura Bay, south-east of Nagasaki, Japan.

Cape Ortegal: a headland on the Atlantic coast of north-west Spain on the entrance to the Bay of Biscay from the south and east.

Cape Palmas: a headland at the extreme south-east of Liberia and midway between the Gulf of Guinea and the Atlantic Ocean.

Cape Pellaro: headland on the east coast of Calabria, nine miles (15 km) south of Reggio di Calabria looking out over the Strait of Messina.

Cape Point: southern extremity of Cape of Good Hope, located at the western entrance into False Bay.

Cape Prior: a promontory 20 miles (36 km) north of La Coruna, Spain, on the Atlantic coast south of the Bay of Biscay.

Cape Race: the southeastern extremity of Newfoundland on the Atlantic coast.

Cape Ray: situated at the southwestern extremity of Newfoundland overlooking Cabot Strait.

Cape Recife: one of the easternmost points of the South American continent and located near the seaport of Recife, Brazil, on the Atlantic coastline.

Cape St Francis: located on the Indian Ocean, 51 miles (85 km) west of Port Elizabeth.

Cape St Vincent: a promontory in south-west Portugal jutting out into the Atlantic Ocean.

Cape Sambro: near Halifax, Nova Scotia, Canada.

Cape Serrat: headland near Tunis, capital of Tunisia.

Cape Spartel: at the western end of the Strait of Gibraltar and the most northeastern point of Morocco, only a short distance from Tangier.

Cape Tenes: on the Mediterranean Sea coast of Algeria.

Capetown: seaport on Table Bay, 29 miles (48 km) north of the Cape of Good Hope, South Africa.

Cape Vado: on the west coast of Italy on the Gulf of Genoa.

Cape Vaticano: on the south-west coast of Italy and facing the Tyrrhenian Sea at the northern tip of the Gulf of Gioia.

Cape Verde: in the Republic of Senegal and is the most western part of the African continent.

Cape Verde Islands: in the mid-Atlantic Ocean, 385 miles (620 km) west of Cape Verde, Senegal.

Cape Wrath: the northeasternmost point of mainland Scotland, some 1,000 feet (330 m) above the Atlantic Ocean at the north end of The Minch, between the Outer Hebrides and the Scottish mainland.

Cap St Vincent: see Cape St Vincent.

Caracas: capital city of Venezuela, with its port of La Guaria seven miles (13 km) away on the north coast, bordering the Caribbean Sea.

Cardiff: port at the mouth of the River Taff on the Bristol Channel, Wales.

Caribbean Sea: a warm sea with its western extremities bounded by South and Central America and the West Indies, and its eastern limit being the Atlantic Ocean.

Cartagena: seaport capital of Murcia province, south-east Spain.

Casablanca: see El Dar-el Beida.

Casablanca Roads: an area of coastal water outside the Casablanca harbour breakwater where ships stand off and moor, awaiting clearance to proceed to a designated berth.

Cascais: coastal town 16 miles (26 km) west of Lisbon and next door to Estoril, both adjacent to the mouth of the River Tagus, Portugal.

Caspian Sea: largest inland sea in the world and sharing coastlines with Kazakhstan, Turkmenistan, Russia, Azerbaijan and Iran.

Castellammare di Stabia: seaport in the Bay of Naples on the west coast of Italy.

Castellon: full name is Castellon de la Plana and is situated on the Mediterranean coast, with its port named El Grao de Castellon where shipbreaking operations take place.

Castries Harbour: a harbour located on the eastern side of the island of St Lucia, part of the Windward group of islands in the Caribbean Sea.

Catalina Island: see Santa Catalina Island.

Cebu: seaport city on Cebu Island, Philippines.

Cebu Island: one of the Visayan Islands group in the Philippines.

Celebes Sea: in the western Pacific Ocean and is bordered by the Sulu Archipelago, the Sulu Sea and Mindanao Island to the north, the Sangi Islands chain to the east, Borneo to the west and Sulawesi Island (formerly known as the Celebes) to the south.

Cephallenia: largest of the Ionian Islands which lie west of the Gulf of Patraikos, Greece. It is also known as Kefallinia and Cephalonia.

Cephalonia: see Cephallenia.

Cerigo: formerly the island of Kithira which is situated off the southeastern tip of the Peloponnesus, Greece, and is separated from that land mass by the Straits of Kithira.

Cesme: a port town at the western extremity of the province of Izmir, which extends out into the Aegean Sea.

Chafer's Passage: a deep water channel leading from Cook Strait into Wellington harbour, New Zealand.

Chalkis (also known as Khalkis & Euripos) an island-located shipbuilding and ship repair town on the Euripos Strait, which separates Euripos Island from the Greek mainland, to which it is joined by a bridge.

Chania: see Khania.

Channel Islands: a group of islands off the coast of north-west France, of which the principle islands are Guernsey, Jersey, Alderney and Sark. The group is self-governing under the British Crown.

Channel-Port aux Basques: seaport town on the extreme south-west of Newfoundland, located on the Cabot Strait separating the Gulf of

St Lawrence from the Atlantic Ocean.

Charleston: industrial capital city of West Virginia, USA, located on the banks of the Kanawha river.

Charlotte Amalie: the port town of St Thomas in the US Virgin Islands group.

Charlottetown: seaport town on Prince Edward Island, Canada, located on Hillsborough Bay, an arm of the Northumberland Strait.

Cheju Island: in the East China Sea off South Korea.

Cherbourg: shipbuilding seaport on the Contentin peninsula in the English Channel, and 77 miles (128 km) from Portsmouth, England.

Chesapeake Bay: an inlet of the Atlantic Ocean extending 190 miles (320 km) from Cape Charles to the mouth of the Susquehanna river, USA.

Chester (USA): shipbuilding port on the Delaware river, Pennsylvania, south-west of Philadelphia.

Chittagong: main port city of Bangladesh, situated on the Karna-fuli river near the Bay of Bengal.

Church Point: a headland in the Scilly Isles which stand off Land's End by 27 miles (45 km) south-west.

Chuuk Islands: a member of the Federated States of Micronesia and located in the western Pacific Ocean. This cluster of volcanic mountains and massive reef structures used to be known as the Truk Islands.

Ciudad Guayana: massive industrial and seaport complex constructed at the confluence of the Rivers Orinoco and Carooni in north-east Venezuela, which saw several industrial towns, mines, ports, hydroelectric plants and dams embraced in a 100 square mile (170 square km) grand plan completed over a 20-year period in 1982. The towns and cities of Puerto Ordaz, San Felix, Matanzas, Caruachi, Castillito, El Pao, Cerro Bolivar, San Isidro, Palua and Ciudad Piar were united with the new region name Santo Tome de Guayana, prior to Ciudad Guayana.

Civitavecchia: seaport for Rome located at Latium on the Tyrrhenian coast, 30 miles (48 km) from the mouth of the River Tiber.

Cleft Island: a rocky projection in the Anser group off the coast of Victoria, Australia, and seven miles (12 km) west of Wilson's Promontory.

Cleveland: shipbuilding city in Ohio, USA, situated on the shore of Lake Erie which is connected to the Great Lakes system.

Clydebank: town adjoining Glasgow, Scotland, on the Clyde river.

Clyde River: flowing into the Firth of Clyde, Scotland, and supporting major shipbuilding operations along its banks.

Coatzacoalcos: seaport on the Gulf of Campeche, Mexico.

Cobh: seaport on the southern side of Great Island, which sits in the middle of Cork harbour.

Colombo: seaport city and capital on the west coast of Sri Lanka. It has an artificial port which was constructed by the British.

Columbia River: a highly complex river system rising in the Canadian Rockies and finally discharging into the Pacific, near the west coast town of Astoria, Oregon, USA.

Concepcion : extensive bay in south-east Newfoundland.

Concepcion Bay: on the Pacific coast of Chile just north of the city of Concepcion.

Congo River: see River Zaire.

Constanta: Black Sea seaport in southeastern Romania on the Danube–Black Sea Canal, which gives oceangoing ships passage from and to the Black Sea along the Trans-European waterway.

Cook Strait: a 14–18 mile (24–29 km)-wide channel between the North and South Islands of New Zealand.

Copenhagen: seaport capital of Denmark and situated on the east coast of Zealand.

Corfu: most northerly of the Ionian Island group belonging to Greece.

Cork: seaport at the mouth of the River Lee, in the south-east of the Republic of Ireland.

Coronel: seaport town in Chile.

Corsewall Point: a headland just outside the Clyde Estuary.

Cowes: town on the River Medina estuary, Isle of Wight, UK.

Crete: the largest island of Greece, situated in the eastern Mediterranean Sea, with her main seaport being Iraklion.

Croatia: independent Balkan state, formerly part of Yugoslavia.

Cromer: seaside resort on the north coast of East Anglia, England.

Cuba: an island state commonly treated as a part of the West Indies,

90 miles (150 km) south of Florida.

Cyclades: a rugged group of 220 islands off Attica, Greece, in the Aegean Sea.

Cyprus: an independent island state, 38 miles (68 km) south of the Turkish mainland. The island is partitioned between Turkey (north) and Greece (south).

Cyrenaica: a province of Libya lying along the coast of the Mediterranean Sea.

Dakar: seaport capital city of Senegal on the Atlantic coast of west Africa.

Dalian: seaport city in Liaoning province, China, with shipbuilding operations.

Dalmuir: former shipbuilding northern suburb of Glasgow, situated on the Clyde river estuary, Scotland.

Danzig: see Gdansk.

Dardanelles: a 38 mile (64 km)-long strait in Turkey between European Turkey and Asian Turkey, and linking the Aegean Sea with the Sea of Marmara.

Dar-es-Salaam: seaport city in Tanzania on the Indian Ocean coast.

Darwin: seaport in northern Australia, with entry into the Arafura Sea via the Van Diemen Gulf and the Dundas Strait, while access to the Timor Sea is direct.

Daunts Rock: a rock outcrop between Kinsale harbour and Cobh in south-east Ireland.

Daytona Beach: town in Florida, USA, involved in shipping and motor sports.

Delagoa Bay: a natural harbour for the port of Maputo, Mozambique.

Delaware Bay: an inlet of the Atlantic Ocean extending from Capes May and Henlopen 78 miles (128 km) inland.

Den Haag: see The Hague.

Den Helder: see Helder.

Denia: town situated at the extreme south of the Gulf of Valencia, Spain, and facing the Mediterranean Sea. It is 48 miles (80 km) east of Alicante.

Devonport: seaport town on the River Mersey, north Tasmania, Australia, adjacent to the Bass Strait.

Diamond Shoals: shallows off the coast of Virginia, USA.

Djakarta: large city in Java in the north-west of Indonesia.

Djibouti: seaport city of the Republic of Djibouti, situated 75 miles (125 km) south of the Strait of Bab-el-Mandeb which separates the Gulf of Aden from the Red Sea.

Dominican Republic: this nation shares half of the island of Hispaniola, West Indies, with Haiti.

Donada: a shipbuilding town on the River Po south of Venice, Italy.

Donegal: county in the north-west of the Republic of Ireland.

Douglas: town on the Michigan state shoreline of Lake Michigan, 40 miles (67 km) north-west of Kalamazoo.

Dover: being the closest English port to France, 20 miles (34 km) away. This is one of England's busiest ports, located on the south coast of Kent on the English Channel.

Drammen: large town standing at the head of Oslo Fjord, 24 miles (40 km) south-west of Oslo, Norway.

Dubai: one of the United Arab Emirates on the Arabian Gulf.

Dubrovnik, a sheltered port on the Dalmatian coast of Croatia, on the southern Adriatic coast.

Dumbarton: shipbuilding town on the northern bank of the River Clyde, 12 miles (19 km) below Glasgow.

Dundee: seaport on the Firth of Tay, Scotland, 48 miles (80 km) north of Edinburgh.

Dunedin: seaport city in the lower half of the South Island of New Zealand, on the Pacific coast.

Dunkirk: seaport on the English Channel coast of northern France.

Durban: seaport city of South Africa, situated on Natal Bay and the Indian Ocean.

Dutch Harbour: on Unalaska Island of the Aleutian group, Alaska, USA.

Dyfed: a county in the south-west of Wales.

Eagle Island: in County Mayo, Ireland.

Eagle Islands: a group of islands south-west of the sub-continent, and lying within the British Indian Ocean Territory which is still administered by Great Britain.

East Cape: massive promontory at the southern extremity of Hawke

Bay, New Zealand.

East Devonport: port town on the Bass Strait coastline of northern Tasmania.

East China Sea: an arm of the Pacific Ocean and the China Sea, bounded by the Cheju Islands in the north, Kyushu in the north-east, the Ryukyu Island chain in the east, Taiwan in the south and mainland China in the west. The Taiwan Strait connects this water mass with the South China Sea.

East London: seaport in Cape province, South Africa, at the mouth of the Buffalo river which empties into the Indian Ocean.

East North Rock: a charted rock hazard eight miles (13 km) north of Bermuda.

East River: a 16 mile (26 km)-long tidal strait with a width ranging from 55 feet (180 m) to 364 feet (1,200 m), separating Long Island from mainland USA in the city of New York.

Eckernforde: seaport on the Baltic Sea, north-west of Kiel, Germany.

Eclaireur Reef: submerged rocks in the Strait of Magellan.

Eddrachillis Bay: on the west coast of Scotland, south of Badcall Bay.

Egersund: a deep sound sheltered from the North Sea by an island at its mouth and lying 33 miles (55 km) south of Stavanger, Norway.

Elbow Bay: on north-east coast of Canada.

Elchat Elmallhoun Reef: a treacherous reef system only three miles (5 km) south of Beirut, Lebanon.

El Dar-el Beida: seaport city with an artificial harbour on the Atlantic Ocean in Algeria. It was formerly known as Casablanca.

Elefsis Bay: see Eleusis Bay.

Eleusis Bay: bay 14 miles (23 km) west of Athens, Greece, in the Aegean Sea and sheltered by Salamis Island.

Elevsis Bay: see Eleusis Bay.

Elsinore: seaport town on The Sound (Oresund) on the north-east coast of Zealand, Denmark. It is sometimes known as Helsingor.

El Grao de Castellon: see Castellon.

Emden: seaport town near the mouth of the River Ems, north Germany.

Empire: river town on the Mississippi river, Louisiana, USA.

English Channel: a narrow stretch of sea from Land's End, Cornwall, UK, to the Strait of Dover, separating England from France. Known by the French as La Manche.

Equatorial Guinea: independent state in west Africa on the Atlantic coast, between Cameroon and Gabon. It was formerly known as Spanish Guinea.

Eregli: town on the Black Sea coast of northern Turkey.

Esbjerg: seaport city on the west coast of Jutland, Denmark, with its harbour on the North Sea.

Espirito Santo: largest and westernmost island in the New Hebrides group in the South Pacific Ocean.

Esquimalt: a shipbuilding suburb of Victoria, Vancouver Island, British Columbia, Canada. Situated on the Esquimalt Lagoon at the convergence of the Strait of Juan de Fuca and Haro Strait.

Estonia: formerly a part of the USSR, with sea borders to the Gulf of Finland, the Gulf of Riga and the Baltic Sea.

Euripos: see Chalkis.

Europoort: a facility linked to the seaport of Rotterdam by the Nieuwe Waterweg and capable of handling ships up to 100,000 grt.

Falconara Marittima: Italian seaport on the Adriatic coast, 11 miles (18 km) north of Ancona.

Falkland Islands: a British Crown dependency in the South Atlantic Ocean.

Fanning Atoll: sometimes referred to as Fanning Island. See Kiribati.

Farilhoes Rocks: hazardous rock cluster 25 miles (42 km) off the Atlantic coast of Portugal, halfway between Peniche and the fishing town of Nazare.

Farne Islands: UK National Trust sanctuary group of islets off the Northumberland coast.

Faroe Islands: a Danish possession 190 miles (320 km) north-west of the Shetland Islands, Scotland.

Faslane: shipbreaking town in the UK.

Fastnet Rock: a jagged projection four miles (7.2 km) south-west of Cape Clear on the Irish coast. A lighthouse is erected on the landmark.

Fedhala: see Mohammedia.

Ferrol: shipbuilding town on the Atlantic coast of Spain south of the Bay of Biscay.

Fevaag: shipbuilding town in Norway.

Finistere: a Department of north-west France in Brittany.

Firth of Clyde: extends 60 miles (102 km) from Dumbarton to the Ailsa Craig, Scotland.

Firth of Forth: on the east coast of Scotland, this estuary is entered by the River Forth after 100 miles (165 km) and is navigable by large vessels for 38 miles (64 km) inland.

Flamborough Head: a high, chalk-cliffed promontory in Yorkshire, England, five miles (8 km) from Bidlington and just north of Bridlington Bay.

Flensburg: Baltic seaport in Germany with shipbuilding operations.

Flores Island: most northerly of the Azores group in the Atlantic Ocean.

Flores Sea: running between the Java and Banda Seas which wash the Indonesian coastline.

Florida Islands: lying 36 miles (60 km) north of Guadalcanal, Solomon Islands, in the Pacific Ocean.

Flushing: see Vlissengen.

Folkestone: seaside resort in Kent and port for the ferry crossing to Boulogne, 28 miles (46 km) across the English Channel.

Foochow: see Fuzhou.

Formby Reef: a rock shelf off Barwon Heads in Port Phillip Bay, Melbourne, Australia.

Formosa Strait: see Straits of Formosa.

Fort Lee: spread along the west bank of the Hudson river, New York state, at a point north-east of New Jersey, USA.

Fort Pierce: situated on the Indian river, which is connected to the Atlantic Ocean by a series of inlets. It is 58 miles (93 km) north of West Palm Beach, Florida, USA.

Foxhol: town six miles (10 km) south-east of Groningen, Netherlands.

Frankfurt: city on the River Main (often referred to as Frankfurt-on-Main to avoid confusion with Franfurt-on-Oder), Germany.

Frankfurt-on-Main: see Frankfurt.

Frankfurt-on-Oder: see Frankfurt.

Fraser Island: one of the world's largest sand dune islands in the Tasman Sea, separated by the Great Sandy Strait from the state of Queensland, Australia, six miles (10 km) away.

Fratelli Island: a minor island just off the Tunisian coast.

Fredericton: capital of New Brunswick, Canada.

Frederikshavn: seaport in north Jutland on the Kattegat, Denmark.

Frederiksted: seaport in St Croix, Virgin Islands (USA).

Freels Rocks: off Cape Race at the entrance to Trepassy Bay, south-east Newfoundland.

Freeport: town on the south-west shore of Grand Bahama Island in the Bahamas.

Freetown: seaport capital of Sierra Leone on the Atlantic coast of west Africa, with one of the largest natural harbours in the world.

Fremantle: seaport city on the Indian Ocean and serving Perth, Western Australia, which is seven miles (12 km) to its east.

Fuerteventura: an island in the Canary group belonging to Spain, lying 60 miles (96 km) off the Moroccan coast.

Fukue Island: one of the Goto Island group lying in the East China Sea, west of Kyushu, Japan.

Fukuoka: seaport city on Hakata Bay, north Honshu, Japan.

Fulda River: a headstream of the Weser river, Germany.

Fuzhou: capital city of Fujian province on the east coast of China, facing the East China Sea. It was formerly known as Foochow.

Gabo Island: lying close to the Australian mainland east coast five miles (8 km) from the New South Wales/Victoria border.

Gadani Beach: on the shore outskirts of Karachi, Pakistan, this is the ships' graveyard where they are cabled up on to the beach and broken up for scrap.

Galapagos: a volcanic wildlife sanctuary island in the Pacific Ocean, 580 miles (960 km) from Ecuador, to whom the island belongs.

Galati: see Galatz.

Galatz: shipbuilding town in Romania. It is also known as Galati.

Galley Head: second major headland to Old Kinsale further up the coast, facing the Irish Sea. It lies 30 miles (50 km) south-east of Cork, Republic of Ireland.

Galveston: seaport city on Galveston Island in Galveston Bay, Texas, USA. The Gulf of Mexico lies along the southern side of Galveston Island.

Gandia: shipbreaking port at the mouth of the Serpis river, which flows into the Mediterranean Sea just south of Valencia, Spain.

Garonne River: stretching 430 miles (720 km) from Mount Maladetta in the Pyrenees to Toulouse in southern France.

Garston: suburb of Liverpool, UK.

Gateshead: on the River Tyne opposite Newcastle, England.

Gdansk: seaport in northern Poland on the Baltic Sea, at the mouth of the Vistula river. Shipbuilding activities. It was formerly known as Danzig before it was ceded to Poland at the end of World War Two.

Gdynia: seaport in northern Poland on the Baltic Sea, competing with Gdansk for Polish industrial and import and export business.

Gedser: port town at the southern tip of a peninsula jutting out from the island of Falster, Denmark.

Geestemunde: see Bremerhaven.

Genoa: seaport city in north-west Italy, on the Gulf of Genoa in the Ligurian Sea.

Ghent: port in Belgium situated on the confluence of the Rivers Scheldt and Lys.

Gibraltar: British territory west of the entrance to the Mediterranean Sea through the eight mile (13 km)-wide Strait of Gibraltar, running from the Atlantic Ocean.

Gijon: seaport on the Bay of Biscay on Spain's north coast.

Glasgow: former major shipbuilding and seaport city of Scotland on the River Clyde.

Golden Horn: the peninsular land formation on the Bosphorus that has formed the harbour in Istanbul, Turkey.

Gorki: see Nizhny Nozgorod.

Gorkiy: see Nizhny Novgorod.

Gorky: see Nizhny Nozgorod.

Gotenhafen: see Gdynia.

Gothenburg: shipbuilding seaport city at the mouth of the River Gota on the Kattegat: Sweden.

Goteborg: see Gothenburg.

Goto Islands: a group of 100 islands in the East China Sea, standing west of Kyushu.

Govan: former shipbuilding suburb west of Glasgow, Scotland.

Grand Bahama Island: lying in the Atlantic Ocean west of Great Abaco Island and 60 miles (100 km) east of West Palm Beach, Floirda, USA.

Grays: former shipbreaking town in Essex, UK.

Great Barrier Island: one of two islands at the head of Hauraki Gulf, 50 miles (84 km) north-east of Auckland, with the South Pacific Ocean to the east and Colville Channel separating it from the mainland of the North Island of New Zealand.

Great Barrier Reef: a 940 mile (1,600 km)-long coral reef running north and south parallel with the north-east Australian coastline, at an average of 82 miles (140 km) distance from the mainland. It contains many island resorts

Great Manan Island: lies off the West Indies island of Antigua.

Greenock: seaport lying 24 miles (40 km) west of Glasgow, Scotland, on the southern shore of the Firth of Clyde.

Groton: a maritime city on the banks of the River Thames, steeped in the history of Connecticut, USA.

Guadalcanal: largest of the Solomon Island group in the Pacific Ocean.

Guangzhou: shipbuilding seaport city and capital of Guangdong province in south China. Formerly known as Canton.

Guantanamo Bay: in the south-west of Cuba, this is an inlet of the Windward Passage which separates Cuba from Haiti in the Caribbean Sea.

Guernsey: one of the Channel Island group in the English Channel.

Gulf of Aden: the link between the Red Sea and the Arabian Sea, lying between the coastlines of Arabia and the Horn of Africa.

Gulf of Alaska: an inlet of the Pacific Ocean in the south of Alaska, USA.

Gulf of Bothnia: shallow, island-strewn sea north of the Baltic Sea, between Sweden and Finland.

Gulf of Campeche: inlet of the Gulf of Mexico on the south-east shoreline of Mexico.

Gulf of Genoa: in the Ligurian Sea which is an inlet of the Mediterranean Sea, this gulf is extensive and takes in the Italian Riviera in a sweep of 90 miles (145 km).

Gulf of Mexico: large inlet of the Atlantic Ocean and connected to it by the Florida Strait, with another link via the Yucatan Strait to the Caribbean Sea.

Gulf of Oman: inlet of the Arabian Sea, linked to the Persian Gulf by the Strait of Hormuz.

Gulf of Sidra: an arm of the Mediterranean Sea stretching between Benghazi in the east to Misratah in the west, a distance of 275 miles (443 km).

Gulf of Taranto: an inlet of the Ionian Sea shaped like the arch of a foot in the Italian 'boot'.

Gulf of Thailand: large inlet of the South China Sea with a length of 370 miles (616 km) and shallow water.

Gulf of Tonkin: an arm of the South China Sea reaching into the south-east of China, where the Red river flows into its waters.

Gulf of Venezuela: an inlet of the Caribbean Sea.

Gulfport: port of entry to Mississippi state, USA, located on the Mississippi Sound and the Gulf of Mexico.

Hachinohe: city on Honshu, Japan.

Haifa: seaport in Israel located on the Bay of Acre at the base of Mount Carmel.

Haikou: on the northern coast of Hainan Island, China, on Hainan Strait which is midway between the South China Sea and the Gulf of Tonkin.

Hainan: Chinese-owned island off the south coast of the mainland.

Haiphong: seaport on the Red river delta, Vietnam.

Hakodate: port city on South Hokkaido, Japan.

Halifax: seaport capital of Nova Scotia.

Halmahera Island: largest island in the Moluccas, Indonesia.

Hamburg: seaport city on the River Elbe close to the North Sea, Germany.

Hamilton: seaport capital of Bermuda, which operates cruise ship schedules on a strict quota system for docking (never more than three vessels at a time).

Hamilton: lake port city on the western end of Lake Ontario, Canada.

Hampton Roads: a complex waterways system based on the James river (Virginia, USA) estuary and the Elizabeth and Nansemond rivers entering the estuary. The roadstead formed connects to Chesapeake Bay via the Thimble Shoal Channel.

Hardinxveld: shipbuilding town east of Rotterdam, Holland.

Harstad: chief town on Lofoten Island in north-west Norway.

Harwich: seaport on the south coast of the River Stour estuary, Essex, England.

Hauraki Gulf: on the eastern approaches to Auckland harbour, with several islands within its area nestling between the east coast of Auckland and the Coromandel peninsula.

Havana: seaport capital city of Cuba.

Haverton Hill-on-Tees: part of the greater Middlesbrough metropolitan area, but is located on the north bank of the River Tees and formerly engaged in shipbuilding.

Hawaiian Islands, state of the USA positioned on the main shipping routes in the Pacific Ocean. It was formerly known as the Sandwich Islands.

Hawke Bay: a wide bay on the east coast of the North Island of New Zealand in the Pacific Ocean.

Hayle: a town situated in a sheltered inlet of St Ives Bay, Cornwall, England.

Hebburn-on-Tyne: shipbuilding town four miles (6 km) below Gateshead, England.

Hebrides: grouped as the Outer and Inner Hebrides, Scotland, these islands are also known as the Western Isles.

Helder: port with a harbour protected by a granite dike six miles (10 km) in length. The town is at the northern end of the North Holland Canal, opposite Texel Island.

Helgoland: small island belonging to Germany in the North Sea, near the mouth of the River Elbe. Also spelt Heligoland.

Heligoland: see Helgoland.

Helsingor: seaport town on The Sound (Oresund) on the north-east coast of Zealand, Denmark Sometimes known as Elsinore.

Helsinki: seaport capital of Finland located in the Gulf of Finland.

Helston: a small town in Cornwall, with its parish taking in the Scilly Isles.

Herakleion: see Iraklion.

Hillyards Reef: a treacherous submerged rock outcrop off St John's, Antigua.

Hiroshima: shipbuilding city in the delta of the Ota river in south-west Honshu, Japan.

Hispaniola: second largest island in the West Indies, and situated between Cuba and Puerto Rico.

Hoboken (Belgium): shipbuilding town near Antwerp.

Hoboken (USA): town in New Jersey, USA, on the Hudson river.

Ho Chi-minh City: largest city in Vietnam and a port on the Saigon river, 50 miles (80 km) from the South China Sea and to the north of the Mekong delta.

Hog Island: shipbuilding region of Pennsylvania, USA.

Hogoleu: see Chuuk Islands.

Holmpton: a small town eight miles (13 km) north of Spurn Head on the Humber river mouth facing the North Sea.

Holyhead: seaport town on Holy Island in north-west Wales, facing Caernarvon Bay to the south and Holyhead Bay to the North, both inlets of the Irish Sea.

Honjiro Rock: treacherous rock formation in the Inland Sea of Japan near Awashima Island.

Hong Kong: an island linked to south-west mainland China by tunnels and bridges to Kowloon and the New Territories, and featuring one of the world's busiest seaports.

Honningsvag: town at the head of the Porsanger Fjord as it opens out into the Artic Ocean, Norway.

Honolulu: seaport capital of Hawaii on Oahu Island.

Hook of Holland: seaport in the Netherlands.

Horn of Africa: the name given to that east coast region of the African continent that is shaped like a rhinoceros horn and includes the countries of the Somali Republic, Djibouti and Ethiopia. Now known as Raas Caseyr.

Horta: harbour town in the Azores.

Howdon-on-Tyne: former shipbuilding centre on the River Tyne, UK.

Hua-lien: the principal harbour on Taiwan's east coast, facing the Philippine Sea.

Huang-p'u river: flows through the seaport city of Shanghai and enters the estuary of the Yangtze on the East China Sea.

Hudson River: rises in the Adirondacks and flows 370 miles (560 km) to New York city, where it enters New York Bay and the Atlantic Ocean.

Huelva: seaport city on the Gulf of Cadiz, Spain, with shipbuilding activities.

Huichon: city in North Korea midway between Dandong to the west and Hamhing in the east.

Hull: see Kingston-upon-Hull.

Humber River: formed by the estuaries of the Rivers Ouse and Trent to become a 36 mile (61 km) long navigable waterway between one mile (2 km) and eight miles (13 km) wide. Several ports are located on the its northern and southern banks, including Grimsby, Goole, Immingham and Kingston-upon-Hull, with its passage ultimately emptying into the North Sea.

Humberside: the district within Yorkshire which includes the city of Hull.

Iceland: an island state in the North Atlantic Ocean.

Igoumenitsa: seaport on the north-west coastline of Greece, east of Corfu.

Ijmuiden: city on the coast of Holland at the mouth of the North Sea Canal.

Ijzer River: see Yser river.

Iles de Lerins: a group of islands standing off the French Riviera coastline , ten miles (17 km) from Cannes. They are positioned off the Pointe de la Croisette, midway between the Gulfs of Napoule and Juan.

Ile d'Yeu: lying off the Bay of Biscay coastline of western France and 50 miles (83 km) south-west of Nantes.

Ilheus: seaport on Ilheus Bay near the mouth of the Cachoeira river and east of the town of Itabuna, 150 miles (250 km) south of Salvador, Brazil.

Imabari: seaport town in the north-west of Shikoku, Japan, facing the Kurushima Strait on the Inland Sea.

Imbui Bay: is at the entrance to Rio de Janeiro's natural harbour on the Atlantic coastline of south-east Brazil.

Inchon: seaport city on the Yellow Sea in South Korea.

Indus River: flows 1,700 miles (2,880 km) from Tibet across Pakistan to the Arabian Sea.

Inhambane: seaport town in south-east Mozambique on Inhambane Bay, an inlet of the Mozambique Channel flowing into the Indian Ocean.

Inishtrahull: an island lying six miles from Malin Head in the Republic of Ireland, with the Inishtrahull Sound separating the two.

Inland Sea of Japan: sheltered, island-strewn sea bounded by the islands of Honshu to the north, Shikoku and Kyushu in the south, and giving access to several major ports.

Innoshima: shipbuilding seaport city on a small offshore island in the Hiroshima prefecture on Honshu, Japan.

Invergordon: seaport on the north side of the Cromarty Firth, 12 miles (19 km) north-east of Dingwall, Scotland.

Inverkeithing: town on the Firth of Forth and engaged in shipbreaking activities.

Iraklion: main port of Crete, Greece, positioned on the Gulf of Iraklion, an arm of the Aegean Sea. It is also known as Herakleion.

Ise Bay: a large inlet of the Pacific Ocean in Honshu, Japan. The city of Nagoya is located at the head of the bay.

Islay: a part of the group of Inner Hebrides, off the west coast of Scotland.

Isle of Lewis: the largest of the islands in the Outer Hebrides, Scotland, surrounded by the Atlantic Ocean on the western side, with The Minch and The Little Minch to its east and south-east sides.

Isle of Man: part of the UK, separated from mainland England by 26 miles (43 km) of the Irish Sea.

Isle of Portland: a craggy peninsula jutting out from Dorset, England, into the English Channel.

Isle of Wight: island lying just off the English coastline in the English Channel, with the Solent and Spithead separating the island from the county of Hampshire, UK.

Ismail: see Izmail.

Istanbul: seaport city on the Golden Horn peninsula at the entry of the Bosphorus into the Sea of Marmara, Turkey.

Iwo Jima: a Japanese island 700 miles (1,170 km) south-east of Tokyo.

Izmail: Russian naval base on the Danube delta in Bessarabia, Ukraine, near the Romanian border. It is also known as Ismail.

Izmir: city at the head of the Gulf of Izmir, Turkey.

Jacksonville: shipbuilding port city on the St John's river, Florida, USA, 20 miles (33 km) from the river mouth on the Atlantic eastern coastline.

Jakarta: major city of Indonesia. It is also known as Djakarta.

Jakobstadt: port town on the Gulf of Bothnia, Finland.

James River: Virginia USA's outlet to Chesapeake Bay for shipping, with the main port being Richmond.

Jarrow: town on the south side of the Tyne river, north-east England.

Java Sea: bordered by Sumatra to the west, Java to the south, Borneo to the north and the Flores Sea to the east.

Jebel Ali: seaport 22 miles (38 km) from Dubai, United Arab Emirates.

Jeddah: seaport in Saudi Arabia, located on the Red Sea, and is the port servicing Mecca. It is also spelt Jiddah.

Jiddah: see Jeddah.

Johnstone Bay: in Prince William Sound, Alaska, an inlet of the Gulf of Alaska.

Johnstone Strait: channel entrance into Prince William Sound, Alaska.

Juelsminde: coastal town on Denmark's mainland at the south-west end of the Kattegat.

Juneau: city capital of Alaska and located on the Gastineau Channel and in sheltered water, with a number of islands between the city and the Pacific Ocean.

Kalamantan: port town on the South China Sea in the Indonesian portion of the island of Borneo.

Kaliningrad: a large city ceded to the Russians under the 1945 Potsdam Agreement. It is connected by a 20 mile (31 km) canal to an outer port on the Baltic Sea.

Kamatero: town on the east coast of Salamis Island, opposite Piraeus.

Kanawha River: important river flowing through West Virginia, USA, which has spawned shipbuilding industries in centres such as Charleston, etc.

Kaohsiung: major seaport in south-west Taiwan engaged in shipbreaking operations.

Karachi: situated on the Arabian Sea close to the Indus delta, Pakistan.

Karm Island: at the mouth of the Bokn Fjord, which opens to the North Sea.

Kattegat: stretch of water from the North Sea to the Baltic Sea, separating Denmark from Sweden.

Kau yi Chau: an island in Hong Kong Island, just west of Green Island.

Kawajiri: shipbuilding town east of Hiroshima, Japan.

Kearny: shipbuilding town in New Jersey, USA.

Keelung: seaport city on the East China Sea coast of north Taiwan.

Kent: a county of England which borders the English Channel and the estuaries of the Thames and Medway rivers.

Kefallinia: see Cephallinia.

Keppel Harbour: Singapore's harbour, lying between Brani and Sentosa islands.

Keratzini: just north of Athen's port, Piraeus, and also known as Keratsinion.

Key West: city on the last island in the Florida Keys which extend out into the Straits of Florida for 140 miles (240 km).

Khabarovsk: city on the Amur river in eastern Russia.

Khalkis: see Chalkis.

Khania: lies in a sheltered bay on the western end of Crete, Greece, facing into the Sea of Crete.

Khawr Fakkar: a natural port for Sharjah, United Arab Emirates.

Kholmsk: shipbuilding town in the south-west of Sakhalin Island, Russia, situated at the junction of Tartary Strait and the La Perouse Strait.

Kiel: shipbuilding city in Germany.

Kiel Canal: a 60 mile (98 km) canal in Germany connecting the Elbe river estuary on the North Sea with the Baltic Sea.

Kilbrannan Sound: an arm of the North Channel on the eastern side of the peninsula of Kintyre, Scotland.

Kinderdjik: shipbuilding port in Holland.

Kingston-upon-Hull: former shipbuilding seaport on the River Humber at the junction with the River Hull.

Kinsale: small fishing port in County Cork, Republic of Ireland.

Kintyre: a peninsula extending down the west coast of Scotland into the North Channel, which is an arm of the Atlantic Ocean.

Kiribati: an island in the west-central Pacific Ocean comprising a main island and numerous islets extending north to Fanning Atoll.

Kitakyushu: city on North Kyushu, Japan.

Kithira: see Cerigo.

Klawock: town on Prince of Wales Island, Alaska, south-east of the Gulf of Esquibel.

Kobe: seaport on Honshu, Japan and outport for Osaka.

Kochi: shipbuilding city on the island of Shikoku, Japan.

Kodiak: a city on Chiniak Bay, Kodiak Island, in Alaska, USA.

Kodiak Island: in the Gulf of Alaska, USA, and separated from the Alaskan peninsula by Shelikof Strait.

Koh Phi Phi Islands: group of islands in the Strait of Malacca, 18 miles (30 km) from the Thai mainland.

Koje: shipbuilding city in South Korea.

Kolobrzeg: harbour city on the Baltic Sea coast, 60 miles (100 km) from the massive shipbuilding centre of Szczcin.

Kotka: Finnish seaport in the Gulf of Finland, located 90 miles (150 km) east of Helsinki.

Kowloon: peninsular mainland city, part of and opposite to Hong Kong. It is joined to Hong Kong Island by tunnel, bridge and ferries.

Kraljevica: shipbuilding town south of Rijeka on the Adriatic Sea coast of Croatia.

Krimpen: shipbreaking and building town east of Rotterdam, Holland.

Krung Thep: see Bangkok.

Kuala Lumpur: major city of Malaysia, with access to port facilities 29 miles (48 km) away at Port Kelang on the Strait of Malacca.

Kuching: a port city on the Sarawak river, and capital of Sarawak, Malaysia.

Kudamasta: a shipbuilding town established on a deep water cove on the Inland Sea of Japan, with shelter provided by Kasado Island six miles (10 km) south-east of Tokuyama.

Kure: seaport city in south-west Honshu, Japan, engaged in shipbuilding.

Kuressaare, town on the east coast of Saaremaa Island in the Gulf of Riga, Baltic Sea.

Kuwait: capital city of Kuwait, with a natural harbour on the Persian Gulf.

Kyle of Lochalsh: village port on mainland Scotland at the north-west entrance to Loch Alsh and immediately opposite the Isle of Skye, less than one mile (1.6 km) distant.

Kyungnam: shipping operations is a major activity in this South Korean city.

Laaland Island: see Lolland Island.

La Ciotat: port city on the Mediterranean Sea, 15 miles (25 km) east of Marseille, France.

La Guaira: seaport in Venezuela servicing the capital, Caracas, seven miles (13 km) inland.

Lake Huron: one of the Great Lakes of North America, with shorelines in both the USA and Canada.

Lake Michigan: third largest of the Great Lakes and entirely within the USA boundaries. It is linked to Lake Huron by the Straits of Mackinac.

La Manche: the French name for the English Channel.

Lampedusa Island: largest of the Pelagi Island group, owned by Italy and lying between Tunisia and Malta.

Landskrona: shipbuilding seaport on the Ore Sund, south-west Sweden.

Lantao Island: see Lantau Island.

Lantau Island: was a part of the New Territories of the British Crown Colony of Hong Kong, but has now been absorbed into the control of China. This island is six miles (10 km) west of Hong Kong Island.

La Pallice: small coastal town facing the Bay of Biscay and west of La Rochelle, France.

La Paz: town on the east coast of Baja, California, facing the Gulf of California.

La Perouse Strait: a water separation between Sakhalin and Hokkaido islands, which is ice-bound during winter and is a highly complex navigation region owing to its strong marine currents.

La Rochelle: town capital of the Charente Maritime Department on the Bay of Biscay, France.

Larvik: seaport south-west of Oslo, Norway.

La Seyne: shipbuilding town near Toulon, France. It is also referred to as La Seyne-sur-Mer.

La Seyne-sur-Mer: see La Seyne.

Las Palmas: chief seaport of the Canary Islands in the north-east of Gran Canaria.

La Spezia: seaport on the Bay of Spezia in the Ligurian province of north-west Italy.

Laurium: shipbreaking seaport town on the Aegean Sea, sheltered by Makronisos Island and Cape Sounion, to the south of Athens.

Lauzon: shipbuilding town on the southern bank of the St Lawrence river, four miles (7 km) from the city of Quebec on the opposite bank.

Lavrion: see Laurium.

Leer: a town three miles (5 km) from the River Ems, Germany.

Leghorn: see Livorno.

Le Havre: seaport on the English Channel at the mouth of the River Seine in northern France.

Leith: outport for Edinburgh, capital of Scotland.

Leixoes: outer harbour serving Oporto, Portugal, lying 12 miles (20 km) to the south-east.

Lena Point: this headland lies 31 miles (52 km) north of Juneau, jutting out into an area where sudden incoming tides can be treacherous.

Leningrad: see St Petersberg.

Lerwick: built around a natural harbour basin, this, the main town in the Shetland Islands, is 130 miles (212 km) north of the Scottish coast and is the most northern town in Britain.

Lesvos: island belonging to Greece in the Aegean Sea, off Turkey.

Le Verdon-Sur-Mer: town on the south bank of the River Gronde estuary in France.

Liberia: west African nation whose capital Monrovia is a specialist ship registration city and a free port.

Lilla Edet: town connected with the shipbuilding industry on the banks of the Gota river, Sweden.

Limassol: seaport city on the south coast of Cyprus with an artificial harbour carved into Akrotiri Bay.

Linz: industrial river port on the River Danube in Austria.

Lisbon: attractive capital city of Portugal with a fine natural harbour, situated eight miles (14 km) from the mouth of the River Tagus.

Littlehampton: seaport town at the mouth of the River Arun, which runs through west Sussex into the English Channel.

Little Minch: passage of water separating the Inner and Outer Hebrides in Scotland.

Liverpool: UK seaport on the norther banks of the River Mersey and once a major facility for the Atlantic passenger liners.

Livorno: seaport capital of Livorno province, Italy. It was formerly known as Leghorn.

Livorno Roads: an area off Livorno in the Bay of Livorno where oceangoing ships can be moored while awaiting berths.

Loano: town lying on the Gulf of Genoa, Italy.

Lodose: town on the banks of the Gota river, Sweden.

Loire River: arising in the Cevennes Mountains and flowing 600 miles (1,000 km) to the Atlantic Ocean where its mouth is in the Bay of Biscay.

Lolland Island, lying in the Baltic Sea, this island is the third largest in Denmark. It is also known as Laaland Island.

London: capital of the UK, formerly a major port.

Londonderry: shipbuilding city on the left bank of the River Foyle, Northern Ireland.

Long Bay: an inlet of the Tasman Sea within the south-east metropolitan suburbs of Sydney, Australia.

Long Beach: resort and exhibition area of Los Angeles, California, USA.

Long Island: an island containing the New York city boroughs of Brooklyn and Queens and separated from the mainland by the East river.

Long Point: a promontory into the Pacific Ocean from the South Island, New Zealand coastline between Dunedin and Bluff.

Longsand Head: promontory on the east coast of England near Harwich.

L'Orient: shipbuilding seaport on the Atlantic coast of north-west France.

Los Angeles: seaport city in southern California, USA, with a fine harbour.

Louisiana: a southern state of the USA with a coastline on the Gulf of Mexico.

Lourenco Marques: see Maputo.

Lowestoft: shipbuilding seaport in Suffolk on the East Anglian coast of the North Sea, at the mouth of the River Waveney.

Lubeck: seaport on the Baltic Sea at the mouth of the Trave river, Germany.

Luda: a special municipality in South Liaoning province comprising Port Arthur and Talien (formerly Dairen), and engaged in shipbuilding. Port Arthur's name changed to Lushun prior to the formation of the new municipality.

Luderitz Bay: a ship shelter on the Atlantic coast of Namibia.

Ludington: city on the east coast of Lake Michigan and linked by ferry to Manitowoc in Wisconsin.

Lundy Island: a wildlife santuary island in the Bristol Channel, England, and 12 miles (20 km) north-west of Hartland Point.

Lungga Point: headland on the Sealark Channel close to Honiara, capital of the Solomon Islands in the Pacific Ocean.

Lushun: see Luda.

Luzon: northernmost and largest of the Philippines with its capital being Manila.

Lys River: a waterway in Belgium joining the River Scheldt at Ghent.

Mackay: port city on the Coral Coast of Queensland, Australia,

Madeira Islands: a group of four islands in the North Atlantic Ocean which belong to Portugal. They are positioned 400 miles (670 km) to the west of Morocco and 300 miles (500 km) north of the Canary Islands.

Madras: seaport city on the Coromandel coast in the Bay of Bengal, India. See Tamil Nadu.

Maiguru: near Kyoto, Japan.

Majorca: see Mallorca.

Malabar: name of a Sydney, Australia, suburb, eight miles (13 km) from downtown Sydney, and named after a ship disaster in 1931.

Malin Head: the northernmost point of the Republic of Ireland, situated in the county of Donegal.

Mallorca: largest of the Balearic Islands, Spain, separated from the Spanish mainland by the Balearic Sea, while its eastern shores are washed by the Mediterranean Sea.

Malmo: shipbuilding seaport city in Sweden at the southern end of the Oresund, which separates the Kattegat from the Baltic Sea.

Malta: independent island state in the Mediterranean, 56 miles (93 km) south of Sicily.

Manchester Ship Canal: opened in 1894, this man-made link between Eastham, Cheshire, and Salford docks near Manchester allowed oceangoing ships to navigate from the Mersey river to Manchester along a 36 mile (58 km) waterway equipped with five locks.

Mangalore: seaport city on the west coast of India, facing into an area where the Arabian Sea and the Indian Ocean meet.

Manila: seaport city on south-west Luzon, Philippines.

Maputo: seaport capital of Mozambique, at the head of Delagoa Bay, with a natural harbour. Formerly known as Lourenco Marques.

Marghera: shipbuilding town within the environs of Venice, Italy.

Maricas Island: lies off the Atlantic coast of Brazil, outside Rio de Janeiro.

Mariehamn: seaport capital of Ahvenanmaan province on the island of Aland in the Baltic Sea, west of Helsinki.

Marina di Carrara: port and beach resort town, south-west of Carrara.

Marseilles: seaport city in southern France on the Mediterranean Sea.

Masella Reef: in the Arafura Sea north of Darwin, Australia.

Massawa: seaport town with an excellent harbour on the Red Sea, Ethiopia.

Matadi: an inland port some 93 miles (155 km) upstream from the Atlantic Ocean and constructed on the banks of the Congo (Zaire) river, opposite the town of Vivi, Zaire.

Matsuyama: seaport city in Japan.

Maud Island: at the entrance to the Seymour Narrows at the north end of Queen Charlotte Strait, Canada.

Mauritius: independent island state of the Commonwealth in the Indian Ocean, 480 miles (800 km) east of Madagascar.

Mayaguez: seaport city on Puerto Rico.

Mecca: holy city in Saudi Arabia to which Islamic pilgrims flock annually.

Mechanics Bay: situated within Auckland's Waitemata harbour. It was formerly of note as the New Zealand terminal for flying boats in the 1930s and 1940s, and for vehicular ferry traffic from the south to the north shore. Today it is involved with container ship movements at Fergusson Wharf.

Medina: the second most important holy city in Saudi Arabia, situated 100 miles (170 km) to the east of its port on the Red Sea, Yanbu'al Bahr.

Medway River: river in Kent, England.

Melbourne: port city and capital of Victoria, Australia. It is the terminus for the Bass Strait ferries to Tasmania.

Melos: this is the most southern of the Cyclades Islands group in the Aegean Sea.

Menam Chao Phraya River: flows into the Gulf of Thailand after passing through Bangkok.

Mersey river: formed by two headstreams in the Pennines and then flows west to Manchester where it enters the man-made Manchester Ship Canal to facilitate safe navigation for the next 36 miles (58 km). It continues to Runcorn where it develops into the River Mersey estuary, an inlet of the Irish Sea.

Messina: seaport city on the northeastern tip of Sicily, opposite Reggio di Calabria on the Strait of Messina.

Miami: city at the mouth of the Miami river, emptying into Biscayne Bay, Florida, USA.

Middle Sands: a sandbar in the River Humber opposite Alexandra Dock.

Middlesbrough: seaport city on the south side of the Tees estuary in the county of Cleveland, England.

Mihara: seaport city at the mouth of the Nuta river, at the Bingo Channel of the Inland Sea of Japan, on the island of Honshu.

Mikonos: see Mykonos.

Mikurajima: town on Mikuka Island in the Pacific Ocean, due south of Tokyo.

Milford Haven: seaport in Wales with shipbreaking operations, south of St George's Channel.

Millwall: suburb in London's dockyards area.

Minch: see The Minch.

Mine Head: coastal town three miles (5 km) south of Helvick Head in County Waterford, Republic of Ireland, and seven miles (12 km) from the seaport of Dungarvan.

Milos: see Melos.

Miranda Point: a cliffy inlet on the eastern coastline of Sydney, Australia.

Mississippi River: rises near Lake Itasca in north Minnesota, USA, and flows for 2,256 miles (3,760 km) until it enters the Gulf of Mexico as a delta.

Mistaken Point: a headland at the extreme south-east corner of Newfoundland, and 60 miles (100 km) south of St John's.

Mitohama Beach: resort near Osezaki, Japan.

Mobile: shipbuilding city and only seaport in Alabama, USA, at the mouth of the Mobile river, emptying into Mobile Bay.

Mobile Bay: an inlet of the Gulf of Mexico and the point of entry by the Mobile river to the open sea.

Mobile River: formed by the confluence of the Tombigbee and Alabama rivers, and entering the open sea via Mobile Bay, Alabama, USA.

Mohammedia: seaport city in north-west Morocco on the Atlantic Ocean, 15 miles (24 km) north-east of Casablanca.

Moko Hinau Island: lies off Whangerei in the far north of the North Island, New Zealand.

Monaco: principality on the Mediterranean Sea between France and Italy.

Mona Island: situated in the centre of the Mona Passage, 45 miles (70 km) west of the seaport of Mayaguez, Puerto Rico.

Mona Passage: a strait separating Puerto Rico from Hispaniola.

Monfalcone: shipbuilding town on the Adriatic Sea in north-east Italy.

Monrovia: Situated at the mouth of the St Paul river on the Atlantic Ocean, this capital of Liberia is a much-favoured port of registration for shipping.

Monte Carlo: the resort town of Monaco.

Montevideo: seaport capital of Uruguay, positioned on the River de la Plata.

Montreal: port city of Quebec, Canada, situated at the confluence of the St Lawrence and Ottawa rivers.

Morecambe: former shipbreaking port town in north Lancashire, England, standing on the south shore of Morecambe Bay.

Morecambe Bay: an wide inlet of the Irish Sea bounded north and south by Barrow-in-Furness and Fleetwood, England, respectively.

Mosbach: town in Germany which acts as headquarters for Operation Mobilisation ships.

Moscow: capital of Russia and situated on the Moskva river. It is connected to a seaport via the 76 mile (128 km)-long Moscow–Volga Canal, built in 1937.

Mostyn: small town on a creek tributary of the River Dee estuary,

Mount Desert Island: an island in Frenchman Bay on the Atlantic coast of southeastern Maine, USA.

Mozambique: positioned on the east coast of Africa with excellent seaports.

Mozambique Channel: a strait in the Indian Ocean separating Madagascar from the African mainland. It is 960 miles (1,600 km) long, and with a width varying between 240 miles (400 km) and 580 miles (960 km).

Mozambique Current: a warm ocean current flowing north-to-south along the east coast of Mozambique and Natal.

Muaco: seaport on the Caribbean coastline in northern Venezuela.

Mudros: seaport on the Greek island of Lemnos in the Aegean Sea.

Muggiaano: shipbuilding port in the Gulf of Trieste near Trieste city.

Mull: an island in the Hebrides off the west coast of Scotland, from which it is separated by the Sound of Mull and the Firth of Lorne.

Mull of Galloway: a promontory into Luce Bay off the district of Galloway, Scotland.

Mumbai: seaport capital of Maharashtra, India. It was formerly known as Bombay.

Murmansk: an ice-free, shipbuilding port on the Kola peninsula in the Barents Sea, north Russia.

Muroran: town on Chikiu Cap at the northern entrance to Touchiura Bay, Hokkaido, Japan.

Mustique: island in the St Vincent and Grenadines group in the Atlantic Ocean, skirting the edge of the Caribbean Sea.

Myanmar: the new name for Burma.

Mykonos: an island in the Cyclades group of Greek islands in the Aegean Sea.

Mytiline: seaport city on the island of Lesvos, Greece, in the Aegean Sea.

Nador: small port town on the Bou Areg Lagoon on the Mediterranean coastline of northeastern Morocco.

Nagasaki: seaport located on a narrow peninsula on the island of Kyushu, Japan.

Nagoya: the third city of Japan and a major port located on Ise Bay in central Honshu.

Naha: seaport city capital of Okinawa, Japan.

Nakhodka: seaport city on the Sea of Japan and the outport for Vladivostok, Russia.

Nakskov: seaport engaged in shipbuilding on Lolland Island, Denmark.

Nantes: seaport city on the River Loire, western France, with the ocean port of St Nazaire on the Atlantic coast 30 miles (50 km) distant. Both cities are involved in shipbuilding operations.

Napa: positioned at the head of the navigable part of the Napa river, California, USA, this city is world-renowned for its wine production. It has been a small port but now relies heavily upon the newly-created seaport of Vallejo, 20 miles (33 km) to the south.

Naples: seaport city on the Bay of Naples, Italy, at the foot of Mount Vesuvius.

Narragansett Bay: an active shipping area on an inlet of the North Atlantic Ocean extending from Rhode Island Sound.

Narvik: ice-free port sheltered by the Lofoten Islands in north-west Norway.

Nash Point: a headland in the Bristol Channel on the south coast of Wales, between Swansea and Cardiff.

Nassau: a port city on the island of Paradise in the Bahamas, 213 miles (350 km) south-east of Miami.

Natal: province of South Africa with a coastline on the Indian Ocean.

Natauna Islands: an Indonesian group of islands in the South China Sea, north-west of Borneo.

Nauplia: port town on the east coast of the Peloponnesus, Greece.

Nauru: independent republic in the Pacific Ocean.

Nazare: seaport fishing town on the Atlantic coastline of Portugal.

Naze: Japanese shipbuilding city on the East China Sea side of Kagoshima, and midway between Okinawa and the Japanese mainland.

Negra Point: headland in Luzon, Philippines.

Nelson: a city at the northern extremity of the South Island of New Zealand.

Neustadt: canal port town on the River Haardt in the Rheinland region of Germany.

New Brunswick: eastern province of Canada.

Newcastle: a seaport north of the central coast of New South Wales, Australia. It lies at the mouth of the Hunter river, 108 miles (180 km) north of Sydney.

Newcastle-upon-Tyne: seaport on the north bank of the River Tyne and ten miles (16 km) from the North Sea, lying along the north-east coast of England.

New Ferry: suburb of Liverpool, England, formerly involved in shipbreaking operations.

New Jersey: a state of the USA adjacent to New York.

New London: deep water seaport in southeastern Connecticut, USA, at the mouth of the Thames river on Long Island Sound.

New Orleans: seaport in the state of Louisiana, located on the Mississippi delta, USA.

Newport: situated on the River Usk five miles (8 km) from its mouth, in the Gwent district of Wales.

Newport News: seaport city in Virginia, USA, on the James river estuary.

Newquay: town on the north Cornish coast of England, facing the Atlantic Ocean.

New York: seaport city on New York Bay at the mouth of the Hudson river, USA.

Nice: seaport capital of the Alpes Maritimes Department, France, in the French Riviera.

Nicobar Islands: see Andaman and Nicobar Islands.

Nieuwe Waterweg (New Waterway): ship canal connecting the River Lek, seven miles (11 km) below Rotterdam, to the North Sea coast at the Hook of Holland.

Niigata: seaport city on the west coast of Honshu, Japan.

Niihama: an industrial city on the Inland Sea coast of Shikoku, Japan.

Nikolayev: port city located at the estuary of the Dneiper and Bug river systems near Odessa, in the Black Sea.

Ninety Mile Beach: an almost unbroken stretch of beach running from 50 miles (84 km) north-east of Wilsons Promontory to Cape Conran, Victoria, Australia.

Nizhny Novgorod: city in western Russia standing on the banks of the confluence of the Volga and Oka rivers. It was formerly known as Gorky.

Normandy: province of France on the English Channel.

North Goodwin Sands: dangerous sandbanks in the English Channel off the east coast of Kent, England.

North Point: in Long Bay just west of Boora Point in Sydney city, Australia.

North Reef: situated 30 miles (50 km) from Rockhampton, Queensland, Australia.

North Sea: bound by the coastlines of Great Britain to the east, Germany, Norway and Denmark to the west, and Holland, France and Belgium to the south.

Northumberland Strait: a crescent-shaped stretch of sea separating Prince Edward Island from Nova Scotia and New Brunswick, Canada, and entering the Gulf of St Lawrence at either end of Prince Edward Island.

North Vancouver: a shipbuilding area of Vancouver city, British Columbia, Canada.

North-West Ledges: a navigation hazard at the northern end of Brier Island in the Bay of Fundy, Nova Scotia, Canada.

Northwest Providence Channel: a sea channel south of Freeport, Great Bahama Island, separating the Straits of Florida from the Atlantic Ocean.

Nova Scotia: eastern maritime province, Canada.

Novorossiisk: seaport on the north-east coast of the Black Sea in Russia.

Numakuma: shipbuilding city six miles (10 km) east of Mihara, located on the Inland Sea of Japan.

Nystad: town in Finland.

Oakland: extension of the greater metropolitan area of San Francisco, California USA.

Odense: shipbuilding seaport on the island of Fyn, Denmark, and connected to the Baltic Sea to the south by the Fehmarns Belt and the North Sea to the north by the Kattegat and Skagerrak.

Odessa: seaport city on the Black Sea coast, Ukraine.

Oita: seaport city on Beppu Bay on north-west Kyushu, Japan.

Okinawa: strategic group of islands governed by Japan since 1972.

Oland: island in the Baltic Sea close to the Swedish coastline.

Old Head of Kinsale: prominent headland jutting well out to sea, five miles (8 km) south of Kinsale harbour, County Cork, Republic of Ireland.

Onomichi: shipbuilding town east of Hiroshima and situated on an island-strewn part of the Inland Sea.

Oporto: also known as Porto, this seaport along the Douro river, two miles (3 km) from its mouth, is the second major city of Portugal. There is also an artificial deep water harbour on the Atlantic coast at Porto de Leixoes, north-west of the city.

Oran: see Ouahran.

Oregon: state of the USA located in the north-west.

Ore Sund: a strait separating Sweden from Denmark.

Orkney Islands: a group of 68 islands, north-east of the Scottish mainland.

Osaka: capital city of Honshu, Japan, built on the shallow Osaka Bay.

Osezaki: town on Nakadari Island in the East China Sea, standing off Nagasaki.

Oskarshamn: town on the Kalmarsund opposite the northern tip of Oland Island and on the western fringe of the Baltic Sea, Sweden.

Oslo: seaport capital of Norway situated at the head of Oslo Fjord.

Otago Heads: at the entrance to the deep water inlet of Port Chalmers, which serves as a port for Dunedin in the South Island of New Zealand.

Otaru: seaport city on Hokkaido, Japan.

Ouahran: seaport in northern Algeria on the Mediterranean Sea.

Outer Hebrides: remote island group off the Scottish mainland, and which stretch for 130 miles (212 km) in length from Barra Head Island in the south to Lewis Island in the north.

Owen Sound: Lake port town on south-west Georgian Bay, Lake Huron, Canada.

Owers Lightship: stands off Selsey Bill, Sussex, England.

Oxnard: a city between Santa Barbara and Los Angeles, California, USA which is serviced for shipping by Port Hueneme on the Pacific Ocean coastline.

Padang: seaport city on the west coast of Sumatra.

Palermo: seaport city at the head of the Bay of Palermo on Sicily's north-west coast, engaged in shipbuilding.

Pallion: former shipyard of Sunderland, UK.

Palma de Mallorca, seaport on Mallorca Island, Spain.

Palm Beach: town in Florida, USA.

Pampatar: seaport town on Margarita Island in northern Venezuela.

Panama: a Central American country featuring the Panama Canal for quick transit from the Caribbean Sea/Atlantic Ocean to the Pacific Ocean. It is a favoured country of registration for shipping.

Papenburg: shipbuilding town 24 miles (40 km) inland from Emden and situated on the banks of the deep water River Ems.

Para: see Belem.

Paris: capital city of France on the River Seine, 106 miles (176 km) from its mouth where the seaport of Le Havre is situated.

Paroikia: see Paros.

Paros: seaport capital of Paros Island in the Cyclades Islands group in the Aegean Sea. It is also known as Paroikia.

Pasajes: small coastal town equidistant between San Sebastian, Spain, and the Spain–France border.

Pascagoula: a shipbuilding and fishing seaport city on Pascagoula Bay of Mississippi Sound at the mouth of the Pascagoula river: Mississippi, USA.

Paternoster Point: a headland 60 miles (100 km) north of Capetown, South Africa.

Patras: seaport capital of the province of Akhaia, Greece.

Peacock Sat: a shipwrecking bar in the Columbia river near Portland, Oregon, USA.

Peloponnesus: the second major land mass that makes up Greece. It was originally joined to the mainland, but artificially made an island when the Corinth Canal was constructed.

Pembroke: small port town at the eastern reach of Milford Haven, Wales.

Pembrokeshire: see Dyfed.

Penang: an island at the northern end of the Strait of Malacca and standing offshore from mainland Malaysia, at a distance of two and a half miles (4 km) at the narrowest point.

Peniche: town located near Lisbon, Portugal, and within sight of Farilhoes Rocks.

Perama Bay: inlet upon which the port of Piraeus is built, serving Athens.

Perim Island: owned by Yemen, this island is in the Strait of Beb-el-Mandeb at the southern entrance to the Red Sea.

Persian Gulf: head of a large inlet from the Arabian Sea through the Gulf of Oman and the Strait of Hormuz.

Perth: city capital of Western Australia, with its port outlet being Fremantle, seven miles (12 km) distant on the Indian Ocean.

Perth Amboy: port on Raritan Bay at the mouth of the Raritan river, New Jersey, USA.

Philadelphia: port city on the Delaware river, Pennsylvania, USA, and active in shipbuilding operations.

Phillippeville: see Skikda.

Phuket: a resort island in southwestern Thailand in the Andaman Sea.

Picton: a deep water port in the Marlborough Sounds of north-east South Island on Waitohi Bay, which is an extension of Queen Charlotte Sound off Davis Strait. The latter finds its way to Cook Strait between the South and North Islands of New Zealand.

Piraeus: seaport city on Perama Bay in the Saronic Gulf serving Athens, five miles (8 km) distant, and occupied with shipbuilding and shipbreaking operations.

Plymouth: seaport in Devon, England.

Point Arguello: a promontory 140 miles (240 km) north-west of Los Angeles, California, USA, on the Pacific coastline.

Pointe-Noire: deep water port city in the Republic of Congo.

Porquerolles Island: an island in the Mediterranean Sea off the southern coast of France, 25 miles (41 km) from Toulouse.

Porsangen Fjord: located at the extreme northern tip of Norway on the Arctic Ocean, this inlet of the Barents Sea extends into the coastline a distance of 80 miles (130 km).

Port Adelaide: deep water port facilities for Adelaide, South Australia.

Port Alma: a town on Keppel Bay, 18 miles (30 km) south of Rockhampton, Queensland, Australia.

Port Arthur: see Luda.

Port aux Basques: see Channel-Port aux Basques.

Port Bacares: lying in the south of France on the shores of the Gulf of Lion, Mediterranean Sea, some 12 miles (20 km) from Perpignan.

Port de Bouc: shipbuilding town 18 miles (30 km) west of Marseilles, France, in the Gulf of Lion.

Port Dickson: coastal town in south-west Malaysia adjacent to the Malacca Straits.

Porter Reef: town on an island cluster lying off the British Columbia shoreline, Canada, on the Queen Charlotte Sound, 270 miles (450 km) north of Vancouver.

Port Gore: an inlet of Cook Strait into the northern tip of the South Island of New Zealand, near Cape Jackson.

Port Hedland: small port town 900 miles (1,500 km) north of Perth, Western Australia.

Port Hueneme: a seaport especially developed to service the growing city of Oxnard, California, USA, which is 45 miles (75 km) north-west of Los Angeles. The port is on the Santa Barbara Channel and opposite Santa Cruz Island.

Port Kelang: major seaport of Malaysia servicing Kuala Lumpur, 29 miles (48 km) east. It is also known as Port Swettenham.

Portland: seaport city in Oregon state, USA

Portland Bill: at the southern tip of the Isle of Portland. It juts out into the English Channel from the Dorset coast, England.

Portland Island: an island lying off the Mahia peninsula, situated at the northern end of Hawke Bay, New Zealand.

Port Louis: seaport capital of Mauritius in the Indian Ocean.

Porto: see Oporto.

Porto de Leixoes: an artificial deep water harbour on the Atlantic coast, just north-west of Oporto, Portugal.

Port of Spain: seaport capital city of Trinidad.

Port Phillip Bay: large bay almost landlocked with Melbourne, Australia, at its head in the north and Geelong city in the west, with a narrow opening of one and three-quarter miles (3 km) into the Bass Strait.

Port Royal: small port town on the south coast of Jamaica, featuring a natural harbour halfway between the city port of Kingston and the Caribbean Sea.

Port Said: seaport city at the northern end of the Suez Canal, Egypt.

Port Sudan: port city, often referred to as Bur-Sudan, in the southern Sudan in the region known as Nubia.

Port Swettenham: see Port Kelang.

Poulo Condor: seaport town in southern Chile in the Magellan and Antarctic region.

Pratas Island: island near a notorious reef in the South China Sea, midway between Hong Kong and the Philippines.

Prince Edward Island: eastern province of Canada.

Prince of Wales Island: in the Northwest Territories of Canada and lying among numerous islands south of the Arctic Ocean. Prince of Wales Island is separated from Victoria Island to its west by the M'Clintock Channel, Somerset Island to its east by Peel Sound, Boothia Peninsula to its south-east by the Franklin Strait and King William Island to its south by Larsen Sound.

Prince William Sound: an inlet of the Gulf of Alaska where the ports of Valdez and Cordova are located.

Puerto Cabello: seaport with excellent harbour on the Caribbean Sea coastline near Valencia, north Venezuela.

Puerto Ordaz: see Ciudad Guayana.

Puerto Rico: a territory of the USA, 1,000 miles (1,650 km) south of Florida.

Puget Sound: inlet of the Pacific Ocean near Seattle, Washington state, USA.

Pula: on the Adriatic Sea coast of Croatia and engages in shipbuilding operations.

Pusan: industrial city at the mouth of the Naktong river which empties into the Korean Strait.

Quebec: seaport capital of Quebec province, Canada, situated on the St Lawrence river at the mouth of the St Charles river.

Queen Charlotte Sound: located at the northern approach to the Inside Passage between British Columbia's shoreline and Vancouver Island. This sound leads straight into the Pacific Ocean and is bounded by the Hecate Strait to the north and the Queen Charlotte Strait to the south.

Quincy: shipbuilding city on Boston harbour just south-west of Boston city, Massachusetts, USA.

Qui Nhon: coastal town in South Vietnam situated on Lang Mai Bay, an arm of the South China Sea.

Quito: capital city of Ecuador and lying 14 miles (24 km) south of the equator.

Raas Caseyr: see Cape Guardafui (the old name).

Rabegh: coastal town in Saudi Arabia 30 miles (50 km) south of Masturah.

Ramsgate: cross-Channel ferry port in Kent, England.

Rangoon: see Yangon.

Rarotonga: volcanic island in the South Pacific Ocean. It is the largest of the Cook Islands group which is situated 2,100 miles (3,400 km) north-east of New Zealand.

Rathlin Island: island off Fair Head, County Antrim in Northern Ireland. A lighthouse on the island is referred to by seafarers as the Rathlin Light.

Rattray Head: located on the North Sea coastline of Scotland, 30 miles (50 km) from Aberdeen.

Rauma: shipbuilding seaport on the south-west coast of Finland on the Baltic Sea.

Rebecca Shoals: dangerous shoals with a lighthouse, 46 miles (77 km) west of Key West, Florida, USA.

Recife: seaport capital of Pernambuco, Brazil.

Red River: see Song-koi.

Red Sea: a narrow sea 1,344 miles (2,240 km) long separating Africa from Arabia and entering the Indian Ocean through the Straits of Bab-el-Mandeb.

Rendova Island: part of the Solomon Islands group in the Pacific Ocean.

Rendsburg: shipbuilding town on the Eider river and the Kiel Canal, Germany.

Reykjavik: capital of Iceland and situated in the south-west.

Rijeka: seaport town on the Adriatic Sea, Croatia.

Richard's Bay: inlet of the Indian Ocean in the coastline of the Zululand region of the province of Natal, South Africa, into which the Umhlatuzi river empties.

Richmond: (1) deep water seaport in California, USA; (2) port and state capital of Virginia, USA, located on the James river.

Rijeka: shipbuilding town in Croatia.

Rio de Janeiro: seaport city in south-east Brazil, with a natural harbour in Guanabara Bay on the Atlantic coastline.

Rio de Oro: lying between Cape Blanco and Cape Bojador, which guard a very narrow inlet from the Atlantic Ocean to the port's berths on the coastline fringing the western Sahara desert.

Rio Grande: seaport eight miles (13 km) from the mouth of the Rio Grande river, Brazil, which empties into the Atlantic Ocean.

Rio Grande do Norte: state in north-east Brazil on the Atlantic Ocean.

Rio Grande River (USA): one of the longest North American rivers, stretching 1,760 miles (2,830 km) from the Rocky Mountains, Colorado, to the Gulf of Mexico where it forms a massive delta region.

Rio Palancia: a river which flows into the Mediterranean Sea north of Valencia, Spain.

Rissa: shipbuilding town near Trondheim, Norway.

Riva Tregoso: shipbuilding port near Genoa on the Gulf of Genoa, Italy.

River Dee: river in north Wales and runs for 86 miles (144 km) through Cheshire, England, and Wales to empty into Liverpool Bay.

River de la Plata: receives the waters of the Rivers Uruguay and Parana and provides seaport locations for Buenos Aires, La Plata and Montevideo.

River Elbe: rising in Riesengebirge and flowing for 690 miles (1,160 km) to Cuxhaven, Germany, on the North Sea. It is navigable for 500 miles (840 km) and is linked to the Rhine and Weser rivers by the Mittelland Canal.

River Ems: rises in the Teutoburger Wald and flows 200 miles (333 km) north to the North Sea where its estuary is at Emden.

River Lee: flows into Lough Mahon which develops into Cork harbour, in the south-east of the Republic of Ireland.

River Mersey: see Mersey river.

River Niger: meanders for 2,494 miles (4,160 km), of which 940 miles (1,600 km) is navigable.

River Nile: the longest river on the African continent at 4,002 miles (6,670 km) and under Egyptian control.

River Ota: flows through south-west Honshu, Japan and enters the Sea of Japan.

River Ottawa: a 600 mile (1,000 km)-long tributary of the St Lawrence river, Canada.

River Ouse: a 125 mile (208 km) long river formed by the Rivers Swale and Ure and emptying into the Humber estuary.

River Parana: formed by the junction of the Rivers Rio Grande and Paranaiba and flowing between Paraguay and Argentina. It is the second largest in South America after the Amazon, with a distance of 3,032 miles (4,880 km) between its rise and its convergence with the Uruguay river.

River Paranaiba: see River Parana.

River Rouge: town sited on the Detroit and Rouge rivers in Michigan state, USA.

River Stour: flows east for 40 miles (67 km) east through Suffolk and Essex to the port of Harwich, England.

River Taff: rises in the Brecon Beacons, South Wales, and flows 38 miles (64 km) to the Bristol Channel at Cardiff.

River Trent: a 140 mile-long (208 km) river flowing from the Pennines to the Humber estuary.

River Tyne: a 76 mile-long (128 km) river formed by the confluence of the North Tyne and the South Tyne rivers at Hexham. It had major shipbuilding activities along its banks near its mouth on the North Sea.

River Zaire: once the mighty Congo river, the new identity doesn't diminish the massive force of this river's rush, 2,900 miles (4,700 km) to the sea after rising in Zambia and traversing the greater part of west Central Africa.

Robben Island: situated at the entrance to Table Bay, Cape province, and once used as a penal colony.

Roca Negra Island: a rocky outcrop in the Atlantic Ocean near Vigo, Spain.

Roche-Bonne Reef: a dangerous reef lying some 50 miles (82 km) off La Rochelle in the Bay of Biscay.

Roches Point: a rocky area on the northern side of the approach to Cork harbour from the Irish Sea, Republic of Ireland.

Rockall: an uninhabited isle in the North Atlantic 220 miles (354 km) west of the Outer Hebrides, Scotland.

Rockhampton: seaport town in Queensland, Australia, and lying on the Tropic of Capricorn.

Ronne: main seaport town on the Danish island of Bornholm in the southern Baltic Sea.

Rosalie Bay: a rocky bay on Great Barrier Island, North Island, New Zealand.

Rostock: seaport lying at the head of the Warnow river estuary, eight miles (13 km) south-south-east of its Baltic Sea outlet at Warnemunde, Germany.

Rosyth: ferry port and former naval dockyard in Scotland.

Rotterdam: Europe's largest seaport on the Nieuwe Maas, part of the Rhine–Maas–Scheldt delta. The Nieuwe Waterweg (New Waterway) links the city with the outport of Europoort.

Royal Sovereign Lightship: stands off the Sussex coastline, England.

Rugen: island in the Baltic Sea off the north German coast, opposite the mainland seaport of Stralsund.

Ryotsu: town on Ryotsu Bay in Niigata Island in the Sea of Japan, 24 miles (41km) from Niigata city on the mainland.

Saaremaa: large island belonging to Estonia, the Gulf of Riga lying to its east and the Baltic Sea to its west and south-west.

Safaga: port town in the Eastern Desert region of Egypt on the Red Sea, 360 miles (600 km) south of Suez.

Sagres: town in south-west Portugal, a few miles from Cape St Vincent on the Atlantic Ocean.

Saigon: see Ho Chi-minh City.

Saigon River: wide waterway emptying into the South China Sea.

Sagunto: a town situated on the western bank of the Palancia river north-north-east of Valencia, Spain.

Saiki: town on coast of Saeki Bay on Bungo Strait between Kyushu and Honshu Islands.

St Catharines: shipbuilding city on the Welland Ship Canal, Ontario, Canada.

St Catherine's Point: one of two headlands at the entrance to False Bay in southwestern Cape Province near Simonstown, West Africa.

St Charles River: short river which converges with the St Lawrence river at Quebec city, which was built around the junction of the two waterways.

St Croix: one of the US Virgin Islands in the Caribbean Sea, 54 miles (90 km) from Puerto Rico.

St George: port town on St George Bay and capital of Grenada, West Indies.

St George Bay: a natural harbour in a submerged volcanic crater in Grenada, West Indies.

St George's Channel: running from the Irish Sea to the Atlantic Ocean and separating Ireland and Wales.

St Govans Head: headland projecting into the Irish Sea and standing at the western entrance to Carmarthen Bay, five miles (8 km) south of Pembroke, Wales.

St Helena: in the South Atlantic Ocean, together with the dependency of Ascension Island, this British island is 1,152 miles (1,920 km) from the west coast of Africa and very isolated.

Saint John: seaport capital of New Brunswick, Canada.

St John's: capital of Antigua, West Indies.

St Kilda: island in the Atlantic Ocean 42 miles (70 km) west of the Outer Hebrides group.

St Lawrence River: a navigable 2,020 mile (3,360 km) waterway from the Great Lakes of North America to the Atlantic Ocean.

St Louis: city in the state of Missouri, USA, situated on the Mississippi river, ten miles (16 km) below the confluence of the the Mississippi and the Missouri rivers.

St Malo: seaport town on the Normandy coast of north-west France.

St Nazaire: seaport shipbuilding centre on the Bay of Biscay at the mouth of the River Loire, serving as an outport for Nantes.

St Paul River: West African river flows through Liberia, with Monrovia located at its mouth on the Atlantic Ocean.

St Petersburg: seaport city of Russia at the mouth of the Neva river. It was formerly named Leningrad.

St Thomas: main island of the US Virgin Islands group in the eastern Caribbean Sea. Its harbour is the crater of an extinct volcano and the port town of Charlotte Amalie houses 80% of the island group's population.

St Vincent: one of the Windward group of West Indian Islands and an independent state.

Sakaide: town on Shikoku Island which is 72 miles (120 km) from Hiroshima across the Hiuchi Gulf.

Skaramangas: seaport town on Eleusis Bay, nine miles (15 km) from Athens, Greece.

Sakhalin Island: lies off the Siberian coastline of Russia and is surrounded by the Sea of Okhotsk to the north and west, the Tartary Strait to the west and La Perouse Strait to the south.

Salamis Island: located in the Saronic Gulf of the Aegean Sea opposite Piraeus, with the seaport town of Salamis located on the west coast.

Salerno: seaport on the Gulf of Salerno, an inlet of the Tyrrhenian Sea, Italy.

Salmaneda Reef: off the coast of Columbia.

Salonika: see Thessaloniki.

Saltwick Nab: rocky outcrop east of Whitby, east Yorkshire, and north of Saltwick Bay, England.

Samarinda: this town has a short road connection to the major port of Balikpapan, plus the ability to navigate from the Makasar Strait up the Mahakam river for 30 miles (48 km) to its own berthing facilities. It is located in southeastern Borneo.

Sambro: an island located three miles (5 km) south of the Atlantic coast of Nova Scotia, 11 miles (18 km) from Halifax.

Samsun: seaport city on the Black Sea coast of northern Turkey.

Sandefjord: shipbuilding port town at the mouth of the Oslo Fjord, south-east Norway.

San Diego: seaport city of southern California, USA, with a natural harbour, ten miles (16 km) from the Mexican border.

Sandwich Islands: see Hawaiian Islands.

Sandy Hook: a peninsula in New Jersey, USA, which projects into the lower bay of New York.

San Esteban de Pravia: shipbreaking town on the central north coast of Spain, facing the Bay of Biscay.

San Francisco: seaport on San Francisco Bay, California, USA.

San Juan: seaport city capital of Puerto Rico and built partially on an island location on the north-east coast.

San Lorenzo: capital of St Vincent.

San Miguel: in the Azores Island group.

San Miguel Island: part of the group of islands lying 40 miles (70 km) off the California, USA, Pacific coast known as the Santa Barbara Islands. San Miguel is separated from the mainland by the Santa Barbara Channel.

San Pablo Bay: at the mouth of the Napa river, 20 miles (34 km) north of San Francisco, California, USA.

San Pedro: shipbuilding seaport near Los Angeles, California, USA.

San Pedro: a shipbreaking suburb of Buenos Aires, Argentina.

San Pedro Channel: separates the Santa Barbara Islands southern group from the California, USA, Pacific coastline.

San Rocco: a town six miles (10 km) across a bay from Trieste, France, on the Gulf of Trieste.

Santa Barbara Islands: an island chain running parallel to the Pacific Ocean coastline of California, USA, extending for 150 miles (240 km) and separated from the mainland by 25–90 miles (40–145 km). The group has the Santa Barbara Channel to the north and the San Pedro Channel to the south between the islands and the mainland.

Santa Barbara Channel: separates the Santa Barbara Islands northern group from the California, USA, Pacific coastline.

Santa Catalina Island: one of the Santa Barbara Islands lying off Los Angeles, California, USA, at a distance of 22 miles (35 km) from the Pacific coast.

Santa Cruz de Tenerife: well-harboured seaport on Tenerife, part of the Canary Islands group, Spain.

Santa Margarita Island: island lying off the Pacific coast of Baja California, Mexico.

Santa Monica: beachside suburb west of Los Angeles on Santa Monica Bay, California, USA.

Santander: resort and seaport city in northern Spain on the Bay of Biscay.

Santos: seaport serving Sao Paulo, Brazil, on the Atlantic coast.

Santo Tome de la Guayana: see Ciudad Guayana.

Sao Paulo: a city of Brazil, 200 miles (338 km) south-west of Rio de Janeiro.

Sarawak: state of Malaysia occupying the eastern and northern areas of the island of Borneo, with the South China Sea washing its western coastline, and the Sulu and Celebes Seas to the north and north-east.

Sardinia: island region of Italy lying 120 miles (200 km) west of the mainland in the Tyrrhenian Sea, with the Mediterranean Sea along its west coast. It is separated from the island of Corsica by the Strait of Bonafacio and a distance of seven and a half miles (12 km).

Sasebo: shipbuilding seaport city on Kyushu, Japan.

Sassnitz: small port town on the island of Rugen, Germany on the Baltic Sea.

Savona: seaport with shipbuilding operations near Genoa, Italy.

Scapa Flow: sheltered anchorage in northern Scotland between Pomona and Hoy, Orkney Islands.

Scheldt River: rises in Aisne, France and flows through France, Belgium and Holland, with the name changing to the River Escaut, Scheldt and Schelde respectively.

Schiedam: shipbuilding town on Nieuwe Maas, just over two and a half miles (4 km) downstream from Rotterdam.

Schleswig-Holstein: a 'land' (state) of Germany located between Denmark and the rest of the German mainland.

Scilly Isles: part of an archipelago 27 miles (45 km) south-west of Land's End, Cornwall, England.

Seagirt: on the coastline of New Jersey, USA, facing the Atlantic Ocean.

Sea of Japan: lying between the Korean and Russian coastlines to the west and the islands of Japan to the east.

Sea of Marmara: almost a lake formation, this sea accesses the Aegean Sea through the Dardanelles to the south and the Black Sea to the north via the Bosphorus, the combination splitting Turkey into European and Asian segments.

Seattle: seaport capital of Washington state, USA, on Puget Sound.

Sebastiao Island: near Santos, Brazil.

Sebastiao Point: on the Isle of Sao Sebastiao which lies off the Brazilian coast, 50 miles (83 km) east of Sao Paulo.

Selsey Bill: headland near Selsey, Sussex, in the English Channel.

Sestri Ponente: shipbuilding area near Genoa on the north-west coast of Italy.

Setoda: Japanese shipbuilding town on an island 24 miles (41 km) south-east of Hiroshima.

Seville: seaport capital city of Seville province and Andalusia, Spain, on the Guadalquivir river, with a canal link to the Atlantic Ocean.

Seychelles: a group of independent islands in the Indian Ocean, with the African continent the closest major landmass.

Seymour Narrows: situated at the northern end of Queen Charlotte Strait, British Columbia, Canada.

Shanghai: major Chinese seaport on the Huang-p'u river where it enters the estuary of the Yangtze river, in the East China Sea.

Sharjah: member of the United Arab Emirates on the Persian Gulf with a natural harbour at Khawr Fakhan.

Shek Kou Bay: on Deep Bay near Hong Kong.

Shimizu: seaport city on the north-west of Suruga Bay, Honshu, Japan, with a harbour protected by the sandspit of Cape Miho.

Shimonoseki: shipbuilding seaport city on the Shimonoseki Strait at the extreme south-west of Honshu, Japan.

Sierra Leone: a nation on the west coast of Africa facing the Atlantic Ocean and with a seaport, Freetown, featuring one of the largest natural harbours in the world.

Simonstown: a naval base on False Bay in southwestern Cape Province, South Africa, 25 miles (40 km) from Capetown.

Singapore: island nation separated from Malaysia by the Johore Strait (now bridged following years using a causeway), with one of the busiest harbours in the world.

Sitka: seaport city located in an island-strewn, mountain-locked harbour on the west coast of Baranof Island, part of the Alexander Archipelago, Alaska, USA.

Skagerrak: arm of the North Sea sparating Norway from Denmark and connecting with the Kattegat.

Skaramangas: suburban beachside town on Eleusis Bay, north-west of Athens and Piraeus.

Skelleftea: seaport on the Gulf of Bothnia, Sweden.

Skikda: seaport town in northern Algeria and the Mediterranean Sea. It was formerly known as Phillippeville.

Skokholm Island: lying in the Broad Sound in the extreme south-west corner of Wales, three miles (5 km) off the Dyfed coast.

Socotra Island: in the Gulf of Aden, Indian Ocean.

Soldier's Reef: a shipping hazard near Paternoster Point, 60 miles (100 km) north of Capetown, South Africa.

Song-koi: The Red river which rises in the Yunnan plateau in south-west China and flows across north Vietnam to the Gulf of Tonkin.

Sorel: a port town at the mouth of the Richelieu river, on the south bank of the St Lawrence river, in southern Quebec province.

Southampton: seaport city in Hampshire, England, located at the head of the Southampton Water on a peninsula between the estuary of the Rivers Test and Itchen.

Southampton Water: an eight mile (14 km) inlet formed by the estuaries of the Rivers Test and Itchen. The inlet gives access from the Solent and Spithead to the port of Southampton.

South Chicago: part of metropolitan Chicago, Illinois, USA, with access to the Atlantic Ocean via the Great Lakes system.

South Kearny: city with shipbreaking operations in New Jersey, USA.

South Stack: a prominent rock projection on the coastline of Caernarvon Bay leading into the Irish Sea, just north of Holyhead, Wales.

Sparrow's Point: town situated on Chesapeake Bay, Maryland, USA.

Split: seaport city in Croatia on the Adriatic Sea.

Spurn Head: a sandspit at the mouth of the Humber river, England, encroaching halfway across the entrance to the estuary, with a lighthouse at its extremity.

Stanley: seaport capital of the Falkland Islands in the South Atlantic Ocean.

Start Point: a cape near Dartmouth, Devon, on the English Channel.

Stavanger: seaport city on the east shoreline of a peninsula in south-west Norway, bounded by the North Sea to the west and the Gand Fjord to the east.

Stettin: see Szczecin.

Stockholm: capital city of Sweden, situated on an island at the outlet of Lake Malar into the Baltic Sea..

Strait of Bab-el-Mandeb: the point at which the Red Sea connects with the Gulf of Aden, thence the Indian Ocean.

Strait of Formosa: lying between the mid-coast of mainland China and Taiwan.

Strait of Georgia: the waterway servicing southern British Columbia and Vancouver Island, Canada, and the north-west of Washington state, USA. This strait is connected to the Pacific Ocean through the Strait of Juan de Fuca.

Strait of Gibraltar: this water stretches 36 miles (58 km) in length and separates the Mediterranean Sea from the Atlantic Ocean. Its narrowest width between Morocco (Point Cires) and Spain (Point Marroqui) is eight miles (13 km).

Strait of Hormuz: between the Persian Gulf and the Gulf of Oman.

Strait of Juan de Fuca: running between the south coast of Vancouver Island, Canada, and the north-west tip of the state of Washington, USA, connecting these areas to the Pacific Ocean.

Strait of Messina: the body of water separating Italy and Sicily, at one point there being only a distance of nine miles (15 km) between the mainland and the island.

Straits of Kithira: separating the island of Cerigo from the Peloponnesus, and running between the Sea of Crete and the Gulf of Lakonia.

Straits of Magellan: the strait between Tierra del Fuego and Chile, separating the Atlantic from the Pacific Ocean.

Straits of Malacca: separate Sumatra, Indonesia, from Malaysia, with its widest point measuring 24 miles (38 km).

Stromo Island: one of the Faroe Islands group north-west of the Shetlands.

Sturgeon Bay: this shipbuilding location is on an inlet from Green Bay, northeastern Wisconsin, USA.

Suez: seaport city in Egypt at the head of the Gulf of Suez , which is an arm of the Red Sea. Suez is at the southern entrance to the Suez Canal.

Suez Canal: a waterway running across the Isthmus of Suez north-to-south, permitting ships to sail from the Mediterranean Sea to the Red Sea and into the Indian Ocean. The canal separates the African continent from Asia.

Suisun Bay: an inner bay in the San Francisco Bay region, connected to the Pacific Ocean through the Carquinez Strait to San Pablo Bay, California, USA.

Sulu Sea: in the western Pacific Ocean, bounded by Borneo in the south-west and the Philippines in the west and north-west.

Sunda Strait: 13 mile-wide (22 km) separation of Java and Sumatra, Indonesia, and linking the Indian Ocean with the Java Sea.

Sunderland: former shipbuilding city at mouth of the River Wear, England.

Surabaya: major industrial and shipbuilding city on the northeastern coastline of Indonesia, opposite Madura Island.

Suruga Bay: an inlet off the Enshu Gulf, Honshu.

Sussex: a southern county of England divided into East and West Sussex and lying on the northern side of the English Channel.

Svendborg: a shipbuilding town on Denmark's Funen Island, which is located on Svendborg Sound.

Swinemunde: see Swinoujscie.

Swinoujscie: a Polish resort town on a flattish island lying off the mouth of the Oder river in the Baltic Sea. It was formerly known as Swinemunde, Germany.

Sydney: a seaport city on the Tasman Sea coast of the state of New South Wales, Australia, with a natural harbour acclaimed by seafarers and visitors.

Syracuse: city on the south-east coast of Sicily. The old town built on Ortygia Island, off the coast, is now joined to the modern city on the mainland by a bridge.

Szczecin: seaport city and province in Poland. It was formerly known as Stettin, East Germany.

Table Bay: inlet of the Atlantic coast of the Cape of Good Hope.

Tabuaeran Atoll: see Kiribati.

Tacoma: seaport city on Puget Sound, Washington state, USA.

Tahiti: largest island in the Windward group of the Society Islands, situated in the central South Pacific, French Polynesia.

Taiwan: island lying off the mainland of China, separated by the Formosa Strait. Taiwan is bordered by the South China Sea, Philippine Sea and East China Sea.

Takamatsu: port city on the north coast of Skikuku, Japan.

Tallin: seaport capital city of Estonia on the Gulf of Finland.

Tamatave Harbour: leading seaport of Madagascar on the Indian Ocean. It is also known as Toamasina.

Tamil Nadu: the new name for Madras, India, which is a seaport city on the Coromandel coast of the Bay of Bengal.

Tam Kan: an island surrounded by rocky outcrops, 20 miles (30 km) south of Hong Kong.

Tampa: resort seaport in Florida, USA, at the mouth of the Hillsborough river, Tampa Bay, in the Gulf of Mexico.

Tampa Bay: an arm of the Gulf of Mexico, east of the Pinellas Peninsula.

Tampico: port city in Mexico on the River Panuco, eight miles (14 km) from the Gulf of Mexico.

Tanega Shima: the most northern island of the Tiukiu Island group, and nearest to the Japanese mainland.

Tangier: seaport on the north-west corner of Morocco, on the Strait of Gibraltar.

Tanjung Priok: a neighbourhood (suburb) of Jakarta, situated on Jakarta Bay.

Tan Tai: seaport on the South China Sea, 30 miles (50 km) south of Cam Lam, Vietnam.

Tatana Island: reef-ringed island off Papua and New Guinea, South Pacific Ocean.

Telukbayur: town on a cape facing the Indian Ocean coast of Sumatra.

Temse: shipbuilding town on the banks of the Schelde river upstream from Antwerp, Belgium.

Tenerife: one of the Canary Islands group in the Atlantic Ocean.

Texel Island: part of the West Frisian Islands off the north-west Netherlands, located on the Marsdiep, a channel linking the North Sea and the Waddenzee.

Thames River: rises in the Cotswold hills in the west of England and flows 200 miles (336 km) across southern England, through London to the North Sea.

The Gates: twin rocky towers three miles (5 km) outside the harbour of the island of Patros, Greece.

The Hague: capital of the Netherlands, situated in the south of the country. It is also referred to as Den Haag.

The Lizard: a cliffy peninsula in the Kerrier district of Cornwall, the southernmost part of the island of Great Britain.

The Minch: lies between the Outer Hebrides and the mainland of Scotland, notorious for its rapid currents and great depth.

Thessaloniki: seaport at the head of the Gulf of Thessaloniki, Greece. It is often referred to as Salonika.

Thorshavn: city on Stromo Island in the Faroe Islands.

Tijucas Rocks: an outcrop that is an extension from the shoreline, only 15 miles (25 km) from Rio de Janeiro, Brazil.

Titana Island: located within the Papua New Guinea Islands.

Tiukiu Islands: a group of islands off the southern Japanese mainland coast, sharing the Pacific Ocean and the East China Sea to its east and west respectively.

Toamasina: see Tamatave.

Toba Bay: a metropolitan bay in the Nagoya, Japan.

Tobermory: seaport on the Isle of Mull at the northern entrance to the Sound of Mull.

Tobruk: seaport on the North African coast of Libya, 210 miles (352 km) east of Benghazi.

Tokyo Bay: a large inlet from the Pacific Ocean with a narrow opening known as the Uraga Channel. Some of the major cities of Honshu, Japan feature on its shoreline.

Tonsberg: shipbuilding port in south-east Norway on the Skagerrak, at the entrace to the Oslo Fjord.

Tory Island: in Tory Sound off the north-west coast of County Donegal, Republic of Ireland.

Toulon: seaport city with a natural harbour on the Mediterranean coast of south-west France.

Toulouse: city in southern France on the banks of the River Garonne.

Townsville: port city on the Coral Sea coast of Queensland, Australia.

Toyama: shipbuilding town on the Etchu plain, east of Noto peninsula on Honshu.

Travemunde: major port on Germany's north coast entering the Baltic Sea.

Trave River: located in Schleswig-Holstein, Germany, and empties into the Baltic Sea at the seaport of Lubeck.

Trelleborg: Swedish seaport on the Baltic Sea coast.

Trepassy Bay: in south-east Newfoundland between Cape Pine and Cape Race, 25 miles (42 km) west on the Atlantic coast.

Trevose Head: promontory on the Atlantic Ocean, ten miles (14 km) north of Newquay, Cornwall, UK.

Trieste: seaport capital of Trieste province, Italy, with large shipbuilding operations.

Trinidad: island in the West Indies group in the Caribbean Sea, north of Venezuela.

Trinity Bay: an inlet of the Coral Sea on the North Queensland coastline, Australia.

Trinity Ledge: town in Newfoundland.

Tripoli: seaport on the Mediterranean coast, and joint capital of Libya with Benghazi.

Trogir: shipbuilding port on the island of Ciovo in the Adriatic Sea, joined to the Dalmatian mainland coast of Croatia by a bridge.

Trondheim: shipbuilding seaport on the west coast of Norway, on the southern side of the Trondheim Fjord.

Troon: shipbuilding seaport on the Firth of Clyde, Scotand, six miles (10 km) north of Ayr.

Truk Atoll: see Chuuk Islands.

Truk Islands: see Chuuk Islands.

Tsingtao: seaport city is located on a fine natural harbour on the south coast of Shantung peninsula, at the eastern entrance to Kiaochow Bay in northern China.

Tsu: capital city of Honshi, Japan, at the mouth of the Ano river in Ise Bay. The city engages in shipbuilding.

Tsugaru Strait: links the Pacific Ocean with the Sea of Japan and separates the Japanese islands of Hokkaido and Honshu.

Tsurumi: town on coast of Sacki Bay on Kyushi Island.

Tung Yung Island: lying north-east off Fuzhou, formerly Foochow, in the East China Sea.

Tunis: seaport city on an inlet of the Mediterranean Sea, Tunisia.

Turku: seaport in south-west Finland on the Baltic Sea. It is sometimes called Abo.

Tuzla: town on a group of islands in the Marmara Denizi, a massive body of water between the Aegean and Black Seas.

Tynemouth: port on the north bank of the Tyne river, England.

Tyneside: general geographic term applied to the whole area of the Tyne river and the many shipbuilding towns along its banks.

Tyrrhenian Sea: bordered by the islands of Corsica, Sardinia and Sicily and the mainland of Italy, this sea is an arm of the Mediterranean Sea.

Uddevalla: seaport town in southern Sweden.

Ulsan: industrial city in southeastern South Korea which merged with the port of Pangojin.

Ulsteinvik: shipbuilding town in Norway.

Umhlatuzi river: flows through the Zululand region of the Natal province of South Africa and empties into the Indian Ocean at Richard's Bay.

Unalaska Island: part of the Aleutian group in the North Pacific Ocean

Uraga: shipbuilding town on the Miura Peninsula separating Tokyo Bay from Sagami Bay.

Ushant: island off the French coast near Finisterre, at the entrance to the English Channel.

US Virgin Islands: islands east of the Greater Antilles which are an external territory of the USA. They are actively involved in the Caribbean cruise industry.

Uto Island: in the Baltic Sea a few kilometres off the Swedish coast, 60 miles (100 km) from Stockholm.

Uyak Bay: an inlet on Kodiak Island, Alaska, USA.

Vaasa: seaport town on the Gulf of Bothnia, Finland.

Vado Ligure: town 18 miles (30 km) south-west of the Lugurian Sea which is also known as the Gulf of Genoa, with both being part of the Mediterranean Sea.

Valencia: seaport and capital of Valencia province, lying at the mouth of the River Turia on the Mediterranean Sea.

Vallejo: shipyard seaport city at the mouth of the Napa river emptying into San Pablo Bay, California, USA.

Valparaiso: situated 84 miles (140 km) north-west of Santiago (the capital of Chile), Valparaiso is located in a very wide bay of the Pacific Ocean, sheltered by high hills surrounding the city.

Vancouver (Canada): seaport city in British Columbia with a natural harbour which is the embarkation point for cruise ships sailing up the coast to Alaska, USA.

Vancouver (USA): shipbuilding seaport on the Columbia river in the state of Washington, opposite Portland, Oregon.

Vancouver Island: an island off the west coast of British Columbia, Canada, featuring numerous natural harbours and the city of Victoria, the capital of British Columbia. It is separated from the mainland by the Strait of Georgia.

Vanuatu: a part of the New Hebrides, South Pacific Ocean, and positioned between New Caledonia and the Fiji Islands.

Vasa: see Vaasa.

Vatulele: town on Koro Island, part of the Fijian Islands group.

Vegesack: shipbuilding town 12 miles (20 km) north of Bremen on the Weser river.

Venezuela: nation with a coastline in the southern Caribbean Sea.

Venice: seaport built on a group of islets in the Gulf of Venezia at the head of the Adriatic Sea, north-east Italy.

Vera Cruz: town in Mexico.

Vianno do Castello: seaport town at the mouth of the Lima river in north-west Portugal, north of Porto (Oporto).

Viareggio: shipbuilding resort on the Tyrrhenian Sea in the Tuscany region of Italy.

Victoria: capital city of British Columbia, Canada, and located on a natural harbour on Vancouver Island at the convergence of the Straits of Georgia and Juan de Fuca.

Vigo: seaport on Vigo Bay, Spain, in the North Atlantic Ocean.

Vigo Bay: an inlet of the North Atlantic Ocean on the north-east shoreline of Spain.

Virginia Capes: an area in Chesapeake Bay historically important but also engaged in shipping activities.

Visby: seaport town on the island of Gotland, Sweden, in the Baltic Sea.

Vitoria: seaport in Brazil.

Vladivostok: seaport in eastern Russia on the Sea of Japan.

Vlissingen: seaport in Zeeland province, south-west Netherlands. It was formerly known as Flushing.

Wake Island: this US possession is a coral atoll between the Mariannas and Hawaii.

Wallsend: shipbuilding town on the north bank of the River Tyne, four miles (6 km) below Newcastle, England.

Warnemunde: ferryport for Berlin and Copenhagen traffic. It is the outport for Rostock which is further downstream on the Warnow river, Germany.

Washington: (1) capital city of the USA, situated on the Potomac river in the District of Columbia; (2) state in the far north-west of the USA, stretching from the Pacific Ocean to the Rocky Mountains.

Waterford: port town on the River Suir, Republic of Ireland, which empties into St George's Channel.

Wear River: rises in the Pennines and flows 60 miles (96 km) into the North Sea at Sunderland, England .

Weland Ship Canal: connects Lakes Erie and Ontario with a 26 mile-long (43 km) two-lane waterway.

Wellington: seaport capital of New Zealand on Port Nicholson harbour, which was once a volcanic crater.

Werra River: the headstream of the Weser river, Germany.

Wesermunde: see Bremerhaven.

Weser River: a 330 mile (550 km) totally navigable river formed by the confluence of the Rivers Fulda and Werra at Munden, and flowing north to Bremerhaven, Germany, where it empties into the North Sea.

West Hartlepool: see Hartlepool.

Western Isles: see Hebrides.

Westkapelle: town on the North Sea coast of Belgium, nine miles (15 km) north-east of Brugges.

West Nangka Point: headland on Banka Island off the south-east coast of Sumatra, Indonesia.

Wexford: a county in the south-east of the Republic of Ireland, bounded south and east by the Irish Sea.

Whangarei: deep water seaport 70 miles (118 km) north of Auckland in the North Island of New Zealand.

Whitby: seaport town in Yorkshire, England.

White Sea: an inlet of Barents Sea and an extension of the Arctic Ocean, indenting the northwestern Russian coastline.

Wick: seaport on the east coast of Scotand, 13 miles (22 km) from John O'Groats.

Wilhelmshaven: seaport on an inlet of the North Sea in Lower Saxony, Germany.

Williamstown: naval base port on the Tasman Sea coast of Victoria, Australia.

Wilmington: (1) seaport with shipbuilding operations on the Delaware river, Delaware, USA; (2) shipbuilding seaport in North

Carolina, USA.

Wilson's Promontory: the southernmost point of the Australian mainland, 110 miles (177 km) south-east of Melbourne, Victoria. This granite projection 2,475 feet (754 m) high juts out into Bass Strait, which separates the Australian mainland from the island state of Tasmania.

Wismar: seaport town in Rostock, Germany.

Wolf Rock: a very isolated rock featuring a lighthouse, eight miles (14 km) south-west of Lands End, Cornwall, England, at the approach from the Atlantic Ocean into the English Channel.

Wyndham: the northernmost port in Western Australia. The town lies at the mouth of the King river.

Yanbu'al Bahr: seaport on the Red Sea, Saudi Arabia, servicing the holy city of Medina.

Yangon: largest city and capital of Myanmar. It is located on the eastern bank of the Yangon river (sometimes referred to as the Hlaing river), 25 miles (40 km) north of the Gulf of Martaban in the Andaman Sea.

Yangtze river: rises in Tibet and flows 3,400 miles (5,600 km) through China until it enters the East China Sea near Shanghai. It is also known as Chang Jiang.

Yap Island: part of the Federated States of Micronesia, this island is part of an archipelago of the western Caroline Islands.

Yarmouth: seaport town in Nova Scotia, Canada.

Yokohama: major seaport on Honshu on the western shore of Tokyo Bay, Japan.

Yokosuka: seaport and resort on Honshu, south of Tokyo, Japan.

Youghal: seaport town on the estuary of the Blackwater river which empties into Youghal Bay, an arm of St George's Channel, which separates the Atlantic Ocean from the Irish Sea.

Yser river: a river system emptying into the North Sea, 12 miles (20 km) south-west of Ostende, Belgium. Over the years, a number of canals have been developed in Belgium, northern France and Holland.

Ystad: coastal town in the extreme south of Sweden, with an outlook to the Baltic Sea.

Zadar: seaport town in Croatia. It features a natural deep water harbour created by the Zadar Channel running between the peninsula upon which Zadar was built and the islands of Pasman and Ugljan.

Zaire River: see River Zaire.

Zanzibar: seaport city on Zanzibar Island, lying 21 miles (35 km) off the east coast of Tanzania.

Zeebrugge: seaport town supporting trade from Brugge, Belgium.

Zeeland: an area covering the Scheldt estuary, Holland.

Zinghua Harbour: located in Shanghai in the People's Republic of China.

Zululand: a region in the province of Natal, South Africa, which has a coastline facing the Indian Ocean.

Zwijndrecht: town in Belgium lying along the Scheldt river, six miles (10 km) from Antwerp.

Glossary

Abaft: towards the aft (rear) end of the ship and commencing amidships.

Aft: rear end of ship from any point from the bow going or looking towards the stern.

Amidships: central area of ship's hull length. Also termed midships.

Armed merchant cruiser: a merchant ship converted to war use by the addition of armaments, coming under the control of a national navy.

Azimuth Electric Propeller Drive: naval architects have dubbed this term for the podded drive which has developed into the shortened term 'Azipod' (a trademark of ABB Azipod Marine Oy of Finland).

Azimuthing drive: see Azipod.

Azimuth Podded Drive: see Azipod.

Azipod: this is a trade-marked azimuth podded drive developed by a joint venture between the Kvaerner-Masa Yard, Helsinki, and ABB Azipod Marine Oy, Finland. It is a 'cowled' screw whereby the screw can rotate 360 degrees and therefore undertake docking manouevres, etc in lieu of outside assistance. It can also take over the tasks of bow and stern thrusters, such is its dexterity. An azimuthing electric propulsion drive screw may eventually take over the duties of a ship's rudder. The appearance of the trademark within some data on specific ships in this book is done so by the author in the absence of an accepted generic term, and is in no way meant to be a breach of copyright or trademark. Various publications have also adopted Azipod as a generic term.

Bareboat charter: a term describing a vessel which is leased or rented from a shipowner on the basis that the charterer provides his own officers and crew.

Base port: the regular port of departure for voyages which return to that port (out-and-back itineraries such as followed by cruise ships). Also referred to as home ports.

Beam: width of ship at widest point, also termed breadth.

Blue Riband: a 'trophy' competed for and held by ships, mainly in the 1920–30 period, for the fastest transatlantic run between New York and Southampton. Also applied to any sea voyage between two ports.

Boat or Ship?: the maritime definition most apt for determining whether a vessel is a boat or a ship is that a ship can carry a boat, but a boat cannot carry a ship!

Boot-topping: a coloured band above the waterline denoting the point where the draft of a ship is measured.

Bow: the 'sharp end'; forward end of ship, also termed stem or prow.

Breadth: width of ship at widest point, also termed beam.

Build date: the year in which a vessel is delivered to her new owners.

Catamaran: twin hulls.

Dayboat: usually a ferry which travels to a destination in broad daylight and thus does not need to be fitted out with sleeping berths or cabins.

Depth: a method of measuring a ship's area from the lowest payload area, such as a hold or passenger deck, to the main deck. A term in vogue at the turn of the century and around 1930, prior to today's terminology of 'draft'.

Dimensions: given as length (overall, perpendicular-to-perpendicular) x beam (at the broadest point at deck level) x loaded draft in both Imperial and metric measurements (in parenthesis).

Delivery date: the year in which an owner accepts delivery of a new, or converted, ship following its sea trials.

Double-ender: reference to a passenger ferry with two wheelhouses and two single propellers at each end. They are usually found only in harbours and sheltered waters.

Draft: depth of a loaded ship in the water and measured from the waterline to the lowest point of the hull. Also spelt draught.

Draught: depth of a loaded ship in the water and measured from the waterline to the lowest point of the hull. Also spelt draft.

Draw: the amount of water required for a specific dimension vessel when navigating close into shore, rivers, lakes or inside reef structures, etc. Draft/draught is considered as the determinant to estimating how much a ship will draw when in shallow water.

DRG: double reduction gears.

Fathom: nautical depth measurement of water equal to six feet (1.82 m).

Fore: the bow section (front of the vessel).

Forward: as in 'fore'. Term applicable to moving towards the bow as in 'go forward'.

GRT: abbreviation for gross registered tonnage.

Gross registered tonnage: a complex calculation of a ship's enclosed spaces (hull, superstructure, etc) measured on the basis of 100 cubic feet to the ton (Imperial), according to which methods of estimation are used by various countries. The International Tonnage Certificate is strictly enforced, except for those nations who did not sign the ITC Agreement in 1969 (ie non-Conference countries).

HMAS: Her/His Majesty's Australian Ship and used as a prefix to vessels of the Royal Australian Navy.

HMNZS: Her/His Majesty's New Zealand Ship and used as a prefix to vessels of the Royal New Zealand Navy.

HMS: Her/His Majesty's Ship and used as a prefix to vessels of the British Royal Navy.

Home port: the regular port of departure for voyages which return to that port (out-and-back itineraries, such as followed by cruise ships). Also referred to as base ports.

Hospital ship: an unarmed ship operating during times of war which is immune to attack by virtue of the terms of the Geneva Convention, under whose auspices the ship operates. Hulls are all-white with a wide horizontal red band broken by a red cross midships, plus a green riband.

HSS: high speed ship. Refers to a smaller vessel with immense power.

Hull: the complete 'shell' which eventually contains machinery, holds, accommodation and public rooms from which the superstructure is formed and fixed.

IHP: indicated horse power.

Inaugural voyage, the first voyage undertaken on behalf of new owners or charterers and not to be confused with her maiden voyage. Also refers to the first voyage on a new route if this differs from her previous itinerary.

Keel: the main central longitudinal 'spine' of a ship to which are affixed the frames of the hull. The exposure of the hull during a ship capsize is the origin of the phrase 'to keel over'.

Knot: maritime measure of speed formulated as 1 knot = 1 nautical mile per hour, or the land equivalent of 1.3 mph (2.2 kph).

Laid down: the act of laying the keel for a brand new ship.

Laid up: an inactive period of a ship when it is moored or berthed at a location for a lengthy period while awaiting sale, charter, rebuilding, etc.

Launched: refers to that moment when the ship enters the water, often after being named at a christening ceremony.

Liner: this is a generic term applied to ships that were engaged on line or long-haul voyages on a regular schedule.

Line voyages: refers to a ship making a voyage between two terminal ports.

Livery: the colours in which a ship is painted on the hull, superstructure, funnel/s and boot-topping.

Long haul: term applied to ships which travel on lengthy voyages on a regular basis between a series of ports.

Maiden voyage: the initial voyage of a new ship on behalf of her original owner/s.

MARAD: acronym for the United States Maritime Administration.

Merchantmen: that group of ships which are not naval or motor yachts.

Merchant Navy: non-military ships of a given national navy (ie armed merchantmen, conversions, etc).

Midships: central area of ship's hull length. Also termed 'amidships'.

Monohull: single hull.

Motor ship: those vessels which are powered by an internal combustion engine (ie diesels) and sometimes have their names prefixed with the letters MV or MS.

MS: abbreviation sometimes prefixed to ship's name as a motor ship in promotional and advertising material.

MV: abbreviation sometimes prefixed to a ship's name to indicate that it is diesel engine-powered.

Nautical mile: a calculation equal to one minute of latitude based on an equatorial bearing and measuring 6080 feet (1853 m). One such sea mile equals 2000 yards (606 m).

NHP: nominal horse power.

Nightboat: usually a ferry which is fitted out with sleeping accommodation for a trip overnight.

Non-monohull: refers to a catamaran, or a hull other than the conventional single unit.

Passenger-cargo vessel: a ship whose mainstream activities are the carriage of freight, but with some passenger accommodation. Within this book, such vessels are included only when their passenger capacity is 50 or greater and with a doctor on board (as opposed to 'twelves' – see below).

Pax: maritime and airline slang term for passengers.

Pilot: a marine officer who is responsible for the entry, movement, and exit of a ship within his control limits, usually a harbour or a passage of water close by. In these circumstances, the pilot has the control of the ship for that temporary period.

Port: the left-hand side of the ship as one looks forward from the bridge to the bow (bears red navigation lights).

Positioning voyage: refers to the delivery of a ship to a new assigned route.

Propeller: the propulsion device beneath the stern and driven by shafts from the internal machinery. Nautically referred to as the 'screw', whether single or multiple.

Power plant: an all-embracing term which refers to the engines.

Prow: alternative term for the bow.

RAN: Royal Australian Navy.

Repositioning voyage: refers to a ship's delivery voyage to a new route.

RMS: a vessel is permitted to embody these initials before the actual ship's name to indicate that it has won a contract for delivering mail from port-to-port.

RN: Royal Navy (UK).

RNZN: Royal New Zealand Navy.

Ro-Pax: classification now given to Ro-Ro ferries which have been designed to give passengers every facility, in addition to having a major freight content.

Ro-Ro: a roll-on, roll-off vessel, mostly associated with freight ferries or ferries transporting a mix of passengers, cars and trailers. A purpose-built ship whereby drivers can simply drive through the stern door at the point of departure and drive off through the bow door without any complicated manoeuvres.

Rudder: the steering device beneath the stern.

Screw: propeller, either single or multiple.

Shakedown: refers to sea trials, or a 'rehearsal cruise' for crew and staff.

SHP: shaft horse power.

Sister ship: a ship built to an identical specification and design as another, usually by the same builder.

SOLAS: an acronym for 'safety of lives at sea' (rigid regulations to prevent loss of life at sea). These regulations are tranched over ten-year periods and call for modifications to ships which must be complied to within specific time periods. The current SOLAS regulation stages are in place up to and including 2010.

SRG: single reduction gears.

Starboard: the right-hand side of the ship as one looks forward from the bridge to the bow (bears green navigation lights).

SS: abbreviation for steamship and often prefixed to a ship's name in promotional material, advertising, etc.

Steamship: those vessels which are powered by steam engines (as opposed to diesel power, etc). The letters SS are often applied as a prefix to the ship's name.

Stem: alternative term for the bow.

Stern: rear end of a ship's hull.

Superstructure: any structure built above the hull and upon the main deck of a ship and having sides flush with those of the hull. Usually the central mass containing the bridge, cabins, public rooms, etc.

SWATH: an acronym for 'small waterplane area twin hull'.

TCL: total constructive loss.

TEU: this refers mainly to containers of 20' (6 m) or 40' (12 m) in length and with a depth and width each of 8'6" (2.6 m) which is termed in shipping circles as a 'Twenty-feet Equivalent Unit'.

Total constructive loss: declared (normally by an insurance company) when a ship has foundered, grounded, become wrecked, caught fire, or other catastrophe which has rendered it incapable of sailing.

Trailers: the 40'-long (12.1 m) vans hauled by prime movers. These are known in Australia as semi-trailers, in the USA as rigs hauled by tractors, and in Europe as trailers.

Troop transport: a ship either purpose-built, or converted, to carry troops on long-haul voyages. Generally, these ships are built to a passenger ship design and emphasis.

TS: abreviation for turbine ship to indicate its machinery and propulsion are via turbine power.

TSS: abbreviation often prefixed to twin screw ship name in promotional or advertising material.

Twelves: those passenger-cargo ships who provide berths for 12 passengers or less and are, under maritime law and regulations, not required to carry a doctor on board.

U-boat: German submarine (unterseebot).

Upperworks: another term for superstructure.

USAF: United States Air Force.

USAT: United States Army Transport.

USN: United States Navy.

USNS: United States Naval Ship.

USS: United States Ship which is used as a prefix to US Navy vessels.

Z-drive: another term for an azimuthing drive (see Azipod).

Builders: Names and Locations

Shipbuilders are akin to ship owners in that many of the companies they operate are an ever-changing kaleidoscope, with takeovers, acquisitions, mergers and bankruptcies keeping the action going. But there is a solid core of shipyards that have specialised in cruise ships as an extension of their past activities constructing passenger liners. Many yards that have been involved in ferry building have maintained their presence and expertise to this day.

There was one period, early in the twentieth century, where the old-and-tried shipyards were very sound and solid, but gradually as wars and depressions altered the very fabric of personal and commercial life, the recognized names were surrounded by newcomers and new operators. Every ship entry within this directory contains the name of the respective builder, as it was so named at the time of the vessel's construction. However, the accuracy of such information does depend upon the original data source.

There is also the added complication that many shipyards, especially those in the UK, gave their locations as a suburb, or a riverbank in a city. This is particularly so in the Clyde river region, the Humber river, the Tees river, the Tyne, etc.

This list is in alphabetical order, with the odd exception caused by name styling where initials or a commencing name peculiar to a specific country are involved. There are what would at first appear to be repeats of a company within the listing; this is in an attempt to cover address variances (eg Astilleros Espanoles SA, Bilbao, Spain; Astilleros Espanoles SA, Ferrol, Spain, etc).

Aalborg Vaerft AS, Aalborg, Denmark.
Adler Werft GmbH, Bremen, Germany.
AG Weser GmbH, Bremen, Germany.
AG Weser Werk Seebeck, Bremerhaven, Germany.
Ailsa Shipbuilding Company Ltd, Troon, Scotland.
A Jdanov Shipyard, St Petersburg, Russia. (See A Zhdanov Shipyard, St Petersburg.)
Aker Finnyards, Rauma, Finland
Aker MTW Werft
Akers AS MV, Oslo, Norway.
Alabama Drydock & Shipbuilding Company, Mobile, Alabama, USA.
Alexander Stephen & Sons Ltd, Glasgow, Scotland.
American International Shipbuilding Corporation, Hog Island, Pennsylvania, USA
Ansaldo SpA, Genoa-Sestri Ponente, Italy.
Ansaldo SpA, La Spezia, Italy.
Ansaldo SpA, Livorno, Italy.
A & P Appledore Ltd, Southampton, England.
Armstrong, Mitchell & Company Ltd, Newcastle, England.
Armstrong, Whitworth & Company Ltd, Newcastle, England.
Arsenal de Brest, Brest, France.
Arsenal de Lorient, Lorient, France.
Asano Shipbuilding Company, Tsurumi, Japan.
Astilleros de Huelva, Spain.
Astilleros Espanoles SA, Bilbao, Spain.
Astilleros Espanoles SA, Ferrol, Spain.
Astilleros Espanoles SA, Santander, Spain.
Astilleros Espanoles SA, Seville, Spain.
Astilleros Principe, Menghi y Penco SA, Avellaneda, Argentina..
Ateliers et Chantiers de Dunkerque et Bordeaux, Dunkirk, France. (See also Chantiers et Ateliers.)
Ateliers et Chantiers de France, Societe des, Dunkirk, France..
Ateliers et Chantiers de la Rochelle-Pallice, La Rochelle-Pallice, France.
Ateliers et Chantiers de la Loire, St Nazaire, France.
Atlantic Marine, Jacksonville, Florida, USA.
Atlantic Marine, Mobile, Alabama, USA.
Austin & Pickersgill Ltd, Sunderland, England.
Avlis Shipyard, Chalkis, Greece.
Avondale Shipyards Inc, Avondale, Louisiana, USA.
A Zdanov Shipyard, St Petersburg, Russia.

Baltic Shipbuilding & Engineering, St Petersburg, Russia.
Barclay, Curle & Company Ltd, Glasgow, Scotland.

Barrow Shipbuilding Ltd, Barrow-in-Furness, England.
Bartram & Sons Ltd, Sunderland, England.
W Beardmore & Company, Dalmuir, Scotland. (See also William Beardmore & Co.)
Bergens AS MV, Bergen, Norway.
Berlin GmbH, Neustadt, Germany.
Bethlehem-Fairfield Shipyard Inc, Baltimore, Maryland, USA.
Bethlehem Shipbuilding Corporation, Sparrows Point, Maryland, USA.
Bethlehem Steel Company: Shipbuilding Division, Alameda, California, USA.
Bethlehem Steel Company: Shipbuilding Division, Quincy, Massachusetts, USA
Bethlehem Steel Corporation: Shipbuilding Division, Alameda, California, USA.
Bethlehem Steel Corporation: Shipbuilding Division, Quincy, Massachusetts, USA.
Bethlehem Steel Corporation: Shipbuilding Division, Sparrows Point, Maryland, USA
Blohm & Voss AG, Hamburg, Germany.
Blyth Drydock & Shipbuilding Company Ltd, Blyth, England.
Blythswood Shipbuilding Company Ltd, Glasgow, Scotland.
Boeles Schps & Mach, Bolnes, Holland.
Boelwerf NV SA, Temse, Belgium.
Boelwerf Vlaanderen NV, Hoboken, Belgium
Bremer Vulkan, Vegesack, Germany.
Brodogradiliste III Maj, Rijeka, Croatia.
Brodogradiliste 'Ivan Cetinic', Korcula, Croatia.
Brodogradiliste 'Split', Split, Croatia.
Brodogradiliste 'Titovo', Kraljevica, Croatia.
Brodogradiliste 'Trogir', Croatia.
Brodogradiliste 'Uljanik', Pula, Croatia.
Brooke Marine Ltd, Lowestoft, England.
Bruce's Shipyard AB, Landskronor, Sweden
Burmeister & Wain, Copenhagen, Denmark
Burmeister and Wain's Skybsbyggeri, Copenhagen, Denmark.
Burntisland SB Company Ltd, Burntisland, Scotland.
Burrard Drydock Company, Vancouver, British Columbia, Canada.
Busumer Schiffs. (W & E Sielaff), Busum, Germany.

Caird & Company, Greenock, Scotland.
Caledon Shipbuilding & Engineering Company Ltd, Dundee, Scotland.
Californian Shipbuilding Corporation, Los Angeles, California, USA.
Cammell Laird & Company (Shipbuilders & Engineers) Ltd, Birkenhead, England.
Cantieri, Breda, Venice, Italy. (See also Fincantieri.)
Cantieri ed Officini Meridionali, Soc. Italiana per Construzioni Navali Meccaniche, Baia, Italy.
Cantieri, Marhera, Venice, Italy.
Cantieri Navali de Tirrenio e Riuniti SpA, Riva Tregoso, Italy.
Cantieri Navali de Visentini Francesco, Donada, Italy.
Cantieri Navali di Muggiano, La Spezia, Italy.
Cantieri Navali di Pietra Ligure, Pietra, Italy.
Cantieri Navali di Taranto, Italy.
Cantieri Navali Felszegi, Muggia, Italy.
Cantieri Navali Italiani SpA, Monfalcone, Italy.
Cantieri Navali Pellegrino, Naples, Italy.
Cantieri Navali Siciliani, Palermo, Italy.
Cantieri Navali Triestino, Monfalcone, Italy.
Cantieri Rinuiti dell'Adriatico, Ancona, Italy.
Cantieri Riuniti dell'Adriatico, Monfalcone, Italy.
Cantieri Riuniti dell'Adriatico, San Marco, Italy.
Cantieri Riuniti dell'Adriatico, Trieste, Italy.
Cantieri Riuniti, Palermo, Italy.
Cantieri Santa Maria, La Spezia, Italy.
Chantiers de l'Atlantique, Penhoet-Loire, France. (See also 'Penhoet' and 'Ateliers et Chantiers'.)
Chantiers et Ateliers de la Gironde, Bordeaux, France.
Chantiers et Ateliers de la Dubigeon, Nantes, France. (See also Dubigeon-Normandie, Nantes.)

Chantiers et Ateliers de Provence S A, Port de Bouc, France.
Chantiers Navales de La Ciotat, France.
Chantiers Navigation de Caen, Blainville, France.
Chas Hill & Sons Ltd, Bristol, England.
Chongjin Shipyards, Huichon, North Korea.
Cia Euskalduna de Construccion y Reparacion de Buques, Bilbao, Spain.
Cia Euskalduna de Construccion y Reparacion de Buques, Ferrol, Spain.
Cockatoo Island Docks & Engineering Company Pty Ltd, Sydney, Australia.
Cockerill-Ougree SA, Hoboken, Belgium. (See also John Cockerill.)
Cockerill Yards Hoboken SA, NV, Hoboken, Belgium.
Collingwood Shipbuilding Co Ltd, Collingwood, Ontario, Canada.
C Connell & Company Ltd, Glasgow, Scotland.
Constructions Navales et Industrielles de la Mediterranee, Bordeaux, France.
Constructions Navales et Industrielles de la Mediterranee, La Seyne, France.
Constructions Navales, Soc Provencale de La Ciotat, La Ciotat, France.
W Cramp & Sons, Philadelphia, Pennsylvania, USA.

Dae Sun Shipbuilding & Engineering Company, Busan, South Korea.
Daewoo Shipbuilding & Heavy Industries, Kyungnam, South Korea.
Danziger Werft, Danzig (Gdansk), Poland.
Davie Shipbuilding Company, Lauzon, Quebec, Canada.
De Haan & Oerlemans, Heusden, Holland.
Der Merwede Shipyard, Hardinxveld, Holland.
De Schelde NV, Koninklijke Mij, Vlissingen, Holland.
Deutsche Werft AG, Hamburg, Germany.
G Dimitrov Shipyard, Varna, Bulgaria.
Doxford & Sons (SB) Ltd. (See William Doxford & Sons.)
Doxford & Sunderland Ltd, Sunderland, England.
Drammen Slip & Verk, Drammen, Norway.
Dubigeon-Normandie, Nantes, France. (See also 'Ateliers' and 'Chantiers').
D & W Henderson Ltd, Glasgow, Scotland.
DW Kromer Sohn, Elmshorn, Germany.

Earles Company Ltd, Hull, England.
Eastern Shipbuilding Corporation, New London, Connecticut, USA.
Elsinor Shipbuilding & Engineering Company, Elsinor, Denmark.
MV Eriksbergs AB, Gotaverken, Sweden.
Evans Deakin & Company, Brisbane, Queensland, Australia.

Fairfield Shipbuilding & Engineering Company Ltd, Glasgow, Scotland.
Federal Shipbuilding & Dry Dock Company, Kearny, New Jersey, USA.
Ferguson-Ailsa Ltd, Troon, Scotland.
Ferguson Shipbuilders Ltd, Port Glasgow, Scotland.
Fijenoord, NV Mij voor Scheeps-en-Werktuigbouw (trading as Wilton-Fijenoord), Rotterdam, Holland.
Fijenoord, NV Mij voor Scheeps-en-Werktuigbouw (trading as Wilton-Fijenoord), Schiedam, Holland.

Finnboda Varf AB, Stockholm, Sweden.
Fincantieri, Ancona, Italy. (See also Cantieri.)
Fincantieri, Castellammare di Stabia, Italy.
Fincantieri, Genoa, Italy.
Fincantieri, Genoa Sestri Ponente, Italy.
Fincantieri, La Spezia, Italy.
Fincantieri, Livorno, Italy.
Fincantieri, Marhera, Venice, Italy.
Fincantieri, Monfalcone, Italy.
Fincantieri, Naples, Italy.
Fincantieri, Palermo, Italy.
Fincantieri, Riva-Tregoso, Italy.
Fincantieri, Trieste, Italy.
Fincantieri, Breda, Venice, Italy.
Finnyards Oy, Raumu, Finland.
F Krupp Shipbuilding, Kiel, Germany. (See also 'Fred Krupp' and 'Krupp'.)

Flender Werft AG, Lubeck, Germany.
Flensburger Aschiffs Ges, Flensburg, Germany.
Forges et Chantiers de la Mediterranee, Bordeaux, France.
Forges et Chantiers de la Mediterranee, La Seyne, France.
Fosen MV AS, Fevaag, Norway.
Fratelli Orlando, Leghorn, Italy.
Frederikshavns V & F AS, Frederikshavn, Denmark.
Fred Krupp Shipbuilding, Kiel, Germany. (See also 'F Krupp' and 'Krupp'.)
F Schichau, Danzig (Gdansk), Poland.
Fujinagata Shipbuilding & Engineering Company Ltd, Osaka, Japan.
Fukuoka Zosen KK, Fukuoka, Japan.
Furness Shipbuilding Company Ltd, Haverton Hill-on-Tees, England.

Germaniawerft, Fried Krupp AG, Kiel, Germany.
Gdynia Stocznia, Poland.
Gotaverken AB, Gothenburg, Sweden.
Govan Shipbuilders Ltd, Govan, Glasgow, Scotland.
W Gray & Company, West Hartlepool, England.

Hakodate Dock Company Ltd, Hakodate, Japan.
Halifax Shipyard Ltd, Halifax, Nova Scotia, Canada.
Hall, Russell & Company Ltd, Aberdeen, Scotland.
Hanseatic Shipyard, Hamburg, Germany.
Harima Zosensho, Aioi, Japan.
Harlan & Hollingsworth, Wilmington, Delaware, USA.
Harland & Wolff Ltd, Belfast, Northern Ireland.
Harland & Wolff Ltd, Govan, Scotland.
Harland & Wolff Ltd, Greenock, Scotland.
Hashihama Zosen, Imabari, Japan.
Haugesund MV AS, Haugesund, Norway.
Hawthorn, Leslie & Company, Hebburn, Newcastle-on-Tyne, England.
Hayashikane Shosen KK, Shimonoseki, Japan.
HDW AG, Hamburg, Germany. (See also Howaldtswerke-Deutsch.)
HDW AG, Kiel, Germany. (See also Howaldtswerke-Deutsch.)
Hellenic General Enterprises Company Ltd, Perama, Greece.
Helsingborgs Varfs AB, Helsingborgs, Denmark.
Helsingor Skibs & Msk, Helsingor, Denmark.
D & W Henderson & Company, Glasgow, Scotland.
Hijos de J Barreras SA, Vigo, Spain.
Hill & Sons, Bristol, England. (See also Chas Hill & Sons.)
Hindustan Shipyard, Vishgapatnam, India.
Hitachi Zosen, Innoshima/Sakai/Mikaishima, Japan.
Hitachi Zosen, Osaka, Japan.
Hong Kong & Whampoa Dock Company Ltd, Hong Kong.
AS Horten Werft, Horten, Norway.
Howaldtswerke-Deutsche Werft AG, Hamburg, Germany. (See also HDW.)
Howaldtswerke-Deutsche Werft AG, Kiel, Germany. (See also HDW.)
Hudong Shipyards, Guangdong Province, China.
Hyundai Shipbuilding Company, Ulsan, South Korea.

Imabari Zosen, Imabari, Japan.
Ingalls SB Corporation, Pascagoula, Mississippi, USA.
INMA, La Spezia, Italy.
Ishikawajima de Brasil-Estaleiros SA, Rio de Janeiro, Brazil.
Ishikawajima-Harima Heavy Industries, Aioi, Japan.
Italcantieri SpA, Genoa, Italy.
Italcantieri SpA, La Spezia, Italy.

M Jansen, Leer, Germany.
JL Thompson & Sons Ltd, Sunderland, England.
John Brown & Company Ltd, Clydebank, Scotland.
John Cockerill SA, Hoboken, Belgium. (See also Cockerill.)
John Elder & Company, Glasgow, Scotland.
Joseph L Meyer Shipyards, Papenburg, Germany.
Jurong Shipyard Ltd, Singapore.

Kaiser Corporation Inc, Richmond, California, USA.
Kaiser Corporation Inc, Vancouver, Washington, USA.
Kaldnes MV AS, Tonsberg, Norway.
Kanasashi Zosensho, Shimizu, Japan.
Kanawa Dock Company Ltd, Kudamatsu, Japan.

Kanda Zosensho KK, Kure, Japan.
Kasado Dock Company Ltd, Kudamatsu, Japan.
Kawasaki Dockyard Company Ltd, Kobe, Japan.
Kawasaki Heavy Industries Ltd, Kobe, Japan.
Kieler Howaldtswerke AG, Kiel, Germany.
Kochiken Zosen, Koochiken, Kapan.
Kockums Shipyard MV AB, Malmo, Sweden.
Koninklijke Maatschappij de Schelde, Flushing, Holland.
Koninklijke Schelde Groep BV, Vlissingen, Holland.
Korea Shipbuilding & Engineering Corporation, Pusan, South Korea.
Koyo Dock, Mihara, Japan.
Krasnoye Sormovo Shipyard, Gorkiy, Russia.
Krogerwerft GmbH, Rendsburg, Germany.
DW Kromer Sohn, Elmshorn, Germany.
F Krupp Shipbuilding, Kiel, Germany.
Kure Zosensho, Kure, Japan.
Kurinoura Dock, Kurinoura, Japan.
Kurushima Dockyard Company Ltd, Imabari, Japan.
Kvaerner Kleven Ulsteinvik AA, Ulsteinvik, Finland.
Kvaerner Masa-Yard Inc, Helsinki, Finland.
Kvaerner Masa-Yard Inc, Turku, Finland.

Laing & Sons.
Lake Washington Shipyards, Seattle, Washington, USA.
Leroux et Lotz Shipyards, St Malo, France.
Lindholmens Varv, Gothenburg, Sweden.
LMG, Orenstein Koppel & Lubecker Maschinenbau AG, Lubeck, Germany.
Lithgows Ltd, Port Glasgow, Scotland.
Lithgows (1969) Ltd, Port Glasgow, Scotland.
Lockheed Shipbuilding Co, Portland, Oregon, USA.
Lodose Varv AB, Lodose, Sweden.
London & Glasgow Engineering & Iron Shipbuilding Company Ltd, Govan, Scotland.

Marine Industries Ltd, Sorel, Quebec, Canada.
Mathias-Thesen-Werft VEB, Wismar, Germany.
Mazagon Dock , Mumbai, India.
Merchant Shipbuilding Corporation, Chester, Pennsylvania, USA.
Meyerwerft, Papenburg, Germany. (See also Joseph Meyer.)
Mitsubishi Dockyard Company, Kobe, Japan.
Mitsubishi Dockyard Company, Nagasaki, Japan.
Mitsubishi Heavy Industries Ltd, Kobe, Japan.
Mitsubishi Heavy Industries, Nagasaki, Japan.
Mitsubishi Heavy Industries Ltd, Shimonoseki, Japan.
Mitsui Zosen KK, Tama, Japan.
M Jansen, Leer, Germany.
Mjellem & Karlsen, Bergen, Norway.
Moss Rosenberg, Stav, Sweden.
MTW Schiffswerft, Wismar, Germany.

Nagoya Zosen, Nagoya, Japan.
Nakai Zosen KK, Setoda, Japan.
Nakai Zosen KK, Taguma, Japan.
Nakskov Skibsvaerft AS, Nakskov, Denmark.
Namura Zosensho, Osaka, Japan.
Napier & Miller Ltd, Glasgow.
Napier, R & Sons, Glasgow, Scotland.
Narazaki Zosen, Muroran, Japan.
Naval Construction & Armaments, Barrow-in-Furness, England.
Navale Meccaniche, Baia, Italy.
Nederlandsche Dok & Scheepsbouwerft Mij VoF, Amsterdam, Holland.
Nederlandsche Scheepsbouw Mij, Amsterdam, Holland.
Neptun Shipyards, Rostock, Germany.
Netherlands Shipbuilding Company, Amsterdam, Holland.
Newport News Shipbuilding & Dry Dock Company, Newport News, Virginia, USA.
New York Shipbuilding Corporation, Camden, New Jersey, USA.
Niigata Engineering Company Ltd, Niigata, Japan.
Nipponkai Heavy Industries Company Ltd, Toyama, Japan.
Nippon Kokan, Shimizu, Japan.
Nippon Kokan, Tsu, Japan.
Nippon Kokan, Tsurumi, Japan.

Nobiskrug GmbH, Rendsburg, Germany.
N Odero Plesandro & Company, Genoa, Italy.
Nordseewerke Rheinstahl GmbH, Emden, Germany.
North Carolina Shipbuilding Corporation, Wilmington, North Carolina, USA.
North East Shipbuilding, Pallion, Sunderland, England.
Northumberland Shipbuilding Company, Newcastle, England.
Nylands Verksted, Oslo, Norway.
Nystads Varv AB, Nystad/Uusikaupunki, Finland.

Odense Staalskibs AS, Lindo, Denmark.
Odero Plesandro & Company, Genoa, Italy.
Officine e Cantieri Liguri-Anconetani, Ancon, Italy.
Okean Shipyard, Nikolayev, Russian Federation.
Onomichi Zosen, Onomichi, Japan.
Oregon Shipbuilding Corporation, Portland, Oregon, USA.
Orenstein Koppel & Lbcr Masch, Lubeck, Germany.
Oresundsvarvet AB, Landskrona, Sweden.
Orskov Christensens Staalskibs AS, Frederikshaven, Denmark.
Osaka Iron Works, Osaka, Japan.
Osaka Tekkosho, Osaka, Japan.
Oshima Dockyard KK, Yoshiumi, Japan
Oskarshamns Varv AB, Oskarshamn, Sweden.

Pacific Islands Shipbuilding Company Ltd, Hong Kong.
Palmers Hebburn Company Ltd, Jarrow, England.
Palmers Shipbuilding & Iron Company Ltd, Jarrow, England.
J Pattje. (See Waterhuizen Scheeps.)
Penhoet, Penhoet-Loire, France. (See also Chantiers de l'Atlantique.)
Port Weller Drydocks Ltd, St Catharines, Ontario, Canada.
J Priestman & Company Ltd, Sunderland, England.
P Smit Jnr, Rotterdam, Holland.
Puget Sound Navy Yard, Seattle, Washington, USA.

Rauma-Repola OY, Rauma, Finland.
Raylton Dixon & Company, Middlesbrough-on-Tees, England.
J Readhead & Sons Ltd, South Shields, Newcastle, England.
Reiherstieg Schiffeswerfte und Maschinenfabrik, Hamburg, Germany.
Rheinstahl Norseewerke, Emden, Germany.
Rickmers Werft, Bremerhaven, Germany.
Robb Caledon Shipbuilders Ltd, Dundee, Scotland.
Rolandwerft GmbH, Bremen, Germany.
Ropner & Sons Ltd, Stockton, England.
AS Rosenberg MV, Stavanger, Norway.
Rotterdamsche Droogdok Mij NV, Rotterdam, Holland.
R & W Hawthorne, Leslie & Company Ltd, Hebburn, Newcastle-on-Tyne, England.
Russell & Company, Glasgow, Scotland.

Saint John Shipbuilding & Dry Dock Company Ltd, Saint John, New Brunswick, Canada.
Samuda Bros, London.
Samuel White Company, Cowes, Isle of Wight, England.
Sandvikins, Helsinki, Finland.
Sanoyasu Dockyard Company Ltd, Mizushimi, Japan.
Sanoyasu Dockyard Company Ltd, Osaka, Japan.
Santierul Naval, Galatz, Roumania.
Sanuki Shipbuilding, Tahma, Japan
Sasebo Heavy Industries, Sasebo, Japan.
Scheepsbouwerft Gebroeders Pot, Bolnes, Holland.
F Schichau, Danzig (Gdansk), Poland.
Schichau Seebeckwerft, Bremerhaven, Germany.
Schiffswerft Neptun, Rostock, Germany.
Schlichting Werft, Travemunde, Germany.
Gebr Schurenstedt, Bardenfleth, Germany.
J Scott, Russell & Company, Millwall, London, England
Scott's Shipbuilding & Engineering Company Ltd, Greenock, Scotland.
Scott's Shipbuilding Company (1969) Ltd, Greenock, Scotland.
Seattle-Tacoma Shipbuilding Corporation, Tacoma, Washington, USA.
Setoda Zosensho, Setoda, Japan.
Severney Shipyards, St Petersburg, Russia.

Shikoku Dock Company Ltd, Takamatsu, Japan.
Shimoda Dockyard Company Ltd, Shimoda, Japan.
Shinhama Anan, Anan, Japan.
Shinkurushima, Onichi, Japan.
Shin Mitsubishi Heavy Industries, Kobe, Japan.
Short Bros, Ltd, Sunderland, England.
JJ Sietas Schiffswerfte, Hamsburg, Germany.
Sir James Laing, Sunderland, England.
Sir Raylton Dixon & Company, Middlesbrough-on-Tees, England.
Sir WG Armstrong, Whitworth & Company, Newcastle, England.
Smith's Dock Company Ltd, Middlesbrough, England.
EJ Smit & Zn's Scheeps, Westerbroek, Holland.
L Smit & Zoon Scheeps, Kinderdijk, Holland.
P Smit Jnr, BV Machinefabriek en Scheepswerf van, Rotterdam, Holland.
P Smit, Jnr, Rotterdam, Holland.
Societa Esercizio Baccini, Riva Trigoso, Italy.
Societa Espanola de Construccion Naval SA, Bilbao, Spain.
Societa Espanola de Construccion Naval SA, Ferrol, Spain.
Societa Italia de Navigazione a Vapori, Genoa, Italy.
Societe des Forges et Chantiers de la Mediterranee, La Seyne, France.
Societe Provencal de Constructions Navales, La Ciotat, France.
Split Brodogradiliste I Tvornika Dizel Motora, Split, Croatia.
SSW Fahr und Specialschiffbaug GmbH, Bremerhaven, Germany.
Stabilimento Technico Triestino, Trieste, Italy.
State Dockyard, Newcastle, New South Wales, Australia.
A Stephen & Sons, Glasgow, Scotland.
Stettiner Oderwerke AG, Stettin, Germany.
Stocznia, Gdansk, Poland.
Stocznia im Komuny Paryskiej, Gdynia, Poland.
Stocznia Szczecinska Shipyard, Szczecin, Poland.
Suez Canal Authority, Port Said, Egypt.
Sumitomo Shipbuilding & Machinery Company Ltd, Uraga, Japan.
Sumitomo Shipbuilding & Machinery Company Ltd, Yokosuka, Japan.
Sunderland Shipbuilders Ltd, Sunderland, England.
Sun Shipbuilding & Dry Dock Company, Chester, Pennsylvania, USA.
Svendborg Skibsv AS, Svendborg, Denmark.
Swan & Hunter, Wallsend, Newcastle-on-Tyne, England.
Swan, Hunter & Wigham Richardson Ltd, Newcastle, England.
Swan Hunter Shipbuilders Ltd, Haverton Hill-on-Tees, England.
Swan Hunter Shipbuilders Ltd, Walker, England.

Taihei Kogyo, Hashihama, Japan.
Taikoo Dockyard & Engineering Company Ltd, Hong Kong.
Taiwan Shipbuilding Corporation, Keelung, Taiwan.
Tama Zosensho KK, Tama, Japan.
Tangen Vaerft, Kragero, Norway.
Joh C Tecklenborg AG, Geestemunde, Germany.
JL Thompson & Sons Ltd, North Sands, Sunderland, England.
J & G Thomson, Glasgow, Scotland.
JJ Thornycroft & Company Ltd, Southampton, England.
Todd-California Shipbuilding Corporation, Richmond, California, USA.
Todd Pacific Shipyards Corporation, Seattle, Oregon, USA.
Tohoku Zosen, Numakuma, Japan.
Trondheims AS MV, Trondheim, Norway.
Turkiye Gemi Halic, Halic, Turkey.

Uddevallavarvet AB, Uddevalla, Sweden.
Ujina Zosen, Hiroshima, Japan.
Uljanik Brodogradiliste, Pula, Croatia.
Ulstein MV AS, Ulsteinvik, Norway.
Union Naval de Levante SA, Barcelona, Spain.
Union Naval de Levante SA, Valencia, Spain.
United Engineers Ltd, Singapore.
United Shipyards, Perama Bay, Greece.
Unterwesser Sciffs, Bremerhaven, Germany.
Upper Clyde Shipbuilders Ltd, Clydebank, Scotland.
Upper Clyde Shipbuilders Ltd, Scotstoun, Scotland.
Upper Clyde Shipbuilders Ltd, Govan, Scotland.
Uraga Heavy Industries Ltd, Yokosuka, Japan.
Uraga Dock Company, Yokosuka, Japan.

Usuki Tekkosho, Saiki, Japan.

C van der Giessen & Zonen's Scheepswerven NV, Krimpen ad Ijssel, Holland.
Valmet oy Helsingen Telakka, Helsinki, Finland.
Van der Werffs Scheeps, Westerbroek, Holland.
Verolme Cork Dockyard Ltd, Cork, Republic of Ireland.
Verolme Scheepswerft., Alblasserdam, Holland.
Versatile Davie Shipyard Inc, Lauzon, Quebec, Canada.
Vickers-Armstrong Ltd, Barrow-in-Furness, England.
Vickers-Armstrong Ltd, Newcastle, England.
Vickers-Armstrong (Shipbuilders) Ltd, Barrow-in-Furness, England.
Vickers Ltd, Barrow-in-Furness, England.
Vickers Ltd, Newcastle, England.
Vickers, Sons & Maxim Ltd, Barrow-in-Furness, England.
Victoria Machinery Depot, Victoria, British Columbia, Canada.
A Vuijk & Zonen, Capelle, Holland.
Vulcan Stettiner Maschinenbau Actien Gesellschaft, Hamburg, Germany.
Vulcan Stettiner Maschinenbau Actien Gesellschaft, Stettin, Germany.

Wallace Shipbuilding & Drydock Company Ltd, Prince Rupert Island, British Columbia, Canada.
Warnowwerft, Warnemunde, Germany.
Wartsila AB Oy, Abo, Finland.
Wartsila AB Oy, Helsinki, Finland.
Wartsila AB Oy, Turku, Finland.
Watanabe Zosen, Watanabe, Japan.
Waterhuizen Scheeps (J Pattje), Waterhuizen, Holland.
Werf de Noord, Alblasserdam, Holland.
Werk Seebeck, Bremerhaven, Germany.
AG Weser Schichau Seebeck Werft, Bremerhaven, Germany.
West Coast Shipbuilding Ltd, Vancouver, Canada.
Western Pipe & Steel Company of California, South San Francisco, California, USA.
W Gray & Company, West Hartlepool, England.
William Beardmore & Company Ltd, Glasgow, Scotland. (See also W Beardmore & Company.)
William Cramp & Sons, Philadelphia, Pennsylvania, USA.
William Denny & Bros, Dumbarton, Scotland.
William Hamilton, Glasgow, Scotland.
Williamstown Naval Dockyard, Williamstown, Victoria, Australia
Wilton-Fijenoord Dok-en Werf Maats NV, Rotterdam, Holland.
Workman, Clark & Company Ltd, Belfast, Northern Ireland.

Xingang Shipyards, Tianjin, China.

Yantar Yard, Kaliningrad, Russia.
Yokohama Dock Company, Yokohama, Japan.

AALBORGHUS (1969) See TIAN E (1985)

AALLOTAR (1972) See ROGALIN (1992)

ABA (1918) See MATRONA (1947)

ABADOL (1915) See OAKLEAF (1917)

ABANGAREZ (1909)
4954 grt; 103 psrs
379' x 50' x 25' (114.8 x 15.2 x 7.6 m)
Triple expansion engine via single screw.
Broken up in Oakland, California in 1947.
Built by Workman, Clark Ltd, Belfast, for the United Fruit Steamship Co.

ABBY (1982) See CLUBSHIP ABEGWEIT (1997)

ABDA (1913)
4331 grt; 118 psrs
391' x 45' x 27'5" depth (118.5 x 13.7 x 8.3 m)
4-cylinder Koninklijke Maatschappij quadruple expansion engine via single screw.
Broken up for scrap in 1931 at Genoa ex-Cie de Navigation Paquet, Marseilles.
Built by Koninklijke Maatschappij for the Nederlands Steamship Co as the KONING WILLEM I (1898).

ABEGWEIT (1947) See CLUBSHIP ABEGWEIT (1997)

ABEGWEIT (1982) See ACCRUED MARINER (1999)

ABEL TASMAN (1985) See THEOFILOS (1995)

ABERDEEN (1881) See HALEP (1912)

ABETO (1977) See MEI ABETO (1984)

ABHA (1978) See NAJD II (1979)

ABINSI (1914)
6365 grt;138 psrs
401' x 53' x 31'5" depth (121.5 x 16.1 x 9.5 m)
8-cylinder quadruple expansion engines via twin screw.
Broken up for scrap in 1934.
Built by Harland & Wolff Ltd, Belfast, for Cie Belge Maritime du Congo as the LEOPOLDVILLE (1908).

ABKHAZIA (1956)
6807 grt; 548 psrs
432' x 59' x 18' (130.9 x 17.9 x 5.5 m)
2 x turbo-electric engines via twin screw.
In service with Black Sea Shipping Co, Odessa prior to the 1990 civil war.
Launched by Stettiner Oderwerke AG, Stettin, for Ostrreussen Baderdienst as the MARIENBURG (1939) and completed by Mathias-Thesen, Wismar, as the LENSOVIET (1946) after the ship was handed to the Russians as a war prize after World War Two.

ABKHAZIYA (1927)
4727 grt; 450 psrs
354' x 51' x 25'3" depth (107.3 x 15.5 x 7.7 m)
12-cylinder Russian Diesel Works diesel engines via twin screw.
Built by the Baltic Shipbuilding & Engineering Works yard at St Petersburg for the Russian government.

ABOITIZ SUPERFERRY I (1989) See SUPERFERRY I (1993)

ABOITIZ SUPERFERRY II (1992) See SUPERFERRY 2 (1996)

ABOITIZ SUPERFERRY III (1993) See SUPERFERRY 3 (1993)

ABOITIZ SUPERFERRY V (1994) See SUPERFERRY 5 (1996)

ABOITIZ SUPERFERRY 2 (1995) See SUPERFERRY 2 (1996)

ABOSSO (1912)
7782 grt; 400 psrs
427' x 57' x 22'6" (129.4 x 17.3 x 6.8 m)
Quadruple expansion engines via twin screw.
Sank on 24 April 24 1917 after being torpedoed, with 65 lives lost, 180 miles (300 km) off Fastnet.
Built by Harland & Wolff Ltd, Belfast, for the African Steamship Co.

ABOSSO (1935)
11330 grt; 550 psrs
481' x 65' x 31'5" depth (145.8 x 19.7 x 9.5 m)
B+W diesel engines via twin screw.
Torpedoed by U-575 and sank on 29 October 1942, 720 miles (1,200 km) north of the Azores. A total of 168 lives were lost, with 31 survivors being picked up from their lifeboat by the British destroyer HMS BIDEFORD on 1 November 1942.
Built by Cammell Laird & Co, Birkenhead, for Elder Dempster Lines as a passenger-cargo ship.

ABOUD (1991) See AL-ABOUD (1994).

ABU-ALIA (1984)
7759 grt; 50 psrs
492' x 65' x 24' (149.1 x 19.7 x 7.3m)
6-cylinder Sulzer geared diesel engines via single screw.
Passenger-cargo ship operating for the Rashid Shipping Co, Alexandria, between the Gulf ports and the US east coast.
Built by Brodogradiliste, Rijeka, for Jugolinija, Rijeka, as KLEK (1965).

ABU-EL-KASSEM (1978)
4410 grt; 81 psrs
385' x 54' x 19' (116.6 x 16.4 x 5.8 m)
Fiat diesel engines via single screw.
Passenger-cargo ship owned by the Arab Navigation Co, Alexandria, and operating between Gulf ports and the US east coast.
Built by Ansaldo Shipyards, Leghorn, for the Adriatica Line as BERNINA (1959).

ABU-HOSNA (1984)
7759 grt; 50 psrs
492' x 65' x 24' (149.1 x 19.7 x 7.3 m)
6-cylinder Sulzer geared diesel engine via single screw.
Passenger-cargo ship operating for the Rashid Shipping Co, Alexandria, and operating between Gulf ports and the US east coast.
Built by Brodogradiliste, Rijeka, for Jugolinija, Rijeka, as VISEVICA (1964).

ABU-RASHID (1984)
7759 grt; 50 psrs
492' x 65' x 24' (149.1 x 19.7 x 7.3 m)
6-cylinder Sulzer geared diesel engine via single screw.
Passenger-cargo ship operating for the Rashid Shipping Co, Alexandria, and operating between Gulf ports and the US east coast.
Built by Brodogradiliste, Rijeka, for Jugolinija, Rijeka, as TUHOBIC (1965).

ABU-YUSSUF (1984)
7759 grt; 50 psrs
492' x 65' x 24' (149.1 x 19.7 x 7.3 m)
6-cylinder Sulzer geared diesel engine via single screw.
Freight-passenger ship operating for the Rashid Shipping Co, Alexandria, operating between Gulf ports and the US east coast.
Built by Brodogradiliste, Rijeka, for Jugolinija, Rijeka, as ZVIR (1966).

ABYSSINIA (1900)
5656 grt; 1110 psrs
452' x 52' x 28'3" depth (137.8 x 15.9 x 8.6 m)
Palmers 3-cylinder triple expansion engine via single screw.
Wrecked near the lighthouse on Farne Islands, Northumberland.

Built by Palmers Co Ltd, Jarrow, for the Hamburg-America Line.

AC-14 (1920) See HUA TONG (1930)

ACADIA (1932)
6185 grt; 744 psrs
403' x 61' x 27' depth (122.1 x 18.5 x 8.2 m)
Turbine engines via twin screw.
Broken up for scrap in Bruges in 1955.
Built by Newport News Shipbuilding & Drydock Co, Newport News, for
Eastern Steamship Lines at a cost of US$3,500,000.

ACAPULCO (1961)
16504 grt; 411 psrs
568' x 71' x 33' (173.1 x 22 x 10 m)
6 x DRG turbines via twin screw.
Broken up for scrap in Osaka in 1964 ex-Navigation Turisticana Mexicana,
Mexico.
Built by Sir WG Armstrong, Whitworth, Vickers & Co, Tyneside, for P&O at
a cost of £1,000,000 as the MONGOLIA (1923). Renamed RIMUTAKA
(1938 – New Zealand Shipping Co Ltd), EUROPA (1950 – Cia de Navigation
Incres SA) and NASSAU (1951 – Incres Line) before being repositioned to
Seattle, Oregon, as an accommodation ship for the Seattle World Fair in 1962.

ACCORN I (1986) See AGIOS SARIDON (1994)

ACCRA (1926)
9337 grt; 313 psrs
451' x 62' x 24' (136.7 x 18.8 x 7.3 m)
2 x 6-cylinder H&W-B+W diesel engines via twin screw.
Sank on 26 July 1940 after being attacked by two U-boats and hit by multiple
torpedoes 300 miles (500 km) off the west coast of Ireland, with 19 lives lost.
Built by Harland & Wolff Ltd, Belfast, for Elder Dempster Lines.

ACCRA (1947)
11644 grt; 313 psrs
471' x 66' x 25'6" (142.7 x 20 x 7.8 m)
Doxford diesel engines via twin screw.
Broken up for scrap in Cartagena in 1967.
Built by Vickers-Armstrong Ltd, Tyneside, for Elder Dempster Lines.

ACCRUED MARINER (1999)
13482 grt; 950 psrs
251 cars & 40 trailers or 20 railroad coaches
402' x 71' x 19' (121.8 x 21.5 x 5.8 m)
6 x 16-cylinder Ruston diesel engines via twin screw.

Ice-strengthened passenger-car-cargo ferry operated by Accruel Investment
Inc.
Built by Saint John Shipbuilding & Drydock Co Ltd, Saint John, for CN
Marine Inc, Halifax, as the ABEGWEIT (1982).

ACHILLE LAURO (1948) See GIULIO CESARE (1922)

ACHILLE LAURO (1965)
23862 grt; 1343 psrs
643' x 82' x 24' (196 x 24.8 x 7.3 m)
8 x 8-cylinder Sulzer diesel engines via twin screw.
Owned by the Lauro Line and operated by the Mediterranean Shipping Co's
Star Lauro cruise division, she sank with the loss of three lives on 2 December
1994 following an explosion and fire off the Horn of Africa two days earlier.

In October 1985 she was subjected to a terrorist attack at sea with the loss of
one life.
Built by NV Koninklijke Maatschappij 'De Schelde', Flushing, for Royal
Rotterdam Lloyd as WILLEM RUYS (1947).

ACHILLES (1920) See BLENHEIM (1940)

ACHILLEUS (1952) See OLYMPIA I (1997)

ACHILLEUS (1969) See REGENCY (1982)

ACHIMOTA (1931) See WANGANELLA (1931)

ACILIA (1900)
5693 grt; 1110 psrs
452' x 52' x 28'3" depth (137.8 x 16 x 8.6 m)
3-cylinder triple expansion engine via single screw.
Disappeared without trace on 27 October 1913 on a voyage from Coronel,
Chile, to Hamburg.
Built by Palmer & Co, Jarrow, for Hapag.

ACONCAGUA (1938) See GIRESUN (1948)

ACROPOLIS (1920) See GREAT CANTON (1923)

ACROPOLIS (1961)
9237 grt; 450 psrs
508' x 72' x 26' (153.9 x 21.8 x 7.9 m)
DRG turbines via twin screw.
Broken up for scrap at Perama Bay in 1972. Ex-Typaldos Lines, Piraeus.
Built by Newport News Shipbuilding & Drydock Co, Newport News,
Virginia, for Grace Lines as the SANTA PAULA (1932).

ADANA (1948)
5236 grt; 306 psrs
404' x 58' x 23' (122.4 x 17.6 x 7 m)
SRG turbine engine via single screw.
Broken up for scrap in Istanbul in 1967. Ex-Turkish Maritime Lines.
Built by Newport News Shipbuilding & Drydock Co, Newport News,
Virginia, for the Columbia Mail Steamship Co as HAITI (1932). Renamed
PUERTO RICO (1938 – Columbia Mail Steamship Co) and MONTEREY
(1939 – Ward Line).

ADDA (1922)
7816 grt; 331 psrs
435' x 57' x 31'3" depth (131.8 x 17.3 x 9.5 m)
Harland & Wolff 16-cylinder diesel engines via twin screw.
Sank on 8 June 1941 after being torpedoed north of Freetown.
Built by Harland & Wolff Ltd, Belfast, for the Elder Dempster Line.

ADELAIDE (1984) See TAMBU EXPRESS (1980)

ADJARIA (1927) See ADJARISTAN (1927)

ADJARIA (1964) See ADZHARIYA (1964)

ADJARISTAN (1927)
4727 grt
354' x 51' x 25'3" depth (107.3 x 15.5 x 7.7 m)
2 x 12-cylinder Russian Diesel Works diesel engines via twin screw.
Built by Baltic Shipbuilding & Engineering Works, St Petersburg, for the
Russian government as the passenger ship ADJARIA (1927).

ADMIRAL (1996)
8974 grt; 800 psrs
150 cars or 11 rail coaches & 30 rail wagons

447' x 58' x 16' (135.5 x 17.7 x 4.8 m)
4 x 9-cylinder Halberstadt geared diesel engines via twin screw.
Ice-strengthened passenger-car-cargo-train RoRo ferry owned and operated by Traghetti Isole Sarde SRL.
Built by VEB Schiffswerft Neptun Shipyard, Rostock, for the East German State Railways as the train ferry WARNEMUNDE (1963).

ADMIRAL BENSON (1927)
3049 grt; 200 psrs
300' x 45' x 22'6" (90.9 x 15.2 x 6.8 m)
Bethlehem Steel Corporation 3-cylinder triple expansion engines via single screw.
Owned by Admiral Lines, she was abandoned as a total constructive loss after being wrecked on Peacock Sat, a notorious bar off Cape Disappointment in the Columbia river near Portland, Oregon, on 15 February 1930.
Built by Bethlehem Shipbuilding Corporation, Wilmington, Delaware, for the US Shipping Board as the passenger ship TIPTON (1918). Renamed ESTHER WEEMS (1922 – Baltimore & Carolina Steamship Co Inc).

ADMIRAL C. F. HUGHES (AP-124) (1945) See GENERAL EDWIN D. PATRICK, USS (T-AP-124) (1950)

ADMIRAL D. W. TAYLOR (1944) See ORIENTAL PRESIDENT (1973)

ADMIRAL E. W. EBERLE (AP-123) (1945) See GENERAL SIMON B. BUCKNER, USS (T-AP-123) (1950)

ADMIRAL F. B. UPHAM (1944) See ORIENTAL EMPRESS (1973)

ADMIRAL H. T. MAYO (AP-125) (1945) See GENERAL NELSON M. WALKER, USS (T-AP-125) (1950)

ADMIRAL HUGH RODMAN (AP-126) (1945) See GENERAL MAURICE ROSE, USS (T-AP-126) (1950)

ADMIRAL LAZAREV (1996)
4575 grt; 150 psrs
297' x 58' x 17'6" (90 x 17.6 x 5.3 m)
6 x Zgoda-Sulzer geared diesel engines via single screw.
Ice-strengthened passenger ship owned by Yuzhmorgeologiya , Novorossiysk, and laid up since July 1998 awaiting a sale at US$4,600,000.
Built by Stocznia in Komuny, Gdynia, for Yuzhmorgeologiya as the NEVA (1991).

ADMIRAL MAKAROV (1975)
14058 grt; 85 psrs
443' x 86' x 36' (135 x 26.1 x 11 m)
9 x 12-cylinder Sulzer diesel engines via triple screw.
Broken up for scrap in 1995 as a passenger-icebreaker cruise ship operated by the Far Eastern Shipping Co, Vladivostok.
Built by Wartsila, Helsinki for the Russian government.

ADMIRAL NAKHIMOV (1949)
17053 grt; 1122 psrs
572' x 69' x 29' (173.3 x 20.1 x 8.8 m)
Triple expansion engine via twin screw.
Sailing for the Black Sea Shipping Co, Odessa, she capsized and sank in 155' (47 m) of water within fifteen minutes of a collision just beyond the harbour limits of the Black Sea port of Novorossisk, on 31 August 1986. At 12.15 am that night, the Russian bulk carrier PYOTR VASEV thrust her deadweight of 32,961 tons into the ADMIRAL NAKHIMOV's starboard side and tore a massive hole, 950 square feet (90 square metres), that exposed the engine room and boilers to the sea. There was a loss of 398 lives.
Built by Bremer Vulkan, Vegesack, for North German Lloyd as the passenger ship BERLIN (1925). She suffered a boiler explosion in 1939 which killed 17 people during a mid-summer cruise, then visited the bottom of the sea during World War Two on 1 February 1945 when she hit a mine off the coast of Swinemunde. She was raised and rebuilt by the Russians over a period of six years after they received her as part of World War Two reparations.

ADMIRAL OF SCANDINAVIA (1997)
18888 grt; 1113 psrs

404 cars
516' x 78' x 17'6" (156.4 x 23.6 x 5.3 m)
2 x 16-cylinder Sulzer diesel engines via twin screw.

Passenger-car ferry operating for Scandinavian Seaways who purchased her for approximately US$30,000,000 from DFDS.
Built by Werft Nobiskrug, Rendsburg, for the Jahre Line as the KRONPRINS HARALD (1976). Renamed HAMBURG (1987 – DFDS).

ADMIRAL PACIFIC (1978) See AL SALAM 89 (1992)

ADMIRAL PEOPLES (1927) See NORTH SEA (1935)

ADMIRAL PIERRE (1922) See LA PEROUSE (1928)

ADMIRAL R. E. COONTZ (AP-122) (1944) See GENERAL ALEXANDER M. PATCH (T-AP 122) (1947)

ADMIRAL VON TIRPITZ (1913) See EMPRESS OF AUSTRALIA (1922)

ADMIRAL WILLIAM S. SIMS (AP-127) (1945) See GENERAL WILLIAM O. DARBY (T-AP 127) (1950)

ADMIRAL W. L. CAPPS (AP-121) (1944) See GENERAL J. GAFFEY (T-AP 121) (1950)

ADMIRAL W. S. BENSON (AP-120) (1944) See GENERAL DANIEL I. SULTAN (T-AP 120) (1947)

ADONIS (1965) See ATLANTIS (1977)

ADRIA (1896) See KHAZAN (1906)

ADRIA (1968) See ODYSSEUS (1969)

ADRIA (1981) See CAPO CARBONARA (1988)

ADRIANA (1988)
4490 grt; 324 psrs
343' x 46' x 14'9" (104 x 14 x 4.5 m)
2 x 8-cylinder Pielstick diesel engines via twin screw.
Cruise ship for Marina Cruises, St Vincent.
Built by United Shipyards, Perama Bay, for Hellenic Mediterranean Lines as the AQUARIUS (1972).

ADRIATIC (1907)
24563 grt; 2825 psrs
726' x 76' x 52'6" depth (220 x 23.1 x 15.9 m)
8-cylinder quadruple expansion engines via twin screw.
Broken up for scrap in Osaka in 1935.
Built by Harland & Wolff, Belfast, for the White Star Line.

ADRIATIC STAR (1984) See TEBAH 2000 (1999)

ADSHARIA (1964) See ADZHARIYA (1964)

ADZHARIYA (1964)
4871 grt; 333psrs
401' x 52' x 17' (121.5 x 15.8 x 5.2 m)
2 x 6-cylinder MAN diesel engines via twin screw.

Broken up for scrap at Aliaga in 1996 as a cruise ship.
Built by Mathias-Thesen, Wismar, for the Black Sea Shipping Co, Odessa.

AEGAEON (1949)
3099 grt; 1200 psrs
291' x 46' x 17' (88.2 x 13.9 x 5.2 m)
4-cylinder reciprocating engine via single screw.
Owned by Typaldos Lines, she sank on 2 December 1966 off the Roman port of Civitavecchia while under tow to the breakers yards in La Spezia.
Built by Swan Hunter Shipbuilders, Newcastle, for the Canadian Pacific Steamship Co as the PRINCESS ALICE (1911).

AEGEAN I (1996)
11563 grt; 576 psrs
420' x 66' x 22' (130 x 20 x 6.7 m)
2 x 14-cylinder Pielstick diesel engines via twin screw.

Cruise ship owned by Dolphin (Hellas) Shipping SA, Piraeus, and operated by Golden Sun Cruises.
Built by Santuerul Naval Galatz, Galatz, for Zim Lines as the freighter NARCIS (1973). Renamed as the passenger-car RoRo ferry ALKYON (1985 – Zea Shipping Co Ltd, Malta), cruise ship AEGEAN DOLPHIN (1986 – Dolphin Hellas Shipping Co), DOLPHIN (1989 – Dolphin Hellas Shipping Co) and AEGEAN DOLPHIN (1990 – Dolphin Hellas Shipping Co).

AEGEAN DOLPHIN (1986) See AEGEAN I (1996)

AEGEAN DOLPHIN (1990) See AEGEAN I (1996)

AEGEAN SPIRIT (2000)
16741 grt; 772 psrs
580' x 73' x 26' (176.7 x 22.3 x 7.9 m)
4 x 16-cylinder Wartsila diesel engines via twin screw.

Cruise ship under long term charter to Golden Sun Cruises.
Built by Swan Hunter & Wigham Richardson, Newcastle, for SCTM, Marseilles, as the passenger ship PROVENCE (1951). Renamed ENRICO C (1965 – Costa Cruises), ENRICO COSTA (Costa Cruises) and SYMPHONY (1995 – Mediterranean Shipping Cruises SpA, following purchase for US$85,000,000).

AEGEO STAR (1995) See NEW YORK FORTUNE I (1997).

AENEAS (1910)
10049 grt; 288 psrs
509' x 60' x 29'6" (155.1 x 18.1 x 8.9 m)
Triple expansion engines via twin screw.
Sank with the loss of 19 lives after being attacked by German aircraft 21 miles

(35 km) south-east of Start Point in the English Channel on 2 July 1940.
Built by Workman, Clark & Co Ltd, Belfast, for the Blue Funnel Line.

AEOLIA (1950)
4285 grt; 115 psrs
342' x 48' x 24'3" (104.2 x 14.5 x 7.4 m)
3-cylinder triple expansion engine via single screw.
Broken up for scrap in Japan in 1960. Ex-Panamanian Lines.
Built by Nederlandsche Scheepsbouw Mij, Amsterdam, for Koninkl Nederlandsche Stoom Maats as the STUYVESANT (1930).

AEOLIS (1967) See SOL PHRYNE (1977)

AEOLUS (1917) See CITY OF LOS ANGELES (1922)

AESAREA (1981)
3992 grt; 1400 psrs
321' x 54' x 13' (97.3 x 16.4 x 3.9 m)
2 x Pametrada DRG turbine engines via twin screw.
Broken up for scrap in South Korea in 1986. Ex-Superluck Enterprises Inc, Panama.
Built by J White & Co Ltd, Cowes, Isle of Wight for the British Transport Commission as CAESAREA (1960) at a cost of £1,500,000.

AETOS (1971) See EXPRESS KARISTOS (1995)

AFFAN OCEANA (1965) See AMBULOMBO (1966)

AFFON (1911)
4865 grt; 1250 psrs
403' x 47' x 27'6" depth (122.8 x 14.4 x 8.4 m)
3- cylinder triple expansion engine via single screw.
Broken up for scrap in 1928. Ex-Russian government.
Built by G Ansaldo & Co, Sestri Ponente, for Navigazione Generale Italiana as the passenger liner LIGURIA (1901).

AFGHANISTAN (1962)
3219 grt; 250 psrs
333' x 48' x 13' (100.9 x 14.5 x 3.9 m)
Russian Diesel Works diesel engines via twin screw.
Built by A Jdanov Shipyards, St Petersburg, for the Russian government.

AFRICA (1952) See PROTEA (1976)

AFRICA (1986)
3392 grt; 904 psrs
340' x 55' x 17' (103 x 16.6 x 5.2 m)
2 x 7-cylinder B+W diesel engines via twin screw.
Passenger ferry for the Ria de Vigo Company.
Built by Union Naval de Levante for Cia Trasmediterranea as VIRGEN DE AFRICA (1953).

AFRICA-CUBA (1978)
14491 grt; 841 psrs
557' x 69' x 27' (169.7 x 21 x 8.2 m)
2 x 10-cylinder Sulzer diesel engines via twin screw.
Broken up for scrap at Barcelona in 1982 ex-Cuban Government.
Built by Soc. Espanola de Construccion Naval SA, Bilbao for Ybarra y Cia as the CABO SAN ROQUE (1957). Renamed GOLDEN MOON (1977 – Growth Marine, Cyprus).

AFRICA MARU (1918)
9476 grt; 71 psrs
475' x 61' x 28'3" (143.9 x 18.5 x 8.6 m)
Triple expansion engines via twin screw.
Sank on 20 October 1942 when hit by a torpedo fired from the USS FINBACK in the Straits of Formosa.
Built by Mitsubishi Dockyard, Kobe, for Mitsui OSK.

AFRICA MARU (1951) See VANLENE (1967)

AFRICA MERCY (1999)
16572 grt; original capacity 450 psrs
469' x 75'6" x 19'6" (143 x 23 x 6 m)

6 x 16-cylinder B+W diesel engines via twin screw.

Ice-strengthened passenger-train ferry purchased for £4,000,000 by Ms Ann Gloag, an Executive Director of Stagecoach Holdings plc., Denmark, and donated to Mercy Ships for use as a seagoing eye hospital for the African continental ports.
Built by Helsingor Vaerft AS, Helsingor, for the Danish government as the DRONNING INGRID (1980 – operated by Scandlines). Renamed INGRID (1999) for handover to Mercy Ships.

AFRICAN COMET (1941) See ARTHUR MIDDLETON, USS (AP-55) (1942)

AFRICAN ENDEAVOUR (1948)
7997 grt; 86 psrs
492' x 66' x 26' (149.1 x 20 x 7.9 m)
General Electric geared turbines via single screw.
Broken up for scrap at Baltimore in 1969. Ex-Farrell Lines.
Built by Bethlehem Steel Corporation, Sparrow's Point, Maryland, for the Mississippi Shipping Co as the DELBRASIL (1939). Renamed GEORGE F. ELLIOTT, USS (AP-105) (1943 – US Navy).

AFRICAN ENTERPRISE (1948)
7997 grt; 86 psrs
492' x 66' x 26' (149.1 x 20 x 7.9 m)
General Electric geared turbines via single screw.
Broken up for scrap at Baltimore in 1969 ex-Farrell Lines.
Built by Bethlehem Steel Corporation, Sparrow's Point, Maryland, for the Mississippi Shipping Co as the DELARGENTINO (1940). Renamed J. W. McANDREW (1941 – US Navy).

AFRICAN METEOR (1941) See SAMUEL CHASE, USS (AP-56) (1942)

AFRICAN PLANET (1941) See GEORGE CLYMER, USS (APA-27) (1942)

AFRICAN TRADER (1980) See CARLA E (1991)

AFRIQUE (1907)
5404 grt; 277 psrs
391' x 48' x 27'7" depth (118.5 x 14.5 x 8.4 m)
Triple expansion engines via twin screw.
Sank in deep water on 12 January 1920 after sliding off Roche-Bonne Reef, 50 miles (83 km) from La Rochelle, France, some hours after hitting them following complete engine failure. She took 533 lives with her.
Built by Swan Hunter Shipyards, Newcastle, for Chargeurs-Reunis, Paris.

AFRODITE II (1995)
9565 grt; 500 psrs
456' x 70' x 15' (138.3 x 21.1 x 4.6 m)
2 x 16-cylinder Lindholmens-Pielstick diesel engines via twin screw.
Passenger-cargo ferry owned by Namora Shipping Ltd, Limassol, and operated by MedLink Lines SA.
Built by Swan Hunter Shipbuilders Ltd, Newcastle, for the Atlantic Steam Navigation Co Ltd, London, as the EUROPIC FERRY (1968). Renamed EUROPEAN FREIGHTER (1992 – P&O European Ferries Ltd).

AGADIR (1974) See GOLFINHO AZUL (1999).

AGAMEMNON (1917) See MONTICELLO (1927).

AGAMEMNON, USS (1953)
5557 grt; 490 psrs
416' x 55' x 17' (126.1 x 16.7 x 5.2 m)
2 x DRG turbine engines via twin screw.
Broken up for scrap in Piraeus in 1968 after capsizing in the harbour. Ex-US Shipping Board.
Built by Ansaldo Shipyards, Leghorn for the Greek government.

AGAPITOS I (1973)
3482 grt; 1400 psrs
28 cars
321' x 51' x 13' (97 x 15.4 x 3.9 m)
4 x Parsons SRG turbine engines via twin screw.
Broken up for scrap in Piraeus in 1980. Ex-Agapitos Bros, Greece.
Built by Cammell Laird & Co, Birkenhead, for the Fishguard & Rosslare Railways & Harbours Co as the St PATRICK (1948) at a cost of £500,000. Renamed THERMOPYLAE (1972 – Gerasimos S Fetouris, Greece).

AGIA METHODIA (1993) See TAXIARCHIS (1999)

AGIOS ANDREAS (1995)
11109 grt; 1120 psrs
300 cars
445' x 70' x 17' (135.6 x 21.3 x 5.2 m)
4 x 12-cylinder Pielstick diesel engines via twin screw., all transferred from the PEGASUS.
Passenger-car ferry operated by the Medlink Line on the Greece-to-Italy service.
Built by the New South Wales State Dockyard, Newcastle, for Australian National Lines as the AUSTRALIAN TRADER (1969). Renamed as the training ship JERVIS BAY, HMAS (AGT-203) (1977 – Royal Australian Navy).

AGIOS SPIRIDON (1994) See ANDROMEDA I (1999)

AGIOS VASSILIOS (1995) See CLYDESDALE (1998)

AGRA (1871) See ASHRUF (1900)

AGUADILLA (1975) See AMOCO VOYAGER (1982).

AGUILA (1912)
3255 grt; 106 psrs
315' x 44' x 25' (95.5 x 13.3 x 7.6 m)
3-cylinder triple expansion engines via single screw.
Sank in less than a minute on 19 August 1941 after two torpedoes from the German U-201 struck her off the Portuguese coast, with 157 lives lost.
Built by Caledon Shipyards, Dundee, for the Yeoward Line.

AGWILEON (1940) See SHAMROCK (1943).

AIDA (1996)
38531 grt; 1186 psrs
578' x 77' x 21' (176.3 x 23.6 x 6.4 m)
4 x 6-cylinder MAN-B+W geared diesel engines via twin screw.
Cruise ship initially chartered by Deutsche Seetouristik, Rostock, from Norwegian Cruise Line, but subsequently re-purchased in 1999 at US$180,000,000 to be operated by the P&O group following its successful

100% control acquisition of Aida Cruises.
Built by Kvaerner-Masa Yard at Turku at a cost of US$185,000,000.

AIDAN (1911)
4550 grt; 146 psrs
376' x 50' x 23' (113.9 x 15.2 x 7 m)
3-cylinder turbine engines via twin screw.
Built by Tyne International Shipbuilding Co Ltd, Newcastle, for the Booth Line as a passenger-cargo ship.

AIKOKU MARU (1939)
10437 grt; 400 psrs
537' x 66' x 40'7" (162.7 x 20 x 12.3 m)
2 x 24-cylinder Tama-B+W diesel engines via twin screw.
Sank on 17 February 1944 after being attacked by US aircraft near Truk Atoll, South Pacific.
Built by Tama Shipbuilding Co for OSK, Tama.

AILSA PRINCESS (1971) See NAIAS EXPRESS (1995)

AISNE (1920) See VILLE DE NAMUR (1940)

AIVAZOVSKY (1976) See CARINA (1996)

AJAX (1901) See HUA TONG (1930)

A & J FAITH (1963) See COSMOS MARINER (1966)

A & J MERCURY (1963) See COSMOS TRADER (1966)

AJWASOWSKIJ (1976) See AIVAZOVSKY (1976)

AKABO (1912) See BALTONIA (1926)

AKADEMIK HESEN ALIYEV (1995)
11450 grt; 202 psrs
50 cars
510' x 60' x 15' (154.5 x 18.3 x 4.5 m)
2 x B+W diesel engines via twin screw.
Passenger-car-cargo RoRo ferry, owned and operated by Caspian Shipping Co, Baki.
Built by Brodogradiliste Uljanik, Pula, for the Russian government as the SOVIETSKAYA KIRGIZIYA (1986). Renamed KIRGIZSTAN (1992 – Russian government).

AKADEMIK IOFFE (1987) See PEREGRINE MARINER (2000)

AKADEMIK KURCHATOV (1966)
5683 grt; 155 psrs
409' x 56' x 20' (123.9 x 17 x 6.1 m)
2 x 6-cylinder MAN diesel engines via twin screw.
Converted to a dedicated ocean research ship owned by Shirshov Oceanological Institute (Atlantic Division), Kaliningrad.
Built by Mathias-Thesen Werft VEB, Wismar, for the Russian government as an ice-strengthened passenger ship.

AKADEMIK M. TOPCHUBASHOV (1995)
11450 grt; 200 psrs
50 cars
513' x 60' x 15' (155.6 x 18.3 x 4.5 m)
2 x 6-cylinder Uljanik-B+W diesel engines via twin screw.
Passenger-car ferry owned and operated by Caspian Shipping Co, Baki.
Built by Brodogradiliste, Pula, for the Caspian Shipping Co, Baki, as the SOVIETSKAYA KALMYKIYA (1985). Renamed KALMYKIYA (1994 – Russian government) and MERCURI-3 (1995 – Russian government).

AKADEMIK NICOLAY PILYU (1999) See SEVEN SEAS NAVIGATOR (1999)

AKADEMIK SERGEY VAVILOV (1988) See MARINE VOYAGER (1995)

AKADEMIK SHIRSHOV (1967)
5754 grt; 90 psrs

409' x 56' x 20' (124 x 17 x 6 m)
2 x 6-cylinder MAN diesel engines via twin screw.
Owned by Far Eastern Regional Hydrometeorological Institute, Vladivostok, and chartered out for cruising ad hoc.
Built by Mathias-Thesen Werft VEB, Wismar, for the Institute as an ice-strengthened dedicated research-cum-passenger ship.

AKARITA (1971) See AKARITA (1981)

AKARITA (1981)
20348 grt; 419 psrs
584' x 78' x 29' (178 x 23.8 x 8.8 m)
2 x 16-cylinder B+W diesel engines via twin screw.
Broken up as a car carrier for scrap at Kaohsiung in 1982. Ex-Ace Navigation Co Ltd.
Built by Harland & Wolff, Belfast, for Royal Mail Lines as the passenger-cargo ship AMAZON (1960). Renamed AKAROA (1968 – Shaw Savill Line), AKARITA (1971 – Uglands Rederi, Norway, as a car carrier) and HUAL AKARITA (1978 – Ace Navigation Co Ltd).

AKAROA (1932)
15320 grt; 200 psrs
570' x 67' x 33' (173.7 x 20.4 x 10 m)
2 x 4-cylinder triple expansion engines via triple screw.
Broken up for scrap. Ex-Shaw Savill Line in Antwerp in 1954 by J. de Smedt & Co.
Built by Harland & Wolff, Belfast, for the Aberdeen Line as the passenger-cargo liner EURIPIDES (1914).

AKAROA (1968) See AKARITA (1981)

AKATSUKI (1981) See MAYNILAD (1992)

AKBAR (1914)
4573 grt; 60 psrs
390' x 47' x 27' (118.2 x 14.2 x 8.2 m)
Triple expansion engine via single screw.
Broken up as a pilgrim ship for scrap in Genoa in 1923. Ex-Mogul Line.
Built by R Napier & Sons Ltd, Glasgow, for the Aberdeen Line as the MORAVIAN (1898).

AKBAR (1971)
8279 grt; 1580 psrs
493' x 62' x 25' (149.4 x 18.8 x 7.6 m)
2 x 7-cylinder B+W diesel engines via twin screw.
Owned and operated by the Shipping Corporation of India Ltd, Mumbai.
Built by the Elsinore Shipyard, Elsinore, as a passenger (pilgrims)-cargo ferry for Turkish Maritime Lines.

AK-DENIZ (1911)
5006 grt; 1988 psrs
415' x 48' x 31'3" (126.5 x 14.6 x 9.5 m)
3-cylinder triple expansion engine via single screw.
Broken up for scrap in 1923 at Aliaga. Ex-Turkish Maritime Lines.
Built by Fairfield Shipbuilding & Engineering Co Ltd, Glasgow, for North German Lloyd as the OLDENBURG (1891).

AK DENIZ (1955)
7864 grt; 444 psrs
475' x 63' x 20' (144 x 19 x 6.1m)
2 x 8-cylinder MAN diesel engines via twin screw.
Training ship since 1997 operated by the Turkish Naval Academy at Tuzla.
Built by AG Weser Shipyards, Bremen, for Turkish Maritime Lines as a passenger-cargo ship.

AKEBONO MARU (1977) See SUPERFERRY 8 (1996)

AKERSHUS (1965) See MAZATLAN (1973)

AKI MARU (1903)
6444 grt; 246 psrs
445' x 49' x 33'6" (135.6 x 14.9 x 10.2 m)
2 x triple expansion engines via twin screw.
Broken up for scrap in 1934.

Built by Mitsubishi Dockyard, Nagasaki, for NYK as a passenger-cargo liner.

AKI MARU (1942)
11409 grt; 137 psrs
535' x 66' x 25' (162.1 x 20 x 7.6 m)
Diesel engines via twin screw.
Sank after being torpedoed on 26 July 1944 by the USS CREVALLE west of Luzon.
Launched by Mitsubishi, Nagasaki, as a passenger ship on 15 May 1942 for NYK, Japan, but completed as a troopship.

AKITSU MARU (1974)
3830 grt; 850 psrs
55 cars & 51 trailers
403' x 65' x 16'6" (122 x 19.6 x 5 m)
2 x 12-cylinder Niigata diesel engines via twin screw.
Passenger-car-cargo ferry operating for Oshima Unyu, KK.
Built by Fukuoka Shipbuilding Co, Fukuoka.

AKROTIRI EXPRESS (1972) See SWITZERLAND (1996)

AKTIV MARINE (1990) See URD (1991)

ALABAMA MARU (1920)
9617 grt; 65 psrs
475' x 61' x 28' (143.9 x 18.5 x 8.5 m)
6 x triple expansion engines via twin screw.
Abandoned as a total constructive loss after she grounded in 1930.
Built by Mitsubishi Zosen, Nagasaki, for OSK, Japan.

AL-ABOUD (1994)
4051 grt; 1200 psrs
130 cars
306' x 55' x 14' (92.7 x 16.7 x 4.2 m)
4 x 12-cylinder B+W diesel engines via twin screw.

Owned by the Red Sea Navigation & Contracting Co Ltd, Jeddah.
Built by Aalborg Vaerft, Aalborg, for Mols-Linien as the ice-strengthened passenger-car ferry MAREN MOLS (1966). Renamed MAREN MO (1975 – Mols-Linien), CARAVAGGIO (1975 – Sicula Regionale di Navigazione SpA, Messina). Laid up during 1990. Renamed ABOUD (1991 – Al Zaher II Marine Co Ltd).

ALA-EDDIN (1987) See LA PATRIA (2000)

ALAMIRA (1997)
5250 grt; 867 psrs
190 cars
377' x 59' x 13' (114.2 x 18 x 3.9 m)
2 x 16-cylinder Pielstick diesel engines via twin screw.
Passenger-car ferry owned & operated by Waad Shipping Co Ltd, Athens.
Built by Ateliers et Chantiers Reunis de la Loire, St Nazair, for SNCF as the COMPIEGNE (1958). Renamed IOANIAN GLORY (1981 – Strintzis Lines), QUEEN VERGINA (1989 – Strintzis Lines), Freedom I (1990 – Ross Shipping Co), KATARINA (1994 – Raneem Shipping) and FREEDOM I (1990 – Ross Shipping Co).

ALANDIA (1972) See ALANDIA (1992)

ALANDIA (1992)
6754 grt; 1200 psrs
220 cars + 26 trailers
359' x 57' x 15' (108.7 x 17.2 x 4.6 m)

2 x 12-cylinder Deutz diesel engines via twin screw.

Ice-strengthened passenger-car-cargo ferry owned by Rederi AB Eckero and operated by Eckero Line.
Built by Jos L Meyer, Papenburg, for the Viking Line as the DIANA (1972). Renamed ALANDIA (1972 – Birka Lines) and BOTNIA EXPRESS (1979 – Wasa Line).

ALANDSFARJAN (1987)
6172 grt; 1500 psrs
250 cars
343' x 62' x 15' (104 x 18.9 x 4.6 m)
2 x 10-cylinder B+W diesel engines via twin screw.

Owned by Finlandsexpressen and operated by the Viking Line as a ferry between Sweden and Finland.
Built by Helsingor Skibsvaerft og Maskinbyg for Jydsk Faergefart AS, Hundestedt as the KATTEGAT (1972). Renamed nf TIGER (1978 – P&O Normandy Ferries) and TIGER (1985 – Townsend Car Ferries Ltd).

ALASKA (1915)
3679 grt; 218 psrs
327' x 45' x 18'6" (99.1 x 13.6 x 5.6 m)
Delaware River Co 3-cylinder triple expansion engines via single screw.
Sank off Cape Mendocino, California, on 6 August 1921, after striking Blunt's Reef in dense fog, with the loss of 42 lives.
Built by Delaware River Co, Chester, Pennsylvania, for the Alaska Steamship Co as the KANSAS CITY (1889).

ALASKA (1923) See MAZATLAN (1955)

ALAUNIA (1913)
13405 grt; 2060 psrs
538' x 65' x 22'6" (163 x 19.7 x 6.8 m)
Scotts 2 x 4-cylinder quadruple expansion engines via twin screw.
Sank on 19 October 1916 with the loss of two lives after hitting a mine laid two miles (3 km) south of the ROYAL SOVEREIGN lightship, off Sussex in the English Channel.
Built by Scotts Shipbuilding & Engineering Co, Greenock, for the Cunard Steamship Co Ltd as a passenger liner.

ALAUNIA (1925) See ALAUNIA, HMS (1941).

ALAUNIA, HMS (1941)
14030 grt; 1673 psrs
540' x 65' x 32' (163.6 x 19.7 x 9.7 m)
4 x John Brown DRG turbines via twin screw.
Broken up for scrap by British Iron & Steel Corporation at Blyth in 1957.
Built by John Brown & Co Ltd, Clydebank, for the Cunard Line as the passenger liner ALAUNIA (1925).

ALAVIA (1903)
4911 grt; 210 psrs
420' x 43' x 34'6" (128.1 x 13.1 x 10.5m)
Compound inverted engine via single screw.
Broken up for scrap in 1906.
Built by Caird & Co, Greenock, for P&O as the passenger-cargo liner VALETTA (1883) at a cost of £137,081 and resold to Shah Steam Navigation Co for £12,199 and renamed ALAVIA.

ALBA (1920) See AMERIQUE (1926)

ALBANIA (1911) See POLERIC (1912)

ALBANIA (1914)
4041 grt; 1330 psrs
364' x 44' x 19' (110.9 x 13.3 x 5.8 m)
3-cylinder triple expansion engine via single screw.
Broken up for scrap in 1933. Ex-Lloyd Triestino.
Built by N Odero fu Alessandro & Co, Sestri Ponente, for La Veloce Navigazioni Italiana as the CITTA DI MILANO (1897).

ALBANIA (1920) See CALIFORNIA (1930)

ALBANO (1895) See BRETON (1911)

ALBANY (1908) See MEGANTIC (1909)

ALBANY (1968) See MISSION VIKING (1974)

ALBATROS (1981) See STAR OF VENICE (1992)

ALBATROS (1993)
24803 grt; 720 psrs
608' x 80' x 29' (185.3 x 24.4 x 8.9 m)
4 x Pametrada DRG steam turbines via twin screw.
Cruise ship owned and operated by Phoenix Reisin, Bonn.
Built by John Brown & Co, Clydebank, for the Cunard Line as the SYLVANIA (1956). Renamed FAIRWIND (1968 – Sitmar Line), SITMAR FAIRWIND (1988 – Sitmar Cruises) and DAWN PRINCESS (1988 – P&O Princess Cruises).

ALBATROSS (1972) See PATMOS (1991)

ALBATROSS (1985) See STAR OF VENICE (1992).

ALBATROSS, HMAS (1929) See HELLENIC PRINCE (1948)

ALBATROSS, HMS (1938) See HELLENIC PRINCE (1948)

ALBERTA (1908) See LAURENTIC (1909)

ALBERT BALLIN (1923) See SOJUS (1980)

ALBERTIC (1927)
18940 grt; 1442 psrs
615' x 71' x 31' (186.4 x 21.5 x 9.4 m)
8-cylinder quadruple expansion engines via twin screw.
Broken up for scrap for US$60,000 in Osaka in 1934. Ex-White Star Line.
Launched by AG Weser, Bremen, for North German Lloyd as the MUNCHEN (1913), but completed as the OHIO (1923 – Royal Mail Lines).

ALBERTO DODERO (1951) See ETAIWI I (1980)

ALBERTVILLE (1906) See CAIRO CITY (1933)

ALBERTVILLE (1927)
11047 grt; 358 psrs
537' x 62' x 25'6" (162.7 x 18.8 x 7.8 m)
Hawthorne-Leslie 8-cylinder quadruple expansion engines via twin screw.
Sank off Le Havre on 11 June 1940 after being attacked by German aircraft.
Built by Ateliers et Chantiers de la Loire, St Nazaire, for Cie Maritime Belge.

ALBERTVILLE (1948)
10901 grt; 207 psrs

505' x 65' x 27'6" (153 x 19.7 x 8.4 m)
B+W-type 8-cylinder diesel engine via single screw.
Broken up for scrap by Nan Feng Steel Enterprise in Kaohsiung in 1973.
Built by John Cockerill SA, Hoboken, Belgium for Cie Maritime Belge.

ALBINGIA (1905) See ARGONAUT (1916)

ALBINGIA (1907) See ARGONAUT (1916)

ALBIREO (1973) See BLUE ISLAND (2000)

ALCA (1927)
3712 grt; 216 psrs
319' x 46' x 20'6" (97.7 x 13.9 x 6.2 m)
Caledon 3-cylinder triple expansion engine via single screw.
The only surviving vessel from the Yeoward Line after World War Two, she was broken up for scrap in 1955. Ex-Greenland government.
Built by Caledon Shipbuilding & Engineering Co Ltd, Dundee, for the Yeoward Line.

ALCAEOS (1981)
6085 grt; 813 psrs
225 cars + 24 trailers
327' x 57' x 16' (99.1 x 17.2 x 4.8 m)
2 x 10-cylinder Sulzer diesel engines via twin screw.

Ice-strengthened passenger-car-cargo ferry operating for the Maritime Co of Lesvos SA and bearing nameboards for the vessel spelt ALCAEOS and ALCAEUS.
Built by Brodogradiliste Titovo, Kraljevica, for the SF Line as the MARELLA (1970).

ALCAEUS (1981) See ALCAEOS (1981)

ALCALA (1913) See VAUBAN (1913)

ALCANTARA (1913)
15831 grt; 1330 psrs
589' x 67' x 33' depth (179.5 x 20.4 x 10 m)
8-cylinder triple expansion engines via triple screw.
Sank in one hour on 29 February 1916 with the loss of 69 lives in the North Sea after being attacked by the guns of the German auxiliary cruiser GREIF which had been heavily disguised as the Norwegian RENA.
Built by Harland & Wolff, Belfast, for Royal Mail Lines.

ALCANTARA (1927) See KAISHO MARU (1958)

ALCOA CAVALIER (1947)
8481 grt; 95 psrs
455' x 62' x 29' (137.9 x 18.8 x 8.8 m)
Westinghouse turbine engines via single screw.
Broken up for scrap in New Orleans, Lousiana, in 1968. Ex-Alco Steamship Co.
Laid down by the Oregon Shipbuilding Corporation, Portland, for Alcoa Steamship Co as a passenger-cargo 'Victory ship' (class VC2-S1-AP7) and named UNITED VICTORY (1943). She was renamed, while the keel was being formed, as the HEMPSTEAD, USS (APA-241) (1943 – US Navy).

ALCOA CLIPPER (1947)
8481 grt; 95 psrs
455' x 62' x 29' (137.9 x 18.8 x 8.8 m)
Westinghouse turbine engines via single screw.
Broken up for scrap in Baltimore in 1969. Ex-Alco Steamship Co.
Laid down by the Oregon Shipbuilding Corporation for the Alcoa Steamship Co as a passenger-cargo "Victory ship" (Class VC2-S1-AP7) for the US Navy

as the IREDELL, USS (APA-242) (1947). She was renamed ALCOA CLIPPER.

ALCOA CORSAIR (1941) See PRIVATE ELDEN H. JOHNSON (1946)

ALCOA CORSAIR (1946) See RYE (1963)

ALCOA COURIER (1941) See SERGEANT CHARLES E. MOWER (1946)

ALCOA CRUISER (1941) See PRIVATE WILLIAM H. THOMAS (1946)

ALCOR, USS (AG-34) (1941)
8188 grt; 379 psrs
427' x 60' x 37" depth (129.4 x 18.2 x 11.2 m)
2 x De Laval triple expansion engines via single screw.
Broken up for scrap in Baltimore in 1950. Ex-US Navy.
Built by Federal Shipbuilding & Drydock Co, Kearny, New Jersey, for the Jutland Line as the DIXIE (1927).

ALDENHAM (1907) See LARNE (1916)

ALDONZA MANRIGUE (1976)
3062 grt; 600 psrs
200 cars or 34 trailers
323' x 59' x 14' (97.9 x 17.8 x 4.2 m)
2 x 10-cylinder MAN diesel engines via twin screw.

Passenger-car-cargo ferry operating for Consolidada de Ferris CA, Pampatar, she was broken up for scrap in 1984 following a fire which gutted her in 1982. Laid down by Schiffswerft Unterweser, Bremerhaven, for Jutland Ferries as the JULLE (1964), completed for Grenaa-Hundested Faergefart AS as the HUNDESTED (1964). Renamed OLAU EAST (1975 – Olau Line).

ALEDA E. LUTZ (1946) See ATLANTICA (1964)

ALEGRO (1984) See STAR OF VENICE (1992)

ALEKOS (1988) See KAPETAN ALEXANDROS A (1993)

ALESIA (1917)
6030 grt; 1260 psrs
403' x 49' x 21' (122.9 x 15 x 6.4 m)
8-cylinder quadruple expansion engines via twin screw.
Owned by the French government, she sank on 6 September 1917 after being torpedoed by the German U-50 near Ushant.
Built by Bremer Vulkan, Vegesack, for the Hamburg-America Line as the PRINZ ADALBERT (1904). Renamed PRINCETON (1916 – British government).

ALESIA (1919)
7112 grt; 1005 psrs
495' x 52' x 34'5" depth (150 x 15.8 x 10.5 m)
6-cylinder quadruple expansion engine via single screw.
Sold to shipbreaker by Cie Sud-Atlantique, but she broke her tow and ran ashore on Texel Island where she became a total constructive loss in December 1923.
Built by Cie General Transport, St Nazaire, for the French Line as the LA BRETAGNE (1886) at a cost of Fr 7,300,000.

ALESIA (1928)
9720 grt; 669 psrs
476' x 56' x 28' (144.2 x 17 x 8.5 m)
8-cylinder quadruple expansion engines via twin screw.
Broken up for scrap in Genoa in 1933. Ex-Fabre Line.
Built by Blohm & Voss, Hamburg, for the Hamburg American Line as the KONIG FRIEDRICH AUGUST (1906). Renamed MONTREAL II (1921 – Canadian Pacific Steamship Co).

ALESSANDRO VOLTA (1957)
11349 grt; 541 psrs
535' x 64' x 28' (163 x 19.5 x 8.5 m)
2 x 8-cylinder Mecan-Sulzer diesel engines via twin screw.
Currently serving as a non-passenger freighter for Italia SAN, Genoa and remeasured at 8086 grt.
Built by Ateliers et Chantiers de la Loire, St Nazaire, for Chargeurs Reunis, Bordeaux, as the passenger ship CLEMENT ADER (1954).

ALEUTIAN (1923)
5708 grt; 280 psrs
360' x 50' x 32' depth (109.1 x 15.2 x 9.7 m)
W Cramp 6-cylinder triple expansion engines via twin screw.
Owned by Alaska Steamship Co, she sank in deep water on 26 May 1929 after striking a rock in Uyak Bay, Kodiak Island, Alaska.
Built by W Cramp & Sons Shipbuilding &Engineering Co, Philadelphia, Pennsylvania, for the New York & Cuba Mail Steamship Co as the passenger-cargo liner HAVANA (1898). Renamed PANAMA (1905 – Isthmian Canal Commission and the Panama Railroad Co).

ALEUTIAN (1929) See TRADEWIND (1954)

ALEXANDER (1983)
5933 grt; 276 psrs
40 cars
390' x 54' x 16'6" (118.2 x 16.4 x 5 m)
2 x 10-cylinder MAN diesel engines via twin screw.
Converted to a luxurious private yacht, with exquisite accommodation for 12 people, by the Greek millionaire shipping tycoon John Latsis, and given as a gift of friendship to the Saudi Arabian Royal family in 1998.
Built by Lubecker Flenderwerke AG, Lubeck, for the Lubeck Line as the passenger-cargo ship REGINA MARIS (1966). Renamed MERCATOR ONE (1976 – Mosswood Co Ltd, Hamilton, Bermuda), FRANKFURT I (1979 – Pieter Deilmann & Co) and then reinstated as the cruise ship REGINA MARIS (1980 – Pieter Deilmann & Co).

ALEXANDER MOZAISKY (1954) See ALEXANDR MOZHAJSKI (1954)

ALEXANDER PUSHKIN (1965) See MARCO POLO (1993)

ALEXANDRA (1988) See COSTA ALLEGRA (1990)

ALEXANDRA WOERMANN (1901) See CALYPSO (1920)

ALEXANDRIA (1901) See KOUANG (1929)

ALEXANDR MOZHAJSKI (1954)
9922 grt; 334 psrs
481' x 57' x 30' (145.8 x 17.3 x 9.1 m)
SRG turbine engines via twin screw.
Broken up for scrap in Hong Kong in 1979. Ex-Far East Shipping Co.
Built by De Schelde , Vlissingen for Rotterdam Lloyd as the passenger liner PATRIA (1919). Renamed SVIR (1935 Russian government).

ALEXANDROS (1970) See JUPITER (1971)

ALEXANDR PUSHKIN (1965) See ALEXANDER PUSHKIN (1965)

ALEXEI RIKOV (1928) See ANDREI ZHDANOV (1937)

ALEXI H (1979)
6962 grt

482' x 62' x 25' (146 x 18.7 x 7.5 m)
2 x 6-cylinder HWD diesel engines via twin screw.
Passenger-cargo ship owned by Amin Kawar & Sons, Panama.
Built by HWD, Hamburg, for the Hamburg-South America Line as the SANTA URSULA (1951). Renamed ANGOL (1964 – Cia. Chilena de Navigacion Interoceanica, Valparaiso), BRIGHT SKY (1969 – C Efstathiou P Pappis, Piraeus) and PAPPIS (1977 – Parpada Maritime Co SA, Piraeus).

ALEX STEPHENS (1973)
10645 grt; 2000 psrs
523' x 71' x 26'6" (159.3 x 21.8 x 8 m)
2 x DRG turbine engines via single screw.
As a container ship conversion, she was broken up for scrap at Kaohsiung in 1980 by Chien Yo Steel Enterprises. Ex-Waterman Carriers, New York.
Built by Kaiser Co, Richmond, California, for the US Maritime Commission as the Class C4-S-A1 troop carrier GENERAL R. M. BLATCHFORD, USS (AP-153) (1945). Reclassified as GENERAL R. M. BLATCHFORD, USAT (1946 – US Army) and GENERAL R. M. BLATCHFORD, USNS (T-AP-153) (1950 – US Navy). Renamed as the container ship STONEWALL JACKSON (1970 – Waterman Carriers, New York).

ALEX VAN OPSTAL (1942) See BLED (1959)

ALEX VAN OPSTAL (1946) See BLED (1959)

AL FAHAD (1986)
6889 grt;1200 psrs
250 cars
360' x 63' x 14' (109.2 x 19 x 4.1 m)
4 x 12-cylinder MAN diesel engines via twin screw.

Pilgrim ferry operating for the Mohammed Sadaka Establishment, Jeddah.
Built by IHC, Schiedam, for Townsend Thoresen as the passenger-car RoRo ferry FREE ENTERPRISE III (1966). Renamed TAMIRA (1984 – Mira Shipping Co) and MONA'S ISLE (1984 – Isle of Man Steam Packet Co).

ALFERDOSS (1984) See AMERICAN STAR (1993)

ALFONSO XIII (1916) See VASCO NUNEZ DE BALBOA (1923)

ALFONSO XIII (1923) See GALICIA (1962)

ALFREDO DA SILVA (1950)
3374 grt; 88 psrs
338' x 45' x 20' (102.4 x 13.6 x 6.1 m)
2 x Atlas-Polar diesel engine via single screw.
Built by Uniao Fabril, Lisbon, for Soc Geral de Comercio Industria e Transportes, Portugal.

ALGAZAYER (1962)
4444 grt; 282 psrs
354' x 55' x 14'6" (107.3 x 16.7 x 4.4 m)
9-cylinder MAN-B+W diesel engine via single screw.
Broken up for scrap in 1994 as a pilgrim ship operated by the Egyptian Navigation Co, Alexandria.
Built by Deutsche Werft, Hamburg, for the United Arab Maritime Co, Alexandria.

ALGERIA (1891) See VIRGINIA (1914)

ALGERIA (1921) See TOLEDO (1922)

ALGONQUIN (1926)
7128 grt; 446 psrs
387' x 55' x 20' (117.3 x 16.7 x 6.1 m)
2 x 3-cylinder triple expansion engines via single screw.
Broken up for scrap in Baltimore in 1957. Ex-US Dept of Commerce.
Built by Newport News Shipbuilding Co, Newport News, Virginia, for operation by the Clyde Steamship Co.

AL HASA (1974) See MARIANNA 9 (1984)

AL HUSSEIN II (1986) See FAGR (1998)

ALICE (1907) See ASIA (1917)

ALICE (1997)
13692 grt; 829 psrs
230 cars or 60 trailers
541' x 71' x 28'6" (164.8 x 21.6 x 8.7 m)
2 x R & W Hawthorne Leslie-Doxford diesel engines via twin screw.
Broken up for scrap in 1998 at Aliaga. Ex-Karageorgios Lines.
Built by Vickers-Armstrong Ltd, Newcastle, for Ellerman Lines as the passenger-cargo ship CITY OF EXETER (1953). Renamed MEDITERRANEAN SEA (1971 – MA Karageorgios) and TUTKU (1996 – Armon Trading Inc).

ALICE PRINCESS (1992) See WANG FU (1993)

ALIYA (1957)
11015 grt; 773 psrs
530' x 61' x 25' (161.5 x 18.3 x 7.6 m)
2 x 4-cylinder quadruple expansion engines via twin screw.
Broken up for scrap by Terrestse Marittima in La Spezia in 1959. Ex-Zim Lines.
Built by Cammell Laird, Birkenhead, for the Norwegian America Line as the passenger liner BERGENSFJORD (1913). Renamed ARGENTINA (1946 – Home Lines) and JERUSALEM (1953 – Zim Lines).

AL JAWAHER (1988)
4911 grt; 1286 psrs
12 cars
439' x 59' x 17' (133 x 17.9 x 5.2 m)
2 x 8-cylinder Kawasaki-MAN diesel engines via twin screw.
Passenger-car ferry owned by Transoceanic Alliance SA, Panama, and operated by Alnaghi Construction, Saudi Arabia. In May 1988 she caught fire and suffered severe structural damage while moored in the inner harbour at Suez. She was then sold to local shipbreakers.
Built by Uraga Heavy Industries Ltd, Yokosuka, for Japanese National Railways as the TSUGARU MARU (1964). Renamed HAE YON (1985 – China Ocean Shipping Co).

AL JUDI (1993)
6925 grt; 1200 psrs
250 cars
379' x 59' x 16' (114.9 x 17.9 x 4.8 m)
2 x 12-cylinder MAN diesel engines via twin screw.

Ice-strengthened passenger-car ferry owned and operated by Dallah Transport (Marine Division), Jeddah.
Built by Schiffbau-ges Unterweser AG, Bremerhaven, for Moltzau AS,

Gedser, as the GEDSER (1968). Renamed MALTA EXPRESS (1976 – Tirrenia) and MOBY WILL (1988 – NavArMa).

AL KAHERA (1986) See LA PATRIA (2000)

AL KHAIRAT (1977)
3303 grt; 510 psrs
40 cars
296' x 50' x 15' (89.7 x 15.2 x 4.5 m)
10-cylinder Sulzer diesel engine via single screw.
Broken up for scrap by AR Mohammed Farooq at Gadani Beach, Karach in 1987i. Ex-Meat & Foodstuffs WLL, Kuwait.
Built by Ailsa Shipbuilding Co Ltd, Troon, for the North of Scotland, Orkney & Shetland Shipping Co Ltd as St CLAIR (1960). Renamed St CLAIR II (1977 – North of Scotland, Orkney & Shetland Shipping Co Ltd).

ALKYON (1978)
3968 grt; 244 psrs
376' x 50' x 18'6" (113.9 x 15.1 x 5.6 m)
2 x 10-cylinder B+W diesel engines via twin screw.
Broken up for scrap as a passenger-cargo ship at Gadani Beach, Karachi, in 1984. Ex-Ventouris Lines.
Built by Helsingor Shipyards, Helsingor, for the United Fruit Steamship Co as the KRONPRINSESSE INGRID (1949). Renamed COPENHAGEN (1967 – DFDS) and MIMIKA L (1969 – Latsis Shipping Co).

ALKYON (1985) See AEGEAN I (1996)

ALLA TARASOVA (1977) See CLIPPER ADVENTURER (1997)

ALLEGHANY (1923) See AMERICAN SEAFARER (1941).

ALLEMANNIA (1905) See OWASCO (1916)

ALLEMANNIA (1907) See OWASCO (1916)

AL MADINA (1995) See AL QAMAR (1999)

AL MAHROUSA (1991) See TEBAH 2000 (1999)

AL MANSOUR (1997)
11717 grt; 1200 psrs
480 cars
399' x 64' x 19' (120.8 x 19.5 x 5.8 m)
2 x 12-cylinder MaK diesel engines via twin screw.

Ice-strengthened passenger-car ferry owned and operated by Comanav.
Built by Rickmers Werft, Bremerhaven, for Stena Line AB as the STENA NORDICA (1975). Renamed HELLAS (1978 – Hellas Ferries), STENA NORDICA (1979 – Canadian National Railways), HELLAS (1980 – Hellas Ferries), STENA NORDICA (1980 – Stena Line), STENA NAUTICA (1981 – Stena Line), REINE ASTRID (1983 – RMT, Belgium) and MOBY KISS (1997 – Nav.Ar.Ma. Moby Lines).

ALMANZORA (1914)
15551 grt; 1390 psrs
589' x 67' x 23'6" (179.5 x 20.4 x 7.1 m)
2 x 4-cylinder triple expansion engines via triple screw.
Broken up for scrap by British Iron & Steel Corporation at Blyth in 1948.
Built by Harland & Wolff Ltd, Belfast, for Royal Mail Lines.

ALMEDA (1926) See ALMEDA STAR (1929)

ALMEDA STAR (1929)
14935 grt; 180 psrs
579' x 68' x 28' (162.1 x 20.6 x 8.4 m)

Geared turbine engines via twin screw.
Sank on 17 January 1941 with the loss of 360 lives 350 miles (584 km) west of the Hebrides after being struck by four torpedoes from the German U-96.
Built by Cammell Laird & Co, Birkenhead for the Blue Star Line as the ALMEDA (1926).

ALMIRANTE (1909)
5010 grt; 103 psrs
379' x 50' x 25' (114.8 x 15.2 x 7.6 m)
Triple expansion engine via single screw.
Sank on 6 September 1918 following a collision with the tanker HISCO off Atlantic City, New Jersey.
Built by Workman, Clark & Co, Belfast, for the United Fruit Steamship Co.

ALMIRANTE IRIZAR (1978)
10065 grt; 100 psrs
399' x 83' x 31' (121 x 25.2 x 9.5 m)
4 x 8-cylinder Pielstick diesel engines via twin screw.
Passenger-icebreaker-hospital ship owned by the Argentine government.
Built by Wartsila, Helsinki.

ALMIRANTE LUIS BRION (1973)
4290 grt; 1000 psrs
140 cars
304' x 55' x 14' (92.4 x 16.7 x 4.2 m)
4 x 9-cylinder MAN diesel engines via twin screw.

Ice-strengthened passenger-car-cargo RoRo ferry operating for Ferrys del Caribe, Muaco, Venezuela.
Built by Aalborg Vaerft AS, Aalborg as the LASSE (1964).

AL NASL (1973) See SAN LORENZO RUIZ (1996)

AL NASR I (1993) See SALEM FLOWER (1996)

ALNWICK CASTLE (1901)
5893 grt; 540 psrs
400' x 50' x 26'6" (121.2 x 15.2 x 8 m)
Beardmore 6-cylinder triple expansion engines via twin screw.
Sank on 19 March 1917 with 40 lives lost after being torpedoed by the German U-81 310 miles (517 km) from Bishop Rock, Scilly Isles.
Built by W Beardmore & Sons Co Ltd, Glasgow, for the Union Castle Line.

ALONDRA (1922)
3445 grt; 120 psrs
319' x 44' x 22' (96.7 x 13.3 x 6.7 m)
3-cylinder triple expansion engine via single screw.
Sold to the Chilean State Railway in 1938.
Built by Caledon Shipyard, Dundee, for the Yeoward Line.

ALPASHA (1974)
5564 grt; 1224 psrs
100 cars
357' x 52' x 17' (108.2 x 15.8 x 5.2m)
4 x 6-cylinder Pielstick diesel engines via twin screw.
Passenger-car ferry owned by Saudi Lines, Jeddah.
Built by Forges et Chantiers de la Mediterranee, La Seyne, for Cie General Transatlantique as the NAPOLEON (1959).

AL QAMAR (1999)
3807 grt; 350 psrs
200 cars
2 x 6-cylinder B+W diesel engines via twin screw.
Passenger-car ferry owned and operated by Maily Vely Shipping Co, Cairo.

Built by Helsingor Shipyards, Helsingor, for the Danish State Railways as the train ferry HALSSKOV (1956). Converted to a pure freight ferry and renamed MELODY (1988 – Navsimar Shipping Co), EUROPEAN SPIRIT (1990 – European Seaways), SHOROUK (1995 – Gulf Cruise & Transport SA), AL MADINA (1995 – Gulf Cruise & Transport SA).

AL QAMAR I (1990) See AL SALAM 89 (1992)

AL-QAMAR AL-SALAM II (1993) See FAGR (1998)

AL-QAMAR AL-SAUDI II (1983) See TIAN E (1985)

AL-QAMAR-AL-SAUDI AL-MISRI I (1991) See FAGR (1998)

AL RASHEED II (1992)
3873 grt; 768 psrs
120 cars
291' x 53' x 13' (88.3 x 16.2 x 4 m)
4 x 9-cylinder MAN diesel engines via twin screw.

Ice-strengthened passenger-car-cargo RoRo ferry owned and operated by Saleh Ahmed Baaboud Establishment, Jeddah.
Built by Adler Werft, Bremen, for Juelsminde-Kalundborg AS, Kalundborg, as the JULLE (1962). Renamed TANGER (1972 – Lignes Maritimes de Ferries, Tangier), CORSICA SERENA (1975 – Corsica Ferries) and GIOTTO (1980 – Sicilia Regionale Marittima SpA).

AL SAFA (1996) See MEDOUSA (1997)

AL SALAM 89 (1992)
6651 grt; 1768 psrs
50 cars + 30 trailers
406' x 69' x 16' (122.9 x 21 x 4.8 m)
2 x 12-cylinder Pielstick diesel engines via twin screw.
Converted to a dedicated 48-passenger-cargo ship owned and operated by Al Salam Shipping & Trading Establishment, Alexandria.
Built by Ishikawajima Ship & Chemical Plant Co, Tokyo, for KS AS Admiral Shipping, Oslo, as the ADMIRAL PACIFIC (1978). Renamed as the passenger-car-cargo ferry SAINT CLAIR (1982 – SNCM, Marseilles), and AL QAMAR I (1990 – Al Salam Shipping & Trading Establishment, Cairo).

AL SALAM 91 (1993)
7738 grt; 48 psrs
465' x 63' x 19'6" (141 x 19 x 5.9 m)
4 x 6-cylinder Fiat diesel engines via twin screw.
Passenger(48)-cargo RoRo ferry following conversion in 1993 for the owners and operators, Saudi Navigation Co SA, Panama.
Built by Cantiere Navale Apuania, Carrara, for Traghetti Isole Sarde SrL as the CANGURO BIONDO (1971). Renamed STAFFETTA TIRRENICA (1973 – Tirrenia) and CONCORD 2 (1993 – Maritime Independence SA).

AL SALAM 93 (1996)
5691 grt; 1350 psrs
210 cars or 20 trailers
361' x 59' x 13' (109.4 x 17.8 x 3.9 m)

2 x 12-cylinder Pielstick diesel engines via twin screw.
Passenger-car-cargo ferry owned by European Maritime Transports SA, Panama, and operated by Al Salam Shipping & Trading Establishment, Cairo. Built by Dubigeon-Normandie, St Nazaire, for SNCF, Paris, as the CHANTILLY (1965). Renamed OLYMPIA (1987 – Olympiada Maritime Co, Greece), EUROPA LINK (1990 – GT Link) and BALTAVIA (1993 – Ali Tabbit & H Baltagi, Beirut).

AL SALAM 97 (1998) See SALAM (1998)

AL SALAM BOCCACCIO 98 (1999)
11779 grt; 1396 psrs
250 cars
432' x 66' x 18'6" (131 x 20 x 5.6 m)
2 x 9-cylinder Fiat diesel engines via twin screw.
Passenger-car ferry owned and operated by Al Salam Shipping & Trading Establishment, Alexandria, after their acquisition of the vessel for US$2,000,000.
Built by Italcantieri SpA, Monfalcone, for Tirrenia as the BOCCACCIO (1970).

AL SALAM CARDUCCI 92 (1999)
11779 grt; 1396 psrs
270 cars
432' x 66' x 18'6" (131 x 20 x 5.6 m)
2 x 9-cylinder Fiat diesel engines via twin screw.
Passenger-car ferry owned by Triton Diamond Shipbuilding SA and operated by Al Salam Maritime Transport Co SA following acquisition of the vessel for US$2,000,000.
Built by Italcantieri SpA, Castellammare di Stabia, for Tirrenia SpA, Naples, as the CARDUCCI (1970).

AL SALAM MANZONI 94 (1999)
11779 grt; 1000 psrs
432' x 66' x 18'6" (131 x 20 x 5.6 m)
2 x 9-cylinder Fiat diesel engines via twin screw.
Passenger ferry owned by Silver Light Shipholding SA and operated by Al Salam Maritime Transport Co SA, Cairo, after acquisition of the vessel for US$2,000,000.
Built by Italcantieri SpA, Castellammare di Stabia, for Tirrenia as the MANZONI (1971).

AL SALAM PASCOLI 96 (1999) See PASCOLI 96 (2000)

AL SALAM PETRARCA 90 (1999)
11779 grt; 1300 psrs
432' x 66' x 18'6" (131 x 20 x 5.6 m)
2 x 9-cylinder Fiat diesel engines via twin screw.
Passenger ferry owned by Sea Gem Maritime Inc and operated by Al Salam Maritime Transport Co SA, Cairo, following acquisition of the vessel for US$2,000,000.
Built by Cantieri Navale del Tirreno e Riuniti, Palermo, for Tirrenia di Navigazioni SpA as the PETRARCA (1971).

AL SALAM TABA I (1998)
5340 grt; 716 psrs
70 cars + 24 trailers
415' x 64' x 17' (125.8 x 19.4 x 5.2 m)
2 x 7-cylinder Fiat diesel engines via twin screw.
Passenger-car ferry owned by Baltic Sea Business SA and operated by Al Salam Shipping & Trading Establishment, Cairo, and Tylos Ferry, Bahrain.
Built by Soc Italiana per Construzione Navali Meccaniche for Linee Canguro SpA, Cagliari, as the CANGURO BIANCO (1968). Renamed TIEPOLO

(1983 – Adriatica), ZAHRET MISR (1993 – Samatour Trading), SALEM FLOWER (1993 – Samatour Shipping) and TABA I (1997 – Al Salam Shipping & Trading Establishment, Cairo).

ALSATIAN (1914) See EMPRESS OF FRANCE (1919)

ALSHAHBA (1990) See BELKIS 1 (1994)

AL SUDAN (1947)
7372 grt; 1450 psrs
417' x 60' x 27' (127.1 x 18.2 x 8.2 m)
2 x Westinghouse DRG turbine engines via twin screw.
Broken up for scrap at Suez in 1984 after being laid up since 1980. Ex-United Arab Maritime Co, Alexandria.
Built by Consolidated Steel Corporation, Wilmington, North Carolina, for the US Maritime Commission as the C-1 type cargo vessel CAPE St VINCENT (1943). Renamed EMPIRE ARQUEBUS (1944 – British Ministry of War Transport), CICERO, HMS (1944 – British Royal Navy) and reinstated to EMPIRE ARQUEBUS (1946 – British Ministry of War Transport).

AL TAHRA (1988) See SALEM EXPRESS (1989)

AL TAIF (1976)
5284 grt; 1908 psrs
397' x 56' x 15' (120.3 x 17 x 4.5 m)
2 x 8-cylinder B+W diesel engines via twin screw.
Operating as a pilgrim ship from Saudi Arabia by Orri Navigation Lines when she sank off Suez in 1980.
Built by Harland & Wolff Ltd, Belfast, for the British Transport Commission as the CAMBRIA (1949).

ALTAIR (1950)
6410 grt; 92 psrs
440' x 60' x 25' depth (133.3 x 18.2 x 7.6 m)
2-stroke engine via single screw.
Abandoned after wrecking herself near the entrance to the Brazilian port of Vitoria on 15 April 1956.
Built by William Gray & Co, West Hartlepool, for the Rotterdam South America Line.

ALTE LIEBE (1966) See HELGOLAND (1985)

ALTENBURG (1903)
3448 grt
350' x 52' x 26'8" depth (106 x 15.8 x 8.1 m)
Caird & Co 3-cylinder triple expansion engines via single screw.
Built by Caird & Co Ltd, Greenock, for Greenock Steamship Co Ltd, Greenock, as the GULF OF GENOA (1891).

AL WADI (1960)
7830 grt; 333 psrs
437' x 59' x 24' (134.5 x 18.1 x 7.3 m)
2 x Parsons SRG turbine engines via twin screw.
Owned by the United Arab Maritime Co, Alexandria, she sank at her berth in Alexandria harbour in 1965 following a long period laid up after she had been declared a total constructive loss as a result of a collision.
Built by Cammell Laird, Birkenhead, for the Canadian National Steamship Co as the LADY NELSON (1928). Renamed GUMHURYAT MISR (1953 – Khedivial Mail Line).

AL ZAHER (1979)
3333 grt; 1500 psrs
120 cars
362' x 61' x 13' (109.7 x 18.5 x 3.9 m)
2 x DRG turbine engines via twin screw.
Broken up for scrap by Karum Shipbreaking Industries at Gadani Beach, Karachi, in 1981. Ex-Ahmed Mohamed Baaboud, Jeddah.
Built by William Denny & Bros, Dumbarton, for the British Transport Commission as the passenger-car ferry LORD WARDEN (1952).

ALZAHRAA (1977) See JIN HU (1993)

AMALFI (1989) See STAR OF VENICE (1992)

AMALIA (1906)
3480 grt; 157 psrs
372' x 40' x 22' (113.2 x 12 x 6.7 m)
3-cylinder Koninklijke Maatschappij triple expansion engines via single screw.
Broken up in 1907 by L Pittaluga, Genoa, after previously winning the tender of £8,000 by JJ King & Co, Garston, UK.
Built by John Elder & Co, Glasgow, for the Nederlands Steamship Co as the passenger-cargo liner PRINSES AMALIA (1874).

AMARAPOORA (1920) See CAPTAIN HOBSON (1951)

AMATISTA (1980) See JI MEI (1983)

AMAZON (1906)
10037 grt; 870 psrs
530' x 60' x 25' (161.5 x 18.2 x 7.6 m)
Quadruple expansion engines via twin screw.
Sank on 15 March 1918 by a torpedo fired from the German U-52 north-east of Northern Ireland, 30 miles (50 km) from Malin Head.
Built by Harland & Wolff Ltd, Belfast, for Royal Mail Lines.

AMAZON (1960) See AKARITA (1981)

AMAZONAS (1923)
3287 grt; 290 psrs
350' x 43' x 25'6" (106.1 x 13 x 7.8m)
3-cylinder compound engine via single screw.
Broken up for scrap in 1934. Ex-Cie Peruana de Vap Y Dique del Callao, Peru.
Built by Barclay, Curle & Co, Glasgow, for the Castle Line as the passenger-cargo liner HARLECH CASTLE (1894). Renamed VERONIQUE (1904 – Earl Fitzwilliam) and IQUITOS (1915 – Peruvian government).

AMAZONE (1905)
6357 grt; 300 psrs
469' x 50' x 36' depth (142 x 15.2 x 10.9 m)
Triple expansion engines via single screw.
Broken up for scrap. Ex-Messageries Maritimes in 1932.
Built by Messageries Maritimes, La Ciotat, for Messageries Maritimes as the passenger liner LAOS (1896).

AMBASSADOR (1993) See AMBASSADOR II (1993)

AMBASSADOR II (1993)
8093 grt; 1040 psrs
240 cars
440' x 69' x 16' (133.3 x 20.9 x 4.9 m)
2 x 16-cylinder Pielstick diesel engines via twin screw.

Ex-passenger-car ferry, now operating as a floating casino ship for Sterling Casino Lines, Florida.
Built by Werft Nobiskrug, Rendsburg, for Prins Ferries as the PRINS OBERON (1970). Renamed PRINZ OBERON (1978 – Prinz Ferry-HAPAG), NORDIC SUN (1984 – Trans Nordic Line), cruise ship CRUISE MUHIBAH (1986 – Perbadanan Berhad & Feri Malaysia), MUNSTER (1990 – B & I Line) and AMBASSADOR (1993 – New Olympic Ferries Ltd, Limassol).

AMBOIM (1925)
3601 grt; 629 psrs
345' x 44' x 25'8" depth (104.5 x 13.3 x 7.8 m)
Fairfield 8-cylinder quadruple expansion engines via single screw.
Broken up for scrap in Rotterdam in 1933. Ex-Cia de Navigacao Colonial,

Portugal.
Built by Blohm & Voss, Hamburg, for the Hamburg-America Line as the Passenger-cargo liner SARDINIA (1898). Renamed SAO JORGE (1916 – after seizure by the Portuguese government).

AMBOISE (1922)
8332 grt; 1620 psrs
469' x 55' x 29'6" (143 x 16.8 x 9m)
8-cylinder quadruple expansion engines via twin screw.
Broken up for scrap at Genoa in 1935. Ex-Messageries Maritimes, Marseilles.
Built by Fairfield Shipbuilding & Engineering Co Ltd, Glasgow, for the Hamburg-America Line as the passenger liner FURST BISMARCK (1905). Renamed FRIEDRICHSRUH (1914 – Hamburg-America Line).

AMBRIA (1896) See PIETRO MARONCELLI (1916)

AMBROSE (1903)
4600 grt 479 psrs
375' x 48' x 18'6" (113.6 x 14.5 x 5.6m)
Triple expansion engine via single screw.
Built by Sir Raylton Dixon, Middlesbrough, for the Booth Line. Acquired in 1915 by the British Admiralty who converted her into a submarine depot ship, later destroyed.

AMBROSE (1990) See QUEEN VERGINA (1990)

AMBROSE SHEA (1967) See QUEEN VERGINA (1990)

AMBULOMBO (1961) See AMBULOMBO (1966)

AMBULOMBO (1966)
11111 grt; 380 psrs
482' x 66' x 24' (146.8 x 20.2 x 7.3 m)
2 x 8-cylinder Kincaid diesel engines via twin screw.
Owned by PT Perusahaan Pelajaran Arafat, Indonesia, this pilgrim ship sank off Luzon on 18 November 1972 while under tow to the breakers yard in Kaohsiung.
Built by Alexander Stephen & Sons, Glasgow, for the Adelaide Steamship Company as the MANOORA (1935). Renamed AMBULOMBO (1961 – Indonesian government) and AFFAN OCEANA (1965 – PT Affan Raya, Indonesia).

AMELIA DE MELLO (1966) See DOLPHIN IV (1987)

AMERICA (1908)
8996 grt; 2650 psrs
506' x 56' x 24'6" (153.3 x 17.1 x 7.5 m)
6-cylinder triple expansion engines via twin screw.
Broken up for scrap in 1928.
Launched in 1908 by Cantieri Navale Riuniti, Muggiano, for La Veloce. Completed for Navigazione Generale Italiana in 1912.

AMERICA (1921) See EDMUND B. ALEXANDER, USS (1941)

AMERICA (1940) See AMERICAN STAR (1993)

AMERICA (1946) See AMERICAN STAR (1993)

AMERICA (1977) See AMERICAN STAR (1993)

AMERICA, USS (1917) See EDMUND B. ALEXANDER, USS (1941)

AMERICA MARU (1950) See VANMINT (1968)

AMERICA XIII (1986) See EUROPA (1988)

AMERICAN (1895) See MARIA GIULIA (1927)

AMERICAN (1900)
5591 grt; 194 psrs
407' x 51' x 30'3" depth (123.3 x 15.5 x 9.2 m)
3-cylinder turbine engines via single screw.
Built by Delaware River Co, Chester, Pennsylvania, for the American

Hawaiian Steamship Co.

AMERICANA (1988)
19203 grt; 80 psrs
1200 containers
580' x 85' x 29' (175.8 x 25.8 x 8.8 m)
Hyundai-MAN-B+W 7-cylinder diesel engine via single screw.
Luxury passenger-freighter, owned and operated by Canadian Pacific, which ceased carrying passengers in May 1999 and is now up for sale at US$24,000,000.
Built by Hyundai Heavy Industries, Ulsan, South Korea, for Ivaran Lines at a cost of US$40,000,000.

AMERICAN ADVENTURE (1993) See COSTA RIVIERA (1994)

AMERICAN BANKER (1924) See AROSA KULM (1952)

AMERICAN BANKER (1941) See BAY STATE (1973)

AMERICAN ENGINEER (1941)
5861 grt; 302 psrs
351' x 52' x 15'2" (106.4 x 15.8 x 4.6 m)
Hooven-Owens 4-cylinder triple expansion engines via single screw.
Broken up for scrap in San Francisco in 1948. Ex-US War Shipping Administration.
Built by Federal Shipbuilding Co, Kearny, New Jersey, for Merchants & Miners Transportation Co Inc as the BERKSHIRE (1923).

AMERICAN FARMER (1924) See VILLE DE LIEGE (1940)

AMERICAN FARMER (1942) See DAVID C. SHANKS (T-AP-180) (1950)

AMERICAN IMPORTER (1924) See VILLE DE GAND (1940)

AMERICAN LEGION (1921) See AMERICAN LEGION, USS (APA-117) (1941)

AMERICAN LEGION, USS (APA-117) (1941)
13736 grt; 430 psrs
516' x 72' x 27'6" depth (156.4 x 21.8 x 8.4 m)
Turbine engines via twin screw.
Broken up for scrap at Portland, Oregon, in 1948. Ex-US Navy.
Laid down by the New York Shipbuilding Corporation for the US Shipping Board as the KODA (1919), but completed as the AMERICAN LEGION (1920).

AMERICAN MERCHANT (1924) See VILLE DE NAMUR (1940)

AMERICAN MERCHANT (1941) See GEORGE W. GOETHALS (T-AP-182) (1950)

AMERICAN NAVIGATOR (1941)
5861 grt; 204 psrs
401' x 52' x 27' depth (121.5 x 15.8 x 8.2 m)
2 x 14-cylinder Busch-Sulzer SRG diesel engines via single screw.
Broken up for scrap in Oakland, California, in 1948. Ex-US War Shipping Administration.
Built by Newport News Shipbuilding Co, Newport News, Virginia, for then Ocean Steamship Co, Savannah, as the CHATTANOOGA (1923).

AMERICAN PIONEER (1994) See THE BIG RED BOAT II (2000)

AMERICAN SEAFARER (1941)
7111 grt; 302 psrs
410' x 54' x 15' (124.2 x 16.4 x 4.5 m)
Hooven-Owens 4-cylinder triple expansion engines via single screw.
Broken up for scrap in San Francisco in 1949. Ex-US War Shipping Administration.
Built by Federal Shipbuilding Co, Kearny, New Jersey, for the Merchants & Miners Transportation Co Inc as the ALLEGHANY (1923).

AMERICAN SHIPPER (1924) See VILLE DE MONS (1940)

AMERICAN SHIPPER (1942) See FRED C. AINSWORTH (1950)

AMERICAN STAR (1993)
34449 grt; 2258 psrs
723' x 93' x 33' (220.3 x 38.3 x 10 m)
8 x W. Cramp & Sons DRG turbines via twin screw.
Owned by the Chapheya Development Transport Co, Thailand, she was abandoned as a total constructive loss when she stranded during a Force 12 storm on the west coast of Fuerteventura, Canary Islands, on 18 January 1994. She had been under tow from Piraeus, Greece, to Phuket, Thailand, where she was scheduled to become a floating hotel. The four people aboard were rescued by helicopter and the ship languished until 9 March 1994 when she finally broke her back.
Built by Newport News Shipbuilding & Drydock Co, Newport News, Virginia, for United States Lines as AMERICA (1940). Renamed WEST POINT, USS (AP-23) (1942 – US Navy), AMERICA (1946 – United States Lines), AUSTRALIS (1964 – Okeania SA Chandris Group), AMERICA (1977 – America Cruise Lines), ITALIS (1978 – Chandris Group), NOGA (1980 – Noga Corporation) and ALFERDOSS (1984 – Silver Moon Ferries).

AMERICAN TRADER (1924) See VILLE DE HASSELT (1940)

AMERICAN TRAVELER (1924) See VILLE D'ARLON (1940)

AMERIGO VESPUCCI (1948)
9774 grt
485' x 62' x 26' (147 x 18.8 x 7.9 m)
2 x 9-cylinder Fiat diesel engines via single screw.
Broken up for scrap as a cargo ship at La Spezia in 1978. Ex-U.S. Maritime Commission.
Launched by Ansaldo Shipyards, Genoa, for Lloyd Triestino as the GIUSEPPE MAJORANA (1942) but completed as the AMERIGO VESPUCCI six years later.

AMERIKA (1905) See EDMUND B. ALEXANDER, USS (1941).

AMERIKA (1929)
10218 grt; 52 psrs
484' x 62' x 28'6" (146.7 x 18.8 x 8.7 m)
6-cylinder B+W diesel engines via twin screw.
Sank on 22 April 1943 by a torpedo fired from the German U-306 in the North Atlantic, with the loss of 86 lives.
Built by Burmeister & Wain, Copenhagen, for the East Asiatic Co, Copenhagen.

AMERIKANIS (1967)
18458 grt; 663 psrs
576' x 74' x 28' (175.5 x 22.6 x 8.5 m)
6 x Parsons DRG turbine engines via twin screw.
Cruise ship owned by Chandris Cruises, Piraeus, and operated by its subsidiary Fantasy Cruises. Laid up in Eleusis Bay since 1997, she was repositioned to a berth in Tampa, Florida, with a sale price tag of US$4,500,000.
Built by Harland & Wolff Ltd, Belfast, for the Union-Castle Line as the KENYA CASTLE (1952).

AMERIQUE (1926)
8396 grt; 1650 psrs
440' x 56' x 35'6" depth (133.3 x 17 x 10.8 m)
Maudsley Sons & Field (London) 6-cylinder triple expansion engines via twin screw.
Broken up for scrap at Blyth in 1936. Ex-Chargeurs Reunis.
Built by Bremer Vulcan, Vegesack, for North German Lloyd as the SIERRA VENTANA (1913). Renamed ALBA (1920 – Cie de Navigation Sud Atlantique by way of World War One reparations).

AMMERLAND (1922) See GENERAL ARTIGAS (1930)

AMOCO TRADER (1982)
13439 grt; 900 psrs
637' x 73' x 29' (192.9 x 22 x 8.9 m)

Geared turbines via single screw.
Owned by the Merchant Terminal Corporation and laid up since 1985.
Built by the Kaiser Co, Richmond, California, for the US Maritime Commission as the Class C4-S-A1 troop transport GENERAL W. G. HAAN (AP-158) (1945). Reclassified as the GENERAL W. G. HAAN, USAT (1947 – US Army) and as the GENERAL W. G. HAAN, USNS (T-AP-158) (1950 – US Navy). Laid up 1958–67 in Beaumont, Texas, by MARAD. Renamed as the container ship TRANSOREGON (1968 – Hudson Waterways, New York) and MAYAGUEZ (1975 – Puerto Rico Maritime Shipping Authority). As the GENERAL W. G. HAAN she became a migrant ship post-World War Two.

AMOCO VOYAGER (1982)
13489 grt; 900 psrs
633' x 73' x 25'6" (191.8 x 22 x 7.8 m)
Geared turbines via single screw.
In service with Merchant Terminal Corporation, USA.
Built by the Kaiser Co, Richmond, California, for the US Maritime Commission as the Class C4-S-A1 troop transport GENERAL J. H. McRAE (AP-149) (1944). Laid up 1960–67. Renamed as the container ship TRANSHAWAII (1968 – Hudson Waterways, New York) and AGUADILLA (1975 – Puerto Rico Maritime Shipping Authority). As the GENERAL H. McRAE, she operated as a migrant ship post-World War Two.

AMORELLA (1988)
34384 grt; 2200 psrs
620 cars + 53 trailers
559' x 91' x 20' (169.4 x 27.6 x 6 m)
4 x 12-cylinder Wartsila-Pielstick diesel engines via twin screw.

Owned by the SF Line and operated as an ice-strengthened passenger-car-cargo ferry by the Viking Line, Sweden, on the Sweden–Aland Islands–Finland service.
Built by Brodogradiliste Shipyard, Split.

AMPHION (1917)
7409 grt; 1997 psrs
429' x 54' x 39'4" depth (130 x 16.6 x 11.9 m)
6-cylinder triple expansion engines via twin screw.
Broken up for scrap in 1923. Ex-US government.
Built by JC Tecklenborg, Geestemunde, for North German Lloyd as the KOLN (1899). Renamed in 1917 after the ship had been seized by the US government.

AMRA (1938)
8314 grt; 959 psrs
467' x 57' x 24' (141.5 x 17.3 x 7.3 m)
SRG turbine engines via twin screw.
Broken up for scrap in Kaohsiung in 1966.
Built by Swan Hunter & Wigham Richardson Ltd, Newcastle, for the British India Line.

AMROTH CASTLE (1915) See ARUNDEL CASTLE (1921)

AMSTERDA (1905)
3629 grt; 960 psrs
410' x 39' x 28'9" (125.1 x 11.9 x 8.8 m)
Triple expansion engine via single screw.
Broken up in 1905. Ex-Italian Line.
Built by Harland & Wolff Ltd, Belfast, for British Shipowners as the BRITISH CROWN (1880). Renamed AMSTERDAM (1887 – Holland America Line).

AMSTERDAM (1887) See AMSTERDA (1905)

AMSTERDAM (1930)
4218 grt; 548 psrs
366' x 50' x 15' (110.9 x 15.2 x 4.5m)

2 x Brown-Curtis SRG turbine engines via twin screw.
Sank as a hospital ship with a heavy loss of life on 7 August 1944 after striking a mine during the Normandy invasion in World War Two.
Built by John Brown & Co Ltd, Clydebank, for the London & Northeastern Railway.

AMSTERDAM (1950) See ARIANE II (1980)

AMSTERDAM (2000)
59000 grt; 1380 psrs
780' x 105' x 25'6" (236.4 x 31.8 x 7.8 m)
5 x 16-cylinder Sulzer diesel engines via twin Azipod screw.

Cruise ship owned by HAL Antillen NV and operated by Carnival Cruises.
Built by Fincantieri, Breda, for Holland America Line.

AMUSEMENT WORLD (1998)
12764 grt; 1300 psrs
275 cars
463' x 69' x 17'6" (140.3 x 21 x 5.3 m)
4 x 6-cylinder Lindholmens-Pielstick diesel engines via twin screw.

Cruise casino ship for New Century Cruise Lines, Singapore.
Built by Lindholmens Varv AB, Gothenburg, for Swedish Lloyd as the passenger-car ferry PATRICIA (1967). Renamed STENA OCEANICA (1978 – Stena Line Ltd), STENA SAGA (1978 – Stena Line Ltd), LION QUEEN (1988 – Lion Ferries), CROWN PRINCESS VICTORIA (1990 – Stena Line of Canada Ltd, Victoria, BC), CROWN PRINCESS (1990 – Stena Line of Canada Ltd), PACIFIC STAR (1990 – Starlite Cruises), SUN FIESTA (1993 – Stena Crown Princess Ltd, Nassau), LION QUEEN (1994 – Lion Ferries) and PUTRI BINTANG (Sembawang Shipmanagement Pte Ltd, Singapore).

ANADIR (1930)
3554 grt
315' x 46' x 26' (95.5 x 13.9 x 7.9 m)
Triple expansion engine via single screw.
Built by Baltic Shipbuilding & Engineering Yard, St Petersburg, for the Russian government (Sovtorgflot).

ANADYR (1930) See ANADIR (1930)

ANAHUAC (1924)
4720 grt; 98 psrs
401' x 47' x 29' (122.2 x 14.3 x 8.8 m)
Palmer Brothers 3-cylinder triple expansion engine via twin screw.
Broken up for scrap in 1925. Ex-government of Mexico.
Built by Palmer Brothers & Co, Jarrow, for P&O at a cost of £78,341 as the BORNEO (1895). Renamed HARIMA MARU (1914 – Shinsan Kisen Kabushiki Kaisha) and NEW CHINA (1922 – The Spain & China Co Ltd).

ANA MAFALDA (1951)
3318 grt; 52 psrs
338' x 45' x 19' (102.4 x 13.6 x 5.8 m)
2 x 7-cylinder Atlas-Polar diesel engines via single screw.
Built by Uniao Fabril, Lisbon for Soc Geral de Comercio Industria e Transportes, Lisbon, as a passenger-cargo ship.

ANANG (1993) See BELLA VISTA (1996)

ANAR (1992) See PRINCESS DANAE (1997)

ANASTASIA V (1996) See BALTIC KRISTINA (1997)

ANASTASIS (1978)
11695 grt; 467 psrs
522' x 68' x 24' (158.2 x 20.7 x 7.2 m)
2 x 10-cylinder Fiat diesel engines via twin screw.

Owned by the 'Youth With A Mission' organisation and operated by their subsidiary Maritime Mercy Ministries Ltd, Malta.
Built by Cantieri Riuniti dell'Adriatico, San Marco, for Lloyd Triestino as the VICTORIA (1953).

ANCERVILLE (1962) See HAI SHANG SHI JIE (1998)

ANCHISES (1911)
10046 grt; 300 psrs
509' x 60' x 29'6" (155.1 x 18.1 x 8.9 m)
Triple expansion engines via twin screw.
Sank on 28 February 28 1941 with the loss of 12 lives near the Aran Islands, west of Galway, Ireland, following a bombing raid by a lone German aircraft.
Built by Workman, Clark & Co Ltd, Belfast, for the Blue Funnel Line.

ANCON (1908) See CONTINENTAL (1948)

ANCON (1939) See STATE OF MAINE (1962)

ANCON (1946) See STATE OF MAINE (1962)

ANCON, USS (AGC-4) (1942) See STATE OF MAINE (1962)

ANCON, USS (AP-66) (1943) See STATE OF MAINE (1962)

ANCONA (1908)
8885 grt; 2680 psrs
482' x 58' x 26' (146.1 x 17.6 x 7.9 m)
6-cylinder triple expansion engines via twin screw.
As a neutral ship, she sank on 8 November 8 1915, with the loss of 194 lives, after being torpedoed by the German U-38 south of Sardinia following a deck gun attack the previous day.
Built by Workman, Clark & Co, Belfast, for Italia Societa di Navigazione a Vapori, Genoa.

ANCONA (1915)
5465 grt; 1120 psrs
400' x 49' x 27' (121.9 x 14.9 x 8.2 m)
4-cylinder quadruple expansion engine via single screw.
Broken up for scrap in 1924. Ex-Italian government.
Built by Harland & Wolff Ltd, Belfast, for the Hamburg-America Line as the passenger liner ARABIA (1897). Renamed BARCELONA (1899 – Sloman

Shipping).

ANCONA (1927) See PIRANCY (1928)

ANCONA (1974) See OCEANOS (1976)

ANDALUCIA (1926) See ANDALUCIA STAR (1929)

ANDALUCIA STAR (1929)
14943 grt; 150 psrs
550' x 68' x 28' (166.7 x 20.6 x 8.5 m)
Geared turbine engines via twin screw.
Owned by the Blue Star Line, she sank on 6 October 1942, with the loss of two lives, 400 miles (667 km) west of Monrovia after being hit by a torpedo from the German U-107.
Built by Cammell Laird & Co, Birkenhead, as the passenger-cargo ship ANDALUCIA (1926).

ANDAMAN PRINCESS (1989)
5145 grt; 350 psrs
60 cars
333' x 56' x 16' (100.9 x 17 x 4.8 m)
2 x MAN 18-cylinder diesel engines via single screw.

Initially a passenger-cargo RoRo ferry, but converted to a cruise ship for Siam Cruise Co Ltd, Bangkok.
Laid down by AB Finnboda Varf, Stockholm, for Rederi AB Svea as the STEN STURE (1959), but completed for the Silja Line as the passenger-car ferry SVEA JARL (1962). Renamed APOLLO III (1976 – Viking Line).

ANDAMANS (1958)
5934 grt; 66 psrs
390' x 52' x 21' (118.2 x 15.8 x 6.4 m)
MAN-B+W 4-cylinder diesel engine via single screw.
Owned by the Shipping Corporation of India, Calcutta.
Launched by Hindustan Shipyard Private for the Shipping Corporation of India as the STATE OF ANDAMAN (1957) and completed as the ANDAMANS.

ANDANIA (1913)
13405 grt; 2060 psrs
519' x 65' x 31' depth (157.3 x 19.7 x 9.4 m)
2 x Scotts 4-cylinder quadruple expansion engines via twin screw.
Sank on 27 January 1918, with the loss of seven lives, after being torpedoed by the German U-46 two miles (3 km) north of Rathlin Island, Northern Ireland.
Built by Scotts Shipbuilding & Engineering Co, Greenock, for the Cunard Steamship Co.

ANDANIA (1922) See ANDANIA, HMS (1939)

ANDANIA, HMS (1939)
13950 grt; 1673 psrs
520' x 65' x 31'6" depth (157.6 x 19.7 x 9.6 m)
4 x Hawthorne Leslie DRG turbines via twin screw.
Sank stern first as an armed merchant cruiser at 6.55 am on 16 June 1940 70 miles (117 km) south-east of Reykjavik, Iceland, the day after being hit with a torpedo from the German U-70. The majority of the crew were rescued by the Icelandic trawler SKALLAGRINUR.
Built by R & W Hawthorn, Leslie & Co, Hebburn-on-Tyne, for the Cunard Line as the passenger liner ANDANIA (1922).

ANDES (1913) See ATLANTIS (1930)

ANDES (1939)
26860 grt; 528 psrs
669' x 83' x 29' (202.7 x 25.2 x 8.8 m)
6 x turbine engines via twin screw.
Broken up for scrap in Ghent in 1971 as a cruise ship by Van Heyghen Freres for a tender price of £300,000.
Built by Harland & Wolff Ltd, Belfast, for the Royal Mail Line as a passenger liner.

ANDORA CASTLE (1920)
5883 grt; 540 psrs
398' x 50' x 26'8" (120.6 x 15.2 x 8.1 m)
Beardmore 6-cylinder triple expansion engines via twin screw.
Broken up for scrap in 1925 after first having caught fire in Kilidini, Mombasa, then being towed to Durban where the hulk was purchased by Andora Soc Anon De Construzioni & Imprese Navale in 1920. Renamed ANDORA CASTLE, then sent to the shipbreakers.
Built by William Beardmore & Co, Glasgow, for the Union Castle Line as the BERWICK CASTLE (1902).

ANDREA C (1948)
8604 grt; 482 psrs
461' x 61' x 23' (139.7 x 18.5 x 7 m)
2 x 7-cylinder Fiat diesel engines via single screw.
Broken up for scrap as a passenger-cargo ship in La Spezia in 1982. Ex-Costa Line.
Built by Todd-California Shipbuilding Corporation, Richmond, California, for the British Ministry of War Transport as the OCEAN VIRTUE (1942).

ANDREA DORIA (1953)
29093 grt; 1241 psrs
700' x 90' x 30' (213.4 x 27.5 x 9 m)
Stabilimento Mekaniko-Parsons geared turbines via twin screw.
Sank with the loss of 51 lives on 26 July 1956 after being rammed amidships by the Swedish vessel STOCKHOLM. The STOCKHOLM's ice-crushing bow ripped 30 feet (9 m) into the ANDRE DORIA's plates the day before and the two ships were locked together until the STOCKHOLM reversed the next day, leaving the ANDRE DORIA vulnerable to the Atlantic Ocean which poured through the gaping hole.
Built by Ansaldo Shipyards, Genoa, for the Italian Line as their flagship.

ANDREA GRITTI (1943) See VERITAS (1967)

ANDRE CHENIER (1921)
5145 grt; 74 psrs
400' x 48' x 28'6" (121.9 x 14.5 x 8.7 m)
North East Marine Engineering 3-cylinder triple expansion engine via single screw.
Broken up for scrap as a passenger-cargo ship by Soc Ligura di Produce Metallica, La Spezia, in 1925. Ex-Messageries Maritimes.
Built by Sunderland Shipbuilding Co, Sunderland, for the Blue Anchor Line as the WILCANNIA (1899). Renamed WAKOOL (1913 – Blue Anchor Line), SHINKOKU MARU (1914 – Goshi Kaisha Kishimoto Shokwai) and DUMONT D'URVILLE (1917 – Messageries Maritimes).

ANDREI ZHDANOV (1937)
3870 grt; 292 psrs
325' x 48' x 25'9" (98.5 x 14.5 x 7.8 m)
Russian Diesel Works 6-cylinder diesel engines via single screw.
Believed to have sunk during World War Two.
Built by Severney Shipbuilding Yard, St Petersburg, for the Russian government as the ALEXEI RIKOV (1928).

ANDRE LEBON (1913)
13682 grt; 565 psrs
508' x 62' x 45'8" depth (153.9 x 18.8 x 13.9 m)
2 x 8-cylinder quadruple expansion engines via twin screw.
Broken up for scrap at La Seyne in 1952.
Built by Constructions Navale, La Ciotat, for Messageries Maritimes, Marseilles.

ANEGAWA (1905) See PECHENGA (1917)

ANEMOS (1989) See MYRTIDIOTISSA (2000)

ANFA (1923)
4436 grt; 120 psrs
398' x 46' x 26'6" (121 x 13.9 x 9 m)
4-cylinder Koninklijke Maatschappij quadruple expansion engine via screw.
Broken up in Genoa in 1936. Ex-Cie de Navigation Paquet, Marseilles.
Built by Koninklijke Maatschappij, Rotterdam, for Nederlands Steamship Co as the passenger-cargo liner ORANJE (1903).

ANGAMOS (1966) See ARMONIA (1993)

ANGARA (1904) See PECHENGA (1917)

ANGARA (1911) See PECHENGA (1917)

ANGELICA ACCAME (1912)
3190 grt; 309 psrs
320' x 43' x 24'6" (97.5 x 13 x 7.5 m)
3-cylinder triple expansion engine via single screw.
Broken up for scrap in 1925. Ex-Flli Accame di L, Italy.
Built by D & W Henderson Ltd, Glasgow, for the Anchor Line as the BOHEMIA (1891).

ANGELIKA (1949)
3061 grt; 1200 psrs
300' x 46' x 17' (90.9 x 13.9 x 5.2 m)
4-cylinder triple expansion engine via single screw.
Broken up for scrap in Genoa in 1967. Ex-Typaldos Bros, Greece.
Built by Fairfield Shipbuilding & Engineering Co Ltd, Glasgow, for the Vancouver–Victoria Ferry Service as the PRINCESS ADELAIDE (1911).

ANGELINA (1978)
24377 grt; 1616 psrs
674' x 83' x 29' (205.5 x 25.1 x 8.8 m)
3 x 12-cylinder Sulzer diesel engines via triple screw.
Owned by the Costa Line, she sank in deep water on 24 September 1979 after listing 60 degrees while under tow to the breaker's yard in Kaohsiung. This followed her refloating in the harbour of St Thomas, US Virgin Islands, where she had been gutted by fire at her berth on 30 March and listed 25 degrees to port, settling 30' (9.1 m) to the harbour bottom. There was no loss of life as the entire passenger list was on the island sightseeing and the crew were evacuated safely.
Built by the Netherlands Shipbuilding Co, Amsterdam, for the Nederland Line as the ORANJE (1939). Renamed ANGELINA LAURO (1964 – Lauro Line).

ANGELINA LAURO (1964) See ANGELINA (1978)

ANGELINA LAURO (1989) See ARCADIA (1991)

ANGERS (1921)
9847 grt; 373 psrs
501' x 55' x 31' depth (151.7 x 16.7 x 9.4 m)
8-cylinder quadruple expansion engines via twin screw.
Broken up for scrap in 1939. Ex-Messageries Maritimes.
Built by Blohm & Voss, Hamburg, for the Hamburg-America Line as the passenger-cargo ship CAP ARCONA (1907).

ANGKOR (1921)
7537 grt; 296 psrs
465' x 52' x 32'8" depth (151 x 15.8 x 9.9 m)
6-cylinder oil engine via single screw.
Passenger ship broken up for scrap at La Seyne in 1933. Ex-Messageries Maritimes.
Launched as the ATLANTIQUE (1899) and advertised for sale.

ANGLIA (1898) See ITONUS (1907)

ANGLIA (1920)
3467 grt; 1505 psrs
383' x 45' x 17' (116 x 13.6 x 5.2 m)
4-cylinder triple expansion engines via twin screw.
Broken up for scrap in 1935.

Built by William Denny & Brothers, Dumbarton, for the London & North-Western Railway Co at a cost of £400,000.

ANGLO-BRAZILIAN (1913) See CHEPSTOW CASTLE (1915)

ANGLO-NORSE (1927) See POLAR CHIEF (1946)

ANGOL (1964) See ALEXI H (1979)

ANGOLA (1949)
13078 grt; 546 psrs
500' x 67' x 27' (166.7 x 20.3 x 8.2 m)
2 x 6-cylinder Doxford diesel engines via twin screw.
Broken up for scrap in Hualian in 1974.
Built by R & W Hawthorne, Leslie & Co Ltd, Hebburn-on-Tyne, for Cia Nacional de Navegacao as a passenger-cargo ship.

ANGRA DO HEROISMO (1966)
9831 grt; 312 psrs
4000 tonnes of cargo
501' x 65' x 27' (151.8 x 19.7 x 8.2 m)
AEG DRG turbine engine via single screw.
Broken up for scrap in Castellon in 1974. Ex-Impresa Insulana, Portugal.
Built by Deutsche Werft AG, Hamburg for Zim Lines as the passenger-cargo ship ISRAEL (1955) as part of German reparations for Jewish losses during World War Two.

ANIVA (1985)
17870 grt; 340 psrs
601' x 74' x 25' (182.2 x 22.4 x 7.6 m)
5 x 8-cylinder & 1 x 6-cylinder MAN diesel-electric engines via twin screw.
Broken up for scrap at Gadani Beach, Karachi, in 1986 after a tender for US$100 per ton was successful. Ex-Russian Northern Fleet, Severomorsk.
Built by Deutsche Werft AG, Hamburg, for the Hamburg-America Line as the PATRIA (1938). Renamed EMPIRE WELLAND (1945 – British Ministry of Transport) and ROSSIA (1946 – Black Sea Shipping Co as a World War Two war prize).

ANJA 11 (1998)
4101 grt; 253 psrs
170 cars
317' x 50' x 16'6" (96 x 15 x 4 m)
Cummins 10-cylinder diesel engines via twin screw.
Passenger-car ferry owned and operated by Easy Line AS, Norway, after a US$10,000,000 acquisition.
Built by North East Ships (BS) Ltd, Pallion, Sunderland, for the Mercandia Line as the passenger-cargo ship MERCANDIA I (1989). Renamed SUPERFLEX KILO (1989 --Superflex Ships). Laid up from May 1989 to June 1992, then renamed EASY 1 (1998 – Easy Line AS).

ANKARA (1948)
6178 grt; 675 psrs
409' x 62' x 21' (123.9 x 18.8 x 6.4 m)
4 x SRG turbine engines via twin screw.
Broken up for scrap in Aliaga in 1982. Ex-Turkish Maritime Lines.
Built by Newport News Shipbuilding & Drydock Co, Newport News, Virginia, for Clyde Mallory Lines as the IROQUOIS (1927). Renamed as the hospital ship SOLACE (1944 – US Navy).

ANKARA (1983)
10552 grt; 752 psrs
214 cars
417' x 64' x 18' (126.4 x 19.4 x 5.5 m)
4 x 6-cylinder Zgoda-Sulzer diesel engines via twin screw.
Ice-strengthened passenger-car ferry operating for Turkish Maritime Lines.
Laid down by Stocznia Szczecinska, Szczecin, Poland for Polish Baltic Lines as the MAZOWIA (1982), but completed as ANKARA.

ANKING (1950) See KLIAS (1970)

ANNA AKHMATOVA (1988)
4575 grt; 150 psrs
297' x 58' x 17'6" (90 x 17.6 x 5.3 m)
Zgoda-Sulzer 6-cylinder diesel engines via single screw.

Passenger ship owned by the Russian government and operated by PO Arktikmoeneftegazrazvedka, Murmansk.
Built by Stocznia im Komuny, Gdynia.

ANNA C (1947)
12030 grt; 1066 psrs
524' x 65' x 28' (158.8 x 19.7 x 8.5 m)
2 x 9-cylinder Fiat diesel engines via twin screw.
Broken up for scrap at La Spezia in 1972. Ex-Costa Line.
Built by Lithgows Ltd, Glasgow, for the Prince Line (Furness Withy) as the passenger-cargo liner SOUTHERN PRINCE (1929).

ANNA K (1996) See REGINA BALTICA (1996)

ANNA KARENINA (1991) See REGINA BALTICA (1996)

ANNAM (1898) See KARNAK (1912)

ANNA NERY (1962) See SALAMIS GLORY (1996)

ANNA SALEN (1946) See UNION RELIANCE (1961)

ANNA V (1997) See JUPITER (1997)

ANNIE JOHNSON (1969) See COSTA ALLEGRA (1990)

ANNOULA (1931)
5432 grt; 1325 psrs
400' x 52' x 25' (121.9 x 15.9 x 7.6 m)
3-cylinder triple expansion engine via single screw.
Owned by GP Cicellis & GA Kambitsis, she foundered off Cape Lookout on 7 October 1933.
Built by Russell & Co, Glasgow, for Unione Austriaca as the COLUMBIA (1908).

ANSELM (1940)
5954 grt
412' x 56' x 25'8" depth (124.8 x 17 x 7.8 m)
3 x William Denny & Bros turbine engines via twin screw.
Passenger liner owned and operated by Booth Steamship Co Ltd, Liverpool.
Built by William Denny & Bros Co Ltd, Dumbarton.

ANSELM (1961) See AUSTRALASIA (1965)

ANSHUN (1951) See SAFINA-E-ABID (1971)

ANTAEUS, USS (AS-21) (1941) See RESCUE, USS (AH-18) (1945)

ANTARTICO (1924) See MARIA GUILIA (1927)

ANTENOR (1925)
11174 grt; 135 psrs
499' x 62' x 35' depth (151.2 x 18.8 x 10.6 m)
Geared turbine engines via twin screw.
Broken up for scrap at Blyth in 1953.
Built by Palmers Shipbuilding Co, Jarrow, for the Henderson Line.

ANTIGONE, USS (1917) See POTOMAC (1921)

ANTIGUA (1931) See TORTUGA (1957)

ANTILLES (1907)
6878 grt; 460 psrs
410' x 53' x 25'6" (124.2 x 16.1 x 7.8 m)
William Cramp & Sons 3-cylinder triple expansion engine via single screw.
Sank on 17 October 1917 after being hit by a torpedo.
Built by William Cramp & Sons Shipbuilding & Engineering Co, Philadelphia, Pennsylvania, for the Southern Pacific Co.

ANTILLES (1953)
19828 grt; 778 psrs
599' x 80' x 26' (181.5 x 24.5 x 7.9 m)
8 x DRG Rateau-geared turbine engines via twin screw.

Broken up by a US breaker's yard where she lay on a reef off the Caribbean island of Mustique, which she struck on 8 January 1971. The reef ripped a hole and pierced the fuel tanks, triggering off a series of explosions and fires which burned for two days before she broke in two on 18 January without any loss of life.
Built by the Arsenal de Brest for the French Line.

ANTINOUS (1923)
7133 grt
414' x 56' x 29'7" (125.5 x 17 x 9 m)
Flensburger 3-cylinder triple expansion engine via single screw.
Broken up for scrap in Genoa in 1931. Ex-Messageries Maritimes.
Built by Flensburger Schiffsbau, Flensburg, for the Hansa Line as the WACHTFELS (1913)

ANTONIA (1922) See WAYLAND, HMS (1942)

ANTONI GARNUSZEWSKI (1974) See YU MEI (1991)

ANTONINA (1898) See PIRANCY (1928)

ANTONINA NEZHDANOVA (1977)
3923 grt; 256 psrs
328' x 53' x 15'6" (99.4 x 16.1 x 4.7 m)
2 x 8-cylinder Uljanik-B+W diesel engines via twin screw.
Ice-strengthened cruise ship owned and operated by the Far Eastern Shipping Co, Vladivostok.
Built by Brodogradiliste Titovo, Kraljevica.

ANTONIO DELFINO (1921) See EMPIRE HALLADALE (1946)

ANTONIO DELFINO (1934) See EMPIRE HALLADALE (1946)

ANTONIO LAZARO (1968) See LOGOS II (1988)

ANTONIO LOPEZ (1900)
5975 grt; 360 psrs
430' x 50' x 31'6" (131.1 x 15.2 x 9.6 m)
Quadruple expansion engine via single screw.
Broken up for scrap in Cadiz in 1946 after a 10-year period laid up in that port. Ex-Cia Trasatlantica.
Built by William Denny & Bros, Dumbarton, for the New Zealand Shipping Co Ltd as the passenger-cargo liner RUAHINE (1891).

ANTONIO MACHADO (1994)
4101 grt; 253 psrs
36 cars + 32 trailers
316' x 56' x 12' (95.8 x 17 x 3.6 m)
10 x 6-cylinder Cummins diesel engines via quadruple screw.
Passenger-car-cargo RoRo ferry owned by Islena de Navegacao SA, Algeciras.
Built by North East Shipbuilders Ltd, Pallion, Sunderland, for Superflex Ships as the SUPERFLEX GOLF (1989), then laid up from June 1989 to December 1991.

ANTONIO PACINOTTI (1957)
11298 grt; 541 psrs
535' x 64' x 28' (163 x 19.5 x 8.5 m)
2 x 8-cylinder Mecan-Sulzer diesel engines via twin screw.
Now a non-passenger cargo ship remeasured at 8086 grt for ItaliaSAN..
Built by Ateliers et Chantiers de la Loire, St Nazaire, for Chargeurs Reunis as the EDOUARD BRANLY (1952).

ANTONIOTTO USODIMARE (1948)
9715 grt; 52 psrs
485' x 62' x 26' (147 x 18.8 x 7.9 m)
2 x 9-cylinder Cantieri diesel engines via single screw.
Broken up for scrap as a freighter in Trieste in 1978. Ex-Italia Line.
Launched by Ansaldo, Genoa, for Italia as the VITTORIO MOCCAGATTA (1942), but completed six years later for Lloyd Triestino as the ANTONIOTTO USODIMARE.

ANTONY (1907)
6300 grt; 500 psrs

419' x 52' x 27'2" (127 x 15.8 x 8.2 m)
Triple expansion engines via twin screw.
Sank on 17 March 1917 after a torpedo attack 20 miles (34 km) from Coningbee Lightship.
Built by Hawthorn, Leslie & Co, Hebburn, for the Booth Line.

ANTRIM PRINCESS (1967) See LAURO EXPRESS (1990).

ANYO MARU (1913)
9257 grt; 92 psrs
466' x 58' x 38' depth (141.2 x 17.6 x 11.5m)
4 x SRG turbine engines via twin screw.
Sank in the Formosa Straits on 8 January 1945 after being torpedoed by the USS BARB.
Built by the Mitsubishi Dockyard , Nagasaki, for Toyo Kisen Kaisha.

AORANGI (1924)
17491 grt; 970 psrs
580' x 72' x 28' (176.8 x 21.9 x 8.5 m)
4 x 6-cylinder Sulzer diesel engines via quadruple screw.

Broken up for scrap at Dalmuir in 1953. Ex-Canadian-Australasian Line.
Built by Fairfield Shipbuilding & Engineering Co, Glasgow, for the Union Steamship Co of New Zealand.

AOTEAROA (1915) See AVENGER, HMS (1916)

APACHE (1901)
4145 grt; 200 psrs
337' x 46' x 20'6" (102 x 13.9 x 6.2 m)
W Cramp & Sons 3-cylinder triple expansion engines via single screw.
Broken up for scrap in Baltimore in 1928.
Built by W Cramp & Sons Shipbuilding & Engineering Co, Philadelphia, Pennsylvania., for the Clyde Steamship Co.

APAPA (1914)
7780 grt; 400 psrs
426' x 67' x 31'3" depth (129.1 x 20.3 x 9.5 m)
Quadruple expansion engines via twin screw.
Sank off Lynes Point 300 miles (500 km) west of Ireland on 28 November 1917 after being torpedoed by the German U-34. Seventy-seven lives were lost.
Built by Harland & Wolff Ltd, Belfast, for Elder Dempster Lines.

APAPA (1926)
9333 grt; 500 psrs
451' x 62' x 24' (136.7 x 18.8 x 7.3 m)
2 x 6-cylinder H&W-B+W diesel engines via twin screw.
Sank within one hour of being bombed by German aircraft off the west coast of Ireland on 15 November 1940, with 23 lives lost.
Built by Harland & Wolff Ltd, Belfast, for Elder Dempster Lines.

APAPA (1948) See TAIPOO SHAN (1969)

APHRODITE (1965) See STELLA OCEANIS (1967)

APHRODITE (1969)
4753 grt; 1500 psrs
25 cars
370' x 50' x 15' (112.1 x 15.2 x 4.6 m)

2 x 10-cylinder B+W diesel engines via twin screw.
Passenger ship owned by Med Sun Lines Ferry Ltd, Limassol, who had her laid up in Perama Bay from 1983 until having her broken up for scrap at Aliaga in 1987.
Built by Harland & Wolff Ltd, Belfast, for the British & Irish Steam Packet Co Ltd as the LEINSTER (1948). Renamed LEINSTER I (1968 –   Med Sun Lines Ferry Ltd).

APOLLO (1952) See REGENCY (1982)

APOLLO (1969) See ARCTIC STAR (1977)

APOLLO (1970) See LANGELAND IV (1999)

APOLLO (1995) See LANGELAND IV (1999)

APOLLO (1998)
28574 grt; 1108 psrs
653' x 83' x 29' (198 x 26 x 8.8 m)
2 x Pametrada Parsons turbine engines via twin screw.
Owned by Athena 2004 SA and operated by Direct Cruises UK who market the ship as APOLLO although the APOLLON nameplates are still in place.
Built by Vickers-Armstrong Ltd, Newcastle, for the Canadian Pacific Steamship Co as the EMPRESS OF CANADA (1960). Renamed MARDIS GRAS (1972 – Carnival Cruise Lines), OLYMPIC (1993 – Royal Olympic Cruises), STAR OF TEXAS (1994 – Marianne Shipping Inc), APOLLON (1995 – Epirotiki Cruises), OLYMPIC 2004 (1997 – Royal Olympic Cruises) and APOLLON (1998 – Athena 2004 SA).

APOLLO III (1976) See ANDAMAN PRINCESS (1982)

APOLLO EXPRESS I (1987) See EXPRESS APOLLON (1996).

APOLLON (1984)
5001 grt; 1094 psrs
130 cars
338' x 53' x 17' (102.4 x 16 x 5.2 m)
2 x 7-cylinder B+W diesel engines via twin screw.
Passenger ferry for Agapitos Bros, Greece.
Built by Union Naval de Levante, Valencia, for Cia Trasmediterranea as the CIUDAD DE TARIFA (1961).

APOLLON (1991) See MINOAN PRINCE (1995)

APOLLON (1998) See APOLLO (1998)

APOLLON II (1969) See REGENCY (1982)

APOLLON EXPRESS 1 (1993) See EXPRESS APOLLON (1996)

APOLLON EXPRESS 2 (1993) See EXPRESS ARTEMIS (2000)

APOLLON HELLAS (1999)
3095 grt; 1000 psrs
303' x 48' x 11'6" (91.8 x 14.5 x 3.5m)
2 x 6-cylinder MAN-B+W diesel engines via twin screw.
Owned and operated by Minoan Flying Dolphins following her purchase for US$2,800,000.
Built by Vassiliadis, Salamis, as the GEORGIOS (1990) for Lepanto Express, Greece. Renamed SUN BEACH (1996 – Han II Leasing Co).

APOLLONIA (1963)
5324 grt; 476 psrs
402' x 54' x 20' (121.8 x 16.4 x 6.1m)
6 x Parsons SRG turbine engines via twin screw.
Passenger ferry owned by Hellenic Mediterranean Lines, Piraeus.
Built by Swan Hunter Shipbuilders Ltd, Haverton, for Soc General de Transport Maritimes as the SIDI-BEL-ABBES (1948).

APOLLONIA (1989) See APOLLONIA II (1990)

APOLLONIA II (1990)
3950 grt; 86 psrs
130 cars

308' x 53' x 14' (93.2 x 16.2 x 4.2 m)
4 x 8-cylinder MWM diesel engines via twin screw.

Ice-strengthened passenger-car-cargo RoRo ferry owned by Halifax Shipping SA, Panama, and operated by Hellenic Mediterranean Ltd, Piraeus.
Built by Orenstein-Koppel und Lubecker Machinebau AG, Lubeck, Germany, for Moltzau Line AS, Gedser, as the TRAVEMUNDE (1964). Renamed EUROFARJAN II (1970 – Sessan Line), CORSICA NOVA (1976 – Tourship SA, Panama), GIRNE SULTANI (1987 – Fergun Shipping Co Ltd, Mersin) and APOLLONIA (1989 – Hellenic Mediterranean Ltd, Piraeus).

APPAM (1912) See APPAM (1919)

APPAM (1919)
7781 grt; 400 psrs
427' x 57' x 22'6" (129.4 x 17.3 x 6.8 m)
Quadruple expansion engines via twin screw.
Broken up in Milford Haven, UK, in 1936. Ex-Elder Dempster Lines.
Built by Harland & Wolff Ltd, Belfast, for the British & African Steam Navigation Co Ltd as the APPAM (1912). Renamed MANDINGO (1916 – Elder Dempster Lines).

APPIA (1961) See FIBI (1992)

APTERA (1987)
12286 grt; 1550 psrs
500 cars
465' x 74' x 18' (140.9 x 22.4 x 5.5 m)
2 x 18-cylinder MAN diesel engines via twin screw.
Passenger-car ferry owned and operated by ANEK.
Built by Hayashikane Shipbuilding & Engineering Co Ltd, Shimonoseki, for the Taiyo Ferry Co, Kanda, as the PEGASUS (1973). Renamed OSAKA (1983), PEGASUS (1984 – Osaka Shosen Mitsu Senpaku KK, Osaka) and CHANIA (1985).

APULIA (1981) See CAPO SPARTIVENTO (1988)

AQUAMARINE (1978) See ODYSSEUS (1988)

AQUAMART (1978) See SAUDI GOLDEN STAR (1979)

AQUARAMA (1955) See MARINE STAR (1994)

AQUARIUS (1972) See ADRIANA (1988)

AQUILA (1941)
30816 grt; 2700 psrs
709' x 83' x 51'5" depth (214.8 x 25.2 x 15.6 m)
8 x Ansaldo SRG turbine engines via quadruple screw.
Broken up as a high-speed aircraft carrier in La Spezia in 1950 after she was refloated from the seabed. She had lain there since the Italian Navy scuttled her with guided torpedoes on 19 April 1945.
Built by Ansaldo Shipyards, Genoa, for Navigazione Generale Italiana as the passenger liner ROMA (1926).

AQUILA UNO (1993) See EL SALAM EL SAUDI (1995)

AQUILEJA (1935)
9448 grt; 312 psrs
481' x 57' x 26'6" (151.8 x 17.4 x 8.1 m)
2 x 4-cylinder Nederlandsche Fabriek quadruple expansion engine via twin

screw.
Broken up for scrap several years after having been scuttled in Marseilles harbour on 26 June 1944. Ex-Lloyd Triestino, Genoa.
Built by Nederlandsche Scheepsbouw, Amsterdam, for the Nederlandsche Steamship Co as the PRINS DER NEDERLANDEN (1914).

AQUILES (1988)
4481 grt; 250 psrs
40 TEUs
340' x 56' x 23' (103 x 17 x 7 m)
2 x 8-cylinder MaK diesel engines via single screw.
Passenger-cargo ferry convertible to a naval auxiliary troopship, owned and operated by the government of Chile, Santiago.
Built by Asmar y Maestranzas de la Armada, Talcahuano.

AQUITAINE (1999) See P&OSL AQUITAINE (1999)

AQUITANIA (1914)
45647 grt; 3230 psrs
901' x 97' x 35' (273 x 29.4 x 10.6 m)
4 x Parsons triple expansion turbine engines via quadruple screw.
Broken up for scrap by British Iron & Steel Corporation at Faslane in 1950 following a successful tender for £125,000 from BISCO.
Built by John Brown & Co, Clydebank, for the Cunard Line.

ARABIA (1897) See ANCONA (1915)

ARABIA MARU (1918)
9480 grt; 167 psrs
475' x 61' x 28' (143.9 x 18.5 x 8.5m)
Mitsubishi 6-cylinder triple expansion engines via twin screw.
Sank on 18 October 1944 after being torpedoed by the USS BLUEGILL 100 miles (167 km) off Luzon.
Built by the Mitsubishi Dockyard for OSK.

ARABIC (1902)
15801 grt; 350 psrs
601' x 66' x 47'6" depth (182.1 x 20 x 14.4 m)
8-cylinder quadruple expansion engines via twin screw.
Sank with 55 lives lost on 19 August 1915 after being torpedoed by the German U-24 off the Old Head of Kinsale, Ireland.
Laid down by Harland & Wolff Ltd, Belfast, for the Atlantic Transport Line as the MINNEWASKA (1902) but completed for the White Star Line as the ARABIC.

ARABIC (1921)
17324 grt; 3212 psrs
590' x 70' x 30'9" (178.8 x 21.2 x 9.4 m)
2 x 4-cylinder quadruple expansion engines via twin screw.
Broken up for scrap in Genoa in 1932 after tender accepted from Cooperativa Demolitori Navi for US$35,000. Ex-White Star Line.
Built by AG Weser Shipbuilders, Bremen, for North German Lloyd as the BERLIN (1909).

ARABUTAN (1940)
7956 grt
410' x 56' x 30'6" (124.2 x 17 x 9.3m)
Union Iron Works 3-cylinder triple expansion engines via single screw.
Under Brazilian ownership, this migrant ship was sunk on 7 March 1942 by a torpedo from the German U-155 70 miles (117 km) off Newport News, Virginia.
Built by Union Iron Works Co, Alameda, California, as the WAR SWORD (1917) for the Shipping Controller, Cunard Steamship Co Ltd. Renamed CAPRERA (1919 – Navigazioni Generale Italiana).

ARACATUBA (1928)
4872 grt; 100 psrs
386' x 56' x 18' (117 x 17 x 5.5 m)
Fiat 8-cylinder diesel engines via twin screw.
Wrecked and abandoned as a total constructive loss in the Rio Grande, Brazil, in February, 1933.
Built by Cantieri Navale Triestino, Monfalcone, for Costeira, Rio de Janeiro.

ARAFURA (1920) See ARAFURA MARU (1930)

ARAFURA LILY (1996)
12308 grt; 348 psrs
255 TEUs
489' x 75' x 20' (148.2 x 22.7 x 6.1 m)
2 x 9-cylinder Sulzer diesel engines via twin screw.
Container-passenger ship managed by Shanghai Haixing Shipping Co Ltd who chartered the vessel to Southern Cross SEA-Australia Line for a cruise-freight programme. However, the inaugural voyage in August 1996 reportedly lost US$390,000 and the ship was repossessed for unpaid fees, etc. As of late 1999, the ship is up for sale at US$42,000,000.
Built by Merwede Shipyard, Hardinxveld for Hoi Wah Shipping SA as the ZI DING XIANG (1996).

ARAFURA MARU (1930)
5597 grt
403' x 49' x 27' (122.1 x 14.8 x 8.2 m)
Bremer Vulkan 3-cylinder triple expansion engines via single screw.
Broken up for scrap in Osaka in 1930. Ex-OSK, Japan.
Built by Bremer Vulkan, Vegesack, for the Argo Line, Germany, as the FLORIDA (1903). Renamed PROFESSOR WOERMANN (1904 – Woermann Line), SWAKOPMUND (1907 – Hamburg-America Line) and ARAFURA (1920 – Eastern & Australian Line).

ARAGON (1905)
9588 grt; 971 psrs
512' x 60' x 25' (155.2 x 18.2 x 7.6 m)
Quadruple expansion engines via twin screw.
Sank with the loss of 610 lives on 30 December 30 1917 after a torpedo attack off Alexandria.
Built by Workman, Clark & Co, Belfast, for the Royal Mail Steam Packet Co.

ARAGON (1960) See TRAVELLER (1981)

ARAGUAYA (1906) See SAVOIE (1940)

ARAHURA (1983)
13621 grt; 997 psrs
100 cars + 27 trailers + 60 rail wagons or 40 trailers
489' x 67' x 18' (148.3 x 20.3 x 5.5m)
4 x 12-cylinder Wartsila-Vasa diesel-electric engines via twin screw.

Passenger-car-cargo train ferry operating for Tranzrail on the Wellington–Picton inter-island service in New Zealand.
Built by Aalborg Vaerft AS, Aalborg, for the New Zealand Railways Corporation, Wellington.

ARAMAC (1964)
13362 grt; 250 psrs
534' x 70' x 30' (162.8 x 21.3 x 9.1 m)
2 x DRG turbines via twin screw.
Broken up for scrap by Chin Ho Fa Steel & Iron Co in Kaohsiung in 1969. Ex-Eastern & Australian Steamship Co Ltd.
Built by Harland & Wolff, Belfast, for the Cunard Line as the PARTHIA (1948). Renamed REMUERA (1962 – New Zealand Shipping Co Ltd).

ARAMIS (1922) See CHENONCEAUX (1925)

ARAMIS (1931) See TEIA MARU (1942)

ARAMOANA (1962) See NIAXCO III (1990)

ARAMOANA (1984) See NIAXCO III (1990)

ARANDA (1968) See TRAVELLER (1981)

ARANDORA (1927) See ARANDORA STAR (1929)

ARANDORA STAR (1929)
15178 grt; 354 psrs
535' x 68' x 28' (162.1 x 20.6 x 8.5 m)
Geared turbine engines via twin screw.
Cruise ship owned by the Blue Star Line, she sank at 7.40 am on 1 July 1940, with 761 lives lost, after being hit by a torpedo from the German U-47 75 miles (125 km) west of Bloody Foreland, Ireland. Seven hours later, the Canadian destroyer HMCS ST LAURENT arrived at the scene and rescued 700 survivors.
Built by Cammell Laird, Birkenhead, for the Blue Star Line as the passenger-cargo liner ARANDORA (1927) with a passenger capacity of 162 – a figure she reverted to when re-converted to a dedicated passenger-cargo ship prior to World War Two.

ARANUI (1966) See NAJD III (1990)

ARANUI (1984) See NAJD III (1990)

ARANUI II (1990)
4200 grt; 60 psrs
343' x 50' x 16'6" (103.9 x 15.2 x 5 m)
12-cylinder Klochner-Humbolt-Deutz diesel engines via single screw.
Ice-strengthened passenger-cargo ship operating for Cie Polynesienne de Transport Maritime, Papeete.
Built by Rolandwerfte GmbH, Bremen, for Bruno Bischoff Reederei, Bremen, for Baltic Sea duty as the cargo ship BREMER HORST BISCHOFF (1971).

ARAPAHOE (1901)
4145 grt; 200 psrs
337' x 46' x 20'6" (102 x 13.9 x 6.2m)
W Cramp 3-cylinder triple expansion engines via single screw.
Broken up for scrap in Baltimore in 1928.
Built by W Cramp & Sons Co, Philadelphia, Pennsylvania, for the Clyde Steamship Co.

ARARANGUA (1927)
4872 grt; 120 psrs
389' x 53' x 18' (117.9 x 16.1 x 5.5 m)
2 x 8-cylinder Fiat diesel engines via twin screw.
Built by Cantieri Navale Triestino, Monfalcone, for Costeira, Rio de Janeiro.

ARARAQUARA (1928)
4872 grt; 100 psrs
386' x 53' x 18' (117 x 16.1 x 5.5 m)
2 x 8-cylinder Fiat diesel engines via twin screw.
Sank on 15 August 1942, with the loss of 131 lives, after being torpedoed by the German U-507.
Built by Cantieri Navale Triestino, Monfalcone, for Lloyd Nacional Soc Anon.

ARATERE (1999)
12596 grt; 355 psrs
160 cars + 60 railway wagons
495' x 67' x 20' (150 x 20.3 x 6 m)
4 x 8-cylinder Wartsila-Vasa diesel-electric geared engines via twin screw.
Passenger-car-cargo train ferry owned by the Wilmington Trust, USA, and leased by Tranzrail Ltd, Wellington, New Zealand, for 15 years.
Built by Hijos de J. Barreras SA, Vigo.

ARATIKA (1974) See VIRGIN MARY (1999)

ARATIMBO (1928)
4872 grt; 100 psrs
389' x 54' x 18' (117.9 x 16.4 x 5.5 m)
2 x 8-cylinder Fiat diesel engines via twin screw.
Built by Cantieri Navale Triestino, Monfalcone, for Costeira, Rio de Janeiro.

ARAUCO (1935)

4449 grt; 280 psrs
351' x 52' x 26'6" (106.4 x 15.8 x 8.1 m)
Central Marine Engineering 3-cylinder triple expansion engines via twin screw.
Broken up for scrap. Ex-Cia Chilena de Navigacion Interoceanica, Valparaiso. Built by W Gray & Co (1918) Ltd, West Hartlepool, for Cie Chilena de Navigacion Interoceanica, Valparaiso, as the REGISTAN (1921). Renamed SAINT ELOI (1929 – Cie Nav et Commerciale de l'Oceanie) and BOUSSOLE (1930 – Messageries Maritimes).

ARAWA (1884) See PORTO SAID (1913)

ARAWA (1907) See GANDIA (1939)

ARAWA (1936)

14491 grt; 274 psrs
552' x 68' x 33' (168.2 x 20.7 x 10 m)
Parsons DRG turbines via twin screw.
Broken up for scrap by John Cashmore Ltd at Newport, Wales, in 1955. Ex-Shaw Savill.
Built by William Beardmore & Co, Dalmuir, for Aberdeen & Commonwealth Lines as the ESPERANCE BAY (1922).

ARAWA (1968) See TROTTER (1981)

ARAYBANK (1940) See NAPOLI (1945)

ARBOREA (1957) See GOLDEN SUN

ARBOREA (1987)

11324 grt; 1200 psrs
409 cars
445' x 68' x 19' (148.3 x 22.8 x 6.3m)
2 x 12-cylinder GMT diesel engines via twin screw.
Passenger-car ferry operating for Tirrenia on the Italy to Sardinia service.
Built by Italcantieri SpA, Genoa, for Tirrenia as the STAFFETTA JONICA (1980).

ARCADI (1971)

5324 grt; 817 psrs
404' x 54' x 19'6" (122.5 x 16.4 x 6 m)
6 x Parsons SRG turbine engines via twin screw.
Owned by the Arcadi Shipping Co, Piraeus.
Built by Swan Hunter Shipbuilding, Newcastle, for Cie Navigation Mixte, Marseilles, as the PRESIDENT DE CAZALET (1948). Renamed MEDITERRANEE (1967 – Cie Navigation Mixte, Marseilles).

ARCADIA (1954)

28734 grt; 1390 psrs
721' x 90' x 31' (219.8 x 27.7 x 9.4 m)
6 x SRG turbine engines via twin screw.

Broken up for scrap by Lee Chang Steel & Iron Works at Kaohsiung in 1979.
Built by John Brown & Co, Clydebank for P&O at a cost of £6,664,000 as a passenger liner.

ARCADIA (1987) See ARCADIA (1991)

ARCADIA (1991)

5113 grt; 342 psrs
362' x 54' x 17'6" (109.6 x 16.3 x 5.3 m)
2 x 10-cylinder B+W diesel engines via twin screw.

Cruise ferry owned and operated by Golden Sun Cruises. There is a firm charter of the ship contracted to the Great Lakes Cruise Inc for one year, commencing June 2001.
Built by Union Naval de Levante SA, Valencia, for Cie Trasmediterranea as the VICENTE PUCHOL (1969). Renamed ARCADIA (1987 – Attica Shipping) and ANGELINA LAURO (1989 – Star Lauro Line).

ARCADIA (1997)

63524 grt; 1470 psrs
804' x 102' x 25' (243.6 x 30.9 x 7.6 m)
4 x 8-cylinder MAN-B+W diesel-electric rubber-dampened engines via twin screw.

Cruise ship owned and operated by P&O Cruises.
Laid down by Chantiers de l'Atlantique, St Nazaire, for Sitmar Cruises as the FAIR MAJESTY (1988) at a cost of US$150,000,000. She was completed as the STAR PRINCESS (1989 – P&O Princess Cruises) at an additional cost of US$50,000,000 to conform to P&O design preferences and renamed ARCADIA (1997 – P&O Cruises).

ARCADIAN (1912)

8939 grt; 320 psrs
500' x 55' x 33'7" depth (152.4 x 16.9 x 10.2 m)
6-cylinder triple expansion engines via twin screw.
Passenger liner owned by Royal Mail Steam Packet Lines, she sank on 15 April 1917 within 10 minutes of being torpedoed near Milos, Greece, losing 279 lives.
Built by Vickers Sons & Maxim Ltd, Barrow-in-Furness, for the Pacific Steam Navigation Co, Liverpool, as the ORTONA (1899).

ARCADIAN (1923)

12002 grt; 800 psrs
520' x 62' x 31'8" depth (157.6 x 18.8 x 9.6 m)
Harland & Wolff 8-cylinder quadruple expansion engines via twin screw.
Broken up for scrap in Japan in 1933. Ex-Royal Mail Lines.
Built by Harland & Wolff Ltd, Belfast, for Royal Mail Lines as the passenger liner ASTURIAS (1907).

ARCHANGELOS (1927) See K. SADIKOGLU (1950)

ARCHER (1919) See FULLER, USS (APA-7) (1943)

ARCHER (1945) See UNION RELIANCE (1961)

ARCHER, HMS (1941) See UNION RELIANCE (1961)

ARCONIA (1905) See IOANNINA (1913)

ARCTIC QUEEN (1928) See PISHCHEVAYA INDUSTRIYA (1935)

ARCTIC STAR (1977)
3288 grt; 1200 psrs
328' x 48' x 13'3" (99.4 x 14.5 x 4 m)
2 x Harland & Wolff 8-cylinder diesel engines via twin screw.
Broken up for scrap at Brownsville, Texas, in 1984. Ex-Zanzibar Inc, Panama.
Built by Harland & Wolff Ltd, Belfast, for Burns & Laird Lines Ltd as the ROYAL SCOTSMAN (1936). Renamed ROYAL SCOTMAN (1967 – Hubbard Explorational Co Ltd, Freetown) and APOLLO (1969 – Institute of Scientology).

ARDEAL (1932)
5695 grt; 50 psrs
410' x 54' x 23'6" (124.9 x 16.4 x 7.2 m)
3-cylinder Marinewerft triple expansion engine via single screw.
Owned by Serv Mar Romania, Braila, and operated by Sovromtransport, she was broken up for scrap in Romania in 1963.
Built by Marinewerfte Wilhelmshaven for the AG Hugo Stinnes Group as the EMIL KIRDORFF (1922).

ARDEOLA (1912)
3140 grt; 106 psrs
310' x 44' x 18'5" (93.9 x 13.3 x 5.6 m)
Caledon 3-cylinder triple expansion engines via single screw.
While under British Royal Navy control, she was impounded by a French craft and escorted to Bizerta, Tunisia.
Built by Caledon Shipyards, Dundee, for the Yeoward Line.

ARDTORNISH CASTLE (1883) See CYRIL (1904)

A. REGINA (1979)
5195 grt; 1300 psrs
300 cars
366' x 61' x 15' (111 x 18.5 x 4.6 m)
2 x 16-cylinder MAN diesel engines via twin screw.

Broken up in 1985 following her running aground on a reef off Mona Island, 40 miles (68 km) west of Puerto Rico, on 15 February 1985. She had been under charter to Dominican Ferries from Armatur SA.
Built by AS Langesunds MV, Langesund, for Stena Lines as the STENA GERMANICA (1967) and also alternatively named SEA CLUB (1981) for promotional purposes.

ARETOUSA (1995)

28417 grt; 1500 psrs
900 cars
585' x 89' x 20'6" (177.3 x 27 x 6.3 m)
4 x 8-cylinder MAN diesel engines via twin screw.
Ice-strengthened passenger-car cargo RoRo ferry operated by Minoan Lines, Heraklion, in the Mediterranean.
Built by Fosen Mek Verksteder, Rissa, Norway, for Minoan Lines at a cost of US$110,000,000.

ARGENTINA (1907)
5526 grt; 1350 psrs
407' x 48' x 22'6" (123.3 x 14.6 x 6.8 m)
Dunsmuir & Jackson 6-cylinder triple expansion engines via twin screw.
Broken up for scrap in 1960. Ex-Tirrenia Line.
Built by Russell & Co, Glasgow, for Unione Austriaca.

ARGENTINA (1931)
11015 grt; 1001 psrs
480' x 60' x 25' (145.5 x 18.2 x 7.6 m)
2 x 4-cylinder combination triple expansion engines & Parsons turbines via quadruple screw.
Owned by Cia Trasatlantica, she was broken up for scrap in 1945 after being raised from the seabed in Barcelona harbour where she had settled after an air attack in 1939.
Built by Swan Hunter & Wigham Richardson, Newcastle, for Cia Trasatlantica as the passenger liner REINA VICTORIA EUGENIA (1913).

ARGENTINA (1938)
20707 grt; 500 psrs
586' x 80' x 20'6" (177.6 x 24.2 x 6.2 m)
Turbo-electric engines via twin screw.
Broken up for scrap by Luria Brothers in South Kearny, New Jersey, in 1964. Ex-Moore McCormack Lines.
Built by Newport News Shipbuilding & Drydock Co, Newport News, Virginia, for the Panama Pacific Line as the passenger liner PENNSYLVANIA (1929).

ARGENTINA (1946) See ALIYA (1957)

ARGENTINA (1956)
12459 grt; 74 psrs
530' x 71' x 27'6" (160.6 x 21.5 x 8.4 m)
Geared turbine engines via twin screw.
Broken up for scrap in Campana, Argentina in 1973. Ex-Empres Lineas Maritimas Argentinas.
Built by Vickers Armstrong, Barrow-in-Furness, for Cia Argentina de Navegaceon Dodero, Buenos Aires, as the passenger-cargo ship PRESIDENTE PERON (1948).

ARGENTINA (1958) See ENCHANTED ISLE (1994)

ARGENTINA MARU (1939) See KAIYO (1943)

ARGENTINA MARU (1958) See NIPPON MARU (1972)

ARGENTINA STAR (1947)
10716 grt; 68 psrs
503' x 68' x 31' (152.4 x 20.6 x 9.4 m)
Parsons geared turbines via single screw.
Broken up for scrap by Hi Yo Steel & Iron Works in Kaohsiung in 1972.
Built by Cammell Laird, Birkenhead, for the Blue Star Line Ltd.

ARGO (1973) See RODOS (1989)

ARGO (1977) See EXPRESS ARIS (2000)

ARGO (1988) See LOGOS II (1988)

ARGONAFTIS (1964) See REGINA MARIS (1996)

ARGONAUT (1916)
4634 grt; 745 psrs
401' x 48' x 27'6" (121.5 x 14.5 x 8.4 m)
Harland & Wolff Ltd 3-cylinder triple expansion engine via single screw.

Operated by the US government when she sank on 5 June 1918 after being torpedoed off Bishop Rock, Scilly Isles.

Built by Harland & Wolff Ltd, Belfast, for the Pacific Steam Navigation Co as the passenger liner ORCANA (1893). Renamed ALBINGIA (1905 – Hamburg-America Line), GRODNO (1906 – Russian American Line) and ALBINGIA (1907 – Hamburg-America Line).

ARGONAUT (1964) See REGINA MARIS (1996)

ARGUAN (1917) See BAYANO (1918)

ARGUS, HMS (1918)
15000 grt
565' x 68' (171.2 x 20 m)
6 x turbine engines via quadruple screw.
Broken up for scrap by TW Ward & Co at Inverkeithing in 1947. Ex-British Royal Navy.
Launched on 2 December 1917 by William Beardmore & Co, Dalmuir, for Lloyd Sabaudo as the passenger ship CONTE ROSSO (1914), but taken over by the British Admiralty and completed as an aircraft carrier.

ARGYLLSHIRE (1911) See CLAN URQUHART (1933)

ARIADNE (1957) See EMPRESS 65 (1997)

ARIADNE (1976) See OURANOS (1999)

ARIAKE (1986) See SUPERFERRY 9 (1995)

ARIAKI (1995)
7910 grt; 200 psrs
451' x 79' x 26' (136.8 x 24 x 8 m)
2 x Pielstick 16-cylinder diesel engines via twin screw.
Passenger-cargo ferry for Oshima Unyu KK.
Built by Hayashikane Dockyard.

ARIANE (1979) See EMPRESS 65 (1997)

ARIANE I (1987) See ATHINA I (1999)

ARIANE II (1980)
5092 grt; 480 psrs
380' x 50' x 15' (115.2 x 15.2 x 4.5 m)
2 x SRG turbine engines via twin screw.
Cruise ship for the Chandris Line, Greece, she sank while acting as a floating hotel under Turkish charter in 1981.
Built by John Brown Ltd, Clydebank, for the British Transport Commission as the AMSTERDAM (1950). Renamed FIORITA (1970 – Chandris Group, following the ship's purchase for £200,000).

ARIEL, USS (AF-22) (1942) See BLUMENTHAL (1957)

ARIES (1998)
11347 grt; 1800 psrs
460 cars or 150 cars + 30 trailers
480' x 72'6" x 13' (145.6 x 22 x 4 m)
2 x General Electric Marine gas turbines + 4 x MTU 20-cylinder diesel engines via quadruple screw.
Passenger-car-cargo ferry owned and operated by Tirrenia, Italy.
Built by Fincantieri, Riva Trigoso.

ARIGUANI (1926)
6850 grt; 60 psrs
425' x 54' x 26' (128.8 x 16.4 x 7.9m)
Triple expansion engines via twin screw.
Broken up for scrap at Briton Ferry, UK, in 1956.
Built by Alex Stephen & Sons, Glasgow, for Elders & Fyffes.

ARION (1976)
7851 grt; 524 psrs
120 cars
450' x 62' x 17' (136.4 x 18.8 x 5.2 m)
2 x 6-cylinder Sulzer diesel engines via twin screw.
Owned by the Maritime Company of Lesvos, Mytilini, she has been laid up in

Haifa since 20 March 1983 after being refloated on 13 January 1982 from the seabed. This followed her 33 degree list to starboard and eventual rolling over and settling on her side after the Captain had purposely beached her. He took this option following a still unexplained explosion and fire that rocked the ship as she was approaching Haifa on 20 December 1981.

Built by Fairfield Shipbuilding & Engineering Co Ltd, Govan, for Somerfin Passenger Lines, Haifa, as the NILI (1965). She performed her sea trials under the name HELSINKI EXPRESS (1965). Renamed JAMAICA QUEEN (1967 – AG Weston Enterprises), then reinstated to NILI (1969 – Somerfin Passenger Lines, Haifa).

ARION (1999)
5634 grt; 340 psrs
383' x 50' x 17' (116.1 x 15.2 x 5.2 m)
2 x 10-cylinder Sulzer diesel engines via twin screw.
Owned by Arcalia Shipping Co Ltd, Lisbon, and operated by Classic International Cruises, Panama, following purchase for US$1,500,000.
Built by Brodogradiliste Uljanik, Pula, for Jadrolinija as the ISTRA (1965). Renamed ASTRA (1992 – Caravella Shipping Co Ltd, Ukraine) and ASTRA II (1994 – Goring Shipping Co Ltd, Ukraine).

ARIZONA (1905) See NEAPOLETANO (1905)

ARIZONA MARU (1920)
9684 grt; 151 psrs
475' x 61' x 28' (143.9 x 18.5 x 8.5 m)
Triple expansion engines via twin screw.
Sank on 14 November 1942 after being attacked by carrier-based US aircraft north of Guadalcanal.
Built by Mitsubishi Dockyard for Mitsui OSK Lines.

ARKADI (1988)
10859 grt; 1500 psrs
180 cars or 50 trailers
369' x 60' x 19'6" (123 x 20 x 6.5 m)
2 x 6-cylinder Pielstick diesel engines via twin screw.

Passenger-car-cargo ferry operating for Cretan Ferries. Placed on the sale lists mid-1999 at US$6,000,000.
Built by Kochi Jyuko KK, Kochi, as the BIZAN MARU (1983) for Kyodo Kisen KK, Komatsushima.

ARKADIA (1958)
20648 grt; 1386 psrs
590' x 76' x 27' (178.8 x 23.2 x 8.2 m)
2 x GEC turbo-electric engines via quadruple screw.
Broken up for scrap by Desguaces Maritimos at Valencia in 1967. Ex-Greek Line.
Built by Vickers-Armstrong Ltd, Newcastle, for the Furness-Bermuda Line as the MONARCH OF BERMUDA (1931). Renamed NEW AUSTRALIA (1949 – British Ministry of Transport) after a complete rebuild. This followed the MONARCH OF BERMUDA being declared a total loss after a fire which gutted her in March 1947, during post-World War Two restoration and reversion to a passenger liner.

ARKADIYA (1996) See ENCHANTED CAPRI (1998)

ARKA MARINE (1991) See ASK (1991)

ARKAS (1972) See BLUE GALAXY (2000)

ARKONA (1985)
18835 grt; 638 psrs
541' x 75' x 20' (162.1 x 22.1 x 6.1 m)
4 x 6-cylinder MAN diesel engines via twin screw.
Owned and operated by P&O after acquisition of 100% of Aida Cruises late in 2000.
Laid down by Howaldtswerke-Deutsche Werft, Hamburg, for Hadag as the HAMMONIA (1980) and completed as ASTOR (1981) at a cost of US$55,000,000.

ARLANZA (1912)
15044 grt; 1390 psrs
589' x 65' x 23'6" (178.5 x 19.7 x 7.1 m)
2 x 4-cylinder triple expansion engines via triple screw.
Broken up at Blyth in 1938.
Built by Harland & Wolff Ltd, Belfast, for the Royal Mail Line.

ARLANZA (1960) See TROTTER (1981)

ARMADALE CASTLE (1882) See REGINA (1904)

ARMADALE CASTLE (1903)
12999 grt; 820 psrs
570' x 65' x 29' depth (172.7 x 19.5 x 8.8 m)
Quadruple expansion engines via twin screw.
Broken up for scrap in 1936 in the UK.
Built by Fairfield Shipbuilding & Engineering Co Ltd, Glasgow, for the Union Castle Line.

ARMAND GRISAR (1945) See BOVEC (1959)

ARMELLE (1968)
7904 grt; 60 psrs
455' x 62' x 28' (137.9 x 18.9 x 8.5 m)
Turbine engines via single screw.
Broken up for scrap at Bilbao in 1973. Ex-Soc D'Avances Commerciales SA.
Built by Permanente Shipyard No 2, Richmond, California, for the US Shipping Administration as the 'Victory' Class freighter St LAWRENCE VICTORY (1945). Renamed ZAGREB (1947 – Yugoslav government) and HRVATSKA (1949 – Yugoslav government).

ARMENIA (1928) See ARMENIYA (1928)

ARMENIA (1963) See ARMENIYA (1963)

ARMENIAN (1903)
8825 grt; 60 psrs
513' x 59' x 35' depth (156.2 x 18 x 10.6 m)
Harland & Wolff 3-cylinder triple engine via single screw.
Sank on 25 June 1915 off Trevose Head, Cornwall, after being captured by the German U-38, then torpedoed point-blank.
Launched by Harland & Wolff Ltd, Belfast, for the White Star Line as the INDIAN (1895) and completed as the ARMENIAN.

ARMENIJA (1963) See ARMENIYA (1963)

ARMENIYA (1928)
4957 grt
356' x 51' x 25' (107.9 x 15.5 x 7.6 m)
Baltic Shipbuilding & Engineering Works 12-cylinder diesel engines via twin screw.
Laid up in Piraeus. Ex-Sovtorgflot.
Built by Baltic Shipbuilding & Engineering Works, St Petersburg.

ARMENIYA (1963)
5169 grt; 333 psrs
401' x 52' x 17' (121.5 x 15.8 x 5.2 m)

2 x 6-cylinder MAN diesel engines via twin screw.
Broken up for scrap in 1995. Ex-Black Sea Shipping Co, Odessa.
Built by Mathias-Thesen, Wismar, as a cruise ship.

ARMIN W. LEUSCHNER (1943) See WILLARD L. HOLBROOK (1944)

ARMONIA (1909)
4977 grt; 1994 psrs
430' x 48' x 29'8" depth (130.3 x 14.6 x 9 m)
Fairfield 3-cylinder triple expansion engine via single screw.
Owned by Canada Steamship Lines, she sank after being torpedoed on 15 March 1918 by a German U-boat near Porquerolles Island, off the south coast of France.
Built by Fairfield Shipbuilding & Engineering Co Ltd, Glasgow, for North German Lloyd as the WEIMAR (1891). Renamed SANTIAGO (1908 – Lloyd del Pacifico).

ARMONIA (1993)
3609 grt; 800 psrs
308' x 53' x 14' (93.3 x 16.1 x 4.2 m)
2 x 8-cylinder Pielstick diesel engines via twin screw.
Broken up for scrap after catching fire in mid-Atlantic and being declared a total constructive loss, in February 1993, while owned by Tina Shipping SA.
Built by Orenstein Koppel for the Norway-Copenhagen Line as the KOBENHAVN (1966). Renamed CERDA (1966), PRES. AGUIRRE (1966), PUERTO MONTT (1966) and ANGAMOS (1966).

ARMORIQUE (1975) See MIN NAN (1993)

ARNECIJK (1947) See ORIENTAL FALCON (1970)

ARNEDIJK (1947) See ORIENTAL FALCON (1970)

ARNEDYK (1947) See ORIENTAL FALCON (1970)

ARNEDYKE (1947) See ORIENTAL FALCON (1970)

ARNHEM (1946)
5008 grt; 750 psrs
377' x 54' x 15' (114.2 x 16.4 x 4.5 m)
2 x Parsons SRG turbine engines via twin screw.
Broken up for scrap by TW Ward Ltd, at Inverkeithing in 1969.
Built by John Brown Ltd, Clydebank, for the London Northeastern Railway.

ARNIS (1975)
8678 grt;
478' x 61' x 25' (144.7 x 18.5 x 24.6 m)
Fiat 6-cylinder diesel engine via single screw.
Broken up for scrap in Shanghai in 1978. Ex-Arnis Bulk Carriers Co Ltd, Cyprus.
Built by Cantieri Riuniti Adriatico, Monfalcone, for Soc Italiana di Armamento as the FRANCESCO MOROSINI (1948).

ARNO (1938)
7785 grt; 518 psrs
429' x 57' x 24'6" (130 x 17.3 x 7.5 m)
Beardmore 8-cylinder quadruple expansion engines via twin screw.
Owned by Lloyd Triestino, she was sunk by British torpedo bombers on 10 September 1942 40 miles (67 km) off Tobruk.
Built by William Beardmore & Co, Dalmuir, for the Adelaide Steamship Co, Australia, as the WANDILLA (1912). Renamed FORT St GEORGE (1921 – Furness Line) and CESAREA (1935 – Lloyd Triestino).

ARONDA (1941)
8396 grt; 1954 psrs
461' x 61' x 24' (139.7 x 18.5 x 7.3 m)
Turbine engines via twin screw.
Broken up for scrap in Kaohsiung in 1964.
Built by Swan Hunter Co Ltd, Newcastle, for the British India Line.

AROOSTOOK (CM-3) (1917) See LUX (1946)

AROSA KULM (1952)

8929 grt; 832 psrs
448' x 58' x 25' (136.6 x 17.6 x 7.6 m)
2 x General Electric DRG turbine engines via single screw.
Broken up for scrap by Van Heyghen Freres in Ghent in 1959 following the ship's arrest in Plymouth for unpaid debts as of December 1958. Ex-Arosa Line.
Built by American International Shipbuilding Corporation, Hog Island, Pennsylvania, for the US Shipping Board as the army transport CANTIGNY (1920). Renamed passenger-cargo ship AMERICAN BANKER (1924 – United States Lines), VILLE D'ANVERS (1940 – Antwerp Navigation Co), CITY OF ATHENS (1946 – Soc Naviera Transatlantic, Honduras) and PROTEA (1948 – Panamanian Lines).

AROSA SKY (1957) See BIANCA C (1958)

AROSA STAR (1954) See LA JENELLE (1969)

AROSA SUN (1955)

20126 grt; 922 psrs or 1502 troops
598' x 68' x 33' (181.2 x 20.6 x 10 m)
2 x 10-cylinder Sulzer-type diesel engines via twin screw.
Broken up for scrap in Bilbao in 1974 after serving as a floating hostel for factory workers in Ijmuiden, Holland, since 1960. Ex-Arosa Line.
Built by Ateliers et Chantiers de la Loire, St Nazaire, for Messageries Maritimes as the FELIX ROUSSEL (1930).

ARRAFIQ (1987) See DELFINI (1996)

ARRAPO (1912) See PORTO SAID (1913)

ARTEMIS (1917) See EMPIRE BITTERN (1942)

ARTEMIS (1973) See PRINCESS (1980)

ARTEMIS I (1996)

4251 grt; 1040 psrs
126 cars
301' x 51' x 13' (91.3 x 15.5 x 4 m)
2 x 7-cylinder Nohab-Polar engines via twin screw.

Ice-strengthened passenger-car-cargo RoRo ferry owned by Petra Navigation and operated by Rainbow Lines.
Built by Aalborg Vaerft, Aalborg, for Rederi AB (Sessan Line) as the PRINSESSAN DESIREE (1965). Renamed FENNO EXPRESS (1970 – Enso-Gutzeit Oy, Vasa), HANH PHUC (1989 – Vietnam Ocean Shipping Co, Haiphong) and JIMY (1991 – World Wide Shipping SA, Panama).

ARTEMISIA (1901)

5739 grt; 1110 psrs
452' x 52' x 28'3" (137.8 x 15.9 x 8.6m)
Palmer's 3-cylinder expansion engine via single screw.
Broken up for scrap in Japan in 1931. Ex- HM Thomson, England.
Built by Palmers & Co, Jarrow, for the Hamburg-America Line.

ARTEMIS K (1973) See PRINCESS (1980)

ARTHUR MIDDLETON, USS (AP-55) (1942)

10812 grt; 100 psrs
465' x 70' x 45'6" depth (140.9 x 21.2 x 13.8 m)
2 x General Electric DRG turbine engines via single screw.
Broken up for scrap in Brownsville, Texas, in 1973.
Built by Ingalls Shipbuilding Corporation, Pascagoula, Mississippi, for the American South African Line as the AFRICAN COMET (1941).

ARTICO (1924) See TRANSILVANIA (1927)

ARTIFEX, HMS (1944)

13984 grt; 1673 psrs
540' x 65' x 31' (163.6 x 19.7 x 9.4 m)
2 x Swan Hunter DRG turbines via twin screw.
Broken up for scrap at La Spezia in 1961 as a heavy repair ship. Ex-British Royal Navy.
Built by Swan Hunter & Wigham Richardson Ltd, Wallsend, for the Cunard Steamship Co as the passenger liner AURANIA (1924). Renamed as the repair ship AURANIA, HMS (1940 – British Royal Navy).

ARTOIS (1915) See IONIAN (1965)

ARTSA (1949)

3213 grt; 394 psrs
339' x 45' x 25'9" (102.7 x 13.6 x 7.8 m)
Triple expansion engine via single screw.
Broken up for scrap in 1963. Ex-Zim Israel Navigation Co, which paid US$1,000,000 for her in 1949. She was engaged for some time in transporting migrants to Israel.
Built by Bremer Vulkan, Vegesack, for Africanische Frucht as the fruit carrier PANTHER (1930). Renamed as the U-Boat tender LECH (1939 – German Navy), and the passenger-cargo ship MARE LIGURIA (1943 – Mare Liguria).

ARTSHIP (1999)

7997 grt; 67 psrs
465' x 66' x 26' (140.9 x 20 x 7.4 m)
General Electric geared turbine engines via single screw.
Floating art gallery owned by The Artship Foundation, Oakland, California.
Laid down by the Bethlehem Steel Company, Sparrow's Point, Maryland, for the Mississippi Shipping Co as the C3P Class passenger-cargo liner DEL ORLEANS (1940) and completed as the attack transport CRESCENT CITY, USS (APA-21) (1941 – US Navy), laid up in Suisin Bay, California, between 1948-1971. Renamed the training ship GOLDEN BEAR (1971 – California Maritime Academy, Vallejo, California) and then retired and laid up from 1995.

ARU MARINER (1964)

3388 grt; 825 psrs
320' x 47' x 19'6" (97 x 14.2 x 5.9 m)
Hong Kong & Whampoa Dock 3-cylinder triple expansion engine via single screw.
Owned by United Marine SA, Liberia.
Built by Hong Kong & Whampoa Dock Co for Rederei M Jebsen AS as the HEINRICH JESSEN (1940).

ARUNDEL CASTLE (1895) See WILBO (1924)

ARUNDEL CASTLE (1921)

19188 grt; 535 psrs
686' x 72' x 33' (207.9 x 21.8 x 10 m)
6 x Parsons SRG turbine engines via twin screw.
Broken up for scrap by Chiap Hua Manufactury Company for a tender of £245,000 in Kowloon, Hong Kong, in 1959.
Laid down by Harland & Wolff Ltd, Belfast, for the Union Castle Line as the passenger liner AMROTH CASTLE (1915) and completed as ARUNDEL CASTLE.

ARVEPRINS KNUD (1963)

8548 grt; 1500 psrs
400 cars
426' x 57' x 15' (129.1 x 17.3 x 4.5 m)
2 x 9-cylinder B+W diesel engines via twin screw.
Ice-strengthened passenger-car-cargo RoRo ferry owned by the Danish

government and operated by DSB on the Danish internal services.
Built by Helsingor Shipyards, Helsingor.

ASAHI MARU (1928)
9754 grt; 2185 psrs
504' x 60' x 25'6" (152.7 x 18.2 x 7.8 m)
Esercizio Baccini 8-cylinder diesel engines via twin screw.
Owned by NYK, she was broken up for scrap in Japan in 1949, five years after being badly damaged in a collision off Bisan Seto, on 5 February 1944.
Built by Soc Esercizio Baccini, Riva Tregoso, for Transatlantica Italiana as the passenger liner DANTE ALIGHIERI (1914).

ASAMA MARU (1929)
16947 grt; 839 psrs
583' x 71' x 28'6" (176.7 x 21.5 x 8.7 m)
4 x 3-cylinder Sulzer diesel engines via quadruple screw.
Sank on 1 November 1944 100 miles (167 km) south of Tungsha, in the South China Sea, after being torpedoed by the USS ATULE at 4.35am. A total of 98 lives were lost.
Built by Mitsubishi Shipbuilding & Engineering Co, Nagasaki, for NYK as a passenger liner.

ASBURY PARK (1903) See LANGDALE QUEEN (1962)

ASCANIA (1911)
9121 grt; 1700 psrs
467' x 56' x 27'6" (141.5 x 17 x 8.4 m)
Palmer's 6-cylinder triple expansion engines via twin screw.
Owned by the Cunard Steamship Co, she was abandoned as a total constructive loss after wrecking herself on 13 June 1918 in Breton Strait, 20 miles (33 km) east of Cape Ray, Newfoundland.
Laid down by Swan Hunter, Wallsend, for the Thompson Line as the GERONA (1910) and completed for the Cunard Steamship Co as the passenger liner ASCANIA.

ASCANIA (1926)
14440 grt; 696 psrs
490' x 60' x 29'6" (148.5 x 18.2 x 9 m)
2 x Armstrong Whitworth DRG turbine engines via twin screw.
Broken up for scrap by John Cashmore Ltd at Newport, Wales, in 1957.
Built by Sir WG Armstrong, Whitworth & Co, Newcastle, for the Cunard Line as a passenger liner.

ASCANIA (1955)
9536 grt; 1247 psrs
490' x 60' x 24' (148.5 x 18.2 x 7.3 m)
SRG turbine engines via twin screw.
Broken up for scrap in 1968. Ex-Grimaldi-Siosa Lines.
Built by Ateliers et Chantiers de la Loire, St Nazaire, for SGTM, France, as the passenger liner FLORIDA (1926).

ASCANIUS (1910) See SAN GIOVANNINO (1949)

ASCUNSION (1956) See MELANESIEN (1958)

ASCUTNEY (1917)
4967 grt; 1240 psrs
389' x 46' x 27'7" (118.6 x 14 x 8.4 m)
A Stephen & Sons 3-cylinder triple expansion engine via single screw.
Broken up for scrap in Boston in 1934. Ex-US government.

Built by Alex Stephen & Sons, Glasgow, for the Sloman Shipping Co as the passenger liner PISA (1897).

ASEAN WORLD (1992) See LEISURE WORLD (1994)

ASHRUF (1900)
4055 grt; 217 psrs
378' x 43' x 33' (114.5 x 13 x 10 m)
2 x 2-cylinder inverted engines via single screw.
Owned by Hajee Cassum Joosub, she was wrecked on 8 May 1905 at the entrance to Tamatave harbour, Madagascar, at the end of a voyage from Port Louis, Mauritius.
Laid down by Caird & Co, Greenock, for the P&O Line as the AGRA (1871), but completed as the passenger-cargo liner PESHAWUR (1872) at a cost of £113,500.

ASIA (1906)
4784 grt; 70 psrs
441' x 44' x 29'2" depth (133.6 x 13.3 x 8.8 m)
Harland & Wolff Ltd 3-cylinder triple expansion engine via single screw.
Owned by the Pacific Mail Steamship Co, she was abandoned as a total constructive loss after being wrecked on Finger Rock on Taichow Island, near Wanchow, China, on 23 April 1911. She was quickly looted and set on fire by local fishermen.
Built by Harland & Wolff Ltd, Belfast, for the White Star Line as the passenger-cargo liner DORIC (1883) and immediately chartered out to the New Zealand Shipping Co.

ASIA (1917)
6122 grt; 1480 psrs
415' x 50' x 25' (125.8 x 15.2 x 7.6 m)
6- cylinder Kincaid triple expansion engines via twin screw.
Owned initially by the Brazilian government, but ceded to France and passed into the ownership of the Fabre Line. She was declared a total constructive loss after fire destroyed her while in the outer harbour of Jeddah on 21 May 1930.
Built by Russell & Co, Port Glasgow, for Unione Austriaca as the ALICE (1907).

ASIA (1946) See SHIRLEY (1963)

ASIA (1953) See NORLEB (1984)

ASIA ANGEL (1988) See PRINCESA CYPRIA (1990)

ASIA CHINA (1995)
3991 grt; 1428 psrs
100 cars
330' x 58' x 15' (100 x 17.7 x 4.5 m)
Niigata 4 x 8-cylinder diesel engines via twin screw.
Passenger-car ferry owned by Trans-Asia Shipping Lines Inc.
Built by Kanda Zosensho KK, Kure, for Sado Kisen KK, Ryotsu, as the OTOME MARU (1973).

ASIAN PRINCESS (1989) See PHILIPPINES (1999)

ASK (1991)
11160 grt; 610 psrs
291 cars
498' x 69' x 19'6" (150.8 x 20.9 x 5.9 m)
4 x 12-cylinder Wartsila-MAN diesel engines via twin screw.

Passenger-car RoRo ferry owned and operated by Scandlines.

Built by Cantieri Navale Apuania, Carrara, for Nordstrum & Thulin as the LUCKY RIDER (1982). Renamed STENA DRIVER (1984 – Stena Challenger Ltd, Nassau), SEAFREIGHT FREEWAY (1985 – Navigation Maritime Bulgare), SERDICA (1988 – So Mejdunaroden Automobilen Transport, Burgas), NORDIC HUNTER (1990) and ARKA MARINE (1991 – Arka Marine II K/S).

ASKA (1939)
8314 grt; 958 psrs
461' x 61' x 24' (139.7 x 18.5 x 7.3 m)
Parsons SRG turbine engines via twin screw.
Sank in September 1940 after being torpedoed off the coast of Ireland.
Built by Swan Hunter Shipbuilders, Haverton, for the British India Line.

ASPASIA (1929) See CHRISTOS (1935)

ASPENLEAF (1916) See PRYGONA (1921)

ASSIMINA (1949)
5751 grt; 190 psrs
436' x 56' x 27'8" depth (132.9 x 17.1 x 8.4 m)
Bremer Vulkan 4-cylinder quadruple expansion engine via single screw.
Broken up for scrap by Hughes Bolckow Ltd at Blyth in 1952. Ex-Cia de Navegacion Dos Oceanos.
Built by Bremer Vulkan, Vegesack, for the German East Africa Line as the cargo ship KAGERA (1915). Renamed INDIANA (1922 – Cie Generale Transatlantique) and DERNA (1948 – Zarati Steamship Co) which acted as a refugee transport.

ASSINIBOIA (1908)
3925 grt; 220 psrs
346' x 44' x 17'6" (104.8 x 13.3 x 5.3 m)
Aft-housed Fairfield 4-cylinder quadruple expansion engine via single screw.
Planned by Assiniboia Steamship Corporation to become a floating display, she was completely destroyed by fire at Philadelphia on 9 November 1969, and broken up for scrap in 1970 after being declared a total constructive loss.
Built by Fairfield Shipbuilding & Engineering Co Ltd, Glasgow, for the Canadian Pacific Railway Co.

ASSYRIA (1898) See EKATERINOSLAV (1906)

ASSYRIA (1921) See BISCO 9 (1950)

ASTI (1915)
5649 grt; 968 psrs
409' x 51' x 27' (124.7 x 15.4 x 8.2 m)
3-cylinder Dickinson triple expansion engine via single screw.
Owned by the Italian government after seizure from Germany, she sank on 13 August 1917 when torpedoed by a German U-boat 220 miles (367 km) south-west of the Scilly Isles.
Built by JL Thompson & Sons Ltd, Sunderland, for the Rickmers Line as the passenger liner ELLEN RICKMERS (1897). Renamed BORKUM (1900 – North German Lloyd).

ASTOR (1981) See ARKONA (1985)

ASTOR (1995)
20606 grt; 656 psrs
578' x 72' x 20' (175.2 x 21.8 x 6.1 m)
4 x 8-cylinder Sulzer SRG diesel engines via twin screw.
Ice-strengthened cruise ship chartered to Aquamarin Kreuzfahrten, Bremen, by the Astor Shipping Co Ltd.
Built by HDW Shipyards, Kiel, for the South African Marine Corporation (Safmarine) as the ASTOR (1987) at a cost of US$65,000,000. Renamed FEDOR DOSTOEVSKIY (1988 – Black Sea Shipping Co, Odessa).

ASTRA (1992) See ARION (1999)

ASTRA II (1995) See OMAR II (2000)

ASTREA (1941) See TJALDUR (1967)

ASTROLABE (1930) See CAPO LENA (1935)

ASTURIAS (1907) See ARCADIAN (1923)

ASTURIAS (1926)
22445 grt; 1407 psrs
666' x 79' x 31' (203 x 24 x 9.4 m)
2 x 8-cylinder H&W-B+W diesel engines via twin screw.
Broken up for scrap at Faslane in 1957.
Built by Harland & Wolff Ltd, Belfast, for Royal Mail Lines.

ASUKA (1991)
28856 grt; 604 psrs
635' x 81' x 20' (192.5 x 24.7 x 6.2 m)
2 x 7-cylinder MAN-B+W diesel SRG engines via twin screw.

Cruise ship owned and operated by NYK Yusen Swire Cruises, Tokyo.
Built by Mitsubishi Heavy Industries, Nagasaki, for NYK.

ATALANTE (1972) See ATALANTE (1992)

ATALANTE (1992)
13562 grt; 815 psrs
548' x 68' x 22' (167.3 x 20.6 x 6.7 m)
2 x 10-cylinder B+W diesel engines via twin screw.
Cruise ship owned by Mediterranean Queen Lines Ltd and chartered to Paradise Cruises, Limassol, while placed on the sales lists late 1999 for US$8,000,000.
Built by Arsenal de Brest, Brest, for Messageries Maritimes as the TAHITIEN (1953). Renamed ATALANTE (1972 – Med Sun Lines) and HOMERICUS (1991 – Med Sun Lines).

ATCHISON VICTORY (1944) See MERCANTILE VICTORY (1963)

ATENAS (1909)
4961 grt; 103 psrs
379' x 50' x 25' (114.8 x 15.2 x 7.6 m)
Triple expansion engine via single screw.
Broken up for scrap at Baltimore in 1942.
Built by Workman, Clark & Co, Belfast, for the United Fruit Steamship Co as a passenger-cargo ship.

ATENE (1913)
4541 grt; 105 psrs
408' x 45' x 23' (123.6 x 13.6 x 7 m)
4-cylinder Koninklijke Maatschaapij quadruple expansion engine via single screw.
Acquired by the Austrian government in 1918, she sank after being wrecked in October, 1918 off Kara Burnu in the Black Sea.
Built by Koninklijke Maatschappij, Vlissingen, for the Nederland Steamship Company as the passenger-cargo ship KONING WILLEM III (1899).

ATHELING, HMS (1943) See ROMA (1950)

ATHENA (1989) See STAR AQUARIUS (1993)

ATHENIA (1904)
8650 grt; 500 psrs
478' x 56' x 32'5" (144.8 x 17 x 9.8 m)
Triple expansion engines via twin screw.
Sank after torpedo attack by the German U-53 on 16 August 1917 near

Inishtrahull.

Built by Vickers & Maxim Ltd, Barrow, for the Donaldson Line as a cargo ship, but was converted to a passenger liner in 1905.

ATHENIA (1923)
13465 grt; 1544 psrs
538' x 66' x 38' (163 x 20 x 11.5 m)
6 x Fairfield DRG turbine engines via twin screw.
Sank within 20 minutes, with the loss of 112 lives, after she was hit by two torpedoes fired from the German U-30 200 miles (334 km) north-west of Rathlin Island and south of Rockall Bank. Nearly 1,300 survivors were picked up out of the water by the British destroyers ELECTRA and ESCORT and the American cargo ship CITY OF FLINT. This incident occurred at 4.00 pm on 3 September 1939, only hours after Britain and France had declared war on Germany, and the ATHENIA thus became the first passenger ship to be sunk in World War Two.
Built by Fairfield Shipbuilding & Engineering Co Ltd, Glasgow, for the Donaldson Line as a passenger liner.

ATHENIA (1989) See MOBY RIDER (1998)

ATHENIC (1902) See PELAGOS (1928)

ATHENIC (1947)
15187 grt; 91 psrs
564' x 71' x 30' (171.9 x 21.6 x 9.1 m)
6 x SRG turbines via twin screw.
Broken up for scrap at Kaohsiung in 1969.
Built by Harland & Wolff Ltd, Belfast, for the Shaw Savill Line as a passenger-cargo ship.

ATHENS EXPRESS (1986)
11003 grt; 1000 psrs
451' x 71' x 21' (136.7 x 21.5 x 6.4 m)
2 x 8-cylinder MAN diesel engines via twin screw.
Passenger-ferry owned by the Grecia Shipping Co, Greece, and chartered to Ventouris Ferries.
Built by Evans Deakin & Co Ltd, Brisbane, for the Australian Coastal Shipping Commission as the cargo RoRo ship BRISBANE TRADER (1969).

ATHESIA (1899) See CHLOE (1924)

ATHINA 1 (1999)
8326 grt; 1200 psrs
421' x 76' x 15" (127.7 x 23 x 4.6 m)
4 x 8-cylinder Wartsila diesel engines via twin screw.
Owned by Starlight Ferries Ltd., Malta, and operated by Five Stars Line, Greece.
Built by Hayashikane Shipbuilding, Shimonoseki, for Hankyu Ferries as the FERRY HANKYU (1968). Renamed SUNBOAT (1985 – Euphoria Navigation Co Ltd, Limassol), ARIANE I (1987 – Iolaos Navigation Co Ltd, Limassol), IERAPETRA (1988 – Falcon Maritime Co, Piraeus), RAFAELLO (1990 – Ayios Efthimios Navigation Co Ltd) and BRINDISI (1995 – owned by Laird Maritime Ltd and chartered by Vergina Ferries Hellas Ltd from 1995 while listed for sale).

ATHINAI (1908)
6742 grt; 2300 psrs
420' x 52' x 27'4'" depth (127.3 x 15.8 x 8.3 m)
North East Marine Engineering 6-cylinder triple expansion engines via twin screw.
Owned by the National Greek Line, she was abandoned in mid-Atlantic on 19 September 1915 after she had been swept from stem to stern by an uncontrollable fire.
Built by Sir Raylton Dixon & Co Ltd, Middlesbrough, for the Hellenic Transatlantic Steam Navigation Co Ltd.

ATHINAI (1961)
9237 grt; 620 psrs
100 cars
584' x 84' x 26' (177.9 x 25.6 x 7.9 m)
4 x General Electric DRG turbine engines via twin screw.
Broken up for scrap as a passenger-car ferry in 1989 after being laid up throughout 1967–89. Ex-Typaldos Bros, Piraeus.

Built by the Federal Shipbuilding & Drydock Co, Kearny, New Jersey, for Grace Lines as the passenger-cargo ship SANTA ROSA (1932) at a cost of US$5,000,000.

ATHIRAH (1992)
12433 grt; 532 psrs
492' x 62' x 18'6" (149.1 x 18.8 x 5.6 m)
2 x 7-cylinder Krupp-B+W diesel engines via twin screw.
Broken up for scrap in India in 1998. Ex-PT Kalla Lines, Indonesia.
Built by Brodogradiliste, Split, for Cia Nacional de Nav Costeira Autarquia Federal, Rio de Janeiro, as the ROSA DA FONSECA (1962). Renamed SEVEN SEAS (1975 – Mitsui-OSK) and NIPPON MARU (1977 – Mitsui-OSK).

ATHLONE CASTLE (1936)
25567 grt; 783 psrs
725' x 82' x 32' (219.7 x 24.8 x 9.7 m)
2 x 10-cylinder B+W diesel engines via twin screw.
Broken up for scrap in Kaohsiung in 1965.
Built by Harland & Wolff Ltd, Belfast, for the Union Castle Line.

ATHOS (1915)
12692 grt; 298 psrs
508' x 62' x 45' depth (153.9 x 18.8 x 13.6 m)
Ateliers et Chantier de France 6-cylinder triple expansion engines via twin screw.
Sank on 17 February 1917 after being hit by a torpedo from the German U-65 200 miles (333 km) south-west of Malta.
Built by Ateliers et Chantier de France, Dunkirk, for Messageries Maritimes.

ATHOS II (1927)
15275 grt; 420 psrs or 526 troops
566' x 66' x 41'6" depth (171.5 x 20 x 12.6 m)
2 x Curtis Reducer turbine engines via twin screw.
Broken up for scrap at La Spezia in 1959.
Built by AG Weser Shipbuilders, Bremen, for Messageries Maritimes.

ATLANTA (1907) See FELTRIA (1916)

ATLANTA (1908) See CHARLOTTE (1943)

ATLANTIC (1949) See QUEEN FREDERICA (1954)

ATLANTIC (1955) See ATLANTICOS (1956)

ATLANTIC (1959) See UNIVERSE (1976)

ATLANTIC (1982) See MELODY (1997)

ATLANTICA (1964)
13803 grt; 578 psrs
100 cars
508' x 67' x 26'6" (153.9 x 20.3 x 8.1 m)
6 x SRG turbine engines via twin screw.
Partially broken up at Perama Bay in 1970, then completed in Barcelona in 1974. Ex-Typaldos Bros, Piraeus.
Built by Ateliers et Chantiers de France, Dunkirk, for the French Line as the COLOMBIE (1931). Renamed as a hospital ship ALEDA E. LUTZ (1946 – US War Shipping Administration), then reverting to COLOMBIE (1946 – French Line).

ATLANTICA I (1991) See HORNBEAM (1992)

ATLANTICOS (1956)
5856 grt; 120 psrs
391' x 55' x 25'5" (119.2 x 16.7 x 7.7 m)
2 x A Stephen & Sons DRG turbine engines via single screw.
Broken up for scrap at La Spezia in 1958. Ex-Typaldos Lines.
Built by Alexander Stephen & Sons, Glasgow, for the Khedivial Mail Steamship Co as the FAMAKA (1922). Renamed ORMISTON (1927 – Australian United Steam Navigation Co) and ATLANTIC (1955 – Typaldos Lines).

ATLANTIDE (1912)
6072 grt; 168 psrs
420' x 54' x 28'7" depth (127.3 x 16.4 x 8.7 m)
Hawthorn Leslie 3-cylinder triple expansion engine via single screw.
Owned by Soc Italiana de Navigazione, she sank on 9 February 1918 after being torpedoed off Madeira island.
Built by Hawthorn Leslie & Co, Hebburn, for the Federal Steam Navigation Co Ltd as the CORNWALL (1896).

ATLANTIQUE (1899) See ANGKOR (1921)

ATLANTIS (1930)
15135 grt; 900 psrs
589' x 67' x 29' (179.5 x 20.4 x 8.8 m)
2 x 4-cylinder H&W triple expansion engines via triple screw.
Broken up for scrap at Faslane in 1952. Ex-Royal Mail Lines.
Built by Harland & Wolff Ltd, Belfast, for Royal Mail Lines as the ANDES (1913).

ATLANTIS (1970) See OCEAN EXPLORER I (1998).

ATLANTIS (1977)
4504 grt; 414 psrs
40 cars
318' x 52' x 14' (96.4 x 15.8 x 4.2 m)
2 x 7-cylinder Sulzer diesel engines via twin screw.
Cruise ship owned by K Lines, Greece, she was broken up for scrap at Perama Bay in 1983 following her gutting by fire, on 7 March 1983, while she was undergoing a refit in the Xaveri Docks. Immediately after the fire, which broke out in the accommodation section, she was towed out to sea and beached at Kamatero, on Salamis Island, to burn completely out before being towed back to the breaker's yard.
Built by Cantieri Riuniti dell'Adriatico, Monfalcone, for Nomikos Lines as the ADONIS (1965).

ATLAS (1972) See COPA CASINO (1993)

ATLAS (1981) See COPA CASINO (1993)

ATLAS I (1981) See ORESTES (1999)

ATLAS II (1981) See KAPETAN ALEXANDROS A (1993)

ATLAS III (1981) See SATURNUS (1991)

ATLAS IV (1983) See VEGA (1990)

ATRATO (1889) See VIKNOR, HMS (1914)

ATSUTA MARU (1909) See ATUTA MARU (1938)

ATTACKER, HMS (1942) See PHILIPPINE TOURIST I (1978).

ATTIKA (1994) See EUROMAGIQUE (1995)

ATUA (1906) See RASHID (1927)

ATUTA MARU (1938)
7974 grt
460' x 56' x 27' (139.4 x 17 x 8.2 m)
Triple expansion engines via twin screw.
Owned by NYK, she sank on 30 May 1942 off Okinawa after being torpedoed by the USS POMPANO.
Built by Mitsubishi Dockyard for NYK as the ATSUTA MARU (1909).

ATZMAUT (1948)
4605 grt; 52 psrs
363' x 59' x 26' (110 x 18 x 7.9 m)
Triple expansion engine via single screw.
Broken up for scrap at Haifa in 1950 as a migrant ship. Ex-Zim Lines.
Built by Newport News Shipbuilding & Drydock Co, Newport News, Virginia, for the Southern Pacific Co as the passenger-cargo liner EL VALLE (1901). Renamed PAN CRESCENT (1941 – Pan Atlantic Steamship Co). In

1946, the PAN CRESCENT was purchased by a Jewish-American businessman, Zeev Shind, then re-registered under Zim Lines.

AUDACIOUS (1941)
7644 grt; 1326 PSRS
438' x 54' x 25'9" (132. x 16.5 x 7.8 m)
North East Marine Engineering 3-cylinder triple expansion engine via single screw.
Scuttled by the US government off the Normandy coast of France as part of the D-Day strategy coded 'Gooseberry #1' in June 1944.
Built by Cantieri Navale Triestino, Monfalcone, for Unione Austriaca as the BELVEDERE (1913).

AUGUST 8TH (1976)
7328 grt; 60 psrs
462' x 62' x 25' (140 x 18.8 x 7.6 m)
2 x 12-cylinder Stork-Werkspoor-Lugt diesel engines via single screw.
Broken up for scrap at Kaohsiung in 1979 as a passenger-cargo ship. Ex-Universal Honolulu Shipping Corporation Inc, Panama.
Built by Boeles Shipbuilding & Engineering Co, Bolnes, for the Oranje Line as the PRINS WILLEM VAN ORANGE (1953). Renamed FERDINAND FREILGRATH (1965 – VEB Deutsche Seereederei), FREIJO (1974 – VEB Deutsche Seereederei) and UNIVERSAL HONOLULU (1974 – Universal Honolulu Shipping Corporation Inc).

AUGUSTA (1924)
5702 grt
421' x 54' x 27' (127.6 x 16.4 x 8.2 m)
North East Marine Engineering triple expansion engines via single screw.
Built by Hawthorn Leslie & Co Ltd, Newcastle, for A Zanchi as the DURHAM (1904).

AUGUSTA VICTORIA (1890) See KUBAN (1904)

AUGUSTE VICTORIA (1897) See KUBAN (1904)

AUGUSTUS (1928) See SPARVIERO (1943)

AUGUSTUS (1952) See PHILIPPINES (1999)

AULONA (1996) See EUROFAST (2000)

AURANIA (1917)
13936 grt; 2060 psrs
538' x 65' x 30' (163 x 19.7 x 9.1 m)
4 x Wilson Slipway SRG turbine engines via twin screw.
After being torpedoed by the German UB-67 15 miles north of Inishtrahull, Ireland, a valiant effort was made to tow her to safety, but she ran aground off Tobermory, Scotland, on 4 February 1918 and had to be abandoned, with eight lives lost.
Launched on 16 July 1916 by Swan Hunter Shipbuilders, Haverton, for the Cunard Steamship Co as the passenger liner AURANIA, she was completed as a troopship and never physically entered commercial service, nor was Cunard's livery applied.

AURANIA (1924) See ARTIFEX, HMS (1944)

AURANIA, HMS (1940) See ARTIFEX, HMS (1944)

AURELIA (1901)
3017 grt; 90 psrs
346' x 38' x 21' (105.4 x 11.7 x 6.4 m)
2-cylinder John Elder steam engines via single screw.
Broken up for scrap in 1904 in Genoa. Ex-GB Lavarello fu P.
Built by John Elder & Co, Glasgow, for the Nederlands Steamship Co as the passenger-cargo liner PRINS ALEXANDER (1881).

AURELIA (1954) See ROMANTICA (1991)

AURELIA (1980)
12523 grt; 2000 psrs
449' x 99' x 19' (136 x 30 x 5.8 m)
2 x 16-cylinder GMT diesel engines via twin screw.
Passenger-car ferry owned by Italimpresit and chartered to Tirrenia for the

Italy–Greek Islands–Greece service.
Built by Italcantieri SpA, Castellammare di Stabia, for Tirrenia.

AURELLA (1972) See VILLE DE SETE (2000)

AUREOL (1951) See MARIANNA VI (1974)

AURIGA (1949)
10758 grt; 220 psrs
497' x 60' x 29' (151.5 x 18.3 x 8.8 m)
Triple expansion engines via twin screw.
Broken up for scrap at Savona in 1957. Ex-Fratelli-Grimaldi.
Built by William Denny & Sons, Dumbarton, for the New Zealand Shipping
Co as the passenger-cargo liner RUAHINE (1909).

AURORA I (1990) See MEGASTAR TAURUS (1995)

AURORA II (1990) See MEGASTAR ARIES (1995).

AURORA (2000)
76000 grt; 1975 psrs
886' x 106' x 26' (270 x 32.2 x 7.9 m)
4 x 14-cylinder MAN-B+W diesel-electric engines via twin screw.

Cruise ship built by Meyer Werft, Papenburg, for P&O Cruises at a cost of
US$324,000,000.

AUSONIA (1911)
7907 grt; 1050 psrs
464' x 54' x 29'2" depth (140.6 x 16.4 x 8.8 m)
6 x Palmers 6-cylinder triple expansion engines via twin screw.
Owned by the Cunard Steamship Co. After purchasing her for £120,000, she
sank on 30 May 1915 after being hit by a torpedo from the German U-55 620
miles (1033 km) off the Fastnet Rock, Ireland, with a loss of life numbering
44.
Built by Swan Hunter Shipbuilding, Haverton, for Thompson Lines as the
passenger-cargo liner TORTONA (1909).

AUSONIA (1915)
11300 grt; 420 psrs
Broken up in 1922 after being launched on 15 April 1915 by Blohm & Voss,
Hamburg, and then partially completed as Germany's first aircraft carrier for
World War One. The project was never completed and when the customer (Soc
Italiano di Servizi Marrittima) was approached by the builder, after the war, to
seek a continuing contract, the Deutschemark collapsed on the currency
exchanges worldwide, leading to Blohm & Voss deciding to cut their losses
and dismantle the vessel. No official dimensions or engine data has been made
available.

AUSONIA (1921) See AUSONIA, HMS (1944)

AUSONIA (1928)
12995 grt; 390 psrs
544' x 66' x 24' (164.8 x 20 x 7.3 m)
Geared turbine engines via twin screw.
Broken up for scrap at Trieste in 1936 after the hulk was salvaged from
Alexandria and towed to Italy following her gutting by a boiler room fire and
explosion, which killed three people, on 18 October 1935. THis incident
happened while she was at her dock.
Built by Ansaldo Shipyards, Sestri Ponente, for Soc Italiano di Servizi
Marrittime.

AUSONIA (1940) See ESPERIA (1949)

AUSONIA (1957) See AUSONIA (2000)

AUSONIA, HMS (1944)
13192 grt; 1649 psrs
540' x 65' x 43' (163.6 x 19.7 x 13 m)
2 x Armstrong Whitworth DRG turbine engines via twin screw.
Broken up for scrap as a heavy repair ship in Castellon in 1965. Ex-British
Admiralty.
Built by Sir WG Armstrong, Whitworth & Co, Newcastle, for the Cunard Line
as the AUSONIA (1921).

AUSONIA (2000)
12609 grt; 701 psrs
522' x 69' x 21' (159.1 x 21.1 x 6.4 m)
2 x Parsons turbine engines via twin screw.

Cruise ship owned and operated by Louis Cruises, Limassol.
Built by Cantieri Riuniti dell'Adriatico for Adriatica SAN, Venice, as the
AUSONIA (1957). Renamed LADY OF FORTUNE (1998 – chartered for two
years to First European Tours as a casino ship).

AUSTRALASIA (1965)
10854 grt; 248 psrs
505' x 65' x 27'6" (153 x 19.7 x 8.4 m)
2 x 8-cylinder B+W diesel engines via single screw.
Broken up for scrap at Hualien in 1973. Ex-Blue Star Line.
Built by John Cockerill Shipyards, Hoboken, Belgium, for Cie Maritime
Belge as the BAUDOUINVILLE (1950). Renamed THYSVILLE (1957 – Cia
Maritime Belge), ANSELM (1961 – Booth Line) and IBERIA STAR (1963 –
Blue Star Line).

AUSTRALASIAN (1884) See SCHAM (1912)

AUSTRALASIAN (1901) See RUAPEHU (1901)

AUSTRAL GLADE (1976) See CARIBE ENTERPRISE (1981)

AUSTRAL GLEN (1976) See PACIFIC ENDEAVOUR (1979)

AUSTRALIA (1904) See GEELONG (1904)

AUSTRALIA (1951) See DONIZETTI (1963)

AUSTRALIAN TRADER (1969) See AGIOS ANDREAS (1995)

AUSTRALIEN (1965) See CHIDAMBARAM (1973)

AUSTRALIS (1964) See AMERICAN STAR (1993)

AUTO TRADER (1981) See HOLGER (1999)

AVALON (1963) See VALON (1980)

AVALON (1990) See INDOCEANIQUE (1994)

AVARE (1945) See SIBIR (1946)

AVELONA (1927) See AVELONA STAR (1929)

AVELONA STAR (1929)
13376 grt; 162 psrs
525' x 68' x 28'6" (162.1 x 20.6 x 8.7 m)
Geared turbine engine via single screw.
Sank as a cargo transport on 1 July 1940 in the Bay of Biscay after being torpedoed the previous day by the German U-43, with the loss of 4 lives.
Built by John Brown & Co Ltd, Clydebank, for the Blue Star Line as the AVELONA (1927).

AVENGER, HMS (1916)
14744 grt; 576 psrs
550' x 66' x 37'6" (167.6 x 20 x 11.4 m)
2 x triple expansion geared engines via twin screw.
Sank on 14 June 1917 with one life lost after being torpedoed in mid-Atlantic, west of Gibraltar, by the German U-69.
Laid down by Fairfield Shipbuilding & Engineering Co Ltd, Glasgow, for the Union Steamship Co of New Zealand as the passenger liner AOTEAROA (1915), but completed as the auxiliary cruiser AVENGER, HMS, after the hull was taken over by the British Admiralty.

AVENIR (1967) See SHAHRAZAD (1985)

AVIATEUR ROLAND GARROS (1921)
4759 grt; 179 psrs
367' x 47' x 25' (111.2 x 14.2 x 7.6 m)
Blohm & Voss 3-cylinder triple expansion engines via single screw.
Broken up for scrap in Italy in 1931. Ex-Messageries Maritimes.
Built by Blohm & Voss, Hamburg, for Cie Woerman as the passenger-cargo ship LUCIE WOERMAN (1902).

AVILA (1927) See AVILA STAR (1929).

AVILA STAR (1929)
14443 grt; 150 psrs
530' x 68' x 27'6" (160.6 x 20.6 x 8.3 m)
2 x Parsons combination SRG turbines via twin screw.
Sank with the loss of 62 lives on 6 July 1942 after multiple torpedo hits from the German U-201 in mid-Atlantic, off San Miguel in the Azores.
Built by John Brown & Co Ltd, Clydebank, for the Blue Star Line as the AVILA (1927).

AVOCA (1891) See FELTRIA (1916)

AVOCA (1896) See FELTRIA (1916)

AVOCA (1908) See FELTRIA (1916)

AVOCA (1916) See AVON (1917)

AVOCETA (1923)
3442 grt; 150 psrs
330' x 44' x 21' (100 x 13.3 x 6.4 m)
Triple expansion engine via single screw.
Sank, with only 20 survivors, on 25 September 1941 after being torpedoed in the Atlantic midway between Gibraltar and England.
Built by Caledon Shipyards, Dundee, for Yeoward Brothers Ltd.

AVON (1907) See AVON (1917)

AVON, HMS (1916) See AVON (1917)

AVON (1917)
11073 grt; 1640 psrs
535' x 62' x 25' (163.1 x 18.8 x 7.6 m)
Quadruple expansion engines via twin screw.
Broken up for scrap by TW Ward at Briton Ferry, UK, in 1930. Ex-Royal Mail Lines.
Built by Harland & Wolff Ltd, Belfast, for Royal Mail Lines as the AVON (1907). Renamed AVOCA, HMS (1916 – British Royal Navy).

AVONDALE CASTLE (1897) See GARONNA (1912)

AVRASYA (1992) See AVRASYA I (1996)

AVRASYA I (1996)
5382 grt; 734 psrs
150 cars
383' x 53' x 17' (116.1 x 16 x 5.2 m)
4 x 6-cylinder Fiat SRG diesel engines via twin screw.
Passenger-car-cargo ferry broken up for scrap in 1997 after a fire in Trabjon.
Ex-Dream Shipping SA, Panama.
Built by Riuniti, Palermo, for Tirrenia as the LAZIO (1953). Renamed SANT ANDREA (1979 – Achaic Lines, Piraeus), MAKEDONIA (1984 – Achaic Lines), SUMMER STAR (1985 – Achaic Lines), LARNACA ROSE (1989 – Megacycle Shipping, Cyprus), CORFU DIAMOND (1987), AVRASYA (1992 – Mirror Holdings SA, Panama) and CORTINA (1996).

AVRISTAN (1923) See CAPO LENA (1935)

AWA MARU (1943)
11249 grt; 137 psrs
535' x 66' (162.1 x 20 m)
Diesel engines via twin screw.
Sank in three minutes with the loss of 2000 lives on 1 April 1945 when she was hit three days out of Singapore by four torpedoes from the USS QUEENFISH, although the Japanese ship was flying the International Red Cross flag at the time. However, she had breached International Red Cross and Allied safe passage agreements by surreptitiously carrying aircraft spare parts, munitions and other ordnance.
Launched on 24 August 1942 by Mitsubishi, Nagasaki, as a passenger liner for NYK, but completed as a troop carrier for the Japanese government.

AWA MARU (1967) See CRUSADER (1993)

AWANI DREAM (1996) See WORLD RENAISSANCE (1998)

AWANI DREAM II (1996) See OLYMPIC COUNTESS (1998).

AWATEA (1936)
13482 grt; 566 psrs
545' x 74' x 26' (166.1 x 22.5 x 7.9 m)
6 x Vickers-Armstrong DRG turbine engines via twin screw.
Sank on 11 November 1942 off Bougie, Algeria, after a constant German bomber attack.
Built by Vickers-Armstrong Ltd, Barrow-in-Furness, for the Union Steamship Co of New Zealand as a passenger liner.

AWU (1991)
6041 grt; 969 psrs
329' x 60' x 14' (99.8 x 18.3 x 4.2 m)
2 x 6-cylinder MaK diesel engines via twin screw.
Passenger ferry operated by PT Pelni, Djakarta.
Built by Jos L Meyer, Papenburg, for the Indonesian government.

AXEL JOHNSON (1969) See COSTA MARINA (1995)

AYVAZOVSKIY (1976) See CARINA (1996)

AYRSHIRE (1903)
9137 grt
460' x 59' x 29' (139.4 x 17.9 x 8.8 m)
North East Marine Engineering 6-cylinder triple expansion engines via twin screw.
Sank in December 1926 during an attempt to tow her back to port after a fire engulfed the ship in the Indian Ocean.
Built by Hawthorn Leslie & Co Ltd, Newcastle, for the Scottish Shire Line.

AZAY LE RIDEAU (1919)
8106 grt; 375 psrs
468' x 55' x 27' (141.8 x 16.7 x 8.2 m)
Blohm & Voss 8-cylinder quadruple expansion engines via twin screw.
Broken up in 1936. This vessel was given to Messageries Maritime as part of German war reparations at the conclusion of World War Two.
Built by Blohm & Voss, Hamburg, for the German East Africa Line as the GENERAL (1911).

AZEMMOUR (1951) See KHALID I (1983)

AZERBAIDZHAN (1975) See AZERBAYDZHAN (1975)

AZERBAIJAN (1985)
11450 grt; 202 psrs
50 cars
510' x 60' x 14'6" (154.6 x 18.3 x 4.5 m)
2 x 6-cylinder Uljanik-B+W diesel engines via twin screw.
Passenger ferry operated by the Caspian Shipping Co.
Built by Brodogradiliste Uljanik, Pula, for the Caspian Shipping Co, Baki, as the SOVIETSKAYA ARMENIYA (1985).

AZERBAYDZHAN (1975) See ENCHANTED CAPRI (1998)

AZROV (1951) See MELINA (1968)

AZTECA (1975)
6823 grt; 1200 psrs
359' x 58' x 15' (108.9 x 17.6 x 4.6 m)
2 x 12-cylinder Deutz diesel engines via twin screw.
Passenger ferry in Mexican waters operated by Transbordadores for the Mexican government.
Built by Jos L Meyer, Papenburg.

AZUR (1975) See THE AZUR (1987)

AZURE SEAS (1980) See IMPERIAL MAJESTY (1999)

BADENIA (1902) See HOLM (1922)

BADGER, USS (1898) See ROSE ISLE (1930)

BADGER (1952)
4244 grt; 620 psrs
180 cars
411' x 60' x 18' (125.1 x 18.1 x 5.7 m)
2 x 4-cylinder Skinner Unaflow engines via twin screw.
Passenger-car-cargo train ferry owned by the Lake Michigan Car Ferry Co, Cleveland, Ohio, and operated on the Great Lakes service.
Built by Christy Corporation, Sturgeon Bay, Wisconsin, for the Chesapeake & Ohio Railroad at a cost of US$5,000,000.

BADGER MARINER (1953) See UNIVERSE (1976)

BAHAMA STAR (1972) See BONAIRE STAR (1975)

BAHAMA STAR (1959) See LA JENELLE (1969)

BAHIA AGUIRRE (1950)
3838 grt; 100 psrs
336' x 47' x 18'6" (101.8 x 14.3 x 5.6 m)
2 x 5-cylinder Nordberg diesel engines via twin screw.
Owned by the Argentine government.
Built by Halifax Shipyards Ltd, Halifax, Nova Scotia.

BAHIA BUEN SUCESO (1950)
3834 grt; 60 psrs
336' x 47' x 18'6" (101.8 x 14.3 x 5.6 m)
2 x 5-cylinder Nordberg diesel engines via twin screw.
Passenger-cargo ship operated by Armada Argentina.
Built by Halifax Shipyards Ltd, Halifax, Nova Scotia, for the Argentine government.

BAHIA CASTILLO (1913) See GENERAL BELGRANO (1922).

BAHIA DE CADIZ (1980) See CIUDAD DE ALGECIRAS (1985).

BAHIA DE CEUTA (1980)
5287 grt; 1300 psrs
328' x 58' x 15' (99.5 x 17.6 x 4.5 m)
2 x 12-cylinder Deutz diesel engines via twin screw.
Passenger-cargo ferry operated by Europa Ferrys SA, Spain.
Built by Astilleros de Santander SA, Santander, for Islena di Navigation, Algeciras.

BAHIA DE MALAGA (1980)
5287 grt; 1300 psrs
328' x 58' x 15' (99.5 x 17.6 x 4.5 m)
2 x 12-cylinder Deutz diesel engines via twin screw.
Passenger-cargo ferry operated by Isnasa.
Built by Astilleros de Santander SA, Santander, for Islena di Navigation, Algeciras.

BAHIA PARAISO (1980)
10000 grt; 350 psrs
438' x 64' x 23' (132.7 x 19.5 x 7 m)
2 x 6-cylinder Sulzer diesel engines via twin screw.
Sank on 31 January 1989 in Antarctica three days after running aground.
Built by Astilleros Principe, Menghi y Penco SA, Avellaneda, for the Argentine government.

BAHIA THETIS (1950)
3838 grt; 100 psrs
336' x 47' x 18'6" (101.8 x 14.3 x 5.6 m)
2 x 5-cylinder Nordberg diesel engines via twin screw.
Owned by the Argentine government.
Built by Halifax Shipyards Ltd, Halifax, Nova Scotia.

BAHRIAHMER (1911)
3603 grt; 828 psrs
345' x 44' x 25'8" (105.2 x 13.3 x 7.8 m)
Wallsend Slipway 3-cylinder triple expansion engine via single screw.
Owned by the Turkish government, she sank on 7 November 1914 when she was attacked by the Russian Navy in the Black Sea, off Eregli.
Built by Armstrong Mitchell & Co Ltd, Newcastle, for North German Lloyd as the ROLAND (1893).

BAIA DE TOGOS DOS SANTOS (1995)
4284 grt; 600 psrs
316' x 56' x 12' (95.8 x 17 x 3.6 m)
10 x 6-cylinder Cummins diesel-electric engines via quadruple screw.
Passenger ferry operating for Top Flag Holdings Corporation, Panama.
Launched by Northeast Shipbuilders Ltd, Southwick, Sunderland, for Superflex Ships as the SUPERFLEX LIMA (1989) and completed as the MERCANDIA II (1989) for Mercandia.

BAIKAL (1962) See BAYKAEL (1962)

BALANGA QUEEN (1993) See DISCOVERY SUN (1995)

BALANGA SISTER (1994) See MOBY MAGIC (1997)

BALBEK (2000)
6576 grt; 985 psrs
250 cars + 35 trailers
371' x 59' x 14'6" (112.5 x 17.2 x 4.4 m)
2 x 12-cylinder Pielstick diesel engines via twin screw.
Passenger-car-cargo ferry operated by Marlines Marine Co Ltd., Limassol, under a leaseback arrangement from Shinedeck Shipping Ltd, Cyprus.
Built by the Taikoo Dockyard & Engineering Co, Hong Kong, for the Union Steamship Co of New Zealand as the WANAKA (1970). Renamed RATA HILLS (1976 – Sea Lanes Transport Co, Piraeus), INIOCHOS EXPRESS (1978 – Inichios Shipping SA, Piraeus), BREIZH-IZEL (1980 – Brittany Ferries) and DUCHESS M (1989 – Marlines Marine Co Ltd).

BALE (1983) See PENELOPE A (2000)

BALFOUR (1923) See KIZAN MARU (1938)

BALHASH (1943)
6806 grt
446' x 54' x 33'6" depth (135.2 x 16.4 x 10.2 m)
Newport News 4-cylinder quadruple expansion engine via single screw.
Owned by Russian government.
Built by Newport News Shipbuilding & Drydock Company, Newport News, Virginia, for Matson Lines as the MANOA (1913).

BALI SEA DANCER (1994) See GALAPAGOS DISCOVERY (1998)

BALKANIJA (1981) See ISTRA (1992)

BALLARAT (1882) See LAARAT (1904)

BALLARAT (1911) See BALLARAT, HMS (A-70) (1914)

BALLARAT, HMS (A-70) (1914)
11120 grt; 1100 psrs
500' x 63' x 38' (152.4 x 19.2 x 11.6 m)
2 x quadruple expansion engines via twin screw.
Sank on 26 April 1917 as an ambulance transport seven miles (12 km) off The Lizard, UK, in 44 fathoms of water. She had been under tow from the area where she had been torpedoed the day before by the German U-32.
Built by Caird & Company, Greenock, for the P&O Line as the BALLARAT (1911) at a cost of £176,109.

BALLARAT (1921)
12996 grt; 490 psrs
537' x 64' x 30' (163.7 x 19.4 x 9.1 m)
2 x quadruple expansion engines via twin screw.
Broken up for scrap at Briton Ferry in 1936 after Thomas W Ward Ltd

submitted a tender for £23,500.
Built by Harland & Wolff Ltd, Greenock, for the P&O Line.

BALMORAL CASTLE (1910)
13361 grt; 807 psrs
590' x 64' x 31' (179.8 x 19.4 x 9.4 m)
Fairfield quadruple expansion engines via twin screw.
Broken up for scrap at Newport, Wales, in 1939 for a tender price of £37,000.
Built by Fairfield Shipbuilding & Engineering Company, Glasgow, for the Union Castle Line.

BALOERAN (1930) See STRASSBURG (1941)

BALRANALD (1922)
13039 grt; 490 psrs
537' x 64' x 30' (163.7 x 19.4 x 9.1 m)
2 xquadruple expansion engines via twin screw.
Broken up for scrap from a tender of £25,000 from Douglas & Ramsey at Troon in 1936.
Built by Harland & Wolff Ltd, Greenock, for the P&O Line.

BALTAVIA (1993) See AL SALAM 93 (1996)

BALTIC (1904)
23884 grt; 2875 psrs
726' x 75'6" x 30'6" depth (162.4 x 21.4 x 9.3 m)
2 x 4-cylinder quadruple expansion engines via twin screw.
Broken up for scrap at Osaka in 1933.
Built by Harland & Wolff Ltd, Belfast, for the White Star Line.

BALTICA (1991) See REGINA BALTICA (1996)

BALTICA (1994) See PRINCESS DANAE (1997)

BALTICA REGINA (1996) See REGINA BALTICA (1996)

BALTIC CLIPPER (1992) See DREAM 21 (1997)

BALTIC FERRY (1980) See PRIDE OF SUFFOLK (1992)

BALTIC KRISTINA (1997)
12281 grt; 578 psrs
359 cars
422' x 73' x 19' (128 x 22 x 5.9 m)
4 x 9-cylinder Sulzer diesel engines via twin screw.

Passenger-car ferry purchased for US$16,625,000 by Scansov and chartered to Estonian Shipping Co, Tallink.
Built by Wartsila-Turku for the Bore Line as the BORE I (1973). Renamed SKANDIA (1980 – Finland Shipping Co), STENA BALTICA (1983 – Stena Line), ILICH (1983 – Baltic Shipping Co), ANASTASIA V (1996 – Scansov Line) and WINDWARD PRIDE (1997 – Windward Venture Shipping Co).

BALTIC STAR (1976)
3001 grt; 1287 psrs
302' x 48' x 13' (91.5 x 14.5 x 3.9 m)
2 x 12-cylinder Deutz diesel engines via twin screw.
Ice-strengthened passenger ferry owned by Seetouristik GmbH, Lubeck.
Built by HWD, Hamburg, for Hafendampfschiffahrt AG, Hamburg, as the HELGOLAND (1963). Renamed STENA FINLANDICA (1972 – Stena Line).

BALTIC STAR (1979)
3564 grt; 918 psrs
25 cars
304' x 47' x 16' (92.1 x 14.2 x 4.9 m)
6-cylinder MAN-B+W diesel engine via single screw.

Passenger-car-cargo ferry owned by Caribbean Shipping Co Inc, Panama, and operated by the Anedin Line, Sweden.
Built by Finnboda Varf AB, Stockholm, for the Svea Line as the BIRGER JARL (1953), BORE NORD (1973 – Jakob Lines) and MINISEA (1977 – Mini Carriers).

BALTIKA (1957)
7494 grt; 437 psrs
445' x 60' x 21' (134.8 x 18.2 x 6.4 m)
2 x Stork turbo-electric engines via twin screw.
Cruise ship for the Baltic Shipping Co.
Built by Nederlandsche Scheepbouw for the Baltic Shipping Co, St Petersburg, as the VYACHESLAV MOLOTOV (1940).

BALTIKA (1990) See BALTICA REGINA (1996)

BALTIMORE (1967) See SAN PEDRO (1970)

BALTONIA (1926)
3839 grt; 330 psrs
352' x 44' x 23' (106.7 x 13.3 x 7 m)
Richardsons-Westgarth 3-cylinder triple expansion engines via single screw.
Broken up for scrap in Belgium in 1936. Ex-United Baltic Corporation.
Built by Sir R Dixon & Co Ltd, Middlesbrough, for Elder Dempster Lines as the AKABO (1912).

BALTROVER (1936) See IONIAN (1965)

BAMBRA (1916)
3302 grt; 500 psrs
327' x 42' x 24' (99.6 x 12.8 x 7.3 m)
Triple expansion engines via twin screw.
Broken up in the UK in 1927. Ex-State Shipping Service, Perth, Western Australia.
Built by AG Weser, Bremen for North German Lloyd as the PRINZ SIGISMUND (1903).

BANADEROS (1994) See BARLOVENTO (2000)

BANASA (1997)
11668 grt; 1750 psrs
420 cars
381' x 66' x 16' (115.4 x 20 x 4.9 m)

4 x 6-cylinder B+W diesel engines via twin screw.
Ice-strengthened passenger-car ferry operating for Comarit.
Built by Helsingor Shipyard, Helsingor, for Mols Linien AS as the METTE
MOLS (1975). Renamed METTE MO (1996 – Mols Linien AS) and
BANASSA (1996 – Fred Olsen Line & Comarit).

BANASSA (1996) See BANASA (1997)

BANCA (1900) See TAIYU MARU (1923)

BANDIRMA (1976)
3213 grt; 1184 psrs
80 cars + 8 trailers
302' x 55' x 15' (91.5 x 16.6 x 4.5 m)
2 x 6-cylinder Stork-Werkspoor diesel engines via twin screw.
Passenger-car-cargo ferry operated by Turkish Maritime.
Built by Denizcilik Bankasi TOA, Camialti, Istanbul.

BANFORA (1933) See BANFORA MARU (1957)

BANFORA MARU (1957)
9615 grt; 337 psrs
478' x 57' x 26'6" (144.8 x 17.3 x 8.1 m)
Triple expansion engines via twin screw.
Broken up for scrap in Yokohama in 1957. Ex-Cie Generale de Navigation,
Marseilles.
Built by Kon Maats de Schelde, Flushing, for Rotterdam Lloyd as the
INSULINDE (1914). Renamed BANFORA (1933 – Cie Generale de
Navigation, Marseilles).

BANG CHUI DAO (1995)
15560 grt; 1107 psrs
226 cars
446' x 77' x 18' (135 x 23.4 x 5.4 m)
2 x 9-cylinder Stork Werkspoor diesel engines via twin screw.
Passenger liner operated by China Shipping.
Built by Van der Giessen, Krimpen, for the Dalian Marine Transport (Group)
Co, Dalian, as a passenger ferry.

BARADINE (1921)
13144 grt; 490 psrs
537' x 64' x 30' (163.7 x 19.4 x 9.1 m)
2 x quadruple expansion engines via twin screw.
Broken up at Dalmuir by WH Arnott for a tender figure of £26,000 in 1936.
Built by Harland & Wolff Ltd, Belfast, for the P&O Line.

BARANOF (1936)
4990 grt; 110 psrs
360' x 52' x 25'6" (109 x 15.8 x 7.8 m)
4-cylinder quadruple expansion engines via single screw.
Broken up for scrap in Sakaide, Japan, in 1955. Ex-D.F Radar.
Built by New York Shipbuilding Corporation, Camden, New Jersey, for the
Alaska Steamship Co as the SANTA ELISA (1919).

BARBAROSSA (1896) See MERCURY, USS (1917)

BARCELONA (1899) See ANCONA (1915)

BARDISTAN (1923) See MADALI (1948)

BARFLEUR (1992)
20133 grt; 1212 psrs
590 cars or 304 cars + 66 trailers

520' x 77' x 18' (157.7 x 23.3 x 5.4 m)
4 x 8-cylinder Wartsila geared diesel engines via twin screw.

Passenger-car-cargo ferry for Brittany Ferries Truckline.
Built by Kvaerner Masa-Yard, Helsinki, for Brittany Ferries at a cost of
£55,000,000.

BARI EXPRESS (1984) See EXPRESS HERMES (1999)

BARLOVENTO (2000)
9735 grt; 1200 psrs
320 cars
425' x 67' x 15' (128.8 x 20.2 x 4.5 m)
3 x 8-cylinder Stork-Werkspoor diesel engines via triple screw.

Passenger-car ferry owned and operated by Olsen Lines.
Built by Aalborg Shipyard, Aalborg, for Stanhope Steamship Co Ltd, London,
as the VIKING VOYAGER (1976). Renamed PRIDE OF CHERBOURG
(1989 – P&O European Ferries Group), PRIDE OF CHERBOURG II (1989
– P&O European Ferries Group) and BANADEROS (1994 – Fred Olsen
Lines).

BARNEGAT, USS (AVP-10) (1941) See KENTAVROS (1962)

BARNES, USS (1942) See PHILIPPINES TOURIST (1978)

BARNETT, USS (APA-11) (1940) See SURRIENTO (1948)

BARNETT, USS (APA-5) (1943) See SURRIENTO (1948)

BARONESSAN (1972) See NAN HU (1983)

BARONESS M (1985) See BARONESS M (1990)

BARONESS M (1987) See BARONESS M (1990)

BARONESS M (1990)
6280 grt; 1200 psrs
160 cars
364' x 58' x 13'6" (110.3 x 17.6 x 4.1 m)
2 x 12-cylinder Crossley-Pielstick diesel engines via twin screw.
Passenger-car ferry operating for the Indonesian government since 1997.
Built by Cammell Laird & Company, Birkenhead, for Burns & Laird as the
LION (1967). Renamed BARONESS M (1985 – Waterstar Marine Ltd),
PORTELET (1987 – BCIF), BARONESS M (1987 – Waterstar Marine Ltd),
and PORTELET (1988 – BCIF).

BARRABOOL (1922)
13148 grt; 490 psrs
537' x 64' x 30' (163.7 x 19.4 x 9.1 m)
Quadruple expansion engines via twin screw.
Broken up for scrap by the Douglas Yard at Barrow-in-Furness in 1936.
Built by Harland & Wolff Ltd, Belfast, for the P&O Line.

BARRETT, USNS (T-AP-196) (1951) See STATE (1990)

BARROW QUEEN (1963) See FIESTA (1964)

BASARABIA (1938) See UKRAINA (1948).

BASHKIRIA (1964) See SILVER STAR (1998)

BASHKIRIYA (1964) See SILVER STAR (1998).

BASS TRADER (1976) See BLUE BRIDGE (2000)

BASTO I (1997)
5505 grt; 550 psrs
200 cars + 18 trailers
360' x 59' x 15'6" (109 x 18 x 4.7 m)
2 x 12-cylinder Wichman diesel engines via twin screw.
Passenger-car-cargo ferry operating for Basto Fosen AS, Norway.
Built by Fosen MV AS, Norway.

BASTO II (1979)
4959 grt; 700 psrs
328' x 59' x 15' (99.5 x 17.8 x 4.6 m)
6-cylinder Bergens-Normo diesel engine via single screw.
Passenger-car ferry owned and operated by Ulisse Shipping SrL.
Built by Moss Rosenberg Stav for Basto Fosen, Trondheim.

BASTO II (1997)
5505 grt; 550 psrs
200 cars + 18 trailers
360' x 61' x 15'6" (109 x 18.5 x 4.7 m)
2 x 12-cylinder Wichman diesel engines via twin screw.
Passenger-car-cargo ferry operating for Basto Fosen AS, Norway.
Built by Fosen MV AS, Fevaag.

BATA (1994)
3238 grt; 250 psrs
333' x 48' x 13' (100.9 x 14.5 x 3.9 m)
2 x 8-cylinder Russian Motor Works diesel engines via twin screw.
Ice-strengthened passenger ferry owned by Intrans, a joint venture company.
Built by A Jdanov Shipyard, St Petersburg, for the Caspian Shipping Company, Baku, as the KIRGHISTAN (1959).

BATAIJSK (1955)
4933 grt
358' x 48' x 22' (108.3 x 14.6 x 6.6 m)
Turbine engines via twin screw.
Built by Stocznia Gdanska for the Russian government as a student education ship.

BATAVIA (1890) See BATAVIA (1919)

BATAVIA (1919)
11464 grt; 2700 psrs
517' x 62' x 42'6" depth (157.4 x 18.8 x 12.9 m)
Blohm & Voss 8-cylinder quadruple expansion engines via twin screw.
Broken up in France in 1924. Ex-Messageries Maritimes.
Built by Blohm & Voss, Hamburg, for the Hamburg-America Line as the BATAVIA (1890). Renamed POLONIA (1913 – Unione Austriaca) and BATAVIA 7 (1917 – Hamburg-America Line).

BATAVIA 7 (1917) See BATAVIA (1919)

BATORY (1936)
14287 grt; 816 psrs
526' x 70' x 24' (159.4 x 21.2 x 7.3 m)
2 x 9-cylinder Sulzer diesel engines via twin screw.
Broken up for scrap by Yau Wing Shipbreaking Co in Hong Kong in 1971 after she had served as a floating hotel in Gdynia since 1969. Ex-Gdynia America Line.
Built by Cantieri Riuniti del'Adriatico, Monfalcone, for the Gdynia-America Line in return for six shipments of coal for the Italian State Railways in lieu of cash.

BATSFORD (1914) See TOZAN MARU (1937)

BAUD (1948) See KUNAK (1960)

BAUDOUINVILLE (1939) See LINDAU (1941)

BAUDOUINVILLE (1950) See AUSTRALASIA (1965)

BAUDOUINVILLE (1957) See SHANGHAI (1978)

BAWTRY (1923) See K. SADIKOGLU (1950)

BAYANO (1913)
6103 grt; 70 psrs
432' x 53' x 26' (130.9 x 16.1 x 7.9 m)
Triple expansion engines via twin screw.
Sank in four minutes, with the loss of 174 lives, on 11 March 1915 after being torpedoed by the German U-27 near Corsewall Point off the Clyde estuary.
Built by A Stephen & Sons, Glasgow, for Elders & Fyffes Ltd

BAYANO (1918)
6788 grt; 99 psrs
440' x 54' x 27' (133.3 x 16.4 x 8.2 m)
Triple expansion engines via single screw.
Broken up for scrap by Van Heygen Freres, Ghent, in 1956.
Laid down by A Stephen & Sons, Glasgow, for Elders & Fyffes as the CAUCA (1917). Renamed ARGUAN (1917) while on the stocks and completed as the BAYANO.

BAYARD (1990) See CHRISTIAN IV (1991)

BAYARDO (1911)
3570 grt; 100 psrs
331' x 47' x 27' (100 x 14.2 x 5.2 m)
3-cylinder Earle's triple expansion engine via single screw.
Her hull was demolished by explosives in March 1912 after grounding on Middle Sands opposite Alexandra Dock in the River Humber, UK and breaking her back on 22 January 1912.
Built by Earles Co Ltd, Humberside, for the Wilson Line.

BAYERN (1921) See SUNLOCK (1955)

BAYERNSTEIN (1955) See ORIENTAL LADY (1967)

BAYKAL (1962)
5236 grt; 333 psrs
402' x 53' x 17' (121.8 x 16 x 5.3 m)
2 x 6-cylinder MAN diesel engines via twin screw.
Ice-strengthened passenger ship owned and operated by the Far Eastern Shipping Line, Vladivostok.
Built by Mathias-Thesen, Wismar, for the Far Eastern Shipping Co.

BAYRAMENTO (1916) See KOUANG (1929)

BAY STATE (1920) See PRESIDENT QUEZON (1939)

BAY STATE (1973)
12069 grt, 360 psrs
489' x 69' x 26' (148.2 x 20.9 x 7.8 m)
Geared turbine engine via single screw.
Broken up for scrap in Kearny, New Jersey, in 1982. Ex-U.S. Navy.
Laid down by Ingall's Shipbuilding Corporation, Pascagoula, Mississippi, for United States Lines as the AMERICAN BANKER (1941), launched for the US government as the BILOXI (1941) and completed for the US Army as the Class C3-In-P&C passenger-cargo carrier HENRY GIBBINS (T-AP-183) (1941). Renamed the EMPIRE STATE IV (1960 – US Maritime Administration).

BAY STATE (1980)
13319 grt; 392 psrs
533' x 73' x 27' (161.5 x 22.1 x 8.2 m)
GE geared turbine engine via single screw.
Broken up for spare parts and bulk scrap in 1986. Ex-US Maritime Administration which had laid the ship up since 1983 in the James river, Virginia, after repairs to major fire damage following an explosion and fire in the engine room on 22 December 1981. This incident had happened while lying at Buzzards Bay, Massachusetts.

Built by the New York Shipbuilding Co, Camden, for American President Lines as the PRESIDENT ADAMS (1950) and renamed as the troop transport GEIGER, USS (T-AP-197) (1951 – US Navy).

BEAR (1909)
4507 grt; 473 psrs
358' x 57' x 26' (108.5 x 14.2 x 7.9 m)
Newport News 3-cylinder triple expansion engine via single screw.
Abandoned as a total loss when wrecked on Cape Mendocino, USA, on 14 June 1916, with five lives lost.
Built by Newport News Shipbuilding, Newport News, Virginia, for the San Francisco & Portlands Steamship Co.

BEAUPORT (1991)
7747 grt; 1038 psrs
220 cars or 30 trailers
391' x 60' x 16'6" (118.5 x 18.2 x 5 m)
2 x 12-cylinder Pielstick diesel engines via twin screw.

Passenger-car-cargo ferry owned by Beauport Shipping Ltd and operated by International Shipping Partners AS, Nassau.
Built by Schiffbau Unterweser, Bremerhaven, for Lion Ferries, Sweden, as the PRINCE OF FUNDY (1970). Renamed PRINCE OF BRITTANY (1978 – Brittany Ferries) and REINE MATHILDE (1989 – Brittany Ferries).

BEAVER (1910) See BEAVER, USS (ARG-19) (1945)

BEAVER, USS (AS-5) (1917) See BEAVER, USS (ARG-19) (1945)

BEAVER, USS (ARG-19 (1945)
4507 grt; 473 psrs
380' x 47' x 26'6" (115.2 x 14.2 x 8 m)
Newport News 3-cylinder triple expansion engines via single screw.
Broken up for scrap in Seattle in 1950. Ex-US government.
Built by Newport News Shipbuilding, Newport News, Virginia, for the Union Pacific Railroad Co as the BEAVER (1910). Renamed BEAVER, USS (AS-5) (1917 – US government).

BEAVERBRAE (1948) See ROMANTICA (1991)

BEAVERDELL (1945) See LUISA COSTA (1963)

BEAVERDELL (1956) See LUISA COSTA (1963)

BEAVERGLEN (1945) See PING AN (1965)

BEAVERHILL (1927)
10041 grt; 138 psrs
523' x 62' x 29'11" (158.5 x 18.8 x 8.8 m)
Parsons geared turbine engines via twin screw.
Abandoned on Hillyards Reef off St John, Antigua, on 24 November 1944 with the only salvageable part of the ship being the stern section. The work was carried out on 11 December 1946 and she rested on the seabed inside St John's harbour until eventually towed out to Great Manan Island where she was sunk to create an artificial reef.
Built by Barclay, Curle & Co, Glasgow, as a passenger-cargo ship for the Canadian Pacific Steamship Co.

BEDWYN (1923) See KIZAN MARU (1938)

BEGONA (1957)
10139 grt; 830 psrs
455' x 62' x 21' (138.7 x 18.4 x 6.4 m)
2 x Westinghouse DRG turbine engines via single screw.
Broken up for scrap at Castellon in 1975 after a major breakdown in mid-

Atlantic under the ownership of Cia Trasatlantica Espanola.
Built by Bethlehem-Fairfield Shipyards, Baltimore, Maryland, for the US government as the Victory Class cargo ship VASSAR VICTORY (1945). Renamed CASTELBIANCO (1947 – Sitmar Line) and CASTEL BIANCO (1952 – Sitmar Line).

BEGONIA (1975) See SONG OF FLOWER (1989)

BELGENLAND (1879) See VENERE (1905)

BELGENLAND (1914) See COLUMBIA (1935)

BELGENLAND (1923) See COLUMBIA (1935)

BELGIA (1899) See IRISHMAN (1900)

BELGIAN FREIGHTER (1942) See KING ABDELAZIZ (1964)

BELGIC (1911) See SAMLAND (1913)

BELGIC (1917) See COLUMBIA (1935)

BELGRAVIA (1899) See TRANSBALT (1920)

BELKIS I (1979) See BELKIS I (1994)

BELKIS I (1994)
3114 grt; 600 psrs
306' x 46' x 14' (92.7 x 14 x 4.2 m)
2 x 8-cylinder Stork-Werkspoor diesel engines via twin screw.
Passenger ferry/pilgrim ship owned and operated by Arabian Ferries Ltd, Jeddah.
Built by Argo Shipbuilding and Repair Co, Perama Bay, as the passenger ferry OINOUSSAI (1973). Renamed BELKIS I (1979 – Arabian Ferries Ltd, Jeddah) and ALSHAHBA (1990 – International Trading Co).

BELLA (1956)
5072 grt; 65 psrs
352' x 52' x 26'6" (106.7 x 15.8 x 8 m)
Central Marine Engineering Works 3-cylinder triple expansion engines via twin screw.
Built by W Gray & Co Ltd, West Hartlepool, for the British India Steam Navigation Co Ltd as the KOHISTAN (1923). Renamed SAINT LUC (1929 – Cie Navale et Commerciale de l'Oceanie) and ESPERANCE (1930 – Messageries Maritime).

BELLA MARIA (1980) See KHALID I (1983)

BELLA VISTA (1996)
13422 grt; 71 psrs
529' x 76' x 26' (161.2 x 23.3 x 7.9 m)
8-cylinder Cockerill-B+W diesel engine via single screw.
Broken up for scrap in Cambodia in 1996.
Built by John Cockerill Shipyards, Hoboken, Belgium, for Cie Mar Congolaise, Matadi, as the passenger-cargo ship KANANGA (1973). Renamed ANANG (1993 – Anglo-Eastern Ship Management Ltd), CHRYSO (1994 – Ahlers Shipping NV) and NORBEL OMAN (1995 – Norbel Shipping Inc).

BELLE ABETO (1966)
12177 grt; 436 psrs
538' x 64' x 28' (163 x 19.4 x 8.5 m)
2 x 8-cylinder Sulzer diesel engines via twin screw.
This pilgrim ship was deliberately sunk by her owners Cia de Navigacion Abeto SA, Panama, on 30 July 1976 at her anchorage in Sasebo, Japan, after an engine room fire had burnt for two days and eventually engulfed the entire vessel.
Built by Chantiers et Ateliers de la Loire, St Nazaire, for Messageries Maritimes as the LAENNEC (1951).

BELOFIN I (1998)
18017 grt; 701 psrs
632' x 79' x 28' (191.5 x 24 x 8.5 m)
6 x SRG turbine engines via twin screw.

Sank on 21 October 2000 in 800 fathoms in the Atlantic, 50 miles (84 km) west of Capetown. At the time she was under tow by the Russian tug IRBIS, en route to Gadani Beach where the ex-cruise ship was to be broken up. Prior to this, she had had a two-year lay up at berth No 206 in Tampa, Florida. She was owned by AG Belofin Investments, Liechtenstein.
Built by Bethlehem Steel Corporation, Quincy, Massachusetts, for the Matson Line as the MONTEREY (1932) at a cost of US$8,300,492. Renamed LURLINE (1932 – Matson Line), MATSONIA (1956 – Matson Line), LURLINE (1963 – Matson Line) and BRITANIS (1970 – Chandris Group).

BELORUS (1994) See PROFESSOR GUL (1995)

BELORUSSIJA (1975) See DELPHIN (1996)

BELORUSSIYA (1975) See DELPHIN (1996)

BELTANA (1912)
11120 grt; 1100 psrs
515' x 63' x 28' (157 x 19.2 x 8.5 m)
2 x quadruple expansion engines via twin screw.
Passenger liner owned by Toyo Hogei KK., Osaka, who sold her to the Japanese breaker's yard Gentaro Kasegawa, Kobe. The yard had tendered £29,500 for her conversion into a whale factory ship, but broke her up for scrap instead in 1933.
Laid down by Caird & Company, Greenock, for the P&O Line as the BENDIGO (1911) and completed as the BELTANA (1912) at a cost of £179,365.

BELTON (1923)
5498 grt
445' x 52' x 25' (134.8 x 15.8 x 7.6 m)
Palmer's 6-cylinder triple expansion engines via twin screw.
Broken up for scrap by Hughes Bolckow in Blyth in 1926.
Built by Palmers Shipbuilding Co, Jarrow, for the Canadian Pacific Steamship Co as the MONTEAGLE (1903).

BELVEDERE (1913) See AUDACIOUS (1941)

BENALLA (1913)
11118 grt; 1100 psrs
515' x 63' x 28' (157 x 19.2 x 8.5 m)
2 x quadruple expansion engines via twin screw.
Broken up for scrap by Gentara Kasegawa, Kobe, in 1931 for a tender offer of £28,300.
Built by Caird & Company, Greenock, for the P&O Line.

BENCHIJIGUA (1994) See BETANCURIA (2000)

BENCHIJIGUA II (1994) See BETANCURIA (2000)

BENDIGO (1911) See BELTANA (1912)

BENDIGO (1923)
13039 grt; 490 psrs
520' x 64' x 30' (158 x 19.5 x 9.1 m)
Quadruple expansion engines via twin screw.
Broken up for scrap by Thomas W Ward for a tender of £26,000 at Barrow-in-Furness in 1936.
Built by Harland & Wolff Ltd, Greenock, for the P&O Line.

BENGAL (1884) See SHAH NAJAM (1905)

BENGORE HEAD (1881) See POMPEI (1900)

BENI ANSAR (1997) See BENI ANSAR (2000)

BENI ANSAR (1998) See DONATELLA D'ABUNDO (2000)

BENI ANSAR (2000)
12046 grt; 1280 psrs
290 cars or 36 trailers
392' x 67' x 15' (218.4 x 20.7 x 4.5 m)
2 x 18-cylinder Pielstick diesel engines via twin screw.
Passenger-car-cargo ferry owned and operated by Limadet Ferries, Morocco.

Built by John Cockerill Shipyards, Hoboken, Belgium, for RMT, Belgium, as the PRINSES MARIA-ESMERALDA (1975). Renamed WISTERIA (1998 – Celine Shipping Consultancies Ltd, London).

BEN-MY-CHREE (1998)
12504 grt; 500 psrs
200 cars
413' x 77' x 16'6" (125.2 x 23.4 x 5 m)
2 x 9-cylinder MaK diesel engines via twin screw.

Passenger-car RoRo ferry owned by Sea Containers Plc, Bermuda, and operated by the Isle of Man Steam Packet Company, Douglas, Isle of Man. Built by Van der Geissen-de-Noord, Krimpen, at a cost of £24,000,000.

BENODET (1984) See LANGELAND IV (1999)

BENWELL TOWER (1890) See PEGLI (1913)

BEPPE (1932)
4859 grt
401' x 52' x 27' (121.5 x 15.8 x 8.2 m)
D Rowan & Co 3-cylinder triple expansion engines via single screw.
Sank on 19 October 1942 28 miles (45 km) off Lampedusa Island, Italy, when hit by a torpedo.
Built by A McMillan & Son Ltd, Dumbarton, for the British & Foreign Steamship Co Ltd as the SAINT HUGO (1912). Renamed FRANKTOR (1915 – Palace Shipping Co Ltd), MATTAWA (1915 – CPR Ocean Lines), BERWYN (1923 – CPR Co) and KINGARTH (1928 – Kintyre Steamship Co).

BERENGARIA (1921)
52226 grt; 2723 psrs
919' x 98' x 35' (278.5 x 29.7 x 10.6 m)
4 x AEG-Vulcan turbine engines via quadruple screw.
Broken up for scrap in two stages for a split tender of US$216,000; firstly at the John Jarvis Yard at Jarrow in 1939; then at Rosyth in 1946 after she had been towed from New York where she had been gutted by a fire on 3 March 1938. At this stage she was under the ownership of the Cunard Line.
Laid down by Bremer Vulkan Shipyards, Hamburg, for the Hamburg-America Line as the EUROPA (1912), she was completed as the IMPERATOR (1913).

BEREZAN (1893) See SOVJETSKAYA ROSSIJA (1921)

BERGAMA (1996) See BOSPORUS (1999)

BERGEN (1993)
16551 grt; 882 psrs
350 cars

444' x 79' x 19' (134.5 x 24 x 5.7 m)
2 x 8-cylinder Wartsila diesel engines via twin screw.
Ice-strengthened passenger-car RoRo ferry owned by Ask Oy, Bergen, and chartered to the Fjord Line for their Norway–Denmark service.
Building completed by Fosen Shipyard after the hull had been constructed by Bruce's Shipyard AB, Landskrona, with the total cost being Norwegian Kronor 350,000,000.

BERGENSFJORD (1913) See ALIYA (1957)

BERGENSFJORD (1956) See RASA SAYANG (1980)

BERKSHIRE (1923) See AMERICAN ENGINEER (1941)

BERLIN (1909) See ARABIC (1921)

BERLIN (1925) See ADMIRAL NAKHIMOV (1949)

BERLIN (1955)
18600 grt; 1120 psrs
590' x 74' x 29' (178.8 x 22.4 x 8.8 m)
2 x 6-cylinder B+W diesel engines via twin screw.
Broken up for scrap at La Spezia in 1966 for a tender price of £203,000. Ex-North German Lloyd.
Built by Sir WG Armstrong, Whitworth & Co Ltd, Newcastle, for the Swedish-American Line as the GRIPSHOLM (1925).

BERLIN (1980) See BERLIN (1985)

BERLIN (1985)
9570 grt; 470 psrs
457' x 57' x 15'6" (138.5 x 17.5 x 4.6 m)
2 x 12-cylinder MaK diesel engines via twin screw.
Ice-strengthened cruise ship owned and operated by Peter Deilmann Cruises, Neustadt.
Built by Howaldtswerk Deutsche Werft, Kiel, for Berlin GmbH & Co, Neustadt, as the BERLIN (1980) and renamed PRINCESS MAHSURI (1982 – Blue Funnel Line).

BERMUDA (1927)
19086 grt; 681 psrs
547' x 74' x 26'9" (165.8 x 22.4 x 8.2 m)
4 x 4-cylinder Doxford diesel engines via a quadruple screw.
Abandoned as a total loss in June 1932 when she was wrecked on Badcall Islands, in Eddrachilles Bay, on the Sutherland coast of Scotland while under tow. This ended a string of bad events, commencing with her catching fire on 17 June 1931 at dockside in Hamilton, Bermuda, with one life lost, then listing heavily to port and allowing the sea to pour into her. She was pumped out and sailed under her own power to Belfast for rebuilding. On 19 November 1931 she caught fire again in the shipbuilder's yard and sank within a week of her scheduled refit programme. She was raised again, on 24 December 1931, but declared a total loss by her insurers. Her engines were removed prior to her being taken to Rosyth for breaking up for scrap.
Built by Workman, Clarke & Company, Belfast, for the Furness-Bermuda Line.

BERMUDA HIBISCUS (1963) See PING AN (1965)

BERMUDA STAR (1984) See ENCHANTED ISLE (1994)

BERMUDIAN (1905) See STELLA d'ITALIA (1926)

BERNARDIN DE SAINT PIERRE (1926) See TEIBI MARU (1942)

BERNINA (1959) See ABU-EL-KASSEM (1978)

BERRIEN (1919) See HUGH L. SCOTT, USS (AP-43) (1942)

BERRIMA (1914)
11137 grt; 1100 psrs
515' x 63' x 28' (157 x 19.2 x 8.5 m)
2 x Caird & Co quadruple expansion engines via twin screw.
Broken up for scrap by Asakichi Kitigawa for a tender price of £29,000 in

Osaka in 1930.
Built by Caird & Company, Greenock, for the P&O Line.

BERTICE (1920) See WILLARD A. HOLBROOK (1944)

BERWICK CASTLE (1902) See ANDORA CASTLE (1920)

BERWYN (1923) See BEPPE (1932)

BETANCURIA (2000)
4731 grt; 1750 psrs
300 cars
353' x 62' x 13' (104 x 18.9 x 3.9 m)
2 x 12-cylinder Stork-Werkspoor diesel engines via twin screw.

Passenger-car ferry owned and operated by the Fred Olsen Line.
Built by Helsingor Skibsvaerft, Helsingor, for Jydsk Faergefart AS as the DJURSLAND II (1974). Renamed DJURSLAND (1980 – Grenaa-Hunderstadt Linien KS), BENCHIJIGUA II (1994 – Transtecina SA) and BENCHIJIGUA (1994 – Fred Olsen Line).

BETHANIA (1899) See TAIHOKU MARU (1934)

BEWA DISCOVERER (1973) See WORLD DISCOVERER (1976)

BEZMI-ALEM (1906)
3950 grt; 90 psrs
400' x 43' x 21'4" (121.2 x 13 x 6.5 m)
Compound engine via single screw.
Owned by the Turkish government when she sank in August 1915 after being fired upon by the Russian fleet near Samsun, Turkey.
Built by Barrow Shipbuilding Co, Barrow-in-Furness, for the Castle Line as the PEMBROKE CASTLE (1883).

BHAMO (1908)
5244 grt; 78 psrs
411' x 52' x 28' (124.5 x 15.8 x 8.5 m)
Denny & Co 3-cylinder compound engine via single screw.
Broken up for scrap in Japan in 1938 by Colvilles Ltd.
Laid down by William Denny & Bros, Dumbarton, for the Henderson Line as the SALWEEN (1907), but completed as the BHAMO at a cost of £79,797.

BIAFRA (1896) See HOMAYUN (1910)

BIANCA C (1957) See MELANESIEN (1958).

BIANCA C (1958)
18427 grt; 1232 psrs
594' x 75' x 27' (180 x 22.7 x 8.2 m)
3 x 11-cylinder Sulzer diesel engines via triple screw.
Cruise ship owned by the Costa Line, she sank in 150 feet of clear water on 22 October 1961 three miles (5 km) off St George, Granada. At the time she was under tow from St George harbour where a series of explosions burst through her bottom hull plates. The tow was devised as an attempt to beach her while she was on fire. Four people died out of 750 on board. She has settled in an upright position and is now highly regarded as a prime dive site. She had already sunk once in her lifetime back in 1945 when the Germans scuttled her.
Laid down by Soc Provencale de Constructions Navales, La Ciotat, for Messageries Maritimes as the MARECHAL PETAIN (1939), which was completed in 1944. Renamed LA MARSEILLAISE (1949 – Messageries Maritimes) and AROSA SKY (1957 – Arosa Line).

BIENVILLE (1924) See EL COSTON (1925)

BIG RED BOAT I (1997) See THE BIG RED BOAT (1997)

BIG RED BOAT II (2000) See THE BIG RED BOAT II (2000)

BIG RED BOAT III (2000) See THE BIG RED BOAT III (2000)

BIG RED BOAT IV (2000) See THE BIG RED BOAT IV (2000)

BIHAR (1993) See LEROS (1997)

BILOXI (1941) See BAY STATE (1973)

BILU (1964) See MIR (1998)

BINTANG SAMUDRA (1951)
5649 grt; 302 psrs
351' x 52' x 36' depth (106.4 x 15.8 x 10.9 m)
Newport News 4-cylinder triple expansion engines via single screw.
Broken up for scrap in Japan in 1956. Ex-PT Perusahaan Relajaran, Indonesia.
Built by Newport News Shipbuilding, Newport News, Virginia, for Merchants & Miners Transportation Co as the FAIRFAX (1926). Renamed CHUNG HSING (1946 – Chung Hsing Steamship Co Ltd) and PACIFIC STAR (1950 – Far Eastern & Panama Transport Corporation).

BIRD CITY (1919) See BUARQUE (1940)

BIRGER JARL (1953) See BALTIC STAR (1979)

BIRKA PRINCESS (1986)
22712 grt; 1100 psrs
80 cars
460' x 81' x 18' (139.4 x 24.5 x 5.5 m)
4 x 12-cylinder Wartsila-Pielstick diesel engines via twin screw.

Ice-strengthened passenger-car-cargo ferry owned by Birka Lines, Finland, and operated by Birka Cruises.
Built by Valmet Oy Helsingin Telakka, Helsinki, for the Birka Line.

BIRKA QUEEN (1992) See HYUNDAI KUMGANG (1998).

BIRMA (1905) See WILBO (1924)

BIRMA (1918) See WILBO (1924)

BISCO 9 (1950)
8142 grt; 1260 psrs
448' x 58' x 28' (136.7 x 17.6 x 8.5 m)
8-cylinder Krupp quadruple expansion engines via twin screw.
Broken up for scrap where she lay after stranding near Campbeltown, Kintyre, during a tow on 17 September 1950. Ex-British Iron & Steel Corporation.
Built by Germania Werft (Krupp), Kiel, for the Hamburg-America Line as the YPIRANGA (1911). Renamed ASSYRIA (1921 – Anchor Line) and COLONIAL (1929 – Cia Colonial de Navegacao).

BISMARCK (1914) See CALEDONIA, HMS (1936)

BISMILLAH (1984)
5213 grt; 900 psrs
150 cars + 6 trailers
351' x 54' x 20' (106.4 x 16.3 x 6.1 m)
2 x 8-cylinder Stork-Werkspoor diesel engines via twin screw.

Ice-strengthened passenger-car-cargo ferry operated by Fred Olsen Lines for Comarit.
Built by Ulstein MVAS, Ulsteinvik, for Amsterdamse Maritiem Transport Maats BV as the BUENAVISTA (1971).

BITHYNIE (1902)
3358 grt; 707 psrs
345' x 41' x 29' (104.5 x 13.6 x 8.8 m)
Forges et Chantiers de la Maditerranee 2-cylinder compound engine via single screw.
Broken up for scrap in Italy in 1907. Ex-Paquet Line.
Built by Forges et Chantiers de la Mediterranee, La Seyne, for Cie National de Navigation, Marseilles, as the passenger ship CACHEMIRE (1884).

BIZAN MARU (1983) See ARKADI (1988)

BLACK ARROW, USS (1919)
6022 grt; 640 psrs
409' x 53' x 28' (124.8 x 16.1 x 8.5 m)
4-cylinder quadruple expansion engine via single screw.
Broken up for scrap at Perth Amboy, New Jersey, in 1924. Ex-New York & Cuba Mail Co.
Built by Bremer Vulkan, Vegesack, for the Hamburg-America Line as the RHAETIA (1905). Renamed BLACK HAWK (1917 – US Shipping Board).

BLACK HAWK (1917) See BLACK ARROW, USS (1919)

BLACK PRINCE (1938) See LOFJORD (1942)

BLACK PRINCE (1966)
11209 grt; 487 psrs
175 cars
469' x 66' x 22'1" (142 x 20 x 6.7 m)
2 x 18-cylinder Pielstick diesel engines via twin screw.

Ice-strengthened cruise ship operating for Fred Olsen Lines, Norway. She underwent a seasonal name change to VENUS every six months until 1986.
Built by Flender Werke, Lubeck.

BLACK WATCH (1938)
5035 grt; 250 psrs
365' x 63' x 26' (110.6 x 16.1 x 7.9 m)
2 x 9-cylinder B+W diesel engines via twin screw.
Owned by Fred Olsen Lines when she sank on 4 May 1945 near Harstad, Norway, after being attacked by British aircraft from HMS TRUMPETER.
Built by Akers Mek Verksted, Oslo.

BLACK WATCH (1966) See BYBLOS (2000)

BLACK WATCH (1996)
28668 grt; 832 psrs
674' x 83' x 24' (205.4 x 25.3 x 7.3 m)
4 x 9-cylinder Wartsila-Sulzer SRG diesel engines via twin screw.

Cruising for Fred Olsen Lines, Norway, following purchase from Royal Cruise Lines for US$55,000,000.
Built by Wartsila, Helsinki, for the Bergen Line and chartered to Royal Viking Line as the ROYAL VIKING STAR (1972). Renamed WESTWARD (1990 – Norwegian Cruise Lines) and STAR ODYSSEY (1994 – Royal Cruise Line).

BLED (1959)
7714 grt; 60 psrs
448' x 57' x 27' (135.8 x 17.3 x 8.2 m)
B+W 5-cylinder diesel engine via single screw.
Broken up for scrap in La Spezia in 1970. Ex-Splosna Plovba.
Laid down by John Cockerill SA, Hoboken, Belgium for Cie Maritime Belge as ALEX VAN OPSTAL (1942) and completed as KANONIER (1945). Renamed ALEX VAN OPSTAL (1946 – Cie Maritime Belge).

BLENHEIM (1940)
11426 grt
507' x 63' x 41' depth (153.6 x 19.1 x 12.4 m)
2 x Scott's Engineering DRG turbine engines via twin screw.
Broken up for scrap at Barrow-in-Furness in 1948. Ex-British Admiralty.
Built by Scott's Shipbuilding & Engineering Co, Greenock, for the Blue Funnel Line as the ACHILLES (1920).

BLENHEIM (1951) See CILAOS (1969)

BLENHEIM (1970) See DISCOVERY I (1986)

BLEXEN (1957)
6692 grt; 100 psrs
446' x 60' x 25' (125.8 x 18.2 x 7.6 m)
Turbo-electric engines via twin screw.
Broken up for scrap in Kaohsiung in 1969. Ex-Scipio & Co, Germany.
Built by Newport News Shipbuilding & Drydock Co, Newport News, Virginia, for the United Fruit Steamship Co as the CHIRIQUI (1932). Renamed TARAZED, USS (AF-13) (1941 – US Navy) and CHIRIQUI (1946 – Scipio & Co, Germany).

BLOEMFONTEIN (1934)
10473 grt; 113 psrs
487' x 63' x 38'6" depth (147.6 x 19.1 x 11.7 m)
2 x 6-cylinder Stork-Werkspoor diesel engines via twin screw.
Broken up in Hong Kong in 1959.
Built by Nederlandsche Shipbuilding Co, Amsterdam, for the Holland Africa Line.

BLOEMFONTEIN CASTLE (1950) See TERRA (1987)

BLUCHER (1901) See SUFFREN (1923)

BLUE BRIDGE (2000)
6374 grt; 800 psrs
60 cars

469' x 77' x 24' (142.2 x 23.3 x 7.2 m)
2 x 9-cylinder MAN diesel engines via twin screw.
Owned and operated by Strintzis Lines, Greece.
Built by the New South Wales Dockyards, Newcastle, Australia, for the Australian National Line as the BASS TRADER (1976). Renamed IONIAN BRIDGE (1997 – Strintzis Lines).

BLUE DIAMOND (1990)
9447 grt; 942 psrs
498' x 83' x 18' (150.9 x 25.2 x 5.5 m)
2 x 14-cylinder Hitachi-Sulzer diesel engines via twin screw.
Passenger ferry operated by Diamond Ferries, Japan.
Built by Shin Kurushima, Onishi.

BLUE GALAXY (2000)
17691 grt; 1612 psrs
600 cars + 65 trailers
551' x 79' x 21' (167 x 24 x 6.3 m)
2 x 18-cylinder B+W diesel engines via twin screw.
Passenger-car-cargo ferry owned and operated by Strintzis Lines, Greece.
Built by Setoda Zosensho, Setoda, for Tauheiyo Ferry KK, Nagoya, as the ARKAS (1972). Renamed IONIAN GALAXY (1990 – Strintzis Lines).

BLUE HEN STATE (1921) See PRESIDENT MADISON (1946)

BLUE HORIZON (2000)
16725 grt; 2000 psrs
105 cars or 30 trailers
618' x 79' x 22' (187.3 x 24.2 x 6.7 m)
2 x 14-cylinder Mitsubishi-MAN diesel engines via twin screw.
Passenger ferry owned and operated by Grimaldi Group's subsidiary Grandi Navi Veloci.
Built by Nakai Zosen KK, Setoda, for Taiheiyo Enkai Ferry KK, Nagoya, as the DAISETSU (1975). Renamed VARUNA (1985 – Strintzis Lines), LATO (1987 – ANEK) and SUPERFERRY HELLAS (1999 – Strintzis Lines).

BLUE ISLAND (2000)
18858 grt; 900 psrs
600 cars
552' x 79' x 20'6" (167.2 x 24 x 6.3 m)
2 x 16-cylinder Hitachi-B+W diesel engines via twin screw.
Passenger-car ferry owned and operated by Strintzis Lines, Greece.
Built by Nakai Shipbuilding Co, Setoda, for Pan Oceanica Galante SA, Chios, as the ALBERTO (1973). Renamed IONIAN ISLAND (1989 – Strintzis Lines).

BLUE NOSE (1955) See MARINE BLUENOSE (   )

BLUE NOSE (1983) See EUROFERRYS ATLANTICA (1999)

BLUE SEA (1977)
21514 grt; 446 psrs
518' x 68' x 27' (158 x 20.8 x 8.2 m)
Ansaldo-Fiat diesel engines via twin screw.
Owned by Ahmed Mohamed Baaboud, Jeddah, she sank in deep water as a pilgrim ship on 14 November 1976 after an uncontrollable fire broke out two days earlier at her anchorage in Jeddah.
Laid down by Ansaldo Yards, La Spezia, for Lloyd Triestino as the KUNGSHOLM (1952) and completed as EUROPA (1953).

BLUE SKY (2000)
11098 grt; 1600 psrs
600 cars
538' x 79' x 22' (164 x 24 x 6.6 m)
2 x 14-cylinder Pielstick diesel engines via twin screw.
Passenger-car ferry owned and operated by Strintzis Lines, Greece.
Built by Hayashikane Shosen KK, Shimonoseki, for Nippon Enkai Car KK, Tokyo, as the SAPPORO MARU (1974). Renamed SUN FLOWER SAPPORO (1991 – Nippon Enkai KK), and IONIAN VICTORY (1998 – Strintzis Lines).

BLUE STAR I (2000)
29415 grt; 1600 psrs
106 cars + 130 trailers

568' x 85' x 21' (172 x 25.7 x 6.4 m)
4 x 8-cylinder MAN-B+W diesel engines via twin screw.
Owned and operated by Strintzis Lines Shipping SA (Blue Ferries) as a passenger-car-cargo ferry.
Built by Van der Giessen de Noord, Krimpen.

BLUE STAR 2 (2000)
29415 grt; 1600 psrs
106 cars + 130 trailers
568' x 85' x 21' (172 x 25.7 x 6.4 m)
4 x 8-cylinder MAN-B+W diesel engines via twin screw.
Owned and operated by Strintzis Lines Shipping SA (Blue Ferries) as a passenger-car-cargo ferry.
Built by Van der Giessen de Noord, Krimpen.

BLUE STAR ITHAKI (2000)
29415 grt; 1500 psrs
300 cars
409' x 62' x 16'8" (123.8 x 18.9 x 5.1 m)
4 x 9-cylinder Wartsila diesel engines via twin screw.
Passenger-car ferry owned and operated by Strintzis Lines Shipping SA (Blue Ferries)
Built by Daewoo Heavy Industries Shipbuilding, Koje.

BLUE ZEPHYR (1990)
12524 grt; 694 psrs
140 cars + 170 trailers
616' x 82' x 23' (186.5 x 24.8 x 6.9 m)
2 x 9-cylinder Pielstick diesel engines via single screw.
Passenger-car-cargo RoRo ferry operating for Kinkai Yusen Kaisha on Japanese internal services.
Built by Kanda Zosensho KK, Kawajiri, for NYK, Tokyo.

BLUMENTHAL (1957)
6982 grt; 100 psrs
442' x 60' x 25' (133.9 x 18.2 x 7.6 m)
Turbo-electric engines via twin screw.
Broken up for scrap at Kaohsiung in 1969. Ex-Scipio & Co, Germany.
Built by Newport News Shipbuilding Corporation, Newport News, Virginia, for the United Fruit Steamship Co as the SEGOVIA (1931). Renamed PETEN (1932 – United Fruit Steamship Co), JAMAICA (1937 – Columbian Line), ARIEL, USS (AF-22) (1942 – US Navy) and JAMAICA (1946 – Columbian Line).

BOCCACCIO (1970) See AL SALAM BOCCACCIO 98 (1999)

BOGUCHAR (1988) See FU JIAN (1994)

BOHEME (1968) See FREEWINDS (1986)

BOHEMIA (1881) See POMPEI (1900)

BOHEMIA (1891) See ANGELICA ACCAME (1912)

BOHEMIA (1913) See EMPIRE BITTERN (1942)

BOHEMIAN (1900)
8548 grt; 90 psrs
512' x 58' x 34'3" depth (155.2 x 17.6 x 10.4 m)
A Stephen & Sons 3-cylinder triple expansion engine via single screw.
Abandoned as a total loss after being wrecked at Cape Sambro, Nova Scotia, on 1 March 1920 while trying to negotiate her approach to Halifax harbour.
Built by Alex Stephen & Son, Glasgow, for the Leyland Line.

BOHINJ (1959)
7746 grt; 70 psrs
448' x 57' x 26' (135.8 x 17.3 x 7.9 m)
B+W 5-cylinder diesel engine via single screw.
Broken up for scrap by Brodospas at Split in 1972. Ex-Splosna Plovba.
Laid down by John Cockerill Yards, Hoboken, for Cie Maritime Belge as the FUSILIER (1941), but completed as the GOUVERNEUR GALOPIN (1946).

BOHUS (1986) See NURA NOVA (1999)

BOHUS (1994)
9149 grt; 1400 psrs
280 cars
405' x 63' x 17' (122.7 x 19.2 x 5.2 m)
8 x 12-cylinder Nohab diesel engines via twin screw.

Passenger-car ferry owned and operated by Scandi-Color Line.
Built by Aalborg Vaerft, Aalborg, for the Sessan Line as the PRINSESSAN DESIREE (1971). Renamed VIKING 2 (1982 – Sally Line), EUROPAFARJAN (1983 – Sessan Line), EUROPAFARJAN II (1985 – Sessan Line) and LION PRINCESS (1987 – Lion Ferries).

BOHUS II (1988) See PETRONILA MATA (1998)

BOISSEVAIN (1937)
14285 grt; 582 psrs
559' x 72' x 30' (169.4 x 21.8 x 9.1 m)
3 x Sulzer 8-cylinder diesel engines via triple screw.
Broken up for scrap for US$500,000 in Kaohsiung in 1968.
Built by Blohm & Voss, Hamburg for Royal Interocean Lines.

BOKUYO MARU (1924)
8619 grt
445' x 58' x 30' (134.8 x 17.6 x 9.1 m)
4 x Mid West Engineering DRG turbine engines via twin screw.
Sank on 18 July 1939 when her load of refined copper ore combusted and started a fire which gutted the ship.
Built by Asano Shipbuilding Company, Tsurumi, for Toyo Kisen Kaisha.

BOLERO (1973) See MAGIC I (1999)

BOLERO (1982) See MAGIC (1999)

BOLERO (1995)
15781 grt; 758 psrs
525' x 75' x 22' (160.1 x 23 x 6.7 m)
2 x 16-cylinder MAN diesel engines via twin screw.
Cruise ship owned by Festival Shipping & Tourist Enterprises Ltd, Piraeus, and chartered to First European Cruises, until the Spanish Cruise Line acquires the charter for three years from 2001.
Built by AG Weser, Bremerhaven, for Klosters Rederi AS, Oslo, as the cruise ship STARWARD (1968).

BOLETTE (1984) See BOUGHAZ (1988)

BOLINGBROKE (1920)
6608 grt
420' x 53' x 36' (127.3 x 16.1 x 10.9 m)
3-cylinder triple expansion engine via single screw.
Broken up for scrap at Troon in 1934. Ex-Canadian Pacific Steamship Co.
Built by Northumberland Shipbuilding Co, Newcastle, for the Canadian Pacific Steamship Co as the MONTCALM II (1917).

BOLLINGTON GRANGE (1915) See MAGICSTAR (1919)

BOMBALA (1904) See CHRISTOS (1935)

BOMBAY (1882) See PROFESSOR GRUVEL (1922)

BONAIRE STAR (1975)
9920 grt; 573 psrs
487' x 65' x 21' (147.6 x 19.7 x 6.4 m)
DRG turbine engines via twin screw.
Owned by Venzolana de Cruceros del Caribe, she sank on 3 October 1979 in mid-Pacific while under tow by the tug JANTAR to the breaker's yard at Kaohsiung.
Built by Deutsche Werft Shipyards, Hamburg, for Zim Lines, Israel, as the JERUSALEM (1957) under the Reparation Payment Scheme at the conclusion of World War Two. Renamed MIAMI (1966 – Peninsular & Occidental Steamship Co, Miami), NEW BAHAMA STAR (1969 – Eastern Steamship Lines) and BAHAMA STAR (1972 – Eastern Steamship Lines).

BONANZA (1992) See ELEFTHERIOS VENIZELOS (1997)

BONN (1895) See GREGO (1913)

BON VIVANT (1974) See EMPRESS 65 (1997)

BOOKER T. WASHINGTON (1924) See MUNORLEANS (1927)

BORDA (1914)
11136 grt; 1100 psrs
515' x 63' x 28' (157 x 19.2 x 8.5 m)
2 x Caird & Co quadruple expansion engines via twin screw.
Broken up for scrap by Tokai Shoji Kabushiki Kaisha for a tender figure of £28,850 at Kobe in 1930.
Built by Caird & Company, Greenock, for the P&O Line at a cost of £208,977.

BORDEN (1923) See PERSEUS (1926)

BORDERER (1884) See YUTE (1916)

BORE (1960) See KRISTINA REGINA (1987)

BORE I (1973) See BALTIC KRISTINA (1997)

BORE III (1952) See ROYAL CLIPPER (1977)

BOREA (1984) See KRISTINA REGINA (1987)

BORE NORD (1973) See BALTIC STAR (1979)

BORE STAR (1975) See WASA QUEEN (1992)

BORGEN (1975) See SKAGEN (1990)

BORINQUEN (1931) See LA JENELLE (1969)

BORINQUEN (1975)
17189 grt; 900 psrs
684' x 71' x 24' (208.5 x 21.7 x 7.3 m)
Geared turbine engine via single screw.
Currently a container ship operating for Puerto Rico Maritime Shipping Authority.
Built by Kaiser Corporation, Vancouver, Canada, for the US Maritime Commission as the Class C4-S-A3 troop transport MARINE FALCON (1945), then converted into a passenger ship by the Matson Line in 1946. Renamed as the container ship TRENTON (1966 – Litton Industries).

BORIS PASTERNAK (1989)
4575 grt; 150 psrs
297' x 58' x 17'6" (90 x 17.6 x 5.3 m)
6-cylinder Sulzer diesel engine via single screw.
Ice-strengthened passenger ship owned and operated by PO Arktikmornefte Gazravedka, Murmansk.
Built by Stocznia Paryskiej, Gdynia.

BORKUM (1900) See ASTI (1915)

BORNEO (1895) See ANAHUAC (1924).

BORNHOLM (1961) See MIN ZHUI (1980)

BORODINO (1948)
3206 grt; 56 psrs
312' x 48' x 18' (94.5 x 14.5 x 5.5 m)
3-cylinder triple expansion engine via single screw.
Broken up for scrap by Van Heyghen Freres at Brugge in 1967.
Built by Ailsa Shipbuilding Co, Troon, for the Wilson Line.

BORUSSIA (1899) See CITY OF HONOLULU (1927)

BORUSSIA (1906)
6951 grt; 1878 psrs
421' x 54' x 32'3" depth (127.6 x 16.4 x 9.8 m)
Quadruple expansion engines via twin screw.
Declared a total loss when she foundered and lost three lives while coaling at a bunker in Lisbon on 22 October 1907.
Built by Fred Krupp AG, Kiel, for the Hamburg-America Line.

BOSNIA (1899) See FRANGESTAN (1922)

BOSNIA (1907) See FRANGESTAN (1922)

BOSPHOR (1994)
4999 grt; 333 psrs
403' x 50' x 17' (122.2 x 16.1 x 5.2 m)
2 x 6-cylinder MAN diesel engine via twin screw.
Broken up for scrap in 1997. Ex-Kamchatka Shipping Co Ltd.
Built by Mathias-Thesen, Rostock, for the Far Eastern Shipping Co, Vladivostok, as the ice-strengthened passenger ship PETROPAVLOVSK (1961).

BOSPORUS (1999)
3809 grt; 1215 psrs
160 cars
385' x 53' x 12'6" (116.7 x 16 x 3.6 m)
2 x 12-cylinder Sulzer diesel engines via twin screw.
Operated by Anatolia Ferries as a floating static casino/restaurant ship at Port Bacares.
Built by J Boel Shipyard for RTM, Belgium, as the KONINGIN FABIOLA (1962). Renamed OLYMPIA (1985 – Agapitos Ferries), LYDIA (1986 – Hellenic Mediterranean Lines), EPHESUS (1996 – Illyria Ferries) and BERGAMA (1996 – Perco Maritime Inc, Greece).

BOSTON (1923)
4989 grt; 900 psrs
385' x 73' x 21' (116.7 x 22.1 x 6.4 m)
4 x Bath Iron Works SRG engines via twin screw.
Sank on 25 September 1942 after being hit by a torpedo in the North Atlantic.
Built by Bethlehem Shipbuilding Corporation, Sparrow's Point, for Eastern Steamship Lines, Inc.

BOSTON (1968)
12544 grt; 2000 psrs
523' x 71' x 26'6" (158.5 x 21.5 x 8 m)
2 x Westinghouse DRG turbine engines via single screw.
Broken up for scrap in the USA in 1975 as a container ship. Ex-Sea Land Services Inc.
Built by Kaiser Corporation, Richmond, California, for the US Navy as the Class C4-S-A1 troop carrier GENERAL M. M. PATRICK, USS (AP-150) (1944). Reclassified as the GENERAL M. M. PATRICK, USAT (1946 – US Army). Reclassified as the GENERAL M. M. PATRICK, USNS (T-AP-150) (1950 – US Navy). She was laid up from 1958 to 1967, moored in Olympia, Washington state.

BOSWORTH (1920)
6672 grt
413' x 56' x 28'6" (125.2 x 17 x 8.7 m)
J Dickinson & Sons 3-cylinder triple expansion engines via single screw.
Broken up for scrap at Dalmuir in 1949.
Built by JL Thompson & Sons Ltd, Sutherland, for HM Thomson as the WAR PERIDOT (1918).

BOTHWELL (1920) See SPERBRECHER (1939)

BOTNIA (1967) See VOLCANO DE TENAGUA (1999)

BOTNIA EXPRESS (1979) See ALANDIA (1992)

BOUGAINVILLEA (1971) See ZERALDA (1976)

BOUGHAZ (1988)
8257 grt; 1200 psrs
300 cars
389' x 57' x 15'6" (118 x 17.3 x 4.7 m)
2 x 12-cylinder Deutz diesel engines via twin screw.

Ice-strengthened passenger-car-cargo RoRo ferry owned by Comarit, Tangier, and operated by Fred Olsen & Co on Morocco–Spain service.
Built by Jos L Meyer Shipyards, Papenburg, for the Sally Line as the VIKING 5 (1974). Renamed THE VIKING (1981 – Viking Line), SALLY EXPRESS (1983 – Sally Line) and BOLETTE (1984 – Fred Olsen Line).

BOUSSOLE (1930) See ARAUCO (1935)

BOVEC (1959)
7724 grt; 70 psrs
448' x 57' x 26' (135.8 x 17.3 x 7.9 m)
B+W 5-cylinder diesel engine via single screw.
Broken up for scrap at Whampoa in 1970. Ex-Splosna Plovba.
Laid down by John Cockerill Shipyards, Hoboken, for Cie Maritime Belge as a yard number in 1940 while under the control of the invading Germans. She was then scuttled by the Germans in 1944, raised from the seabed in 1945 and completed as the ARMAND GRISAR (1945).

BOVIC (1892) See COLONIAN (1922)

BOWDITCH, USS (AGS-4) (1940)
4576 grt; 117 psrs
370' x 53' x 20' (112.1 x 16.1 x 6.1 m)
B+W diesel engines via twin screw.
Broken up for scrap in Baltimore in 1959. Ex-US Navy.
Built by Burmeister & Wain, Copenhagen, for the Grace Line as the SANTA INEZ (1928).

BOYANA (1989) See URD (1991)

BRABANTIA (1920) See LOMBARDIA (1935)

BRACCIANO (1925)
4201 grt; 96 psrs
385' x 45' x 28' (117 x 13.8 x 8.5 m)
Triple expansion engine via single screw.
Broken up for scrap in 1925.
Built by Caird & Company, Greenock, for the P&O Line as the MANILA (1892) at a cost of £72,295. Renamed MARIA C (1910 – U Serra fuL).

BRAEMAR (1953) See THE PHILIPPINE TOURIST I (1978)

BRAEMAR (1985) See REGINA BALTICA (1996)

BRAEMAR CASTLE (1952)
17029 grt; 453 psrs
576' x 74' x 28' (175.5 x 22.6 x 8.5 m)
DRG turbine engines via twin screw.
Broken up for scrap by Shipbreaking Industries Ltd at Faslane in 1966.
Built by Harland & Wolff Ltd, Belfast, for the Union Castle Line.

BRAGA (1920)
6122 grt; 1480 psrs
415' x 50' x 26' (125.8 x 15.2 x 7.9 m)
6-cylinder Kincaid triple expansion engines via twin screw.
Owned by the Fabre Line, she was abandoned after being wrecked on Aspro Island, Greece, on 16 November 1926.
Built by Russell & Co, Glasgow, for Unione Austriaca as the LAURA (1907). Renamed EUROPA (1917 – Lloyd Nacional, Brazil, after the Brazilian government had seized her).

BRANDENBURG (1902) See HECUBA (1922)

BRANDON (1923)
6655 grt
412' x 56' x 28' (124.8 x 17 x 8.5 m)
Blair & Co 3-cylinder turbine engines via single screw.
Sank on 8 December 1939 after being torpedoed by the German U-48 south of Cork. Ex-Canadian Pacific Railway Co.
Built by JL Thompson & Sons Ltd, Sunderland, for the South Georgia Co Ltd as the HOLBROOK (1917). Renamed BREDON (1923 – Canadian Pacific Railway Co).

BRANKSOME HALL (1888) See FAKHRI (1909)

BRASIL (1948) See HOMELAND (1951)

BRASIL (1958) See UNIVERSE EXPLORER (1996)

BRASIL (1974) See ENCHANTED ISLE (1994)

BRASILE (1912) See VENEZUELA (1912)

BRASILIA (1898) See NORSEMAN (1900)

BRASIL STAR (1947)
10723 grt; 53 psrs
503' x 68' x 31' (152.4 x 20.6 x 9.4 m)
3 x Parsons DRG turbine engines via single screw.
Broken up for scrap at Kaohsiung in 1972.
Built by Cammell Laird & Company, Birkenhead, for the Blue Star Line.

BRAVE MERCHANT (1998)
22150 grt; 214 psrs
200 cars + 170 trailers
594' x 80' x 28'6" (180 x 24.3 x 8.7 m)
4 x 9-cylinder Wartsila diesel engines via twin screw.
Passenger-car-cargo Ropax ferry owned and operated by Merchant Ferries (a Cenargo International subsidiary).
Built by Astilleros Espanoles, Seville, at a cost of US$65,000,000.

BRAZIL (1938)
20683 grt; 650 psrs
613' x 80' x 20'6" (185.8 x 24.2 x 6.2 m)
2 x turbo-electric engines via twin screw.
Broken up for scrap by the Peck Transportation Company in Kearny New Jersey in 1964. Ex-Moore McCormick Lines.
Built by Newport News Shipbuilding & Drydock Company, Newport News, Virginia, for the Panama Pacific Line as the VIRGINIA (1928).

BRAZIL (1974)
10216 grt; 982 psrs
512' x 64' x 28'6" (155.2 x 19.4 x 8.7 m)
Mitsubishi-Sulzer diesel engine via single screw.
Broken up for scrap in 1996 in China after serving as a floating museum with restaurant and recreation facilities in Toba Bay, Nagoya. However, a sighting near Guangzhou in 1999, operating as an accommodation vessel, has not been confirmed or denied. Owned by NYK.
Built by Mitsubishi Heavy Industries, Kobe, for Mitsui OSK, Osaka, as the BRAZIL MARU (1954).

BRAZILIAN (1891) See POTENGY (1938)

BRAZIL MARU (1939)
12752 grt; 901 psrs

544' x 68' x 41'3" depth (164.8 x 23.6 x 12.5 m)
Sulzer diesel engines via twin screw.
Sank on 5 August 1942 by a torpedo fired from the USS GREENLING (SS-213) north-east of Chuuk Island in the western Pacific.
Built by Mitsubishi Heavy Industries, Kobe, for OSK as a passenger-cargo ship.

BRAZIL MARU (1954) See BRAZIL (1974)

BRAZOS (1908) See SAN LORENZO (1920)

BRAZZA (1927)
10387 grt; 367 psrs
453' x 59' x 36' depth (137.3 x 17.9 x 10.9 m)
Sulzer diesel engines via twin screw.
Owned by Chargeurs Reunis, Le Havre, she sank on 28 May 1940 after being torpedoed by the German U-37 100 miles (167 km) west of Oporto.
Built by Ateliers et Chantiers de la Loire, Nantes, for Chargeurs Reunis, Le Havre, as the CAMRANH (1923).

BRAZZA (1948) See MAURIENNE (1964)

BRECON (1923) See FRANGOULA B. GOULANDRIS (1928)

BREDON (1923) See BRANDON (1923)

BREIZH-IZEL (1980) See BALBEK (2000)

BREMEN (1897) See KING ALEXANDER (1923)

BREMEN (1923) See KARLSRUHE (1928)

BREMEN (1929)
51731 grt; 2200 psrs
938' x 102' x 33'6" (284.2 x 30.9 x 10.2 m)
12 x SRG turbine engines via quadruple screw.
Broken up for scrap in Bremerhaven in 1953 after capsizing in that city as an accommodation ship, following her being gutted by fire on 16 March 1944. The fire was believed to have been the work of saboteurs. Some parts of the ship are still at the bottom of the Weser river.
Built by AG Weser, Bremen, for North German Lloyd.

BREMEN (1959) See FILIPINAS SAUDI I (1980)

BREMEN (1995)
6752 grt; 184 psrs
370' x 56' x 16' (112 x 17 x 4.8 m)
2 x 8-cylinder Daihatsu diesel engines via twin screw.
Ice-strengthened cruise ship chartered by Hapag-Lloyd Cruises, Germany.
Built by Mitsubishi Heavy Industries Ltd, Kobe, for NYK as the FRONTIER SPIRIT (1990) at a cost of US$42,000,000.

BREMERHAVEN (1961) See VIKING BORDEAUX (1998)

BREMER HORST BISCOFF (1989) See ARANUI (1990)

BRENNERO (1959) See EL HASSAN (1979)

BRESIL (1888) See DUMBEA (1903)

BRESLAU (1901) See BRIDGEPORT (1946)

BRETAGNE (1937) See MASSALIA (1958)

BRETAGNE (1937)
10108 grt; 440 psrs
470' x 59' x 27' (143.4 x 17.9 x 8.2 m)
4 x Curtis DRG turbine engines via twin screw.
Passenger ship owned by the French Line, she sank on 14 October 1939 in the Atlantic 300 miles (500 km) west of the English Channel, with the loss of seven lives, after being torpedoed by the German U-45.
Built by Barclay, Curle & Co, Glasgow, for Royal Holland Lloyd as the FLANDRIA (1922).

BRETAGNE (1952) See BRITTANY (1962)

BRETAGNE (1989)
24534 grt; 2056 psrs
650 cars or 200 cars + 62 trailers
499' x 86' x 20' (151.2 x 26 x 6 m)
4 x 12-cylinder Wartsila diesel engines via twin screw.

Passenger-car-cargo ferry owned by Sabemen and operated by Brittany Ferries between the UK, France and Spain.
Built by Chantiers et Ateliers de l'Atlantique, St Nazaire, for Sabemen at a cost of US$55,000,000.

BRETON (1911)
3747 grt; 791 psrs
380' x 43' x 27'4" (115.9 x 13.1 x 8.3 m)
Harland & Wolff 3-cylinder triple expansion engine via single screw.
Owned by Messageries Maritimes, Marseilles, she sank on 8 August 1917 after hitting a mine laid by the German U-37 near Fratelli Island, Tunisia.
Built by Harland & Wolff Ltd, Belfast, for the Iran Steamship Co, Britain, as the IRAN (1886). Renamed ALBANO (1895 – Sloman Shipping Co).

BRIDGEPORT (1917) See BRIDGEPORT (1946)

BRIDGEPORT (1946)
7524 grt; 1720 psrs
429' x 54' x 23'6" (130.8 x 16.6 x 7.2 m)
Bremer Vulcan 8-cylinder quadruple expansion engine via twin screw.
Broken up for scrap in 1948. Ex-HH Buncher of Pittsburgh and ex-US Army as a troop transport.
Built by Bremer Vulkan, Vegesack, for North German Lloyd as the BRESLAU (1901). Seized and renamed by the US Navy as the BRIDGEPORT (1917) and hospital ship LARKSPUR (1943 – US government).

BRIGHT SKY (1969) See ALEXI H (1979)

BRINDISI (1995) See ATHINA I (1999)

BRINDISI EXPRESS (1974) See OCEANOS (1976)

BRISBANE TRADER (1969) See ATHENS EXPRESS (1986)

BRITANIS (1970) See BELOFIN -I (1998)

BRITANNIA (1914)
4898 grt; 1514 psrs
408' x 46' x 28' (123.6 x 14.1 x 8.5 m)
3-cylinder triple expansion engine via single screw.
Broken up for scrap at La Seyne in 1927.
Built by Chantiers et Ateliers de Provence, Port de Bouc, for the Fabre Line as the GERMANIA (1903). Renamed BRITANNIA upon Germany's declaration of war in 1914.

BRITANNIA (1929) See CYNTHIA (1966)

BRITANNIC (1915)
48158 grt; 2573 psrs
903' x 95' x 34'6" (273.6 x 28.5 x 10.5 m)
8-cylinder triple expansion engines via triple screw.
Sank in one hour, on 21 November 1916, with the loss of 21 lives after she had

been torpedoed by the German U-73. When she went under, south of Athens in the Zea Channel in the Aegean Sea, she was recorded as the largest merchant vessel to go down in World War One.
Built by Harland & Wolff Ltd, Belfast, as a passenger ship for the White Star Line, but she never saw service as a passenger liner as she was converted into a hospital ship while still on the stocks.

BRITANNIC (1932)
27666 grt; 993 psrs
712' x 82' x 35' (215.8 x 24.8 x 10.6 m)
2 x 10-cylinder B+W diesel engines via twin screw.
Broken up for scrap by British Iron & Steel Co in Inverkeithing in 1961.
Built by Harland & Wolff Ltd, Belfast, for the White Star Line.

BRITISH CROWN (1880) See AMSTERDA (1905)

BRITISH EMPIRE (1901) See FLAVIA (1916)

BRITISH EXHIBITOR (1931) See ZAMZAM (1933)

BRITISH KING (1881) See HARBIN (1900)

BRITISH MAPLE (1920)
7044 grt
470' x 56' x 32' depth (142.4 x 17 x 9.7 m)
Broken up for scrap by Metal Industries Ltd at Rosyth in 1933. Ex-British Tanker Co Ltd.
Built by CS Swan Hunter, Newcastle, for the Beaver Line as the MOUNT ROYAL (1898). Renamed RANGOL (1914 – Canadian government) and MAPLELEAF (1916 – Lane & MacAndrew Ltd).

BRITISH PRINCE (1899) See NAPOLI (1913)

BRITISH PRINCESS (1899) See PALERMO (1913)

BRITISH QUEEN (1881) See ONEGA (1914)

BRITISH TRADE (1922) See ORONTES (1924)

BRITTANY (1962)
16644 grt; 1200 psrs
581' x 73' x 26' (177 x 22.2 x 7.9 m)
Geared turbine engines via twin screw.
Broken up for scrap by Cantieri Santa Maria at La Spezia in 1964 following her complete destruction by fire on 23 March 1963, while undergoing engines repairs at Skaramana. She was beached at Vasilika Bay on 9 April, then refloated on 10 May for towing to the breaker's yard.. Ex-Chandris Group.
Built by Chantiers de l'Atlantique, St Nazaire, for SGTM as the BRETAGNE (1952).

BRODFIELD (1915)
5455 grt; 162 psrs
420' x 54' x 32' depth (127.3 x 16.4 x 9.7 m)
Hawthorne Leslie 3-cylinder triple expansion engine via single screw.
Owned by Brodfield Steamship Co Ltd, she was abandoned as a total loss when she was wrecked on 13 November 1916 near Church Point, Scilly Isles, while in ballast.
Built by Hawthorn Leslie, Newcastle, for the Beaver Line as the SURREY (1899).

BRODLEA (1915) See SAXON STAR (1929)

BRODLIFFE (1916) See LUGANO (1942)

BROOKLYN (1906) See ONEGA (1914)

BROOKLYN (1968) See EASTERN LIGHT (1981)

BRUIZER, USN (LST-1) (1943) See CIUDAD DE SANTA FE (1963)

BRUNETTE (1921)
3704 grt; 698 psrs
365' x 44' x 31'3" (110.6 x 13.3 x 9.5 m)

3-cylinder triple expansion engine via single screw.
Broken up for scrap in Italy in 1923. Ex-Italian Line.
Built by J Elder & Co, Glasgow, for the Union-Castle Line as the GARTH CASTLE (1880). Renamed the ISMAILIA (1901 – Khedivial Mail).

BRUTON (1923)
7397 grt; 940 psrs
430' x 54' x 28'2" depth (131 x 16.5 x 8.5 m)
Workman, Clark 3-cylinder triple expansion engine via single screw.
Broken up for scrap in Italy in 1925 as a cargo ship. Ex-Canadian Pacific.
Built by Workman, Clark, Belfast, for the Allan Line as the SICILIAN (1899), then chartered out as TRANSPORT 57 (1899 – British government) and SICILIAN (1917 – Canadian Pacific).

BRUXELLESVILLE (1897) See CALYPSO (1920)

BRUXELLESVILLE (1906) See LEGAZPI (1911)

BUARQUE (1940)
5301 grt; 74 psrs
401' x 54' x 28' (121.5 x 16.4 x 8.5 m)
General Electric DRG turbine engine via single screw.
Passenger-cargo ship owned by Lloyd Brasileiro, she sank on 15 February 1942 after being torpedoed by the German U-432 off Cape Hatteras, North Carolina.
Built by American International Shipbuilding Corporation, Hog Island, Pennsylvania, for the US Shipping Board as the BIRD CITY (1919). Renamed SCANPENN (1932 – American Scantic Line).

BUCEPHALOS (1966)
7607 grt
439' x 62' x 28'6" (133 x 18.8 x 8.7 m)
2 x Westinghouse DRG turbine engines via single screw.
Broken up for scrap in Kaohsiung in 1969. Ex-Magellan Strait Development Corporation.
Built by Bethlehem-Fairfield Shipyard Inc, Baltimore, for the US War Shipping Administration as the LA CROSSE VICTORY (1945). Renamed TUCUMAN (1947 – Dodero Line) and KISMET (1965 – Magellan Strait Development Corporation).

BUCKEYE STATE (1921) See WILLARD L. HOLBROOK (1944)

BUENAVISTA (1971) See BISMILLAH (1984)

BUENOS AIRES (1912) See CEPHEE (1922)

BUENOS AIRES (1947) See FAIRWIND (1963)

BUENOS AIRES MARU (1929)
9626 grt
461' x 62' x 26' (139.7 x 18.8 x 7.9 m)
2 x Mitsubishi diesel engines via twin screw.
Sank on 27 November 1943 after an attack by US aircraft.
Built by Mitsubishi Dockyard for Mitsui OSK.

BUKIT RAYA (1994)
6041 grt; 969 psrs
329' x 60' x 14' (99.8 x 18.3 x 4.2 m)
2 x 6-cylinder MaK SRG diesel engines via twin screw.
Passenger ship operated by PT Pelni in Indonesian waters.
Built by Jos L Meyer, Papenburg, for the Indonesian government.

BUKIT SIGUNTANG (1996)
14800 grt; 1973 psrs
440' x 71' x 17'6" (146.5 x 23.7 x 5.9 m)
2 x 6-cylinder MaK via twin screw.
Passenger ship operated by PT Pelni in Indonesian waters.
Built by Jos L Meyer, Papenburg, for the Indonesian government.

BUKOVINA (1962)
3435 grt; 250 psrs
333' x 50' x 13' (102 x 15 x 3.9 m)
2 x 8-cylinder Skoda diesel engines via twin screw.
Ice-strengthened passenger-cargo ferry operating on Black Sea routes.

Built by A Jdanov, St Petersburg, for the Northern Shipping Co, Arkhangelsk.

BULUWAYO (1895) See KATHIAWAR (1912)

BULGARIA (1898) See PHILIPPINES (1919)

BULGARIA (1913) See PHILIPPINES (1919)

BULOLO (1938)
6397 grt; 180 psrs
412' x 58' x 23' (125.6 x 17.6 x 7 m)
2 x 6-cylinder Kincaid diesel engines via twin screw.
Broken up for scrap in Kaohsiung in 1968.
Built by Barclay, Curle & Company, Glasgow, for Burns Philp & Co Ltd, Sydney.

BULOW (1906) See NYASSA (1924)

BUNKER HILL (1907) See LUX (1946)

BUNKER HILL (1943) See LUX (1946)

BURDIGALA (1912)
12481 grt; 1350 psrs
600' x 64' x 37'9" depth (182.9 x 19.5 x 11.5 m)
Schichau 10-cylinder quadruple expansion engines via twin screw.
Passenger ship owned by Cie Sud Atlantique, Bordeaux, she sank in 35 minutes on 14 November 1916 in the Aegean Sea two miles (3 km) south-west of St Nicolo near Mykonos. She had entered a minefield laid by the German U-73.
Built as the KAISER FRIEDRICH (1898) by Schichau Shipyards, Danzig, for North German Lloyd.

BURGEMEESTER DEN TEX (1883) See ILE DE FRANCE (1914)

BURGUNDY (1999) See P&OSL BURGUNDY (1999)

BURMA (1914) See SAFINA-E-NUSRAT (1953)

BURUTU (1902)
3850 grt; 80 psrs
360' x 44' x 14'3" depth (109.1 x 13.3 x 4.3 m)
A Stephen 3-cylinder triple expansion engine via single screw.

Sank in the Irish Sea on 3 October 1918, with the loss of 148 lives, after colliding with the 7500 grt CITY OF CALCUTTA.
Built by A Stephen & Sons Ltd, Glasgow, for the British & African Steam Navigation Co.

BUTESHIRE (1893) See MAGICSTAR (1919)

BYBLOS (2000)
11497 grt; 1800 psrs
175 cars
469' x 56' x 22' (142 x 20 x 6.7 m)
2 x 18-cylinder Pielstick diesel engines via twin screw.

Ice-strengthened passenger-car ferry owned and operated by Philpot Shipping Ltd, Cyprus, after acquisition from Marlines, Greece, who had laid the vessel up in Eleusis Bay since October 1999.
Built by Flenderwerke, Lubeck, for Fred Olsen as the BLACK WATCH (1966). Renamed JUPITER (1966) when the vessel was put in seasonal rotation every six months in a joint venture with the Bergen Line until 1985. She was then laid up between 1990 and 1997 for an average of eight months at a time. Renamed again as the CROWN M (1990 – Marlines).

BYELORUSSIYA (1975) See BELORUSSIYA II (1975)

BYRON (1902) See SANTIAGO (1916)

BYRON (1924)
9272 grt; 1860 psrs
470' x 58' x 24' (142.4 x 17.6 x 7.3 m)
Quadruple expansion engines via twin screw.
Broken up for scrap in La Spezia for a tender figure of US$58,000 in 1937.
Ex-Byron Steamship Co Ltd.
Launched by Cammell Laird & Company, Birkenhead, for the National Steam Navigation Company of Greece as the VASILEFS CONSTANTINOS (1914) and completed as the MEGALI HELLAS (1920 – National Steam Navigation Co Ltd of Greece).

CABO DE BUENA ESPERENZA (1940)
14124 grt; 560 psrs
535' x 72' x 30'6" (162.1 x 21.8 x 9.3 m)
Geared turbine engines via twin screw.
Broken up for scrap in Barcelona in 1958. Ex-Ybarra y Cia.
Built by the New York Shipbuilding Co, Camden, New Jersey for the US Shipping Board as the Type '535' transport HOOSIER STATE (1922). Renamed PRESIDENT LINCOLN (1922 – Pacific Mail Line) and MARIA DEL CARMEN (1940 – Berge y Cia).

CABO DE HORNOS (1940)
15124 grt; 560 psrs
535' x 72' x 30'6" (162.1 x 21.8 x 9.3 m)
Geared turbine engines via twin screw.
Broken up for scrap in Aviles in 1959. Ex-Ybarra y Cia.
Built by the New York Shipbuilding Co, Camden, New Jersey for the US Shipping Board as the Type '535' transport EMPIRE STATE (1920). Renamed PRESIDENT WILSON (1922 – Pacific Mail Line) and MARIA PIPA (1940 – Berge y Cia).

CABO IZZARA (1967) See XINGHU (1979)

CABO SAN AGUSTIN (1931) See DNEPR (1939)

CABO SAN ANTONIO (1930)
12275 grt; 250 psrs
483' x 63' x 25'6" (146.4 x 19.1 x 7.8 m)
MAN diesel engines via twin screw.
Sank on 31 December 1939 south-west of Dakar from deliberate gunfire from the French destroyer CASSARD to force her under. This followed an uncontrollable blaze throughout the vessel in which five lives were lost two days earlier.
Built by Soc Espanola Construccion Naval, Bilbao, for Ybarra y Cia, Seville.

CABO SAN ROQUE (1957) See AFRICA-CUBA (1978)

CABO SAN SEBASTIAN (1972) See CIUDAD DE SANTA CRUZ DE LA PALMA (1982)

CABO SANTA PAULA (1969) See EUROSTAR (1977)

CABO SANTO TOME (1931)
12589 grt; 512 psrs
483' x 63' x 25'6" (146.4 x 19.1 x 7.8 m)
MAN diesel engines via twin screw.
Sunk by Spanish gunboats DATO and CANOVAS on 10 October 1937 when one shell scored a direct hit on the ammunition room and the resultant explosion blew the keel off the ship. One life was lost.
Built by Soc Espanolas de Construccion Naval, Bilbao, for Ybarra y Cia, Seville.

CABO SAN VINCENTE (1959) See NOOR JEHAN (1975)

CACHEMIRE (1884) See BITHYNIE (1902)

CAESAREA (1960) See AESAREA (1981)

CAIRNRONA (1908) See POLERIC (1912)

CAIRO (1908) See ROYAL EDWARD (1910)

CAIRO CITY (1933)
4792 grt; 120 psrs
380' x 47' x 22'9" (115.2 x 14.2 x 6.9 m)
A Stephen & Sons 3-cylinder triple expansion engines via single screw. Laid down by A Stephen & Sons Ltd, Glasgow, for the Fenton Steamship Co Ltd, as IPHIGENIA (1906) and completed for Cie Belge Maritime as the ALBERTVILLE (1906). Renamed ELMINA (1910 – Elder Dempster).

CALABAR (1957)
8305 grt; 105 psrs
468' x 61' x 25' (141.8 x 18.5 x 7.6 m)
Triple expansion engines via twin screw.
Broken up for scrap in Inverkeithing in 1963. Ex-Elder Dempster Lines.
Built by Swan Hunter Shipbuilding, Newcastle, for Bullard, King & Co (the Natal Line) as the UMTALI (1936).

CALABRIA (1901)
4376 grt; 1170 psrs
376' x 47' x 27'6" (134 x 14.1 x 8.4 m)
D & W Henderson 4-cylinder triple expansion engine via single screw.
Broken up for scrap in 1923 by Gracechurch Transport Ltd, London.
Built by D & W Henderson Ltd, Glasgow, for the Anchor Line as a passenger liner.

CALABRIA (1952)
5230 grt; 560 psrs
383' x 52' x 17' (116.1 x 15.8 x 5.2 m)
4 x 6-cylinder Fiat diesel engines via twin screw.
Passenger ferry owned and operated by Tirrenia.
Built by Cantieri Riuniti, Palermo.

CALAMARES (1913) See CALAMARES, USS (AF-18) (1941)

CALAMARES, USS (AF-18) (1941)
7782 grt; 143 psrs
470' x 55' x 29' (142.4 x 16.7 x 8.8 m)
Quadruple expansion engines via twin screw.
Broken up for scrap in Baltimore, New Jersey, in 1947. Ex-US Navy.
Built by Workman, Clark & Co, Belfast for the United Fruit Steamship Co as the passenger-cargo ship CALAMARES (1913).

CALAWAII (1923)
7271 grt; 230 psrs
445' x 49' x 30' (134.8 x 14.8 x 9.1 m)
6-cylinder triple expansion engines via twin screw.
Broken up for scrap in Osaka in 1933. Ex-Los Angeles Steamship Co.
Built by Harland & Wolff Ltd, Belfast, for Elder Dempster Lines as the freighter MOBILE (1893). Renamed as the transport SHERMAN (1898 – US Army).

CALCHAS (1921)
10305 grt
491' x 62' x 39'6" depth (148.8 x 18.8 x 12 m)
2 x Cammell Laird DRG turbine engines via twin screw.
Sank on 21 April 1941 off West Africa, with 31 lives lost, after a torpedo hit from the German U-107.
Built by Workman, Clark & Co Ltd, Belfast, for A Holt & Co.

CALDERON (1900)
4083 grt
378' x 47' x 20'7" depth (114.5 x 14.2 x 6.3 m)
Triple expansion engine via single screw.
Sank after breaking in half in the River Mersey, Liverpool, after a collision with the MUSKETEER on 23 January 1912.
Built by Workman, Clark & Co, Belfast, for Lamport & Holt, Liverpool.

CALEDONIA (1904)
9223 grt; 1428 psrs
500' x 58' x 33'4" depth (151.5 x 17.6 x 10.1 m)
D & W Henderson 6-cylinder triple expansion engines via twin screw.
Sank as a troopship on 4 December 1916 after being torpedoed by the German U-65 125 miles (208 km) south-east of Malta.
Built by D & W Henderson, Glasgow, for the Anchor Line.

CALEDONIA (1925) See SCOTSTOUN, HMS (1939)

CALEDONIA, HMS (1936)
56551 grt; 3500 psrs
950' x 100' x 35' (287.9 x 30.3 x 10.6 m)
8 x Parsons turbine engines via quadruple screw.
Owned by the British Admiralty, and used as a training ship, she was broken

up for scrap by TW Ward & Co in Inverkeithing in 1943. She had been refloated following a fire at Rosyth, on 29 September 1939, which saw her settle on the seabed when she was completely gutted. Wards had tendered successfully in 1936 (£115,000) to break her up for scrap.
Launched by Blohm & Voss, Hamburg, for the Hamburg-America Line as the BISMARCK (1914), but completed for the White Star Line as the MAJESTIC (1922) under the World War Two reparations rules.

CALEDONIA (1948)
11255 grt; 304 psrs
506' x 66' x 27'6" (180.6 x 20 x 8.4 m)
2 x 4-cylinder Doxford diesel engines via twin screw.
Broken up for scrap by Ritcher Shipbreakers at Hamburg in 1970 after serving as an accommodation ship since 1965 for students of the University of Amsterdam.
Built by the Fairfield Shipbuilding & Engineering Co, Glasgow, for the Anchor Line.

CALEDONIA (1997)
3523 grt; 156 psrs
50 cars + 10 trailers
249' x 49' x 14' (75.6 x 14.7 x 4.3 m)
2 x 9-cylinder MAN-B+W-Alpha diesel engines via twin screw.
Passenger-car trailer ferry owned and operated by UKR FERRI State Shipping Co, Ukraine.
Built by Dubigeon-Normandie, Grand Quevilly, as the POOLE ANTELOPE (1973). Renamed QORMI (1976), PANAGIA FANEROMENI (1989 – Almar Shipping Co Ltd), YEYE (1991), PRESIDENTE YEIWENE (1992), CASABLANCA (1992) and PRESIDENTE YEIWENE (1993 – Societe de Development et d'Investissement des Iles).

CALEDONIAN ISLES (1993)
5221 grt; 1000 psrs
132 cars
312' x 52' x 10' (94.5 x 15.8 x 3.1 m)
2 x 8-cylinder Mirrlees diesel engines via twin screw.

Passenger-car ferry operated by Caledonian MacBrayne, Scotland.
Built by Richards Shipyard, Lowestoft, for Caledonian MacBrayne at a cost of £10,000,000.

CALEDONIAN PRINCESS (1961) See TUXEDO PRINCESS (1983)

CALEDONIAN STAR (1983)
3095 grt; 132 psrs
294' x 46' x 21' (89 x 14 x 6.4 m)
2 x 8-cylinder MaK diesel engines via single screw.
Ice-strengthened passenger ship owned by the Caledonian Steamship Co and chartered to Lindblad Special Expeditions, New York, from 1997.
Laid down by AG Weser, Bremerhaven, for a German fishing fleet as the mother ship MARBURG (1966), but completed as the NORTH STAR (1966). Renamed LINDMAR (1982 – Salen Linblad).

CALEDONIEN (1952) See ISLAND OF CYPRUS (1972)

CALGARIAN (1914)
17515 grt; 1680 psrs
590' x 70' x 41'6" depth (178.8 x 21.2 x 12.6 m)
4 x Fairfield turbine engines via quadruple screw.
Owned by Canadian Pacific Steamship Co, she sank on 1 March 1918 off

Rathlin Island, Northern Ireland, with 49 lives lost after being torpedoed by the German U-19.
Built by Fairfield Shipbuilding & Engineering Co, Glasgow, for the Allan Line as a passenger liner.

CALGARIC (1927)
16063 grt; 1170 psrs
550' x 67' x 43' depth (166.7 x 20.3 x 13 m)
2 x 4-cylinder combination triple expansion engine & turbines via triple screw.
Broken up for scrap at Rosyth in 1935 for £31,000. Ex-White Star Line passenger liner.
Built by Harland & Wolff Ltd, Belfast, for the Pacific Steam Navigation Co as the cargo ship ORCA (1918).

CALIFORNIA (1907)
8669 grt; 1214 psrs
470' x 58' x 34' depth (143.3 x 17.8 x 10.3 m)
2 x 3-cylinder Henderson triple expansion engines via twin screw.
Sank in seven minutes, with 43 lives lost, on 7 February 1917 38 miles (63 km) south-west of Fastnet after being torpedoed by a German U-boat.
Built by D & W Henderson Ltd, Glasgow, for the Anchor Line as a passenger liner.

CALIFORNIA (1923)
16792 grt; 1760 psrs
579' x 69' x 38'8" depth (175.5 x 20.9 x 11.8 m)
Turbine engines via twin screw.
Sank as a troopship following a fire which erupted during an aircraft bombing attack off Cape St Vincent, Portugal, 320 miles (533 km) west of Oporto, and then a single torpedo fired from her convoy escort destroyer on 11 July 1943. Forty-six lives were lost.
Built by Alexander Stephen & Sons, Glasgow, for the Anchor Line as a passenger liner.

CALIFORNIA (1928) See URUGUAY (1938)

CALIFORNIA (1930)
12768 grt; 160 psrs
539' x 64' x 31'9" depth (163.3 x 19.4 x 9.7 m)
4 x Scotts Shipbuilding & Engineering DRG turbine engines via twin screw.
Owned by Navigation Liberia Triestina, she sank as a hospital ship on 11 August 1941 with one dead following a British torpedo-bomber attack near Syracuse, Italy.
Laid down by Scotts Shipbuilding & Engineering Co, Greenock, for the Cunard Line as the passenger-cargo ship ALBANIA (1914), but not completed until 1920.

CALIFORNIAN (1898) See COAMO (1901)

CALIFORNIAN (1902)
6223 grt; 410 psrs
448' x 54' x 30'5" depth (136.4 x 16.4 x 9.2 m)
3-cylinder triple expansion engine via single screw.
Sank off Cape Matapan with one fatality after being torpedoed by an enemy submarine on 9 November 1915.
Built by Caledon Shipbuilding & Engineering Co, Dundee, for the Dominion Line.

CALIFORNIE (1905)
5152 grt; 960 psrs
370' x 47' x 25' (112.7 x 14.4 x 7.6 m)
3-cylinder Union Iron Works triple expansion engine via single screw.
Broken up for scrap in 1934.
Built by Ateliers et Chantiers de France, Dunkirk, for the French Line as a passenger liner.

CALLAO (1917) See RUTH ALEXANDER (1922)

CALMAR (1964) See ORINOCO (1975)

CALMAR NYCKEL (1964) See SHOROK 1 (1998)

CALPEAN STAR (1959)
14232 grt; 439 psrs

544' x 69' x 28' (165.8 x 21.1 x 8.5 m)
2 x 8-cylinder B+W diesel engines via twin screw.
Owned by the Calpean Shipping Co Ltd, Gibraltar, as a whaling fleet mother ship, she was abandoned as a total constructive loss after grounding on 1 June 1960 two miles (3 km) from the harbour of Montevideo. At the time she had been under tow following a massive engine room explosion.
Built by Harland & Wolff Ltd, Belfast, for the Nelson Line as the passenger-cargo ship HIGHLAND CHIEFTAIN (1928).

CALVERT, USS (AP-65) (1942) See CALVERT, USS (APA-32) (1943)

CALVERT, USS (APA-32) (1943)
7997 grt
465' x 66' x 39'7" depth (140.9 x 20 x 12 m)
General Electric DRG turbine engines via single screw.
Broken up for scrap in Richmond, California in 1977.
Built by Bethlehem Steel Co (Shipbuilding Division), Sparrow's Point, for the Missouri Shipping Co Inc, as the DELORLEANS II (1942). Renamed CALVERT, USS (AP-65) (1942 – US Navy).

CALVIN AUSTIN (1903)
3826 grt
299' x 61' x 17'8" (90.6 x 20 x 5.4 m)
Harlan & Hollingsworth 3-cylinder triple expansion engines via single screw.
Broken up for scrap in Baltimore in 1934.
Built by Harlan & Hollingsworth Co, Wilmington, Delaware, for the Eastern Steamship Co.

CALYPSO (1920)
3817 grt; 140 psrs
354' x 44' x 23' (107.3 x 13.3 x 7 m)
Richardson 3-cylinder triple expansion engine via single screw.
Broken up for scrap by Van Heyghen Freres in Bruges in 1936. Ex-Wilson Line.
Built by Raylton Dixon, Middlesbrough, for Soc Maritime de Congo as the BRUXELLESVILLE (1897). Renamed ALEXANDRA WOERMANN (1901 – Woermann Line).

CALYPSO (1973) See IMPERIAL MAJESTY (1999).

CALYPSO (1988) See EUROFAST (2000)

CALYPSO II (1996) See EUROFAST (2000)

CALYPSO (1995)
11162 grt; 594 psrs
454' x 63' x 20' (137.5 x 19 x 6.1 m)
2 x 12-cylinder Wartsila-Vasa diesel engines via twin screw.

Cruise ship owned and operated by Louis Cruises, Cyprus, after her purchase from auction at US$14,000,000 in 2000.
Built by Navali Meccaniche, Baia, for Linee Canguro SpA, Cagliari, as the passenger-car train ferry CANGURO VERDE (1967). Renamed DURR (1981 – Fayez Trading & Shipping Establishment, Jeddah), IONIAN HARMONY (1989 – Strintzis Lines SA, Valetta), SUN FIESTA (1990 – Ferry Charter St Thomas Ltd, Nassau, with a charter to SeaEscape Cruise Ltd) and REGENT JEWEL (1993 – Regency Cruises).

CALYPSO I (1980) See IMPERIAL MAJESTY (1999)

CAMBODGE (1953) See STELLA SOLARIS (1970)

CAMBRIA (1921) See VILLE D'ARLON (1940)

CAMBRIA (1949) See ALTAIF (1976)

CAMELLIA (1990)
9707 grt; 445 psrs
250 cars
548' x 79' x 21'6" (166.5 x 24 x 6.5 m)
2 x 18-cylinder MAN SRG expansion engines via twin screw.
Passenger-car-cargo RoRo ferry on the Japan-to-Korea service.
Built by Nakai Shipbuilding & Engineering Co Ltd, Setoda, for NYK, Tokyo, as the SAROMA MARU (1975).

CAMERONIA (1911)
10963 grt; 1700 psrs
532' x 62' x 25'7" depth (162.1 x 19 x 7.8 m)
D & W Henderson 8-cylinder triple expansion engines via twin screw.
Sank on 15 April 1917, with the loss of 210 lives, 150 miles (250 km) east of Malta after being torpedoed by the German U-33.
Built by D & W Henderson, Glasgow, for the Anchor Line.

CAMERONIA (1921) See EMPIRE CLYDE (1953)

CAMILLE MARCOUX (1974)
6122 grt; 600 psrs
313' x 63' x 16'6" (94.8 x 19 x 5 m)
4 x 16-cylinder Ruston diesel engines via twin screw.
Ice-strengthened passenger ferry operated by the Societe des Trav, Quebec, Canada, on the St Lawrence river.
Built by Marine Industries Ltd, Sorel, Quebec, for the Ministry of Transport for Quebec.

CAMITO (1956)
8687 grt; 113 psrs
448' x 62' x 26' (135.8 x 18.8 x 7.9 m)
Geared turbine engines via twin screw.
Broken up for scrap in Kaohsiung in 1973.
Built by Alexander Stephen & Sons, Glasgow, for Elders & Fyffes Ltd.

CAMMELL LAIRD (1968) See SOUNION (1970)

CAMPANA (1929) See IRPINIA (1955)

CAMPANA (1946) See IRPINIA (1955)

CAMPANELLO (1910) See FLAVIA (1916)

CAMPANIA (1893) See CAMPANIA, HMS (1915)

CAMPANIA (1906) See FLAVIA (1916)

CAMPANIA FELIX (1952)
5208 grt; 560 psrs
383' x 52' x 17' (116.1 x 15.8 x 5.2 m)
4 x 6-cylinder Fiat SRG diesel engines via twin screw.
Built by Navali Meccaniche, Baia, for Tirrenia.

CAMPANIA, HMS (1915)
12950 grt; 1460 psrs
601' x 65' x 37'8" depth (182.1 x 19.7 x 11.5 m)
Fairfield 10-cylinder triple expansion engines via twin screw.
Owned by the British Admiralty as an aircraft carrier, she sank stern-first on 5 November 1918 off Burntisland in the Firth of Forth. She had dragged her anchors during a storm and collided with the battleship HMS ROYAL OAK and then crashed into the aircraft carrier HMS GLORIOUS.
Built by Fairfield Shipbuilding & Engineering Co, Glasgow, for the Cunard Line as the passenger liner CAMPANIA (1893).

CAMPERDOWN (1917) See KIZAN MARU (1938)

CAMPHUYS (1948)

4497 grt; 250 psrs
357' x 53' x 22'6" (108.2 x 16.1 x 6.8 m)
Hawthorn-Werkspoor 8-cylinder diesel engine via single screw.
Built by Wilton-Fijenoord for Koninkl Paket Maats.

CAMRANH (1923) See BRAZZA (1927)

CANADA (1912)
9684 grt; 344 psrs
476' x 57' x 26'3" (148.5 x 19 x 8 m)
6-cylinder Dickinson triple expansion engines via twin screw.
Broken up for scrap in Newport, Wales, in 1952.
Laid down by Forges et Chantiers de la Mediterranee, La Seyne, for the Fabre Line as SANTA LUCIA (1911), but completed as the passenger-cargo liner CANADA.

CANADA (1913) See PHILIPPINES (1919)

CANADA (1935)
11108 grt; 55 psrs
493' x 64' x 28'8" (149.4 x 19.4 x 8.7 m)
2 x 6-cylinder B+W diesel engines via twin screw.
Sank on 3 November 1939 after striking a rock two miles (3 km) east of Holmpton near Spurn Head, UK.
Built by Nakskov Skibsvaerft for the East Asiatic Company.

CANADA MARU (1911)
5760 grt
408' x 50' x 26' (123.6 x 15.2 x 7.9 m)
Triple expansion engines via twin screw.
Broken up for scrap in 1935.
Built by Mitsubishi Dockyard for OSK, Japan.

CANADA STAR (1986) See UNIVERSE EXPLORER (1996)

CANADIAN (1900)
9301 grt; 60 psrs
530' x 59' x 35' depth (176.7 x 19.7 x 10.6 m)
R & W Hawthorn, Leslie compound engine via single screw.
Sank on 5 April 1917 47 miles (79 km) off Fastnet after being torpedoed by the German U-59. One life was lost
Built for the Leyland Line by R & W Hawthorn, Leslie Co Ltd.

CANBERRA (1913) See ESPANA (1954)

CANBERRA (1961)
49073 grt; 1641 psrs
818' x 102' x 35'6" (249.3 x 31 x 10.8 m)
2 x AEI turbo-electric engines via twin screw.

Broken up for scrap at Gadani Beach, Karachi, in 1998.
Built by Harland & Wolff Ltd, Belfast, for the P&O Line at a cost of £17,021,000.

CANDI (1990) See REGAL VOYAGER (1994)

CANDIA (1972)
5788 grt; 1450 psrs
350 cars
426' x 72' x 18' (129.1 x 21.8 x 5.5 m)
2 x 14-cylinder MAN diesel engines via twin screw.

Owned by Cretan Marine and operated as a passenger-car-cargo RoRo ferry on the Greece-Crete service by ANEK. Towards the end of 2000 the United Arab Emirates purchased her for US$1,250,000 for delivery in 2001.
Built by Sumitomo Shipbuilding & Machinery Co Ltd, Uraga Shipyard, Yokosuka, for the Central Ferry Co, Kobe, as CENTRAL NO. 2 (1971).

CANDLER (1923)
5672 grt; 80 psrs
445' x 49' x 30' depth (135.6 x 15 x 9.1 m)
6-cylinder triple expansion engines via twin screw.
Broken up for scrap in 1924. Ex-US government.
Built by Harland & Wolff Ltd, Belfast, for the Atlantic Transport Co of West Virginia as the MANITOBA (1892). Renamed LOGAN (1898 – US Army).

CANGURO AZZURO (1965) See ESPRESSO AZZURO (1978)

CANGURO BIANCO (1968) See AL SALAM TABA I (1998)

CANGURO BIONDO (1971) See AL SALAM 91 (1993)

CANGURO BRUNO (1968) See LEROS (1998)

CANGURO CABO SAN SEBASTIAN (1972) See DONATELLA D'ABUNDO (2000)

CANGURO GIALLO (1969) See CONCORD (1992)

CANGURO ROSSO (1965) See SINDIBAD I (1982)

CANGURO VERDE (1967) See CALYPSO (1995)

CANONESA (1916) See MAGICSTAR (1919)

CANOPIC (1903)
11394 grt; 1277 psrs
594' x 59' x 30' (181 x 18 x 9.1 m)
2 x 8-cylinder triple expansion engines via twin screw.
Broken up for scrap by TW Ward Ltd at Briton Ferry, UK, in 1925. Ex-White Star Line.
Built by Harland & Wolff Ltd, Belfast, for the Dominion Line as the passenger liner COMMONWEALTH (1900).

CANTERBURY (1929)
3017 grt; 1400 psrs
342' x 47' x 12'10" depth (103 x 14.2 x 3.7 m)
2 x Parsons SRG steam turbine engines via twin screw.
Passenger ferry owned and operated by Southern Railways. Broken up for scrap by Brussels Shipbreaking Company in 1965.
Built by William Denny and Brothers, Dumbarton.

CANTERBURY (1999) See POSL CANTERBURY (1999)

CANTIGNY (1920) See AROSA KULM (1952)

CANTON (1930) See CARTHAGE MARU (1961)

CANTON (1938)
16033 grt; 542 psrs
568' x 73' x 42' depth (173 x 22.1 x 12.7 m)
Parsons SRG steam turbine engines via twin screw.
Broken up for scrap by Leung Yau Shipbreaking Co in Hong Kong in 1962.
Built by Alexander Stephen & Sons, Glasgow, for the P&O Line.

CANTUARIA (1940)
5312 grt; 74 psrs
390' x 54' x 28' depth (118.2 x 16.4 x 8.5 m)
General Electric DRG turbine engine via single screw.
Broken up for scrap in 1958. Ex-Lloyd Brasileiro.
Built by American International Shipbuilding Corporation, Hog Island, Pennsylvania, for the US Shipping Board as the SAGUACHE (1919). Renamed SCANSTATES (1932 – American Scantic Line).

CAOBANG (1902)
6762 grt

446' x 47' x 37'7" depth (135.2 x 14.2 x 11.4 m)
Forges et Chantiers de la Mediterranee triple expansion engines via twin screw.
Owned by Messageries Maritimes, she was abandoned as a total constructive loss on 4 January 1906 after becoming wrecked in a dense fog at Poulo Condor.
Built by Forges et Chantiers de la Mediterranee, La Seyne, for Cie Nationale de Navigation.

CAP ARCONA (1907) See ANGERS (1921)

CAP ARCONA (1927)
27561 grt; 1315 psrs
676' x 84' x 28'6" (204.8 x 25.5 x 8.7 m)
SRG turbine engines via twin screw.
Broken up in the Bay of Lubeck in 1946 after one of the great tragedies of World War Two. Unbeknown to the British Royal Air Force, she was transporting 5,000 Allied prisoners-of-war, plus about 1,000 crew and guards, when British aircraft attacked her with rockets which ripped into her on 3 May 1945, only five days before the war ceased in Europe. She capsized and sank with all lives lost.
Built by Blohm & Voss, Hamburg, for the Hamburg-South American Line as a passenger liner.

CAPELLA (1982) See FINNMAID (1997)

CAPELLA AV STOCKHOLM (1986) See FINNMAID (1997)

CAPE St VINCENT (1943) See AL SUDAN (1947)

CAPE St ROQUE (1943) See MISR (1947)

CAPETOWN CASTLE (1938)
27002 grt; 796 psrs
734' x 82' x 32' (222.4 x 24.8 x 9.7 m)
2 x 10-cylinder B+W diesel engines via twin screw.
Broken up for scrap at La Spezia in 1967.
Built by Harland & Wolff Ltd, Belfast, for the Union Castle Line.

CAPE VERDE (1923) See KIZAN MARU (1938)

CAP FINISTERRE (1911) See TAIYO MARU (1920)

CAP FRIO (1900)
5732 grt; 580 psrs
411' x 48' x 29' depth (125.4 x 14.7 x 8.8 m)
Reiherstieg 4-cylinder quadruple expansion engine via single screw.
Sank on 30 August 1908 near Bahia, Brazil, after running aground in a violent storm and holing her hull beyond repair.
Built by Reiherstieg, Hamburg, for HAPAG.

CAPITAINE POTIE (1946) See KING ABDELAZIZ (1964)

CAP LAY (1925)
8169 grt; 850 psrs
418' x 55' x 34'5" depth (126.7 x 16.7 x 10.5 m)
3 x Ateliers et Chantiers de la Loire DRG turbine engines via single screw.
Lost in a typhoon on 15 July 1928 in the Bay of Along.
Built by Ateliers et Chantiers de la Loire, Nantes, for Cie des Chargeurs Reunis, Marseilles, as the HALGAN (1921).

CAP NORTE (1922) See EMPIRE TROOPER (1940)

CAP NORTE (1934) See EMPIRE TROOPER (1940)

CAPO BIANCO (1974) See SHOROK 1 (1998)

CAPO CARBONARA (1988)
12167 grt; 1508 psrs
425 cars
489' x 75' x 21'6" (148.3 x 22.7 x 6.6 m)
2 x 12-cylinder GMT diesel engines via twin screw.
Passenger-car-cargo RoRo ferry which operated for Tirrenia in Italy, but sold to US buyers for US$6,500,000 in August 2000.

Built by Cantieri Navale Riuniti SpA, Ancona, for Lloyd Triestino as the ADRIA (1981).

CAPO FALCONARA (1978)
3119 grt; 946 psrs
327' x 46' x 17' (99.1 x 14 x 5.2 m)
2 x 7-cylinder B+W diesel engines via twin screw.
Broken up for scrap in Medina, Saudi Arabia, in 1986. Ex-Libera Navagazione Lauro SpA, Naples.
Built by Helsingor Shipyards, Helsingor, for the United Steamship Co as the KRONPRINS OLAV (1937). Renamed FRANKFURT (1940 –), CORSICA EXPRESS (1967 – Corsica Ferries) and EXPRESS FERRY ANGELINA LAURO (1975 – Liberia Navagazioni Lauro SpA).

CAPO LENA (1935)
5106 grt
351' x 53' x 24'6" (106.4 x 16.1 x 7.5 m)
Central Marine Engineering Works 3-cylinder triple expansion engines via single screw.
Sank on 17 August 1945. Ex-Cia Genovese di Navegazione a Vapores SA.
Built by W Gray & Co Ltd, West Hartlepool, for Sov Nav de l'Quest as the SAINT RENE (1921). Renamed AYRISTAN (1923 – Strick Line Ltd), SAINT AUGUSTIN (1929 – Cie Navale et Commerciale de l'Oceanie) and ASTROLABE (1930 – Messageries Maritimes).

CAPO MANARA (1948)
7510 grt; 1294 psrs
457' x 57' x 29' (138.5 x 17.3 x 8.8 m)
Westinghouse turbine engine via single screw.
Broken up for scrap in Yokohama in 1954. Ex-Cia de Navegazioni Stellamaris.
Built by Merchant Shipbuilding Corporation, Chester, Pennsylvania, for Shawmut Steamship Co, New York, as the MOUNT CLINTON (1921). Renamed MAUNALEI (1925 – Matson Lines) and SANTA ROSA (1948 – Paiaggio & Ravano).

CAPO OLMO (1935) See MADALI (1948)

CAP ORTEGAL (1903) See CHAMBORD (1923)

CAPO SANDALO (1988)
17961 grt; 1508 psrs
425 cars
489' x 75' x 23'6" (148.3 x 22.7 x 7.1 m)
2 x 12-cylinder GMT diesel engines via twin screw.
Passenger-car-cargo RoRo ferry for Tirrenia, but is for sale at US$6,300,000.
Built by Cantieri Navale Riuniti SpA, Ancona, for Lloyd Triestino as the TORRE DEL GRECO (1982).

CAPO SPARTIVENTO (1988)
17971 grt; 1508 psrs
425 cars
489' x 75' x 23'6" (148.3 x 22.7 x 7.1 m)
2 x 12-cylinder GMT diesel engines via twin screw.
Passenger-car-cargo ferry operated by Tirrenia.
Built by Italcantieri SpA, Genoa, for Lloyd Triestino as the cargo RoRo APULIA (1981).

CAP PADARAN (1926)
8009 grt; 224 psrs
417' x 55' x 34'4" depth (126.4 x 16.7 x 10.4 m)
3 x Ateliers et Chantiers de la Loire DRG turbine engines via single screw.
Sank on 9 December 1943 after being torpedoed by the German U-596 in the Adriatic Sea. At the time she was under the management of Ellerman Lines following the seizure of the ship in 1941 by the British Ministry of War Transport.
Built by Ateliers et Chantiers de la Loire, St Nazaire, for Chargeurs Reunis as the D'IBERVILLE (1922).

CAP POLONIO (1913) See CAP POLONIO (1914)

CAP POLONIO (1914)
20576 grt; 1555 psrs
638' x 72' x 39'6" depth (193.3 x 21.8 x 12 m)
Triple expansion engine via twin screw.

Broken up for scrap in Bremerhaven in 1935 after several lengthy periods laid up in Hamburg, during which she was used on a number of occasions as a German trade exhibition ship.
Laid down by Blohm & Voss, Hamburg, for the Hamburg-South American Line as the passenger liner CAP POLONIO (1913), but completed for the German Navy as the armed cruiser VINETA (1913). The conversion was not a success and the vessel reverted to her original design and name of CAP POLONIO.

CAPRERA (1919) See ARABUTAN (1940)

CAPRICORN (1999)
11347 grt; 1800 psrs
460 cars or 150 cars + 30 trailers
480' x 73' x 13' (145.6 x 22 x 4 m)
2 x General Electric Marine gas turbine engines + 4 x MTU 20-cylinder diesel engines via quadruple screw.
Passenger-car-cargo ferry owned and operated by Tirrenia, Italy.
Built by Fincantieri, Riva Trigoso.

CAPTAIN CONSTANTINOS (1979) See ARTEMIS (1994)

CAPTAIN COOK (1951)
13876 grt; 1088 psrs
538' x 66' x 28' (164 x 20.1 x 8.5 m)
DRG turbine engines via twin screw.
Broken up for scrap by British Iron & Steel Corporation at Inverkeithing in 1960. Ex-British Ministry of Transport.
Built by Fairfield Shipbuilding & Engineering Co, Glasgow, for Donaldson Lines as the LETITIA (1925). Renamed EMPIRE BRENT (1946 – British Ministry of Transport).

CAPTAIN HOBSON (1951)
9306 grt; 580 psrs
482' x 59' x 27' (147 x 18 x 8.2 m)
Triple expansion engine via single screw.
Owned by Shaw Savill, she was broken up for scrap by Okushogi & Co in Osaka in 1959. This followed a major mechanical breakdown at sea and being towed to Auckland, then taken to Mumbai for laying up.
Built by William Denny & Bros, Dumbarton, for the Henderson Line as the passenger liner AMARAPOORA (1920).

CAPTAIN MARCOS (1948) See CORSICA (1951)

CAPTAIN NICOLAS V (1984) See NIAXCO III (1990)

CAPTAIN OMAR See COLUMBUS CARAVELLE (1991)
(This casino vessel also sailed under the name of LIDO STAR which was painted on her hull sides, amidships, and has been referred to as CAPTAIN OMAR since 1999, but is not registered as such.)

CAPTAIN ZAMAN I (1998)
12394 grt; 1532 psrs
100 cars or 10 trailers
460' x 68' x 17'6" (139.4 x 20.6 x 5.3 m)
4 x 6-cylinder Lindholmen-Pielstic diesel engines via twin screw.

Passenger-car-cargo ferry owned by Sirene Shipping & Trading Inc, and operated by Ferro Ferryboat & RoRo Transportation Co.
Built by Lindholmens Varv, Gothenburg, for Swedish Lloyd as the SVEA (1966). Renamed HISPANIA (1969). Renamed SAGA (1972 – Swedish Lloyd), FESTOS (1984 – Minoan Lines) and ZAMAN II (1998 – Sirene Shipping & Trading Inc).

CAPTAIN ZAMAN II (1998)
12374 grt; 130 psrs
340 cars
467' x 66' x 18' (141.2 x 20 x 5.5 m)
4 x 6-cylinder Lindholmens-Pielstick diesel engines via twin screw.

Owned by Sirene Shipping & Trading Inc and operated by Ferro Ferryboat & RoRo Transportation Co.
Built by Lindholmens Varv, Gothenburg, for Swedish Lloyd as the SAGA (1966). Renamed STENA ATLANTICA (1971 – Stena Line), FINNPARTNER (1973 – Finncarriers), OLAU FINN (1976 – Olau Line), KNOSSOS (1978 – Minoan Lines) FOLKLINER (1982 – Folkline) and ZAMAN I (1998 – Serene Shipping & Trading Inc).

CAP TOURANE (1925)
8009 grt; 224 psrs
418' x 55' x 34'4" depth (126.7 x 16.7 x 10.4 m)
3 x Ateliers et Chantiers de la Loire turbine engines via single screw.
Broken up for scrap in 1953 at Zeebrugge. Ex-Ellerman Lines.
Built by Ateliers et Chantiers de la Loire, St Nantes, for Chargeurs Reunis as the JOUFFROY D'ABBANS (1923).

CAP TRAFALGAR (1914)
18805 grt; 1586 psrs
613' x 72' x 39'6" depth (187 x 22 x 12 m)
AG Vulcan 8-cylinder triple expansion engines via triple screw.
Sank on 14 September 1914 with the loss of 15 lives after withstanding two hours of solid gunfire from the British Cunard merchantman CARMANIA, off Trinidad. This was the first recorded sinking of a passenger ship by another passenger vessel during World War One.
Built by Bremer Vulcan Shipyards, Hamburg, for the Hamburg-South America Line.

CAP VILLANO (1906) See GENERAL METZINGER (1924)

CARACAS (1927) See SOUTHERN CROSS (1955)

CARALIS (1957) See REYNA FILIPINA (1978)

CARALIS (1988) See FUDI (2000)

CARAQUET (1913)
4917 grt; 178 psrs
401' x 47' x 31' (121.5 x 14.2 x 9.4 m)
Triple expansion engines via twin screw.
Passenger-cargo ship owned by the Royal Mail Steam Packet Co, she was abandoned as a total constructive loss after becoming shipwrecked on 25 June 1923 near Hamilton, Bermuda.
Built by Harland & Wolff Ltd, Belfast, for the Union Line as the GUELPH (1894).

CARARE (1926)
6850 grt; 60 psrs
425' x 55' x 29'9" depth (128.8 x 16.7 x 9.1 m)
Triple expansion engines via twin screw.
Sank on 28 May 1940 in the Bristol Channel, south-west of Nash Point, after sailing into a minefield.
Built by Cammell Laird Ltd, Birkenhead, for Elders & Fyffes as a passenger-cargo liner.

CARAVAGGIO (1975) See AL-ABOUD (1994)

CARAVAN (1985) See MEDIA II (1993)

CARAVAN (1986) See KARDEN (1995)

CARDUCCI (1970) See AL SALAM CARDUCCI 92 (1999)

CAR FERRY CHEJU No. 2 (1991) See DONG YANG EXPRESS FERRY No. 6 (1999)

CARIBA VIVA (1994) See HAPPY DOLPHIN (1999)

CARIBBEAN (1913)
5625 grt; 350 psrs
420' x 50' x 33' (127.3 x 15.2 x 10 m)
Fairfield 3-cylinder triple expansion engine via single screw.
Owned by Royal Mail Steam Packet Co, she sank as an armed merchant cruiser on 26 September 1915, with 15 lives lost, after foundering in foul weather off Cape Wrath, Scotland.
Built by Fairfield Shipbuilding & Engineering Co Ltd, Glasgow, for Castle Line as the DUNOTTAR CASTLE (1889).

CARIBE (1976) See DISCOVERY SUN (1995)

CARIBE (1982) See REGAL EMPRESS (1993)

CARIBE I (1982) See REGAL EMPRESS (1993)

CARIBE BREMEN (1981) See DISCOVERY SUN (1995)

CARIBE ENTERPRISE (1981)
11447 grt; 2000 psrs
523' x 71' x 33' (159.3 x 21.7 x 10 m)
Geared turbine engine via single screw.
Owned by Vanessa Trading Co, she sank on 25 July 1986 as a container ship in mid-Pacific, while under tow to be broken up in Kaohsiung.
Built by Kaiser Corporation, Richmond, California, for the US Maritime Commission as the Class C4-S-A1 troop transport GENERAL A. W. GREELY, USS (AP-141) (1945). Reclassified as the GENERAL A. W. GREELY, USAT (1947 – US Army). Reclassified as the GENERAL A. W. GREELY, USNS (T-AP-141) (1950 – US Navy). Laid up in Olympia, Washington state, from 1955 to 1967 (US Maritime Commission). Renamed HAWAII BEAR (1968 – Pacific Far East Line), AUSTRAL GLADE (1976 – Farrell Lines) and PACIFIC ENTERPRISE (1979 – Farrell Lines).

CARIBIA (1933) See ILYICH (1946)

CARIBIA (1965)
24496 grt; 1370 psrs
631' x 79' x 29' (191.2 x 23.9 x 8.8 m)
2 x 10-cylinder Fiat diesel engines via twin screw.
Owned by Grimaldi-Siosa Lines, she sank on 20 July 1974 while waiting off Kaohsiung to be broken up for scrap. She had been towed from Barcelona when she suffered heavy damage after going out of control following starboard engine failure. She struck submerged rocks in the Baie des Anges off Nice on 23 September 1972 and was declared a total constructive loss, after which she was sold quickly to a Spanish shipbreaker who, in turn, resold her to a Taiwanese breaking yard.
Laid down by Cantieri Navale Triestino, Monfalcone, for the Cosulich Line as the URANIA (1926) and completed as VULCANIA (1928).

CARIBIA (1968)
34172 grt; 600 psrs
715' x 91' x 31'6" (216.7 x 27.6 x 9.5 m)

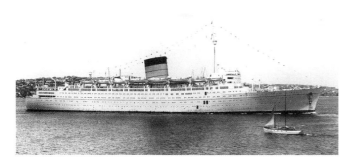

1 x SRG + 1 x DRG John Brown Ltd turbine engines via twin screw.
Owned by the Franchard Corporation, she was broken up for scrap at Apra, Guam, in 1974. She had caught fire on 25 March 1969 near St Thomas, West Indies, and had been towed to New York where she was laid up for five years as a hull for sale. Taiwanese shipbreakers offered the owner US$3,500,000 and the ship was under tow by the German tug HAMBURG to Kaohsiung when a violent storm broke her cables and she hit a breakwater, heeled over and broke into three sections.
Built by John Brown & Co Ltd, Clydebank, for the Cunard Line as the CARONIA (1948). Renamed COLUMBIA (1968 – Star Line).

CARIBIA 2 (1973)
14986 grt; 1113 psrs
492' x 69' x 29' (150 x 21 x 8.8 m)
2 x General Electric SRG turbine engines via single screw.
Broken up for scrap by Terrestre Marittima at La Spezia for Lira 760,000,000 in 1975. Ex-Marimina Shipping Co.
Laid down by Western Pipe & Steel Co, San Francisco, for the US Navy as the aircraft carrier CROATIAN, USS (1942) and completed as FENCER, HMS (1942 – British Royal Navy). Renamed SYDNEY (1950 – Flotto Lauro), ROMA (1967 x Flotto Lauro), GALAXY QUEEN (1971 – Sovereign Cruises Ltd) and LADY DINA (1972 – George Kotzovilis).

CARIBOU (1985)
27213 grt; 1342 psrs
350 cars or 18 cars + 91 trailers
591' x 83' x 22' (179 x 25 x 6.6 m)
4 x 8-cylinder MaK SRG diesel engines via twin screw.

Ice-strengthened passenger-car-cargo ferry operated by Marine Atlantic on the Nova Scotia-to-Newfoundland service.
Built by Versatile Davie Shipyard Inc, Lauzon, Quebec, for Marine Atlantic at a cost of Can$135,000,000.

CARIDDI (1932)
3123 grt; 1800 psrs
15 cars + 36 rail coaches
409' x 57' x 13'6" (124 x 17.2 x 4.1 m)
3 x Stablimento Tecnico 8-cylinder diesel engines via twin screw.
Passenger-car-train ferry owned by the Italian State Railways and chartered to Ferrovie Stato.
Built by Cantieri Riuniti dell'Adriatico, Trieste.

CARIGNANO (1920)
5359 grt
400' x 52' x 28'8" (121.2 x 15.8 x 8.7 m)
Harland & Wolff Ltd 3-cylinder triple expansion engines via single screw.
Broken up for scrap. Ex-Lloyd Sabaudo.
Built by Ropner & Sons Ltd, Stockton, for the British Shipping Controller as the WAR PIDGEON (1918). As CARIGNANO, she was a post-World War One immigrant ship.

CARINA (1964) See FIESTA (1964)

CARINA (1967)
4055 grt; 350 psrs
330' x 51' x 16' (100 x 15.5 x 4.8 m)
6 x SRG turbine engines via twin screw.

Operated by International Cruises SA (subsidiary of Chandris Group).
Built by William Denny & Bros, Dumbarton, for the Canadian Pacific Steamship Co as PRINCESS HELENE (1930). Renamed HELENE (1963 – Marvic Navigation Inc, Monrovia) and CARINA II (1965 – Marvic Navigation Inc, Monrovia).

CARINA (1996)
7727 grt; 328 psrs
399' x 59' x 14'6" (121 x 18 x 4.4 m)
2 x 8-cylinder SEMT-Pielstick diesel engines via twin screw.
Ice-strengthened cruise ship for Phoenix Reisen and Ukrainian Danube Shipping Co.
Built by Ateliers et Chantiers Dubigeon-Normandie, Nantes, for the Soviet Danube Steamship Co, Ismail, as the AYVAZOVSKIY (1976).

CARINA II (1965) See CARINA (1967)

CARINTHIA (1925)
20277 grt; 1650 psrs
624' x 73' x 32' (189 x 22.1 x 9.7 m)
2 x Vickers DRG turbine engines via twin screw.
Sank stern first at 9.40 pm on 8 June 1940 off the west coast of Ireland, with the loss of three lives, two days after being hit by a torpedo fired from the German U-46.
Laid down by Vickers-Armstrong Ltd, Barrow-in-Furness, for the Cunard Line as the SERVIA (1924), she was completed as the cruise ship CARINTHIA.

CARINTHIA (1956) See CHINA SEA DISCOVERY (2000)

CARISSIMA (1963) See FIESTA (1964)

CARLA (1995) See SALEM FLOWER (1998)

CARLA C (1968) See PALLAS ATHENA (1992)

CARLA COSTA (1987) See PALLAS ATHENA (1992)

CARLA E (1991)
4092 grt; 130 psrs
432' x 63' x 21'6" (131 x 19.2 x 6.6 m)
2 x 14-cylinder Crossley diesel engines via twin screw.
Passenger ferry owned by CoNar Tir, SpA, Trapani.
Built by Robb Caledon, Dundee, for the Union Steamship Co of New Zealand as the MAHENO (1969). Renamed JOLLY GIALLO (1976 – V-Ships Management Inc, Monaco), AFRICAN TRADER (1980 – Thames Marine Ltd, SA, Panama), JUNE LADY (1985 – Oyster Shipping Ltd), OLBIAS (1987 – V-Ships Management Inc) and TIERRA DEL FUEGO (1987 – Naviera Magallenes, Chile).

CARLO R (1990)
13102 grt; 1080 psrs
500 cars
502' x 71' x 22' (152.4 x 21.6 x 6.7 m)
2 x AEI turbo-electric engines via twin screw.
Passenger-car ferry owned and operated by Alimar, with frequent periods laid up in Naples.
Built by Swan Hunter Shipbuilders Ltd, Walker, for the Union Steamship Co of New Zealand Ltd as the RANGATIRA (1972). Renamed QUEEN M (1986 – Marlines).

CARL SCHURZ (1913) See CHANGUINOLA (1914)

CARMANIA (1905)
19524 grt; 1440 psrs
650' x 72' x 33' depth (197 x 21.8 x 10 m)
3 x Parsons turbine engines via triple screw.
Broken up for scrap by Hughes Bolckow Ltd at Blyth in 1932.
Built by John Brown & Co Ltd, Clydebank, for the Cunard Steamship Co Ltd as a passenger liner.

CARMANIA (1962) See LEONID SOBINOV (1973)

CARMARTHENSHIRE (1908) See CHALEUR (1913)

CARMIA (1925) See DRACHENSTEIN (1930)

CARNARVON CASTLE (1926)
20148 grt; 1283 psrs
686' x 74' x 32' (198.8 x 22.4 x 9.7 m)
2 x 8-cylinder H&W-B+W diesel engines via twin screw.
Broken up for scrap at Mihara in 1962.
Built by Harland & Wolff Ltd, Belfast, for the Union Castle Line.

CARNIVAL DESTINY (1996)
101353 grt; 3350 psrs
899' x 116' x 27' (272.4 x 35.5 x 8.3 m)
6 x 16-cylinder Sulzer diesel-electric engines via twin screw.

Cruise ship for Carnival Cruise Lines.
Built by Fincantieri Navegazione Italiana SpA, Monfalcone, for Futura Cruises Inc (a Carnival Corporation subsidiary) at a cost of US$400,000,000.

CARNIVALE (1969) See THE FIESTA (1991)

CARNIVALE (1975) See THE TOPAZ (1998)

CARNIVAL TRIUMPH (1999)
101672 grt; 2758 psrs
893' x 116' x 27' (270.6 x 35.2 x 8.2 m)
4 x 16-cylinder + 2 x 12-cylinder Sulzer diesel-electric engines via twin screw.

Cruise ship owned and operated by Carnival Cruise Lines.
Built by Fincantieri, Monfalcone, at a cost of US$410,000,000.

CARNIVAL VICTORY (2000)
101672 grt; 2758 psrs
898' x 117' x 27' (272 x 35.5 x 8.2 m)
6 x 16-cylinder Sulzer diesel engines via twin screw.

Cruise ship built for Carnival Cruise Lines by Fincantieri, Monfalcone, at a cost of US$430,000,000.

CAROLINA (1905)
5093 grt; 240 psrs
404' x 48' x 36'5" depth (122.4 x 14.5 x 11.1 m)
Newport News 8-cylinder quadruple expansion engines via twin screw.
Sank on 2 June 1918 off Delaware Capes after a gunfire attack by the German U-151.
Built by Newport News Shipbuilding Co, Newport News, Virginia, for Plant Investment Company as the LA GRANDE DUCHESSE (1899). Renamed CITY OF SAVANNAH (1901 – Ocean Steamship Co).

CAROLINA (1975)
13489 grt; 2000 psrs
637' x 73' x 29'4" depth (193 x 22 x 8.9 m)
2 x Westinghouse DRG turbine engines via single screw.
Passenger ship owned by New Puerto Rico Marit Shipping Authority.
Built by Kaiser Corporation, Richmond, California, for the US Maritime Commission and US Navy as the Class C4-S-A1 troop transport GENERAL W.F. HASE, USS (AP-146) (1944). Reclassified as the GENERAL W.F. HASE, USAT (1947 – US Army). Reclassified as the GENERAL W.F. HASE, USNS (T-AP-146) (1950 – US Navy). Laid up in Suisin Bay, Benecia, California from 1960 to 1969 (US Maritime Commission). Renamed TRANSIDAHO (1969 – Hudson Waterways Corporation, New York). Underwent a conversion by the addition of cargo holds in 1970.

CAROLINE (1908) See JACQUES CARTIER (1929)

CARONI (1975)
11538 grt; 3000 psrs
523' x 71' x 33' (158.5 x 21.5 x 10 m)
Westinghouse geared turbine engine via single screw.
Broken up for scrap in 1979 in Kaohsiung. Ex-Cia An Venezolana de Navegacion, Caracas.
Built by Kaiser Corporation, Richmond, California, for the US Navy as the Class C4-S-A1 troop transport GENERAL TASKER H. BLISS (1941). Renamed GENERAL T. H. BLISS (APA-131) (1944) and SEAMAR (1964 – Bethlehem Steel Corporation.

CARONIA (1905) See TAISEIYO MARU (1932)

CARONIA (1948) See CARIBIA (1968)

CARONIA (1999)
24492 grt; 717 psrs
627' x 90' x 27' (191.1 x 24.4 x 8.2 m)
2 x 9-cylinder Clark-Sulzer diesel engines via twin screw.

Ice-strengthened cruise ship owned and operated by Cunard Line.
Built by Swan Hunter's Neptune Yards at Low Walker, Newcastle, for the Norwegian American Line as the VISTAFJORD (1973) at a cost of US$27,000,000.

CAROUSEL (1995)
23149 grt; 1194 psrs
644' x 80' x 22' (195.2 x 24.2 x 6.7 m)
4 x 9-cylinder Wartsila-Sulzer diesel engines via twin screw.
Cruise ship for Airtours, UK, following its purchase of the ship from Royal Caribbean Lines for US$55,000,000.

Built as the NORDIC PRINCE (1972) by Wartsila-Helsinki for Royal Caribbean Cruise Lines.

CARPATHIA (1902)
13603 grt; 1704 psrs
558' x 66' x 37'4" depth (170.1 x 20 x 11.3 m)
2 x 4-cylinder Wallsend Slipway quadruple expansion engines via twin screw.
Sank at 12.40am on 17 July 1918 after three torpedoes fired from the German U-55 tore into her 170 miles (283 km) west of Bishop Rock, Scilly Isles. Five lives were lost and all other passengers and crew were rescued by HMS SNOWDROP. Recent expeditions have found her to be in an upright position at a depth of 600' (182 m), but she has settled south of the Scilly Isles.
Built by Swan Hunter & Wigham Richardson Ltd, Newcastle, for the Cunard Steamship Co.

CARRILLO (1911)
5012 grt; 103 psrs
379' x 50' x 25' (114.8 x 15.2 x 7.6 m)
Triple expansion engine via single screw.
Broken up for scrap in Baltimore in 1948.
Laid down by Workman, Clark & Co, Belfast, for United Fruit Steamship Co as LA SENORA (1911) and completed as CARRILLO.

CARTAGO (1908) See CARTAGO (1938)

CARTAGO (1938)
4937 grt; 103 psrs
379' x 50' x 25' (114.8 x 15.2 x 7.6 m)
Triple expansion engine via single screw.
Broken up for scrap in Tampa, Florida, in 1949. Ex-United Fruit Steamship Co.
Built by Workman, Clarke & Co Ltd, Belfast, for United Fruit Steamship Co as the CARTAGO (1908). Renamed GENERAL LEE (1932 – States Steamship Co, Portland, Oregon).

CARTER (1968) See MOBY RIDER (1998)

CARTHAGE (1931) See CARTHAGE MARU (1961)

CARTHAGE (1999)
31647 grt; 2208 psrs
594' x 91' x 21'6" (180 x 27.5 x 6.5 m)
4 x 12-cylinder Sulzer diesel engines via twin screw.
Passenger-cargo ship built by Fosen AS, Fevaag, for Cotunav under charter from the Tunisian government.

CARTHAGE MARU (1961)
14280 grt; 394 psrs
545' x 71' x 26' (166.1 x 21.6 x 7.9 m)
6 x Parsons SRG turbine engines via twin screw.
Broken up for scrap by Mitsui Bussan KKK in Osaka in 1961.
Laid down by Alexander Stephen & Sons, Glasgow for the P&O Line as the CANTON (1930) and completed as CARTHAGE (1931).

CARVALHO ARAUJO (1930)
4469 grt; 354 psrs
346' x 50' x 26'6" (104.8 x 15.2 x 8.1 m)
2 x 3-cylinder Kincaid triple expansion engines via twin screw.
Built by Cantieri Navale Triestino, Monfalcone, for Empresa Insulana de Navegacao, Portugal, as a passenger-cargo ship.

CASERTA (1914) See VENEZUELA (1923)

CASSANDRA (1906) See DRACHENSTEIN (1930)

CASSEL (1901) See MARECHAL GALLIENI (1919)

CASSIOPEIA (1972) See SUPERFERRY (1991)

CASSIUS (1898) See SUMNER (1900)

CASTALIA (1906) See URANIA II (1950)

CASTALIA (1974) See ENCHANTED SUN (1999)

CASTELBIANCO (1947) See BEGONA (1957)

CASTEL BIANCO (1952) See BEGONA (1957)

CASTEL FELICE (1952)
12478 grt; 1405 psrs
493' x 64' x 25' (150.3 x 19.5 x 7.6 m)
SRG turbine engines via twin screw.
Broken up for scrap at Kaohsiung in 1970. Ex-Sitmar Line.
Built by Alexander Stephen & Sons, Glasgow, for the British India Line as the KENYA (1930). Renamed HYDRA (1940 – British India Line), KEREN, HMS (1940 – British Ministry of Transport), KEREN (1949 – British Ministry of Transport), KENYA (1949 – Sitmar Line), KEREN (1949 – Sitmar Line), KENYA (1949 – Sitmar Line), FAIRSTONE (1950 – Sitmar Line), KENYA (1950 – Sitmar Line) and KEREN (1951 – Sitmar Line).

CASTELFORTE (1949) See PHILIPPINE TOURIST (1978)

CASTEL FORTE (1952) See PHILIPPINE TOURIST (1978)

CASTELVERDE (1947) See MONTSERRAT (1957)

CASTEL VERDE (1950) See MONTSERRAT (1957)

CASTILLA (1927)
4087 grt; 58 psrs
342' x 48' x 28' (103.6 x 14.5 x 8.5 m)
Workman, Clark 4-cylinder triple expansion engine via single screw.
Built by Workman, Clark & Co, Belfast, for United Fruit Steamship Co

CATHAY (1925)
15104 grt; 306 psrs
545' x 70' x 31' (166.1 x 21.3 x 9.4 m)
2 x quadruple expansion engines via twin screw.
Sank quickly on 11 November 1942 with the loss of one life during a severe aircraft bombing attack off Bougie, Algeria. One bomb fell into her ammunition room and the resulting explosion and fire blew her stern completely off.
Built by Barclay, Curle & Co Ltd, Glasgow, for the P&O Line.

CATHAY (1961) See SHANGHAI (1978)

CATLIN, USS (AP-19) (1940) See GEORGE WASHINGTON (1941)

CATUSHA (1957)
6907 grt; 60 psrs
425' x 54' x 30'3" depth (128.8 x 16.4 x 9.2 m)
2 x A Stephen & Sons 3-cylinder triple expansion engines via twin screw.
Broken up for scrap in Hong Kong in 1958. Ex-Cia Navigation Lavena Ltd, Panama.
Built by Alex Stephen & Son, Glasgow, for Elders & Fyffes as the CAVINA (1924).

CAUCA (1917) See BAYANO (1918)

CAVINA (1915)
6539 grt; 60 psrs
425' x 54' x 30' (128.8 x 16.4 x 9.1 m)

2 x 3-cylinder Workman, Clark triple expansion engines via twin screw.
Sank 45 miles (75 km) off Fastnet, Ireland, on 1 June 1917 after being torpedoed by the German U-88.
Built by Workman, Clarke & Co Ltd, Belfast, for Elders & Fyffes.

CAVINA (1924) See CATUSHA (1957)

CAVOUR (1911)
5018 grt; 1625 psrs
381' x 48' x 25'7" depth (116.2 x 14.7 x 7.8 m)
Esercizio Bacini 6-cylinder triple expansion engines via twin screw.
Owned by Ligure Brasiliana, Genoa, she sank on 12 December 1917 after a collision with the Italian auxiliary cruiser CAPRERA near Armevilla.
Built by Soc Esercizio Bacini, Riva Tregoso, for Lloyd Italiano as the passenger liner FLORIDA (1905).

CAWDOR CASTLE (1902)
6243 grt; 540 psrs
415' x 51' x 28' (125.8 x 15.5 x 8.5 m)
Barclay Curle 6-cylinder triple expansion engines via twin screw.
Abandoned as a total constructive loss after running aground in 1926 at Conception Bay, South West Africa.
Built by Barclay, Curle & Co Ltd, Glasgow, for the Union-Castle Mail Steamship Co Ltd.

CAYRU (1940)
5301 grt; 74 psrs
401' x 54' x 32' depth (121.5 x 16.4 x 9.7 m)
Turbine engine via single screw.
Owned by Lloyd Brasileiro, she sank on 8 March 1942 off Long Island, New York, after being torpedoed by the German U-94.
Built by American International Shipbuilding Corporation, Hog Island, Pennsylvania, for the US Shipping Board as the passenger-cargo ship CHICKASAW (1919). Renamed SCANMAIL (1932 – American Scantic Line).

c. COLUMBUS (1997)
14903 grt; 418 psrs
475' x 71' x 17' (145 x 21.5 x 5.1 m)
4 x 6-cylinder Wartsila diesel engines via twin screw.

A purpose-built cruise ship for Great Lakes cruising constructed by MTW Schiffswerft, Wismar, for Conti 1 Kreuzfahrt GmbH & Co, KG, as the COLUMBUS (1997) at a cost of US$70,000,000. The shipyard then chartered her out to HAPAG-Lloyd.

CEDRIC (1903)
20904 grt; 2857 psrs
681' x 75' x 44' depth (206.4 x 22.7 x 13.3 m)
Harland & Wolff 8-cylinder quadruple expansion engines via twin screw.
Broken up for scrap by TW Ward Ltd at Inverkeithing in 1932 for £22,000.
Built by Harland & Wolff Ltd, Belfast, for the White Star Line

CEFALONIAN SKY (1991) See EUROFAST (2000)

CEIJHUN (1914) See DJEYHUN (1914)

CELEBRATION (1987)
47262 grt; 1896 psrs
733' x 94' x 25'6" (222.1 x 28.5 x 7.8 m)
2 x 7-cylinder Sulzer diesel engines via twin screw.

Cruise ship for Carnival Cruise Lines Inc.
Built by Kockums, Malmo, at a cost of US$131,000,000.

CELT (1900) See WALMER CASTLE (1902)

CELTIC (1901)
21035 grt; 2857 psrs
697' x 75' x 44' depth (212.1 x 22.7 x 13.3 m)
2 x Harland & Wolff 8-cylinder quadruple expansion engines via twin screw.
Broken up where she lay on the rocks of Roches Point, Cobh Harbour, Ireland, after being driven on to them on 10 December 1928 by a violent storm (with gales at 70 mph (116 kmph). The rocks tore a gaping hole in her side and she settled in shallow water. All lives were saved, including 25 passengers who had been rescued from the sinking VESTRIS by the CELTIC four weeks earlier.
Built by Harland & Wolff Ltd, Belfast, for the White Star Line.

CELTIC PRIDE (1987) See ROGALIN (1992)

CELTIC PRIDE (1991) See ROGALIN (1992)

CELTIC PRIDE II (1990) See IONIAN SUN (1994)

CENPAC ROUNDER (1972)
3179 grt; 306 psrs
300' x 52' x 15'6" (90.8 x 15.8 x 4.7 m)
2 x 10-cylinder Fairbanks-Morse diesel engines via single screw.
Owned by Nauru Corporation Local Government Council (Victoria, Australia) Inc.
Built by Port Weller Drydocks Ltd, St Catherines, Ontario, for Furness Withy & Co Ltd as the FEDERAL PALM (1961).

CENTAUR (1924)
3066 grt
316' x 48' x 21'6" (95.8 x 14.5 x 6.5 m)
B+W 6-cylinder diesel engine via single screw.
Sank in three minutes on 13 May 1943 in 94 fathoms in the Pacific Ocean after being hit by a torpedo abaft of hatch No 2 on the port side, while running fully illuminated as a hospital ship 40 miles (66 km) east of Brisbane, near Cape Moreton. The attack was from the Japanese submarine I-177 commanded by Y Nakagawa and cost 268 lives. The I-177 was herself sunk by the USS SAMUEL S. MILES on 3 October 1944.
Built by Scotts Shipbuilding & Engineering Co Ltd, Greenock, for A Holt & Co.

CENTAUR (1964) See HAI DA (1986)

CENTAURO (1951)
8674 grt; 176 psrs
490' x 62' x 32' depth (148.5 x 18.8 x 9.7 m)
Quadruple expansion engines via single screw.
Broken up for scrap at Savona in 1955 after running aground in Bermuda. Ex-Fratelli Grimaldi.
Laid down by Earles Shipyards, Hull, for the Wilson Line as the COLORADO (1923), but completed for Ellerman Lines as the CITY OF HONG KONG (1924) at a cost of £2,500,000.

CENTENNIAL STATE (1921) See PRESIDENT GRANT (1940)

CENTRAL NO. 1 (1971) See TASSILI (1973)

CENTRAL NO. 2 (1971) See CANDIA (1972)

CENTRAL NO. 3 (1971) See EL-DJAZAIR (1973)

CENTRAL NO. 5 (1971) See RETHIMNON (1972)

CENTRAL NO. 6 (1971) See TAMPOMAS II (1980)

CENTURION, HMS (1914) See PRYGONA (1921)

CENTURY (1995)
70666 grt; 1750 psrs
815' x 105' x 25' (247 x 31.8 x 7.6 m)
4 x 9-cylinder MAN-B+W diesel engines via twin screw.

Cruise ship for Celebrity Cruises (subsidiary of Royal Caribbean Cruise Lines).
Built by Jos L Meyer Yards, Papenburg, for the Chandris Group at a cost of US$318,000,000.

CEPHALONIA (1882) See HAI LOR (1900)

CEPHEE (1922)
9680 grt
492' x 59' x 35' depth (149.1 x 17.9 x 10.6 m)
Bremer Vulcan 6-cylinder triple expansion engines via twin screw.
Broken up for scrap in Blyth in 1936.
Built by Bremer Vulcan, Vegesack, for Hamburg-South America Line as the BUENOS AIRES (1912).

CERAMIC (1913)
18713 grt; 340 psrs
679' x 69' x 35' (205.8 x 21 x 10.7 m)
2 x 4-cylinder triple expansion engines via triple screw.
Sank within minutes of being torpedoed by the German U-515 at dawn on 6 December 1942, west of the Azores, with the loss of 655 lives.
Built by Harland & Wolff Ltd, Belfast, for the White Star Line.

CERAMIC (1948)
15896 grt; 85 psrs
564' x 72' x 30' (171.9 x 21.9 x 9.1 m)
6 x DRG turbine engines via twin screw.
Broken up for scrap by Boel & Fils in Tamise in 1972.
Built by Cammell Laird & Co, Birkenhead, for Shaw Savill Albion.

CERDA (1966) See KOBENHAVN (1966)

CERDIC FERRY (1961) See ORESTES (1999)

CERDIC FERRY (1986) See EUROPEAN FREEWAY (1994)

CESAREA (1935) See ARNO (1938)

CESAREE (1962)
8799 grt; 495 psrs
449' x 58' x 24' (136.1 x 17.6 x 7.3 m)
6 x Parsons SRG turbine engines via twin screw.
Owned by Cie Francaise de Navigation, Paris.
Built by Forges et Chantiers de la Mediterranee, La Seyne, for Cie de Navigation Paquet as the DJENNE (1931).

CESME STERN (1996)

5739 grt; 600 psrs
138 cars
326' x 58' x 14'6" (98.8 x 17.7 x 4.4 m)
2 x 12-cylinder Lindholmens-Pielstick diesel engines via twin screw.

Owned by Lucky Shipping SA.
Built by Kaldnes MV, Tronsberg, for Thoresen Ferries as the VIKING II (1964). Renamed EARL WILLIAM (1977 – Sealink UK), WILLIAM (1992 – Sealink UK), PEARL WILLIAM (1992 – Adonis Shipping Co Ltd, Valetta) and MAR. JULIA (1996 – P & L Ferries Shipping Co SA).

C. F. TIETGEN (1906) See DWINSK (1913)

CHAGRES (1912)

5288 grt; 50 psrs
400' x 51' x 29'6" depth (121.2 x 15.5 x 9 m)
A Stephen & Sons 6-cylinder triple expansion engines via twin screw.
Sank on 10 March 1918, with the loss of one life, after being torpedoed by the German U-74 62 miles (103 km) off Cape Drepano, Crete.
Built by Alex Stephens & Sons, Glasgow, for Elders & Fyffes as a passenger-cargo ship.

CHALEUR (1913)

4745 grt; 178 psrs
401' x 47' x 26'6" (121.5 x 14.2 x 8.1 m)
Triple expansion engines via twin screw.
Broken up for scrap in Holland in 1927. Ex-Royal Mail Line.
Built by Harland & Wolff Ltd, Belfast, for Union Steamship Co as the passenger-cargo ship GAUL (1893). Renamed SABUR (1906 – Royal Mail Line) and CARMARTHENSHIRE (1908 – Shire Line).

CHAMBORD (1923)

7818 grt; 222 psrs
441' x 52' x 29'8" depth (133.6 x 15.8 x 9 m)
Blohm & Voss 6-cylinder triple expansion engines via twin screw.
Broken up for scrap in 1932. Ex-Messageries Maritimes.
Built by Blohm & Voss, Hamburg, for Hamburg Sud America Line as the CAP ORTEGAL (1903).

CHAMPAGNE (1915)

5303 grt; 135 psrs
421' x 49' x 27' (127.6 x 14.8 x 8.2 m)
Triple expansion engines via twin screw.
Sank in 1917 after being torpedoed in the Irish Sea as a French armed merchant cruiser.
Built by Harland & Wolff Ltd, Belfast, for Pacific Steam Navigation Co as the OROPESA (1895).

CHAMPLAIN (1932)

28124 grt; 800 psrs
641' x 83' x 46' depth (194.2 x 25.2 x 14 m)
2 x 3 Penhoet-Parsons SRG turbine engines via twin screw.
Broken up for scrap in 1946 on the spot off La Pallice, France, where she had sunk within 15 minutes of striking a magnetic mine and losing 330 lives on 17 June 1940. She was finally broken up in 1963 where she lay.
Built by Chantiers de l'Atlantique, St Nazaire, for the French Line.

CHAMPOLLION (1925)

13619 grt; 499 psrs
495' x 63' x 40'6" depth (150 x 19.1 x 12.3 m)
2 x 6-cylinder triple expansion engines via twin screw.

Broken up in Lebanon on the Elchat Elmallhoun Reef three miles south of Beirut and only 200 yards (60 m) from shore where she had gone aground on 21 December 1952, with the loss of 15 lives. She broke in half two days later. Subsequent evidence at a maritime court revealed that the officers on the bridge had picked up on the Haede Airport (Beirut) beacon, during a bad storm, mistaking it for the Ras Beirut lighthouse.
Built by Soc Provencal de Constructions Navales, La Ciotat, for Messageries Maritimes.

CHAMPS ELYSEE (1984) See SEAFRANCE MANET (1996)

CHAMS (1993) See IONIAN SUN (1994)

CHANCELLOR (1891) See PALLANZA (1901)

CHANEA (1965) See SIRIUS (1972)

CHANG BENG (1978)

5926 grt; 850 psrs
455' x 58' x 19'8" (138 x 17.6 x 6 m)
2 x 6-cylinder Hudong diesel engines via twin screw.
Owned by China PR Ocean Shipping Co, Beijing.
Built by Hudong Shipyard, Shanghai, as a passenger-cargo ship.

CHANG CHENG (1974)

5926 grt; 850 psrs
455' x 58' x 19'8" (138 x 17.6 x 6 m)
2 x 6-cylinder Hudong diesel engines via twin screw.
Owned by China PR Ocean Shipping Co, Beijing.
Built by Hudong Shipyard, Shanghai, as a passenger-cargo ship.

CHANGCHOW (1951) See RESURGENT (1953)

CHANG GENG (1979)

5926 grt; 850 psrs
455' x 58' x 19'8" (138 x 17.6 x 6 m)
2 x 6-cylinder Hudong diesel engines via twin screw.
Owned by China PR Ocean Shipping Co, Beijing.
Built by Hudong Shipyard, Shanghai, as a passenger-cargo ship.

CHANG HE (1974)

5926 grt; 850 psrs
455' x 58' x 19'8" (138 x 17.6 x 6 m)
2 x 6-cylinder Hudong diesel engines via twin screw.
Owned by China PR Ocean Shipping Co, Beijing.
Built by Hudong Shipyard, Shanghai, as a passenger-cargo ship.

CHANG HU (1974)

5926 grt; 850 psrs
455' x 58' x 19'8" (138 x 17.6 x 6 m)
2 x 6-cylinder Hudong diesel engines via twin screw.
Owned by China PR Ocean Shipping Co Beijing.
Built by Hudong Shipyard, Shanghai, as a passenger-cargo ship.

CHANG JIN (1974)

5926 grt; 850 psrs
455' x 58' x 19'8" (138 x 17.6 x 6 m)
2 x 6-cylinder Hudong diesel engines via twin screw.
Owned by China PR Ocean Shipping Co, Beijing.
Built by Hudong Shipyard, Shanghai, as a passenger-cargo ship.

CHANG KEN (1974)

5926 grt; 850 psrs
455' x 58' x 19'8" (138 x 17.6 x 6 m)
2 x 6-cylinder Hudong diesel engines via twin screw.
Owned by China PR Ocean Shipping Co, Beijing.
Built by Hudong Shipyard, Shanghai, as a passenger-cargo ship.

CHANG LI (1974)

5926 grt; 850 psrs
455' x 58' x 19'8" (138 x 17.6 x 6 m)
2 x 6-cylinder Hudong diesel engines via twin screw.
Broken up for scrap in 1996. Ex-China PR Ocean Shipping Co, Beijing.
Built by Hudong Shipyard, Shanghai, as a passenger-cargo ship.

CHANGSHA (1949) See KOTA PANJANG (1969)

CHANG SHAN (1973)
5926 grt; 850 psrs
455' x 58' x 19'8" (138 x 17.6 x 6 m)
2 x 6-cylinder Hudong diesel engines via twin screw.
Broken up in 1996. Ex-China PR Ocean Shipping Co, Beijing.
Built by Hudong Shipyard, Shanghai, as a passsenger-cargo ship.

CHANG SHEN (1974)
5926 grt; 850 psrs
455' x 58' x 19'8" (138 x 17.6 x 6 m)
2 x 6-cylinder Hudong diesel engines via twin screw.
Owned by China PR Ocean Shipping Co, Beijing.
Built by Hudong Shipyard, Shanghai, as a passenger-cargo ship.

CHANG SHENG (1989) See WANG FU (1993)

CHANGTE (1925)
4324 grt; 191 psrs
352' x 48' x 23'6" (106.7 x 14.6 x 7.2 m)
Triple expansion engine via single screw.
Broken up for scrap in Hong Kong in 1961.
Built by the Hong Kong & Whampoa Dockyard Co for the Australian-Oriental Line.

CHANGUINOLA (1914)
5978 grt; 72 psrs
411' x 51' x 26' (124.5 x 15.5 x 7.9 m)
Wallsend Slipway 6-cylinder triple expansion engine via twin screw.
Broken up in 1933. Ex-Elders & Fyffes.
Built by Swan Hunter Shipyards, Newcastle, for the Hamburg-America Line as the passenger-cargo ship CARL SCHURZ (1912). Renamed KARL SHURZ (1913 – Hamburg American Line).

CHANG XIU (1974)
5926 grt; 850 psrs
455' x 58' x 19'8" (138 x 17.6 x 6 m)
2 x 6-cylinder Hudong diesel engines via twin screw.
Owned by China PR Ocean Shipping Co, Beijing.
Built by Hudong Shipyard, Shanghai, as a passenger-cargo ship.

CHANG ZHENG (1974)
5926 grt; 850 psrs
455' x 58' x 19'8" (138 x 17.6 x 6 m)
2 x 6-cylinder Hudong diesel engines via twin screw.
Total constructive loss in May 1994. Ex-China PR Ocean Shipping Co, Beijing.
Built by Hudong Shipyard, Shanghai, as a passenger-cargo ship.

CHANIA (1965) See SIRIUS (1971)

CHANIA (1985) See APTERA (1987)

CHANNEL ENTENTE (1989) See MOBY LOVE II (1998)

CHANNEL SEAWAY (1982) See SEAFRANCE CEZANNE (1996)

CHANTILLY (1924)
9986 grt; 450 psrs
479' x 59' x 27' (145.2 x 17.9 x 8.2 m)
6 x engines via twin screw.
Broken up for scrap at Marseilles in 1952.
Built by Ateliers et Chantiers de la Loire, St Nazaire, for Messageries Maritimes as the passenger-cargo ship KERGUELEN (1922).

CHANTILLY (1965) See AL SALAM 93 (1996)

CHAOUIA (1911)
4249 grt; 98 psrs
382' x 45' x 27'6" (120.7 x 13.7 x 8.9 m)
4-cylinder Koninklijke Maatschappij quadruple expansion engines via single screw.

Owned by Cie de Navigation Marocaine et Armenienne, Marseilles, she sank on 15 January 1919 after hitting a mine in the Strait of Messina.
Built by Koninklijke Maatschappij, Vlissingen, for the Nederlands Steamship Co as the KONINGIN WILHELMINA (1896).

CHARGER, USS (CVE-30) (1942) See FAIRSEA (1949)

CHARLES, USS (1916) See HARVARD (1920).

CHARLES A. STAFFORD (1944)
7582 grt; 304 psrs
423' x 60' x 32' depth (128.2 x 18.2 x 9.7 m)
4 x William Cramp SRG turbine engines via twin screw.
Broken up for scrap at Baltimore in 1957.
Ex-US War Shipping Administration.
Laid down by W Cramp & Sons Shipbuilding & Engineering Co, Philadelphia, Pennsylvania, for the New York & Cuba Mail Steamship Co as the ORIENTE (1917), but completed as the SIBONEY (1918).

CHARLES CARROLL, USS (AP-58) (1942)
7997 grt; 67 psrs
492' x 66' x 32' depth (149.1 x 20 x 9.7 m)
General Electric geared turbine engines via twin screw.
Broken up for scrap at Tacoma, Washington, in 1977. Ex-US Navy.
Built by Bethlehem Steel Corporation, Sparrow's Point, for the Mississippi Shipping Co as the passenger-cargo ship DELURUGUAY (1942).

CHARLES PLUMIER (1938) See PLEIAS (1964).

CHARLES PLUMIER (1948) See PLEIAS (1964)

CHARLES TELLIER (1952) See LE HAVRE ABETO (1967)

CHARLESTON (1968)
11389 grt; 550 psrs
523' x 72' x 24' (158.5 x 21.8 x 7.3 m)
Geared turbine engine via single screw.
Owned by Sea Land Services Inc, she was broken up for scrap as a container ship in the USA after going aground off Block Island on 4 April 1980.
Built by Kaiser Corporation, Vancouver, for the US Shipping Administration as the Class C4-S-A3 troop transport MARINE SHARK (1945). She operated as a migrant ship after World War One.

CHARLESVILLE (1951) See GEORG BUCHNER (1967)

CHARLOTTE (1943)
4897 grt; 1280 psrs
385' x 50' (117.3 x 15.2 m)
3-cylinder triple expansion engine via single screw.
Owned by a German company, she sank on 11 January 1945 after an Allied bombing attack off Egersund, Norway.
Built by Russell & Co, Glasgow, for Unione Austriaca as the passenger liner ATLANTA (1908).

CHARLTON MONARCH (1948)
6892 grt; 377 psrs
366' x 57' x 16'6" (110.9 x 17.3 x 5 m)
Geared turbine engines via twin screw.
Broken up for scrap in Newport, Wales, in 1951. Ex-Charlton Steam Shipping Co.
Built by Cammell Laird & Company, Birkenhead, for the Canadian National Steamship Co as the PRINCE DAVID (1930).

CHARLTON SOVEREIGN (1948) See LUCANIA (1951)

CHARLTON STAR (1950) See MARISTRELLA (1958)

CHARM M (1995) See MILLENNIUM EXPRESS II (2000)

CHARON (1936) See SENG KONG No. 1 (1964)

CHARTRES (1974) See EXPRESS SANTORINI (1993)

CHATHAM (1926)

5649 grt; 317 psrs
350' x 52' x 36' depth (106.1 x 15.8 x 10.9 m)
Newport News 4-cylinder triple expansion engines via single screw.
Sank, with 23 lives lost, on 28 August 1942 after being hit by a torpedo from the German U-517 in the Belle Isle Strait, Canada.
Built by Newport News Shipbuilding Co, Newport News, Virginia, for the Merchant & Miners Transportation Co.

CHATTANOOGA (1923) See AMERICAN NAVIGATOR (1941)

CHAUDIERE (1914)

4100 grt; 160 psrs
370' x 46' x 22'8" (112.1 x 13.9 x 6.9 m)
Triple expansion engines via twin screw.
Lost during World War One. Ex-Elder Dempster Lines.
Built by Sir Raylton Dixon Shipbuilding, Middlesbrough, for the British & African Steam Navigation Co as the PHILIPPEVILLE (1899). Renamed MANDINGO (1906 – African Steamship Co).

CHEFOO (1931) See CORFU MARU (1961)

CHEMNITZ (1902)

7542 grt; 2064 psrs
428' x 54' x 39'7" depth (130.5 x 16.6 x 12 m)
Tecklenborg 6-cylinder triple expansion engines via twin screw.
Broken up for scrap in Holland in 1923 after the ship was surrendered by Germany at the conclusion of World War One.
Built by JC Tecklenborg, Geestemunde, for North German Lloyd.

CHENONCEAUX (1925)

14825 grt; 317 psrs
543' x 65' x 41' depth (164.5 x 19.7 x 12.4 m)
6-cylinder triple expansion engines via twin screw.
Broken up for scrap in 1948 at Toulon after raising her from the seabed in Marseilles harbour where she had been scuttled by the Germans in August 1944. Ex-Messageries Maritimes.
Built by Chantiers et Ateliers de la Gironde, Bordeaux, for Messageries Maritimes as the ARAMIS (1923).

CHEPSTOW CASTLE (1915)

7494 grt; 100 psrs
426' x 56' x 28'3" depth (129.1 x 17 x 8.6 m)
North East Marine Engineering 4-cylinder quadruple expansion engines via single screw.
Broken up for scrap in 1933 after stranding on Toward Point in April 1932. Ex-Union-Castle Mail Steamship Co Ltd.
Built by Short Bros Ltd, Sunderland, for the Nitrate Producers Steamship Co Ltd as the ANGLO BRAZILIAN (1913).

CHEROKEE (1925)

5896 grt; 446 psrs
387' x 54' x 20' (122.1 x 16.4 x 6 m)
2 x Newport News SRG turbine engines via single screw.
Sank on 15 June 1942 after being torpedoed by the German U-87 off Cape Cod, Massachusetts, with the loss of 85 lives.
Built by Newport News Shipbuilding, Newport News, Virginia, for the Clyde Steamship Co.

CHESHIRE (1889) See SEANG CHOON (1911)

CHESHIRE (1927)

10623 grt; 650 psrs
502' x 60' x 30' (153 x 18.3 x 9.1 m)
2 x 8-cylinder Sulzer diesel engines via twin screw.
Broken up for scrap by John Cashmore Ltd in Newport, Wales, in 1957.
Built by Fairfield Shipbuilding & Engineering Co Ltd, Glasgow, for the Bibby Line.

CHESTER (1893) See NEAPOLITANO (1905)

CHICAGO (1898) See ETONIAN (1904)

CHICAGO (1906)

17000 grt
Name formally registered by Hamburg-America Line for a passenger liner and firm order placed upon AG Vulcan, Stettin, but cancelled prior to keel being laid.

CHICAGO (1908) See GUADELOUPE (1928)

CHICAGO (1968) See SAN JUAN (1975)

CHICAGO MARU (1910)

5863 grt
420' x 50' x 25'6" (127.3 x 15.2 x 7.8 m)
Kawasaki Dockyard 6-cylinder triple expansion engines via twin screw.
Sank on 15 October 1943 after being torpedoed by the USS TULLIBEE (SS-284) in the Formosa Straits.
Built by Kawasaki Dockyard for OSK, Japan.

CHI-CHEMAUN (1974)

6991 grt; 613 psrs
173 cars
368' x 63' x 13'6" (111.4 x 19 x 4.1 m)
2 x 6-cylinder Ruston diesel engines via twin screw.
Passenger-car ferry owned by Ontario Northland Transportation Commission and operated by Owen Sound Transportation Co Ltd, Owen Sound.
Built by Collingwood Shipyard, Collingwood, Ontario.

CHICHIBU MARU (1930) See KAMAKURA MARU (1939)

CHICKASAW (1919) See CAYRU (1940)

CHIDAMBARAM (1973)

17226 grt; 430 psrs
571' x 79' x 26' (174 x 24 x 7.9 m)
2 x 9-cylinder Sulzer diesel engines via twin screw.
Passenger-cargo ship owned by the Shipping Corporation of India, Mumbai, she was broken up for scrap in Mumbai in 1986 after limping back to port in two days with 40 bodies of passengers and crew following a galley fire. This had rapidly spread throughout the ship on 12 February 1985, 300 miles (500 km) east of Tamil Nadu.
Laid down by Ateliers et Chantiers de Dunquerque et Bordeaux, Dunkirk, for Messageries Maritimes as the AUSTRALIEN (1965) but completed as the PASTEUR (1966).

CHIEF SKIDEGATE (1930) See TAIHOKU MARU (1934)

CHIGNECTO (1913)

4747 grt; 178 psrs
401' x 47' x 26'9" depth (121.5 x 14.2 x 8.2 m)
Triple expansion engines via twin screw.
Broken up in Holland for scrap in 1927. Ex-Royal Mail Lines.
Built by Harland & Wolff Ltd, Belfast, for the Union Steamship Co as the GREEK (1893). Renamed SEGURA (1906 – Royal Mail Lines) and PEMBROKESHIRE (1908 – Shire Line).

CHINA (1899) See CHINA (1915)

CHINA (1915)

5060 grt; 691 psrs
440' x 48' x 32'8" depth (133.3 x 14.5 x 9.9 m)
Fairfield 3-cylinder triple expansion engines via single screw.
Broken up for scrap in 1925. Ex-China Mail Steamship Co.
Built by Fairfield Shipbuilding & Engineering Co Ltd, Glasgow, for the Pacific Mail Line as the CHINA (1889). She was registered as the JOHN BARNESON (1915) for sale before reverting to CHINA (1915).

CHINA SEA DISCOVERY (2000)

19887 grt; 925 psrs
608v x 80' x 29' (185.3 x 24.2 x 8.7 m)
4 x Pametrada DRG turbine engines via twin screw.
Delivered in November 2000 to Emerald Cruises (a consortium comprised of Great Canadian Casinos, Allegiance Capital Corporation, Dallas, and Lake City Casinos), and to be managed by V-ships, Monaco, after the ship's

purchase for US$15,500,000 from P&O Holidays, Sydney.
Built by John Brown & Co Ltd, Clydebank, for the Cunard Line as the CARINTHIA (1956). Renamed FAIRLAND (1968 – Sitmar Line), FAIRSEA (1969 – Sitmar Line), REGENT ISLE (1995 – Regency Cruises) and FAIR PRINCESS (1997 – P&O Holidays, Sydney).

CHINDWIN (1910) See ROD-EL-FARAG (1938)

CHINOOK (1904)
5658 grt; 80 psrs
445' x 49' (135.6 x 15 m)
6-cylinder triple expansion engines via twin screw.
Broken up for scrap in 1946 as a dredger converted for the US Army in 1942.
Built by Harland & Wolff Ltd, Belfast, for the African Steamship Co as the MOHAWK (1892). Renamed GRANT (1898 – US Army).

CHINOOK (1947) See MUSKEGON CLIPPER (1989)

CHINOOK II (1955) See SECHELT QUEEN (1963)

CHIRIKOF (1928) See RADNIK (1947)

CHIRIQUI (1932) See BLEXEN (1957)

CHIRIQUI (1946) See BLEXEN (1957)

CHITRAL (1925)
15248 grt; 334 psrs
548' x 70' x 31' (167 x 21.3 x 9.4 m)
2 x quadruple expansion engines via twin screw.
Broken up for scrap by British Iron & Steel Corporation in Dalmuir for £167,500 in 1953.
Built by Alexander Stephen & Sons, Glasgow, for the P&O Line.

CHITRAL (1961)
13821 grt; 240 psrs
558' x 70' x 28' (170.1 x 21.3 x 8.5 m)
2 x Parsons DRG turbine engines via single screw.
Broken up for scrap by Chou's Iron & Steel Co Ltd, in Kaohsiung in 1976. Ex-P&O Group.
Built by Penhoet, St Nazaire, for Cie Maritime Belge as the JADOTVILLE (1956).

CHIYO MARU (1908)
13426 grt; 1150 psrs
575' x 62' x 35'5" depth (175.3 x 18.9 x 10.8 m)
3 x Parsons turbine engines via triple screw.
Abandoned as a total constructive loss after running aground, on 31 March 1916, on rocks near the island of Tam Kan, 20 miles (33 km) south of Hong Kong, and then breaking in two.
Built by Mitsubishi Dockyard, Nagasaki, for Toyo Kisen Kaisho.

CHLOE (1924)
5751 grt; 1120 psrs
431' x 55' x 27" (131.4 x 16.6 x 8.5 m)
Reiherstieg 4-cylinder quadruple expansion engine via single screw.
Foundered on 13 September 1932 near Ushant during her voyage from Cardiff to the breakers' yard in Italy. Ex-ND Ylkiardopulo, Greece.
Built by Reiherstieg, Hamburg, for the Hamburg-America Line as the passenger liner ATHESIA (1899). Renamed UARDA (1902 – Kosmos) and

SALAVERRY (1917 – Peruvian government).

CHONG MING DAO (1998)
18777 grt; 1600 psrs
500 cars
498' x 79' x 20' (151 x 24 x 6 m)
2 x 12-cylinder Pielstick diesel engines via twin screw.

Passenger-car ferry owned and operated by the government of China, Shanghai.
Built by Hyundai Shipbuilding Co, Ulsan, for the Stena Line as the truck-cargo ferry STENA SHIPPER (1977). Renamed NORSKY (1978 – North Sea Ferries), STENA SHIPPER (1980 – Stena Line), MERZARIO IONIA (1980 – Merzario Line), CONSTELLATION ENTERPRISE (1981 – Enterma Shipping Co SA, Piraeus), STENA SHIPPER (1986 – Stena Line), N & T 700 (1987 – Nordstrom & Thulin) and GRAIP (1987 – N & T Gotlands Linjen).

CHORAN MARU (1942)
7392 grt; 680 psrs
460' x 52' x 28' (139.4 x 15.8 x 8.5 m)
6-cylinder triple expansion engines via twin screw.
Broken up for scrap at Dalmuir in 1949. Ex-British government.
Built by Barclay, Curle & Co, Glasgow, for Elder Dempster's Beaver Line as the LAKE CHAMPLAIN (1900). Renamed RUTHENIA (1913 – Canadian Pacific Steamship Co). She was converted during World War One as a replica of the British battleship HMS KING GEORGE V.

CHRISSI AMMOS III (1980) See AGIOS SPIRIDON (1994)

CHRISTIAAN HUYGENS (1928)
16286 grt; 572 psrs
570' x 68' x 36' (172.7 x 20.6 x 12 m)
2 x 10-cylinder Sulzer diesel engines via twin screw.
Abandoned as a total constructive loss after beaching at Zuid Steenbank, in the Schelde estuary near Westkapelle, on 26 August 1945 following her breaking her back shortly after hitting a mine. One life was lost.
Built by the Netherlands Shipbuilding & Drydock Co, Amsterdam, for the Nederland Line.

CHRISTIAN IV (1968) See LOBO MARINHO (1996)

CHRISTIAN IV (1991)
21699 grt; 1600 psrs
530 cars or 60 cars + 60 trailers
506' x 80' x 19' (153.4 x 24.2 x 5.8 m)
4 x 8-cylinder Pielstick diesel engines via twin screw.

Passenger-car-cargo ferry owned by Kosmos and chartered to the Color Line for the UK to Norway service.
Built by AG Weser Schichau Seebeckwerft, Bremerhaven, for the Olau Line as the OLAU BRITANNIA (1982) at a cost of £23,000,000. Renamed

BAYARD (1990 – Fred Olsen Lines).

CHRISTIAN X (1914) See HOI HUNG (1954)

CHRISTOBAL (1948) See TASIKMALAGA (1951)

CHRISTOS (1935)
3571 grt; 300 psrs
348' x 44' x 24'6" (106 x 13.4 x 7.5 m)
Triple expansion engine via single screw.
Broken up for scrap in Savona in 1935. Ex-Ditta Trivero.
Built by Sir James Laing & Sons, Sunderland, for Howard Smith Ltd, Sydney, as the BOMBALA (1904). Renamed ASPASIA (1929 – Mrs M Vardy, Greece).

CHROBRY (1939)
11030 grt; 1154 psrs
506' x 67' x 27' (153.3 x 20.3 x 8.2 m)
2 x 16-cylinder B+W diesel engines via twin screw.
Sank on 15 May 1940, with 12 lives lost, after continued heavy bombing by the Germans the day before, off Narvik, Norway.
Built by Nakskov Skibsvaerft, Nakskov, for the Gdynia America Line.

CHRYSO (1994) See BELLA VISTA (1996)

CHRYSSOVALANDOU (1976) See PANAGIA PAXON (1996)

CHRYSSOVALANDOU II (1978) See EROS (1979)

CHUKOTKA (1946)
7848 grt
419' x 56' x 24' (127 x 17 x 7.3 m)
4 x Blohm & Voss SRG turbine engines via single screw.
World War Two prize to Russia.
Built by Blohm & Voss, Hamburg, for the Woermann Line as the WANGONI (1920).

CHUNG HSING (1946) See BINTANG SUMUDRA (1951)

CHUNGKING (1950) See RETAINER (A329) (1953)

CHUNG MING (1965) See HONG Qi 144 (1977)

CHUSAN (1884) See SHAH NAJAF (1906).

CHUSAN (1950)
24318 grt; 1005 psrs
673' x 85' x 29' (205.1 x 25.9 x 8.8 m)
6 x DRG turbine engines via twin screw.
Broken up for scrap by Chou's Iron & Steel Co Ltd in Kaohsiung in 1973.
Built by Vickers-Armstrong Ltd, Barrow-in-Furness, for the P&O Line at a cost of £3,492,000.

CHUYO (1942)
7150 grt; 283 psrs
562' x 73' x 29' (170.3 x 22.1 x 8.8 m)
2 x Zoelly geared turbine engines via twin screw.
Sank as an aircraft carrier for the Japanese Imperial Navy on 4 December 1943 after being torpedoed the previous day by the USS SAILFISH, 260 miles (433 km) south-west of Yokosuka, Japan.
Built by Mitsubishi Shipbuilding & Engineering Company, Nagasaki, for NYK, Japan as the passenger-cargo ship NITTA MARU (1940).

CICERO, HMS (1944) See AL SUDAN (1947)

CILAOS (1969)
4766 grt; 242 psrs
40 cars
374' x 53' x 18' (113.3 x 16.1 x 5.5 m)
8-cylinder B+W diesel engine via single screw.
Broken up for scrap at Gadani Beach, Karachi, as a car carrier in 1981. Ex-AS Uglands Rederi.
Hull constructed by J.J Thornycroft and ship completed by Akers Mek Verksted, Oslo, for the Fred Olsen Line as the BLENHEIM (1951).

CILICIA (1938) See CILICIA (1980)

CILICIA (1980)
11172 grt; 298 psrs
506' x 66' x 27'6" (153.3 x 20 x 8.4 m)
2 x 4-cylinder Doxford diesel engines via twin screw.
Broken up for scrap in Bilbao in 1980. Ex-Anchor Line.
Built by Fairfield Shipbuilding & Engineering Co, Glasgow, for the Anchor Line as the CILICIA (1938). Renamed JAN BACKX (1966 – college for maritime training of stevedores and ships' agents operated by Stichting Havenbedrijf, Rotterdam).

CINCINNATI (1909) See COVINGTON, USS (1917)

CINDERELLA (1989)
46398 grt; 2500 psrs
480 cars or 60 trailers
627' x 96' x 22' (190 x 29 x 6.6 m)
4 x 12-cylinder Sulzer diesel engines via twin screw.

Passenger-car-cargo ferry owned by the SF Line and chartered to the Viking Line, Mariehamn, for the Sweden to Norway service.
Built by Wartsila-Turku for the SF Line at a cost of US$100,000,000.

CIRCASSIA (1903)
6717 grt; 60 psrs
450' x 55' x 30' (136.4 x 16.7 x 9.9 m)
D & W Henderson 3-cylinder triple expansion engine via single screw.
Broken up for scrap in 1931.
Built by DW Henderson & Co Ltd, Glasgow, for the Anchor Line as a passenger-cargo ship.

CIRCASSIA (1937)
11170 grt; 298 psrs
506' x 66' x 27'6" (153.3 x 20 x 8.4 m)
2 x 4-cylinder Doxford diesel engines via twin screw.
Broken up for scrap at Alicante in 1966.
Built by Fairfield Shipbuilding & Engineering Co, Glasgow, for the Anchor Line.

CIREMAI (1993)
14610 grt; 1737 psrs
483' x 78' x 19'6" (146.5 x 23.7 x 5.9 m)
2 x 6-cylinder MaK diesel engines via twin screw.
Passenger ferry owned by the Indonesian government and operated by PT Pelni, Jakarta.
Built by Jos L Meyer, Papenburg.

CITTA DE CATANIA (1910)
3261 grt
364' x 42' x 19' (110.8 x 12.8 x 5.7 m)
Turbine engines via triple screw.
Sank in August 1943 after being torpedoed by a British submarine off Brindisi.Built by Ansaldo, Armstrong & Co, Sestri Ponte, for Tirrenia Lines.

CITTA DI GENOVA (1921)
8081 grt; 2102 psrs
454' x 56' x 35'8" depth (138.3 x 17 x 10.8 m)
AG Vulcan 6-cylinder triple expansion engines via twin screw.
Broken up for scrap in Italy in 1930. Ex-Navigazione Generale Italiana.
Built by AG Vulcan, Stettin, for North German Lloyd as the GNEISENAU (1903).

CITTA DI MILANO (1897) See ALBANIA (1914).

CITTA DI NAPOLI (1902)
4125 grt; 1166 psrs
420' x 41' x 31' depth (128 x 12.5 x 9.4 m)
Forrester & Co 4-cylinder triple expansion engine via single screw.
Broken up for scrap in Genoa, in 1910. Ex-La Veloce, Genoa.
Built by Harland & Wolff Ltd, Belfast, for the White Star Line as the passenger liner REPUBLIC (1871). Renamed MAASDAM (1889 – Holland America Line) and VITTORIA (1902 – Italian Line).

CITTA DI NAPOLI (1962)
5770 grt; 955 psrs
36 cars
395' x 52' x 18' (119.7 x 15.7 x 5.5 m)
2 x 9-cylinder Fiat diesel engines via twin screw.
Passenger-car ferry operated by Tirrenia on the ItalytoSardinia service.
Built by Naval Meccaniche, Castellammare di Stabia.

CITTA DI NUORO (1962)
5200 grt; 955 psrs
36 cars
395' x 52' x 18' (119.7 x 15.7 x 5.5 m)
2 x 9-cylinder Fiat diesel engines via twin screw.
Passenger-ferry operated by Tirrenia on the Italy to Sardinia service.
Built by Cantieri Riuniti dell'Adriatico, Ancona.

CITTA DI TORINO (1901) See CONSTANTINOPOLIS (1914)

CITTA DI TRIPOLI (1958)
3479 grt; 234 psrs
329' x 44' x 20' (99.7 x 13.3 x 6.1 m)
2 x 6-cylinder Fiat diesel engines via twin screw.
Passenger ferry owned and operated by Tirrenia.
Built by Stabilimento Technico Triestino, Trieste, for Tirrenia as the FILIPPO GRIMANI (1927).

CITTA DI TUNISI (1929)
5474 grt; 446 psrs
411' x 51' x 22' (124.5 x 15.5 x 6.7 m)
Fiat 12-cylinder diesel engines via twin screw.
Passenger ferry in Italy operated by Tirrenia.
Built by Cantieri Navale del Tirreno, Genoa.

CITY OF ANDROS (1976) See ROYAL STAR (1991)

CITY OF ATHENS (1901)
5594 grt; 96 psrs
430' x 50' x 28'5" depth (130.3 x 15.2 x 8.6 m)
Workman, Clark 3-cylinder triple expansion engine via single screw.
Foundered on 10 August 1917 after hitting a mine laid by the German raider WOLF 20 miles (33 km) north of Cape Town.
Built by Workman, Clark & Co Ltd, Belfast, for the Ellerman City Line.

CITY OF ATHENS (1917)
3648 grt
309' x 46' x 19' (93.6 x 13.9 x 5.8 m)
New York Shipbuilding Co 3-cylinder triple expansion engines via single screw.
Sank on 1 May 1918 after being rammed by the French cruiser GLOIRE.
Built by New York Shipbuilding Co, Camden, New Jersey, for the Merchants & Miners Transportation Co as the SOMERSET (1911).

CITY OF ATHENS (1946) See AROSA KULM (1952)

CITY OF ATLANTA (1904)
5433 grt
378' x 49' x 15'8" (114.5 x 14.8 x 4.8 m)
Delaware River Co 3-cylinder triple expansion engines via single screw.
Sank on 19 January 1942 after being torpedoed off Cape Hatteras, North Carolina.
Built by Delaware River Co, Chester, Pennsylvania, for the Ocean Steamship Co of Savannah.

CITY OF BALTIMORE (1919) See HAYWOOD, USS (APA-6) (1941)

CITY OF BARODA (1918)
7129 grt; 113 psrs
433' x 57' x 30'6" depth (131.2 x 17.3 x 9.3 m)
Triple expansion engine via single screw.
Sank on 2 April 1943, with the loss of 14 lives, after being torpedoed by the German U-509 in Luderitz Bay off south-west Africa.
Built by Barclay, Curle & Co, Glasgow, for City & Ellerman Lines.

CITY OF BENARES (1902)
6722 grt; 91 psrs
460' x 55' x 31' depth (139.4 x 16.7 x 9.4 m)
Workman, Clark 3-cylinder triple expansion engine via single screw.
Built by Workman, Clark & Co, Belfast for the City Line.

CITY OF BENARES (1936)
11081 grt; 219 psrs
486' x 63' x 39' depth (147.3 x 19.1 x 11.8 m)
3 x Cammell Laird SRG turbine engines via single screw.
Sank on 17 September 1940, with the loss of 312 lives, after being torpedoed by the German U-48 in the North Atlantic 600 miles (1,000 km) off the west coast of Ireland. The British destroyer HMS HURRICANE picked up 80 survivors.
Built by Barclay, Curle & Co, Glasgow, for Ellerman Lines.

CITY OF BIRMINGHAM (1911)
7498 grt; 170 psrs
452' x 56' x 31'5" depth (137 x 17 x 9.5 m)
Palmer's 4-cylinder quadruple expansion engine via single screw.
Sank on 27 November 1916 after being torpedoed 90 miles (150 km) east of Malta.
Built by Palmer Shipbuilding Co, Jarrow, for the Hall Line.

CITY OF BIRMINGHAM (1923)
5861 grt; 204 psrs
382' x 52' x 27' (115.8 x 15.8 x 8.2 m)
Newport News 3-cylinder triple expansion engines via single screw.
Sank on 30 June 1942 after being torpedoed off the east coast of the USA.
Built by Newport News Shipbuilding, Newport News, Virginia, for the Ocean Steamship Co of Savannah.

CITY OF CAIRO (1915)
8034 grt; 150 psrs
450' x 56' x 28' (136.4 x 17 x 8.5 m)
4-cylinder quadruple expansion engines via single screw.
Sank on 6 November 1942 after being torpedoed by the German U-68 in the South Atlantic, 500 miles (834 km) south of St Helena.
Built by Earle's Co Ltd, Hull, for Ellerman Lines as a passenger-cargo liner.

CITY OF CALCUTTA (1903)
7679 grt; 146 psrs
472' x 56' x 31'9" depth (143 x 17 x 9.7 m)
Workman, Clark 3-cylinder triple expansion engine via single screw.
Built by Workman, Clark & Co Ltd, Belfast, for City & Ellerman Lines.

CITY OF CANDIA (1929)
4212 grt; 1430 psrs
346' x 45' x 26' (105.5 x 13.7 x 7.9 m)
J Redhead & Sons 3-cylinder triple expansion engine via single screw.
Broken up for scrap in 1929. Ex-Anglo Maritime.
Built by J Readhead & Sons, South Shields, for Unione Austriaca as the cargo vessel GERTY (1904).

CITY OF CANTERBURY (1922)
8331 grt; 176 psrs
466' x 56' x 28' (141.2 x 17 x 8.5 m)
Quadruple expansion engine via single screw.
Broken up for scrap in 1953.
Built by Swan Hunter & Wigham Richardson Ltd, Newcastle, for the Ellerman City Line.

CITY OF CHATTANOOGA (1923) See AMERICAN NAVIGATOR (1941)

CITY OF CHESTER (1873) See NEAPOLITANO (1905)

CITY OF COLUMBUS (1904)
5433 grt; 50 psrs
378' x 49' x 27' (114.5 x 14.8 x 8.2 m)
Delaware River Co 3-cylinder triple expansion engines via single screw.
Broken up for scrap in Trieste in 1935.
Built by Delaware River Co, Chester, Pennsylvania, for the Ocean Steamship Co of Savannah as a passenger-cargo ship.

CITY OF CORINTH (1898) See SEQUANA (1912)

CITY OF DURBAN (1954) See MEDITERRANEAN DOLPHIN (1971)

CITY OF EXETER (1914)
9373 grt; 180 psrs
487' x 59' x 28'6" (147.6 x 17.9 x 8.6 m)
Quadruple expansion engines via twin screw.
Broken up for scrap in 1950.
Built by Workman, Clark & Co, Belfast, for the City Line as a passenger-cargo liner.

CITY OF EXETER (1953) See ALICE (1996)

CITY OF FAMAGUSTA (1990) See KARDEN (1995)

CITY OF GLASGOW (1906)
6450 grt; 147 psrs
443' x 54' x 30'3" depth (134.2 x 16.4 x 11.9 m)
Workman, Clark 4-cylinder quadruple expansion engine via single screw.
Sank on 1 September 1918 after being torpedoed 20 miles (33 km) east of Tuskar Rock.
Built by Workman, Clark & Co, Belfast, for the City Line as a passenger-cargo liner.

CITY OF HAMBURG (1931) See WILLIAM P. BIDDLE, USS (APA-8) (1943)

CITY OF HAVRE (1931) See GEORGE F. ELLIOT, USS (AP-13) (1941)

CITY OF HONG KONG (1924) See CENTAURO (1951)

CITY OF HONOLULU (1922)
10771 grt; 2132 psrs
546' x 60' x 30' (166.4 x 18.3 x 9.1 m)
2 x 4-cylinder quadruple expansion engines via twin screw.
Operated by the Los Angeles Steamship Co, she was sunk on 17 October 1922 by deliberate gunfire from the US Army Transport THOMAS after she had caught fire from stem to stern five days earlier, 670 miles (1118 km) southwest of San Pedro, California.
Built by Vulkan Shipyards, Stettin, for North German Lloyd as the FRIEDRICH DER GROSSE (1897). Renamed HURON (1917 – US Navy, after seizure from German government post-World War One).

CITY OF HONOLULU (1927)
10981 grt; 2036 psrs
540' x 60' x 30' (163.6 x 18.2 x 9.1 m)
2 x 4-cylinder quadruple expansion engines via twin screw.
Operated by the Los Angeles Steamship Co, she was broken up for scrap in Osaka in 1933 following her being gutted by fire while berthed at Honolulu pier on 25 May 1930. She sailed from Honolulu to Los Angeles under her own power to undergo survey, but repairs were not considered to be economical and she was sold to the breakers' yard.
Laid down by AG Vulkan, Stettin, for the Hamburg-America Line as the passenger liner BORUSSIA (1899). Renamed on the slips as TEUTONIA (1899), but completed for the Hamburg-America Line as the KIAUTSCHOU (1900). Renamed PRINZESS ALICE (1903 – North German Lloyd), seized by the US government and renamed as the US Navy transport PRINCESS

MATOIKA, USS (1917 – US Shipping Board), PRESIDENT ARTHUR (1922 – United States Lines), WHITE PALACE (1924 – American Palestine Line) and PRESIDENT ARTHUR (1924 – United States Lines).

CITY OF KARACHI (1905)
5547 grt; 94 psrs
414' x 52' x 29'2" depth (125.5 x 15.8 x 8.8 m)
Workman, Clark 4-cylinder quadruple expansion engine via single screw.
Built by Workman, Clark & Co, Belfast, for City & Ellerman Lines as a passenger-cargo liner.

CITY OF LISBON (1946) See PARTIZANKA (1947)

CITY OF LONDON (1903)
8917 grt; 260 psrs
491' x 58' x 26' (148.8 x 17.6 x 7.9 m)
Quadruple expansion engine via single screw.
Broken up for scrap by Arnott Young & Co in 1946.
Built by Workman, Clark & Co, Belfast, for the City Line.

CITY OF LOS ANGELES (1922)
13182 grt; 446 psrs
561' x 62' x 35'9" depth (170 x 18.8 x 10.9 m)
SRG turbine engines via twin screw.
Owned by Matson Line when she was broken up for scrap, in Yokohama, in 1937 after last serving as a floating hotel at the 1935 San Diego Exposition.
Built by F Schichau, Danzig, for North German Lloyd as the GROSSER KURFURST (1899). Renamed as a transport AEOLUS (1917 – US Navy).

CITY OF LOS ANGELES (1938) See GEORGE F. ELLIOTT, USS (AP-13) (1941)

CITY OF MACON (1903) See MACONA (1916)

CITY OF MEMPHIS (1902)
5252 grt; 50 psrs
378' x 49' x 15'8" (114.5 x 14.8 x 4.8 m)
Delaware River Co 3-cylinder triple expansion engines via single screw.
Sank on 17 March 1917 by a submarine in mid-Atlantic.
Built by Delaware River Co, Chester, Pennsylvania, for the Ocean Steamship Co of Savannah as a passenger-cargo liner.

CITY OF MIDLAND (1941)
3969 grt; 200 psrs
76 cars
389' x 58' x 20'6" (117.9 x 17.6 x 6.2 m)
Skinner 10-cylinder Unaflow engines via twin screw.
Built by Manitowoc Shipbuilding Co, Manitowoc, Wisconsin, for the Pere Marquette Railroad Co as a passenger-car ferry.

CITY OF MIKONOS (1977) See CITY OF MYKONOS (1977)

CITY OF MONTGOMERY (1910)
5040 grt; 329 psrs
372' x 50' x 27' (112.7 x 15.2 x 8.2 m)
Newport News 3-cylinder triple expansion engines via single screw.
Broken up for scrap in the USA in 1957.
Built by Newport News Shipbuilding Co, Newport News, Virginia, for the Ocean Steamship Co of Savannah.

CITY OF MYKONOS (1977)
4755 grt; 370 psrs
370' x 53' x 17'6" (112 x 16 x 5.3 m)
2 x 7-cylinder Fiat diesel engines via twin screw.
Cruise ship owned by Cycladic Cruises, Greece, she sank at her moorings in Perama Bay on 29 December 1996 while laid up following the aborted sale to Vinland Cruise Line (who proposed renaming her VINLAND STAR).
Built by Cantieri Riuniti dell'Adriatico for the Adriatic Line as the SAN MARCO (1956).

CITY OF NAGPUR (1914)
8138 grt; 195 psrs
465' x 58' x 31'6" depth (140.9 x 17.6 x 9.6 m)
Workman, Clark 4-cylinder quadruple engine via single screw.

Abandoned as a total constructive loss when wrecked in Delagoa Bay, Mozambique on 23 August 1917.
Built by Workman, Clark & Co, Belfast, for the City Line as a passenger-cargo liner.

CITY OF NAGPUR (1922)
10146 grt; 318 psrs
470' x 59' x 30'6" depth (142.4 x 17.9 x 9.3 m)
Quadruple expansion engine via single screw.
Sank on 29 April 1941 after being torpedoed by the German U-75, with 11 lives lost, 900 miles (1500 km) west of Fastnet.
Built by Workman, Clark & Co, Belfast, for the Ellerman City Line as a passenger-cargo liner.

CITY OF NEWPORT NEWS (1931) See FULLER, USS (APA-7) (1943)

CITY OF NEW YORK (1888) See NEW YORK (1921)

CITY OF NEW YORK (1929)
8272 grt; 60 psrs
450' x 62' x 24' (136.4 x 16.6 x 7.3 m)
Sun 8-cylinder diesel engine via single screw.
Sank on 29 March 1942 after being torpedoed off Cape Hatteras, Massachusetts.
Built by Sun Shipbuilding & Drydock Co for Farrell Lines as a passenger-cargo liner.

CITY OF NORFOLK (1931) See NEVILLE, USS (APA-9) (1941)

CITY OF PARIS (1889) See PHILADELPHIA (1920)

CITY OF PARIS (1922)
10877 grt; 199 psrs
485' x 59' x 32' (147 x 17.9 x 9.7 m)
3 x turbine engines via single screw.
Broken up for scrap in Newport, Wales, in 1956.
Built by Swan Hunter Shipbuilding, Newcastle, for the Ellerman City Line as a passenger-cargo liner.

CITY OF PORT ELIZABETH (1952) See MEDITERRANEAN SUN (1976)

CITY OF RHODOS (1979) See CITY OF RODOS (1979)

CITY OF RODOS (1979) See JOYWAVE (2000)

CITY OF ROME (1917) See SOMERSET (1928)

CITY OF SACRAMENTO (1953) See LANGDALE QUEEN (1962)

CITY OF St LOUIS (1910)
5040 grt; 229 psrs
477' x 58' x 27' (112.7 x 17.6 x 8.2 m)
Newport News 3-cylinder triple expansion engines via single screw.
Broken up for scrap in 1946.
Built by Newport News Shipbuilding, Newport News, Virginia, for the Ocean Steamship Co of Savannah as a passenger-cargo liner.

CITY OF SAN FRANCISCO (1938) See WILLIAM P. BIDDLE, USS (APA-8) (1941)

CITY OF SAVANNAH (1901) See CAROLINA (1905)

CITY OF SIMLA (1921)
9468 grt; 243 psrs
477' x 58' x 28'6" (144.5 x 17.6 x 8.7 m)
Quadruple expansion engine via twin screw.
Sank on 21 September 1940 after being torpedoed south of the Outer Hebrides.
Built by W Gray & Co Ltd (1918), West Hartlepool, for the City Line as a passenger-cargo liner.

CITY OF TARANTO (1989)
10714 grt; 860 psrs
505' x 66' x 28' (154 x 20.2 x 8.6 m)
6-cylinder Smit-B+W diesel engine via single screw.
Broken up for scrap at Aliaga in 1998. Ex-Marlines.
Laid down by P Smit, Rotterdam, for PHS van Ommeren NV, but completed for the Finnish Tankship Company as the oil tanker WIRAKEL (1953). Renamed as the passenger ferry KYDON (1968 – Cretan Maritime Co, SA, Canea).

CITY OF VANCOUVER (1962) See QUEEN OF VANCOUVER (1963)

CITY OF VENICE (1923)
8762 grt; 165 psrs
473' x 58' x 28' (143.3 x 17.6 x 8.5 m)
Quadruple expansion engine via single screw.
Sank on 4 June 1943 after being torpedoed off Ouahran, Algeria.
Built by Workman, Clark & Co, Belfast, for the City Line as a passenger-cargo ship.

CITY OF VICTORIA (1962) See QUEEN OF VICTORIA (1963)

CITY OF VIENNA (1889) See THESSALONIKI (1914)

CITY OF YORK (1953) See SITERRANEAN SKY (1987)

CIUDAD DE ALGECIRAS (1985)
5287 grt; 1300 psrs
140 cars
328' x 58' x 15' (99.5 x 17.6 x 4.5 m)
2 x 12-cylinder Deutz diesel engines via twin screw.
Passenger-car ferry operated by Trasmediterranea, but for sale at US£3,000,000.
Built by Astilleros Espanolas SA, Santander, for Islena di Navigacion SA, Algeciras, as the BAHIA DE CADIZ (1980).

CIUDAD DE BADAJOZ (1979)
7419 grt; 982 psrs
455' x 68' x 19' (137.9 x 20.6 x 5.7 m)
2 x 16-cylinder MAN diesel engines via twin screw.
Passenger ferry operated by Cia Trasmediterranea, Valencia.
Built by Union Naval de Levante, Valencia.

CIUDAD DE BARCELONA (1929)
3946 grt
332' x 49' x 25'6" (100.6 x 14.8 x 7.8 m)
B+W 16-cylinder diesel engines via twin screw.
Sank in May 1937 after being attacked by an Italian submarine during the Spanish Civil war.
Built by Cantieri Navigazioni, Monfalcone, for Cia Trasmediterranea as the INFANTE DON JAIME (1929).

CIUDAD DE BARCELONA (1956)
5195 grt; 708 psrs
14 cars + 2 trailers.
348' x 51' x 16'6" (105.5 x 15.5 x 5 m)
2 x 7-cylinder B+W diesel engines via twin screw.
Built by Union Naval de Levante, Valencia, for Cia Trasmediterranea, Barcelona, as the passenger-car-cargo ferry PLAYA DE FORMENTOR (1955).

CIUDAD DE BUENOS AIRES (1964) See TONG HU (1992)

CIUDAD DE BURGOS (1956)
5245 grt; 698 psrs
321' x 51' x 16'6" (97.3 x 15.5 x 5 m)
2 x 7-cylinder B+W diesel engines via twin screw.
Launched by Union Naval de Levante SA, Valencia, for Cia Trasmediterranea SA, Palma de Mallorca, as the PLAYA DE PALMANOVA (1956) and completed as the passenger ferry CIUDAD DE BURGOS.

CIUDAD DE CADIZ (1951)
6514 grt; 207 psrs

397' x 55' x 24' (120.3 x 16.7 x 7.3 m)
2 x 7-cylinder B+W diesel engines via twin screw.
Passenger ferry laid up since 1998.
Built by Union Naval de Levante, Valencia, for Trasmediterranea.

CIUDAD DE COMPOSTELA (1967) See SARAY STAR (1994)

CIUDAD DE GRANADA (1960)
4944 grt; 1094 psrs
351' x 51' x 16'6" (106.4 x 15.5 x 5 m)
2 x 7-cylinder B+W diesel engines via twin screw.
Built by Union Naval de Levante, Valencia, for Cia Trasmediterranea, Valencia.

CIUDAD DE IBIZA (1947)
3059 grt; 400 psrs
324' x 44' x 18' (98.2 x 13.3 x 5.5 m)
2 x 6-cylinder B+W diesel engines via twin screw.
Broken up for scrap by D Ricardo Villanova Companhia, Valencia, in 1978.
Ex-Cia Trasmediterranea.
Built by Helsingor Shipyards, Helsingor, for the United Steamship Co as the ESBJERG (1929). She had been sunk by an Allied mine on 24 July 1945, but raised and sold to Trasmediterranea in 1947.

CIUDAD DE LA LAGUNA (1975) See VOLCANO DE TENAGUA (1999)

CIUDAD DE MALAGA (1998)
8845 grt; 1584 psrs
440 cars or 45 trailers
461' x 61' x 22'6" (139.7 x 18.4 x 6.9 m)
2 x 12-cylinder Deutz diesel engines via twin screw.
Passenger-car-cargo ferry owned and operated by Trasmediterranea.
Built by Ast De HuelvaSA, Huelva, for Isnasa, Algeciras, as the JULIAN BESTEIRO (1996). Renamed CIUDAD DE MALAGA.

CIUDAD DE MAR LA PLATA (1963)
3956 grt; 458 psrs
345' x 59' x 12' (104.5 x 17.9 x 3.7 m)
3 x 8-cylinder B+W diesel engines via twin screw.
Built by Union Naval de Levante, Valencia, for the Argentine government.

CIUDAD DE MONTEVIDEO (1915)
3872 grt; 500 psrs
365' x 46' x 12'6" (110.6 x 13.9 x 3.8 m)
4 x Cammell Laird SRG turbine engines via twin screw.
Built by Cammell Laird & Co, Birkenhead, for Argentine Navegacion Fluvial.

CIUDAD DE OVIEDO (1957)
5251 grt; 90 psrs
379' x 52' x 25' (114.8 x 15.8 x 7.6 m)
B+W 7-cylinder diesel engines via single screw.
Ferry operating for Cia Trasmediterranea, Spain.
Built by Union Naval de Levante, Valencia.

CIUDAD DE PALMA (1930)
3959 grt; 370 psrs
348' x 49' x 19' (105.5 x 14.8 x 5.8 m)
B+W 16-cylinder diesel engines via twin screw.
Laid down by Cantieri Navale Triestino, Monfalcone, for Cia Trasmediterranea as the PRINCIPE ALFONSO (1930), but completed as the CIUDAD DE PALMA.

CIUDAD DE PALMA (1982) See DONATELLA D'ABUNDO (2000)

CIUDAD DE PAMPLONA (1964) See KOTA SINGAPURA (1981)

CIUDAD DE SALAMANCA (1982)
7112 grt; 1500 psrs
220 cars + 24 trailers
455' x 68' x 18'6" (137.9 x 20.6 x 5.6 m)
2 x 16-cylinder MAN diesel engines via twin screw.

Passenger-car-cargo ferry operated by Trasmediterranea.
Built by Union Naval de Levante, Valencia.

CIUDAD DE SANTA CRUZ DE LA PALMA (1982) See DONATELLA D'ABUNDO (2000)

CIUDAD DE SANTA FE (1963)
5101 grt; 492 psrs
492' x 49' x 15'6" (127.9 x 14.8 x 4.7 m)
Turbine engines via twin screw.
Owned by Flota Argentina de Navegacion Fluvial.
Built by Harland & Wolff Ltd, Belfast, for the US Navy as the BRUIZER, USN (LST-1) (1943).

CIUDAD DE SEVILLA (1932)
7240 grt; 250 psrs
410' x 52' x 22' (124.2 x 15.8 x 6.7 m)
2 x 6-cylinder Krupp diesel engines via twin screw.
Owned by Cia Trasmediterranea, she was broken up on site after running aground during bad weather, on 19 October 1982, beside the breakwater ringing the Palma de Majorca harbour.
Built by Fred. Krupp AG, Kiel, for Cia Trasmediterranea, Madrid, as the INFANTA BEATRIX (1928).

CIUDAD DE SEVILLA (1980)
7535 grt; 1500 psrs
225 cars
456' x 68' x 18' (138.3 x 20.5 x 5.5 m)
2 x 16-cylinder MAN diesel engines via twin screw.
Passenger-car ferry owned by Trasmediterranea.
Built by Union Naval de Levant, Valencia.

CIUDAD DE TANGER (1998)
9481 grt; 1200 psrs
283 cars
383' x 62' x 23'6" (116 x 18.9 x 7.2 m)
2 x 8-cylinder MAN diesel engines via twin screw.
Passenger-car ferry owned and operated by Trasmediterranea, but for sale at US$22,000,000.
Built by Barreras, Vigo, for Limadet Ferry, Tangiers, as the IBN BATTOUTA 2 (1993).

CIUDAD DE TARIFA (1961) See APOLLON (1984)

CIUDAD DE TOLEDO (1956)
9835 grt; 52 psrs
487' x 62' x 24'6" (147.6 x 18.8 x 7.5 m)
Sulzer 10-cylinder diesel engine via single screw.
Built by Euskalduna, Bilbao, for Cia Trasmediterranea.

CIUDAD DE VALENCIA (1984)
7053 grt; 1500 psrs
220 cars
457' x 68' x 18'6" (138.5 x 20.5 5.6 m)
2 x 16-cylinder MAN diesel engines via twin screw.
Passenger-car ferry operated by Trasmediterranea.
Built by Union Naval de Levante SA

CLAN COLQUHOUN (1933) See DJATINEGARA (1952)

CLANSMAN (1998)

5499 grt; 666 psrs
91 cars or 10 cars + 10 trailers
327' x 52' x 10'6" (99 x 15.8 x 3.2 m)
2 x 8-cylinder MaK diesel engines via twin screw.
Passenger-car-cargo ferry owned and operated by Caledonian MacBrayne.
Built by Appledore Shipyards, North Devon, at a cost of £15,500,000.

CLAN URQUHART (1933)
9564 grt; 130 psrs
526' x 61' x 30' (159.4 x 18.5 x 9.1 m)
John Brown 8-cylinder quadruple expansion engines via twin screw.
Broken up for scrap by TW Ward Ltd at Briton Ferry, UK, in 1936. Ex-Clan
Line Steamers, Glasgow.
Built by John Brown & Co Ltd, Clydebank, for the Scottish Shire Line Ltd as
the passenger-cargo ship ARGYLLSHIRE (1911).

CLARIDON (1959) See FURANSU MARU (1958)

CLAUDE BERNARD (1950) See PEGANCIA (1979)

CLAUDE CHAPPE (1925)
4394 grt; 142 psrs
370' x 47' x 26'6" (112.1 x 14.2 x 8.1 m)
G Clarke 6-cylinder triple expansion engine via twin screw.
Broken up for scrap in 1939.
Built by Northumberland Shipbuilding Co Ltd, Newcastle, for National Steam
Navigation Ltd of Greece as the PATRIS (1909).

CLELIA C (1922) See HOI HUNG (1954)

CLELIA II (1996)
4077 grt; 50 psrs
290' x 53' x 12' (88 x 16 x 3.6 m)
2 x 12-cylinder MAN-B+W diesel engines via twin screw.
Owned by Haji-Ioannou after being purchased from Renaissance Cruises for
US$12,000,000 and now operating as a cruise ship for Classical Cruises.
Built by Cantieri Navale Ferrari Shipyards, La Spezia, for Renaissance
Cruises at a cost of US$28,000,000 as the RENAISSANCE 4 (1990).

CLEMENT (1900) See FRESHFIELD (1915)

CLEMENT ADER (1954) See ALESSANDRO VOLTA (1957)

CLEOPATRA (1956)
8193 grt; 100 psrs
455' x 62' x 28' (137.9 x 18.8 x 8.5 m)
2 x DRG Westinghouse turbine engine via single screw.
Operated as a passenger-cargo ship by the United Arab Maritime Co,
Alexandria, but she has been laid up in Alexandria since 1975 following a
boiler explosion during a voyage from the UK to Egypt.
Built by Oregon Shipbuilding Corporation, Portland, for the US Maritime
Commission as the UNITED VICTORY (1944). Renamed KHEDIVE
ISMAIL (1948 – Furness, Withy Group).

CLEVELAND (1909) See CLEVELAND (1923)

CLEVELAND (1923)
16971 grt; 1600 psrs
607' x 63' x 46'7" depth (185 x 19.9 x 14.2 m)
Blohm & Voss 8-cylinder quadruple expansion engines via twin screw.
Broken up for scrap by Blohm & Voss, Hamburg, in 1933. Ex-Hamburg-
America Line.
Built by Blohm & Voss, Hamburg, for the Hamburg-America Line as the
CLEVELAND (1909). Renamed MOBILE, USS (1919 – US Navy) and
KING ALEXANDER (1920 – Byron Steamship Co).

CLIMAX GARNET (1974)
7723 grt; 50 psrs
490' x 63' x 26' (148.6 x 19 x 7.9 m)
2 x 10-cylinder Soc Espanola de Construccion Naval diesel engines via single
screw.
Broken up for scrap at Gadani Beach, Karachi, in 1978. Ex-Climax Shipping
Corporation, Monrovia.
Launched by Soc Espanola de Construccion Naval, Bilbao, for Naviera Aznar

SA as the GUADALUPE (1949) and completed as the MONTE URQUIOLA
(1949 – Naviera Aznar).

CLIMAX OPAL (1977)
10123 grt; 50 psrs
487' x 62' x 26' (148.5 x 18.8 x 7.9 m)
2 x 10-cylinder Sulzer diesel engines via single screw.
Passenger-cargo ship owned by Climax Shipping Corporation, she was broken
up in Santander in 1977 after towing from Belfast, where she had completely
burnt out on 3 April 1977.
Launched by Soc Espanola de Construccion Naval, Bilbao, for Empresa
Nacional Elcano SA as the MONASTERIO DE EL ESCORIAL (1951) and
completed as the MONTE ULIA (1952 – Empresa Nacional Elcano SA).
Renamed EL ESCORIAL (1952 – Empresa Nacional Elcano SA).

CLIPPER (1977) See MILWAUKEE CLIPPER (1990)

CLIPPER ADVENTURER (1997)
4575 grt; 122 psrs
328' x 54' x 15' (99.4 x 16.4 x 4.5 m)
2 x 8-cylinder MAN-B+W diesel engines via twin screw.

Ice-strengthened cruise expedition ship owned by Clipper Cruise Line, St
Louis, Missouri, a subsidiary of Kuoni Travel, and operated by New World
Ship Management, USA.
Built by Brodogradiliste Titovo, Kraljevica, for the Murmansk Shipping Co,
Murmansk, as the ALLA TARASOVA (1977). Renamed MARINE
DISCOVERER (1995 – under charter).

CLIPPER ODYSSEY (1999)
5218 grt; 128 psrs
339' x 51' x 13' (102.9 x 15 x 3.9 m)
2 x 16-cylinder Wartsila-Vasa diesel engines via twin screw.

Owned by Clipper Cruise Line, St Louis, Missouri, a subsidiary of Kuoni
Travel, and operated by new World Ship Management, USA.
Built by Nippon Kokan KK Shipyard, Tsu, for Oceanic Cruise Ltd (Showa
Line) as the OCEANIC GRACE (1989). Renamed OCEANIC ODYSSEY
(1997 – Spice Island Cruises).

CLODIA (1980)
12413 grt; 728 psrs
488' x 84' x 20' (147.9 x 25.4 x 6 m)
2 x 16-cylinder GMT diesel engines via twin screw.
Passenger ferry operated by Tirrenia.
Built by Italcantieri SpA, Genoa,.

C. LOPEZ Y LOPEZ (1905)
4171 grt; 472 psrs

396' x 43' x 28'5" depth (120.7 x 13.1 x 8.6 m)
Barclay Curle 3-cylinder triple expansion engine via single screw.
Broken up for scrap in Italy in 1931. Ex-Cia Trasatlantica.
Built by Barclay, Curle & Co, Glasgow, for the Castle Line as the LISMORE CASTLE (1891). Renamed WESTMOUNT (1902 – Barclay Curle & Co Ltd).

CLUB I (1998) See VAN GOGH (1999)

CLUB CRUISE I (1999) See VAN GOGH (1999)

CLUB MED (1989) See WIND SURF (1997)

CLUB MED I (1990) See WIND SURF (1997)

CLUB MED II (1992) See WIND SPIRIT (1998)

CLUB SEA (1987) See WASA QUEEN (1992)

CLUBSHIP ABEGWEIT (1997)
7000 grt; 950 psrs
60 cars or 19 railway freight cars
372' x 61' x 18'6" (112.7 x 18.5 x 5.6 m)
8 x Dominion Engineering Works diesel-electric engines via quadruple screw.
(2 in the stern plus 2 in the bow to assist in ice-crushing).

Clubhouse for the Columbia Yacht Club, Chicago, since 1983.
Built by Marine Industries Ltd, Sorrel, Quebec for the Ministry of Transport, Ottawa, and operated by Marine Atlantic as the ice-strengthened passenger-car ferry ABEGWEIT (1947) at a cost of US $4,750,000. Renamed ABBY (1982).

CLUNY CASTLE (1903) See UMKUZI (1924)

CLYDE (1881) See SHAH NOOR (1901).

CLYDESDALE (1998)
4275 grt; 650 psrs
125 cars or 18 trailers.
315' x 52' x 14' (95.5 x 15.9 x 4.2 m)
2 x 6-cylinder Nohab-polar diesel engines via twin screw.

Ice-strengthened passenger-car-cargo ferry owned by Clydesdale Shipping Corporation, Panama, and operated by Ventouris Shipping.
Built by Hanseatic Shipyard, Hamburg, for OY Finnlines Ltd as the HANSA EXPRESS (1962). Renamed FINNDANA (1966 – Finnlines), GRYF (1967 – Polska Zegluga Baltycka, Kolobrzeg), EOLOS (1981 – Fragline Ferries) and AGIOS VASSILIOS (1995 – Ventouris Group).

C. M. SCHWAB (1918) See PRESIDENT JEFFERSON (1946)

COAMO (1901)
4244 grt; 140 psrs
386' x 46' x 21'9" (117.6 x 14.1 x 6.6 m)
A Stephen 3-cylinder triple expansion engine via single screw.
Broken up for scrap in 1925. Ex-New York & Puerto Rico Steamship Co.
Built by Alex Stephen & Sons, Glasgow, for the State Line as the STATE OF CALIFORNIA (1891). Renamed CALIFORNIAN (1898 – Allan Line).

COAMO (1925)
7057 grt; 361 psrs
429' x 60' x 25' (130 x 18.2 x 7.6 m)
2 x Newport News DRG turbine engines via single screw.
Sank at 8.00 pm on 9 December 1942, with all lives lost, after being torpedoed by the German U-604 off Bermuda.
Built by Newport News Shipyards, Newport News, Virginia, for the New York & Puerto Rico Co as a passenger liner.

COBEQUID (1913)
4738 grt; 178 psrs
401' x 47' x 26'8" depth (121.5 x 14.2 x 8.1 m)
Triple expansion engine via single screw.
Abandoned as a total constructive loss by her owners, Royal Mail Lines, after becoming wrecked on 13 January 1914 on Trinity Ledge, Newfoundland, in the Bay of Fundy.
Built by Harland & Wolff Ltd, Belfast, for the Union Line as the GOTH (1893).

COBLENZ (1897) See CUBA (1920)

COBLENZ (1923)
9449 grt
459' x 58' x 30'8" depth (139.1 x 17.6 x 9.3 m)
2 x AG Weser DRG turbine engines via twin screw.
Sank in April 1943.
Built by AG Weser, Bremen, for North German Lloyd.

COHO (1959)
5315 grt; 750 psrs
125 cars
342' x 72' x 12'6" (103.6 x 21.8 x 3.8 m)
2 x 8-cylinder Cooper-Bessemer diesel engines via twin screw.
Passenger-car ferry for the Black Ball Transport Line, Seattle.
Built by Puget Sound Shipyards.

COL. FREDERICK C. JOHNSON (1948) See GALILAH (1948)

COLLINGWOOD, HMS (1914)
4979 grt
400' x 47' x 26'2" (122 x 14.4 x 7.9 m)
3-cylinder triple expansion engine via single screw.
Passenger ship converted into a dummy battleship for the British Admiralty in World War One, she was purposely beached in the Dardanelles as a breakwater and salvaged for scrap after the war.
Built by Harland & Wolff Ltd, Belfast, for George Warren & Co as the passenger ship MICHIGAN (1887).

COLOMBIA (1930)
10782 grt; 309 psrs
430' x 62' x 36' depth (130.3 x 18.8 x 10.9 m)
Stork-Werkspoor 16-cylinder diesel engines via twin screw.
Sank on 27 February 1942 after being torpedoed by the German U-516 off Simonstown, South Africa.
Built by P Smit Jnr, Rotterdam for the Royal Netherlands Steamship Co.

COLOMBIE (1931) See ATLANTICA (1964)

COLOMBIE (1946) See ATLANTICA (1964)

COLOMBO (1921)
12087 grt; 2800 psrs

518' x 64' x 27'9" (157 x 19.4 x 8.5 m)
Palmer's 8-cylinder quadruple expansion engines via twin screw.
Passenger liner owned by the Italian Line, she was broken up in 1949 after raising her from the seabed at Massawa, Ethiopia, where she had been scuttled by the Italians on 8 April 1941.
Built by Palmers Shipbuilding & Iron Co, Jarrow-on-Tyne, for the Sicula American Line as the cargo vessel SAN GENNARO (1917).

COLON (1885) See PORTO SAID (1913)

COLON (1905) See YUKON (1923)

COLONIAL (1929) See BISCO 9 (1950)

COLONIAN (1902)
6440 grt; 410 psrs
451' x 54' x 30'6" depth (137.3 x 16.5 x 9.3 m)
3-cylinder triple expansion engine via single screw.
Wrecked on 20 May 1917 at the south end of Bishop Rock, Pembrokeshire.
Built by Hawthorn, Leslie & Co, Newcastle, for the Dominion Line.

COLONIAN (1922)
6583 grt; 150 psrs
470' x 53' x 23'9" depth (143.3 x 16.2 x 7.2 m)
Harland & Wolff 6-cylinder triple expansion engines via twin screw.
Broken up for scrap in Rotterdam in 1928. Ex-Leyland Steamship Co.
Built by Harland & Wolff Ltd, Belfast, for the White Star Line as the BOVIC (1892).

COLORADO (1923) See CENTAURO (1951)

COLOR FESTIVAL (1994)
34471 grt; 1937 psrs
350 cars or 40 cars + 60 trailers
554' x 91' x 21' (168 x 27.6 x 6.5 m)
4 x 12-cylinder Wartsila-SEMT-Pielstick diesel engines via twin screw.

Ice-strengthened passenger-car-cargo RoRo ferry operated by the Color Line.
Built by Wartsila-Helsinki for the Svea Line, Finland, as the SVEA (1984).
Renamed SILJA KARNEVAL (1992 – Silja Line).

COLOR VIKING (1994) See JUPITER (1998)

COLOR VIKING (2000)
19763 grt; 1750 psrs
403 cars or 152 cars + 37 trailers
442' x 83' x 18'6" (134 x 25 x 5.7 m)
2 x 8-cylinder MAN-B+W diesel engines via twin screw.
RoRo passenger ship owned and operated by Color Line after purchasing her for US$16,000,000.
Built by AS Nakskov Skibsvaerft, Nakskov, for the Danish State Railways as the PEDER PAARS (1985) at a cost of £40,000,000. Renamed STENA INVICTA (1991 – Stena Line) and WASA JUBILEE (1998 – Vaasanlaivat, Sweden).

COLUMBELLA, HMS (1914) See MOREAS (1926)

COLUMBIA (1889) See TEREK (1904)

COLUMBIA (1899) See TEREK (1904)

COLUMBIA (1902) See MOREAS (1926)

COLUMBIA (1908) See ANNOULA (1931)

COLUMBIA (1915)
5643 grt; 189 psrs
380' x 48' (115.2 x 14.5 m)
Triple expansion engine via single screw.
Abandoned as a total constructive loss when she was wrecked on 13 September 1931 on Santa Margarita Island, Baja, California.
Built by Nederlandsche Scheepsbouw Maats for Koninklijke Wesr-Indiosohe Maildienst, Amsterdam.

COLUMBIA (1917) See GEORGE S. SYMONDS (1942)

COLUMBIA (1919) See MOREAS (1926)

COLUMBIA, USS (AG-9) (1921) See GEORGE S. SYMONDS (1942)

COLUMBIA (1932) See ISTANBUL (1947)

COLUMBIA (1935)
24578 grt; 2600 psrs
697' x 78' x 36'3" (211.2 x 23.6 x 11 m)
Harland & Wolff combination 2 x 4-cylinder triple expansion engines & turbines via triple screw.
Broken up for scrap at Barrow-in-Furness in 1936. Ex-Panama Pacific Line.
Launched by Harland & Wolff Ltd, Belfast, for the White Star Line as the cargo ship BELGENLAND (1914); completed as the cargo and troop ship BELGIC (1917); and then rebuilt as a passenger ship and reverted to her original name BELGENLAND (1923 – Red Star Line).

COLUMBIA (1938) See PORTUGAL (1946)

COLUMBIA (1949)
9424 grt; 804 psrs
468' x 60' x 23'6" (142.6 x 18.2 x 7.1 m)
Combination geared triple expansion engines & turbines via triple screw.
Broken up for scrap in Nagasaki in 1959. Ex-Greek Line.
Built by Harland & Wolff Ltd, Belfast, for McIlwraith McEachern, Melbourne, as the passenger liner KATOOMBA (1913).

COLUMBIA (1968) See CARIBIA (1968)

COLUMBIA (1974)
3946 grt; 625 psrs
134 cars
420' x 86' x 21' (127.4 x 26 x 6.4 m)
2 x 16-cylinder De Laval diesel engines via twin screw.
Passenger-car ferry operated by Alaska Marine Highway, Juneau.
Built by the Lockheed Shipbuilding & Construction Co, Seattle, for the Public Works Department of the state of Alaska.

COLUMBUS (1903) See REPUBLIC (1903)

COLUMBUS (1913) See HOMERIC (1922)

COLUMBUS (1924)
32581 grt; 1724 psrs
775' x 83' x 36' (234.9 x 25.2 x 10.9 m)
2 x 8-cylinder SRG turbine engines via twin screw.
Scuttled by her German crew on 19 December 1939 to avoid capture by the British warship HMS HYPERION 320 miles (533 km) east of Norfolk, Virginia.
Laid down by Schichau Shipyards, Danzig, for North German Lloyd as the HINDENBURG (1914) but completed as the COLUMBUS.

COLUMBUS (1997) See C. COLUMBUS (1997)

COLUMBUS C (1982)
21164 grt; 400 psrs
600' x 77' x 26' (182.9 x 23.5 x 7.9 m)
2 x 8-cylinder B+W diesel engines via twin screw.
Owned by Costa Line, she was broken up for scrap in Barcelona in 1985 after refloating her from the seabed beneath her berth in Cadiz on 2 November 1984. She had been blown against the harbour breakwater by galeforce winds on 29 July 1984 and was badly holed through to the engine room. Water cascaded into her as she attempted to dock alongside, a manoeuvre which was successful, but she then gracefully settled to the bottom.
Built by De Schelde Shipyards, Vlissingen, for the Swedish American Line as the passenger liner KUNGSHOLM (1953). Renamed EUROPA (1964 – North German Lloyd).

COLUMBUS CARAVELLE (1991)
7560 grt; 330 psrs
384' x 57' x 14'6" (116.4 x 17.2 x 4.4 m)
2 x 8-cylinder Wartsila diesel engines via twin screw.
Cruise casino ship owned by Kong Wing Ltd., Hong Kong, and operated by Conning Shipping Ltd, Hong Kong.
Built by Rauma Yards Oy, Rauma, for Delfin Cruises Ltd, Turku, as the ice-strengthened cruise ship DELFIN CARAVELLE (1990). Renamed SALLY CARAVELLE (1990 – Sally Lines). She reverted to COLUMBUS CARAVELLE for Sander Shipping Ltd, Virgin Islands, and during the short stay in the role of a casino ship, she had the name "LIDO STAR" painted on her hull amidships. In 1999 the promotional name was changed to CAPTAIN OMAR for casino cruise operations out of Singapore.

COLUSA (1913) See LYNGENFJORD (1933)

COMFORT, USS (AH-3) (1917) See SHAMROCK (1943)

COMMANDANT QUERE (1948)
4401 grt; 994 psrs
363' x 50' x 17' (110 x 15.2 x 5.2 m)
2 x Thorncroft DRG turbine engines via twin screw.
Owned by Cie Generale Transatlantique.
Built by JJ Thornycroft & Co, Southampton.

COMMISSAIRE RAMEL (1920)
10061 grt; 552 psrs
479' x 59' x 33'4" depth (145.2 x 17.9 x 10.1 m)
3-cylinder triple expansion engine via single screw.
Sank on 17 September 1940 in the Indian Ocean, with three lives lost, after an attack by the German raider ATLANTIS.

Built by Chantiers Navals de La Ciotat for Messageries Maritimes.

COMMODORE (1999)
8909 grt; 1305 psrs
360 cars
405' x 63' x 17' (122.7 x 19.2 x 5.1 m)
8 x 12-cylinder Nohab-Polar diesel engines via twin screw.

Passenger-car ferry owned by Freedom Ferries and operated by Traghetti Isole Sarde SrL, Genoa.
Built by Aarborg Vaerft, Aalborg, for Rederi AB Goteborg-Fredrikshavn Linjen as the PRINSESSAN CHRISTINA (1969). Renamed SAFE CHRISTINA (1981 – Safe Ship Rederi), PRINSESSAN CHRISTINA (1982 – Stena Line), STENA NORDICA (1983 – Stena Line), EUROPAFARJAN I (1985 – Lion Ferry A.B), LION PRINCE (Lion Ferry A.B) and STENA PRINCE (1997 – Stena Line).

COMMODORE CLIPPER (1999)
13465 grt; 524 psrs
100 trailers
426' x 77' x 19' (129 x 23.4 x 5.8 m)
2 x 9-cylinder MaK diesel engines via twin screw.
Passenger-cargo ferry owned and operated by Commodore Shipping.
Built by Van Der Geissen-de-Noord, Krimpen, at a cost of US$48,000,000.

COMMODORE HOTEL, St PETERSBURG (1993) See ENCHANTED ISLE (1994)

COMMONWEALTH (1900) See CANOPIC (1903)

COMMONWEALTH (1902)
6616 grt; 450 psrs
450' x 52' x 30'6" (137.2 x 15.9 x 9.3 m)
2 x triple expansion engines via twin screw.
Broken up for scrap by Stabilimento Metallurgica Ligure Societa for a tender fee of £14,100 at La Spezia in 1923.
Built by Barclay, Curle & Co, Glasgow, for the Blue Anchor Line.

COMORIN (1925) See COMORIN, HMS (1939)

COMORIN, HMS (1939)
15116 grt; 306 psrs
545' x 70' x 31' (166.1 x 21.3 x 9.4 m)
2 x quadruple expansion engines via twin screw.
Purposely sunk by a torpedo fired from HMS BROKE, on 7 April 1941, as fire raged out of control on the armed merchant cruiser COMORIN during a fierce storm off Sierra Leone. Twenty lives were lost.
Built by Barclay, Curle & Co, Glasgow, for the P&O Line as the CORMORIN (1939).

COMPIEGNE (1923)
9986 grt; 326 psrs
479' x 59' x 27'3" (145.2 x 17.9 x 8.3 m)
4 x Ateliers et Chantiers de la Loire turbine engines via twin screw.
Broken up for scrap at La Seyne in 1954.
Launched by Ateliers et Chantiers de la Loire, St Nazaire, for Messageries Maritimes as the JAMAIQUE (1922) but completed as COMPIEGNE.

COMPIEGNE (1958) See ALAMIRA (1997)

COMRIE CASTLE (1903) See UMVOTI (1924)

COMTE DE NICE (1966) See NAIAS II (1983)

COMUS (1900) See WESTERN OCEAN (1930)

CONCEPCION MARINO (1978)
6213 grt; 1500 psrs
346' x 54' x 13' (105 x 16.5 x 4 m)
2 x 6-cylinder Deutz diesel engines via twin screw.
Owned by Consolidada de Ferrys, Pampatar, Venezuela.
Built by AS Trondheims MV, Trondheim.

CONCORD (1992)
4736 grt; 2464 psrs
465' x 63' x 19' (141 x 19 x 5.9 m)
4 x 6-cylinder Fiat diesel engines via twin screw.
Passenger-cargo RoRo ferry owned by Maritime Independence SA and
operated by Petra Navigation and Transportation Trading Co Ltd, Panama.
Built by Cantieri Navale Apuania, Carrara, for Traghetto as the CANGURO
GIALLO (1969). Renamed STAFFETTA ADRIATICA (1973 – Tirrenia).

CONCORD 2 (1993) See AL SALAM 91 (1993)

CONDE DE ARGELEJO (1949) See ISLA DE FORMENTERA (1973)

CONFEDERATION (1993)
8060 grt; 600 psrs
214 cars
377' x 62' x 14'6" (114.2 x 18.8 x 4.4 m)
2 x 10-cylinder Wartsila diesel engines via twin screw.
Passenger-car-cargo RoRo ferry owned by Transport Canada and chartered to
Northumberland Ferries.
Built by Port Weller Shipyards, St Catherines, Ontario, for Transport Canada
at a cost of C$22,000,000.

CONGRESS (1913) See EMPIRE WOODLARK (1941)

CONNACHT (1978) See DUBROVNIK (1996)

CONQUEST (2002) See CARNIVAL CONQUEST (2002)

CONSTANTINOPLE (1920) See KING ALEX ANDER (1923)

CONSTANTINOUPOLIS (1920)
8174 grt; 1460 psrs
454' x 56' x 36' depth (138.2 x 17 x 10.9 m)
JC Tecklenborg 6-cylinder triple expansion engines via twin screw.
Broken up for scrap in Germany in 1925. Ex-Greek government.
Built by JC Tecklenborg, Geestemunde, for North German Lloyd as the
ROON (1902).

CONSTANZA (1903)
3123 grt
380' x 38' x 28'5" (115.2 x 11.5 x 8.6 m)
William Denny & Co 3-cylinder triple expansion engines via single screw.
Broken up for scrap in Genoa in 1903.
Built by Barrow Shipbuilding Ltd, Barrow, for the Duke of Devonshire
Steamship Co Ltd as the DUKE OF DEVONSHIRE (1873).

CONSTELLATION (1978) See SALAMIS GLORY (1996)

CONSTELLATION ENTERPRISE (1981) See CHONG MING
DAO (1998)

CONSTITUTION (1951) See CONSTITUTION (1982)

CONSTITUTION (1982)
30090 grt; 798 psrs
683' x 89' x 30' (208 x 27 x 9 m)
4 x DRG turbine engines via twin screw.
Sank 700 miles (1170 km) north of the island of Hawaii on 10 November 1997
while under tow from being laid up in the Cascade General Shipyard, Portland,
Oregon, to shipbreakers in Kaohsiung. Ex-America Hawaii Cruises Inc.
Built by the Bethlehem Steel Co, Quincy, Massachusetts, for American Export
Lines as the CONSTITUTION (1951). Renamed OCEANIC
CONSTITUTION (1974 – CY Tung Group's Atlantic Far East Line) and then
laid up from 1975 t0 1981.

CONSUELO (1900) See POLERIC (1912)

CONSUELO (1925) See HUA TONG (1930)

CONSUL HORN (1939)
6845 grt
454' x 56' x 30'5" (137.6 x 17 x 9.2 m)
Quadruple expansion engines via twin screw.
Sank in July 1942 after hitting a mine laid off Borkum Island, Germany.
Built by Harland & Wolff Ltd, Belfast, for the Shaw Savill Line as the
MAMARI (1904). Renamed as the cargo ship GEROLSTEIN (1928 – Red
Star Line), with passenger accommodation added in 1931.

CONTE AZZURO (1932) See CONTE DI SAVOIA (1932)

CONTE BIANCAMANO (1925) See CONTE BIANCAMANO (1947)

CONTE BIANCAMANO (1947)
23842 grt; 1578 psrs
665' x 76' x 26' (201.5 x 23 x 7.9 m)
4 x Parsons DRG turbine engines via twin screw.
Broken up for scrap at La Spezia in 1960. Ex-Italian Line.
Built by William Beardmore & Co, Dalmuir, for Lloyd Sabaudo as the
CONTE BIANCAMANO (1925). Renamed HERMITAGE, USS (AP-54)
(1942 – US Navy). The ship was returned to the Italian navy in 1947.

CONTE DI SAVOIA (1932)
48502 grt; 2200 psrs
814' x 96' x 27'7" (246.7 x 29.1 x 8.4 m)
12 x Parson turbine engines via quadruple screw.
Broken up for scrap at Monfalcone in 1950. She had been refloated on 16
October 1945 from the Venice seabed where she had lain since being sunk by
Allied bombs on 11 September 1943.
Laid down by Cantieri Riuniti dell'Adriatico, Trieste, for Lloyd Sabaudo as
the passenger liner CONTE AZZURO (1932) but completed as CONTE DI
SAVOIA for the Italian Line.

CONTE GRANDE (1928) See CONTE GRANDE (1947)

CONTE GRANDE (1947)
23562 grt; 1379 psrs
667' x 78' x 27' (203.3 x 23.8 x 8.2 m)
4 x DRG turbine engines via twin screw.
Broken up for scrap at La Spezia in 1962. Ex-Lloyd Triestino.
Built by Stabilimento Tecnico Shipyards, Trieste, for Lloyd Sabaudo as the
CONTE GRANDE (1928). Renamed MONTICELLO, USS (AP-61) (1942 –
US Navy).

CONTE ROSSO (1914) See ARGUS, HMS (1918)

CONTE ROSSO (1922)
17856 grt; 640 psrs
588' x 74' x 35'9" depth (178.2 x 22.4 x 10.9 m)
4 x Beardmore DRG turbine engines via twin screw.
Passenger liner owned by Lloyd Triestino, she sank with 1,212 lives lost on 24
May 1941 after two torpedoes from the HMS UPHOLDER hit her 15 miles
(25 km) off Syracuse, Sicily.
Built by William Beardmore & Co, Glasgow, for Lloyd Sabaudo.

CONTESSA I (1997)
11259 grt; 506 psrs
165 cars + 18 trailers

400' x 69' x 20' (121.2 x 20.9 x 6.2 m)
8 x 12-cylinder Fairbanks-Morse diesel engines via twin screw.
Ice-strengthened vessel converted to a cruising casino ship owned and operated by Contessa International Cruise Line, Inc, Panama.
Built by Marine Industries Ltd, Port Sorel, for CN Marine Inc, Halifax, as the passenger-car-cargo ferry JOHN HAMILTON GRAY (1968) at a cost of US$14,000,000.

CONTE VERDI (1923) See KOTOBUKI MARU (1943)

CONTINENTAL (1948)
9006 grt; 250 psrs
489' x 58' x 28'9" depth (149.1 x 17.7 x 8.8 m)
Maryland Steel Corporation 6-cylinder triple expansion engines via twin screw.
Broken up for scrap in Genoa in 1951. Ex-Tidewater Commercial Co Inc, San Francisco.
Built by Maryland Steel Corporation, Sparrow's Point, for the Boston Steamship Co as the cargo ship SHAWMUT (1902). Renamed ANCON (1908 – Panama Railroad Co), PERMANENTE (1940 – Permanente Steamship Co) and TIDEWATER (1946 – Tidewater Commercial Co Inc, San Francisco).

CONTINENTAL WORLD (1993) See LEISURE WORLD (1994)

COOK, HMAS (1981) See MARIA KOSMAS (1992)

COOMA (1907)
3839 grt; 300 psrs
330' x 46' x 21'4" (100.6 x 14 x 6.5 m)
Triple expansion engine via single screw.
Abandoned after becoming wrecked on 7 July 1926 on North Reef, 60 miles (100 km) north of Port Alma, Rockhampton, Queensland. Although she could possibly have been salvaged, she was gutted by fire on 26 January 1927.
Built by Alex ander Stephen & Sons, Glasgow, for Howard Smith Ltd, Sydney.

COOPERATZIA (1929)
3767 grt; 292 psrs
332' x 48' x 16' (100.6 x 14.5 x 4.8 m)
6-cylinder Russki diesel engine via single screw.
Built by A Jdanov Shipyards, St Petersburg, for the Russian government (Sovtorgflot).

COPA CASINO (1993)
9114 grt; 731 psrs
503' x 69' x 29' (153.3 x 21 x 8.8 m)
2 x General Electric DRG turbine engines via single screw.
Operating as a stationary casino ship at a mooring near Gulfport, Mississippi, for Gulfside Casino Inc, USA.
Laid down by Wilton Fijenoord, Schiedam, for Holland America Lines as the passenger-cargo ship DINTELDYK (1951) and completed as the RYNDAM (1951). Renamed WATERMAN (1968 – Transocean Steamship Co), RYNDAM (1968 – Holland America Line), ATLAS (1972 – Epirotiki Cruise Lines), ROYAL PRINCE (1980 – Intercontinental Shipping Co, Mexico), ATLAS (1981 – Epirotiki Cruise Lines), PRIDE OF MISSISSIPPI (1988 – Pride Cruise Line, USA) and PRIDE OF GALVESTON (1991 – Pride Cruise Line, USA).

COPENHAGEN (1967) See ALKYON (1978)

COPENHAGEN (1974) See ODESSA I (1999)

COPIAPO (1937) See ORDU (1948)

COPTIC (1881) See PERSIA MARU (1915)

CORAL PRINCESS (1970) See CORAL PRINCESS (2000)

CORAL PRINCESS (2000)
9766 grt; 530 psrs
478' x 61' x 18' (145.7 x 18.5 x 5.5 m)
2 x 8-cylinder B+W diesel engines via twin screw.
Cruise ship owned by Universal Summit Ltd (Stanley Ho) and chartered to Sinba International Cruises as a floating casino until laid up in 2000 in Port Kelang, Malaysia. She was then entered on the sale lists at US$4,250,000.

Built by Cia Euskalduna, Bilbao, for the Costiera Line as the PRINCESA LEOPOLDINA (1962) at a cost of US$5,000,000. Renamed CORAL PRINCESS (1970 – China Navigation Co, Hong Kong), as a floating casino ship CORA PRINCESS (1990 – Universal Summit Ltd) and MILLENNIUM QUEEN (1999).

CORAL RIVIERA (1973) See RASA SAYANG (1980)

CORA PRINCESS (1990) See CORAL PRINCESS (1993)

CORBIERE (1985) See LANGELAND IV (1999)

CORCOVADO (1907) See MOUZINHO (1930)

CORCOVADO (1910) See POTENGY (1938)

CORDILLERA (1933) See RUSS (1952)

CORDOBA (1947)
7604 grt
439' x 62' x 34'5" depth (133 x 18.8 x 105 m)
2 x Westinghouse DRG turbine engines via single screw.
Broken up at Campana in 1962. Ex-Dodero Line.
Built by Bethlehem-Fairfield, Baltimore, for the US War Shipping Administration as the NYU VICTORY (1945).

CORFU (1931) See CORFU MARU (1961)

CORFU DIAMOND (1987) See AVRASYA (1996)

CORFU MARU (1961)
14280 grt; 394 psrs
545' x 70' x 26' (166.1 x 21.3 x 7.9 m)
6 x Parsons geared turbine engines via twin screw.
Broken up for scrap by Miyachi Salvage Co Ltd in Osaka in 1961. Ex-Mitsui Bussan Kaisha.
Laid down by Alex ander Stephen & Sons, Glasgow, for the P&O Line as the CHEFOO (1931) and completed as CORFU (1931).

CORFU SEA (1985) See EXPRESS KARISTOS (1996)

CORINTHIA (1939)
3879 grt; 93 psrs
338' x 44' x 23' (102.9 x 13.5 x 7 m)
3-cylinder triple expansion engine via single screw.
Broken up for scrap at Genoa, in 1959. Ex-Greek Line.
Built by De Schelde, Flushing, for the Royal West Indian Mail Service as the passenger-cargo liner ORANJE NASSAU (1911).

CORINTHIA (1987) See ZENITH ((1995)

CORINTHIAN (1900)
7333 grt; 940 psrs
430' x 54' x 28'2" depth (131 x 16.5 x 8.5 m)
Workman, Clark 3-cylinder triple expansion engine via single screw.
Abandoned as a total constructive loss after she wrecked herself upon the north-west ledges of Brier Island in the Bay of Fundy, Canada, on 14 December 1918.
Built by Workman, Clark & Co, Belfast, for the Allan Line as a passenger liner.

CORINTHIC (1902)
12231 grt; 688 psrs
530' x 63' x 31' (161.5 x 19.2 x 9.4 m)
Quadruple expansion engines via twin screw.
Broken up for scrap at Blyth in 1931 for £10,250.
Built by Harland & Wolff Ltd, Belfast, for the White Star Line as a passenger liner.

CORINTHIC (1947)
15682 grt; 85 psrs
560' x 71' x 30' (169.7 x 21.6 x 9.1 m)
6 x SRG turbine engines via twin screw.
Broken up for scrap in Kaohsiung in 1969.

Built by Cammell Laird & Co, Birkenhead, for the Shaw Savill Line as a passenger-cargo liner.

CORMORAN (1969) See ETAIWI I (1980)

CORNELIA (1912) See KENKOKU MARU (1914)

CORNISHMAN (1903)
5749 grt
461' x 49' x 31' depth (139.7 x 14.8 x 9.4 m)
6-cylinder triple expansion engine via single screw.
Passenger ship owned and operated by the British and North Atlantic Steam Navigation Co Ltd.
Built by Harland & Wolff Ltd, Belfast, as the steam schooner NOMADIC (1890) for the Oceanic Steam Navigation Co Ltd.

CORNOUAILLES (1977) See SVETI STEFAN (2000)

CORNWALL (1896) See ATLANTIDE (1912)

COROMANDEL (1884) See SHAH NOOR (1905)

COROMUEL (1973)
7234 grt; 650 psrs
225 cars
359' x 58' x 15' (108.9 x 78.6 x 4.6 m)
2 x 12-cylinder Deutz diesel engines via twin screw.
Passenger-car Ro Ro ferry operating in Mexico by Transbordadores, La Paz , for the Mexican government.
Built by Jos L Meyer, Papenburg.

CORONADO (1915)
6539 grt; 100 psrs
425' x 54' x 30' (128.8 x 16.4 x 9.1 m)
Triple expansion engines via twin screw.
Broken up in Italy in 1935.
Built by Workman, Clarke & Co Ltd, Belfast, for Elders & Fyffes.

CORONEL (1942) See TOPEKA (1976)

CORRIENTES (1949)
12053 grt; 1379 psrs
468' x 70' x 39'7" depth (141.8 x 21.2 x 12 m)
2 x Allis-Chalmers DRG turbine engines via single screw.
Owned by Dodero Line, she was broken up at Antwerp in 1964 after major engine damage.
Laid down by Seattle-Tacoma Shipbuilding Corporation, Tacoma, for Moore-McCormack Lines as the passenger-cargo liner MORMACMAIL (1941) but completed for the British Royal Navy as the auxiliary aircraft carrier TRACKER, HMS (1943).

CORSE (1908) See NIAGARA (1910)

CORSE (1966) See EXPRESS SAMINA (2000)

CORSE (1983)
12686 grt; 2262 psrs
680 cars + 43 trailers
479' x 77' x 21' (145 x 23.3 x 6.3 m)
4 x 16-cylinder Pielstick diesel engines via twin screw.
Passenger-car-cargo ferry owned by SNCM and operated by Corsica Maritti.
Built by Dubigeon-Normandie, Nantes.

CORSICA (1951)
7475 grt; 925 psrs
426' x 59' x 35'2" depth (129 x 17.9 x 10.7 m)
Reiherstieg Maschinenf quadruple expansion engines via twin screw.
Broken up for scrap in Ghent in 1954. Ex-Cia de Navigation Baru SA.
Launched by Reiherstieg Co, Hamburg, for the Woermann Line as HILDA WOERMANN (1914) but completed as WAHEHE (1914 – British Ministry of Transport). Renamed MARELLA (1920 – Burns, Philp & Co Ltd, Sydney), CAPTAIN MARCOS (1948 – Cia Naviera Baru, Panama) and LIGURIA (1950 – Cia Naviera Baru, Panama).

CORSICA (1980) See HAPPY DOLPHIN (1999)

CORSICA EXPRESS (1967) See CAPO FALCONARA (1978)

CORSICA MARINA (1977) See NORTIA (1999)

CORSICA MARINA II (1986) See CORSICA MARINE SECONDA (1999)

CORSICA MARINE SECONDA (1999)
12120 grt; 140 psrs
479 cars
399' x 64' x 19'2" (120.8 x 19.5 x 5.8m)
2 x 12-cylinder MaK diesel engines via twin screw.

Ice-strengthened passenger-car ferry owned and operated by Medcharter SpA, Genoa.
Built by Rickmers Werft, Bremerhaven, for Stena AB, Gothenburg, as the STENA NAUTICA (1974). Renamed MARINE NAUTICA (1974 m–chartered to CN Marine) and CORSICA MARINA II (1986 – Dominican Ferries SA, Panama).

CORSICAN (1907) See MARVALE (1922)

CORSICA NOVA (1976) See APOLLONIA II (1990)

CORSICA REGINA (1989) See SARDINIA REGINA (1996)

CORSICA SERENA (1975) See AL RASHEED II (1992)

CORSICA SERENA II (1983) See CORSICA SERENA SECONDA (2000)

CORSICA SERENA SECONDA (2000)
8798 grt; 1200 psrs
404 cars
392' x 61' x 16'6" (118.7 x 18.6 x 5 m)
4 x 9-cylinder MaK diesel engines via twin screw.

Passenger-car ferry owned by Tourship SA, Panama, and operated by Corsica Ferries.
Built by Werft Nobiskrug, Rendsburg, for Lion Ferry AB as EUROPAFARJAN III (1974) at a cost of S.krona 60,000,000. Renamed CORSICA SERENA II (1983 – Corsica Ferries).

CORSICA VERA (1986) See SARDINIA VERA (1987)

CORSICA VICTORIA (1989)
13085 grt; 1700 psrs
300 cars
484' x 69' x 17'6" (146.6 x 20.9 x 5.3 m)
6 x 16-cylinder Nohab-Polar diesel engines via twin screw.

Ice-strengthened passenger-car-cargo RoRo ferry operated by Tourship Italia SPa.
Built by Brodogradiliste, Trogir, for Rederi AB, Gotland, as the GOTLAND (1973).

CORSICA VIVA (1993) See HAPPY DOLPHIN (1999)

CORSICA VIVA I (1988) See HAPPY DOLPHIN (1999)

CORSICA VIVA II (1985) See SARDINIA REGINA (1987)

CORTINA (1996) See AVRASYA I (1996)

COSMOS MARINER (1966)
8610 grt; 52 psrs
459' x 63' x 27' (139.1 x 19.1 x 8.2 m)
2 x General Electric DRG turbine engines via single screw.
Broken up for scrap in Kaohsiung in 1970. Ex-Cosmos Navigation Corporation.
Built by Federal Shipbuilding & Drydock Co, Kearny, New Jersey, for the Grace Line as the passenger-cargo liner SANTA SOFIA (1946). Renamed A & J FAITH (1963 – Pacific Seafarers Inc) and SANTA SOFIA (1964 – Grace Line Inc).

COSMOS TRADER (1966)
8610 grt; 52 psrs
459' x 63' x 27' (139.1 x 19.1 x 8.2 m)
2 x General Electric DRG turbine engines via single screw.
Broken up for scrap in Kaohsiung in 1969. Ex-Cosmos Navigation Corporation.
Built by Federal Shipbuilding & Drydock Company, Kearny, New Jersey, for the Grace Line as the passenger-cargo liner SANTA MONICA (1946). Renamed MAXIMUS (1963 – Grace Line), A & J MERCURY (1963 – Pacific Seafarers Inc) and SANTA MONICA (1964 – Grace Line Inc).

COSTA ALLEGRA (1990)
28430 grt; 1066 psrs
615' x 83' x 27' (186.4 x 25.2 x 8.2 m)
8 x 6-cylinder Wartsila-Pielstick diesel engines via twin screw.

Cruise ship owned by Prestige Cruises (Carnival Cruises subsidiary).
Built by Wartsila-Turku for the Johnson Line as the container ship ANNIE JOHNSON (1969). Renamed REGENT MOON (1986 – Regency Cruises) and ALEXANDRA (1988 – Mediterranean Shipping Co, SA).

COSTA ATLANTICA (2000)
84000 grt; 2112 psrs
963' x 106' x 25'6" (291.7 x 32.2 x 7.8 m)
6 x 9-cylinder Wartsila diesel engines via twin Azipod screw.
Cruise ship built by Kvaerner-Masa Yards, Helsinki, for Costa Cruises at a cost of US$375,000,000.

COSTA CLASSICA (1991)
52926 grt; 1300 psrs
773' x 98' x 25' (234.2 x 29.7 x 7.6 m)
4 x 8-cylinder Sulzer diesel engines via twin screw.
Cruise ship owned by the Costa Line.
Built by Fincantieri, Venice, at a cost of US$325,000,000.

COSTA MARINA (1990)
25558 grt; 780 psrs

572' x 84' x 27' (173.3 x 25.5 x 8.2 m)
4 x 16-cylinder Pielstick diesel engines via twin screw.

Cruise ship owned and operated by the Costa Line (subsidiary of Carnival Cruise Lines).
Built by Wartsila, Turku, for the Johnson Line as the container ship AXEL JOHNSON (1969). Renamed REGENT SUN (1986 – Regency Cruises) and ITALIA (1987 – The Navy Club, Rome).

COSTA OLYMPIA (1998) See NORWEGIAN SKY (1999)

COSTA PLAYA (1995) See JOY WAVE (1999)

COSTA RICA (1910)
8672 grt; 254 psrs
455' x 55' x 29' (144.2 x 16.8 x 8.9 m)
4-cylinder Nederlandsche Fabriek van Werktuigen quadruple expansion engine via single screw.
Sank on 29 April 1941 after attack by German dive bombers north of Crete.
Built by Nederlandsche Scheepsbouw Maatschappij, Amsterdam, for the Nederlands Steamship Co as the PRINSES JULIANA (1910).

COSTA RICA VICTORY (1944) See MARIANNA IV (1968)

COSTA RIVIERA (1983) See COSTA RIVIERA (1994)

COSTA RIVIERA (1994)
30361 grt; 974 psrs
702' x 94' x 28' (214 x 28.6 x 8.5 m)
2 x 2-cylinder De Laval DRG turbine engines via twin screw.

Cruise ship owned and operated by Costa Cruises (Carnival Cruise Lines subsidiary).
Built by Cantieri Riuniti dell'Adriatico, Monfalcone, for Lloyd Triestino as the GUGLIELMO MARCONI (1963). Renamed COSTA RIVIERA (1983 – Costa Armatori) and AMERICAN ADVENTURE (1993 – American Family Cruises).

COSTA ROMANTICA (1993)
53049 grt; 1905 psrs
773' x 98' x 26' (234.2 x 29.7 x 7.3 m)
4 x 8-cylinder Sulzer diesel engines via twin screw.
Cruise ship for Costa Cruises (subsidiary of Carnival Cruise Lines).
Built by Fincantieri, Venice, at a cost of US$269,000,000.

COSTA VICTORIA (1996)
75166 grt; 2350 psrs
824' x 106' x 26' (249.7 x 32 x 7.8 m)
6 x 6-cylinder MAN-B+W diesel-electric engines via twin screw.

Cruise ship for Costa Cruises.
Built by Bremer Vulkan, Vegesack, at a cost of US$300,000,000.

COTABATO PRINCESS (1988)
7977 grt; 1193 psrs
120 cars
492' x 76' x 16'6" (149.1 x 22.9 x 5 m)
2 x 14-cylinder MAN diesel engines via twin screw.
Passenger-car ferry operating in the Philippines for Sulpicio Lines, Cebu City.
Built by Hayashikane Zosen, Shimonoseki, for Hankyu Ferry KK, Shimonoseki, as the FERRY HARIMA (1970).

COTE D'AZUR (1951)
3998 grt; 1450 psrs
365' x 51' x 12' (110.6 x 15.5 x 3.6 m)
Geared turbine engines via twin screw.
Passenger ferry operating between UK and France for French State Rail.
Built by Forges et Chantiers de la Mediterranee, La Seyne.

COTE D'AZUR (1981) See SEAFRANCE RENOIR (1996)

COUNTESS M (1986) See DIMITRA A (2000)

COVADONGA (1953)
10226 grt; 353 psrs
487' x 62' x 26' (148.5 x 19 x 7.9 m)
10-cylinder Sulzer diesel engine via single screw.
Broken up for scrap at Castellon in 1973. Ex-Cia Trasatlantica.
Built by Soc Euskalduna, Bilbao, for Empresa Nacional Elcano SA as the cargo vessel MONASTERIO DE LA RABIDA (1951).

COVINGTON, USS (1917)
16339 grt; 2827 psrs
603' x 65' x 46'5" depth (183.9 x 19.7 x 14 m)
F Schichau 8-cylinder quadruple expansion engines via twin screw.
Seized by the US Shipping Board and transferred to the US Navy, she sank on 1 July 1918 after being torpedoed by the German U-86 off France's North Atlantic coast.
Built by Schichau Shipyards, Danzig, for the Hamburg-America Line as the passenger liner CINCINNATI (1909).

COZY ISLAND (1999)
4388 grt; 370 psrs

100 trailers + 274 TEUs
398' x 76' x 19' (120.6 x 23.1 x 5.7 m)
Mitsubishi 8-cylinder diesel engine via twin screw.
Passenger-cargo ferry owned by Korea Development Leasing Corporation, South Korea.
Built by Fukuoka Zosen KK as a shipyard asset named the HIRYU 3 (1986). Renamed SEMO EXPRESS FERRY 2 (1998 – Semo Marine Co Ltd, South Korea).

CRACOVIA (1920) See GERUSALEMME (1934)

CRANSTON VICTORY (1944) See ZUIDERKRUIS (1947)

CREFELD (1895) See TEIDE (1925)

CREFELD (1921)
9573 grt; 900 psrs
474' x 61' x 32'8" (144.5 x 18.6 x 9.9 m)
3-cylinder triple expansion engine via single screw.
Scuttled as a cargo ship on 4 April 1941 to block the harbour at Massawa, Ethiopia. The hulk ultimately had to be raised in peacetime to clear the port.
Built by Flensburger Schiffbau, Flensburg, for North German Lloyd.

CREMONA (1916) See IRAN CREMONA (1976)

CRENELLA (1916) See POLAR CHIEF (1946)

CREOLE STATE (1920) See PRESIDENT TYLER (1940)

CRESCENT CITY, USS (APA-40) (1941) See ARTSHIP (1999)

CRESCENT CITY, USS (APA-21) (1943) See ARTSHIP (1999)

CRETA SKY (1992) See VERGINA SKY (1993)

CRETE (1971) See KRITI (1971)

CRETIC (1903) See DEVONIAN (1923)

CRETIC (1955)
11151 grt
512' x 70' x 30'10" depth (155.2 x 21.2 x 9.1 m)
2 x 6-cylinder Wallsend Slipway diesel engines via twin screw.
Built by Swan Hunter & Wigham Richardson, Wallsend, for Shaw Savill Ltd.

CRIJNSSEN (1919)
4321 grt; 130 psrs
343' x 48' x 24'5" (104.5 x 14.5 x 7.4 m)
3-cylinder triple expansion engine via single screw.
Sank on 10 June 1942 after being torpedoed in the Caribbean.
Built by Wilton Fijenoord, Rotterdam, for the Royal West Indian Mail Service, Amsterdam.

CRISTOBAL (1908) See ESMERALDA (1950)

CRISTOBAL (1939)
9978 grt; 202 psrs
493' x 64' x 26' (149.4 x 19.4 x 7.9 m)
4 x DRG turbine engines via twin screw.
Broken up by Consolidated Andy Inc at Brownsville, Texas, in 1981.
Built by Bethlehem Steel Co, Quincy, for the Panama Railroad Steamship Co at a cost of US$4,000,000.

CRISTOBAL COLON (1923)
10833 grt; 1100 psrs
481' x 61' x 25'9" (145.8 x 18.5 x 7.8 m)
4 x SRG turbine engines via twin screw.
Abandoned as a total constructive loss after she wrecked herself on East North Rock, eight miles (13 km) north of Bermuda at 12.30 am on 24 October 1936. She had been hopelessly off course and it was suspected that her crew purposely let her run aground.
Built by Soc Espanola de Construccion Naval, Ferrol, for Cia Trasatlantico Espanol.

CRISTOFORO COLOMBO (1954)

29429 grt; 862 psrs
700' x 90' x 30' (213.4 x 27.5 x 9 m)
6 x Parsons DRG turbine engines via twin screw.
Broken up for scrap at Kaohsiung in 1983. She had been laid up in 1981 following four years service in Puerto Ordaz, Venezuela, as an accommodation ship for a massive government 'new city' incorporating a huge steelworks. She had been purchased for US$6,800,000.
Built by Ansaldo Shipyards, Genoa, for the Italian Line.

CROATIAN (1942) See CARIBIA 2 (1973)

CROWN DEL MAR (1987) See RIVIERA II (2000)

CROWN DYNASTY (1993) See CROWN DYNASTY (1999)

CROWN DYNASTY (1999)

19089 grt; 820 psrs
525' x 73' x 18' (159.1 x 22.1 x 5.4 m)
4 x 8-cylinder Wartsila diesel engines via twin screw.
Cruise ship owned by Crown Cruises Panama Inc and operated by Commodore Ship Management following the ship's acquisition for US$74,500,000.
Built by Union Navale de Levante SA, Valencia, for Crown Dynasty Inc, as the CROWN DYNASTY (1993). Renamed CROWN MAJESTY (1997 -- Effjohn International BV) and NORWEGIAN DYNASTY (1997 – after being chartered to the Neptun Maritime Group with purchase option and operated in 1999 by a joint venture between Commodore Holdings Ltd, Crown Cruise Line, Apple Vacations and the Bermudan government).

CROWN JEWEL (1992) See SUPERSTAR GEMINI (1995)

CROWN M (1990) See BYBLOS (2000)

CROWN MAJESTY (1997) See CROWN DYNASTY (1999)

CROWN MONARCH (1990) See WALRUS (1996)

CROWN ODYSSEY (1988) See CROWN ODYSSEY (2000)

CROWN ODYSSEY (2000)

34242 grt; 1052 psrs
614' x 92' x 23' (186.1 x 27.9 x 7 m)
4 x MaK diesel engines via twin screw.
Cruise ship owned by Norwegian Cruise Line and operated by Orient Lines.

Built by Meyer Werft, Papenburg, for Royal Cruise Lines at a cost of US$160,000,000 as the CROWN ODYSSEY (1988). Renamed NORWEGIAN CROWN (1996 – Norwegian Cruise Line).

CROWN OF SCANDINAVIA (1994)

35498 grt; 2170 psrs
450 cars
564' x 91' x 21' (171 x 27.6 x 6.3 m)
4 x 12-cylinder SEMT-Pielstick diesel engines via twin screw.
Ice-strengthened cruise ship operated by Scandinavian Seaways.
Laid down as THOMAS MANN (1993), launched as FRANS KOCKUM (1994) for Euroway (subsidiary of Sealink AB, Stockholm) and completed by Brodogradiliste, Split, as the CROWN OF SCANDINAVIA for DFDS at a cost of US$131,000,000.

CROWN PRINCESS (1990)

70285 grt; 1590 psrs
804' x 105' x 26'6" (243.6 x 31.8 x 8 m)
4 x MAN-B+W diesel engines via twin screw.
Cruise ship owned by P&O Steam Navigation and cruising for P&O Princess Cruises.
Built by Fincantieri, Monfalcone, for the P&O Group at a cost of US$200,000,000.

CROWN PRINCESS VICTORIA (1990) See AMUSEMENT WORLD (1998)

CRUCERO EXPRESS (1994) See MAGIC I (1999)

CRUISE FERRY HIRYU (1995)

10351 grt; 430 psrs
100 cars + 145 trailers
551' x 73' x 19'6" (167 x 22 x 6 m)
2 x 18-cylinder Pielstick diesel engines via twin screw.
Passenger-car-cargo ferry owned and operated by Arimura Sangyo KK, Naha.
Built by Mitsubishi Heavy Industries, Shimonoseki, as the HIRYU (1995 – Arimura Sangyo KK).

CRUISE FERRY HIRYU 21 (1996)

9225 grt; 324 psrs
124 trailers
551' x 73' x 19'6" (167 x 22 x 6 m)
2 x 16-cylinder Pielstick diesel engines via twin screw.
Passenger-cargo ferry operated by Arimura Sangyo KK, Naha.
Built by Mitsubishi Heavy Industries, Shimonoseki.

CRUISE MUHIBAH (1986) See AMBASSADOR (1993)

CRUSADER I (1993)

3080 grt; 1800 psrs
293' x 52' x 12' (88.9 x 15.8 x 3.7 m)
2 x 14-cylinder B+W diesel engines via twin screw.
Passenger ferry owned by Supernat Shipping SA, Panama, and operated by Taruna Kusan Explosive.
Built by Mitsubishi Heavy Industries Ltd, Shimonoseki, for Hayashi Marine as the AWA MARU (1967).

CRYSTAL HARMONY (1990)

48621 grt; 960 psrs
791' x 97' x 24' (239.7 x 29.4 x 7.3 m)
4 x 8-cylinder MAN diesel-electric engines via twin screw.

Cruise ship for Crystal Cruises, an NYK subsidiary.
Built by Mitsubishi Heavy Industries, Nagasaki, for NYK, Japan, at a cost of US$300,000,000.

CRYSTAL SYMPHONY (1995)
51044 grt; 975 psrs
780' x 100' x 25' (236.4 x 30.3 x 7.6 m)
6 x 9-cylinder Wartsila-Sulzer diesel-electric engines via twin screw.

Cruise ship for Crystal Cruises, an NYK subsidiary.
Built by Kvaerner Masa-Yard, Turku, for NYK, Japan, at a cost of US$250,000,000.

C S ABEGWEIT (1983) See CLUBSHIP ABEGWEIT (1997)

CUBA (1920)
3168 grt; 700 psrs
308' x 43' x 24'7" (93.3 x 13 x 7.5 m)
Blohm & Voss 6-cylinder triple expansion engines via twin screw.
Owned by Pacific Mail Steamship Co, she was wrecked on San Miguel Island, in California's Santa Barbara Channel, on 8 September 1923.
Built by Blohm & Voss, Hamburg, for North German Lloyd as the COBLENZ (1897); seized by the US government and renamed SACHEM (1917 – US Shipping Board).

CUBA (1921) See SASSARI (1960)

CUBA (1923)
11420 grt; 406 psrs
476' x 62' x 25' depth (144.2 x 18.8 x 7.6 m)
4 x Rateau DRG turbine engines via twin screw.
Sank on 6 April 1945 when torpedoed by the German U-1195 in the English Channel.
Built by Swan Hunter Shipbuilding, Newcastle, for the French Line.

CUBA (1955) See SOUTHERN CROSS (1955)

CUFIC (1904) See MARIA GIULIA (1927)

CUNARD ADVENTURER (1971) See TRITON (1991)

CUNARD AMBASSADOR (1972) See RASLAN (1983)

CUNARD CONQUEST (1975) See RHAPSODY (1995)

CUNARD COUNTESS (1976) See OLYMPIC COUNTESS (1998)

CUNARD PRINCESS (1976) See RHAPSODY (1995)

CUNDALL (1891) See PALLANZA (1902)

CURONIA (1904) See SUSANNA II (1919)

CYNTHIA (1966)
4216 grt; 265 psrs
376' x 50' x 20' (114.6 x 15 x 6 m)
3 x Parsons SRG turbine engines via single screw.
Broken up for scrap by Vado Ligure in Savona in 1973. Ex-Hellenic Mediterranean Lines.
Built by Swan Hunter & Wigham Richardson Ltd, Newcastle, for Swedish Lloyd as the BRITANNIA (1929).

CYNTHIA I (1993) See KRALJICA MIRA (1994)

CYRENIA (1947)
7527 grt; 499 psrs
447' x 56' x 25' (136.2 x 17 x 7.6 m)
2 x quadruple expansion engines via twin screw.
Broken up for scrap in Savona in 1957. Ex-Hellenic Mediterranean Lines.
Built by Fairfield Shipbuilding & Engineering Co, Glasgow, for the Union Steamship Co of New Zealand as the MAUNGANUI (1911).

CYRIL (1904)
4380 grt; 400 psrs
381' x 48' x 31'4" depth (115.5 x 14.5 x 9.5 m)
Fairfield 3-cylinder triple expansion engines via single screw.
Owned by the Booth Line, she sank on 5 September 1905 in the Amazon river near Para, Brazil, after colliding with another Booth Line vessel, the ANSELM.
Built by John Elder & Co, Glasgow, for the Castle Line as the HAWARDEN CASTLE (1883), although all preceding publicity and newspaper advertisements referred to her as the ARDTORNISH CASTLE.

CYRILL (1912) See VIRGINIA (1914)

CYRNOS (1979) See ILE DE BEAUTE (1990)

CZAR (1912) See EMPIRE PENRYN (1946)

CZARITZA (1915) See EMPIRE HELFORD (1946)

DAEDALUS (1989)

15039 grt; 1414 psrs
800 cars
465' x 74' x 21' (140.9 x 22.4 x 6.3 m)
2 x 18-cylinder MAN diesel engines via twin screw.
Passenger-car ferry operated by Minoan Lines, Iraklion.
Built by Hayashikane Shipbuilding & Engineering Company Ltd, Shimonoseki, for Kyushu Kyuko KK, Tokyo, as the ORION (1973). Renamed NISHIKI MARU (1980 – Kurushima Dockyard KK, Osaka), ORION (1984 – Kyushu Kyuko KK, Tokyo), and VIEW OF NAGASAKI (1989 – Kyushu Kyuko KK, Tokyo).

DAGISTAN (1984)

11450 grt; 2021 psrs
510' x 60' x 15' (154.5 x 18.3 x 4.5 m)
2 x 6-cylinder B+W diesel engines via twin screw.
Passenger ship operating for the Caspian Shipping Co.
Built by Brodogradiliste Uljanik, Pula, for the Caspian Shipping Company as the SOVIETSKAYA DAGESTAN (1984).

DAHAB (1994)

9042 grt; 813 psrs
89 cars or 34 trailers
391' x 66' x 18'6" (118.4 x 20 x 5.6 m)
2 x 9-cylinder MaK diesel engines via twin screw.
Ice-strengthened passenger-car-cargo RoRo ferry for Misr Shipping Company, Alexandria, Egypt, with an increased passenger capacity to 1098 when carrying pilgrims.
Built by Suez Canal Authority, Port Said, for the Egyptian Navigation Co as the RoRo cargo ship SHARM EL-SHEIKH (1987).

DA-IN (1995)

12365 grt; 600 psrs
20 cars + 96 trailers
444' x 70'6" x 18'6" (134.6 x 21.4 x 5.7 m)
2 x 14-cylinder Pielstick diesel engines via twin screw.
Passenger-car-cargo RoRo ferry owned by HMC Maritime and operated by DA-IN Ferry, South Korea.
Built by Mitsubishi Heavy Industries, Shimonoseki, for Higashi Nippon Ferry Co Ltd as the VENILIA (1988).

DAISETSU (1975) See BLUE HORIZON (2000)

DAISETSU MARU (1965)

8300 grt; 1200 psrs
48 rail coaches
433' x 59' x 17' (131.2 x 17.9 x 5.2 m)
Mitsui-B+W diesel engines via quadruple screw.
Passenger-train ferry operated by Japanese Railways for the Japanese government.
Built by Mitsubishi Heavy Industries.

DAITEN MARU (1913)

4248 grt; 1150 psrs
491' x 45' x 28' depth (122.1 x 13.8 x 8.5 m)
3-cylinder triple expansion engine via single screw.
Owned by Shoshu Kisen KK, Dairen, she sank on 6 March 1918 after being torpedoed in the Mediterranean Sea.
Built by Harland & Wolff Ltd, Belfast, for the Bibby Line as the LANCASHIRE (1889). Renamed KINA (1905 – East Asiatic Co), LITUANIA (1907 – Russian American Line).

DAKOTA (1905)

20714 grt; 2700 psrs
630' x 73' x 41'5" depth (192 x 22.1 x 12.6 m)
Midvale Steel 6-cylinder triple expansion engines via twin screw.
Broken up where she lay after striking a submerged reef on 3 March 1907 40 miles (67 km) from Yokohama. She broke her back 27 days later and was abandoned by crew and passengers.
Built by the Eastern Shipbuilding Company, New London, Connecticut, for the Great Northern Steamship Company.

DALERDYK (1949) See PRESVIA (1963)

DALIANA (1988)

5528 grt; 2300 psrs
80 cars + 55 trailers
388' x 68' x 14'6" (117.5 x 20.7 x 4.4 m)
4 x 16-cylinder MAN diesel engines via twin screw.
Owned by Keffalonia Shipping and operated as a passenger-cargo RoRo ferry by GA Ferries, Piraeus.
Built by Hayashikane Zosen, Shimonoseki, for KK Diamond Ferry, Matsuyama, as the FERRY PEARL (1970).

DALMACIJA (1969)

5634 grt; 217 psrs
386' x 56' x 17' (117 x 7 x 5.2 m)
2 x 10-cylinder Sulzer diesels via twin screw.
Cruise ship owned by Jadrolinija, Rijeka, and operated by Seeadler Cruises.
Built by Brodogradiliste Uljanik, Pula.

DALMATIA (1892) See KENKOKU MARU (1914)

DAMAN (1976)

4867 grt; 1154 psrs
382' x 55' x 23'6" (115.8 x 16.7 x 7.2 m)
2 x 5-cylinder Doxford diesel engines via single screw.
Broken up for scrap by Ghaziram Gokulchand & Co in Mumbai in 1979. Ex-Damodar Bulk Carriers Ltd, Mumbai.
Built by Barclay, Curle & Co, Glasgow, for the British India Line as the passenger-cargo ship DUMRA (1946).

DAME M (1994) See SALAMIS STAR (2000)

DAMSTERDIJK (1930) See PRESVIA (1963)

DAN (1967) See MIR (1998)

DANA ANGLIA (1978)

19321 grt; 1372 psrs
470 cars
506' x 78' x 20' (152.9 x 23.7 x 6.1 m)
2 x 18-cylinder Pielstick diesel engines via twin screw.

Owned by DFDS and operated as a ferry by Scandinavian Seaways between Denmark and the UK.
Built by the Aalborg Shipyard, Aalborg.

DANA CORONA (1979) See TIAN E (1985)

DANAE (1974) See PRINCESS DANAE (1997)

DANA FUTURA (1975) See POLARIS (1992)

DANA GLORIA (1975) See VENUS (1989)

DANA GLORIA (1977) See ISTRA (1992)

DANA GLORIA (1981) See JUPITER (1998)

DANA GLORIA (1984) See NEW YORK FORTUNE I (1997)

DANA GLORIA (1985) See JUPITER (1998)

DANA HAFNIA (1977) See VENUS (1989)

DANAOS (1978) See SALAMIS GLORY (1996)

DANA REGINA (1974) See VANA TALLINN (1997)

DANA SIRENA (1971) See TIAN E (1985)

DANA SIRENA (1977) See TIAN E (1985)

DANIA MARINE (1991) See VITTORE CARPACCIO (1992)

DANIA MARINE (1992) See SHOROK I (1998)

DANIELLE CASANOVA (1989)
21317 grt; 2366 psrs
804 cars
546' x 90' x 21' (165.5 x 27.4 x 6.4 m)
4 x 18-cylinder Pielstick diesel engines via twin screw.
Passenger-car ferry owned by SNCM and operated by Ferryterranee on the France to Corsica service.
Laid down by Chantiers de l'Atlantique, St Nazaire, for SNCM, Ajaccio, as the ILE DE BEAUTE (1988) and completed as DANIELLE CASANOVA.

DANMARK (1968)
10350 grt; 1500 psrs
260 cars
477' x 57' x 18' (144.5 x 17.4 x 5.5 m)
2 x 10-cylinder B+W diesel engines via twin screw.
Broken up for scrap in 1999 by Fornaes, Grena. Ex-Scandlines Consortium.
Built by Helsingor Skisvaerft, Helsingor, for Dansk Statbaner as an ice-strengthened passenger-car ferry.

DAN NOH (1989) See SUPERFERRY 6 (1993)

DANTE ALIGHIERI (1914) See ASAHI MARU (1928)

DAPHNE (1975) See SWITZERLAND (1996)

DARA (1948)
5030 grt; 1028 psrs
399' x 55' x 22' (120.9 x 16.7 x 6.7 m)
Doxford 5-cylinder diesel engine via single screw.
Sank in 60' (18 m) of water on 10 April 1961 while under tow from Dubai to Bahrain. This followed a terrorist bomb explosion between decks two days earlier which caused a fire to engulf the ship, killing 338 people.
Built by Barclay, Curle & Company, Glasgow, for the British India Line.

DARESSA (1950) See KIM HWA (1968)

DARESSA (1964) See KIM HWA (1968)

DARESSALAM (1939)
6130 grt
386' x 53' x 28'1" (117 x 16.1 x 8.5 m)
Blohm & Voss 6-cylinder triple expansion engines via twin screw.
Broken up for scrap in England in 1953.
Built by Blohm & Voss, Hamburg, for TC Munakalat Vekaleti Devlet Denizyollari Isletme UM as the SAVAS (1939).

DARMSTADT (1890) See KARADENIZ (1910)

DARNIA (1978) See NEPTUNIA (1997)

DARRO (1912)
11484 grt; 990 psrs
517' x 62' x 26' (157.5 x 18.8 x 7.9 m)
Quadruple expansion engines via twin screw.

Broken up for scrap in Japan in 1933.
Built by Harland & Wolff Ltd, Belfast, for Royal Mail Lines.

D'ARTAGNAN (1924) See TEIKO MARU (1942)

DAUPHIN, USS (APA-97) (1944) See STEVENS (1967)

DAVAO PRINCESS (1987) See ILOILO PRINCESS (1994)

DAVID C. SHANKS (1943) See DAVID C. SHANKS (T-AP 180) (1950)

DAVID C. SHANKS (T-AP-180) (1950)
12097 grt; 165 psrs
489' x 69' x 34'9" depth (148.2 x 20.9 x 10.6 m)
2 x DRG turbine engines via single screw.
Broken up at Kaohsiung in 1973. Ex-Inter-Ocean Grain Storage Co, Washington.
Laid down by Ingall's Shipbuilding Corporation, Pascagoula, Mississippi, for United States Lines as the AMERICAN FARMER (1942); launched for the US government as the GULFPORT (1942); and completed for the US Army as the Class C3-IN-P&C passenger-cargo carrier DAVID C. SHANKS (1943).

DAVID W. BRANCH (1937) See NEGBAH (1948)

DAWN MERCHANT (1998)
22152 grt; 214 psrs
170 trailers
594' x 80' x 28'6" (180 x 24.3 x 8.7 m)
2 x 9-cylinder Wartsila diesel engines via twin screw.
Passenger-cargo RoRo ferry owned by Cenargo International, London, and operated by their subsidiary Merchant Ferries.
Built by Astilleros Espanoles, Seville at a cost of US$65,000,000.

DAWN PRINCESS (1988) See ALBATROS (1993)

DAWN PRINCESS (1997)
77441 grt; 1950 psrs
862' x 107' x 26'6" (259 x 30.9 x 8.1 m)
4 x 16-cylinder Sulzer diesel engines via twin screw.

Cruise ship owned by Fairlane Shipping International Corporation, Panama and operated by P&O Princess Cruises.
Built by Fincantieri Navale Italiani SpA, Monfalcone at a cost of US$295,000,000.

DE GRASSE (1924) See VENEZUELA (1956)

DE GRASSE (1971) See RASA SAYANG (1980)

DE KALB, USS (1917) See MOUNT CLAY (1920)

DELARGENTINO (1940) See AFRICAN TRADER (1948)

DE LA SALLE (1921)
8400 grt; 291 psrs
440' x 57' x 34'6" depth (134.1 x 17.3 x 10.5 m)
6-cylinder triple expansion engines via twin screw.
Sank after being torpedoed by the German U-508 on 9 July 1943 in the Bight of Benin, West Africa.
Built by Barclay, Curle & Co, Glasgow, for the French Line.

DELBRASIL (1939) See AFRICAN ENDEAVOUR (1948)

DELEDDA (1978)
7222 grt; 1000 psrs
432' x 66' x 18'6" (131 x 20 x 5.6 m)
2 x 16-cylinder G.M.T. diesel engines via twin screw.
Passenger ferry operated by Tirrenia.
Built by Italcantieri SPa, Castellammare de Stabia.

DELFIN CARAVELLE (1990) See COLUMBUS CARAVELLE (1994)

DELFIN CLIPPER (1989) See WORLD DISCOVERER II (2000)

DELFINI (1996)
4405 grt; 1200 psrs
10 cars + 300 trailers
308' x 54' x 17'6" (93.2 x 16.4 x 5.4 m)
4 x 16-cylinder Werkspoor diesel engines via twin screw.
Owned and operated by Acanthus International.
Built by Merwede NV, SA, Hardinxveld, for Rederi AB, Gotland, as the GOTLAND (1964). Renamed THJELVAR (1973 – Rederi AB, Gotland), ARRAFIQ (1987 – ComP Marocaine de Navigation, Casablanca) and DIVA (1993 – Louris Shipping Co Ltd, Valetta).

DELFIN STAR (1995) See WORLD DISCOVERER II (2000)

DELFINO (1959) See WOOLAMBI (1961)

DELFTDYK (1929) See TUNG LONG (1966)

DELHI (1905)
8090 grt; 240 psrs
470' x 56'6" x 31'6" (143.3 x 17.3 x 9.6 m)
2 x quadruple expansion engines via twin screw.
Abandoned as a total loss, and losing three lives in the process, on 13 December 1911 after running aground at 2.00 am two days earlier during a gale two miles (3 km) south of Cape Spartel near Tangier. In March 1912 she broke her back and shipbreakers eventually removed the remains.
Built by Workman, Clark & Co Ltd, Belfast, for the P&O Line.

DEL MAR (1947)
10073 grt; 120 psrs
495' x 70' x 28' (150 x 21.2 x 8.5 m)
2 x General Electric DRG turbine engines via single screw.
Broken up for scrap in Kaohsiung in 1972.
Built by the Ingalls Shipyard, Pascagoula, Mississippi, for the Mississippi Shipping Co Inc.

DEL NORTE (1948)
10073 grt; 120 psrs
495' x 70' x 28' (150 x 21.2 x 8.5 m)
General Electric geared turbines via single screw.
Broken up for scrap in Kaohsiung in 1972.Built by the Ingalls Shipyard, Pascagoula, Mississippi, for the Delta Steamship Line.

DELORLEANS (1940) See ARTSHIP (1999)

DELORLEANS II (1940) See CALVERT, USS (APA-32) (1943)

DELOS (1969) See KHALID I (1983)

DELOS (1986)
5543 grt; 1200 psrs
180 cars or 18 trailers
344' x 58' x 13' (104.2 x 17.7 x 3.9 m)
2 x 16-cylinder Pielstick diesel engines via twin screw.
Broken up for scrap in 1998. Ex-Ionian Lines.
Built by Dubigeon-Normandie, Nantes, for French State Rail (SNCF) as the passenger-car-cargo train ferry VILLANDRY (1964). Renamed OLYMPIA (1985 – Agapitos, Piraeus).

DELPHI (1969) See LA PALMA (1980).

DELPHIN (1996)
16214 grt; 554 psrs
256 cars + 23 trailers
515' x 72' x 19'6" (157 x 21.8 x 5.9 m)
2 x 18-cylinder Wartsila-Pielstick geared diesel engines via twin screw.
Cruise ship owned by Lady Lou Shipping and operated by Delfin Cruises.
Built by Wartsila, Helsinki, for the Black Sea Shipping Co, Odessa, as the BELORUSSIYA (1975) at a cost of US$25,000,000. Renamed KAZAKHSTAN II (1994 – Delphin Seereisen).

DEL SUD (1947)
10073 grt; 120 psrs
495' x 70' x 28' (150 x 21.2 x 8.5 m)
2 x General Electric geared turbine engines via single screw.
Broken up in Kaohsiung in 1972.
Built by the Ingalls Shipbuilding Corporation, Pascagoula, Mississippi, for the Delta Steamship Line.

DELTA (1905)
8053 grt; 240 psrs
470' x 56'6" x 31'6" (143.3 x 17.3 x 9.6 m)
2 x quadruple expansion engines via twin screw.
Broken up by Sakaguchi Sadakichi Shosen KK for scrap in Japan in 1929 for a tender fee of £25,500.
Built by Workman, Clark & Co Ltd, Belfast, for the P&O Line.

DELTA FILIPINE DREAM (1995)
9318 grt; 548 psrs
48 rail coaches
435' x 59' x 18' (131.8 x 17.9 x 5.5 m)
8 x 16-cylinder MAN diesel engines via twin screw.
Trading as a floating hotel owned and operated by Philippine Dream Co Inc in Cebu.
Built by Uraga Heavy Industries Ltd, Uraga, for Japan National Railways as the train ferry TOWADA MARU (1966). Renamed JAPANESE DREAM (1990 – Nippon Ryokyakusen).

DELTARGENTINO (1940) See AFRICAN ENTERPRISE (1948)

DELTARGENTINO II (1942) See MONROVIA, USS (APA-31) (1942)

DELURUGUAY (1942) See CHARLES CARROLL, USS (AP-58) (1942)

DEMERARA (1912)
11484 grt; 993 psrs
517' x 62' x 26' (157.5 x 18.8 x 7.9 m)
Harland & Wolff quadruple expansion engines via twin screw.
Broken up for scrap in Japan in 1933.
Built by Harland & Wolff Ltd, Belfast, for Royal Mail Lines.

DEMOSTHENES (1911)
11233 grt; 350 psrs
517' x 62' x 29'6" (157.5 x 18.8 x 8.9 m)
Triple expansion engines via triple screw.
Broken up by Hughes Bolckow & Company for scrap on River Tyne, UK, in 1931.
Built by Harland & Wolff Ltd, Belfast, for the Aberdeen Line.

DEMPO (1931)
16979 grt; 634 psrs
573' x 70' x 41'6" depth (173.6 x 21.2 x 12.6 m)
2 x 20-cylinder Sulzer diesel engines via twin screw.
Sank on 17 March 1944, with the loss of 498 lives, after being torpedoed by the German U-371 off Algeria.
Built by de Schelde Shipyards, Flushing, for Rotterdam Lloyd.

DENALI (1938) See SOUTHERN CROSS (1955).

DENIS (1911)
4450 grt; 146 psrs
376' x 50' x 23'6" (113.9 x 15.2 x 7.2 m)

North East Marine Engineering 3-cylinder triple expansion engine via single screw.
Built by Hawthorne Leslie & Co Ltd, Newcastle, for the Booth Line.

DENVER (1901)
4549 grt; 136 psrs
373' x 48' x 24'5" depth (113 x 14.5 x 7.4 m)
Harlan & Hollingsworth 3-cylinder triple expansion engines via single screw.
Abandoned as a total loss after colliding with an iceberg in mid-Atlantic on 23 March 1915.
Built by Harlan & Hollingsworth Co, Wilmington, Delaware, for Mallory Steamship Co.   .

DERBYSHIRE (1935)
10641 grt; 115 psrs
501' x 66' x 29' (151.8 x 20 x 8.8 m)
2 x 8-cylinder Sulzer diesel engines via twin screw.
Broken up for scrap in Hong Kong in 1964.
Built by Fairfield Shipbuilding & Engineering Company, Glasgow, for the Bibby Line.

DER DEUTSCHE (1934) See SHIRLEY (1963)

DERECKTOR (1948) See GALILAH (1948)

DERFFLINGER (1907) See DERFFLINGER (1923)

DERFFLINGER (1923)
9144 grt; 1460 psrs
481' x 57' x 35'8" depth (145.8 x 17.3 x 10.8 m)
F Schichau 8-cylinder quadruple expansion engines via twin screw.
Broken up for scrap in Bremerhaven in 1932. Ex-North German Lloyd.
Laid down by F Schichau Shipyards, Danzig, for North German Lloyd as the DERFFLINGER (1907) but completed as the HUNTSGREEN (1914) after seizure by Great Britain.

DERNA (1948) See ASSIMINA (1949)

DESEADO (1911)
11477 grt; 995 psrs
517' x 62' x 26' (157.2 x 18.8 x 7.9 m)
Quadruple expansion engines via twin screw.
Broken up for scrap in Japan in 1934.
Built by Harland & Wolff Ltd, Belfast, for Royal Mail Lines.

DESNA (1912)
11484 grt; 995 psrs
517' x 62' x 26' (157.5 x 18.8 x 7.9 m)
Harland & Wolff quadruple expansion engines via twin screw.
Broken up for scrap in Japan in 1933.
Built by Harland & Wolff Ltd, Belfast, for Royal Mail Lines.

DEUTSCHLAND (1900) See HANSA (1921)

DEUTSCHLAND (1924)
21046 grt; 1558 psrs
678' x 73' x 41'9" (205.5 x 22.1 x 12.7 m)
SRG turbines via twin screw.
Broken up for scrap in 1948 after raising her from the seabed in the Bay of Lubeck, off Neustadt, where she sank on 3 May 1945 after an Allied air attack There was no loss of life as the ship had just arrived with a skeleton crew, and dropped anchor in the harbour roads, in preparation for her conversion into a hospital ship.
Built by Blohm & Voss, Hamburg, for the Hamburg-America Line.

DEUTSCHLAND (1953) See NISSOS RODOS (1977)

DEUTSCHLAND (1972) See SALAM (1999)

DEUTSCHLAND (1998)
22496 grt; 650 psrs
570' x 75' x 19' (172.7 x 22.7 x 5.8 m)
4 x 8-cylinder MaK diesel engines via twin screw.
Cruise ship assembled by Howaldswerke-Deutsche Werft, Kiel, from a bow constructed at Rendsburg; stern sections from Bremerhaven and Helsinki; and mid-sections and engines built by HWD for Peter Dielmann Reederei, Germany, at a total cost of Dm 225,000,000.

DEVANHA (1906)
8092 grt; 240 psrs
470' x 56'6" x 31'6" (143.3 x 17.3 x 9.6 m)
2 x quadruple expansion engines via twin screw.
Broken up Sakaguchi Sadakichi Shosen KK for a scrap tender of US$42,000 in Osaka in 1928.
Built by Caird & Company, Greenock, for the P&O Line at a cost of £159,249.

DEVON (1967)
10574 grt; 160 psrs
528' x 63' x 30' (160 x 19 x 9.1 m)
2 x 9-cylinder Sulzer diesel engines via twin screw.
Broken up for scrap in Kaohsiung in 1967. Ex-Embajada Cia Naviere SA, Piraeus.
Laid down by de Schelde Shipyards, Flushing, for the Holland-Africa Line as the RIETFONTEIN (1939) and completed as the ELANDSFONTEIN (1940). Renamed JAGERSFONTEIN (1947 – Holland-Africa Line).

DEVONIA (1962)
12796 grt; 1026 psrs
517' x 63' x 24'6" (156.7 x 19.1 x 7.5 m)
2 x 8-cylinder Sulzer diesel engines via twin screw.
Broken up for scrap at La Spezia in 1967. Ex-British India Line.
Built by Fairfield Shipbuilding & Engineering Co Ltd, Glasgow, for the Bibby Line as the DEVONSHIRE (1939).

DEVONIAN (1900)
10418 grt; 135 psrs
570' x 59' x 31' (173.6 x 18 x 9.4 m)
Triple expansion engine via single screw.
Sank on 21 August 1917 with the loss of two lives after being torpedoed by the German U-53 20 miles (33 km) north-east of Tory Island, near Donegal, Ireland.
Built by Harland & Wolff Ltd, Belfast, for F Leyland, Liverpool.

DEVONIAN (1923)
13507 grt; 1300 psrs
601' x 60' x 32'10" depth (183.2 x 18.2 x 9.7 m)
Hawthorne Leslie 6-cylinder triple expansion engines via twin screw.
Broken up for scrap at Barrow-in-Furness in 1929. Ex-Red Star Line.
Built by R & W Hawthorn, Leslie & Co Ltd, Newcastle, for F Leyland, Liverpool, as the HANOVERIAN (1903). Renamed MAYFLOWER (1903 – Dominion Line) and CRETIC (1903 – White Star Line).

DEVONSHIRE (1939) See DEVONIA (1962)

DE WITT CLINTON (1919) See GALILAH (1948)

DIAMOND ISLAND (1990) See THE EMERALD (1996)

DIAMOND OKINAWA (1975) See NEW UTOPIA (1982)

DIANA (1972) See ALANDIA (1992)

DIANA II (1979) See MELOODIA (1996)

D'IBERVILLE (1922) See CAP PADARAN (1926)

DIEMERDYK (1950) See ORIENTAL AMIGA (1969)

DIFKO FYN (1995)
4101 grt; 253 psrs
32 cars + 8 trailers or 16 trailers
316' x 56' x 12' (95.8 x 17 x 3.6 m)
10 x 6-cylinder Cummins diesel engines via quadruple screw.
Passenger-car-cargo ferry owned by KS Difko, but laid up in 1997, then placed on the sales lists minus her engines from mid-1999 for US$1,650,000.
Built by North East Shipbuilding Co, Pallion, for Superflex Ships as the SUPERFLEX ECHO (1989).

DIFKO NYBORG (1990)
4104 grt; 253 psrs
36 cars + 30 trailers
314' x 58' x 12' (95 x 17 x 3.6 m)
10 x 6-cylinder Cummins diesel engines via quadruple screw.
Passenger-car ferry operated by Difko Lxxi, Denmark, but laid up from mid-2000.
Built by North East Shipbuilders, Pallion, for Superflex Ships as the SUPERFLEX ALFA (1987).

DIFKO STOREBAELT (1990) See GITTE 3 (1999)

DIGBY (1913) See IONIAN (1965)

DIGBY (1918) See IONIAN (1965)

DIGNITY (1995) See IONIS (1998)

DILWARA (1935) See KUALA LUMPUR (1960)

DIMBOOLA (1912) See EMPIRE LONGFORD (1951)

DIMITRA (1989) See NAIAS EXPRESS (1995)

DIMITRA (1994) See LEROS (1997)

DIMITRA A (2000)
10093 grt; 1600 psrs
350 cars or 60 trailers
442' x 72' x 16' (133.9 x 21.8 x 4.8 m)
2 x 12-cylinder Pielstick diesel engines via twin screw.
Passenger-car-cargo ferry owned and operated by Dimitra Navigation Co Ltd, Malta.
Built by Ateliers et Chantiers de Bretagne & Dubigeon-Normandie SA, Nantes, for Normandy Ferries as the LEOPARD (1968). Renamed COUNTESS M (1986 – Marlines).

DIMITRIOS EXPRESS (1990) See EXPRESS POSEIDON (1999)

DIMITRIOS EXPRESS (1994) See EXPRESS POSEIDON (1999)

DIMITRIOS MIRAS (1988)
3883 grt; 941 psrs
220 cars
332' x 53' x 13'2" (100.5 x 16 x 4 m)
2 x 12-cylinder MAN diesel engines via twin screw.
Passenger-car ferry owned and operated by Domitrios Miras & Co ENE, Piraeus.
Built by Ateliers et Chantiers du Havre, Le Havre, as the MONACO (1972). Renamed ION (1983) and OLYMPIA (1986).

DIMITRI SHOSTAKOVICH (1980) See DMITRI SHOSTAKOVICH (1980)

DIMITROS (1958)
9589 grt
498' x 65' x 29'9" (150.9 x 19.7 x 6 m)
2 x 6-cylinder Kincaid diesel engines via single screw.
Built by Lithgows Ltd, Port Glasgow, for Cia Mar Marmara SA, Piraeus, as the EMPIRE RAWLINSON (1944). Renamed MONKAY (1946 – Messageries Maritimes).

DIMITROULA (1997)
7222 grt; 1000 psrs
432' x 66' x 18'6" (131 x 20 x 5.6 m)
2 x 12-cylinder MAN diesel engines via twin screw.
Passenger ferry owned and operated by GA Ferries.
Built by Italcantieri SpA, Castellarmare di Stabia, as the VERGA (1978).

DINTELDYK (1951) See COPA CASINO (1993)

DINTELDYK (1957) See HONG KONG SUCCESS (1972)

DIOGENES (1922) See MATAROA (1926)

DIOMED (1922)
10374 grt
491' x 62' x 31' depth (148.8 x 18.8 x 9.4 m)
4 x Workman, Clark DRG turbine engines via twin screw.
Broken up for scrap at Dalmuir in 1952.
Built by Workman, Clark & Co Ltd, Belfast, for A Holt & Co.

DIONISIOS SOLOMOS (1999)
8847 grt; 600 psrs
72 trailers
381' x 69' x 15' (115.6 x 21 x 4.5 m)
2 x 8-cylinder Pielstick diesel engines via twin screw.
Passenger-cargo ferry operated by Anonimos Naftiliaki.
Built by Sanoyas Corporation, Mitsushima, for Shikoku Chuo as the ROYAL KAWANOE (1990).

DIPOLOG PRINCESS (1989)
3501 grt; 1002 psrs
367' x 50' x 18' (111.2 x 15.2 x 5.5 m)
8-cylinder Hitachi-B+W diesel engines via single screw.
Passenger-ship operated by Sulpicio Lines, Cebu City.
Built by Onomichi Zosen for Ryukyu Kaiun as the TOKYO MARU (1969). Renamed DON EUSEBIO (1978 – Sulpicio Lines Inc, Cebu City).

DIPONEGORO (1951) See DJAKARTA RAYA (1952)

DISCOVERER (1974) See WORLD DISCOVERER (1976)

DISCOVERER II (1972)
5678 grt; 188 psrs
381' x 70' x 19' (115.5 x 21.2 x 5.8 m)
2 x 12-cylinder Alco diesel engines via twin screw.
Cruise ship owned by Discoverer Reederei and chartered to Society Expeditions.
Built by Mitsui Shipbuilding & Engineering Co Ltd, Tama, for Offshore International SA, Panama.

DISCOVERY I (1986)
12244 grt; 446 psrs
489' x 68' x 20' (149.2 x 20.8 x 6.1 m)
2 x 18-cylinder Crossley-Pielstick diesel engines via twin screw.

Broken up for scrap at Alang in 1998 after being declared a total constructive loss following a serious fire in Freeport Harbour in May 1996. This occurred during the period of ownership by Bajamar Shipping Co, Panama, and cruising for Discovery Cruises.
Built by Upper Clyde Shipbuilders Ltd, Glasgow, for Fred Olsen Ltd, London, as the cruise ship BLENHEIM (1970). Renamed SCANDINAVIAN SEA (1982 – Scandinavian World Cruises) and VENUS VENTURER (1984 – Venus Cruise Lines).

DISCOVERY DAWN (1996) See TEXAS TREASURE (2000)

DISCOVERY SUN (1995)
11979 grt; 1150 psrs
220 cars

441' x 70' x 18' (133.6 x 21.2 x 5.5 m)
2 x 16-cylinder Pielstick diesel engines via twin screw.
Ice-strengthened passenger cruise ferry owned by Discovery Cruises and operated by V Ships Leisure.
Launched by Orensten & Koppel, Lubeck, for Freeport Cruise Lines as the cruise ship FREEPORT (1963) and completed as the FREEPORT I (1968). Renamed FREEPORT (1973 – Birka Line), SVEA STAR (1974 – Svea Line), CARIBE (1976 – owned by Bremer Schiffahrts and chartered to Commodore Cruise Line), CARIBE BREMEN (1981 – Bremer Schiffarhrts), SCANDINAVIAN SUN (1982 – owned by DFDS and chartered to Scandinavian World Cruises Inc, Nassau) and BALANGA QUEEN (1993 – owned by Belle Meade Shipping, Monrovia, and chartered to the Corona Line).

DISNEY MAGIC (1998)
83338 grt; 1760 psrs
964' x 104' x 26' (272.7 x 31.5 x 5.5 m)
5 x 16-cylinder Sulzer diesel-electric engines via twin screw.
Cruise ship operated by the Disney Cruise Line, Miami.
Built by Fincantieri in both their Trieste and Monfalcone shipyards, the bow and stern sections constructed 100 miles (167 km) apart and joined in June 1997. The total cost of the vessel was US$380,000,000.

DISNEY WONDER (1999)
83308 grt; 1760 psrs
964' x 104' x 26' (272.7 x 31.5 x 5.5 m)
5 x 16-cylinder Sulzer diesel-electric engines via twin screw.
Cruise ship operated by the Disney Cruise Line, Miami.
Built by Fincantieri in both their Trieste and Monfalcone shipyards, the bow and stern sections constructed 100 miles (167 km) apart and joined in June 1997. The total cost of the vessel was US$380,000,000.

DIVA (1993) See DELFINI (1996)

DIVONA (1912)
6812 grt; 581 psrs
482' x 52' x 19' (146.9 x 15.9 x 5.8 m)
Triple expansion engine via single screw.
Broken up for scrap partially by Lefevre-Des Peaux in France and completed in Genoa, in 1922. Ex-Cie Sud Atlantique.
Built by Fairfield Shipbuilding & Engineering Co Ltd, Glasgow, for the Orient Line as the ORMUZ (1886).

DIXIE (1927) See ALCOR, USS (AG-34) (1941)

DJAKARTA RAYA (1952)
8582 grt
449' x 60' x 28' (136 x 18.2 x 8.5 m)
Geared turbines via twin screw.
Broken up for scrap. Ex-Djakarta Lloyd.
Built by the Sun Shipbuilding Co, Chester, Pennsylvania, for the US government as the SOUTH BEND (1919). Renamed JL LUKENBACH (1923 – Lukenbach Steamship Co), SAN FRANCISCO (1948 – Republic Steamship Corporation) and DIPONEGORO (1951 – Djakarta Lloyd).

DJATINEGARA (1952)
7914 grt; 290 psrs
465' x 58' x 29' (141.7 x 17.7 x 8.8 m)
2 x Workman, Clark 3-cylinder triple expansion engines via twin screw.
Owned by Djakarta Lloyd, she was broken up for scrap in Hong Kong in 1956 after having to be beached at Lingayen. She had started to leak badly on 1 December 1955 while under tow for repairs. She was refloated on 21 February 1956.
Built by Workman, Clark & Co Ltd, Belfast, for the British government as the WAR ARGUS (1918). Renamed GALLIC (1920 – White Star Line), CLAN COLQUHOUN (1933 – Clan Line), IOANNIS LIVANOS (1947 – Zarati Steamship Co), JENNY (1948 – Dos Oceanos Cia de Navigation) and IMAM BONDJOL (1951 – Djakarta Lloyd).

DJEBEL DIRA (1948) See MELODY (1979)

DJENNE (1931) See CESAREE (1962)

DJEYHUN (1914)
3509 grt; 84 psrs
360' x 43' x 27'6" (109.7 x 13 x 8.9 m)
Caird 3-cylinder steam engines via single screw.
Under ownership of the Turkish government, she sank on 7 June 1915 by a torpedo from the British submarine E-11.
Built by Caird & Co Ltd, Greenock, for Nederlands Steamship Co as the PRINSES SOPHIE (1890). Renamed ELLA (1907 – M Jebsen, Hamburg). Note: ship's 1914 name often spelt CEIJHUN.

D. JUAN (1998) See RIVIERA II (2000)

DJURSLAND (1972) See ST. SUNNIVA (1987)

DJURSLAND (1980) See BETANCURIA (2000)

DJURSLAND II (1974) See BETANCURIA (2000)

DMITRI SHOSTAKOVICH (1980) See GEORG OTS (1995)

DMITRIY SHOSTAKOVICH (1980) See DMITRI SHOSTAKOVICH (1980)

DNEPR (1939)
12589 grt; 512 psrs
483' x 63' x 25'6" (146.4 x 19.1 x 7.8 m)
MAN diesel engines via twin screw.
Sank on 3 October 1941 after being hit by an aircraft-launched torpedo off Annaba.
Built by Soc Espanola de Construccion Naval, Bilbao, for Ybarra y Cia as the CABO SAN AGOSTIN (1931).

DOBONSOLO (1993)
14610 grt; 1737 psrs
483' x 78' x 19'6" (146.5 x 23.7 x 5.9 m)
2 x 6-cylinder MaK geared diesel engines via twin screw.
Passenger ferry owned by the Indonesian government and operated by PT Pelni.
Built by Jos L Meyer, Papenburg.

DODEKANISSOS (1987) See EXPRESS KARISTOS (1996)

DOGU (1939) See PETR VELIKI (1949)

DOLCE VITA (1999)
4437 grt; 800 psrs
125 cars
361' x 511' x 14' (109.4 x 15.6 x 4.2 m)
2 x 10-cylinder Pielstick diesel engines via twin screw.
Owned and operated by Coral Investments, Seychelles.
Built by Hanseatic Werft, Hamburg, for KS Jens C Hagen & Co, Oslo, as the HOLGER DANSK (1961). Renamed FRIENDSHIP (1989 – Ross Sea Shipping Co) and MONTE CARLO (1996 – Symphony Shipping Corporation).

DOLPHIN (1987) See DOLPHIN IV (1978)

DOLPHIN (1989) See AEGEAN I (1996)

DOLPHIN IV (1978) See DOLPHIN IV (1987)

DOLPHIN IV (1987)
13007 grt; 718 psrs
501' x 65' x 27' (152.7 x 20 x 8.2 m)
2 x AEG DRG turbines via single screw.
Cruise ship owned by Ulysses Shipping Co, and chartered to Cape Canaveral Cruise Lines, until the financial collapse of the latter company and the seizure of this solus ship by the Commissioner of the Bahamas Supreme Court. She was sold for US$950,000 by the court, with the purchaser's identity and funds disbursement to be released in February 2001.
Built by Deutsche Werft, Hamburg, for Zim Lines as the passenger-cargo ship ZION (1956) under the Reparation Payment Scheme whereby Germany had to atone for any war losses sustained by the Jewish people during World War

Two. Renamed AMELIA DE MELLO (1966 – Soc Geral de Commercio Inde Transportes, Lisbon), ITHACA (1972 – Cia de Vapores Realma SA, Paraeus, and chartered to the Ulysses Line) and DOLPHIN (1987 – South Pacific Cruises Pty Ltd, Sydney, although the name registration was terminated following litigation between the charterer and the owner over the contracted service speed of the vessel, with the ship being reinstated to the owner in 1987).

DOMALA (1922) See EMPIRE ATTENDANT (1940)

DOMINE (1935)
6914 grt; 137 psrs
407' x 54' x 22' (123.3 x 16.4 x 6.7 m)
2 x 12-cylinder Krupp diesel engines via twin screw.
Built by Espanola de Construccion Naval, Bilbao, for Trasmediterranea.

DOMINICA (1925) See IONIAN (1965)

DOMINICAN (1985) See HAPPY DOLPHIN (1999)

DOMINION MONARCH (1939) See DOMINION MONARCH MARU (1962)

DOMINION MONARCH MARU (1962)
26463 grt; 508 psrs
682' x 84' x 33' (207.8 x 25.5 x 10 m)
2 x 5-cylinder Doxford + 2 x 5-cylinder Swan Hunter diesel engines via quadruple screw.s.
Broken up for scrap in Osaka in 1963 by the Mitsui Breakers' Yard.
Built as the DOMINION MONARCH (1939) by Swan Hunter & Wigham Richardson Ltd, Newcastle, for Shaw Savill.

DOMIZIA (1979) See DOMIZIANA (1979)

DOMIZIANA (1979)
12523 grt; 2000 psrs
610 cars
432' x 76' x 19' (131 x 23 x 5.8 m)
2 x 16-cylinder GMT diesel engines via twin screw.
Passenger-car RoRo ferry operated by Tirrenia on the Italy–Sardinia service.
Launched by Italcantieri SPa, Castellammare de Stabia, for Tirrenia as the DOMIZIA (1979) and completed as the DOMIZIANA.

DOM PEDRO I (1926)
6338 grt; 450 psrs
403' x 54' x 30'6" (122 x 16.4 x 9.3 m)
A Stephen & Sons 6-cylinder triple expansion engines via twin screw.
Broken up for scrap in Rio de Janiero in 1958. Ex-Lloyd Brasileiro, Rio de Janeiro.
Built by A Stephen & Sons Ltd, Glasgow, for the Australasian United Steam Navigation Company as the WYREEMA (1908).

DOM PEDRO II (1926)
6129 grt; 450 psrs
403' x 55' x 30'7" (122 x 16.7 x 9.3 m)
A Stephen & Sons 8-cylinder quadruple expansion engine via single screw.
Broken up for scrap in Rio de Janiero in 1963. Ex-Lloyd Brasileiro, Rio de Janeiro.
Built by A Stephen & Sons Ltd, Glasgow, for the Australasian United Steam Navigation Company as the LEVUKA (1910).

DON (1904) See SAN GIUSTO (1918).

DONA MONTSERRAT (1975) See XINGHU (1979)

DONATELLA D'ABUNDO (2000)
11799 grt; 900 psrs
455' x 68' x 18'8" (137.8 x 20.5 x 5.7 m)
240 cars
2 x 16-cylinder MAN diesel engines via twin screw
Passenger-cargo ferry owned and operated by a joint venture between Linee Lauro SRL and Agostino Lauro SRL after purchase for US$6,000,000.
Built by Union Levante, Valencia, for y Barra Cia SA, Seville, as the CANGURO CABO SAN SEBASTIAN (1972). Renamed CIUDAD DE PALMA (1981 – Trasmediterranee), CIUDAD DE SANTA CRUZ DE LA PALMA (1982 – Trasmediterranee) and BENI ANSAR (1998 – Limadet, Morocco).

DON ENRIQUE (1978) See ILOILO PRINCESS (1994)

DON EUSEBIO (1978) See DIPOLOG PRINCESS (1989)

DONG CHUN (2000)
5410 grt; 798 psrs
152 cars + 129 TEUs or 57 trailers
481' x 67' x 19'8" (146 x 20.4 x 6 m)
2 x 12-cylinder Mitsubishi-MAN diesel engines via twin screw.
Passenger-car-cargo container ship owned by Dae A Express Shipping Co Ltd, South Korea.
Built by Mitsubishi Heavy Industries, Shimonoseki, as the HIRYU II (1980) for Arimura Sangyo KK, Naha. Renamed TIAN IN 2 (1995 – Dae A Express Shipping Co Ltd, South Korea).

DONGEDYK (1952) See TUNG LONG (1966)

DONGOLA (1905)
8038 grt; 240 psrs
470' x 56'6" x 23' (143.3 x 17.3 x 7 m)
2 x quadruple expansion engines via twin screw.
Broken up for scrap by Thomas Ward Ltd at Barrow in 1926 for a tender of £15,500.
Built by Barclay, Curle & Co Ltd, Glasgow, for P&O Lines at a cost of £160,167.

DONG YANG EXPRESS FERRY No. 2 (1979) See KAMOME I (1998)

DONG YANG EXPRESS FERRY No. 6 (1999)
5999 grt; 670 psrs
65 cars + 68 trailers
378' x 65' x 15' (114.5 x 19.8 x 4.5 m)
2 x 6-cylinder Makita diesel engines via twin screw.
Passenger-car-cargo ferry owned and operated by Dong Yang Express Ferry Co Ltd, Busan.
Built by Sanuki Shipbuilding Co, Takuma, for Shinkoku Ferry Co as the KOBE MARU (1982). Renamed KOBE MARU No. 1 (1991 – Korea Industrial Leasing Co Ltd), and CAR FERRY CHEJU No.2 (1991 – Dong Yang Express Ferry Co Ltd).

DONIZETTI (1963)
13140 grt; 672 psrs
528' x 69' x 27' (161 x 21 x 8.2 m)
2 x 10-cylinder Sulzer diesel engines via twin screw.
Broken up for scrap at La Spezia for a tender of Lira 300,000,000 in 1977. Ex-Italian Line.
Built by Cantieri Riuniti dell 'Adriatico for Lloyd Triestino as the AUSTRALIA (1951). Renamed GAETANO DONEZETTI (1963 – Italian Line).

DON JUAN (1994) See RIVIERA II (2000)

DORCHESTER (1926)
5649 grt; 302 psrs
368' x 52' x 36' depth (111.5 x 15.8 x 10.9 m)

Newport News 4-cylinder triple expansion engines via single screw.
Sank on 3 February 1943 in the North Atlantic, 150 miles (250 km) south of Cape Farewell, with the loss of 675 lives and the survival of 229 people. She had been torpedoed by the German U-233.
Built by Newport News Shipbuilding Co, Newport News, Virginia, for Merchants & Miners Transportation Co.

DORIC (1883) See ASIA (1906)

DORIC (1923)
16484 grt; 2300 psrs
601' x 67' x 34' (182.1 x 20.3 x 10.3 m)
4 x SRG turbines via twin screw.
Broken up for scrap at Newport, Wales, for a tender of £35,000 in 1935 following a collision on 5 September 1935 off Cape Finisterre with the 2166 grt French cargo ship FORMIGNY. She was first taken to Vigo, Spain, for temporary repairs before returning to England under her own power.
Built by Harland & Wolff Ltd, Belfast, for the White Star Line.

DORIC (1973) See SUN (1996)

DORIC FERRY (1962) See KAPETAN ALEX ANDROS A (1993)

DORIC FERRY (1982)
5100 grt; 429 psrs
335' x 50' x 15' (102.1 x 15.2 x 4.5 m)
6 x SRG turbines via twin screw.
Passenger ferry broken up for scrap at Aliaga in 1989.
Built by A Stephens & Sons Ltd, Glasgow, for Tasmanian Steamers Pty Ltd as the TAROONA (1933). Renamed HELLAS (1959 – Typaldos Lines, Greece). The ship was laid up from 1966 to 1982 while Typaldos Lines were fully engaged in legal proceedings over the HERAKLION sinking tragedy.

DOROTHY ALEX ANDER (1916) See PORTUGAL (1946)

DORSET (1903)
7630 grt; 324 psrs
460' x 58' x 31' depth (139.4 x 17.6 x 9.4 m)
2 x John Brown triple expansion engines via twin screw.
Broken up for scrap at Barrow-in-Furness in 1927. Ex-Federal Steam Navigation Co Ltd.
Built by John Brown Ltd for Birt, Trinder & Bethell.

DORSETSHIRE (1920)
9645 grt; 550 psrs
450' x 57' x 23' (137.1 x 17.4 x 7 m)
2 x 6-cylinder B+W diesel engines via twin screw.
Broken up for scrap by John Cashmore Ltd at Newport, Wales, in 1954.
Built by Harland & Wolff Ltd, Belfast, for the Bibby Line.

DOUKKALA (1912)
4293 grt; 107 psrs
393' x 45' x 30' (120.1 x 13.7 x 9 m)
4-cylinder Maatschippij Voor-Scheeps-En Werktuigbouw quadruple expansion engines via single screw.
Broken up at Genoa, in 1935.
Built by Maatschippij Voor-Scheeps-En Werktuigbouw, Rotterdam, as the KONING WILLEM II (1900).

DOULOS (1978)
6822 grt; 570 psrs

427' x 54' x 18' (125 x 16.4 x 5.5 m)
18-cylinder Fiat diesel engine via single screw.
Missionary ship owned by Gute Bucher Fur Alle eV and operated by Operation Mobilisation, Malta.
Built by Newport News Shipbuilding & Drydock Company, Newport News, Virginia, for the Mallory Steamship Company as the cargo ship MEDINA (1914). Renamed ROMA (1948 – International Catholic Travel Committee) and FRANCA C (1952 – Costa Line).

DOUNE CASTLE (1883) See OLYMPIA (1904)

DOUNE CASTLE (1890) See SUSANNA II (1919)

DOVER (1965) See TUXEDO ROYALE (1988)

DOVER (1999) See P&O SL DOVER (1999).

DOVER CASTLE (1904)
8271 grt; 800 psrs
476' x 57' x 31' (144.2 x 17.3 x 9.4 m)
Barclay, Curle & Co quadruple expansion engines via twin screw.
Sank on 17 May 1917 as a hospital ship which was torpedoed by the German UC-67 in the Mediterranean, 50 miles (84 km) north of Annaba.
Built by Barclay, Curle & Co, Glasgow, for the Union-Castle Line.

DRACHENFELS (1976) See VENUS (1989)

DRACHENSTEIN (1930)
8135 grt; 1200 psrs
455' x 53' x 29'1" (138.7 x 16.2 x 8.8 m)
Scott & Co 6-cylinder triple expansion engine via twin screw.
Owned by Bernstein Line when it was broken up for scrap in Germany in 1934.
Built by Scotts Shipbuilding Co, Greenock, for the Donaldson Line as the CASSANDRA (1906). Renamed as the cargo vessel CARMIA (1925 – Donaldson Line Ltd).

DRAGO (1952)
5617 grt; 1216 psrs
421' x 48' x 28'6" (128.3 x 14.6 x 8.7 m)
6-cylinder Hawthorn Leslie triple expansion engine via twin screw.
Broken up for scrap in Spain in 1959 as a cargo ship. Ex-Cia Trasatlantica. Launched by Sir WG Armstrong, Mitchell & Co, Walker-on-Tyne, for MacIver Shipping as the LUCANIA (1891) and completed as the H.H. MEIER (1892 – North German Lloyd). Renamed MANUEL CALVO (1901 – Cia Trasatlantica, Espanola).

DRAGON (1967) See MILLENNIUM EXPRESS II (2000)

DRAYTON GRANGE (1902) See TYRONE (1912)

DREAM 21 (1997) See WORLD DISCOVERER II (2000)

DREAMWARD (1992) See NORWEGIAN DREAM (1998)

DRESDEN (1888) See TIRIMUJGHIAN (1906)

DRESDEN (1927)
14690 grt; 971 psrs
570' x 67' x 29' (173.7 x 20.4 x 8.8 m)
2 x 4-cylinder quadruple expansion engines via twin screw.
Owned by North German Lloyd, she sank following capsizing on 21 June 1934 after striking a submerged rock at 7.30 pm the previous day. The incident happened off Karmoy Island in the Boknfjord, Norway. Four lives wer lost. The Norwegian coastal ferry CROWN PRINCESS MARTHA rescued 333 people in a very dangerous situation, for which her Captain (Pallesen) was decorated by Adolf Hitler. Salvage attempts were made in 1937.
Launched by Bremer Vulkan, Vegesack, for North German Lloyd as the ZEPPELIN (1915) and completed as the ORMUZ (1920 – Orient Line).

DRINA (1912)
11483 grt; 995 psrs
517' x 62' x 26' (157.5 x 18.8 x 7.9 m)
Quadruple expansion engines via twin screw.

Sank on 1 March 1917 after being torpedoed by the German U-65 two miles (3 km) west of Skokholm Island, off the Pembrokeshire coast of Wales. Fifteen lives were lost.
Built by Harland & Wolff Ltd, Belfast, for Royal Mail Lines.

DRONNING INGRID (1980) See AFRICA MERCY (1999)

DRONNING MARGRETHE II (1973)

10850 grt; 1286 psrs
260 cars
477' x 58' x 14'6" (144.6 x 17.7 x 4.4 m)
2 x 10-cylinder B+W diesel engines via twin screw.

Ice-strengthened passenger-car ferry owned by the Danish government and operated by DSB on the Danish coastal service.
Built by Nakskov Skibsvaerft, Nakskov.

DROSSELFELS (1976) See POLARIS (1992)

DROTTEN (1980) See SARDINIA REGINA (1996)

DROTTNINGEN (1968) See JIN HU (1993)

DROTTNINGHOLM (1920) See HOMELAND (1951)

DROTTNING SILVIA (1982) See NORMANDY (1997)

DROTTNING VICTORIA (1909)

3594 grt; 530 psrs
70 cars or 8 rail coaches
371' x 51' x 17'6" (112.4 x 15.5 x 5.3 m)
2 x 3-cylinder Swan Hunter & Wigham, Richardson triple expansion engines via twin screw.
Broken up for scrap in 1968 by Personer AB, Ystad
Passenger train ferry built by Swan,Hunter & Wigham Richardson Ltd, Newcastle for Swedish State Rail.

DUALA (1945) See PETR VELIKI (1949)

DUBA 94 (1995) See EL SALAM EL SAUDI (1995)

DUBROVNIK (1996)

9795 grt; 1500 psrs
332 cars or 39 trailers
403' x 61' x 16'6" (122 x 18.5 x 5 m)
4 x 8-cylinder MaK diesel engines via twin screw.

Passenger-car ferry owned and operated by Jadrolinija, Rijeka.
Built by the Verolme Shipyard, Cork, for British & Irish Steam Packet Co at a cost of £15,000,000 as the CONNACHT (1978). Renamed DUCHESSE ANNE (1988 – Brittany Ferries).

DUCA D'AOSTA (1909)

7804 grt; 836 psrs
476' x 53' x 18'9" (144.2 x 16.2 x 5.7 m)
N Odero 8-cylinder quadruple expansion engine via twin screw.
Broken up for scrap in 1929.
Built by Cantieri Navale Siciliani, Palermo for Navigazione Generale Italia.

DUCA DEGLI ABRUZZI (1908)

7793 grt; 1836 psrs
476' x 53' x 18'7" (145 x 16.3 x 5.7 m)
8-cylinder quadruple engines via twin screw.
Broken up for scrap in 1929.
Built by Cantieri Navale Riuniti, La Spezia, for Navigazione Generale Italia.

DUCA DI GENOVA (1908)

7893 grt; 1836 psrs
476' x 53' x 18'7" (145 x 16.3 x 5.7 m)
Odero 8-cylinder quadruple engines via twin screw.
As an Italian troopship, she sank on 6 February 1918 after being torpedoed by the German U-64 near Cape Canet, France.
Built by Cantieri Siciliani, Palermo, for Navigazione Generale Italia as a passenger ship.

DUC DE NORMANDIE (1986)

9677 grt; 1500 psrs
354 cars + 48 trailers
432' x 76' x 17' (131 x 22.6 x 5.2 m)
4 x 8-cylinder Stork-Werkspoor diesel engines via twin screw.

Ferry operated by Brittany Ferries.
Built by Rijn-Schelde-Verolme for Zeeland Steamship Co as the PRINSES BEATRIX (1978).

DUCHESS, USS (APA-98) (1944) See ORIENTAL JADE (1965)

DUCHESSE ANNE (1988) See DUBROVNIK (1996)

DUCHESS M (1989) See BALBEK (2000)

DUCHESS OF ATHOLL (1928)

20119 grt; 2070 psrs
582' x 75' x 27'6" (176.4 x 22.7 x 8.4 m)
6 x Beardmore SRG turbines via twin screw.
Sank on 10 October 1942 after being torpedoed by the German U-178 200 miles (333 km) east of Ascension Island in the Atlantic, with four lives lost.
Built by William Beardmore & Company, Dalmuir, for the Canadian Pacific Steamship Company.

DUCHESS OF BEDFORD (1928) See EMPRESS OF FRANCE (1948)

DUCHESS OF CORNWALL (1927) See DUCHESS OF YORK (1929)

DUCHESS OF RICHMOND (1928) See EMPRESS OF CANADA (1947)

DUCHESS OF YORK (1929)

20021 grt; 1570 psrs
601' x 75' (182.1 x 22.7 m)
6 x John Brown & Co SRG turbines via twin screw.

Sank on 12 July 1943, off Cape St Vincent, Portugal, after being hit by a German torpedo following a Luftwaffe bombing attack and raging fire the day before. Eleven lives were lost.

Laid down by John Brown & Co Ltd, Clydebank, for the Canadian Pacific Steamship Company as the passenger ship DUCHESS OF CORNWALL (1927), but completed as the DUCHESS OF YORK.

DUILIO (1923)
23635 grt; 757 psrs
602' x 76' x 46'3" depth (182.4 x 23 x 14 m)
4 x Ansaldo turbine engines via quadruple screw.
Broken up for scrap at Trieste, in 1948, after raising her from the harbour seabed following her sinking by British bombers on 10 July 1944. Ex-Lloyd Triestino.
Launched by Ansaldo Shipyards, Genoa, in 1916 but not completed for Navigazione Generale Italiana until 1923.

DUKE OF ARGYLL (1873) See RINA (1902)

DUKE OF ARGYLL (1928)
3604 grt; 510 psrs
349' x 53' x 18'6" (105.8 x 16.1 x 5.6 m)
4 x William Denny SRG turbine engines via twin screw.
Broken up for scrap in 1918.
Built by William Denny & Bros, Dumbarton, for the London Midland & Scottish Railway as a passenger ferry at a cost of £216,000.

DUKE OF ARGYLL (1956) See ZENITH (1995)

DUKE OF DEVONSHIRE (1873) See CONSTANZA (1903)

DUKE OF FIFE (1898) See ITSUKISHIMA MARU (1903)

DUKE OF LANCASTER (1928)
3608 grt; 510 psrs
349' x 53' x 18'6" (105.8 x 16.1 x 5.6 m)
SRG turbine engines via twin screw.
Broken up for scrap in 1956.
Built by William Denny & Bros, Dumbarton, for the London, Midland & Scottish Railway as a passenger train ferry at a cost of £216,000.

DUKE OF LANCASTER (1956) See DUKE OF LLANERCH-Y-MOR (1979)

DUKE OF LLANERCH-Y-MOR (1979)
4797 grt; 1200 psrs
376' x 57' x 15' (113.9 x 17.3 x 4.5 m)
2 x Pametruda DRG turbine engines via twin screw.
Ex-passenger ferry operated by Empirewise Ltd, Liverpool, as a static leisure and shopping centre on the coast of north Wales in a creek off the River Dee, near Mostyn.
Built by Harland & Wolff Ltd, Belfast, for the British Transport Commission as the DUKE OF LANCASTER (1956).

DUKE OF NORFOLK (1899) See PERICLES (1914)

DUKE OF PORTLAND (1898) See HIGHLAND FLING (1905)

DUKE OF ROTHESAY (1928)
3606 grt; 510 psrs
349' x 53' x 18'6" (105.8 x 16.1 x 5.6 m)
4 x William Denny SRG turbine engines via twin screw.
Broken up for scrap in 1957.
Built by William Denny & Bros, Dumbarton, for the London Midland & Scottish Railway as a passenger ferry at a cost of £216,000.

DUKE OF ROTHESAY (1956)
4780 grt; 1800 psrs
110 cars
376' x 57' x 15' (113.9 x 17.3 x 4.5 m)
2 x Pametrada DRG turbine engines via twin screw.
Broken up for scrap at Faslane in 1975.
Built by William Denny & Bros Ltd, Dumbarton, for the British Transport Commission as a passenger ferry.

DUKE OF SUTHERLAND (1873) See HANAMET (1906)

DUKE OF WELLINGTON, HMS (1942) See FANTASIA (1964)

DUKE OF WESTMINSTER (1882) See WESTMINSTER (1903)

DUKE OF YORK (1935) See FANTASIA (1964)

DUMANA (1923)
8450 grt; 220 psrs
450' x 58' x 33' (136.4 x 17.6 x 10 m)
2 x 8-cylinder North British Ltd diesel engines via twin screw.
Sank, with 40 lives lost, between Port Etienne and Takoradi on 24 December 1943 after being hit by a torpedo.
Laid down by Barclay, Curle & Co for British India Steam Navigation Co as the passenger-cargo ship MELMA (1923), but completed as the DUMANA.

DUMBEA (1903)
5809 grt; 310 psrs
464' x 46' x 32' depth (140.6 x 13.9 x 9.7 m)
Forges et Chantiers de la Mediterranean 3-cylinder triple expansion engines via single screw.
Broken up for scrap at Marseilles in 1928 after refloating her from the position where she had capsized, while berthing, on 19 September 1919.
Built by Forges et Chantiers de la Mediterranean, La Seyne, for Messageries Maritimes as the BRESIL (1888).

DUMONT D'URVILLE (1917) See ANDRE CHENIER (1921)

DUMRA (1946) See DAMAN (1976)

DUNBAR CASTLE (1883) See OLYMPIA (1904)

DUNBAR CASTLE (1930)
10002 grt; 460 psrs
471' x 61' x 29'6" (142.7 x 18.5 x 9 m)
2 x 6-cylinder H&W-B+W diesel engines via twin screw.
Demolished in 1946 following her settling in shallow water 30 minutes after striking a magnetic mine and wrecking herself on the North Goodwin Sands in the English Channel, off Deal. Disaster struck during a beaching attempt on 9 January 1940. Nine lives were lost.
Built by Harland & Wolff Ltd, Belfast, for the Union Castle Line.

DUNBRIDGE (1917) See FRANGOULA B. GOULANDRIS (1928)

DUNDALK BAY (1948) See WESTBAY (1957)

DUNERA (1937)
12615 grt; 1022 psrs
517' x 63' x 24'6" (156.7 x 19.1 x 7.5 m)
2 x 5-cylinder Doxford diesel engines via twin screw.
Broken up for scrap at Bilbao in 1967 as an education ship for students.
Built by Barclay, Curle & Co, Glasgow, for the British India Line as a dedicated troopship.

DUNGENESS, HMS (1945) See TRIADIC (1948)

DUNLUCE CASTLE (1897) See St DOMINGO (1905)

DUNLUCE CASTLE (1904)
8114 grt; 800 psrs
476' x 57' x 31' (144.2 x 17.3 x 9.4 m)
Quadruple expansion engines via twin screw.
Broken up for scrap at Inverkeithing in 1945.
Built by Harland & Wolff Ltd, Belfast, for the Union-Castle Line.

DUNNOTTAR CASTLE (1936) See PRINCESA VICTORIA (1993)

DUNNOTTAR CASTLE, HMS (1939) See PRINCESA VICTORIA (1993).

DUNOLLY CASTLE (1897) See IOANNINA (1913)

DUNOTTAR CASTLE (1889) See CARIBBEAN (1913)

DUNTROON (1935) See LYDIA (1966)

DUNVEGAN CASTLE (1936) See DUNVEGAN CASTLE, HMS (1939)

DUNVEGAN CASTLE, HMS (1939)
15007 grt; 508 psrs
540' x 72' x 37'8" depth (163.6 x 21.8 x 11.5 m)
Harland & Wolff diesel engines via twin screw.
Sank as an armed merchantman on 27 August 1940 after being torpedoed four weeks earlier by the German U-46, 120 miles (200 km) south-west of Ireland.
Built by Harland & Wolff Ltd, Belfast, for the Union Castle Line as the DUNVEGAN CASTLE (1936).

DUQUE DE CAXIAS (1945)
6937 grt; 304 psrs
423' x 60' x 24'4' (128.2 x 18.2 x 7 m)
4 x William Cramp & Sons SRG turbine engines via twin screw.
Broken up for scrap in 1963. Ex-Lloyd Brasileiro.
Built by W Cramp & Sons Shipbuilding & Engineering Co, Philadelphia, Pennsylvania, for Lloyd Brasileiro Patrimonio Nacional as the ORIZABA (1918). Renamed ORIZABA (SP-1536) (1918 – US Navy) and ORIZABA, USS (AP-24) (1941 – US Shipping Administration).

DURBAN CASTLE (1938)
17382 grt; 539 psrs
594' x 76' x 29' (181.2 x 23.2 x 8.8 m)
2 x 8-cylinder H&W-B+W diesel engines via twin screw.
Broken up for scrap at Hamburg, Germany, in 1962.
Built by Harland & Wolff Ltd, Belfast, for the Union Castle Line.

DURHAM (1904) See AUGUSTA (1924)

DURHAM CASTLE (1904)
8217 grt; 800 psrs
476' x 57' x 31' (144.2 x 17.3 x 9.4 m)
Quadruple expansion engines via twin screw.
Sunk in 1940 by either a mine or torpedo off Invergordan, Cromarty, while under tow to Scapa Flow.
Built by Fairfield Shipbuilding & Engineering Co Ltd, Glasgow, for the Union-Castle Line.

DURR (1981) See CALYPSO (1995)

DVD No. 1 (1995) See DVD No. I (1999)

DVD No. I (1999)
4284 grt; 300 psrs
316' x 50' x 12' (95.8 x 15 x 3.6 m)
10 x 6-cylinder Cummins diesel engines via quadruple screw.
Passenger ferry owned and operated by Dalian Vivid Dream Shipping Co Ltd, Dalian.
Built by North East Shipbuilders, Southwick, for Per Henriksen as the SUPERFLEX JULIET (1988). Renamed MERCANDIA VI (1990 – Mercandia), DVD No. 1 (1995 – Dalian Vivid Dream Shipping Co Ltd) and YONG LIAN (1997 – Dalian Vivid Dream Co Ltd).

DVD No. II (1995) See DVD No. II (1999)

DVD No. II (1999)
4101 grt; 253 psrs
316' x 50' x 12' (95.8 x 15 x 3.6 m)
10 x 6-cylinder Cummins diesel engines via quadruple screw.
Passenger ferry owned and operated by Dalian Vivid Dream Shipping Co Ltd, Dalian, but has been laid up since October 2000.
Built by Appledore Ferguson Ltd, Appledore, for Per Henriksen as the SUPERFLEX WHISKEY (1988). Renamed MERCANDIA VII (1990 – Mercandia), DVD No. II (1995 – Dalian Vivid Dream Shipping Co Ltd) and YONG QIANG (1997 – Dalian Vivid Dream Shipping Co Ltd).

DVD No. III (1995)
4101 grt; 253 psrs
316' x 50' x 12' (95.8 x 15 x 3.6 m)
10 x 6-cylinder Cummins diesel engines via quadruple screw.
Passenger ferry owned and operated by Dalian Vivid Dream Shipping Co Ltd, Dalian.
Built by North East Shipbuilders, Pallion, for Per Henriksen as the SUPERFLEX MIKE (1989). Renamed MERCANDIA III (1989 – Mercandia).

DVD No. IV (1995)
4101 grt; 253 psrs
316' x 50' x 12' (95.8 x 15 x 3.6 m)
10 x 6-cylinder Cummins diesel engines via quadruple screw.
Owned and operated by Dalian Vivid Dream Shipping Co Ltd, Dalian.
Built by North East Shipbuilders, Pallion, for Per Henriksen as the SUPERFLEX INDIA (1988). Renamed MERCANDIA V (1990 – Mercandia).

DWARKA (1947)
4851 grt; 1082 psrs
399' x 55' x 22' (120.9 x 16.7 x 6.7 m)
5-cylinder Doxford diesel engine via single screw.
Broken up for scrap by Zulfiqar Metals Ltd at Gadani Beach, Karachi, in 1982.
Built by Swan Hunter, Newcastle, for the British India Line as a passenger-cargo liner.

DWINSK (1913)
8302 grt; 2350 psrs
470' x 53' x 22'3" (143.3 x 16.2 x 6.8 m)
Harland & Wolff 6-cylinder triple expansion engines via twin screw.
Owned by Russian American Line, but under Cunard Line management from 1917 when she sank after being torpedoed by the German U-151 on 18 June 1918, 400 miles (666 km) from Bermuda.
Built by Harland & Wolff Ltd, Belfast, for Holland America Line as the ROTTERDAM (1897). Renamed C.F. TIETGEN (1906 – Scandinavian American Line).

EAGLE (1971) See THE AZUR (1987)

EARL GODWIN (1975) See MOBY BABY (1990)

EARL GRANVILLE (1980) See EXPRESS OLYMPIA (1990)

EARL HAROLD (1985) See NAIAS EXPRESS (1995)

EARL LEOFRIC (1976)
3521 grt; 850 psrs
371' x 57' x 13' (102.5 x 17.3 x 3.9 m)
2 x DRG turbine engines via twin screw.
Broken up for scrap at San Esteban de Pravia, Spain, in 1982. Ex-Sealink UK.
Built by Hawthorn, Leslie & Co, Hebburn, for British Railways as the HOLYHEAD FERRY I (1965).

EARL SIWARD (1977) See TUXEDO ROYALE (1988)

EARL WILLIAM (1977) See CESME STERN (1997)

EASTERN (1899) See TERUKUNI MARU (1924)

EASTERN (1946)
9896 grt; 51 psrs
475' x 64' x 29'8" (143.9 x 19.4 x 9 m)
2 x Richardson-Westgarth DRG turbine engines via single screw.
Passenger-cargo ship owned by Eastern & Australian Steamship Co.
Built by JL Thompson & Sons, Sunderland, for British Ministry of War Transport as the EMPIRE DYNASTY (1944).

EASTERN LIGHT (1981)
11369 grt; 2000 psrs
523' x 71' x 30'7" (159.3 x 21.7 x 9.3 m)
2 x Westinghouse DRG turbine engine via single screw.
Broken up as a passenger ship for scrap at Kaohsiung in 1981. Ex-Eastern Star Maritime.
Built by Kaiser Corporation, Richmond, California, for the US Maritime Commission as the Class C4-S-A1 troop carrier GENERAL C. C. BALLOU (AP-157) (1945). Laid up for the period 1954–1967. Renamed as the container ship BROOKLYN (1968 – Sea Land Service Inc) and HUMACAO (1975 – Puerto Rico Maritime Shipping Authority).

EASTERN PEACE (1974)
3382 grt; 96 psrs
302' x 49' x 17'6" (92 x 14.9 x 5.3 m)
7-cylinder British Polar diesel engine via single screw.
Broken up in Kaohsiung in 1980. Ex-Lye Shipping (Panama) SA.
Built by William Denny & Brothers, Dumbarton, for the State Shipping Service, Western Australia, as the passenger-cargo ship KOOLAMA (1957). Renamed GRAIN TRADER (1974 – O'Sheas (Dublin) Ltd.

EASTERN PRINCE (1929) See EMPIRE MEDWAY (1950)

EASTERN PRINCESS (1974) See OCEANOS (1976)

EASTERN QUEEN (1950) See WICKLOW (1970)

EASTERN QUEEN (1972) See SHAHEED SALAHUDDIN (1981)

EASTERN TRADER (1919) See GIOVANNA C (1946)

EASY 1 (1998) See ANJA 11 (1998)

EASY RIDER (1981) See URD (1991)

EBINO (1976) See SAN LORENZO RUIZ (1996)

EBRO (1896) See QUEBEC (1903)

EBRO (1914) See SERPA PINTO (1940)

ECLIPSE (1920) See WILLIAM P BIDDLE (1946)

ECSTASY (1991)
70367 grt; 2634 psrs
860' x 102' x 26' (260.6 x 30.9 x 7.9 m)
6 x 12-cylinder Sulzer diesel-electric engines via twin screw.

Cruise ship for Carnival Cruise Line, USA.
Built by Wartsila-Masa Yard, Helsinki, for Carnival Cruise Line at a cost of US$275,000,000.

ECUADOR (1915) See NEGBAH (1948)

EDAM (1921)
8871 grt; 974 psrs
450' x 58' x 30' (136.4 x 17.6 x 9.1 m)
3 x John Brown DRG turbine engines via single screw.
Broken up for scrap in Hong Kong in 1954.
Built by de Schelde Koninklijke Maatschaapij, Flushing, for the Holland America Line.

EDAM (1976) See ENCHANTED ISLE (1994)

EDDA (1983) See ROGALIN (1992)

EDINBURGH CASTLE (1910)
13326 grt; 388 psrs
570' x 64' x 31'6" (172.7 x 19.5 x 9.6 m)
Quadruple expansion engines via twin screw.
Owned by the British Admiralty, she was sunk in September 1945 as a target vessel 60 miles (100 km) off Sierra Leone. It had been estimated that the cost of towing the broken down ship to European repair yards would not be economical.
Built by Harland & Wolff Ltd, Belfast, for the Union Castle Line.

EDINBURGH CASTLE (1948)
28625 grt; 642 psrs
747' x 84' x 32' (226.4 x 25.5 x 10 m)
DRG turbine engines via twin screw.
Broken up at Kaohsiung in 1976.
Built by Harland & Wolff Ltd, Belfast, for the Union Castle Line at a cost of £3,000,000.

EDINBURGH CASTLE (1997) See THE BIG RED BOAT II (2000)

EDISON (1924)
10785 grt; 1799 psrs
552' x 60' x 29' (168.2 x 18.3 x 8.8 m)
2 x 4-cylinder quadruple expansion engines via twin screw.
Broken up in Genoa, in 1935. Ex-National Steam Navigation Co, Greece.
Built by AG Vulkan, Stettin, for North German Lloyd as the KONIGIN LOUISE (1897). Renamed OMAR (1921 – Orient Steam Navigation Co).

EDMUND B. ALEX ANDER USS (1941)
21329 grt; 1748 psrs
700' x 74' x 33'6" (212.1 x 22.4 x 10.2 m)
2 x 4-cylinder quadruple expansion engines via twin screw.
Owned by the US Shipping Board, she was broken up as a troopship at

Baltimore in 1958 by Bethlehem Steel Corporation after being laid up for eight years.
Built by Harland & Wolff Ltd, Belfast, for the Hamburg-America Line as the AMERIKA (1905). Renamed AMERICA, USS (1917 – US Navy) and AMERICA (1921 – United States Lines).

EDOUARD BRANLY (1952) See ANTONIO PACINOTTI (1957)

EDUARD REGEL (1905) See MINSK (1909)

EDWARD RUTLEDGE, USS (AP-52) (1941)
9360 grt; 147 psrs
474' x 61' x 42'3" depth (143.6 x 18.5 x 12.8 m)
New York Shipbuilding Co turbine engine via single screw.
Owned by US Navy, she sank on 12 November 1942 after being torpedoed off Fedhala, Morocco.
Built by the New York Shipbuilding Company, Camden, New York, for the American Export Isbrandtsen Line as the EXETER (1931).

EFTHYCOSTA II (1969) See ZAKROS (1971)

EGE (1955) See ERKIN (A-590) (1984)

EGEMEN (1939)
6000 grt
386' x 53' x 20'6" (117 x 16 x 6.2 m)
2 x 6-cylinder Blohm & Voss triple expansion engines via twin screw.
Built by Blohm & Voss, Hamburg, for TC Munakalat Vekaleti Devlet Denizyollari Isletme UM.

EGITTO EXPRESS (1991)
8975 grt; 822 psrs
221 cars or 45 cars + 30 trailers
415' x 61' x 17' (125.7 x 18.5 x 5.2 m)
2 x 14-cylinder Fiat diesel engines via twin screw.
Passenger-car-cargo ferry operated by Adriatica Line.
Built by Cantieri Navale Luigi Orlando, Livorno, for Adriatica Line, Cagliari, as the ESPRESSO CAGLIARI (1974). Renamed ESPRESSO EGITTO (1980).

EGNATIA (1960)
5725 grt; 638 psrs
145 cars
379' x 57' x 13'6" (114.8 x 17.2 x 4.1 m)
2 x 8-cylinder Sulzer diesel engines via twin screw.
Owned by Hellenic Mediterranean Lines Ltd, Piraeus, and chartered to HML as a passenger-car ferry on the Italy–Greek Islands–Greece service.
Built by Loire-Normandie.

EGNATIA II (1998) See VILLE DE SETE (2000)

EINAR TAMBARSKJELVE (1995) See PETRONILA MATA (1998)

EISENACH (1908) See SANTAREM (1917)

EKARI (1920) See STANLEYVILLE (1926)

EKATERINA II (1993)
5330 grt; 333 psrs
401' x 53' x 17' (121.5 x 16 x 5.2 m)
2 x 6-cylinder MAN diesel engines via twin screw.
Broken up in Russia in 1997 as a cruise ship. Ex-Gals-T Joint Stock Co, Novorossiysk.
Built by Mathias-Thesen, Wismar, for Black Sea Shipping Co, Odessa, as the ice-strengthened passenger ship ESTONIYA (1960).

EKATARINI P (1999)
3200 grt
384' x 59' x 14'9" (116.5 x 18 x 4.5 m)
2 x 6-cylinder Daihatsu diesel engines via twin screw.
Owned and operated by Olympic Flame-Fast Ferry Shipping Co.
Built by Shin Kurushima Dockyard Co Ltd, Akitsu.

EKATERINOSLAV (1906)
6581 grt; 1250 psrs
421' x 54' x 34'4" depth (128.2 x 16.6 x 10.4 m)
JC Tecklenborg 4-cylinder quadruple expansion engine via single screw.
Broken up for scrap at Kiel in 1928. Ex-Russian Volunteer Fleet.
Built by JC Tecklenborg, Geestemunde, for Hamburg-America Line as the passenger ship ASSYRIA (1898). Renamed SVEABORG (1905 – Russian Volunteer Fleet).

EKMA (1911)
5108 grt
410' x 53' x 24'6" (124.2 x 16 x 7.5 m)
Workman, Clark 6-cylinder triple expansion engine via twin screw.
Broken up for scrap in Mumbai in 1948.
Built by Workman, Clark & Co Ltd, Belfast, for the British India Steam Navigation Co, Ltd.

EL AMIR SAID (1952) See ROMANTICA (1960)

ELANDSFONTEIN (1940) See DEVON (1967)

EL ARISH (1980) See VITTORE CARPACCIO (1992)

EL ARISH (1999)
4609 grt; 596 psrs
80 cars + 16 trailers
346' x 57' x 13'6" (105 x 17.3 x 4.1 m)
4 x 12-cylinder Normo diesel engines via twin screw.
Passenger-car-cargo RoRo ferry on the Egypt–Jordan service for Sayed Nasr Navigation Lines, Saudi Arabia.
Built by AS Bergens MV, Bergen, for Misr Edco Shipping Co Ltd as the EL TOR (1981). Renamed EL ARISH EL-TOR (1991 – Misr Edco Shipping Co Ltd).

ELATION (1998)
70390 grt; 2040 psrs
863' x 133' x 25'6" (261 x 32 x 7.8 m)
6 x 12-cylinder Wartsila diesel-electric engines via twin Azipod screw.

Cruise ship owned and operated by Carnival Cruise Lines.
Built by Kvaerner-Helsinki, Turku, at a cost of US$300,000,000.

ELBA NOVA (1992) See NURA NOVA (1999)

EL COSTON (1925)
7286 grt; 347 psrs
427' x 57' x 26'6" (129.4 x 17.3 x 8 m)
2 x De Laval DRG turbine engines via single screw.
Sank, after colliding with the MURFREESBORO on 26 February 1944, a few years following her conversion to a cargo vessel by Southern Pacific Steamship Co.
Built by Todd Drydock & Construction Corporation, Tacoma, Washington state, for Southern Pacific Steamship Co as the BIENVILLE (1924).

EL DIA (1901) See KOMMIYUT (1949)

EL-DJAZAIR (1952) See FLORIANA (1970)

EL-DJAZAIR (1973)
12529 grt; 776 psrs
220 cars or 99 trailers
428' x 72' x 18' (130.4 x 22 x 5.6 m)

2 x 14-cylinder Kawasaki-MAN diesel engines via twin screw.
Passenger-car-cargo ferry owned by ENTMV and operated by EMTV on the France–Algeria service.
Built by Kanasashi Zosensho, Shimizu, for the Central Ferry Co, Kobe, as the CENTRAL No.3 (1971). She was listed for sale in July 1999.

ELECTRA (1964)
4232 grt; 300 psrs
40 cars
312' x 51' x 22' (112.7 x 15.5 x 6.7 m)
3 x JS White & Co DRG turbine engines via single screw.
Owned by Typaldos Shipping Co Ltd.
Built by J Samuel White Co, Cowes, for Soc Generale de Transports Maritime as the SIDI OKBA (1947). Renamed MEDITERRANEAN II (1963 – Aegean Steam Navigation Co).

ELEFTHERIOS VENIZELOS (1997)
38261 grt; 3000 psrs
750 cars or 540 cars + 26 trailers
578' x 94' x 22' (175.2 x 28.5 x 6.7 m)
4 x 16-cylinder Zgoda-Sulzer diesel engines via twin screw.

Passenger-car-cargo ferry operated by ANEK Lines, Cyprus.
Laid down by Styocznia Shipyard, Gydnia, as the STENA POLONICA (1987 – Stena Line); launched as the BOHUS (1989 – Fred Olsen Ltd); and completed by Bremer Vulkan, Vegesack, as the EL VENIZELOS (1990 – ANEK Lines). Renamed BONANZA (1992 – Fred Olsen Ltd).

ELEKTRA (1964) See ELECTRA (1964)

EL ESCORIAL (1952) See CLIMAX OPAL (1977)

EL GRECO (1976) See MIR (1998)

EL GRECO (1981)
14425 grt; 1320 psrs
500 cars
465' x 76' x 19' (140.8 x 22.9 x 5.7 m)
2 x 18-cylinder MAN diesel engines via twin screw.
Passenger-car ferry owned by Minoikai Grammai and operated by Minoan Lines on the Italy–Greek Islands–Greece service.
Built by Hayashikane Zosen, Shimonoseki, for Meimon Car Ferry KK, Nagoya, as the FERRY ATSUTA (1972).

EL HASSAN (1979)
4406 grt; 81 psrs
385' x 54' x 19' (116.7 x 16.4 x 5.8 m)
2 x 5-cylinder Fiat diesel engines via twin screw.
Owned and operated as a passenger ferry by the Arab Navigation Co, Alexandria.
Built by the Ansaldo Shipyard, Leghorn, for the Adriatica Line as the BRENNERO (1959).

EL HIND (1948) See STATE OF BOMBAY (1954)

EL HORRIA (1865) See MAHROUSSA (1905)

ELISABETH RICKMERS (1898) See NORDERNEY (1900)

ELISABETHVILLE (1921) See MARISTRELLA (1958)

ELISABETHVILLE (1948)
10901 grt; 179 psrts
505' x 65' x 27'6" (153 x 19.7 x 8.4 m)

B+W-type 8-cylinder diesel engine via single screw.
Broken up for scrap at Antwerp in 1968 after the ship was gutted by fire at her Antwerp berth on 20 March 1968.
Built by John Cockerill Shipyards, Hoboken, Belgium, for Cie Maritime Belge.

ELIZABETH (1969) See SEAWISE UNIVERSITY (1970)

ELIZABETH A (1967)
5043 grt; 751 psrs
379' x 55' x 20' (114.8 x 16.7 x 6.1 m)
Turbine engine via single screw.
Broken up for scrap at Lavrion, Greece, in 1979. Ex-Hellenic International Lines.
Built by William Cramp & Sons Shipbuilding & Enginebuilding Co, Philadelphia, Pennsylvania, for the Eastern Steamship Co as the passenger ship YARMOUTH (1926). Renamed YARMOUTH CASTLE (1954 – Eastern Steamship Co), QUEEN OF NASSAU (1954 – Eastern Steamship Co), YARMOUTH CASTLE (1957 – Eastern Steamship Co), YARMOUTH (1958 – Yarmouth Cruise Lines) and SAN ANDRES (1966 – Columbian Co).

EL KANTARA (1904)
6888 grt; 94 psrs or 1200 troops
447' x 53' x 32'6" depth (135.5 x 16.1 x 9.9 m)
2 x triple expansion reciprocating engines via twin screw.
Broken up for scrap at Dunkirk in 1926.
Built by Soc Provencale de Constrations Navales, La Ciotat, for Messageries Maritimes.

ELLA (1907) See DJEYHUN (1914)

ELLEN RICKMERS (1896) See ASTI (1915)

ELLINIS (1963)
24351 grt; 1642 psrs
642' x 79' x 28' (195.6 x 24 x 8.5 m)
6 x Bethlehem Shipbuilding Corporation SRG turbine engines via twin screw.
Broken up for scrap at Kaohsiung in 1987.
Ex-Australia Line SA, Piraeus, after being laid up for seven years in Eleusis Bay.
Built by the Bethlehem Steel Company, Quincy, Massachusetts, for the Matson Line as the LURLINE (1932).

EL MADINA (1937)
3962 grt
360' x 50' x 22' (109 x 15.2 x 6.7 m)
Barclay Curle 6-cylinder triple expansion engines via twin screw.
Sank on 16 March 1944 after being torpedoed in the Bay of Bengal.
Built by Barclay Curle & Co Ltd, Glasgow, for Scindia Steam Navigation Co Ltd.

EL MALEK FOAD (1947) See EL MALEK FOUAD (1948).

EL MALEK FOUAD (1948) See OLBIA (1961)

ELMINA (1910) See CAIRO CITY (1933)

EL SALAM 94 (1994) See GURGEN 2 (1996)

EL SALAM 93 (1995) See EL SALAM EL SAUDI (1995)

EL SALAM 97 (1998) See SALAM (1999)

EL SALAM EL SAUDI (1995)
4447 grt; 905 psrs
74 cars + 45 trailers or 30 rail coaches
393' x 57' x 18' (119.1 x 17.3 x 5.5 m)
2 x 6-cylinder Fiat diesel engines via twin screw.
Passenger ferry owned by Saudi-Egyptian Maritime Transport SA, Panama, and operated by El Salam Maritime Transport Co SA, Cairo.
Built by Riuniti, Palermo, for the Italian State Railways as the TYRSUS (1961). Renamed AQUILA UNO (1993 – Soc Di Frestazioni Servizi Aquila), TYRSUS (1994 – Soc di Frestazioni Servizi Aquila. SNC, Civitavecchia) and EL SALAM 93 (1995 – Saudi-Egyptian Maritime TransportSA, Cairo).

EL SALVADOR (1928) See MOUNT McKINLEY (1936)

EL TOR (1980) See EL ARISH-EL TOR (1981)

EL-TOR (1998)
8167 grt; 987 psrs
194 cars
419' x 65' x 17' (126.9 x 19.6 x 5.2 m)
2 x 16-cylinder Pielstick diesel engines via twin screw.

Passenger-car ferry owned by Salam International Transport & Trading Co Ltd, Amman, and operated as a pilgrim ship.
Built by Dubigeon-Normandie, Nantes, for Rederi AB Svea as the ice-strengthened passenger-car ferry SVEA REGINA (1972). Renamed REGINA (1978 – Finska Angfartyes AB), MEDITERRANEAN SUN (1979 – Transatlantic Navigation Ltd), ODYSSEAS ELYTIS (1982 – Brittany Ferries), SCANDINAVIAN SKY (1985 – Siamaa Lines, Finland), TALLINK (1989 – FG Shipping Oy AB) and MAMA TANZANIA (1998).

EL VALLE (1901) See ATZMAUT (1948)

EL VENIZELOS (1990) See ELEFTHERIOS VENIZELOS (1997)

ELYSIA (1908)
6757 grt; 90 psrs
441' x 53' x 29'6" (134.3 x 15 x 9 m)
D & W Henderson 3-cylinder triple expansion engine via single screw.
Sank on 5 June 1942 after an attack by Japanese armed merchant raiders, 30 miles (50 km) east-nor-east of Durban.
Built by D & W Henderson Ltd, Glasgow, for the City Line.

EMERAL (1975) See ZAMBOANGA (1989)

EMERALD (1953) See ZAKROS (1971)

EMERALD (1980) See TAMPOMAS II (1980)

EMERALD (1996) See THE EMERALD (1996)

EMERALD AMAMI (1975) See ZAMBOANGA (1989)

EMERALD EMPRESS (1997) See ENCHANTED SUN (1999)

EMERALD SEAS (1972) See OCEAN EXPLORER I (1998)

EMILIA (1979)
12523 grt; 2000 psrs
470 cars
488' x 75' x 19' (147.9 x 23 x 5.8 m)
2 x 16-cylinder GMT diesel engines via twin screw.
Passenger-car ferry operated by Tirrenia on the Italy–Sardinia service.
Built by Italcantieri SPa, Castellammare di Stabia.

EMILIA PELLEGRINA (1926) See JANUA (1928)

EMIL KIRDORFF (1922) See ARDEAL (1932)

EMIL L. BOAS (1913) See MOTAGUA (1912)

EMILY H. M. WEDER (1941) See PRESIDENT BUCHANAN (1945).

EMMA (1987) See EUROPA (1988)

EMMA ALEXANDER (1923) See EMPIRE WOODLARK (1941)

EMPEROR ALEXANDER III (1914) See KHAI DINH (1939)

EMPEROR OF INDIA (1921) See KAISER-I-HIND (1922)

EMPIRE (1902) See VOLUBILIS (1919)

EMPIRE ARQUEBUS (1944) See AL SUDAN (1947)

EMPIRE ARQUEBUS (1946) See AL SUDAN (1947)

EMPIRE ATTENDANT (1940)
8441 grt; 1460 psrs
464' x 58' x 33' (140.6 x 17.6 x 10 m)
2 x 8-cylinder North British Ltd diesel engines via twin screw.
Operated during World War Two by the British Ministry of Supply, her fate has never been revealed. She was requisitioned as the DOMALA for secret operations and was attacked by German bombers at 5.00 am on 2 March 1940 resulting in an onboard explosion and raging fire off St Catherine's Point. One hundred lives were lost. The ship survived and was taken by the Ministry of Supply to an undisclosed location and underwent a complete transformation in late 1940 to become the EMPIRE ATTENDANT.
Launched by Barclay Curle & Co Ltd, Glasgow, for British India Steam Navigation Co as the passenger-cargo liner MAGVANA (1920) but completed as the DOMALA (1921).

EMPIRE BITTERN (1942)
8370 grt; 1200 psrs
501' x 58' x 30' (152.5 x 17.6 x 9.1 m)
Harland & Wolff Ltd 6-cylinder triple expansion engine via twin screw.
Owned by the British Ministry of Transport when she was purposely sunk on 7 June 1944 as a blockship off Arromanches during the Normandy landings.
Built by Harland & Wolff Ltd, Belfast, for the Warren Line as the IOWA (1902). Renamed BOHEMIA (1913 – HAPAG) and ARTEMIS (1917 – US government seizure).

EMPIRE BRENT (1946) See CAPTAIN COOK (1951)

EMPIRE BURE (1947) See MARISTRELLA (1958)

EMPIRE CHIEF (1941) See POLAR CHIEF (1946)

EMPIRE CHIVALRY (1941) See PLANTER (1946)

EMPIRE CLYDE (1953)
16584 grt; 1266 psrs
578' x 70' x 31' (176.2 x 21.3 x 9.4 m)
8-cylinder DRG turbine engines via twin screw.
Broken up for scrap at Newport, Wales, in 1957. Ex-British Ministry of Transport.
Built by William Beardmore & Co, Dalmuir, for the Anchor Line as the CAMERONIA (1921), but fitting out to completion was carried out in Cherbourg owing to industrial action in the UK.

EMPIRE DEBEN (1945)
11251 grt; 562 psrs
473' x 61' x 41'9" depth (143.3 x 18.5 x 12.7 m)
DRG turbine engine via single screw.
Broken up for scrap at Newport, Wales, in 1949. Ex-British Ministry of Transport.
Laid down by Howaldtswerke, Kiel, for the Hamburg-America Line as the HAVELLAND (1922) and completed as THURINGIA (1923). Renamed GENERAL SAN MARTIN (1930 – Hamburg South American Line).

EMPIRE DOON (1945) See KRI TANJUNG PANDAN (1977)

EMPIRE DYNASTY (1944) See EASTERN (1946)

EMPIRE EVENLODE (1947)
10224 grt; 600 psrs
506' x 60' x 39'5" depth (153.3 x 18.1 x 12 m)
Triple expansion engines via twin screw.

Broken up for scrap at Briton Ferry, UK, in 1949. Ex-British Ministry of Transport.
Built by Scotts Shipbuilding & Engineering Co Ltd, Greenock, for the Blue Funnel Line as the TALTHYBIUS (1911). Renamed TARUYASU MARU (1942 – Japanese government).

EMPIRE EXPLORER (1941)
5985 grt; 80 psrs
407' x 52' x 25'8" (123.3 x 15.8 x 7.8 m)
Compound single engine via single screw.
Sank on 8 July 1942 after being torpedoed near the West Indies. She had previously been sunk by German bombers while she was berthed in London docks on 7 September 1940, but was raised and converted into an armed merchantman by the British Ministry of Transport.
Built by Swan Hunter & Wigham Richardson Ltd, Newcastle, for the Harrison-Rennie Line as the INANDA (1925).

EMPIRE FOWEY (1935) See SAFINA-E-HUJJAJ (1961)

EMPIRE GOVERNOR (1940)
8657 grt; 360 psrs
450' x 57' x 27' (137.2 x 17.4 x 8.2 m)
12-cylinder Stablimento Tecnico diesel engines via twin screw.
Broken up for scrap at Dalmuir in 1946. Ex-British Ministry of War Transport.
Built by Cantieri San Rocca SA, Trieste, for Lloyd Triestino as the ESQUILINO (1925).

EMPIRE GRACE (1942) See WAIRANGI (1946).

EMPIRE GULL (1958)
4258 grt
348' x 55' x 27' (105.5 x 16.7 x 8.2 m)
2 x 8-cylinder CPR triple expansion engines via single screw.
Broken up for scrap at Santander in 1980. Ex-Atlantic Steam Navigation Co.
Built by SB Davy Ltd, Levis, for British Secretary of State for Defence as the TROUNCER, HMS (1945). Renamed LST 3525, HMS (1945).

EMPIRE HALLADALE (1946)
14056 grt; 518 psrs
500' x 64' x 38'7" depth (151.5 x 19.4 x 11.7 m)
Vulcan Werke 6-cylinder triple expansion engines via twin screw.
Broken up for scrap at Dalmuir in 1956. Ex-Ministry of Transport & Anchor Line.
Built by AE Vulcan Werke, Hamburg, for Hamburg South America Line as the ANTONIO DELFINO (1921). Renamed SIERRA NEVADA (1932 – Hamburg South America Line) and ANTONIO DELFINO (1934 – Hamburg South America Line).

EMPIRE HELFORD (1946)
6598 grt; 790 psrs
440' x 53' x 24'4" (133.3 x 16.1 x 7.4 m)
8-cylinder quadruple expansion engines via twin screw.
Broken up for scrap in Blyth in 1950. Ex-British Admiralty.
Built by Barclay, Curle & Co, Glasgow, for the Russian-American Line as the CZARITZA (1915). Renamed LITUANIA (1921 – Baltic American Line), KOSCIUSZKO (1930 – Gdynia America Line) and GDYNIA (1939 – Polish Navy).

EMPIRE JEWEL (1945) See SAFINA-E-HUJJAJ(1961)

EMPIRE JOY (1945) See NELLORE (1946)

EMPIRE KENT (1945)
9523 grt; 300 psrs
469' x 60' x 29'7" depth (149 x 18.2 x 9 m)
4 x Blohm & Voss SRG turbine engines via single screw.
Broken up for scrap at Dalmuir in 1957. Ex-Royal Mail Lines.
Built by Blohm & Voss, Hamburg, for Deutsche Ost Afrika Linie as the UBENA (1928).

EMPIRE LAGAN (1946) See UNION RELIANCE (1961)

EMPIRE LONGFORD (1951)
3886 grt; 146 psrs

360' x 50' x 23' (109.7 x 15.2 x 7 m)
Quadruple expansion engine via single screw.
Broken up for scrap in Dover, UK, in 1953. Ex-British Ministry of Transport.
Built by Swan Hunter & Wigham Richardson Ltd, Newcastle, for Melbourne Steamship Co as the DIMBOOLA (1912). Renamed HONG SIANG (1935 – Ho Hung Steamship Co, Singapore).

EMPIRE MACE (1944) See MISR (1947)

EMPIRE MACE (1946) See MISR (1947)

EMPIRE MEDWAY (1950)
10926 grt; 102 psrs
496' x 65' x 26'6" (155.3 x 19.7 x 8.1 m)
Kincaid-B+W diesel engines via twin screw.
Broken up for scrap at Faslane in 1953. Ex-British Ministry of Transport.
Built by Napier & Miller Ltd, Glasgow, for Furness, Withy & Co, London, as the EASTERN PRINCE (1929).

EMPIRE MERCIA (1946) See EMPIRE STAR (1946)

EMPIRE OCK (1945) See PETR VELIKI (1949)

EMPIRE ORWELL (1949) See KRI TANJUNG PANDAN (1977)

EMPIRE PAKEHA (1941) See PAKEHA (1946)

EMPIRE PARKESTON (1947)
6893 grt; 404 psrs
366' x 57' x 16'6" (107.9 x 17.3 x 5 m)
2 x Parsons SRG turbine engines via twin screw.
Broken up for scrap by Lotti SpA at La Spezia in 1962. Ex-British Admiralty.
Built by Cammell Laird & Company, Birkenhead, for Canadian National Steamships Ltd as the PRINCE HENRY (1930). Renamed NORTH STAR (1937 – Clarke Steamship Co, Quebec) and PRINCE HENRY, HMCS (1940 – Canadian Royal Navy).

EMPIRE PENRYN (1946)
6503 grt; 790 psrs
425' x 53' x 24'6" (128.8 x 16.1 x 7.5 m)
Barclay, Curle & Co 8-cylinder quadruple expansion engines via twin screw.
Broken up for scrap at Blyth in 1949. Ex-British government.
Built by Barclay, Curle & Company, Glasgow, for the Russian-American Line as the CZAR (1912). Renamed ESTONIA (1921 – Gdynia America Line) and PULASKI (1930 – Baltic America Line).

EMPIRE RAWLINSON (1944) See DIMITROS (1958)

EMPIRE STAR (1946)
11085 grt; 128 psrs
540' x 70' x 29'8" (163.6 x 21.2 x 9 m)
H&W diesel engines via twin screw.
Broken up for scrap in Kaohsiung in 1971 as a cargo only ship.
Launched by Harland & Wolff Ltd, Belfast, for the Blue Funnel Line as the EMPIRE MERCIA (1946), but completed as the EMPIRE STAR.

EMPIRE STATE (1920) See CABO DE HORNOS (1940)

EMPIRE STATE (1973) See STATE (1990)

EMPIRE STATE III (1956)
6750 grt; 900 psrs
Geared turbine engine via single screw.
Broken up for scrap at Valencia in 1971 after serving as a maritime college for the State University of New York.
Laid down by the Consolidated Steel Co, Wilmington, California, and completed by the Los Angeles Shipbuilding & Drydock Co as the US Navy hospital ship Class C1-B MERCY (1943).

EMPIRE STATE IV (1960) See BAY STATE (1973)

EMPIRE SWAN (1940) See KING ABDELAZIZ (1964)

EMPIRE TAMAR (1940)

6558 grt; 1012 psrs

448' x 57' x 30'5" depth (135.8 x 17.3 x 9.2 m)

2 x 3-cylinder Workman, Clark triple expansion engines via twin screw.

Lost in July 1944 while under the control of the British Ministry of War Transport.

Built by Workman, Clark & Co Ltd, Glasgow, for Shaw Savill & Albion Co Ltd as the KIA ORA (1907). Renamed VERBANIA (1935 – Ditta Pittaluga, Genoa).

EMPIRE TARN (1945) See SIBIR (1946)

EMPIRE TRADER (1940)

9957 grt; 414 psrs

499' x 61' x 30' (152.1 x 18.6 x 9.1 m)

Triple expansion engines via twin screw.

Under the control of the British Ministry of War Transport, she sank on 21 February 1943 after being torpedoed by the German U-92 in mid-Atlantic.

Built by Workman, Clark & Company, Belfast, for Shaw Savill & Albion as the TAINUI (1908).

EMPIRE TROOPER (1940)

14106 grt; 518 psrs

503' x 64' x 38'6" depth (15.2 x 19.4 x 11.7 m)

Vulcan Werke 6-cylinder triplee expansion engines via twin screw.

Controlled by the British Ministry of War Transport, she was broken up for scrap at Inverkeithing in 1955 after raising her from the Inverkeithing seabed. One month earlier she had caught fire and sank.

Built by AG Vulcan, Hamburg, for the Hamburg-America Line as the CAP NORTE (1922). Renamed SIERRA SALVADA (1932 – North German Lloyd) and CAP NORTE (1934 – Hamburg-America Line).

EMPIRE WAIMANA (1941) See WAIMANA (1946)

EMPIRE WANSBECK (1945) See ESPEROS (1964)

EMPIRE WAVENEY (1945)

16754 grt; 559 psrs

547' x 72' x 42'2" depth (165.8 x 21.8 x 12.8 m)

2 x 6-cylinder MAN diesel engines via twin screw.

Owned by the British Ministry of Transport, she was broken up at Glasgow in 1947. Fire had gutted the ship on 1 March 1946 during her conversion to a troop carrier at Liverpool.

Built by Blohm & Voss, Hamburg, for the Hamburg-America Line as the MILWAUKEE (1929).

EMPIRE WELLAND (1945) See ANIVA (1985)

EMPIRE WESSEX (1946) See PORT HOBART (1946)

EMPIRE WINDRUSH (1946)

14651 grt; 2408 psrs

523' x 66' x 37'8" (158.5 x 20 x 11.5 m)

4 x 8-cylinder MAN diesel engines via twin screw.

Owned by the British Ministry of Transport, she sank stern first on 29 March 1954 north-west of Algiers after an engine room explosion and fire, off Cape Caxine. She had been under tow to Gibraltar by the British Royal Navy destroyer HMS SAINTES. Four lives lost.

Built by Blohm & Voss, Hamburg, for the Hamburg-South America Line as the MONTE ROSA (1930).

EMPIRE WOODLARK (1941)

7793 grt; 536 psrs

442' x 55' x 17' (133.0 x 16.7 x 5.2 m)

Triple expansion engines via twin screw.

Owned by the British Ministry of Transport, she was purposely scuttled in November 1946 to ensure that her cargo of gas bombs was sent to the bottom.

Built by the New York Shipbuilding Company, Camden, New York, for the Pacific Coast Steamship Company as the CONGRESS (1913). Renamed NANKING (1918 – China Mail) and EMMA ALEX ANDER (1923 – Admiral Line).

EMPIRE YARE (1946) See GOGOL (1946)

EMPRESS (1985) See ROYAL PACIFIC (1992)

EMPRESS (1994) See THE EMPRESS (1994)

EMPRESS 65 (1997)

6725 grt; 380 psrs

454' x 58' x 19' (137.6 x 17.6 x 5.8 m)

3 x Parsons SRG turbine engines via single screw.

Broken up for scrap in 1997 at Alang after being laid up in Manila following her arrest in Singapore while owned by the Daphne Shipping Co (T Pattichis), Cyprus. Ex-Thanfil Shipping & Trading, SA.

Built by Swan Hunter & Wigham Richardson Ltd, Newcastle, for Swedish Lloyd as the ice-strengthened passenger ship PATRICIA (1951). Renamed ARIADNE (1957 – Hamburg-American Line), FREEPORT II (1973 – Bon Vivant Cruises, a Chandris Group subsidiary), BON VIVANT (1974 – Bon Vivant Cruises), ARIANE (1979 – Gilda Maritime Corporation) and EMPRESS KATERINA (1989 – Thanfil Shipping & Trading, SA).

EMPRESS ABETO (1970) See MALAYSIA RAYA (1971)

EMPRESS KATERINA (1989) See EMPRESS 65 (1997)

EMPRESS OF ASIA (1913)

16909 grt; 1238 psrs

592' x 68' x 29' (179.4 x 20.6 x 8.8 m)

Turbine engines via quadruple screw.

Her hulk was salvaged in 1952 by International Salvage Association Ltd after negotiating the rights to do so with the insurance underwriters. She had been sunk on 5 February 1942 by incessant bombing from the Japanese air force nine miles (15 km) off Singapore, with a loss of 19 lives.

Built by Fairfield Shipbuilding & Engineering Co Ltd, Glasgow, for the Canadian Pacific Steamship Co.

EMPRESS OF AUSTRALIA (1922)

21860 grt; 1139 psrs

590' x 75' x 29'3" (178.8 x 22.7 x 8.9 m)

8 x Brown-Curtis SRG turbine engines via twin screw.

Broken up for scrap by British Iron & Steel Corporation at Inverkeithing in 1952. Ex-Canadian Pacific Steamship Co.

Laid down by Vulcan Shipbuilding, Stettin, for the Hamburg-America Line as the ADMIRAL VON TIRPITZ (1913) and completed as the TIRPITZ (1914). Renamed EMPRESS OF CHINA (1921 – Canadian Pacific Steamship Co).

EMPRESS OF AUSTRALIA (1953) See VENEZUELA (1956)

EMPRESS OF AUSTRALIA (1965) See ROYAL PACIFIC (1992)

EMPRESS OF BRITAIN (1906) See MONTROYAL (1924).

EMPRESS OF BRITAIN (1931)

42348 grt; 1195 psrs

733' x 97' x 32'8" depth (222.1 x 29.4 x 9.9 m)

12 x geared turbine engines via quadruple screw.

Sank on 28 October 1940 off the Irish coast while under tow by the Polish destroyer BURZA. She had been hit by two torpedoes from the German U-32 which had shadowed the ship for two days. This followed an enemy air attack which had set her on fire and made her uncontrollable, 100 miles (167 km) north-west of the Irish coast. Forty-nine lives were lost.

Built by John Brown & Co Ltd, Clydebank, for the Canadian Pacific Steamship Co.

EMPRESS OF BRITAIN (1956) See THE TOPAZ (1998)

EMPRESS OF CANADA (1922)

21517 grt; 1758 psrs

627' x 77' x 30' (190 x 23.3 x 9.1 m)

Geared turbine engines via twin screw.

Sank 400 miles (667 km) off Cape Palmas, at 11.54 pm on 14 March 1943, by a single torpedo fired by the Italian submarine LEONARDO DA VINCI. The previous day another Italian submarine, the TAZZOLI, had torpedoed her, but had failed to finish her off. Unbeknown to either submarine crew, the ship was transporting Italian prisoners of war from North Africa, and 592 of them were lost in the second attack. Another 754 prisoners were rescued by the British destroyer HMS BOREAS and two corvettes, CROCUS and PETUNIA, while

the Ellerman Line's CORINTHIAN assisted.
Built by Fairfield Shipbuilding & Engineering Co Ltd, Glasgow, for the Canadian Pacific Steamship Co.

EMPRESS OF CANADA (1947)
20325 grt; 700 psrs
601' x 75' x 27' (182.1 x 22.7 x 8.2 m)
SRG turbine engines via twin screw.
Owned by the Canadian Pacific Steamship Co, she was broken up for scrap at La Spezia in 1954. She had been refloated on 3 June 1954 and towed from Gladstone Dock, Liverpool, where she had caught fire, capsized and sunk on 25 January 1953.
Built by John Brown & Co Ltd, Clydebank, for the Canadian Pacific Steamship Co as the DUCHESS OF RICHMOND (1928).

EMPRESS OF CANADA (1960) See APOLLO (1998)

EMPRESS OF CHINA (1921) See EMPRESS OF AUSTRALIA (1922)

EMPRESS OF CHINA (1921) See MONTNAIRN (1925)

EMPRESS OF ENGLAND (1956) See OCEAN MONARCH (1970)

EMPRESS OF FRANCE (1919)
18452 grt; 1639 psrs
571' x 72' x 42'2" depth (173 x 21.8 x 12.8 m)
4 x Parsons turbine engines via quadruple screw.
Owned by the Canadian Pacific Steamship Co, she was broken up for scrap at Dalmuir in 1934 following a three-year period laid up.
Built by William Beardmore & Co Ltd, Dalmuir, for the Allan Line as the ALSATIAN (1914).

EMPRESS OF FRANCE (1948)
20448 grt; 700 psrs
601' x 75' x 27'6" (181.8 x 22.7 x 8.4 m)
6 x John Brown-Parsons geared turbine engines via twin screw.
Broken up for scrap by John Cashmore & Sons Ltd at Newport, Wales, in 1960. Ex-Canadian Pacific Steamship Co.
Built by John Brown & Co Ltd, Clydebank, for Canadian Pacific Steamship Co as the DUCHESS OF BEDFORD (1928).

EMPRESS OF INDIA (1890) See LOYALTY (1915)

EMPRESS OF INDIA (1921) See MONTNAIRN (1925

EMPRESS OF IRELAND (1905)
14191 grt; 1581 psrs
570' x 66' x 27'6" (173.7 x 20 x 8.4 m)
8-cylinder quadruple expansion engines via twin screw.
Sank bow first on 29 May 1914 within 14 minutes of a gaping 25' x 14' (7.6 x 4.2 m) hole being torn open by the fully-laden Norwegian coal carrier STORSTADT. The incident occured at 2.30 am in the St Lawrence river, near Father Point, with 1,012 lives lost.
Built by Fairfield Shipbuilding & Engineering Co Ltd, Glasgow, for the Canadian Pacific Steamship Co .

EMPRESS OF JAPAN (1930) See HANSEATIC (1958)

EMPRESS OF RUSSIA (1913)
16810 grt; 1238 psrs
592' x 68' x 29' (179.4 x 20.6 x 8.8 m)
4 x Parsons turbine engines via quadruple screw.
Broken up for scrap by TW Ward Ltd at Barrow-in-Furness in 1946. This followed her being gutted by fire and capsizing during a refit on 8 September 1945.
Built by Fairfield Shipbuilding & Engineering Co Ltd, Glasgow, for the Canadian Pacific Steamship Co.

EMPRESS OF SCOTLAND (1921)
25037 grt; 1897 psrs
678' x 77' x 50'2" depth (205.5 x 23.4 x 15.2 m)
AG Vulcan 8-cylinder quadruple expansion engines via twin screw.

Salvage pieces broken up for scrap by Hughes Bolckow & Co at Blyth in 1931 after catching fire, sinking and breaking apart on the seabed. Ex-Canadian Pacific Steamship Co.
Laid down by Vulcan Shipyards, Stettin, for the Hamburg-America Line as the EUROPA (1905); completed as KAISERIN AUGUSTE VICTORIA (1906).

EMPRESS OF SCOTLAND (1942) See HANSEATIC (1958)

EMS (1884) See LAKE SIMCOE (1901)

EMSLAND (1977) See NURA NOVA (1999)

ENCHANTED CAPRI (1998)
15410 grt; 650 psrs
260 cars + 23 trailers
515' x 73' x 19'6" (156.2 x 22 x 5.9 m)
2 x 18-cylinder Wartsila-Pielstick diesel engines via twin screw.

Cruise ship owned by Norsong Shipping and operated by Commodore Cruise Line.
Built by Wartsila, Turku, for the Black Sea Shipping Co, Odessa, as the ice-strengthened cruise RoRo ferry vessel AZERBAYDZHAN (1975) at a cost of US$25,000,000. Renamed ARKADIYA (1996 – Ocean Agencies Ltd) and ISLAND HOLIDAY (1997 – New Escape Cruises).

ENCHANTED ISLE (1990) See ENCHANTED ISLE (1994)

ENCHANTED ISLE (1994)
23875 grt; 731 psrs
617' x 86' x 27' (188.2 x 26.2 x 8.2 m)
General Electric geared turbine engines via twin screw.
Cruise ship operated by Commodore Cruise Line.
Built by Ingalls Shipbuilding Corporation, Pascagoula, Mississippi, for the Grace-McCormack Line as the passenger liner ARGENTINA (1958) at a cost of US$25,000,000. Renamed VEENDAM (1972 – Holland America Line), BRASIL (1974 – Agence Maritime International, Brazil), VEENDAM (1975 – Holland America Line), EDAM (1976 – Holland America Line), MONARCH STAR (1976 – Monarch Cruise Lines), VEENDAM (1978 – Holland America Line), BERMUDA STAR (1984 – Bahama Cruise Lines), ENCHANTED ISLE (1990 – Commodore Cruise Line) and COMMODORE HOTEL, St PETERSBERG (1993 – Commodore Cruise Line).

ENCHANTED ODYSSEY (1990) See UNIVERSE EXPLORER (1996)

ENCHANTED SEAS (1990) See UNIVERSE EXPLORER (1996)

ENCHANTED SUN (1999)
5259 grt; 1050 psrs
430' x 62' x 17' (130.3 x 18.8 x 5.2 m)
2 x 8-cylinder MaK diesel engines via twin screw.
Cruise ship converted from the owners of SOFIA at a total cost of US$14,250,000 by Commodore Holdings Ltd and operated by Commodore Day Cruises.
Built by Kynoscoura Dockyard, Salamis, for Hellenic Mediterranean Lines Co Ltd, Piraeus, as the CASTALIA (1974). Renamed SCANDINAVIAN SAGA (1988 – Stena Gulf Line Ltd), PRIDE OF SAN DIEGO (1991 – SeaEscape Ltd, Nassau), TROPIC STAR II (1992 – Starlight Cruises, USA), STENA

ARCADIA (1995 – Stena America Line Ltd), EMERALD EXPRESS (1997 – Yacata Shipping Inc, Nassau) and SOFIA (1998 – Albuferra Investments Inc).

ENCHANTMENT OF THE SEAS (1997)
74136 grt; 2430 psrs
921' x 106' x 25'6" (279.1 x 32.2 x 7.8 m)
4 x 12-cylinder MAN diesel-electric engines via twin screw.

Cruise ship for Royal Caribbean International.
Built by Kvaerner Masa-Yards, Helsinki, at a cost of US$300,000,000.

ENGLAND (1964) See EUROPA (1988)

ENGLESTAN (1927)
4850 grt; 114 psrs
386' x 48' x 25' (117 x 14.5 x 7.6 m)
Hall Russell 3-cylinder triple expansion engines via single screw.
Built by Hall, Russell & Co, Aberdeen, for the Rennie Line as the INTABA (1910). Renamed as the Q-ship WAITOMO (1916 – British Royal Navy) and INTABA (1917 – Rennie Line).

ENNA G (1970)
9423 grt; 108 psrs
456' x 61' x 28' (139 x 18.5 x 8.5 m)
10-cylinder MAN-type diesel engine via single screw.
Broken up for scrap in Thailand in 1992. Owned by Nauru Local government Council.
Built by de Merwede, Hardinxveld, for the Oranje Line as the PRINSES MARGRIET (1961).

ENOTRIA (1951) See ZAM ZAM (1975)

ENRICO C (1965) See AEGEAN SPIRIT (2000)

ENRICO COSTA (1987) See AEGEAN SPIRIT (2000)

ENTRE RIOS (1947)
7604 grt
455' x 62' x 28'6" (137.9 x 18.8 x 8.7 m)
2 x Westinghouse DRG turbine engines via single screw.
Broken up for scrap in Campana as a Dodero Line cargo ship in 1977.
Built by Bethlehem-Fairchild, Baltimore, for the US War Shipping Administration as the ROCK HILL VICTORY (1945).

EOLOS (1981) See CLYDESDALE (1998)

EPHESUS (1996) See BOSPORUS (1999)

EQUATOR (1984) See TEBAH 2000 (1999)

EQUATORE (1926) See HOI HUNG (1954)

ERIDAN (1929)
9928 grt; 570 psrs
475' x 61' x 27' (144.7 x 18.6 x 8.2 m)
2 x 8-cylinder Sulzer diesel engines via twin screw.
Broken up for scrap in Marseilles in 1957.
Built by Soc Provencale de Constructions Navales, La Ciotat, for Messageries Maritimes.

ERIDANIA (1931) See OCEANIA (1931)

ERIMO MARU (1972) See KING MINOS (1987)

ERIMO MARU (1989) See SUNFLOWER ERIMO (1991)

ERINPURA (1911)
5142 grt; 90 psrs
411' x 52' x 25' (124.5 x 15.8 x 7.6 m)
Denny 6-cylinder triple expansion engines via twin screw.
Sank bow first in four minutes in the Mediterranean, 30 miles (50 km) north of Benghazi, after a vital hit by one bomb from an attacking German aircraft on 1 May 1943. A total of 664 lives were lost.
Built by William Denny & Bros, Dumbarton, for the British India Steam Navigation Co Ltd.

ERKIN (1923)
9415 grt; 900 psrs
459' x 58' x 30'8" depth (139.8 x 17.6 x 9.3 m)
6-cylinder triple expansion engines via twin screw.
Turkish Navy submarine escort ship.
Built by AG Weser, Bremen, for North German Lloyd as the TRIER (1923).

ERKIN 2 (1967)
6790 grt; 526 psrs
443' x 59' x 24' (134.3 x 17.8 x 7.2 m)
6-cylinder Fiat diesel engine via single screw.
Owned by the government of Turkey.
Built by Nakskov Skibsvaerft, Nakskov, for Cia Sud Americana de Vapore as the IMPERIAL (1938). Renamed TRABZON (1949 – Turkish Maritime Lines).

ERKIN (A-590) (1984)
6042 grt; 590 psrs
402' x 55' x 19' (121.8 x 16.6 x 5.8 m)
8-cylinder MAN diesel engine via single screw.
In Turkish Navy service.
Built by AG Weser, Bremen, for Turkish Maritime Lines as the EGE (1955).

ERNEST HINDS (1941) See ERNEST HINDS (1942)

ERNEST HINDS (1942)
4858 grt; 110 psrs
360' x 52' x 24'6" (109 x 15.8 x 7.5 m)
William Cramp & Sons 4-cylinder quadruple expansion engines via single screw.
Operated by US Shipping Administration. Broken up for scrap in Baltimore in 1957.
Built by William Cramp & Sons Co, Philadelphia, Pennsylvania, for Grace Steamship Co Inc as the SANTA TERESA (1918). Renamed KENT (1936 – Merchants & Miners Transportation Co), ERNEST HINDS (1941 – Grace Steamship Co Inc) and KENT USS (AP-28) (1941 – US Navy).

ERNESTO ANASTASIO (1955)
7295 grt; 255 psrs
413' x 55' x 24' (125.2 x 16.7 x 7.3 m)
2 x 7-cylinder B+W diesel engines via twin screw.
Sold for scrap in 1980 after going aground on 24 April 1980, off the Spanish coast near Pasajes, then being towed to Bilbao for survey. No official confirmation exists that she was ever broken up.
Built by Union Navale de Levante, Valencia, for Trasmediterranea.

ERNIE PYLE (1945) See GREEN LAKE (1965)

EROS (1965) See IASON (1995)

EROS (1979)
10945 grt; 400 psrs
492' x 64' x 24'6" (150 x 14.5 x 7.5 m)
2 x 10-cylinder Pennhoet-B+W diesel engines via twin screw.
Broken up for scrap in Greece in 1986. Ex-Amelia Martin Cia Navigation.
Built by Arsenal de Brest, Brest, for Messageries Maritimes as the PIERRE LOTI (1953). Renamed OLYMPIA (1969 – Efthymiadis Lines), PATRA (1972 – Efthymiadis Lines) and CHRYSOVALANDOU II (1978 – Vanieros Ultramar Armadora SA, Piraeus).

EROTOKRITOS (1991)
23870 grt; 905 psrs
105 cars or 130 trailers
622' x 79' x 21' (188.4 x 24.2 x 6.3 m)
2 x 14-cylinder Mitsubishi-MAN diesel engines via twin screw.
Owned by Minoan Lines.
Built by Nakai Zosen KK, Setodoa, for Teiheiyo Enkai Ferry KK, Nagoya, as the ISHIKARI (1974).

ERRIA (1932)
7670 grt; 74 psrs
463' x 62' x 25' (140.3 x 18.8 x 7.6 m)
2 x 12-cylinder B+W diesel engines via twin screw.
Broken up for scrap in Osaka in 1962.
Built by Nakskov Skibsvaerft, Nakskov, for the East Asiatic Co, Copenhagen.

ESBJERG (1929) See CIUDAD DE IBIZA (1947)

ESCAPADE (1967) See SAMA 1 (2000)

ESCORIAL (1945) See EUROSTAR (1977)

ESKIMO (1910) See ESKIMO (1919)

ESKIMO, HMS (1914) See ESKIMO (1919)

ESKIMO (1919)
3326 grt; 700 psrs
331' x 45' x 25'6" (100 x 13.6 x 7.7)
Earle's Co 2 x 4-cylinder quadruple expansion engines via twin screw.
Broken up for scrap in 1930. Ex-Wilson Line.
Built by Earles Co Ltd, Humberside, for the Wilson Line as the ESKIMO (1910). Renamed ESKIMO, HMS (1914 – British Admiralty).

ESMERALDA (1950)
9606 grt; 82 psrs
490' x 58' x 28'9" depth (148.5 x 17.6 x 8.8 m)
Triple expansion engines via twin screw.
Broken up for scrap in Italy in 1951. Ex-Cia de Navagacion Penonme.
Built by Maryland Steel Co for the Boston Steamship Co as the TREMONT (1902). Renamed CRISTOBAL (1908 – Panama Railroad Steamship Line) and as a bulk cement carrier PHILIPPA (1940).

ESPAGNE (1910)
11155 grt; 488 psrs
561' x 60' x 39' depth (171 x 18.5 x 11.8 m)
Chantiers et Ateliers de Provence 8-cylinder quadruple expansion engines via twin screw.
Broken up for scrap at St Nazaire in 1934.
Built by Chantiers et Ateliers de Provence, Port de Bouc, for the French Line.

ESPANA (1921) See GENERAL BAGRATSION (1946)

ESPANA (1954)
7707 grt; 804 psrs
426' x 57' x 23'6" (129.8 x 17.3 x 7.2 m)
2 x 4-cylinder A Stephen quadruple expansion engines via single screw.
Broken up for scrap in the Dominican Republic in 1959. Ex-the Dominican Republic Navy.
Built by A Stephen & Sons, Glasgow, for Howard Smith Ltd, Sydney, as the CANBERRA (1913).

ESPANA No.4 (1918) See REIDE (1925)

ESPERANCE BAY (1922) See ARAWA (1936)

ESPERANCE BAY (1930) See BELLA (1956)

ESPERANCE BAY (1937)
14343 grt; 290 psrs
549' x 68' x 33' (167.3 x 20.7 x 10 m)
4 x Vickers DRG turbine engines via twin screw.
Broken up for scrap at Faslane in 1955. Ex-Australian Commonwealth Line.

Built by Vickers-Armstrong Ltd, Barrow-in-Furness, for the Aberdeen & Commonwealth Line as the HOBSONS BAY (1922).

ESPERANZA (1901)
4764 grt; 194 psrs
341' x 48' x 16'9" (103.3 x 14.5 x 5.1 m)
W Cramp & Sons 3-cylinder triple expansion engines via twin   screw.
Wrecked off Tampico, Mexico, on 20 November 1924.
Built by W Cramp & Sons Co, Philadelphia, Pennsylvania, for New York & Cuba Mail Steamship Co.

ESPERIA (1921)
11398 grt; 479 psrs
528' x 62' x 34' (160 x 18.8 x 10.3 m)
4 x Odero SRG turbine engines via twin screw.
Sank on 20 August 1941 after being hit by three torpedoes fired from the British submarine UNIQUE, mid-Mediterranean, with three lives lost.
Built by Soc Esercizio Bacini, RWA Tregoso, for Soc Italia di Servizi Maritima.

ESPERIA (1949)
9314 grt; 472 psrs
488' x 63' x 21'8" (147.9 x 19 x 6.6 m)
2 x 10-cylinder Sulzer diesel engines via twin screw.
Launched by Cantieri Riuniti dell'Adriatico, Monfalcone, for Adriatica as the AUSONIA (1940), but completed as the ESPERIA.

ESPEROS (1964)
3964 grt; 500 psrs
60 cars
336' x 46' x 18' (101.8 x 13.9 x 5.5 m)
6-cylinder MAN diesel engine via single screw.
Broken up for scrap at Gandia, Spain, in 1980. Ex-Kavounides Shipping Co Ltd, Piraeus.
Hull constructed by Danziger Werft, Danzig, in 1940, but completed by Odense Steel Shipyards, Odense, for North German Lloyd as the LINZ (1939). Renamed EMPIRE WANSBECK (1945 – British Ministry of Transport).

ESPEROS I (1977) See EUROSTAR (1977)

ESPRESSO AZZURO (1978)
5299 grt; 713 psrs
70 cars + 24 trailers
417' x 63' x 18' (126.4 x 19.1 x 5.5 m)
2 x 7-cylinder Fiat diesel engines via twin screw.
Ferry operated by Adriatica, Cagliari.
Built by Soc Italiana per Construzioni Navali Meccaniche, Baia, for Traghetto as the CANGURO AZZURO (1965).

ESPRESSO CAGLIARI (1974) See EGITTO EXPRESS (1991)

ESPRESSO CATANIA (1994)
14398 grt; 74 psrs
496' x 77' x 19'6" (150.4 x 23.4 x 6 m)
2 x 8-cylinder Zgoda-Sulzer diesel engines via twin screw.
Owned and operated by Tirrenia Navigation, Naples.
Built by Fincantieri, Palermo, for Tirrenia as the VIA MEDITERRANEO (1993).

ESPRESSO CORINTO (1976) See SHAHRAZAD (1985)

ESPRESSO EGITTO (1980) See EGITTO EXPRESS (1991)

ESPRESSO GRECIA (1980) See GRECIA (2000)

ESPRESSO LIVORNO (1972) See GRECIA (2000)

ESPRESSO MALTA (1990) See PEGASUS (1998)

ESPRESSO OLBIA (1976) See SARDINIA NOVA (1989)

ESPRESSO RAVENNA (1978) See ESPRESSO VENEZIA (1990)

ESPRESSO ROSSO (1978) See SINDIBAD I (1982)

ESPRESSO VENEZIA (1977) See PEGASUS (1998)

ESPRESSO VENEZIA (1990)
8069 grt; 834 psrs
203 cars
414' x 61' x 17' (125.5 x 18.6 x 5.2 m)
2 x 12-cylinder GMT diesel engines via twin screw.
Passenger-car ferry owned by Adriatica, Cagliari, and operated by Tirrenia, Naples.
Built by Cantieri Navali Luigi Orlando, Livorno, for Adriatica di Navigazione SpA, Venice, as the ESPRESSO RAVENNA (1978).

ESQUILINO (1925) See EMPIRE GOVERNOR (1940)

ESSEQUIBO (1914) See NEVA (1935)

ESSEX (1902) See VAN (1927)

ESTEREL (1981) See MISTRAL (1997)

ESTHER DOLLAR (1918) See TAIHOKU MARU (1934)

ESTHER WEEMS (1922) See ADMIRAL BENSON (1927)

ESTONIA (1907)
4269 grt; 1150 psrs
401' x 45' x 28'2" (122.1 x 13.8 x 8.5 m)
Harland & Wolff 3-cylinder triple expansion engine via single screw.
Owned by Russian American Line, she was purposely sunk by explosives on 23 January 1913 after abandoning ship one week earlier, when she caught fire off Port Sudan.
Built by Harland & Wolff Ltd, Belfast, for the Bibby Line as the YORKSHIRE (1889). Renamed INDIEN (1905 – East Asiatic Co, Copenhagen).

ESTONIA (1921) See EMPIRE PENRYN (1946)

ESTONIA (1960) See EKATERINA II (1993)

ESTONIA (1993)
15567 grt; 2000 psrs
370 cars + 52 trailers
513' x 80' x 18' (155.4 x 24.2 x 5.5 m)
4 x 8-cylinder MAN diesel engines via twin screw.

Owned by Estline, she sank at 1.00 am on 28 September 1994 after her bow door was torn off en route from Tallinn to Stockholm during a gale with winds of 80 mph (135 kph) and 18' (5.5 m) waves. This passenger-car-cargo ferry went down so quickly that 852 lives were lost. She was 20 miles (34 km) south of the island of Uto. A subsequent joint accident investigation delivered its findings on 3 December 1994, blaming faulty design bow doors, poor distribution of vehicles on the ship's garage deck, slow crew reaction to events overtaking them, the helmsman and the captain's persevering with continuing the ship's course into the wind.
Built by Jos L Meyer, Papenburg, for Rederi Sally AB as the VIKING SALLY (1980). Renamed SILJA STAR (1990 – Silja Line) and WASA KING (1990 – Wasa Line, subsidiary of Effjohn International).

ESTONIYA (1960) See ESTONIA (1960)

ETAIWI I (1980)
11521 grt; 753 psrs

520' x 64' x 26' (158.6 x 19.4 x 7.9 m)
2 x 10-cylinder Sulzer diesel engines via twin screw.
Broken up for scrap in Kaohsiung as a livestock carrier in 1985. Ex-Mr Ahmed Awad Etaiwi, Saudi Arabia.
Built by Royal de Schelde, Flushing, for Cia Argentina de Navigation Dodero as the ALBERTO DODERO (1951). Renamed as the livestock carrier CORMORAN (1969 – Transportes Oceanicos).

ETOLIN (1937)
9402 grt; 324 psrs
501' x 58' x 31' (151.8 x 17.6 x 9.4 m)
Triple expansion engines via twin screw.
Broken up for scrap in Baltimore in 1957. Ex-Alaska Packers Association.
Built by Newport News Shipbuilding & Drydock Co, Newport News, Virginia, for Matson Lines as the MATSONIA (1913).

ETONIAN (1904)
6438 grt
476' x 52' x 23'2" (144.2 x 15.8 x 7 m)
Central Marine Engineering 3-cylinder triple expansion engines via single screw.
Owned by the Leyland Line, she sank on 23 March 1918, with the loss of seven lives, after being torpedoed by the German U-61 off the Old Head of Kinsale.
Built by Furness, Withy & Co Ltd, West Hartlepool, for the Wilson Line as the CHICAGO (1898).

ETRUSK (1938)
3090 grt; 81 psrs
307' x 44' x 21'6" (93 x 13.3 x 6.5 m)
Neptunwerft 6-cylinder triple expansion engines + turbines via twin screw.
Owned by Turkish Maritime Lines.
Built by NeptunWerft, Rostock.

ETTRICK (1938)
11279 grt; 194 psrs
497' x 63' x 31' (151.4 x 19 x 9.5 m)
2 x 5-cylinder Doxford diesels via twin screw.
Under the control of the British Ministry of War Transport, she sank in November 1942 after being torpedoed by the German U-155 120 miles (200 km) north-west of Gibraltar. A total of 24 lives were lost.
Built by Barclay, Curle & Company, Glasgow, for the P&O Line as a troopship.

EUBEE (1921)
9645 grt; 225 psrs
483' x 59' x 34'6" depth (146.4 x 17.9 x 10.5 m)
Chantiers de France 3-cylinder triple expansion engines via twin screw.
Sank on 16 August 1936 two days after a collision with the British steamer CORINALDO in dense fog, 90 miles (150 km) north of Rio Grande, Brazil.
Built by Ateliers et Chantiers de France, Dunkirk, for Cie des Chargeurs.

EUGENIA (1907)
4835 grt; 1215 psrs
385' x 50' x 18'4" (117.3 x 15.2 x 5.6 m)
3-cylinder Rowan triple expansion engine via single screw.
Sank on 6 August 1917 after being torpedoed by a German U-boat south-west of Ireland.
Built by Russell & Co, Port Glasgow, for Unione Austriaca.

EUGENIO C (1966) See THE BIG RED BOAT II (2000)

EUGENIO COSTA (1987) See THE BIG RED BOAT II (2000).

EURIPIDES (1914) See AKAROA (1932)

EUROFAST (2000)
5998 grt; 1100 psrs
130 cars or 24 trailers
363' x 59' x 14'6" (110 x 17.9 x 4.4 m)
2 x 8-cylinder and 2 x 9-cylinder MAN diesel engines via twin screw.
Passenger-car-cargo ferry owned by Whitecliff Shipping, Italy, and operated by Globetrotter, Italy
Built by Werft Nobiskrug, Rendsburg, as the GUSTAV VASA (1965) for Lion

Ferries. Renamed WAWEL (1973 – Pol Ferries), CALYPSO (1988 – Lea Shipping Co Ltd, Nassau), CEFALONIAN SKY (1991 Strintzis Lines), LUCINDA (1994 – Endeavour Shipping Co SA, Piraeus), CALYPSO II (1996 – Aulona Maritime Ltd) and AULONA (1996 – owned by New Fortune Shipping SA and operated by Aragon Shipping & Trading Co).

EUROFERRYS ATLANTICA (1999)
13179 grt; 1100 psrs
425 cars + 51 trailers
412' x 76' x 18' (124.9 x 23.4 x 5.5 m)
2 x 18- cylinder Lindholmen-Pielstick diesel engines via twin screw.

Passenger-car ferry owned and operated by Europa Ferrys SA.
Built by Brodogradiliste, Trogir, for Stena Lines at a cost of US$12,000,000 as the STENA JUTLANDICA (1973). Renamed JUTLANDICA (1982 – Stena-Canadian National Railways joint venture), BLUENOSE (1983 – Bay Ferries Ltd), Hull 309 (Bay Ferries Ltd) and EUROWAYS ATLANTICA (1999 – Europa Ferrys SA).

EUROMAGIQUE (1995)
11591 grt; 350 psrs
109 cars + 115 trailers
535' x 59' x 22' (162 x 18 x 6.6 m)
2 x 8-cylinder Sulzer SRG diesel engines via twin screw.
Ice-strengthened passenger-car-cargo RoRo ferry operating for Eurolineas Maritimos SAL, Denia, Spain.
Built by Lodose Varv AB, Lodose, for AB Lilla Edets Virkes Export, Lilla Edet, Sweden, as the KAPRIFOL (1977). Renamed NAESBORG (1988 – Vendila Rederi AS, Rungsted), DANA CORONA (1990 – Vendila Rederi AS, Rungsted), NAESBORG (1991 – Vendila Rederi AS, Rungsted) and ATTIKA (1994 – Remel Shipping Co Ltd & AK Ventouris Inc, Limassol). For sale since May 1999.

EUROMANTIQUE (1995) See TAXIARCHIS (1999)

EUROPA (1905) See EMPRESS OF SCOTLAND (1921)

EUROPA (1907)
7870 grt; 2516 psrs
455' x 53' x 20'5" (138.6 x 16.3 x 6.2 m)
Ansaldo 6-cylinder triple expansion engines via twin screw.
Broken up for scrap in 1927. Ex-Navale Generale Italia.
Built by Cantieri Navale Siciliana, Palermo, for La Veloce Lines.

EUROPA (1912) See BERENGARIA (1921)

EUROPA (1917) See BRAGA (1920)

EUROPA (1930) See LIBERTE (1946)

EUROPA (1931)
10224 grt; 64 psrs
465' x 62' x 28'4" (140.9 x 18.8 x 8.6 m)
2 x 6-cylinder B+W diesel engines via single screw.

Broken up for scrap at New Ferry, UK, in 1941 following a German air raid on Liverpool on 3 May 1941. During the raid the ship was hit numerous times and finally burnt out.
Built by Burmeister & Wain, Copenhagen, for the East Asiatic Co, Copenhagen.

EUROPA, USS (1945) See LIBERTE (1946)

EUROPA (1950) See ACAPULCO (1961)

EUROPA (1953) See BLUE SEA (1977)

EUROPA (1964) See COLUMBUS C (1982)

EUROPA (1981) See SUPERSTAR ARIES (1999)

EUROPA (1986) See VEGA (1990)

EUROPA (1988)
8221 grt; 463 psrs
100 cars
459' x 63' x 18' (139.1 x 19.1 x 5.5 m)
2 x 10-cylinder B+W diesel engines via twin screw.

Passenger-car cruise ship operating for Belinder Marine Corporation SA, Piraeus.
Built by Helsingor Shipyards, Helsingor, for the United Steamship Co Ltd, Denmark, as the ENGLAND (1964). Renamed as the pilgrim ship AMERICA XIII (1986 – Petrola Inc, Panama) and EMMA (1987 – Belinder Marine Corporation SA, Piraeus).

EUROPA (1993) See SILJA EUROPA (1993).

EUROPA (1999)
28600 grt; 410 psrs
655' x 79' x 19'6" (198.6 x 24 x 6 m)
4 x 8-cylinder MAN-B+W diesel-electric engines via twin screw.

Built by Kvaerner-Masa Yards, Helsinki, for HAPAG Lloyd at a cost of US$260,000,000.

EUROPA I (1998)
3983 grt; 525 psrs
100 cars + 10 trailers
291' x 53' x 14' (88.3 x 16.2 x 4.2 m)

4 x 9-cylinder MAN diesel engines via twin screw.
Owned and operated by Inver Shipping Ltd, Kingstown, St Vincent.
Built by Bartram & Sons Ltd, Sunderland, UK, for Bornholms Faergen as the JENS KOFOED (1963). Renamed SKIPPER CLEMENT (1965 – DFDS), SLAVIJA (1976) and SLAVIJA I (1976 – Jadrolinija, Rijeka).

EUROPAF SYD (1967) See HERMES (1999)

EUROPA II (1987) See SATURNUS (1991)

EUROPAFARJAN (1983) See BOHUS (1994)

EUROPAFARJAN I (1985) See COMMODORE (1999)

EUROPAFARJAN II (1970) See APOLLONIA II (1990)

EUROPAFARJAN II (1985) See BOHUS (1994)

EUROPAFARJAN III (1974) See CORSICA SERENA SECONDA (2000)

EUROPAFARJAN IV (1978) See HERMES (1999)

EUROPAFARJAN IV (1983) See HERMES (1999)

EUROPAFARJAN SYD (1984) See HERMES (1999)

EUROPA LINK (1990) See AL SALAM 93 (1996)

EUROPEAN (1896) See TRANSILVANIA (1927)

EUROPEAN CAUSEWAY (2000)
20800 grt; 410 psrs
375 cars or cars + trailer mix
526' x 77' x 18'2" (159.5 x 18.2 x 5.5 m)
4 x 12-cylinder Wartsila diesel engines via twin screw.
Ro-pax ferry owned and operated by P&O Management Irish Sea.
Built by Mitsubishi Heavy Industries, Shimonoseki, at a cost of US$45,000,000.

EUROPEAN EXPRESS (1975) See PENELOPE A (2000)

EUROPEAN FREEWAY (1994)
21162 grt; 538 psrs (originally)
556' x 56' x 14'6" (108 x 16.6 x 4.4 m)
MAN 9-cylinder diesel engines via single screw.
Owned and operated by P&O North Sea Ferries Ltd.
Passenger ferry laid down by Deutsche Werft AG, Hamburg, as the ALPHA ENTERPRISE (1978) and completed as the SYRIA (1979) for United Arab Maritime Co, Alex andria. Renamed STENA TRANSPORTER (1983 – Stena Lines) and CERDIC FERRY (1986).

EUROPEAN FREIGHTER (1992) See AFRODITE II (1995)

EUROPEAN GATEWAY (1975) See PENELOPE A (2000)

EUROPEAN GLORY (1990) See MEDIA II (1993)

EUROPEAN PRIDE (1994) See HERMES (1999)

EUROPEAN SPIRIT (1990) See AL QAMAR (1999)

EUROPEAN STAR (1992) See SARAY STAR (1994)

EUROPIC FERRY (1968) See AFRODITE II (1995)

EUROSTAR (1977)
10142 grt; 390 psrs
487' x 62' x 20' (147.6 x 18.8 x 7.9 m)
2 x 10-cylinder Sulzer diesel engines via single screw.
Broken up for scrap in Beirut in 1977. Ex-Cypriot owners.
Laid down by Soc Espanola de Construccion Naval, Bilbao, for Empresa Nacional Elcano as the freighter ESCORIAL (1945) and completed for the Aznar Line as the MONTE URBASA (1948). Renamed CABO SANTA

PAULA (1969 – Ybarra y Cia) and ESPEROS (1977 – Seamanager Navigation Co Ltd, Limassol).

EUROSUN (1989) See WASA QUEEN (1992)

EUROSUN (1990) See WASA QUEEN (1992)

EUROTRAVELLER (1997) See LARKSPUR (1999)

EUROVOYAGER (1998)
12599 grt; 1300 psrs
250 cars + 55 trailers
391' x 68' x 15' (118.4 x 20.7 x 4.5 m)
2 x 18-cylinder Pielstick diesel engines via twin screw.
Passenger ferry owned by Denval, London, and chartered to Sally Line.
Built by John Cockerill Shipyards, Hoboken, for RMT, Belgium, as the PRINS ALBERT (1978).

EUROWAYS ATLANTICA (1999) See EUROFERRYS ATLANTICA (1999)

EVANGELINE (1900) See VALPARAISO (1917)

EVANGELINE (1927) See YARMOUTH CASTLE (1964)

EVA PERON (1950) See URUGUAY (1956)

EVERTON GRANGE (1903) See NORDICO (1926)

EVITA (1952) See RIO TUNUYAN (1955)

EXCALIBUR (1931) See JOSEPH HEWES, USS (AP-50) (1941)

EXCALIBUR (1948) See ORIENTAL JADE (1965)

EXCAMBION (1931) See JOHN PENN, USS (APA-23) (1943)

EXCAMBION (1948) See TEXAS CLIPPER (1998)

EXCELLENT (1998)
39739 grt; 2250 psrs
140 cars + 50 trailers
667' x 92' x 22' (202.2 x 28 x 6.7 m)
4 x 8-cylinder Wartsila diesel engines via twin screw.
Passenger-car-cargo ferry owned by the Grimaldi Group and operated by their subsidiary, Grandi Navi Veloce.
Built by Apuania Nuovi, Carrara, at a cost of US$116,000,000.

EXCELSIOR (1882) See MUNEASTERN (1924)

EXCELSIOR (1990)
5071 grt; 250 psrs
401' x 52' x 17' (121.5 x 15.8 x 5.2 m)
2 x 6-cylinder MAN diesel engines via twin screw.
Broken up for scrap by Ege Celik Endustrisi AS at Aliaga in 1996.
Built by Mathias-Thesen, Wismar, for Black Sea Shipping Co, Odessa, as the ice-strengthened LATVIYA (1963).

EXCELSIOR (1999)
39500 grt; 2250 psrs
140 cars + 50 trailers
667' x 92' x 22' (202.2 x 28 x 6.7 m)
4 x 8-cylinder Wartsila Sulzer diesel engines via twin screw.
Passenger-car-cargo ferry owned by the Grimaldi Group and operated by their subsidiary, Grandi Navi Veloce.
Built by Kvaerner-Masa Shipyard at a cost of US$116,000,000.

EXCELSIOR MERCURY (1990)
4871 grt; 333 psrs
401' x 52' x 17' (121.5 x 15.6 x 5.2 m)
2 x 6-cylinder MAN diesel engines via twin screw.
Cruise ship owned by Excelsior Shipping Co Ltd.
Built by Mathias-Thesen, Wismar, for the Far Eastern Shipping Co, Vladivostok, as the ice-strengthened vessel MARIA ULYANOVA (1959).

I

I

I

I

I

EXCELSIOR NEPTUNE (1990)
4195 grt; 250 psrs
401' x 52' x 17' (122.2 x 15.8 x 5.2 m)
2 x 6-cylinder MAN diesel engines via twin screw.
Owned by Excelsior Third Marine Transport Inc, Panama, and operated by Far East Shipping Co, Vladivostok.
Built as the FELIX DZERJINSKY (1958) by Veb Mathias-Thesen, Wismar, for the Black Sea Shipping Company.

EXETER (1931) See EDWARD RUTLEDGE, USS (AP-52) (1941)

EXETER (1948) See ORIENTAL PEARL (1965)

EXOCHORDA (1931) See TARSUS (1946)

EXOCHORDA (1947) See STEVENS (1967)

EXPLORADOR IRADIER (1948) See SATRUSTEGUI (1953)

EXPLORATEUR GRANDIDIER (1924)
10268 grt; 299 psrs
456' x 61' x 38' depth (138.2 x 18.5 x 11.5 m)
Triple expansion engines via twin screw.
Broken up for scrap in 1946 after having been scuttled by the Germans, in August 1944, as a block ship to the port of Marseilles.
Built by Ateliers et Chantiers de la Loire, St Nazaire, for Messageries Maritimes.

EXPLORER OF THE SEAS (2000)
137308 grt; 3114 psrs
1020' x 157' x 28' (309 x 47.6 x 8.6 m)
6 x 12-cylinder Wartsila diesel engines via triple Azipod screw.

Cruise ship built by Kvaerner-Masa Yards Inc, Turku, for Royal Caribbean International at a cost of US$500,000,000.

EXPLORER STARSHIP (1986) See SONG OF FLOWER (1989)

EXPRES ATHINA (1998)
5643 grt; 1302 psrs
310 cars
389' x 65' x 14' (118 x 19.8 x 4.2 m)
2 x 18-cylinder Pielstick diesel engines via twin screw.
Passenger-car ferry owned and operated by Minoan Flying Dolphins.
Built by NV Boelwerf SA, Tamise, for RMT, Belgium, as the PRINS PHILIPPE (1973). Renamed MOBY LOVE (1986 – Nav Ar Ma, Italy) and PANAGIA TINOU 2 (1993 – Ventouris Sea Lines).

EXPRESS ANEMOS (1989) See MYRTIDIOTISSA (2000)

EXPRESS APHRODITE (1997)
11690 grt; 1700 psrs
335 cars or 36 trailers
424' x 70' x 15' (128.5 x 21.2 x 4.5 m)
2 x 16-cylinder Stork-Werkspoor diesel engines via twin screw.
Passenger-car-cargo RoRo ferry owned and operated by Minoan Flying Dolphins.
Built by Aalborg Vaerft, Aalborg, for British Rail at a cost of £13,000,000 as the St COLUMBA (1977). Renamed STENA HIBERNIA (1991 – Stena Line) and STENA ADVENTURER (1996 – Stena Line).

EXPRESS APOLLON (1977)
5284 grt; 1908 psrs
397' x 57' x 15' (120.3 x 17.2 x 4.5 m)
2 x 8-cylinder B+W diesel engines via twin screw.
Broken up for scrap in Mumbai in 1981. Ex-Agapitos Bros, Piraeus.
Built by Harland & Wolff Ltd, Belfast, for British Transport Commission as the HIBERNIA (1949).

EXPRESS APOLLON (1997)
7849 grt; 2800 psrs
217 cars
390' x 65' x 13'6" (118.1 x 19.8 x 4.1 m)
2 x 16-cylinder Pielstick SRG diesel engines via twin screw.

Ferry owned and operated by Minoan Flying Dolphins.
Built by Arsenal de la Marine National Francaise, Brest, for Sealink UK Ltd as the SENLAC (1973). Renamed APOLLO EXPRESS (1987 – Ventouris) and APOLLON EXPRESS 1 (1993 – Ventouris Group).

EXPRESS ARIS (2000)
11334 grt; 1700 psrs
446' x 73' x 17' (135 x 22 x 5.2 m)
2 x 16-cylinder MAN diesel engines via twin screw.
Passenger ferry owned and operated by Minoan Flying Dolphins.
Built by Kanda Kure, Kure, for Hiroshima Green Ferry KK, Hiroshima, as the GREEN ARROW (1972). Renamed ARGO (1977 – Tai Heiyo Ferry KK, Osaka), KRITI (1978 – Cretan Marine and ANEK) and SUPER NAIAS (1996 – Super Naias Shipping and Agapitos Lines).

EXPRESS ARTEMIS (2000)
5596 grt; 1400 psrs
390' x 65' x 13'6" (118.1 x 19.8 x 4.1 m)
2 x 16-cylinder diesel engines via twin screw.

Passenger-car ferry owned and operated by Minoan Flying Dolphins.
Built by Arsenal de la Marine National Francaise, Brest, for Sealink UK as the HENGIST (1972). Renamed STENA HENGIST (1991 – Sealink-Stena Line),

ROMILDA (1992 – GA Ferries), APOLLON EXPRESS 2 (1993 – Ventouris Sea Lines) and PANAGIA EKATONTAPYLIANI (1996 – Agapitos Express Ferries).

EXPRESS FERRY ANGELINA LAURO (1975) See CAPO FALCONARA (1978).

EXPRESS HERMES (1999)
3397 grt; 1800 psrs
180 cars
389' x 53' x 12'6" (118 x 16 x 3.8 m)
2 x 12-cylinder Sulzer diesel engines via twin screw.
Passenger-car-cargo RoRo ferry owned and operated by Minoan Flying Dolphins.
Built by NV Boelwerf, Tamise, for RTM, Belgium, as the PRINCESS ASTRID (1968). Renamed GEORGIOS II (1983 – Ventouris Ferries) and BARI EXPRESS (1984 – Ventouris Ferries).

EXPRESS KARISTOS (1996)
3017 grt; 600 psrs
285' x 46' x 12' (86.3 x 13.8 x 3.7 m)
2 x 8-cylinder MWM diesel engines via twin screw.
Passenger ferry owned and operated by Karistos Maritime Co.
Built by D Kamitsis Shipyard & Machine Shop & Co Ltd, Perama Bay, as the AETOS (1971). Renamed CORFU SEA (1985 – Aktoploikai Grammai Agapitos) and DODEKANISSOS (1987 – Pyraki Shipping Co).

EXPRESS MILOS (2000)
7627 grt; 1400 psrs
40 cars
378' x 63' x 13'6" (114.6 x 19.2 x 4.1 m)
2 x 16-cylinder Pielstick diesel engines via twin screw.
Passenger-car ferry owned and operated by Minoan Flying Dolphins.
Built by Swan Hunter Shipbuilding, Newcastle, for Sealink, UK, as the VORTIGERN (1969). Renamed MILOS EXPRESS (1988 – Minoan Flying Dolphins).

EXPRESS OLYMPIA (1990)
4358 grt; 1200 psrs
300 cars
359' x 57' x 15' (108.7 x 17.3 x 4.6 m)
2 x 12-cylinder Pielstick diesel engines via twin screw.

Ice-strengthened passenger-car ferry owned and operated by Minoan Flying Dolphins.
Built by Jos L Meyer, Papenburg, for Viking Lines as the VIKING 4 (1973). Renamed EARL GRANVILLE (1980 – Sealink UK).

EXPRESS PENELOPE (2000)
5109 grt; 1400 psrs
220 cars
390' x 65' x 13'6" (118.1 x 19.8 x 4.1 m)
2 x 16-cylinder Pielstick diesel engines via twin screw.

Passenger-car ferry owned and operated by Minoan Flying Dolphins.
Built by Arsenal de la Marine National Francaise, Brest, for Sealink UK as the HORSA (1972). Renamed STENA HORSA (1991 – Stena Line) and PENELOPE A (1992 – Agoudimos Lines).

EXPRESS POSEIDON II (1999)
7819 grt; 1874 psrs
210 cars or 30 trailers
389' x 60' x 16'6" (118 x 18.2 x 5 m)
2 x 12-cylinder Pielstick diesel engines via twin screw.

Passenger-car-cargo ferry owned and operated by Hellas Ferries.
Built by Schichau Unterweser, Bremerhaven, for Irish-Continental Group, Wexford, as the SAINT PATRICK (1973) at a cost of £5,500,000. Renamed SAINT COLUMB (1982 – Belfast Car Ferries Ltd), SAINT COLUM I (1982 – Belfast Car Ferries Ltd), DIMITRIOS EXPRESS (1990 – Strathakis Shipping Co), KADIA EXPRESS (1993 – short charter), DIMITRIOS EXPRESS (Arkadia Lines) and POSEIDON EXPRESS 2 (1997 – Arkadia Lines).

EXPRESS SAMINA (2000)
4555 grt; 1300 psrs
180 cars
377' x 59' x 15'6" (114.2 x 18 x 4.7 m)
2 x 16-cylinder Pielstick diesel engines via twin screw.
Owned and operated by Minoan Flying Dolphins after purchase for US$2,250,000. At 10.00 pm on the night of 27 September 2000, she crashed bow-on at full speed into two 60' (18.2 m) high rocky outcrops known as 'The Gates' three miles (5 km) outside the harbour of Patros, and equipped with a beacon which was highly visible for seven miles (12 km). She sank within 45 minutes, taking 94 people with her. As a result of initial court hearings on the matter, the Greek authorities clamped down and quarantined almost the entire Greek ferry fleet for rigid inspections and surveys. As this book goes to press, the hearings have not reached a final conclusion; however, Mr Pandelis Sfinias, the general manager of Minoan Lines, parent company of Minoan Flying Dolphins which operated EXPRESS SAMINA, jumped six floors to his death from the Minoan office building on 29 November 2000.
Built by Chantiers de l'Atlantique, St Nazaire, for the French Line as the CORSE (1966). Renamed GOLDEN VERGINA (1982 – Agapitos Lines, Piraeus).

EXPRESS SANTORINI (1993)
4140 grt; 1400 psrs
250 cars + 20 trailers or 335 rail wagons
381' x 63' x 14' (115.4 x 19.2 x 4.2 m)
2 x 16-cylinder Pielstick diesel engines via twin screw.

Passenger-car-cargo-train ferry owned and operated by Minoan Flying Dolphins.
Built by Dubigeon-Normandie, Nantes, for SNCF, Calais, as the CHARTRES (1974).

FABIOLAVILLE (1972) See HAI HUA (1989)

FAGR (1998)
5993 grt; 1200 psrs
260 cars
359' x 57' x 15' (108.7 x 17.3 x 4.6 m)
2 x 12-cylinder Deutz diesel engines via twin screw.
Ice-strengthened passenger-car ferry owned and operated by Brave Commander SA, San Lorenzo.
Built by Jos L Meyer, Papenburg, for the Sally Line, Mariehamn, as the VIKING I (1970). Renamed WASA EXPRESS (1983 – Sally Line), VIKING I (1984 – Khalid Shipping Co Ltd, Jeddah), KHALID (1984 – Khalid Shipping Co Ltd, Jeddah), MECCA I (Brave Commander SA, Panama), AL HUSSEIN II (1986 – Khaled Fouda, Cairo), AL-QAMAR AL-SAUDI AL-MISR I (1990 – El Salam Trading & Shipping Co, Cairo), MECCA I (1992 – El Salam Trading & Shipping Establishment), AL QAMAR AL SAUDI II (1993 – El Salam Trading & Shipping Establishment) and MECCA I (1994 – El Salam Trading & Shipping Establishment).

FAIRFAX (1926) See BINTANG SAMUDRA (1951)

FAIRLAND (1968) See CHINA SEA DISCOVERY (2000)

FAIR MAJESTY (1989) See ARCADIA (1997)

FAIR PRINCESS (1997) See CHINA SEA DISCOVERY (2000)

FAIRSEA (1949)
13432 grt; 925 psrs
492' x 70' x 24' (150 x 21.3 x 7.3 m)
2 x 6-cylinder Doxford diesel engine via single screw.
Owned by Sitmar Cruises Inc, she was broken up for scrap for a tender price of US$300,000 at La Spezia in 1969 after catching fire on 24 January 24 1969, 900 miles west of Balboa, Panama.
Laid down by the Sun Shipbuilding & Drydock Company, Chester, Pennsylvania, for the Moore McCormack Line as the Class C3-type cargo ship RIO DE LA PLATA (1941) and completed by Newport News Shipbuilding, Newport News, Virginia, as the auxiliary aircraft carrier CHARGER, USS (CVE-30) (1942 – US Navy).

FAIRSEA (1969) See CHINA SEA DISCOVERY (2000)

FAIRSKY (1957) See PHILIPPINE TOURIST (1978)

FAIRSKY (1980) See MARIANNA 9 (1984)

FAIRSKY (1984) See PACIFIC SKY (2000)

FAIRSTAR (1963) See RIPA (1997)

FAIRSTONE (1949) See CASTEL FELICE (1952)

FAIRWIND (1963)
7696 grt
439' x 62' x 28'6" (133 x 18.8 x 8.7 m)
Geared turbine engine via single screw.
Broken up for scrap at Bilbao, Spain, in 1968 after she grounded very severely in the Bahamas. Ex-Southwind Shipping Corporation.
Built by Bethlehem-Fairfield Shipyards, Baltimore, for the US War Shipping Administration as the SMITH VICTORY (1945). Renamed BUENOS AIRES (1947 – Dodero Line).

FAIRWIND (1968) See ALBATROS (1993).

FAIRY PRINCESS (1995) See ZENITH (1995)

FAITH POWER (1993) See ZENITH (1995)

FAKHRI (1909)
3950 grt; 116 psrs
380' x 45' x 27'6" (115.8 x 13.8 x 8.4 m)
Triple expansion engine via single screw.
Owned by Bombay & Hujaz Steam Navigation Co of India Ltd, she was abandoned as a total constructive loss as a pilgrim ship when wrecked on 20 December 1911 on Perim, an island at the southern entrance to the Red Sea in Yemen territory.
Built by Palmer Brothers Shipyard, Jarrow, for the Sun Shipping Line as the BRANKSOME HALL (1888). Renamed TIENTSIN (1898 – after the P&O Line acquired it for £32,802) and SHAH NASIR (1906 – Shah Steam Navigation Co of India Ltd).

FALABA (1906)
4806 grt; 120 psrs
381' x 47' x 22'9" (115.5 x 14.2 x 6.9 m)
A Stephen & Sons 3-cylinder triple expansion engine via single screw.
Sank with the loss of 104 lives on 28 March 1915, after the German U-28 gave the ship a five minute warning prior to firing a torpedo into her side off the south coast of Ireland.
Built by A Stephen & Sons Ltd, Glasgow, for Elder Dempster Lines.

FALAISE (1948)
3710 grt; 700 psrs
100 cars
314' x 51' x 23'3" (95.2 x 15.5 x 7.1 m)
4 x William Denny SRG turbine engines via twin screw.
Broken up at Bilbao in 1975 as a passenger-car ferry.
Built by William Denny & Bros, Dumbarton, for the Southern Railway as a train ferry at a cost of £560,000.

FALSTER (1975) See VEGA (1990)

FALSTER LINK (1988) See TAG EL SALAM (1998)

FALSTRIA (1941) See VERYR (1964)

FAMAKA (1922) See ATLANTICOS (1956)

FANTAASIA (1998)
16630 grt; 1700 psrs
554 cars
449' x 80' x 17'6" (136.1 x 24.2 x 5.4 m)
4 x 12-cylinder Wartsila-Pielstick diesel engines via twin screw.

Ice-strengthened passenger-car ferry acquired for US$31,000,000 by Hansatee Shipping Oy, Estonia, and operated by Tallink.
Built by Wartsila, Turku, for the Viking Line as the TURELLA (1979). Renamed STENA NORDICA (1988 – Stena Line) and LION KING (1996 – Lion Ferry).

FANTASIA (1964)
4325 grt; 380 psrs
359' x 52' x 15' (108.8 x 15.8 x 4.5 m)
2 x Parsons SRG turbine engines via twin screw.
Broken up for scrap by Prodromos Sariktzis at Piraeus in 1976 after being gutted by fire while owned by Chandris Cruises Ltd.
Built by Harland & Wolff Ltd, Belfast, for the British Transport Commission as the ferry DUKE OF YORK (1935). Renamed DUKE OF WELLINGTON, HMS (1942 – British Royal Navy), YORK (1963 – Chandris subsidiary, Marivic).

FANTASIA (1990) See P&OSL CANTERBURY (1999)

FANTASTIC (1996)
25186 grt; 2060 psrs
760 cars
621' x 92' x 22' (188.2 x 28 x 6.8 m)
4 x 9-cylinder Sulzer diesel engines via twin screw.
Passenger-car ferry operated by Grandi Navi Veloci, a subsidiary of the Grimaldi Group.
Built by Nuovi Cantieri Apuania, Marina di Carrara.

FANTASTICA (1992) See OCEAN EXPLORER I (1998).

FANTASY (1990)
70367 grt; 2634 psrs
860' x 102' x 26' (260.6 x 30.9 x 7.9 m)
6 x 12-cylinder Wartsila-Sulzer diesel-electric engines via twin screw.

Cruising for Carnival Cruise Line, USA.
Built by Kvaerner-Masa Shipyards, Helsinki, for Carnival Cruise Line at a cost of US$205,000,000.

FANTASY WORLD (1992) See LEISURE WORLD (1994)

FANTEE (1899) See ROLLO (1920)

FARAH I (1983) See TIAN PENG (1991)

FARAH I (1993) See GURGEN-2 (1996)

FARJA (1979) See VISBY (1980)

FASCINATION (1994)
70367 grt; 2040 psrs
860' x 102' x 26' (260.6 x 30.9 x 7.8 m)
6 x 12-cylinder Sulzer diesel-electric engines via twin screw.

Cruising for Carnival Cruise Lines.
Built by Kvaerner-Masa Shipyards, Helsinki, for Carnival Cruise Line at a cost of US$315,000,000.

FAVORITA (1964) See KIM HWA (1968)

FEDERAL MAPLE (1961)
3171 grt; 250 psrs
298' x 52' x 16' (90.3 x 15.8 x 4.8 m)
2 x 10-cylinder Fairbanks-Morse diesel engine via single screw.
Operating for Furness Withy & Co Ltd, Port of Spain.
Built by Canadian Vickers Ltd, Montreal.

FEDERAL PALM (1961) See CENPAC ROUNDER (1972)

FEDERICO C (1958) See SEABREEZE I (1989)

FEDOR DOSTOEVSKIY (1988) See ASTOR (1995)

FEDOR DOSTOJEWSKIJ (1988) See ASTOR (1995)

FEDOR SHALYAPIN (1991)
22296 grt; 943 psrs
608' x 80' x 29' (185.3 x 24.3 x 8.8 m)
4 x DRG turbine engines via twin screw.
Owned by the the Far Eastern Shipping Company, Vladivostok, she was scheduled for scrapping when an unnamed Russian company chartered her in 1996 and commenced a US$3,5000,000 refurbishment programme to prepare her for troop transportation. However, that company was declared bankrupt midway through the programme and the ship has been laid up at the Iliychevsk Shipyard since March 1997.
Built by John Brown & Co Ltd, Clydebank, for the Cunard Line as the IVERNIA (1955). Renamed FRANCONIA (1962 – Cunard Line) and FYODOR SHALYAPIN (1973 – Far Eastern Shipping Co).

FEDRA (1987)
17879 grt; 1800 psrs
470 cars or 45 trailers
490' x 79' x 16'6" (149.4 x 24 x 5.1 m)
2 x 6-cylinder Pielstick diesel engines via twin screw.

Ferry operating for Minoan Lines.
Built by Werft Nobiskrug, Rendsburg, for TT-Line, Lubeck, as the PETER PAN (1974). Renamed ROBIN HOOD (1986 – TT-Line).

FELICIA (1999)
7009 grt; 1185 psrs
495' x 76' x 16' (150 x 22.9 x 4.8 m)
2 x 16-cylinder MAN diesel engines via twin screw.
Passenger ferry owned by Fidelity Maritime SA.
Built by Kanda Zosensho KK, Kure, for Hankyu Ferry KK, Shimonoseki, as the FERRY NAGATO (1972). Laid up 1991–94. Renamed GRACE M (1994 – Marlines).

FELICITY (1989) See VISBY (1997)

FELIKS DZERSHINSKI (1958) See FELIX DZERJINSKY (1958)

FELIX DZERINSKY (1929)
3767 grt; 292 psrs
333' x 48' x 25'6" (100.9 x 14.5 x 7.8 m)
Russian Diesel Works 6-cylinder diesel engine via single screw.
Believed lost during World War Two.
Built by Severney Shipbuilding Yard, St Petersburg, for Sovtorgflot (Russian government).

FELIX DZERJINSKY (1958) See EXCELSIOR NEPTUNE (1990)

FELIX DZERJINSKY (1963)
5169 grt; 333 psrs
401' x 52' x 17' (121.5 x 15.8 x 5.2 m)
2 x 6-cylinder MAN diesel engines via twin screw.
Built by Mathias-Thesen, Wismar, for the Russian government.

FELIX ROUSSEL (1930) See AROSA SUN (1955)

FELTRE (1915)
6403 grt; 140 psrs

409' x 53' x 28' (124.8 x 16.1 x 8.5 m)
4-cylinder quadruple expansion engine via single screw.
Seized by Italian government at Naples in 1915, but sank on 25 May 1916 after hitting a mine near Flamborough, Yorkshire.
Built by Bremer Vulkan, Vegesack, for Hapag as the RHENANIA (1909).

FELTRIA (1916)
5254 grt; 400 psrs
420' x 48' x 22'4" (128 x 14.7 x 6.8 m)
William Denny & Brothers 4-cylinder quadruple expansion engine via single screw.
Owned by the Cunard Steamship Co Ltd, she sank on 5 May 1917, with the loss of 45 lives, after being torpedoed by the German U-48 eight miles south-east of the Irish coast near Mine Head, Waterford.
Built by William Denny & Bros, Dumbarton, for the British India Associated Steamers as the AVOCA (1891). Renamed SAN FERNANDO (1896 – Cia Trasatlantica), AVOCA (1896 – British India Associated Steamers), ATLANTA (1907 – East Asiatic Shipping Co), AVOCA (1908 – New York & Continental Line) and URANIUM (1908 – Northwest Transport).

FENCER, HMS (1942) See CARIBIA (1973)

FENJA (1999)
10404 grt; 600 psrs
111 cars + 414 TEUs
435' x 66' x 20'6" (131.7 x 20.1 x 6.2 m)
12-cylinder Krupp-MaK diesel engine via single screw.

Passenger-car-container ship owned by James Fisher & Co, Liverpool.
Built by Frederikshavn Vaerft, Frederikshavn, for Mercandia as the MERCANDIAN PRESIDENT (1982). Renamed LODBROG (1988 – owned by Mercandia and operated by the Danish government). Currently being converted by the Cammell Laird Group, Tyneside, for Global Marine Systems as a cable-laying ship at a cost of £8,500,000.

FENNIA (1966)
10515 grt; 1200 psrs
225 cars or 32 trailers
421' x 65' x 16'6" (127.6 x 19.7 x 5 m)
4 x 9-cylinder MaK diesel engines via twin screw.

Passenger-car-cargo ferry for the Silja Line.
Built by Oresundevarvet AB, Landskrona for the O.Y Svea Line AB, Mariehamn.

FENNO EXPRESS (1970) See ARTEMIS I (1996)

FENNO STAR (1990) See SANDEFJORD (1992)

FEODOR SHALYAPIN (1973) See FEDOR SHALYAPIN (1973)

FERDINAND DE LESSEPS (1952) See LA PALMA (1980)

FERDINANDO FREILIGRATH (1964) See AUGUST 8th (1976)

FERDINANDO PALASCIANO (1917) See ITALIA (1923)

FERMITA (1964) See ZAKROS (1971)

FERNANDO POO (1935)
6914 grt; 99 psrs
407' x 54' x 22' (150.6 x 16.4 x 6.7 m)
Krupp diesel engines via twin screw.
Sank in July 1937 by gunfire off Bata, Spanish New Guinea, during the Spanish Civil War.
Built by Soc Espanola de Construccion Naval SA, Bilbao, for Cia Trasmediterranea.

FERNHILL (1974) See SONG OF FLOWER (1989)

FERRANIA (1927)
6998 grt
460' x 58' x 30'9" depth (139.4 x 17.6 x 9.4 m)
John Brown 6-cylinder triple expansion engines via twin screw.
Broken up for scrap in 1928. Ex-Ditta L Pittalunga.
Built by John Brown & Co Ltd, Glasgow, for the New Zealand Shipping Co Ltd as the KAIKOURA (1903). Renamed GIANO (1926).

FERRUCCIO BUONAPACE (1945) See UGOLINO VIVALDI (1947)

FERRY AKASHI (1972) See SALAMIS STAR (2000)

FERRY AKASHIA (1973) See FILIPINA PRINCESS (1988)

FERRY AKEBONO (1989)
6466 grt; 695 psrs
469' x 73' x 20'6" (142.1 x 22.1 x 6.2 m)
2 x 12-cylinder Pielstick diesel engines via twin screw.
Passenger ferry operated by Oshima Unyu, Japan.
Built by Mitsubishi Heavy Industries, Shimonoseki, for Oshima Unyu KK

FERRY AMAMI (1987) See ZAMBOANGA (1989)

FERRY ATSUTA (1972) See EL GRECO (1981)

FERRY AZALEA (1994)
20554 grt; 926 psrs
80 cars
645' x 97' x 22' (195.5 x 29.4 x 6.8 m)
2 x 9-cylinder Pielstick diesel engines via twin screw.
Passenger-car ferry operated by Shin Nihonkai.
Built by Ishikawajima Heavy Industries, Tokyo.

FERRY COSMO (1992) See SUPERFERRY 5 (1996)

FERRY DIAMOND (1986)
9023 grt; 965 psrs
50 cars + 105 trailers
498' x 82' x 18' (150.9 x 25 x 5.5 m)
2 x 8-cylinder MAN diesel engines via twin screw.
Passenger-car-cargo ferry operated by Diamond Ferry, Japan.
Built by Kurushima Dockyard Company Ltd, Onishi, for KK Diamond Ferry.

FERRY FUKUOKA (1992)
9320 grt; 780 psrs
100 cars + 155 trailers
528' x 82' x 21' (160 x 25 x 6.3 m)
2 x 8-cylinder Pielstick diesel engines via twin screw.
Passenger-car-cargo ferry operated by the Blue Highway Line.
Built by Onomichi Zosen KK, Onomichi, for Meimon Taiyo Ferry, Osaka, as the NEW ORION (1989).

FERRY GOLD (1970) See MILENA (1990)

FERRY HACHINOHE (1979) See HANIL CAR FERRY No. 2 (1991)

FERRY HACHINOHE (1989)
4967 grt; 444 psrs

418' x 68' x 18' (126.6 x 20.7 x 5.5 m)
2 x 9-cylinder Pielstick diesel engines via twin screw.
Passenger ferry operated by Silver Higashi Nippon, Japan.
Built by Naikai Setoda, Setoda.

FERRY HAKOZAKI (1973) See SUPERFERRY 5 (1996)

FERRY HAMANASAU (1972) See LISSOS (1989)

FERRY HANKYU (1968) See ATHINA I (1999)

FERRY HARIMA (1970) See COTABATO PRINCESS (1988)

FERRY HAYATOMO II (1987)
4159 grt; 756 psrs
376' x 69' x 16'5" (113.9 x 21 x 5 m)
2 x 8-cylinder Mitsubishi diesel engines via twin screw.
Ferry operated by Kansai Kisen, Japan.
Built by Kurushima Dockyard Co Ltd, Onishi.

FERRY IZU (1970) See POSEIDON (1994)

FERRY KAMPU
5169 grt; 1200 psrs
421' x 63' x 14'6" (127.7 x 19.2 x 4.4 m)
2 x 16-cylinder MAN diesel engines via twin screw.
Owned by Kampu Ferry KK., Shimonoseki.
Built by Hayashikane Zosen, Shimonoseki, for the Hankyu Ferry KK,
Shimonoseki, as the HANKYU No.6 (1968).

FERRY KAMPU (1984) See FERRY PUKWAN (1998)

FERRY KATSURA (1971) See SWEET GLORY (1988)

FERRY KIKAI (1979) See OUR LADY OF GOOD VOYAGE (1999)

FERRY KOGANE MARU (1980) See RODOS (1989)

FERRY KUROSHIO (1978) See SEATRAILER (1998)

FERRY KURUSHIMA (1987)
4273 grt; 756 psrs
393' x 69' x 16'6" (119.1 x 20.9 x 5 m)
2 x 8-cylinder Mitsubishi diesel engines via twin screw.
Passenger ferry operated by Kansai Kisen Kaisha Ltd.
Built by Shin Kurushima, Onichi.

FERRY KYOTO (1989)
9320 grt; 780 psrs
100 cars + 155 trailers
528' x 83' x 21' (160 x 25 x 6.3 m)
2 x 8-cylinder Pielstick diesel engines via twin screw.
Passenger-car-cargo ferry owned and operated by Blue Highway Line.
Built by Harima Heavy Industries, Onomichi, for Meimon Taiyo Ferry, Tokyo,
as the NEW PEGASUS (1989), but renamed FERRY KYOTO the same year.

FERRY LAVENDER (1991)
19904 grt; 796 psrs
266 cars
632' x 96' x 22' (191.5 x 29.1 x 6.7 m)
2 x 8-cylinder Pielstick diesel engines via twin screw.
Passenger-car ferry operating for Shin-Nihonkai Ferry, Osaka.
Built by Ishikawajima Heavy Industries, Tokyo.

FERRY LILAC (1970) See POSEIDON (1994)

FERRY LILAC (1984)
19329 grt; 554 psrs
136 cars + 152 trailers
637' x 97' x 22'6" (193 x 29.4 x 6.8 m)
2 x 8-cylinder Pielstick geared diesel engines via twin screw.
Ferry operated by Shin Nihonkai Ferry KK, Japan.
Built by Ishikawajima Harima Heavy Industries, Aioi.

FERRYMAR I (1988) See HEIMDAL (1989)

FERRY MUROTO (1975) See MYRTIDIOTISSA (2000)

FERRY MUROTO (1982) See SANTA ANA (1993)

FERRY MUROTO (1987)
6472 grt; 867 psrs
53 cars + 88 trailers
420' x 76' x 18' (127.4 x 23 x 5.5 m)
2 x 7-cylinder Pielstick diesel engines via twin screw.
Passenger ferry operated by Muroto Kisen, Japan.
Built by Kurushika, Onishi.

FERRY NAGATO (1972) See GRACE M (1994)

FERRY NAMINOUE (1994)
6586 grt; 804psrs
480' x 73' x 21' (145.6 x 22 x 6.3 m)
2 x 12-cylinder Pielstick diesel engines via twin screw.
Passenger ferry operated by Oshima Unyu KK, Okinawa.
Built by Hayashikane Dock, Nagasaki.

FERRY NANIWA (1971) See IONIS (1998)

FERRY NISHIKI MARU (1980) See DAEDALUS (1989)

FERRY ORANGE (1976) See MANILA PRINCESS (1991)

FERRY ORANGE No. 2 (1980) See PREVELIS (2000)

FERRY PEARL (1970) See DALIANA (1988)

FERRY PUKWAN (1983) See STARTRAILER (1998)

FERRY PUKWAN (1998)
10729 grt; 770 psrs
446' x 73' x 17' (135 x 22 x 5.2 m)
2 x 16-cylinder Pielstick diesel engines via twin screw.
Passenger ferry operated by Pukwan Ferry Co Ltd, Panama.
Built by Kanda Zosensho KK, Kure, for Kampu Ferry KK, Shimonoseki, as
the HAKATU (1973). Renamed HANKYU No. 17 (1973 – Hankyu Ferry
KK) and FERRY KAMPU (1984 – Kampu Ferry).

FERRY RAIRAKKU (1970) See UTOPIA (1980)

FERRY SETO (1970) See NASIPIT PRINCESS (1980)

FERRY SETTSU (1995)
15188 grt; 810 psrs
77 cars
624' x 89' x 22' (189 x 27 x 6.7 m)
2 x 9-cylinder Pielstick diesel engines via twin screw.
Passenger ferry operated by Hankyu Ferry.
Built by Kanda Kawajiri Shipyard for US$50,000,000.

FERRY SHIRAKABA (1994)
20552 grt; 926 psrs
80 cars
645' x 97' x 22' (195.5 x 29.4 x 6.8 m)
2 x 9-cylinder Pielstick diesel engines via twin screw.
Passenger ferry operated by Shin Nihonkai Ferry Co Ltd.
Built by Ishikawajima Heavy Industries, Tokyo..

FERRY SHIRAYURI (1976) See SUPERFERRY 6 (1995)

FERRY SUMIYOSHI (1976) See SUPERFERRY 2 (1996)

FERRY SUZURAN (1995) See UTOPIA 3 (1995)

FERRY TENRYU (1973) See UTOPIA 3 (1995)

FERRY TONE (1973) See SUPERFERRY 6 (1993)

FERRY YAKUSHIMA No. 2 (1993)
3392 grt; 494 psrs
96 cars + 16 trailers
404' x 59' x 17' (122.4 x 17.8 x 5.2 m)
Pielstick 18-cylinder diesel engine via single screw.
Passenger-car-cargo ferry operated by Orita Kisen.
Built by Yamanishi Shipyard.

FESTIVALE (1978) See THE BIG RED BOAT III (2000)

FESTOS (1984) See CAPTAIN ZAMAN II (1998)

FEZARA (1923) See ORUNGAL (1927)

FIBI (1993)
7820 grt; 1130 psrs
120 cars or 6 coaches
406' x 62' x 18' (123 x 18.8 x 5.5 m)
2 x 6-cylinder Fiat diesel engines via twin screw.
Broken up for scrap in 1995. Ex-Sea World Lines SA, Panama.
Built by Cantieri Navale, Breda, for Adriatica Ferries as the passenger-car ferry APPIA (1961).

FIESTA (1964)
3659 grt; 378 psrs
345' x 47' x 18' (104.5 x 14.2 x 5.5 m)
4 x SRG turbine engines via twin screw.
Broken up for scrap in Piraeus in 1981. Ex-Chandris Group.
Built by Cammell Laird & Company, Birkenhead, for the Isle of Man Steam Packet Company as the MONA'S QUEEN (1946). Renamed BARROW QUEEN (1963 – Chandris Group), CARISSIMA (1963 – Chandris Group) and CARINA (1964 – Chandris Group).

FIESTA (1988) See P&OSL CANTERBURY (1999)

FIESTA (1990) See SEAFRANCE CEZANNE (1996)

FIESTA (1991) See THE FIESTA (1991)

FIESTAMARINA (1993) See THE TOPAZ (1998)

FIFESHIRE (1887) See ITSUKISHIMA MARU (1903)

FIGUIG (1916)
3655 grt; 240 psrs
350' x 45' x 27'2" (106.7 x 13.7 x 8.2 m)
Triple expansion engine via single screw.
Broken up for scrap in Italy in 1934. Ex-French Line.
Built by Armstrong Whitworth & Company, Newcastle, for Adelaide Steamship Co as the GRANTALA (1903).

FILIPINA PRINCESS (1988)
13705 grt; 727 psrs
150 cars + 19 trailers
592' x 87' x 16'6" (180.5 x 26.4 x 5 m)
2 x 16-cylinder Kawasaki-MAN diesel engines via twin screw.
Passenger-car-cargo ferry operating for Sulpicio Lines Inc.
Built by Kanda Shipbuilding Company, Kure, for Shin Nihonkai Ferry Co Ltd, Otaru, as the FERRY AKASHIA (1973).

FILIPINAS SAUDI I (1980)
32336 grt; 1122 psrs
699' x 88' x 31' (211.8 x 26.7 x 9.4 m)
4 x Parsons SRG turbine engines via quadruple screw.
Sank in the Indian Ocean on 9 June 1980 while under tow to Taiwan from Jeddah, where she had been a floating hostel owned by Philippine Singapore Ports Corporation since 1976.
Built by Chantiers de l'Atlantique, St Nazaire, for Cie Navigation du Sud-Atlantique as the PASTEUR (1939). Renamed BREMEN (1959 – North German Lloyd), REGINA MAGNA (1972 – Chandris Group), and SAUDI PHIL I (1977 – Philippine Singapore Ports Corporation).

FILIPPO GRAMANI (1927) See CITTA DI TRIPOLI (1958)

FINLAND (1902)
12760 grt; 1537 psrs
560' x 60' x 38'4" depth (169.7 x 18.2 x 11.6 m)
W Cramp & Son 6-cylinder triple expansion engines via twin screw.
Broken up for scrap by Hughes Bolckow at Blyth in 1928. Ex-Panama-Pacific Line.
Built by William Cramp & Sons, Philadelphia, Pennsylvania, for Red Star Line.

FINLANDIA (1967) See GOLDEN PRINCESS (2000)

FINLANDIA (1980) See QUEEN OF SCANDINAVIA (1990)

FINNARROW (1997)
25996 grt; 200 psrs
800 cars
554' x 93' x 20' (168 x 28.3 x 6 m)
4 x 6-cylinder Sulzer diesel engines via twin screw.

Ice-strengthened passenger-car ferry operated by Finnlines Ltd following their purchase of the vessel for SwKr 400,000,000.
Built by PT Dok & Perkapalan Kodja Bahari, Tanjung Priok, for Rederi AB Gotland, Visby, as the GOTLAND (1996).

FINNCARRIER (1975) See SCANDINAVIA (1984)

FINNCLIPPER (1999)
30500 grt; 450 psrs
160 trailers
620' x 95' x 21'6" (188.3 x 28.7 x 6.5 m)
4 x 8-cylinder Sulzer diesel engines via twin screw.
RoPax ferry owned by Finnlines Deutschland and operated by Finnlines.
Laid down by Espanoles Puerto Real for Stena Ferries Ltd as the STENA SEAPACER 1 but sold three months prior to completion to Finnlines for £50,000,000 and renamed FINNCLIPPER (1999).

FINNDANA (1966) See CLYDESDALE (1998)

FINNEAGLE (1999)
29841 grt; 440 psrs
160 trailers
620' x 95' x 20'5" (188.3 x 28.7 x 6.2 m)
4 x 8-cylinder Sulzer diesel engines via twin screw.
RoPax ferry owned by Finnlines Deutschland and operated by Finnlines.
Laid down by Espanoles Puerto for Stena Ferries Ltd as the STENA SEA PACER 2, but sold to Finnlines three months prior to completion for £50,000,000 and renamed FINNEAGLE (1999).

FINNHANSA (1966) See PRINCESA MARISSA (1986)

FINNHANSA (1994)
32534 grt; 90 psrs
195 trailers
604' x 95' x 22' (183 x 28.7 x 6.8 m)
4 x 8-cylinder Zgoda diesel engines via twin screw.

Ice-strengthened passenger-RoRo-cargo ferry owned by the Finnlines Group

Oy, Helsinki, and operated by Finncarriers.
Built by Stocznia Gdanska SA, Gdansk, at a cost of Finmark 330,000,000.

FINNHAWK (1980) See MALMO LINK (1990)

FINNJET (1977)
32940 grt; 1686 psrs
380 cars or 30 trailers
692' x 83' x 21' (212.8 x 25.4 x 6.4 m)
2 x Pratt & Whitney gas-turbine engines plus 2 x 18-cylinder Wartsila-Pielstick diesel engines via twin screw.
Ice-strengthened passenger-car ferry owned by Sea Containers Ltd, UK, and operated by Silja Line on the Finland–Germany service.
Built by Wartsila, Helsinki, for Finnlines. This ship is unique in that she has two different types of propulsion equipment installed, using the diesel engines during off-season periods.

FINNMAID (1997)
13730 grt; 50 psrs
453' x 81' x 20' (137.4 x 24.6 x 6.1 m)
2 x 14-cylinder Pielstick diesel engines via twin screw.
Owned by Finnlines Oy, Kotka.
Built by Wartsila, Turku, for Finnlines Oy, Kotka, as the passenger-cargo ship HANS GUTZEIT (1972). Renamed CAPELLA (1982) and CAPELLA av STOCKHOLM (1986).

FINNPARTNER (1966) See IALYSSOS (1982)

FINNPARTNER (1973) See CAPTAIN ZAMAN I (1998)

FINNPARTNER (1994)
32534 grt; 90 psrs
195 trailers
604' x 95' x 22' (183 x 28.7 x 6.8 m)
4 x Zgoda diesel engines via twin screw.

Passenger-cargo RoRo ferry operated by Finncarriers.
Built by Stocznia Gdanska, Gdansk, for the Finnlines Group Oy, Helsinki, at a cost of FinMark 330,000,000.

FINNROSE (1980) See LUBECK LINK (1990)

FINNSAILOR (1987)
20783 grt; 119 psrs
230 cars
523' x 83' x 24' (158.4 x 25.3 x 7.3 m)
2 x 12-cylinder Sulzer diesel engines via twin screw.
Owned by the Finnlines Group and operated by FG Shipping.
Built by Stocznia Gdanska, Gdansk.

FINNSTAR (1978) See GOLDEN PRINCESS (2000)

FINNTRADER (1995)
32534 grt; 112 psrs
195 trailers + 293 teuS
604' x 95' x 22' (183 x 28.7 x 6.8 m)
4 x Zgoda diesel engines via twin screw.
Passenger-cargo-RoRo ferry owned by the Finnlines Group Oy, Helsinki, and operated by Finncarriers.
Built by Stocznia Gdanska, Gdansk, for FinMark 330,000,000.

FIONIA (1912) See HOI HUNG (1954)

FIORITA (1970) See ARIANE II (1980)

FIUME (1900)
3500 grt; 170 psrs
364' x 43' x 31'4" depth (110.3 x 13 x 9.5 m)
2-cylinder compound engine via single screw.
Broken up for scrap in 1902.
Built by J & G Thomson, Glasgow for the Union Line as the SPARTAN (1882).

FJORDVEIEN (1988) See HOLGER (1999)

FIVE DE AGUSTO (1952) See 5 DE AGUSTO (1952)

5 DE AGUSTO (1952) See VICTORIA (1952)

FIVOS (1973) See PANAGIA PAXON (1996)

FLAMENCO (1950) See PACIFIC ABETO (1966)

FLAMENCO (1997)
17370 grt; 736 psrs
536' x 75' x 25'6" (163.3 x 23 x 7.8 m)
4 x 10-cylinder geared Fiat diesel engines via twin screw.

Owned by Festival Cruise Lines after purchase from the Receivers of the collapsed cruise line CTC, for US$22,500,000, and chartered to First European Cruises.
Laid down by Cantieri del Terreno & Riniti, Genoa, for Norwegian Cruise Lines as the SEAWARD 1970) and completed for the P&O Group as the SPIRIT OF LONDON (1972). Renamed SUN PRINCESS (1974 – P&O Princess Cruises), STARSHIP MAJESTIC (1989 – Premier Cruise Line) and SOUTHERN CROSS (1994 – CTC).

FLAMINIA (1955) See KING ABDELAZIZ (1964)

FLAMINIA (1981)
12523 grt; 2000 psrs
470 cars
488' x 76' x 19' (148 x 23 x 5.8 m)
2 x 16-cylinder GMT diesel engines via twin screw.
Passenger-car ferry operated by Tirrenia, Naples.
Built by Italcantieri Stabia, Castellammare di Stabia.

FLAMINIA NOUVA (1971) See SHOROK 1 (1998)

FLANDRE (1952) See PALLAS ATHENA (1992)

FLANDRIA (1922) See BRETAGNE (1937)

FLAVIA (1916)
9001 grt; 2270 psrs
470' x 57' x 32' depth (143.3 x 17.3 x 9.7 m)
Palmers 6-cylinder triple expansion engine via twin screw.
Owned by Cunard Line when she sank on 24 August 1918 after being torpedoed by the German U-107 off Tory Island, Ireland.
Launched in 1900 by Palmers Shipbuilding Co, Jarrow, for British Shipowners as the BRITISH EMPIRE, but completed and delivered to the Phoenix Line in 1901. Renamed CAMPANIA (1906 – Navigazione Generale Italia) and CAMPANELLO (1910 – Uranium Steamship Co).

FLAVIA (1961) See LAVIA (1986)

FLAVIA (1984) See PENELOPE A (2000)

FLAVIA II (1987) See MOBY RIDER (1998)

FLAVIAN (1982) See LAVIA (1986)

FLEISS (1918) See VULCAIN (1921)

FLORENTIA (1949) See SAFINA-E-NUSRAT (1953)

FLORIA (1970) See VILLA DE AGAETE (1975)

FLORIANA (1970)
7608 grt; 344 psrs
433' x 59' x 19' (131.2 x 17.9 x 5.8 m)
SRG turbine engines via twin screw.
Broken up for scrap in Spain in 1973. Ex-Sovereign Cruises, Cyprus.
Built by Forges et Chantiers de la Mediterranee, La Seyne, for Mix te, Marseille, as the EL DJAZAIR (1952).

FLORIDA (1882) See ORN (1909)

FLORIDA (1903) See ARAFURA MARU (1930)

FLORIDA (1905) See CAVOUR (1911)

FLORIDA (1926) See ASCANIA (1955)

FLORIDA (1931) See LA PALAIS FLOTTANT (1967)

FLORIDE (1907)
6693 grt; 836 psrs
413' x 52' x 35' depth (125.9 x 15.9 x 10.6 m)
3-cylinder triple expansion engine via single screw.
Sank on 19 February 1915 after being attacked by the German raider PRINZ EITEL FRIEDRICH off the West African coast near Dakar.
Built by Chantiers et Ateliers de Provence de St Nazaire, St Nazaire, as a passenger ship for the French Line.

FLUSHING RANGE (1987)
7951 grt; 1326 psrs
350 cars or 60 trailers
437' x 77' x 19' (132.5 x 23.2 x 5.7 m)
3 x 12-cylinder Sulzer diesel engines via triple screw.

Broken up for scrap at Kaohsiung in 1988.
Built by Schischau Unterweser AG, Bremerhaven, for Townsend Car Ferries Ltd as the passenger-car ferry HERALD OF FREE ENTERPRISE (1980). As the HERALD OF FREE ENTERPRISE, she sank with the loss of 193 lives on 6 March 1987 as she drew away from her berth at Zeebrugge. A subsequent marine enquiry found, on 24 July 1987, that the cause of her demise was gross negligence on the part of her crew in not securing the bow door prior to getting under way. The sea literally flowed into the ship at 6.46 pm. Her name was changed prior to the hulk being removed from the entrance to Zeebrugge harbour.

FOCH (1951) See JIAN HUA (1961)

FOLIA (1916)
6560 grt; 2020 psrs

430' x 53' x 25' (131 x 16.1 x 7.6 m)
James Laing 6-cylinder triple expansion engines via twin screw.
Owned by the Cunard Steamship Co Ltd when she sank on 11 March 1917 after being torpedoed by the German U-53 near Yougal, Ireland, with the loss of seven lives.
Built by Sir J Laing & Sons Ltd, Sunderland, for Lloyd Sabaudo as the passenger ship PRINCIPE DI PIEMONTE (1907). Renamed PRINCIPELLO (1914 – Uranium Steamship Co).

FOLKLINER (1982) See CAPTAIN ZAMAN II (1998)

FONTEIN (1967)
10544 grt; 160 psrs
527' x 63' x 30' (159.7 x 19.1 x 9.1 m)
B+W diesel engines via twin screw.
Broken up for scrap in Bilbao in 1967.
Built by P Smit Jnr, Rotterdam, for the Holland-Africa Line as the ORANJEFONTEIN (1939).

FONTAINEBLEU (1924)
10015 grt; 346 psrs
501' x 59' x 27'3" (151.8 x 17.9 x 8.3 m)
Geared turbine engines via twin screw.
Caught fire on 12 July 1926 and was deliberately sunk to form a breakwater to Djibouti harbour.
Launched by Ateliers et Chantiers de la Loire, St Nazaire, for Messageries Maritimes as the ISLANDE (1923) and completed as the FONTAINEBLEU.

FORFAR, HMS (1939)
16402 grt; 1810 psrs
549' x 70' x 28' (166.4 x 21.2 x 8.5 m)
6 x Harland & Wolff SRG turbine engines via twin screw.
Owned by the British Admiralty as an armed merchant cruiser when she sank, with the loss of 185 lives, on 2 December 1940 after being torpedoed five times by the German U-99 400 miles (666 km) off the west coast of Ireland.
Laid down by Fairfield Shipbuilding & Engineering Co, Glasgow, for the Canadian Pacific Steamship Company as the MONTMORENCY (1919) and completed as the MONTROSE (1922).

FORT HAMILTON (1919) See STELLA D'ITALIA (1926)

FORT St GEORGE (1921) See ARNO (1938)

FORT SALISBURY (1895) See GUJARAT (1913)

FORT TOWNSHEND (1936) See ROMANTICA (1960)

FORTUNE MARINER (1968)
4041 grt; 824 psrs
345' x 48' x 18' (104.5 x 14.5 x 5.5 m)
DRG turbine engines via twin screw.
Built by Chantiers de Provence, Port de Bouc, for Cie Generale Transatlantique as the SAMPIERO CORSO (1936).

FORTUNE STAR (1929) See LUGANO (1942)

FORT VICTORIA (1920)
7784 grt; 429 psrs
412' x 57' x 34' (124.8 x 17.3 x 10.3 m)
8-cylinder quadruple expansion engines via twin screw.
Owned by Furness Group when she was demolished underwater after sinking in three and a half hours in the main channel to New York, near the Ambrose Light. This followed her being rammed amidship on the port side by the liner ALGONQUIN on 18 December 1929.
Built by William Beardmore & Co, Dalmuir, for the Adelaide Steamship Co as the WILLOCHRA (1913).

FOUCAULD (1929)
11028 grt; 225 psrs
483' x 59' x 34'9" depth (146.4 x 17.9 x 10.6 m)
Triple expansion engines via twin screw.
Owned by Chargeurs Reunis, Le Havre, when she sank on 20 June 1940 during a German aircraft attack off La Pallice, France.
Built by Forges et Chantiers de la Mediterranee as the HOEDIC (1922).

FOUCAULD (1948)
9095 grt; 458 psrs
479' x 62' x 23' (138.8 x 18.8 x 7 m)
2 x 4-cylinder Doxford diesel engines via twin screw.
Built by Swan Hunter, Newcastle, for Paquet Line.

FRANCA C (1952) See DOULOS (1978)

FRANCE (1912) See FRANCE (1919)

FRANCE (1919)
23769 grt; 1623 psrs
713' x 75' x 30' (217.2 x 23 x 9.1 m)
4 x Parsons turbine engines via quadruple screw.
Owned by French Line when she was broken up for scrap at Dunkirk in 1935 after having caught fire in Le Havre in February 1935.
Laid down by Chantiers de Penhoet, St Nazaire, for the French Line as the PICARDIE (1912) and completed as the FRANCE (1912). Renamed FRANCE IV (1914 – French government).

FRANCE (1961) See NORWAY (1979)

FRANCE IV (1914) See FRANCE (1919)

FRANCESCA (1905)
4946 grt; 1580 psrs
360' x 48' x 17'3" (109.7 x 14.6 x 5.2 m)
3-cylinder triple expansion engine via single screw.
Broken up for scrap in 1926. Ex-Cosulich Lines.
Built by Russell & Co, Port Glasgow, for Union Austriaca.

FRANCESCA (1996)
12668 grt; 520 psrs
25 cars + 4 trailers
452' x 69' x 18'6" (137.1 x 21 x 5.6 m)
4 x 6-cylinder Sulzer diesel engines via twin screw.

Ice-strengthened passenger-car-cargo ferry owned by Trilby Shipping, Venezuela, and operated by Pakartin Shipping. She is now for sale at US$8,500,000 and has been laid up at Wilhelmshaven since September 1999. Built by Szczecinska Warskie, Poland, for the Black Sea Shipping Co, Odessa, as the KONSTANTIN SIMONOV (1982).

FRANCESCO CARACCHILIO (1920)
Launched by the Italian Navy on 12 May 1920, but onsold to Navigazione Generale Italiana for completion as a luxury high-speed passenger liner. However, the project was abandoned and the hull broken up for scrap that same year.

FRANCESCO MOROSINI (1948) See ARNIS (1975)

FRANCIS DRAKE (1962)
7438 grt; 130 psrs
440' x 61' x 26' (134.1 x 18.5 x 7.9 m)
DRG & SRG geared turbine engines via single screw.
Broken up for scrap at Kaohsiung in 1971. Ex-Dominion Far East Line.
Built by Vickers-Armstrong Ltd, Barrow-in-Furness, for the Furness, Warren Line as the pasenger-cargo ship NOVA SCOTIA (1947).

FRANCIS Y. SLANGER USS (1944) See SATURNIA (1946)

FRANCONIA (1911)
18150 grt; 2850 psrs
625' x 71' x 40'4" depth (190.5 x 21.5 x 12.2 m)
2 x Wallsend Slipway 4-cylinder quadruple expansion engines via twin screw.
Sank in 50 minutes after being torpedoed by the German U-47 on 4 October 1916, with the loss of 12 lives, 200 miles north-east of Malta.
Built by Swan Hunter & Wigham Richardson Ltd, Newcastle, for the Cunard Steamship Co as a passenger ship.

FRANCONIA (1923)
20341 grt; 853 psrs
601' x 74' x 32'7" depth (182.1 x 22.4 x 9.9 m)
6 x Brown & Curtis DRG turbine engines via twin screw.
Broken up for scrap by TW Ward Ltd at Inverkeithing in 1956 after continual boiler problems throughout 1955.
Built by John Brown & Co Ltd, Clydebank, for the Cunard Line as a passenger liner.

FRANCONIA (1962) See FEDOR SHALYAPIN (1991)

FRANGESTAN (1922)
9683 grt; 2500 psrs
485' x 57' x 32'9" depth (147.8 x 17.5 x 10 m)
3-cylinder triple expansion engine via single screw.
Destroyed by fire in the Red Sea on 2 April 1924 while serving the British government.
Built by Palmer & Co, Jarrow, for the Hamburg-America Line as the cargo ship BOSNIA (1899) and converted into the passenger ship BOSNIA (1907).

FRANGOULA B. GOULANDRIS (1928)
6650 grt
412' x 56' x 26'5" (124.8 x 17 x 8 m)
Blair & Co 3-cylinder triple expansion engines via single screw.
Sank on 7 June 1940 after being torpedoed by the German U-26 off Cape Clear, Ireland.
Built by JL Thompson & Sons Ltd, Sunderland, for Century Shipping Co Ltd as the passenger ship DUNBRIDGE (1917). Renamed BRECON (1923 – Canadian Pacific Railway Co).

FRANK (1997)
20064 grt; 750 psrs
578' x 77' x 26' (176.2 x 23.5 x 7.9 m)
2 x 7-cylinder Sulzer diesel engines via twin screw.
Broken up for scrap at Alang in 1997.
Built by Mathias Thesen Werft Shipyards, Wismar, for the Black Sea Shipping Company, Odessa, as the ice-strengthened cruise ship IVAN FRANKO (1964).

FRANKENWALD (1908) See TARI (1934)

FRANKFURT (1940) See CAPO FLACONARA (1978)

FRANKFURT (1954) See ORIENTAL HERO (1966)

FRANKFURT ONE (1979) See ALEX ANDER (1983)

FRANKMOUNT (1912) See MEDORA (1915)

FRANKTOR (1915) See BEPPE (1932)

FRANS KOCKUM 1994) See CROWN OF SCANDINAVIA (1994)

FRANS SUELL (1992) See GABRIELLA (1997)

FRATELLI BANDIERA (1915) See HOI HUNG (1954)

FRED (1986) See MOBY RIDER (1998)

FRED C. AINSWORTH (1950)
12093 grt; 426 psrs
489' x 69' x 32' depth (148.2 x 20.9 x 9.7 m)
Geared turbine engine via single screw.

Broken up for scrap as a passenger-cargo ship at Kaohsiung in 1973. Ex-Inter-Ocean Grain Storage Co, Washington.
Laid down by Ingalls Shipbuilding Corporation, Pascagoula, Mississippi, for United States Lines as the AMERICAN SHIPPER (1942). Launched for the US government as the PASS CHRISTIAN (1942) and completed for the US Army as the Class C3-IN-P & C passenger-cargo ship FRED C. AINSWORTH (T-AP 181) (1943).

FRED C. AINSWORTH (T-AP 181) (1943) See FRED C. AINSWORTH (1950)

FREDERICK CARTER (1968) See MOBY RIDER (1998)

FREDERIK VIII (1914)
11850 grt; 1208 psrs
524' x 62' x 31'8" (158.8 x 18.8 x 9.6 m)
AG Vulkan 8-cylinder triple expansion engines via twin screw.
Broken up for scrap at Blyth in 1937 by Hughes Bolckow Ltd.
Built by AG Vulkan, Stettin, for the Scandinavian-American Line as a passenger ship.

FREDERICK FUNSTON (T-AP-178) (1950)
11971 grt; 300 psrs
492' x 69' x 26'6" (149.1 x 20.9 x 8 m)
Geared turbine engine via single screw.
Laid up since 1992 by the US Maritime Administration.
Built by Seattle-Tacoma Shipbuilding Co, Tacoma, for the US Army as a Class C3-S1-A3 troop transport FREDERICK FUNSTON (T-AP 178) (1941) and redesignated to US Navy as the FREDERICK FUNSTON (A-AP-89) (1943).

FREDERICK FUNSTON (T-AP 178) (1941) See FREDERICK FUNSTON (1950)

FRED SCAMARONI (1965) See SALEM EXPRESS (1989)

FREEDOM (1919)
5640 grt; 1540 psrs
446' x 46' x 27'4" (135.9 x 14 x 8.3 m)
6-cylinder triple expansion engines via twin screw.
Broken up for scrap as a passenger ship in 1924. Ex- US government.
Built by Blohm & Voss, Hamburg, for North German Lloyd as the WITTEKIND (1894). Renamed IROQUOIS (1917 – after seizure by the US government).

FREEDOM I (1990) See ALAMIRA (1997)

FREE ENTERPRISE II (1965) See MOBY BLU (1982)

FREE ENTERPRISE III (1966) See AL FAHAD (1986)

FREE ENTERPRISE IV (1969) See TAG AL SALAM (1998)

FREE ENTERPRISE V (1970) See LABURNAM (1993)

FREE ENTERPRISE VI (1972) See PRIDE OF ALSALM 95 (1996)

FREE ENTERPRISE VII (1973) See PRIDE OF RATHLIN (1992)

FREE ENTERPRISE VIII (1974) See ROMILDA (1993)

FREEPORT (1963) See DISCOVERY SUN (1995)

FREEPORT (1973) See DISCOVERY SUN (1995)

FREEPORT (1976) See THE FIESTA (1991)

FREEPORT I (1968) See DISCOVERY SUN (1995)

FREEPORT II (1973) See EMPRESS 65 (1997)

FREE STATE MARINER (1952) See MONTEREY (1955)

FREEWINDS (1986)
10328 grt; 480 psrs
441' x 69' x 18' (134.3 x 21 x 5.5 m)
2 x 8-cylinder Wartsila-Sulzer diesel engines via twin screw.

Owned by the International Association of Scientologists and operated by Majestic Cruises, San Donata, Panama, for scientologist members only.
Built by Wartsila, Turku, for Wallenius Bremen as the BOHEME (1968).

FREJA SCARLETT (1993) See MIGUEL HERNANDEZ (1995)

FRENGENFJORD (1983) See PETRONILA MATA (1998)

FRESHFIELDS (1915)
3450 grt; 340 psrs
345' x 44' x 24'6" (104.5 x 13.3 x 7.5 m)
Triple expansion engine via single screw.
Built by Napier & Miller Ltd, Glasgow, for the Royal Mail Line as the passenger ship LA PLATA (1896). Renamed CLEMENT (1900 – Booth Line).

FRIDTJOF NANSEN (1986) See VALTUR PRIMA (1999)

FRIEDRICH DER GROSSE (1896) See CITY OF HONOLULU (1922)

FRIEDRICHSRUHE (1914) See AMBOISE (1922)

FRIENDSHIP (1989) See DOLCE VITA (1998)

FRIESLAND (1889) See LA PLATA (1910)

FRIESLAND (1989)
3583 grt; 1790 psrs
122 cars and 16 trailers
228' x 55' x 9' (69 x 16.6 x 2.7 m)
2 x 8-cylinder MaK diesel engines via twin screw.
Passenger ferry owned by G Doeksen and operated by Rederij Doeksen, Holland.
Built by Van Der Giessen-De Noord, Krimpen.

FRIGGA (1999)
7955 grt; 500 psrs

Purchased by James Fisher & Co, Liverpool, for DKR35,000,000, following the vessel's two-year period laid up in Naksov. Ex-Mercandia charter to DSB. Built for Mercandia as the MERCANDIAN GOVERNOR (1982). Renamed GOVERNOR (1984 – Mercandia) and KRAKA (1988 – DSB).

FRITZ HECKERT (1961) See GULF FANTASY (1994)

FRONTIER SPIRIT (1990) See BREMEN (1995)

FRYDERYK CHOPIN (1951) See KASZUBY (1957)

FUDI (2000)
11315 grt; 1200 psrs
409 cars
489' x 75' x 21' (148.3 x 22.8 x 6.3 m)
2 x 12-cylinder GMT diesel engines via twin screw.
Passenger-car ferry owned and operated by PT Pelni, Indonesia, after acquisition for US$6,660,000.
Built by Italcantieri SpA, Genoa, for Tirrenia Navigazione as the STAFFETTA LIGURE (1979). Renamed CARALIS (1988 – Tirrenia).

FU JIAN (1994)
4992 grt; 333 psrs
401' x 52' x 17' (121.5 x 15.8 x 5.2 m)
2 x 6-cylinder MAN diesel engines via twin screw.
Cruise ship owned by Fu Jian United Shipping Co, China.
Built by Mathias-Thesen Werft, Wismar, for the Black Sea Shipping Company, Odessa, as the ice-strengthened passenger ship LITVA (1960). Renamed BOGUCHAR (1988 – Brave Commander SA, San Lorenzo).

FUJI MARU (1989)
23340 grt; 603 psrs
548' x 78' x 22' (166.1 x 23.6 x 6.6 m)
2 x 8-cylinder Mitsubishi diesel engines via twin screw.
Cruising for Mitsui OSK Lines and Club Med.
Built by Mitsubishi Heavy Industries, Kobe, for Mitsui OSK.

FULLER, USS (AP-14) (1941) See FULLER, USS (APA-7) (1943 – US Navy)

FULLER, USS (APA-7) (1943)
8378 grt; 80 psrs
487' x 56' x 35'2" depth (147.6 x 17 x 10.7 m)
De Laval geared steam turbine engine via single screw.
Broken up for scrap at Seattle in 1957. Ex-US Navy.
Built by Bethlehem Shipbuilding Corporation, Alameda, California, for the US Shipping Board as the ARCHER (1919). Renamed the passenger-cargo ship CITY OF NEWPORT NEWS (1931 – Baltimore Mail Line) and FULLER, USS (APA-14) (1941 – US Navy).

FULVIA (1969)
16923 grt; 721 psrs
577' x 72' x 26' (174.8 x 21.8 x 7.9 m)
2 x 7-cylinder Stork-Werkspoor diesel engines via twin screw.
Chartered to the Costa Line when she sank on 20 July 1970. She had been under tow 140 miles north of the Canary Islands, after an explosion and fire erupted at 1.00 am in the number two engine room. The fire's intensity melted the ship's funnel.
Built by the Netherlands Shipbuilding Company, Amsterdam, for the Norwegian-America Line as the OSLOFJORD (1949).

FUNCHAL (1961)
9845 grt; 370 psrs
506' x 63' x 20' (153 x 19 x 6.1 m)
2 x 9-cylinder Stork-Werkspoor diesel engines via twin screw.
Owned by Great Warwick Shipping Company Inc, Panama, and operated as a cruise ship by Arcalia Shipping Co from 1999.
Built by Elsinor Shipbuilding & Engineering Company, Elsinor, for Cia Transportes Maritimos.

FUNTASTICA (1992) See OCEAN EXPLORER I (1998)

FURANSU MARU (1958)
44356 grt; 1262 psrs
791' x 91' x 32' (239.7 x 27.6 x 9.7 m)
4 x Parsons turbine engines via quadruple screw.
Owned by Yamamoto, Japan, she was broken up for scrap at Osaka in 1959. She had just been refloated from the seabed where she had settled following a sequence in the movie *The Last Voyage* where she was deliberately sunk.
Built by Chantiers de l'Atlantique, St Nazaire, for the French Line as the ILE DE FRANCE (1927). Renamed CLARIDON (1959) for the movie and then reverted to FURANSU MARU.

FURST BISMARCK (1891) See SAN GIUSTO (1918)

FURST BISMARCK (1905) See AMBOISE (1922)

FUSHIMI MARU (1914)
10936 grt; 372 psrs
513' x 64' x 29' (155.5 x 19.4 x 8.9 m)
2 x 6-cylinder Mitsubishi triple expansion engines via twin screw.
Owned by the Japanese government, she sank on 1 February 1943 after being torpedoed by the USS TARPON off Honshu.
Built by the Mitsubishi Shipbuilding & Engineering Works for NYK as a passenger-cargo ship.

FUSILIER (1941) See BOTHINJ (1959)

FUSO MARU (1924) See HUSO MARU (1938)

FUTURE SEAS (1990) See NORDIC EMPRESS (1989)

FYODOR SHALYAPIN (1973) See FEDOR SHALYAPIN (1991)

GABRIELLA (1997)

35492 grt; 2300 psrs
480 cars 8 coaches
556' x 91' x 21' (168.5 x 27.6 x 6.4 m)
4 x 12-cylinder Pielstick diesel engines via twin screw.

Ice-strengthened passenger-car ferry acquired by the Viking Line from Silja Line for US$91,000,000.
Built by Brodogradiliste, Split, for Sealink as the FRANS SUELL (1992) at a cost of US$131,000,000. Renamed SILJA SCANDINAVIA (1992 – Silja Line).

GAEA (1913) See SAN GIUSTO (1918)

GAETANO DONAZETTI (1963) See DONIZETTI (1963)

GALAPAGOS DISCOVERY (1998)

3852 grt; 148 psrs
333' x 50' x 15'6" (101 x 15 x 4.7 m)
2 x 6-cylinder Fiat diesel engines via twin screw.
Owned by Conodros SA, Quito, she sank on 19 October 1999 near the Miraflores locks in the Panama Canal. She had caught fire while at berth No 3, Rodman Pier, Balboa, where she had been under repair.
Built by Cantieri Navigazioni Pelligrino, Naples, for the Adriatica Line as the ILLIRIA (1962). Renamed BALI SEA DANCER (1994 – Owned by P&O Cruises and operated by Spice Island Cruises).

GALAPAGOS EXPLORER II (1998)

4077 grt; 111 psrs
290' x 53' x 12' (88 x 16 x 3.6 m)
2 x 12-cylinder MAN-B+W diesel engines via twin screw.
Owned by Canodros SA, Quito.
Built by Cantieri Navale Ferrari Shipyards, La Spezia, for Renaissance Cruises at a cost of US$28,000,000 as the RENAISSANCE 3 (1990).

GALAXIAS (1969) See PRINCESA AMOROSA (1989)

GALAXY (1996)

76522 grt; 1896 psrs
857' x 106' x 26' (259.7 x 32.1 x 7.9 m)
4 x 6-cylinder MAN-B+W diesel engines via twin screw.

Owned by Royal Caribbean International and operated by their subsidiary Celebrity Cruises.
Built by Meyer-Weft Shipyards, Papenburg, at a cost of US$317,000,000.

GALAXY QUEEN (1971) See CARIBIA (1973)

GALICIA (1962)

10413 grt; 112 psrs
500' x 61' x 28' (151.5 x 18.5 x 8.5 m)
SRG turbine engines via twin screw.
Broken up for scrap in Spain in 1978 as a fish factory ship. Ex-Pescanova SA.
Built by Soc Espanola de Construccion Naval, Bilbao, for Cia Trasatlantica Espanola as the ALFONSO XIII (1923). Renamed HABANA (1931 – Cia Trasatlantica Espanola, Madrid).

GALICIAN (1900) See GLENART CASTLE (1914)

GALILAH (1948)

3899 grt
320' x 48' x 22' (97 x 14.5 x 6.7 m)
Triple expansion engine via twin screw.
Broken up for scrap in Italy in 1953. Ex-Zim Lines.
Built by Harlan & Hollingsworth, Wilmington, Delaware, for the Central Vermont Transportation Company as the MANHATTAN (1913). Renamed NOPATIN (1917 – US Navy), DE WITT CLINTON (1919 – Hudson River Day Line), COL. FREDERICK C. JOHNSON (1948 – Samuel Derecktor, New York) and DERECKTOR (1948 – Samuel Derecktor, New York) which operated from 1948 as a migrant ship.

GALILEE (1966) See LINDOS (1967)

GALILEO (1984) See MERIDIAN (1989)

GALILEO FERRARIS (1957)

11349 grt; 643 psrs
535' x 64' x 28' (163 x 19.5 x 8.5 m)
2 x 8-cylinder Construccion Mecan-Sulzer diesel engines via twin screw.
Currently a non-passenger cargo ship for C Italia San, Genoa.
Built by Penhoet, St Nazaire, for Chargeurs Reunis, Bordeaux, as the passenger-cargo ship HENRI POINCARE (1953).

GALILEO GALILEI (1963) See SUN VISTA (1997)

GALLIA (1900)

4035 grt; 1250 psrs
387' x 41' x 22'8" (117.3 x 12.4 x 6.9 m)
2-stroke motor via single screw.
Broken up for scrap in Italy in 1910. Ex-Fabre Line.
Built by Chantiers et Ateliers de la Gironde, Bordeaux, for Cie Bordelaise de Navigation a Vapeur, Bordeaux, as the CHATEAU YQUEM (1884).

GALLIA (1913)

14966 grt; 1086 psrs
574' x 64' x 40'2" depth (173.9 x 19.4 x 12.2 m)
Turbine engines via triple screw.
Sank on 4 October 1916 in 15 minutes, with the loss of 1750 lives, following a hit by a torpedo fired from the German U-35 35 miles (58 km) west of Sardinia.
Built by Forges et Chantiers de la Mediterranee, La Seyne, for Cie de Navigation Sud Atlantique.

GALLIC (1920) See DJATINEGARA (1952)

GALLOWAY PRINCESS (1980) See STENA GALLOWAY (1990)

GALLURA (1968)

4938 grt; 1000 psrs
170 cars + 30 rail wagons
406' x 58' x 18' (123 x 17.7 x 5.5 m)
2 x 6-cylinder Fiat diesel engines via twin screw.
Passenger-train ferry owned by the Italian State Railways and operated by Ferrovie Stato on the Italy–Sardinia service.
Built by Tirreno Riuniti, Ancona.

GALTEEMORE, HMS (1944) See MISR (1947)

GALVESTON (1968)
11389 grt; 3800 psrs
523' x 71' x 30' (158.5 x 21.5 x 9.1m)
Geared turbine engine via single screw.
Owned by Sea Land Service Inc, Portland, Oregon, as a container ship.
Built by J Hendy Ironworks for the US Maritime Commission as the Class C4-S-A3 troop transport MARINE SERPENT (1945) which assisted with the migrant problem after World War Two.

GALWAY CASTLE (1911)
7988 grt; 412 psrs
470' x 56' x 27' (142.4 x 17 x 8.2 m)
Quadruple expansion engines via twin screw.
Sank on 12 September 1918, with 143 lives lost, following a torpedo hit from the German U-82 three days earlier. This broke her back 160 miles (267 km) south-west of Fastnet Rock in the English Channel. She was bearing the name RHODESIA in an effort to confuse the enemy's identification.
Built by Barclay, Curle & Co, Glasgow, for the Union-Castle Line.

GAMBELA (1965) See HYSAN (1971)

GAMID SULTANOV (1963)
8840 grt; 290 psrs
30 rail freight cars
441' x 60' x 14'6" (133.7 x 18.3 x 4.4 m)
4 x 10-cylinder Fairbanks-Morse diesel engines via triple screw.
Passenger-cargo ferry operated by Caspian Shipping Co, Baku.
Built by Krasnoye Sormovo Shipyard, Gorkiy.

GAMSOLO (1970) See HYSAN (1971)

GANDIA (1939)
9372 grt; 220 psrs
480' x 60' x 29' (146.3 x 18.3 x 8.8 m)
Triple expansion engines via twin screw.
Owned by Cie Maritime Belge, she sank on 22 January 1942 after being torpedoed by the German U-135 in the North Atlantic, north-west of the Azores. Sixty-five lives were lost.
Built by Swan Hunter & Wigham Richardson Ltd, Newcastle, for Shaw Savill & Albion as the passenger-cargo liner ARAWA (1907). Renamed KONIGSTEIN (1928 – Bernstein Line).

GANGE (1929) See MARCO POLO (1936)

GARIBALDI (1911)
5181 grt; 1625 psrs
381' x 48' x 25'7" (116.2 x 14.7 x 7.8 m)
6-cylinder Ansaldo-Armstrong-Sampier-Darena triple expansion engines via twin screw.
Broken up for scrap in 1946 after raising her from the Genoa harbour seabed. She had settled there on 2 August 1944 following an Allied air attack. Ex-Ligure Brasiliana, Genoa.
Built by Soc Esercizio Baccini, Riva Trigoso, for Lloyd Triestino as the passenger liner VIRGINIA (1906).

GARNATA (1977)
13868 grt; 1000 psrs
300 cars
497' x 68' x 22' (151.5 x 20.7 x 6.6 m)
2 x 16-cylinder Bazan-MAN geared diesel engines via twin screw.
Passenger-car ferry operated by GMTC, Tripoli.
Built by Union Naval de Levante, Valencia, for Naviera Aznar, Bilbao, as the MONTE GRANADA (1974).

GARONNA (1912)
5531 grt; 500 psrs
425' x 50' x 22'2" (128.8 x 15.2 x 6.7 m)
Compound engine via single screw.
Broken up for scrap at Bordeaux in 1923. Ex-Cie de Navigation Sud Atlantique.
Built by Fairfield Co Ltd, Glasgow, for the Castle Line as the passenger ship AVONDALE CASTLE (1897).

GARTH CASTLE (1880) See BRUNETTE (1921)

GARTH CASTLE (1910)
7612 grt; 385 psrs
453' x 54' x 30'7" (137.3 x 16.4 x 9.3 m)
Quadruple expansion engines via twin screw.
Broken up for scrap in 1939.
Built by Barclay, Curle & Co, Glasgow, for the Union-Castle Line.

GARYOUNIS (1977)
15505 grt; 679 psrs
549' x 81' x 21' (166.5 x 24.4 x 6.4 m)
2 x 16-cylinder Pielstick diesel engines via twin screw.
Passenger ferry owned by GMTC, Tripoli.
Built by Nakai Zosen, Setoda, for Kinkai Yusen KK, Tokyo, as the MASHU (1973).

GASCOGNE (1948)
5184 grt; 380 psrs
390' x 54' x 29'9" depth (118.2 x 16.4 x 9.1 m)
2 x Newport News SRG turbine engines via single screw.
Broken up for scrap in Hong Kong in 1955. Ex-CGT.
Built by Newport News Shipbuilding, Newport News, Virginia, for Dominion Steamship Co as the GEORGE WASHINGTON (1924).

GAUCHO MARTIN FIERRO (1965) See MINOTAUROS (1966)

GAUL (1893) See CHALEUR (1913)

GAVINA (1964) See HYSAN (1971)

GDANSK (1921) See SIERRA (1923)

GDYNIA (1939) See EMPIRE HELFORD (1946)

GEDSER (1968) See AL JUDI (1993)

GEDSER (1976) See LARKSPUR (1999)

GEDSER (1986) See VENUS (1989)

GEDSERLINK (1986) See VENUS (1989)

GEELONG (1904)
7951 grt; 540 psrs
450' x 55' x 27' (137.2 x 16.7 x 8.2 m)
2 x triple expansion engines via twin screw.
Sank on 1 January 1916 after colliding with the 2866 grt British collier BONVILSTON while in convoy 96 miles (160 km) north-west of Alexandria. Laid down by Barclay, Curle & Co, Glasgow, for Wilhelm Lund, London, as the AUSTRALIA (1904) and completed as the GEELONG.

GEIGER, USNS (T-AP-197) (1951) See BAY STATE (1980)

GELRIA (1913) See GRADISCA (1935)

GELTING NORD (1981) See LANGELAND IV (1999)

GELTING SYD (1982)
6672 grt; 800 psrs
145 cars
380' x 59' x 15' (115.2 x 17.9 x 4.5 m)

4 x 9-cylinder Ruston-Pax ton diesel engines via twin screw.
Passenger-car-cargo-RoRo ferry owned by Nordisk Faergefart and operated by Faborg-Gelting on the Denmark–Germany service.
Built by Jos L Meyer, Papenburg, for Stockholms Rederi AB Svea, Landskrona, as the STELLA SCARLETT (1974).

GENERAL (1911) See AZAY LE RIDEAU (1919)

GENERAL A. E. ANDERSON (AP-111) (1943)
17833 grt; 5200 psrs
622' x 76' x 26' (188.5 x 23 x 7.9 m)
De Laval geared turbine engines via twin screw.
Laid up in Suisin Bay since 1958.
Built by Federal Shipbuilding & Drydock Co, Kearny, New Jersey, for the US Navy as a Class P2-S2-R2 troop carrier.

GENERAL ALEXANDER M. PATCH, USAT (1947) See GENERAL ALEXANDER M. PATCH, USS (T-AP 122) (1950)

GENERAL ALEXANDER M. PATCH, USS (T-AP 122) (1950)
17100 grt; 4680 psrs
609' x 76' x 26' (184.5 x 23 x 7.9 m)
Turbo-electric engines via twin screw.
Laid up in the James river, Virginia, reserve fleet at Fort Eustis since 5 March 1993 by US Maritime Administration.
Built by Bethlehem Steel Co, Alameda, California, for the US Navy as the Class P2-SE2-R1 troop transport ADMIRAL R. E. COONTZ (1944). Renamed GENERAL ALEXANDER M. PATCH (1947 – US Army).

GENERAL ARTIGAS (1930)
11254 grt; 561 psrs
473' x 61' x 41'9" depth (143.3 x 18.5 x 12.7 m)
DRG turbine engine via single screw.
Broken up for scrap at Hamburg in 1946 after raising her from the harbour where she had sunk after a raid by British bombers on 25 July 1943.
Laid down by HDW, Kiel, for the Hamburg-America Line as the AMMERLAND (1922) and completed as the WESTPHALIA (1923).

GENERAL A. W. BREWER (AP-155) (1945) See PHILADELPHIA (1968)

GENERAL A. W. GREELY, USS (AP-141) (1945) See CARIBE ENTERPRISE (1981)

GENERAL A. W. GREELY, USAT (1947) See CARIBE ENTERPRISE (1981)

GENERAL A. W. GREELY, USS (T-AP-141) (1950) See CARIBE ENTERPRISE (1981)

GENERAL BAGRATSION (1946)
7465 grt
413' x 55' x 36' depth (125.2 x 16.7 x 10.9 m)
HDW 3-cylinder triple expansion engine via single screw.
World War Two prize awarded to Russia.
Built by HDW, Kiel, for Hamburg South America Line as the ESPANA (1921).

GENERAL BELGRANO (1922)
10121 grt; 202 psrs
492' x 59' x 35'6" (149 x 17.9 x 10.8 m)
Triple expansion engines via twin screw.
Broken up for scrap at Hamburg, Germany, in 1932. Ex-Hamburg-America Line.
Built by Reiherstag Schiffeswerke, Hamburg, for Hamburg South America Line as the BAHIA CASTILLO (1913).

GENERAL C. C. BALLOU (AP-157) (1945) See EASTERN LIGHT (1981)

GENERAL C. G. MORTON (AP-138) (1944) See GREEN WAVE (1967)

GENERAL C. G. MORTON, USAT (1946) See GREEN WAVE (1967)

GENERAL C. G. MORTON, USNS (T-AP-138) (1950) See GREEN WAVE (1967)

GENERAL C. H. MUIR (AP-142) (1945) See SAN JUAN (1975)

GENERAL DANIEL I. SULTAN (T-AP 120) (1947)
17100 grt; 4680 psrs
609' 76' 26' (184.5 x 23 x 7.9 m)
Turbo-electric engines via twin screw.
Laid up in reserve fleet by MARAD since 1968.
Built by Bethlehem Steel Co, Alameda, California, for the US Navy as the Class P2-SE2-R1 troop carrier ADMIRAL W. S. BENSON, USS (AP-120) (1944).

GENERAL DIAZ (1919) See MARCO POLO (1936)

GENERAL EDWIN D. PATRICK, USAT (1946) See GENERAL EDWIN D. PATRICK (T-AP-124) (1947)

GENERAL EDWIN D. PATRICK (T-AP-124) (1950)
17100 grt; 4680 psrs
609' x 76' x 26' (184.5 x 23 x 7.9 m)
Turbo-electric engines via twin screw.
Laid up in reserve fleet at Benecia, California, in Suisun Bay since 1968 and placed under the control of the US Maritime Administration on 28 September 1992.
Built by Bethlehem Steel Co, Alameda, California, for the US Navy as the Class P2-SE2-R1 troop carrier ADMIRAL C. F. HUGHES, USS (AP-124) (1945). Reclassified as the GENERAL EDWIN D. PATRICK, USAT (1946 – US Army).

GENERAL E. T. COLLINS (AP-147) (1944) See GUAYAMA (1975)

GENERAL G. M. RANDALL (AP-115) (1944)
17833 grt; 5200 psrs
622' x 76' x 26' (188.5 x 23 x 7.9 m)
De Laval geared turbine engines via twin screw.
Broken up by Union Minerals & Alloys Corporation, New York, in 1975.
Built by Federal Shipbuilding & Drydock Co, Kearny, New Jersey, for the US Maritime Administration.

GENERAL GEORGE S. SIMONS (1942) See H. F. ALEXANDER (1945)

GENERAL G. O. SQUIER, USS (APA-130) (1942) See PENNY (1978)

GENERAL G. W. GOETHALS (1917) See MUNORLEANS (1927)

GENERAL G. W. GOETHALS (1925) See MUNORLEANS (1927)

GENERAL HARRY TAYLOR, USS (AP-145) (1945) See GENERAL HOYT S. VANDENBERG (1963)

GENERAL HARRY TAYLOR, USAT (1946) See GENERAL HOYT S. VANDENBERG (1963)

GENERAL HARRY TAYLOR, USNS (T-AP-143) (1950) See GENERAL HOYT S. VANDENBERG (1963)

GENERAL H. B. FREEMAN, USS (AP-143) (1945) See NEWARK (1968)

GENERAL H. B. FREEMAN, USAT (1946) See NEWARK (1968)

GENERAL H. B. FREEMAN, USNS (1950) See NEWARK (1968)

GENERAL H. F. HODGES, USS (AP-144) (1945) See JAMES (1968)

GENERAL H. F. HODGES, USAT (1946) See JAMES (1968)

GENERAL H. F. HODGES, USNS (T-AP-144) (1950) See JAMES (1968)

GENERAL H. H. ARNOLD (T-AGM 9) (1963)
12351 grt; 2000 psrs
523' x 71' x 26'6" (159.3 x 21.7 x 8 m)
Geared turbine engine via single screw.
Owned by the US Navy.
Built by Kaiser Corporation, Richmond, California, for the US Navy as the Class C4-S-A1 troop transport GENERAL R.E. CALLAN, USS (AP-139) (1944). Reclassified as the GENERAL R.E. CALLAN, USAT (1947 – US Army), the GENERAL R.E. CALLAN, USNS (T-AP-139) (1950 – US Navy) and GENERAL H. H. ARNOLD (1961 – US Air Force).

GENERAL H. L. SCOTT (AP-136) (1944) See YORK MARU (1974)

GENERAL HOYT S. VANDENBERG (T-AGM 10) (1963)
10645 grt; 2000 psrs
523' x 71' x 26'6" (159.3 x 21.7 x 8 m)
Westinghouse geared turbine engine via single screw.
Under the control of the US Maritime Administration from 1 May 1999 and laid up with the James river reserve fleet at Fort Eustis, Virginia.
Built by Kaiser Corporation, Richmond, California, for the US Navy as the Class C4-S-A1 troop carrier GENERAL HARRY TAYLOR, USS (AP-145) (1945) which acted as a refugee transport after World War Two. Reclassified as the GENERAL HARRY TAYLOR, USAT (1946 – US Army) and the GENERAL HARRY TAYLOR, USNS (T-AP-145) (1950 – US Navy). Laid up in Beaumont, Texas, by MARAD from 1958 to 1961. Renamed GENERAL HOYT S. VANDENBERG (1961 – USAF) and GENERAL HOYT S. VANDENBERG (T-AGM-10) (1963 – US Navy).

GENERAL HUGH J. GAFFEY (T-AP-121) (1947)
17100 grt; 4680 psrs
609' x 76' x 26' (184.5 x 23 x 7.9 m)
Turbo-electric engines via twin screw.
Laid up from 1968 to 2000 in Pearl Harbor. In 2000 she became a target ship, and was sunk by a missile during exercise RIMPAC 2000, sinking to a depth of 2730 fathoms.
Built by Bethlehem Steel Co, Alameda, California, for the US Maritime Administration as the Class P2-SE2-R1 troop transport ADMIRAL W.L. CAPPS (AP-121) (1944).

GENERAL HUGH L. SCOTT (1941) See HUGH L. SCOTT (1942).

GENERAL H. W. BUTNER (AP-113) (1943)
17800 grt; 5200 psrs
622' x 75' x 26' (188.5 x 23 x 7.9 m)
De Laval geared turbine engines via twin screw.
Laid up in the James river, Virginia, since 1960 and placed under the control of the US Maritime Administration on 17 November 1976.
Built by Federal Shipbuilding & Drydock Co, Kearny, New Jersey, for the US Navy.

GENERAL J. C. BRECKENRIDGE, USNS (T-AP-176) (1949)
17833 grt; 5200 psrs
622' x 76' x 26' (188.5 x 23 x 7.9 m)
De Laval geared turbine engines via twin screw.
Laid up in Suisun Bay, California, since 1966 and then placed under the control of the US Maritime Administration on 28 September 1992.
Laid down by the Federal Shipbuilding & Drydock Co, Kearny, New Jersey, for the US Maritime Administration as Class P2-S2-R2 troop transport and completed as the GENERAL J. C. BRECKENRIDGE, USS (AP-176) (1945).

GENERAL J. H. McRAE (AP-149) (1944) See AMOCO VOYAGER (1982)

GENERAL JOHN POPE (T-AP-110) (1943)
17833 grt; 5200 psrs
622' x 76' x 26' (188.5 x 23 x 7.9 m)
De Laval geared turbine engines via twin screw.
Laid up in Suisin Bay with the reserve fleet since 1966, but recently listed for disposal by the US Shipping Corporation.
Built by Federal Shipbuilding & Drydock Co, Kearny, New Jersey, for the US Maritime Administration as Class P2-S2-R2 troop transport.

GENERAL J. R. BROOKE (1944) See MARY (1976)

GENERAL LECLERC (1951) See SAFINA-E-SIAHAT (1970)

GENERAL LEE (1932) See CARTAGO (1938)

GENERAL LEROY ELTINGE, USS (AP-154) (1945) See ROBERT TOOMBS (1973)

GENERAL LEROY ELTINGE, USNS (T-AP-154) (1950) See ROBERT TOOMBS (1973)

GENERAL MANGIN (1953) See SHAHEED SALAHUDDIN (1981)

GENERAL MAURICE ROSE, USAT (1947) See GENERAL MAURICE ROSE (T-AP-126) (1950)

GENERAL MAURICE ROSE (T-AP-126) (1950)
17100 grt; 4680 psrs
609' x 76' x 26' (184.5 x 23 x 7.9 m)
Turbo-electric engines via twin screw.
Laid up in James river, Virginia, since 1970 by the US Navy, but under the control of the US Maritime Administration since 17 September 1992.
Built by Bethlehem Steel Co, Alameda, California for the US Navy as the Class P2-SE2-R1 troop transport ADMIRAL HUGH RODMAN, USS (AP-126) (1945). Renamed GENERAL MAURICE ROSE, USAT (1947 US Army).

GENERAL M. B. STEWART, USS (AP-140) (1945) See MISSION VIKING (1974)

GENERAL M. B. STEWART, USAT (1947) See MISSION VIKING (1974)

GENERAL M. B. STEWART, USNS (T-AP-140) (1950) See MISSION VIKING (1974)

GENERAL M. C. MEIGS (AP-116) (1944)
17707 grt; 5200 psrs
622' x 76' x 26' (188.5 x 23 x 7.9 m)
De Laval geared turbine engines via twin screw.
Laid up since 1958. She was being towed to a new mooring by Murphy Marine Salvage Co when misfortune struck on 1 September 1972 – the line snapped and she grounded on a beach and broke in two off Cape Flattery.
Built by Federal Shipbuilding & Drydock Co, Kearny, New Jersey, for the US Navy as a Class P2-S2-R2 troop transport.

GENERAL METZINGER (1924)
9467 grt; 297 psrs
476' x 55' x 30'9" depth (144.2 x 16.7 x 9.4 m)
Blohm & Voss 8-cylinder quadruple expansion engines via twin screw.
Built by Blohm & Voss, Hamburg, for the Hamburg Sud-America Line as the passenger-cargo ship CAP VILLANO (1906).
Renamed SOBRAL (1918 – government of Brazil as a World War One requisition).

GENERAL M. L. HERSEY, USS (AP-148) (1944) See ST. LOUIS (1969)

GENERAL M. L. HERSEY, USAT (1946) See ST. LOUIS (1969)

GENERAL M. L. HERSEY, USNS (T-AP-148) (1950) See ST. LOUIS (1969)

GENERAL M. M. PATRICK, USS (AP-150) (1944) See BOSTON (1968)

GENERAL M. M. PATRICK, USAT (1946) See BOSTON (1968)

GENERAL M. M. PATRICK, USNS (T-APA-150) (1950) See BOSTON (1968)

GENERAL NELSON M. WALKER (T-AP 125) (1950)
17100 grt; 4680 psrs
609' x 76' x 26' (184.5 x 23 x 7.9 m)
Turbo-electric engines via twin screw.
Laid up with the reserve fleet at Fort Eustis in the James river, Virginia, since 1970 and then placed under the control of the US Maritime Administration from 23 December 1994.
Built by Bethlehem Steel Co, Alameda, California, for the US Navy as the Class P2-SE2-A1 troop transport ADMIRAL H.T. MAYO (AP-125) (1945). Renamed GENERAL NELSON M. WALKER, USAT (1947 – US Army).

GENERAL O. H. ERNST (AP-133) (1944) See ORINOCO (1975)

GENERAL OMAR BUNDY (AP-152) (1944) See POET (1979)

GENERAL OSORIO (1929)
11590 grt; 980 psrs
499' x 66' x 32'8" depth (151.2 x 20 x 9.9 m)
2 x 12-cylinder Vulkan-MAN diesel engines via twin screw.
Broken up for scrap in the UK in 1947 after raising her from the seabed in Kiel harbour where she had been sunk twice during Allied air raids – on 27 July 1944 and 9 April 1945.
Built by Bremer Vulkan, Vegesack, for Hamburg-America Line.

GENERAL PERSHING (1932) See HEREDIA (1937)

GENERAL R. E. CALLAN, USS (AP-139) (1944) See GENERAL H. H. ARNOLD (T-AGM 9) (1963)

GENERAL R. E. CALLAN, USAT (1947) See GENERAL H. H. ARNOLD (T-AGM 9) (1963)

GENERAL R. L. HOWZE (1945) See PACIFIC ENDEAVOUR (1979)

GENERAL R. M. BLATCHFORD (AP-118) (1944) See OCEAN EXPLORER I (1998)

GENERAL R. M. BLATCHFORD, USS (AP-153) (1945) See ALEX STEPHENS (1973)

GENERAL R. M. BLATCHFORD, USAT (1946) See ALEX STEPHENS (1973)

GENERAL R. M. BLATCHFORD, USNS (T-AP-153) (1950) See ALEX STEPHENS (1973)

GENERAL ROBERT L. HOWZE (AP-134) (1944) See PACIFIC ENDEAVOUR (1979)

GENERAL SAMUEL D. STURGIS (AP-137) (1944) See GREEN PORT (1967)

GENERAL SAN MARTIN (1930) See EMPIRE DEBEN (1945)

GENERAL S. D. STURGIS, USS (AP-137) (1944) See GREEN PORT (1967)

GENERAL S. D. STURGIS (1946) See GREEN PORT (1967)

GENERAL S. D. STURGIS, USNS (T-AP-137) (1950) See GREEN PORT (1967)

GENERAL SHERMAN (1932) See PARISMINA (1938)

GENERAL SIMON B. BUCKNER, USAT (1947) See GENERAL SIMON B. BUCKNER (T-AP 122) (1950)

GENERAL SIMON B. BUCKNER, USS (T-AP 122) (1950)
17100 grt; 4680 psrs
609' x 76' x 26" (184.5 x 23 x 7.9 m)
Turbo-electric engines via twin screw.
Laid up since 1968, but placed under the control of the US Maritime Administration from 14 July 1993.
Built by Bethlehem Steel Co, Alameda, California, for the US Navy as the Class P2-SE2-R1 troop transport ADMIRAL E.W. EBERLE, USS (AP-123) (1945). Renamed GENERAL SIMON B. BUCKNER, USAT (1947 – US Army).

GENERAL STUART HEINTZELMAN (AP-159) (1945) See MOBILE (1968)

GENERAL TASKER H. BLISS (1941) See TASKER H. BLISS, USS (AP-42) (1942)

GENERAL T. H. BLISS (APA-131) (1944) See CARONI (1975)

GENERAL VON STEUBEN (1931) See STEUBEN (1938)

GENERAL W. A. MANN, USS (AP-112) (1943) See GENERAL W. A. MANN, USS (T-AP-112) (1949)

GENERAL W. A. MANN, USS (T-AP-112) (1949)
17833 grt; 5200 psrs
622' x 76' x 26' (188.5 x 23 x 7.9 m)
De Laval geared turbine engines via twin screw.
Laid up in the Hudson river, New York, since 1966.
Built by Federal Shipbuilding & Drydock Co, Kearny, New Jersey, for the US Maritime Commission as a Class P2-S2-R1 troop transport, GENERAL W. A. MANN, USS (1943 – US Navy).

GENERAL W. C. GORGAS (1945) See MIKHAIL LOMONOSOV (1945)

GENERAL W. C. LANGFITT, USS (AP-151) (1945) See TRANSINDIANA (1969)

GENERAL W. C. LANGFITT, USNS (T-AP-151) (1950) See TRANSINDIANA (1969)

GENERAL WERDER (1874) See MIDNIGHT SUN (1901)

GENERAL W. F. HASE, USS (AP-146) (1944) See CAROLINA (1975)

GENERAL W. F. HASE, USAT (1947) See CAROLINA (1975)

GENERAL W. F. HASE, USNS (T-AP-146) (1950) See CAROLINA (1975)

GENERAL W. G. HAAN (T-AP-158) (1945) See AMOCO TRADER (1982)

GENERAL W. H. GORDON, USS (AP-117) (1944) See GENERAL W. H. GORDON, USAT (AP-117) (1948)

GENERAL W. H. GORDON, USAT (AP-117) (1948)
17707 grt; 900 psrs
622' x 76' x 26' (188.5 x 23 x 7.9 m)
De Laval geared turbine engines via twin screw.
Laid up by the US Navy in the James river, Virginia, since 1970.
Built by Federal Shipbuilding & Drydock Co, Kearny, New Jersey, for the US Maritime Administration as a Class P2-S2-R2 troop transport, GENERAL W. H. GORDON, USS (T-AP-117) (1944 – US Navy). Reclassified as the GENERAL W. H. GORDON, USAT (1948 – US Army).

GENERAL WILLARD A. HOLBROOK (1941) See
WILLARD A. HOLBROOK (1944)

GENERAL WILLIAM M. BLACK (1944) See GREEN
FOREST (1967)

GENERAL WILLIAM MITCHELL, USS (AP-114) (1944)
See GENERAL WILLIAM MITCHELL, USNS (T-AP-114) (1950)

**GENERAL WILLIAM MITCHELL, USNS (T-AP-114)
(1950)**
17233 grt; 5200 psrs
622' x 76' x 26' (188.5 x 23 x 7.9 m)
De Laval geared turbo-electric engines via twin screw.
Laid up in Suisin Bay since 1966.
Built by the Bethlehem Steel Co, Alameda, California, for the US Maritime
Administration as a Class P2-S2-R2 troop transport. Reclassified as the
GENERAL WILLIAM MITCHELL, USS (AP-114) (194 – US Navy).

GENERAL W. M. BLACK, USAT (T-AP-135) (1946) See
GREEN FOREST (1967)

GENERAL W. M. BLACK, USNS (1950 – US Army) See
GREEN FOREST (1967)

GENERAL WILLIAM O. DARBY, USAT (1946) See
GENERAL WILLIAM O. DARBY, USNS (T-AP-127) (1950)

**GENERAL WILLIAM O. DARBY, USNS (T-AP-127)
(1950)**
17100 grt; 4680 psrs
609' x 76' x 26' (184.5 x 23 x 7.9 m)
Turbo-electric engines via twin screw.
Laid up as a troop accommodation ship at the Norfolk Naval Shipyard,
Portsmouth, Virginia, since 1981.
Built by Bethlehem Steel Co, Alameda, California, for the US Navy as the
Class P2-S2-R2 troop carrier ADMIRAL W.S. SIMS (AP-127) (1945).
Reclassified as the GENERAL WILLIAM O. DARBY, USAT (1946 – US
Army).

GENERAL WILLIAM WEIGEL (AP-119) (1943)
17833 grt; 4657 psrs
622' x 76' x 26' (188.5 x 23 x 7.9 m)
De Laval geared turbo-electric engines via twin screw.
Laid up in Suisun Bay since 1970.
Built by Federal Shipbuilding & Drydock Co, Kearny, New Jersey, for the US
Maritime Administration   .

GENERAL W. P RICHARDSON (AP-118) (1944) See
OCEAN EXPLORER (1998)

GENNARGENTU (1965)
4887 grt; 1000 psrs
84 cars or 45 trailers or 30 rail coaches
401' x 58' x 16' (121.5 x 17.5 x 4.8 m)
2 x 6-cylinder Fiat diesel engines via twin screw.
Passenger-car-train ferry owned by the Italian State Railways and operated
by Ferrovie Stato on the Italy–Sardinia service.
Built by Riuniti.

GENOVA (1948) See KING ABDELAZIZ (1964)

GEORG BUCHNER (1967)
11060 grt; 248 psrs
505' x 65' x 27'6" (153 x 19.7 x 8.4 m)
2 x 8-cylinder B+W-type diesel engines via single screw.
Education ship owned by VEB Deutsche Seereederei, Rostock, and moored
permanently adjacent to the museum.
Built by John Cockerill Shipyard, Hoboken, Belgium, for Cie Maritime Belge
as the CHARLESVILLE (1951).

GEORGE ANSON (1962)
7437 grt; 130 psrs

440' x 61' x 26' (134.1 x 18.5 x 7.9 m)
DRG & SRG turbine engines via single screw.
Broken up for scrap at Kaohsiung in 1971. Ex-Dominion Far East Line.
Built by Vickers-Armstrong Ltd, Barrow-in-Furness, for Furness, Warren Line
as the NEWFOUNDLAND (1948).

GEORGE CLYMER, USS (AP-57) (1942) See GEORGE
CLYMER, USS (APA-27) (1943)

GEORGE CLYMER, USS (APA-27) (1942)
7997 grt; 100 psrs
422' x 57' x 26'1" (127.9 x 17.3 x 7.9 m)
2 x 3-cylinder Doxford diesel engines via single screw.
Broken up for scrap at San Pedro, California, in 1968.
Built by Furness Shipbuilding Co Ltd, Haverton Hill-on-Tees, for Prince Line
Ltd as the AFRICAN PLANET (1941). Renamed GEORGE CLYMER, USS
(AP-57) (1942 – US Navy).

GEORGE F. ELLIOTT, USS (AP-13) (1941)
8378 grt; 80 psrs
495' x 56' x 26' (150 x 17 x 7.9 m)
De Laval geared steam turbine engine via single screw.
Owned by the US Navy, she sank on 8 August 1942 after a Japanese aircraft
attack at Florida Island, off Guadalcanal.
Built by Bethlehem Shipbuilding Corporation, Alameda, California, for the
US Shipping Board as the VICTORIOUS (1919). Renamed CITY OF
HAVRE (1931 – Baltimore Mail Line) and CITY OF LOS ANGELES (1938
– Panama Pacific Line).

GEORGE F. ELLIOTT, USS (AP-105) (1943) See AFRICAN
ENDEAVOUR (1948)

GEORGE H. EVANS (1967)
6911 grt; 914 psrs
419' x 58' x 17' (127.7 x 17.6 x 5.2 m)
Turbo-electric engines via twin screw.

Broken up for scrap at Hong Kong in 1971. She had been acting as a staff
dormitory ship for the Tasmanian Hydro-electric Commission from 19
October 1967.
Built by Vickers-Armstrong Ltd, Barrow-in-Furness, for the Union Steamship
Company of New Zealand as the HINEMOA (1946).

GEORGE OTS (1995)
12549 grt; 416 psrs
150 cars
410' x 69' x 18' (124.8 x 21 x 5.5 m)
4 x 6-cylinder Cegielski-Sulzer diesel engines via twin screw.
Owned by the Estonian Shipping Co and operated by Tallink.

Built by Stocznia Szczecinska, Szczecin, for the Estonian Shipping Co as the
GEORG OTS (1979). Renamed DMITRI SHOSTAKOVICH (1980 –
chartered by the Black Sea Shipping Company, Odessa).

GEORGES PHILIPPAR (1930)
17539 grt; 1045 psrs
543' x 68' x 46'9" depth (164.5 x 20.6 x 14.2 m)
2 x 20-cylinder Sulzer diesel engines via twin screw.
Sank on 19 May 1932 145 miles (242 km) north-east of Cape Guardafui on her return maiden voyage, with a loss of life numbering 54. She was engulfed by fire which started off as a short circuit in Cabin No 6, lost her electric power and drifted out of control for four days and 160 miles (267 km) in the Gulf of Aden.
Built by Ateliers et Chantiers de la Loire, St Nazaire, for Messageries Maritimes.

GEORGE S. SYMONDS (1942)
8357 grt; 510 psrs
524' x 63' x 21' (158.8 x 19.1 x 6.4 m)
3 x William Cramp & Sons turbine engines via triple screw.
Broken up for scrap by the Sun Shipbuilding & Drydock Co at Philadelphia, Pennsylvania in 1948. Ex-Canadian Pacific Steamship Co.
Built by the Sun Shipbuilding & Drydock Company, Chester, Pennsylvania, for the Great Northern Pacific Steamship Co at a cost of US$1,945,000 as the GREAT NORTHERN (1914). Renamed COLUMBIA (1917), COLUMBIA, USS (AG-9) (1921 – US Navy) and H. F. ALEX ANDER (1922 – Admiral Line).

GEORGE WASHINGTON (1908) See GEORGE WASHINGTON (1941)

GEORGE WASHINGTON (1917) See GEORGE WASHINGTON (1941)

GEORGE WASHINGTON (1920) See GEORGE WASHINGTON (1941)

GEORGE WASHINGTON (1924) See GASCOGNE (1948)

GEORGE WASHINGTON (1941)
25570 grt; 2679 psrs
699' x 78' x 50'1" depth (211.8 x 23.6 x 15.2 m)
2 x AG Vulcan 4-cylinder quadruple expansion engines via twin screw.
Owned by the US government, she was broken up for scrap at Baltimore, Maryland, in 1951 after initially catching fire at her berth at a New York pier. She was then totally consumed by another fire at Baltimore on 17 January 1931.
Built by Vulcan Shipyards, Stettin, for North German Lloyd as the GEORGE WASHINGTON (1908). Renamed GEORGE WASHINGTON, USS (1917 – US Navy), GEORGE WASHINGTON (1920 – US government) and CATLIN,USS (AP-19) (1940 – US Navy).

GEORGE W. GOETHALS (1942) See GEORGE W. GOTHALS (T-AP 182) (1950)

GEORGE W. GOETHALS (T-AP-182) (1950)
12090 grt; 360 psrs
489' x 69' x 27'4" (148.2 x 20.9 x 8 m)
Geared turbine engine via single screw.
Broken up for scrap by I Varela at Castellon, in 1971. Ex-US Maritime Administration.
Laid down by Ingalls Shipbuilding Corporation, Pascagoula, Mississippi, for United States Lines as the AMERICAN MERCHANT (1941). Launched for the US government as the PASCAGOULA (1942) and completed for the US Army as the Class C3-IN-P&C passenger-cargo ship GEORGE W. GOETHALS (1942).

GEORGIA (1895) See HOUSATONIC (1915)

GEORGIC (1932)
27469 grt; 993 psrs
712' x 82' x 35' (217 x 25 x 10.7 m)
2 x 10-cylinder B+W diesel engines via twin screw.
Owned by the British government, and chartered to the Cunard Line for the period 1950–56.
Broken up for scrap by Shipbreaking Industries at Faslane in 1956.
Built by Harland & Wolff Ltd, Belfast, for the White Star Line.

GEORGIOS (1990) See APOLLON HELLAS (1999)

GEORGIOS II (1983) See EXPRESS HERMES (1999)

GEORGIOS EXPRESS (1983)
3023 grt; 1700 psrs
160 cars
389' x 53' x 13' (117.8 x 16 x 3.8 m)
2 x 12-cylinder Sulzer diesel engines via twin screw.
Passenger-car ferry owned by Santorini Shipping Co and operated by Ventouris Sea Lines.
Built by John Cockerill SA, Hoboken, for RMT, Belgium, as the ROI BAUDOUIN (1965).

GEORG OTS (1979) See GEORGE OTS (1995)

GERA (1890) See VALPARAISO (1908)

GERMAN (1898) See GLENGORM CASTLE (1914)

GERMANIA (1903) See BRITANNIA (1914)

GERMANIC (1875) See GULCEMAL (1928)

GEROLSTEIN (1928) See CONSUL HORN (1939)

GERONA (1910) See ASCANIA (1911)

GERTY (1904) See CITY OF CANDIA (1929).

GERUSALEMME (1934)
8052 grt
444' x 53' x 25' (134.5 x 16.1 x 7.6 m)
4 x geared turbine engines via twin screw.
Broken up for scrap at Savona in 1952. Ex-Lloyd Triestino.
Built by Cantieri San Rocco, San Rocco, for Lloyd Triestino as the CRACOVIA (1920).

GHAWDEX (1979) See VIRGEM DE FATIMA (2000)

GIANO (1926) See FERRANIA (1927)

GINYO MARU (1921)
8613 grt
445' x 58' x 28' (134.8 x 17.6 x 8.5 m)
Turbine engines via twin screw.
Sank on 16 December 1943 after being torpedoed by the USS FLYING FISH off Taiwan.
Built by Ansano Shipbuilding Company, Tsurumi, for Toyo Kisen Kaisha.

GIOACCHINO ROSSINI (1963) See ROSSINI (1963)

GIORGIOS EXPRESS (1983) See GEORGIOS EXPRESS (1983)

GIOTTO (1980) See AL RASHEED II (1992)

GIOVANNA (1924)
6660 grt; 160 psrs
450' x 52' x 30' (137.2 x 15.9 x 9.1 m)
2 x triple expansion engines via twin screw.
Broken up for scrap by Cognati Schiaffino, La Spezia, after John Cashmore of Newport, Wales, had made the original purchase for scrap at £16,000.
Built by A Stephen & Sons, Glasgow, for the P&O Line as the passenger-cargo ship SYRIA (1901) at a cost of £151,694

GIOVANNA C (1946)
6475 grt
445' x 58' x 27'6" (134.8 x 17.6 x 8.4 m)
Kubota Iron Works 6-cylinder triple expansion engines via twin screw.
Broken up for scrap in 1953 as a cargo ship. Ex-Costa Line.
Built by Ansano Shipbuilding Co, Tsurumi, for the US Shipping Board as the EASTERN TRADER (1919). Renamed HORACE LUCKENBACH (1923 – Luckenbach Steamship Co)

GIOVENTU (1999)

10850 grt; 1500 psrs
211 cars
478' x 58' x 14'6" (144.7 x 17.7 x 4.4 m)
4 x 12-cylinder B+W diesel engines via twin screw.

Ice-strengthened passenger-car ferry owned and operated by Traghetti Isole Sarde.
Built by AS Nakskov Skibsvaerft, Nakskov, for the Danish government as the PRINS HENRIK (1974).

GIRESUN (1948)

6790 grt; 528 psrs
441' x 58' x 24' (133.6 x 17.6 x 7.3 m)
2 x 5-cylinder Fiat diesel engines via single screw.
Cruise ship operating for Turkish Maritime Lines.
Built by Nakskov for Cia Sud Americana de Vapores, Chile, as the ACONCAGUA (1938).

GIRNE SULTANI (1987) See APOLLONIA II (1990)

GIROLATA (1989) See SAGA STAR (1993)

GISELLA (1974) See HORNBEAM (1992)

GITTE B (1999) See GITTE 3 (1999)

GITTE 3 (1999)

4296 grt 300 psrs
316' x 58' x 12' (95.8 x 17 x 3.6 m)
10 x 6-cylinder Cummins diesel engines via quadruple screw.
Passenger ferry owned and operated by Easy Line, Denmark
Built by North East Shipbuilders, Southwick, for Supereflex Ships as the SUPERFLEX DELTA (1989). Renamed DIFKO STREBAELT (1990 – Difko, Denmark) and GITTE B (1999 – Easy Line).

GIULIA (1904)

4337 grt; 1460 psrs
346' x 45' x 25'3" (105.5 x 13.7 x 7.7 m)
3-cylinder triple expansion engine via single screw.
Owned by Cosulich, she was abandoned in the North Atlantic when she foundered on 22 March 1923.
Built by Russell & Co, Glasgow, for Unione Austriaca.

GIULIO CESARE (1922)

21658 grt; 2373 psrs
634' x 76' x 30'2" (192.1 x 23 x 9.2 m)
4 x SRG turbine engines via quadruple screw.
Broken up for scrap at Trieste in 1948 under the name ACHILLE LAURO after being raised from the Trieste harbour seabed. She had settled there on 11 September 1944 after being bombed by Beaufighters from No 16 Squadron of the South African Air Force.
Laid down as the GIULIO CESARE (1913) by Swan Hunter & Wigham Richardson, Newcastle, for Navigazione Generale Italiana.

GIULIO CESARE (1951)

27078 grt; 1183 psrs
681' x 87' x 28' (207.6 x 26.6 x 8.5 m)
2 x 12-cylinder Fiat diesel engines via twin screw.
Broken up for scrap at La Spezia in 1973.
Built by Cantieri Riuniti dell'Adriatico, Monfalcone, for the Italian Line.

GIUSEPPE CANERA (1953) See HONG Qi 144 (1977)

GIUSEPPE MAJORANA (1942) See AMERIGO VESPUCCI (1948)

GLACIER (1942) See ROMA (1950)

GLACIER, USS (1943) See ROMA (1950)

GLENAPP (1918) See MATRONA (1947)

GLENART CASTLE (1914)

6575 grt; 195 psrs
440' x 53' x 26' (133.3 x 16.1 x 7.9 m)
Triple expansion engines via twin screw.
Owned by the Union-Castle Line, she sank on 26 February 1918, with the loss of 162 lives, ten miles (17 km) west of Lundy Island in the Bristol Channel . She had been torpedoed by the German U-56 despite the fact that she was in hospital ship colours.
Built by Harland & Wolff Ltd, Belfast, for the Union Line which merged with Castle Line during the ship's construction as the GALICIAN (1900).

GLENGORM CASTLE (1914)

6763 grt; 195 psrs
440' x 53' x 21'6" (133.3 x 16.1 x 6.5 m)
Harland & Wolff Ltd 6-cylinder turbine engines via twin screw.
Broken up for scrap in Holland in 1930. Ex-Union-Castle Line.
Built by Harland & Wolff Ltd, Belfast, for Union-Castle Mail Steamship Co Ltd as the GERMAN (1898).

GLOUCESTER CASTLE (1911)

7999 grt; 412 psrs
470' x 50' x 27' (142.4 x 17 x 8.2 m)
Quadruple expansion engines via twin screw.
Sank on the night of 15 July 1942, with the loss of 93 lives, after the German raider SCHIFF had opened fire on her north-east of Ascension Island.
Built by Fairfield Shipbuilding & Engineering Co, Glasgow, for the Union-Castle Line.

GLOUCESTERSHIRE (1909)

8124 grt; 235 psrs
467' x 54' x 28' (141.5 x 16.4 x 8.5 m)
Quadruple expansion engines via twin screw.
Broken up for scrap at Barrow-in-Furness in 1936 by TW Ward Ltd for a tender of £16,500.
Built by Harland & Wolff Ltd, Belfast, for the Bibby Line.

GNEISENAU (1903) See CITTA DI GENOVA (1921)

GNEISENAU (1935)

18160 grt; 293 psrs
651' x 74' x 29' (197.3 x 22.4 x 8.8 m)
2 x geared turbine engines via twin screw.
Broken up for scrap in Denmark in 1946 after she had hit a British mine on 21 May 1943 east of Gedser, Denmark. She was beached on the island of Lloland where she became a submerged hulk.
Built by AG Weser, Bremen, for North German Lloyd.

GOEBEN (1906) See ROUSSILION (1919)

GOELO (1980) See SARDEGNA BELLA (1993)

GOENTOER (1902)

5894 grt; 159 psrs
442' x 50' x 26' (133.9 x 15.2 x 7.0 m)
Maats de Schelde 8-cylinder quadruple expansion engines via twin screw.
Built by Kon Maats de Schelde for Rotterdam Lloyd.

GOGOL (1946)

4701 grt
376' x 50' x 23'7" (113.1 x 15.2 x 7.2 m)
Reiherstieg 4-cylinder quadruple expansion engine via single screw.
War prize awarded to Russia.

Built by Reiherstieg Schiffeswerft, Hamburg, for Woermann Line as the WADAI (1922). Renamed EMPIRE YARE (1945 – British Shipping Controller).

GOKOKU MARU (1942)
10438 grt; 400 psrs
length 537' x beam 66' (162.7 x 20 m)
B+W diesel engines via twin screw.
Sank on 10 October 1944 after being torpedoed by the US submarine BARB north-west of Hiroshima.
Launched by Tama Shipbuilding Co for OSK, Japan, in 1941 as a passenger liner, but converted into a troop transport.

GOLDEN BEAR (1971) See ARTSHIP (1999)

GOLDEN BRIDGE (1990)
4317 grt; 500 psrs
426' x 65' x 16' (129 x 19.8 x 4.9 m)
2 x 6-cylinder Niigata diesel engines via twin screw.
Passenger ferry owned by Arimura Sangyo and operated by Wei Dong, but has been laid up since 1994.
Built by Usuki Tekkosho, Saiki, for Arimura Sangyo KK, Naha, as the GYOKURYU (1975). Renamed WEI DONG (1990 – Wei Dong Ferry Co Ltd, China).

GOLDEN CITY (1967)
7173 grt; 76 psrs
451' x 59' x 26' (136.7 x 17.9 x 7.9 m)
2 x 3-cylinder Doxford diesel engines via twin screw.
Broken up for scrap in Hong Kong in 1973. Ex-Guan Guan Shipping (Pte) Co, Singapore.
Built by Cammell Laird & Co, Birkenhead, for Elder Dempster Lines as the TAMELE (1945).

GOLDEN GLORY (1976)
3709 grt; 75 psrs
344' x 49' x 18' (104.8 x 14.9 x 5.5 m)
6-cylinder B+W diesel engine via single screw.
Broken up for scrap by Gi Yuen Steel Enterprises Co Ltd, Kaohsiung, in 1979. Ex-Guan Guan Shipping (Pte) Co, Singapore.
Built by Dubigeon-Normandie, Nantes, for Messageries Maritimes as the POLYNESIE (1955).

GOLDEN ISLES (1952)
3504 grt; 250 psrs
317' x 50' x 15' (96.1 x 15.2 x 4.5 m)
Parsons SRG turbine engines via twin screw.
Broken up for scrap by John Cashmore Ltd at Newport, Wales, in 1956. Ex-Harris & Dixon.
Built by Vickers Ltd, Barrow-in-Furness, for the Straits Steamship Company as the KEDAH (1927). Renamed KEDAH, HMS (1942 – British Royal Navy) and KEDMAH (1946 – Kedem Israel Lines).

GOLDEN LION (1967)
7414 grt; 72 psrs
451' x 59' x 26' (136.7 x 17.9 x 7.9 m)
4 x 8-cylinder Kincaid-B+W-type diesel engines via twin screw.
Broken up for scrap at Shanghai in 1971. Ex-Guan Guan Shipping (Pte) Co, Singapore.
Built by Cammell Laird & Co, Birkenhead, for Elder Dempster Lines as the TARKWA (1944).

GOLDEN MOON (1977) See AFRICA-CUBA (1978)

GOLDEN MOON (1978) See RASA SAYANG (1980)

GOLDEN ODYSSEY (1974) See OMAR II (2000)

GOLDEN OKINAWA (1972) See ORIENTAL PEARL (1998).

GOLDEN PRINCESS (1993) See HYUNDAI KUMGANG (1998)

GOLDEN PRINCESS (2000)
12704 grt; 725 psrs

69 cars + 4 trailers
520' x 66' x 18'5" (157.7 x 20 x 5.6 m)
2 x 14-cylinder MAN diesel engines via twin screw.

Casino cruise ship owned by Pleasure Hotels and Profits Ltd, and operated by Farsco Nice, Hong Kong.
Passenger-car-cargo ferry built by Wartsila, Helsinki, as the FINLANDIA (1967). Renamed FINNSTAR (1978 – Lauritzen & Skaugen Joint venture), INNSTAR (1981 – Lauritzen & Skaugen joint venture), PEARL OF SCANDINAVIA (1982 – Pearl Cruises), OCEAN PEARL (1988 – Ocean Cruise Lines), PEARL (1993 – Martinol SAM), COSTA PLAYA (1995 – Prestige Cruises NV), ORIENTAL PEARL (1998 – Mega Wave International Ltd) and JOY WAVE (1999).

GOLDEN SKY (1979) See MIR (1998)

GOLDEN STAR (1979) See SAUDI GOLDEN STAR (1979)

GOLDEN STATE (1921) See TASKER H. BLISS, USS (AP-42) (1942)

GOLDEN SUN (1976)
5485 grt; 440 psrs
395' x 53' x 17' (119.7 x 16 x 5.2 m)
4 x 7-cylinder Fiat SRG diesel engines via twin screw.
Broken up for scrap at Piraeus in 1981. Ex-Prospect Marine Investments Ltd, Limassol.
Built by Soc Italiana per Construzioni Navale Meccaniche for Tirrenia as the ARBOREA (1957).

GOLDEN VERGINA (1982) See EXPRESS SAMINA (2000)

GOLFINHO AZUL (1999)
3797 grt; 460 psrs
cars
358' x 57' x 16' (108.5 x 17.4 x 4.8 m)
2 x 12-cylinder MAN diesel engines via twin screw.
Passenger-car ferry owned and operated by the government of the Azores.
Built by Jos L Meyers, Papenburg, for Heinrich Th Moller and chartered to Fred Olsen Lines as the VIKINGFJORD (1969). Renamed PRINZ HAMLET II (1973), AGADIR (1974 – Comonav, Casablanca) and OURANOS (1986 – Fragline Ferries).

GOLFITO (1949)
8740 grt; 111 psrs
447' x 62' x 26' (135.5 x 18.8 x 7.9 m)
DRG turbine engines via twin screw.
Broken up for scrap at Faslane in 1971.
Built by A Stephen & Sons, Glasgow, for Elder & Fyffes Ltd.

GONG NONG BING (1966) See TIAN 2 (1985)

GOOD SAVIOUS I (1997) See SANUKI MARU (1997)

GORGON (1933)
3678 grt; 84 psrs
320' x 51' x 216" (97 x 15.5 x 6.5 m)
2 x 6-cylinder B+W diesel engine via single screw.
Broken up for scrap in Hong Kong in 1964.
Built by Caledon Shipbuilding & Engineering Co, Dundee, for the Blue Funnel Line & WA Steam Navigation Co

GORIZONT (1961)
4404 grt; 154 psrs

347' x 48' x 20' (105 x 14.4 x 6.2 m)
MAN 6-cylinder diesel engine via single screw.
Built by Neptunwerft, Rostock, for the Russian government as an ice-strengthened education ship.

GOSTA BERLING (1967) See SAMA 1 (2000)

GOSTA BERLING (1975) See SAMA 1 (2000)

GOTALAND (1973)
18060 grt; 400 psrs
35 cars + 18 trailers + 44 rail wagons
604' x 74' x 19' (183.1 x 22.5 x 5.8 m)
4 x 8-cylinder Pielstick diesel engines via twin screw.

Passenger-car-cargo-train ferry owned by Scandlines AB and operated by Scandlines-Hansa.
Built by Nakskov for Swedish Ferry as a pure freight ferry.

GOTH (1893) See COBEQUID (1913)

GOTHA (1907)
6974 grt
429' x 55' x 27'9" depth (130 x 16.7 x 8.5 m)
Bremer Vulkan 4-cylinder quadruple expansion engines via single screw.
Broken up for scrap in 1932.
Built by Bremer Vulkan, Vegesack, for North German Lloyd.

GOTHIC (1893) See GOTHLAND (1914)

GOTHIC (1911) See GOTHLAND (1914)

GOTHIC (1948)
15911 grt; 85 psrs
561' x 72' x 30' (171 x 21.9 x 9.1 m)
6 x DRG turbine engines via twin screw.
Broken up for scrap at Kaohsiung in 1969. This followed a fire in the superstructure, on 2 August 1968, which cost seven lives in the Tasman Sea, 800 miles (1335 km) from Wellington, New Zealand.
Built by Swan Hunter & Wigham Richardson, Newcastle, for Shaw Savill & Albion.

GOTHLAND (1907) See GOTHLAND (1914)

GOTHLAND (1914)
7669 grt; 875 psrs
491' x 53' x 33'5" (148.8 x 16.1 x 10.2 m)
6 x triple expansion engines via twin screw.
Broken up for a tender fee of £16,000 at Barrow-in-Furness in 1926. Ex-White Star Line.
Built by Harland & Wolff Ltd, Belfast, for the White Star Line as the GOTHIC (1893). Renamed GOTHLAND (1907 – Red Star Line) and GOTHIC (1911 – White Star Line).

GOTLAND (1964) See DELFINI (1996)

GOTLAND (1973) See CORSICA VICTORIA (1989)

GOTLAND (1980) See PETER WESSEL (1984)

GOTLAND (1996) See FINNARROW (1997)

GOUVERNEUR GALOPIN (1946) See BOTHINJ (1959)

GOVERNOR (1907)
5474 grt; 438 psrs
392' x 48' x 19'7" (118.8 x 14.5 x 6 m)
New York Shipbuilding Co 6-cylinder triple expansion engines via twin screw.
Sank on 31 March 1921 off Point Wilson, Washington, after being rammed by the freighter WEST HARTLAND.
Built by New York Shipbuilding Co, Camden, New Jersey, for Pacific Coast Steamship Co.

GOVERNOR (1984) See FRIGGA (1999)

GOYA (1947) See MELINA (1964)

GRACE M (1994) See FELICIA (1998)

GRADISCA (1935)
13868 grt; 1520 psrs
541' x 66' x 28'9" (163.9 x 20 x 8.8 m)
A Stephen & Sons 8-cylinder quadruple expansion engines via twin   screw.
Broken up for scrap in Venice in 1950. Ex-Lloyd Triestino.
Built by A Stephen & Sons Ltd, Glasgow, for Koninkl Nederlandsche Lloyd as the GELRIA (1913).

GRAFTON (1901) See TOTOMI MARU (1905)

GRAIN TRADER (1974) See EASTERN PEACE (1974)

GRAIP (1987) See CHONG MING DAO (1998)

GRAMPIAN (1907)
10947 grt; 1460 psrs
486' x 60' x 38' depth (147.3 x 18.2 x 11.5 m)
6-cylinder triple expansion engines via twin screw.
Broken up for scrap by F Rijsdijk at Rotterdam in 1926 following her being gutted by fire on 14 March 1921. She had been undergoing a refit in Antwerp and subsequently had her hulk condemned by maritime inspection teams.
Built by A Stephen & Sons, Glasgow for the Allan Line.

GRANDEUR OF THE SEAS (1996)
73817 grt; 2340 psrs
891' x 106' x 27' (270 x 32.1 x 8.2 m)
4 x 12-cylinder MAN-B+W diesel-electric engines via twin screw.

Cruise ship for Royal Caribbean International.
Built by Kvaerner Masa-Yards, Helsinki, at a cost of US$300,000,000.

GRAND FLOTEL (1977) See THE EMPRESS (1994)

GRAND MANAN V (1990)
3833 grt; 320 psrs
248' x 51' x 11'6" (75 x 15.4 x 3.6 m)
2 x 6-cylinder Wartsila Kromhaut diesel engines via twin screw.
Passenger ferry owned by the Canadian government (Ministry of Transportation for the Province of New Brunswick) and operated by Marine Atlantic Inc.
Built by Bodewes Volh Fh Bv, Fox Hol.

GRAND PRINCESS (1998)
108806 grt; 3100 psrs
956' x 118' x 26' (289.7 x 35.8 x 7.9 m)
6 x 16-cylinder Sulzer diesel-electric engines via twin screw.

Cruise ship owned by Fairlane Shipping Co and operated by P&O Princess Cruises.
Built by Fincantieri, Monfalcone, at a cost of US$418,000,000.

GRANITE STATE (1921) See PRESIDENT TAYLOR (1938)

GRANT (1898) See CHINOOK (1904)

GRANTALA (1903) See FIGUIG (1916)

GRANTULLY CASTLE (1910)
7612 grt; 385 psrs
451' x 54' x 27'3" (136.7 x 16.4 x 8.2 m)
Barclay Curle 8-cylinder quadruple expansion engines via twin screw.
Broken up in 1939. Ex-Union-Castle Line.
Built by Barclay, Curle & Co, Glasgow, for the Union-Castle Line.

GREAT CANTON (1923)
8001 grt; 850 psrs
491' x 56' x 25' (148.8 x 17 x 7.6 m)
Fawcet-Preston 6-cylinder triple expansion engine via single screw.
Broken up for scrap in Italy in 1924. Ex-TC Phelps, New York.
Built by Harland & Wolff Ltd, Belfast, for Atlantic Transport Co Ltd, England, as the passenger-cargo ship MICHIGAN (1890). Renamed KILPATRICK (1898 – US government), ACROPOLIS (1920 – American Black Sea Line) and WASHINGTON (1923 – Booras Steamship Company).

GREAT EMERALD (1980) See TAMPOMAS (1980)

GREAT NORTHERN (1914) See GEORGE S. SIMONDS (1942)

GREAT SEA (1976) See PHILIPPINES (1999)

GRECIA (2000)
7873 grt; 835 psrs
221 cars + 30 trailers
414' x 61' x 17' (125.5 x 18.5 x 5.2 m)
2 x 14-cylinder Fiat diesel engines via twin screw.
Passenger-car-cargo ferry owned and operated by Halkyon Shipping Co after purchasing her for a figure believed to have been US$2,000,000.
Built by Cantieri Navali Lugi Orlando, Livorno, for Adriatica, Cagliari, as the ESPRESSO LIVORNO (1972) and renamed ESPRESSO GRECIA (1980 – Adrriatica).

GRECIA EXPRESS (1987)
4112 grt; 250 psrs
265 cars + 65 trailers
357' x 63' x 16' (108.2 x 19 x 4.8 m)
2 x 14-cylinder Bolnes diesel engines via twin screw.
Broken up for scrap in Turkey in 1994 after raising her from the seabed where she had sunk mysteriously in March 1994. Ex-Ventouris Group.   Built by AG Weser, Stettin, for North Sea Ferries Ltd, Rotterdam, as the NORWIND (1966).

GREEK (1893) See CHIGNECTO (1913)

GREEN ACE (1971) See MARINA (1990)

GREEN ARCH (1975) See IERAPTERA L (1999)

GREEN ARROW (1973) See EXPRESS ARIS (2000)

GREEN BAY (1965)
11021 grt; 920 psrs
523' x 72' x 24' (158.5 x 21.8 x 7.3 m)
Geared turbine engine via single screw.
Owned by Central Gulf Steamship Co, New Orleans, she was broken up as a passenger-cargo ship in Hong Kong in 1972. She had been raised and towed from the Qui Nhon harbour bed, South Vietnam, where she sank on 17 August 1971 following several explosions from underwater magnetic mines attached to the ship's hull by Viet Cong frogmen.
Built by Kaiser Corporation, Vancouver, Washington, for the US Maritime Administration as the Class C4-S-A3 troop carrier MARINE MARLIN (1945).

GREEN EMERALD (1980) See OUR LADY OF BANNEUX (1999)

GREEN FOREST (1967)
10645 grt; 2000 psrs
523' x 71' x 24' (159.3 x 21.7 x 7.3 m)
Geared turbine engine via single screw.
Owned by the Central Gulf Steamship Co, New Orleans, she was broken up as a cargo ship for scrap at Kaohsiung in 1980.
Built by Kaiser Corporation, Richmond, California, for the US Maritime Corporation as the Class C4-S-A1 troop carrier GENERAL WILLIAM M. BLACK (AP-135) (1944). Renamed GENERAL W. M. BLACK, USAT (1946 – US Army) and GENERAL W. M. BLACK, USNS (T-AP-135) (1950). She acted as a refugee transport ship after World War Two until she was laid up for the years 1956–66.

GREEN LAKE (1965)
11021 grt; 920 psrs
523' x 71' x 24' (158.5 x 21.8 x 7.3 m)
Geared turbine engine via single screw.
Owned by the Central Gulf Steamship Co, New Orleans, she was broken up as a cargo ship for scrap at Kaohsiung in 1978.
Built by Kaiser Corporation, Vancouver, Washington, for the US Shipping Administration as the Class C4-S-A3 troop carrier ERNIE PYLE (1945). After World War Two she was converted to a passenger liner involved in migrant transportation.

GREEN PORT (1967)
10645 grt; 2000 psrs
523' x 71' x 24' (159.3 x 21.7 x 7.3 m)
Westinghouse geared turbine engine via single screw.
Owned by the Central Gulf Steamship Co, New Orleans, she was broken up for scrap at Kaohsiung in 1980.
Built by Kaiser Corporation, Vancouver, Washington, for the US Maritime Corporation as the Class C4-S-A1 troop carrier GENERAL S. D. STURGIS, USS (AP-137) (1944). Renamed GENERAL S. D. STURGIS, USAT (1946 – US Army) and reclassified as the GENERAL S. D. STURGIS, USNS (T-AP-137) (1950 – US Navy). She acted as a refugee transport ship after World War Two until being laid up for the period 1958–66.

GREEN SPRINGS (1968)
10575 grt; 920 psrs
523' x 71' x 24' (158.5 x 21.5 x 7.3 m)
Geared turbine engine via single screw.
Owned by the Central Gulf Steamship Co, New Orleans, she was broken up for scrap at Kaohsiung in 1979.
Built by Kaiser Corporation, Vancouver, Washington, for the US Shipping Administration as the Class C4-S-A3 troop carrier MARINE CARP (T-AP-199) (1945). After World War Two she operated as a migrant ship until she was laid up for the years 1958–66.

GREEN WAVE (1967)
10562 grt; 2000 psrs
523' x 71' x 24' (159.3 x 21.5 x 7.3 m)

Geared turbine engine via single screw.
Owned by the Central Gulf Steamship Co, New Orleans.
Built by Kaiser Corporation, Richmond, California, for the US Navy as the Class C4-S-A1 troop carrier GENERAL C. G. MORTON, USS (AP-138) (1944). Reclassified as the GENERAL C. G. MORTON, USAT (1946 – US Army) and the GENERAL C. G. MORTON, USNS (T-AP-138) (1950 – US Navy).

GREGOR (1913)
3969 grt; 1243 psrs
355' x 44' x 25'6" (108.2 x 13.3 x 7.8 m)
AG Germaniawerft 3-cylinder triple expansion engine via single screw.
Owned by Jebsen & Diederichsen following seizure of the German vessel at Odessa in 1918. She was abandoned as a total constructive loss after stranding in the Black Sea in February 1920.
Built by Germaniawerft, Kiel, for North German Lloyd as the BONN (1895).

GREGORY MORCH (1902) See MUNCHEN (1910)

GREGORY ORDJONIKIDZE (1959) See GRIGORI ORDZHONIKIDZE (1959)

GRENAA (1964) See NORTIA (1999)

GREYHOUND, USS (IX-106) (1943)
3818 grt
376' x 61' x 20'2" (113.9 x 18.5 x 6.1 m)
Fletcher 3-cylinder turbine engines via triple screw.
Broken up for scrap at Stockton, California, in 1949. Ex- the US Navy, via the scrap merchant Walter W Johnson Company, San Francisco.
Built by Delaware River International Shipbuilding & Engine Works, Chester, Pennsylvania, for the Pacific Navigation Co as the YALE (1907). The US Navy acquired her at a cost of US$1,000,000.

GREY MASTER (1973) See HUA LU (1994)

GRIGORI ORDZHONIKIDZE (1959)
4871 grt; 333 psrs
401' x 52' x 17' (121.5 x 15.8 x 5.2 m)
2 x 6-cylinder MAN diesel engines via twin screw.
Built by Mathias-Thesen, Wismar, for Far Eastern Shipping Co, Vladivostok.

GRIPEN VON MALMO (1984) See HELGOLAND (1985)

GRIPSHOLM (1925) See BERLIN (1955)

GRIPSHOLM (1957) See SEA (1996)

GRIPSHOLM (1996) See SAGA ROSE (1997)

GRODNO (1906) See ARGONAUT (1916)

GROOTE BEER (1947) See MARIANNA IV (1968)

GROOTE BEER (1965) See MARIANNA IV (1968)

GROSSER KURFURST (1899) See CITY OF LOS ANGELES (1922)

GROTIUS (1907)
5867 grt; 167 psrs
420' x 48' x 30' (132.3 x 14.6 x 9.1 m)
4-cylinder Maatschappij quadruple expansion engine via single screw.
Broken up in 1931 by Firma Simons, Hendrik Ido Ambacht.
Built by Maatschappij, Rotterdam, for Nederlandsche Steamship Co

GRUNEWALD (1911) See MUNORLEANS (1927)

GRUSIJA (1928)
4857 grt
363' x 51' x 25'2" (110 x 15.5 x 7.6 m)
2 x 12-cylinder Krupp diesel engines via twin screw.
Built by Fred Krupp, Kiel, for the Russian government (Sovtorgflot).

GRUZIA (1928) See GRUSIJA (1928)

GRUZIA (1950)
11030 grt; 904 psrs
518' x 73' x 26' (157 x 22 x 7.9 m)
2 x 8-cylinder Kincaid diesel engines via twin screw.
Broken up for scrap at La Spezia in 1975. Ex-Sovtorflot.
Built by Swan Hunter & Wigham Richardson Ltd, Newcastle, for Gdynia-America Line as the SOBIESKI (1939).

GRUZIYA (1928) See GRUSIJA (1928)

GRUZIYA (1950) See GRUZIA (1950)

GRUZIYA (1975) See VAN GOGH (1999)

GRYF (1967) See CLYDESDALE (1998)

GUADALUPE (1945) See CLIMAX GARNET (1974)

GUADALUPE (1953)
10226 grt; 349 psrs
487' x 62' x 26' (148.5 x 19 x 7.9 m)
10-cylinder Sulzer diesel engine via single screw.
Broken up for scrap at Castellon in 1973.
Laid down by Soc Espanola de Construccion Naval, Bilbao, for Empresa Nacional Eccano SA as the cargo ship MONASTERIO DE GUADALUPE (1951) and completed as GUADALUPE for Cia Trasatlantica.

GUADELOUPE (1928)
10502 grt; 1608 psrs
508' x 58' x 39'5" depth (153.9 x 17.7 x 12 m)
2 x Chantiers de l'Atlantique 3-cylinder triple expansion engines via twin screw.
Broken up for scrap at St Nazaire in 1937. Ex-French Line.
Built by Penhoet, St Nazaire, for CGT as the CHICAGO (1908).

GUAM BEAR (1968) See PACIFIC ENDEAVOUR (1979)

GUANG HUA (1960)
14216 grt; 444 psrs
544' x 69' x 29' (165.8 x 21.1 x 8.8 m)
2 x 8-cylinder B+W diesel engines via twin screw.
Broken up for scrap in 1981. Ex-China Ocean Shipping.
Built by Harland & Wolff Ltd, Belfast, for the Nelson Line as the HIGHLAND PRINCESS (1930). Renamed MARIANNA (1959 – John S. Latsis) and SLAPY (1960 – Czechoslovak Ocean Shipping).

GUARUJA (1921)
4282 grt
362' x 46' x 23'6" (109.7 x 13.9 x 7.2 m)
2 x Sauter-Harle DRG turbine engines via single screw.
Abandoned after grounding ashore and breaking in two at Punta Polacra on 2 January 1938.
Built by Forges et Chantiers de la Mediterranee, La Seyne, for Cie de Navigation France-Amerique, Marseilles.

GUATEMALA (1928) See JOHN L. CLEM (1941)

GUAYAMA (1975)
11400 grt; 2000 psrs
526' x 73' x 31' (159.4 x 22 x 9.3 m)
2 x Westinghouse DRG turbine engines via single screw.
Owned by the Puerto Rico Maritime Shipping Authority.
Built by Kaiser & Co, Richmond, Virginia, for the US Navy as a Class C4-S-A1 troop transport GENERAL E. T. COLLINS (AP-147) (1944). Renamed as a container ship NEW ORLEANS (1969 – Container Ship Chartering Service, Wilmington).

GUELPH (1894) See CARAQUET (1913)

GUGLIELMO MARCONI (1963) See COSTA RIVIERA (1994)

GUGLIELMO PIERCE (1920) See MOUZINHO (1930)

GUILDFORD CASTLE (1911)
7995 grt; 412 psrs
470' x 56' x 27' (142.4 x 17 x 8.2 m)
Quadruple expansion engines via twin screw.
Sank on 1 June 1933, with the loss of two lives, after colliding with the Blue Funnel steamer STENTOR in the River Elbe, Germany.
Built by Barclay, Curle & Co, Glasgow, for the Union-Castle Line.

GUISEPPE VERDI (1963) See VERDI (1963)

GUJARAT (1913)
4148 grt; 60 psrs
370' x 48' x 25'6" (112.1 x 14.5 x 7.8 m)
Harland & Wolff 6-cylinder compound engine via single screw.
Built by Harland & Wolff Ltd, Glasgow, for Bucknall Line as the FORT SALISBURY (1895). Renamed VINCENT (1912 – Booth Line).

GU LANG YU (1979) See TONG HU (1992)

GU LANG YU (1984) See NEW ORIENT PRINCESS (1992)

GULCEMAL (1928)
5071 grt; 1700 psrs
455' x 46' x 24'6" (137.9 x 13.9 x 7.4 m)
3-cylinder triple expansion engine via single screw.
Broken up for scrap at Messina in 1950 after spending her last days as a floating hotel. Ex-Turkish Maritime Lines.
Built by Harland & Wolff Ltd, Belfast, for the White Star Line at a cost of £100,000 as the GERMANIC (1875). Renamed OTTAWA (1905 – Dominion Line) and GUL DJEMAL (1910 – Imperial Ottoman government).

GUL DJEMAL (1910) See GULCEMAL (1928)

GULF FANTASY (1994)
8115 grt; 377 psrs
463' x 58' x 18' (140.3 x 17.6 x 5.5 m)
2 x 8-cylinder MAN diesel engines + 2 x Turbinfabrik DRG gas turbines via twin screw.
Broken up for scrap in Mumbai in 1999 after being a hotel accommodation ship in Dubai.
Built by Mathias-Thesen, Wismar, for the East German government as the FRITZ HECKERT (1961) and used as a floating army barracks from 1970.

GULF OF GENOA (1891) See ALTENBURG (1903)

GULF OF MEXICO (1893) See YAHIKO MARU (1904)

GULFPORT (1942) See DAVID C. SHANKS (T-AP-180) (1950)

GULLFOSS (1950) See MECCA (1975)

GUMHURYAT MISR (1953) See AL WADI (1960)

GUNUNG DJATI (1959) See KRI TANJUNG PANDAN (1977)

GURGEN-2 (1996)
42178 grt; 950 psrs
150 cars
328' x 50' x 14' (99.4 x 15 x 4.2 m)
5-cylinder Fiat diesel engines via twin screw.
Owned by Gurgen Turizm ve Ticaret AS.
Built by Cantieri Navale Apuania, Carrara, for the Adriatic Line as the passenger-car ferry JACAPO TINTORETTO (1966 – Adriatic Line). Renamed TINTORETTO (1983 – Adriatic Line), SARA I (1990 – Baltic Sea Co), FARAH I (1993 – El Salam Shipping & Trading Establishment) and EL SALAM 94 (1994 – El Salam Shipping & Trading Establishment).

GUSTAVUS VICTORY (1945) See SANTA FE (1947)

GUSTAV VASA (1965) See EUROFAST (2000)

GUSTAV VASA (1973) See NORRONA (1996)

GWALIOR (1900)
4219 grt; 300 psrs
389' x 46' x 23'7" (117.9 x 13.9 x 7.2 m)
J Elder 2-cylinder inverted compound engine via single screw.
Broken up for scrap in Italy in 1911. Ex-British India Line.
Built by John Elder & Co, Glasgow, for New Zealand Shipping Co as the RUAPEHU (1884). Renamed ZAYATHIA (1899 – British India Line).

GYOKURYU (1975) See GOLDEN BRIDGE (1990)

HABANA (1931) See GALICIA (1962)

HABIB (1978)
16168 grt; 1150 psrs
350 cars or 76 trailers
470' x 77' x 20' (144.5 x 23.3 x 6.2 m)
4 x 8-cylinder Wartsila diesel engines (installed in 2000) via twin screw.
Ice-strengthened passenger ferry operated by Cotunav.
Built by Nobiskrug Werft, Rendsburg, for Vie Tunisienne de Navigation SA, Tunis.

HACKNESS (1913) See MINIOTA (1916)

HAE YON (1985) See AL JAWAHER (1988)

HAI DA (1986)
7989 grt; 188 psrs
481' x 66' x 23' (146.6 x 20 x 7 m)
2 x 11-cylinder B+W diesel engines via twin screw.
Passenger-cargo ship owned by China Shipping Passenger Liner Co Ltd and operated by the Shanghai Hai Xing Shipping Company, Shanghai. She was broken up for scrap in southern China in 1999.
Built by John Brown & Co Ltd, Clydebank, for the Blue Funnel Line, Singapore, at a cost of £2,000,000 as the CENTAUR (1964). Renamed HAO LONG (1985 – Richown Shipping & Enterprise Ltd).

HAI HUA (1989)
13547 grt; 71 psrs
529' x 76' x 26' (161.2 x 23.1 x 7.9 m)
8-cylinder Cockerill-B+W diesel engines via twin screw.
Passenger-cargo ship owned by China Shipping Passenger Liner Co Ltd and operated by Shanghai Hai Xing Shipping Company, Shanghai. She was broken up for scrap in southern China in 1999.
Built by John Cockerill Shipyards, Hoboken, Belgium, for Cie Maritime Belge as the FABIOLAVILLE (1972).

HAI LOR (1900)
5606 grt; 1700 psrs
431' x 47' x 34'5" depth (131.2 x 14.2 x 10.5 m)
Laird Brothers 2-cylinder compound engine via single screw.
Under the ownership of the Chinese Eastern Railway Co, she was deliberately sunk as a block ship in Port Arthur in 1904.
Built by Laird Bros, Birkenhead, for Cunard Steamship Co as the CEPHALONIA (1882).

HAIMON (1922) See PIRANGY (1928)

HAI SHANG SHI JIE (1998)
14225 grt; 450 psrs
549' x 71' x 21' (167.3 x 21.6 x 6.4 m)
2 x 12-cylinder B+W diesel engines via twin screw.
Built by Chantiers de l'Atlantique, St Nazaire, for Cie De Navigation Paquet as the passenger-cargo ship ANCERVILLE (1962). Renamed MINGHUA (1973 – China Ocean Shipping Co) and SEA WORLD (1984 – Sea World Ltd as a floating hotel in the Pearl River Holiday Resort at Shek Kou Bay).

HAITI (1932) See ADANA (1948)

HAI XING (1981) See HERBERT (1996)

HAI YANG DAO (1995)
15560 grt; 938 psrs
226 cars
446' x 77' x 18' (135 x 23.4 x 5.4 m)
2 x 9-cylinder Stork-Werkspoor diesel engines via twin screw.
Passenger-car ferry operating on the China–South Korea service for the Dalian Steam Shipping Company, Dalian.
Built by Van der Geissen, Krimpen, for the Dalian Steam Shipping Company, Dalian.

HAI YING (1985) See OUR LADY OF BANNEUX (1999)

HAKATU (1973) See FERRY KANPU (1984)

HAKKODA MARU (1964)
8300 grt; 1200 psrs
48 rail coaches
433' x 59' x 17' (131.2 x 17.9 x 5.2 m)
8 x 16-cylinder MAN diesel engines via twin screw.
Passenger-train ferry owned by the Japanese government and operated by the Seikan Railway Ferry Co as a floating museum in Aomori harbour.
Built by Mitsubishi Heavy Industries Ltd, Kobe.

HAKONE MARU (1921)
10423 grt; 307 psrs
498' x 62' x 29' (150.9 x 18.9 x 8.0 m)
6 x Mitsubishi turbine engines via twin screw.
Sank in the Straits of Formosa on 27 November 1943 after being attacked by US aircraft.
Built by Mitsubishi Dockyard, Nagasaki, for NYK as a passenger-cargo ship.

HAKONE MARU (1956)
8853 grt; 312 psrs
448' x 60' x 35'6" (136.5 x 18.2 x 10.8 m)
Harland & Wolff Ltd 16-cylinder diesel engines via twin screw.
Broken up for scrap in Japan in 1957. Ex-Okadagumi Ltd, Japan.
Built by William Beardmore & Company, Dalmuir, for the Adelaide Steamship Company as the MANUNDA (1929).

HAKOZAKI MARU (1922)
10413 grt; 307 psrs
495' x 62' x 29' (150 x 18.9 x 8.9 m)
6 x Mitsibishi turbine engines via twin screw.
Sank on 19 March 1945 after being torpedoed by the US submarine BALAO in the East China Sea, north of Shanghai.
Built by Mitsubishi Dockyard, Nagasaki, for NYK as a passenger-cargo ship.

HAKUSAN MARU (1923)
10380 grt; 307 psrs
495' x 62' x 29' (150 x 18.9 x 8.9 m)
6 x Mitsubishi turbine engines via twin screw.
Sank on 4 June 1944 after being torpedoed by the US submarine FLIER, south-west of Iwo Jima and west of Io Island.
Built by Mitsubishi Dockyard, Nagasaki for NYK as a passenger-cargo ship.

HALEAKALA (1923) See TASIKMALAJA (1951)

HALEP (1912)
3684 grt; 695 psrs
362' x 44' x 28'5" depth (109.7 x 13.3 x 8.6 m)
R Napier & Sons 3-cylinder triple expansion engine via single screw.
Broken up under the ownership of the Turkish government after refloating her from where she beached in the Sea of Marmora. This followed followed a torpedo attack by the British submarine E-11 on 25 August 1915.
Built by Napier & Miller, Glasgow, for the Aberdeen Line as the ABERDEEN (1881).

HALGAN (1821) See CAP LAY (1925)

HALIFAX (1903) See MONTREAL (1905)

HALLE (1896) See IRIS (1924)

HA LONG (1975) See MEDOUSA (1997)

HALSSKOV (1956) See AL QAMAR (1999)

HAMAROY (1993)
3695 grt; 399 psrs
105 cars
277' x 50' x 13'6" (84 x 15 x 4.1 m)
Bergen-Normo 6-cylinder diesel engine via twin screw.
Passenger-car ferry owned and operated by Finnmark Fylkes. Features include

aft uptake vents and a stern bridge in a pseudo-double ender profile.
Built by Ofotens.

HAMAYU (1971) See SUPERFERRY 3 (1993)

HAMAYUU (1998)
16187 grt; 500 psrs
41 cars + 76 trailers
535' x 78' x 18'5" (162 x 23.6 x 5.6 m)
2 x 8-cylinder Daihatsu diesel engines via twin screw.
Passenger-car-cargo ferry owned and operated by Kampu Ferry, Japan.
Built by Mitsubishi Industries, Shimonoseki.

HAMBURG (1900) See PRESIDENT FILLMORE (1922)

HAMBURG (1914) See PRESIDENT FILLMORE (1922)

HAMBURG (1926) See YURI DOLGORUKI (1950)

HAMBURG (1954) See ORIENTAL WARRIOR (1967)

HAMBURG (1969) See MAXIM GORKI (1974)

HAMBURG (1987) See ADMIRAL OF SCANDINAVIA (1997)

HAMDALE (1927) See TOZAN MARU (1937)

HAMILTON (1899) See HAMILTON (1922)

HAMILTON (1922)
3723 grt; 145 psrs
350' x 42' x 17' (106.1 x 12.7 x 5.2 m)
Delaware River Co 3-cylinder triple expansion engines via single screw.
Broken up for scrap at Baltimore in 1932. Ex-Old Dominion Steamship Co.
Built by Delaware River Co, Chester, Pennsylvania, for Old Dominion Co as the HAMILTON (1899). Renamed SARANAC, USS (1919 – U.S. Navy).

HAMLET (1968)
3693 grt; 800 psrs
85 cars
246' x 54' x 12'6" (74.4 x 16.5 x 3.8 m)
2 x 8-cylinder MaK diesel engines via twin screw.

Passenger-car ferry owned and operated by Traghetti Pozzuoli and Agostino Lauro.
Built by Vulkan, Vegesack.

HAMMERSHUS (1965) See KRALJICA MIRA (1994)

HAMMONIA (1980) See ARKONA (1985)

HAMONIC (1909)
5265 grt
350' x 50' x 32' depth (106 x 15.2 x 9.7 m)
Collingwood 4-cylinder quadruple expansion engines via single screw.
Burnt out as a total constructive loss at Sarnia in 1945.
Built by Copllingwood Shipbuilding Co Ltd, Collingwood, Ontario, for Canada Steamship Lines Ltd.

HANAA (1992)
7963 grt; 706 psrs

130 cars
424' x 56' x 17' (128.6 x 17.4 x 5.2 m)
2 x 18-cylinder Pielstick diesel engines via twin screw.
Passenger-car ferry owned by General National Maritime Transport Co, Tripoli, and operated by the Libyan government.
Built by Hayashikane Shipbuilding, Nagasaki, for Terukini Yusan KK, Kagoshima, as the QUEEN CORAL (1972). Renamed QUEEN VERGINA (1987 – Comanav) and RIF (1988 – Comanav).

HANAMET (1906)
3013 grt
380' x 38' x 28'5" depth (115.2 x 11.5 x 8.6 m)
William Denny & Brothers 3-cylinder triple expansion engines via single screw.
Broken up for scrap at in Danzig in 1925. Ex-W Katz.
Built by R Duncan & Co, Port Glasgow, for Duke of Sutherland Steamship Co Ltd as the DUKE OF SUTHERLAND (1873). Renamed MACQUARIE (1904 – W & A McArthur Ltd).

HANH PHUC (1989) See ARTEMIS I (1996)

HANIA (1965) See SIRIUS (1971)

HANIL CAR FERRY No. 2 (1991)
3195 grt; 439 psrs
347' x 63' x 15'6" (105 x 19 x 4.7 m)
2 x 12-cylinder Pielstick diesel engines via twin screw.
Owned and operated by Hanil Express Co Ltd, South Korea.
Built by Imabari Shipbuilding, Imabari, for Silver Ferry KK, Higashihinon, as the FERRY HACHINOHE (1979).

HANKYU No. 6 (1968) See FERRY KAMPU ( )

HANKYU No. 16 (1976) See FERRY PUKWAN (1983)

HANKYU No. 17 (1973) See FERRY KAMPU (1984)

HANKYU No. 24 (1976) See St JOSEPH THE WORKER (1995)

HANKYU No. 32 (1976) See St PETER THE APOSTLE (1993)

HANNA (1905) See READY (1931)

HANNOVER (1955) See ORIENTAL INVENTOR (1966)

HANOVERIAN (1903) See DEVONIAN (1923)

HANSA (1921)
16703 grt; 1386 psrs
684' x 67' x 40'4" depth (208.5 x 20.3 x 12.3 m)
AG Vulkan 12-cylinder (later changed to 4-cylinders)
Quadruple expansion engines via twin screw.
Broken up for scrap in Hamburg in 1925. Ex-Hamburg-America Line.
Built by Vulkan Shipyards, Stettin, for the Hamburg-America Line as the DEUTSCHLAND (1900). Renamed VICTORIA LUISE (1911 – Hamburg-America Line).

HANSA (1935) See SOJUS (1980)

HANSA EXPRESS (1962) See CLYDESDALE (1998)

HANSA LINK (1990) See MOBY RIDER (1998)

HANSEATIC (1958)
30029 grt; 1252 psrs
672' x 83' x 30' (203.6 x 25.2 x 9.1 m)
6 x Parsons SRG turbine engines via twin screw.
Broken up for scrap by Eisen-und-Metall AG at Hamburg in 1967 for a tender fee of Dm.15,000,000. She had been towed from New York where a severe fire virtually destroyed the ship following a diesel oil lcak from a ruptured fuel line. This had ignited the engine room at 7.30 am on 7 September 1966. Ex-Hamburg-America Line.
Built by Fairfield Shipbuilding & Engineering Co Ltd, Glasgow, for the Canadian Pacific Steamship Company as the EMPRESS OF JAPAN (1930).

Renamed EMPRESS OF SCOTLAND (1942 – Hamburg-America Line) and SCOTLAND (1958 – British Ministry of Transport).

HANSEATIC (1967) See SUN (1996)

HANSEATIC (1973) See MAXIM GORKI (1974)

HANSEATIC (1993)
8378 grt; 188 psrs
406' x 59' x 15'6" (123 x 18 x 4.7 m)
2 x 8-cylinder Krupp-MaK diesel engines via twin screw.
Ice-strengthened cruise ship owned by a group of German investors headed by Herr A Bolten, Hamburg, and cruising for Hanseatic Cruises, Hamburg.
Built by Rauma Repola for Society Expedition Cruises as the SOCIETY ADVENTURER (1990) at a cost of US$68,000,000.

HANSEATIC RENAISSANCE (1991) See MEGASTAR SAGITTARIUS (2000)

HANS GUTZEIT (1972) See FINNMAID (1997)

HAO LONG (1985) See HAI DA (1986)

HAPPY DOLPHIN (1999)
7187 grt; 1149 psrs
280 cars
390' x 59' x 14'6" (118.2 x 17.8 x 4.4 m)
4 x 7-cylinder MAN diesel engines via twin screw.

Ice-strengthened passenger-car ferry owned by Millennium Shipping Ltd and operated by Happy Lines.Built by Werft Nobiskrug, Rendsburg, for British & Irish Steam Packet Company as the INNISFALLEN (1969). Renamed CORSICA (1980 – Corsica Ferries, Panama), CORSICA VIVA (1980 – Corsica Ferries, Panama), DOMINICAN (1985 – on charter from Corsica Ferries), CORSICA VIVA I (1988 – Corsica Ferries, Panama), SARDINIA VIVA (1992 – Sardinia Ferries), CARIBA VIVA (1994 – Tourship Italia SpA) and SPIRIT OF INDEPENDENCE (1995 – Meridian Ferries).

HAPPY PRINCESS (1987) See PRINCESS OF NEGROS (1994)

HARBIN (1900)
3559 grt; 732 psrs
410' x 39' x 27'9" (124.2 x 11.8 x 8.5 m)
Palmer 3-cylinder compound engine via single screw.
Owned by the Chinese Eastern Railway, she was scuttled by the Russians in March 1904 at Port Arthur.
Built by Harland & Wolff Ltd, Belfast, for the British Shipowners Company as the BRITISH KING (1881). Renamed WERKENDAM (1889 – Holland America Line).

HARIMA MARU (1914) See ANAHUAC (1924)

HARLECH CASTLE (1894) See AMAZONAS (1923)

HARMODIUS (1900) See KUT (1919)

HARMONIDES (1901) See KHARTUM (1919)

HARNETT, USS (APA-240) (1945) See RYE (1963)

HARRIS, USS (AP-8) (1940) See PRESIDENT GRANT (1946)

HARRIS, USS (T-AP-2) (1943) See PRESIDENT GRANT (1946)

HARRISBURG, USS (1917) See PHILADELPHIA (1920)

HARRY LEE, USS (AP-17) (1940) See TARSUS (1946)

HARRY LEE, USS (APA-10) (1943) See TARSUS (1946)

HARSHA VARDHANA (1974)
8871 grt; 753 psrs
438' x 71' x 23' (132.6 x 21.5 x 7 m)
6-cylinder Sulzer diesel engines via single screw.
Passenger ferry operated by the Shipping Corporation of India Ltd.
Built by Mazagon Dock Ltd, Mumbai.

HARUNA MARU (1922)
10421 grt; 307 psrs
495' x 62' x 29' (150 x 18.8 x 8.9 m)
6 x Mitsubishi turbine engines via twin screw.
Abandoned as a total constructive loss after stranding herself off Surga Bay and finally sinking on 7 July 1942.
Built by Mitsubishi Dockyard, Nagasaki, for NYK as a passenger-cargo ship.

HARVARD, USS (1898) See NEW YORK (1921)

HARVARD (1916) See HARVARD (1920)

HARVARD (1920)
3818 grt
376' x 61' x 20'2" (113.9 x 18.5 x 6.1 m)
3 x W & A Fletcher turbine engines via triple screw.
Owned by the Matson Line and operated by the Los Angeles Steamship Co (LASSCO), she was wrecked on Point Arguello, California, near Santa Barbara on 30 May 30 1931.
Built by the Delaware River International Shipbuilding & Engine Works, Chester, Pennsylvania, for the Metropolitan Steamship Company as the HARVARD (1916). Renamed CHARLES, USS (1916 – US Navy acquisition for US$1,000,000).

HAVANA (1898) See ALEUTIAN (1923)

HAVANA (1906) See SHAMROCK (1943)

HAVANA (1927) See SHAMROCK (1943)

HAVELET (1989) See SVETI STEFAN (2000)

HAVELLAND (1922) See EMPIRE DEBEN (1945)

HAVEN (1948)
4088 grt; 140 psrs
361' x 47' x 22'9" (109 x 14.4 x 6.9 m)
Clyde Shipbuilding & Engineering 3-cylinder triple expansion engine via single screw.
Broken up for scrap in Japan in 1955. Ex-Wah Sing Shang Steamship Company, Singapore.
Built by Clyde Shipbuilding & Engineering Company, Glasgow, for the Burns Philp & Co Ltd, Sydney, as the MONTORO (1910).

HAVERFORD (1901)
11635 grt; 1850 psrs
550' x 59' x 27'2" (167.6 x 18 x 8.2 m)
John Brown Ltd 6-cylinder triple expansion engines via twin screw.
Broken up for scrap in Italy in 1925. Ex-Dominion Line.
Built by John Brown & Co Ltd, Clydebank, for the American Line.

HAWAII BEAR (1968) See CARIBE ENTERPRISE (1981)

HAWAII MARU (1915)
9482 grt
475' x 61' x 27'9" (143.9 x 18.5 x 8.5 m)
Kawasaki 6-cylinder triple expansion engines via twin screw.
Sank on 2 December 1944 after being torpedoed by the US SEA DEVIL in

the East China Sea.
Built by the Kawasaki Dockyard, Nagasaki, for the OSK Line.

HAWARDEN CASTLE (1883) See CYRIL (1904)

HAWKES BAY (1912) See MAR BIANCO (1938)

HAWKEYE STATE (1921) See HUGH L. SCOTT, USS (AP-43)
(1942)

HAYATOMO MARU (1977) See OUR LADY OF MANAOAG
(1992)

HAYWOOD, USS (APA-6) (1941)
8378 grt; 80 psrs
495' x 56' x 35'2" depth (150 x 17 x 10.7 m)
2 x Westinghouse DRG turbine engines via single screw.
Broken up for scrap at Baltimore in 1956. Ex-US Navy.
Built by Bethlehem Shipbuilding Corporation, Alameda, California, for the
US Shipping Board as the STEADFAST (1919). Renamed CITY OF
BALTIMORE (1919 – Baltimore Mail Line).

HEBRIDEAN ISLES (1985)
3040 grt; 507 psrs
68 cars
281' x 54' x 10' (85.2 x 16.3 x 3.1 m)
2 x 8-cylinder Mirrlees diesel engines via twin screw.
Passenger-car ferry owned and operated by Caledonian MacBrayne, Scotland.
Built by Cochrane Shipbuilders Ltd, Selby.

HEBRIDES (2000)
5500 grt; 595 psrs
110 cars
327' x 52' x 10'6" (99 x 15.8 x 3.2 m)
2 x 8-cylinder MaK diesel engines via twin screw.
Passenger-car ferry owned and operated by Caledonian MacBrayne.
Built by Ferguson Shipbuilding.

HECTOR (1924)
11198 grt; 175 psrs
499' x 62' x 26'4" (151.2 x 18.8 x 8 m)
3 x Harland & Wolff DRG turbine engines via twin screw.
Broken up for scrap in 1946 after raising her from Colombo harbour. She sank
here on 5 April 1942 following an attack by Japanese bombers.
Built by Scotts Shipbuilding Co, Greenock, for the Blue Funnel Line.

HECTOR (1950)
10125 grt; 53 psrs
523' x 69' x 31' depth (158.5 x 20.9 x 9.4 m)
Mitsubishi 16-cylinder geared turbine engine via single screw.
Broken up for scrap at Kaohsiung in 1972.
Built by Harland & Wolff Ltd, Belfast, for the Blue Funnel Line.

HECUBA (1922)
7532 grt; 1720 psrs
429' x 54' x 39'6" depth (130.8 x 16.6 x 12 m)
Bremer Vulkan 8-cylinder quadruple expansion engines via twin screw.
Broken up for scrap in 1925. Ex-Alfred Holt.
Built by Bremer Vulkan, Vegesack, for North German Lloyd as the
BRANDENBURG (1902).

HEIAN MARU (1930)
11616 grt; 330 psrs
523' x 69' x 30' (155.9 x 20 x 9.2 m)
2 x 8-cylinder B+W diesel engines via twin screw.
Sank on 18 February 1944 after being attacked at night by US aircraft from an
aircraft carrier in Truk Lagoon, South Pacific.
Built by the Osaka Iron Works, Osaka, for NYK, Japan, as a passenger-cargo
ship.

HEIMDAL (1989)
9975 grt; 500 psrs
290 cars
435' x 66' x 18'6" (131.7 x 20.1 x 6.2 m)

12-cylinder MaK diesel engines via single screw.

Passenger-car ferry owned by Mercandia and operated by International
Maritime, although the ship has been laid up in Scandlines livery since mid-
1999.
Built by Frederikshavn Y & F, Frederikshavn, for Mercandia as the RoRo
cargo vessel MERCANDIAN PRINCE II (1982). Renamed FERRYMAR I
(1988 – KS Mercandia-Scandia XXXV, Copenhagen) and ADMIRAL II
(1988 – KS Mercandia).

HEINRICH JESSEN (1940) See ARU MARINER (1964)

HEIYO MARU (1930)
9816 grt
460' x 60' x 30'2" (139.4 x 18.2 x 9.2 m)
2 x Mitsubishi 16-cylinder diesel engines via single screw.
Sank on 17 January 1943 after being struck by a torpedo fired from the USS
WHALE north-east of Truk Island, South Pacific.
Built by Osaka Iron Works, Osaka, for NYK.

HEKLA (1884) See MINSK (1909)

HEKTORIA (1928)
13797 grt; 320 psrs
570' x 63' x 32'6" (173.7 x 19.2 x 9.8 m)
Quadruple expansion engines via twin screw.
Owned by AS Hektor (N. Bugge), Tonsberg, she sank on 12 September 1942,
with the loss of one life, after being torpedoed by the German U-608 in the
mid-Atlantic as a whaling mother ship.
Built by Harland & Wolff Ltd, Belfast, for the White Star Line as the MEDIC
(1899).

HELEANNA (1966)
11674 grt; 620 psrs
220 cars
549' x 66' x 30'2" (167.3 x 20 x 9.2 m)
2 x 9-cylinder Gotaverken diesel engines via single screw.
Currently a dumb lighter in Toulon following the purchase of the hulk by the
port authorities from the shipbreakers, Siana Lotti. Owned by CF Efthymiadis,
Piraeus, the vessel was destroyed by a raging inferno started by a kitchen gas
cylinder explosion on 28 August 1971, 25 miles (42 km) off Brindisi. She was
towed to the latter port where 24 bodies were taken from the ship.
Built by Gotaverken, Gothenburg, for the Munkedals AB Line as the oil tanker
MUNKEDAL (1954).

HELENE (1963) See CARINA II (1967)

HELENUS (1949)
10129 grt; 53 psrs
523' x 69' x 31' (158.5 x 20.9 x 9.4 m)
3 x Harland & Wolff DRG turbine engines via single screw.
Broken up at Kaohsiung in 1972.
Built by Harland & Wolff Ltd, Belfast, for the Blue Funnel Line.

HELGOLAND (1900) See POLYXENA (1914)

HELGOLAND (1963) See BALTIC STAR (1976)

HELGOLAND (1985)
3464 grt; 1890 psrs
344' x 50' x 13' (104.1 x 15.2 x 4 m)

2 x 16-cylinder Pielstick diesel engines via twin screw.

Ice-strengthened passenger ferry owned and operated by Bremerhaven & Helgoland Line GmbH & Co.
Built by Blohm & Voss, Hamburg, for the Hamburg-America Line as the WAPPEN VON HAMBURG (1962). Renamed WAPPEN (1964 – Skagen Line), ALTO LIEBE (1966 – Hamburg-America Line), HELGOLAND (1984 – Rederi D Altmann) and GRIPEN VON MALMO (1984 – Rederi AB Gripen).

HELIOPOLIS (1907) See ROYAL GEORGE (1910)

HELIOPOLIS (1916) See PERSEUS (1926)

HELIPOLIS (1905) See PERSEUS (1926)

HELIUS (1903) See TIRIMUJGHIAN (1906)

HELLAS (1959) See DORIC FERRY (1982)

HELLAS (1978) See AL MANSOUR (1997)

HELLAS (1980) See AL MANSOUR (1997)

HELLENIC PRINCE (1948)
6558 grt; 1000 psrs
444' x 61' x 28'2" (135.3 x 18.5 x 8.5 m)
4 x Parsons SRG turbine engines via twin screw.
Broken up for scrap by Pacific Salvage Co Ltd in Hong Kong in 1954. Ex-China Hellenic Lines.
Built by the Cockatoo Island Dockyard, Sydney, for the Royal Australian Navy as the seaplane carrier ALBATROSS, HMAS (1929). Renamed ALBATROSS, HMS (1938 – British Royal Navy) and PRIDE OF TORQUAY (1947 – South Western Steam Navigation Co). Acted in the role of a migrant ship after World War Two.

HELLIG OLAV (1903)
10085 grt; 1170 psrs
520' x 58' x 29'2" (158.5 x 17.7 x 8.8 m)
A Stephen & Sons 6-cylinder triple expansion engines via twin screw.
Broken up for scrap by Hughes Bolckow at Blyth, Scotland, in 1934.
Built by Alexander Stephen & Sons, Glasgow, for Det Forenede DS, Copenhagen.

HELSINKI EXPRESS (1965) See ARION (1976)

HEMPSTEAD, USS (APA-241) (1943) See ALCOA CAVALIER (1947)

HENGIST (1972) See EXPRESS ARTEMIS (2000)

HENG LI (1993)
16653 grt; 365 psrs
563' x 70' x 30' (171.6 x 21.3 x 9 m)
2 x Bethlehem Steel Corporation DRG turbine engines via twin screw.
Broken up for scrap in Alang, India, in 1996. Ex-Beihai Hai Tai International Shipping Co Ltd, China.
Built by Bethlehem Shipyards, Quincy, Massachusetts, for the US Maritime Commission as the Class C4 cargo ship PINE TREE MARINER (1952). Renamed MARIPOSA (1956 – Matson Line), JIN JIANG (1984 – Guangzhou Ocean Shipping Co) and QUEEN OF JIN JIANG (1993 – Guangzhou Ocean Shipping Company).

HENRIETTA (1959) See MARIANNA (1960)

HENRIETTA LATSIS (1964) See MARIANNA LATSIS (1966)

HENRIETTA LATSIS (1966)
23580 grt; 1200 psrs
665' x 82' x 30' (202.7 x 24.8 x 9.1 m)
6 x SRG turbine engines via twin screw.
Broken up as a pilgrim ship for scrap by Terrestre Marittima SpA at La Spezia, Italy, in 1969. Ex-Latsis Lines.
Built by Vickers-Armstrong Ltd, Newcastle, for the P&O Line as the STRATHMORE (1935). Renamed MARIANNA LATSIS (1963 – Latsis Lines).

HENRI POINCARE (1953) See GALILEO FERRARIS (1957)

HENRY GIBBINS (T-AP 183) (1950) See BAY STATE (1973)

HENRY OSBORNE (1972)
6787 grt; 750 psrs
358' x 62' x 14'6" (108.5 x 18.8 x 4.4 m)
4 x SRG turbine engines via twin screw.
Broken up for scrap at Bilbao in 1974. Ex-Union Pipe & Machinery Co Ltd, Montreal.
Built by Fairfield Shipbuilding & Engineering Co Ltd, Glasgow, for Canadian Pacific Railway Co as the NANAIMO (1950). Renamed PRINCESS OF NANAIMO (1951 – Canadian Pacific Railway Co), PRINCESS OF ACADIA (1963 – Canadian Pacific Railway Co)) and PRINCESS OF NANAIMO (1971 – Canadian Pacific Railway Co).

HENRY R. MALLORY (1916)
6063 grt; 100 psrs
440' x 54' x 33'9" depth (133.3 x 16.4 x 10.3 m)
Newport News 3-cylinder triple expansion engine via single screw.
Sank on 7 February 1943, after being hit by single torpedoes from the German submarines U-609 and U-625 patrolling the North Atlantic. A total of 263 lives were lost, but 232 were rescued by the US Coastguard cutter BIBB.
Built by Newport News Shipbuilding, Newport News, Virginia, for Mallory Steamship Co.

HENRY T. ALLEN (1940) See PRESIDENT JEFFERSON (1947)

HENRY T. ALLEN, USS (APA-15) (1942) See PRESIDENT JEFFERSON (1947)

HENRY T. ALLEN, USS (AG-90) (1945) See PRESIDENT JEFFERSON (1947)

HERA (1988) See SUPERFERRY 6 (1993)

HERAKLION (1965)
8922 grt; 300 psrs
498' x 60' x 27'6" (150.9 x 18.2 x 8.4 m)
Geared turbine engine via single screw.
Owned by Typaldos Lines, she sank in 15 minutes on 8 December 1966, with 241 lives lost, near Falconcra in the Cyclades (Greek Islands). A 16-ton refrigerated trailer had broken away from its restraining chains on the motor vehicle deck and smashed through the Ro-Ro doors, letting the Aegean Sea pour into the ship.
Built as the LEICESTERSHIRE (1949) by Fairfield Shipbuilding & Engineering Co Ltd, Glasgow, for the Bibby Line.

HERALD OF FREE ENTERPRISE (1980) See FLUSHING RANGE (1987)

HERAN MARU (1923)
3460 grt; 895 psrs
25 railway wagons
362' x 52' x 14' (109.7 x 15.9 x 4.3 m)
Passenger-train ferry sunk by US bombers outside Aomori harbour on 14 July 1945.
Built by Mitsubishi Heavy Industries, Nagasaki, for the Seikan Railway Ferries Co.

HERBERT (1996)
12191 grt; 289 psrs
585' x 70' x 27' (178.3 x 21.3 x 8.2 m)
2 x 6-cylinder MAN diesel engines via twin screw.
Broken up in Alang, India, in 1996. Ex-China Ocean Shipping.
Built by Wilton-Fijenoord, Schiedam, for Holland Africa Line as the passenger-cargo ship RANDFONTEIN (1958). Renamed NIEUW HOLLAND (1971 – Royal Interocean Lines), YU HUA (1975 – China Ocean Shipping) and HAI XING (1981 – China Ocean Shipping).

HERCULES (1917) See PHILIPPINES (1919)

HERCULES (1992) See LEFKA ORI (2000)

HEREDIA (1908) See HEREDIA (1937)

HEREDIA (1937)
4943 grt; 103 psrs
379' x 50' x 25' (114.8 x 15.2 x 7.6 m)
Triple expansion engine via single screw.
Owned by United Fruit Steamship Co, she sank on 19 May 1942 after being hit by a torpedo in the Gulf of Mexico.
Built by Workman, Clark & Co Ltd, Belfast, for the United Fruit Steamship Company, London, as the HEREDIA (1908). Renamed GENERAL PERSHING (1932 – States Steamship Co).

HERMAEA (1962)
4447 grt; 905 psrs
74 cars + 45 trailers or 30 rail coaches
393' x 57' x 16' (119.1 x 17.3 x 4.8 m)
2 x 6-cylinder Fiat diesel engines via twin screw.
Passenger-car train ferry owned by the Italian State Railways and operated by Ferrovie Stato.
Built by Riuniti, Palermo.

HER MAJESTY M (1990) See TARA II (1997)

HERMES (1961)
5271 grt; 470 psrs
375' x 52' x 18'6" (113.6 x 15.8 x 5.6 m)
Quadruple expansion engines via twin screw.
Broken up for scrap at Inverkeithing by TW Ward Ltd in 1974. Ex-Epirotiki Cruises.
Built by Fairfield Shipbuilding & Engineering Co Ltd, Glasgow, for Canadian Pacific Railways as the PRINCESS JOAN (1930).

HERMES (1990) See SOPHOCLES V (1999)

HERMES (1999) See HERMES V (2000)

HERMES V (2000)
4391 grt; 850 psrs
407' x 59' x 15'6" (123,3 x 18 x 4.7 m)
2 x 12-cylinder Ottensener-Eisenwerk diesel engines via twin screw.

RoRo passenger ship owned by Access Ferries, Malta, and for sale at US$1,500,000.
Built by Lubecker-Flender-Werk, Lubeck, for the TT-Line, Hamburg, as the EUROPAF SYD (1967). Renamed NILS HOLGERSSON (1967 – TT-Line), OLIVER TWIST (1975 – TT-Line, Hamburg), EUROPAFARJAN IV (1978 – Lion ferry), EUROPAFARJAN IV (1983 – Helsingborg-Grena Line), EUROPAFARJAN SYD (1984 – Kopersune Johanson), LANCUT (1985 – Pol Ferries), EUROPEAN PRIDE (1994 – European Seaways, Malta) and NETTUNO (1998 – Ocean Crest Shipping Co Ltd).

HERMINIUS (1926) See WAIMANA (1946)

HERMIONE (1903)
4011 grt
360' x 45' x 24'3" (109 x 13.6 x 7.4 m)
Wigham-Richardson 3-cylinder triple expansion engine via single screw.
Broken up in Ireland after a mine blast off Waterford destroyed her. Ex-RP Houston & Co.
Built by JL Thompson & Sons. Ltd, Sunderland, for W Lund as the YARRAWONGA (1891).

HERMITAGE, USS (AP-54) (1942) See CONTE BIANCARNANO (1947)

HERO (1972)
4489 grt; 66 psrs
371' x 53' x 20' (112.3 x 16.2 x 6.1 m)
6-cylinder Stork-Werkspoor diesel engine via single screw.
Passenger-cargo ship owned by Joint Maritime Co Ltd, Panama.
Launched by Nederlandsche Dok & Scheepsbouw, Amsterdam, as the VAN RIEMSDIJ K (1940) and completed in 1948. Renamed KEERKRING (1960 – Joint Maritime Co Ltd) and VENICE (1967 – Venders Navigation Corporation (Liberia) Ltd).

HESPARIAN (1908)
10920 grt; 1460 psrs
502' x 60' x 30' (153 x 18.2 x 9.1 m)
6-cylinder triple expansion engines via twin screw.
Sank on 6 September 1915 130 miles (220 km) west of Malin Head, Donegal, two days after being hit by a torpedo from the German U-20, 80 miles (135 km) south-west of Fastnet, Ireland. Thirty-two lives were lost.
Built by Alex ander Stephen & Sons, Glasgow, for the Allan Line.

HESSENSTEIN (1954) See ORIENTAL MUSICIAN (1967)

HESTIA (1993)
13539 grt; 703 psrs
100 cars
634' x 89' x 22' (192 x 27 x 6.7 m)
2 x 12-cylinder Pielstick diesel engines via twin screw.
Built by Mitsubishi Heavy Industries, Shimonoseki, for Higashi Nippon Ferry at a cost of US$89,000,000.

H. F. ALEX ANDER (1922) See GEORGE S. SIMONDS (1942)

H. H. MEIER (1892) See DRAGO (1952)

HIBERNIA (1920)
3458 grt; 1505 psrs
381' x 45' x 17'2" (115.5 x 13.6 x 5.2 m)
4 x William Denny SRG turbine engines via twin screw.
Broken up for scrap in 1949.
Built by William Denny & Bros Ltd for the London & North Eastern Railway at a cost of £400,000.

HIBERNIA (1949) See EXPRESS APOLLON (1977)

HIBISCUS (1971) See HOGGAR (1976)

HIDAKA MARU (1969)
4089 grt; 2266 psrs
477' x 61' x 17' (144.6 x 18.5 x 5.1 m)
8 x 8-cylinder MAN diesel engines via twin screw.
Owned by the government of Japan (Japanese National Railways Department), Tokyo.
Built by Mitsubishi Heavy Industries Ltd, Kobe.

HIE MARU (1938)
11622 grt; 331 psrs
514' x 66' x 30' (155.9 x 20 x 9.2 m)
2 x 16-cylinder B+W diesel engines via twin screw.
After acquisition by the Japanese Navy, she sank on 17 November 1943 after being torpedoed by the US DRUM north-west of Truk Island.
Built by the Yokohama Dockyard Company for NYK, Japan, as the HIYE

MARU (1930).

HIGHLAND BRAE (1911)
7490 grt; 122 psrs
414' x 56' x 26' (125.5 x 17 x 7.9 m)
Rankin & Blackmore 3-cylinder triple expansion engine via single screw.
Scuttled on 31 January 1915 after her capture 17 days earlier by the German KRONPRINZ WILHELM, 630 miles (1050 km) north of Recife.
Built by Cammell Laird & Company, Birkenhead, for Nelson Steam Navigation Co Ltd, Liverpool.

HIGHLAND BRIGADE (1929) See MARIANNA (1960)

HIGHLAND CHIEFTAIN (1928) See CALPEAN STAR (1959)

HIGHLAND CORRIE (1910)
7490 grt; 122 psrs
414' x 56' x 26' (125.5 x 17 x 7.9 m)
Rankin & Blackmore 3-cylinder triple expansion engine via single screw.
Sank on 16 May 1917 by a torpedo four miles (7 km) off the Owers Lightship in the English Channel.
Built by Russell & Company, Glasgow, for Nelson Steam Navigation Co Ltd, Liverpool.

HIGHLAND FLING (1905)
3822 grt
351' x 48' x 24' (106.4 x 14.5 x 7.3 m)
Hawthorne Leslie 3-cylinder triple expansion engines via single screw.
Converted into a refrigerated cargo vessel by the Nelson Line, she was abandoned after running aground near the Lizard, UK.
Built by Hawthorne Leslie & Co Ltd, Newcastle, for Elderslie Steamship Co Ltd as the passenger-cargo ship MORAYSHIRE (1890). Renamed DUKE OF PORTLAND (1898 – Duke of Portland Steamship Co).

HIGHLAND GLEN (1910) See JAMAICA PRODUCER (1929)

HIGHLAND HOPE (1929)
14137 grt; 801 psrs
544' x 69' x 28' (165.8 x 21.1 x 8.5 m)
B+W 16-cylinder diesel engines via twin screw.
One life was lost when she was abandoned as a total loss after striking the Farilhoes Rocks near Peniche, 60 miles (100 km) north of Lisbon, in dense fog on 19 November 1930. She sank in her maiden year.
Built by Harland & Wolff Ltd, Govan, for the Nelson Line, Liverpool.

HIGHLAND LADDIE (1910) See JAMAICA SETTLER (1929)

HIGHLAND LOCH (1911) See JAMAICA PLANTER (1929)

HIGHLAND MONARCH (1928)
14216 grt; 700 psrs
544' x 69' x 28' (164.8 x 20.9 x 8.5 m)
Harland & Wolff 16-cylinder diesel engines via twin screw.
Broken up for scrap by WH Arnott Young at Dalmuir in 1960.
Built by Harland & Wolff Ltd, Belfast, for the Nelson Line.

HIGHLAND PATRIOT (1931)
14157 grt; 701 psrs
544' x 69' x 28' (165.8 x 21.1 x 8.5 m)
B+W 16-cylinder diesel engines via twin screw.
Sank with the loss of three lives on 1 October 1940 after being torpedoed by the German U-38 500 miles (835 km) west of Bishop Rock, Scilly Isles.
Built by Harland & Wolff Ltd, Belfast, for Nelson Steam Navigation Co Ltd, Liverpool.

HIGHLAND PIPER (1911) See JAMAICA MERCHANT (1929)

HIGHLAND PRIDE (1910)
7469 grt; 122 psrs
405' x 56' x 26' (122.7 x 17 x 7.9 m)
Rankin & Blackmore 3-cylinder triple expansion engine via single screw.
Following her grounding on Roca Negra Island near Vigo, Spain, and successfully refloating, she had to be abandoned when she broke her back two days later (10 September 1929) on the same rocky outcrop in heavy fog.

Built by Russell & Company, Glasgow, for Nelson Steam Navigation Co Ltd, Liverpool.

HIGHLAND PRINCESS (1930) See GUANGHUA (1960)

HIGHLAND QUEEN (1973)
5275 grt; 470 psrs
353' x 52' x 18'6" (113.6 x 15.8 x 5.6 m)
2 x 8-cylinder Harland & Wolff quadruple expansion engines via twin screw.
Broken up for scrap at Zeebrugge by Brugge Scheepssloperij NV in 1976. Ex-North Sea Oil Co charter from Epirotiki Cruises, during which she acted as an oil platform personnel accommodation ship from 1973.
Built by Fairfield Shipbuilding & Engineering Co, Glasgow, for Canadian Pacific Railways as the PRINCESS ELIZABETH (1930). Renamed PEGASUS (1961 – Hellenic Mediterranean Cruise and Car Ferry Services SA, Piraeus).

HIGHLAND ROVER (1910)
7490 grt; 122 psrs
405' x 56' x 26' (122.7 x 17 x 7.9 m)
Rankin & Blackmore 3-cylinder triple expansion engine via single screw.
Broken up for scrap in 1932 by Thos W Ward, Grays, Essex.
Built by Russell & Company, Glasgow, for Nelson Steam Navigation Co Ltd, Liverpool.

HIGHLAND SCOT (1910)
7604 grt; 122 psrs
414' x 56' x 26' (125.5 x 17 x 7.9 m)
Rankin & Blackmore 3-cylinder triple expansion engine via single screw.
Abandoned after being wrecked on Maricas Island, Brazil, on 6 May 1918.
Built by Russell & Company, Glasgow, for Nelson Steam Navigation Co Ltd, Liverpool.

HIGHLAND WARRIOR (1911)
7604 grt; 122 psrs
414' x 56' x 26' (125.5 x 17 x 7.9 m)
Rankin & Blackmore 3-cylinder triple expansion engine via single screw.
Abandoned as a total loss after being wrecked on the north-west coast of Spain, north of Cape Prior, on 3 October 1915.
Built by Russell & Company, Glasgow, for Nelson Steam Navigation Co Ltd, Liverpool.

HIKARI (1972)
4679 grt; 1003 psrs
368' x 46' x 16' (111.4 x 13.9 x 4.8 m)
2 x Mitsubishi 8-cylinder diesel engines via twin screw.
Owned by Oshima Unyu KK, Nase.
Built by Mitsubishi Heavy Industries Ltd, Shimonoseki.

HIKAWA MARU (1930)
11625 grt; 331 psrs
536' x 66' x 30' (155.9 x 20 x 9.2 m)
2 x 8-cylinder B+W diesel engines via twin screw.
Passenger-cargo ship owned by NYK, she is the only Japanese ocean-going passenger-cargo ship to have survived World War Two. She has been a floating museum since her conversion at Yokohama in 1961, followed by a period as a youth hostel and then reverting to a museum on a permanent basis.
Built by Yokohama Dockyard Company, Yokohama.

HILARY (1908)
6329 grt; 500 psrs
419' x 52' x 27'3" (126.7 x 15.8 x 8.3 m)
Caledon 6-cylinder triple expansion engines via twin screw.
Sank on 25 May 1917 as an armed merchant cruiser after being torpedoed by the German U-88 40 miles (69 km) north-east of Lerwick.
Built by Caledon Shipbuilding & Engineering Co, Dundee, for the Booth Line.

HILARY (1931)
7403 grt; 294 psrs
424' x 56' x 24'8" (128.5 x 17 x 7.5 m)
Cammell Laird 3-cylinder triple expansion engine via single screw.
Built by Cammell Laird, Birkenhead, for the Booth Line as a passenger.cargo ship.

Sold as scrap by the Booth Line in 1959.

HILDA WOERMANN (1914) See CORSICA (1951)

HILDE (1963) See MELINA (1964)

HILDEBRAND (1911)
6991 grt; 624 psrs
440' x 54' x 27'3" (133.3 x 16.4 x 8.3 m)
Scott's 8-cylinder quadruple expansion engines via twin screw.
Broken up for scrap in 1934. Ex-Booth Line.
Built by Scott's Shipbuilding Co, Greenock, for the Booth Line.

HILDEBRAND (1951)
7735 grt; 173 psrs
421' x 60' x 25'4" (127.6 x 18.2 x 7.7 m)
Abandoned as a total loss after running aground in fog on 25 September 1957 near Cascais, 18 miles (30 km) west of Lisbon, despite several attempts to refloat her. She broke her back two months later.
Built by Cammell Laird & Co, Birkenhead, for the Booth Line.

HIMALAYA (1949)
28047 grt; 1416 psrs
709' x 91' x 31' (216.1 x 27.7 x 9.4 m)
6 x Parsons SRG + DRG turbine engines via twin screw.
Broken up for scrap by Tong Cheng Steel Manufacturing Co Ltd at Kaohsiung in 1975.
Built by Vickers-Armstrong Ltd, Newcastle, for the P&O Line at a cost of £3,600,000.

HIND (1997) See MILLENNIUM EXPRESS (2000)

HINDENBURG (1914) See COLUMBUS (1924)

HINDENBURG (1923) See HOMERIC (1923)

HINEMOA (1946) See GEORGE H. EVANS (1967)

HINRICH-WILHELM KOPF (1998)
5148 grt; 785 psrs
100 cars
341' x 57' x 15' (103.4 x 17.2 x 4.6 m)
2 x 9-cylinder B+W diesel engines via twin screw.
Passenger-car ferry owned by Elbe-Ferry GmbH & Co KG and operated by Harms EH.
Built by Aalborg Vaerft, Aalborg, for the Danish government and operated by DSB as the PRINSESSE ELISABETH (1964).

HIRYU (1974) See PRINCESS OF PARADISE (1994)

HIRYU (1995) See CRUISE FERRY HIRYU (1995).

HIRYU II (1980) See DONG CHUN (2000)

HIRYU 3 (1986) See COZY ISLAND (1999)

HISPANIA (1969) See CAPTAIN ZAMAN I (1998)

HITAKA MARU (1955)
3061 grt
387' x 52' x 16'5" (117.3 x 15.8 x 5 m)
2 x Hitachi DRG turbine engines via twin screw.
Owned by government of Japan (Department of Railways).
Built by Uraga Dockyard Co, Uraga.

HITAKA MARU (1970)
4089 grt; 2286 psrs
TEUs
477' x 61' x 17' (144.6 x 18.5 x 5.1 m)
8 x 8-cylinder Kawasaki-MAN diesel engines via single screw.
Passenger-cargo ship owned and operated by government of Japan (Department of Railways).
Built by Mitsubishi Dockyard Co, Kobe.

HITTFELD (1908) See IOANNINA (1913)

HIYAMA MARU (1955)
3393 grt; 1722 psrs
43 rail coaches
393' x 58' x 15'6" (119.2 x 17.5 x 4.7 m)
2 x 8-cylinder Sulzer diesel engines via twin screw.
Passenger train ferry owned by the Japanese government (Department of Railways), but sold on 21 July 1977.
Built by Mitsubishi Heavy Industries Ltd, Kobe.

HIYE MARU (1930) See HIE MARU ((1938)

HIYO (1942)
27500 grt; 880 psrs
719' x 88' x 45'9" depth (218 x 26.7 x 13.9 m)
Geared turbine engines via twin screw.
Sank as a Japanese aircraft carrier on 20 June 1944 after aircraft from the US aircraft carrier USS BELLEAUWOOD attacked her 450 miles (750 km) north-west of Yap, in the Mariana Sea.
Launched by Kawasaki, Kobe, for NYK, Japan, on 12 April 1941 as the IZUMO MARU (1941), but completed as the aircraft carrier HIYO for the Japanese Navy.

HIZBUHL BAHR (1977) See SHAHEED SALAHUDDIN (1981)

HOBSONS BAY (1922) See ESPERANCE BAY (1937)

HOEDIC (1922) See FOUCAULD (1929)

HOEGH TRANSIT (1971) See TROTTER (1981)

HOEGH TRAVELLER (1971) See TRAVELLER (1981)

HOEGH TROTTER (1972) See TROTTER (1981)

HOGGAR (1976)
8668 grt; 1145 psrs
190 cars
389' x 68' x 19' (118 x 20.5 x 5.7 m)
4 x 12-cylinder Pielstick engines via twin screw.
Passenger-car ferry operated by ENTMV, Algeria.
Built by Mitsubishi Heavy Industries Ltd, Kobe, for Japan Car Ferry KK, Tokyo, as the HIBISCUS (1971).

HOHENZOLLERN (1900)
6668 grt; 1200 psrs
451' x 52' x 27'2" (136.7 x 15.8 x 8.2 m)
AG Vulcan 3-cylinder triple expansion engine via single screw.
Broken up for scrap in Italy in 1908 after she ran aground at Alghero, Sardinia, on 10 May 1908, and was refloated. She had previously sunk at her berth in Genoa, as the KAISER WILHELM II, on 5 June 1893. Ex-North German Lloyd .
Built by A G Vulcan, Stettin, for North German Lloyd as the KAISER WILHELM II (1890).

HOI HOUW (1949)
3394 grt; 700 psrs
341' x 46' x 25'3" (103.3 x 13.9 x 7.7 m)
B+W 7-cylinder diesel engine via single screw.
Built by Helsingors Shipyards, Helsingor, for HM Wrangell & Co AS, Norway.

HOI HUNG (1954)
5219 grt
414' x 53' x 24'6" (125.5 x 16.1 x 7.5 m)
B+W 4-stroke single action heavy oil engine via twin screw.
Broken up for scrap in 1955. Ex-Shun Kee Navigation Co Ltd.
Built by Burmeister & Wain, Copenhagen, for the East Asiatic Co, Copenhagen, as the FIONIA (1912). Renamed CHRISTIAN X (1914 – Hamburg-America Line), FRATELLI BANDIERA (1915 – requisitioned by the Italian State Railways), CLELIA C (1922 – Tito Campanella) and EQUATORE (1926 – Navigazione Generale Italiana).

HOI KUNG (1964) See LUO DING (1977)

HOI WONG (1949)
3405 grt; 700 psrs
341' x 46' x 19' (103.3 x 13.9 x 5.8 m)
B+W 7-cylinder diesel engine via single screw.
Built by Helsingors Shipyard, Helsingors, for HM Wrangell & Co AS, Norway.

HOI YING (1955)
4000 grt; 900 psrs
358' x 50' x 20' (108.5 x 15.2 x 6.1 m)
B+W 8-cylinder diesel engine via single screw.
Built by Helsingor Ship.yard, Helsingor, for HM Wrangell & Co AS, Norway.

HOKOKU MARU (1914)
4674 grt; 98 psrs
401' x 47' x 28' (122.2 x 14.3 x 8.5 m)
Caird 3-cylinder triple expansion engine via single screw.
Under the ownership of Minamimanshu KKK, she disappeared without trace in 1917 while en route from Portland, Oregon, to England with a cargo of wheat.
Laid down by Caird & Company, Greenock, for the P&O Line as the MADRAS (1895) and completed as the SUNDA (1895) at a cost of £77,566.

HOKOKU MARU (1939)
10438 grt; 400 psrs
492' x 66' x 40'7" depth (149.1 x 20 x 12.3 m)
B+W 24-cylinder diesel engines via twin screw.
Sank on 11 November 1942 after the Allied merchantman ONDINA fired upon her in the Indian Ocean.
Built by Tama Shipbuilding Co for OSK, Japan.

HOLBROOK (1917) See BRANDON (1923)

HOLGER (1999)
4979 grt; 500 psrs
150 cars or 45 trailers
350' x 53' x 16'6" (106 x 16 x 5 m)
4 x 8-cylinder Bergens-Normo diesel engines via twin screw.

Passenger-car-cargo ferry owned and operated by Meridiano Sr L.
Built by Kristiansands Shipbuilder, Kristiansand, for Stena AB, Gothenburg, as the STENA CARRIER (1970). Renamed ULIDIA (1974 – Barclays Export & Finance Co Ltd, London), AUTO TRADER (1981 – Corvo Shipping Inc, Piraeus), RAGA QUEEN (1986 – International Agency for Shipping & Trading Co, Alexandria), FJORDVEIEN (AS Rogaland Kystferger AB, Stavanger), FJARDVAGEN (1994 – Rederi AB Lillgaard) and HOLGERSTJERN (1995 – Basto Fosen AS).

HOLGER DANSKE (1961) See DOLCE VITA (1999)

HOLIDAY (1985)
46052 grt; 1452 psrs
727' x 93' x 24'6" (220.3 x 28.2 x 7.5 m)
2 x 7-cylinder Sulzer diesel engines via twin screw.
Cruise ship for Carnival Cruise Line.
Built by Aalborg Vaerft, Aalborg, for Carnival Cruise Line at a cost of US$170,000,000.

HOLIDAY ISLAND (1971)
3037 grt; 487 psrs
155 cars + 16 trailers
323' x 69' x 16'6" (97.9 x 20.8 x 5 m)
2 x 16-cylinder Rushton diesel engine via single screw.
Passenger ferry operating for Northumberland Ferries.
Launched by Port Weller Drydocks Ltd, St Catherines, Ontario, for CN Marine Inc, Charlottetown, Prince Edward Island, as the WILLIAM POPE (1971), but completed as HOLIDAY ISLAND.

HOLLAND EXPO (1979) See PRINCESS OF SCANDINAVIA (1991)

HOLM (1922)
7442 grt; 1210 psrs
451' x 53' x 31'2" depth (136.7 x 16.2 x 9.5 m)
Richardsons, Westgarth 3-cylinder triple expansion engine via single screw.
Broken up for scrap at Hamburg in 1929. Ex-Hamburg-America Line.
Built by Furness Shipbuilding Co Ltd, Haverton Hill-on-Tees, for Hamburg-America Line as the BADENIA (1902).

HOLMIA (1965) See SHOROK I (1998)

HOLYHEAD (1970)
3783 grt; 1400 psrs
50 cars
321' x 51' x 13' (97.3 x 15.4 x 3.9 m)
4 x Parsons SRG turbine engines via twin screw.
As a Chandris Line ship, laid up in Perama Bay since 1971. She was eventually broken up for scrap.
Built by Cammell Laird & Co, Birkenhead, for the Fishguard & Rosslare Railways & Harbours Co as the St DAVID (1947) at a cost of £500,000.

HOLYHEAD FERRY I (1965) See EARL LEOFRIC (1976)

HOMAYUN (1910)
3350 grt; 116 psrs
332' x 43' x 23' (100.6 x 13 x 7 m)
T Richardson & Sons 3-cylinder turbine engine via single screw.
Broken up for scrap by the British Admiralty in 1923, after earlier acquiring her from the ownership of the Bombay & Persia Steam Navigation Co Ltd.
Built by Sir Raylton Dixon & Co Ltd, Middlesbrough, for Cie Belge Maritime du Congo as the LEOPOLDVILLE (1895). Renamed BIAFRA (1896 – Elder Dempster Lines).

HOMELAND (1951)
11182 grt; 951 psrs
539' x 60' x 32' (163.3 x 18.4 x 9.7 m)
3 x Parsons SRG turbine engines via triple screw.
Broken up for scrap by Sidarma at Trieste in 1955. Ex-Home Lines.
Built by Alexander Stephen & Sons, Glasgow, for the Allan Line as the VIRGINIAN (1905). Renamed DROTTNINGHOLM (1920 – Swedish American Line) and BRASIL (1948 – Home Lines).

HOMERIC (1922)
34351 grt; 2766 psrs
774' x 82' x 48'6" depth (234.5 x 24.8 x 14.7 m)
2 x Schichau Engineering 4-cylinder triple expansion engines via twin screw.
Broken up for scrap at Inverkeithing in 1936. Ex-Cunard White Star Line.

Laid down by Schichau Shipyards, Danzig, for North German Lloyd as the COLUMBUS (1913). Launched as the HOMERIC (1920 – White Star Line), but not completed until 1922.

HOMERIC (1953)
18563 grt; 1243 psrs
632' x 79' x 28' (192.6 x 24 x 8.6 m)
SRG turbine engines via twin screw.
Broken up for scrap at Kaohsiung in 1974 after incurring extensive fire damage 90 miles (150 km) off the east coast of the USA, near New Jersey. A blaze had erupted at 4.00 am in the ship's galley.
Built by the Bethlehem Steel Corporation, Quincy, Massachusetts, for the Matson Line as the MARIPOSA (1932).

HOMERIC (1977) See WORLD RENAISSANCE (1998)

HOMERIC (1986) See WESTERDAM (1988)

HOMERIC (1995) See APOLLON (1998)

HOMERICUS (1991) See APOLLON (1991)

HOMERUS (1977) See NISSOS KYPROS (1993)

HONG KHENG (1904) See TAI WAY FOONG (1923)

HONG KONG FIR (1973) See YARA (1974)

HONG KONG PRODUCER (1963) See ORIENTAL FALCON (1970)

HONG KONG SUCCESS (1972)
10417 grt; 60 psrs
504' x 69' x 30' (153.7 x 21.1 x 9.1 m)
2 x Wilton-Fijenoord DRG turbine engines via single screw.
Broken up for scrap at Kaohsiung in 1979. Ex-Pacific Union Lines.
Built by Wilton-Fijenoord, Schiedam, for the Holland America Line as the DINTELDYK (1957). Renamed ORIENTAL FANTASIA (1970 – Orient Overseas Lines).

HONG Qui 144 (1977)
7121 grt; 700 psrs
473' x 62' x 26'10" (143.3 x 18.9 x 7.9 m)
7-cylinder Fiat diesel engine via single screw.
In Chinese government service.
Built by Ansaldo SA, Genoa, for the Garibaldi Group as the LUCIANO MANARA (1941) which acted as a migrant ship after World War Two. Renamed as the cargo ship GIUSEPPE CANEPA (1953 – Soc Anonima Cooperativa di Navigazione Garibaldi), MALGORZATA FORNALSKA (1955 – Polish Ocean Lines) and CHUNG MING (1965 – China Ocean Shipping Co).

HONG SIANG (1935) See EMPIRE LONGFORD (1951)

HONNINGSVAG (1993)
3780 grt; 544 psrs
104 cars
277' x 50' x 17' (84 x 15 x 5 m)
Bergen Ulstein AS 6-cylinder diesel engine via single screw.
Passenger-car ferry owned and operated by Finnmark Fylkes and equipped with aft raked exhaust vents and a stern bridge, giving it a semblance of a 'double-ender' profile.
Built by Slipen Mik at a cost of US$23,000,000.

HOOSIER STATE (1922) See CABO DE BUENA ESPERENZA (1940)

HORACE LUCKENBACH (1923) See GIOVANNA C (1946)

HORAI MARU (1924)
9735 grt; 843 psrs
451' x 60' x 27' (137.5 x 18.2 x 8.2 m)
Quadruple expansion engines via twin screw.
Owned by OSK, she was broken up for scrap by a Japanese salvage team in

1947. She had been raised from the position in which she sank in the Sunda Strait, on 1 March 1942, following an intense Allied sea and air bombardment. Built by William Denny & Brothers, Dumbarton, for the Australasian United Steam Navigation Company as the INDARRA (1912). Renamed PAYS DE WAES (1920 – Lloyd Royal Belge Ltd).

HORIZON (1990)
46811 grt; 1354 psrs
682' x 95' x 24' (205.7 x 28.8 x 7.3 m)
4 x 9-cylinder MAN-B+W diesel engines via twin screw.

Owned by Chandris Group and operated by their subsidiary Celebrity Cruises Inc.
Built by Jos L Meyer, Papenburg, at a cost of US$185,000,000.

HORNBEAM (1992)
7818 grt; 492 psrs
380' x 62' x 20' (115.1 x 18.8 x 6 m)
2 x 9-cylinder Stork-Werkspoor diesel engines via twin screw.
Passenger ferry owned by Colibri Maritime Co Ltd, Limassol, and operated by Celine Shipping Co Ltd, Limassol.
Built by Cantieri Navale Cassaro, Messina, for Soc Armatoriale Touristica Mediterranea SpA as the ferry MONICA RUSSOTTI (1973). Renamed GISELLA (1974), SEASPEED CHALLENGER (1974), MERENGUE EXPRESS (1980 – Nosira Shipping Ltd, London), OLEANDER (1988 – Celine Shipping Co Ltd, Limassol) and ATLANTICA I (1991).

HORORATA (1914) See WAROONGA (1939)

HORSA (1972) See EXPRESS PENELOPE (2000)

HORUS (1994)
7192 grt; 600 psrs
20 cars
451' x 69' x 19' (136.6 x 21 x 5.7 m)
2 x 14-cylinder NKK-SEMT-Pielstick diesel engines via twin screw.
Passenger-car ferry operated by the Higashi Nippon Ferry, Hakodate, Japan.
Built by Mitsubishi Heavy Industries Ltd, Shimonoseki.

HOSPITAL SHIP No. 5 (1914)
7267 grt; 165 psrs
456' x 56' x 29'8" depth (138.2 x 17 x 9 m)
3 x Parsons turbine engines via triple screw.
Sank on 4 January 1918 after being torpedoed in the Bristol Channel.
Built by William Denny & Brothers, Dumbarton, for the British India Steamship Co as the passenger-cargo liner ROHILLA (1906). Upon conversion to a hospital ship., she carried 300 doctors and nurses as permanent medical staff and cared for over 7,000 casualties during her service.

HOUSATONIC (1915)
3143 grt; 630 psrs
331' x 41' x 19'2" (100.9 x 12.5 x 5.8 m)
Barclay Curle 3-cylinder triple expansion engine via single screw.
Owned by US War Shipping Board when she sank, on 3 February 1917,. after being torpedoed by the German U-53 south of the Scilly Isles.
Built by Barclay, Curle, Glasgow for HANSA as the cargo ship PICKHUBEN (1892). Renamed GEORGIA (1895 – Hamburg-America Line).

HOWARD A. McCURDY (1945) See PRESIDENT TYLER (1945)

H. P PRIOR (1950) See SWEET FAITH (1970)

HRVATSKA (1949) See ARMELLE (1968)

HUAL AKARITA (1978) See AKARITA (1981)

HUALALAI (1929) See MOIZ (1955)

HUA LIEN (1975)
9317 grt; 1420 psrs
390' x 68' x 19' (118.1 x 20.5 x 5.7 m)
2 x 10-cylinder diesel engines via twin screw.
Owned by Taiwan Car Ferry Co Ltd, Keelung.
Built by Hayashikane Zosen, Shimonoseki, for Miyazaki Car Ferry Co Ltd, Hyuga, as the LUPINUS (1971).

HUAL TRAVELLER (1978) See TRAVELLER (1981)

HUAL TROTTER (1978) See TROTTER (1981)

HUA LU (1994)
6036 grt; 500 psrs
409' x 53' x 16'6" (124 x 16 x 5 m)
4 x 9-cylinder Bergens-Normo diesel engines via twin screw.
Passenger ferry owned and operated by Yantai Marine Shipping Co, Tan Tai.
Built by Trosvik, Brevik, Norway, for SA Golden West, Oslo, as the ice-strengthened passenger ferry GREY MASTER (1973). Renamed SIR CARADOC (1983 – Nitre Shipping Ltd, London) and STAMVEIEN (1988 – Askoy Bergen).

HUASCARAN (1938) See ROMANTICA (1991)

HUA TONG (1930)
4358 grt; 1155 psrs
375' x 46' x 27' (114.3 x 14.1 x 8.2 m)
D & W Henderson 3-cylinder triple expansion engine via single screw.
Broken up for scrap in 1933.
Built by D & W Henderson Ltd, Glasgow, for Henderson Brothers as the SCINDIA (1890). Renamed AJAX (1901 – US government), AC-14 (1920 – US government) and CONSUELO (1925 – Madrigal Co).

HUBERT (1955) See KHALEEJ EXPRESS (1976)

HUDSON (1905)
5558 grt; 760 psrs
391' x 51' x 28'5" (118.5 x 15.5 x 8.7 m)
Penhoet 3-cylinder triple expansion engine via single screw.
Broken up for scrap at Ghent in 1930 by Van Heyghen Freres.
Built by Chantiers de Normandie, Grand Quevilly, for the French Line.

HUDSON (1921) See PRESIDENT FILLMORE (1922)

HUGH L. SCOTT, USS (AP-43) (1942)
14124 grt; 561 psrs
535' x 72' x 28' (162.1 x 21.8 x 8.5 m)
4 x turbine engines via twin screw.
Owned by the US Navy, she sank on 12 November 1942 after being torpedoed by the German U-130 while the ship was standing off Fedala, Morocco, during an assault landing.
Laid down by Bethlehem Shipbuilding Corporation, Sparrow's Point, Maryland, for the US Shipping Board as the BERRIEN (1919) and completed as the HAWKEYE STATE (1921). Renamed PRESIDENT PIERCE (1922 – Pacific Mail Steamship Co), GENERAL HUGH L. SCOTT (1941 – US Army) and HUGH L. SCOTT (1942 – US Navy).

HUI HSING (1974)
8516 grt; 800 psrs
475' x 62' x 29' (143.9 x 18.8 x 8.8 m)
8-cylinder Mitsubishi-Sulzer diesel engine via single screw.
Broken up for scrap at Kaohsiung in 1976. Ex-Sincere Navigation Co, Taiwan.
Built by Shin Mitsubishi Heavy Industries, Kobe, for OSK, Japan, as the

SANTOS MARU (1952). Renamed WINONA (1972 – Liberty Maritime Corporation).

HULL No 309 (1999) See EUROFERRYS ATLANTICA (1999)

HUMACAO (1975) See EASTERN LIGHT (1981)

HUNDESTED (1964) See ALDONZA MANRIGUE (1976)

HUNTER LIGGETT (1939) See HUNTER LIGGETT, USS (APA-14) (1943)

HUNTER LIGGETT, USS (APA-14) (1943)
13712 grt; 430 psrs
535' x 72' x 31'3" (162.1 x 21.8 x 9.5 m)
4 x Bethlehem Steel DRG turbine engines via twin screw.
Broken up for scrap at San Pedro, California, in 1948 by Boston Metals Co, Baltimore, Maryland. Ex-US Army.
Launched by Bethlehem Shipbuilding Corporation, Sparrow's Point, Maryland, for the Matson Line as the PALMETTO STATE (1921) and completed as the PAN AMERICA (1922 – Munson Line). Renamed as the troopship HUNTER LIGGETT (1939 – US Army). Reclassified as the HUNTER LIGGETT, USS (AP-27) (1941 – US Navy).

HUNTSEND (1914) See LUTZOW (1924)

HUNTSGREEN (1914) See DERFFLINGER (1923)

HURON (1917) See CITY OF HONOLULU (1922)

HURONIC (1902)
3330 grt; 600 psrs
321' x 43' x 23'4" (97.3 x 13 x 7.1 m)
J Inglis & Sons 3-cylinder triple expansion engines via single screw.
Sank after a shipboard blaze on the Great Lakes in 1949.
Built by Collingwood Shipbuilding Co, Collingwood, Ontario, for Canada Steamship Lines.

HURUNUI (1912)
8901 grt
495' x 63' x 31'7" depth (150 x 19.1 x 9.6 m)
D Rowan & Co 8-cylinder quadruple expansion engines via twin screw.
Sank on 18 May 1918 after being torpedoed off the Lizard Rock, UK.
Built by Russell & Co, Port Glasgow, for New Zealand Shipping Co Ltd.

HUSO MARU (1938)
9216 grt; 308 psrs
475' x 58' x 32'6" depth (143.9 x 17.7 x 9.9 m)
Barclay, Curle 6-cylinder triple expansion engines via twin screw.
Owned by OSK when she sank after being torpedoed by the USS STEELHEAD on 31 July 1944 off Luzon.
Built by Barclay, Curle, Glasgow, for the Russian American Line as the RUSSIA (1908). Renamed ROSSIJA (1917 – Russian American Line), RUSS (1917 – Russian American Line), LATVIA (1921 – Baltic American Line) and FUSO MARU (1924 – OSK).

HWA LIEN (1946)
3488 grt; 630 psrs
350' x 47' x 17' (106.7 x 14.3 x 5.2 m)
Geared turbine engines via triple screw.
Owned by United Corporation of China Ltd, Shanghai, she was broken up for scrap at Kaohsiung in 1951. She had been raised from the Keelung harbour sea bed in May of that year, having settled there on 13 January 1951 following stormwater entering her open portholes during a raging cyclone.
Built as the MAORI (1907) by William Denny & Brothers, Dumbarton, for the Union Steamship Company of New Zealand.

HYDRA (1940) See CASTEL FELICE (1952)

HYSAN (1971)
4272 grt; 55 psrs
376' x 52' x 22' (114.6 x 15.8 x 6.1 m)
Stork-Werkspoor 8-cylinder diesel engines via single screw.
Broken up for scrap at Kaohsiung in 1974. Ex-Cia Navigation Thompson SA,

Panama.
Built by Netherlands Drydock Co, Amsterdam, for the KPM Co as the MAETSUYCKER (1937). Renamed TONG HAN (1960 – Kie Hock Shipping Co Ltd, Hong Kong), GAVINA (1964 – Kie Hock Shipping Co Ltd, Hong Kong), PACECO (1965 – Cia Naviera Thompson, Hong Kong), GAMBELA (1965 – Cia Naviera Thompson, Hong Kong) and GAMSOLO (1970 – Cia Naviera Thompson, Hong Kong).

HYUNDAI KUMGANG (1998)
28388 grt; 1396 psrs
674' x 83' x 24' (205.4 x 25.3 x 7.3 m)
4 x 9-cylinder Wartsila-Sulzer geared diesel engines via twin screw.
Cruise ship chartered by Hyundai Merchant Marine, Seoul, until 2003, following short charter to Manhattan Cruises as a floating casino ship.
Built by Wartsila-Helsinki for the Royal Viking Line as the ROYAL VIKING SKY (1973). Renamed SUNWARD (1991 – Norwegian Cruise Lines), BIRKA QUEEN (1992 – Birka Line), SUNWARD (1992 – Norwegian Cruise Lines), GOLDEN PRINCESS (1993 – P&O Cruise Lines) and SUPERSTAR CAPRICORN after purchase for US$50,000,000 (1997 – Star Cruises, Singapore).

HYUNDAI PONGNAE (1998)
18556 grt; 724 psrs
552' x 79' x 22' (168.3 x 23.9 x 6.7 m)
4 x 9-cylinder Wartsila-Sulzer diesel engines via twin screw.

Cruise ship owned and operated by Hyundai Merchant Marine, Seoul, Korea. Built by Wartsila-Helsinki for Royal Caribbean International as the SUN VIKING (1973). Renamed SUPERSTAR SAGITTARIUS (1998 – Star Cruises, Singapore, following the ship's purchase for US$30,000,000).

HYUNDAI PUNGAK (1999)
20186 grt; 610 psrs
550' x 80' x 24'6" (167.6 x 24.4 x 7.5 m)
4 x 10-cylinder Fiat diesel engines via twin screw.
Cruise ship chartered to Hyundai Merchant Marine, Seoul, Korea.
Built by Noordseewerke Rheinstahl GmbH, Emden, for the Norwegian Cruiseships AG subsidiary, Flagship Cruises, as the ISLAND VENTURE (1972) at a cost of £7,500,000. Renamed ISLAND PRINCESS (1975 – P&O Princess Cruises).

HYUNDAI SEALBONG (2000)
9258 grt; 472 psrs
58 cars + 36 trailers
378' x 66' x 15'8" (114.5 x 20 x 4.8 m)
2 x 16-cylinder Sjang Yong-Alpha diesel engines via twin screw.
Passenger-car-cargo ferry owned and operated by Dong Yang Express, Seoul, and chartered to Hyundai Merchant Marine, Seoul, Korea.
Built by Daewoo Heavy Industries, Koje, for Dong Yang Shipping SA as TREASURE ISLAND (1998).

IALYSSOS (1982)

7586 grt; 1243 psrs
340 cars + 38 trailers
441' x 74' x 17' (133.6 x 22.5 x 5.2 m)
2 x 8-cylinder Wartsila-Sulzer diesel engines via twin screw.

Ice-strengthened ferry operated by DANE Sea Line, Greece.
Built by Wartsila, Helsinki, for Finnlines as the FINNPARTNER (1966).
Renamed SVEABORG (1977 – Svea Line), PEER GYNT (1977 –
Stockholms Rederi AB Svea) and STENA BALTICA (1978 – Stena Line).

IAN RUDZUTAK (1928) See MARIJA ULYANOVA (1937)

IASON (1995)

4561 grt; 325 psrs
40 cars
321' x 53' x 14'6" (97.2 x 16.1 x 4.5 m)
2 x 7-cylinder Sulzer diesel engines via twin screw.
Owned by Sarah Shipping, Piraeus, and operated by Royal Olympic Cruises,
Piraeus.
Built by Cantieri Riuniti dell'Adriatico, Monfalcone, for Typaldos Lines as the
EROS (1965). Renamed JASON (1966 – Epirotiki Cruises).

IBERIA (1934) See PEBEDA (1946)

IBERIA (1954)

29614 grt; 1406 psrs
719' x 91' x 31' (219 x 27.7 x 9.4 m)
6 x Harland & Wolff SRG and DRG turbine engines via twin screw.
Broken up for scrap by Tung Chen Steel Corporation in Kaohsiung in 1973.
Built by Harland & Wolff Ltd, Belfast, for P&O Lines at a cost of £6,930,000.

IBERIA STAR (1963) See AUSTRALASIA (1965)

IBN BATTOUTA (1993) See CIUDAD DE TANGER (1998)

IBN BATOUTA (1998)

12711 grt; 1200 psrs
425 cars or 45 trailers
428' x 71' x 18' (129.6 x 21.6 x 5.5 m)
Passenger-car-cargo ferry owned and operated by Limadet, Morocco.
Built by Harland & Wolff Ltd, Belfast, for Sealink UK Ltd as the ST.
CHRISTOPHER (1981). Renamed STENA ANTRIM (1991 – Stena Line
Ltd).

ICARUS (1997) See IKARUS (1997)

IERAPETRA (1988) See ATHINA I (1999)

IERAPETRA (1999)

12891 grt; 1300 psrs
400 cars
452' x 74' x 18'6" (137 x 22.5 x 5.6 m)
2 x Mitsubishi-MAN diesel engines via twin screw.
Joint ownership and operation by Lane Lines and ANEK.
Built by Kanda Kure, Kure, for Hiroshima Green Ferry Co, Hiroshima, as the
GREEN ARCH (1975). Renamed OKUDOGO No. 8 (1982), the cargo ship
KYDON (1991) and passenger-car ferry TALOS (1995 – ANEK).

IGINIA (1969)

5768 grt; 2000 psrs
467' x 62' x 20' (141.5 x 18.8 x 6.1 m)
4 x 6-cylinder Fiat diesel engines via twin screw.
Passenger ferry owned by the Italian State Railways and operated by Ferrovie
Stato on the Italy–Sicily service.
Built by Cantieri Riuniti dell'Adriatico, Ancona.

IGNIS (1998) See IONIS (1998)

IGOUMENITSA EXPRESS (1995) See ORESTES (1998)

IJSTROOM (1926)

5934 grt; 85 psrs
394' x 52' x 26'6" (124.2 x 15.6 x 8.9 m)
D Rowan 3-cylinder triple expansion engines via single screw.
Broken up for scrap in 1934 by Van Heyghen Freres, Ghent. Ex-NV
Hollandsche Stoomboot Maatschappij, Amsterdam.
Built by William Hamilton & Co Ltd, Glasgow, for Nederlandsche Steamship
Co as the LOMBOK (1907).

IKARUS (1997)

30010 grt; 1500 psrs
800 cars or 150 trailers
661' x 85' x 20'6" (200.4 x 25.8 x 6.3 m)
4 x 8-cylinder MAN diesel engines via twin screw.
Passenger-car-cargo ferry owned and operated by Minoan Lines.
Hull constructed by Bruces Shipyard, Landskrona, and completed by Fosen
Fevaag, at a total cost of US$110,000,000.

ILE DE BEAUTE (1973) See THE EMPRESS (1994)

ILE DE BEAUTE (1988) See DANIELLE CASANOVA (1989)

ILE DE BEAUTE (1990)

20564 grt; 1564 psrs
520 cars
525' x 76' x 19' (159 x 23 x 5.7 m)
4 x 12-cylinder Pielstick diesel engines via twin screw.
Passenger-car ferry owned by SCNM and operated by FerryTerranee on the
France-Sardinia service.
Built by Dubigeon-Normandie, Nantes, for SNCM as the CYRNOS (1979).

ILE DE CUBA (1914) See MEXIQUE (1928)

ILE DE FRANCE (1927) See FURANSU MARU (1959)

ILICH (1983) See BALTIC KRISTINA (1997)

ILITCH (1946) See ILYICH (1946)

ILLIRIA (1962) See GALAPAGOS DISCOVERY (1998)

ILMATAR (1964) See PALM BEACH PRINCESS (1997)

ILOILO PRINCESS (1994)

3935 grt; 1031 psrs
368' x 50' x 17'6" (111.5 x 15.2 x 5.3 m)
Mitsubishi 14-cylinder diesel engine via single screw.
Passenger ferry owned and operated by Sulpicio Lines Inc, Cebu City.
Built by Onomichi Zosen, Onomichi, for Ryukyu Kaiun KK, Naha, as the
OKINAWA MARU (1973). Renamed DON ENRIQUE (1978 – Sulpicio
Lines) and DAVAO PRINCESS (1987 – Sulpicio Lines Inc, Cebu City).

IL PIEMONTE (1904) See JANUA (1928)

IL PIEMONTE (1908) See JANUA (1928)

ILSENSTEIN (1928)

6518 grt; 190 psrs
448' x 57' x 30'6" depth (135.8 x 17.3 x 9.3 m)
Workman, Clark 6-cylinder triple expansion engines via twin screw.
Owned and operated by A Bernstein, she was deliberately sunk by a

demolition team in 1950 in the Scapa Flow, Scotland, where she had been placed as a block ship during World War Two. She was broken up where she lay the following year.
Built by Workman, Clark, Belfast, for Shaw, Savill as the MATATUA (1904).

ILYCH (1946) See ILYICH (1946)

ILYICH (1946)
13101 grt; 409 psrs
498' x 66' x 25' (150.9 x 20 x 7.6 m)
2 x 8-cylinder diesel engines via twin screw.
Broken up for scrap in Hong Kong in 1979. Ex-Russian government.
Built by Blohm & Voss, Hamburg, for the Hamburg-America Line as the CARIBIA (1933).

ILYICH (1983) See ILITCH (1983)

IMAGINATION (1998)
70367 grt; 2624 psrs
860' x 102' x 26' (260.6 x 31 x 7.8 m)
6 x 12-cylinder Sulzer diesel-electric engines via twin screw.

Cruising for Carnival Cruise Line Inc, USA.
Built by Kvaerner-Masa Ship.yard, Helsinki, for Carnival Cruise Line at a cost of US$330,000,000.

IMAM BONDJOL (1951) See DJATINEGARA (1952)

IMO (1912) See GUVERNOREN (1920)

IMPERATOR (1913) See BERENGARIA (1921)

IMPERATOR PETR VELIKY (1913) See MORSKAJA II (1913)

IMPERIAL (1938) See ERKIN 2 (1967)

IMPERIAL BAHAMA HOTEL (1964)
21532 grt; 1440 psrs
609' x 78' x 29' (184 x 23.6 x 8.8 m)
2 x 8-cylinder B+W diesel engines via twin screw.
Broken up as a floating hotel (at Freeport) for a tender of £265,000 for scrap at Bilbao in 1965. Ex-Canaveral International Corporation, Bahamas.
Built by Blohm & Voss, Hamburg, for the Swedish-American Line as the KUNGSHOLM (1928). Renamed JOHN ERICCSON, USS (1941 – US War Shipping Administration) and ITALIA (1948 – Home Lines).

IMPERIAL MAJESTY (1999)
21486 grt; 946 psrs
604' x 78' x 26' (184 x 23.9 x 7.9 m)
2 x Pametrada DRG turbine engines via twin screw.
Owned by Premier Cruises and chartered on 21 December 1998 to the Imperial Majesty Ocean Cruise Line, a subsidiary of the Ramada Hotel Group, until December 2000.
Built by Harland & Wolff Ltd, Belfast, for Shaw Savill Line as the SOUTHERN CROSS (1955). Renamed CALYPSO (1973 – Ulysses Line), CALYPSO I (1980 – Pacquet-Ulysses Line), AZURE SEAS (1980 – Western Cruise Lines) and OCEAN BREEZE (1992 – Premier Cruises).

IMPERIO (1948)
13186 grt; 590 psrs

532' x 68' x 28' (161.2 x 20.6 x 8.5 m)
4 x Parsons DRG turbine engines via twin screw.
Broken up for scrap by Chi Shun Hwa Steel & Iron Company at Kaohsiung in 1974.
Built by John Cockerill Shipyards, Hoboken, Belgium, as a passenger-cargo ship for Cia Colonial, Portugal.

INANDA (1904) See ORLANDO (1920)

INANDA (1925) See EMPIRE EXPLORER (1941)

INCHANGA (1934)
7069 grt; 70 psrs
404' x 57' x 25'3" (122.4 x 17.3 x 7.7 m)
2 x 6-cylinder Workman, Clark-Sulzer type diesel engines via twin screw.
Broken up for scrap at Ghent in 1964.
Built by Workman, Clark, Belfast, for the Bank Line.

INCOMATI (1934)
7100 grt; 70 psrs
412' x 57' x 25'3" (124.8 x 17.3 x 7.7 m)
2 x 6-cylinder Workman, Clark-Sulzer-type diesel engines via twin screw.
Sank on 18 July 1943 after being torpedoed by a German U-boat 300 miles (500 km) south of Lagos.
Built by Workman, Clark, Belfast, for the Bank Line.

INDARRA (1912) See HORAI MARU (1924)

INDEPENDENCE (1918) See NEVILLE, USS (APA-9) (1941)

INDEPENDENCE (1950) See INDEPENDENCE (1982)

INDEPENDENCE (1982)
30293 grt; 867 psrs
683' x 89' x 30' (208 x 27.2 x 9 m)
4 x DRG turbine engines via twin screw.

Cruising Hawaiian Island waters for America Hawaii Cruises Inc, USA.
Built by Bethlehem Steel Company, Quincy, Massachusetts, for American Export Lines as the INDEPENDENCE (1950) at a cost of US$25,000,000. Renamed OCEANIC INDEPENDENCE (1974 – Atlantic Far East Lines), SEA LUCK I (1976 – Atlantic Far East Lines) and OCEANIC INDEPENDENCE (1979 – America Hawaii Cruises Inc).

INDIA (1951) See KIM HOCK (1971)

INDIAN (1895) See ARMENIAN (1903)

INDIAN (1900)
9121 grt; 60 psrs
483' x 57' x 31'8" depth (146.4 x 17.3 x 9.6 m)
Workman, Clark 6-cylinder triple expansion engines via twin screw.
Broken up for scrap in Germany in 1923.
Built by Workman, Clark, Belfast, for E Leyland & Co as a passenger-cargo liner.

INDIANA (1905) See ROMANIA (1924)

INDIANA (1922) See ASSIMINA (1949)

INDIAN REEFER (1939) See ROLAND VON BREMEN (1966)

INDIAN REEFER (1946) See ROLAND VON BREMEN (1966)

INDIA VICTORY (1944) See ORIENTAL FALCON (1970)

INDIEN (1905) See ESTONIA (1907)

INDIEN (1907)
5554 grt
390' x 49' x 25'3" (118.2 x 14.8 x 7.7 m)
Flensburger 3-cylinder triple expansion engines via single screw.
Owned by the East Asiatic Company, she sank on 31 March 1918 after being torpedoed by a German U-boat in the Atlantic.
Built by Flensburger Schiffbau, Flensburg, for the East Asiatic Company as the PRINCE VALDEMAR (1902). Renamed LIVONIA (1907 – Russian-American Line).

INDOCEANIQUE (1994)
3144 grt; 93 psrs
331' x 48' x 18' (100.8 x 14.6 x 5.5 m)
6-cylinder Stork-Werkspoor diesel engine via single screw.
Broken up for scrap in 1996 while in the ownership of Indoceanic Maritime Enterprises Ltd, Port Louis, Mauritius.
Built by the Burrard Drydock Company, North Vancouver, BC, for Northland Navigation Company, Vancouver, as the passenger-cargo ship NORTHLAND PRINCE (1963). Renamed St HELENA (1977 – Curnow Shipping Company, Helston), St HELENA ISLAND (1990 – Curnow Shipping Co, Helston) and AVALON (1990 – Curnow Shipping Co, Helston).

INDRAPOERA (1926) See MELANESIEN (1958)

INDRAPURA (1911) See PORT ADELAIDE (1916)

INFANTA BEATRIX (1928) See CIUDAD DE SEVILLA (1932)

INFANTA ISABEL (1912) See MIZUHO MARU (1926)

INFANTA ISABEL DE BORBON (1913) See URUGUAY (1931)

INFANTE DOM HENRIQUE (1961) See SEAWIND CROWN (1990)

INFANTE DON HAIME (1929) See CIUDAD DE BARCELONA (1929)

INGOMA (1913) See SAN GIOVANNI BATTISTA (1937)

INGRID (1999) See AFRICA MERCY (1999)

INIOCHOS EXPRESS (1978) See BALBEK (2000)

INKOSI (1902)
3576 grt; 88 psrs
350' x 43' x 20' (106 x 13 x 6.1 m)
Hall, Russell 3-cylinder triple expansion engine via single screw.
Sank on 28 March 1918 after being hit by a torpedo off the Mull of Galloway.
Built by Hall, Russell & Company, Aberdeen, for the Rennie Line.

INKOSI (1937) See PLANTER (1946)

INNISFALLEN (1948) See POSEIDONIA (1969)

INNISFALLEN (1969) See HAPPY DOLPHIN (1999)

INNISFALLEN (1980) See IONIAN SUN (1994)

INNISFALLEN I (1969) See POSEIDONIA (1969)

INNSTAR (1981) See GOLDEN PRINCESS (2000)

INSIZWA (1899) See TOLEMAIDE (1913)

INSPIRATION (1996)
70367 grt; 2594 psrs
860' x 102' x 29' (260.6 x 30.9 m x 8.8 m)
6 x 12-cylinder Sulzer diesel-electric engines via twin screw.
Cruise ship for Carnival Cruise Lines Inc, USA.
Built by Kvaerner-Masa Yards, Helsinki, for Carnival Cruise Lines at a cost of US$270,000,000.

INSULINDE (1882) See BANFORA MARU (1957)

INSULINDE (1914) See BANFORA MARU (1957)

INTABA (1910) See ENGELSTAN (1927)

INTABA (1917) See ENGELSTAN (1927)

INVICTA (1940)
4178 grt; 1300 psrs
348' x 52' x 13' (105.5 x 15.8 x 3.9 m)
2 x Parsons SRG turbine engines via twin screw.
Passenger ferry sold for scrap in 1972.
Built by William Denny & Bros, Dumbarton, for the Southern Railway at a cost of £290,000.

IOANNINA (1913)
4603 grt; 1820 psrs
368' x 46' x 20' (112.2 x 14.1 x 6.1 m)
Barclay Curle 3-cylinder triple expansion engine via single screw.
Sank on 15 December 1917 after being torpedoed by the German U-156 off the Azores while in the ownership of the National Greek Line.
Built by Barclay, Curle & Company, Glasgow, for the Castle Line as the DUNOLLY CASTLE (1897). Renamed JULIETTE (1905 – East Asiatic Company), ARCONIA (1905 – Russian-American Line) and HITTFELD (1908 – Continetali Rederei Act Ges,Germany).

IOANNIS EXPRESS (1992) See PANAGIA PAXON (1996)

IOANNIS LIVANOS (1947) See DJATINEGARA (1952)

ION (1983) See DIMITRIOS MIRAS (1988)

IONIAN (1901)
8268 grt; 1092 psrs
470' x 58' x 37' depth (142.4 x 17.6 x 11.2 m)
6-cylinder triple expansion engines via twin screw.
Owned by Canadian Pacific Lines, she sank on 21 October 1917 with the loss of seven lives after striking a mine laid a week earlier by the German UC-51. The incident occurred two miles west of St Govans Head, south of Pembroke.
Built by Workman, Clark & Co Ltd, Belfast, for the Allan Line.

IONIAN (1946) See IONIAN (1965)

IONIAN (1965)
4916 grt; 194 psrs
351' x 50' x 25' (106.9 x 15.2 x 7.6 m)
Wallsend Slipway 3-cylinder triple expansion engine via single screw.
Broken up in the Far East. Ex-Ellerman Lines.
Built by Irvine's Shipbuilding & Drydock Company, West Hartlepool, for the Furness Line as the DIGBY (1913). Renamed ARTOIS (1915 – French Navy), DIGBY (1918 – Furness, Warren Line), DOMINICA (1925 – Furness Line), BALTROVER (1936 – United Baltic Corporation) and IONIAN (1946, Greece).

IONIAN (1972)
3277 grt; 870 psrs
284' x 48' x 12' (86.2 x 14.5 x 3.6 m)
Stork-Werkspoor 6-cylinder diesel engines via twin screw.
Passenger ferry owned and operated by Strathakis Brothers & Valskios Manoussos, Piraeus.
Built by Hellenic General Enterprises Co Ltd, Perama.

IONIAN BRIDGE (1997) See BLUE BRIDGE (2000)

IONIAN EXPRESS (1992) See SUPERFERRY II (1993)

IONIAN EXPRESS (1994)
13275 grt; 843 psrs
290 cars
499' x 73' x 19' (152.1 x 22.3 x 5.8 m)
4 x 12-cylinder Pielstick geared diesel engines via twin screw.

Operated by Strintzis Lines, Greece, after having been reported to have been broken up for scrap following a fire which gutted her at her Venice berth on 4 June 1991. Instead, she was laid up in Aliaga while her future was being determined by her owners Epirotiki Lines.
Built by Dubigeon-Normandie Shipyards, Nantes, for the Johnson Line as the ice-strengthened passenger-car ferry SVEA CORONA (1975). Renamed SUNDANCER (1983 – Sundance Cruises), and PEGASUS (1985 – Epirotiki Lines).

IONIAN FANTASY (1988) See LEROS (1997)

IONIAN GALAXY (1990) See BLUE GALAXY (2000)

IONIAN GLORY (1981) See ALAMIRA (1997)

IONIAN HARMONY (1990) See CALYPSO (1995)

IONIAN ISLAND (1989) See BLUE ISLAND (2000)

IONIAN SEA (1991) See LEROS (1997)

IONIAN SEA (1993) See LEROS (1997)

IONIAN STAR (1976) See TIAN KUN (1991)

IONIAN STAR (1991) See SUPERFERRY (1991)

IONIAN STAR (1994) See SCANDOLA (1999)

IONIAN SUN (1986) See IONIAN SUN (1994)

IONIAN SUN (1994)
4976 grt; 1200 psrs
250 cars + 5 trailers or 30 cars + 35 trailers
390' x 59' x 15' (118.3 x 17.8 x 4.5 m)
4 x 18-cylinder MAN diesel engines via twin screw.

Ice-strengthened passenger-car ferry owned by Strintzis Lines, Greece, but operated by Swansea Cork Ferries on the UK–Eire service and on the sales lists for offers.
Built by the Verolme Shipyard, Cork, for British & Irish Steam Packet Company as the LEINSTER (1969). Renamed INNISFALLEN (1980 – Irish Ferries), IONIAN SUN (1986 – Strintzis Lines), CELTIC PRIDE II (1990 – Swansea-Cork Ferries) and CHAMS (1993 – Minoan and Strintzis Lines joint venture).

IONIAN VICTORY (1984) See JIN HU (1993)

IONIAN VICTORY (1998) See BLUE SKY (2000)

IONIC (1883) See SOPHOCLES (1900)

IONIC (1902)
12232 grt; 688 psrs
530' x 63' x 31' (161.5 x 19.2 x 9.4 m)
Quadruple expansion engines via twin screw.
Broken up for scrap at Osaka in 1937 for a tender price of US$63,000.
Built by Harland & Wolff Ltd, Belfast, for the White Star Line.

IONIC FERRY (1986) See MILLENNIUM EXPRESS II (2000)

IONION (1972)
3277 grt; 870 psrs
284' x 48' x 12' (86.2 x 14.5 x 3.6 m)
6-cylinder Stork-Werkspoor diesel engine via single screw.
Ferry owned by Strathakis Bros & Valskios Manoussos, Piraeus.
Built by Hellenic General Enterprises Company Ltd, Perama.

IONIS (1998)
8135 grt; 810 psrs
54 cars
399' x 68' x 16' (120.8 x 20.5 x 4.9 m)
4 x 6-cylinder Niigata diesel engines via twin screw.
Passenger-car ferry owned by Tyrogalas and operated by Strintzis Lines.
Built by Koyo Dockyard Co Ltd, Mihara, as the passenger-car vessel FERRY NANIWA (1971). Renamed VIGNESSWARA (1990 – Green Seas Shipping, Singapore), DIGNITY (1995 – European Seaways) and IGNES (1998 – Ionisus Maritime Co Ltd).

IOWA (1902) See EMPIRE BITTERN (1942)

IPHIGENIA (1906) See CAIRO CITY (1933)

IQUITOS (1915) See AMAZONAS (1923)

IRAKLION (1965)
8922 grt; 300 psrs
498' x 60' x 27' (150.9 x 18.2 x 8.2 m)
DRG turbine engine via single screw.
Owned by Typaldos Lines, Greece.
Built by Fairfield Shipbuilding & Engineering Company, Glasgow, for the Bibby Line as the LEICESTERSHIRE (1949).

IRAN (1886) See BRETON (1911)

IRAN CREMONA (1976)
11450 grt; 753 psrs
520' x 64' x 26' (158.6 x 19.4 x 7.9 m)
2 x 10-cylinder Sulzer diesel engines via twin screw.
Broken up for scrap as a livestock carrier at Kaohsiung in 1980. Ex-Cormoran Steamship Company.
Built by Van der Giessen, Krimpen, for Cia Argentina de Navigation Dodero as the passenger-cargo ship YAPEYU (1951). Renamed the livestock carrier PETREL (1969 – Transportes Oceanicos) and CREMONA (1974 – Cormoran Steamship Company).

IREDELL, USS (APA-242) (1947) See ALCOA CLIPPER (1947)

IRIONA (1927)
4250 grt; 58 psrs
342' x 48' x 28'2" (103.6 x 14.5 x 8.5 m)
Workman, Clark 8-cylinder triple expansion engines via twin screw.
Passenger-cargo ship owned and operated by the United Fruit Company.
Built by Workman, Clark Ltd, Belfast.

IRIS (1924)
3960 grt; 1090 psrs
357' x 48' x 24'11" (108.2 x 14.5 x 7.3 m)
3-cylinder triple expansion engine via single screw.
Broken up for scrap in 1926. Ex-A Lauro.
Built by Germaniawerfte, Kiel, for North German Lloyd as the HALLE

(1896). Renamed PAWEL (1913 – Jebsen & Diederichsen), WOUDRICHEM (1915 – De Doordtsche Stoomschip Maatschappij) and LLOYD (1919 – D Pace).

IRISH COAST (1953) See REGENCY (1982)

IRISHMAN (1900)
9510 grt; 2700 psrs
501' x 62' x 34' depth (151.8 x 18.8 x 10.3 m)
Harland & Wolff 8-cylinder quadruple expansion engines via twin screw.
Broken up for scrap in Holland in 1925. Ex-Dominion Line.
Built by Blohm & Voss, Hamburg, for the Hamburg-America Line as the BELGIA (1899). Renamed MICHIGAN (1899 – Atlantic Transport Line).

IROQUOIS (1917) See FREEDOM (1919)

IROQUOIS (1927) See ANKARA (1948)

IRPINIA (1955)
13204 grt; 1181 psrs
537' x 67' x 23' (162.7 x 20.3 x 10 m)
2 x 10-cylinder Fiat diesel engines via twin screw.
Broken up for scrap at La Spezia, Italy, in 1983. Ex-Grimaldi Siosa Lines.
Built by Swan Hunter & Wigham Richardson Ltd, Newcastle, for Soc Generale de Transports Maritimes a Vapeur as the CAMPANA (1929). Renamed RIO JACHAL (1943 – Argentine government) and CAMPANA (1946 – SGTM).

IRWIN (1936) See JOHN L.CLEM (1941)

ISABELLA (1989)
34386 grt; 2200 psrs
420 cars or 53 trailers
559' x 91' x 21' (169.4 x 27.6 x 6.3 m)
4 x 12-cylinder Wartsila-Pielstick diesel engines via twin screw.

Ice-strengthened passenger-car ferry owned by SF Line and operated by the Viking Line.
Built by Brodogradiliste, Split, for the Viking Line.

ISE MARU (1973) See St EZEKIEL MORENO (1996)

ISHIKARI (1974) See EROROKRITOS (1991)

ISHIKARI MARU (1977) See SEA HARMONY (1993)

ISHIKARI II (1991)
14257 grt; 850 psrs
632' x 89' x 23' (191.5 x 27 x 7 m)
2 x 14-cylinder Mitsubishi-MAN diesel engines via twin screw.
Passenger ferry owned and operated by Taiheiyo Ferry KK, Nagoya (Pacific Ferry Co Ltd), Japan.
Built by Mitsubishi Heavy Industries Ltd, Kobe.

ISIPINGO (1934)
7069 grt; 70 psrs
404' x 57' x 25'3" (122.4 x 17.3 x 7.7 m)
2 x 6-cylinder Workman, Clark-Sulzer-type diesel engines via twin screw.
Broken up for scrap in Hong Kong in 1964.
Built by Workman, Clark, Belfast, for the Bank Line.

ISKENDERUN (1950)
6570 grt; 416 psrs
433' x 57' x 19' (131.2 x 17.4 x 5.8 m)
4 x DRG turbine engines via twin screw.
Broken up for scrap at Aliaga, Turkey, in 1982. Ex-Turkish Maritime Lines.
Built by Ansaldo SpA, Genoa,.

ISKENDERUN (1991)
10583 grt; 610 psrs
610 cars or 7 cars + 26 trailers
421' x 64' x 18' (127.5 x 19.4 x 5.4 m)
4 x 6-cylinder Zgoda-Sulzer diesel engines via twin screw.
Passenger-car-cargo ferry owned and operated by Turkish Maritime Lines. She was placed on the sales lists as of 31 December 2000.
Built by Turkiye Gemi Camialti, Camielti, for TDI Deniz.

ISLA DE BOTAFOC (1999)
12705 grt; 1350 psrs
310 cars or 40 cars + 62 trailers
425' x 71' x 15'6" (128.8 x 21.5 x 4.7 m)
2 x 16-cylinder Crossley-Pielstick diesel engines via twin screw.

Passenger-car-cargo ferry owned by Umafisa Cataluna SA and operated by Umafisa Lines.
Built by Harland & Wolff Ltd, Belfast, for Sealink UK Ltd, Dover, as the St ANSELM (1980). Renamed STENA CAMBRIA (1990 – P&O-Stena Line Ltd).

ISLA DE CABRERA (1974)
6518 grt; 236 psrs
401' x 55' x 23'10" (121.5 x 16.7 x 7 m)
2 x 7-cylinder B+W diesel engines via twin screw.
Broken up for scrap at Castellon in 1974, following her gutting by fire while her new owners were actually registering her in her new name after a change of ownership. Ex-Trasmediterranea.
Built by Union Naval de Levante, Valencia, for Empresa Nacional Elcano as the passenger-cargo ship EXPLORADOR IRADIER (1948). Renamed SATRUSTEGUI (1952 – Spanish Line).

ISLA DE COCHE (1974) See THEOSKEPASTI (1986)

ISLA DE CUBAGUA (1975)
3733 grt; 1100 psrs
175 cars
333' x 61' x 15' (100.9 x 18.6 x 4.5 m)
2 x 9-cylinder Wartsila-Vasa diesel engines via twin screw.
Sank on 14 April 1986 720 miles (1,200 km) south-west of the Azores. She had been on her delivery voyage to Piraeus for the handover to her new owners of four weeks, CA Consilidado de Ferrys, Caracas.
Built by Wartsila-Helsinki for the Silja Line as the SKANDIA (1961).

ISLA DE FORMENTERA (1973)
6518 grt; 236 psrs
402' x 55' x 24' (121.8 x 16.7 x 7.3 m)
2 x 7-cylinder B+W diesel engines via twin screw.
Broken up for scrap at Barcelona in 1979. Ex-Cia Trasmediterranea.
Built by Union Naval de Levante, Valencia, for Empresa Nacional Elcano as the CONDE DE ARGELEJO (1949). Renamed VIRGIN DE CHURRUCA (1952 – Cia Trasatlantica Espanol).

ISLAM (1902)
3662 grt; 710 psrs
365' x 43' x 28'6" (111.1 x 13 x 8.7 m)

Richardson & Sons 3-cylinder triple expansion engine via single screw. Broken up for scrap in Marseille in 1903. Ex-French Line. Built by J & G Thompson, Glasgow, for the Union Steamship Co Ltd as the TROJAN (1880). Renamed WASSAU (1901 – Elder Dempster Lines).

ISLAMI (1934)
5876 grt; 98 psrs
429' x 56' x 26' (130 x 17.7 x 9 m)
Triple expansion engine via single screw.
Owned and operated by the Mogul Line Ltd, India.
Built by Lithgows Ltd, Port Glasgow.

ISLAND ADVENTURE (1998)
15409 grt; 650 psrs
518' x 73' x 19'6" (157 x 22 x 5.9 m)
2 x 18-cylinder Wartsila-Pielstick diesel engines via twin screw.
Casino ship owned by Marvest Shipholding Corporation and operated by SeaEscape Cruises.
Built by Wartsila-Turku for Black Sea Shipping Co, Odessa, as the KAZAKHSTAN (1976). Renamed UKRAINA (1994 – Ocean Agencies Ltd) and ROYAL SEAS (1996 – Royal Seas Cruise Line).

ISLAND BREEZE (1996) See THE BIG RED BOAT III (2000)

ISLAND DAWN (1998) See TEXAS TREASURE (2000)

ISLANDE (1923) See FONTAINEBLEU (1924)

ISLAND FIESTA (1984) See REGAL VOYAGER (1994)

ISLAND HOLIDAY (1997) See ENCHANTED CAPRI (1998)

ISLAND OF CYPRUS (1972)
12712 grt; 363 psrs
549' x 68' x 22' (167.3 x 20.7 x 6.7 m)
2 x 10-cylinder B+W diesel engines via twin screw.
Broken up for scrap at Kaohsiung in 1975. Ex-Efthymiadis Line.
Built by Ateliers et Chantiers de France, Dunkirk, for Messageries Maritimes as the CALEDONIEN (1952). Renamed NISOS KYPROS (1972 – Efthymiadis Line).

ISLAND PRINCESS (1975) See HYUNDAI PUNGAK-HO (1998)

ISLAND SUN (1984) See UNIVERSE EXPLORER (1996)

ISLAND VENTURE (1972) See HYUNDAI PUNGAK (1999)

ISLE OF ARRAN (1984)
3296 grt; 446 psrs
68 cars
280' x 52' x 10'6" (84.9 x 15.8 x 3.2 m)
2 x 8-cylinder Mirrlees diesel engines via twin screw.

Passenger-car ferry operated by Caledonian MacBrayne.
Built by the Ferguson Ailsa Shipyard, Port Glasgow, for Caledonian MacBrayne at a cost of £7,000,000.

ISLE OF INISHMORE (1993) See MADELEINE (1997)

ISLE OF INISHMORE (1997)
34031 grt; 2200 psrs

856 cars + 122 trailers
598' x 92' x 19' (182.5 x 27.8 x 5.8 m)
4 x 8-cylinder Zgoda-Sulzer diesel engines via twin screw.

Passenger-car-cargo RoRo ferry operated by Irish Ferries.
Built by Van der Giessen-de Noord Shipyard, Krimpen, for Irish Ferries at a cost of £63,000,000.

ISLE OF INISHTURK (1996) See MADELEINE (1997)

ISLE OF INNISFREE (1992) See STENA NAUTICA (1996)

ISLE OF INNISFREE (1995)
22365 grt; 1650 psrs
600 cars or 108 trailers or 142 coaches
599' x 77' x 19' (181.6 x 23.4 x 5.8 m)
4 x 8-cylinder Sulzer diesel engines via twin screw.

Owned and operated by Irish Ferries.
Built by Van der Giessen de Noord Shipyards, Krimpen, for Irish Continental Ltd at a cost of £46,000,000.

ISLE OF LEWIS (1995)
6753 grt; 680 psrs
123 cars
334' x 59' x 14' (101.3 x 18 x 4.2 m)
2 x 6-cylinder Mirrlees diesel engines via twin screw.

Passenger-car ferry operated by Caledonian MacBrayne.
Built by Ferguson Shipbuilders Ltd, Port Glasgow, for Caledonian MacBrayne at a cost of US$30,000,000.

ISLE OF MULL (1988)

4719 grt; 1000 psrs
80 cars
297' x 52' x 10'6" (90.4 x 15.8 x 3.2 m)
2 x 8-cylinder Mirrlees diesel engines via twin screw.

Ferry operating for Caledonian MacBrayne.
Built by Appledore Ferguson Ltd, Port Glasgow, for Caledonian MacBrayne at a cost of £6,500,000.

ISMAILIA (1901) See BRUNETTE (1921)

ISOLA DI LEVANZO (1901) See LEVANZO (1902)

ISRAEL (1955) See ANGRA DO HEROISMO (1966)

ISTANBUL (1947)

5236 grt; 306 psrs
404' x 58' x 23' (122.4 x 17.6 x 7 m)
SRG turbine engine via single screw.
Broken up for scrap in Turkey in 1966. Ex-Turkish Maritime Lines.
Built by Newport News Shipbuilding & Drydock Company, Newport News, Virginia, for Colombian Mail Steamship Company as the COLOMBIA (1932). Renamed MEXICO (1938 – New York & Cuba Mail Steamship Company).

ISTANBUL (1973)

3445 grt; 413 psrs
303' x 54' x 14' (91.7 x 16.5 x 4.2 m)
2 x 9-cylinder Werkspoor diesel engines via twin screw.
Sank in 1993, with the loss of one life, in the Sea of Marmara where she had caught fire while en route to Izmir.
Built by Denizcilik Bankasi TAO., Camialti, for Turkish Marine.

ISTHMIA (1966)

4216 grt; 265 psrs
376' x 50' x 28' (113.9 x 15.2 x 8.5 m)
3 x Parsons SRG turbine engines via single screw.
Broken up for scrap in Turkey in 1973. Ex-Hellenic Mediterranean Lines.
Built by Swan Hunter & Wigham Richardson Ltd, Newcastle, for Swedish Lloyd Line as the SUECIA (1929). She had previously been sunk in March 1937 when a berthing hawser snapped and she swung into the path of a new tanker being launched.

ISTRA (1965) See ARION (1999)

ISTRA (1992)

4258 grt; 800 psrs
306' x 53' x 14' (92.7 x 16.7 x 4.2 m)
4 x 12-cylinder B+W diesel engines via twin screw.

Owned and operated by Jadrolinija.

Built by Aalborg Vaerft, Aalborg, for Mols Linien AS as the METTE MOLS (1966). Renamed METTE MO (1974 – Mols Linien), DANA GLORIA (1977 – DFDS) and BALKANIJA (1981 – Jadrolinija).

ITAHITE (1928)

4998 grt; 280 psrs
386' x 52' x 20'6" (117 x 15.8 x 6.2 m)
Penhoet 6-cylinder triple expansion engines via twin screw.
Broken up for scrap. Ex-CNNC, Brazil.
Built by Penhoet, St Nazaire, for Cia Nacional de Navegacao Costeira, Brazil.

ITAIMBE (1928)

4998 grt; 280 psrs
386' x 52' x 20'6" (117 x 15.8 x 6.2 m)
Pennhoet 3-cylinder triple expansion engines via twin screw.
Broken up for scrap. Ex-CNNC, Brazil.
Built by Penhoet, St Nazaire, for Cia Nacional de Navegacao Costeira, Brazil.

ITALIA (1889) See TENEDOS (1903)

ITALIA (1904)

4806 grt; 1420 psrs
400' x 49' x 27'7" (121.9 x 15 x 8.4 m)
D & W Henderson 3-cylinder triple expansion engine via single screw.
Broken up for scrap in 1923.
Built by D & W Henderson Ltd, Glasgow, for the Anchor Line.

ITALIA (1905) See MASANIELLO (1917)

ITALIA (1905)

5018 grt; 2516 psrs
394' x 48' x 27' (120 x 14.5 x 8.2 m)
Odero 6-cylinder triple expansion engines via twin screw.
Owned by Lloyd Triestino, she was broken up for scrap at La Spezia in 1950 after raising her from the harbour bed at Arsa (Trieste). She had sank here on 6 July 1944 during an intensive air raid by Allied bombers.
Built by N Odero & Company, Genoa, for La Veloce.

ITALIA (1923)

10484 grt; 2145 psrs
521' x 60' x 34'6" (158.6 x 18.2 x 10.5 m)
2 x 4-cylinder AG Vulcan quadruple expansion engines via twin screw.
Broken up for scrap in Italy in 1926 after serving as an exhibition ship. Ex-Italian government.
Built by Vulcan, Stettin, for North German Lloyd as the KONIG ALBERT (1899). Renamed as the hospital ship FERDINANDO PALASCIANO (1917 – Italian government, after seizing the vessel).

ITALIA (1948) See IMPERIAL BAHAMA HOTEL (1964)

ITALIA (1967) See SAPPHIRE (1996)

ITALIA (1987) See COSTA MARINA (1990)

ITALIA I (1993) See VALTUR PRIMA (1999)

ITALIA EXPRESS (1987)

4300 grt; 249 psrs
200 cars or 70 cars and 65 trailers
357' x 62' x 16' (108.2 x 18.8 x 4.8 m)
2 x 14-cylinder Bolnes diesel engines via twin screw.
Passenger-car ferry operated by Ventouris Co Ltd, Piraeus. She capsized and sank, on 24 March 1988, 328 yards (300 m) from the FIESTA at Kynosoura while berthing at Drapetzona for repairs.
Built by AG Weser, Bremerhaven, for North Sea Ferries as the passenger-car ferry NORWAVE (1965).

ITALIAN (1915) See ROLLO (1920)

ITALIA PRIMA (1994) See VALTUR PRIMA (1999)

ITALIS (1978) See AMERICAN STAR (1993)

ITANAGE (1928)
4966 grt; 280 psrs
386' x 52' x 20'6" (117 x 15.8 x 6.2 m)
Beardmore-Tosi 12-cylinder diesel engines via twin screw.
Broken up for scrap. Ex-CNNC, Brazil.
Built by William Beardmore & Company, Dalmuir, for Costeira, Brazil.

ITAPAGE (1927)
4998 grt; 280 psrs
386' x 52' x 20'6" (117 x 15 x 6.2 m)
Beardmore-Tosi 12-cylinder diesel engines via twin screw.
Sank on 26 September 1943 after being torpedoed by the German U-161.
Built by William Beardmore & Company, Dalmuir, for Cia Nacional de Navegacao Costeira, Brazil.

ITAPE (1928)
4998 grt; 280 psrs
386' x 52' x 20'6" (117 x 15.8 x 6.2 m)
Triple expansion engines via twin screw.
Broken up for scrap. Ex-CNNC, Brazil.
Built by Penhoet, St Nazaire, for Cia Nacional de Navegacao Costeira, Brazil.

ITAQUICE (1928)
4966 grt; 280 psrs
386' x 52' x 20'6" (117 x 15.8 x 6.2 m)
Beardmore 12-cylinder triple expansion engines via twin screw.
Sank in the mid-1950s.
Built by William Beardmore & Co Ltd, Glasgow, for Cia Nacional Navegacao Costeira, Brazil.

ITHACA (1972) See DOLPHIN IV (1987)

ITONUS (1907)
6630 grt; 2000 psrs
449' x 54' x 24'7" (136.9 x 16.5 x 7.5 m)
Vickers & Maxim 6-cylinder triple expansion engine via twin screw.
Owned by the British India Line when she sank on 20 December 1916 after being torpedoed by U-38 off Malta.
Built by Vickers Sons & Maxim, Barrow-in-Furness, for British India Steam Navigation Co Ltd as the ANGLIA (1898).

ITSUKISHIMA MARU (1903)
3860 grt
345' x 48' x 24' (104.5 x 14.5 x 7.3 m)
Blair & Co 3-cylinder triple expansion engines via single screw.
Owned and operated by Maroto Mortoka, Japan.
Built by CS Swan Hunter Ltd, Newcastle, for Elderslie Steamship Vco Ltd as the FIFESHIRE (1887). Renamed DUKE OF FIFE (1898 – Duke of Fife Steamship Co Ltd).

IVAN FRANKO (1964) See FRANK (1997)

IVAN ZAJC (1992)
5124 grt; 900 psrs
334' x 53' x 14' (101.2 x 16 x 4.3 m)
2 x 16-cylinder Fiat diesel engines via twin screw.
Owned and operated by Jadrolinija, Rijeka.
Built by Cantieri Navale Apuania, Carrara, for Jadrolinija, Rijeka, as the passenger ferry TIZIANO (1970).

IVER HEATH (1918)
9674 grt; 75 psrs
470' x 56' x 31'9" (143.1 x 17.1 x 9.7 m)
Richardson, Westgarth 6-cylinder triple expansion engines via twin screw.
Broken up for scrap in 1924. Ex-Crete Shipping Company.
Built by CS Swan Hunter, Newcastle, for Beaver Line as the LAKE MANITOBA (1901).

IVERNIA (1900)
14278 grt; 1730 psrs
582' x 65' x 37'8" depth (176.4 x 19.8 x 11.5 m)
2 x 4-cylinder Wallsend Slipway quadruple expansion engines via twin screw.
Sank on 1 January 1917 after being torpedoed by the German U-47 58 miles (98 km) off Cape Matapan, Greece. A total of 222 lives were lost.
Built by CS Swan Hunter Ltd, Newcastle, for the Cunard Steamship Company.

IVERNIA (1955) See FEDOR SHALYAPIN (1991)

IVORY MARU (1967) See VERGINA CITY (1992)

IXION (1912)
10221 grt; 600 psrs
518' x 60' x 39'5" depth (157.9 x 18.1 x 12 m)
Scotts 6-cylinder triple expansion engines via twin screw.
Sank on 7 May 1941 200 miles (334 km) south of Reykjavik, after a torpedo hit her from the German U-94.
Built by Scotts Shipbuilding & Engineering Co Ltd, Greenock, for the Blue Funnel Line.

IXION (1951)
10125 grt; 53 psrs
523' x 69' x 31' (158.5 x 20.9 x 9.4 m)
3 x Harland & Wolff DRG turbines engine via single screw.
Broken up for scrap at Barcelona in 1972.
Built by Harland & Wolff Ltd, Belfast, for the Blue Funnel Line.

IYO MARU (1901)
6320 grt
445' x 49' x 26'3" (134.8 x 14.8 x 8 m)
Mitsubishi 6-cylinder triple expansion engines via twin screw.
Broken up for scrap in 1933.
Built by Mitsubishi Dockyard, Nagasaki, for NYK.

IYO MARU (1965)
3071 grt; 2350 psrs
27 rail coaches
276' x 52' x 12' (83.6 x 15.9 x 3.6 m)
2 x 14-cylinder Mitsui-B+W diesel engines via twin screw.
Built by Hitachi Zosen, Sakurajima, for Japan National Railways and operated by Hayashi Marine as a train ferry.

IZMIR (1955)
6049 grt; 476 psrs
402' x 54' x 19' (121.8 x 16.4 x 5.8 m)
2 x 8-cylinder MAN diesel engines via single screw.
Sank in Turkish waters in 1957 and, although declared a total constructive loss, she was raised, refloated and refurbished.
Built by AG Weser, Bremen, for Turkish Maritime Line.

IZU 3 (1976) See SUPERFERRY (1991)

IZU No. 11 (1972) See PATMOS (1991)

IZU MARU No. 3 (1976) See SUPERFERRY (1991)

IZUMO MARU (1941) See HIYO (1942)

JABAL ALI 1 (1999)
6399 grt; 1180 psrs
160 cars
361' x 58' x 14'9" (109.5 x 17.5 x 4.5 m)
2 x 12-cylinder Pielstick diesel engines via twin screw.
Passenger-car ferry owned and operated by Naif Marine Services (Pvt), Dubai, United Arab Emirates.
Built by Soc Nouvelle des Ateliers at Chantiers de la La Rochelle-Pallice for Brittany Ferries as the PENN-AR-BED (1974). Renamed SVENO MARINA (1984 – Seveno Line), PRINCESS M (1985 – JNC Cruising), LILLY R (1989 – Alimar), and PRINCESS (1996 – Alimar Ferries Service Ltd, Nicosia).

JACK DALTON (1960) See SUNSHINE COAST QUEEN (1967)

JACOPO TINTORETTO (1966) See GURGEN-2 (1996)

JACQUES CARTIER (1929)
6693 grt; 156 psrs
413' x 52' x 36' depth (125.2 x 15.8 x 10.9 m)
6-cylinder triple expansion engine via twin screw.
Broken up for scrap in Genoa in 1934 after being laid up since 1931. She had served in the French Navy as an officers' training ship. Ex-French Line.
Built by Chantiers et Ateliers de Provence, Port de Bouc, for the French Line as the CAROLINE (1908).

JADOTVILLE (1956) See CHITRAL (1961)

JAGERSFONTEIN (1934)
10083 grt; 113 psrs
457' x 63' x 30'10" (138.5 x 19.1 x 9.1 m)
2 x 6-cylinder Stork diesel engines via twin screw.
Sank on 26 June 1942 after being torpedoed by the German U-107 500 miles east of Bermuda.
Built by Nederlandsche Shipbuilding Mij, Amsterdam, for the Holland Africa Line.

JAGERSFONTEIN (1947) See DEVON (1967)

JAGIELLO (1947) See PETR VELIKI (1949)

JAKUTIA (1913) See MORSKAJA II (1913)

JAL-AZAD (1948) See STATE OF BOMBAY (1954)

JALJAWAHAR (1948) See STATE OF MADRAS (1954)

JAMAICA (1937) See BLUMENTHAL (1957)

JAMAICA (1946) See BLUMENTHAL (1957).

JAMAICA MERCHANT (1929)
7490 grt; 122 psrs
414' x 56' x 26' (125.5 x 17 x 7.9 m)
Triple expansion engine via single screw.
Broken up for a tender fee of £25,000 at Trieste, Italy, in 1937. Ex-the Jamaica Direct Fruit Line.
Built by Cammell Laird & Company, Birkenhead, for the Nelson Steam Navigation Company Ltd as the HIGHLAND PIPER (1911).

JAMAICA PLANTER (1929)
7490 grt; 122 psrs
414' x 56' x 26' (125.5 x 17 x 7.9 m)
Triple expansion engine via single screw.
Broken up for scrap in 1935. Ex-the Jamaica Direct Fruit Line.
Built by Cammell Laird & Company for the Nelson Steam Navigation Co Ltd as the HIGHLAND LOCH (1911).

JAMAICA PRODUCER (1929)
7490 grt; 122 psrs
414' x 56' x 26' (125.5 x 17 x 7.9 m)

Triple expansion engine via single screw.
Broken up for scrap in 1934. Ex-the Jamaica Direct Fruit Line.
Built by Russell & Company, Glasgow, for the Nelson Steam Navigation Co Ltd as the HIGHLAND GLEN (1910).

JAMAICA QUEEN (1967) See ARION (1976).

JAMAICA SETTLER (1929)
7490 grt; 122 psrs
405' x 56' x 26' (122.7 x 17 x 7.9 m)
Triple expansion engine via single screw.
Broken up for scrap in 1935. Ex-the Jamaica Direct Fruit Line.
Built by Cammell Laird & Co, Glasgow, for the Nelson Steam Navigation Co Ltd as the HIGHLAND LADDIE (1910).

JAMAIQUE (1922) See COMPIEGNE (1923)

JAMAIQUE (1928)
10123 grt; 400 psrs
484' x 59' x 27'2" (146.7 x 17.9 x 8.2 m)
4 x Wallsend Slipway DRG turbine engines via twin screw.
Broken up for scrap at Ghent, Belgium, in 1954.
Built by Swan Hunter & Wigham Richardson Ltd, Newcastle, for Cie de Navigation Sud Atlantique as the MOSELLA (1922).

JAMES (1968)
10530 grt; 2000 psrs
520' x 72' x 32'10" (157.6 x 21.8 x 9.7 m)
Westinghouse SRG turbine engines via single screw.
Owned by James River Transport Inc, New York, which converted her into a passenger ship after she had been laid up in the Hudson River, New York, by the US Maritime Commission.
Built by Kaiser Corporation, Richmond, California, for the US Navy as the Class A4-S-A1 troop transport GENERAL H. F. HODGES, USS (AP-144) (1945). Reclassified as the GENERAL H. F. HODGES, USAT (1946 – US Army) and the GENERAL H. F. HODGES, USNS (T-AP-144) (1950 – US Navy).

JAMES L. PARKER (1941) See REGINA PRIMA (1973)

JAMES O'HARA (1941) See JAMES OHARA (T-APA 179) (1950)

JAMES O'HARA (T-APA 179) (1950)
11471 grt; 300 psrs
492' x 69' x 26'6" (149.1 x 20.9 x 8 m)
Geared turbines via single screw.
Laid up in 1992 with the reserve fleet in Puget Sound by the US Shipping Board.
Built by the Seattle-Tacoma Shipbuilding Company, Tacoma, Washington, for the US Army as the Class C3-S1-A3 troop transport and then redesignated for the US Navy in 1942 as an AP-90 ship.

JAMES SCREVEN (1944) See OLIMPIA (1947)

JAN (1968) See ORIENTAL ESMERALDA (1969)

JAN BAKX (1966) See CILICIA (1980)

JANINA (1966) See JI MEI (1983)

JAN PIETERSZOON COEN (1915)
11692 grt; 412 psrs
503' x 61' x 35'6" (152.4 x 18.5 x 10.8 m)
2 x 3-cylinder Nederlandsche Fabriek triple expansion engines via twin screw.
Broken up in 1945, where she lay, after being scuttled on 14 May 1940 to make a block ship between the pier heads at Ijmuiden, Holland.
Built by Nederlandsche Scheepsbouw Maatschappij, Amsterdam, for the Nederlands Steamship Co.

JANUA (1928)
5601 grt; 1650 psrs
389' x 52' x 26'3" (118.7 x 16 x 8 m)
Richardson-Westgarth 3-cylinder triple expansion engine via single screw.
Broken up for scrap in 1931. Ex-Italian Line.

Built by Cantieri Navale Di Muggiano, La Spezia, for Navigazione Generale Italiana as the IL PIEMONTE (1904). Renamed PRESIDENT P MONTT (1908 – chartered to Lloyd del Pacifico), IL PIEMONTE (1908 – Navigazione Generale Italiana), SAN ROSSORE (1916 – Lloyd Sabaudo) and EMILIA PELLEGRINA (1926 – Italian Line).

JAN WELLEM (1935)
11776 grt; 766 psrs
469' x 71' x 32'7" depth (142.1 x 21.5 x 9.9 m)
Bremer Vulkan 3-cylinder triple expansion engine via single screw.
Broken up for scrap at Blyth in 1947 as a whaling ship. Ex-Henkel & Cie GmbH, Germany.
Built by Bremer Vulkan, Vegesack, for Hapag as the WURTEMBURG (1921).

JAPAN (1893) See WALTER HOLKEN (1919)

JAPANESE DREAM (1990) See DELTA FILIPINE DREAM (1992)

JASON (1950)
10160 grt; 53 psrs
523' x 69' x 31' (158.5 x 20.9 x 9.4 m)
3 x Wallsend Slipway DRG turbines via single screw.
Broken up for scrap at Kaohsiung in 1972.
Built by Swan Hunter & Wigham Richardson Ltd, Newcastle, for the Blue Funnel Line.

JASON (1966) See IASON (1995)

JATRA IBPS (1995)
5057 grt; 628 psrs
309' x 59' x 14' (93.5 x 18 x 4.2 m)
4 x 6-cylinder Daihatsu diesel engines via twin screw.
Passenger ferry owned and operated by PT Samudera Perkasa Wlsma Budi.
Built by Kurushima Dock Co Ltd for Shikoku Chuo, Niihama, as the NIIHAMA (1973).

JATTEN FINN (1964) See WAPPEN VON HAMBURG (1984)

JAVA (1892) See UME MARU (1910)

JEAN LABORDE (1929)
11591 grt; 900 psrs
497' x 62' x 28'3" (150.6 x 18.8 x 8.6 m)
Schneider 16-cylinder diesel engines via twin screw.
Broken up for scrap at Le Seyne, France, in 1946 after raising her from the Marseilles harbour bed. She had settled here following her scuttling by the Germans in August 1944.
Built by Constructions Navales, La Ciotat, for Messageries Maritimes.

JEAN LABORDE (1953) See OCEANOS (1976)

JEAN MERMOZ (1957) See SERENADE (1999)

JEDDAH (1914)
4686 grt; 98 psrs
401' x 47' x 29' (122.3 x 14.3 x 8.8 m)
Triple expansion engine via single screw.
Broken up for scrap by GBA Lambardo, Genoa, in 1924.
Built as the PALAWAN (1895) by Caird & Company, Greenock, for the P&O Line at a cost of £78,317. Sold to the Arab Steamship Company in 1914 for £17,279.

JEFFERSON (1899) See JEFFERSON (1920)

JEFFERSON (1920)
3723 grt
352' x 42' x 17' (106.7 x 12.7 x 5.2 m)
Delaware River Co 3-cylinder triple expansion engine via single screw.
Broken up for scrap at Baltimore, USA, in 1932 after colliding with the liner MOHAWK off the New Jersey coast on 19 May 1928.
Built by Delaware River Co, Chester, Pennsylvania, for Eastern Steamship Lines Inc as the JEFFERSON (1899). Renamed QUINNEBAUG, USS (1918 – US Navy).

JEHANGIR (1914)
5186 grt; 122 psrs
411' x 48' x 30'5" depth (124.5 x 14.5 x 9.2 m)
Compound engine via single screw.
Broken up for scrap in 1923 by her Indian owners at Mumbai.
Built by William Denny & Brothers, Dumbarton, for the British India Steam Navigation Company as the JELUNGA (1890). Renamed LEON XIII (1893 – Cia Trasatlantica), JELUNGA (1894 – British India Steam Navigation Company), SANTIAGO (1896) and JELUNGA (1896 – British India Steam Navigation Company).

JELUNGA (1890) See JEHANGIR (1914)

JELUNGA (1894) See JEHANGIR (1914)

JELUNGA (1896) See JEHANGIR (1914)

JENNY (1948) See DJATINEGARA (1952)

JENS BANG (1950) See NAIAS (1970)

JENS KOFOED (1963) See EUROPA I (1998)

JENS KOFOED (1979)
12131 grt; 1500 psrs
300 cars
400' x 73' x 17' (121.2 x 22 x 5.2 m)
4 x 16-cylinder Alpha diesels via twin screw.

Ice-strengthened ferry owned and operated by Bornholmstrafikken.
Built by Aalborg Vaerft AS, Aalborg.

JEROME (1897) See KERASOUNDE (1911)

JEROUSALIM (1911)
4815 grt; 1360 psrs
403' x 47' x 27'7" (122.8 x 14.2 x 8.4 m)
Ansaldo 3-cylinder triple expansion engine via single screw.
Broken up for scrap in 1928. Ex-the Russian government.
Built by G Ansaldo & Company, Sestri Ponente, for Navigazione Generale Italiana as the LOMBARDIA (1901).

JERUSALEM (1953) See ALIYA (1957)

JERUSALEM (1957) See BONAIRE STAR (1975)

JERVIS BAY (1922)
14164 grt; 542 psrs
549' x 68' x 33' (167.3 x 20.7 x 10 m)
DRG turbines via twin screw.
Sank at twilight on 5 November 1940 in the South Atlantic from the intense gunfire of the German pocket battleship ADMIRAL SCHEER. Loss of life numbered 180.
Built by Vickers-Armstrong Ltd, Barrow-in-Furness, for the Aberdeen & Commonwealth Line.

JERVIS BAY, HMAS (AGT-203)(1977) See AGIOS ANDREAS (1995)

J. FRANKLIN BELL (1940) See J. FRANKLIN BELL, USS (APA-16) (1942)

J. FRANKLIN BELL, USS (APA-16) (1942)
14127 grt; 550 psrs
length 535' x beam 72' (162.1 x 21.8 m)
Turbines via twin screw.
Broken up for scrap at San Pedro, California, USA, in 1949. Ex-US Navy.
Built by the New York Shipbuilding Company, Camden, New York, for the Admiral Line as the KEYSTONE STATE (1921). Renamed PRESIDENT McKINLEY (1922 – Admiral Line) and J. FRANKLIN BELL (1940 – US Army).

J. G. FICHTE (1963) See PEGANCIA (1979)

JIAN HUA (1967)
9505 grt; 314 psrs
481' x 62' x 23' (145.9 x 18.8 x 6.9 m)
2 x 8-cylinder B+W diesel engines via twin screw.
Owned by the China Ocean Shipping Company, Canton.
Built by Pennhoet, St Nazaire, for Paquet Lines as the FOCH (1951).

JIAN ZHEN (1985) See PRINCESS OF PARADISE (1994)

JI MEI (1981) See NAN HU (1983)

JI MEI (1983)
7694 grt; 614 psrs
230 cars
467' x 56' x 19' (140.8 x 20 x 5.8 m)
2 x 9-cylinder MAN diesel engines via twin screw.
Operated by Xiamen Lutong Shipping Co, Hong Kong, as a passenger-car ferry and casino ship.
Built by HWD for the Jahre Line as the PRINSESSE RAGNHILD (1966). Renamed JANINA (1966), AMATISTA (1980 – Amatista Shipping Corporation, Monrovia), JIN JIANG (1981 – government of China).

JIMY (1991) See ARTEMIS I (1996)

JIN HU (1993)
5625 grt; 1400 psrs
175 cars
382' x 62' x 16' (115.8 x 18.8 x 4.9 m)
4 x 6-cylinder Pielstick diesel engines via twin screw.

Passenger-car ferry and casino ship owned and operated by Shantou Shipping Company, Canton.
Built by Uddevalla Varvet AB, Uddevalla, for the State Jaravagar, Trelleborg as the DROTTNINGEN (1968). Renamed ALZAHRAA (1977- Federal Arab Maritime Company, Alex andria), IONIAN VICTORY (1984 – Strintzis Lines SA, Limassol) and PALOMA (1985 – Arkadia Lines).

JIN JIANG (1981) See JI MEI (1983)

JIN JIANG (1984) See HENG LI (1993)

JINYO (1942) See SHINYO MARU (1943)

JJ LUCKENBACH (1900) See MADISON (1923).

JJ SISTER (1975) See MOBY MAGIC (1997)

JJ SISTER (1995) See MOBY MAGIC (1997)

J. L. LUCKENBACH (1923) See DJAKARTA RAYA (1952)

JOCHEN STEFFEN (1999)
5293 grt; 785 psrs
100 cars
341' x 57' x 15' (103.4 x 17.2 x 4.6 m)
2 x 9-cylinder B+W diesel engines via twin screw.
Passenger-car ferry owned by Elbe Ferry GmbH & Co KG and operated by Harms EH, Germany.
Built by Aalborg Vaerft, Aalborg, for the Danish government to be operated by DFDS as the PRINSESSE ANNE-MARIE (1960).

JOHAN DE WITT (1920) See NEPTUNIA (1948)

JOHANNA (1908) See PERICLES (1914)

JOHANNESBURG (1895) See SURAT (1912)

JOHANN HEINRICH BURCHARD (1914) See RELIANCE (1926)

JOHAN VAN OLDENBARNEVELT (1930) See LAKONIA (1963)

JOHN BARNESON (1915) See CHINA (1915)

JOHN ERICCSON, USS (1941) See IMPERIAL BAHAMA HOTEL (1964)

JOHN HAMILTON GRAY (1968) See CONTESSA I (1997)

JOHN L. CLEM (1941)
4900 grt; 132 psrs
length 360' x beam 52' (109.1 x 15.8 m)
Quadruple expansion engine via single screw.
Broken up at Baltimore, USA, in 1948.
Built by William Cramp & Sons, Philadelphia, for the Grace Line as the SANTA ANA (1917). Renamed GUATEMALA (1928 – Panama Mail Line), SANTA CECILIA (1931 – Grace Line) and IRWIN (1936 – Merchant & Miners).

JOHN PENN, USS (AP-51) (1942) See JOHN PENN, USS (T-AP-23) (1943)

JOHN PENN, USS (T-AP-23) (1943)
9359 grt; 147 psrs
length 474' x beam 61' (143.6 18.5 m)
Turbine engine via single screw.
Sank on 13 August 1943 after a Japanese aircraft attack off Lungga Point, Guadalcanal. Ex-US Navy.
Built by the New York Shipbuilding Company, Camden, New York, for American Export Isbrandtsen Lines as the EXCAMBION (1931). Renamed JOHN PENN, USS (AP-51) (1942 – US Navy).

JOLLY GIALLO (1976) See CARLA E (1991)

JON (1992) See NURA NOVA (1999)

JOSEF PILSUDSKI (1921) See WILBO (1924)

JOSEPH AND CLARA SMALLWOOD (1989)

27614 grt; 1223 psrs
350 cars or 18 cars + 90 trailers
591' x 84'6" x 22' (179 x 25.6 x 6.8 m)
4 x 8-cylinder MaK diesel engines via twin screw.
Ice-strengthened ferry operated by Marine Atlantic, Canada.
Built by Versatile Davie Inc, Lauzon, at a cost of Can$146,000,000

JOSEPH HEWES, USS (AP-50) (1941)
9359 grt; 147 psrs
474' x 61' x 42'3" depth (143.6 x 18.5 x 12.8 m)
New York Shipbuilding Co SRG turbine engines via single screw.
Sank on 11 November 1942 after being torpedoed off Fedala, Morocco. Ex-US Navy.
Built as the EXCALIBUR (1931) by the New York Shipbuilding Company, Camden, New York, for American Export Isbrandtsen Lines.

JOSEPH T. DICKMAN, USAT (1940) See JOSEPH T. DICKMAN, USS (AP-13) (1943 – US Army)

JOSEPH T. DICKMAN, USNS (AP-26) (1941 – US Navy)
See JOSEPH T. DICKMAN, USS (AP-13) (1943)

JOSEPH T. DICKMAN, USS (AP-13) (1943)
13869 grt; 644 psrs
535' x 72' x 28' (162.1 x 21.8 x 8.5 m)
4 x Curtis SRG turbine engines via twin screw.
Broken up for scrap at Oakland, California, USA, in 1948. Ex-US Navy.
Built by the New York Shipbuilding Company, Camden, New York, for United States Lines as the Class "535" troopship PENINSULA STATE (1922). Renamed PRESIDENT ROOSEVELT (1922 – United States Lines) and JOSEPH T. DICKMAN, USAT (1940 – US Army). Reclassified as the JOSEPH T. DICKMAN, USS (AP-13) (1941 – US Navy).

JOUFFREY D'ABBANS (1923) See CAP TOURANE (1925)

JOY WAVE (1999) See GOLDEN PRINCESS (2000)

JOYWAVE (2000)
5994 grt; 510 psrs
429' x 56' x 14' (130 x 17 x 4.2 m)
2 x 10-cylinder B+W diesel engines via twin screw.
Cruise ferry owned by New Marathon Lines, Cyprus, and operated by Legend Cruises, Puerto Rico.
Built by Soc Espanola de Construccion Naval SA, Cadiz, for Flota Argentina de Navigacion, Fluvial, as the 33 ORIENTALES (1966). Renamed CITY OF RODOS (1979 – Atlantis Naviera SA, Piraeus, & Cycladic Cruises), QUEEN ELENI (1995 – Vergina Cruises Hellas Co Ltd.) and QUEEN CONSTANTINA (2000 – Legend Cruises).

JUAN DE GARAY (1947)
9880 grt; 316 psrs
480' x 61' x 29' (145.5 x 18.5 x 8.8 m)
2 x 8-cylinder Schichau-Sulzer diesel engines via twin screw.
Broken up for scrap at Castellon, Spain, in 1963. Ex-Cia Transoceanic Argentina, Buenos Aires.
Built by Bremer Vulkan, Vegesack, as the ORINOCO (1928). Renamed PUEBLA (1941- government of Mexico).

JUAN J. SISTER (1993)
22409 grt; 550 psrs
150 cars + 92 trailers
49' x 86' x 20' (151.1 x 26 x 6 m)
4 x 8-cylinder Wartsila diesel engines via twin screw.
Passenger-car-cargo ferry operated by Trasmediterranea.
Built by Kvaerner-Masa Yards, Turku, for Trasmediterranea at a cost of US$110,000,000.

JUAN MARCH (1966) See OCEAN MAJESTY (1991)

JUAN SEBASTION ELCANO (1928) See VOLGA (1939)

JUBILEE (1986)
47262 grt; 1486 psrs
733' x 94' x 25' (222.1 x 28.4 x 7.6 m)

2 x 7-cylinder Sulzer diesel engines via twin screw.
Cruising for Carnival Cruise Line, Inc, Miami.
Built by Kockums, Malmo, at a cost of US$131,000,000.

JULIA (1968)
8357 grt; 52 psrs
459' x 63' x 28' (139.1 x 19.1 x 8.5 m)
Turbine engine via single screw.
Broken up for scrap at Kaohsiung in 1970. Ex-Anchor Shipping Corporation.
Built by the North Carolina Shipbuilding Corporation for the Grace Line as the SANTA CECILIA (1946).

JULIAN BESTREIRO (1996) See CIUDAD DE MALAGA (1998)

JULIETTE (1905) See IOANNINA (1913)

JULLE (1962) See AL RASHEED II (1992)

JULLE (1964) See ALDONZA MANRIGEO (1976)

JUNE LADY (1985) See CARLA E (1991)

JUNIATA (1905) See MILWAUKEE CLIPPER (1990)

JUNYO MARU (1942)
27700 grt; 890 psrs
719' x 88' x 45'9" depth (218 x 26.7 x 13.9 m)
2 x geared turbines via twin screw.
Broken up for scrap at Sasebo, Japan, in 1947 after being torpedoed on 9 December 1944 by USS REDFISH and USS SEADEVIL off Cape Nomozaki, near Nagasaki.
Launched on 26 June 1941 by Mitsubishi, Nagasaki, for NYK as the passenger ship KASHIWARA MARU (1941), but converted into an aircraft carrier for the Japanese Navy.

JUPITER (1966) See BYBLOS (2000)

JUPITER (1971)
6306 grt; 590 psrs
415' x 65' x 20' (125.8 x 19.7 x 6.1 m)
2 x 9-cylinder SEMT-Pielstick diesel engines via twin screw.
Sank while operating for Epirotiki Lines after a collision with the Italian car carrier ADIGE (5054 grt) on 21 October 1988, off Piraeus. Four lives were lost.
Built by Chantiers de l'Atlantique, St Nazaire, for the Zim Line as the MOLEDET (1961). Renamed ALEX ANDROS (1970 – although it had ZEUS on the stern in 1971).

JUPITER (1990) See MAGIC I (1999)

JUPITER (1997)
10524 grt; 880 psrs
420 cars
438' x 63' x 19'6" (132.7 x 19 x 5.9 m)
2 x 8-cylinder B+W diesel engines via twin screw.
Passenger-car ferry owned by Priority Shipping, Athens, and operated by Perco Maritime Inc, Athens.

Built by Helsingor SV, Helsingor, for DFDS as the SURREY (1969). Renamed PATRAS (1992 – DFDS) and ANNA V (1997 – Perco Maritime Inc, Athens).

JUPITER (1998)

20581 grt; 1250 psrs
360 cars
578' x 73' x 19' (175.3 x 22.3 x 5.8 m)
4 x 12-cylinder LAtlantique-Pielstick geared diesel engines via twin screw.

Ice-strengthened passenger-car ferry owned and operated by the Fjord Line, Bergen.
Built by Dubigeon-Normandie Yards, Nantes, for the Finland Steamship Company, Helsinki, as the WELLAMO (1975). Renamed DANA GLORIA (1981 – DFDS), SVEA CORONA (1984 – Johnson Line), DANA GLORIA (1985 – DFDS), KING OF SCANDINAVIA (1989 – DFDS) and COLOR VIKING (1994 – Color Line).

JUSTICIA (1917)

32234 grt; 3430 psrs
776' x 86' x 28' (235.2 x 26.1 x 8.5 m)
6 x SRG turbines via triple screw.
Sank on 20 July 1918, with the loss of ten lives, after a follow-up two torpedo attack by the German U-124 the day after she was hit by six torpedoes from the U-64, 20 miles north-west of Skerryvore, Northern Ireland.
Launched by Harland & Wolff Ltd, Belfast, for the Holland-America Line as the STATENDAM (1914) and completed as the troopship JUSTICIA for the British government.

JUTLANDIA (1934)

8542 grt; 69 psrs
460' x 61' x 25' (139.4 x 18.5 x 7.6 m)
B+W 10-cylinder diesel engines via twin screw.
Broken up for scrap at Bilbao in 1965.
Built by Nakskov Skibsvaerft, Nakskov, for the East Asiatic Company, Copenhagen.

JUTLANDICA (1982) See EUROFERRYS ATLANTICA (1999)

J. W. McANDREW (1941) See AFRICAN ENTERPRISE (1948)

KACHIDOKI MARU (1942)
10496 grt; 78 psrs
523' x 62' x 28'3" (158.5 x 18.8 x 8.6 m)
Triple expansion engines via twin screw.
After acquisition by the Japanese government, she sank on 12 September 1944 when she was torpedoed by the USS PAMPANITO in the South China Sea, 50 miles (83 km) east of Hainan. Of the allied prisoners of war aboard the ship, 656 were saved.
Built by the New York Shipbuilding Company, Camden, New Jersey, for the US Shipping Board as the WOLVERINE STATE (1921). Renamed PRESIDENT HARRISON (1923 – Pacific Mail Steamship Company) and KAKO MARU (1941) after the Japanese captured the ship on 8 December 1941, following her running aground at Sha Wai Shan in the East China Sea.

KADES (1938)
3089 grt; 135 psrs
325' x 44' x 16' (98.5 x 13.3 x 4.8 m)
Triple expansion engines coupled with turbines via twin screw.
Operating for Turkish Maritime Lines.
Built by Neptun, Rostock.

KADIA EXPRESS (1993) See EXPRESS POSEIDON (1999)

KAGA MARU (1901)
6301 grt; 220 psrs
445' x 49' x 34' (134.8 x 14.8 x 10.2 m)
2 x triple expansion engines via twin screw.
Broken up for scrap in Japan in 1934.
Built by Mitsubishi Dockyard, Nagasaki, for NYK, Japan, as a passenger-cargo ship costing Yen 1,157,000.

KAGERA (1915) See ASSIMINA (1949)

KAHLOKE (1953) See LANGDALE QUEEN (1962)

KAIJO MARU (1913) See SUSANNA II (1919)

KAIKOURA (1903) See FERRANIA (1927)

KAIPARA (1903)
7392 grt
460' x 58' x 31' depth (139.4 x 17.6 x 9.4 m)
John Brown 6-cylinder triple expansion engines via twin screw.
Sank on 16 August 1914, 170 miles (280 km) south-west of Tenerife, after an attack by the German raider KAISER WILHELM DER GROSSE.
Built by John Brown & Co Ltd, Glasgow, for the New Zealand Shipping Co Ltd.

KAIROUAN (1950)
8589 grt; 423 psrs
468' x 60' x 29'5" (141.8 x 18.2 x 8.9 m)
Construction Electric & Mechanic Alsthom turbo-electric engines via twin screw.
Built by Forges et Chantiers de la Mediterranee, La Seyne, for Mix te, Marseille.

KAISAR-I-HIND (1914) See KAISAR-I-HIND (1921)

KAISAR-I-HIND (1921)
11430 grt; 548 psrs
520' x 61' x 33' (158.5 x 18.6 x 10 m)
2 x 8-cylinder quadruple expansion engines via twin screw.
Broken up for scrap by Hughes Bolckow at Blyth in 1938 for a tender fee of £28,500. Ex-P&O Lines.
Built by Caird & Company, Greenock, for the P&O Line at a cost of £363,176 as the KAISAR-I-HIND (1914). Renamed EMPEROR OF INDIA (1921 – Cunard Steamship Company Ltd).

KAISER FRANZ JOSEF I (1912) See MARCO POLO (1936)

KAISER FRIEDRICH (1898) See BURDIGALA (1912)

KAISERIN AUGUSTE VICTORIA (1906) See EMPRESS OF SCOTLAND (1921)

KAISERIN MARIA THERESIA (1899) See URAL (1904)

KAISER WILHELM II (1890) See HOHENZOLLERN (1900)

KAISER WILHELM II (1903) See MONTICELLO (1927)

KAISHO MARU (1958)
22608 grt; 1430 psrs
656' x 78' x 40'5" depth (198.8 x 23.6 x 12.3 m)
6 x turbine engines via twin screw.
Broken up for scrap at Osaka in 1958. Ex-Royal Mail Lines.
Built as by Harland & Wolff Ltd, Belfast, for Royal Mail Lines as the ALCANTARA (1927).

KAIYO (1943)
12755 grt; 901 psrs
544' x 68' x 29' (164.8 x 20.6 x 8.8 m)
2 x Mitsubishi-B+W 22-cylinder diesel engines via twin screw.
Broken up for scrap on site outside Beppu harbour, Japan, in 1946 where, as an aircraft carrier for the Japanese government, she ran aground and capsized in 1945. She had been attempting to escape bombs and torpedoes during a raid.
Built by Mitsubishi Heavy Industries, Nagasaki, for OSK, Japan, as the passenger liner ARGENTINA MARU (1939).

KAKO MARU (1941) See KACHIDOKI MARU (1942)

KALLE (1962) See VIRGEM DE FATIMA (2000)

KALLE (1971) See NORTIA (1999)

KALLE III (1974) See PEDER OLSEN (1992)

KALLISTE (1993)
12418 grt; 196 psrs
120 cars + 150 trailers
545' x 96' x 21'5" (165 x 29.3 x 6.5 m)
4 x 16-cylinder Wartsila-Vasa diesel engines via twin screw.

Passenger-car-cargo ferry owned and operated by Meridionale de Navigation. Built by Aker Finnyards, Rauma.

KALMYKIYA (1994) See AKADEMIK M. TOPCHUBASHOV (1995)

KALYAN (1915)
9118 grt; 147 psrs
481' x 58' x 34' (146.5 x 17.7 x 10.3 m)
2 x quadruple expansion engines via twin screw.
Broken up for scrap by Taminosuki Miyaji for a tender fee of US$33,500 in Osaka in 1932.
Laid down by Cammell Laird & Company, Birkenhead, for the P&O Line as the KHORASSAN (1914) and completed as KALYAN (1915) at a cost of £199,012.

KALYPSO (1990) See STAR PISCES (1994)

KAMAKURA MARU (1939)
17498 grt; 838 psrs
584' x 74' x 28'6" (177.8 x 22.6 x 8.7 m)
2 x 8-cylinder B+W diesel engines via twin screw.
Following acquisition by the Japanese Navy, she sank on 28 April 1943 after being torpedoed by the USS GUDGEON in the Sulu Sea, south-east of Lagayan and west of Panay Island, Philippines, with the loss of 176 lives.
Built by Yokohama Dockyard Company, Yokohama, for NYK, Japan, as the passenger ship CHICHIBU MARU (1930). Renamed TITIBU MARU (1938 – NYK).

KAMARIMA (1919)
4508 grt
393' x 47' x 29'6" (119.1 x 14.2 x 9 m)
Hall, Russell 3-cylinder triple expansion engine via single screw.
Broken up for scrap at Trieste, Italy, in 1924. Ex-Canada Steamship Lines.
Built by Hall, Russell & Company, Aberdeen, for the Aberdeen Line as the SALAMIS (1899).

KAMBUNA (1984)
13921 grt; 1596 psrs
472' x 77' x 19'6" (143 x 23.3 x 5.9 m)
2 x 6-cylinder MaK geared diesel engines via twin screw.
Passenger ferry owned by the government of Indonesia and operated by P T Pelni, Indonesia.
Built by Meyer Werft, Papenburg, for P T Pelni.

KAMIROS (1980) See THESSALONIKI (1997)

KAMO MARU (1908)
8524 grt; 265 psrs
474' x 54' x 33' (141.7 x 17.3 x 10.5 m)
2 x triple expansion engines via triple screw.
Sank on 3 July 1944 after being torpedoed by the USS TINOSA off the west coast of Japan and south of Fukue Island in the Goto Island group.
Built by Mitsubishi Dockyard for NYK, Japan, as a passenger-cargo ship.

KAMOME (1975) See KAMOME II (1998)

KAMOME II (1998)
3007 grt; 1100 psrs
300' x 53' x 13' (91 x 16 x 4 m)
4 x 6-cylinder Niigata diesel engines via twin screw.
Passenger ferry owned by Trust Bank of Japan and operated by Hayashi Marine.
Built by Naikai Zosen-Taguma Shipyard, Innoshima, for Hayashi Marine as the KAMOME (1975). Renamed DONG YANG EXPRESS FERRY No. 2 (1979 – Dong Yang Express Ferry Co Ltd, Busan).

KAMPALA (1947)
10304 grt; 1065 psrs
507' x 66' x 27' (153.6 x 20 x 8.2 m)
Parsons geared turbine engines via twin screw.
Broken up for scrap by China Steel Company in Kaohsiung in 1971.
Built by Alex ander Stephen & Sons, Glasgow, for the British India Line.

KANAGAWA MARU (1906)
6151 grt; 160 psrs
445' x 49' x 30'5" depth (134.8 x 14.8 x 9.2 m)
Henderson 6-cylinder triple expansion engines via twin screw.
Built by D & W Henderson, Glasgow, for NYK, Japan.

KANANGA (1973) See BELLA VISTA (1996)

KANDAHAR (1913) See KARMALA (1914)

KANGAROO (1915) See NORAH MOLLER (1938)

KANGAROO (1962) See YARA (1974)

KANIMBLA (1936) See ORIENTAL QUEEN (1961)

KANJU MARU (1940)
7267 grt; 800 psrs
430' x 56' x 25'3" (130.3 x 17 x 7.7 m)
2 x 6-cylinder Sulzer diesel engines via twin screw.
Owned by OSK, she sank in January 1945 after a US aircraft bombing attack on Saigon harbour.
Built by Mitsubishi Dockyard for OSK, Japan, as the passenger liner LA PLATA MARU (1926).

KANNON MARU (1961)
10329 grt; 286 psrs
483' x 64' x 29'3" (146.4 x 19.4 x 8.9 m)
2 x Fairfield-Sulzer diesel engines via twin screw.
Broken up for scrap at Osaka in 1961 by C Itoh & Company. Ex-Bibby Line.
Built by Fairfield Shipbuilding & Engineering Company, Glasgow, for the Bibby Line as the WORCESTERSHIRE (1931).

KANONIER (1945) See BLED (1959)

KANOWNA (1902)
6942 grt; 511 psrs
416' x 53' x 28'6" (126 x 16 x 8.7 m)
William Denny 8-cylinder quadruple expansion engines via twin screw.
Sank stern first at 7.30 am on 18 February 1929. She had gone out of control in the Bass Strait to where she had drifted after striking a rock off Cleft Island in the Anser Group, seven miles west of Wilson's Promontory, Victoria, Australia.
Built by William Denny & Bros, Dumbarton, for the Australasian United Steam Navigation Company.

KANSAS CITY (1889) See ALASKA (1915)

KAPELLA (1967) See NISSOS CHIOS (1979)

KAPETAN ALEX ANDROS (1989) See KAPETAN ALEXANDROS A (1993)

KAPETAN ALEXANDROS A (1993)
4908 grt; 1200 psrs
364' x 55' x 13' (110.2 x 16.8 x 3.9 m)
4 x 12-cylinder MAN-Sulzer diesel engines via twin screw.
Passenger ferry owned by Richmond Shipping Ltd, Greece, and operated by Flanmare Shipping, Greece. Placed on the sales list at US$2,500,000.
Built by Ailsa Shipbuilding Co, Troon, for Transport Ferry Service as the freighter DORIC FERRY (1962). Renamed ATLAS II (1981 – Cie Armordora de Sud-America SA, Piraeus), ALEKOS (1988 – Endeavour Shipping Co, SA, Panama) and KAPETAN ALEX ANDROS (1989 – Agoudimos Lines).

KAPITAN DRANITSYN (1980)
12919 grt; 106 psrs
437' x 88' x 28' (132.4 x 26 x 8.5 m)
6 x 9-cylinder Wartsila diesel-electric engines via triple screw.

Ice-breaker cruise ship specialising in Antarctic expeditions for the Far East Shipping Company, Vladivostok.
Built by Wartsila-Helsinki.

KAPITAN KHLEBNIKOV (1981)
12288 grt; 112 psrs
437' x 88' x 28' (132.4 x 26 x 8.5 m)
6 x 9-cylinder Wartsila diesel-electric engines via triple screw.

Icebreaker ship specialising in Antarctic expedition cruises for the Far Eastern Shipping Co, Vladivostok.
Built by Wartsila-Helsinki.

KAPITAN LEDOCHOWSKI (1974)
5975 grt; 180 psrs
403' x 56' x 24' (122 x 17 x 7.4 m)
2 x 5-cylinder Sulzer diesel engines.
Ice-strengthened education ship owned by the Polish Steamship Company.
Built by Stocznia Sczecinska, Szczec.

KAPITAN NIKOLAYEV (1978)
14264 grt; 114 psrs
440' x 88' x 28' (134.2 x 26 x 8.5 m)
6 x 9-cylinder Wartsila diesel-electric engines via triple screw.
Icebreaker cruise ship operating for the Murmansk Shipping Company, Murmansk.
Built by Wartsila Yard, Helsinki.

KAPITAN SOROKIN (1977)
15385 grt; 114 psrs
437' x 88' x 28' (132.4 x 26 x 8.5 m)
6 x 9-cylinder Wartsila diesel engines via triple screw.
Icebreaker cruise ship for the Murmansk Shipping Company, Murmansk.
Built by Wartsila Yard, Helsinki.

KAPRIFOL (1977) See EUROMAGIQUE (1995)

KAPUNDA (1908)
3097 grt; 100 psrs
330' x 45' x 21'3" (100.6 x 13.6 x 6.5 m)
Central Marine Engineering 3-cylinder triple expansion engine via single screw.
Sank on 12 November 1916 after being torpedoed by a German U-boat.
Built by W Gray & Company, West Hartlepool, for the Melbourne Steamship Company.

KARADENIZ (1910)
5012 grt; 1991 psrs
415' x 48' x 31'3" depth (126.5 x 14.6 x 9.5 m)
Fairfield 3-cylinder triple expansion engine via single screw.
Broken up for scrap, in 1923, following a nine-year period laid up after having been seized by the Turkish government as a war prize while the vessel was in Mumbai.
Built by Fairfield Shipbuilding & Engineering Company, Glasgow, for North German Lloyd as the DARMSTADT (1890).

KARADENIZ (1956)
8809 grt; 452 psrs
474' x 61' x 20' (143.6 x 18.5 x 6.1 m)
2 x 8-cylinder MAN diesel engines via twin screw.
Broken up for scrap at Aliaga in 1987.
Built by AG Weser, Bremen, for Turkish Maritime Lines as a cruise ship.

KARAMEA (1900) See MONGIOIA (1925)

KARANJA (1948) See NANCOWRY (1976)

KARAPARA (1914)
7117 grt; 500 psrs
425' x 56' x 26'5" (128.8 x 17 x 8 m)
Engines via twin screw.
Broken up in Mumbai in 1950 by the Steel Corporation of India. Ex-British government.
Laid down by Swan Hunter & Wigham Richardson, Newcastle, as the passenger ship KARUNGA (1913) for British India Steam Navigation Company and completed as the hospital ship. KARAPARA.

KARDEN (1995)
3614 grt; 650 psrs
302' x 52' x 12' (91.5 x 15.9 x 3.7 m)
2 x 9-cylinder British Polar diesel engines via twin screw.
Passenger-cargo ship owned by Karden Gemicilik, Turkey, and operated by Tem Trading and Shipping Co, Denizcilik, Turkey.
Built by Evans, Deakin & Co, Brisbane, for the Adelaide Steamship Co Ltd, Port Adelaide, as the TROUBRIDGE (1961). Renamed CITY OF FAMAGUSTA (1990 – Jenny Shipping Inc) and SEA WAVE (1990 – Poseidon Lines Shipping Co).

KARELIYA (1976) See OLVIA (1995)

KARELIYA (1989) See OLVIA (1995)

KARINA (1905)
4200 grt; 170 psrs
370' x 46' x 23'3" (112.1 x 13.9 x 7.1 m)
A Stephen & Co 3-cylinder triple expansion engine via single screw.
Sank on 8 August 1917 after being torpedoed off Wexford.
Built by Alex Stephen & Sons, Glasgow, for the Elder Dempster Line.

KARIYUSHI OKINAWA (1988)
6613 grt; 150 psrs
139 TEUs + 160 cars
481' x 74' x 20'8" (145.8 x 22.4 x 6.3 m)
8-cylinder MAN diesel engine via single screw.
Passenger-car-container ferry owned and operated by Ryukyu Kaiun, Japan.
Built by Onomichi Zosen, Onomichi.

KARL CARSTENS (1986)
12829 grt; 1500 psrs
156 cars + 25 rail rolling stock
544' x 57' x 19'6" (164.8 x 17.4 x 5.9 m)
6 x 12-cylinder MaK-Siemens diesel-electric engines via twin screw.

Ice-strengthened passenger-car-train ferry operating for Scandlines AG and has been for sale since mid-1999 for US$7,200,000.
Built by HWD, Kiel, for the Deutsche Bundesbahn.

KARLSRUHE (1928)
10893 grt; 2356 psrs
524' x 60' x 34'7" depth (158.8 x 18.3 x 10.5 m)
2 x 4-cylinder Vulkan quadruple expansion engines via twin screw.
Broken up for scrap at Bremerhaven in 1932. Ex-North German Lloyd.
Built by Vulkan Shipyards, Stettin, for North German Lloyd as the passenger liner PRINZESS IRENE (1900). Seized by the US government and renamed POCAHONTAS (1917 – US Navy) and BREMEN (1923 – North German Lloyd).

KARMALA (1914)

9128 grt; 147 psrs
481' x 58' x 33'8" depth (146.5 x 17.7 x 10.2 m)
2 x 4-cylinder Cammell Laird quadruple expansion engines via twin screw.
Broken up for scrap by Amakasu Gomei Kaisha in Japan in 1932 for a tender fee of £14,100.
Laid down by Cammell Laird & Company, Birkenhead, for the P&O Line as the passenger-cargo ship KANDAHAR (1913) and completed as the KARMALA at a cost of £196,724.

KARNAK (1912)

6343 grt; 348 psrs
469' x 51' x 36' (142 x 15.5 x 10.9 m)
Triple expansion engines via twin screw.
She sank on 27 November 1916 after being torpedoed by the German U-32 off Malta.
Built by Messageries Maritimes, La Ciotat, for Messageries Maritimes as the ANNAM (1898). Renamed TOURANE (1904 – Messageries Maritimes).

KAROOLA (1909)

7391 grt; 430 psrs
437' x 56' x 25'5" (132.4 x 17 x 7.7 m)
Harland & Wolff 8-cylinder quadruple expansion via twin screw.
Broken up for scrap at Shanghai in 1937.
Built by Harland & Wolff Ltd, Belfast, for McIlwraith McEachern.

KARUNGA (1913) See KARAPARA (1914)

KASHGAR (1914)

9005 grt; 147 psrs
481' x 58' x 34' (146.5 x 17.7 x 10.3 m)
2 x quadruple expansion engines via twin screw.
Broken up for scrap by Tamizo Okushoji for a tender fee of £16,400 in Osaka in 1932.
Built by Caird & Company, Greenock, for the P&O Line at a cost of £186,391.

KASHIMA MARU (1913) See KASIMA MARU (1938)

KASHIWARA MARU (1941) See JUNYO (1942)

KASHMIR (1915)

8985 grt; 148 psrs
480' x 58' x 33'7" depth (146.4 x 17.7 x 10.2 m)
Caird 8-cylinder quadruple expansion engines via twin screw.
Broken up for scrap by Mitshiwa Kabushiki Kaisha for a tender fee of £14,400 in Osaka in 1932.
Built by Caird & Company, Greenock, for the P&O Line at a cost of £189,396.

KASIMA MARU (1938)

10559 grt; 355 psrs
492' x 60' x 28'6" (149.1 x 18.2 x 8.7 m)
Triple expansion engines via twin screw.
Sank on 27 September 1943 after being torpedoed by the USS BONEFISH 200 miles (334 km) east of Saigon.
Built by Kawasaki Dockyard, Kobe, for NYK as the passenger-cargo ship KASHIMA MARU (1913).

KASUGA MARU (1940) See TAIYO (1941)

KASZUBY (1957)

8061 grt; 76 psrs
length 494' x beam 61' (149.7 x 18.7 m)
Bremer Vulkan 4-cylinder triple expansion engine via single screw.
Owned by the Polish government.
Built by Bremer Vulkan, Vegesack, as the WISCONSIN (1929). Seized twice as a war prize – first by the US government, and then by the French government in 1945, to be operated by the French Line. Renamed FRYDERYK CHOPIN (1951 – Polish Ocean Line).

KATARINA (1994) See ALAMIRA (1997)

KATHIAWAR (1912)

4400 grt; 60 psrs

370' x 48' x 25' (112.1 x 14.5 x 7.6 m)
Harland & Wolff 6-cylinder compound engine via single screw.
Passenger-cargo ship owned and operated by the Bank Line, UK.
Built by Harland & Wolff Ltd, Govan, for the Ellerman Line as the BULAWAYO (1895).

KATOOMBA (1913) See COLUMBIA (1949)

KATORI MARU (1913)

10513 grt; 380 psrs
500' x 60' x 28'6" (151.5 x 18.2 x 8.7 m)
Mitsubishi 6-cylinder turbine engines via single screw.
Sank on 23 December 1941 after being torpedoed by a Dutch submarine off Kuching, Sarawak.
Built by Mitsubishi Dockyard & Engineering Works, Nagasaki, for NYK, Tokyo.

KATTEGAT (1972) See ALANDSFARJAN (1987)

KATTEGAT II (1974) See MOBY LALLI (2000)

KAWANOE (1973) See MUFIDAH (1990)

KAWANOE 2 (1984)

3623 grt; 400 psrs
62 trailers
381' x 69' x 13' (115.6 x 21 x 4.5 m)
2 x 6-cylinder MaK diesel engines via twin screw.
Passenger-cargo ferry operated in Japan by Shikoku Chuo.
Built by Kochi Jyuko, Kochi.

KAWTHER (1975)

5207 grt; 268 psrs
383' x 54' x 19' (116 x 16.4 x 5.8 m)
2 x 8-cylinder Fiat diesel engines via twin screw.
Broken up for scrap at Piraeus in October 1980. She had been under tow to a breakers' yard in Spain, but sprang a leak one hour out of Piraeus and then hit rocks at the Piraeus harbour entrance on her return.
Built by Cantieri Navale di Taranto for the Adriatica Line as the MESSAPIA (1952).

KAZAKHSTAN (1976) See ISLAND ADVENTURE (1998)

KAZAKHSTAN II (1994) See UKRAINA (1999)

KEDAH (1927) See GOLDEN ISLES (1952)

KEDAH, HMS (1942) See GOLDEN ISLES (1952)

KEDMAH (1946) See GOLDEN ISLES (1952)

KEEMUN (1890) See PATRICIA (1906)

KEERKRING (1960) See HERO (1972)

KEEWATIN (1908)

3856 grt; 220 psrs
346' x 44' x 17'6" (104.8 x 13.3 x 5.3 m)
4-cylinder Fairfield quadruple expansion engine via single screw.
Preserved at a berth in Douglas on Lake Michigan, USA, since 1967 as a museum and gift shop.
Built by Fairfield Shipbuilding & Engineering Ltd, Glasgow, for Canadian Pacific Railway Company as a passenger-cargo ship.

KEFALONIA (1995)

3924 grt; 1012 psrs
45 trailers
363' x 57' x 16' (110 x 17.2 x 4.9 m)
2 x 14-cylinder NYK-Pielstick diesel engines via twin screw.
Passenger-cargo ferry owned and operated by Strintzis Lines.
Built by Nakai Shipbuilding, Innoshima, for Higashi Nippon Ferry Co Ltd as the VENUS (1975).

KELIBIA (1990) See NORTIA (1999)

KELIMUTU (1986)
5684 grt; 920 psrs
329' x 59' x 14' (99.8 x 18 x 4.2 m)
2 x 6-cylinder Krupp-MaK diesel engines via twin screw.
Passenger ship owned by the Indonesian government and operated by PT Pelni, Indonesia.
Built by Meyer Werft, Papenburg.

KELUD (1998)
14716 grt; 1906 psrs
484' x 77' x 19'6" (146.5 x 23.4 x 5.9 m)
2 x 8-cylinder MaK diesel engines via twin screw.
Passenger ship owned by the Indonesian government and operated by PT Pelni.
Built by Meyer Werft, Papenburg.

KEMAL SADIKOGLU (1950)
5692 grt
413' x 52' x 25' (125.2 x 15.8 x 7.6 m)
Northeast Marine Engineering 3-cylinder triple expansion engine via single screw.
Built by W Dobson & Co, Newcastle, for Harris & Dixon Ltd as the MOTTISFONT (1917). Renamed BAWTRY (1923 – Canadian Pacific Railway Co), ARCHANGELOS (1927 – Levanos Brothers) and K SADIKOGLU (1950).

KEMMENDINE (1924)
7850 grt; 180 psrs
454' x 59' x 30'7" depth (137.6 x 17.9 x 9.3 m)
William Denny 3-cylinder triple expansion engine via single screw.
Sank on 13 July 1940 in the Indian Ocean after being attacked by the German raider ATLANTIS.
Built by William Denny & Bros, Dumbarton, for the Henderson Line, UK.

KENGHSHIN (1976) See SHANGHAI (1978)

KENILWORTH CASTLE (1904)
12975 grt; 810 psrs
570' x 64'6" x 31'6" (172.7 x 19.6 x 9.6 m)
Harland & Wolff 8-cylinder quadruple expansion engines via twin screw.
Broken up for scrap in 1936.
Built by Harland & Wolff Ltd, Belfast, for the Union Castle Line.

KENINGAU (1960)
4856 grt; 520 psrs
375' x 53' x 20' (113.6 x 16 x 6.1 m)
Hawthorn Leslie-Werkspoor 8-cylinder diesel engine via single screw.
Owned and operated by Straits Steamship Company, Singapore.
Built by Wilton Fijenoord, Rotterdam, for NV Koninklijke Paketvaart Maats as the REYNIERSZ (1948).

KENKOKU MARU (1914)
3317 grt; 621 psrs
320' x 43' x 24'5" (97.5 x 13 x 7.4 m)
D & W Henderson 3-cylinder triple expansion engine via single screw.
Owned by the Japanese government, she sank on 29 December 1915 after being torpedoed by a submarine 75 miles (125 km) south-west of Glado Island.
Built by D & W Henderson Ltd, Glasgow, for the Anchor Line as the DALMATIA (1892). Renamed CORNELIA (1912 – U Serra ful, Italy).

KENMORE, USS (AP-62) (1942) See PRESIDENT MADISON (1946)

KENNIKOTT (1998)
12635 grt; 748 psrs
120 cars + 20 trailers
382' x 85' x 17'6" (115.8 x 25.8 x 5.3 m)
2 x 12-cylinder Wartsila diesel engines via twin screw.
Passenger-car-cargo ferry owned and operated by the Alaska Marine Highway.
Built by Halter Marine Group, Moss Point, Mississippi, at a cost of US$80,000,000.

KENT (1899) See SAXON STAR (1929)

KENT (1936) See ERNEST HINDS (1942)

KENT (1999) See P&O SL KENT (1999).

KENTAVROS (1962)
3600 grt; 230 psrs
311' x 41' x 15' (94.2 x 12.4 x 4.5 m)
Fairbanks-Morse diesel engines via twin screw.
Passenger ferry owned by Kavounides Shipping Company Ltd, Piraeus, but broken up for scrap in Eleusis in 1986.
Built by Puget Sound Navy Yard for the US Navy as the seaplane tender BARNEGAT, USS (AVP-10) (1941).

KENT, USS (AP-28) (1941) See ERNEST HINDS (1942)

KENYA (1930) See CASTEL FELICE (1952)

KENYA (1949) See CASTEL FELICE (1952)

KENYA (1950) See CASTEL FELICE (1952)

KENYA (1951)
14464 grt; 297 psrs
540' x 71' x 27'6" (164.5 x 21.7 x 8.4 m)
Parsons geared turbine engines via twin screw.
Broken up for scrap by Cantieri di Portovenere at La Spezia in 1969.
Built by Barclay, Curle & Company, Glasgow, for the British India Line.

KENYA CASTLE (1952) See AMERIKANIS (1967)

KENYA, HMS (1940) See CASTEL FELICE (1952)

KERASOUNDE (1911)
3006 grt; 338 psrs
349' x 39' x 28'8" (105.8 x 11.8 x 8.7 m)
Fairfield 3-cylinder triple expansion engine via single screw.
Broken up for scrap in 1986 as a training ship in Turkey. Ex-Naval Administrator, Turkey.
Built by Napier, Glasgow, for the Castle Line as the WARWICK CASTLE (1877). Renamed JEROME (1897 – Booth Line).

KEREN (1949) See CASTEL FELICE (1952)

KEREN (1951) See CASTEL FELICE (1952)

KEREN (1983) See SCIROCCO (1993)

KEREN, HMS (1940) See CASTEL FELICE (1952)

KERGUELEN (1922) See CHANTILLY (1924)

KERGUELEN (1928) See KERGUELEN (1945)

KERGUELEN (1945)
10241 grt; 400 psrs
484' x 59' x 35' (146.7 x 17.9 x 10.6 m)
4 x Wallsend Slipway SRG turbine engines via twin screw.

Broken up for scrap at Antwerp, Belgium, in 1955.
Launched by Swan Hunter & Wigham Richardson for Chargeurs Reunis as the MEDUANA (1920). Completed after refloating her as a result of the ship catching fire and sinking at her fitting out berth in 1922. Renamed KERGUELEN (1928) and WINRICH VON KNIPRODE (1940).

KERINCI (1983)
13954 grt; 1596 psrs
472' x 77' x 19'6" (143 x 23.3 x 5.9 m)
2 x 6-cylinder MaK geared diesel engines via twin screw.
Passenger ferry operated by PT Pelni, Indonesia, on the inter-island service.
Built by Meyer Werft, Papenburg, for PT Pelni. Resurrected after hitting rocks off Teluk Bayur, Padang, on 2 November 1997 and being declared a total constructive loss.

KEYSTONE STATE (1921) See J. FRANKLIN BELL, USS (APA-16) (1942)

KHABAROVSK (1932)
3553 grt
315' x 46' x 26' (95.5 x 13.9 x 7.9 m)
Baltic Shipbuilding & Engineering Works 3-cylinder triple expansion engines via single screw.
Built by Baltic State Shipbuilding Yard, St Petersburg, for the USSR government.

KHABAROVSK (1962)
5235 grt; 333 psrs
401' x 52' x 17' (122.2 x 15.8 x 5.2 m)
2 x 6-cylinder DMR diesel engines via twin screw.
Passenger liner operated by the Far East Shipping Company, Vladivostok, mainly on the Nakhodka–Yokohama service.
Built by Mathias-Thesen Werft, Wismar, for the Far East Shipping Company.

KHAI DINH (1939)
5100 grt; 144 psrs
396' x 52' x 27'8" depth (120 x 15.8 x 8.4 m)
Engines via twin screw.
Owned and operated by Messageries Maritimes, she sank on 22 November 1942 following an attack by American bombers in the Bay of Along, with seven killed.
Built by William Denny & Brothers, Dumbarton, for Messageries Maritimes as the EMPEROR ALEX ANDER III (1914). Renamed LAMARTINE (1922).

KHALEEJ EXPRESS (1976)
8062 grt; 170 psrs
439' x 60' x 25' (133.8 x 18.3 x 7.6 m)
DRG turbine engine via single screw.
Broken up for scrap as a sheep carrier in Karachi, Pakistan, in 1984.
Built by Cammell Laird & Company, Birkenhead, for the Booth Line as the HUBERT (1955). Renamed MALAYSIA (1965 – Austasia Line), and the livestock carrier UNITED CHALLENGER (1976 – Atlas Shipping Agency, Singapore).

KHALID I (1983)
3921 grt; 450 psrs
373' x 49' x 23' (113 x 14.8 x 7 m)
2 x DRG turbine engines via single screw.
Broken up for scrap at Piraeus in 1991. Ex-Arab Emirates.
Built by Chantiers de Bretagne, Nantes, for Paquet Lines as the AZZEMOUR (1951). Renamed DELOS (1969 – Epthymiadis Lines) and BELLA MARIA (1980 – Acquaviva Shipping Company).

KHALID (1984) See FAGR (1998)

KHARTUM (1919)
3521 grt
360' x 44' x 24'6" (109.7 x 13.5 x 7.5 m)
Wigham Richardson 3-cylinder triple expansion engine via single screw.
Broken up for scrap in Genoa, Italy, in 1926. Ex-the "K" Steamship Co Ltd.
Built by Wigham Richardson Ltd, Newcastle, for the Blue Anchor Line as the WOOLLOOMOOLOO (1891). Renamed HARMONIDES (1901 – Howton Steamship Company).

KHAZAN (1906)
5458 grt; 1120 psrs
399' x 50' x 27'3" (121.7 x 15.3 x 8.3 m)
3-cylinder triple expansion engine via single screw.
Wrecked near Colombo on 19 April 1906 while serving with the Russian Volunteer Fleet.
Built by Palmers & Company Ltd, Jarrow, for the Hamburg-America Line as the ADRIA (1896). Renamed NARVA (1905 – Russian Navy).

KHEDIVE ISMAIL (1948) See CLEOPATRA (1956)

KHERSON (1896) See RAETORIA (1920)

KHERSON (1906) See RAETORIA (1920)

KHIVA (1914)
8947 grt; 148 psrs
481' x 58' x 33'7" depth (146.5 x 17.7 x 10.2 m)
Cammell Laird 8-cylinder quadruple expansion engines via twin screw.
Broken up for scrap for a tender fee of US$31,000 in Japan in 1931, following the ship being gutted by fire.
Built by Cammell Laird & Company, Birkenhead, for the P&O Line at a cost of £197,658.

KHORASSAN (1914) See KALYAN (1915)

KHYBER (1914)
9114 grt; 148 psrs
481' x 58' x 33'7" depth (146.5 x 17.7 x 10.2 m)
Cammell Laird 8-cylinder quadruple expansion engines via twin screw.
Broken up for scrap by Tamizo Okushoja for a tender fee of £16,250 in Osaka in 1931.
Built by Cammell Laird & Company, Birkenhead, for the P&O Line at a cost of £196,346.

KIA ORA (1907) See VERBANIA (1935)

KIAUTSCHOU (1900) See CITY OF HONOLULU (1927)

KIBBUTZ GALUYOT (1947) See KOMMIYUT (1949)

KIGOMA (1914) See TOLEDO (1922)

KILDONAN CASTLE (1900)
9652 grt; 586 psrs
515' x 59' x 34'7" depth (156 x 17.9 x 10.5 m)
Fairfield 8-cylinder quadruple expansion engines via twin screw.
Broken up for scrap at Stavanger, Norway, in 1931.
Built by Fairfield Shipbuilding & Engineering Company Ltd, Glasgow, for the Union Castle Line.

KILPATRICK (1898) See GREAT CANTON (1923)

KIMANIS (1951)
3189 grt; 536 psrs
314' x 51' x 19' (95.2 x 15.6 x 5.8 m)
2 x 8-cylinder British Polar diesel engines via twin screw.
Built by Caledon Shipbuilding & Engineering Company Ltd, Dundee, for Straits Shipping Ltd, Singapore.

KIM ANN (1974)
7656 grt; 403 psrs
432' x 59' x 26' (130.9 x 18 x 7.9 m)
2 x 4-cylinder Doxford diesel engines via twin screw.
Passenger-cargo ship operating for Guan Guan Shipping Ltd, Singapore.
Built by Bartram & Sons, Sunderland, for Cia Nacional de Navegacao, Lisbon, as the TIMOR (1951).

KIMBERLEY (1958)
4227 grt; 90 psrs
330' x 50' x 18'8" (100.6 x 15.2 x 5.7 m)
Harland & Wolff 8-cylinder diesel engines via twin screw.
Broken up for scrap in Hong Kong as a livestock carrier in 1960. Ex-

Australian Pacific Shipping Pty Ltd.
Built by Harland & Wolff Ltd, Belfast, for the State Shipping Company, Perth, Western Australia, as the KOOLINDA (1926).

KIM HOCK (1971)
7631 grt; 403 psrs
432' x 59' x 26' (130.9 x 17.9 x 7.9 m)
2 x 4-cylinder Doxford diesel engines via twin screw.
Broken up for scrap at Kaohsiung in 1977. Ex-Guan Guan Shipping (Pte) Ltd, Singapore.
Built by Bartram & Sons, Sunderland, for Cia Nacional de Navegacao, Portugal, as the passenger-cargo ship INDIA (1951).

KIM HWA (1968)
4180 grt; 586 psrs
399' x 55' x 22' (120.9 x 16.7 x 6.7 m)
Doxford 5-cylinder diesel engine via single screw.
Broken up for scrap in Hong Kong in 1974. Ex-Guan Guan Shipping (Pte) Ltd, Singapore.
Built by Barclay, Curle & Company, Glasgow, for the British India Line as the DARESSA (1950). Renamed FAVORITA (1964 – Chandris Group) and DARESSA (1964 – Chandris Group).

KINA (1905) See DAITEN MARU (1913)

KINFAUNS CASTLE (1880) See PRUT (1914)

KING ABDELAZIZ (1964)
8776 grt; 1024 psrs
461' x 59' x 27' (140.5 x 17.9 x 8.2 m)
2 x 5-cylinder Sulzer diesel engines via twin screw.
Broken up for scrap in Kaohsiung in 1970 after stranding on the Algahan Reef five miles (9 km) off Jeddah on 30 April 1965. At the time she was under the ownership of Saudi Lines.
Built by Merchant Shipbuilding Corporation, Chester, Pennsylvania, for the American Hawaiian Steamship Company as the MISSOURIAN (1922). Renamed EMPIRE SWAN (1940 – British Ministry of War Transport), BELGIAN FREIGHTER (1942 – Belgian government-in-exile), CAPITAINE POTIE (1946 – Cie Maritime Belge), GENOVA (1948 – Cogedar Line) and FLAMINIA (1955 – Cogedar Line).

KING ALEX ANDER (1920) See CLEVELAND (1923)

KING ALEX ANDER (1923)
11570 grt; 2358 psrs
550' x 60' x 34'9" depth (167.6 x 18.3 x 10.6 m)
2 x 4-cylinder Schichau quadruple expansion engines via twin screw.
Broken up for scrap in Venice in 1929. Ex-Byron Steam Navigation Company.
Built by Schichau, Danzig, for North German Lloyd as the BREMEN (1897). Renamed CONSTANTINOPLE (1921 – Byron Steam Navigation Company).

KINGARTH (1928) See BEPPE (1932)

KING MINOS (1987)
10164 grt; 1500 psrs
300 cars
512' x 75' x 20' (155 x 22.9 x 6 m)
2 x 18-cylinder MAN diesel engines via twin screw.
Passenger-car-ferry owned by Minoikai Grammai and operated by Minoan Lines, Iraklion.
Built by Kanasashi Zosensho, Shimizu, for Nippon Enkai Ferry KK, Tokyo, as the ERIMO MARU (1972).

KING OF SCANDINAVIA (1989) See JUPITER (1998)

KING OF SCANDINAVIA (1995)
13336 grt; 1040 psrs
300 cars or 38 trailers
505' x 66' x 18'6" (153 x 20 x 5.6 m)
2 x 18-cylinder Wartsila-SEMT-Pielstick diesel engines via twin screw.
Passenger-car-cargo ferry owned by DFDS and operated by DFDS-Scandinavian Seaways on the Denmark–Germany–UK service.
Built by Wartsila Yard, Turku, for Sessan Line as the PRINSESSAN BIRGITTA (1974). Renamed STENA SCANDINAVICA (1982 – Stena

Line), SCANDINAVICA (1987 – Cotunav, Tunisia), TARAK L (1989 – Cotunav, Tunisia), KING OF SCANDINAVIA (1989 – DFDS), SCANDINAVICA (1989 – Stena Line) and VENUS (1990 – Norway Line).

KING OLAV V(1961) See NAN HU (1983)

KING OLAV (1968) See NEW ORIENT PRINCESS

KING ORRY (1990) See MOBY LOVE II (1998)

KIRCHBERG (1907) See PEGLI (1913)

KIRGHISTAN (1959) See BATA (1994)

KIRGIZSTAN (1992) See AKADEMIK HESEN ALIYEV (1995)

KIRGIZTAN (1959) See KIRGHISTAN (1959)

KISMET (1965) See BUCEPHALOS (1966)

KISO (1987)
13730 grt; 850 psrs
110 cars + 65 trailers
635' x 90' x 22' (192.5 x 27.3 x 6.7 m)
2 x 8-cylinder Mitsubishi-MAN diesel engines via twin screw.
Passenger-car-cargo ferry owned and operated by Taiheiyo Enkai.
Built by Mitsubishi Heavy Industries Ltd, Shimonoseki.

KISTAN (1988) See WANG FU (1993)

KITAKAMI (1989)
13937 grt; 842 psrs
635' x 90' x 22'6" (192.5 x 27.3 x 6.9 m)
2 x 8-cylinder Mitsubishi-MAN diesel engines via twin screw.
Passenger ferry owned and operated by Taiheiyo Enkai.
Built by Mitsubishi Heavy Industries Ltd, Shimonoseki.

KITANO MARU (1909)
8512 grt; 247 psrs
474' x 54' x 34'6" (141.7 x 17.1 x 10.5 m)
2 x triple expansion engines via twin screw.
Sank on 27 March 1942 in the Lingayen Gulf after striking a mine.
Built by Mitsubishi Dockyard for NYK, Japan.

KIZAN MARU (1938)
5038 grt
405' x 53' x 27'4" (122.7 x 16.1 x 8.3 m)
Kincaid 3-cylinder triple expansion engines via single screw.
Destroyed on 27 September 1943 by British underground forces in Singapore during the Japanese occupation of that country.
Built by R Duncan & Co Ltd, Port Glasgow, as the CAMPERDOWN (1917). Renamed MONTEZUMA II (1918), BEDWYN (1923), BALFOUR (1923), CAPE VERDE (1923) and SHANG No. 7 (1935).

KLAVDIYA YELANSKAYA (1977)
4329 grt; 256 psrs
332' x 53' x 15' (100.6 x 16.1 x 4.6 m)
2 x 8-cylinder B+W diesel engines via twin screw.
Cruise ship for the Murmansk Shipping Company.
Built by Brodogradiliste Titovo, Kraljevica.

KLEIST (1906) See YOSHINO MARU (1919)

KLEK (1965) See ABU ALIA (1984)

KLIAS (1970)
5450 grt; 166 psrs
418' x 57' x 22'6" (127.4 x 17.3 x 6.8 m)
2 x 4-cylinder Doxford diesel engines via single screw.
Broken up for scrap in Hong Kong in 1977 as a pilgrim ship. Ex-Straits Steamship Company, Singapore.
Built by Scotts Shipbuilding & Engineering Company, Greenock, for the China Navigation Company as the ANKING (1950).

KLIPFONTEIN (1939)
10544 grt; 148 psrs
527' x 63' x 30'2" (159.7 x 19.1 x 9.2 m)
2 x 5-cylinder B+W diesel engines via twin screw.
Sank within 45 minutes on 8 January 1953 after striking a submerged object, which set off an explosion in the ship's forward bunker, five miles (8.2 km) off Cape Barra near Inhambane, Mozambique.
Built by P Smit Jnr, Rotterdam, for United Netherlands Navigation Company, The Hague.

KNOSSOS (1968)
10886 grt; 346 psrs
492' x 64' x 24'6" (150 x 19.5 x 7.4 m)
2 x 10-cylinder Penhoet-B+W diesel engines via twin screw.
Broken up for scrap in Spain in 1976 after being laid up in Piraeus for three years. This followed a fire (ignited by leaking fuel oil on to a generator) on 3 May 1973 while at sea en route from Piraeus to Limassol. Ex-Efthymiadis Lines.
Built by Arsenal de LOrient for Messageries Maritimes as the LA BOURDONNAIS (1953).

KNOSSOS (1978) See CAPTAIN ZAMAN I (1998)

KNOSSOS PALACE (2000)
37482 grt; 2190 psrs
700 cars or 110 cars + 120 trailers
706' x 87' x 23' (214 x 26.4 x 7 m)
4 x 16-cylinder Wartsila diesel engines via twin screw.
Built by Fincantieri subsidiary Sestri Cantieri Navale, Genoa, for Minoan Shipping Lines as a cruise ferry at a cost of US$130,000,000.

KNOXVILLE, USS (1914) See St PAUL (1919)

KNUD (1997)
3882 grt; 1500 psrs
200 cars or 10 rail coaches
359' x 58' x 15' (108.5 x 17.6 x 4.5 m)
2 x 7-cylinder B+W diesel engines via twin screw.

Broken up for scrap at Alang in 1998 after purchase by Canberra Ltd, Kingston.
Built by Helsingors Shipbuilding Company, Helsingor, for Dansk Statsbaner and operated by the Danish State Railways on the Denmark–Germany service as the passenger-car-train ferry KNUDSHOVED (1961).

KNUDSHOVED (1961) See KNUD (1997)

KOAN MARU (1936)
7125 grt; 2500 psrs
435' x 57' x 21' (131.8 x 17.3 x 6.4 m)
4 x Mitsubishi SRG turbine engines via twin screw.
Built by Mitsubishi, Nagasaki, for Toyo Yusen.

KOBE MARU (1974) See OUR LADY OF BANNEUX (1995)

KOBE MARU (1980) See OUR LADY OF BANNEUX (1995)

KOBE MARU (1982) See DONG YANG EXPRESS FERRY No.6 (1999)

KOBE MARU (1991)
3717 grt; 470 psrs
51cars + 50 trailers
383' x 73' x 15'6" (116 x 22 x 4.7 m)
2 x 8-cylinder B+W diesel engines via twin screw.
Owned and operated by Shikoku Ferry.
Built by Sanuki Shipbuilding, Tahma.

KOBE MARU No. 1 (1991) See DONG YANG EXPRESS FERRY No. 6 (1999)

KOBENHAVN (1966) See ARMONIA (1993)

KODA (1919) See AMERICAN LEGION, USS (APA-117) (1941)

KOGANE MARU (1972) See TRANS ASIA (1993)

KOGANE MARU (1995)
9504 grt; 1133 psrs
151 cars
398' x 65' x 17'6" (120.5 x 19.8 x 5.3 m)
2 x 9-cylinder Pielstick diesel engines via twin screw.
Passenger-car ferry operating for Sado Kisen KK, Japan.
Built by Kanda Shipyards.

KOHISTAN (1923) See BELLA (1956)

KOHSO MARU (1917) See KOSO MARU (1938)

KOLCHIDA (1961)
3219 grt; 250 psrs
333' x 48' x 13' (100.9 x 14.5 x 3.9 m)
2 x 8-cylinder Russian diesel engines via twin screw.
In service in Russia.
Built by A Jdanov, St Petersburg, for the Black Sea Shipping Company, Odessa.

KOLKHIDA (1961) See KOLCHIDA (1961)

KOLN (1899) See AMPHION (1917)

KOLN (1921)
9265 grt; 900 psrs
474' x 61' x 32'8" depth (144.8 x 18.5 x 9.9 m)
Bremer Vulkan 3-cylinder triple expansion engine via single screw.
Abandoned after becoming wrecked in the Gulf of Bothnia on the Swedish coast in 1940.
Built by Bremer Vulkan, Vegesack, for North German Lloyd.

KOMATI (1960)
8194 grt; 1500 psrs
438' x 60' x 23' (132.7 x 18.2 x 7 m)
2 x Parsons SRG turbine engines via twin screw.
Owned by United Arab Maritime Company, Alexandria, and scuttled as a pilgrim ship in the Suez Canal on the orders of the Egyptian government during the Arab–Israeli war in July 1967.
Built by Cammell Laird & Company, Birkenhead, for Canadian National Steamship Company as the LADY RODNEY (1928). Renamed MECCA (1953 – United Arab Maritime Company).

KOMEMIUT (1948) See KOMIYUT (1948)

KOMMIYUT (1949)
4570 grt
392' x 48' x 24'4" (118.8 x 14.5 x 7.4 m)
Triple expansion engine via single screw.
Broken up for scrap at Briton Ferry, UK, in 1952. Ex-Ships & Vessels Ltd.
Built by Newport News Shipbuilding & Drydock Company, Newport News, Virginia, for the Southern Pacific Company as the EL DIA (1901). Renamed ROANOKE (1901 – Southern Pacific Steamship Lines), EL DIA (1901 –

Southern Pacific Steamship Lines), PAN YORK (1941 – Pan Atlantic Steamship Company) and KIBBUTZ GALIYOT (1947).

KONG FREDERIK IX (1954)
6592 grt; 1500 psrs
115 cars
375' x 57' x 15' (113.6 x 17.3 x 4.5 m)
2 x 10-cylinder B+W diesel engines via twin screw.

Passenger-car-train ferry owned by the Danish government and operated by DSB until 1997, when it was installed as the centrepiece in the Danish Ferry Museum.
Built by Helsingor Shipbuilding Company, Helsingor.

KONG HARALD (`1993)
11204 grt; 691 psrs
402' x 63' x 16' (121.8 x 19.2 x 4.9 m)
2 x 6-cylinder MaK diesel engines via twin screw.
Passenger-car ferry in service for TFDS, Tromso.
Built by Volkswerft for Troms Fyles at a cost of US$63,000,000 and chartered to the Hurtigruten Group for the Norwegian coastal service.

KONG OLAV V (1957) See NAN HU (1983)

KONG OLAV V (1961) See JI MEI (1981)

KONG OLAV V (1968) See NEW ORIENT PRINCESS (1992)

KONGO MARU (1936)
7125 grt; 2500 psrs
435' x 57' x 21' (131.8 x 17.3 x 6.4 m)
4 x Mitsubishi SRG turbine engines via twin screw.
Built by Mitsubishi, Nagasaki, for Toyo Yusen.

KONIG ALBERT (1899) See ITALIA (1923)

KONIG BOUDEWIJN (1990) See P&OSL AQUITAINE (1999)

KONIG FRIEDRICH AUGUST (1906) See ALESIA (1928)

KONIGIN LUISE (1897) See EDISON (1924)

KONIGSTEIN (1928) See GANDIA (1939)

KONING ALBERT (1948)
3701 grt; 1600 psrs
373' x 49' x 12'6" (113 x 14.8 x 3.8 m)
Sulzer 24-cylinder diesel engines via twin screw.
Broken up for scrap at Antwerp, Belgium, in 1978.
Built by John Cockerill SA, Hoboken, for RMT, Belgium.

KONINGIN BEATRIX (1986)

31189 grt; 2100 psrs
485 cars or 220 cars + 80 trailers
534' x 91' x 20'6" (161.7 27.6 6.2 m)
4 x 8-cylinder MAN-B+W diesel engines via twin screw.
Multi-purpose ferry owned and operated by Stena Line.
Built by Van der Giessen-De Noord Yards, Rotterdam, for the Stena Line Holland BV at a cost of £40,000,000.

KONINGIN BEATRIX (1993)
7910 grt; 1000 psrs
210 cars
375' x 63' x 15'6" (113.6 x 19.1 x 4.7 m)
4 x 9-cylinder Stork-Wartsila diesel engines via twin screw. (also with bow twin screw.).
Passenger-car ferry owned by Veerboot Westerschelde and chartered long-term to PS D, Vlissingen.
Built by Royal Schelde Shipyard.

KONINGIN DER NEDERLANDEN (1911)
8280 grt; 254 psrs
455' x 55' x 33' (144.2 x 16.7 x 9 m)
4-cylinder Nederlandsche Fabriek quadruple expansion turbine engines via twin screw.
Broken up for scrap by Frank Rijsdijk, Hendrik Ido Ambacht in 1932.
Built by Nederlandsche Scheepsbouw for the Nederland Steamship Co.

KONINGIN ELISABETH (1957) See NAJD II (1979)

KONINGIN EMMA (1913)
9181 grt
470' x 57' x 35' (143.3 x 17.4 x 11.6 m)
4-cylinder Maatschappij Voor Scheepsbouw quadruple expansion engines via single screw.
Sank on 22 September 1915 nex t to the Sunk Lightship after hitting a mine laid by the German U-7.
Built by Maatschappij Voor Scheepsbouw, Rotterdam, for Nederlandsche Steamship Co.

KONINGIN EMMA (1939) See KONINGIN EMMA (1948)

KONINGIN EMMA (1948)
4353 grt; 1200 psrs
25 cars
380' x 47' x 18'6" (115.2 x 14.2 x 4.1 m)
2 x 10-cylinder Sulzer diesel engines via twin screw.
Broken up for scrap by Jos de Smedt at Antwerp, Belgium in 1969. Ex-Zeeland Line.
Built by Kon Maats de Schelde, Flushing, for the Zeeland Line as the KONINGIN EMMA (1939). Renamed QUEEN EMMA (1940 – British Admiralty).

KONINGIN FABIOLA (1962) See BOSPORUS (1999)

KONINGIN JULIANA (1968) See MOBY PRINCE (1985)

KONINGIN REGENTES (1894) See KOWA MARU (1937)

KONINGIN WILHELMINA (1896) See CHAOUIA (1911)

KONINGIN WILHELMINA (1960) See PANAGIA TINOY (1981)

KONING WILLEM I (1898) See ABDA (1913)

KONING WILLEM II (1900) See DOUKKALA (1913)

KONING WILLEM III (1899) See ATENE (1913)

KONPIRA No. 2 (1989)
3560 grt; 475 psrs
347' x 66' x 15' (105 x 20 x 4.6 m)
2 x Daihatsu diesel engines via twin screw.
Passenger-cargo ferry operated by Kato Kisen, Japan.
Built by Hayashikane Dockyard Co Ltd, Nagasaki.

KONSTANTIN CHERNENKO (1987) See RUSS (1988)

KONSTANTIN SIMONOV (1981) See FRANCESCA (1996)

KONUNG GUSTAF V (1910)
3264 grt; 530 psrs
374' x 51' x 17'6" (113.3 x 15.6 x 5.3 m)
2 x 3-cylinder Motala Verkstads engine via single screw.
Broken up for scrap by Personer AB, Ystad, in 1968.
Built by Lindholmens Vaerv, Goteborg for SJ Trelleborg as a passenger ferry.

KOOLAMA (1936)
4068 grt; 280 psrs
362' x 54' x 18' (110.3 x 16.4 x 5.5 m)
Harland & Wolff 12-cylinder diesel engines via twin screw.
Scuttled at sea off Wyndham, Western Australia, in 1946 after a year or so had passed following a Japanese aircraft attack which left her crippled and partially foundering.
Built by William Denny & Bros, Dumbarton, for the State Shipping Service, Western Australia.

KOOLAMA (1957) See EASTERN PEACE (1974)

KOOLINDA (1926) See KIMBERLEY (1958)

KOOMBANA (1909)
3668 grt; 188 psrs
340' x 48' x 28' (103.7 x 14.6 x 8.5 m)
A Stephen & Sons 3-cylinder triple expansion engine via single screw.
Sank with all hands on 21 March 1912 during a cyclone off Port Hedland, Western Australia.
Built by Alex Stephen & Sons Ltd, Glasgow, for the Adelaide Steamship Company.

KOREA (1901) See KOREA MARU (1916)

KOREA MARU (1916)
11810 grt; 1560 psrs
572' x 63' x 40' (173.3 x 19.1 x 12.1 m)
Quadruple expansion engines via twin screw.
Broken up for scrap at Kobe in 1934. Ex-NYK, Japan.
Built as the passenger-cargo ship KOREA (1901) by Newport News Shipbuilding & Engineering Company, Newport News, Virginia, for the Pacific Fast Mail Steamship Company.

KOSADO MARU (1983)
8754 grt; 1500 psrs
164 cars or 48 cars + 28 trailers
393' x 67' x 17' (119 x 20.4 x 5.2 m)
2 x 9-cylinder Pielstick diesel engines via twin screw.
Passenger-car-cargo ferry operated by Sado Kisen, Japan.
Built by Kanda Kawajiri, Kawajiri.

KOSCIUSZKO (1930) See EMPIRE HELFORD (1946)

KOSO MARU (1938)
3178 grt
305' x 44' x 23'2" (92.4 x 13.3 x 7 m)
Osaka Iron Works 3-cylinder triple expansion engines via single screw.
Built by Osaka Iron Works Ltd, Osaka, for Osaka Shosen KK as the KHOSO MARU (1917).

KOTA AGOENG (1930)
7356 grt
450' x 61' x 26'9" (136.4 x 18.5 x 7 m)
2 x Maats Fyenoord SRG diesel engines via single screw.
Built by Maats Fyenoord, Rotterdam, for Rotterdam Lloyd.

KOTA BALI (1971)
9020 grt; 235 psrs
479' x 63' x 23' (146 x 19.2 x 7 m)
2 x 8-cylinder Stork-Werkspoor diesel engines via twin screw.
Broken up for scrap at Shanghai in 1984. Ex-Pacific International Line, Singapore.

Built as the TJIWANGI (1950) by C Van der Geissen & Zonen, Krimpen, for Royal Interocean Lines.

KOTA BAROE (1929)
7281 grt
449' x 61' x 26'8" (136 x 18.5 x 8.1 m)
Maats de Schelde 8-cylinder diesel engine via single screw.
Built by Kon Maats De Schelde, Flushing, for Rotterdam Lloyd.

KOTA GEDE (1928)
7323 grt
450' x 61' x 26'9" (136.4 x 18.5 x 8.2 m)
Maats Fyenoord 7-cylinder diesel engine via single screw.
Built by Maats Fyenoord, Rotterdam, for Rotterdam Lloyd.

KOTA INTEN (1927)
7191 grt
450' x 61' x 26'8" (136.4 x 18.5 x 8.1 m)
Maats Fyenoord 7-cylinder diesel engines via twin screw.
Broken up for scrap in Hong Kong in 1957.
Built by Wilton-Fijenoord, Rotterdam, for Rotterdam Lloyd.

KOTA NOPAN (1931)
7322 grt
450' x 61' x 26'9" (136.4 x 18.5 x 8.2 m)
Maats De Schelde 8-cylinder diesel engine via single screw.
Built by Kon Maats De Schelde, Rotterdam, for Rotterdam Lloyd.

KOTA PANJANG (1969)
7412 grt; 561 psrs
440' x 57' x 23'6" (134.1 x 17.3 x 7.2 m)
5-cylinder Doxford diesel engine via single screw.
Broken up for scrap at Gadani Beach in 1981. Ex-Pacific International Line, Singapore.
Built as the CHANGSHA (1949) by Scotts Shipbuilding & Engineering Company, Greenock, for China Navigation Company.

KOTA PINANG (1930)
7277 grt
450' x 61' x 26'9" (136.4 x 18.5 x 8.2 m)
Maats Fyenoord 7-cylinder diesel engine via single screw.
Built by Nederland Shipyard, Amsterdam, for Rotterdam Lloyd.

KOTA RADJA (1927)
7177 grt
449' x 61' x 26'8" (136 x 18.5 x 8.1 m)
Maats De Schelde 8-cylinder diesel engine via single screw.
Built by Kon Maats De Schelde, Flushing, for Rotterdam Lloyd.

KOTA SAHABAT (1972)
6160 grt; 156 psrs
440' x 57' x 23'6" (134.1 x 17.3 x 7.2 m)
5-cylinder Doxford diesel engine via single screw.
Broken up for scrap in Kaohsiung in 1980. Ex-Pacific International Lines, Singapore.
Built by Scotts Shipbuilding & Engineering Company, Greenock, for China Navigation Company.

KOTA SINGAPURA (1972)
9849 grt; 235 psrs
479' x 63' x 23' (146 x 19.2 x 7 m)
Stork-Werkspoor diesel engines via twin screw.
Broken up for scrap at Kaohsiung in 1980. Ex-Pacific International Lines, Singapore.
Built by C Van der Geissen & Zonen, Krimpen, as the passenger-cargo liner TJILUWAH (1951) for Royal Interocean Lines.

KOTA SINGAPURA (1981)
7760 grt; 136 psrs
440' x 59' x 25' (133.2 x 17.9 x 7.6 m)
6-cylinder B+W diesel engines via twin screw.
Broken up for scrap in China in 1986. Ex-Pacific International Lines (Pte) Ltd, Singapore. Built by Union Naval de Levante, Valencia, for Cia Trasmediterranea as the CIUDAD DE PAMPLONA (1964).

KOTA TJANDI (1930)
7295 grt
450' x 61' x 26'9" (136.4 x 18.5 x 8.2 m)
Maats Fyenoord 7-cylinder diesel engine via single screw.
Built by Wilton's Engineering & Slipway Co, Rotterdam, for Rotterdam Lloyd.

KOTOBUKI MARU (1943)
18383 grt; 2234 psrs
570' x 74' x 30' (172.7 x 22.4 x 9.1 m)
DRG turbine engines via twin screw.
Broken up for scrap in Japan in 1951. Ex-Japanese government.
Built by William Beardmore & Company, Dalmuir, for Lloyd Sabaudo as the CONTE VERDI (1923). Renamed KOTABUKI MARU after the Japanese salvaged the ship from the Shanghai harbour bed where she had been scuttled, on 9 September 1943, to thwart the Japanese from capturing her intact. The Japanese refloated the vessel and converted her into a troop carrier until she sank in Maiguru, Japan, during an American air raid. In 1949 she was again refloated by the Mitsui Line and surveyed for rebuilding, but the company opted for scrapping her instead.

KOTO RATU (1975) See SANG FAJAR (1975)

KOUANG (1929)
7633 grt; 1110 psrs
452' x 52' x 28'5" (137.8 x 15.9 x 8.6 m)
Palmer 3-cylinder triple expansion engine via single screw.
Broken up for scrap in 1936. Ex-Messageries Maritimes,Marseilles.
Built by Palmers Shipbuilding Company Ltd, Jarrow, for Hamburg-America Line as the ALEX ANDRIA (1901). Renamed SACRAMENTO (1914), BAYRAMENTO (1916 – The Bay Steamship Co Ltd, Britain), PORT DE St NAZAIRE (1921) and PYTHEAS (1922).

KOUFRA (1946) See MADALI (1948)

KOWA MARU (1937)
3331 grt; 85 psrs
331' x 43' x 22'4" (100 x 13 x 6.8 m)
Clyde 3-cylinder triple expansion engine via single screw.
While owned by Nippon KKK, she sank on 19 March 1943 after being torpedoed by the USS WAHOO, south of Darien.
Built by Clyde Shipbuilding & Engineering Co Ltd, Glasgow, for Burns Philp & Company Ltd, Sydney as the MATARAM (1909). Renamed KWAN HO (1935 – VK Song, China).

KOWEIT (1911)
3618 grt; 84 psrs
376' x 43' x 27'6" (114.6 x 13.1 x 9.1 m)
Caird 3-cylinder steam engine via single screw.
Broken up for scrap in Italy in 1925. Ex-Egyptian Maritime Enterprise.
Built by Caird & Co, Glasgow, for the Nederlands Steamship Co as the KONINGIN REGENTES (1894).

KOWNO (1906) See OWASCO (1916)

KRAKA (1988) See FRIGGA (1999)

KRALJICA MIRA (1994)
3984 grt; 1000 psrs
78 cars
287' x 53' x 14' (87 x 16 x 4.2 m)
2 x 12-cylinder Deutz diesel engines via twin screw.

Passenger-car ferry owned by United Shipping Co, Panama, and operated by

SEM Maritime Co, Split.
Built by Jos L Meyer, Papenburg, for AS Dampskibselskabet as the HAMMERSHUS (1965). Renamed CYNTHIA I (1993 – Hellenic Mediterranean Lines).

KRALJIKA MARIJA (1930) See SAVOIE (1940)

KRASIN (1976)
14058 grt; 55 psrs
443' x 86' x 36' (135 x 26.1 x 11 m)
9 x 12-cylinder Sulzer diesel-electric engines via triple screw.
Passenger-icebreaker operated by the Far East Shipping Company, Vladivostok.
Built by Wartsila, Helsinki, for the Russian government.

KRASNOYARSK (1939)
3554 grt
315' x 46' x 26' (95.5 x 13.9 x 7.9 m)
Baltic Shipbuilding & Engineering Works 3-cylinder triple expansion engine via single screw.
Built by Baltic Shipbuilding & Engineering Works, St Petersburg, for the Russian government as the SAKHALIN (1930).

KRIM (1928)
4867 grt; 450 psrs
363' x 51' x 19' (110 x 15.5 x 5.8 m)
2 x 6-cylinder Krupp diesel engines via twin screw.
In USSR service.
Built by F Krupp, Kiel, for the Russian government.

KRISTIANIAFJORD (1913)
10669 grt; 1117 psrs
512' x 61' x 26' (155.2 x 18.3 x 7.9 m)
2 x 4-cylinder Cammell Laird quadruple expansion engines via twin screw.
Abandoned as a total loss after running aground on 15 July 1917 seven miles (12 km) from Cape Race, near Mistaken Point, Newfoundland.
Built by Cammell Laird & Company, Birkenhead, for the Norwegian America Line.

KRISTINA REGINA (1987)
4295 grt; 350 psrs
65 cars + 6 trailers
328' x 50' x 16'6" (99.4 x 15.2 x 5 m)
2 x 12-cylinder Wartsila-Vasa diesel engines via single screw. (Replaced original Gotaverken quadruple expansion engine.)

Ice-strengthened cruise ferry owned by Rannikkolinjat, Finland, and cruising for Kristina Cruise Ltd, Kotka.
Built by Oskarshavns, Sweden, for Bore Steamship Company Ltd, Turku, as the BORE (1960). Renamed BOREA (1977 – Aura Line, Finland).

KRI TANJUNG OISINA (1978)
8533 grt; 1063 psrs
456' x 61' x 28' (138.2 x 18.5 x 8.5 m)
4 x 9-cylinder MAN diesel engine via single screw.
Military transport operated by the Indonesian government.
Built by De Merwede, Hardinxveld, for the Oranje Line as the passenger ferry PRINSES IRENE (1960).

KRI TANJUNG PANDAN (1977)
17891 grt; 2106 psrs
577' x 72' x 26'6" (174.8 x 21.8 x 8.1 m)
2 x 6-cylinder MAN-type diesel engines via twin screw.
Broken up for scrap at Kaohsiung in 1987 after serving as a military accommodation and training ship for the Indonesian Navy.
Built by Blohm & Voss, Hamburg, for the German East Africa Line as the

PRETORIA (1936). Renamed EMPIRE DOON (1945 – British government), EMPIRE ORWELL (1949 – British government) and GUNUNG DJATI (1959 – Blue Funnel Line).

KRITI (1978) See EXPRESS ARIS (2000)

KRITI I (1997)
27667 grt; 1600 psrs
1200 cars
629' x 96' x 22'6" (190.6 x 29.1 x 6.8 m)
2 x 16-cylinder MAN diesel engines via twin screw.
Passenger-car ferry operated by ANEK, Greece.
Built by Koyo Dock Co Ltd, Mihara, for Shin Nipponkai KK, Osaka, as the NEW SUZURAN (1979).

KRITI II (1997)
27239 grt; 1600 psrs
1200 cars
629' x 96' x 22'6" (190.6 x 29.1 x 6.8 m)
2 x 16-cylinder MAN diesel engines via twin screw.
Passenger-car ferry operated by ANEK, Greece.
Built by Koyo Dock Company Ltd, Mihara, for Shin Nipponkai KK, Osaka, as the NEW YUKARI (1979).

KRITI III (2000) See OLYMPIC CHAMPION (2000)

KRITI V (2000) See LEFKA ORI (2000)

KRONPRINS CARL GUSTAF (1966) See SPLIT 1700 (1997)

KRONPRINSESSAN VICTORIA (1981) See STENA EUROPE (1998)

KRONPRINSESSE INGRID (1949) See ALKYON (1978)

KRONPRINS FREDERIK (1946) See PATRA (1976)

KRONPRINS FREDERIK (1981)
16071 grt; 2280 psrs
200 cars
499' x 75' x 19'6" (151.2 x 22.7 x 6 m)
6 x 16-cylinder B+W diesel engines via twin screw.

Ice-strengthened passenger-car ferry owned and operated by Scandlines.
Built by AS Nakskov Skibsvaerft, Nakskov, for the Danish government.

KRONPRINS HARALD (1961) See MEDOUSSA (1997)

KRONPRINS HARALD (1976) See ADMIRAL OF SCANDINAVIA (1997)

KRONPRINS HARALD (1987)
31914 grt; 1454 psrs

700 cars
543' x 94' x 21'6" (164.5 x 28.4 x 6.5 m)
4 x 12-cylinder Wartsila-Sulzer diesel engines via twin screw.
Ice-strengthened passenger-car ferry owned and operated by Color Line, Norway.
Built by Wartsila, Turku, for Jahre Line.

KRONPRINS OLAV (1937) See CAPO FALCONARA (1978)

KRONPRINZESSIN CECILIE (1907) See MOUNT VERNON, USS (1914)

KRONPRINZ WILHELM (1901) See VON STEUBEN (1917)

KRONSTADT (1904) See VULCAIN (1921)

KRONSTADT (1919) See VULCAIN (1921)

KROONLAND (1902)
12241 grt; 1420 psrs
560' x 60' x 38'4" depth (169.7 x 18.2 x 11.6 m)
William Cramp 6-cylinder triple expansion engines via twin screw.
Broken up for scrap at Genoa, in 1927. Ex-American Lines.
Built by William Cramp & Sons, Philadelphia, Pennsylvania, for the Red Star Line.

K. SADIKOGLU (1950) See KEMAL SADIKOGLU (1950)

KUALA LUMPUR (1960)
12555 grt; 1911 psrs
517' x 63' x 25' (157.5 x 19.2 x 7.6 m)
2 x 5-cylinder Doxford diesel engines via twin screw.
Broken up for scrap as a pilgrim ship at Kaohsiung in 1971. Ex-China Navigation Company.
Built by Barclay, Curle & Company, Glasgow, for the British India Line as the troopship DILWARA (1935).

KUBAN (1904)
8479 grt; 1100 psrs
521' x 56' x 33'8" (157.9 x 17 x 10.2 m)
AG Vulcan 6-cylinder triple expansion engines via twin screw.
Broken up as an auxiliary cruiser for scrap at Szczecin, Poland, in 1907. Ex-Russian Navy.
Laid down by AG Vulcan, Stettin, for the Hamburg-Amerikan Line as the NORMANNIA (1887) and completed as the incorrectly-spelt and registered AUGUSTA VICTORIA (1890). Correctly renamed AUGUSTE VICTORIA (1897 – Hamburg-Amerikan Line).

KUBAN (1976)
4722 grt; 333 psrs
401' x 52' x 17' (121.5 x 15.8 x 5.2 m)
2 x 6-cylinder MAN diesel engines via twin screw.
Broken up for scrap in 1998 as a troop transport for the Russian Navy.
Built by Mathias-Thesen, Wismar, for the Black Sea Shipping Company as the NADEZHDA KRUPSKAYA (1963).

KUKJAE EXPRESS FERRY No. 2 (1994)
4225 grt; 200 psrs
62 trailers
381' x 69' x 15' (115.6 x 21 x 4.5 m)
2 x 6-cylinder MaK diesel engines via twin screw.
Passenger-cargo ferry owned by Dong Nam Leasing Co Ltd and operated by Kuk Jae Express Co Ltd.
Built by Kochi Jyuko, Koshi, for Shikoku Chuo, Japan, as the NIIHAMA II (1984).

KUMANO MARU (1901)
4654 grt; 225 psrs
400' x 49' x 27' (121.2 x 14.8 x 8.2 m)
Fairfield 3-cylinder triple expansion engine via single screw.
Broken up for scrap in 1927.
Built by Fairfield Shipbuilding & Engineering Co Ltd, Glasgow, for NYK.

KUNAK (1960)
4874 grt; 520 psrs
375' x 53' x 20' (113.6 x 16 x 6.1 m)
Hawthorn Leslie 8-cylinder diesel engine via single screw.
In Malaysian service for the Straits Steamship Company.
Built by Wilton Fijenoord for NV Koninklijke Paketvaart Maats as the BAUD (1948).

KUNGSHOLM (1922) See NOORDAM (1926)

KUNGSHOLM (1928) See IMPERIAL BAHAMA HOTEL (1964)

KUNGSHOLM (1952) See BLUE SEA (1977)

KUNGSHOLM (1953) See COLUMBUS C (1982)

KUNGSHOLM (1966) See VICTORIA (1995)

KURFURST (1901)
5655 grt; 100 psrs
length 411' x beam 48' (124.5 x 14.5 m)
Triple expansion engines via twin screw.
Abandoned as a total loss after becoming wrecked on 6 May 1904 in dense fog on the Portuguese coast near Sagres.
Built by Reicherstieg Werft, Hamburg, for the Dutch East Africa Line.

KUROSHIO MARU (1971) See OUR LADY OF LIPA (1995)

KURSK (1910) See POLONIA (1921)

KURUSHIMA MARU (1982) See MYRTIDIOTISSA (2000)

KURUSHIMA No.7 (1984) See OUR LADY OF LIPA (1995)

KUT (1919)
3515 grt
360' x 44' x 26' (109.1 x 13.3 x 7.9 m)

Triple expansion engine via single screw.
Broken up for scrap at Briton Ferry, UK, in 1926. Ex-"K" Steamship Company Ltd.
Built by Sunderland Shipbuilding Company, Sunderland, for the Blue Anchor Line as the WARRNAMBOOL (1892). Renamed HARMODIUS (1900 – British & South American Steam Navigation Company Ltd).

KUWAIT MARRIOTT HOTEL (1976) See RAMADA AL-SALAM HOTEL SHIP. (1990)

KWAN HO (1935) See KOWA MARU (1937)

KWANTO MARU (1912) See LE MYRE DE VILLIERS (1917)

KYARRA (1903)
6952 grt; 511 psrs
416' x 53' x 28'6" (126 x 16 x 8.7 m)
Quadruple expansion engines via twin screw.
Sank as a hospital ship, within one hour, on 26 May 1918 after being torpedoed three miles (5 km) off the Isle of Wight, UK. Five lives were lost.
Built by William Denny & Bros, Dumbarton, for the Australasian United Steam Navigation Company.

KYDON (1968) See CITY OF TARANTO (1989)

KYDON (1991) See IERAPETRA L (1999)

KYPROS (1944) See PRINCESS (1980)

KYPROS STAR (1986) See OCEAN MAJESTY (1991)

KYSTVEIEN (1984) See PETRONILA MATA (1998)

KYSTVEIEN (1988) See WADI ALNEEL (1993)

LAARAT (1904)
4764 grt; 208 psrs
420' x 43' x 26' (127.3 x 13 x 7.9 m)
2-cylinder steam inverted compound engine via single screw.
Broken up for scrap at Genoa in 1904 for a tender figure of £9350.
Built by Caird & Company, Greenock, for the P&O Line as the BALLARAT (1882).

LA BOURDONNAIS (1921)
8287 grt; 1460 psrs
472' x 56' x 24'6" (143 x 17 x 7.5 m)
6-cylinder triple expansion engines via twin screw.
Broken up for scrap at Genoa in 1934. Ex-Messageries Maritimes.
Built by JC Tecklenborg, Geestemunde, for North German Lloyd as the SCHARNHORST (1904) which was seized by France in 1919.

LA BOURDONNAIS (1953) See KNOSSOS (1968)

LABRADOR (1953)
3823 grt; 66 psrs
271' x 64' x 30' (82 x 19.5 x 9.2 m)
6 x 10-cylinder Fairbanks-Morse diesel engines via twin screw.
Owned by the Canadian Ministry of Transport.
Built by Marine Industries Ltd, Sorel, Quebec as a passenger-icebreaker.

LA BRETAGNE (1886) See ALESIA (1919)

LABURNUM (1993)
7838 grt; 1152 psrs
202 cars
389' x 64' x 14'6" (117.8 x 19.4 x 4.4 m)
3 x 12-cylinder MAN diesel engines via triple screw.
Passenger-car ferry owned by Charterhall Shipping Co.
Built by NV Scheepswerf Gusto, Schiedam, for Townsend Car Ferries Ltd as the FREE ENTERPRISE V (1970). Renamed PRIDE OF HYTHE (1988 – P&O European Ferries Ltd) and MILDA (1993 – G.A Ferries).

LACASIELLE (1968) See TOPEKA (1976)

LACONIA (1912)
18099 grt; 2850 psrs
625' x 71' x 29' (190.5 x 21.5 x 8.8 m)
2 x Wallsend Slipway 4-cylinder quadruple expansion engines via twin screw.
Sank in one hour on 25 February 1917, with 12 lives lost, after being hit by two torpedoes from the German U-50 160 miles (265 km) north-west of Fastnet.
Built by Swan Hunter & Wigham Richardson Ltd, Newcastle, for the Cunard Steamship Co Ltd.

LACONIA (1922)
19695 grt; 2197 psrs
601' x 74' x 32'8" (182.1 x 22.4 x 9.9 m)
6 x Wallsend Slipway DRG turbine engines via twin screw.
Sank as a troopship within one hour, on 12 September 1942, after being torpedoed twice by the German U-156 500 miles (835 km) south of Cape Palmas, Liberia. The loss of life numbered 1750, including a massive percentage of 2,700 Italian prisoners-of-war being transported to land-based camps.
Built by Swan Hunter & Wigham Richardson for the Cunard Line.

LA CROSSE VICTORY (1945) See BUCEPHALOS (1966)

LADY CARIBE I (1998)
4245 grt; 1000 psrs
120 cars + 14 trailers
284' x 55' x 13' (86 x 16.6 x 3.9 m)
2 x 12-cylinder Deutz diesel engines via twin screw.
Casino cruise ferry operated by Robbie Shipping & Port Services Inc, San

Lorenzo.
Built by Ateliers et Chantiers de le Seine-Maritime, Le Trait for the Stena Line as the STENA DANICA (1965). Renamed LUCY MAUD MONTGOMERY (1970 – Canadian National Railways).

LADY CLEMENTINE (1974) See VANA TALLINN (1997)

LADY CONNAUGHT (1938) See LADY KILLARNEY (1947)

LADY DINA (1972) See CARIBIA 2 (1973)

LADY DRAKE (1928)
8194 grt; 259 psrs
438' x 60' x 23' (132.7 x 18.2 x 7 m)
2 x Parsons DRG turbine engines via twin screw.
Sank on 3 May 1942 after being torpedoed near Bermuda.
Built by Cammell Laird & Co, Birkenhead, for Canadian National Steamship Co.

LADY HAWKINS (1928)
8194 grt; 259 psrs
438' x 60' x 23' (132.7 x 18.2 x 7 m)
2 x Parsons DRG turbine engines via twin screw.
Sank on 19 January 1942 when torpedoed twice by the German U-66 off Bermuda, with the loss of 250 lives. Seventy-one survivors were rescued by the ss COAMO and several other ships in the vicinity.
Built by Cammell Laird & Co, Birkenhead, for Canadian National Steamship Co.

LADY KILLARNEY (1947)
3222 grt; 200 psrs
325' x 42' x 16'6" (98.5 x 12.7 x 5 m)
2 x 4-cylinder triple expansion engines via twin screw.
Broken up for scrap in 1947 by Smith & Houston Ltd, Glasgow. Ex-Coast Lines Ltd.
Built by Harland & Wolff Ltd, Belfast, for Belfast Steamship Co as the passenger ferry PATRIOTIC (1912). Renamed LADY LEINSTER (1930 – British & Irish Steam Packet Co) and LADY CONNAUGHT (1938 – British & Irish Steam Packet Co).

LADY LEINSTER (1930) See LADY KILLARNEY (1947)

LADY M (1982) See MANAR (2000)

LADY NELSON (1928) See AL WADI (1960)

LADY OF FORTUNE (1998) See AUSONIA (2000)

LADY OF MANN (1930)

3104 grt; 2853 psrs
371' x 50' x 18'6" (112.4 x 15.2 x 5.6 m)
Geared turbine engines via twin screw.
Broken up for scrap at Dalmuir in 1972.
Built by Vickers-Armstrong Ltd, Barrow-in-Furness, for the Isle of Man Steam Packet Company as a passenger ferry at a cost of £249,000.

LADY OF MANN (1976)
4482 grt; 1000 psrs
105 cars
345' x 55' x 12' (104.4 x 16.7 x 3.6 m)
2 x 12-cylinder Pielstick diesel engines via twin screw.

Passenger-car ferry operating for Sea Containers Ltd between the Isle of Man and the UK mainland.
Built by Ailsa Shipbuilding Company, Troon, for the Isle of Man Steam Packet Co Ltd.

LADY RODNEY (1928) See KOMATI (1960)

LADY SOMERS (1928)
8194 grt; 125 psrs
438' x 60' x 23' (132.7 x 18.2 x 7 m)
2 x Parsons SRG turbine engines via twin screw.
Sank on 15 July 1941 while serving as an armed boarding vessel in mid-Atlantic.
Built by Cammell Laird & Co, Birkenhead, for the Canadian National Steamship Co.

LADY TERRY (1990) See SEA SERENADE (1992)

LAENNEC (1951) See BELLE ABETO (1966)

LAESOFAERGEN (1996) See MARGRETHE LAESOE (1997)

LA FAYETTE (1915) See MEXIQUE (1928)

LA FAYETTE (1930)
25178 grt; 1067 psrs
577' x 77' x 27'9" (174.8 x 23.3 x 8.5 m)
4 x 4-cylinder MAN diesel engines via quadruple screw.
Broken up for scrap at Rotterdam in 1938. She had been destroyed by fire on 4 May 1938 while being refurbished in dry dock in Le Havre.
Built by Chantiers de l'Atlantique, St Nazaire, for the French Line.

LA FAYETTE (1941)
82799 grt; 1972 psrs
1028' x 117' x 36'6" (311.5 x 35.5 x 11.1 m)
Turbo-electric engines via quadruple screw.
Owned by the US Navy, she was broken up for scrap for a tender price of US$161,000 at Port Newark, New Jersey, in 1946. This followed her catching fire during conversion into a troopship, on 9 February 1942, and then capsizing at her New York berth as a result of the amount of firehose water pumped into her.
Built by Chantiers de l'Atlantique, St Nazaire, for the French Line as the NORMANDIE (1935) at a cost of US$5,000,000.

LAFAYETTE (1988) See CLUB MED II (1989)

LAGAN VIKING (1997)
21856 grt; 340 psrs

70 cars + 162 trailers
614' x 84' x 18'6" (186 x 25.6 x 5.6 m)
2 x 8-cylinder Wartsila diesel engines via twin screw.
Operated by Norse Irish Ferries as a passenger-car-cargo ferry.
Built by Visentini Shipyards, Donada, at a cost of £90,000,000.

LA GRANDE DUCHESSE (1896) See CAROLINA (1905)

LA GRANDE VICTORY (1945) See MARGARITA (1963)

LA GUARDIA (1949) See OCEAN EXPLORER I (1998)

LAHN (1888) See RUSS (1904)

LA JANELLE (1969)
9070 grt; 806 psrs
466' x 60' x 23' (142 x 18.3 x 7 m)
Geared turbine engines via single screw.
Owned by Western Steamship Co, she was partially broken up for scrap on site as a floating restaurant at Port Hueneme, Oxnard, California, after she dragged her anchor and moorings during a hurricane on 13 April 1970. A breakwater was constructed over the remaining hulk.
Built by Bethlehem Shipbuilding Corporation, Quincy, Massachusetts, for the New York & Porto Rico Steamship Company as the BORINQUEN (1931). Renamed PUERTO RICO (1949 – Bull Line), AROSA STAR (1954 – Arosa Line) and BAHAMA STAR (1959 – McCormick Shipping Corporation).

LAKE CHAMPLAIN (1900) See CHORAN MARU (1942)

LAKE ERIE (1899) See PRYGONA (1921)

LAKE MANITOBA (1901) See IVER HEATH (1918)

LAKEMBA (1947)
7459 grt; 98 psrs
441' x 57' x 27' (134.4 x 17.3 x 8.2 m)
Triple expansion engine via single screw.
Owned by Pacific Shipowners Ltd, Suva, she sank on 9 October 1967 after grounding on a reef off Vatulele, Fiji, four days earlier.
Built by Burrard Drydock Company, North Vancouver, BC, for the British Royal Navy as the SPURN POINT, HMS (1945).

LAKE MEGANTIC (1900) See PORTO SAID (1913)

LAKE MICHIGAN (1901)
8200 grt; 513 psrs
470' x 56' x 31'9" depth (143.1 x 17.1 x 9.7 m)
Richardson, Westgarth 6-cylinder triple expansion engines via twin screw.
Sank on 16 April 1918 after being torpedoed by the German U-100 93 miles (155 km) north-west of Eagle Island, off County Mayo.
Built by CS Swan Hunter, Wallsend, for the Elder Dempster Line.

LAKE SIMCOE (1901)
4966 grt; 1255 psrs
430' x 47' x 34'3" depth (131 x 14.3 x 10.4 m)
3-cylinder compound engine via single screw.
Broken up for scrap at Genoa in 1905. Ex-Elder Dempster.
Built by John Elder & Co, Glasgow, for North German Lloyd as the EMS (1884).

LAKONIA (1963)
20314 grt; 1186 psrs
609' x 75' x 29' (185.6 x 22.9 x 8.8 m)
2 x 10-cylinder Sulzer diesel engines via twin screw.
Owned by the Greek Line, she sank on 29 December 1963, with the loss of 128 lives, after capsizing while under tow by the Norwegian tug HERKULES, 250 miles (417 km) west of Gibraltar. The hairdresser's salon had erupted in fire which swept throughout the vessel one week earlier, 180 miles (300 km) north of Madeira in the Bay of Biscay. Many lives were saved by the crews from the CENTAUR, MONTCALM, CHARLESVILLE and SALTA.
Built by Netherlands Shipbuilding & Drydock Company for the Nederland Line as the JOHAN VAN OLDENBARNEVELT (1930).

LALANDIA (1915) See NORAH MOLLER (1938)

LA LORRAINE (1900) See LA LORRAINE (1917)

LA LORRAINE (1917)
11372 grt; 1114 psrs
580' x 60' x 35'9" (176.8 x 18.3 x 10.9 m)
2 x 4-cylinder CGT triple expansion engines via twin screw.
Broken up for scrap at St Nazaire in 1922. Ex-French Line.
Built by Penhoet, St Nazaire, for CGT, France, as the LA LORRAINE (1900).
Renamed as the armed merchant cruiser LORRAINE II (1914 – French Navy).

LA MARSELLAISE (1949) See BIANCA C (1958)

LAMARTINE (1922) See KHAI DINH (1939)

LAMBELU (1997)
14701 grt; 2000 psrs
483' x 78' x 19'6" (146.5 x 23.7 x 5.9 m)
2 x 6-cylinder MaK diesel engine via single screw.
Passenger ship owned and operated by the Indonesian government's Ministry of Sea Communications.
Built by Jos L Meyer, Papenburg.

LAMPEDUSA (1988) See TEBAH 2000 (1999)

LANCASHIRE (1889) See DAITEN MARU (1913)

LANCASHIRE (1914)
10331 grt; 190 psrs
500' x 57' x 28' (151.5 x 17.3 x 8.5 m)
Quadruple expansion engines via twin screw.
Broken up for scrap by TW Ward & Co at Barrow-in-Furness in 1956.
Launched by Harland & Wolff Ltd, Belfast, for the Bibby Line as the OXFORDSHIRE (1913) and completed as the LANCASHIRE.

LANCASTRIA (1924)
16243 grt; 1580 psrs
579' x 70' x 31'4" (175.5 x 21.2 x 9.5 m)
6 x Beardmore DRG turbine engines via twin screw.
Owned by the Cunard Steamship Co, she capsized and sank in 20 minutes, bow first, as a troopship at 4.00 pm on 17 June 17, 1940. This followed an attack by German Dornier 17 twin-engined bombers, while evacuating over 5,000 Allied troops from St Nazaire. The ferocity of the attack lifted the ship out of the water several times before the hull split open and the sea flooded her, taking 2,833 lives. Another 2,477 lives were saved by a flotilla of ships, including HMS HAVELOCK.
Built by William Beardmore & Co Ltd, Glasgow, for the Anchor Line as the TYRRHENIA (1922).

LANCUT (1985) See HERMES (1999)

LANFRANC (1907)
6300 grt; 500 psrs
length 419' x beam 52' (127 x 15.8 m)
Triple expansion engine via twin screw.
Sank as a hospital ship on 17 April 1917 after a torpedo hit from a German U-boat 40 miles (67 km) north-east of Lerwick.
Built by Caledon Shipyard, Dundee for the Booth Line.

LANGDALE QUEEN (1962)
3911 grt; 1000 psrs
100 cars
307' x 57' x 13' (93 x 17.3 x 3.9 m)
4 x 16-cylinder General Motors diesel-electric engines via twin screw.
Built by William Cramp & Son, Philadelphia, Pennsylvania, for the British Columbia Toll Authority Ferry System as the ASBURY PARK (1903). Renamed CITY OF SACRAMENTO (1953) and KAHLOKE (1962).

LANGELAND III (1989) See PETAR HEKTOROVIC (1999)

LANGELAND IV (1999)

6480 grt; 870 psrs
260 cars or 23 trailers
359' x 57' x 15' (108.7 x 17.3 x 4.6 m)
2 x 12-cylinder Deutz diesel engines via twin screw.

Passenger-car-cargo ferry owned by Labrador Marine Inc, Canada, following their March 2000 purchase from Birka Line for US$4,200,000.
Built by Jos L Meyer Shipyards, Papenburg, for Rederi AB Slite as the APOLLO (1970). Renamed OLAU KENT (1976 – Olau Line), GELTING NORD (1980 – Nordisk Faergefart), BENODET (1984 – Brittany Ferries), CORBIERE (1985 – British Channel Islands Ferries), LINDA (1991 – Eckero Line), CORBIERE (1992 – British Channel Islands Ferries) and APOLLO (1994 – Birka Line).

LANGKAPURI STAR AQUARIUS (1993) See STAR AQUARIUS (1993)

LAOS (1896) See AMAZONE (1905)

LAOS (1903)
6145 grt; 1230 psrs
413' x 50' x 26'6" (125 x 15.2 x 8.1 m)
B+W 3-cylinder triple expansion engines via single screw.
Sank after breaking in two on 9 February 1907.
Built by Burmeister & Wain, Copenhagen, for Cie de l'Est Asiatique.

LAOS (1954) See MALAYSIA RAYA (1971)

LA PALAIS FLOTTANT (1967)
4923 grt; 742 psrs
388' x 56' x 20' (117.6 x 17 x 6.1 m)
Turbine engines via twin screw.
Broken up for scrap at Santander in 1968 after she served as a floating hotel during Expo '67 in Montreal under the ownership of the Peninsular & Occidental Steamship Co.
Built by Newport News Shipbuilding & Drydock Company, Newport News, Virginia, for P&O Steamship Co as the FLORIDA (1931).

LA PALMA (1980)
11951 grt; 785 psrs
492' x 64' x 23' (150 x 19.5 x 7 m)
2 x 10-cylinder Creusot-B+W diesel engines via twin screw.
Cruise ship owned by Louis Cruise's subsidiary Intercruise Ltd, Cyprus, and has been laid up in Eleusis Bay since 8 April 1999 waiting for a sale.
Built by Chantiers de la Gironde, Bordeaux, for Messageries Maritimes as the FERDINAND DE LESSEPS (1952). Renamed DELPHI (1969 – Efthymiadis Shipping Co SA, Piraeus) and LA PERLA (1977 – Intercruises SA).

LAPATAIA (1951)
4153 grt; 100 psrs
335' x 51' x 23' (101.5 x 15.4 x 7 m)
2 x 6-cylinder Fiat diesel engines via twin screw.
Operated as a troop carrier by the Argentine government.
Built by Cantieri Riuniti dell Adriatico.

LA PATRIA (2000)
6009 grt; 1274 psrs
140 cars + 55 TEUs
377' x 54' x 13'6" (114.2 x 16.4 x 4.1 m)

2 x 12-cylinder Pielstick diesel engines via twin screw.
Passenger-car-container ferry owned by Founders Shipping Co and operated by Hellenic Mediterranean Lines.
Built by Cammell Laird & Co, Birkenhead, for the Belfast Steamship Co as the ULSTER QUEEN (1967). Renamed MED SEA (1982 – Pangloss Navigation Co Ltd, Limassol), AL KAHERA (1986 – Pangloss Navigation Co Ltd, Limassol), ALA-EDDIN (1987) and POSEIDONIA (1988 – owned by Silkwave Marine and operated by Hellenic Mediterranean Lines).

LA PERLA (1977) See LA PALMA (1980)

LA PEROUSE (1928)
4928 grt; 102 psrs
length 370' (112 m)
Quadruple engines via twin screw.
Broken up for scrap in 1936.
Built by Flensburger Aschiffs, Flensburg, for the Hamburg-America Line as the STEIGERWALD (1912). Renamed ADMIRAL PIERRE (1922 – Messageries Maritimes).

LAPLAND (1907)
18694 grt; 2350 psrs
606' x 70' x 32'10" (183.6 x 21.2 x 9.7 m)
Harland & Wolff 8-cylinder quadruple expansion engines via twin screw.
Broken up for scrap at Osaka in 1934 for a tender fee of £30,000. Ex-Red Star Line.
Built by Harland & Wolff Ltd, Belfast, for the White Star Line.

LA PLATA (1888) See NERA (1903)

LA PLATA (1896) See FRESHFIELDS (1915)

LA PLATA (1901) See THE VIKING (1908)

LA PLATA (1910)
7116 grt; 928 psrs
437' x 51' x 35' (132.4 x 15.5 x 10.6 m)
J & G Thompson 3-cylinder triple expansion engine via single screw.
Broken up for scrap in 1912.
Built by J & G Thomson, Glasgow, for the Red Star Line as the FRIESLAND (1889).

LA PLATA MARU (1926) See KANJU MARU (1940)

LA PROVENCE (1906) See PROVENCE II (1914)

LARGS BAY (1922)
14362 grt; 290 psrs
552' x 68' x 33' (168.2 x 20.7 x 10 m)
Geared turbine engines via twin screw.
Broken up for scrap at Barrow-in-Furness in 1957.
Built by William Beardmore & Company, Dalmuir, for the Aberdeen & Commonwealth Line as a passenger ship.

LARGS BAY, HMS (1940) See PLEIAS (1964)

LARKSPUR (1943) See BRIDGEPORT (1946)

LARKSPUR (1999)
14558 grt; 1143 psrs
325 cars or 60 trailers

475' x 68' x 16' (143.9 x 20.5 x 4.9 m)
2 x 9-cylinder SWD diesel engines via twin screw.
Passenger-car-cargo ferry operated by the Denval Shipping Co.
Built by Schichau Seebeckwerft, Bremerhaven, for GT-Ruten AS as the GEDSER (1976). Renamed VIKING 2 (1986 – Sally Line), SALLY SKY (1988 – Sally Line) and EUROTRAVELLER (1997 – Sally Line Ltd).

LARNACA ROSE (1989) See AVRASYA I (1996)

LARNE (1916)
3808 grt; 695 psrs
365' x 45' x 28'6" (110.6 x 13.6 x 8.7 m)
Triple expansion engine via single screw.
Broken up for scrap at Wilhelmshaven in 1923 as a meat carrier for Zurbaran Steamship Co.
Built by R Napier & Sons, Glasgow, for the Aberdeen Line as the NINEVAH (1894). Renamed ALDENHAM (1907 – Eastern & Australian Steamship Co).

LA SAVOIE (1900)
11168 grt; 953 psrs
563' x 60' x 35'9" depth (170.6 x 18.3 x 10.9 m)
CGT 8-cylinder triple expansion engines via twin screw.
Broken up for scrap at Dunkirk in 1928.
Built by Penhoet, St Nazaire, for the French Line.

LA SENORA (1911) See CARRILLO (1911)

LASITHI (1990) See SEA HARMONY (1993)

LAS PALMAS DE GRAN CANARIA (1967) See RIVIERA II (2000)

LAS PALMAS DE GRAN CANARIA (1993)
10473 grt; 878 psrs
280 cars
385' x 68' x 17' (116.8 x 20.7 x 5.2 m)
2 x 12-cylinder MAN-B+W diesel engines via twin screw.
Built by Union Naval de Levante, Bilbao, as an ice-strengthened passenger-car ferry for Trasmediterranea at a cost of US$50,000,000. Has been laid up since December 1998.

LASSE (1964) See ALMIRANTE LUIS BRION (1973)

LASSE II (1974) See ST. SUNNIVA (1987)

L'ATLANTIQUE (1931)
42512 grt; 1156 psrs
length 742' x beam 92' (224.8 x 27.9 m)
4 x SRG turbine engines via quadruple screw.
Broken up for scrap at Glasgow in 1936 after three years of legal battles over salvage of her hulk. A fire at sea on 4 January 1933 had put her out of control for three days, as she drifted towards the Dorset coast off Portland Bill, UK. She was carrying a reduced crew and no passengers for the short voyage from Bordeaux to Le Havre, but 17 lives were lost.
Built by Chantiers de l'Atlantique, St Nazaire, for Cie de Navigation Sud Atlantique at a cost of £3,200,000.

LATO (1987) See BLUE HORIZON (2000)

LATONA (1906)
4387 grt
400' x 48' x 26'6" depth (133.3 x 16 x 8.9 m)
Wigham, Richardson 4-cylinder quadruple expansion engine via single screw.
Sank on 20 May 1908 after a collision off Wolf Rock in the English Channel.
Built by Sunderland Shipbuilding Co Ltd for W Lund as the WARRIGAL (1893).

LATVIA (1921) See HUSO MARU (1938)

LATVIA (1963) See LATVIYA (1963)

LATVIYA (1963) See EXCELSIOR (1990)

LAURA (1907) See BRAGA (1920)

LAURANA (1992)
10977 grt; 1100 psrs
272 cars
403' x 64' x 17'6" (122 x 19.4 x 5.3 m)
2 x 6-cylinder GMT diesel engines via twin screw.
Passenger-car ferry owned and operated by Adriatica di Navigazione.
Built by Fincantieri, Palermo.

LAURA RUSSOTTI (1975) See TAMBU EXPRESS (1980)

LAURENTIA (1949)
8323 grt; 55 psrs
455' x 62' x 28' (137.9 x 18.8 x 8.5 m)
Geared turbine engine via single screw.
Broken up for scrap in Kaohsiung in 1967 as a passenger-cargo liner. Ex-Donaldson Line.
Built by Permanente Metals Corporation, Richmond, California, for the US Maritime Commission as the cargo ship MEDINA VICTORY (1945).

LAURENTIC (1909)
14892 grt; 1670 psrs
565' x 67' x 27'6" (172.2 x 20.4 x 8.3 m)
8-cylinder triple expansion engines via triple screw.
Owned by the White Star Line, she sank quickly in 120' (36.4 m) of water on 25 January 1917 after hitting two mines laid by the German U-80 off Malin Head, Co Donegal. She cost 354 lives and took gold bullion valued at £5,000,000 to the seabed, for which an R Cossum of Derby, UK, acquired salvage rights in 1969 for an undisclosed sum.
Laid down by Harland & Wolff Ltd, Belfast, for the Dominion Line as the ALBERTA (1908).

LAURENTIC (1927)
18724 grt; 1500 psrs
603' x 75' x 29' (182.7 x 22.7 x 8.8 m)
2 x 2 x Harland & Wolff Ltd 4-cylinder combination triple expansion and turbine John Brown Ltd engines via triple screw.
Sank, with 49 lives lost, as an armed merchant cruiser at 9.00 pm on 3 November 1940 after being hit by three torpedoes from the German U-99 off Bloody Foreland, Ireland.
Built by Harland & Wolff Ltd, Belfast, for the White Star Line.

LAURO EXPRESS (1990)
6037 grt; 690 psrs
155 cars
372' x 57' x 12' (112.4 x 17.3 x 3.7 m)
2 x 16-cylinder Pielstick geared diesel engines via twin screw.
Passenger-car ferry operated by Linee Lauro SRL, Italy.
Built by Hawthorn Leslie, Hebburn, for British Railways as the ANTRIM PRINCESS (1967). Renamed TYNWALD (1986 – Isle of Man Steam Packet Co Ltd).

LA VALETTA (1971) See MISTRAL II (1992)

LAVIA (1986)
15465 grt; 1224 psrs
557' x 69' x 26' (172.5 x 20.9 x 7.9 m)
2 x DRG turbine engines via twin screw.
Owned by Virtue Shipping Co, Hong Kong, she was broken up for scrap at Kaohsiung in 1989. She had been gutted by fire on 7 January 1989 while at anchor off Kau Yi Chau Island, Hong Kong, and then settled on her side in shallow water next to the position where the QUEEN ELIZABETH caught fire and capsized 16 years before.
Built by John Brown & Co Ltd, Clydebank, for the Cunard Line as the passenger-cargo ship MEDIA (1947). Renamed FLAVIA (1961 – Cogedar Line) and FLAVIAN (1982 – Flavian Cruises, a CY Tung subsidiary).

LAVOISIER (1950) See VIKING PRINCESS (1965)

LAWIT (1986)
5684 grt; 920 psrs
329' x 59' x 14' (99.8 x 18 x 4.2 m)
2 x 6-cylinder Krupp-MaK diesel engines via twin screw.

Passenger ship owned by the Indonesian government and operated by P T Pelni, Indonesia.
Built by Meyer Werft, Papenburg.

LAWTON (1900) See ROSE ISLE (1930)

LAWTON, USS (1902) See ROSE ISLE (1930)

LAZIO (1906) See PALERMO (1913)

LAZIO (1953) See AVRASYA I (1996)

LEADER PRINCE (1988) See NEW ORIENT PRINCESS (1992)

LEASOWE CASTLE (1917)
9737 grt; 2110 psrs
488' x 58' x 24'7" depth (147.9 x 17.6 x 7.5)
Cammell Laird 8-cylinder quadruple expansion engines via twin screw.
Sank on 27 May 1918, with the loss of 104 lives, after being torpedoed 104 miles (174 km) north-west of Alexandria, Egypt.
Built by Cammell Laird & Co Ltd, Birkenhead, as the VASILISSA SOPHIA (1917).

LECH (1939) See ARTSA (1949)

LECONTE DE LISLE (1922) See LECONTE DE LISLE (1950)

LECONTE DE LISLE (1950)
9876 grt; 232 psrs
455' x 61' x 28' (137.9 x 18.5 x 8.5 m)
Sank after catching fire in the Indian Ocean in 1956.
Built by Soc Provencale de Construction Naval, La Ciotat, for Messageries Maritimes as the LECONTE DE LISLE (1922). Renamed TEIRITU MARU (1944).

LEDA (1953) See STAR OF VENICE (1992)

LEEDSTOWN, USS (AP-73) (1942)
9135 grt; 290 psrs
484' x 72' x 25'8" (146.7 x 21.8 x 7.8 m)
2 x General Electric DRG turbine engines via twin screw.
Owned by the US Navy, she sank on 9 November 1942 after being torpedoed the previous day by what was probably the German U-331 off Cape Matifou, Algiers.
Built by Federal Shipbuilding & Drydock Co for the Grace Line as the SANTA LUCIA (1933) at a cost of US$5,000,000.

LEERDAM (1921)
8854 grt; 974 psrs
450' x 58' x 30'3" (136.4 x 17.6 x 9.2 m)
3 x J Brown DRG turbine engines via single screw.
Broken up for scrap in Japan in 1954.
Built by Nieuwe Waterweg, Schiedam, for the Holland America Line.

LEEWARD (1995) See SUPERSTAR TAURUS (2000)

LEFKA ORI (2000)
29429 grt; 703 psrs
77 cars + 145 trailers
634' x 89' x 23' (192 x 27 x 6.7 m)
2 x 12-cylinder Nippon-Pielstick diesel engines via twin screw.
Passenger-car-cargo ferry owned and operated by ANEK Lines, Greece.
Built by Mitsubishi Heavy Industries, Shimonoseki, for ANEK Lines as the HERCULES (1992). Renamed KRITI V (2000 – ANEK Lines)

LEGAZPI (1911)
4349 grt; 533 psrs
376' x 47' x 22'7" (114.4 x 14.3 x 6.9 m)
Wallsend Slipway 6-cylinder triple expansion engines via twin screw.
Owned by Cia Trasatlantica, she was broken up for scrap at Sagunto following a dramatic salvage attempt on a beach near Benicassim. Her captain had purposely beached her here on 19 May 1937 after being heavily bombed by aircraft during the Spanish Civil War.
Built by Sir Raylton Dixon & Co, Middlesbrough, for the African Steamship

Co as the ZUNGERU (1904). Renamed BRUXELLESVILLE (1906 – Cie Maritime Belge) and ZUNGERU (1908 – African Steamship Co).

LEGEND OF THE SEAS (1995)
69490 grt; 2064 psrs
875' x 106' x 24' (264.6 x 32 x 7.3 m)
5 x 12-cylinder Wartsila-Vasa diesel-electric engines via twin screw.

Cruising for Royal Caribbean International.
Built by Chantiers de l'Atlantique, St Nazaire, for Royal Caribbean International at a cost of US$317,000,000.

LE HAVRE ABETO (1967)
12177 grt; 436 psrs
538' x 64' x 28' (163 x 19.4 x 8.5 m)
2 x 8-cylinder Sulzer diesel engines via twin screw.
Broken up for scrap as a pilgrim ship at Chittagong in 1984. Ex-Cia de Navigacion Abeto SA, Panama.
Built by Chantiers et Ateliers de la Loire, St Nazaire, for Messageries Maritimes as the CHARLES TELLIER (1952).

LEICESTERSHIRE (1909) See ZAMZAM (1933)

LEICESTERSHIRE (1949) See HERAKLION (1965)

LEIF ERIKSSON (1966) See TIAN KUN (1991)

LEILANI (1956) See OCEAN EXPLORER I (1998)

LEINSTER (1937) See ODYSSEUS (1969)

LEINSTER (1948) See APHRODITE (1969)

LEINSTER (1969) See IONIAN SUN (1994)

LEINSTER (1981) See MADELEINE (1997)

LEINSTER I (1968) See APHRODITE (1969)

LEISURE WORLD (1994)
16254 grt; 920 psrs
525' x 75' x 22' (160.1 x 23 x 6.7 m)
2 x 16-cylinder MAN diesel engines via twin screw.
Cruise casino ship owned by a joint venture between Norwegian Cruise Line and Queenston Investment Ltd, and operated by New Century Cruise Lines, Singapore.
Built by AG Weser Shipyards, Bremerhaven, for Norwegian Cruise Lines as the SKYWARD (1969). Renamed SHANGRI-LA WORLD (1991 – Constantine Ltd, Singapore), ASEAN WORLD (1992 – Sembawang Ship Management Co), FANTASY WORLD (1992 – Sembawang Ship Management Co) and CONTINENTAL WORLD (1993 – Sembawang Ship Management Co).

LE JEUNE, USS (1943) See LE JEUNE, USS (AP-74) (1944)

LE JEUNE, USS (AP-74) (1944)
16662 grt; 490 psrs
577' x 72' x 31'5" depth (174.8 x 21.8 x 9.5 m)
6 x Blohm & Voss SRG turbine engines via single screw.
Broken up for scrap at Portland, Oregon, in 1966 after being laid up out of commission since July 1957. Ex-US Maritime Commission.

Built by Blohm & Voss, Hamburg, for the German East Africa Line as the WINDHUK (1937). Renamed LE JEUNE, USS (1943 – US Army). She had been disguised by the Germans in 1939 as the 'neutral' Japanese liner SANTOS MARU to avoid capture by the Allies. However, she was seized in Brazil in 1942.

LE LEVANTE (1998)
4500 grt; 95 psrs
327' x 46' x 10'6" (99.6 x 13.9 x 3.3 m)
2 x 9-cylinder Wartsila diesel engines via twin screw.

Ice-strengthened, yacht-like cruise ship owned by Cie des Isles du Ponant and chartered to Classical Cruises International.
Built by Leroux et Lotz Shipyard, St Malo.

LE MAIRE (1951)
4153 grt; 100 psrs
340' x 50' x 22' (103 x 15.2 x 6.7 m)
2 x Fiat 6-cylinder diesel engines via twin screw.
Operated by the Argentine government.
Built by Cantieri Riuniti dell Adriatico, Monfalcone.

LEME (1925) See LEME (1948)

LEME (1948)
8059 grt
468' x 57' x 27'6" (141.8 x 17.3 x 8.4 m)
Soc Anon Franco Tosi 12-cylinder diesel engines via twin screw.
Broken up for scrap in 1961. Ex-Italia.
Built by Stabilimento Tecnico, Trieste, for Navigation Libera Triestina as the passenger-cargo ship LEME (1925). Renamed LOWLANDER (1941 – British Ministry of War Transport).

LE MYRE DE VILLERS (1917)
5111 grt; 50 psrs
400' x 47'6" x 28'6" (121.9 x 14.5 x 8.7 m)
Northeast Marine Engineering 3-cylinder triple expansion engine via single screw.
Broken up for scrap by S Bertorello at La Spezia in 1925.
Built by Sunderland Shipbuilding Company, Sunderland, for Wilhelm Lund, London, as the WAKOOL (1898). Renamed KWANTO MARU (1912 – Goshi Kaisha Kishimoto Shokai).

LENA (1903) See RAETORIA (1920)

LENAPE (1913)
5179 grt; 393 psrs
399' x 50' x 20'6" (120.1 x 15.2 x 9.1 m)
Newport News 3-cylinder triple expansion engines via single screw.
Sank on 18 November 1925 after catching fire off the Delaware Bay breakwater.
Built by Newport News Shipbuilding Co, Newport News, Virginia, for the Clyde Steamship Co.

LENSOVIET (1946) See ABKHAZIA (1956)

LEONA (1889) See SABINE (1900)

LEONARDO DA VINCI (1960)
33340 grt; 1326 psrs
761' x 92' x 30' (233.9 x 28.1 x 9 m)

4 x Parsons DRG turbine engines via twin screw.
Broken up for scrap at La Spezia in 1982. She had been raised from her resting place just outside La Spezia harbour on 3 March 1981, having been towed there following her catching fire on 3 July 1980. The fire had broken out at her berth, to which she had been attached since 23 September 1978. During the tow to open sea she had heeled over to port by 60 degrees before sinking.
Built by Ansaldo Shipyards, Genoa, for the Italian Line.

LEONARD WOOD (1939) See LEONARD WOOD, USS (APA-12) (1943)

LEONARD WOOD, USS (AP-25) (1941) See LEONARD WOOD, USS (APA-12) (1943)

LEONARD WOOD, USS (APA-12) (1943)
13712 grt; 430 psrs
517' x 72' x 41' depth (156.7 x 21.8 x 12.4 m)
4 x Bethlehem Steel Co SRG turbine engines via twin screw.
Broken up for scrap by Consolidated Builders, Vancouver, Washington, in 1948. Ex-US Maritime Commission.
Launched by Bethlehem Shipbuilding Corporation, Sparrow's Point, Maryland, for the Matson Line as the NUTMEG STATE (1921) and completed as the WESTERN WORLD (1922 – Munson Line). Renamed as the troop transport LEONARD WOOD (1939 – US Army). Reclassified as the LEONARD WOOD, USS (AP-25) (1941).

LEONID BREZHNEV (1976) See OLVIA (1995)

LEONID SOBINOV (1973)
22592 grt; 936 psrs
608' x 80' x 29' (185.3 x 24.3 x 8.8 m)
2 x DRG turbine engines via twin screw.
Broken up for scrap in Alang in 1998. Ex-Black Sea Shipping Co, Odessa.
Built by John Brown & Co Ltd, Clydebank, for the Cunard Line as the SAXONIA (1954). Renamed CARMANIA (1962 – Cunard Line).

LEON XIII (1893) See JEHANGIR (1914)

LEOPARD (1968) See DIMITRA A (2000)

LEOPARDI (1971) See SANTA CATHERINE (1994)

LEOPOLDINA (1917) See SUFFREN (1923)

LEOPOLDVILLE (1895) See HOMAYUN (1910)

LEOPOLDVILLE (1908) See ABINSI (1914)

LEOPOLDVILLE (1928)
11509 grt; 360 psrs
517' x 62' x 25'10" (156.7 x 18.8 x 7.6 m)
John Cockerill 8-cylinder quadruple expansion engines via twin screw.
Sank in ten minutes in 30 fathoms of the Atlantic Ocean, following the collapse of a bulkhead which had remained intact and kept the ship afloat for an hour while HMS BRILLIANT rescued 1,500 lives. The ship had been torpedoed by the German U-486 on 24 December 1944 only five miles (8 km) from her destination, Cherbourg, and took 808 lives with her.
Built by John Cockerill, Hoboken, for Cie Maritime Belge.

LEOPOLDVILLE (1948) See P E. LUMUMBA (1967)

LE PALAIS FLOTTANT (1967)
4956 grt; 500 psrs
388' x 56' x 20' (117.6 x 17 x 6.1 m)
4 x Newport News DRG turbine engines via twin screw.
Broken up for scrap at Valencia in 1968. She had served as a hotel ship during the Expo '67 World's Fair in Montreal.
Built by Newport News Shipbuilding & Drydock Co, Newport News, Virginia, for Peninsular & Occidental Steamship Co as the FLORIDA (1931).

LEROS (1992)
1244 psrs
50 cars + 34 trailers
length 417' x beam 64' (126.4 x 19.3 m)

Gutted by a night fire which raced through the vessel while she was berthed in Piraeus on 15 December 1998.
Built as a passenger-car-cargo ferry.

LEROS (1997)
5477 grt; 1165 psrs
417' x 64' x 18' (126.4 x 19.4 x 5.5 m)
2 x 7-cylinder Fiat diesel engines via twin screw.
Passenger ferry operated by DANE Sea Line.
Built by Italcantieri SpA, Castellammare di Stabia, for Linee Canguro SpA as the CANGURO BRUNO (1968). Renamed YUM (1982), IONIAN FANTASY (1988 – Strintzis Lines), IONIAN SEA (1991 – Strintzis Lines) BIHAR (1993), IONIAN SEA (1993 – Strintzis Lines) and DIMITRA (1994 – GA Ferries).

LES ECLAIREURS (1951)
4153 grt; 100 psrs
340' x 50' x 22' (103 x 15.2 x 6.7 m)
2 x 6-cylinder Fiat diesel engines via twin screw.
Operated by the Argentine government.
Built by Cantieri Riuniti dell'Adriatico, Trieste.

LETITIA (1912)
8991 grt; 300 psrs
470' x 57' x 28'8" depth (142.4 x 17.3 x 8.7 m)
Scott & Co 6-cylinder triple expansion engines via twin screw.
Owned by the British Ministry of Transport, she was abandoned after being wrecked on 1 August 1917 as a hospital ship near Halifax.
Built by Scotts Shipbuilding Co, Greenock, for the Donaldson Line as a passenger ship.

LETITIA (1925) See CAPTAIN COOK (1951)

LEUSER (1994)
6041 grt; 969 psrs
329' x 60' x 13' (99.8 x 18.3 x 4.2 m)
2 x 6-cylinder Krupp-MaK diesel engines via twin screw.
Passenger ferry operated by PT Pelni, Indonesia, she sank in shallow water near Samarinda, East Kalamantan on 20 November 1999. The cause of the sinking was a collision with the 3936 grt bulk carrier KAYU LAPUS LIMA (operated by Dasalines, Indonesia) which pierced the LEUSER's hull amidships. She was resurrected from a total constructive loss.
Built by Jos L Meyer, Papenburg, for the Indonesian government.

LEUTHEN (1942)
6846 grt; 94 psrs
450' x 52' x 28' (137.2 x 15.8 x 8.5 m)
2 x quadruple expansion engines via twin screw.
Destroyed as a German supply ship, on 30 November 1942, by an explosion and fire in Yokohama when the tanker UCKERMARK exploded next to her during bunkering operations. She had been captured by the German raider THOR in May 1942 and taken to Japan.
Built by Caird & Company, Greenock, for the P&O Line at a cost of £115,127 as the passenger-cargo ship. NANKIN (1912).

LEVANT (1998) See LE LEVANT (1998)

LEVANZO (1902)
3713 grt; 900 psrs
340' x 46' x 17'7" (103.5 x 14.1 x 5.4 m)
Fratelli Orlando 3-cylinder triple expansion engine via single screw.
Wrecked in the Red Sea on 14 March 1923.
Built by Fratelli Orlando, Leghorn, for Navigazione Generale Italia as the ISOLA LEVANZO (1901), but the name was condensed to LEVANZO the following year.

LEVIATHAN (1919)
59956 grt; 3008 psrs
950' x 100' x 35' (287.9 x 30.3 x 10.6 m)
4 x Blohm & Voss turbine engines via quadruple screw.
Broken up by Thomas W Ward at Rosyth in 1938. Ex-United States Lines.
Built by Blohm & Voss, Hamburg, for the Hamburg-America Line as the VATERLAND (1914). Renamed LEVIATHAN, USS (1917 – US government, after seizure).

LEVIATHAN, USS (1917) See LEVIATHAN (1919)

LEV TOLSTOI (1981) See LEV TOLSTOY (1981)

LEV TOLSTOY (1981) See PALMIRA (1998)

LEVUKA (1910) See DOM PEDRO II (1926)

LEVUKA (1947) See TRIADIC (1948)

LIBAN (1975)
9971 grt; 580 psrs
508' x 62' x 26' (153.9 x 18.8 x 7.9 m)
Sulzer 10-cylinder diesel engine via single screw.
Broken up for scrap at Gadani Beach in 1979. Ex-Dem Line, Beirut.
Built by Cia Euskalduna, Bilbao, for Aznar Lines as the MONTE UMBE (1959).

LIBERTAD (1955)
12653 grt; 96 psrs
530' x 71' x 27'6" (160.6 x 21.5 x 8.4 m)
4 x Vickers-Armstrong DRG turbine engines via twin screw.
Broken up for scrap at Campana, Argentina, in 1974. Ex-Elma Lines.
Built by Vickers-Armstrong Ltd, Newcastle, for Elma Lines as the 17 DE OCTUBRE (1950).

LIBERTE (1946)
51839 grt; 1513 psrs
936' x 102' x 34' (283.6 x 30.9 x 10.3 m)
12 x Blohm & Voss SRG turbine engines via quadruple screw.
Broken up for scrap at La Spezia in 1962 after raising her from the Le Havre harbour bed. She had been scuttled on 15 April 1947 to prevent her from capsizing at her refitting berth when the moorings broke. Five months earlier, on 9 December 1946, she had rammed the sunken hull of the PARIS (sank in 1939) and severely damaged her starboard side. Ex-CGT, France.
Built by Blohm & Voss, Hamburg, for North German Lloyd as the EUROPA (1930). Renamed EUROPA, USS (1945 – US Navy).

LIBERTE (1980)
18913 grt; 1240 psrs
500 cars
543' x 72' x 18' (164.5 x 21.8 x 5.5 m)
2 x 18-cylinder Pielstick diesel engines via twin screw.
Passenger-car ferry owned by SNCM and operated by Ferryterranee on the France–Algeria service.
Built by Chantiers Dubigeon-Normandie, Nantes, for SNCM.

LIBERTE (1985) See UNIVERSE EXPLORER (1996)

LIBURNIJA (1965)
3910 grt; 700 psrs
110 cars
293' x 54' x 14' (88.8 x 16.4 x 4.2 m)
2 x 8-cylinder Sulzer diesel engines via twin screw.
Passenger-car ferry operated by Jadrolinija Rijeka on the Yugoslavia–Greece–Italy service.
Built by De Merwede, Hardinxveld.

LIDO STAR (1991) See COLOMBUS CARAVELLE (1991)

LIGER (1912)
5531 grt; 500 psrs
425' x 50' x 30' depth (128.8 x 15.2 x 9.1 m)
Fairfield 3-cylinder compound engine via single screw.
Broken up for scrap at Genoa in 1923. Ex-Cie de Navigation Sud Atlantque.
Built by Fairfield & Co, Glasgow, for the Castle Line as the TINTAGEL CASTLE (1896).

LIGURIA (1901) See AFFON (1911)

LIGURIA (1935)
15183 grt; 1750 psrs
546' x 67' x 50'3" depth (165.5 x 20.3 x 15.2 m)

2 x Harland & Wolff 4-cylinder combined triple expansion engines and turbines via triple screw.
Owned by the Italian government, she was broken up for scrap at Savona in 1950, after salvaging her from Tobruk harbour where she was scuttled on 22 January 1941 as a troop transport.
Laid down by Barclay, Curle & Company, Glasgow, for Canadian Steamship Company unnamed (1916) and completed by Harland & Wolff Ltd, Belfast, as the passenger ship MELITA (1918).

LIGURIA (1950) See CORSICA (1951)

LILLY R (1989) See JABAL ALI I (1999)

LIMA (1916)
4056 grt; 217 psrs
368' x 45' x 25' (111.6 x 13.7 x 7.5 m)
3-cylinder Richardson-Westgarth triple expansion engine via single screw.
Broken up for scrap in 1969. Ex-Empresa Insulana de Navegacao, Lisbon.
Built by Furness, Withy & Co Ltd, West Hartlepool, as the passenger-cargo ship WESTERWALD (1908).

LIMBURGIA (1920) See RELIANCE (1926)

LINDA (1991) See LANGELAND IV (1999)

LINDA CLAUSEN (1975) See RASLAN (1983)

LINDA Jnr (1968)
3310 grt; 77 psrs
328' x 47' x 21' (99.9 x 14.3 x 6.4 m)
8-cylinder B+W diesel engine via single screw.
Broken up for scrap by Chin Ho Fu Steel & Iron Co at Kaohsiung in 1971. Ex-Jaguar Shipping Co Ltd.
Built by Barclay, Curle & Company, Glasgow, for Burns Philp & Co Ltd, Sydney, as the MALAITA (1933). Renamed PILAR REGIDOR (1965 – San Fernando Steamship Co, Panama).

LINDAU (1941)
13761 grt; 495 psrs
542' x 68' x 39' depth (164.2 x 20.6 x 11.8 m)
B+W 18-cylinder diesel engines via twin screw.
Broken up for scrap at Boom, Belgium, in 1947 after raising her from the Nantes harbour bed where the Germans had scuttled her on 10 August 1944. Ex-German Africa Line.
Built by John Cockerill Shipyards, Hoboken, for Cie Maritime Belge as the BAUDOUINVILLE (1939).

LINDMAR (1982) See CALEDONIAN STAR (1983)

LINDOS (1967)
9931 grt; 545 psrs
465' x 64' x 22' (140.9 x 19.4 x 6.7 m)
2 x Forges et Chantier de la Mediterranee SRG turbine engines via twin screw.
Cruise ship operated by Paquet Line.
Built by Forges et Chantiers de la Mediterranee, La Seyne, for Efthymiadis, Greece, as the LYAUTEY (1952). Renamed GALILEE (1966 – Paquet Line) and LYAUTEY (1966 – Paquet Line).

LINK (1988) See MYRTIDIOTISSA (2000)

LINNET (1977)
12420 grt; 550 psrs
523' x 71' x 33' (158.5 x 21.5 x 10 m)
2 x Westinghouse SRG turbine engines via single screw.
Broken up as a bulk carrier for scrap at Kaohsiung in 1978. Ex-Meadowbank Transport.
Built by Kaiser Corporation, Richmond, California, for the US Shipping Administration as the Class C4-S-A3 troop carrier MARINE SWALLOW (1945). Renamed MISSOURI (1965 – Meadowbank Transport) and OGDEN MISSOURI (1974 – Meadowbank Transport). As the MARINE SWALLOW she operated as a migrant ship after World War Two.

LINZ (1939) See ESPEROS (1964)

LION (1967) See BARONESS M (1990)

LION EUROPE (1997) See STENA EUROPE (1998)

LION KING (1995) See FANTAASIA (1998)

LION KING II (1996) See STENA NAUTICA (1996)

LION PRINCE (1987) See COMMODORE (1999)

LION PRINCESS (1987) See BOHUS (1994)

LION QUEEN (1988) See AMUSEMENT WORLD (1998)

LISBOA (1910)
7412 grt; 1328 psrs
432' x 54' x 24'5" depth (130.9 x 16.4 x 7.4 m)
Triple expansion engines via twin screw.
Abandoned as a total loss on her second only voyage when she ran aground on Soldier's Reef near Paternoster Point, 60 miles (100 km) north of Cape Town. Disaster struck at 10.50 pm on 23 October 1910. Seven lives were lost.
Built by D & W Henderson & Co Ltd, Clydebank, for Empresa Nacional de Navegacao, Lisbon.

LISMORE CASTLE (1891) See C. LOPEZ Y LOPEZ (1905)

LISMORIA (1948) See NEON (1966)

LISSOS (1989)
20454 grt; 1600 psrs
600 cars
535' x 87' x 21' (162 x 26.5 x 6.3 m)
2 x 18-cylinder Pielstick diesel engines via twin screw.
Passenger-car ferry operated by ANEK.
Built by Koyo Dockyard Co Ltd, Mihara, for Shin Nipponkai Ferry KK, Kitakyusho, as the FERRY HAMANASU (1972).

LITUANIA (1907) See DAITEN MARU (1913)

LITUANIA (1921) See EMPIRE HELFORD (1946)

LITVA (1960) See FU JIAN (1994)

LIVONIA (1907) See INDIEN (1907)

LJUBOV ORLOVA (1974) See LYUBOV ORLOVA (1974)

LLANDAFF CASTLE (1926)
10786 grt; 410 psrs
490' x 62' x 27'4" (148.5 x 18.8 x 8.3 m)
Workman, Clark 8-cylinder quadruple expansion engines via twin screw.
Sank on 30 November 1942 after being hit by three torpedoes from the German U-177 100 miles (168 km) off Lourenco Marques, on the Zululand coast of Africa. Two lives were lost.
Built by Workman, Clark & Co, Belfast, for the Union-Castle Line.

LLANDOVERY CASTLE (1914)
10639 grt; 429 psrs
501' x 63' x 28'8" (151.8 x 19.1 x 8.7 m)
Barc;lay Curle 8-cylinder quadruple expansion engines via twin screw.
Sank in ten minutes on 27 June 1918 as a hospital ship by the German U-86. Firstly the submarine crippled her with a torpedo, and then sank her at 9.30 am with gunfire aimed at both the ship and the lifeboats hurrying from her side. The action took place 116 miles (193 km) west of Fastnet Rock, with the loss of 234 lives.
Built by Barclay, Curle & Co, Glasgow, for the Union-Castle Line.

LLANDOVERY CASTLE (1925)
10640 grt; 410 psrs
487' x 62' x 27'4" (147.6 x 18.8 x 8.3 m)
Barclay Curle 8-cylinder quadruple expansion engines via twin screw.
Broken up for scrap by British Iron & Steel Corporation at Inverkeithing in 1953.
Built by Barclay, Curle & Co, Glasgow, for the Union-Castle Line.

LLANGIBBY CASTLE (1929)
12039 grt; 450 psrs
507' x 66' x 27' (153.6 x 20 x 8.2 m)
2 x 8-cylinder H&W-B+W diesel engines via twin screw.
Broken up for scrap at Newport, Wales, in 1954.
Built by Harland & Wolff Ltd, Govan, for the Union-Castle Line.

LLANSTEPHAN CASTLE (1914)
11348 grt; 411 psrs
501' x 63' x 28'8" (151.8 x 19.1 x 8.7 m)
Fairfield 8-cylinder quadruple expansion engines via twin screw.
Broken up for scrap at Newport, Wales, in 1952.
Built by Fairfield Shipbuilding & Engineering Co Ltd, Glasgow, for the Union-Castle Line.

LLOYD (1919) See IRIS (1924)

LOANDA (1925)
5139 grt; 1043 psrs
402' x 47' x 28'2" depth (122.6 x 14.4 x 8.5 m)
3-cylinder triple expansion engine via single screw.
Broken up for scrap in Italy in 1938. Ex-Cia Colonial de Navegacao, Lisbon.
Built by Bremer Vulkan, Vegesack, for North German Lloyd as the WURZBURG (1900). Seized by Portugal and renamed SAO VICENTE (1916).

LOBO MARINHO (1996)
4163 grt; 840 psrs
130 cars or 15 trailers/coaches
288' x 52' x 13' (87.3 x 15.7 x 4 m)
4 x 12-cylinder B+W diesel engines via twin screw.

Owned by Portline, Portugal, and operated by Porto Santo Line, Madiera.
Built by Aalborg Vaerft, Aalborg, for AS Kristiansands Dampskippselscap as the passenger-cargo ferry CHRISTIAN IV (1968). Renamed PERNAS SAFARI (1985 – Perbadanan Shipping Line Berhad, Port Kelang) and SAFARI (1994 – Endeavour Shipping Co, Panama).

LOCKSLEY HALL (1887) See NAJMI (1909)

LOCKSLEY HALL (1901)
3600 grt; 80 psrs
345' x 44' x 27'3" (104.5 x 13.3 x 8.3 m)
William Denny 3-cylinder compound engine via single screw.
Sank on 12 May 1917 after being torpedoed 30 miles (50 km) east-south-east of Malta. Ex-Hall Line.
Built by William Denny & Brothers, Dumbarton, for Burmah Steamship Co Ltd, as the PROME (1894).

LODBROG (1988) See FENJA (1999)

LOFJORD (1942)
5035 grt; 250 psrs
365' x 53' x 26' (110.6 x 16.1 x 7.9 m)
2 x 9-cylinder B+W diesel engines via twin screw.
Broken up for scrap by Dohmen & Abetz at Burcht in 1951. She had been extensively damaged by Allied aircraft over Danzig on 21 December 1942.
Built by Akers Mek Verksted, Oslo, for the Fred Olsen Line as the passenger-cargo ship BLACK PRINCE (1938).

LOGAN (1898) See CANDLER (1923)

LOGOS II (1988)
4804 grt; 400 psrs
348' x 53' x 16'6" (105.5 x 16.1 x 5 m)

2 x 10-cylinder B+W diesel engines via twin screw.
Missionary ship owned by Operation Mobilisation for Gute Bucher fur Alle eV, Mosbach.
Built by Union Naval de Levante, Valencia, for Cia Trasmediterranea as the passenger-car-cargo ferry ANTONIO LAZARO (1968). Renamed ARGO (1988 – Operation Mobilisation).

LOGUDORO (1989)
6505 grt; 998 psrs
80 cars + 45 rail coaches
479' x 62' x 19'6" (145 x 18.8 x 5.9 m)
2 x 6-cylinder GMT diesel engines via twin screw.
Passenger-car-train ferry owned by the Italian State Railways and operated by Ferrovie Stato.
Built by Fincantieri, Palermo.

LOMBARDIA (1901) See JEROUSALIM (1911)

LOMBARDIA (1935)
19696 grt; 1945 psrs
616' x 72' x 40'2" depth (186.7 x 21.8 x 12.2 m)
8-cylinder combination triple expansion engine and turbines via triple screw.
Owned by the Italian government and managed by Lloyd Triestino, she was broken up for scrap at La Spezia in 1947. Her hulk had been raised from its resting place in Naples harbour where she was sunk by Allied aircraft on 4 August 1943, breaking into three sections.
Launched by AG Weser Shipbuilders, Bremen, for the Hamburg-America Line as the WILLIAM OSWALD (1914) and completed as the BRABANTIA (1920 – Royal Holland Lloyd). Renamed RESOLUTE (1922 – United American Lines).

LOMBOK (1907) See IJSTROOM (1926)

LONE STAR STATE (1922) See VILLE DE BRUGES (1940)

LONG BEACH (1966)
17814 grt; 920 psrs
523' x 72' x 24' (158.5 x 21.8 x 7.3 m)
Joshua Hendy Iron Works DRG turbine engine via single screw.
Container ship owned by Litton Industries Corporation when she was abandoned as a total loss in 1988 after running aground near San Juan, Puerto Rico.
Built as the Class C4-S-A3 troop carrier MARINE FLASHER (1945) by Kaiser Corporation, Vancouver, Washington, for the US Shipping Administration. Engaged in some migration work after World War Two.

LONG HU (1988) See MANAR (2000)

LONG ISLAND, USS (CVE-1) (1941) See SEVEN SEAS (1954)

LORD OF SINAI (1982) See SALEM EXPRESS (1989)

LORD OF THE ISLES (1989)
3504 grt; 506 psrs
56 cars
213' x 52' x 10'6" (84.6 x 15.8 x 3.2 m)
2 x 8-cylinder Mirrlees-Blackstone diesel engines via twin screw.

Passenger-car ferry owned by the Scottish Transport Group and operating for Caledonian MacBrayne, Scotland.
Built by Appledore Ferguson Ltd, Port Glasgow.

LORD SINAI (1982) See SALEM EXPRESS (1989)

LORD WARDEN (1952) See AL ZAHER (1979)

LORRAINE II (1914) See LA LORRAINE (1917)

LOTUS (1912)
6246 grt; 394 psrs
469' x 51' x 36'1" depth (142 x 15.5 x 10.9 m)
Messageries Maritimes 6-cylinder triple expansion engines via twin screw.
Broken up for scrap in Italy in 1932.
Built by Messageries Maritimes, La Ciotat, for the Ex treme Orient Line as the TONKIN (1898).

LOUISE LUMIERE (1952) See MEI ABETO (1984)

LOUISIANE (1905)
5104 grt; 760 psrs
370' x 47' x 25'2" depth (112.7 x 14.4 x 7.6 m)
Caillard & Co 3-cylinder triple expansion engine via single screw.
Sank on 3 September 1916 when she was torpedoed by the German U-18 while riding at anchor in the Havre Roads.
Built by Ateliers et Chantiers de France, Dunkirk, for CGT.

LOUISVILLE, USS (1917) See St LOUIS (1920)

LOUQSOR (1904)
6889 grt; 94 psrs
447' x 53' x 32'6" (140.6 x 16.1 x 9.9 m)
Messageries Maritimes 6-cylinder triple expansion engines via twin screw.
Broken up for scrap in Belgium in 1930.
Built by Messageries Maritimes, La Ciotat, for Messageries Maritimes.

LOWELL THOMAS EXPLORER (1976) See ROYAL CLIPPER (1977)

LOWLANDER (1941) See LEME (1948)

LOYALIST (1901) See SANTIAGO (1916)

LOYALTY (1915)
5905 grt; 600 psrs
456' x 51' x 33'1" depth (152 x 17 x 10 m)
Compound engines via single screw.
Broken up for scrap at Mumbai in 1923. Ex-the Maharajah of Gwalior.
Built by Naval Construction & Armaments, Barrow-in-Furness, for Canadian Pacific Steamship Co as the EMPRESS OF INDIA (1890).

LST 3525, HMS (1945) See EMPIRE GULL (1958)

LUBECK LINK (1990)
33163 grt; 240 psrs
800 cars + 1132 TEUs
636' x 89' x 22'6" (192.6 x 27 x 6.8 m)
2 x 6-cylinder Sulzer diesel engines via twin screw.

Passenger-car-cargo ferry owned by Lubeck Link and operated by Sea-link.
Built by Oskarshamns Varv., Oskarshamn, for OT Redlererna, Sweden, as the RoRo freighter FINNROSE (1980).

LUCANIA (1891) See DRAGO (1952)

LUCANIA (1951)
6723 grt; 700 psrs
366' x 57' x 16'6" (110.5 x 17.3 x 5 m)
Geared turbine engines via twin screw.
Broken up for scrap at Livorno in 1962. Ex-Fratelli Grimaldi.
Built by Cammell Laird & Co, Birkenhead, for Canadian National Railways as the PRINCE ROBERT (1930). Renamed CHARLTON SOVEREIGN (1948 – Charlton Steam Shipping Co).

LUCAYA (1965) See WAPPEN VON HAMBURG (1984)

LUCIA, HMS (1914) See SINAI (1948)

LUCIANO MANARA (1941) See HONG Qi 144 (1977)

LUCIE WOERMAN (1902) See AVIATEUR ROLAND GARROS (1921)

LUCINDA (1994) See EUROFAST (2000)

LUCKENBACH (1908) See ONEGA (1914)

LUCKY RIDER (1981) See ASK (1991)

LUCKY STAR (1994) See HOMERIC (1995)

LUCY MAUD MONTGOMERY (1970) See LADY CARIBE I (1998)

LUGANO (1942)
6942 grt; 50 psrs
420' x 54' x 28'6" depth (127.3 x 16.4 x 8.7 m)
Hawthorne Leslie 3-cylinder triple expansion engine via single screw.
Broken up for scrap at Savona in 1952.
Built by R & W Hawthorn Leslie, Newcastle, for the Elderslie Steamship Co as the cargo ship MORAYSHIRE (1898). Renamed BRODLIFE (1916 – Blue Star Line), TUSCANSTAR (1920 – Union Cold Storage Co), FORTUNE STAR (1929 – Fratelli Rizzuto) and SEMIEN (1936 – Ignazio Messina).

LUISA (1968)
8357 grt; 52 psrs
459' x 63' x 28' (139.1 x 19.1 x 8.5 m)
Turbine engine via single screw.
Broken up for scrap at Kaohsiung in 1969. Ex-Central Gulf Steamship Co.
Built by North Carolina Shipbuilding Corporation, Wilmington, for the Grace Line as the SANTA LUISA (1946),

LUISA COSTA (1963)
9901 grt
498' x 64' x 29'10" (150.1 x 19.4 x 8.8 m)
2 x Parsons turbine engines via single screw.
Broken up for scrap at La Spezia in 1972.
Built by Lithgows Ltd, Port Glasgow, for Canadian Pacific Steamship Ltd as the BEAVERDELL (1945). Renamed MAPLEDELL (1952 – Canadian Pacific Steamship Ltd) and BEAVERDELL (1956 – Giacomo Costa fu Andrea).

LUISIANA (1906)
4983 grt; 1625 psrs
394' x 48' x 25'6" depth (120 x 14.7 x 7.8 m)
Soc Esercizio Bacini 6-cylinder triple expansion engines via twin screw.
Sank on 6 February 1917 after being torpedoed near Almeria.
Built by Soc Esercisio Bacini for Lloyd Italiano.

LU JIANG (1985) See PRINCESA CYPRIA (1990)

LUMINOUS KOBE 2 (1994)
4778 grt; 700 psrs
350' x 53' x 15'8" (106 x 16 x 4.8 m)
8-cylinder Mitsubishi diesel engine via single screw.
Passenger ferry owned and operated by Hoya Sangyo, Japan.
Built by Mitsubishi Heavy Industries, Kobe.

LUO DING (1977)
3233 grt; 1130 psrs
365' x 52' x 25' (110.6 x 15.9 x 7.6 m)
7-cylinder B+W diesel engine via single screw.
Ice-strengthened cruise ship owned by China Ocean Shipping Co, Canton.
Built by Moss Vaerft & Dokk AS, Moss, for CH Wrangell & Co, Norway, as the HOI KUNG (1964).

LUPINUS (1971) See HUA LIEN (1975)

LURLINE (1908) See RADNIK (1947)

LURLINE (1932) See ELLINIS (1963)

LURLINE (1963) See BELOFIN I (1998)

LUSITANIA (1900)
3912 grt; 855 psrs
380' x 41' x 35'2" depth (115.2 x 12.4 x 10.7 m)
T Richardson & Sons 3-cylinder triple expansion engine via single screw.
While under charter to Dempster's Beaver Line, she was wrecked near Cape Race, without loss of life, on 26 June 1901.
Built by Laird Bros, Birkenhead, for Pacific Steam Navigation Co Ltd.

LUSITANIA (1906)
5537 grt; 800 psrs
421' x 51' x 19'9" (127.6 x 15.5 x 6 m)
Northeast Marine Engineering 6-cylinder triple expansion engines via twin screw.
Sank on 18 April 1911, with four lives lost, after grounding on the Bellowes Rocks at the entrance to Table Bay, Cape Town, at midnight. Four days later she slid into deep water. An enquiry later recorded, among several complaints, that the lighthouse, constructed at a high level on these rocks, was often shrouded in cloud and indiscernible at those times.
Built by Sir Raylton Dixon & Company, Middlesbrough, for Empresa de Navegacao, Lisbon.

LUSITANIA (1907)
31550 grt; 2165 psrs
787' x 87' x 46'2" depth (238.5 x 26.4 x 14 m)
4 x Parsons turbine engines via quadruple screw.
Sank bow first in 18 minutes at 2.15 pm on 7 May 1915, with 1,198 lives lost. She had been torpedoed by the German U-20 off Old Head of Kinsale, Ireland, while approaching St George's Channel en route from New York to Liverpool.
Built by Laird Brothers, Birkenhead, for the Cunard Line at a cost of £1,300,000.

LUTETIA (1913)
14561 grt; 912 psrs
579' x 64' x 36'7" depth (175.5 x 19.4 x 11.1 m)
Ateliers et Chantiers de l'Atlantique 8-cylinder triple expansion engines via quadruple screw.
Broken up for scrap at Blyth in 1938.
Built by Chantiers et Ateliers de St Nazaire for Cie de Navigation Sud Atlantique.

LUTZOW (1908) See LUTZOW (1924)

LUTZOW (1924)
8818 grt; 1460 psrs
462' x 58' x 35'7" depth (140 x 17.6 x 10.8 m)
AG Weser 8-cylinder quadruple expansion engines via twin screw.
Broken up for scrap at Bremen in 1933. Ex-North German Lloyd.
Laid down by AG Weser, Bremen, for North German Lloyd as LUTZOW (1908). Renamed HUNTSEND (1914 – British government, after seizure).

LUX (1919)
3528 grt; 779 psrs
336' x 46' x 27'6" depth (101.8 x 13.9 x 8.4 m)
Union Iron Works 3-cylinder triple expansion engines via single screw.
Sank with all hands on 16 March 1920 following a collision off the Balearic Islands.
Built by Union Iron Works, San Francisco, for Pacific Mail Steamship Co as the PERU (1892).

LUX (1946)

4779 grt
375' x 52' x 31'6" depth (113.6 x 15.8 x 9.6 m)
W Cramp & Sons 8-cylinder triple expansion engines via twin screw.
Broken up for scrap at Napa, California, in 1948 after serving as a floating casino off Santa Monica since 1946.
Built by W Cramp & Sons, Philadelphia, Pennsylvania, for Eastern Steamship Corporation as the BUNKER HILL (1907). Renamed AROOSTOOK, USS (CM-3) (1917 – US Navy) and BUNKER HILL (1943).

LUXOR (1947) See NEGBAH (1948)

LYAUTEY (1952) See LINDOS (1967)

LYAUTEY (1966) See LINDOS (1967)

LYDIA (1966)

10514 grt; 361 psrs
472' x 65' x 25'6" (143.9 x 19.9 x 7.7 m)
2 x 6-cylinder Kincaid diesel engines via twin screw.
Broken up for scrap by Hua Eng Copper & Iron Industrial Co at Kaohsiung in 1968. Ex-Africa Shipping Co.
Built by Swan Hunter & Wigham Richardson Ltd, Newcastle, for the Melbourne Steamship Company as the DUNTROON (1935). Renamed TONG HOO (1961 – Kie Hock Shipping Co, Hong Kong).

LYDIA (1986) See BOSPORUS (1999)

LYNGENFJORD (1933)

5873 grt
408' x 55' x 23'10" (123.6 x 16.7 x 7 m)
D Rowan & Co 4-cylinder quadruple expansion engine via single screw.
Owned by Den Norske Amerikalinje, she was abandoned as a total loss when wrecked on 14 January 1938 off Cape Francis, South Africa.
Built by William Hamilton & Co, Glasgow, for Grace Lines as the COLUSA (1913). Renamed SANTA CECILIA (1921 – Grace Line) and NIDAROS (1931 – AS Krogstads Dampskibrederei, Norway).

LYUBOV ORLOVA (1976) See MARINE DISCOVERY (1999)

MAASDAM (1889) See CITTA DI NAPOLI (1902)

MAASDAM (1921)
8850 grt; 974 psrs
454' x 58' x 30'2" (137.6 x 17.6 x 9.2 m)
3 x J Brown turbine engines via single screw.
Sank on 26 June 1941 after being torpedoed in the North Atlantic.
Built by Wilton Fijenoord, Schiedam, for Holland America Line.

MAASDAM (1952) See STEFAN (1988)

MAASDAM (1993)
55451 grt; 1266 psrs
720' x 90' x 25' (218.2 x 27.3 x 7.5 m)
2 x 12-cylinder Sulzer diesel-electric engines via twin screw.

Cruise ship owned and operated by the Holland-America Line.
Built by Fincantieri Shipyard, Monfalcone, at a cost of US$225,000,000.

MABUHAY (1996) See MABUHAY SUNSHINE (1996)

MABUHAY SUNSHINE (1996)
7262 grt; 1211 psrs
491' x 56' x 16' (127 x 17 x 4.9 m)
2 x 8-cylinder Pielstick diesel engines via twin screw.
Cruise ship owned by WG & A Jebsens Ship Management Inc and operated by Mabuhay Holiday Cruises International. She has been laid up since 1998.
Built by Mitsubishi Heavy Industries, Shimonoseki, for Oshima Unyu KK as the SUNSHINE FUJI (1984). Renamed MABUHAY (1996).

MACAU (1964)
3670 grt; 300 psrs
325' x 49' x 12' (98.5 x 14.8 x 3.lm)
4 x William Denny SRG turbine engines via twin screw.
Operated by Shun Tak Shipping Co Ltd, Hong Kong.
Built by William Denny & Bros, Dumbarton, for the London and North Eastern Railway as the PRINCESS MARGARET (1931).

McCAWLEY, USS (AP-10) (1940) See McCAWLEY, USS (APA-4) (1943)

McCAWLEY, USS (APA-4) (1943)
8153 grt; 157 psrs
486' x 64' x 25'6" (147.3 x 19.4 x 7.8 m)
2 x 8-cylinder Sulzer diesel engines via twin screw.
Owned by the US Navy, she sank on 30 June 1943 after a Japanese aircraft attack off Rendova Island, South Pacific.
Built by Furness Shipbuilding Co Ltd, Haverton Hill-on-Tees, for the Grace Line as the passenger-cargo ship SANTA BARBARA (1928).

MACDHUI (1931)
4561 grt; 167 psrs
342' x 51' x 21' (104.2 x 15.5 x 6.4 m)
Kincaid 8-cylinder diesel engine via single screw.
Sank on 18 June 1942 after she drifted on to a reef and rolled over, off Titana

Island near Port Moresby, Papua & New Guinea .
Built by Barclay, Curle & Co, Glasgow, for Burns Philp & Co Ltd, Sydney.

MACEDONIA (1904)
10512 grt; 564 psrs
545' x 60' x 27' (166.1 x 18.3 x 8.2 m)
2 x quadruple expansion via twin screw.
Broken up for scrap by Amakasu Gomei Kaisha for a tender of £25,000 in Japan in 1931.
Built by Harland & Wolff Ltd, Belfast, for the P&O Line at a cost of £344,296.

MACMOSA (1988) See MANAR (2000)

MACONA (1916)
5252 grt; 50 psrs
378' x 49' x 27' depth (114.5 x 14.8 x 8.2 m)
Delaware River Co 3-cylinder triple expansion engine via single screw.
Abandoned as a total constructive loss after being wrecked off the Swedish coast on 17 January 1920.
Built by Delaware River Co, Chester, Pennsylvania, for Ocean Steamship Co of Savannah as the CITY OF MACON (1903).

McPHERSON (1898) See ONEGA (1914)

MACQUARIE (1904) See HANAMET (1906)

MADALI (1948)
4888 grt
351' x 53' x 26'8" depth (106.4 x 16.1 x 8.1 m)
Central Marine Engineering 3-cylinder triple expansion engines via twin screw.
Broken up for scrap. Ex-Les Cargos Algeriens Soc Anon.
Built by W Gray & Co Ltd, West Hartlepool, for Strick Line Ltd as the BARDISTAN (1923). Renamed SAINT ROCH (1929 – Cie Navale et Commerciale de l'Oceanie), RECHERCHE (1930 – Messageries Maritimes), CAPO OLMO (1935 – Cia Genovese de Navigation a Vapore SA) and KOUFFRA (1946 – government of France).

MADELEINE (1997)
9700 grt; 1200 psrs
403' x 62' x 16'6" (122 x 18.8 x 5 m)
4 x 8-cylinder Krupp-MaK diesel engines via twin screw.

Passenger ferry owned by the government of Canada and operated by Transport Canada.
Built by Verolme Dockyard, Cork, for the British & Irish Steam Packet Co as the LEINSTER (1981) at a cost of £23,500,000. Renamed ISLE OF INISHMORE (1993 – B & I Line) and ISLE OF INISHTURK (1996 – Ministry of Public Works & Services, Ottawa).

MADISON (1911) See MADISON (1926)

MADISON (1923)
4967 grt; 1340 psrs
429' x 48' x 34'4" depth (130 x 14.5 x 10.4 m)
Townsend & Downey 3-cylinder triple expansion engine via single screw.
Broken up for scrap in Italy in 1924.
Built by Fairfield Shipbuilding & Engineering Co Ltd, Glasgow, for North German Lloyd as the SAALE (1886). Renamed as the passenger-cargo ship JJ LUCKENBACH (1900 – Luckenbach Transport & Wrecking Co) and PRINCESS (1921 – AM Ostram). As the JJ LUCKENBACH she had sunk with the loss of 99 lives after catching fire on 30 June 1900, and subsequent ships have been constructed within her same hull design.

MADISON (1926)
4321 grt; 263 psrs
374' x 42' x 16'8" (113.3 x 12.7 x 5.1 m)
Newport News 3-cylinder triple expansion engine via single screw.
Broken up for scrap at Quincy, Massachusetts, in 1948. Ex-Eastern Steamship Lines.
Built by Newport News Shipbuilding, Newport News, Virginia, for Ocean Steamship Co as the MADISON (1911). Renamed WARSZAWA (1920 – Holland America Line).

MADONNA (1905)
5537 grt; 1764 psrs
431' x 48' x 21'5" (131.3 x 14.6 x 6.5 m)
Swan Hunter 6-cylinder triple expansion engines via twin screw.
Broken up for scrap in Italy in 1934.
Built by Swan Hunter Shipbuilding, Wallsend, for Fabre Line, Marseilles.

MADRAS (1895) See HOKOKU MARU (1914)

MADRAS (1914) See TANDA (1919)

MADRID (1925) See MADRID (1935)

MADRID (1935)
8736 grt; 637 psrs
length 440' x beam 57' (134 x 17.3 m)
6-cylinder triple expansion engines via twin screw.
Owned by Hamburg South American Line, she sank during an air attack on 9 December 1941 off Den Helder, Holland.
Built by AG Vulcan, Stettin, for North German Lloyd as the passenger liner SIERRA NEVADA (1922).

MADURA (1921)
9032 grt; 168 psrs
length 465' x beam 58' (141.7 x 17.4 m)
Geared turbine engines via twin screw.
Broken up in 1953.
Built by Barclay, Curle & Company, Glasgow, for the British India Line.

MAETSUYCKER (1937) See HYSAN (1971)

MAGALLANES (1928)
9689 grt; 903 psrs
467' x 56' x 25' (141.5 x 17 x 7.6 m)
SRG turbine engines via twin screw.
Broken up at Bilbao in 1957.
Built by Soc Espanola Construccion Naval, Cadiz, for Cia Trasatlantica Espanola.

MAGDALENA (1928) See POBEDA (1946)

MAGDALENA (1949)
17547 grt; 479 psrs
570' x 73' x 28'6"(172.7 x 22.1 x 8.7 m)
Geared turbine engines via twin screw.
After grounding on the Tijucas Rocks 15 miles (25 km) from Rio de Janiero, on 25 April 1949, the ship was successfully refloated. However, she had sustained major damage and a few hours into the tow back to a naval drydock the bow section broke away, followed an hour later by the stern and mid-section. Her end came in Imbui Bay, at the entrance to Rio's harbour, in June 1949.
Built by Harland & Wolff Ltd, Belfast, for Royal Mail Lines.

MAGIC I (1999)
14264 grt; 1600 psrs
425 cars
466' x 72' x 19' (142.1 x 22 x 5.7 m)
2 x 12-cylinder l'Atlantique-Pielstick diesel engines via twin screw.
Passenger-car ferry owned and operated by Lance Shipping Co Ltd following purchase for US$3,900,000.
Built by Dubigeon-Normandie, Nantes, for Fred Olsen Lines as the BOLERO (1973). Renamed SCANDINAVICA (1978 – Stena Line), BOLERO (1982 – Fred Olsen Lines), JUPITER (1990 – Color Line ASA), CRUCERO

EXPRESS (1994 – Color Line AS, Bergen) and SEMINOLE EXPRESS (1998 – Skaugen Holdings). As CRUCERO EXPRESS, another name had been registered – TREGOR (1980) – and marketing brochures, etc had been produced under this name, but the acquisition failed to be completed.

MAGICSTAR (1919)
5574 grt
420' x 54' x 28'7" depth (127.3 x 16.4 x 8.7 m)
Hawthorne Leslie 3-cylinder triple expansion engines via single screw.
Built by Hawthorne Leslie & Co Ltd, Newcastle, for Elderslie Steamship Co Ltd as the BUTESHIRE (1893). Renamed BOLLINGTON GRANGE (1915 – Houlder Brothers Co Ltd) and CANONESA (1916 – Furness-Houlder Argentine Lines Ltd).

MAGVANA (1920) See EMPIRE ATTENDANT (1940)

MAHANA (1917)
11796 grt
501' x 63' x 29' (151.8 x 19.1 x 8.8 m)
4 x Parsons SRG turbine engines via twin screw.
Broken up for scrap at Dalmuir in 1953 as a migrant ship.
Built by W Hamilton & Co Ltd, Port Glasgow, for Thos & Jno Brocklebank Ltd.

MAHENO (1905)
5323 grt; 489 psrs
403' x 50' x 23' (122 x 15 x 7 m)
Geared turbine engines via triple screw.
Abandoned as a total constructive loss after beaching on Fraser Island off the Queensland coast on 8 July 1935. A towline had snapped while en route to Japan following her sale.
'Built by William Denny & Bros, Dumbarton, for the Union Steamship Co of New Zealand.

MAHENO (1969) See CARLA E (1991)

MAHROUSSA (1905)
3762 grt
478' x 43' x 26'5" depth (144.8 x 13 x 8 m)
3 x A & J Inglis turbine engines via triple screw.
Owned by the government of Egypt and operated as a student education ship.
Built by Samuda Brothers, London, for HH The Khedive of Egypt as the paddle-wheeler EL HORRIA (1865).

MAID OF KENT (1959)
4413 grt; 1000 psrs
190 cars
375' x 61' x 13' (113.7 x 18.4 x 3.9 m)
2 x DRG turbine engines via twin screw.
Broken up for scrap at Pasajes in 1982.
Built by William Denny & Bros, Dumbarton, for the British Transport Commission.

MAID OF ORLEANS (1949)
3777 grt; 1404 psrs
35 cars
342' x 52' x 12'6" (103.6 x 15.8 x 3.8 m)
2 x Parsons SRG turbine engines via twin screw.
Broken up for scrap at Bilbao in 1975.
Built by William Denny & Bros, Dumbarton, for the British Transport Commission.

MAIN (1927)
7624 grt

503' x 63' x 28'3" depth (152.4 x 19 x 8.6 m)
Bremer Vulkan 4-cylinder triple expansion engines via single screw.
Built by Bremer Vulkan, Vegesack, for North German Lloyd.

MAINE (1920)
5768 grt; 605 psrs
401' x 52' x 33'7" depth (121.5 x 15.8 x 10.2 m)
Fairfield 6-cylinder triple expansion engines via twin screw.
Broken up as a Royal Navy hospital ship at Barrow-in-Furness in 1948. Ex-British Royal Navy.
Built by Fairfield, Glasgow, for Pacific Steam Navigation Co as the PANAMA (1902).

MAINE II (1914) See PERSEUS (1926)

MAINZ (1897) See LYDIA (1912)

MAIPU (1951)
11515 grt; 753 psrs
480' x 64' x 38' depth (145.5 x 19.4 x 11.5 m)
2 x 10-cylinder Sulzer diesel engines via twin screw.
Sank in three hours on 4 November 1951 (only six months after her completion) when she collided with the USS GENERAL M. L. HERSEY north-west of the Weser lightship, in the Elbe river estuary, Germany. There was no loss of life.
Built by De Schelde, Vlissingen for Cia Argentina de Navigation Dodero.

MAITAI (1909)
3393 grt; 364 psrs
345' x 42' x 25' (105.2 x 12.8 x 7.6 m)
Triple expansion engine via single screw.
Abandoned as a total constructive loss on 25 December 1916. Her anchor chain snapped while waiting to enter Avarua harbour, in Rarotonga, during strong currents and heavy swells. She was thrown on to the Avarua Reef and began breaking up.
Built by CS Swan & Hunter, Wallsend, for the New Zealand & Australian Steamship Co as the MIOWERA (1892).

MAJESTIC (1922) See CALEDONIA, HMS (1936)

MAJESTIC (1993)
32746 grt; 1800 psrs
760 cars
621' x 91' x 22' (214 x 27.6 x 6.7 m)
4 x 8-cylinder Sulzer diesel engines via twin screw.
Cruise ferry owned by the Grimaldi Group, Italy, and operated by their subsidiary Grandi Navi Veloci.
Built by Nuovi Cantieri Apuania Yard for the Grimaldi Group at a cost of US$120,000,000.

MAJESTY OF THE SEAS (1992)
73937 grt; 2354 psrs
874' x 106' x 25' (264.8 x 32.1 x 7.6 m)
4 x 9-cylinder Pielstick diesel engines via twin screw.

Cruise ship for the Royal Caribbean Cruise Line.
Built by Chantiers de l'Atlantique, St Nazaire, for Royal Caribbean Cruise Line.

MAJORCA ROSE (1984) See TEBAH 2000 (1999)

MAKARINI (1912) See PORT NICHOLSON (1914)

MAKEDONIA (1984) See AVRASYA I (1996)

MAKSIM GORKIY (1974) See MAXIM GORKI (1974)

MAKURA (1908)
8075 grt; 402 psrs
466' x 58' x 26' (142 x 17.7 x 7.9 m)
Triple expansion engines via twin screw.
Broken up for scrap at Shanghai in 1936.
Built by Alexander Stephen & Sons Ltd, Glasgow, for the Union Steamship Co of New Zealand.

MALABAR (1925)
4512 grt; 156 psrs
351' x 49' x 22'3" (107 x 14.6 x 6.8 m)
B+W-Kincaid diesel engine via single screw.
Partially broken up where she lay in May 1931 after she struck rocks off Miranda Point, Sydney, at 7.00 am on 2 April 1931. The helmsman had made an error in steering five degrees to port in lieu of starboard. She remained firmly wedged in the rocks 50' (15.2 m) from the cliff face of a Sydney suburb (which now bears the ship's name) and slowly was destroyed by the pounding waves.
Built by Barclay, Curle & Company, Glasgow, for Burns Philp & Co Ltd, Sydney.

MALAITA (1933) See LINDA Jnr (1968)

MALASPINA (1963)
9121 grt; 500 psrs
88 cars
408' x 74' x 16' (123.6 x 22.4 x 4.8 m)
2 x 12-cylinder Enterprise diesel engines via twin screw.

Laid up in the Allen Marine Dock near Auke Bay since September 1999.
Built by Lockheed Shipbuilding Co, Portland, Oregon, for the Alaska Marine Highway System.

MALAYSIA (1964)
8062 grt; 170 psrs
439' x 60' x 25' (133 x 18.2 x 7.6 m)
Geared turbine engine via single screw.
Broken up for scrap in India in 1984. Ex-Austasia Line Ltd.
Built by Cammell Laird & Co, Birkenhead, for the Booth Line as the HUBERT (1955).

MALAYSIA (1965) See KHALEEJ EXPRESS (1976)

MALAYSIA BARU (1971)
11792 grt; 441 psrs
532' x 72' x 26' (162 x 22 x 7.9 m)
Parsons DRG turbine engines via twin screw.
Owned by Cia de Navegacion Abeto SA, Hong Kong, she was broken up for scrap at Kaohsiung in 1976 after being towed from Singapore. She had been raised from shallow water there on 26 June 1975, following a fire which had erupted in the repair yards on 12 May 1974.
Built by Chantiers Navigation de la Ciotat for Messageries Maritimes as the passenger-cargo ship VIET-NAM (1952). Renamed PACIFIQUE (1967 – Messageries Maritimes), MALAYSIA KITA (1968 – Cia de Navegacion Abeto) and PRINCESS ABETO (1970 – Cia de Navegacion Abeto).

MALAYSIA KITA (1968) See MALAYSIA BARU (1971)

MALAYSIA RAYA (1971)
11792 grt; 1696 psrs
532' x 72' x 26' (162 x 22 x 7.9 m)
Parsons DRG turbine engines via twin screw.
Owned by Cia de Navegacion Abeto, she was broken up for scrap at Kaohsiung in 1977. She had been completely destroyed by fire while lying at anchor on 23 August 1976, near Port Kelang, and beached the next day.
Built by Chantiers Navigation de la Ciotat for Messageries Maritimes as the LAOS (1954). Renamed EMPRESS ABETO (1970 – Cia de Navegacion Abeto).

MALDA (1913)
7900 grt; 68 psrs
450' x 58' x 33' (136.4 x 17.6 x 10 m)
Triple expansion engines via twin screw.
Sank on 25 August 1917 after being torpedoed by the German U-70 off Plymouth, with the loss of 64 lives.
Built by Barclay, Curle & Co, Glasgow, for British India Steam Navigation Co as a passenger-cargo ship.

MALDA (1922)
9000 grt; 168 psrs
465' x 58' x 33'5" depth (140.9 x 7.9 x 11.2 m)
6 x Barclay Curle DRG turbine engines via twin screw.
Sank on 6 April 1942, with 25 lives lost, after being captured in the Bay of Bengal by the Japanese who then torpedoed her at point-blank range.
Built by Barclay, Curle & Co, Glasgow, for British India Steam Navigation Co.

MALGORZATA FORNALSKA (1955) See HONG Qi 144 (1977)

MALMO LINK (1990)
33163 grt; 240 psrs
800 cars + 1132 TEUs
636' x 89' x 22'6" (192.6 x 27 x 6.8 m)
2 x 6-cylinder Sulzer diesel engines via twin screw.
Passenger-car-cargo ferry owned by Lubeck Link and operated by Sea Link.
Built by Oskarshamns Varv, Oskarshamn, for OT Redlererna, Sweden, as the Ro Ro freighter FINNHAWK (1980).

MALOJA (1911)
12431 grt; 670 psrs
550' x 63' x 34' (166.7 x 19.2 x 10.3 m)
Quadruple expansion engines via twin screw.
Sank in 20 minutes on 27 February 1916, with the loss of 122 lives, after hitting a mine that had been laid by the German U-6 two miles (3 km) south-west of Dover pier. The hulk was demolished by explosives in 1964.
Built by Harland & Wolff Ltd, Belfast, for the P&O Line at a cost of £328,202.

MALOJA (1923)
21036 grt; 656 psrs
625' x 73' x 32' (189.4 x 22.2 x 9.7 m)
2 x quadruple expansion engines via twin screw.
Broken up for scrap by British Iron & Steel Corporation at Inverkeithing in 1954 for a tender figure of US$340,000.
Built by Harland & Wolff Ltd, Belfast, for the P&O Line.

MALOLO (1927) See QUEEN FREDERICA (1954)

MALOU (1903) See VIRGINIE (1907)

MALTA EXPRESS (1976) See AL JUDI (1993)

MALWA (1909)
10883 grt; 607 psrs
560' x 61' x 27' (170.7 x 18.6 x 8.2 m)
2 x quadruple expansion engines via twin screw.
Broken up for scrap by Kishimoto Kisen KK for a tender of £20,000 at Osaka in 1932.
Built by Caird & Company, Greenock, for the Peninsular & Oriental Steam Navigation Co Ltd at a cost of £308,455.

MAMARI (1904) See CONSUL HORN (1939)

MAMARI (1932)
8090 grt; 1006 psrs
478' x 63' x 28'7" (144.8 x 19.1 x 8.7 m)
Harland & Wolff 8-cylinder quadruple expansion engines via twin screw.
Owned by Shaw Savill & Albion, she was abandoned as a total constructive loss after going aground off Cromer, UK, on 4 June 1941 while trying to evade a heavy German air attack.
Built by Harland & Wolff Ltd, Belfast, for the White Star Line as the ZEALANDIC (1911). Renamed MAMILIUS (1926 – Aberdeen Line). At the commencement of World War Two she was heavily employed with transporting migrants and then was converted into a duplicate of the British aircraft carrier HMS HERMES, in an attempt to confuse the enemy.

MAMA TANZANIA (1998) See EL-TOR (1998)

MAMILIUS (1926) See MAMARI (1932)

MANAR (2000)
6008 grt; 1311 psrs
140 cars
377' x 54' x 13'6" (114.2 x 16.4 x 5 m)
2 x 12-cylinder Pielstick diesel engines via twin screw.
Passenger-car ferry owned and operated by Manar Marine Services Inc.
Built by Harland and Wolff Ltd, Belfast, for the Belfast Steamship Co as the ULSTER PRINCE (1967). Renamed LADY M (1982 – Panmar Ferry Services, Nicosia), TANGPAKORN (1984 – Varsity SA, Panama), LONG HU (1988), MACMOSA (1988 – Chin Hing Ltd, Nassau), NEPTUNIA II (1994 – Aquila Maritime Services Inc), NEPTUNIA (1995 – Panther Marine Corporation) and VATAN (2000).

MANCHURIA (1904) See TAGUS (1949)

MANDALA (1915)
8246 grt; 129 psrs
450' x 58' x 27'11" (136.4 x 17.6 x 8.2 m)
Barclay Curle 6-cylinder triple expansion engines via twin screw.
Broken up for scrap in Italy in 1934 for a tender of £9,500.
Built by Barclay, Curle & Co, Glasgow, for the British India Steam Navigation Co.

MANDINGO (1906) See CHAUDIERE (1914)

MANDINGO (1916) See APPAM (1919)

MANELA (1921)
8300 grt; 129 psrs
450' x 58' x 33' (136.4 x 17.6 x 10 m)
Geared turbine engines via twin screw.
Broken up for scrap in Holland. Ex-British Royal Air Force accommodation ship following her requisition in 1939.
Built by Barclay, Curle & Co, Glasgow, for the British India Steam Navigation Co as a passenger-cargo liner.

MANGYONGBONG (1971)
3574 grt; 300 psrs
length 333' x beam x depth 33' (100 x beam x 10.1 m)
Chongjin Shipyard diesel engine via twin screw.
Passenger-cargo ship owned by the North Korean government.
Built by Chongjin Shipyard, Huichon.

MANHATTAN (1913) See GALILAH (1948)

MANHATTAN (1932) See WAKEFIELD, USS (AP-21) (1941)

MANILA (1892) See BRACCIANO (1925)

MANILA MARU (1915)
9486 grt
475' x 61' x 27'10" (143.9 x 18.5 x 8.2 m)
Mitsubishi 6-cylinder triple expansion engines via twin screw.

Sank on 25 November 1944 after being torpedoed by the USS MINGO off the coast of Sarawak.
Built by Mitsubishi Dockyard for OSK.

MANILA PRINCESS (1991)
4149 grt; 470 psrs
60 cars + 60 trailers
406' x 63' x 16'6" (123 x 19.6 x 5 m)
4 x 6-cylinder Hanshin diesel engines via twin screw.
Passenger-car-cargo ferry owned and operated by Sulpicio Lines Inc.
Built by Imabari Zosen, Imabari, for Shikoku Kaihatsu Ferry KK, Tokyo, as the FERRY ORANGE (1976).

MANITOBA (1892) See CANDLER (1923)

MANITOU (1898) See NATALE (1925)

MANMASCO (1919) See WHARTON, USS (AP-7) (1939)

MANOA (1913) See BALHASH (1943)

MANOORA (1935) See AMBULOMBO (1966)

MANORA (1913)
7875 grt; 68 psrs
450' x 58' x 33' depth (136.4 x 17.6 x 10 m)
Barclay Curle 6-cylinder triple expansion engines via twin screw.
Broken up for scrap in Italy in 1932 for a tender of £3,650.
Built by Barclay, Curle & Co, Glasgow, for British India Steam Navigation Co as a passenger-cargo liner.

MANSOUR (1956) See ROMANTICA (1960)

MANTOLA (1916)
8246 grt; 69 psrs
450' x 58' x 33'3" depth (136.4 x 17.6 x 10.1 m)
Triple expansion engines via twin screw.
Sank with seven lives lost on 8 February 1917 after being torpedoed 140 miles (234 km) off Fastnet by the German U-81.
Built by Barclay, Curle & Co, Glasgow, for the British India Steam Navigation Co.

MANTOLA (1921)
9065 grt; 168 psrs
465' x 58' x 33'5" depth (140.9 x 17.6 x 10.2 m)
6 x Barclay Curle triple expansion engines via twin screw.
Broken up for scrap in 1953 by the British Iron & Steel Co, UK.
Built by Barclay Curle & Co Ltd, Glasgow, for the British India Steam Navigation Co Ltd.

MANTUA (1909)
10885 grt; 607 psrs
560' x 61' x 27' (170.7 x 18.6 x 8.2 m)
2 x Caird & Co 8-cylinder quadruple expansion engines via twin screw.
Broken up for scrap by China Shipbreakers Ltd for a tender figure of £32,000 at Shanghai in 1935.
Built by Caird & Company, Greenock, for the P&O Line at a cost of £308,053.

MANUEL ALFREDO (1954)
3468 grt; 92 psrs
338' x 46' x 19' (102.4 x 13.9 x 5.8 m)
2 x 7-cylinder Atlas diesel engines via single screw.
Broken up for scrap in 1973.
Built by Cia Uniao Fabril, Lisbon, for Soc de Geral Comercio Industria e Transportes as a passenger-cargo ship.

MANUEL AZANA (1995)
8851 grt; 1184 psrs
460 cars
461' x 61' x 12'6" (139.7 x 18.4 x 3.8 m)
2 x 12-cylinder Deutz-MWM diesel engines via twin screw.
Passenger-car ferry operated by Isnasa, Algeciras.
Built by AST de Huelva for Isnasa.

MANUEL CALVO (1901) See DRAGO (1952)

MANUEL SOTO (1976) See MOBY FANTASY (1997)

MANUKA (1903)
4534 grt; 367 psrs
373' x 46' x 23' (113 x 14 x 7 m)
Triple expansion engines via twin screw.
Sank on 17 December 1929 after running aground on the previous day in dense fog and breaking in two at Long Point, which lies between Dunedin and Bluff, New Zealand.
Built by William Denny & Bros, Dumbarton, for the Union Steamship Co of New Zealand.

MANUNDA (1929) See HAKONE MARU (1956)

MANX (1987) See NINDAWAYMA (1993)

MANX VIKING (1978) See NINDAWAYMA (1993)

MANZONI (1971) See AL SALAM MANZONI 94 (1999)

MAORI (1907) See HWA LIEN (1946)

MAORI (1953)
8303 grt; 790 psrs
455' x 63' x 17' (138.7 x 19.2 x 5.2 m)
2 x British-Thomson-Houston turbo-electric engines via twin screw.

Broken up for scrap as a RoRo ferry at Kaohsiung in 1974.
Built by Vickers-Armstrong Ltd, Newcastle, for the Union Steamship Co of New Zealand as a passenger ferry.

MAPINDUZI (1974)
3999 grt; 707 psrs
363' x 53' x 15'6" (109.9 x 16 x 4.7 m)
2 x 6-cylinder Niigata diesel engines via single screw.
Owned by the government of Tanzania (Ministry of Shipping, Zanzibar).
Built by Niigata Engineering Co Ltd, Niigata.

MAPLEDELL (1952) See LUISA COSTA (1963)

MAPLELEAF (1916) See BRITISH MAPLE (1920)

MARAMA (1907)
6496 grt; 461 psrs
436' x 53' x 25' (132.9 x 16.1 x 7.6 m)
Triple expansion engines via twin screw.
Broken up for scrap at Kobe in 1938.
Built by Caird & Co, Greenock, for the Union Steamship Co of New Zealand.

MARATHON (1904) See ORUBA (1921)

MAR BIANCO (1938)
8491 grt; 750 psrs
508' x 61' x 30' (154.9 x 18.6 x 9 m)
Workman, Clark 6-cylinder triple expansion engines via twin screw.
Owned by the German Navy, she sank on 7 December 1943 after an attack by Allied bombers in Zadar harbour, Croatia.
Built by Workman, Clark & Co Ltd, Belfast, for the Tyser Line, London, as the

HAWKES BAY (1912). Renamed PORT NAPIER (1916 – Commonwealth & Dominion Line), MARTANO (1936 – T & J Brocklebank, Liverpool) and MARTANO (1938 – A Zanchi, Genoa,). She was extensively used as a migrant ship.

MARBURG (1966) See NORTH STAR (1983)

MARBURN (1922)
10743 grt; 1460 psrs
501' x 59' x 39'8" depth (151.8 x 18 x 12.1 m)
S Stephen & Sons 6-cylinder triple expansion engines via twin screw.
Broken up for scrap by SA Coop Ligure Demolitori Navi at Genoa in 1928.
Ex-Canadian Pacific Steamship Co.
Built as the TUNISIAN (1900) by Alexander Stephen & Sons, Glasgow, for the Allan Line.

MARCELLUS (1905) See PERICLES (1914)

MARCO POLO (1936)
12272 grt; 374 psrs
477' x 60' x 29' (145.5 x 18.8 x 8.8 m)
2 x 4-cylinder Rowan quadruple expansion engines via twin screw.
Owned by Mediterranean Reederei GmbH, Germany, she was broken up for scrap at La Spezia in 1950. She had been raised from the harbour seabed where she had settled following her scuttling by the Germans on 12 May 1944.
Built by Cantieri Navale Triestino, Monfalcone, for Unione Austriaca, Trieste, as the KAISER FRANZ JOSEF I (1912). Renamed GENERALE DIAZ (1919 – Cosulich Line), PRESIDENTE WILSON (1920 – Cosulich Line) and GRANGE (1929 – Lloyd Triestino).

MARCO POLO (1949)
8949 grt
485' x 62' x 26' (147 x 18.8 x 7.9 m)
Cantieri Riuniti 9-cylinder diesel engine via single screw.
Broken up for scrap at La Spezia in 1978 as a cargo ship.
Launched by Ansaldo Shipyards, Genoa, for Italia SpA, Genoa, as the NICOLO GIANI (1942) and completed for Lloyd Triestino as the MARCO POLO.

MARCO POLO (1969) See ODYSSEUS (1988)

MARCO POLO (1993)
22080 grt; 850 psrs
577' x 77' x 27' (176.2 x 23.5 x 8.2 m)
2 x 9-cylinder Sulzer diesel engines via twin screw.
Cruise ship for Orient Lines.

Built by Mathias-Thesen Werft, Wismar, for the Baltic Shipping Co as the ice-strengthened passenger ship ALEXANDER PUSHKIN (1965).

MARDI GRAS (1972) See APOLLO (1998)

MARE BALTICUM (1994) See MELOODIA (1996)

MARECHAL GALLIENI (1919)
7543 grt; 2078 psrs
429' x 54' x 39'7" depth (130.7 x 16.6 x 12 m)
JC Tecklenborg 6-cylinder triple expansion engines via twin screw.

Broken up for scrap at La Seyne in 1926. Ex-Messageries Maritimes, who operated the vessel after she was handed back to France as war reparations. Built by JC Tecklenborg, Geestemunde, for North German Lloyd as the CASSEL (1901).

MARECHAL JOFFRE (1931) See MARECHAL JOFFRE (1945)

MARECHAL JOFFRE (1945)
11680 grt; 301 psrs
472' x 64' x 28'3" depth (143 x 19.4 x 8.6 m)
2 x 8-cylinder B+W diesel engines via twin screw.
Broken up for scrap at Osaka in 1960. Ex-Messageries Maritimes.
Built by Constructions Navales, La Ciotat, for Messageries Maritimes as the MARECHAL JOFFRE (1931). Renamed ROCHAMBEAU (1942 – US Army).

MARECHAL PETAIN (1939) See BIANCA C (1958)

MARE LIGURIA (1943) See ARTSA (1949)

MARELLA (1920) See CORSICA (1951)

MARELLA (1970) See ALCAEUS (1981)

MARENGO (1949) See URANIA II (1950)

MAREN MO (1975) See AL-ABOUD (1994)

MAREN MOLS (1966) See AL-ABOUD (1994)

MAREN MOLS (1975) See VOLCAN DE TAMASITE (1996)

MAREN MOLS (1996)
14221 grt; 616 psrs
344 cars + 65 trailers
450' x 79' x 18' (136.4 x 24 x 5.5 m)
2 x 9-cylinder MAN-B+W diesel engines via twin screw.

Built by Orskov Christensens Stalskipsvaerft, Frederikshaven, for Mols Linien.

MARGARET JOHNSON (1969) See REGENT SKY (1993)

MARGARITA (1963)
9374 grt; 800 psrs
455' x 62' x 28' (138.7 x 18.9 x 8.5 m)
Geared turbine engine via single screw.
Broken up for scrap at Onimichi in 1970. Ex-John S Latsis Line.
Built by Oregon Shipbuilding Corporation, Portland, Oregon, for the US Maritime Commission as the LA GRANDE VICTORY (1945). Renamed WATERMAN (1947 – Royal Rotterdam Lloyd).

MARGARITA L (1977)
37640 grt; 782 psrs
783' x 93' x 32' (238.7 x 28.2 x 9.7 m)
4 x 3-cylinder Pametrada DRG turbine engines via twin screw.
Owned by John S Latsis and laid up in Eleusis Bay since 1991 awaiting a sale for US$8,000,000. She had alternated as a pilgrim ship and a floating hotel moored at Jeddah for Petrola International SA from 1979.
Built as the WINDSOR CASTLE (1960) by Cammell, Laird & Co Ltd, Birkenhead, for the Union Castle Line.

MARGHA (1918)

8278 grt; 70 psrs
450' x 58' x 33'3" depth (136.4 x 17.6 x 10.1 m)
2 x Barclay Curle triple expansion engines via twin screw.
Broken up for scrap in the UK in 19934 for a tender of £9750.
Built by Barclay, Curle & Co, Glasgow, for British India Steam Navigation Co.

MARGLEN (1922)

10417 grt; 846 psrs
534' x 60' x 29' (162.8 x 18.3 x 8.8 m)
Harland & Wolff 6-cylinder triple expansion engines via twin screw.
Broken up for scrap by DL Pittaluga at Genoa in 1927. Ex-Canadian Pacific Steamship Co.
Built by Harland & Wolff Ltd, Belfast, for the Holland America Line as the STATENDAM (1898). Renamed SCOTIAN (1911 – Allan Line).

MARGRETHE LAESO (1997)

3688 grt; 586 psrs
75 cars
228' x 54' x 9' (69 x 16.3 x 2.8 m)
2 x 6-cylinder MAN-B+W diesel engines via twin screw.
Ice-strengthened passenger-car ferry owned by Andelsfaergeselskabet.
Built by Nordsovaerflet AS, Ringkobing, and chartered to Laeso Faergen as the LAESOFAERGEN (1996).

MARIA (1900)

3019 grt; 87 psrs
321' x 40' x 29' (100.5 x 12 x 9 m)
John Elder compound 2-cylinder engine via single screw.
Broken up for scrap as a freighter by Fratelli Bruzzo in 1903. Ex-GB Lavarello Pu P, Genoa.
Built by John Elder & Co, Glasgow, for Nederland Steamship Co as the PRINS VAN ORANJE (1871).

MARIA C (1910) See BRACCIANO (1925)

MARIA CHRISTINA (1927) See MOUZINHO (1930)

MARIA DEL CARMEN (1940) See CABO DE BUENA ESPERENZA (1940)

MARIA ERMOLOVA (1974) See MARIA YERMOLOVA (1974)

MARIA G (1998)

12338 grt; 845 psrs
429' x 76' x 20' (130 x 23.5 x 6 m)
2 x 14-cylinder MAN diesel engines via twin screw.
Passenger ferry owned by Maria Shipping and operated by Med Link Lines.
Built by Kochi Yuko KK, Kochi, for Kurushima Dockyard as the OKUDOGO 3 (1976).

MARIA GORTHON (1951) See PHAISTOS (1964)

MARIA GIULIA (1927)

8196 grt; 50 psrs
491' x 55' x 28'9" (148.8 x 16.7 x 8.8 m)
Harland & Wolff 6-cylinder triple expansion engines via twin screw.
Broken up for scrap at Genoa in 1932.
Built by Harland & Wolff Ltd, Belfast, for West India & Pacific Steamship Co Ltd as the AMERICAN (1895). Renamed CUFIC (1904 – Oceanic Steam Navigation Co) and ANTARTICO (1924 – Soc Anon Ligure di Navigation a Vapore).

MARIA KOSMAS (1992)

6384 grt; 318 psrs
424' x 58' x 29' (128.5 x 17.6 x 8.8 m)
4 x 12-cylinder Caterpillar diesel engines via twin screw.
As a cruise ship owned by Dido Shipping Co, Cyprus, and operated by Stability Lines, Greece, this ship has been laid up since 1995 and is for sale at US$3,400,00 as of late 2000.
Built by the Williamstown Naval Dockyard, Victoria, for the Royal Australian Navy as the oceanographic research ship COOK, HMAS (GOR 291) (1981).

MARIANNA (1959) See GUANG HUA (1960)

MARIANNA (1960)

14216 grt; 439 psrs
544' x 69' x 29' (165.8 x 21.1 x 8.8 m)
2 x 8-cylinder B+W diesel engines via twin screw.
Broken up for scrap at Kaohsiung in 1965. Ex-John S Latsis, Greece.
Built by Harland & Wolff Ltd, Belfast, for the Nelson Line as the HIGHLAND BRIGADE (1929). Renamed HENRIETTA (1959 – John S Latsis).

MARIANNA IV (1963) See MARIANNA IV (1968)

MARIANNA IV (1968)

9892 grt; 828 psrs
455' x 62' x 28' (138.7 x 18.9 x 8.5 m)
2 x General Electric DRG turbine engines via single screw.
Broken up for scrap at Eleusis in 1970. Ex-John S. Latsis, Greece.
Built by Permanente Metal Corporation, Richmond, California, for the US Maritime Commission as the 'Victory' Class troopship COSTA RICA VICTORY (1944). Renamed GROOTE BEER (1947 – Nederland Line), MARIANNA IV (1963 – John S Latsis) and GROOTE BEER (1965 – Holland America Line) until laid up in 1968.

MARIANNA V (1965)

9255 grt; 96 psrs
492' x 70' x 27' (149.1 x 21.2 x 8.2 m)
Turbine engine via single screw.
Broken up for scrap at Hong Kong in 1969.
Built by Newport News Shipbuilding & Drydock Co, Newport News, Virginia, for American President Lines as the PRESIDENT MONROE (1940). Renamed PRESIDENT MONROE, USS (AP-103) (1943 – US Navy) and PRESIDENT MONROE (1946 – American President Lines).

MARIANNA VI (1974)

14083 grt; 353 psrs
537' x 70' x 25' (163.6 x 21.4 x 7.6 m)
2 x 4-cylinder Doxford diesel engines via twin screw.
Laid up in Eleusis Bay near Piraeus since 1992. She had served as a hotel ship at Rabegh and Jeddah from 1986 to 1991 for Marianna Shipping & Trading Co, Panama. She was scrapped in 2001.
Built by Alexander Stephen & Sons, Glasgow, for Elder Dempster Lines as the AUREOL (1951) at a cost of US$4,00,000.

MARIANNA IX (1982) See MARIANNA 9 (1993)

MARIANNA LATSIS (1963) See HENRIETTA LATSIS (1966)

MARIANNA LATSIS (1966)

23372 grt; 1200 psrs
664' x 82' x 30' (202.7 x 24.8 x 9.1 m)
6 x Parsons SRG turbine engines via twin screw.
Broken up as a pilgrim ship for scrap by Terrestre Marittima SpA at La Spezia in 1969. Ex-Latsis Line.
Built by Vickers-Armstrong Ltd, Barrow-in-Furness, for the P&O Line as the STRATHEDEN (1937). Renamed HENRIETTA LATSIS (1963 – Latsis Line).

MARIANNA 9 (1984)

19393 grt; 1000 psrs
625' x 78' x 25'6" (190.5 x 23.9 x 7.8 m)
4 x Parsons DRG turbine engines via twin screw.
Laid up in Eleusis Bay in 1992 after alternating as an accommodation ship and a cruise ship, operating out of Rebagh for the John L Latsis Group.
Built by Swan Hunter & Wigham Richardson Ltd, Newcastle, for Cia Nacional de Navegacao, Lisbon, as the passenger ship PRINCIPE PERFEITO (1961). Renamed as the accommodation ship AL HASA (1974 – Global Transportation Inc, Panama), FAIRSKY (1980 – Sitmar Line – registered but sold prior to inaugural voyage), VERA (1980 – Sitmar Line) and MARIANNA IX (1982 – Latsis Group).

MARIA PA (1997)

3249 grt; 362 psrs
293' x 46' x 15' (88.8 x 13.9 x 4.5 m)

2 x 12-cylinder Ansaldo diesel engines via twin screw.
Passenger ferry owned and operated by Golden Ferries Maritime, Piraeus.
Built by Dubigeon-Normandie, Nantes, for SNCM as the LA VALETTA (1971). Renamed MISTRAL II (1992 – Saronic Cruises, a subsidiary of Royal Olympic Cruises).

MARIA PIPA (1940) See CABO DE HORNOS (1940)

MARIA RICKMERS (1896) See POLYXENA (1914)

MARIA SAVINA (1975)
3923 grt; 256 psrs
328' x 53' x 15'6" (99.4 x 16.1 x 4.7 m)
2 x 8-cylinder B+W diesel engines via twin screw.
Ice-strengthened cruise ship operating for the Far East Shipping Co, Vladivostok.
Built by Brodogradiliste, Kraljevica.

MARIA ULJANOVA (1959) See EXCELSIOR MERCURY (1990)

MARIA ULYANOVA (1937)
3870 grt; 292 psrs
Believed to have been lost during World War Two.
Built as the RUZZUTAK (1928).

MARIA ULYANOVA (1959) See EXCELSIOR MERCURY (1990)

MARIA YERMOLOVA (1974)
3941 grt; 256 psrs
332' x 53' x 15'6" (100.6 x 16.1 x 4.7 m)
2 x 8-cylinder B+W diesel engines via twin screw.
Ice-strengthened expeditionary cruise ship engaged by charter seasonally. When cruising in ecologically-delicate regions, her passenger capacity is reduced to 148 persons.
Built by Mathias-Thesen, Wismar, for the Murmansk Shipping Co.

MARIELLA (1985)
37799 grt; 2500 psrs
580 cars or 62 trailers
584' x 94' x 22' (177 x 28.4 x 6.5 m)
4 x 12-cylinder Wartsila-Pielstick diesel engines via twin screw.

Ice-strengthened passenger-car-cargo ferry owned by SF Line and operated by the Viking Line on the Sweden–Finland service.
Built by Wartsila-Turku for the SF Line.

MARIENBURG (1939) See ABKHAZIA (1956)

MARIETTA PACHA (1925)
12239 grt; 949 psrs
495' x 63' x 40'5" depth (150 x 19.1 x 12.3 m)
Provencale de Construction Navales 6-cylinder triple expansion engines via twin screw.
Broken up for scrap in 1946 after raising her from the position where the Germans scuttled her in August 1944.
Built by Constructions Navales, La Ciotat, for Messageries Maritimes.

MARIE WOERMANN (1914) See TJERIMAI (1921)

MARIGOLD (1944) See PRESIDENT FILLMORE (1946)

MARIJA ERMOLOVA (1974) See MARIA YERMOLOVA (1974)

MARIJA SAVINA (1976) See MARIA SAVINA (1976)

MARIMO (1972) See PRINCESS OF THE WORLD (1996)

MARINA (1990)
7895 grt; 1500 psrs
446' x 73' x 17' (135.1 x 22.1 x 5.2 m)
2 x 16-cylinder MAN diesel engines via twin screw.
Passenger ferry operated by G.A Ferries, Greece.
Built by Kanda Zosensho, Kure, for Hiroshima Green Ferry KK as the GREEN ARROW (1971). Renamed OKUDODO N0. 6 (1982 – Kurushima Dockyard Co Ltd).

MARINE ADDER (1945) See TRANSCOLORADO (1967)

MARINE ADVENTURER (1995) See PEREGRINE MARINER (2000)

MARINE ATLANTICA (1975) See SARDINIA VERA (1987)

MARINE BLUENOSE (1955)
6524 grt; 615 psrs
150 cars + 18 trailers
346' x 66' x 17' (104.8 x 20 x 5.2 m)
6 x 12-cylinder Fairbanks-Morse diesel engines via twin screw.
Passenger-car-cargo ferry owned by General Dynamics Inc, and operated as a floating shop in the River Thames near Groton, Connecticut, USA.
Built by Davie Shipbuilding Co, Lauzon, Quebec, for Canadian National Railroads as the BLUE NOSE (1955).

MARINE CARDINAL (1945) See SAN PEDRO (1970)

MARINE CARP (T-AP-199) (1945) See GREEN SPRINGS (1968)

MARINE CRUISER (1975) See TEBAH 2000 (1999)

MARINE DISCOVERER (1995) See CLIPPER ADVENTURER (1997)

MARINE DISCOVERY (1999)
3941 grt; 256 psrs
332' x 53' x 16' (100.6 x 16.1 x 4.7 m)
2 x 8-cylinder B+W diesel engines via twin screw.

Marketed by Marine Expeditions as the ice-strengthened cruise ship MARINE DISCOVERY, but is registered as the LYUBOV ORLOVA and operated by the Far East Shipping Co, Vladivostok.
Built by Titovo Kraljevica for the Far East Shipping Co as the LYUBOV ORLOVA (1976).

MARINE FALCON (1945) See BORINQUEN (1975)

MARINE FLASHER (1945) See LONG BEACH (1966)

MARINE JUMPER (1945) See PANAMA (1966)

MARINE LYNX (T-AP-194) (1945) See TRANSCOLUMBIA (1967)

MARINE MARLIN (1945) See GREEN BAY (1965)

MARINE NAUTICA (1974) See CORSICA MARINE SECONDA (1999)

MARINE PERCH (1945) See YELLOWSTONE (1965)

MARINE PHOENIX (1945) See MOHAWK (1968)

MARINE SERPENT (1945) See GALVESTON (1968)

MARINE SHARK (1945) See CHARLESTON (1968)

MARINE STAR (1945) See MARINE STAR (1994)

MARINE STAR (1994)
12733 grt; 2500 psrs
165 cars
523' x 72' x 17' (159.3 x 21.8 x 5.2 m)
2 x General Electric DRG turbine engines via single screw.
Laid up at a derelict berth alongside abandoned grain silos in Buffalo as of early 1990.
Built by Sun Shipbuilding & Drydock Co, Chester, Pennsylvania, for the US Maritime Commission as the Class C4 cargo ship MARINE STAR (1945). Renamed AQUARAMA (1955 – Sand Products Corporation, Wilmington, Delaware) and then laid up by Sand Products Corporation between 1977 and 1993.

MARINE SWALLOW (1945) See LINNET (1977)

MARINE TIGER (1945) See OAKLAND (1965)

MARINE VOYAGER (1995)
6231 grt; 82 psrs
386' x 59' x 19'6" (117 x 17.9 x 5.9 m)
2 x Pielstick diesel engines via twin screw.
Marketed for polar cruises as the MARINE VOYAGER for Marine Expeditions, but is still registered as the AKADEMIK SERGEY VAVILOV and operated by Russian government officers and crew.
Built by Hollming RS, Finland, for the Russian government as the ice-strengthened oceanographic research ship AKADEMIK SERGEY VAVILOV (1988).

MARINO (1894) See UMZINTO (1921)

MARIO VISENTINI (1947) See SEBASTIANO CABOTO (1947)

MARIPOSA (1932) See HOMERIC (1953)

MARIPOSA (1956) See HENG LI (1993)

MARISTRELLA (1958)
8178 grt; 700 psrs
457' x 57' x 25'7" (138.5 x 17.3 x 7.8 m)
John Cockerill 8-cylinder quadruple expansion engines via twin screw.
Broken up for scrap at Osaka in 1960. Ex- Maristrella Naviera SA.
Built by John Cockerill Shipyards, Hoboken, for Cie Belge Maritime as the ELISABETHVILLE (1921). Renamed EMPIRE BURE (1947 – British Ministry of Transport) and CHARLTON STAR (1950 – Charlton Steam Shipping Co).

MARITZBERG (1904) See VENEZUELA (1923)

MARIYA SAVINA (1975) See MARIA SAVINA (1975)

MARIYA YERMOLOVA (1974) See MARIA YERMOLOVA (1974)

MAR. JULIA (1996) See CESME STERN (1997)

MARKOMANNIA (1890) See PEGLI (1913)

MARKO POLO (1988)
10154 grt; 1500 psrs
270 cars or 26 trailers
423' x 66' x 18' (128.1 x 20 x 5.5 m)
4 x 8-cylinder Stork-Werkspoor diesel engines via twin screw.

Ice-strengthened passenger-car-cargo ferry owned by Adriatic General and operated by Jadrolinija, Croatia.
Built by Soc Nouvelle des Ateliers et Chantiers du Havre for AS Larvik-Frederikshavnferjen as the PETER WESSEL (1973).
Renamed ZEELAND (1984 – Stoomvaart Maatschappij Zeeland NV) and STENA NORDICA (1986 – Stena Line).

MARLIN (1976) See MARY (1976)

MARLOCH (1922)
10687 grt; 984 psrs
540' x 60' x 29'6" (164.6 x 18.2 x 8.9 m)
Workman, Clark & Co turbine engines via triple screw.
Broken up for scrap by TW Ward & Co in Pembroke Dock, Milford Haven, in 1929. Ex-Canadian Pacific Steamship Co.
Built by Workman, Clarke & Co Ltd, Belfast, for the Allan Line as the VICTORIAN (1905).

MARMARA (1956)
6041 grt; 590 psrs
402' x 54' x 19' (121.8 x 16.4 x 5.8 m)
MAN 8-cylinder diesel engine via single screw.
Sank on 5 March 1972 when a fire broke out during repairs and engulfed the ship at the Golden Horn, Turkey.
Built by AG Weser, Bremen, for Turkish Maritime Lines.

MARMORA (1903)
10509 grt; 564 psrs
530' x 60' x 25'6" (161.6 x 18.3 x 7.8 m)
2 x quadruple expansion engines via twin screw.
Sank as an auxiliary cruiser on 23 July 1918 after being torpedoed by the German U-64 south of Ireland, with ten lives lost.
Built by Harland & Wolff Ltd, Belfast, for the P&O Line at a cost of £344,084.

MARNE (1920) See VILLE DE HASSELT (1940)

MARNIX VAN SINT ALDEGONDE (1920)
19355 grt; 683 psrs
608' x 74' x 36' (184.2 x 22.4 x 10.9 m)
2 x 10-cylinder Sulzer diesel engines via twin screw.
Sank on 6 November 1943 after being hit by aerial torpedoes fired from German aircraft the previous day, off Phillippville, Algeria.
Built by Netherlands Shipbuilding & Drydock Co, Amsterdam, for the Nederland Line.

MAROC (1956) See VILLE DE MARSEILLES (1956)

MARQUES DE COMILLAS (1928)
9922 grt; 390 psrs
467' x 56' x 25' (141.5 x 17 x 7.6 m)

SRG turbine engines via twin screw.
Broken up for scrap at Bilbao in 1962. Fire had gutted her on 6 November 1961 while waiting for repair work at Ferrol, Spain.
Built by Soc Espanola Construccion, Ferrol, for Cia Trasatlantica Espanola.

MARRAKECH (1986)
11515 grt; 634 psrs
418' x 67' x 16'6" (126.8 x 20.4 x 5 m)
2 x 9-cylinder B+W diesel engines via twin screw.
Passenger ferry owned by Cia Marockanian Navigation and operated by Comanav.
Built by Chantiers de l'Atlantique, St Nazaire.

MARTANO (1936) See MAR BIANCO (1938)

MARTANO (1938) See MAR BIANCO (1938)

MARTHA WASHINGTON (1908) See TEL AVIV (1928)

MARTINIQUE (1903)
4241 grt; 400 psrs
380' x 48' x 31'4" depth (115.2 x 14.5 x 9.5 m)
Elder & Co 2-cylinder compound engine via single screw.
Broken up for scrap in Italy in 1932.
Built by Elders Shipyards for the Castle Line as the NORHAM CASTLE (1883).

MARVALE (1922)
11439 grt; 1506 psrs
516' x 61' x 38' depth (157.3 x 18.5 x 11.5 m)
Barclay Curle 6-cylinder triple expansion engines via twin screw.
Owned and operated by Canadian Pacific Steamship Co, she was abandoned as a total constructive loss when she grounded on Freel Rock at the entrance to Trepassy Bay, 20 miles (33 km) west of Cape Race, on 21 May 1923.
Built by Barclay, Curle & Co, Glasgow, for the Allan Line as the CORSICAN (1907).

MARY (1976)
11513 grt; 3000 psrs
523' x 71' x 33' depth (158.5 x 21.5 x 10 m)
2 x Westinghouse DRG turbine engines via single screw.
Broken up for scrap in 1979. Ex-Calmar Steamship Co.
Built by Kaiser Corporation, Richmond, California, for the US Navy as the GENERAL J. R. BROOKE (APA-132) (1944). Renamed MARYMAR (1964 – Bethlehem Steel Corporation) and MARLIN (1976 – Calmar Steamship Co).

MARYMAR (1964) See MARY (1976)

MARY POPPINS (1975) See SAMA 1 (2000)

MARY QUEEN OF PEACE (1997)
9551 grt; 982 psrs
526' x 71' x 20' (159.5 x 21.5 x 6.2 m)
2 x 18-cylinder MAN diesel engines via twin screw.
Passenger ferry owned and operated by Negros Corporation Co Inc.
Built by Naikai Zosen, Setoda, for Nippon Car Ferry KK, Setoda, as the MIMITSU MARU (1974).

MARY WEEMS (1922) See NORTH SEA (1935)

MASANIELLO (1917)
6366 grt; 1958 psrs
392' x 52' x 33'4" depth (119.4 x 15.9 x 10.1 m)
G Clark Ltd 3-cylinder triple expansion engine via single screw.
Broken up for scrap in 1933. Ex-Transoceanica.
Built by Cantieri Navale Siciliana, Palermo, for Navigazione Generale Italia as the passenger liner ITALIA (1905).

MASBATE I (1987) See OUR LADY OF MANAOAG (1992)

MASHOBRA (1914)
8200 grt; 129 psrs
450' x 58' x 27'11" (136.4 x 17.6 x 8.2 m)

Barclay Curle 6-cylinder triple expansion engines via twin screw.
Sank on 15 April 1917 after being torpedoed 140 miles (233 km) from Cape Matapan.
Built by Barclay, Curle & Co, Glasgow, for the British India Steam Navigation Co.

MASHOBRA (1920)
8200 grt; 129 psrs
450' x 58' x 32'9" depth (136.4 x 17.6 x 10 m)
Barclay Curle 6-cylinder triple expansion engines via twin screw.
Destroyed as a British Fleet Air Arm depot vessel by a massive German bomber attack at Narvik on 25 May 1940.
Built by Barclay, Curle & Co, Glasgow, for the British India Steam Navigation Co.

MASHU (1973) See GARYOUNIS (1977)

MASHU MARU (1948)
5796 grt; 389 psrs
276' x 52' x 12' (83.6 x 15.8 x 3.6 m)
Geared turbine engines via twin screw.
Passenger-train ferry operated by the Japanese government (Department of Railways) until she was sold on 25 January 1966.
Built by Uraga Dockyard Co.

MASHU MARU (1965)
8327 grt; 1286 psrs
8 rail coaches
433' x 59' x 17' (131.2 x 18 x 5.2 m)
2 x 12-cylinder B+W diesel engines via quadruple screw.
Passenger-train ferry operated by as a Seikan Railway Ferries museum in Hakodate.
Built by Mitsubishi Heavy Industries Ltd, Kobe, for the Japanese government (Department of Railways).

MASSACHUSETTS (1907) See OGLALA, USS (1928)

MASSALIA (1958)
3285 grt; 346 psrs
315' x 46' x 18' (95.5 x 13.9 x 5.5 m)
9-cylinder B+W diesel engine via single screw.
Broken up for scrap by P Skounis & I Efthimiou at Eleusis Bay in 1974. Ex-Hellenic Mediterranean Lines Co Ltd, Piraeus.
Built by AS Akers Mek, Oslo, for Fred Olsen Line as the BRETAGNE (1937).

MASSALIA (1971) See REGAL VOYAGER (1994)

MASSILIA (1902)
5156 grt; 60 psrs
401' x 49' x 27'8" depth (122 x 15 x 8.4 m)
A Stephen 3-cylinder triple expansion engine via single screw.
Broken up for scrap in 1930.
Built by Alex Stephens & Sons, Glasgow, for the Anchor Line.

MASSILIA (1920)
15363 grt; 846 psrs
577' x 64' x 37' depth (174.8 x 19.4 x 11.2 m)
Forges et Chantiers de la Mediterranee 6-cylinder triple expansion engines via quadruple screw.
Broken up for scrap in 1946. The retreating Germans had scuttled her in shallow water as a harbour block in 1944 close to the Basin Mirabeau, Marseilles.
Launched in 1914 by Forges et Chantiers de la Mediterranee, La Seyne, for Cie de Navigation Sud-Atlantique, but not completed until 1920.

MATAI (1908)
3393 grt; 360 psrs
Wrecked beyond salvage on 25 December 1916 when the combined force of a strong current and heavy swell drove her on to a coral reef at Avarua, Rarotonga, when her mooring lines and anchor chain snapped.

MATANUSKA (1963)
3029 grt; 756 psrs
88 cars

411' x 74' x 16' (124.4 x 22.5 x 4.9 m)
2 x 12-cylinder Krupp-MaK diesel engines via twin screw.

Passenger-car ferry in Alaska operated by the Alaska Marine Highway
(Division of the Dept of Public Works, State of Alaska).
Built by Puget Sound Bridge & Dockyard Co, Seattle.

MATARAM (1909) See KOWA MARU (1937)

MATAROA (1926)
12390 grt; 372 psrs
519' x 63' x 33' (158.2 x 19.2 x 10 m)
DRG turbine engines via twin screw.
Broken up for scrap at Faslane in 1957. Ex-Shaw Savill Line.
Built by Harland & Wolff Ltd, Belfast, for the Aberdeen Line as the
DIOGENES (1922).

MATATUA (1904) See ILSENTSTEIN (1928)

MATIANA (1922)
8965 grt; 168 psrs
465' x 58' x 28'2" (140.1 x 17.6 x 8.5 m)
6 x Barclay Clark geared turbine engines via twin screw.
Broken up for scrap in 1952 by the British Iron & Steel Co, UK.
Built by Barclay, Curle & Co, Glasgow, for the British India Steam Navigation
Co.

MATRONA (1947)
7937 grt; 360 psrs
451' x 56' x 24' (136.7 x 17 x 7.3 m)
2 x 8-cylinder B+W diesel engines via twin screw.
Broken up for scrap at Barrow-in-Furness in 1948 after towing her from
Bidston Dock, Birkenhead, UK, where she had capsized and settled during a
refit ordered by her new owners, Bawtry Steamship Co Ltd.
Laid down by Barclay, Curle & Co, Glasgow, for the Tsarist government of
Russia as a passenger ship. Listed by Job Number only, it was completed for
the Glen Line, London, as the cargo ship GLENAPP (1918). Renamed as the
passenger-cargo ship ABA (1918 – British & African Steamship Co).

MATSONIA (1913) See ETOLIN (1937)

MATSONIA (1938) See QUEEN FREDERICA (1954)

MATSONIA (1956) See BELOFIN I (1998)

MATSUMAE MARU (1924)
3484 grt; 895 psrs
25 railway wagons
362' x 52' x 14' (109.7 x 15.9 x 4.3 m)
Passenger-train ferry which was bombed incessantly by US aircraft on 14 July
1945, until she caught fire and ran aground just outside Hakodate harbour.
Built by Mitsubishi Heavy Industries, Nagasaki.

MATSUMAE MARU (1964)
5376 grt; 1286 psrs
48 rail coaches
433' x 59' x 17' (131.2 x 17.9 x 5.2 m)
8 x 16-cylinder MAN diesel engines via twin screw.
Passenger-train ferry operated by Japanese National Rail until sold to Korean
interests in 1984.
Built by Hakodate Dock Co Ltd, Hakodate.

MATTAWA (1915) See BEPPE (1932)

MATUA (1937) See SULTAN KL (1968)

MAUA (1939)
5312 grt; 74 psrs
length 401' x beam 54' (121.5 x 16.4 m)
Turbine engine via single screw.
Owned by Lloyd Brasileiro, she was abandoned as a total constructive loss in
1952.
Built by American International Shipbuilding Corporation, Hog Island, for the
US Shipping Board as the SCHENECTADY (1919). Renamed SCANYORK
(1932 – American Scantic Line).

MAUI (1917)
9801 grt; 352 psrs
484' x 58' x 30'6" (146.7 x 17.6 x 9.3 m)
4 x Westinghouse geared turbine engines via twin screw.
Broken up for scrap as a freight ship at Portland, Oregon, in 1948. Ex-US
Maritime Commission which acquired her in 1941.
Built by the Union Iron Works, San Francisco, for the Matson Line.

MAUNALEI (1925) See CAPO MANARA (1948)

MAUNGANUI (1911) See CYRENIA (1947)

MAUNIWILI (1925) See PORTARITISSA (1955)

MAURETANIA (1907)
31938 grt; 2335 psrs
790' x 88' x 25' (239.4 x 26.7 x 7.6 m)
4 x Parsons turbine engines via quadruple screw.
Broken up for scrap by Metal Industries Ltd at Rosyth for a tender figure of
£80,000 in 1935.
Built by Swan Hunter & Wigham Richardson Ltd, Newcastle, for the Cunard
Steamship Co Ltd.

MAURETANIA (1939)
35738 grt; 1360 psrs
772' x 89' x 30' (233.9 x 27 x 9.1 m)
6 x Cammell Laird SRG turbine engines via twin screw.
Broken up for scrap by TW Ward Ltd at Inverkeithing in 1965.
Built by Cammell Laird & Co, Birkenhead, for the Cunard-White Star Line.

MAURIENNE (1964)
9100 grt
458' x 62' x 22' (138.8 x 18.8 x 6.7 m)
2 x Swan Hunter & Wigham Richardson 4-cylinder diesel engines via twin
screw.
French government training vessel.
Built by Swan Hunter Shipbuilding, Newcastle, for Cie Maritime des
Chargeur Reunis as the BRAZZA (1948).

MAURITIUS PRIDE (1990)
5234 grt; 452 psrs
328' x 56' x 21'6" (99.5 x 17 x 6.5 m)
2 x 9-cylinder MAN-B+W-Alpha diesel engines via twin screw.
Passenger-cargo ship owned by the Mauritian government and operated by
Mauritius Shipping Corporation Ltd (Coraline).
Built by Husumer Schiffswerft, Germany.

MAVI MARMARA (1994)
4142 grt; 1500 psrs
307' x 63' x 18' (93 x 19 x 5.5 m)
2 x 6-cylinder Wartsila diesel engines via twin screw.
Cruise ship base-ported in Istanbul and operated by TDI Deniz Yollari
Isletmesi. Listed for sale as of 31 December 2000.
Built by Turkiye Gemi Halic, Halic.

MAXIM GORKI (1974) See MAXIM GORKIY (1992)

MAXIM GORKIY (1992)
24981 grt; 652 psrs

639' x 87' x 27' (194.7 x 26.6 x 8.2 m)
4 x AEG DRG turbine engines via twin screw.
Cruise ship owned by Sovcomflot, Moscow, with registration in the Bahamas, managed by Lothian Shipping Services, London, and chartered to Phoenix Reisen GmbH, Bonn.
Built by Howaldtswerke-Deutsche Werft, Hamburg, for the German Atlantic Line as the HAMBURG (1969). Renamed HANSEATIC (1973 – Home Lines Ltd). Named "BRITANNIC" in February 1974 for the making of the movie *Juggernaut*. Name restyled to MAKSIM GORKI (1974–92).

MAXIM GORKY (1974) See MAXIM GORKIY (1992)

MAXIMUS (1963) See COSMOS TRADER (1966)

MAXSIM GORKI (1974) See MAXIM GORKIY (1992)

MAYAGUEZ (1975) See AMOCO TRADER (1982)

MAYA MARU (1971) See SOUTHERN QUEEN (1996)

MAYAN EMPRESS (1996)
10513 grt; 850 psrs
180 cars or 13 trailers
464' x 68' x 18' (140.9 x 20.5 x 5.5 m)
2 x 10-cylinder B+W diesel engines via twin screw.

Cruise ship owned by Emerald Empress Holding Co, St Vincent, and operated by Empress Cruise Line. She was rebuilt from a fire-gutted hull, after an engine room blaze.
Built by Cantieri Navale del Tirreno e Riuniti SpA, Riva Trigoso, for DFDS as the WINSTON CHURCHILL (1967).

MAYFLOWER (1903) See DEVONIAN (1923)

MAYNILAD (1992)
4997 grt; 1032 psrs
47 cars
422' x 62' x 16' (140.5 x 20.5 x 5.4 m)
2 x 8-cylinder Niigata-Pielstick diesel engines via twin screw.
Passenger-car ferry owned and operated by WG & A Philippines Inc.
Built by Towa Shimonoseki, Shimonoseki, for Oshima Unyu as the AKATSUKI (1981).

MAZAGON (1894) See SAINT NICHOLAS (1918)

MAZATLAN (1955)
4515 grt
350' x 50' x 15'6" (106.1 x 15.2 x 4.5 m)
Hooven Owen & Rentschler 6-cylinder triple expansion engines via twin screw.
Broken up for scrap in Japan in 1956.
Built by Todd Drydock & Construction Co, Tacoma, for Alaska Steamship Co as the ALASKA (1923).

MAZATLAN (1973)
5012 grt; 800 psrs
150 cars or 22 trailers
359' x 57' x 15' (108.9 x 17.3 x 4.6 m)
2 x 7-cylinder B+W diesel engines via twin screw.
Owned by the Mexican government, she sank on 3 October 1973 between La Paz and Topolobampo after a blaze had erupted.
Built by Helsingor Shipyards, Helsingor, for DFDS as the AKERSHUS (1965).

MAZOWIA (1982) See ANKARA (1983)

MECCA (1953) See KOMATI (1960)

MECCA (1975)
3858 grt; 209 psrs
355' x 48' x 18' (107.6 x 14.5 x 5.5 m)
B+W 12-cylinder diesel engines via twin screw.
Owned by Orri Navigation Lines, she sank on 19 December 1976 as a pilgrim ship after catching fire the day before, running aground out of control and rolling over, 17 miles (28 km) from Jeddah. All 1,100 pilgrims and crew survived.
Built by Burmeister & Wain, Copenhagen, for the Iceland Steamship Co, Reykjavik, as the GULLFOSS (1950).

MECCA I (1985) See FAGR (1998)

MECCA I (1992) See FAGR (1998)

MECCA I (1994) See FAGR (1998)

MECKLENBURG (1904)
3431 grt
350' x 42' x 26'8" (106.1 x 12.7 x 8.1 m)
Caird & Co 3-cylinder triple expansion engines via single screw.
Built by Caird & Co Ltd, Greenock, for Gulf Line Association Ltd as the GULF OF TARANTO (1892).

MECKLENBURG-VORPOMMERN (1996)
36185 grt; 887 psrs
440 cars
660' x 95' x 21'6" (200 x 28.9 x 6.5 m)
4 x 6-cylinder MAN-B+W diesel engines via twin screw.

Owned by Scandlines GmbH and operated by Scandlines-Hansa.
Built by Schichau Seebeckswerft, Bremerhaven.

MEDIA (1947) See LAVIA (1986)

MEDIA II (1993)
5440 grt; 940 psrs
150 cars
326' x 60' x 14'6" (98.8 x 18.2 x 4.4 m)
2 x 12-cylinder Lindholmens-Pielstick diesel engines via twin screw.
Passenger-car ferry owned by Regonti Navigation Ltd, Piraeus, and operated by the Hellenic Mediterranean Line.
Built by Kaldnes MV, Tonsberg, for Thoresen Ferries Ltd as the VIKING (1964). Renamed VIKING I (1964 – Thoresen Ferries Ltd.), VIKING VICTORY (1976 – Townsend Thoresen Ferries), SUN BOAT (1983 – Euphoria Navigation Co, Limassol), CARAVAN (1985 – Red Sea Line),

VASMED (1986 – Bluebird Shipping Co, Limassol), EUROPEAN GLORY (1990 – European Seaways) and NEPTUNIA (1991 – Regonti Navigation Ltd, Piraeus).

MEDIATOR (1913) See PERSEUS (1926)

MEDIC (1899) See HEKTORIA (1928)

MEDINA (1893) See MAROMORA (1900)

MEDINA (1911)
12350 grt; 670 psrs
562' x 61' x 24'6" (171.3 x 18.6 x 7.4 m)
2 x quadruple expansion engines via twin screw.
Sank in three hours on 28 April 1917 after being torpedoed at 4.00 pm by the German U-31, three miles (5 km) east-north-east of Start Point, near Plymouth, Devon. Six lives were lost.
Built by Barclay, Curle & Co, Glasgow, for the P&O Line at a cost of £332,377.

MEDINA (1914) See DOULOS (1978)

MEDINA STAR (1999)
13638 grt; 2000 psrs
418 cars or 26 trailers
515' x 64' x 17' (156.1 x 19.4 x 5.1 m)
2 x 18-cylinder Lindholmen-Pielstick diesel engines via twin screw.

Ice-strengthened passenger-car-cargo ferry owned by CaP Enterprises (Marintas) Ltd, Piraeus, and operated by Newshipco SA.
Built by Brodogradiliste Titovo, Kraljevica, for the Stena Line as the STENA SCANDINAVICA (1973). Renamed SAINT KILLIAN (1978 – Irish Continental Lines) and SAINT KILLIAN II (1982 – Irish Ferries).
As this book was going to press, the MEDINA STAR was placed on the sales lists for US$3,900,000.

MEDINA VICTORY (1945) See LAURENTIA (1947)

MEDITERRANEAN (1950)
3844 grt; 1200 psrs
330' x 46' x 23' (100 x 13.9 x 7 m)
8-cylinder triple expansion engine via twin screw.
Broken up for scrap by Sidireboriki SA at Perama Bay. Ex-Typaldos Bros.
Built by Fairfield Shipbuilding & Engineering Co Ltd, Glasgow, for the Canadian Pacific Steamship Co as the PRINCESS CHARLOTTE (1908).

MEDITERRANEAN II (1963) See ELECTRA (1964)

MEDITERRANEAN DOLPHIN (1971)
13345 grt; 107 psrs
541' x 71' x 28'6" (164.8 x 21.6 x 8.7 m)
2 x 6-cylinder Hawthorne Leslie-Doxford diesel engines via twin screw.
Broken up for scrap at Kaohsiung in 1974. Ex-MA Karageorgios, Piraeus.
Built by Vickers-Armstrong Ltd, Newcastle, for Ellerman Lines as the CITY OF DURBAN (1954).

MEDITERRANEAN ISLAND (1971) See MEDITERRANEAN SUN (1976)

MEDITERREANEAN ISLAND (1979) See TERRA (1987)

MEDITERRANEAN SEA (1971) See ALICE (1997)

MEDITERRANEAN SKY (1971) See SITERRANEAN SKY (1987)

MEDITERRANEAN STAR (1982) See TERRA (1987)

MEDITERRANEAN SUN (1976)
13363 grt; 850 psr
350 cars
541' x 71' x 28'6" (164.8 x 21.6 x 8.7 m)
2 x Doxford diesel engines via twin screw.
Broken up for scrap at Kaohsiung in 1980. Ex-Karageorgios Lines.
Built by Vickers-Armstrong Ltd, Newcastle, for Ellerman Lines as the CITY OF PORT ELIZABETH (1952). Renamed MEDITERRANEAN ISLAND (1971 – MA Karageorgios) and MEDITERRANEAN SUN (1976 – MA Karageorgios).

MEDITERRANEAN SUN (1979) See EL TOR (1998)

MEDITERRANEE (1967) See ARCADI (1971)

MEDORA (1915)
5135 grt
410' x 52' x 29' (124.2 x 15.8 x 8.8 m)
D Rowan & Co 3-cylinder triple expansion engine via single screw.
Owned by Canadian Pacific Steamship Co, she sank on 2 May 1918 after being torpedoed by the German U-86 11 miles (18 km) west-south-west of Mull, Scotland.
Built by Russell & Co, Glasgow, for the Palace Shipping Co as the FRANKMOUNT (1912).

MEDOUSA (1997)
7034 grt; 577 psrs
120 cars
454' x 59' x 18' (137.6 x 18 x 5.5 m)
2 x 9-cylinder MAN diesel engines via twin screw.
Passenger-car ferry owned by Mediterranean Cruise Maritime SA.
Built by HWD, Kiel, for Jahre Line as the KRONPRINS HARALD (1961). Renamed HA LONG (1975 – Vietnam Ocean Shipping Co, Saigon), THONG NHAT (1978 – Vietnam Coastal Shipping Co), PANAGIA (1991 – Oriental Glory Maritime, Valetta) and AL SAFA (1996 – Global Union Maritime, San Lorenzo).

MED SEA (1982) See LA PATRIA (2000)

MEDUANA (1922) See KERGUELEN (1945)

MEGALI HELLAS (1920) See BYRON (1924)

MEGA EXPRESS I (2000)
23700 grt; 1756 psrs
550 cars
581' x 81' x 21'8" (176 x 24.5 x 6.6 m)
Wartsila 12-cylinder diesel engines via screw.
Built by Cantieri Navale Fratellia Orlandi for the Tourship Group, Italy.

MEGALONISSOS KRITI (1967)
9226 grt; 977 psrs
466' x 61' x 20' (141.2 x 18.5 x 61 m)
Geared turbine engines via twin screw.
Built by Arsenal de Lorient for Cie General Transatlantique, Paris, as the VILLE DE TUNIS (1952).

MEGANTIC (1909)
14878 grt; 1262 psrs
565' x 67' x 27'6" (172.2 x 20.4 x 8.3 m)
8-cylinder quadruple expansion engines via twin screw.

Broken up for scrap at Osaka in 1933.
Laid down by Harland & Wolff Ltd, Belfast, for the Dominion Line as ALBANY (1908) and completed as MEGANTIC for the White Star Line.

MEGASTANIS (1995) See MEGI (2000)

MEGASTAR ARIES (1995)
3264 grt; 72 psrs
271' x 53' x 11' (82 x 16 x 3.3 m)
2 x 16-cylinder MWM diesel engines via twin screw.
Cruise ship for Star Cruises, Singapore.
Launched by Flender Werft, Lubeck, for the Windsor Cruise Line (Ionian Maritime) as the LADY SARAH (1989). Renamed AURORA II (1991 – New Frontier Cruises, Hamburg).

MEGASTAR ASIA (1999) See SUPERSTAR ARIES (1999)

MEGASTAR CAPRICORN (2000)
4280 grt; 114 psrs
297' x 50' x 12' (90 x 15 x 3.6 m)
2 x 8-cylinder MAN-B+W diesel engines via twin screw.
Cruise ship owned by Hebridean Island Cruises and chartered by Star Cruises until March 2001, when she is renamed HEBRIDEAN SPIRIT and fully operated by Hebridean Island Cruises.
Built by Nuovi Cantieri Apuania Shipyard for Renaissance Cruises Inc as the RENAISSANCE 6 (1991) at a cost of US$25,000,000. Renamed SUN VIVA 2 (1997 – Sun Cruises).

MEGASTAR SAGITTARIUS (2000)
4200 grt; 114 psrs
297' x 50' x 12' (90 x 15 x 3.6 m)
2 x 8-cylinder MAN-B+W diesel engines via twin screw.
Cruise ship owned and operated by Star Cruises, Singapore, but sold for delivery to Cruise West Inc, USA, in April 2001 and scheduled for a name change to SPIRIT OF OCEANUS.
Launched by Nuovi Cantieri Apuania Shipyard for Renaissance Cruises Inc as the cruise ship RENAISSANCE 5 (1991) at a cost of US$28,000,000. Renamed HANSEATIC RENAISSANCE (1991 – Hanseatic Tours, Hamburg), RENAISSANCE 5 (1992 – Renaissance Cruises Inc) and SUN VIVA (1997 – Sun Cruises).

MEGASTAR TAURUS (1995)
3264 grt; 72 psrs
271' x 53' x 11' (82 x 16 x 3.3 m)
2 x 16-cylinder MWM diesel engines via twin screw.
Cruise ship for Star Cruises, Singapore.
Built by Flender Werft, Lubeck, for the Windsor Cruise Line as the LADY DIANA (1989). Renamed LADY DI (1989 – Windsor Cruise Line, Ionian Maritime subsidiary) and AURORA I (1991 – New Frontier Cruises, Hamburg).

MEGI (2000)
9940 grt; 1400 psrs
115 cars + 45 trailers
454' x 61' x 19' (137.5 x 18.4 x 5.8 m)
4 x 9-cylinder Halberstadt diesel engines via twi screw.
Broken up for scrap at Aliaga in 2000 after being laid up for five years in

Eleusis Bay. Ex-Arcadia Lines.
Built by Neptun Shipyards, Rostock, for the German State Railways as the ice-strengthened passenger-car-cargo ferry SASSNITZ (1959). Renamed SILVER PALOMA (1986 – Afroessa Lines SA, Piraeus) and MEGASTANIS (1995 – Arcadia Lines).

MEI ABETO (1967) See MEI ABETO (1984)

MEI ABETO (1984)
12654 grt; 411 psrs
537' x 64' x 28' (163.6 x 19.5 x 8.5 m)
2 x 8-cylinder Mecan-Sulzer diesel engines via twin screw.
Broken up as a pilgrim ship for scrap at Chittagong in 1984. Ex-PT Perusahaan Pelajaran Arafat, Djakarta.
Built by Chantiers et Ateliers de France, St Nazaire, for Chargeurs Reunis, Le Havre, as the LOUIS LUMIERE (1952). Renamed MEI ABETO (1967 – Cia de Navegacao Abeto) and ABETO (1977 – PT Perusahaan Pelajaran Arafat).

MELANESIEN (1958)
9585 grt; 96 psrs
506' x 60' x 28' (154.2 x 18.3 x 8.5 m)
2 x 6-cylinder Sulzer diesel engines via twin screw.
Broken up for scrap at Genoa in 1963. Ex-Messageries Maritimes.
Built by De Schelde NV, Vlissingen, for Royal Rotterdam Lines as the INDRAPOERA (1926). Renamed ASCUNCION (1956 – Providencia Shipping Co, Panama) and BIANCA C (1957 – Costa Line).

MELINA (1964)
6996 grt; 900 psrs
439' x 59' x 24' (133 x 17.9 x 7.3 m)
8-cylinder MAN diesel engine via single screw.
Broken up for scrap at Kaohsiung in 1969. Ex-Meldaf Shipping Co, Greece.
Built by Bremer Vulkan, Vegesack, for the Woermann Line as the cargo ship KAMERUN (1939). Renamed GOYA (1947 – Johann Ludwig Mowinckels Rederi) which acted as a refugee transport after World War Two, REINA (1961 – TJ Skogland), SVANHOLM (1962 – Trygve Matland Jnr) and HILDE (1963 – Skibs AS Hilde).

MELINA (1968)
3920 grt; 342 psrs
373' x 49' x 23' (113 x 14.8 x 7 m)
2 x DRG turbine engines via single screw.
Broken up for scrap at Perama Bay in 1980, but her engines were transferred to the DELOS (1969) belonging to Ionian Lines. Ex-Efthymiadis Lines, Piraeus.
Built by Ateliers et Chantiers de Bretagne, Nantes, for Paquet Lines as the AZROV (1951).

MELITA (1918) See LIGURIA (1935)

MELMA (1923) See DUMANA (1923)

MELODY (1979)
5551 grt; 188 psrs
372' x 51' x 24' (112.7 x 15.6 x 7.3 m)
3 x Parsons DRG turbine engines via single screw.
Owned by Athens Marine, she was declared a total constructive loss after catching fire during repairs at Keratsini, Greece, and being beached in the Piraeus roads on 6 July 1990.
Built by Swan Hunter & Wigham Richardson Ltd, Newcastle, for Cie de Navigation Mixte, Marseilles, as the ferry DJEBEL-DIRA (1948). Renamed PHOENIX (1970 – Spiros Billinis, Piraeus).

MELODY (1988) See AL QAMAR (1999)

MELODY (1997)
35143 grt; 1600 psrs

672' x 90' x 25'6" (204.2 x 27.3 x 7.8 m)
2 x 10-cylinder Fiat diesel engines via twin screw.
Cruise ship owned by Mediterranean Shipping Cruises after acquisition for US$75,000,000.
Built by CNIM, La Seyne, for Home Lines as the ATLANTIC (1982) at a cost of US$100,000,000. Renamed STARSHIP ATLANTIC (1988 – Premier Cruise Line).

MELOODIA (1996)
17955 grt; 1340 psrs
480 cars or 70 cars + 45 trailers
452' x 80' x 18' (137 x 24.2 x 5.5 m)
4 x 8-cylinder MAN diesel engines via twin screw.

Ice-strengthened cruise ship owned by the Estonian Shipping Co and chartered to Hansatee (associated with Tallink) by Est Line.
Built by Jos L Meyer, Papenburg, for the Viking Line as the DIANA II (1979). Renamed but never entered service as VIRONIA (1994 – Est Line) and MARE BALTICUM (1994 – Est Line).

MEMED ABACHIDZE (1998) See MILLENNIUM EXPRESS II (2000)

MENDI (1905)
4200 grt; 800 psrs
370' x 46' x 23'3" (112.2 x 13.9 x 7.1 m)
A Stephen & Sons 3-cylinder triple expansion engine via single screw.
Sank on 21 February 1917, with the loss of 655 lives, off St Catherine's Point after colliding with the Royal Mail Line's 11484 grt passenger liner DARRO.
Built by Alex, Stephen & Sons, Glasgow, for British & African Steamship Co as a passenger liner.

MENDOZA (1905) See VENEZUELA (1922)

MENDOZA (1947)
7722 grt
439' x 62' x 34'5" (133 x 18.8 x 10.5 m)
2 x Westinghouse DRG turbine engines via single screw.
Broken up for scrap as a cargo ship at Campana in 1972. Ex-Dodero Line.
Built by Bethlehem-Fairchild, Baltimore, for the US Shipping Administration as the WILLIAM AND MARY VICTORY (1945).

MENELAUS (1923)
10278 grt
496' x 62' x 39'6" depth (150.3 x 19.1 x 12 m)
4 x Northeast Marine Engineering DRG turbine engines via twin screw.
Broken up for scrap at Dalmuir in 1952.
Built by Caledon Shipbuilding & Engineering Co Ltd, Dundee, for the Ocean Steamship Co Ltd.

MERAC, USS (AF-21) (1942) See SINALOA (1958)

MERCANDIA I (1989) See ANJA 11 (1998)

MERCANDIA II (1989) See BAIA DE TOGOS DOS SANTOS (1995)

MERCANDIA III (1989) See DVD No. III (1995)

MERCANDIA IV (1989)
4296 grt; 300 psrs
316' x 50' x 12' (95.8 x 15 x 3.6 m)
10 x 6-cylinder Cummins diesel engines via twin screw. + twin bow screw.

Passenger ferry owned and operated by HH-Ferries AS, Denmark.
Built by Northeast Shipbuilders, Southwick, for Per Henriksen as the SUPERFLEX NOVEMBER (1989).

MERCANDIA V (1990) See DVD No. IV (1995)

MERCANDIA VI (1990) See DVD No. I (1999)

MERCANDIA VII (1990) See DVD No. II (1999)

MERCANDIA VIII (1993)
4296 grt; 300 psrs
200 cars or 85 cars + 16 trailers
316' x 56' x 12' (95.8 x 17 x 3.6 m)
10 x 6-cylinder Cummins diesel engines via twin screw. + twin bow screw.

Passenger-car-cargo ferry owned and operated by HH Ferries, Denmark.
Built by Northeast Shipbuilding, Southwick, for Superflex Ships as the SUPERFLEX BRAVO (1987). Renamed SVEA SCARLETT (1993 – International Shipping Partners AS).

MERCANDIAN ADMIRAL (1988) See HEIMDAL (1982)

MERCANDIAN ADMIRAL II (1983) See HEIMDAL (1982)

MERCANDIAN GOVERNOR (1982) See FRIGGA (1999)

MERCANDIAN PRESIDENT (1982) See FENJA (1999)

MERCANTILE VICTORY (1963)
8190 grt; 100 psrs
455' x 62' x 28' (135.8 x 18.8 x 8.5 m)
Turbine engine via single screw.
Broken up for scrap at Castellon in 1965. Ex-Salvador Investment Co.
Built by the Californian Shipbuilding Corporation, Los Angeles, for the US Shipping Board as the ATCHISON VICTORY (1944). Renamed MOHAMMED ALI EL KEBIR (1947 – Renfrew Navigation Co) and SALAH EL DIN (1960 – United Arab Marine Co).

MERCATOR ONE (1976) See ALEX ANDER (1983)

MERCURI-3 (1995) See AKADEMIK M. TOPCHUBASHOV (1995)

MERCURY (1997)
76522 grt; 1870 psrs
866' x 106' x 25'6" (262.4 x 32 x 7.8 m)
4 x 6-cylinder MAN-B+W diesel engines via twin screw.

Cruise ship owned by Royal Caribbean International and operated by Celebrity Cruises.
Built by Meyer Werft, Papenburg, at a cost of US$317,000,000.

MERCURY (1998) See THE MERCURY (1998)

MERCURY, USS (1917)
10984 grt; 2373 psrs
548' x 60' x 34'6" depth (167.1 x 18.3 x 10.5 m)
2 x 4-cylinder Blohm & Voss quadruple expansion engines via twin screw.
Broken up for scrap by Boston Iron & Metals Co, Boston, in 1924. Ex-US Navy.
Built by Blohm & Voss, Hamburg, for North German Lloyd as the BARBAROSSA (1897).

MERCURY-1 (1995)
11450 grt; 81 psrs
509' x 60' x 27'4" (154.3 x 18.3 x 8.3 m)
2 x 6-cylinder B+W diesel engines via twin screw.
Passenger ferry built by Uljanik, Pula, for the Caspian Shipping Co, Baki, as the SOVIETSKAYA GRUZIYA (1986).

MERCURY 3 (1995) See AKADEMIK M. TOPCHUBASHOV (1995)

MERCURY BAY (1978)
50 psrs
Broken up for scrap in 1988
Built in Rotterdam as the passenger-cargo ship STRAAT MAKASTAR (1951).

MERCURY LAKE (1977) See UNITED VANTAGE (1978)

MERCY, USS (AH-4) (1917)
6391 grt; 280 psrs
413' x 50' x 17'5" (137.7 x 16.7 x 5.8 m)
W Cramp 6-cylinder triple expansion engines via twin screw.
Broken up for scrap at Baltimore USA in 1939.
Built by W Cramp & Sons Shipbuilding & Engineering Co, Philadelphia, Pennsylvania, for New York & Cuba Mail Steamship Co as the SARATOGA (1907).

MERCY (1943) See EMPIRE STATE III (1956)

MERENGUE EXPRESS (1980) See HORNBEAM (1992)

MERIDA (1906)
6207 grt; 261 psrs
416' x 50' x 30' depth (126 x 15.2 x 10 m)
W Cramp 6-cylinder triple expansion engines via twin screw.
Sank in five hours on 12 May 1911 after being rammed by the freighter ADMIRAL FARRAGUT at 12.30 am in dense fog, 50 miles (83 km) north-east of Cape Charles, Vancouver.
Built by William Cramp & Sons, Philadelphia, Pennsylvania, for New York & Cuba Mail Steamship Co.

MERIDIAN (1962)
4404 grt; 154 psrs
344' x 48' x 20' (115.3 x 16 x 6.7 m)
2 x 8-cylinder Gorlitzer diesel engines via single screw.
Built by Neptun Werft, Rostock, for the Russian government as a training ship.

MERIDIAN (1990) See SUN VISTA (1997)

MERION (1902) See TIGER, HMS (1914)

MERKARA (1914)
8228 grt; 129 psrs
450' x 58' x 33'3" depth (136.4 x 17.6 x 11.1 m)
Barclay Curle triple expansion engines via twin screw.
Broken up for scrap in Italy in 1932 after a UK firm had initially won the tender for £4,000, but sold the contract to the Italians.
Built by C Connell & Co Ltd, Glasgow, for the British India Steam Navigation Co.

MERKUR (1934)
5952 grt; 105 psrs
411' x 52' x 21'8" (125.3 x 15.8 x 7.3 m)
2 x 6-cylinder Krupp diesel engines via twin screw.
Broken up for scrap at Osaka in 1954. Ex-Burns Philp & Co Ltd, Sydney.
Built by Fred Krupp Shipyards, Kiel, for Ozean Linie, Flensburg, as the RIO BRAVO (1924).

MERMOZ (1970) See SERENADE (1999)

MERSEY VIKING (1997)
21856 grt; 340 psrs
100 cars + 164 trailers
614' x 86' x 18'6" (186 x 26 x 5.6 m)
2 x 8-cylinder Wartsila diesel engines via twin screw.
Passenger-car-cargo RoRo ferry operating for Norse-Irish Ferries.
Built by Cantieri Visentini Francesco & Co, Donada, at a cost of £90,000,000.

MERZARIO ESPANIA (1978) See PRIDE OF FLANDERS (1992)

MERZARIO HISPANIA (1979) See PRIDE OF FLANDERS (1992)

MERZARIO IONIA (1980) See CHONG MING DAO (1998)

MESSAPIA (1952) See KAWTHER (1975)

METAGAMA (1915)
12420 grt; 1654 psrs
520' x 64' x 27'7" (157.6 x 19.4 x 8.4 m)
Barclay Curle 8-cylinder quadruple expansion engines via twin screw.
Broken up for scrap by PW McLennan Ltd at Barrow-in-Furness in 1934.
Built by Barclay, Curle & Co, Glasgow, for the Canadian Pacific Line.

METAPAN (1909)
4937 grt; 103 psrs
379' x 50' x 25' (114.8 x 15.2 x 7.6 m)
Triple expansion engine via single screw.
Sank on 1 October 1943 when she was torpedoed in the eastern Mediterranean.
Built by Workman, Clark & Co, Belfast, for the United Fruit Steamship Co.

METAPEDIA (1921) See MONTCLARE, HMS (1942)

METEOR (1904)
3613 grt; 283 psrs
329' x 44' x 26'5" depth (99.7 x 13.3 x 8 m)
Blohm & Voss 6-cylinder triple expansion engines via twin screw.
Built by Blohm & Voss, Hamburg, for the Hamburg-America Line.

METEOR (1954) See NEPTUNE (1972)

METHVEN (1917) See PERSEUS (1926)

METTE MO (1966) See ISTRA (1992)

METTE MO (1996) See BANASA (1997)

METTE MOLS (1975) See BANASA (1997)

METTE MOLS (1996)
14221 grt; 616 psrs
344 cars or 65 trailers
450' x 79' x 20' (136.4 x 24 x 6.1 m)
2 x 9-cylinder MAN-B+W diesel engines via twin screw.
Passenger-car-cargo ferry owned and operated by Mols Linien.
Built by Orskov Stalskipbvaerft, Frederikshaven.

MEXICO (1900)
4173 grt
380' x 45' x 29'2" (115.2 x 13.6 x 8.8 m)
Palmer 3-cylinder triple expansion engine via single screw.
Abandoned as a total loss when she was wrecked on 7 July 1901 on rocks six miles (10 km) south of Viano do Castelo, Portugal.
Built by Palmer's Co, Newcastle, for the Sun Shipping Co Ltd as the TRENTHAM HALL (1875).

MEXICO (1906) See TRADEWIND (1954)

MEXICO (1905)
4885 grt; 836 psrs
354' x 48' x 27'3" depth (108 x 14.5 x 8.3 m)
Forges et Chantiers de la Mediterranee 3-cylinder triple expansion engine via single screw.
Broken up for scrap in 1925.
Built by Forges et Chantiers de la Mediterranee, Havre, for the French Line.

MEXICO (1938) See ISTANBUL (1947)

MEXICO CITY (1913)
5078 grt; 50 psrs
400' x 48' x 20' (121.9 x 14.5 x 6.1 m)
Quadruple expansion engine via single screw.
Owned by Mexico City Steamship Co Ltd, she sank on 5 February 1918 after being torpedoed by the German U-101 15 miles (25 km) off South Stack, near Holyhead, Wales. Twenty-nine lives were lost.
Built by the Doxford & Sunderland Shipbuilding Co for the Blue Anchor Line (Wilhelm Lund), London, as the NARRUNG (1896).

MEXICO MARU (1910)
5785 grt
408' x 50' x 26' (123.6 x 15.2 x 7.9 m)
Mitsibishi 6-cylinder triple expansion engines via twin screw.
Sank on 29 August 1944 after being torpedoed by the USS JACK in the Celebes Sea.
Built by Mitsubishi Dockyard, Nagasaki, for OSK.

MEXIQUE (1928)
12220 grt; 536 psrs
563' x 54' x 24' (170.6 x 16.4 x 7.3 m)
2 x reciprocating engines via quadruple screw.
Owned by the French Line, she sank on 19 June 1940 when she hit a mine laid in the Geronde Estuary off Le Verdon, France.
Laid down by Chantiers et Ateliers de Provence, Port de Bouc, for the French Line as the ILE DE CUBA (1914) and completed as the LA FAYETTE (1915).

MIAMI (1966) See BONAIRE STAR (1975)

MICHELANGELO (1965)
45911 grt; 1775 psrs
906' x 99' x 34' (276.2 x 30.1 x 10.3 m)
4 x DRG turbine engines via twin screw.
Broken up for scrap at Gadani Beach, Karachi, in 1992 after the ship had suffered severe war damage during the Iraq–Iran war. She had been permanently berthed as an Iranian Navy dormitory ship at Bandar Abbas, following her purchase by the Iranian government in 1976 for US$9,000,000.
Built by Ansaldo, Sestri Ponente, for the Italian Line.

MICHIGAN (1887) See COLLINGWOOD, HMS (1914)

MICHIGAN (1890) See GREAT CANTON (1923)

MICHIGAN (1899) See IRISHMAN (1900)

MIDHAT PACHA (1911)
4450 grt; 150 psrs
370' x 46' x 22' (112.1 x 13.9 x 6.7 m)
Richardson, Westgarth 6-cylinder triple expansion engine via single screw.
While operating for the Turkish government as a Black Sea naval transport, she sank on 7 November 1914, near Eregli, after an attack by a group of Russian warships patrolling the blockaded harbour and sea roads of Istanbul.
Built by Sir Raylton Dixon & Co Ltd, Middlesbrough, for the Imperial Direct Line as the PORT ROYAL (1901).

MIDNATSOL (1982)
6167 grt; 410 psrs
40 cars
358' x 54' x 15' (108.6 x 16.5 x 4.5 m)
2 x 16-cylinder Bergens-Normo diesel engines via twin screw.

Passenger-car ferry owned and operated by Troms Fylkes DS AS as part of the Hurtigurten Group.
Built by Ulstein Hatlo, Ulsteinvik.

MIDNIGHT MERCHANT (2000)
22152 grt; 250 psrs
594' x 80' x 21'6" (180 x 24.3 x 6.5 m)
4 x 9-cylinder Wartsila diesel engines via twin screw.
Owned by Merchant Ferries (a Cenargo International Ltd subsidiary) and chartered to the Norfolk Line, UK.
Built by Astilleros Espanoles, Seville.

MIDNIGHT SUN (1893) See MIDNIGHT SUN (1901)

MIDNIGHT SUN (1901)
3020 grt; 714 psrs
352' x 39' x 31'2" depth (106.7 x 11.9 x 9.5 m)
Wallsend Slipway 3-cylinder triple expansion engine via single screw.
Broken up for scrap as a cruise ship on the River Tyne in 1912. Ex-Armstrong, Mitchell & Co.
Built by Caird & Co, Greenock, for North German Lloyd as the GENERAL WERDER (1874). Renamed MIDNIGHT SUN (1893 – Armstrong, Mitchell & Co) and PRINCESS OF WALES (1899 – British government).

MIDZUHO MARU (1926) See MIZUHO MARU (1926)

MIGUEL HERNANDEZ (1995)
4296 grt; 300 psrs
85 cars + 16 trailers or 200 cars
316' x 56' x 12' (95.8 x 17 x 3.6 m)
10 x 6-cylinder Cummins diesel engines via quadruple screw.
Passenger-car-cargo ferry owned and operated by Islena de Navagacion SA.
Built by Northeast Shipbuilding, Southwick, for Superflex Ships as the SUPERFLEX HOTEL (1980). Renamed FREJA SCARLETT (1993 – International Shipping Partners Inc).

MIIKE MARU (1941)
11738 grt; 236 psrs
length 535' x beam 66' (162.1 x 20 m)
2 x diesel engines via twin screw.
Sank on 29 April 1944 after being torpedoed two days earlier by the USS TRIGGER south-west of Yap, in the Caroline Islands group.
Launched on 12 April 1941 by Mitsubishi Heavy Industries, Nagasaki, as the passenger liner MISHIMA MARU (1941) and completed on 30 September 1941 as the troopship MIIKE MARU.

MIKHAIL BULGAKOV (1989)
9805 grt; 412 psrs
440' x 70' x 17' (133.3 x 21.1 x 5.3 m)
4 x 6-cylinder Sulzer diesel engines via twin screw.
Cruise ship converted into a floating eye surgery in Russia.
Built by Stocznia Szczecinska Shipyard, Poland, for the Russian government as the passenger ferry MIKHAIL SUSLOV (1983).

MIKHAIL KALININ (1958)
5243 grt; 333 psrs
401' x 52' x 17' (121.5 x 15.8 x 5.2 m)
2 x 6-cylinder MAN diesel engines via twin screw.
Broken up for scrap in India in 1994.
Built by Mathias-Thesen Werft, Wismar, for the Baltic Shipping Co, St Petersburg, as an ice-strengthened cruise ship.

MIKHAIL LERMONTOV (1972)
20352 grt; 750 psrs
578' x 77' x 26' (176.2 x 23.5 x 7.9 m)
2 x 7-cylinder Sulzer diesel engines via twin screw.
Owned and operated by the Baltic Shipping Co.
Sank on 16 February 1986 in 100 feet (30 m) of water as her captain, V Vorobyev, vainly attempted to beach the ship. Her hull had been split open by a submerged rock while under the control of the Picton, New Zealand, harbour pilot, Captain Don Jamison. The ship had listed 12 degrees before wallowing in a position off Port Gore on the extreme northern tip of New Zealand's South Island. One life was lost. Legal controversy raged over the area of responsibility between the ship's captain and the pilot regarding the decision

taken to pass on the inside passage of a rock pinnacle protruding from some very difficult waters, along the southern edge of the notorious Cook Strait. A finding was eventually handed down, laying full responsibility with the pilot who was in sole command on the bridge while the captain was in his cabin. Built by Mathias-Thesen Werft, Wismar, for the Baltic Shipping Co.

MIKHAIL LOMONOSOV (1945)
4636 grt; 93 psrs
370' x 45' x 26'8" depth (112.1 x 13.6 x 8.1 m)
4-cylinder quadruple expansion engine via single screw.
Owned by the Russian government as a World War Two prize.
Built by AG Neptun, Rostock, for the Hamburg-America Line as the PRINZ SIGISMUND (1902). Renamed GENERAL W. C. GORGAS (1945 – US Army).

MIKHAIL LOMONOSOV (1957) See VETERAN MORYA (1994)

MIKHAIL SHOLOKOV (1986)
12798 grt; 350 psrs
150 cars
462' x 69' x 18'6" (140 x 21 x 5.6 m)
4 x 6-cylinder Sulzer diesel engines via twin screw.
Cruise ferry operated by the Far East Shipping Co, Vladivostok.
Built by Adolph Warski Shipyards, Szczecin, for the Far East Shipping Co.

MIKHAIL SUSLOV (1983) See MIKHAIL BULGAKOV (1989)

MIKHAIL URITZKIJ (1959) See M. URITZKIJ (1959)

MIKKE MOLS (1969) See MOBY ALE (1997)

MILANO (1900) See TENEDOS (1903)

MILDA (1993) See LABURNAM (1993)

MILENA (1990)
9856 grt; 2300 psrs
388' x 66' x 14'6" (117.5 x 20 x 4.4 m)
4 x 16-cylinder Kawasaki diesel engines via twin screw.
Passenger ferry owned by Patos, Greece and operated by GA Ferries.
Built by Hayashikane Zosen, Shimonoseki for KK Diamond Ferry, Oita as the FERRY GOLD (1970).

MILLENNIUM I (2000)
90228 grt; 2524 psrs
965' x 106' x 26' (292.4 x 32 x 7.9 m)
2 x General Electric gas-turbines via twin Mermaid azimuthing screw.

Cruise ship operated by Celebrity Cruises.
Built by Chantiers de l'Atlantique, St Nazaire, for Celebrity Cruises at a cost of US$376,600,000.

MILLENNIUM EXPRESS (2000)
5304 grt; 982 psrs
526' x 71' x 20' (159.5 x 21.5 x 6.2 m)
2 x 18-cylinder MAN diesel engines via twin screw.
Passenger ferry owned and operated by Access Ferries.
Built by Nippon Kokan KK, Tokyo, as the TAKACHIHO MARU (1975). Renamed OCEAN SKY (1990 – Adriatic Lines) and HIND (1997 – Valpores Ultramar SS, Panama).

MILLENNIUM EXPRESS II (2000)
6141 grt; 1300 psrs
350 cars + 65 TEUs
442' x 72' x 16' (134 x 21.8 x 4.8 m)
2 x 12-cylinder Pielstick diesel engines via twin screw.
Passenger-car ferry owned and operated by Access Ferries.
Built by Chantiers et Ateliers de Bretagne, Nantes, for the General Steam Navigation Co Ltd, London, as the DRAGON (1967). Renamed IONIC FERRY (1986 – P&O European Ferries), VISCOUNTESS M (1992 – Marlines), CHARM M (1995 – Marlines) and MEMED ABACHIDZE (1998 – Superferries, London).

MILLENNIUM QUEEN (1999) See CORAL PRINCESS (2000)

MILOS EXPRESS (1988) See EXPRESS MILOS (2000)

MILTIADES (1903) See ORCANA (1922)

MILWAUKEE (1903)
7317 grt
470' x 56' x 32' (142.4 x 17 x 9.7 m)
Northeast Marine Engineering 3-cylinder triple expansion engine via single screw.
Sank on 31 August 1918 with one life lost after an attack by the German U-105 200 miles (333 km) south-west of Fastnet.
Launched by CS Swan & Hunter, Wallsend, on 7 November 1896 for Beaver Line, but not completed until 1903.

MILWAUKEE (1929) See EMPIRE WAVENEY (1945)

MILWAUKEE CLIPPER (1941) See MILWAUKEE CLIPPER (1990)

MILWAUKEE CLIPPER (1990)
4272 grt; 350 psrs
363' x 45' x 25' (110 x 13.8 x 7.6 m)
4 x Detroit Shipbuilding Co quadruple expansion steam engine via single screw.
Owned by the Hammond Port Authority, she has been berthed since 1988 at the former train ferry dock in Muskegon, Michigan, where she is cared for by the Great Lakes Clipper Preservation Association.
Built by American Shipbuilding Co, Cleveland, Ohio, for the Anchor Line (Erie & Western Transportation Co) as the passenger-cargo ship JUNIATA (1905). Renamed MILWAUKEE CLIPPER (1941 – Wisconsin & Michigan Co) and CLIPPER (1977 – Illinois Steamship Co, Chicago).

MIMIKA L (1969) See ALKYON (1978)

MIMITSU MARU (1974) See MARY QUEEN OF PEACE (1997)

MINERVA (1996)
12331 grt; 330 psrs
439' x 66' x 17' (133 x 20 x 5.2 m)
2 x 8-cylinder Pielstick diesel engines via twin screw.
Cruise ship owned by V-Ships, Monaco, and chartered to Swan Hellenic for cruising.
Laid down by the Okean Shipyard, Nikolayev, as the minesweeper-research ship OKEAN (1991) and completed by the Mariotti Shipyard, Genoa, as the MINERVA.

MIN FUNG (1980) See NAN HU (1983)

MINGHUA (1973) See HAI SHANG SHI JIE (1998)

MING YI (1979) See TONG HU (1992)

MINHO (1896) See MONTREAL (1905)

MINIOTA (1916)
4928 grt
420' x 55' x 24' (127.3 x 16.7 x 7.3 m)
3-cylinder triple expansion engine via single screw.
Owned by the Canadian Pacific Steamship Co, she lost three lives when she sank on 31 August 1917 after being torpedoed by the German U-62 30 miles (50 km) south-east of Start Point, UK.
Built by W Gray & Co, West Hartlepool, for the London & Northern Steamship Co as the HACKNESS (1913).

MINISEA (1977) See BALTIC STAR (1979)

MIN NAN (1993) See SHENG SHENG (1998)

MINNEAPOLIS (1900)
13401 grt; 228 psrs
601' x 66' x 39'7" depth (182.1 x 20 x 12 m)
Harland & Wolff 8-cylinder quadruple expansion engines via twin screw.
Sank on 23 March 1916, with 12 lives lost, after being torpedoed by the German U-35 200 miles (333 km) north-east of Malta.
Built by Harland & Wolff Ltd, Belfast, for the Atlantic Transport Line, Belfast.

MINNEDOSA (1918) See PIEMONTE (1935)

MINNEFLORA (1904) See PANAMANIAN (1940)

MINNEHAHA (1900)
13403 grt; 228 psrs
601' x 66' x 39'5" depth (182.1 x 20 x 12 m)
Harland & Wolff 8-cylinder quadruple expansion engine via twin screw.
Sank in four minutes, taking 42 lives with her, on 7 September 1917 after being torpedoed by the German U-48 12 miles off Fastnet.
Built by Harland & Wolff Ltd, Belfast, for the Atlantic Transport Line, Belfast.

MINNEKAHDA (1904) See TAGUS (1949)

MINNEKAHDA (1917)
17281 grt; 750 psrs
621' x 66' x 47'3" depth (188.2 x 20 x 14.3 m)
Harland & Wolff combination turbines and 8-cylinder triple expansion engines via triple screw.
Broken up at Dalmuir in 1936 after a five-year period laid up in New York.
Laid down in 1914 by Harland & Wolff Ltd, Belfast, as a cargo ship, but completed as a conversion into a passenger liner in 1919 for the Atlantic Transport Line, Belfast.

MINNESOTA (1904) See MINNESOTA (1919)

MINNESOTA (1919)
20718 grt; 2644 psrs
622' x 73' x 41'5" depth (188.5 x 22.1 x 12.6 m)
Midvale Steel Co 6-cylinder steam engines via twin screw.
Broken up for scrap as a cargo ship at Wilhelmshaven in 1924. Ex-Atlantic Transport Line, Belfast.
Built by Eastern Shipbuilding Co, New London, Connecticut, for the Great Northern Steamship Co as the passenger liner MINNESOTA (1904) at a cost of US$5,000,000. Renamed TROY, USS (1919 – US Navy), but reverted to her original name to avoid confusion with a major US battleship of the same name.

MINNESOTA (1927)
11667 grt; 1162 psrs
561' x 60' x 38'2" depth (170 x 18.2 x 11.6 m)
J Brown 8-cylinder quadruple expansion engines via twin screw.
Broken up for scrap by TW Ward Co Ltd at Inverkeithing in 1930. Ex-Atlantic Transport Line.
Built by John Brown & Co Ltd, Clydebank, for the Red Star Line as the ZEELAND (1901). Renamed NORTHLAND (1915 – British Ministry of War Transport) and ZEELAND (1920 – Red Star Line).

MINNETONKA (1901)
13398 grt; 250 psrs
601' x 66' x 39'7" depth (182.1 x 24.2 x 12 m)
Harland & Wolff 8-cylinder quadruple expansion engine via twin screw.
Sank on 31 January 1918, with four lives lost, after being torpedoed by the German U-64 40 miles (66 km) north-east of Malta.
Built by Harland & Wolff Ltd, Belfast, for the Atlantic Transport Line, Belfast.

MINNETONKA (1924)
21998 grt; 369 psrs
626' x 80' x 36' (187.8 x 20 m)
Brown-Curtis SRG quadruple expansion engines via twin.
Broken up for scrap at Barrow-in-Furness in 1934 for a tender figure of £35,000.
Built by Harland & Wolff Ltd, Belfast, for the Atlantic Transport Line, Belfast.

MINNEWASKA (1902) See ARABIC (1903)

MINNEWASKA (1909)
14317 grt; 326 psrs
601' x 65' x 39'6" (182.1 x 19.7 x 12 m)
Harland & Wolff quadruple expansion engine via twin screw.
Broken up in 1918 where she beached herself in Soudhas Bay, Mundros, in the Aegean Sea. She had struck a mine on 29 November 1916 laid by the German U-23.
Built by Harland & Wolff Ltd, Belfast, for the Atlantic Transport Line, Belfast.

MINNEWASKA (1923)
21716 grt; 369 psrs
626' x 80' x 37' (189.7 x 24.2 x 11.2 m)
Brown-Curtis SRG turbine engines via twin screw.
Broken up for scrap by Douglas & Ramsey at Glasgow in 1934 for a tender figure of £35,000.
Built by Harland & Wolff Ltd, Belfast, for the Atlantic Transport Line, Belfast.

MINOAN PRINCE (1995)
7735 grt; 805 psrs
407' x 56' x 19' (123.3 x 17 x 5.8 m)
2 x 8-cylinder Pielstick diesel engines via single screw.
Passenger ferry owned and operated by Minoan Lines.
Built by Usuki Tekkosho, Saiki, for Kansai Kisen KK, Kobe, as the cargo ferry WAKASHIO MARU (1973). Renamed as the passenger-cargo ferry SUNFLOWER 7 (1979 – Kansai Kosen KK, Osaka), APOLLON (1991 – Epirotiki Cruise Lines) and PRINCE (1995 – Minoan Lines).

MINOS (1964)
9517 grt; 1000 psrs
537' x 63' x 16' (162.5 x 19.2 x 4.9 m)
6-cylinder MAN diesel engine via single screw.
Broken up for scrap in Spain in 1984 as a passenger-car ferry. Ex-Minoan Lines, Greece.
Built by Kockums, Malmo, for the Wallenius Group, Sweden, as the oil tanker SOYA-MARGARETA (1952).

MINOTAUROS (1966)
9260 grt; 96 psrs
492' x 70' x 27' (149.1 x 21.2 x 8.2 m)
Turbine engine via single screw.
Broken up for scrap at Kaohsiung in 1970. Ex-Ganderos del Mar SA.
Built by Newport News Shipbuilding & Drydock Co, Newport News, Virginia, for the American President Line as the PRESIDENT POLK (1941). Renamed PRESIDENT POLK, USS (AP-104) (1943 – US Navy) and the cattle carrier GAUCHO MARTIN FIERRO (1965 – Ganderos del Mar SA).

MINSK (1909)
3258 grt; 870 psrs
330' x 42' x 29'9" depth (100 x 12.7 x 9.1 m)
Scott & Co 2-cylinder compound engine via single screw.
Broken up for scrap in 1910. Ex-Russian government.
Built by Scotts Shipbuilding Co, Greenock, for the Thingvalla Line, Copenhagen, as the HEKLA (1884). Renamed EDUARD REGEL (1905 – Northern Steamship Co Ltd, Denmark).

MIN ZHUI (1980)
4071 grt; 1500 psrs
78 cars
322' x 52' x 15' (97.6 x 15.7 x 4.5 m)
B+W 8-cylinder diesel engine via single screw.

Passenger ferry operated by the China Ocean Shipping Company.
Built by Burmeister & Wain, Copenhagen, for Bornholms as the BORNHOLM (1961).

MIOWERA (1892) See MAITAI (1909)

MIR (1998)
8039 grt; 673 psrs
120 cars + 2 coaches
422' x 61' x 17' (127.8 x 18.6 x 5.2 m)
2 x 7-cylinder Fiat diesel engines via twin screw.
Passenger-ferry owned and operated by Stability Line Inc, but laid up each year from 1989 to 1998 for an average period of six months.
Built by John Cockerill Shipyards, Hoboken, Belgium, for Somerfin Passenger Lines, Haifa, as the BILU (1964). Renamed DAN (1967 – Kavim Hevrat Oniyot BM, Haifa), EL GRECO (1976), SAUDI MOON (1976), GOLDEN SKY (1979) and VERGINA (1979 – Stability Lines).

MIRIAM B (1967)
5091 grt; 152 psrs
378' x 50' x 22' (114.5 x 15.2 x 6.7 m)
Stork-Werkspoor 7-cylinder diesel engine via single screw.
Broken up for scrap in 1974.
Built by Van der Giessen du Noord, Krimpen, as the PERICLES (1938). Renamed ORANJESTAD (1950 – Koninkl Nederlandsche Stoom Maats).

MISHIMA MARU (1908)
7905 grt
465' x 56' x 27' (140.9 x 17 x 8.2 m)
Kawasaki 6-cylinder triple expansion engines via twin screw.
Broken up for scrap in 1934.
Built by Kawasaki Dockyard, Kobe, for NYK, Japan.

MISHIMA MARU (1941) See MIIKE MARU (1941)

MISR (1947)
7400 grt; 1450 psrs
417' x 60' x 27' (127.1 x 18.2 x 8.2 m)
Geared turbine engine via single screw.
Broken up as a pilgrim ship for scrap by Millwala Sons Ltd at Gadani Beach, Karachi, in 1982. Ex-United Arab Maritime Co.
Built by Consolidated Steel Corporation, Wilmington California, for the US Maritime Commission as the Class C1-type cargo ship CAPE St ROQUE (1943). Renamed EMPIRE MACE (1944 – British Ministry of War Transport), GALTEE MORE, HMS (1944 – British Royal Navy) and EMPIRE MACE (1946 – British Ministry of Transport).

MISSANABIE (1915)
12469 grt; 1654 psrs
500' x 64' x 38' (152.5 x 19.6 x 11.5 m)
8-cylinder quadruple expansion engines via twin screw.
Sank on 9 September 1918, with the loss of 45 lives, after being torpedoed by the German U-87 52 miles (87 km) south-east of Daunts Rock, near Kinsale, Ireland.
Built by Barclay, Curle & Co, Glasgow, for the Canadian Pacific Railway Co.

MISSION VIKING (1974)
10645 grt; 2000 psrs
523' x 71' x 26' (159.3 x 21.5 x 7.9 m)

2 x Westinghouse DRG turbine engines via single screw.
Broken up as a drilling barge in 1987. Ex-Avondale Shipyards Inc, New York. Built by Kaiser Corporation, Richmond, California, for the US Maritime Commission as the Class C4-S-A1 troop transport GENERAL M. B. STEWART, USAT (1947 – US Army). Reclassified as the GENERAL M. B. STEWART, USNS (T-AP-140) (1950 – US Navy) which acted as a refugee transport ship after World War Two. Renamed as a cargo ship ALBANY (1968 – Albany River Transport, New York).

MISSISSIPPI (1902) See SAMLAND (1913)

MISSOURI (1965) See LINNET (1977)

MISSOURIAN (1922) See KING ABDELAZIZ (1964)

MISTRAL (1997)
20220 grt; 2286 psrs
700 cars + 43 trailers
479' x 77' x 21' (145 x 23.3 x 6.3 m)
4 x 16-cylinder Pielstick diesel engines via twin screw.

Passenger-car-cargo ferry owned by Cenargo Navigation Ltd, UK, and operated by V-Ships (UK) Ltd.
Built by Dubigeon-Normandie, Nantes, for SNCM as the ESTEREL (1981).

MISTRAL (1999)
47276 grt; 1200 psrs
708' x 95' x 22'6" (216 x 28.8 x 6.9 m)
4 x 12-cylinder Wartsila diesel-electric engines via twin screw.

Cruise ship owned by Auxiliage Maritime, operated by Festival Cruises and chartered to First European.
Built by Chantiers de l'Atlantique, St Nazaire, at a cost of US$250,000,000.

MISTRAL II (1992) See MARIA PA (1997)

MITAU (1909) See WILBO (1924)

MIYASAKI (1976) See St EZEKIEL MORENO (1996)

MIZAR, USS (AF-12) (1941) See SAMALA (1958)

MIZUHO MARU (1926)
8182 grt
460' x 58' x 26' (139.4 x 17.6 x 7.9 m)
2 x 8-cylinder Rowan quadruple expansion engines via twin screw.
Sank in September 1944 after being torpedoed by a US submarine north of Luzon.
Built by Russell & Co, Glasgow, for Pinollus, Izquiero y Cia as the INFANTA ISABEL (1912). Renamed MIDZUHO MARU (1926).

MOBILE (1893) See CALAWAII (1923)

MOBILE USS (1919) See CLEVELAND (1923)

MOBILE (1968)
11302 grt; 2000 psrs
533' x 71' x 30'6" depth (159.3 x 21.7 x 9.3 m)
2 x Westinghouse DRG turbine engine via single screw.
Broken up for scrap as a container ship at Inchon in 1984. Ex-Sea Land Services Inc.
Built by Kaiser Corporation, Richmond, California, for the US Maritime Commission as the Class C4-S-A1 troop transport GENERAL STUART HEINTZELMAN (AP-159) (1945) and acted as a refugee transport ship after World War Two.

MOBY ALE (1997)
3937 grt; 800 psrs
160 cars
306' x 55' x 14' (92.7 x 16.7 x 4.2 m)
4 x 14-cylinder B+W diesel engines via twin screw.

Passenger-car ferry owned and operated by Moby Trader SrL.
Built by Aalborg Vaerft, Aalborg, for DFDS as the MIKKE MOLS (1969).
Renamed TEISTIN (1980 – government of Faroe Islands).

MOBY BABY (1990)
5667 grt; 1244 psrs
220 cars
333' x 59' x 14'6" (101 x 18 x 4.4 m)
2 x 12-cylinder + 2 x 6-cylinder Deutz diesel engines via twin screw.

Passenger-car ferry owned and operated by Moby Trader SrL, Italy.
Built by Oresunds for Svea Lines as the SVEA DROTT (1966). Renamed EARL GODWIN (1975 – British Rail).

MOBY BIG (1989) See MOBY KING (1990)

MOBY BLU (1982)
5956 grt; 1200 psrs
235 cars
356' x 59' x 13' (107.9 x 18 x 3.9 m)
2 x 12-cylinder MAN diesel engines via twin screw.

Passenger-car ferry operated by Moby Trader SrL, Italy, but available for purchase at US$1,500,000 as at 31 December 2000.
Built by NV Scheepswerf Gusto, Schiedam, Holland, for Stanhope Steamship Co Ltd, Dover, as the FREE ENTERPRISE II (1965).

MOBY DREAM (1986) See SARDEGNA BELLA (1993)

MOBY FANTASY (1997)
13284 grt; 1080 psrs
350 cars
469' x 66' x 21' (142 x 22 x 6.4 m)
4 x 12-cylinder MAN diesel engines via twin screw.
Passenger-car ferry operated by Moby Lines.
Built by Union Naval de Levante SA, Valencia, for Cia Trasmediterranea as the MANUEL SOTO (1976).

MOBY KING (1990)
12377 grt; 1830 psrs
570 cars
488' x 69' x 17'6" (148 x 21 x 5.3 m)
4 x 6-cylinder Lindholmens-Pielstick diesel engines via twin screw.

Passenger-car ferry owned and operated by Fion SA, Italy.
Built by Uddevallavarvet, Uddevalla, for the government of Sweden as the SKANE (1966). Renamed MOBY BIG (1989 – NavArMar Line).

MOBY KISS (1997) See AL MANSOUR (1997)

MOBY LALLI (2000)
8586 grt; 1150 psrs
284 cars
389' x 62' x 16'6" (118 x 18.9 x 5 m)
2 x 12-cylinder MAN diesel engines via twin screw.

Ice-strengthened passenger-car ferry owned and operated by Moby Line.
Launched by AG Weser, Bremerhaven, for Jydsk Faergefart, Juelsminde, as the KATTEGAT II (1974) and completed as the KALLE III (1974). Renamed THE VIKING (1983 – Sally Viking Line), WASA PRINCE (1988 – Bornholmstrafikken), PRINCE (1991 – Bornholmstrafikken) and PEDER OLSEN (1992 – Bornholmstrafikken).

MOBY LOVE (1986) See EXPRES ATHINA (1998)

MOBY LOVE II (1998)
7555 grt; 1000 psrs

110 cars
378' x 61' x 13'6" (114.6 x 18.6 x 4.1 m)
2 x 16-cylinder Pielstick diesel engines via twin screw.
Passenger-car ferry owned and operated by Moby Trader SrL.
Built by Cantieri Navali di Pietra , Genoa, for SCNF as the SAINT ELOI (1975). Renamed CHANNEL ENTENTE (1989 – Angleterre Lorraine-Alsace S A de Navigation, Dunkirk) and KING ORRY (1990 – Isle of Man Steam Packet Co Ltd).

MOBY MAGIC (1997)
13331 grt; 1080 psrs
250 cars
465' x 73' x 21' (144 x 22 x 6.4 m)
4 x 12-cylinder MAN diesel engines via twin screw.

Passenger-car ferry acquired for US$10,000,000 by Moby Lines, but now owned by Sardegna Lines SpA.
Built by Union Naval de Levant SA, Valencia, for Cia Trasmediterranea as the J. J. SISTER (1975). Renamed BALANGA SISTER (1994 – Corona Line) and J. J. SISTER (1995 – Trasmediterranea).

MOBY PRINCE (1985)
6187 grt; 1200 psrs
235 cars
432' x 66' x 16'6" (131 x 20.5 x 5 m)
4 x 9-cylinder MAN diesel engines via twin screw.

Broken up for scrap in 1998 at Aliaga after raising her from the seabed off Livorno following a disaster-packed few days in 1991. A fire totally engulfed the vessel upon her ramming the stationary 98545 grt naphtha-loaded oil tanker AGIP ABRUZZO, which was anchored in the Livorno Roads in the Bay of Livorno, Italy, during the night of 15 April 1991. Only one person aboard the ferry survived. The death toll numbered 140, despite the fact that all lifeboats got away, but the surface of the sea caught fire and enveloped the survivors' boats and rafts. The charred remains of the MOBY PRINCE were towed into an inner berth at Livorno and immediately sank.
Built by Cammell Laird & Co Ltd, Birkenhead, for Stoomvaart Maatschappij Zeeland (SMZ) as the passenger RoRo ferry KONINGIN JULIANA (1968). Renamed as a trade exhibition ship TROMP (1984 – BV Tromp, Amsterdam)

MOBY RIDER (1998)
21717 grt; 800 psrs
480 cars
486' x 71' x 20' (187 x 24 x 6.1 m)
4 x 12-cylinder Pielstick diesel engines via twin screw.

Passenger-car-cargo ferry owned and operated by NavArMa, Italy.
Built by Davie Shipbuilder, Lauzon, for the Canadian government as the RoRo freight vessel FREDERICK CARTER (1968). Renamed FRED (1986 – Anco Ferries, Cyprus), FLAVIA II (1987 – Harma Shipping Co Ltd, Limassol), ATHENIA (1987 – Olympic Ferries), THENIA (1988 – Windepoint Shipping Ltd, Nassau), HANSA LINK (1990 – Rederi AB Nordo-Link) and NORSE LAGAN (1991 – Norse Irish Ferries).

MOBY VINCENT (1990)
12108 grt; 1400 psrs
550 cars or 107 trailers
403' x 66' x 19' (122 x 22 x 5.9 m)
2 x 12-cylinder MaK diesel engines via twin screw.

Passenger-car-cargo RoRo ferry operated by NavArMa., Italy.
Built by Rickmers Werft, Bremerhaven, for Stena Line as the STENA NORMANDICA (1974). Renamed St BRENDAN (1985 – Sealink UK).

MOBY WILL (1988) See AL JUDI (1993)

MOCAMBIQUE (1949)
12976 grt; 749 psrs
550' x 67' x 27' (166.7 x 20.3 x 8.2 m)
2 x 6-cylinder Doxford diesel engines via twin screw.
Broken up for scrap at Kaohsiung in 1972.
Built by Swan Hunter Shipbuilding, Newcastle, for Cia Nacional de Navegacao, Portugal, as a passenger-cargo liner.

MOCCASIN (1917) See PORTO RICO (1920)

MODASA (1921)
9000 grt; 168 psrs
465' x 58' x 33'5" depth (140.9 x 17.6 x 10.2 m)
4 x Swan Hunter & Wigham Richardson DRG turbine engines via twin screw.
Broken up for scrap in 1954 at Blyth.
Built by Swan Hunter Shipbuilding, Newcastle, for the British India Steam Navigation Co.

MOERAKI (1902)
4392 grt; 365 psrs
373' x 46' x 31' (113 x 14 x 9.4 m)
2 x triple expansion engines via twin screw.
Broken up for scrap at Osaka in 1933.
Built by William Denny & Bros, Dumbarton, for the Union Steamship Co of New Zealand.

MOHAMMED-ALI EL KEBIR (1947) See MERCANTILE VICTORY (1963)

MOHAMMEDI (1951)
7026 grt; 62 psrs
451' x 60' x 25' (137.5 x 18.3 x 7.6 m)
Rankin & Blackmore triple expansion engine via single screw.
Broken up for scrap as a pilgrim ship at Mumbai in 1978. Ex-Mogul Line.
Built by Lithgows Ltd, Glasgow, for the Mogul Line as the MOHAMMEDI (1947). Renamed OCEAN TRIUMPH (1950 – Mogul Line).

MOHAWK (1892) See CHINOOK (1904)

MOHAWK (1908)
4623 grt; 375 psrs
367' x 48' x 20'4" (111.2 x 14.5 x 6.2 m)
W Cramp 3-cylinder triple expansion engines via single screw.
Scuttled on 2 January 1925 after catching fire in Delaware Bay, USA.

Built by W Cramp & Sons Shipbuilding & Engineering Co, Philadelphia, Pennsylvania, for the Clyde Steamship Co.

MOHAWK (1926)
5896 grt; 446 psrs
404' x 54' x 20' (122.4 x 16.4 x 9.6 m)
2 x Newport News SRG turbine engines via single screw.
Sank on 24 January 1935 after a collision with the Norwegian freighter TALISMAN off Sea Girt, New Jersey.
Built by Newport News Shipbuilding, Newport News, Virginia, for the Clyde Steamship Co.

MOHAWK (1968)
12420 grt; 520 psrs
523' x 71' x 29' (159.3 x 21.7 x 8.8 m)
Geared turbine engine via single screw.
Broken up for scrap as a cargo ship at Kaohsiung in 1980. Ex-Mohawk Shipping.
Built as the Class C4-S-A3 troop carrier MARINE PHOENIX (1945) by the Kaiser Corporation, Richmond, California, for the US Maritime Commission. The ship was acquired by the Matson Line after the end of World War Two and converted into a passenger liner.

MOIZ (1955)
3566 grt; 314 psrs
295' x 48' x 25'6" (89.4 x 14.6 x 7.8 m)
2 x Westinghouse DRG turbine engines via twin screw.
Broken up for scrap in Karachi in 1959. Ex-Gulf Steamship Co, Karachi.
Built by Bethlehem Shipbuilding Corporation, San Francisco, for the Matson Line subsidiary, Inter-Island Steam Navigation Co as the HUALALAI (1929). Renamed NGAIO (1949 – Anchor Shipping & Foundry Co Ltd, Nelson, New Zealand).

MOLDAVIA (1903)
9505 grt; 514 psrs
545' x 58' x 33' (166.1 x 17.7 x 10.1 m)
2 x triple expansion engines via twin screw.
Sank in 15 minutes on 23 May 1918, with the loss of 56 lives, after being torpedoed by the German U-57 in the English Channel off Beachy Head.
Built by Caird & Co, Greenock, for the P&O Line at a cost of £336,178.

MOLDAVIA (1923)
16556 grt; 830 psrs
573' x 71' x 33' (174.6 x 21.6 x 10 m)
DRG turbine engines via twin screw.
Broken up for scrap by John Cashmore Ltd in the UK in 1938.
Built by Cammell Laird &Co, Birkenhead, for the P&O Line.

MOLDAVIA (1961)
3219 grt; 250 psrs
333' x 48' x 13' (100.9 x 14.5 x 3.9 m)
2 x 8-cylinder Russki diesel engines via twin screw.
Ice-strengthened cruise ship operated by the Black Sea Shipping Co, Odessa.
Built by A Jdavnov, St Petersburg.

MOLDAVIJA (1903) See MOLDAVIA (1903)

MOLDAVIJA (1923) See MOLDAVIA (1923)

MOLDAVIJA (1961) See MOLDAVIA (1961)

MOLDAVIYA (1903) See MOLDAVIA (1903)

MOLDAVIYA (1923) See MOLDAVIA (1961)

MOLEDET (1961) See JUPITER (1971)

MOLENGAT (1980)
3254 grt; 1200 psrs
292' x 61' x 12'6" (88.4 x 18.5 x 3.8 m)
2 x 8-cylinder MaK diesel engines via twin screw.
Passenger ferry operated by Texels Eigene Stoomb, Den Hoorn.
Built by Verolme Scheefswerf, Heusden.

MOLENO (1947)
3092 grt; 314 psrs
310' x 48' x 27'6" (93.9 x 14.5 x 8.4 m)
2 x Westinghouse DRG turbine engines via twin screw.
Broken up for scrap at Yokohama in 1956. Ex-De La Rama Steamship Co.
Built by Bethlehem Steel Corporation, Alameda, California, for Inter-Island Steam Navigation Co as the WAIALEALE (1928).

MOLTKE (1901) See PESARO (1915)

MOMUS (1906)
6878 grt; 460 psrs
410' x 53' x 25'6" (124.2 x 16.1 x 7.8 m)
W Cramp 3-cylinder triple expansion engines via single screw.
Broken up for scrap at Osaka in 1935.
Built by W Cramp & Sons Shipbuilding & Engineering Co, Philadelphia, Pennsylvania, for the Southern Pacific Steamship Lines.

MONACO (1972) See DIMITRIOS MIRAS (1988)

MONACO (1987) See NEW YORK FORTUNE I (1997)

MONARCH OF BERMUDA (1931) See ARKADIA (1958)

MONARCH OF THE SEAS (1991)
73937 grt; 2353 psrs
874' x 106' x 25' (264.8 x 32.1 x 7.6 m)
4 x 9-cylinder Pielstick diesel engines via twin screw.

Cruise ship operated by Royal Caribbean International.
Built by Chantiers de l'Atlantique, St Nazaire, for Royal Caribbean Cruise Lines at a cost of US$335,000,000.

MONARCH STAR (1976) See ENCHANTED ISLE (1994)

MONARCH SUN (1975) See UNIVERSE EXPLORER (1996)

MONA'S ISLE (1984) See AL FAHAD (1986)

MONA'S QUEEN (1946) See FIESTA (1964)

MONASTERIO DE EL ESCORIAL (1951) See CLIMAX OPAL (1977)

MONASTERIO DE GUADALUPE (1951) See GUADALUPE (1953)

MONASTERIO DE LA RABIDA (1951) See COVADONGA (1953)

MONCALIERI (1920)
5267 grt
400' x 52' x 25'3" (121.2 x 15.8 x 7.7 m)
Central Marine Engineering 3-cylinder triple expansion engine.
Owned by Lloyd Sabaudo.
Built by Craig Taylor & Co Ltd, Stockton, for the British Shipping Controller as the WAR LINNET (1918) which served as a post-World War One migrant ship.

MONCENISIO (1924)
5715 grt; 26 psrs
420' x 54' x 27'3" (127.3 x 16.4 x 8.3 m)

Hawthorne Leslie 3-cylinder triple expansion engine via single screw.
Broken up in Italy in 1929. Ex-Soc Anon Anonima de Navagazione Alta Italia.
Built by Hawthorne Leslie & Co, Hebburn, for New Zealand Shipping Co as
the WHAKATANE (1900). Note that this ship does not meet the criteria set
for inclusion within this book, but it is a known fact that she was used as a
migrant ship after World War One and accommodated a passenger capacity far
in excess of her registered number.

MONGARA (1914)
8200 grt; 129 psrs
450' x 58' x 27'11" (136.4 x 17.6 x 8.2 m)
Wallsend Slipway 6-cylinder triple expansion engines via twin screw.
Sank on 3 July 1917 after being torpedoed off Messina.
Built by Swan Hunter & Wigham Richardson Ltd, Newcastle, for the British
India Steam Navigation Co.

MONGIOIA (1925)
5564 grt; 224 psrs
429' x 54' x 27'4" (141.6 x 16.4 x 8.3 m)
Hawthorne Leslie 3-cylinder triple expansion engine via single screw.
Broken up for scrap in 1929. Ex-Navigazione Alta Italia SpA.
Laid down by Hawthorn Leslie & Co, Hebburn, for the Federal Steam
Navigation Co Ltd as the SUSSEX (1899), but completed for Shaw Savill &
Albion as the KARAMEA (1900).

MONGOLIA (1903)
9505 grt; 514 psrs
545' x 58' x 25' (166.1 x 17.7 x 7.6 m)
2 x triple expansion engines via twin screw.
Broken up for scrap at Shanghai in 1947. The hulk was removed from where
she had sunk in 13 minutes on 28 June 1917, with the loss of 23 lives. She had
hit a mine laid by the German raider WOLF 58 miles (99 km) off Mumbai.
Built by Caird & Co, Greenock, for the P&O Line at a cost of £336,024.

MONGOLIA (1904) See PANAMANIAN (1940)

MONGOLIA (1923) See ACAPULCO (1961)

MONICA RUSSOTTI (1973) See HORNBEAM (1992)

MONKAY (1946) See DIMITROS (1958)

MONMOUTH (1903) See TRETI KRABOLOV (1929)

MONOWAI (1930)
11037 grt; 401 psrs
519' x 63' x 26' (158.2 x 19.2 x 7.9 m)
2 x quadruple expansion engines via twin screw.

Broken up for scrap by the Far East Metal Industry & Shipping Co at Hong
Kong in 1960 for a tender figure of US$330,000. Ex-Union Steamship Co of
New Zealand.
Built by Harland & Wolff Ltd, Belfast, for P&O Lines as the RAZMAK
(1925).

MONROE (1903)
4704 grt; 276 psrs
366' x 46' x 29'4" depth (110.9 x 13.9 x 8.9 m)
Newport News 3-cylinder triple expansion engine via single screw.
Sank on 30 January 1914 following a collision with the steamer
NANTUCKET off Virginia Capes.

Built by Newport News Shipbuilding, Newport News, Virginia, for the
Dominion Steamship Co.

MONROVIA, USS (AP-64) (1944) See MONROVIA, USS (APA-31) (1946)

MONROVIA, USS (APA-31) (1946)
7997 grt
Broken up for scrap at Kaohsiung in 1969.
Built as the DELTARGENTINO II (1942). Renamed MONROVIA, USS (AP-64) (1944 – US Navy).

MONTCALM (1921) See WOLFE, HMS (1939)

MONTCALM (1903) See POLAR CHIEF (1946)

MONTCALM II (1917) See BOLINGBROKE (1920)

MONTCLARE (1922) See MONTCLARE, HMS (1942)

MONTCLARE, HMS (1942)
16314 grt; 1810 psrs
575' x 70' x 27'6" (174.2 x 21.2 x 8.4 m)
Brown-Curtis DRG turbine engines via twin screw.
Broken up for scrap at Inverkeithing in 1958. Ex-British Admiralty.
Laid down by John Brown & Co Ltd for the Canadian Pacific Steamship Co
as the METAPEDIA (1921) and completed as the MONTCLARE (1922).

MONTEAGLE (1903) See BELTON (1923)

MONTE ANAGA (1959) See PRIMERO DE JUNIO (1974)

MONTE CARLO (1976) See NINDAWAYMA (1993)

MONTE CASTILLO (1976) See MANX VIKING (1978)

MONTE CERVANTES (1928)
13913 grt; 2492 psrs
501' x 66' x 37'9" depth (151.8 x 20 x 11.5 m)
MAN 24-cylinder geared diesel engines via twin screw.
Sank bow first with her captain on 24 January 1930 after striking submerged
rocks in the Straits of Magellan two days earlier. She was then driven onto the
Eclaireur Reef where she capsized before sinking. In 1954 she was raised and
was under tow to Ushuaia, Argentina, when she sank for the last time.
Built by Blohm & Voss, Hamburg, for the Hamburg South America Line

MONTE CRUCETA (1976) See NINDAWAYMA (1993)

MONTE D'ORO (1990)
22070 grt; 508 psrs
130 cars or 80 trailers
479' x 85' x 20'6" (136 x 22.5 x 6.2 m)
4 x 12-cylinder Wartsila diesel engines via twin screw.
Passenger-car-cargo RoRo ferry owned and operated by SNCM.
Built by Ateliers et Chantiers du Havre, Le Havre.

MONTE GRANADA (1974) See GARNATA (1977)

MONTEITH (1925) See MONTNAIRN (1925)

MONTE OLIVIA (1924)
13750 grt; 2528 psrs
501' x 66' x 37'9" depth (151.8 x 20 x 11.5 m)
4 x 6-cylinder MAN diesel engines via twin screw.
Broken up for scrap in 1946 after she had been sunk on 3 April 1945 by an
Allied air attack on Kiel harbour.
Built by Blohm & Voss, Hamburg, for the Hamburg-South America Line.

MONTE PASCOAL (1930)
13870 grt; 2408 psrs
501' x 66' x 37'8" depth (151.8 x 20 x 11.5 m)
4 x 6-cylinder MAN geared diesel engines via twin screw.
Purposely sunk in the Skagerrak on 31 December 1946 by the British Navy as
a war prize. She contained a load of chemical and conventional war weapons

and ammunition.
Built by Blohm & Voss, Hamburg, for the Hamburg South American Line.

MONTEREY (1901)
4729 grt; 208 psrs
341' x 48' x 16'9" (103.3 x 14.5 x 5.1 m)
W Cramp 6-cylinder triple expansion engines via twin screw.
Broken up for scrap at Baltimore in 1931.
Built by W Cramp & Sons Shipbuilding & Engineering Co, Philadelphia, Pennsylvania, for the New York & Cuba Mail Steamship Co.

MONTEREY (1932) See BELOFIN I (1998)

MONTEREY (1939) See ADANA (1948)

MONTEREY (1955)
20046 grt; 639 psrs
564' x 76' x 30' (171 x 23.2 x 9 m)
2 x Bethlehem Steel DRG turbine engines via single screw.

Cruise ship owned by Cia Naviera Pan Ocean S A, Panama, and chartered for cruising to Mediterranean Shipping Cruises, Italy.
Built by Bethlehem Steel Corporation, Sparrow's Point, Maryland, for the US Maritime Commission as the Class C4 cargo vessel FREE STATE MARINER (1952).

MONTE ROSA (1930) See EMPIRE WINDRUSH (1946)

MONTE SARMIENTO (1924)
13625 grt; 2470 psrs
501' x 66' x 37'9" depth (151.8 x 20 x 11.5 m)
MAN 24-cylinder diesel engines via twin screw.
Broken up for scrap at Hamburg in 1943 after raising her from the bottom of Kiel harbour. She had sank on 26 February 1942 during an Allied air attack.
Built by Blohm & Voss, Hamburg, for the Hamburg South American Line.

MONTE STELLO (1979) See PALANGA (1996)

MONTE TOLEDO (1974) See TOLETELA (1977)

MONTE UDALA (1948)
10170 grt; 392 psrs
487' x 62' x 26' (148.5 x 19 x 7.9 m)
10-cylinder Sulzer diesel engine via single screw.
Sank on 8 September 1971 after she sprang a leak in the engine room and capsized 70 miles (117 km) off Ilheus, Brazil.
Laid down as a cargo vessel by Cie Euskalduna de Construccion, Bilbao, for Naviera Aznar SA, Bilbao, but completed as a passenger-cargo ship.

MONTE ULIA (1952) See CLIMAX OPAL (1977)

MONTE UMBE (1959) See LIBAN (1975)

MONTE URBASA (1948) See EUROSTAR (1977)

MONTE URQUIOLA (1949) See CLIMAX GARNET (1974)

MONTEVIDEO MARU (1926)
7267 grt; 800 psrs
430' x 56' x 25'3" (130.3 x 17 x 7.7 m)
Mitsubishi 12-cylinder diesel engines via twin screw.

Sank on 1 July 1942 after being hit by two torpedoes from the USS STURGEON in the South China Sea, off Cape Bojidoru, Luzon.
Built by Mitsubishi Dockyard for OSK, Japan.

MONTEZUMA (1899) See OAKLEAF (1917)

MONTEZUMA II (1918) See KIZAN MARU (1938)

MONTICELLO (1927)
19361 grt; 1791 psrs
707' x 72' x 40'2" depth (215.3 x 21.8 x 12.2 m)
AG Vulcan 4 x 4-cylinder quadruple expansion engines via twin screw.
Broken up for scrap at Baltimore in 1940 for a tender figure of US$183,500.
Ex-US Shipping Board.
Built by Vulcan Shipyards, Stettin, for North German Lloyd as the KAISER WILHELM II (1903). Seized by the US government and renamed as the troop carrier AGAMEMNON, USS (1917 – US Navy).

MONTICELLO, USS (AP-61) (1942) See CONTE GRANDE (1947).

MONTLAURIER (1922) See MONTNAIRN (1925)

MONTMORENCY (1919) See FORFAR, HMS (1939)

MONTNAIRN (1925)
17282 grt; 2480 psrs
590' x 68' x 38'6" depth (178.8 x 20.8 x 11.7 m)
2 x 4-cylinder quadruple expansion engines via twin screw.
Broken up for scrap by SA Co-op Ligure Demolitori Navi at Genoa in 1930.
Ex-Canadian Pacific Steamship Co.
Built by JC Tecklenborg Shipyard, Geestemunde, for North German Lloyd as the PRINZ FRIEDRICH WILHELM (1908). Renamed EMPRESS OF CHINA (1921 – Canadian Pacific Steamship Co), EMPRESS OF INDIA (1921 – Canadian Pacific Steamship Co), MONTLAURIER (1922 – Canadian Pacific Steamship Co) and MONTEITH (1925 – Canadian Pacific Steamship Co).

MONTORO (1910) See HAVEN (1948)

MONTREAL (1900)
8644 grt; 1000 psrs
470' x 56' x 42'9" depth (142.4 x 17 x 13 m)
Wallsend-Slipway 6-cylinder triple expansion engines via twin screw.
Sank 14 miles (24 km) from Liverpool's Bar Lightship, on 30 January 1918, while under tow after colliding with the White Star liner CEDRIC the day before. No lives were lost.
Built by CS Swan & Hunter, Wallsend, for Elder Dempster's Beaver Line as a passenger liner.

MONTREAL (1905)
3342 grt; 800 psrs
346' x 44' x 24'6" depth (105.4 x 13.4 x 7.5 m)
3-cylinder triple expansion engine via single screw.
Owned by the French Line, she sank on 24 March 1917 after being torpedoed by the German U-46 77 miles (128 km) north-east of Cape Ortegal, Spain.
Launched by R Napier & Sons, Glasgow, for the Royal Mail Steam Packet Co as the MINHO (1896). Renamed HALIFAX (1903 – French Line).

MONTREAL (1921) See ALESIA (1928)

MONTROSE (1922) See FORFAR, HMS (1939)

MONTROYAL (1924)
15646 grt; 1300 psrs
549' x 66' x 31' (166.4 x 20 x 9.4 m)
Fairfield 8-cylinder quadruple expansion engines via twin screw.
Broken up for scrap by the Stavanger Shipbreaking Co at Stavanger in 1930.
Ex-Canadian Pacific Steamship Co.
Built as the EMPRESS OF BRITAIN (1906) by Fairfield Shipbuilding & Engineering Co Ltd, Glasgow, for the Canadian Pacific Steamship Co.

MONTSERRAT (1957)
9001 grt; 708 psrs

455' x 62' x 28' (138.7 x 18.9 x 8.5 m)
Allis-Chalmers geared turbine engine via single screw.
Broken up for scrap at Castellon in 1975. Ex-Cia Trasatlantica Espanola.
Built by Bethlehem-Fairfield Shipbuilding Inc, Baltimore, for the US Maritime Commission as the Victory Class cargo ship WOOSTER VICTORY (1945). Renamed CASTELVERDE (1947 – Sitmar Line) and CASTEL VERDE (1950 – Sitmar Line).

MOOLTAN (1905)
9621 grt; 514 psrs
545' x 58' x 25' (166.1 x 17.7 x 7.6 m)
2 x quadruple expansion engines via twin screw.
Sank on 26 July 1917 after being torpedoed by the German U-27 53 miles (88 km) north-north-west of Cape Serrat, Tunis.
Built by Caird & Co, Greenock, for the P&O Line at a cost of £314,982.

MOOLTAN (1923)
21039 grt; 656 psrs
625' x 73' x 32' (190.5 x 22.2 x 9.7 m)
2 x Harland & Wolff quadruple expansion engines via twin screw.
Broken up for scrap by the British Iron & Steel Corporation Ltd for a tender fee of £150,000 at Faslane in 1954.
Built by Harland & Wolff Ltd, Belfast, for the P&O Line.

MOOR (1881) See THE VIKING (1908)

MOOR B (1967)
5088 grt; 152 psrs
378' x 50' x 22' (114.5 x 15.2 x 6.7 m)
Stork-Werkspoor diesel engine via single screw.
Broken up for scrap in 1974.
Built by Van der Geissen Shipyards, Krimpen, for the Royal Netherlands Steamship Co as the SOCRATES (1938). Renamed WILLEMSTAD (1950 – Royal Netherlands Steamship Co).

MORAITIS (1907) See THEMISTOCLES (1908)

MORAVIAN (1898) See AKBAR (1914)

MORAYSHIRE (1890) See HIGHLAND FLING (1905)

MORAYSHIRE (1898) See LUGANO (1942)

MOREA (1908)
10890 grt; 607 psrs
562' x 61' x 27' (171.3 x 18.6 x 8.2 m)
Quadruple expansion engines via twin screw.
Broken up for scrap for a tender of £32,500 at Kobe in 1932.
Built by Barclay, Curle & Co Ltd, Glasgow, for the P&O Line at a cost of £309,692.

MOREAS (1926)
8292 grt; 1303 psrs
486' x 56' x 33'4" depth (147.3 x 17 x 10.1 m)
D & W Henderson 6-cylinder triple expansion engines via twin screw.
Broken up for scrap at Venice in 1929. Ex-Byron Shipping Line, although it had been sold to the National Greek Line, but never commissioned by the latter.
Built by D & W Henderson & Co, Glasgow, for the Anchor Line as the COLUMBIA (1902). Renamed COLUMBELLA, HMS (1914 – British Royal Navy) and COLUMBIA (1919 – Anchor Line).

MORETON BAY (1922)
14376 grt; 724 psrs
549' x 68' x 33' (167.3 x 20.7 x 10 m)
Vickers-Armstrong DRG turbine engines via twin screw.
Broken up for scrap at Barrow-in-Furness in 1957. Ex-Shaw Savill & Albion.
Built by Vickers-Armstrong Ltd, Barrow-in-Furness, for the Aberdeen & Commonwealth Line.

MORGEDAL (1962) See ZAKROS (1971)

MORMACLAND (1939) See UNION RELIANCE (1961)

MORMACMAIL (1940) See SEVEN SEAS (1954)

MORMACMAIL (1941) See CORRIENTES (1949)

MORNING STAR (1992) See SALAMIS GLORY (1996)

MORRO CASTLE (1900)
6004 grt; 208 psrs
400' x 50' x 26' (121.2 x 15.2 x 7.9 m)
W Cramp & Sons 8-cylinder triple expansion engines via twin screw.
Broken up for scrap at Genoa in 1929.
Built by W Cramp & Sons Shipbuilding & Engineering Co, Philadelphia, Pennsylvania, for the New York & Cuba Mail Steamship Co.

MORRO CASTLE (1930)
11520 grt; 530 psrs
508' x 71' x 39' depth (153.9 x 21.5 x 11.8 m)
2 x General Electric turbo-electric engines via twin screw.
Broken up for scrap at Baltimore in 1935. She sank on 8 September 1934 after completely burning out six miles (10 km) off the New Jersey coast. Hordes of sightseers gathered to watch the spectacle which claimed 137 lives. It is believed that a small fire erupted in the ship's stationery locker and the poorly-trained crew had not contained the blaze before it got out of control. The captain had died of a heart attack while taking a bath the previous evening.
Built by Newport News Shipbuilding & Engineering Co, Newport News, Virginia, for the Ward Line.

MORSKAJA II (1913)
5878 grt
395' x 52' x 22'6" (131.7 x 17.3 x 7.5 m)
3-cylinder triple expansion engines via twin screw.
Broken up for scrap in Korea in 1987.
Built by John Brown & Co Ltd, Clydebank, for the Russian Steam Navigation Co as the IMPERATOR PETR VELIKY (1913 – Russian Steam Navigation Co) Renamed JAKUTIA (1913 – Russian Steam Navigation Co).

MORTEN MOLS (1969) See SMYRIL (1975)

MORVADA (1914)
8193 grt; 129 psrs
450' x 58' x 32'7" (136.4 x 17.6 x 9.9 m)
Wallsend Slipway 6-cylinder triple expansion engines via twin screw.
Broken up in 1933 by Van Heyghen Freres, Ghent, for a tender of £8,900.
Built by Swan Hunter & Wigham Richardson Ltd, Newcastle, for the British India Steam Navigation Co.

MOSELLA (1922) See JAMAIQUE (1928)

MOSKVA (1898) See PECHANGA (1917)

MOSKVA (1906) See SAN GIUSTO (1918)

MOSKWA (1883) See PRUT (1914)

MOSSAMEDES (1915)
4607 grt; 74 psrs
400' x 47' x 29' (121.9 x 14.3 x 8.8 m)
Triple expansion engine via single screw.
Owned by Cia Colonial de Navigacao, Lisbon, she was abandoned after running aground on 23 April 1923 on False Cape Frio on the Angolan coast, with 31 lives lost.
Built as the SUMATRA (1895) by Alexander Stephen & Sons, Glasgow, for the P&O Line at a cost of £78,843.

MOTAGUA (1912)
5977 grt; 72 psrs
411' x 51' x 26' (124.5 x 15.5 x 7.9 m)
Wallsend Slipway 6-cylinder compound engine via single screw.
Built by Swan Hunter Shipbuilding, Newcastle, for the Hamburg-America Line as the EMIL L. BOAS (1913).

MOTOHIRA MARU No. 2 (1904)
3950 grt; 116 psrs
380' x 45' x 27'6" (115.8 x 13.8 x 8.4 m)

Triple expansion engine via single screw.

Owned by a Japanese consortium, she was partially broken up on site in 1907 following her becoming wrecked in the Soya Strait on 12 September 1907.

Built by Palmer Brothers, Jarrow, for the Sun Shipping Co Ltd as the RUFFORD HALL (1888). Renamed NANKIN (1898 – P&O Steam Navigation Co Ltd).

MOTTISFONT (1917) See KEMAL SADIKOGLU (1950)

MOUNT CARROLL (1921) See PORTARITISSA (1955)

MOUNT CLAY (1920)
8865 grt; 1452 psrs
488' x 56' x 32'1" depth (147.9 x 17 x 9.7 m)
AG Vulcan 8-cylinder quadruple expansion engines via twin screw.
Broken up for scrap in 1934. Ex-United American Lines.
Built by Vulcan Shipyards, Stettin, for North German Lloyd as the PRINZ EITEL FRIEDRICH (1904). Renamed DE KALB, USS (1917 – US Navy).

MOUNT CLINTON (1921) See CAPO MANARA (1948)

MOUNT McKINLEY (1936)
4932 grt; 245 psrs
360' x 52' x 24'6" (109.1 x 15.8 x 7.5 m)
W Cramp & Sons 4-cylinder quadruple expansion engine via single screw.
Owned by Alaska Steamship Co, she was wrecked beyond salvage on 11 March 1942 near Scotch Cap Light, Alaska.
Built by William Cramp & Sons, Philadelphia, Pennsylvania, for the Grace Line as the passenger-cargo ship SANTA LUISA (1918). Renamed EL SALVADOR (1928 – Panama Mail Line) and SANTA ANA (1931 – Grace Line).

MOUNT OLYMPOS (1965)
10172 grt; 1184 psrs
40 cars
484' x 63' x 21'6" (146.7 x 19.1 x 6.5 m)
Parsons geared turbine engines via twin screw.
Broken up for scrap at Trieste in 1970. Ex-Typaldos Lines.
Built by Constructions Navales, La Ciotat, for CGT, Marseilles, as the VILLE DORAN (1936).

MOUNT OSSA (1937) See SPERBRECHER (1939)

MOUNT PARNASSUS (1937)
5334 grt
400' x 52' x 28'5" (121.2 x 15.8 x 8.6 m)
John Inglis & Co 3-cylinder triple expansion engine via single screw.
Built by Wallace Shipbuilding & Drydock Co Ltd, Prince Rupert, for Canadian Scottish Ltd as the passenger ferry CANADIAN SCOTTISH (1921).

MOUNT ROYAL (1898) See BRITISH MAPLE (1920)

MOUNT TEMPLE (1901)
8790 grt; 500 psrs
485' x 59' x 30'4" (147.8 x 18 x 9.2 m)
Wallsend Slipway 6-cylinder triple expansion engines via twin screw.
Owned by the Canadian Pacific Steamship Co, she sank on 6 December 1916 after the German raider MOEWE had captured the ship 620 miles (1033 km) west of Fastnet, then turned her guns on the vessel at point blank range to send her to the bottom.
Built by Armstrong, Whitworth & Co Ltd, Walkerton-on-Tyne, for Elder Dempster.

MOUNT VERNON, USS (1914)
19503 grt; 1741 psrs
707' x 72' x 33' (215.3 x 21.8 x 10 m)
4 x 4-cylinder quadruple expansion engines via twin screw.
Broken up for scrap for a tender figure of US$35,000 at Baltimore, Maryland in 1940. Ex-US Shipping Board, which had kept the ship laid up in Chesapeake Bay since 1919.
Built by AG Vulcan Shipyards, Stettin, for North German Lloyd as the KRONPRINZESSIN CECILIE (1907), which was a ship of 8689 grt and 200 passenger capability.

MOUNT VERNON, USS (AP-22) (1941) See WASHINGTON (1946)

MOUZINHO (1930)
8512 grt; 1260 psrs
448' x 55' x 25'11" (136.6 x 16.8 x 7.6 m)
Krupp 8-cylinder quadruple expansion engines via twin screw.
Broken up for scrap at Savona in 1954. Ex-Cia Colonial de Navegacao, Lisbon.
Built by Krupp, Kiel, for the Hamburg-America Line as the passenger liner CORCOVADO (1907). Renamed SUEH (1914 – government of Turkey), GUGLIELMO PIERCE (1920 – Sicula Americana) and MARIA CHRISTINA (1927 – Lloyd Sabaudo).

MOYSALEN (1993)
3638 grt; 544 psrs
104 cars
277' x 50' x 17' (84 x 15 x 5 m)
Wichmann 8-cylinder diesel engine via single screw.
Passenger-car ferry owned and operated by Finnmark Fylkes.
Built by Slipen Mik at a cost of US$23,000,000.

MOZAFFARI (1948) See MOZAFFARI (1951)

MOZAFFARI (1951)
7024 grt; 62 psrs
451' x 60' x 25' (137.5 x 18.3 x 7.6 m)
Rankin & Blackmore triple expansion engine via single screw.
Broken up as a pilgrim ship for scrap at Mumbai in 1977. Ex-Mogul Line.
Built by Lithgows Shipyards, Glasgow, for the Mogul Line as the passenger-cargo ship MOZAFFARI (1948). Renamed OCEAN VICTORY (1950 – Mogul Line).

MUKOGAWA (1990) See NEFELI (1999)

MULBERA (1922)
9032 grt; 168 psrs
466' x 60' x 33'3" (141.2 x 18.2 x 10 m)
6 x A Stephen & Sons DRG turbine engines via twin screw.
Broken up for scrap at Inverkeithing in 1954.
Built by Alexander Stephen & Sons, Glasgow, for the British India Line as a passenger-cargo ship.

MUNAMAR (1915)
3440 grt
353' x 48' x 24'9" (107 x 14.5 x 7.5 m)
Maryland Steel Co 3-cylinder triple expansion engine via single screw.
Broken up for scrap at Baltimore in 1938.
Built by the Maryland Steel Co for the Matson Line as a passenger-cargo ship.

MUNARGO (1921) See THISTLE (1944)

MUNARGO, USS (AP-20) (1941) See THISTLE (1944)

MUNCHEN (1889) See MUNCHEN (1910)

MUNCHEN (1910)
4691 grt; 1798 psrs
391' x 47' x 31'1" depth (119 x 14.2 x 9.4 m)
3-cylinder triple expansion engine via single screw.
Broken up for scrap by the new owner, Thos W Ward, at Morecombe in 1910.
Built by Fairfield Shipbuilding & Engineering Co, Glasgow, for North German Lloyd as the passenger ship MUNCHEN (1889). Renamed GREGORY MORCH (1902 – Northern Steamship Co).

MUNCHEN (1913) See ALBERTIC (1927)

MUNCHEN (1923) See STEUBEN (1938)

MUNEASTERN (1924)
3542 grt; 100 psrs
340' x 43' x 23'5" (103 x 13 x 7.1 m)
Harlan & Hollingworth 2-cylinder compound engine via single screw.

Broken up for scrap at Baltimore in 1927. Ex-Munson Steamship Line.
Built by Harlan & Hollingworth, Wilmington, Delaware, as the EXCELSIOR (1882 – Morgan's L & TRR and Steamship Co).

MUNKEDAL (1954) See HELEANNA (1966)

MUNORLEANS (1927)
4418 grt
353' x 49' x 25' (107 x 14.8 x 7.6 m)
Bremer Vulkan 4-cylinder quadruple expansion engines via single screw.
Broken up for scrap at Ardrossan in 1936.
Built by Bremer Vulcan, Vegesack, as the GRUNEWALD (1911). Renamed GENERAL G. W. GOETHALS (1917 – US Army), BOOKER T. WASHINGTON (1924) and GENERAL G. W. GOETHALS (1925 – Winthrop Waite).

MUNSTER (1938)
4320 grt
353' x 50' x 14'6" (107 x 15.2 x 4.4 m)
Harland & Wolff 2-cylinder diesel engines via twin screw.
Sank after hitting a mine in February 1940 off the Bar at Liverpool while en route to Belfast.
Built by Harland & Wolff Ltd, Belfast, for the British & Irish Steam Packet Co (1936) Ltd, Dublin.

MUNSTER (1948) See ORPHEUS (1969)

MUNSTER (1969) See TIAN PENG (1991)

MUNSTER (1990) See AMBASSADOR II (1993)

MUNSTER I (1968) See ORPHEUS (1969)

M. URITSKIY (1959)
4871 grt; 333 psrs
401' x 52' x 17' (121.5 x 15.8 x 5.2 m)
2 x 6-cylinder MAN diesel engines via twin screw.
Broken up for scrap in 1996.
Built by Mathias-Thesen, Wismar, for the Far Eastern Shipping Co, Vladivostok, as an ice-strengthened cruise ship.

M. URITZKIJ (1959) See M. URITSKIY (1959)

MUSKEGON CLIPPER (1989)
4979 grt; 480 psrs
83 cars

318' x 66' x 13' (96.4 x 20 x 3.9 m)
4 x 16-cylinder General Motors diesel-electric engines via twin screw.
Passenger-car ferry owned and operated by Sea World Processors, USA.
Built by Todd Shipbuilding Corporation for British Columbia Ferries as the CHINOOK (1947). Renamed CHINOOK II (1955 – British Columbia Ferries) and SECHELT QUEEN (1989 – British Columbia Ferries).

MYCONOS (1964) See PRINCESS (1980)

MYKINAI (1971) See OCEANOS (1976)

MYREEMA (1908) See DOM PEDRO I (1926)

MYRTIDIOTISSA (2000)
3484 grt; 645 psrs
230 cars
319' x 59' x 15' (96.6 x 18 x 4.5 m)
4 x 6-cylinder Daihatsu diesel engines via twin screw.
Passenger-car ferry owned and operated by ANEK Lines.
Built by Kochi Jyuko KK, Kochi, for Muroto Kisen KK, Kochi, as the FERRY MUROTO (1975). Renamed KURUSHIMA MARU (1982 – Kurushima KK), LINK (1988 – South Aegean Lines Maritime Co), ANEMOS (1989 – Bluebird Maritime Co Ltd) and EXPRESS ANEMOS (2000 – ANEK Lines).

MYTILENE (1990)
10737 grt; 1735 psrs
50 cars + 75 trailers
451' x 74' x 18'6" (136.7 x 22.4 x 5.6 m)
2 x 16-cylinder Pielstick diesel engines via twin screw.

Passenger-car-cargo ferry operated by Maritime Company of Lesvos SA (NEL Lines).
Built by Naikai Zosen, Setoda, for Higashi Nippon Ferry KK, Tomakomai, as the VEGA (1973).

NADEZHDA KRUPSKAYA (1963) See KUBAN (1976)

NAESBORG (1988) See EUROMAGIQUE (1995)

NAESBORG (1991) See EUROMAGIQUE (1995)

NAGASAKI MARU (1922)
5272 grt; 355 psrs
395' x 54' x 20' (119.7 x 16.4 x 6.1 m)
4 x William Denny & Brothers SRG turbine engines via twin screw.
Built by William Denny & Brothers Co Ltd, Dumbarton, for NYK.

NAGASAKI SHANGHAI (1995) See ORIENTAL PEARL (1998)

NAGOYA (1913)
6874 grt; 94 psrs
450' x 52' x 30'6" (137 x 15.9 x 9.3 m)
2 x quadruple expansion engines via twin screw.
Broken up for scrap by Amakasu Gomei at Yokohama in 1932 for a tender figure of US$14,500.
Built by Caird & Co, Greenock, for P&O Lines at a cost of £120,741.

NAHA MARU (1972) See PHILIPPINE PRINCESS (1981)

NAIAS (1970)
3284 grt; 1200 psrs
341' x 49' x 16' (103.3 x 14.9 x 4.8 m)
2 x 9-cylinder B+W diesel engines via twin screw.

Broken up for scrap at Eleusis Bay in 1984. Ex-Naias Shipping Co SA, Piraeus.
Built by Elsingor Shipyards, Elsingor, for the United Steamship Co Ltd as the JENS BANG (1950).

NAIAS II(1983)
6712 grt; 1894 psrs
176 cars
377' x 60' x 15'6" (114.2 x 18.1 x 4.7 m)
2 x 16-cylinder Pielstick diesel engines via twin screw.
Passenger-car ferry owned by Syros Shipping, Greece, and operated by Agapitos on the Greece–Greek Islands service.
Launched by Chantiers et Ateliers de Provence, Port de Bouc, for Soc Nationale Maritime Corse Mediterranee as the PROVENCE (1966) and completed as the COMTE DE NICE (1966).

NAIAS EXPRESS (1995)
6177 grt; 1600 psrs
372' x 58' x 12' (112.6 x 17.5 x 3.7 m)
2 x 16-cylinder Pielstick diesel engines via twin screw.
Passenger ferry owned by Naias Express NE and operated by Agapitos Lines.
Built by Ansaldo, Genoa, for Sealink UK as the AILSA PRINCESS (1971). Renamed EARL HAROLD (1985 – Sealink UK Ltd) and DIMITRA (1989 – GA Ferries, Greece).

NAIRANA (1917)
3042 grt; 392 psrs
length 330' x beam 46' (100.6 x 14.1 m)

Geared turbine engines via twin screw.
Broken up where she lay in 1954 in Port Phillip Bay, Melbourne, following her running aground after breaking her moorings on 18 February 1951.
Built by William Denny & Bros, Dumbarton, for Huddart Parker Ltd.

NAIRNSHIRE (1898) See PERICLES (1914)

NAJD (1978)
3794 grt; 1700 psrs
374' x 50' x 13' (113.3 x 15.2 x 3.9 m)
2 x 12-cylinder Sulzer diesel engines via twin screw.
Owned by Najd Marine Agency, Jeddah.
Built by John Cockerill Shipyards, Hoboken, for RMT, Belgium, as the ROI LEOPOLD III (1956).

NAJD II (1979)
3389 grt; 1700 psrs
374' x 50' x 13' (113.3 x 15.2 x 3.9 m)
2 x 12-cylinder Sulzer diesel engines via twin screw.
Broken up for scrap at Elleusis Bay in 1985. Ex-Abha Marine Co Ltd, Limassol.
Built by John Cockerill Shipyards, Hoboken, for RMT, Belgium, as the KONINGIN ELISABETH (1957). Renamed ABHA (1978 – Abha Marine Co Ltd, Limassol).

NAJD II (1986) See NIAXCO III (1990)

NAJD III (1990)
3821 grt; 800 psrs
80 cars or 20 cars + 25 rail wagons
369' x 61' x 16' (112.4 x 18.6 x 4.8 m)
6 x 16-cylinder English-Electric diesel-electric engines via twin screw.
Broken up for scrap at Chittagong in 1994. Ex-Najd Marine Agency, Jeddah.
Built by Vickers-Armstrong Ltd, Newcastle, for New Zealand Railways as the passenger-car-cargo-rail RoRo ferry ARANUI (1966) at a cost of NZ$4,000,000. Renamed ARANUI I (1984 – Najd Marine Agency, Jeddah) and NUI (1985 – Najd Marine Agency, Jeddah).

NAJLA (1979) See STAR OF VENICE (1992)

NAJMI (1909)
3957 grt; 116 psrs
380' x 45' x 27'6" (115.8 x 13.8 x 8.4 m)
Triple expansion engine via single screw.
Broken up for scrap at Mumbai in 1911.
Built as the LOCKSLEY HALL (1887) for the Sun Shipping Co Ltd. Renamed PEKIN (1899 – P&O Steam Navigation Co Ltd) and SHAH NAWAZ (1906).

NALDERA (1920)
15825 grt; 673 psrs
605' x 67' x 30' (184.4 x 20.4 x 9.1 m)
2 x quadruple expansion engines via twin screw.
Broken up for scrap by P & W MacLellan Ltd for a tender price of £36,000 at Barrow-in-Furness in 1938.
Laid down by Caird & Co, Greenock, for the P&O Line in 1914 but not completed until 1920.

NAMINOUE MARU (1980) See SUPERFERRY 7 (1994)

NAMUR (1906)
6694 grt; 94 psrs
450' x 52' x 30'6" (137 x 15.9 x 9.3 m)
2 x quadruple expansion engines via twin screw.
Sank in 40 minutes, with one life lost, after being torpedoed by the German U-35 55 miles (92 km) south-east of Gibraltar.
Built by Caird & Co, Greenock, for the P&O Line at a cost of £104,871.

NANCOWRY (1976)
10294 grt; 1040 psrs
515' x 66' x 27' (156.1 x 20 x 8.2 m)
6 x Parsons geared turbine engines via twin screw.
Owned and operated by the Shipping Corporation of India Ltd. Broken up in 1089.

Built by Alexander Stephen & Sons, Glasgow, for the British India Line as the KARANJA (1948).

NANCOWRY (1992)
14176 grt; 1200 psrs
39 TEUs
518' x 69' x 22' (157 x 21 x 6.7 m)
2 x 6-cylinder B+W diesel engines via twin screw.
Passenger-cargo ship owned and operated by the Shipping Corporation of India Ltd.
Built by Stocznia Szczecinska, Szczecin.

NAN HAI MING ZHU (1993)
8836 grt; 984 psrs
150 cars or 32 trailers + 28 rail wagons
416' x 63' x 15' (126.1 x 19.1 x 4.5 m)
4 x 12-cylinder General Motors diesel engines via twin screw.

Passenger-car-cargo-train ferry owned by Kangda Shipping Co Ltd, China. Built by Alexander Stephen & Sons Ltd, Glasgow, for Canadian Pacific Railways as the PRINCESS OF VANCOUVER (1955). Renamed VANCOUVER ISLAND PRINCESS (1987 – British Columbia Steamship Co).

NAN HU (1983)
4996 grt; 1117 psrs
399' x 53' x 17' (121 x 16.2 x 5.2 m)
2 x 8-cylinder B+W diesel engines via twin screw.

Passenger ferry owned by the government of the People's Republic of China and operated by Shantou Navigation Co, Hong Kong. Built by Aalborg Vaerft, Aalborg, for DFDS as the KING OLAV V (1961). Renamed OLAV (1968 – DFDS), TAIWAN (1969 – China Navigation Co), BARONESSAN (1972 – Birka Line), MIN FUNG (1980 – Yick Fung Shipping & Enterprise Co Ltd, Panama) and JI MEI (1981 – China Ocean Shipping Ltd, Taiwan).

NANKIN (1898) See MOTOHIRA MARU No. 2 (1904)

NANKIN (1912) See LEUTHEN (1942)

NANKING (1918) See EMPIRE WOODLARK (1941)

NANSEMOND (1917)
13333 grt; 2604 psrs
579' x 62' x 29' (176.5 x 18.9 x 8.8 m)
Harland & Wolff 8-cylinder quadruple expansion engines via twin screw.
Broken up for scrap in 1924 as an ex-US Navy transport via the US Shipping Board.
Built by Harland & Wolff Ltd, Belfast, for the Hamburg-America Line as the PENNSYLVANIA (1896).

NAPOLEON (1959) See ALPASHA (1974)

NAPOLEON (1976)
14918 grt; 1896 psrs
500 cars
508' x 79' x 20' (155 x 24 x 6.1 m)

2 x 18-cylinder Pielstick geared diesel engines via twin screw.
Passenger-car ferry owned by SNCM and operated by Ferrymediterranee on the France–Corsica service.
Built by Chantiers Dubigeon-Normandie, Nantes, for SNCM.

NAPOLEON BONAPARTE (1996)
43307 grt; 2462 psrs
708 cars
568' x 100' x 22' (172 x 30.4 x 6.6 m)
4 x 18-cylinder Pielstick diesel engines via twin screw.
Passenger-car ferry owned by SNCM and operated by Corsica Marittima.
Built by Chantiers de l'Atlantique, St Nazaire, at a cost of US$173,000,000.

NAPOLI (1913)
9203 grt; 2270 psrs
470' x 57' x 32'1" depth (143.3 x 17.3 x 9.7 m)
Palmer's 6-cylinder triple expansion engines via twin screw.
Sank on 4 July 1918 after colliding with the Norwegian OTTO SVERDRUP in the Mediterranean Sea.
Launched by Palmer's Shipbuilding & Iron Co, Jarrow, for British Shipowners as the BRITISH PRINCE (1899) and completed for the Phoenix Line in 1900. Renamed SANNIO (1906 – Navigazione Generale Italiana, Genoa).

NAPOLI (1921)
6392 grt; 1890 psrs
406' x 52' x 26'6" depth (123 x 15.8 x 8.1 m)
G Clark Ltd 6-cylinder triple expansion engines via twin screw.
Broken up for scrap in Italy in 1926. Ex-Navagazione Generale Italiana.
Built by Sir James Laing Shipyards, Sunderland, for Sicula Americana as the passenger ship SAN GIORGIO (1907).

NAPOLI (1945)
8082 grt; 650 psrs
451' x 57' x 26' (137.5 x 17.3 x 7.9 m)
9-cylinder diesel engine via single screw.
Broken up for scrap at La Spezia in 1971. Ex-Achille Lauro.
Built by Harland & Wolff Ltd, Belfast, for the Bank Line as the ARAYBANK (1940), which sank in shallow water after being bombed in Suda Bay, Crete. She was raised and rebuilt five years later.

NARCIS (1973) See AEGEAN I (1996)

NARKUNDA (1920)
16227 grt; 673 psrs
606' x 70' x 33' (184.7 x 21.3 x 10 m)
2 x quadruple expansion engines via twin screw.
Sank on 14 November 1942, with 31 lives lost, after surviving a torpedo attack from the Italian submarine PLATINO the day before. However, she succumbed to heavy bombing by enemy aircraft during the North African landings the next morning.
Laid down by Harland & Wolff Ltd, Belfast, for the P&O Line in 1914, but not completed until 1920.

NARRAGANSET (1913) See PASSENGER No.3 (1966)

NARRUNG (1896) See MEXICO CITY (1913)

NARVA (1905) See KHAZAN (1906)

NARVIK (1982)
6257 grt; 410 psrs
40 cars
358' x 54' x 12' (109 x 16.5 x 3.6 m)
2 x 16-cylinder Bergens-Normo diesel engines via twin screw.
Passenger ferry operated by OVDS, Narvik.
Built by Aker Trondelag, Trondheim.

NASHVILLE, USS (1917)
11629 grt; 1370 psrs
536' x 53' x 26'8" (162.4 x 16.1 x 8.1 m)
W Cramp & Sons 12-cylinder quadruple expansion engines via twin screw.
Broken up for scrap in Italy in 1923 after catching fire during a refit in 1920.
Built by W Cramp & Sons Co, Philadelphia, Pennsylvania, for the International Navigation Co as the passenger ship ST. LOUIS (1895).

NASIPIT PRINCESS (1989)

8209 grt; 1193 psrs
492' x 75' x 16'6" (149.1 x 22.8 x 5 m)
2 x 14-cylinder MAN diesel engines via twin screw.
Passenger ferry operating for the Gothong Line, Philippines.
Built by Hayashikane Zosen, Shimonoseki, for Hankyu Ferry KK, Shimonoseki, as the FERRY SETO (1970)

NASSAU (1951) See ACAPULCO (1961)

NATALE (1925)

6849 grt; 1000 psrs
476' x 52' x 27'6" (144.9 x 15.9 x 8.4 m)
T Richardson & Sons 3-cylinder triple expansion engine via single screw.
Broken up for scrap in Italy in 1925 for a tender figure of US$36,000. Ex-Atlantic Transport Link.
Built by Furness, Withy & Co Ltd, West Hartlepool, for Wilson's & Furness-Leyland Line as the VICTORIA (1898). Renamed MANITOU (1898 – Atlantic Transport Link) and POLAND (1920 – Red Star Line).

NATASHI (1998) See PALMIRA 91998)

NAUTICAN (1994) See WALRUS (1996)

NAVAL HOSPITAL SHIP No. 4 (1939)

5767 grt; 613 psrs
390' x 53' x 24' (130 x 17.7 x 8 m)
A Stephen & Sons 6-cylinder triple expansion engines via twin screw.
Broken up for scrap in Blyth in 1951. Ex-British Royal Navy.
Built by Alexander Stephen & Sons Ltd, Glasgow, for the British India Steam Navigation Co as the passenger-cargo ship VASNA (1917).

NAVARINO (1975) See SEA (1998)

NAVARINO (1983) See SEA (1998)

NEA HELLAS (1939) See NEW YORK (1955)

NEAPOLETANO (1905)

4566 grt; 1442 psrs
length 445' x beam 44' (135.5 x 13.5 m)
2-cylinder compound engine via single screw.
Broken up for scrap in Italy in 1907.
Built by Caird & Co, Greenock, for the Inman Line as the CITY OF CHESTER (1873). Renamed CHESTER (1893 – American Line), SEDGWICK (1898 – US Army) and ARIZONA (1905).

NECKAR (1901) See POTOMAC (1921)

NEFELI (1999)

3756 grt; 716 psrs
30 cars + 31 trailers
297' x 55' x 13'6" (90 x 16.6 x 4.1 m)
2 x 6-cylinder Daihatsu diesel engines via twin screw.
Passenger-car- cargo ferry owned by Argosaronikos Lines Shipping Co.
Built by Shinhama Anan, Anan, for Koshien Kosoku Ferry KK as the MUKOGAWA (1990).

NEFERTITI (1956) See OLBIA (1961)

NEGBAH (1948)

5444 grt; 189 psrs
395' x 48' x 25' (119.7 x 14.5 x 7.6 m)
Triple expansion engine via single screw.
Broken up for scrap at Savona in 1956. Ex-Zim Israel Line.
Built by De Schelde, Vlissingen, for the Dutch Royal West Indian Mail Line as the passenger-cargo ship ECUADOR (1915). Renamed SANTA OLIVIA (1931 – Grace Line), DAVID W. BRANCH (1937 – Libby, McNeil & Libby) and LUXOR (1947 – Cia Victoria de Vapores, Panama).

NELLORE (1913)

6856 grt; 94 psrs
450' x 52' x 28' (137.2 x 15.8 x 8.5 m)

2 x quadruple expansion engines via twin screw.
Passenger-cargo ship owned by the Eastern & Australian Line, she sank on 29 June 1944 after being torpedoed by the Japanese submarine I-8 in the Indian Ocean while en route from Mumbai to Australia. There were no casualties durink the sinking, all 47 survivors drifting for 28 days in an open boat across 2,500 miles (4,167 km) to eventual rescue in Madagascar. However, 38 persons perished during the open boat voyage.
Built by Caird & Company, Greenock, for the P&O Line at a cost of £120,433.

NELLORE (1946)

9895 grt; 51 psrs
500' x 64' x 29'8" (151.5 x 19.4 x 9 m)
2 x Parsons DRG turbine engines via single screw.
Sold by Eastern & Australian Steamship Co in 1966.
Built by JL Thompson & Sons Ltd, Sunderland, for the British Ministry of War Transport as the EMPIRE JOY (1945).

NELLY (1949) See SEVEN SEAS (1954)

NEON (1966)

8323 grt; 55 psrs
455' x 62' x 28' (137.9 x 18.8 x 8.5 m)
Geared turbine engines via single screw.
Broken up for scrap at Kaohsiung in 1967. Ex-Cia Astro Guardia, Panama.
Built by the Californian Shipbuilding Corporation, Los Angeles, for the US Maritime Administration as the cargo ship TAOS VICTORY (1945). Renamed as the passenger-cargo ship LISMORIA (1948 – Astroguarda Cia Navigation SA).

NEPTUN (1934) See NEPTUNA (1935)

NEPTUN (1976)

5975 grt; 180 psrs
403' x 56' x 24' (122.2 x 17 x 7.4 m)
Sulzer 5-cylinder diesel engine via single screw.
Education and training ship owned by IMC Mircea Cel Batrin since 1992.
Built by Stocznia Szczecinska, Szczecin, for Navrom, Constantza.

NEPTUNA (1935)

5592 grt; 105 psrs
411' x 52' x 25'3" (125.3 x 15.8 x 7.7 m)
2 x 6-cylinder Krupp diesel engines via twin screw.
Passenger-cargo ship owned by Burns, Philp & Co Ltd, Sydney, she was broken up on site in 1959 by a Japanese salvage team. She had broken in two and sunk at her berth in Darwin as a result of a Japanese bomber attack on 19 February 1942.
Built by Fried Krupp Shipyards, Kiel, for Ozean Linie, Flensburg, as the RIO PANUCO (1924). Renamed NEPTUN (1934 – North German Lloyd).

NEPTUNE (1972)

4007 grt; 192 psrs
297' x 46' x 16' (90 x 14 x 4.8 m)
9-cylinder B+W diesel engine via single screw.
Cruise ship operated by Royal Olympic Cruises, but has been laid up in Piraeus since 1995.
Built by Aalborg Vaerft, Aalborg, for the Bergen Line as the METEOR (1954). Renamed ZEPHIROS (1972 – Epirotiki Cruise Lines).

NEPTUNE (1998) See THE NEPTUNE (1998)

NEPTUNE (2000) See WALRUS (1996)

NEPTUNIA (1945) See SIBIR (1946)

NEPTUNIA (1932)

19475 grt; 884 psrs
590' x 77' x 27'6" (178.8 x 23.3 x 8.4 m)
2 x 8-cylinder & 2 x 9-cylinder Sulzer diesel engines via twin screw.
Sank on 18 September 1941, with the loss of 384 lives, after being torpedoed by the British submarine HMS UPHOLDER, which also sank her sister OCEANIA in the same action, 58 miles (97 km) north of Tripoli.
Built by Cantieri Riuniti dell'Adriatico, Monfalcone, for the Cosulich Line.

NEPTUNIA (1948)
10519 grt; 787 psrs
523' x 59' x 29' (159.4 x 18.1 x 8.8 m)
2 x 3-cylinder NV Werkspoor triple expansion engines via twin screw.
Passenger ship owned by Cia Maritima del Este, she was broken up for scrap at Hendrick Ido Ambacht, Rotterdam, in 1958 after being towed from Ireland. She had been beached there following her striking Daunt's Rock off Cobh and developing a bad leak on 2 November 1957, which threatened to sink her.
Built by the Netherland Shipbuilding Co, Amsterdam, for the Nederland Line as the JOHAN DE WITT (1920).

NEPTUNIA (1951) See ROSSINI (1963)

NEPTUNIA (1975) See ZENITH (1995)

NEPTUNIA (1991) See MEDIA II (1993)

NEPTUNIA (1995) See MANAR (2000)

NEPTUNIA (1997)
8457 grt; 426 psrs
376' x 60' x 19' (114 x 18.1 x 5.8 m)
2 x 12-cylinder Deutz diesel engines via twin screw.

Passenger ferry owned by the Estonian Shipping Co, Tallin, and operated by Estline.
Launched after fabrication by Oosterreichische Schiffswerften AG, Linz, as the freight ferry STENA TOPPER for the Stena Line, but completed by Galati, Romania, as the DARNIA (1977 – James Fisher & Sons Plc, Barrow). Renamed NORD NEPTUNUS (1991 – Nordstrom & Thulin).

NEPTUNIA II (1994) See MANAR (2000)

NERA (1903)
5540 grt; 967 psrs
453' x 46' x 32'9" depth (137.3 x 13.9 x 10 m)
Messageries Maritimes 3-cylinder triple expansion engines via single screw.
Broken up for scrap in Italy in 1923. Ex-Messageries Maritimes.
Built by Messageries Maritimes, La Ciotat, for Messageries Maritimes as the LA PLATA (1888).

NERISSA (1926)
5583 grt; 229 psrs
350' x 54' x 30' (106.1 x 16.4 x 9.1 m)
4-cylinder triple expansion engine via single screw.
Owned by the Bermuda & West Indies Steamship Co, she sank on 30 April 1941 after being torpedoed by a German U-boat north-west of Ireland, off Inishtrahull.
Built by William Hamilton & Co Ltd, Port Glasgow, for the Red Cross Line.

NESSEBAR (1964)
6458 grt; 391 psrs
14 cars
421' x 55' x 19' (127.6 x 16.7 x 5.8 m)
4 x 8-cylinder Gotaverken diesel engines via twin screw.
Broken up for scrap by Brodospas at Split in 1976. Ex-Navigation Maritime Bulgare.
Hull constructed by Lindholmens and completed by Gotaverken for Swedish Lloyd as the SAGA (1940). Renamed VILLE DE BORDEAUX (1956 – Cie Generale Transatlantique).

NESTOR (1913)
14501 grt; 175 psrs

563' x 68' x 31'2" depth (170.6 x 20.8 x 9.5 m)
Workman, Clark 6-cylinder triple expansion engines via triple screw.
Broken up for scrap as a passenger-cargo ship at Faslane in 1950.
Built by Workman, Clark & Co Ltd, Belfast, for the Blue Funnel Line.

NETLEY (1912) See NOVARA (1912)

NETTUNO (1998) See HERMES (1999)

NEURALIA (1912)
9082 grt; 230 psrs
480' x 58' x 30'8" depth (145.5 x 17.6 x 9.3 m)
Barclay Curle 8-cylinder quadruple expansion engines via twin screw.
Sank on 1 May 1945 as a troopship after striking a mine in the Gulf of Taranto.
Built by Barclay, Curle & Co, Glasgow, for the British India Steam Navigation Co.

NEVA (1935)
8464 grt; 498 psrs
450' x 57' x 25'6" (136.4 x 17.3 x 7.7 m)
8-cylinder quadruple expansion engines via twin screw.
Broken up for scrap as a submarine tender in the late 1970s. Ex-Russian government.
Built by Workman, Clark & Co, Belfast, for the Royal Mail Steam Packet Co as the ESSEQUIBO (1914).

NEVA (1991) See ADMIRAL LAZAREV (1996)

NEVASA (1913)
9100 grt; 230 psrs
480' x 58' x 30'8" depth (145.5 x 17.6 x 9.3 m)
Barclay Curle 8-cylinder quadruple expansion engines via twin screw.
Broken up for scrap at Barrow-in-Furness in 1948 by the British Iron & Steel Co.
Built by Barclay, Curle & Co, Glasgow, as a passenger-cargo ship for the British India Steam Navigation Co.

NEVASA (1956)
20746 grt; 1400 psrs
609' x 78' x 26' (185.6 x 23.8 x 7.9 m)
6 x Parsons SRG turbines via twin screw.
Broken up for scrap as a school ship by Nan Feng Steel Enterprise Co Ltd at Kaohsiung in 1975.
Built by Barclay, Curle & Co, Glasgow, as a passenger ship for the British India Line.

NEVILLE, USS (APA-9) (1941)
8378 grt; 80 psrs
487' x 56' x 35'2" depth (147.6 x 17 x 10.7 m)
De Laval DRG turbine engines via single screw.
Broken up for scrap at Wilmington, Delaware, in 1957. Ex-US Navy.
Built by Bethlehem Shipbuilding Corporation, Alameda, California, for the US Shipping Board as the INDEPENDENCE (1918). Renamed as the passenger-cargo ship CITY OF NORFOLK (1931 – Baltimore Mail Line).

NEW AKASHI (1991)
14988 grt; 1066 psrs
110 cars 180 trailers
612' x 88' x 22' (185.5 x 26.8 x 6.7 m)
2 x 9-cylinder Pielstick diesel engines via twin screw.
Passenger-car-cargo ferry owned and operated by Hankyu Ferry KK, Japan.
Built by Kanda Zosen, Kawajiro.

NEW AKASHIA (1988)
19796 grt; 800 psrs
637' x 97' x 22'4" (193 x 29.4 x 6.8 m)
Passenger ferry operated on the Japanese inter-island service by Shin Nihonkai.
Built by Ishikawajima Heavy Industries, Tokyo.

NEW AKATSUKI (1992)
6412 grt; 580 psrs
54 cars + 70 trailers
480' x 73' x 20'6" (145.6 x 22 x 6.3 m)

2 x 12-cylinder Pielstick diesel engines via twin screw.
Owned and operated by Oshima Unyu KK, Naze.
Built by Hayashikane Dockyard, Nagasaki.

NEWARK (1968)
11522 grt; 2000 psrs
523' x 72' x 30'8" (158.5 x 21.8 x 9.3 m)
2 x Westinghouse DRG turbine engines via single screw.
Passenger ship owned by Sea Land Services Inc.
Built by Kaiser Corporation, Richmond, California, for the US Navy as the Class A4-S-A1 troop carrier GENERAL H.B. FREEMAN (AP-143) (1945). Reclassified as the GENERAL H.B. FREEMAN, USAT (1946 – US Army) and as the GENERAL H.B. FREEMAN, USNS (T-AP-143) (1950 – US Navy). Laid up at Olympia, Washington state, by the US Maritime Commission from 1958 to 1967.

NEWARK CASTLE (1902)
6224 grt; 540 psrs
414' x 51' x 28' (125.5 x 15.5 x 8.5 m)
Triple expansion engines via twin screw.
Abandoned after becoming wrecked on a sandbank in the mouth of the Umhlatuzi river in Richards Bay, Zululand, on 12 March 1908. This followed a successful refloating operation from a position seven miles (12 km) up the coast where she had run aground a few days earlier. Three lives were lost.
Built by Barclay, Curle & Co, Glasgow, for the Union-Castle Line.

NEW AUSTRALIA (1949) See ARKADIA (1958)

NEW BAHAMA STAR (1969) See BONAIRE STAR (1975)

NEW CHINA (1922) See ANAHUAC (1924)

NEW ENGLAND (1898) See SCANDINAVIAN (1912)

NEWFOUNDLAND (1925)
6791 grt; 185 psrs
406' x 55' x 25'4" (123 x 16.7 x 7.7 m)
Vickers 4-cylinder quadruple expansion engines via twin screw.
Sank on 13 September 1943 as a hospital ship when she was attacked by German aircraft off Salerno.
Built by Vickers-Armstrong Ltd, Barrow-in-Furness, as a passenger-cargo ship for the Furness-Warren Line.

NEWFOUNDLAND (1948) See GEORGE ANSON (1962)

NEW GOLDEN BRIDGE (1994)
16352 grt; 673 psrs
548' x 74' x 21'6" (166 x 22.5 x 6.5 m)
2 x 18-cylinder MAN diesel engines via twin screw.
Owned by Fair Lease, South Korea, and operated by Weidong Ferry Co Ltd.
Built by Koyo Dockyard, Mihara, for Nippon Car Ferry KK, Tokyo, as the OSUMI (1980). Renamed OLYMPIA 88 (1986 – Kuk Gae Ferry Co).

NEW GULANGYU (1984) See NEW ORIENT PRINCESS (1992)

NEW HAMANASU (1987)
17304 grt; 920 psrs
103 cars + 15 trailers
609' x 87' x 22'6" (184.5 x 26.5 x 6.8 m)
2 x 9-cylinder Pielstick diesel engines via twin screw.
Passenger-car-cargo ferry operated by Shin Nihonkai.
Built by Ishikawajima Shipbuilding, Aioi.

NEW HARIMA (1988)
12589 grt; 1104 psrs
75 cars + 166 trailers
576' x 88' x 20'6" (174.5 x 26.8 x 6.2 m)
2 x 8-cylinder Mitsubishi diesel engines via twin screw.
Passenger-car-cargo ferry operated by Hankyu Ferry.
Built by Kanda Zosensho KK, Kawajiri.

NEW KATSURA (1981)
16772 grt; 1070 psrs
48 cars + 99 trailers

466' x 75' x 18' (141.3 x 22.7 x 5.4 m)
2 x 12-cylinder Pielstick diesel engines via twin screw.
Passenger-car-cargo ferry operated by Osaka Kochi.
Built by Naikai Zosen KK, Setoda.

NEW MIYAKO (1984) See SUPERFERRY 12 (1996)

NEW NAGATO (1991)
14988 grt; 1066 psrs
110 cars + 180 trailers
612' x 88' x 22' (185.5 x 26.8 x 6.7 m)
2 x 9-cylinder Pielstick diesel engines via twin screw.
Passenger-car-cargo ferry operated by Hankyu Ferry KK, Japan.
Built by Kanda Zosensho KK, Kawajiri.

NEW NORTHLAND (1927) See NUEVO DOMINICANO (1947)

NEW ORANGE (1983)
6840 grt; 550 psrs
465' x 69' x 28'4" (141 x 21 x 8.6 m)
2 x 12-cylinder Ishikawajima diesel engines via twin screw.
Passenger ferry operated by Shikoku Kaihatsu Ferry KK.
Built by Imabari Zosen, Imabari.

NEW ORIENT PRINCESS (1992)
8669 grt; 900 psrs
413' x 64' x 17' (125 x 19.3 x 5.1 m)
2 x 10-cylinder B+W diesel engines via twin screw.

Owned by Gatmore Enterprises SA, she was broken up for scrap in August 1993 after she had been gutted by fire while operating for Sovereign Super Shipping Co as a casino ship, based in Hong Kong. She was beached on Junk Island, Kowloon, to prevent her sinking.
Built by Cantieri Navali de Tirrenio, Riva Trigoso, for DFDS as the ice-strengthened passenger ferry KONG OLAV V (1968). Renamed NEW GULANGYU (1984 – government of China), GULANGYU (1984 – government of China) and LEADER PRINCE (1988 – Strida Navigation, Panama).

NEW ORION (1989) See FERRY FUKUOKA (1992)

NEW ORLEANS (1969) See GUAYAMA (1975)

NEW PEGASUS (1989) See FERRY KYOTO (1989)

NEW PHOENIX (1981) See TONG AN (1983)

NEW QUEEN CORAL (1983) See PRINCESS OF THE PACIFIC (1993)

NEW ROCHELLE (1920) See PRESIDENT FILLMORE (1922)

NEW SETO (1988)
12589 grt; 1104 psrs
75 cars + 166 trailers
576' x 88' x 20'6" (174.5 x 26.7 x 6.2 m)
2 x 8-cylinder Mitsubishi-MAN diesel engines via twin screw.
Passenger-car-cargo ferry operated by Hankyu Ferry.
Built by Kanda Zosensho KK, Kawajiri.

NEW SEVILLA (1930)
12482 grt; 400 psrs

565' x 63' x 33' (172.2 x 19.2 x 10 m)
Harland & Wolff quadruple expansion 8-cylinder engines via twin screw.
Owned by Sevilla Whaling Co as a whaling factory ship, she sank on 20 September 1940, with two lives lost, after being torpedoed 30 miles (50 km) north of Malin Head, Ireland, by the German U-138.
Built by Harland & Wolff Ltd, Belfast, for the White Star Line as the passenger-cargo ship RUNIC (1901).

NEW SHIRAYURI (1987)
17305 grt; 920 psrs
103 cars + 150 trailers.
609' x 87' x 22'6" (184.5 x 26.5 x 6.8 m)
2 x 9-cylinder Pielstick diesel engines via twin screw.
Passenger-car-cargo ferry operated by Shin Nihonkai.
Built by Ishikawajima KK, Aoio.

NEW SOYA (1989)
3178 grt; 650 psrs
56 cars + 21 trailers
314' x 50' x 13' (95.7 x 15.1 x 4 m)
2 x 8-cylinder Daihatsu diesel engines via twin screw.
Passenger-car-cargo ferry operated by Higashi Nippon, Japan.
Built by Naikai Zosen KK, Setoda.

NEW SUZURAN (1979) See KRITI I (1997)

NEW TOSA (1990)
6939 grt; 1070 psrs
35 cars + 103 trailers
467' x 76' x 19' (141.5 x 23 x 5.7 m)
2 x 12-cylinder Pielstick diesel engines via twin screw.
Passenger-car-cargo ferry operated by Osaka Kocho Tokyo Ferry, Japan.
Built by Naikai Zosen KK, Setoda.

NEW UTOPIA (1982)
12344 grt; 650 psrs
594' x 69' x 20' (180 x 20.9 x 6.1 m)
2 x 18-cylinder MAN diesel engines via twin screw.
Cruise ship for Nishi Nihon Shosen, Japan.
Built by Onomichi Zosen, Onomichi, for Ryukyu Kaiun KK., Naha, as the ferry DIAMOND OKINAWA (1975).

NEW YAMATO (1983) See PRINCESS OF THE UNIVERSE (1996)

NEW YORK (1893) See NEW YORK (1921)

NEW YORK (1899) See NEW YORK (1921)

NEW YORK (1906)
16967 grt; 2886 psrs
length 615' x beam 68' (186.4 x 20.6 m)
Built by Harland & Wolff Ltd, Belfast, for the Holland-America Line.

NEW YORK (1921)
10798 grt; 1265 psrs
560' x 64' x 30'4" (170.7 x 19.4 x 9.2 m)
6-cylinder triple expansion engines via twin screw.
Broken up for scrap at Genoa in 1923. Ex-US government.
Built by J & G Thomson, Glasgow, for the Inman Line as the CITY OF NEW YORK (1888). Renamed NEW YORK (1893 – American Line), HARVARD, USS (1898 – as an armed cruiser for the US Navy), NEW YORK (1899 – American Line) and PLATTSBURG, USS (1919 – as a transport for the US Navy).

NEW YORK (1924)
4989 grt; 900 psrs
385' x 73' x 20'9" (116.7 x 22.1 x 6.3 m)
4 x Bath Ironworks SRG turbine engines via twin screw.
Sank on 25 September 1942 after being torpedoed in the North Atlantic.
Built by Bethlehem Shipbuilding Corporation, Sparrow's Point, Maryland, for Eastern Steamship Lines.

NEW YORK (1927)
22337 grt; 960 psrs

603' x 72' x 42'1" depth (182.7 x 21.8 x 12.8 m)
8 x Blohm & Voss SRG turbine engines via twin screw.
Broken up for scrap in England in 1949. She had been raised and towed from the harbour bed at Kiel where she had capsized and sunk following a heavy attack by British bombers on 3 April 1945.
Built by Blohm & Voss, Hamburg, for the Hamburg-America Line as a passenger ship.

NEW YORK (1955)
16991 grt; 1130 psrs
580' x 70' x 29' (176.8 x 21.4 x 8.8 m)
6 x DRG turbine engines via twin screw.
Owned by the Greek Line, she was broken up for scrap at Onomichi, Japan, in 1961 for a tender of £312,000.
Built by Fairfield Shipbuilding & Engineering Company, Glasgow, for the Anchor Line as the passenger ship TUSCANIA (1922). Renamed NEA HELLAS (1939 – Greek Line).

NEW YORK FORTUNE I (1997)
7632 grt; 852 psrs
375' x 56' x 16'6" (131.8 x 17 x 5 m)
4 x 6-cylinder Wartsila-Vasa diesel engines via twin screw.
Operated by Fortune Ship Investments Ltd.
Built by Helsingor Skibsvaerft, Helsingor, for DFDS as the ice-strengthened passenger-cargo ferry STAFFORD (1967). Renamed DANA GLORIA (1984 – DFDS), passenger-car ferry VOYAGER (1985 – TZA Marine Corporation, Limassol), MONACO (1987 – Cross Med Maritime Co, Piraeus), SITIA (1998 – Cross Med Maritime Co, Piraeus), converted to the passenger ship TROPIC STAR (1991 – Cross Med Maritime Co, Piraeus), PACIFIC STAR (1993 – Cross Med Maritime Co, Piraeus) and AEGEO STAR (1995 – Tony Travel Agency Ltd).

NEW YUKARI (1979) See KRITI II (1997)

NEW ZEALAND BEAR (1975) See PACIFIC ENDEAVOUR (1979)

nf PANTHER (1979) See ST. SUNNIVA (1987)

nf TIGER (1978) See ALANDSFARJAN (1987)

NGAIO (1949) See MOIZ (1955)

NIAGARA (1910)
8481 grt; 1142 psrs
485' x 56' x 33'8" (147.9 x 17.1 x 10.2 m)
3-cylinder triple expansion engines via twin screw.
Broken up for scrap in 1931.
Launched by Ateliers et Chantiers de la Loire, St Nazaire, for the French Line as the CORSE (1908), but completed as the NIAGARA (1910).

NIAGARA (1913)
13415 grt; 691 psrs
543' x 66' x 28' (165.5 x 20.2 x 8.5 m)
John Brown 4-cylinder triple expansion engines via triple screw.
Sank in one hour and 52 minutes on 19 June 1940 in 75 fathoms of water. She had struck a mine laid between Bream Head and Moko Hinau Island near Whangarei, New Zealand, by the German raider ORION five days earlier. There was no loss of life as all the passengers were transferred to the Huddart Parker's WANGANELLA and the vessel KAPITI. The vessel was carrying £2,500,000 worth of gold bullion which was later salvaged by a New Zealand team headed by diver JE Johnstone in two dives, in 1942 and 1953.
Laid down by John Brown & Co Ltd, Clydebank, for the Union Steamship Company of New Zealand as the SICAMOUS (1912) and completed as the NIAGARA.

NIASSA (1953)
10742 grt; 306 psrs
497' x 64' x 27'6" (151.5 x 19.5 x 8.4 m)
Ansaldo-Doxford 6-cylinder diesel engine via single screw.
Broken up for scrap at Bilbao in 1979.
Built by John Cockerill Shipyards, Hoboken, Belgium, for Cia Nacional de Navegacao, Portugal, as a passenger-cargo ship.

NIAXCO III (1990)
4343 grt; 800 psrs
80 cars or 20 cars + 25 rail wagons
368' x 61' x 15'6" (112.2 x 18.6 x 4.7 m)
6 x 16-cylinder English-Electric diesel-electric engines via twin screw.
Broken up for scrap at Alang in 1994. Ex-Najd Trading & Construction Establishment, Jeddah.
Built by William Denny & Brothers, Dumbarton, for New Zealand Railways as the passenger-car-cargo-train ferry ARAMOANA (1962) at a cost of NZ$4,000,000. Renamed CAPTAIN NICOLAS V (1984), ARAMOANA (1984 – New Zealand Railways) and NAJD II (1986 – Najd Marine Agency, Jeddah).

NICHINAN MARU (1973) See SANTA ANA (1993)

NICOBAR (1991)
14195 grt; 1200 psrs
39 TEUs
518' x 69' x 22' (157 x 21 x 6.7 m)
2 x 6-cylinder B+W diesel engines via twin screw.
Operated by the Shipping Corporation of India Ltd.
Built by Szczecinska Warskie, Szczecin.

NICOLAS PAQUET (1928)
8517 grt; 1100 psrs
428' x 57' x 25'8" (130 x 17.3 x 7.8 m)
Forges et Chantiers de la Mediterranee 6-cylinder triple expansion engines via twin screw.
Abandoned as a total loss after becoming wrecked on 6 July 1933 four miles (7 km) off Cape Spartel, North Africa.
Built for Forges et Chantiers de la Mediterranee, La Seyne, for Cie de Navigation Paquet.

NICOLO GIANI (1942) See MARCO POLO (1949)

NICOS KAZANTZAKIS (1990) See N. KAZANTZAKIS (1990)

NIDAROS (1931) See LYNGENFJORD (1933)

NIEBOROW (1989)
8697 grt; 1100 psrs
225 cars or 20 trailers
392' x 61' x 16'6" (118.7 x 18.6 x 5 m)
4 x 6-cylinder Stork-Werkspoor diesel engines via twin screw.

Passenger-car-cargo ferry owned by Stena and operated by Pol Ferries on the Sweden–Poland service.
Built by Werft Nobiskrug, Rendsburg, for Prinz Ferry as the PRINZ HAMLET (1973). Renamed PRINS HAMLET (1987 – Prins Ferries) and STENA BALTICA (1988 – Polish Baltic Shipping Co).

NIELS KLIM (1986) See STENA NAUTICA (1996)

NIEUW AMSTERDAM (1906)
17149 grt; 2886 psrs
615' x 68' x 35'6" (187.4 x 20.9 x 10.8 m)
2 x Harland & Wolff 4-cylinder quadruple expansion engines via twin screw.
Broken up for scrap at Osaka in 1932.
Built by Harland & Wolff Ltd, Belfast, for the Holland America Line.

NIEUW AMSTERDAM (1938)
36982 grt; 1220 psrs
758' x 88' x 31' (229.7 x 26.7 x 9.4 m)

8 x SRG turbine engines via twin screw.
Broken up for scrap at Kaohsiung in 1974.
Laid down by Rotterdam Drydock Co, Rotterdam, for the Holland-America Line as the PRINSENDAM (1936), but completed as the NIEUW AMSTERDAM.

NIEUW AMSTERDAM (1983) See PATRIOT (2000)

NIEUW HOLLAND (1928)
11215 grt; 173 psrs
541' x 63' x 32'3" depth (163.9 x 19 x 9.8 m)
4 x Stork & Co SRG turbine engines via twin screw.
Broken up for scrap at Hong Kong in 1959.
Built by Nederlandsche Shipbuilding Mij, Amsterdam, for the Royal Packet Company.

NIEUW HOLLAND (1971) See HERBERT (1996)

NIEUW ZEELAND (1928)
11069 grt; 173 psrs
559' x 63' x 26' (169.4 x 19.1 x 7.9 m)
SRG turbine engines via twin screw.
Sank on 11 November 1942 after being torpedoed by the German U-407 off Gibraltar, losing 15 lives in the action.
Built by the Rotterdam Drydock Co for the Royal Packet Line.

NIGERIA (1902)
4650 grt; 150 psrs
365' x 44' x 22' (110.6 x 13.3 x 6.7 m)
Richard Westgarth and Co Ltd 3-cylinder triple expansion engine via single screw.
Built by Sir Raylton Dixon and Co Ltd, Middlesbrough, for Elder Dempster Lines.

NIIHAMA (1973) See JATRA IBPS (1995)

NIIHAMA II (1984) See KUKJAE EXPRESS FERRY No. 2 (1994)

NIKKO MARU (1903)
5539 grt; 275 psrs
428' x 49' x 26'7" (129.7 x 14.8 x 8.1 m)
Mitsubishi 3-cylinder triple reduction engine via single screw.
Sank in the Pacific Ocean on 9 April 1945 after being torpedoed by the US submarine TIRANTE.
Built by Mitsubishi Dockyard, Nagasaki, for NYK as a passenger-cargo ship.

NIKOLAJEFF (1904) See NORODOVOLETZ (1917)

NIKOLA VAPTZAROV (1976)
6140 grt; 180 psrs
403' x 56' x 24' (122.2 x 17 x 7.4 m)
Sulzer 5-cylinder diesel engine via single screw.
Education ship owned by Navigation Maritime Bulgare.
Built by Stocznia Szczecinska, Szczecin.

NIKOLAYEVSK (1962)
5236 grt; 333 psrs
401' x 52' x 17' (121.5 x 15.8 x 5.2 m)
2 x 6-cylinder MAN diesel engines via twin screw.
Broken up for scrap in 1995.
Built by Mathias-Thesen, Wismar, for Kamchatka Shipping Co, Petropavlovsk-Kamcharskiy, as an ice-strengthened cruise ship.

NILE (1906)
6694 grt; 94 psrs
450' x 52' x 30'6" (137 x 15.9 x 9.3 m)
2 x quadruple expansion engines via twin screw.
Abandoned as a total loss after striking the Hojiro Rock, Awashima Island, in the Inland Sea of Japan on 11 January 1915. She sank within two hours.
Built by Caird & Co, Greenock, for the P&O Line at a cost of £105,057.

NILI (1965) See ARION (1976)

NILI (1969) See ARION (1976)

NILS DACKE (1975) See QUIBERON (1982)

NILS DACKE (1988) See PETER PAN (1993)

NILS DACKE (1995)
26790 grt; 308 psrs
155 cars
593' x 91' x 20' (179.6 x 27.9 x 6 m)
4 x 6-cylinder MaK diesel-electric engines via twin screw.

Passenger-car ferry owned and operated by TT Line GmbH, Hamburg.
Built by Finnyards, Rauma.

NILS HOLGERSSON (1962) See SAMA 1 (2000)

NILS HOLGERSSON (1967) See HERMES (1999)

NILS HOLGERSSON (1975) See THEOFILOS (1995)

NILS HOLGERSSON (1987) See VAL DE LOIRE (1993)

NILS HOLGERSSON (1993)
24728 grt; 1044 psrs
535 cars or 110 trailers
585' x 86' x 19' (177.2 x 26 x 5.8 m)
2 x 6-cylinder & 2 x 8-cylinder MAN-B+W DRG diesel engines via twin screw.

Owned and operated by TT-Line GmbH, Hamburg.
Built by Schichau Seebeckwerft AG, Bremerhaven, for the TT-Line as the ROBIN HOOD (1989).

NINDAWAYMA (1993)
3589 grt; 777 psrs
250 cars
304' x 55' x 15'6" (92.2 x 16.8 x 7.6 m)
2 x 12-cylinder Pielstick diesel engines via twin screw.
Passenger ferry owned and operated by Ontario Northland Marine Services, Owen Sound.
Launched by Juliana Construction Gijonesa SA, Gijon, as the MONTE CRUCETA (1976) and completed as the MONTE CASTILLO (1976). Renamed MANX VIKING (1978), MANX (1987), SKUDENES (1987 – Det Stavangerske Dampskibesselskab AS, Stavanger) and ONTARIO No. 1 (1989 – Ontario Northland Marine Services).

NINEVAH (1894) See LARNE (1916)

NIOBE I (1993)
5648 grt; 800 psrs
192 TEUs
343' x 62' x 17' (104 x 18.7 x 5.2 m)
2 x 8-cylinder MWM diesel engines via twin screw.
Owned by Cascade Navigation, Panama, and operated by Ikaria Lines, Brindisi.
Built by CNIM, La Seyne, for SNCF, Denmark, as the TRANSCONTAINER 1 (1969). Renamed NOUR I (1991 – Corporate Transactions SA, Panama).

NIPPON MARU (1972)
10908 grt; 1055 psrs
514' x 67' x 28'6" (156.6 x 20.5 x 8.7M)
Westinghouse geared turbine engine via single screw.
Broken up for scrap at Kaohsiung in 1977. Ex-Mitsui-OSK.
Built by Mitsubishi Heavy Industries, Kobe, for OSK as the ARGENTINA MARU (1958).

NIPPON MARU (1977) See ATHIRAH (1992)

NIPPON MARU (1990)
21903 grt; 607 psrs
546' x 78' x 22' (165.5 x 23.6 x 6.6 m)
2 x 8-cylinder Mitsubishi diesel engines via twin screw.
Cruise ship for Mitsui OSK, Japan.
Built by Mitsubishi Heavy Industries, Kobe.

NISHIKI MARU (1980) See DAEDALUS (1989)

NISOS KYPROS (1972) See ISLAND OF CYPRUS (1972)

NISSOS CHIOS (1979)
5260 grt; 1200 psrs
220 cars
322' x 60' x 16' (97.5 x 18.2 x 4.8 m)
2 x 8-cylinder Jugo-Sulzer diesel engines via twin screw.

Ice-strengthened passenger-car ferry owned by Chios Shipping Co SA and operated by Hellenic Coastal, Greece.
Built by Brodogradiliste, Kraljevica, for the Viking Line as the KAPELLA (1967).

NISSOS KYPROS (1993)
9965 grt; 983 psrs
30 cars + 40 rail coaches
452' x 62' x 18' (137 x 18.8 x 5.5 m)
2 x 8-cylinder B+W diesel engines via twin screw.

Passenger-car-cargo-train ferry owned and operated by Kyprohellenic Shipping Co Ltd, Limassol.
Built by Helsingor Shipyards, Helsingor, for Swedish Rail as the train ferry TRELLEBORG (1958). Renamed HOMERUS (1977 – Maritime Company, Lesvos).

NISSOS RODOS (1977)

6694 grt; 1200 psrs
90 cars + 24 rail wagons or 10 rail coaches
377' x 57' x 15' (114.2 x 17.3 x 4.5 m)
2 x 8-cylinder MAN diesel engines via twin screw.

Gutted by fire in June 1978.
Built by HWD for German State Rail as the train ferry DEUTSCHLAND (1953). Renamed RENETTA (1972 – government of Greenland).

NITTA MARU (1940) See CHUYO (1942)

NJEGOS (1980) See St CLAIR (1992)

N. KAZANTZAKIS (1989)

12500 grt; 1800 psrs
300 cars
512' x 76' x 20' (155 x 22.9 x 6 m)
2 x 18-cylinder Kawasaki-MAN diesel engines via twin screw.
Passenger-car ferry for Minoan Lines, but sold to Pacific Cruises, Hainan Island, China, for US$12,000,000 for a May 2001 delivery as the MING FAI PRINCESS.
Built by Kanashi Zosensho, Shimizu, for Nippon Enkai Ferry KK, Tokyo, as the SHIRETOKO MARU (1972). Renamed NICOS KAZANTZAKIS (1989 – Minoan Lines).

NOAH'S ARK (1999) See OCEAN HOME (1999)

NOGA (1980) See AMERICAN STAR (1993)

NOMADIC (1890) See CORNISHMAN (1903)

NOMENTANA (1980)

14834 grt; 728 psrs
645 cars
449' x 99' x 19' (136 x 30 x 5.9 m)
2 x 16-cylinder GMT diesel engines via twin screw.
Passenger-car ferry operated by Tirrenia.
Built by Italcantieri SpA, Castellammare di Stabia.

NOMI (1984) See TEBAH 2000 (1999)

NOORDAM (1902) See NOORDAM (1926)

NOORDAM (1926)

12528 grt; 2278 psrs
575' x 62' x 34' depth (175.3 x 19 x 10.3 m)
2 x Harland & Wolff 3-cylinder triple expansion engines via twin screw.
Broken up for scrap by F Rijsdijk at Rotterdam in 1928.
Built by Harland & Wolff Ltd, Belfast, for the Holland America Line as the NOORDAM (1902). Renamed KUNGSHOLM (1922 – Swedish America Line) when on charter.

NOORDAM (1938) See OCEANIEN (1963)

NOORDAM (1984)

33933 grt; 1214 psrs
704' x 90' x 24'6" (213.3 x 27.3 x 7.5 m)
2 x 7-cylinder Sulzer diesel engines via twin screw.
Cruise ship for Holland America Lines.
Built by Chantiers de l'Atlantique, St Nazaire, for the Holland America Line at a cost of US$160,000,000.

NOOR JEHAN (1975)

14569 grt; 841 psrs
557' x 69' x 27' (169.7 x 21 x 8.2 m)
2 x 10-cylinder Sulzer diesel engines via twin screw.
Broken up for scrap as a pilgrim ship at Mumbai in 1985. Ex-Mogul Line Ltd, Mumbai.
Built by Soc Espanola de Construccion Naval, Bilbao, for Ybarra Y Cia, Seville, as the CABO SAN VINCENTE (1959).

NOPATIN (1917) See GALILAH (1948)

NORAH MOLLER (1938)

4433 grt; 70 psrs
365' x 50' x 23'3" (111.2 x 15.2 x 7.1 m)
B+W 18-cylinder diesel engine via single screw.
Owned by Moller & Co, Shanghai, she sank on 3 February 1942 after Japanese aircraft had attacked her and left her on fire, with engines disabled, off West Nangka Point, in the Banka Strait.
Laid down by Harland & Wolff Ltd, Belfast, for the East Asiatic Company, Denmark, as the passenger-cargo ship LALANDIA (1915), but completed as the KANGAROO (1915) for the State Shipping Service, Western Australia.

NORBEL OMAN (1995) See BELLA VISTA (1996)

NORDERNEY (1900)

5211 grt; 994 psrs
410' x 51' x 27'1" (125 x 15.4 x 8.2 m)
Wigham Richardson 4-cylinder quadruple expansion engine via single screw.
Owned by North German Lloyd, she was lost without trace on 25 July 1916 near Sassnitz in the Baltic Sea.
Built by Wigham Richardson Ltd, Newcastle, for North German Lloyd as the passenger ship ELISABETH RICKMERS (1898).

NORD ESTONIA (1990) See VANA TALLINN (1997)

NORD GOTLANDIA (1989) See NORDLANDIA (1998)

NORDIA (1962) See THEOSKEPASTI (1986)

NORDIC EMPRESS (1990)

48563 grt; 2274 psrs
692' x 100' x 23' (209.7 x 30.3 x 7 m)
4 x 12-cylinder Wartsila diesel engines via twin screw.
Cruise ship for Royal Caribbean International.
Laid down by Chantiers de l'Atlantique, St Nazaire, for Admiral Cruises as the FUTURE SEAS (1989), but completed for Royal Caribbean International as the NORDIC EMPRESS at a cost of US$200,000,000.

NORDIC FERRY (1979) See PRIDE OF FLANDERS (1992)

NORDIC HUNTER (1990) See ASK (1991)

NORDICO (1926)

7204 grt
475' x 56' x 32'4" depth (143.9 x 17 x 9.8 m)
Richardsons Westgarth 6-cylinder triple expansion engines via twin screw.
Broken up for scrap in Italy in 1931.
Built by Furness, Withy & Co Ltd, West Hartlepool, as the EVERTON GRANGE (1903) for the Empire Transport Co. Renamed WESTMEATH (1912 – New Zealand Shipping Co Ltd).

NORDIC PRINCE (1972) See CAROUSEL (1995)

NORDIC SUN (1984) See AMBASSADOR (1993)

NORDKAPP (1996)

11386 grt; 691 psrs

50 cars
403' x 67' x 16' (122.1 x 20.3 x 4.9 m)
2 x 6-cylinder Krupp-MaK diesel engines via twin screw.
Cruise ferry owned and operated by Ofotens Vesteraalens.
Built by Kvaerner Kleven Ulstein, Ulsteinvik.

NORDLANDIA (1998)
21473 grt; 2048 psrs
550 cars or 60 cars + 65 trailers
502' x 80' 18' (152 x 24.2 x 5.8 m)
4 x 8-cylinder Pielstick diesel engines via twin screw.

Passenger-car-cargo ferry owned by Rederi AB, Eckero, and operated by Eckero Line.
Built by AG Weser Schichau Seebeckwerfte, Bremerhaven, for the Olau Line as the OLAU HOLLANDIA (1981). Renamed NORD GOTLANDIA (1989 – N & T Gotlands-Linjen, Sweden).

NORDLYS (1994)
11204 grt; 691 psrs
50 cars
402' x 63' x 16' (121.8 x 19.2 x 4.9 m)
2 x MaK diesel engines via twin screw.
Operated by Tromso Fylkes DS, Tromso, on the Norwegian coastal cruise service.
Built by Volkswerft Shipyard, Strasland, at a cost of US$63,000,000

NORD NEPTUNUS (1991) See NEPTUNIA (1997)

NORDNORGE (1997)
11384 grt; 691 psrs
50 cars
407' x 64' x 16' (123.3 x 19.5 x 4.9 m)
2 x 6-cylinder MaK diesel engines via twin screw.
Cruise ferry operated by the Bergen Line.
Built by Kvaerner Kleven Ulsteinvik AS, Ulsteinvik, for Ofotens OG Vesteraalens Dampskibsselskab AS, Narvik.

NORD PAS DE CALAIS (1987) See SEAFRANCE NORD PAS-DE-CALAIS (1996)

NORE (1907)
6696 grt; 94 psrs
450' x 52' x 30'6" (137 x 15.9 x 9.3 m)
2 x quadruple expansion engines via twin screw.
Broken up for scrap by TW Ward Ltd, Hayle, Cornwall, in 1926 for a tender of £14,400.
Built by Caird & Company, Greenock, for the P&O Line at a cost of £104,790.

NORFOLK (1900)
5310 grt; 64 psrs
421' x 54' x 28'8" depth (127.6 x 16.4 x 8.7 m)
Northeast Marine Engineering 3-cylinder triple expansion engine via single screw.
Abandoned after the captain beached her on fire on 8 November 1914 on the Ninety Mile Beach, Victoria, Australia, where she broke her back.
Built by Sunderland Shipping Co, Sunderland, for the Federal Steam Navigation Co, London.

NORHAM CASTLE (1883) See MARTINIQUE (1903)

NORILSK (1951)
3498 grt; 346 psrs
334' x 47' x 18' (101.2 x 14.2 x 5.5 m)
2 x 6-cylinder Fiat diesel engines via twin screw.

Cruise ship operated by the Russian government.
Built by Camtieri del Mediterraneo.

NORLAND (1974)
26290 grt; 881 psrs
520 cars or 179 trailers
572' x 83' x 20' (173.3 x 25.2 x 6 m)
2 x 16-cylinder Stork Werkspoor diesel engines via twin screw.

Passenger-car-cargo ferry owned and operated by P&O North Sea Ferries Ltd, Hull, on the UK–Belgium service.
Built by AG Weser, Bremerhaven.

NORLEB (1984)
11693 grt; 467 psrs
520' x 68' x 25' (158.4 x 20.7 x 7.6 m)
2 x 10-cylinder Ansaldo-Fiat Diesel engines via twin screw.
Broken up for scrap as a sheep carrier at Gadani Beach, Karachi, in 1985. Ex-Norleb Shipping Enterprises, Beirut.
Built by Cantieri Riuniti dell'Adriatico, San Marco, for Lloyd Triestino as the ASIA (1953). Renamed PERSIA (1975 – Rashid Fares Enterprises, Beirut).

NORMANDIE (1935) See LA FAYETTE (1941)

NORMANDIE (1992)
27541 grt; 2263 psrs
680 cars
533' x 88' x 18'6" (161.4 x 26.6 x 5.7 m)
4 x 12-cylinder Wartsila-Vasa diesel engines via twin screw.

Passenger-car ferry operating for Brittany Ferries.
Built by Kvaerner Masa-Yard, Turku, for Brittany Ferries at a cost of £88,000,000.

NORMANDY (1997)
24872 grt; 2100 psrs
480 cars or 52 trailers
492' x 86' x 20' (149 x 26 x 6.1 m)
4 x 12-cylinder Nohab-Wartsila-Vasa diesel engines via twin screw.
Passenger-car-cargo ferry owned and operated by Irish Continental Ferries following their purchase from Rederi AB Gotland for US$18,400,000 in early 2000.
Laid down by Gotaverken-Arendal, Gothenburg, for Sessan Line as Job No 909, launched as the DROTTNING SILVIA (1982) and completed for the Stena Line as the PRINSESSAN BIRGITTA (1982). Renamed St NICHOLAS (1983 – Sealink UK) and STENA NORMANDY (1991 – Stena Line).

NORMANNIA (1887) See KUBAN (1904)

NORMANNIA (1952)
3543 grt; 500 psrs
110 cars
309' x 50' x 12'6" (93.6 x 15.2 x 3.8 m)
Pametrada DRG turbine engines via twin screw.
Broken up for scrap in Spain in 1978.
Built by William Denny & Bros Co Ltd, Dumbarton, for British Transport Commission.

NORODOVOLETZ (1917)
7326 grt; 2060 psrs
460' x 52' x 31'9" depth (140.2 x 15.9 x 9.7 m)
AG Vulcan 6-cylinder triple expansion engine via twin screw.
Broken up for scrap at St Petersburg, in 1925. Ex-Russian Navy.
Built by AG Vulcan, Stettin, for the Hamburg-America Line as the PALATIA (1895). Renamed NIKOLAJEFF (1904 – Russian Navy).

NORONIC (1913)
6905 grt; 600 psrs
362' x 52' x 24'8" (109.7 x 15.8 x 7.5 m)
American Shipbuilding Co 4-cylinder triple expansion engine via single screw.
Burnt out in Toronto in 1949 with a loss of 118 lives. She was broken up in Hamilton, Ontario.
Built by Western Drydock & Shipbuilding Co Ltd, Port Arthur, Ontario, for Northern Navigation Company.

NORRONA (1983) See NORRONA (1996)

NORRONA (1996)
11999 grt; 1050 psrs
300 cars or 44 trailers
426' x 69' x 17' (129 x 21 x 5.2 m)
4 x 6-cylinder Stork-Werkspoor diesel engines via twin screw.

Ice-strengthened passenger-car-cargo ferry owned and operated by Smyril Line.
Built by Werft Nobiskrug GmbH, Rendsburg, for the Saga Line as the GUSTAV VASA (1973). Renamed NORRONA (1983 – Smyril Line) and WISMAR II (1994 – North Sea Baltic Ferries as a charter).

NORSEA (1987)
31785 grt; 1258 psrs
850 cars or 180 trailers

591' x 83' x 20' (179 x 25.1 x 6.2 m)
2 x 9-cylinder & 2 x 6-cylinder Wartsila-Sulzer diesel engines via twin screw.

Passenger-car-cargo ferry owned and operated by P&O North Sea Ferries Ltd, Hull, on the UK–Holland service.
Built by Govan Shipbuilders Ltd, Glasgow, for the P&O Line at a cost of £40,000,000.

NORSE LAGAN (1991) See MOBY RIDER (1998)

NORSEMAN (1900)
9546 grt; 2700 psrs
516' x 62' x 33'9" depth (157.1 x 18.8 x 10.3 m)
8-cylinder quadruple expansion engines via twin screw.
Owned by Dominion Line, Liverpool, she was broken up for scrap by Soc Italiana di Salvataggi e Navigazione in Italy in 1920. She had been raised from the seabed of Mudros harbour, Greece, where she sank after being torpedoed in the Gulf of Salonika by the German U-39 on 22 January 1916.
Built by Harland & Wolff Ltd, Belfast, for the Hamburg-America Line as the BRASILIA (1897).

NORSKY (1978) See CHONG MING DAO (1998)

NORSTAR (1974)
26919 grt; 889 psrs
520 cars
571' x 83' x 19'6" (173 x 25.2 x 6 m)
2 x 16-cylinder Stork- Werkspoor diesel engines via twin screw.

Passenger-car ferry owned and operated by P&O North Sea Ferries Ltd, Hull, on the UK–Belgium service.
Built by AG Weser, Bremerhaven, for North Sea Ferries.

NORSUN (1987)
31598 grt; 1258 psrs
850 cars or 180 trailers
591' x 84' x 20' (179 x 25.4 x 6.1 m)
4 x 6-cylinder Wartsila-Sulzer diesel engines via twin screw.
Ferry owned and operated by P&O North Sea Ferries Ltd, Hull, on the UK–Holland service.
Built by Nippon Kokan KK, Yokohama, for Nedlloyd at a cost of £40,000,000.

NORTHERN MERCHANT (2000)
24046 grt; 250 psrs
260 cars
594' x 80' x 21'6" (180 x 24.3 x 6.5 m)
4 x 9-cylinder Wartsila diesel engines via twin screw.
Owned by Cenargo International Ltd subsidiary Merchant Ferries, and

chartered to the Norfolk Line, UK.
Built by Astilleros Espanoles, Seville.

NORTHERN PACIFIC (1914)
8255 grt; 850 psrs
524' x 63' x 21' (158.8 x 19.1 x 6.4 m)
3 x W Cramp & Sons turbine engines via triple screw.
Sank on 9 February 1922 after catching fire off Cape May, New Jersey.
Built by the Sun Shipbuilding & Drydock Co, Chester, Pennsylvania, for the Great Northern Pacific Steamship Company at a cost of US$1,950,000.

NORTHERN PRINCE (1929)
10917 grt; 101 psrs
496' x 65' x 26'6" (150.3 x 19.7 x 8.1 m)
Kincaid-B+W diesel engines via twin screw.
Sank on 3 April 1941 after a German aircraft attack in the Straits of Kithira (anti-Kithira Channel), Greece.
Built by Lithgows Ltd, Port Glasgow, for Furness, Withy & Co, London.

NORTHERN STAR (1962)
23983 grt; 1437 psrs
650' x 83' x 26' (198.1 x 25.3 x 7.9 m)
Parsons DRG turbine engines via twin screw.
Broken up for scrap by Li Chong Steel & Iron Works at Kaohsiung in 1976.
Built by Vickers-Armstrong Ltd, Newcastle, for the Shaw Savill Line.

NORTHLAND (1915) See MINNESOTA (1927)

NORTHLAND (1926) See NUEVO DOMINICANO (1947)

NORTHLAND PRINCE (1963) See INDOCEANIQUE (1994)

NORTH SEA (1935)
3133 grt; 180 psrs
299' x 45' x 22'8" (90.6 x 13.6 x 6.9 m)
Bethlehem Shipbuilding Corporation 3-cylinder triple expansion engines via single screw.
Abandoned as a total loss after wrecking herself on Porter Reef, Bella Bella, BC, Canada, on 13 February 1947. Ex-Northland Transportation Co.
Built by Bethlehem Shipbuilding Corporation Ltd, Elizabeth Port, for the US Shipping Board as the PLAINFIELD (1918). Renamed MARY WEEMS (1922 – Baltimore & Carolina Steamship Co) and ADMIRAL PEOPLES (1927 – Admiral Lines).

NORTH STAR (1901)
3159 grt; 108 psrs
299' x 46' x 22'8" (90.6 x 13.9 x 6.9 m)
Delaware Shipbuilding & Engineering Co 3-cylinder triple expansion engine via single screw.
Abandoned as a total loss after becoming wrecked on Green Island, Nova Scotia, on 8 August 1919.
Built by Delaware Shipbuilding & Engineering Co for the Maine Steamship Co.

NORTH STAR (1937) See EMPIRE PARKESTON (1947)

NORTH STAR (1966) See CALEDONIAN STAR (1983)

NORTH STAR (1983)
3095 grt; 170 psrs
288' x 46' x 18'5" (87.3 x 13.9 x 5.6 m)
2 x 8-cylinder MaK diesel engines via single screw.
Cruise ship owned by North Star Line, Oslo, she was declared a total constructive loss after being holed in two compartments as she grounded off Klawock, Prince of Wales Island on 8 August 1986. The US Coastguard evacuated her 143 passengers and crew.
Built by AG Weser, Bremerhaven as the stern trawler MARBURG (1966). Renamed LINDMAR (1982).

NORTHWESTERN (1906)
3497 grt; 150 psrs
336' x 43' x 22' (101.8 x 13 x 6.7 m)
Delaware River Co 3-cylinder triple expansion engines via single screw.
Broken up for scrap in Dutch Harbour, Alaska, in 1946 where she had been badly damaged by Japanese bombers on 3 June 1942. Ex-Alaska Steamship Co Inc.
Built by Delaware River Co, Chester, Pennsylvania, for the New York & Cuba Mail Steamship Co as the ORIZABA (1890).

NORTIA (1999)
3450 grt; 1008 psrs
185 cars
305' x 59' x 14'5" (92.4 x 17.8 x 4.4 m)
2 x 10-cylinder MAN diesel engines via twin screw.

Ice-strengthened passenger-car ferry for Etruria Shipping, Italy.
Built by Schichau Unterweser, Bremerhaven, for Grenaa-Hundested Faergefart AS as the GRENAA (1964). Renamed KALLE (1971 – Jutland Line), OLAU WEST (1975 – Olau Line), CORSICA MARINA (1977 – Tourship Co Ltd, Panama), KELIBIA (1990 – Alimar Shipping Co Ltd) and SCENT OF SEA (1998 – Carretel Malta Shipping Co Ltd).

NORWAVE (1965) See ITALIA EXPRESS (1987)

NORWAY (1979)
76049 grt; 2022 psrs
1035' x 110' x 34'4" (315.5 x 33.7 x 10.5 m)
8 x Parsons SRG turbine engines via twin screw. (The original forward engine compartment was sealed and the outboard shafts and screw removed for economy of operation.)

Cruise ship owned and operated by Norwegian Cruise Lines.
Built by Chantiers de l'Atlantique, St Nazaire, for the French Line as the FRANCE (1961).

NORWEGIAN CROWN (1996) See CROWN ODYSSEY (2000)

NORWEGIAN DREAM (1998)
50760 grt; 1726 psrs
754' x 94' x 22' (228.5 x 28.5 x 6.7 m)

4 x 8-cylinder MAN-B+W diesel engines via twin screw.
Cruise ship for Orient Cruise Lines.
Built by Chantiers de l'Atlantique, St Nazaire, for Norwegian Cruise Lines as the DREAMWARD (1992) at a cost of US$240,000,000.

COSTA OLYMPIA (1998), but then purchased for US$27,000,000 by NCL for completion by Kvaerner Masa-Yards, Turku, as the NORWEGIAN SKY at a cost of US$225,000,000.

NORWEGIAN DYNASTY (1997) See CROWN DYNASTY (1999)

NORWEGIAN MAJESTY (1997)
40876 grt; 1462 psrs
680' x 91' x 20'6" (206.1 x 27.6 x 6.2 m)
4 x 6-cylinder Wartsila diesel engines via twin screw.

NORWEGIAN STAR (1997)
28018 grt; 880 psrs
674' x 83' x 24' (205.4 x 25.3 x 7.3 m)
4 x 9-cylinder Wartsila-Sulzer geared diesel engines via twin screw.

Cruise ship for Norwegian Cruise Lines.
Partially built to an unfinished ferry hull stage for Birka Line by Kvaerner Masa-Yards, Turku, but purchased on the slips by Majesty Cruise Line Inc and completed as the ROYAL MAJESTY (1992) at a cost of US$229,000,000.

NORWEGIAN SEA (1997)
42276 grt; 1534 psrs
709' x 96' x 21' (214.8 x 29.1 x 6.4 m)
4 x 8-cylinder Wartsila-Sulzer diesel engines via twin screw.

Cruise ship owned and operated by Norwegian Capricorn Lines, a joint venture between Norwegian Cruise Line and Star Cruises, Singapore.
Built by Wartsila, Helsinki, for the Royal Viking Line as the ROYAL VIKING SEA (1973). Renamed ROYAL ODYSSEY (1991 – Royal Cruise Line).

NORWEGIAN WIND (1998)
50760 grt; 1748 psrs
754' x 94' x 22' (228.5 x 28.5 x 6.8 m)
4 x 8-cylinder MAN-B+W diesel engines via twin screw.
Cruise ship owned and operated by Norwegian Cruise Lines.
Built by Chantiers de l'Atlantique, St Nazaire, for Norwegian Cruise Lines as the WINDWARD (1993) at a cost of US$243,000,000.

NORWIND (1966) See GRECIA EXPRESS (1987)

NOUR I (1991) See NIOBE I (1993),

NOVARA (1912)
6875 grt; 94 psrs
450' x 52' x 30'6" (128.2 x 15.9 x 9.3 m)
2 x quadruple expansion via twin screw.
Broken up for scrap by Tamizo Okushoji for a tender of £9,500 at Osaka in 1932.
Laid down by Caird & Company, Greenock, for the P&O Line at a cost of £115,056 as the NETLEY (1912), but completed as the NOVARA.

N & T 700 (1987) See CHONG MING DAO (1998)

NOVA SCOTIA (1926)
6796 grt; 185 psrs
406' x 55' x 25'4" (123 x 16.7 x 7.6 m)
Vickers-Armstrong 4-cylinder quadruple expansion engines via twin screw.
Owned by the Warren Line, she sank on 4 December 1942 after being torpedoed by the German U-177 off Laurenco Marques, Mozambique, while transporting Italian prisoners-of-war, of whom 508 were lost.
Built by Vickers-Armstrong Ltd, Barrow-in-Furness, as a passenger-cargo ship.

Cruise ship for Norwegian Cruise Lines.
Built by Wartsila-Turku for Norwegian Cruise Lines as the SEAWARD (1988) at a cost of US$120,000,000.

NORWEGIAN SKY (1999)
77104 grt; 2002 psrs
842' x 105' x 26' (255.2 x 31.8 x 7.9 m)
6 x 7-cylinder MAN B+W diesel engines via twin screw.
Cruise ship owned and operated by Norwegian Cruise Line.
Hull partially built by Bremer Vulkan, Vegesack, for Costa Cruises as the

NOVA SCOTIA (1947) See FRANCIS DRAKE (1962)

NUBIA (1882) See SAO LUIZ (1906)

NUEVO DOMINICANO (1947)
3445 grt; 175 psrs
315' x 47' x 18' (95.5 x 14.2 x 5.5 m)
Swan Hunter & Wigham Richardson steam reciprocal engines via single screw.
Foundered on 27 November 1953 off the north coast of Cuba.
Built by Swan Hunter & Wigham Richardson Ltd, Newcastle, for the Clarke Steamship Company, Canada, as the ice-strengthened passenger cargo ship NORTHLAND (1926). Renamed NEW NORTHLAND (1927 – Clarke Steamship Co, Canada).

NUI (1985) See NADJ III (1990)

NUITS ST GEORGES (1980) See SALEM EXPRESS (1989)

NURA NOVA (1999)
3134 grt; 450 psrs
104 cars
259' x 45' x 12' (78.5 x 13.6 x 3.7 m)
2 x 6-cylinder Niigata diesel engines via twin screw.
Passenger-car ferry owned and operated by Cia Iscomar SA, Palma de Mallorca.
Built by Usuki Ironworks Ltd, Saiki, for AG Ems Schiffarts KG, Emden, as the EMSLAND (1977). Renamed BOHUS (1986 – Scandi Line), St JULIEN (1989 – Sealink UK), JON (1992 – Armatur SA, Panama) and ELBA NOVA (1992 – Sardinia Ferries SrL, Genoa).

NURNBERG (1936) See WESTBAY (1957)

NUSA PEJUANG (1992)
4468 grt; 945 psrs
240 cars or 30 cars + 22 trailers
404' x 61' x 16' (122.4 x 18.5 x 4.8 m)
2 x 12-cylinder Pielstick diesel engines via twin screw.
Broken up for scrap by RK Engineering in Mumbai in 1998. Ex-Perabadanan Nasional Shipping Line Berhad, Kuala Lumpur.
Built by Lubecker Flender-Werke, Lubeck, for the TT Line as the ice-strengthened passenger-car-cargo ferry PETER PAN (1965). Renamed s.f. PANTHER (1973 – Southern Ferries), TERJE VIGEN (1975 – Dano Line charter) and ST CLAIR (1977 – P&O Ferries).

NUTMEG STATE (1921) See LEONARD WOOD, USS (APA-12) (1943)

NYANZA (1907)
6695 grt; 94 psrs
450' x 52' x 30'6" (137 x 15.9 x 9.3 m)
2 x quadruple expansion engines via twin screw.
Broken up for scrap in Osaka in 1927 by Sakaguchi Sadakichi Shoten KK, for a tender of £17,000.
Built by Caird & Company, Greenock, for the P&O Line at a cost of £104,680.

NYASSA (1924)
9028 grt; 1460 psrs
462' x 58' x 34'6" depth (140.9 x 17.6 x 10.5 m)
Tecklenborg 8-cylinder quadruple expansion engines via twin screw.
Broken up for scrap in 1952 at Blyth. Ex-Cia Nacional de Navegacao, Lisbon.
Built by JC Tecklenborg, Geestemunde, for North German Lloyd as the BULOW (1906). Renamed TRAS-OS-MONTES (1916 – after seizure by Portuguese government).

NYU VICTORY (1945) See CORDOBA (1947)

OAKLAND (1965)
17184 grt; 920 psrs
684' x 72' x 24' (158.5 x 21.8 x 7.3 m)
Geared turbine engine via single screw.
Owned by Sea Land Service Inc as a container ship, she was wrecked off Vietnam while being delivered to be broken up for scrap in 1988.
Built by Kaiser Corporation, Vancouver, Washington, for the US Shipping Administration as the Class C4-S-A3 troop transport MARINE TIGER (1945). As the MARINE TIGER, she operated as a migrant ship after World War Two, prior to being laid up for the period 1949–64.

OAKLEAF (1917)
7345 grt; 500 psrs
485' x 59' x 31' (146.7 x 17.9 x 9.4 m)
6-cylinder triple expansion engines via twin screw.
Owned by Lane & MacAndrew Ltd, she sank on 25 July 1917 after being torpedoed by the German U-41 64 miles (107 km) north-west of the Butt of Lewis, Scotland.
Built by Alex Stephen & Sons, Glasgow, for the Beaver Line as the MONTEZUMA (1899). Renamed ABADOL (1915 – British Admiralty).

OARI MARU (1987) See SUNFLOWER OARI (1991)

OBDAM (1889) See ONEGA (1914)

OCEANA (1927) See SIBIR (1946)

OCEAN BREEZE (1992) See IMPERIAL MAJESTY (1999)

OCEAN BUILDER (1964)
10998 grt; 1700 psrs
552' x 67' x 31'8" (168.1 x 20.2 x 9.6 m)
2 x 9-cylinder Kieler HDW diesel-electric engines via twin screw.
Owned by Ocean Shipping Enterprises Ltd, Monrovia, as a cargo ship, she was broken up for scrap by Chien Tai Iron Works at Kaohsiung in 1972.
Launched initially by Germaniawerft, Kiel, as a cargo ship, but converted to a passenger ship by Howaldtswerke, Kiel, for the Hamburg-America Line as the OSTMARK (1940). Renamed SKAUGUM (1948 – IM Skaugum, Oslo).

OCEAN EAST (1991)
11523 grt; 452 psrs
75 cars + 101 trailers
548' x 83' x 20'6" (166 x 25 x 6.2 m)
2 x 8-cylinder pielstick diesel engines via twin screw.
Passenger-car-cargo ferry operated by Ocean Tokyo Ferry, Japan.
Built by Saiki Jukoyo, Saiki, for Ocean Tokyo.

OCEAN ENDURANCE (1966)
7795 grt; 276 psrs
503' x 66' x 29' (153.3 x 20.2 x 8.1 m)
6-cylinder Hawthorne-Sulzer diesel engine via single screw.
Broken up for scrap in Pakistan in 1984. Ex-Ocean Shipping Enterprises Ltd, Monrovia.
Built by Bartram & Sons, Sunderland, for the Pakistan National Shipping Corporation, Karachi.

OCEAN EXPLORER I (1998)
20071 grt; 1069 psrs
622' x 75' x 26' (226.4 x 22.7 x 7.9 m)
2 x De Laval turbine engines via twin screw.
Cruise ship owned by Excellence Holdings, Greece, and up for charter following the collapse of the World Cruise Company, Toronto. The latter had chartered the ship in November 1999 on a long-term contract following an earlier six-month period laid up in Eleusis Bay, Greece. In 2000 she was returned to be laid up in Eleusis Bay again.
Laid down by the Federal Shipbuilding & Drydock Company, Kearny, New Jersey, for the US government as the Ps-S2-R2 troop transport GENERAL R. M. BLATCHFORD (AP-118) (1944), but completed as the GENERAL W. P

RICHARDSON (AP-118) (1944) at a cost of US$7,000,000. Renamed LA GUARDIA (1949 – American Export Lines), LEILANI (1956 – Textron Inc), PRESIDENT ROOSEVELT (1961 – American President Lines), ATLANTIS (1970 – Chandris Group), EMERALD SEAS (1972 – Eastern Steamship Lines), SAPPHIRE SEAS (1993 – Ambassador Cruises) and RIVIERA STAR (1996 – Cyprus businessman). In 1992, her eventual charterer (Ambassador Cruises) registered SUN FIESTA, FANTASTICA, FUNTASTICA and TERRIFICA, but she never cruised under any of these names.

OCEAN HOME (1999)
12000 grt; 550 psrs
498' x 56' x 14'6" (151 x 17 x 4.5 m)
2 x Wartsila diesel engines via twin screw.
Cruise ship built by MEKAP, Perama, as the TAYGETOS (!980). Renamed SEA VENTURE (1991 – Sea Venture Cruises), SEAWIND ROYALE (1991 – Seawind Cruise Line) and NOAH'S ARK (1999 – Palm Beach Shipping & Trading Co SA, Piraeus).

OCEANIA (1906) See VASCO NUNEZ DE BALBOA (1916)

OCEANIA (1908)
5497 grt; 391 psrs
391' x 50' x 23'2" (119.2 x 15.2 x 7 m)
A Stephen & Sons 6-cylinder triple expansion engines via twin screw.
Scuttled by the Austrians on 15 October 1918 to prevent her capture by the Italians. This followed damage from a mine at sea and her eventual beaching 12 days earlier near Cape Rondoni.
Built by Alex Stephen & Sons, Glasgow, for Unione Austriaca.

OCEANIA (1909) See STAMPALIA (1912)

OCEANIA (1933)
19507 grt; 1250 psrs
590' x 77' x 27'6" (178.8 x 23.3 x 8.4 m)
4 x 8-cylinder Fiat diesel engines via quadruple screw.
Sank simultaneously with her sister ship NEPTUNIA on 18 September 1941, with the loss of 2,500 lives, after being torpedoed by the British submarine HMS UPHOLDER, 58 miles (97 km) north of Tripoli.
Laid down by Cantieri Riuniti dell'Adriatico, Monfalcone, for the Cosulich Line as the ERIDANIA (1931) and completed as the OCEANIA.

OCEANIA (1951) See VERDI (1963)

OCEANIC (1965) See THE BIG RED BOAT I (1997)

OCEANIC (1997) See THE BIG RED BOAT I (1997)

OCEANIC CONSTITUTION (1974) See CONSTITUTION (1982)

OCEANIC GRACE (1989) See CLIPPER ODYSSEY (1999)

OCEANIC INDEPENDENCE (1974) See INDEPENDENCE (1982)

OCEANIC INDEPENDENCE (1979) See INDEPENDENCE (1982)

OCEANIC ODYSSEY (1997) See CLIPPER ODYSSEY (1999)

OCEANIC RELIANCE (1956)
8254 grt; 120 psrs
494' x 61' x 26'4" (150.5 x 18.6 x 8 m)
2 x 5-cylinder MAN diesel engines via twin screw.
Owned by Pacific Bulk Carriers Inc, she was broken up for scrap at Mihara in 1959.
Built by Bremer Vulkan, Vegesack, for Cie Generale Transatlantique as the WASHINGTON (1929). Renamed SAGITTAIRE (1938 – Messageries Maritimes) and the bulk carrier PACIFIC GLORY (1954 – Cia Maritime Asiatic Panamense, Hong Kong).

OCEANIEN (1963)
10726 grt; 123 psrs
502' x 64' x 31' (153 x 19.5 x 9.4 m)

2 x 12-cylinder B+W diesel engines via twin screw.
Owned by the Costa Line subsidiary Cielomar SA, she was broken up for scrap by Brodospas at Split in 1967.
Built by Van P Smit Jr, Rotterdam, for the Holland America Line as the NOORDAM (1938).

OCEAN ISLANDER (1985) See ROYAL STAR (1991)

OCEAN KING (1980) See PHILIPPINES (1999)

OCEAN MAJESTY (1986) See OCEAN MAJESTY (1991)

OCEAN MAJESTY (1995)
10417 grt; 613 psrs
100 cars
431' x 63' x 18' (130.6 x 19 x 5.4 m)
4 x 16-cylinder Wartsila diesel engines via twin screw.
Cruise ship chartered to Indian Ocean Cruise Line, Mumbai, in 2000 by her owners, Majestic International Cruises.
Built by Union Navale de Levante, Espanol, for Trasmediterranea as the passenger-car ferry JUAN MARCH (1966). Renamed SOL CHRISTIANA (1985 – Sol Lines Ltd, Limassol), KYPROS STAR (1986 – Opal Lines), OCEAN MAJESTY (1989 – Majestic International Cruises), OLYMPIC (1994 – Epirotiki Lines), OCEAN MAJESTY (1995 – Majestic International Cruises) and HOMERIC (1995 – chartered to Page & Moy, UK). She was not operational between 1991 and 1994 while undergoing a major reconstruction and replacement of engines for her original 2 x 7-cylinder B+W diesels.

OCEAN MONARCH (1951) See REINA DEL MAR (1979)

OCEAN MONARCH (1970)
25971 grt; 1372 psrs
640' x 85' x 29' (195.1 x 25.9 x 8.8 m)
DRG turbine engines via twin screw.
Owned by Shaw Savill, she was broken up for scrap by Chi Shun Hwa Steel Co Ltd at Kaohsiung in 1975.
Built by Vickers-Armstrong Ltd, Newcastle, for the Canadian Pacific Steamship Company as the EMPRESS OF ENGLAND (1956).

OCEAN NORTH (1996)
11114 grt; 148 psrs
71 cars + 130 trailers
548' x 83' x 21' (166 x 25 x 6.4 m)
2 x 8-cylinder Pielstick diesel engines via twin screw.
Passenger-car-cargo ferry owned and operated by Ocean Tokyu.
Built by Onomichi Zosen, Onomichi.

OCEANOS (1976)
14000 grt; 516 psrs
492' x 64' x 24'6" (150 x 19.5 x 7.5 m)
2 x 10-cylinder B+W diesel engines via twin screw.
Owned by Epirotiki Cruise Lines, Greece, she was under charter for once-only cruise itinerary for TFC Tours, Johannesburg, when she sank on 4 August 1991. Her engine room had unaccountably flooded a few days earlier in huge seas 100 miles (167 km) north-east of East London, South Africa. The behaviour of the ship's captain, who left his ship by helicopter while his crew and passengers were attempting to survive, has been much criticised subsequently. No loss of life was involved from the 580 people on board.
Built by Chantiers de la Gironde, Bordeaux, for Messageries Maritimes as the JEAN LABORDE (1953). Renamed MYKINAI (1971 – Efthymiadis Line), ANCONA (1974 – Efthymiadis Line), EASTERN PRINCESS (1974 – Far East Travel Centre) and BRINDISI EXPRESS (1974 – Efthymiadis Line).

OCEAN PEARL (1988) See GOLDEN PRINCESS (2000)

OCEAN PRINCESS (1983) See SAPPHIRE (1995)

OCEAN PRINCESS (2000)
77441 grt; 1950 psrs
856' x 106' x 26' (259.4 x 32 x 7.9 m)
4 x 16-cylinder Sulzer diesel engines via twin screw.
Cruise ship owned and operated by P&O Princess Cruises.
Built by Fincantieri, Monfalcone, at a cost of US$300,000,000.

OCEAN QUEEN (1976) See SINDBAD I (1978)

OCEAN SKY (1990) See MILLENNIUM EXPRESS (2000)

OCEAN SOUTH (1996)
11114 grt; 148 psrs
71 cars + 130 trailers
548' x 83' x 21' (166 x 25 x 6.4 m)
2 x 8-cylinder Pielstick diesel engines via twin screw.
Passenger-car-cargo ferry owned and operated by Ocean Tokyu.
Built by Onomichi Zosen, Onomichi.

OCEAN SPIRIT (1988) See THE EMPRESS (1994)

OCEAN TRIUMPH (1950) See MOHAMMEDI (1951)

OCEAN VICTORY (1950) See MOZZAFFRI (1951)

OCEAN VIRTUE (1942) See ANDREA C (1948)

OCEAN WEST (1991)
11522 grt; 452 psrs
75 cars + 101 trailers
512' x 83' x 20'6" (155 x 25 x 6.2 m)
2 x 8-cylinder Pielstick diesel engines via twin screw.
Passenger-car-cargo ferry operated by Ocean Tokyo Ferry, Japan.
Built by Saiki Jukogyo.

OCTANS, USS (AF-26) (1943)
6305 grt; 131 psrs
425' x 54' x 29' (128.8 x 16.4 x 8.8 m)
2 x triple expansion engines via twin screw.
Broken up for scrap at Baltimore in 1947. Ex-US Navy.
Built by Workman, Clark & Co, Belfast, for the Unifruit Co as the ULUA (1917).

OCTORARA (1910)
4272 grt
363' x 45' x 28' (110 x 13.6 x 8.5 m)
Detroit Shipbuilding Co 4-cylinder quadruple expansion engine via single screw.
Broken up for scrap at San Francisco in 1952 as a Great Lakes cruise ship.
Built by Detroit Shipbuilding Co, Wyandotte, Michigan, for the Anchor Line (Erie & Western Transportation Company).

ODESSA (1975) See ODESSA I (1999)

ODESSA I (1999)
11889 grt; 470 psrs
446' x 71' x 19' (136 x 21.5 x 5.8 m)
2 x 16-cylinder Crossley-Pielstick diesel engines via twin screw.
Cruise ship owned by Black Sea Shipping Co and chartered to Eastmar Management Inc.
Laid down by Vickers-Armstrong Ltd, Barrow-in-Furness for AS Nordline as the PRINS HENRIK AF DANMARK (1969), but following Nordline's inability to proceed with the contract, the vessel was completed for international sale by Swan, Hunter & Wigham Richardson, Newcastle, as the COPENHAGEN (1974). A sale to the Black Sea Shipping Co, Odessa, in 1975 saw the ship renamed ODESSA. She was last chartered to Transocean

Cruises until 1996 and then laid up at Imperia (1996–99) until Eastmar Marine chartered her under the name ODESSA I.

ODESSA SKY (1995) See VAN GOGH (1999)

ODESSA SONG (1992) See SILVER STAR (1998)

ODESSA SUN (1991) See OMEGA (2000)

ODYSSEAS ELYTIS (1982) See EL-TOR (1998)

ODYSSEUS (1969)
4307 grt; 350 psrs
52 cars
367' x 52' x 15' (111.2 x 15.8 x 4.5 m)
2 x 8-cylinder B+W diesel engines via twin screw.
Owned by Epirotiki Steamship Co Ltd, Famagusta, she was broken up for scrap at Faslane in 1979 after serving as an accommodation ship to an oil platform crew off the Kyle of Lochalsh. She was then laid up for two years. Built by Harland & Wolff Ltd, Belfast, for the British & Irish Steam Packet Company as the LEINSTER (1937). Renamed ULSTER PRINCE (1946 – Belfast Steamship Co) and ADRIA (1968).

ODYSSEUS (1988)
12000 grt; 452 psrs
478' x 61' x 18' (145.7 x 18.5 x 5.5 m)
2 x 8-cylinder B+W diesel engines via twin screw.

Cruise ship owned by Royal Olympic Cruises, Greece, and chartered to Legend Cruises, Gibraltar, for three years with a guaranteed purchase in 2004. Built by Soc Espanola de Construccion Naval, Bilbao, for Cia Nacional de Navigacao Costeira, Brazil, as the passenger-cargo (72500cf) ship PRINCESA ISABEL (1962) at a cost of US$5,000,000. Renamed as the cruise ship MARCO POLO (1969 – Dominion Far East Line) and AQUAMARINE (1978 – owned by Arkley Navigation Co, Monrovia, a subsidiary of Aquamarine Ltd, Greece). Chartered to John N Strathakis Co Ltd, Piraeus, until financial difficulties forced the Commercial Bank of Greece to lay the ship up for the period 1981–87. Currently for sale at US$12,000,000.

OFELIA (1968)
3638 grt; 600 psrs
110 cars
246' x 55' x 12'6" (74.4 x 16.8 x 3.8 m)
2 x 8-cylinder Atlas-MaK diesel engines via twin screw.
Passenger-car ferry owned by Hoiupanga Liisingu, Estonia, and operated by Saaremaa Shipping Co Ltd, Saaremaa.
Built by Kroegerwerft, Rendsburg.

OGASAWARA MARU (1979) See PRINCESS OF THE CARIBBEAN (1997)

OGASAWARA MARU (1997)
6679 grt; 833 psrs
432' x 57' x 19' (131 x 17.2 x 5.7 m)
2 x 18-cylinder Pielstick diesel engines via twin screw.
Built by Mitsubishi Heavy Industries Ltd, Shimonoseki, for Ogasawara Kaiun KK, Tokyo, as a passenger-cargo ferry.

OGDEN MISSOURI (1974) See LINNET (1977)

OGLALA, USS (1928)
5131 grt
Broken up for scrap at Richmond, California, in 1965 by the US Navy.
Built as the MASSACHUSETTS (1907). Renamed SHAWMUTT, USS (CM-4) (1917 – US Navy).

OHIO (1923) See ALBERTIC (1927)

OHRMAZD (1968)
11046 grt; 276 psrs
520' x 67' x 29' (158.6 x 20.5 x 8.8 m)
Clark-Sulzer diesel engines via single screw.
Broken up for scrap at Gadani Beach in 1994 as a passenger-cargo ship owned by Pakistan National Shipping Corporation, Karachi.
Built by Burntisland Shipbuilding Co Ltd, Burntisland, for the East + West Steamship Company, Karachi.

OINOUSSAI (1973) See BELKIS I (1994)

OKEAN (1989) See MINERVA (1996)

OKESA MARU (1993)
12419 grt; 1520 psrs
290 cars
445' x 69' x 18' (134.7 x 21 x 5.4 m)
2 x 12-cylinder Niigata-Pielstick diesel engines via twin screw.
Passenger-car ferry operating for Sado Kisen KK, Japan.
Built by Kanda Shipyard for Sado Kisen, Kawajiri.

OKINAWA MARU (1973) See ILOILO PRINCESS (1994)

OKUDOGO (1972) See SANTA FLORENTINA (1983)

OKUDOGO 2 (1973) See PRINCESS OF NEGROS (1994)

OKUDOGO 3 (1976) See MARIA G (1998)

OKUDOGO No. 6 (1982) See MARINA (1990)

OKUDOGO No. 8 (1982) See IERAPETRA L (1999)

OLAU BRITANNIA (1982) See CHRISTIAN IV (1991)

OLAU BRITANNIA (1990) See PRIDE OF PORTSMOUTH (1994)

OLAU DANA (1975) See TIAN E (1985)

OLAU EAST (1975) See ALDONZA MANRIGUE (1976)

OLAU FINN (1976) See CAPTAIN ZAMAN II (1998)

OLAU HOLLANDIA (1981) See NORDLANDIA (1998)

OLAU HOLLANDIA (1989) See PRIDE OF LE HAVRE (1994)

OLAU KENT (1976) See LANGELAND IV (1999)

OLAU WEST (1975) See NORTIA (1999)

OLAV (1968) See NAN HU (1983)

OLBIA (1961)
3975 grt; 326 psrs
358' x 50' x 21' (108.5 x 15.2 x 6.4 m)
SRG turbine engines via twin screw.
Passenger ferry owned and operated by Tirrenia.
Built by Thornycroft, Southampton, for Khedivial Mail Line as the EL MALEK FOAD (1947). Renamed EL MALEK FOUAD (1948 – Khedivial Mail Line) and NEFERTITI (1956 – Khedivial Mail Line).

OLBIAS (1987) See CARLA E (1991)

OLD COLONY (1907)
4779 grt
375' x 52' x 31'6" depth (113.6 x 15.8 x 9.6 m)
3 x William Cramp & Sons turbine engines via triple screw.
Broken up for scrap in Germany in 1922.
Built by William Cramp & Sons Shipbuilding & Engineering Co Ltd, Philadelphia, Pennsylvania.

OLDENBURG (1891) See AK-DENIZ (1911)

OLD NORTH STATE (1920) See PRESIDENT FILLMORE (1946)

OLEANDER (1988) See HORNBEAM (1992)

OLGA ANDROVSKAYA (1976)
4258 grt; 256 psrs
328' x 53' x 16' (99.4 x 16.1 x 4.7 m)
2 x 8-cylinder B+W diesel engines via twin screw.
Cruise ship broken up for scrap in 1998.
Built by Brodogradiliste, Kraljevica, for the Far East Shipping Co, Vladivostok.

OLGA SADOVSKAYA (1977) See ORIENT STAR (1993)

OLIMPIA (1947)
7716 grt
442' x 57' x 34'8" depth (133.9 x 17.3 x 10.5 m)
General Machinery Corporation 3-cylinder triple expansion engine via single screw.
Broken up for scrap at La Spezia in 1968 as a cargo ship operating for Achille Lauro.
Built by St John's River Shipbuilding Co, Jacksonville, Florida, for the US Maritime Commission as the "Liberty"-class cargo ship SHAULA (1943). Renamed JAMES SCREVEN (1944 – for the US Maritime Commission as a refugee transport, for which she was fitted out with temporary accommodation).

OLIVER TWIST (1975) See HERMES (1999)

OLVIA (1995)
15791 grt; 750 psrs
256 cars + 23 trailers
518' x 73' x 20' (157 x 22 x 6 m)
2 x 18-cylinder Pielstick diesel engines via twin screw.
Owned by Maddock Trading Inc and chartered to Peace Boat Cruises, Tokyo.
Built by Wartsila-Turku for the Black Sea Shipping Co, Odessa, as the cruise ship KARELIYA (1976). Renamed LEONID BREZHNEV (1982 – Black Sea Shipping Co), KARELIYA (1989 – Black Sea Shipping Co) and OLVIYA (1995).

OLVIYA (1995) See OLVIA (1995)

OLYMPIA (1902)
5197 grt; 70 psrs
400' x 49' x 27'8" depth (121.9 x 15 x 8.4 m)
D & W Henderson 3-cylinder triple expansion engine via single screw.
Broken up for scrap in 1926.
Built by D & W Henderson Ltd, Glasgow, for the Anchor Line.

OLYMPIA (1946) See JUAN DE GARAY (1947)

OLYMPIA (1953) See REGAL EMPRESS (1993)

OLYMPIA (1969) See EROS (1979)

OLYMPIA (1984) See DELOS (1986)

OLYMPIA (1985) See BOSPORUS (1999)

OLYMPIA (1986) See DIMITRIOS MIRAS (1988)

OLYMPIA (1986) See PRIDE OF BILBAO (1993)

OLYMPIA (1987) See AL SALAM 93 (1996)

OLYMPIA I (1997)
6064 grt; 328 psrs
416' x 55' x 17' (126.1 x 16.7 x 5.2 m)
2 x Nordberg 9-cylinder diesel engines via twin screw.
Owned by Royal Olympic Cruises and operated by Olympic Short Cruises.
Built by Ansaldo Shipyards, Livorno, for Nomikos Lines as the ACHILLEUS (1952). Renamed ORION (1968 – Hellenic Cruises SA, Piraeus). Laid up between 1987 and 1995 and then named THOMAS II (1995 – Thomas Cruises, UK).

OLYMPIA 88 (1986) See NEW GOLDEN BRIDGE (1994)

OLYMPIC (1911)
46359 grt; 2764 psrs
882' x 92' x 34'6" (268.8 x 28 x 10.6 m)
2 x Harland & Wolff Ltd 4-cylinder triple expansion and turbine engines via triple screw.
Broken up for scrap finally in 1937 at Inverkeithing by Metal Industries Ltd. She had been partially dismantled at Jarrow, UK, in 1935 following her collision with the 630 ton Nantucket Lightship, USA, on 16 May 1934. All aboard OLYMPIC survived, but all seven hands on the lightship were lost when it sank. White Star Line paid the US Department of State US$350,000 as loss compensation.
Built by Harland & Wolff Ltd, Belfast, for the White Star Line.

OLYMPIC (1946) See JUAN DE GARAY (1947)

OLYMPIC (1993) See APOLLO (1998)

OLYMPIC (1994) See THE TOPAZ (1998)

OLYMPIC 2004 (1997) See APOLLO (1998)

OLYMPIC CHAMPION (2000)
32694 grt; 1850 psrs
654 cars or 106 cars + 157 trailers
673' x 85' x 22' (204 x 25.8 x 6.7 m)
4 x 12-cylinder Wartsila diesel engines via twin screw.
Passenger-car-trailer ferry owned and operated by ANEK Lines.
Built by Bruces Shipyards, Landskronor, and Mek Verksteder, Fevaag, at a cost of US$90,000,000.

OLYMPIC COUNTESS (1998)
16795 grt; 750 psrs
535' x 75' x 19' (163 x 22.8 x 5.8 m)
4 x 7-cylinder B+W geared diesel engines via twin screw.

Cruise ship for Royal Olympic Cruises, but for sale since mid-2000.
Laid down by Burmeister & Wain, Copenhagen, for the Cunard Line as the CUNARD COUNTESS (1976), but completed by Industrie Navale Meccaniche Affini Shipyard, La Spezia, at a cost of £12,000,000. Renamed AWANI DREAM II (1996 – owned by P T Modern Hotel Group and operated by its subsidiary, Klub Awani, after being purchased from Cunard for US$23,000,000).

OLYMPIC FLAME (1988) See WANG FU (1993)

OLYMPIC VOYAGER (2000)
24500 grt; 820 psrs

590' x 84' x 24' (178.8 x 25.5 x 7.3 m)
4 x 9-cylinder Wartsila diesel engines via twin screw.

Owned by Royal World Cruises and operated by Royal Olympic Cruises.
Built by Blohm & Voss, Hamburg, at a cost of US$175,000.000.

OMAR (1921) See EDISON (1924)

OMAR II (2000)
9848 grt; 509 psrs
429' x 63' x 17' (130 x 19 x 5.2 m)
2 x 12-cylinder MaK diesel engines via twin screw.
Casino cruise ship owned by Liberty Investment Worldwide Management Ltd,
Hong Kong, and operated by Conning Shipping, Hong Kong, after purchase
at US$13,000,000.
Built by Elsinore Shipbuilding & Engineering Co, Elsinore, for Royal Cruise
Line as the GOLDEN ODYSSEY (1974) at a cost of US$22,000,000.
Renamed ASTRA II (1995 – Astra II Shipping Co Ltd, and chartered to
Caravella Shipping Co Ltd).

OMEGA (2000)
3696 grt; 250 psrs
337' x 50' x 13' (102 x 15 x 3.9 m)
2 x 8-cylinder Russian diesel engine via single screw.
Cruise ship owned by Odessa Sun Ltd, Greece.
Built by A Jdanov, St Petersburg, for the Black Sea Shipping Co, Odessa, as
the UZBEKISTAN (1962) and renamed ODESSA SUN (1991) following sale
to a Ukranian consortium. Laid up from 1997 to 2000, and broken up for scrap
in the latter year.

ONEGA (1914)
3558 grt; 940 psrs
401' x 40' x 21'3" (121.5 x 12.1 x 6.5 m)
Nederland Shipbuilding Co 3-cylinder compound engine via single screw.
Owned by the US government, she sank on 30 August 1918 after being
torpedoed by the German U-123 in the English Channel.
Built by Harland & Wolff Ltd, Belfast, for British Shipowners as the
passenger-cargo ship BRITISH QUEEN (1881). Renamed OBDAM (1889 –
Holland America Line), troop transport ship McPHERSON (1898 – US
Army), BROOKLYN (1906 – Frank Steamship Company trading as the Zotti
Line, New York) and troop transport ship LUCKENBACH (1908 – US Army).

ONTARIO (1904)
3082 grt; 164 psrs
292' x 42' x 15'9" (88.5 x 12.7 x 4.8 m)
New York Shipbuilding Co 3-cylinder triple expansion engine via single
screw.
Sank on 6 May 1942 after being torpedoed near Mobile, Alabama.
Built by New York Shipbuilding Co, Camden, New Jersey, for the Merchant
& Miners Transportation Co.

ONTARIO No. 1 (1989) See NINDAWAYMA (1993)

OP ten NOORT (1927)
6076 grt; 190 psrs
425' x 55' x 22'2" (128.8 x 16.7 x 6.7 m)
Werkspoor 8-cylinder compound engines via twin screw.
Sank as a hospital ship after a Japanese attack.
Built by the Nederland Shipbuilding Co for Koninkijke Pakkervaart
Maatschappij.

ORAMA (1911)
12927 grt; 1080 psrs
551' x 64' x 39' (168 x 19.5 x 11.9 m)
Turbine engines via triple screw.
Sank in four hours on 19 October 1917 after being torpedoed by the German
U-62 south of Ireland.
Built by John Brown & Co Ltd, Clydebank, for the Orient Line.

ORAMA (1924)
19777 grt; 1836 psrs
660' x 75' x 30' (201.1 x 22.9 x 9.1 m)
6 x Parsons SRG turbine engines via twin screw.
Sank 300 miles (500 km) west of Narvik on 8 June 1940, with the loss of 19
lives, after the combined massive firepower of the German battleships
SCHARNHORST, GNEISENEN and ADMIRAL HIPPER destroyed her.
Laid down by Vickers-Armstrong Ltd, Barrow-on-Furness, for the Orient Line
as the ORIANA (1923) and completed as the ORAMA.

ORANGE ACE (1989)
7318 grt; 604 psrs
486' x 78' x 14'6" (147.2 x 23.5 x 4.5 m)
2 x 12-cylinder Pielstick diesel engines via twin screw.
Passenger ferry operated by Shikoku Kaihatsu.
Built by Imabari Shipyards, Imabari.

ORANGE 7 (1994)
9917 grt; 604 psrs
138 cars
540' x 84' x 18' (163.6 x 25.6 x 5.5 m)
2 x 18-cylinder Pielstick diesel engines via twin screw.
Passenger-car ferry operated by Shikoku Kaihatsu.
Built by Imabari Zosen, Imabari.

ORANIA (1922)
9763 grt; 1192 psrs
450' x 59' x 28' (136.4 x 17.9 x 8.5 m)
4 x Workman, Clark DRG turbine engines via twin screw.
Sank on 19 December 1934 after being rammed amidships by the Portuguese
liner LOANDA while ORANIA was at anchor in Leixoes harbour, Oporto.
Built by Workman, Clark & Co, Belfast, for Royal Holland Lloyd.

ORANJE (1903) See ANFA (1923)

ORANJE (1939) See ANGELINA (1978)

ORANJEFONTEIN (1939) See FONTEIN (1967)

ORANJE NASSAU (1911) See CORINTHIA (1939)

ORANJE NASSAU (1957) See XX ANIVERSARIO (1973)

ORANJE S. A. (1966) See S. A. ORANJE (1966)

ORANJESTAD (1950) See MIRIAM B (1967)

ORAZIO (1932)
11669 grt; 640 psrs
506' x 62' x 27'2" (153.3 x 18.8 x 8.2 m)
2 x 8-cylinder B+W diesel engines via twin screw.
Broken up for scrap after an explosion off Marseilles on 21 January 1940
which gutted the ship and cost 106 lives.
Built by Cantieri ed Officini Meridionali, Baia, for the Italian Line.

ORBITA (1915)
15486 grt; 887 psrs
550' x 67' x 32'7" (166.7 x 20.5 x 9.9 m)
Harland & Wolff combination triple expansion engine and turbines via triple
screw.
Broken up for scrap at Newport, Wales, in 1950.
Built by Harland & Wolff Ltd, Belfast, for the Pacific Steam Navigation
Company.

ORCA (1918) See CALGARIC (1927)

ORCADES (1921)
9764 grt; 599 psrs
492' x 58' x 27' (150 x 17.7 x 8.2 m)
Quadruple expansion engines via twin screw.
Broken up for scrap by M Stern at Bremerhaven in 1925. Ex-Orient Line.
Built by Vulkan SMAE, Stettin, for North German Lloyd as the PRINCE LUDWIG (1903).

ORCADES (1937)
23456 grt; 1068 psrs
664' x 82' x 30' (201.2 x 25 x 9.1 m)
6 x Parsons SRG turbine engines via twin screw.
Sank on 10 October 1942, with the loss of 48 lives, after being hit early in the day by two torpedoes from the German U-172, 300 miles (500 km) west-south-west of the Cape of Good Hope. As she struggled to reach port under her own power, reduced to a mere 5 knots, the U-172 shadowed her for two and a half hours and then fired six more torpedoes which sent her to the bottom.
Built by Vickers-Armstrong Ltd, Barrow-in-Furness, for the Orient Line.

ORCADES (1948)
28399 grt; 1635 psrs
709' x 90' x 31' (216.1 x 27.3 x 9.4 m)
6 x SRG turbine engines via twin screw.
Broken up for scrap by Feng Steel Enterprise Co Ltd at Kaohsiung in 1973.
Built by Vickers-Armstrong Ltd, Barrow-in-Furness, for the Orient Line at a cost of £3,418,000.

ORCANA (1893) See ARGONAUT (1916)

ORCANA (1922)
7814 grt; 257 psrs
504' x 55' x 26'11" (152.7 x 16.7 x 7.9 m)
A Stephen & Sons 6-cylinder triple expansion engines via twin screw.
Broken up for scrap in Holland in 1924. Ex-Royal Mail Line.
Built by Alexander Stephen & Sons, Glasgow, for the Aberdeen Line as the MILTIADES (1903).

ORCOMA (1908)
11533 grt; 1150 psrs
512' x 62' x 29'8" (155.2 x 19 x 9 m)
Beardmore 8-cylinder quadruple expansion engines via twin screw.
Broken up for scrap by Hughes Bolckow & Company at Blyth in 1933.
Built by William Beardmore & Company, Dalmuir, for the Pacific Steam Navigation Company.

ORDU (1948)
6790 grt; 528 psrs
441' x 58' x 24' (133.6 x 17.6 x 7.2 m)
Fiat diesel engine via single screw.
In service with Turkish Maritime Lines.
Built by Nakskov Skibsvaerft, Nakskov, for Denizcilik Bankasi Tao, Chile, as the COPIAPO (1937).

ORDUNA (1914)
15499 grt; 1100 psrs
550' x 67' x 35'10" (166.7 x 20.3 x 10.6 m)
Harland & Wolff 2 x 4-cylinder combination triple expansion engines and turbines via triple screw.
Broken up for scrap at Dalmuir in 1951 as a troopship. Ex-Cunard Steamship Co.
Laid down as the ORMEDA (1913) by Harland & Wolff Ltd, Belfast, for the Pacific Steam Navigation Company and launched and completed as the ORDUNA for the Pacific Steam Navigation Co.

OREGON (1929) See PACIFIC HARMONY (1955)

ORELLANA (1893) See OWASCO (1916)

ORESTES (1998)
5796 grt; 166 psrs
100 trailers
361' x 55' x 13' (109.4 x 16.7 x 3.9 m)

4 x 6-cylinder Paxman diesel engines via twin screw.
Passenger-cargo ferry owned and operated by Orestes Sea Trade Corporation. Built by Ailsa Shipbuilding Co, Troon, for Atlantic Steam Navigation Co Ltd, London, as the CERDIC FERRY (1961). Renamed ATLAS I (1981 – Barracuda Maritime Co SA), SUFNOS (1987 – Ventouris Lines), SIFNOS EXPRESS (1990 – Ventouris Sea Lines) and IGOUMENITSA EXPRESS (Medlink Lines).

ORFORD (1928)
19941 grt; 500 psrs
658' x 75' x 30' (199.4 x 22.9 x 9.1 m)
6 x Parsons SRG turbine engines via twin screw.
Broken up for scrap at Savona in 1947. She was refloated from the bottom of Marseilles harbour where she settled on 1 June 1940 in an air raid that claimed 14 lives.
Built by Vickers-Armstrong Ltd, Barrow-in-Furness, for the Orient Line.

ORIANA (1923) See ORAMA (1924)

ORIANA (1960)
41923 grt; 1677 psrs
804' x 97' x 32' (245 x 29.4 x 9.7 m)
6 x SRG turbine engines via twin screw.

Purchased in 1997 by China International Travel Services for Chinese US$5,700,000 and towed to a site in the Huang-P'u river in Shanghai's Zinghua Harbour. She was there converted into a tourist and cultural centre funded by West Lake International Travel Culture. Prior to this, the Daiwa House Group, Japan, had successfully tendered to P&O Group for the acquisition of the ship for US$9,400,000. They had converted her into a convention centre, with accommodation, at a permanent berth in Beppu Spa, Japan, from 1986 to 1997. As this book goes to press, it was announced by China International Travel Services that the ORIANA was being listed for sale again.
Built by Vickers-Armstrong Ltd, Wallsend, for the Orient Line at a cost of £14,764,000.

ORIANA (1995)
69153 grt; 1975 psrs
850' x 105' x 26' (257.6 x 31.8 x 7.9 m)
4 x 9-cylinder MAN-B+W diesel engines via twin screw.

Cruise ship owned and operated by the P&O Line.
Built by Meyer Werft, Papenburg, at a cost of US$344,000,000.

ORIC (1910)
5453 grt; 550 psrs
460' x 46' x 35' (140.2 x 14.1 x 10.7 m)
Compound expansion engine and turbine via single screw.
Broken up for scrap in Italy in 1910 after a name change and sale to the

shipbreakers for a tender figure of £12,500.
Built by John Elder, Glasgow, for the Orient Line at a cost of £150,000 as the ORIENT (1879).

ORIENT (1879) See ORIC (1910)

ORIENTAL (1889) See TAI WAY FOONG (1923)

ORIENTAL AMIGA (1969)
10150 grt; 61 psrs
494' x 69' x 30' (149.7 x 20.9 x 9.1 m)
General Electric DRG turbine engine via single screw.
Broken up for scrap at Kaohsiung in 1979. Ex-Orient Overseas Lines.
Built by Wilton Fijenoord Shipyards, Schiedam, for the Holland America Line as the DIEMERDYK (1950).

ORIENTAL CARNAVAL (1969)
19567 grt; 300 psrs
609' x 78' x 32' (185.6 x 23.8 x 9.7 m)
2 x 6-cylinder Doxford diesel engines via twin screw.
Broken up for scrap by Lee Sing Shipbreaking Co Ltd at Hong Kong in 1976. Ex-Orient Overseas Line.
Built by Vickers-Armstrong Ltd, Newcastle, for the New Zealand Shipping Company as the RANGITOTO (1949).

ORIENTAL EMPRESS (1973)
15446 grt; 511 psrs
609' x 75' x 26'6" (185.6 x 23 x 8.1 m)
2 x General Electric turbo-electric engines via twin screw.
Broken up for scrap at Kaohsiung in 1984. Ex-Orient Overseas Line.
Laid down by Bethlehem Steel Company, Alameda, California, for American President Lines as the Class P2-SE2-R1 troop transport ADMIRAL F. B. UPHAM (1944) and completed as the PRESIDENT WILSON (1948 – American President Lines) at a cost of US$8,000,000.

ORIENTAL ESMERALDA (1969)
19567 grt; 350 psrs
609' x 78' x 32' (185.6 x 23.8 x 9.7 m)
2 x 6-cylinder Doxford diesel engines via twin screw.
Broken up for scrap by I Shing Steel & Iron Works Co Ltd at Kaohsiung in 1976. Ex-Orient Overseas Line.
Built by John Brown & Co Ltd, Clydebank, for the New Zealand Shipping Company as the RANGITANE (1949). Renamed JAN (1968 – Astroguarda Cia Navigation).

ORIENTAL FALCON (1970)
7658 grt
455' x 62' x 28'6" (137.9 x 18.8 x 8.7 m)
2 x General Electric DRG turbine engines via single screw.
Built as a "Victory" ship by Permanente Metals Corporation, Richmond, Virginia, for the US Shipping Administration as the INDIA VICTORY (1944). Renamed ARNECIJK (1947 – Holland America Line), SAN MARINO (1962) and as a container ship HONG KONG PRODUCER (1963 – HK Whampoa Drydock Company, Hong Kong).

ORIENTAL FANTASIA (1970) See HONG KONG SUCCESS (1972).

ORIENTAL HERO (1966)
8244 grt; 86 psrs
538' x 64' x 26' (163 x 19.4 x 7.9 m)
2 x 7-cylinder MAN diesel engines via single screw.
Owned by Orient Overseas Line, she sank on 28 June 1971 after a collision with the Greek tanker CASTOR in the North Pacific.
Built by Bremer-Vulkan Shipyards, Bremen, for North German Lloyd as the FRANKFURT (1954).

ORIENTAL INVENTOR (1966)
8245 grt; 86 psrs
538' x 64' x 26' (163 x 19.4 x 7.9 m)
2 x 7-cylinder MAN diesel engines via single screw.
Broken up for scrap at Kaohsiung in 1978. Ex-Orient Overseas Line.
Built by Bremer-Vulkan, Bremen, for the Hamburg-American Line as the HANNOVER (1955).

ORIENTAL JADE (1965)
9645 grt; 125 psrs
473' x 56' x 27' (143.3 x 20 x 8.2 m)
2 x Bethlehem Steel Corporation DRG turbine engines via single screw.
Broken up for scrap at Kaohsiung in 1974. Ex- Orient Overseas Line.
Built by Bethlehem Shipbuilding Corporation, Sparrow's Point, Maryland, for the US Navy as the attack transport DUCHESS, USS (APA-98) (1944). Renamed as the passenger-cargo ship EXCALIBUR (1948 – American Export Lines).

ORIENTAL LADY (1967)
8999 grt; 96 psrs
538' x 64' x 26' (163 x 19.4 x 7.9 m)
2 x 7-cylinder MAN diesel engines via single screw.
Broken up for scrap at Kaohsiung in 1978. Ex-Orient Overseas Line.
Built by Bremer-Vulkan Shipyards, Bremen, for North German Lloyd as the BAYERNSTEIN (1955).

ORIENTAL MUSICIAN (1967)
8213 grt; 86 psrs
538' x 64' x 26' (163 x 19.4 x 7.9 m)
2 x 7-cylinder MAN diesel engines via single screw.
Broken up for scrap at Kaohsiung in 1978. Ex-Orient Overseas Line.
Built by Bremer-Vulkan Shipyards, Bremen, for North German Lloyd as the HESSENSTEIN (1954).

ORIENTAL PEARL (1965)
9645 grt; 125 psrs
473' x 66' x 27' (143.3 x 20 x 8.2 m)
2 x Bethlehem Steel Corporation DRG turbine engines via single screw.
Broken up for scrap at Kaohsiung in 1974. Ex-Orient Overseas Line.
Built by Bethlehem Shipbuilding Company, Sparrow's Point, Maryland, for the US Navy as the SHELBY, USS (APA-105) (1945). Renamed as the passenger-cargo ship EXETER (1948 – American Export Lines).

ORIENTAL PEARL (1998)
11003 grt; 631 psrs
69 cars + 4 trailers
418' x 73' x 19'6" (126.8 x 22.1 x 6 m)
2 x 14-cylinder MAN diesel engines via single screw.

Passenger-car-cargo ferry owned and operated by Hayashi Marine Co Ltd. Built by Onomichi Zosen KK, Onomichi, as the GOLDEN OKINAWA (1972). Renamed TIEN IN (1991 – Retin International SA, Panama) and NAGASAKI SHANGHAI (1995 – Nagasaki Ferry Co (SA), Panama).

ORIENTAL PEARL (1998) See GOLDEN PRINCESS (2000)

ORIENTAL PEARL II (2000)
5087 grt; 52 psrs
22 cars + 27 trailers
416' x 66' x 18' (126.1 x 20 x 5.5 m)
2 x 12-cylinder Pielstick diesel engines via twin screw.
Passenger-car-cargo ferry owned by Asia International Ferry and operated by Daewoo Marine, South Korea.
Built by Naikai Setoda, Setoda, for Higashi Nippon Ferry Co Ltd, Hakodate, as the VEDA (1986).

ORIENTAL PRESIDENT (1973)
15456 grt; 511 psrs
609' x 75' x 26'6" (185.6 x 23 x 8.1 m)
General Electric turbo-electric engines via twin screw.
Broken up for scrap at Kaohsiung in 1974. Ex-Orient Overseas Line.

Laid down by Bethlehem Steel Corporation, Alameda, California, for American President Lines as the Class P2-SE2-R1 troop transport ADMIRAL D. W. TAYLOR (1944) and completed as the PRESIDENT CLEVELAND (1947) at a cost of US$8,000,000.

ORIENTAL QUEEN (1961)
10985 grt; 364 psrs
494' x 66' x 23' (150.6 x 20.2 x 7 m)
H&W-B+W 8-cylinder diesel engines via twin screw.
Broken up for scrap at Kaohsiung in 1973. Ex-Toyo Yusen KK.
Built by Harland & Wolff Ltd, Belfast, for McIlwraith McEachern as the KANIMBLA (1936).

ORIENTAL RIO (1968)
17730 grt; 220 psrs
548' x 75' x 30' (178 x 22.9 x 9 m)
2 x 6-cylinder Doxford diesel engines via twin screw.
Broken up for scrap at Kaohsiung in 1974. Ex-Orient Overseas Line.
Built by John Brown & Co Ltd, Clydebank, for the New Zealand Shipping Company as the RUAHINE (1951).

ORIENTAL RULER (1967)
8269 grt; 86 psrs
538' x 64' x 26' (163 x 19.4 x 7.9 m)
2 x 7-cylinder MAN diesel engines via single screw.
Broken up for scrap at Kaohsiung in 1978. Ex-Orient Overseas Line.
Built by Bremer-Vulcan Shipyards, Bremen, for North German Lloyd as the SCHWABENSTEIN (1954).

ORIENTAL WARRIOR (1967)
8269 grt; 84 psrs
538' x 64' x 26' (163 x 19.4 x 7.9 m)
2 x 7-cylinder MAN diesel engines via single screw.
Deliberately sunk off the US east coast of Florida on 1 October 1972. She had been refloated in Jacksonville where she had settled on the seabed during a tow from a position 30 miles (50 km) north-east of Daytona Beach, where she was abandoned by passengers and crew following an engine room explosion and fire on 25 May 1972.
Built by Bremer-Vulcan Shipyards, Bremen, for the Hamburg-American Line as the passenger-cargo ship HAMBURG (1954).

ORIENTE (1917) See CHARLES A. STAFFORD (1944)

ORIENTE (1930) See THOMAS H. BARRY (1941)

ORIENT EXPRESS (1986) See WASA QUEEN (1992)

ORIENT EXPRESS (1987) See WASA QUEEN (1992)

ORIENT EXPRESS (1990) See WASA QUEEN (1992)

ORIENT PRINCESS (1987)
10151 grt; 318 psrs
491' x 69' x 22' (148.8 x 21 x 6.7 m)
2 x 9-cylinder Sulzer diesel engines via twin screw.
Cruise casino ship owned and operated by the Pallister Group of Companies, Panama, but currently laid up in China.
Built by Chantiers de l'Atlantique, St Nazaire, for the China National Ocean Shipping Co as the passenger-cargo ship YAO HUA (1967).

ORIENT STAR (1990) See TIAN KUN (1991)

ORIENT STAR (1993)
3923 grt; 256 psrs
328' x 53' x 16' (99.4 x 16.1 x 4.7 m)
2 x 8-cylinder B+W diesel engines via twin screw.
Cruise ship owned and operated by American Pacific Cruises, Khabarovsk.
Built by Brodogradiliste, Kraljevica, for the Far East Shipping Co, Vladivostok, as the OLGA SADOVSKAYA (1977).

ORIENT SUN (1992) See WASA QUEEN (1992)

ORIENT VENUS (1990)
21906 grt; 626 psrs

574' x 78' x 21' (173.9 x 23.6 x 6.3 m)
2 x 12-cylinder Pielstick diesel engines via twin screw.
Cruise ship owned jointly by Nihonkai Ferry Co, Hankyu Ferry Co and Kanko Kisen KK and cruising for Japan Cruise Ship Ltd, Osaka.
Built by Ishikawajima-Harima Heavy Industries Co Ltd, Tokyo, for the joint venture partners at a cost of US$150,000,000.

ORINOCO (1928) See JUAN DE GARAY (1947)

ORINOCO (1975)
11424 grt; 3000 psrs
497' x 72' x 10' (150.6 x 21.8 x 3 m)
2 x Westinghouse DRG turbine engines via single screw.
Broken up for scrap at Puerto Cabello, Brazil, in 1981. Ex-Cia An Venezolana de Navigation, Caracas.
Built by the Kaiser Corporation for the US Navy as the GENERAL O. H. ERNST (AP-133) (1944). Renamed CALMAR (1964 – Bethlehem Steel Corporation).

ORION (1917)
6026 grt; 1260 psrs
403' x 49' x 27' (123 x 15 x 8.2 m)
Bremer Vulkan 8-cylinder quadruple expansion engines via twin screw.
Broken up for scrap in 1929 in Baltimore, Maryland. Ex-US Shipping Board.
Built by Bremer Vulkan, Vegesack, for the Hamburg-America Line as the PRINZ OSKAR (1902).

ORION (1929) See REGINA MARIS (1996)

ORION (1935)
23696 grt; 1691 psrs
665' x 82' x 30' (202.7 x 25.5 x 9.1 m)
6 x Parsons SRG turbine engines via twin screw.
Broken up for scrap as a Hamburg-based hotel ship by Jos Boel et Fils SA at Tamise in 1963.
Built by Vickers-Armstrong Ltd, Barrow-in-Furness, for the Orient Line.

ORION (1950) See REGINA MARIS (1996)

ORION (1968) See OLYMPIA I (1997)

ORION (1973) See DAEDALUS (1989)

ORION (1984) See DAEDALUS (1989)

ORITA (1903)
9239 grt; 910 psrs
496' x 58' x 32' (150.3 x 17.6 x 9.7 m)
Quadruple expansion engines via twin screw.
Broken up for scrap by Thos W Ward & Co at Morecambe in 1932 after being laid up for four years.
Built by Harland & Wolff Ltd, Belfast, for the Pacific Steam Navigation Company.

ORIZABA (1890) See NORTHWESTERN (1906)

ORIZABA (SP-1536) (1918) See DUQUE DE CAXIAS (1945)

ORIZABA, USS (AP-24) (1941) See DUQUE DE CAXIAS (1945)

ORLANDO (1920)
4233 grt; 140 psrs
370' x 46' x 18'6" (112.1 x 13.9 x 5.6 m)
3-cylinder triple expansion engine via single screw.
Broken up for scrap by Thos W Ward & Co at Briton Ferry in 1932. Ex-Ellerman's Wilson Line.
Built by Hall Russell & Co, Aberdeen, for the John T Rennie Line as the INANDA (1904).

ORMEDA (1913) See ORDUNA (1914)

ORMISTON (1927) See ATLANTICOS (1956)

ORMONDE (1918)

14853 grt; 1070 psrs
580' x 67' x 27'4" (176.9 x 20.3 x 8.3 m)
4 x John Brown & Co SRG quadruple reduction steam turbine engines via twin screw.
Broken up for scrap at Dalmuir in 1953.
Built by John Brown & Co Ltd, Clydebank, for the Orient Line.

ORMUZ (1886) See DIVONA (1912)

ORMUZ (1920) See DRESDEN (1927)

ORN (1909)

3138 grt
337' x 41' x 26'5" depth (102.1 x 12.4 x 8 m)
Blair & Co 3-cylinder triple expansion engines via single screw.
Abandoned after becoming wrecked in November 1913.
Built by C Mitchell & Co, Newcastle, for Nelson, Donkin & Co as the FLORIDA (1882).

ORO (1909)

6357 grt; 692 psrs
460' x 49' x 19'4" (140.2 x 15 x 5.9 m)
Barrows 3-cylinder triple expansion engine via single screw.
Broken up for scrap in 1909 at Genoa. Ex-Royal Mail Steam Packet Co.
Built by Barrow Shipbuilding Co Ltd, Barrow-in-Furness, for the Pacific Steam Navigation Co, Liverpool, as the OROYA (1886).

ORONSA (1906)

8067 grt; 1080 psrs
476' x 56' x 29' (144.2 x 17 x 8.8 m)
Quadruple expansion engines via twin screw.
Sank in 1915 after being torpedoed off Bardsey Island, UK.
Built by Harland & Wolff Ltd, Belfast, for the Pacific Steam Navigation Company.

ORONSAY (1925)

20001 grt; 1836 psrs
660' x 75' x 30' (201.1 x 22.9 x 9.1 m)
6 x Parsons SRG turbine engines via twin screw.
Sank on 9 October 1942, with five lives lost, after being hit by four torpedoes from the Italian submarine ARCHIMEDE, 800 miles (1334 km) south-west of Monrovia.
Built by John Brown & Co Ltd, Clydebank, for the Orient Line.

ORONSAY (1951)

27632 grt; 1416 psrs
708' x 93' x 31' (215.8 x 28.3 x 9.4 m)
6 x SRG turbine engines via twin screw.
Broken up for scrap by Nan Feng Steel Enterprise Co Ltd at Kaohsiung in 1975.
Built by Vickers-Armstrong Ltd, Barrow-in-Furness, for the Orient Line at a cost of £4,228,000.

ORONTES (1902) See ORONTES (1924)

ORONTES (1924)

9028 grt; 1000 psrs
514' x 58' x 34'6" (156.6 x 17.7 x 10.5 m)
Quadruple expansion engines via twin screw.
Broken up for scrap in 1926. Ex-Orient Line.
Built by Fairfield Shipbuilding & Engineering Co Ltd, Glasgow, for the Orient Line as the ORONTES (1902). Renamed BRITISH TRADE (1922 – British National Exhibition Ship Ltd).

ORONTES (1929)

20186 grt; 1410 psrs
664' x 75' x 30' (201.2 x 22.9 x 9.1 m)
6 x Parsons SRG turbine engines via twin screw.
Broken up for scrap by Ordaz Y Cia at Valencia, Spain, in 1962.
Built by Vickers-Armstrong Ltd, Barrow-in-Furness, for the Orient Line.

OROPESA (1895) See CHAMPAGNE (1915)

OROPESA (1920)

14072 grt; 632 psrs
530' x 66' x 34'4" depth (160.6 x 20 x 10.4 m)
6 x Parsons DRG turbine engines via twin screw.
Sank as a troop transport in two and a half hours on 16 January 1941, with 113 lives lost, after surviving one torpedo from the German U-106, but then being hit by two more torpedoes later from the same U-boat, 100 miles (170 km) north-west of Bloody Foreland, Northern Ireland.
Built by Cammell Laird &Co, Birkenhead, for the Pacific Steam Navigation Co.

OROYA (1886) See ORO (1909)

OROYA (1923)

12257 grt; 723 psrs
525' x 63' x 33' (159.1 x 19.1 x 10 m)
4 x Harland & Wolff SRG turbine engines via twin screw.
Broken up for scrap at La Spezia in 1939 following being laid up from 1931 to 1939.
Built by Harland & Wolff Ltd, Belfast, for the Pacific Steam Navigation Company.

ORPHEUS (1968) See REGENCY (1982)

ORPHEUS (1969)

5092 grt; 280 psrs
25 cars
376' x 50' x 15' (114 x 15 x 4.5 m)
2 x Harland & Wolff 10-cylinder diesel engines via twin screw.
Cruise ship sold for scrap for an estimated price of US$400,000 in 2000 by Royal Olympic Cruises, Piraeus, and broken up in India.
Built by Harland & Wolff Ltd, Belfast, for British & Irish Steam Packet Co Ltd as the MUNSTER (1948). Renamed MUNSTER I (1968 – British & Irish Steam Packet Co Ltd) and THESEUS (1968 – Epirotiki Cruise Lines).

ORSOVA (1909)

12036 grt; 660 psrs
536' x 63' x 28' (163.3 x 19.2 x 8.5 m)
John Brown & Co quadruple expansion engines via twin screw.
Broken up for scrap at Barrow-in-Furness in 1936.
Built by John Brown & Co Ltd, Clydebank, for the Orient Line.

ORSOVA (1954)

29091 grt; 1503 psrs
723' x 91' x 30' (220.4 x 27.7 x 9 m)
6 x SRG turbine engines via twin screw.
Broken up for scrap by Nan Feng Steel Enterprise Co Ltd at Kaohsiung in 1974.
Built by Vickers-Armstrong Ltd, Barrow-in-Furness, for the Orient Line at a cost of £5,776,000.

ORTEGA (1906)

8075 grt; 1080 psrs
476' x 56' x 29' (144.2 x 17 x 8.8 m)
Quadruple expansion engines via twin screw.
Broken up for scrap at Briton Ferry in 1927.
Built by Harland & Wolff Ltd, Belfast, for the Pacific Steam Navigation Company.

ORTONA (1899) See ARCADIAN (1912)

ORUBA (1921)

7848 grt; 257 psrs
459' x 56' x 30' (139 x 17 x 9.1 m)
Triple expansion engines via twin screw.
Broken up for scrap in Germany in 1924. Ex-Pacific Steam Navigation Company.
Built by Alex Stephen & Sons, Glasgow, for the Aberdeen Line as the MARATHON (1904).

ORUNGAL (1927)

5826 grt; 199 psrs
391' x 55' x 23'8" (119.2 x 16.7 x 7.2 m)

2 x A Stephen & Sons SRG turbine engines via single screw.
Owned by Australian United Steam Navigation Co, she was broken up on 13 December 1940 where she lay on Formby Reef, off Barwon Heads in Port Phillip Bay, Melbourne. She had run aground, broken in half and caught fire on 21 November 1940.
Built by Alexander Stephen & Sons, Glasgow, for the Khedivial Mail Steamship Company as the FEZARA (1923).

ORVIETO (1909) See ORVIETO (1919)

ORVIETO, HMS (1914) See ORVIETO (1919)

ORVIETO (1919)
12133 grt; 1117 psrs
554' x 64' x 28' (168.8 x 19.5 x 8.5 m)
2 x Workman, Clark quadruple expansion engines via twin screw.
Broken up for scrap in the UK in 1931. Ex-Orient Steam Navigation Co.
Built by Workman, Clark & Co Ltd, Belfast, for the Orient Steam Navigation Company as the ORVIETO (1909). Renamed ORVIETO, HMS (1914 – British Royal Navy).

OSADO MARU (1988)
11085 grt; 1525 psrs
190 cars + 30 trailers
435' x 69' x 17' (131.9 x 21 x 5.2 m)
2 x 9-cylinder Pielstick diesel engines via twin screw.
Passenger-car-cargo ferry owned and operated by Sado Kisen KK.
Built by Kanda Kawajiri, Kawajiri.

OSAKA (1983) See APTERA (1987)

OSCAR II (1902)
10012 grt; 1170 psrs
501' x 58' x 37'6" depth (151.8 x 17.7 x 11.4 m)
A Stephen 6-cylinder triple expansion engines via twin screw.
Broken up for scrap by Hughes Bolckow & Co at Blyth in 1934.
Built by Alexander Stephen & Sons, Glasgow, for the Scandinavian American Line, Copenhagen.

OSETIYA (1963)
3219 grt; 237 psrs
333' x 48' x 13' (100.9 x 14.5 x 3.9 m)
2 x 8-cylinder Russki diesel engines via single screw.
Broken up in 1997. Ex-Russian government.
Built by A Jdanova Shipyard, St Petersburg, for the Ukrainian-Danube Shipping Co, Izmail.

OSLOFJORD (1938)
18673 grt; 860 psrs
length 590' x beam 73' (178.8 x 22.1 m)
4 x 7-cylinder Stork-Werkspoor diesel engines via twin screw.
Abandoned as a total loss after hitting a mine on 13 December 1940, beaching and breaking her back at Tynemouth, UK, with one life lost.
Built by AG Weser Shipbuilders, Bremen, for the Norwegian America Line.

OSLOFJORD (1949) See FULVIA (1969)

OSTERLEY (1909)
12129 grt; 1090 psrs
535' x 67' x 28' (163 x 19.2 x 8.5 m)
London & Glasgow Co Ltd quadruple expansion engines via twin screw.
Broken up for scrap at Glasgow in 1930.
Built by London & Glasgow Shipbuilding Company, Govan, for the Orient Steam Navigation Company.

OSTERSJON (1989) See NURA NOVA (1999)

OSTMARK (1940) See OCEAN BUILDER (1964)

OSUMI (1980) See NEW GOLDEN BRIDGE (1994)

OSWESTRY GRANGE (1902) See ROSCOMMON (1912)

OTOME MARU (1973) See ASIA CHINA (1995)

OTRANTO (1909)
12124 grt; 1117 psrs
535' x 64' x 30' (163 x 19.5 x 9.1 m)
Parsons quadruple expansion engines via twin screw.
Abandoned after attempts to beach her on the island of Islay off Scotland failed when she became hopelessly wrecked on 6 October 1918. This followed a collision with P&O's KASHMIR, during which 431 lives were lost.
Built by Workman, Clark & Co Ltd, Belfast, for the Orient Line.

OTRANTO (1925)
20032 grt; 1686 psrs
660' x 75' x 30' (201.1 x 22.9 x 9.1 m)
6 x Parsons SRG turbine engines via twin screw.
Broken up for scrap at Faslane in 1957.
Built by Vickers-Armstrong Ltd, Barrow-in-Furness, for the Orient Line.

OTTAWA (1905) See GULCEMAL (1928)

OTWAY (1909)
12077 grt; 1090 psrs
536' x 63' x 34' (163.3 x 19.2 x 10.4 m)
Quadruple expansion engines via twin screw.
Sank on 22 July 1917, with the loss of 12 lives, after being torpedoed by the German U-49 in the Minches, north of the Hebrides.
Built by Fairfield Shipbuilding & Engineering Co Ltd, Glasgow, for the Orient Line.

OURANOS (1986) See GOLFINHO AZUL (1999)

OURANOS (1999)
7748 grt; 1420 psrs
300 cars
453' x 71' x 18' (137.3 x 21.5 x 5.5 m)
4 x 12-cylinder Pielstick diesel engines via twin screw.

Passenger-car ferry owned and operated by Fraglines.
Built by Flender Werke, Lubeck, for Tor Line as the TOR HOLLANDIA (1967). Renamed SAUDI MOON (1976 – Saudi Maritime Transport Co Ltd) and ARIADNE (1976 – Fraglines).

OURCQ (1922) See VILLE DE LEIGE (1940)

OUR LADY OF AKITA (1995) See OUR LADY OF BANNEUX (1999)

OUR LADY OF BANNEUX (1999)
4929 grt
473' x 55' x 21'6" (143.4 x 16.8 x 6.5 m)
2 x 8-cylinder Mitsubishi diesel engines via twin screw.
Owned and operated by Cebu Ferries, Cebu City.
Built by Mitsibishi Heavy Industries Ltd, Shimonoseki, for Oshima Unyu KK, Naha, as the passenger-cargo ship KOBE MARU (1974). Renamed GREEN EMERALD (1980 – Komodo Marine SA), KOBE MARU (1980 – Oshima Unyu KK, Naha), HAI YING (1985), OUR LADY OF AKITA 2 (1995 – Rio Grande Shipping Overseas Corporation SA) and SUPERFERRY 11 (1996 – WG & A Philippines Inc).

OUR LADY OF GOOD VOYAGE (1999)
5463 grt; 258 psrs
30 cars
360' x 59' x 15'5" (109.2 x 17.9 x 4.7 m)

2 x 6-cylinder Mitsubishi diesel engines via twin screw.
Owned by WG & A Philippines Inc, and operated by Cebu Ferries.
Built by Fukuoka Zosen KK, Fukuota, as the FERRY KIKAI (1979) and renamed WILLINES MABUHAY 6 (1995 – WG & A Philippines Inc).

OUR LADY OF LIPA (1995)
6911 grt; 1280 psrs
32 TEUs
409' x 56' x 18' (124 x 16.9 x 5.4 m)
2 x 18-cylinder NYK-Pielstick diesel engines via twin screw.
Passenger-cargo ship owned and operated by WG & A Philippines Inc.
Built by Hayashikane Zosen, Shimonoseki, for Kansai Kisen KK, Osaka, as the KUROSHIO MARU (1971). Renamed KURUSHIMA No. 7 (1984 – Kurushima Kosan Co Ltd).

OUR LADY OF MANAOAG (1992)
6496 grt; 1376 psrs
345' x 66' x 14'6' (104.6 x 20 x 4.4 m)
2 x 8-cylinder Mitsubishi diesel engines via twin screw.
Passenger ferry owned and operated by Cebu Ferries, Cebu City.

Built by Shikoku Dockyard Co Ltd, Takamatsu, as the TOSA (1971). Renamed HAYATOMO MARU (1977 – Kansai Kisen KK) and MASBATE I (1987 – William Lines, Manila).

OWASCO (1916)
4630 grt; 745 psrs
401' x 48' x 27'6" (121.5 x 14.5 x 8.4 m)
3-cylinder triple expansion engine via single screw.
Broken up for scrap in Spain in 1919 after being torpedoed on 5 June 1918 near Alicante and being beached. Ex-US government.
Built by Harland & Wolff Ltd, Belfast, for the Pacific Steam Navigation Co as the ORELLANA (1893). Renamed ALLEMANNIA (1905 – Hamburg-America Line) KOWNO (1906 – Russian American Line) and ALLEMANNIA (1907 – Hamburg-America Line).

OXFORDSHIRE (1914) See LANCASHIRE (1914)

OXFORDSHIRE (1920) See SAFINA-E-ARAB (1951)

OXFORDSHIRE (1957) See RIPA (1997)

PACE (1947) See SASSARI (1960)

PACECO (1965) See HYSAN (1971)

PACIFIC ABETO (1966)
8491 grt; 12 psrs
Broken up for scrap in Chittagong in 1980 after a three-year period laid up as a pilgrim ship. Ex-Cia de Navigacion Abeto SA, Hong Kong.
Built by Greenock Dockyard for the Pacific Steam Navigation Co as the passenger ship FLAMENCO (1950) which had a passenger capacity of several hundred. When she carried pilgrims after 1966, the official number of berths was 12 but, of course, many more than that figure were transported.

PACIFIC ENDEAVOUR (1979)
12544 grt; 2000 psrs
523' x 71' x 33' (159.3 x 21.7 x 10 m)
2 x Westinghouse DRG turbine engines via single screw.
Broken up for scrap as a container ship at Gadani Beach, Karachi, in 1980. Ex-Farrell Lines.
Built by the Kaiser Corporation, Richmond, California, for the US Maritime Commission as the Class C4-S-A1 troop transport GENERAL ROBERT L. HOWZE (AP-134) (1944). Renamed GENERAL R. L. HOWZE (1945 – US Army) which acted as a migrant ship after World War Two, laid up 1958–67, container ship GUAM BEAR (1968 – Pacific Far East Line), NEW ZEALAND BEAR (1975 – Pacific Far East Line) and AUSTRAL GLEN (1976 – Farrell Lines).

PACIFIC ENTERPRISE (1979) See CARIBE ENTERPRISE (1981)

PACIFIC GLORY (1954) See OCEANIC RELIANCE (1956)

PACIFIC HARMONY (1955)
7706 grt; 76 psrs
473' x 61' x 27'5" depth (144.3 x 18.7 x 8.3 m)
2 x 5-cylinder Bremer Vulkan diesel engines via twin screw.
Sank in October 1955 five months after running aground on 23 May at Murmagao under the ownership of Cia Maritima Asiatic Panamerise.
Built by Bremer Vulkan, Vegesack, for CGT as the OREGON (1929) and claimed as a war prize for the French Line by the French government at the conclusion of World War Two.

PACIFIC PRINCESS (1975)
20636 grt; 750 psrs
550' x 80' x 25' (167.6 x 24.4 x 7.6 m)

4 x 10-cylinder geared Fiat diesel engines via twin screw.
Cruise ship owned and operated by P&O Princess Cruises.
Built by Nordseewerke Rheinstahl Shipyards, Emden, for Flagship Cruises (a Norwegian Cruiseships AS subsidiary) as the SEA VENTURE (1971) at a cost of £7,500,000.

PACIFIC SKY (2000)
46087 grt; 1212 psrs
790' x 92' x 27' (239.4 x 27.8 x 8.2 m)
4 x General Electric DRG turbine engines via twin screw.

Cruise ship owned by the P&O Group and operated by P&O Holidays, Sydney.
Built by CNIM Shipyards, La Seyne, for Sitmar Cruises as the FAIRSKY (1984) at a cost of US$170,000,000. Renamed SKY PRINCESS (1988 – P&O Princess Cruises).

PACIFIC STAR (1950) See BINTANG SAMUDRA (1951)

PACIFIC STAR (1990) See AMUSEMENT WORLD (1998)

PACIFIC STAR (1993) See NEW YORK FORTUNE I (1997)

PACIFIC SUN (1991) See THE EMERALD (1996)

PACIFIC VENUS (1998)
26518 grt; 720 psrs
605' x 83' x 21'6" (183.4 x 25 x 6.5 m)
2 x 12-cylinder United-Pielstick diesel engines via twin screw.
Cruise ship operating for Japan Cruise Line Ltd, Osaka.
Built by Ishikawa Heavy Industries, Tokyo, for joint venture partners Nihonkai Ferry Co, Hankyu Ferry Co and Kanko Kisen KK, Osaka, at a cost of US$114,000,000.

PACIFIQUE (1967) See MALAYSIA BARU (1971)

PAGLIA ORBA (1994)
29718 grt; 196 psrs
120 cars
547' x 95'6" x 21'8" (165.8 x 29 x 6.6 m)
4 x 16-cylinder Wartsila diesel engines via twin screw.
Passenger-car-cargo RoRo ferry operating for SNCM.
Built by Ateliers et Chantiers du Havre, Le Havre.

PAKEHA (1910) See PAKEHA (1946)

PAKEHA (1946)
8115 grt; 1000 psrs
494' x 63' x 31'2" (149.7 x 19 x 9.5 m)
Harland & Wolff 8-cylinder quadruple expansion engines via twin screw.
Broken up for scrap at Briton Ferry UK in 1950. Ex-Shaw Savill & Albion.
Built by Harland & Wolff Ltd, Belfast, for Shaw Savill & Albion as the PAKEHA (1910). Renamed EMPIRE PAKEHA (1941 – British Admiralty). During World War Two, she was rebuilt to look identical to HMS REVENGE to confuse the enemy. After World War Two she was used extensively as a migrant ship.

PALANGA (1996)
11630 grt; 133 psrs
440 cars + 95 trailers
419' x 69' x 19'6" (126.9 x 21 x 5.9 m)
2 x 12-cylinder Pielstick diesel engines via twin screw.
Passenger-car-cargo ferry owned and operated by Lisco Line (subsidiary of Krantas Shipping) after purchase for $10,700,000.

Built by Ateliers et Chantiers du Havre, Le Havre, for SNCM as the cargo ship MONTE STELLO (1979).

PALATIA (1895) See NORODOVOLETZ (1917)

PALAWAN (1895) See JEDDAH (1914)

PALERMO (1913)
9203 grt; 2270 psrs
470' x 57' x 32'1" depth (143.3 x 17.3 x 9.7 m)
Palmer 6-cylinder triple expansion engines via twin screw.
Owned by Navali Generale Italia, she sank on 2 December 1916 after being torpedoed by a German U-boat off San Sebastian.
Launched by Palmers Shipbuilding Ltd, Jarrow, for British Shipowners as the cargo ship BRITISH PRINCESS (1899), but completed for the Phoenix Line as a conversion to a passenger ship and renamed LAZIO (1906).

PALERMO (1921)
6999 grt; 1890 psrs
430' x 53' x 25' (130.3 x 16 x 7.6 m)
G Clark 6-cylinder triple expansion engines via twin screw.
Broken up for scrap in 1928. Ex-Navale Generale Italia.
Built by Sir James Laing, Sunderland, for Sicula Americana, Italy, as the SAN GIOVANNI (1907).

PALLADIO (1989)
10977 grt; 1100 psrs
272 cars
403' x 64' x 17' (122 x 19.4 x 5.2 m)
2 x 6-cylinder GMT diesel engines via twin screw.
Passenger-car ferry operated by Adriatica di Navigazione.
Built by Fincantieri, Ancona.

PALLANZA (1901)
4606 grt; 850 psrs
399' x 47' x 28'4" (121.4 x 14.4 x 8.6 m)
Wallsend Slipway 3-cylinder triple expansion engine via single screw.
Acquired from Sloman Lines by the German Navy, she was acting as a naval auxiliary when she hit a mine near Borkum and sank on 11 December 1915.
Built by Swan Hunter Shipbuilders Ltd, Haverton, for the Harrison-Rennie Line as the CHANCELLOR (1891)

PALLAS ATHENA (1992)
19942 grt; 732 psrs
600' x 80' x 26' (182.8 x 24.4 x 7.9 m)
2 x 20-cylinder Stork-Werkspoor diesel engines via twin screw.
Cruise ship owned by Epirotiki Cruise Lines, she was broken up for scrap at Aliaga in December 1994. She had been towed from just outside Piraeus where she had been beached following her being gutted amidships by fire at her berth on 24 March 1994, just prior to embarking passengers for her next cruise.
Built by Ateliers et Chantiers de France, Dunkirk, for the French Line as the FLANDRE (1952). Renamed CARLA C (1968 – Costa Line) and CARLA COSTA (1987 – Costa Line).

PALM BEACH PRINCESS (1997)
6659 grt; 520 psrs
50 cars
421' x 54' x 15'6" (127.6 x 16.4 x 4.7 m)
2 x 12-cylinder Nohab diesel engines via triple screw.

Cruise ship owned by Leo Equity Group Corporation Inc, Panama, and operated by Palm Beach Cruise Line.
Built by Wartsila, Helsinki, for Finnlines as the ILMATAR (1964). Renamed VIKING PRINCESS (1984 – Grundstad Maritime Overseas Inc, Florida).

PALMETTO STATE (1921) See HUNTER LIGGETT, USS (APA-14) (1943)

PALMIRA (1998)
12602 grt; 333 psrs
150 cars
442' x 69' x 17' (134 x 21 x 5.2 m)
4 x 6-cylinder Sulzer diesel engines via twin screw.

Ice-strengthened passenger-car ferry owned by Blasplan Marine, Odessa, and chartered to Columbus Leisure Cruises, Hamilton.
Built by Stocznia Szczecinska Shipyards for the Black Sea Shipping Co as the LEV TOLSTOY (1981). Renamed NATASHA (1998 – Blasplan Marine, Odessa).

PALOMA (1985) See JIN HU (1993)

PANAGIA (1991) See MEDOUSA (1997)

PANAGIA EKATONTAPYLIANI (1996) See EXPRESS ARTEMIS (2000)

PANAGIA FANEROMENI (1989) See CALEDONIA (1997)

PANAGIA PAXON (1996)
3978 grt; 935 psrs
80 cars
297' x 48' x 13'6" (90 x 14.6 x 4.1 m)
2 x 6-cylinder Stork-Werkspoor diesel engines via twin screw.
Owned by Ventouris Northwest Ionian Lines Shipping Co and operated by the Ventouris Group.
Built by United Perama Shipyards, Perama Bay, for Labout SA, Piraeus, as the FIVOS (1973). Renamed CHRYSSOVALANDOU (1976 – Cross Ferry Lines), PAROS (1979) and IOANNIS EXPRESS (1992 – Arkadia Lines).

PANAGIA TINOU (1981) See ARTEMIS (1994)

PANAGIA TINOU 2 (1993) See EXPRES ATHINA (1998)

PANAMA (1902) See MAINE (1920)

PANAMA (1905) See ALEUTIAN (1923)

PANAMA (1939) See REGINA PRIMA (1973)

PANAMA (1946) See REGINA PRIMA (1973)

PANAMA (1966)
17184 grt; 850 psrs
684' x 71' x 29' (208.5 x 21.7 x 8.8 m)
2 x geared turbine engines via single screw.
Broken up for scrap as a container ship in 1987. Ex-Sea Land Services Inc.
Built by the Kaiser Corporation, Richmond, California, for the US Maritime Commission as the Class C4-S-A3 troop carrier MARINE JUMPER (1945). World War Two ended shortly after the ship's completion and she was converted into a migrant ship by the United States Line.

PANAMA MARU (1910)
6058 grt
408' x 50' x 29'8" depth (123.6 x 15.2 x 9 m)
Mitsubishi 6-cylinder triple expansion engines via twin screw.
Broken up for scrap in 1935.
Built by Mitsubishi Dockyard for OSK.

PANAMANIAN (1940)
15575 grt; 1074 psrs
616' x 65' x 31' (187.8 x 19.8 x 9.4 m)
8-cylinder quadruple expansion engines via twin screw.
Broken up for scrap at Shanghai in 1947. Ex-Cia Transatlantica Centroamericana, Panama.
Laid down by New York Shipbuilding Co, Camden, New Jersey, for the Pacific Mail Steamship Co as the MINNEFLORA (1904) and completed as the MONGOLIA (1904). Renamed PRESIDENT FILLMORE (1929 – Dollar Line).

PAN AMERICA (1922) See HUNTER LIGGETT, USS (APA-14) (1943)

PANCRAS (1911)
4436 grt; 146 psrs
376' x 50' x 23'6" (113.9 x 15.2 x 7.2 m)
Northeast Marine Engineering 8-cylinder triple expansion engines via twin screw.
Broken up in 1933.
Built by Hawthorne Leslie & Co Ltd, Newcastle, for the Booth Line.

PAN CRESCENT (1941) See ATZMAUT (1948)

PANHANDLE STATE (1920) See PRESIDENT BUCHANAN (1945)

PANNONIA (1903)
9851 grt; 2157 psrs
487' x 59' x 33' depth (147.6 x 17.9 x 10 m)
2 x John Brown 3-cylinder triple expansion engines via twin screw.
Broken up for scrap at Hamburg in 1922.
Built by John Brown & Co Ltd, Clydebank, for the Cunard Steamship Co.

PANORAMA (1987)
5330 grt; 700 psrs
150 cars + 32 TEUs
344' x 58' x 13' (101.3 x 17.5 x 4 m)
4 x 6-cylinder Wartsila diesel engines via twin screw.
Passenger-car-cargo ferry owned and operated by Port Arthur Authority of Trinidad & Tobago.
Built by M Jansen, Leer.

PANTHER (1930) See ARTSA (1949)

PANTHER (1973) See NUSA PEJUANG (1992)

PANTHER (1985) See BENCHIJIGUA (1994)

PANTHER (1995) See VATAN (2000)

PANTHER, N. F. (1979) See ST. SUNNIVA (1987)

PANTOKRATOR (1997)
6000 grt; 234 psrs
280 cars + 34 trailers
360' x 50' x 13' (109.2 x 15 x 4 m)
2 x Pielstick diesel engines via twin screw.
Passenger-car-cargo ferry owned by a Greek consortium which has had the ship on sale since the end of 1999 for US$8,500,000, with delivery in 2001.
Built by Northeast Marine Shipbuilding, Southwick, for Superflex Ships as the SUPERFLEX FOXTROT (1989).

PAN YORK (1941) See KOMMIYUT (1949)

PAOLO TOSCANELLI (1949)
8967 grt; 620 psrs
485' x 62' x 26' (149.2 x 19 x 7.9 m)
Fiat 9-cylinder diesel engines via twin screw.
Broken up for scrap at La Spezia in 1973. Ex-Lloyd Triestino.
Built by Ansaldo Shipyards SA, Genoa, for the Italian Line.

PAPPIS (1977) See ALEXI H (1979)

PARADISE (1998)
70367 grt; 2634 psrs
861' x 106' x 25' (261 x 32 x 7.6 m)
6 x 12-cylinder Wartsila-Sulzer diesel-electric engines via twin Azipod screw.

Cruise ship owned and operated by Carnival Cruise Lines.
Built by Kvaerner Masa-Yards, Helsinki, at a cost of US$310,000,000.

PARAGUAY STAR (1948)
10723 grt; 53 psrs
503' x 68' x 31' (152.4 x 20.6 x 9.4 m)
Parsons geared turbine engine via single screw.
Broken up for scrap by Eckardt & Co at Hamburg in 1969. She had been gutted by fire which started in her engine room on 12 August 1969 in London.
Built by Cammell Laird & Co, Birkenhead, for the Blue Star Line as a passenger-cargo ship.

PARIS (1893) See PHILADELPHIA (1920)

PARIS (1898) See PHILADELPHIA (1920)

PARIS (1921)
34569 grt; 1934 psrs
764' x 85' x 59'1" depth (231.5 x 25.8 x 17.9 m)
4 x Parsons turbine engines via quadruple screw.
Sold for scrap in 1947 after she had caught fire at her Le Havre berth on 19 April 1939, then capsized and sunk the next day. Twenty months later, the LIBERTE broke away from her moorings at Le Havre and rammed the hulk of the PARIS as a coup de grace. The PARIS had previously been gutted by fire in 1929 at Le Havre, but had been refurbished and resumed service.
Laid down by Chantiers de l'Atlantique, St Nazaire, for the French Line in 1913 as the PARIS, but not completed until 1921.

PARISIAN (1916) See TAIHOKU MARU (1934)

PARISMINA (1908) See PARISMINA (1937)

PARISMINA (1937)
4937 grt; 103 psrs
379' x 50' x 29'6" depth (114.8 x 15.2 x 9 m)
Workman, Clark 3-cylinder triple expansion engine via single screw.
Passenger-cargo ship owned by United Fruit Co, she sank on 18 November 1942 after being torpedoed in the North Atlantic.
Built by Workman, Clarke & Co Ltd, Belfast, for the United Fruit Steamship Company as the PARISMINA (1908). Renamed GENERAL SHERMAN (1932 – States Steamship Co, Portland, Oregon).

PAROS (1979) See PANAGIA PAXON (1996)

PARTHIA (1870) See STRAITS MARU (1956)

PARTHIA (1948) See ARAMAC (1964)

PARTIZANKA (1947)
6209 grt; 754 psrs
395' x 62' x 19' (120.4 x 18.9 x 5.8 m)
4 x geared turbine engines via twin screw.
While owned by Jugolinija, a fire destroyed 70% of her at Split, Croatia, on 12 August 1949 while in dry dock. The ship was declared a total constructive

loss on 13 September 1949.

Built by Newport News Shipbuilding & Drydock Co, Newport News, Virginia, for the Clyde Steamship Co as the SHAWNEE (1927). Renamed CITY OF LISBON (1946 – Iberian Star Line).

PASCAGOULA (1942) See GEORGE W. GOETHALS (T-AP 182) (1950)

PASCOLI (1971) See PASCOLI 96 (2000)

PASCOLI 96 (2000)

11779 grt; 1300 psrs
370 cars
432' x 66' x 18'6" (131 x 20 x 5.6 m)
2 x 9-cylinder Fiat diesel engines via twin screw.
Passenger-car ferry owned and operated by Tirrenia.
Built by Cantieri Navale del Terrino e Riuniti, Palermo, for Tirrenia di Navigazioni SpA as the passenger-car ferry PASCOLI (1971). Renamed AL SALAM PASCOLI 96 (1999 – El Salam Shipping & Trading Establishment) and TERTIUM MILLENIUM (2000 – El Salam Shipping & Trading Establishment).

PASIPHAE (1998)

31000 grt; 1500 psrs
1000 cars
661' x 85' x 22'6" (200.4 x 25.8 x 6.8 m)
4 x 8-cylinder MAN-B+W diesel engines via twin screw.

Ice-strengthened passenger-car ferry owned and operated by Minoan Lines. Hull built by Bruces Shipyard, Landskrona, and completion by Fosen mek Verksteder, Rissa, at a cost of US$110,000,000.

PASS CHRISTIAN (1942) See FRED C. AINSWORTH (1950)

PASSENGER No. 1 (1966)

7013 grt; 466 psrs
358' x 70' x 21' (108.5 x 21.2 x 6.4 m)
Triple expansion engines via twin screw.
Broken up for scrap by Jos de Smedt at Antwerp in 1966 after being towed from Canada by the German tug ROBBENPLATE. Ex-Canadian Steamship Lines.
Built by Davie Shipyards, Lauzon, Quebec, for Canadian Steamship Lines as the TADOUSSAC (1928). Renamed QUEBEC (1928).

PASSENGER No. 2 (1966)

6328 grt; 466 psrs
330' x 68' x 17'9" (100 x 20.6 x 5.4 m)
Richardson Westgarth 8-cylinder triple expansion engines via twin screw.
Embedded in sand as a static hotel at Sharjah (1975). Ex-Canadian Steamship Lines.
Built by Davie Shipyards, Lauzon, Quebec, for Canadian Steamship Lines as the St LAWRENCE (1927).

PASSENGER No. 3 (1966)

5528 grt; 466 psrs
323' x 48' x 19'1" (100.6 x 14.5 x 5.8 m)
Triple expansion engines via twin screw.
Broken up for scrap by Jos de Smedt at Antwerp in 1966 after being towed from Canada by the German tug ROBBENPLATE. Ex-Canada Steamship Lines Ltd.
Built by Harlaw & Hollingsworth for Canadian Steamship Lines as the NARRAGANSETT (1913). Renamed RICHELIEU (1913 – Canada Steamship Lines Ltd).

PASTEUR (1939) See FILIPINAS SAUDI I (1980)

PASTEUR (1966) See CHIDAMBARAM (1973)

PASTORES (1912) See PASTORES, USS (AF-16) (1941)

PASTORES, USS (AF-16) (1941)

7781 grt; 143 psrs
470' x 55' x 29' (142.4 x 16.7 x 8.8 m)
2 x quadruple expansion engines via twin screw.
Broken up for scrap at Oakland, California, in 1947. Ex-US Navy.
Built by Workman, Clarke & Co, Belfast, for the United Fruit Steamship Co as the passenger-cargo ship PASTORES (1912).

PATIA (1913)

6103 grt; 60 psrs
417' x 53' x 26' (126.4 x 16.1 x 7.9 m)
Triple expansion engines via twin screw.
Sank on 13 June 1918 after being torpedoed by the German U-49 in the Bristol Channel.
Built by Workman, Clark & Co Ltd, Belfast, for Elders & Fyffes as a passenger-cargo ship.

PATMOS (1991)

8992 grt; 1400 psrs
343 cars or 260 cars + 62 trailers
455' x 77' x 18' (137.9 x 23.4 x 5.6 m)
2 x 18-cylinder Pielstick diesel engines via twin screw.
Passenger-car-cargo ferry operating for DANE Sea Lines.
Built by Hashihama Zosen, Imabari, as the ALBATROSS (1972). Renamed IZU No.11 (1976 – Ocean Tokyo Ferry KK, Kitakyushu).

PATRA (1972) See EROS (1979)

PATRA (1976)

3985 grt; 284 psrs
35 cars
376' x 50' x 26' (113.9 x 15.2 x 7.9 m)
2 x 10-cylinder B+W-type diesel engines via twin screw.
While operating as a pilgrim ship for the Arab Navigation Co, Alex andria, she sank on 25 December 1976, with the loss of 102 lives, after an engine room explosion and fire 50 miles from her embarkation port of Jeddah. She had previously been destroyed by fire on 19 April 1953 while berthed at Parkeston Quay, Harwich, and had capsized and settled on the harbour bed following the massive amount of water pumped into her by the local fire brigade.
Launched by Helsingor Shipyard, Helsingor, for DFDS as the KRONPRINS FREDERIK (1941), but hidden from the German occupation troops and completed in 1946 at a cost of £300,000.

PATRA EXPRESS (1984) See TEXAS TREASURE (2000)

PATRIA (1901) See PATRICIA (1906)

PATRIA (1914)

11885 grt; 2240 psrs
512' x 59' x 40'1" (155.2 x 17.9 x 12.2 m)
Forges et Chantiers de la Mediterranee 6-cylinder triple expansion engines via twin screw.
Broken up where she lay in 1952, twelve years after she had been sabotaged by three explosions at her moorings in Haifa, where she heeled over and settled in shallow water on 25 November 1940. The loss of life numbered 729, mostly Jewish refugees.
Built by Forges et Chantiers de la Mediterranee, La Seyne, as a passenger ship for the Fabre Line.

PATRIA (1919) See ALEX ANDR MOZHAJSKI (1954)

PATRIA (1938) See ANIVA (1985)

PATRIA (1948)

13196 grt; 798 psrs
532' x 68' x 28' (161.2 x 20.6 x 8.5 m)
4 x Parsons DRG turbine engines via twin screw.

Broken up for scrap at Kaohsiung in 1973.
Built by John Brown & Co Ltd, Clydebank, for Cia Colonial de Navegacao,
Portugal, as a passenger-cargo ship.

PATRICIA (1906)
3162 grt; 790 psrs
362' x 42' x 24'5" (110.2 x 12.8 x 7.4 m)
J Dickinson 3-cylinder triple expansion engines via single screw.
Under the ownership of the Greek Line, she sank on 18 January 1907 after a
collision seven miles (11 km) off Haisboro Light, Norfolk.
Launched by JL Thompson & Sons, Sunderland, for Alfred Holt & Co,
Liverpool, as the KEEMUN (1890). Renamed PATRIE (1900 – Belgian
Marine) and PATRIA (1901 – Andresen).

PATRICIA (1920)
14466 grt; 2551 psrs
length 560' x beam 62' (169.7 x 18.8 m)
Broken up for scrap in 1921. Ex-Ellerman Line.
Built by AG Vulcan, Stettin, for the Hamburg-America Line as a passenger
ship.

PATRICIA (1935)
3902 grt; 244 psrs
336' x 48' x 20' (101.8 x 14.5 x 6.1 m)
2 x 3-cylinder triple expansion engines via twin screw.
Broken up for scrap in 1971. Ex-Swedish Lloyd as a Swedish Navy depot ship
for submarines.
Built by Swan Hunter & Wigham Richardson Ltd, Newcastle, for the Byron
Steamship Co as the PATRIS II (1926).

PATRICIA (1951) See EMPRESS 65 (1997)

PATRICIA (1967) See AMUSEMENT WORLD (1998)

PATRIE (1900) See PATRICIA (1906)

PATRIOT (2000)
33930 grt; 1214 psrs
704' x 90' x 31'6" (213.3 x 27.3 x 9.5 m)
2 x Sulzer diesel engines via twin screw.

Cruise ship for United States Lines from October 2000 after paying
US$114,500,000 for her from Holland America Lines.
Built by Chantiers de l'Atlantique, St Nazaire, for Holland America Lines as
the NIEUW AMSTERDAM (1983) at a cost of US$160,000,000.

PATRIOTIC (1912) See LADY KILLARNEY (1947)

PATRIOT STATE (1984)
14442 grt; 125 psrs
547' x 79' x 29' (166.7 x 24.1 x 8.9 m)
2 x General Electric DRG turbine engines via single screw.
US Maritime Commission training ship at the Massachusetts Maritime
Academy, Buzzard's Bay, Massachusetts.
Built by the Bethlehem Shipbuilding Corporation, Sparrow's Point, Maryland,
for the Grace Line as the passenger-cargo-container ship SANTA
MERCEDES (1964).

PATRIS (1909) See CLAUDE CHAPPE (1925)

PATRIS (1959) See TERRA (1987)

PATRIS II (1926) See PATRICIA (1935)

PATROCLUS (1923)
11314 grt; 140 psrs
499' x 62' x 26'4" (151.2 x 18.8 x 8 m)
2 x Scott & Co SRG turbine engines via twin screw.
Sank on 4 November 1940 after being torpedoed five times by the German U-
99, 150 miles (250 km) west of Ireland. She remained afloat for five hours as
her holds were full of empty barrels which created incredible buoyancy.
Ironically, she had been hove to while rescuing survivors of another ship
torpedoed earlier in the day. There were 76 lives lost between the two vessels.
Built by Cammell Laird &Co, Birkenhead, for the Blue Funnel Line as a
passenger-cargo ship.

PATUCA (1913)
6103 grt; 60 psrs
417' x 53' x 26' (126.4 x 16.1 x 7.9 m)
Triple expansion engines via twin screw.
Broken up for scrap at Rotterdam in 1935.
Built by Workman, Clark & Co Ltd, Belfast, for Elders & Fyffes.

PAUL GAUGUIN (1997)
19170 grt; 320 psrs
513' x 71' x 16'9" (155.5 x 21.5 x 5.2 m)
2 x 6-cylinder and 2 x 9-cylinder MAN diesel-electric engines via twin screw.

Cruise ship owned and operated by Radisson Seven Seas Cruises.
Built by Chantiers de l'Atlantique, St Nazaire, at a cost of US$154,000,000.

PAUL LECAT (1911)
12989 grt; 493 psrs or 826 troops
511' x 62' x 42' depth (154.8 x 18.8 x 12.7 m)
Messageries Maritimes 8-cylinder quadruple expansion engines via twin
screw.
Broken up for scrap a La Spezia in 1929 after she was gutted by fire in
Marseilles on 30 December 1928.
Built by Constructions Navales, La Ciotat, for Messageries Maritimes as a
passenger-cargo ship.

PAWEL (1913) See IRIS (1924)

PAYS DE WAES (1920) See HORAI MARU (1924)

PEARL (1993) See JOY WAVE (1999)

PEARL OF SCANDINAVIA (1982) See GOLDEN PRINCESS
(2000)

PEARL WILLIAM (1993) See CESME STERN (1997)

PECHENGA (1917)
7267 grt; 1100 psrs
length 467' x beam 58' (141.5 x 17.6 m)
Triple expansion engines via twin screw.
Broken up for scrap at Vladivostok in 1923. Ex-Bolshevik Russian
government.
Built by John Brown & Co Ltd, Clydebank, for the Russian Volunteer Fleet
Association as the MOSKVA (1898). Renamed ANGARA (1904 – Russian
Volunteer Fleet Association), ANEGAWA (1905 – Japanese government) and
ANGARA (1911 – Russian Volunteer Fleet Association).

PEDER OLSEN (1992) See MOBY LALLI (2000)

PEDER PAARS (1985) See COLOR VIKING (2000)

PEDRO GOMES (1922)
5795 grt; 462 psrs.
424' x 50' x 26' (128.5 x 15.2 x 7.9 m)
Maats de Schelde 8-cylinder expansion engines via twin screw.
Passenger-cargo ship broken up for scrap in Kobe in 1932.
Built by Kon Maats de Schelde, Flushing, for Rotterdam Lloyd as the SINDORO (1900).

PEER GYNT (1945) See SIBIR (1946)

PEER GYNT (1977) See IALYSSOS (1982)

PEGANCIA (1979)
11045 grt; 324 psrs
537' x 64' x 28' (162.7 x 19.4 x 8.5 m)
Sulzer diesel engines via twin screw.
Broken up for scrap in Karachi in 1981.
Built by Ateliers et Chantiers de la Loire, St Nazaire, for Chargeurs Reunis as the CLAUDE BERNARD (1950). Renamed J. G. FICHTE (1963 – VEB Deutsche Seereederei, Rostock) and SUNRISE IV (1979 – Estrella Christal Navegacaon SA, Panama).

PEGASUS (1961) See HIGHLAND QUEEN (1973)

PEGASUS (1972)
7171 grt; 154 psrs
465' x 74' x 18' (141 x 22.4 x 5.5 m)
2 x 18-cylinder MAN diesel engines via twin screw.
Owned by Kyushu Kyuko Ferry KK, Tokyo.
Built by Hayashikane Zosen, Shimonoseki.

PEGASUS (1973) See APTERA (1987)

PEGASUS (1984) See RODOS (1989)

PEGASUS (1985)
13275 grt; 843 psrs
290 cars
499' x 73' x 19' (152.1 x 22.3 x 5.8 m)
4 x 12-cylinder Pielstick geared diesel engines via twin screw.
Broken up for scrap at Aliaga in 1995 (minus her engines, which had been stripped out and reinstalled in the AGIOS ANDREAS) after catching fire at her berth in Venice, Italy, on 4 June 1991. Initially, she was towed to Eleusis Bay, then sold as a hulk to Strintzis Ferries, but caught fire again during her rebuild and was sold to Turkish shipbreakers in 1995.
Built by Dubigeon-Normandie Shipyards, Nantes, for the Johnson Line (a subsidiary of Stockholm Rederi AB Svea, Stockholm) as the ice-strengthened passenger-car ferry SVEA CORONA (1975). Renamed SUNDANCER (1983 – Sundance Cruises). As the latter, she had grounded in Menzies Bay, north of Vancouver, Canada, and settled on the seabed, had been refloated and then smashed into the dry dock allocated for her. She was immediately put up for sale.

PEGASUS (1998)
8069 grt; 834 psrs
414' x 61' x 17' (125.5 x 18.6 x 5.2 m)
2 x 12-cylinder GMT diesel engines via twin screw.

Passenger ferry built by Cantieri Navale Luigi Orlando, Livorno, for Adriatica, Cagliari, as the ESPRESSO VENEZIA (1977). Renamed ESPRESSO MALTA (1990 – Ventouris Enterprises, Piraeus).

PEGLI (1913)
3335 grt; 50 psrs
321' x 42' x 18'9" (97.3 x 12.7 x 5.7 m)
R Stephenson 3-cylinder triple expansion engine via single screw.
Broken up for scrap at La Spezia in 1922.
Launched by Edward's Shipbuilding Co, Howdon-on-Tyn,e for F Stumore & Co Ltd, London, as the passenger-cargo ship BENWELL TOWER (1890) and completed as the MARKOMANNIA (1890 – Hamburg-America Line). Renamed KIRCHBERG (1907 – Seetransport GmbH, Germany).

PEGU (1913)
6339 grt; 106 psrs
446' x 55' x 28'8" depth (135.2 x 16.7 x 8.7 m)
William Denny 3-cylinder triple expansion engine via single screw.
Sank off Galley Head on 8 July 1917 after hitting a mine.
Built by William Denny & Bros, Dumbarton, for the Henderson Line as a passenger-cargo ship.

PEGU (1921)
8016 grt; 150 psrs
466' x 59' x 30'5" (141.2 x 17.9 x 9.2 m)
William Denny 3-cylinder triple expansion engine via single screw.
Abandoned in the mid-Atlantic on 29 December 1939 as fire swept through the vessel and claimed five lives.
Built by William Denny & Bros, Dumbarton, for the Burmah Steamship Co Ltd and the British & Burmese Steam Navigation Co Ltd.

PEKIN (1899) See NAJMI (1909)

PELAGOS (1928)
12067 grt; 688 psrs
530' x 63' x 31' (161.5 x 19.2 x 9.4 m)
Quadruple expansion engines via twin screw.
Broken up for scrap at Hamburg in 1962. Ex-Hvalfanger-Selskapet Pelagos AS, Tonsberg, as a whaling mother ship.
Built by Harland & Wolff Ltd, Belfast, for the White Star Line as the passenger liner ATHENIC (1902).

P. E. LUMUMBA (1967)
10877 grt; 217 psrs
505' x 65' x 27'6" (153 x 19.7 x 8.4 m)
B+W 8-cylinder diesel engine via single screw.
Broken up for scrap by Siderurgica Riograndese SA in Rio Grande in 1974. Ex-Cie Mar Congolaise, Matadi.
Built as the passenger-cargo liner LEOPOLDVILLE (1948) by John Cockerill Shipyards, Hoboken, Belgium, for Cie Maritime Belge.

PEMBROKE CASTLE (1883) See BEZMI-ALEM (1906)

PEMROKESHIRE (1908) See CHIGNECTO (1913)

PENDENNIS CASTLE (1959) See SINBAD I (1978)

PENELOPE A (1992) See EXPRESS PENELOPE (2000)

PENELOPE A (2000)
16829 grt; 1859 psrs
440 cars
453' x 67' x 19' (137.4 x 20.3 x 5.8 m)
2 x 9-cylinder Stork-Werkspoor diesel engines via twin screw.

Passenger-car ferry owned and operated by Minoan Flying Dolphins.
Laid down by Schichau Unterweser AG (SUAG), Bremerhaven, for the Monarch Steamship Co Ltd, London, as the EUROPEAN GATEWAY (1974),

launched as the EUROPEAN EXPRESS (1975) and completed as the TRAVEMUNDE (1981 – GT Ruten AS, Gedser). Renamed TRAVEMUNDE LINK (1981 – Monarch Steamship Co Ltd), BALE (1983), FLAVIA (1984 – Alliance Navigation), SALLY STAR (1988 – Sally Line), ROSTOCK LINK (1992 – GT-Link), WASA EXPRESS (painted on hull sides in 1997) and THJELVAR (1997 – Rederi AB Gotland).

PENINSULA STATE (1922) See JOSEPH T. DICKMAN, USS (AP-13) (1943)

PENN (1976) See PENNY (1978)

PENN-AR-BED (1974) See JABAL ALI I (1999)

PENNLAND (1926)
16322 grt; 550 psrs
601' x 67' x 28' (182.1 x 20.3 x 8.5 m)
8-cylinder combination triple expansion engine and turbines via triple screw.
Owned by the British Ministry of War Transport, she sank on 25 April 1941 after being hit by seven bombs from German aircraft in the Gulf of Athens, off Crete.
Laid down by Harland & Wolff Ltd, Belfast, for the American Line as the passenger liner PITTSBURGH (1913), but completed for the White Star Line in 1922.

PENNMAR (1964) See PENNY (1978)

PENNSYLVANIA (1896) See NANSEMOND (1917)

PENNSYLVANIA (1929) See ARGENTINA (1938)

PENNY (1978)
11538 grt; 1000 psrs
523' x 71' x 26'6" (159.3 x 21.7 x 8 m)
2 x Westinghouse DRG turbine engines via single screw.
Broken up for scrap in 1984. Ex-American Coastal & Foreign Shipping Inc, New York.
Built by the Kaiser Corporation, Richmond, California, for the US Maritime Commission and ultimately the US Navy as the Class C4-S-A1 troop transport GENERAL G. O. SQUIER, USS (AP-130) (1942). Laid up in the James river by the US Maritime Commission from 1946 to 1964. Renamed PENNMAR (1964 – Bethlehem Steel Corporation) and PENN (1976 – Alpine Steamship Co Inc, Wilmington, Delaware).

PEOTR VELIKI (1946) See PETR VELIKI (1949)

PERALTA (1911) See TIVIVES (1911)

PEREGRINE MARINER (2000)
6450 grt; 117 psrs
386' x 59' x 19'6" (117 x 17.9 x 5.9 m)
2 x 6-cylinder Russian diesel engines via twin screw.

Owned by the Institute of Oceanology, Moscow, and chartered for five years to Peregrine Adventures, Melbourne, who specialise in cold water cruising expeditions.
Built by Holming Shipyards, Rauma, for the Russian Academy of Sciences as the ice-strengthened passenger-oceanographic research ship AKADEMIK IOFFE (1987) and renamed MARINE ADVENTURER (1995 – Peregrine Adventures).

PERE NOUVEL (1962) See SUNSHINE COAST QUEEN (1967)

PERICLES (1908)
10925 grt; 500 psrs
518' x 62' x 25' (157.9 x 19 x 7.6 m)
Quadruple expansion engines via twin screw.
Sank bow first in two and a half hours in 16 fathoms of water, on 31 March 1910, after striking an uncharted reef six miles (10 km) south of Cape Leeuwin, Western Australia.
Built by Harland & Wolff Ltd, Belfast, for the Aberdeen Line.

PERICLES (1914)
5673 grt
Sank after foundering on 24 May 1914 off Ushant.
Built by Clydebank Engineering & Shipbuilding Co Ltd, Glasgow, for the Elderslie Steamship Co Ltd as the NAIRNSHIRE (1898). Renamed DUKE OF NORFOLK (1899), MARCELLSIUS (1905) and JOHANNA (1908).

PERICLES (1938) See MIRIAM B (1967)

PERMANENTE (1940) See CONTINENTAL (1948)

PERNAS SAFARI (1985) See LOBO MARINHO (1996)

PERSEUS (1923)
10276 grt
491' x 63' x 39'6" depth (148.8 x 19.1 x 12 m)
Parsons DRG turbine engines via twin screw.
Sank on 16 January 1944 after being torpedoed by the Japanese submarine I-165 off Madras.
Built by the Caledon Shipbuilding & Engineering Co Ltd, Dundee, for the Blue Funnel Line.

PERSEUS (1926)
4852 grt
390' x 53' x 26'2" (118.2 x 16.1 x 7.9 m)
D & W Henderson 3-cylinder triple expansion engines via single screw.
Broken up for scrap at Genoa in 1932.
Built by D & W Henderson & Co Ltd, Glasgow, as the HELIPOLIS (1905). Renamed MEDIATOR (1913), MAINE II (1914), HELIOPOLIS (1916), METHVEN (1917) and BORBEN (1923).

PERSIA (1900)
7974 grt; 480 psrs
500' x 54' x 24'5" (151.5 x 15.2 x 7.4 m)
Caird & Co 4-cylinder triple expansion engine via single screw.
Sank on 30 December 1915, with 334 lives lost, after being torpedoed by the German U-38 70 miles (117 km) east of Crete.
Built by Caird & Co, Greenock, for the P&O Line.

PERSIA (1906) See PERSIA MARU (1915)

PERSIA (1975) See NORLEB (1984)

PERSIA MARU (1915)
4367 grt; 1080 psrs
430' x 42' x 29' (130.3 x 12.7 x 8.8 m)
Triple expansion engine via single screw.
Broken up for scrap at Osaka in 1926. Ex-Toyo Kisen, Kaisha.
Built by Harland & Wolff Ltd, Belfast, for the White Star Line as the passenger liner COPTIC (1881). Renamed PERSIA (1906 – Pacific Mail Steamship Co).

PERSIC (1901)
11973 grt; 350 psrs
550' x 63' x 32'6" (166.7 x 19.1 x 9.8 m)
Quadruple expansion engines via twin screw.
Broken up for scrap in 1927 at Hendrik Ido Ambacht.
Built by Harland & Wolff Ltd, Belfast, for the White Star Line.

PERU (1892) See LUX (1919)

PERUGIA (1901)

4348 grt; 1170 psrs
375' x 47' x 27'6" depth (114.3 x 14.4 x 8.4 m)
D & W Henderson 3-cylinder triple expansion engine via single screw.
Sank on 3 December 1916 as a 'Q' ship for the British Admiralty, after being torpedoed by an enemy submarine in the Gulf of Genoa.
Built by D & W Henderson Ltd, Glasgow, for the Anchor Line.

PESARO (1915)

12335 grt; 2102 psrs
526' x 60' x 35'6" depth (159.4 x 18.9 x 10.8 m)
Blohm & Voss 8-cylinder quadruple expansion engines via twin screw.
Broken up for scrap at Genoa in 1925. Ex-Lloyd Sabaudo.
Built by Blohm & Voss, Hamburg, for the Hamburg-America Line as the MOLTKE (1901).

PESHAWUR (1872) See ASHRUF (1900)

PETAR HEKTOROVICH (1999)

6721 grt; 1100 psrs
140 cars
303' x 59' x 12'6" (91.8 x 18 x 3.8 m)
2 x 6-cylinder Krupp-MaK diesel engines via twin screw.
Passenger-car ferry owned and operated by Jadrolinija, Croatia.
Built by Svendborg Skibsvaerft AS, Svendborg, for the Langeland-Kiel Line as the LANGELAND III (1989).

PETEN (1932) See BLUMENTHAL (1957)

PETER PAN (1965) See NUSA PEJUANG (1992)

PETER PAN (1974) See FEDRA (1987)

PETER PAN (1986) See SPIRIT OF TASMANIA (1993)

PETER PAN (1993)

30825 grt; 1044 psrs
535 cars or 110 trailers
584' x 86' x 18'6" (177 x 26 x 5.7 m)
4 x 8-cylinder MAN-B+W diesel engines via twin screw.

Passenger-car-cargo RoRo ferry owned and operated by the TT Line GmbH, Hamburg.
Built by Schichau Seebeckwerft, Bremerhaven, for the TT-Line as the NILS DACKE (1988).

PETER PERVYY (1990) See PETR PERVYY (1990)

PETERSBURG (1878) See SOVJETSKAJA ROSSIJA (1921)

PETER WESSEL (1968) See YESILADA (1971)

PETER WESSEL (1973) See MARKO POLO (1988)

PETER WESSEL (1984)

29706 grt; 2180 psrs
650 cars
556' x 79' x 18' (168.5 x 24 x 5.5 m)
4 x 8-cylinder B+W diesel engines via twin screw.
Ice-strengthened passenger-car ferry owned and operated by the Color Line on the Denmark–Norway service.
Laid down by Oresundbolaget, Landskrona, for Rederi AB Gotland (Larvik Line) as the GOTLAND (1980) and completed for Vaasanlaivat & Karageorgios as the WASA STAR (1981).

PETRARCA (1971) See AL SALAM PETRARCA 90 (1999)

PETREL (1969) See IRAN CREMONA (1976)

PETRONILA MATA (1998)

6665 grt; 650 psrs
170 cars
412' x 55' x 16' (124.7 x 16.8 x 4.9 m)
2 x 9-cylinder Wichman diesel engines via twin screw.

Ice-strengthened passenger-car ferry owned and operated by Consolidada de Ferrys.CA, Caracas.
Built by Trosvik Verksted AS, Brevik, for the Stena Line as the STUBBENKAMMER (1971). Renamed FRENGENFJORD (1983 – Fosen Mekaniske Verkstad AS), KYSTVEIEN (1984 – Askoy-Bergen AS), BOHUS II (1988 – KS AS Scandi Line, Sandefjord), SUBIC ADVENTURE (1994 – Elcana Marine Inc, Panama), and EINER TAMBARSKJELVE (1995 – Basto Fosen AS, Trondheim).

PETROPAVLOVSK (1961) See BOSPHOR (1994)

PETR PERVYY (1990)

12602 grt; 412 psrs
440' x 69' x 18'6" (133.3 x 21.1 x 5.6 m)
4 x 6-cylinder Zgoda-Sulzer diesel engines via twin screw.
Floating eye hospital in Russia.
Built by Szczecinskaya Warskie, Szczecin, for the Black Sea Shipping Co, Odessa, as the passenger ship VASILIY SOLOVYEV SEDOY (1982). Renamed MIKHAIL SUSLOV (1982 – Black Sea Shipping Co) and PYOTR PERVYY (1989 – Black Sea Shipping Co).

PETR VELIKI (1949)

6261 grt; 600 psrs
400' x 53' x 28'1" depth (121.2 x 16.1 x 8.5 m)
Blohm & Voss 6-cylinder triple expansion engines with turbines via twin screw.
Cruise ship in Russian waters.
Built by Blohm & Voss for Turkish Maritime Lines as the DOGU (1939), but not physically delivered, owing to the outbreak of World War Two. She was commandeered by the German Navy. Renamed DUALA (1945 – AS Castillo), EMPIRE OCK (1945), PEOTR VELIKI (1946 – USSR government) and JAGIELLO (1947 – Gdynia America Line).

PHAISTOS (1964)

8100 grt; 1000 psrs
499' x 63' x 15' (151.3 x 19 x 4.6 m)
7-cylinder MAN diesel engine via single screw.
Passenger-car ferry owned by Efthymiadis Lines, Piraeus.
Built by Kockums MV AB, Malmo, for Rederi AB Gylfe Stig Gorthon as the MARIA GORTHON (1951).

PHENIX (1971) See TIPASA (1974)

PHILADELPHIA (1899) See PHILADELPHIA (1920)

PHILADELPHIA (1920)

10786 grt; 1740 psrs
560' x 63' x 39' (169.7 x 19.1 x 11.8 m)
6-cylinder triple expansion engines via twin screw.
Broken up for scrap at Genoa in 1923. Ex-New York-Naples Steamship Co.
Built by J & G Thomson & Co, Glasgow, for the Inman Line as the CITY OF PARIS (1889). Renamed PARIS (1893 – American Line), YALE, USS (1898 – US Navy, as an armed cruiser), PARIS (1898 – American Line), PHILADELPHIA (1899 – American Line) and HARRISBURG, USS (1917 – US Navy, as a transport).

PHILADELPHIA (1968)

10979 grt; 2000 psrs
523' x 72' x 30'7" (158.5 x 21.8 x 9.3 m)
2 x Westinghouse DRG turbine engines via single screw.
Passenger ship owned by Sea Land Services Inc, New York.
Built by the Kaiser Corporation, Richmond, California, for the US Navy as the Class A4-S-A1 troop transport GENERAL A.W. BREWER (AP-155) (1945).

PHILIPPA (1940) See ESMERALDA (1950)

PHILIPPEVILLE (1899) See CHAUDIERE (1914)

PHILIPPINE PRINCESS (1981)

4717 grt; 1367 psrs
432' x 55' x 18' (130.9 x 16.8 x 5.6 m)
2 x 12-cylinder B+W diesel engines via single screw.
Passenger ferry owned and operated by Sulpicio Lines.
Built by Onomichi Zosen, Onomichi, for Ryukyu Kaiun KK, Naha, as the NAHA MARU (1972).

PHILIPPINES (1919)

11440 grt; 2700 psrs
501' x 62' x 34'6" depth (151.8 x 18.9 x 10.5 m)
Blohm & Voss 8-cylinder quadruple expansion engines via twin screw.
Broken up for scrap at New York in 1924. Ex-US Shipping Board.
Built by Blohm & Voss, Hamburg, for the Hamburg-America Line as the BULGARIA (1898). Renamed CANADA (1913 – Canadian Pacific Railway Co), BULGARIA (1913 – Hamburg-America Line) and HERCULES (1917 – US Army).

PHILIPPINES (1983) See PHILIPPINES (1999)

PHILIPPINES (1999)

27090 grt; 1174 psrs
680' x 87' x 28' (207.4 x 26.6 x 8.5 m)
2 x 12-cylinder Fiat diesel engines via twin screw.

Floating restaurant in Manila Bay adjacent to the Manila Hotel, who own and operate her.
Built by Cantieri Riuniti dell'Adriatico, Trieste, for the Italian Line as the

AUGUSTUS (1952). Renamed GREAT SEA (1976 – Great Shipping & Investment Ltd, Hong Kong), OCEAN KING (1980 – Philtrust, Manila), PHILIPPINES (1983 – Philtrust, Manila, who placed her on sale at US15,000,000 in 1984), PRESIDENT (1985 – Philippine President Line) and ASIAN PRINCESS (Philtrust Finance Ltd, Manila).

PHILIPPINE TOURIST (1975) See PHILIPPINE TOURIST I (1978)

PHILIPPINE TOURIST I (1978)

12464 grt; 1050 psrs
492' x 70' x 26' (150 x 21.3 x 7.9 m)
2 x General Electric DRG turbine engines via single screw.
Broken up for scrap as a casino ship at Hong Kong in 1980, after towing her from Manila following her gutting by fire on 3 November 1978. Ex-Peninsula Tourist Shipping Corporation, Manila.
Laid down by Western Pipe & Steel Company, San Francisco, California, for Isthmian Lines as a Class C3 cargo ship STEEL ARTISAN (1942), but commandeered by the US Maritime Commission and completed as the auxiliary aircraft carrier BARNES, USS (1942). Renamed ATTACKER, HMS (1942 – British Royal Navy), CASTELFORTE (1949 – Sitmar Line), CASTEL FORTE (1952 – Sitmar Line), FAIRSKY (1957 – Sitmar Line) and PHILIPPINE TOURIST (1975 – Peninsula Tourist Shipping Corporation, Manila).

PHILOCTETES (1922)

11446 grt
512' x 63' x 41'1" depth (155.2 x 19.1 x 12.5 m)
4 x Scott & Co DRG turbine engines via twin screw.
Broken up for scrap at Newport, Wales, in 1948.
Built by Scott's Shipbuilding & Engineering Co Ltd, Greenock, for the China Mutual Steam Navigation Co Ltd. She was a migrant ship after World War Two.

PHOENICIA (1895) See VULCAIN (1921)

PHOENICIAN SEA (1995) See SALEM FLOWER (1998)

PHOENIX (1970) See MELODY (1979)

PHOENIX EXPRESS (1993)

11578 grt; 900 psrs
90 cars
561' x 83' x 21' (170 x 25 x 6.5 m)
2 x 14-cylinder Pielstick diesel engines via twin screw.
Passenger-car ferry owned by Marine Express, Tokyo.
Built by Mitsubishi Heavy Industries Ltd, Shimonoseki, for Marine Express, Tokyo.

PHOENIX WORLD CITY (2001) See AMERICA WORLD CITY (2001)

PICARDIE (1912) See FRANCE (1912)

PICARDY (1999) See P&OSL PICARDY (1999)

PICKHUBEN (1892) See HOUSATONIC (1915)

PIEMONTE (1935)

15186 grt; 1339 psrs
520' x 67' x 34'4" (157.6 x 20.3 x 10.4 m)
2 x Harland & Wolff 4-cylinder combination triple expansion engines and turbines via triple screw.
Owned by the Italian government as a troop carrier, she was broken up for scrap at La Spezia in 1949. She had been salvaged from Messina where she capsized after being bombed by Allied aircraft on 15 August 1943.
Laid down as a Job Number in 1939 by Barclay, Curle & Co, Glasgow, for the Hamburg-America Line, but completed for the Canadian Pacific Line as the MINNEDOSA (1918).

PIERO DELLA FRANSCESCA (1980)

4419 grt; 700 psrs
300' x 53' x 13' (91 x 16 x 4 m)
2 x 18-cylinder GMT diesel engines via twin screw.

Owned by Si Re Mar, Palermo, and operated by Tirrenia, Naples.
Built by Cantieri Riuniti, Palermo.

PIERRE LOTI (1953) See EROS (1979)

PIETER CORNELISZOON HOOFT (1926)
14729 grt; 639 psrs
540' x 68' x 29' (163.6 x 20.6 x 8.8 m)
2 x 9-cylinder Sulzer diesel engines via twin screw.
Broken up for scrap by Firma Simons, Hendrik Ido Ambacht, Rotterdam, in 1932 after being gutted by fire while berthed at Sumatra Quay, Amsterdam, on 14 November 1932. She had previously caught fire during her construction and on a second occasion during her fit out.
Built by Ateliers et Chantiers de la Loire, St Nazaire, for the Nederland Line.

PIETRO CALVI (1915)
6595 grt; 1175 psrs
455' x 50' x 29'8" depth (138.8 x 15.3 x 9 m)
F Schichau 6-cylinder triple expansion engines via twin screw.
Broken up for scrap in 1928. Ex-Banco di San Giorgio.
Built by F Schichau, Danzig, for North German Lloyd as the PRINZ REGENT LUITPOLD (1894).

PIETRO MARONCELLI (1916)
5463 grt; 285 psrs
404' x 50' x 21'2" (123.1 x 15.2 x 6.4 m)
Flensburger Schiffbau 6-cylinder triple expansion engine via twin screw.
Following seizure by the Italian government in 1915, she sank on 30 May 1918 after being torpedoed by a submarine near Alghero, Sardinia.
Built by Flensburger Schiffbau, Flensburg, as the AMBRIA (1896).

PILAR REGIDOR (1965) See LINDA Jnr (1968)

PILSUDSKI (1935)
14294 grt; 759 psrs
526' x 70' x 24' (159.4 x 21.2 x 7.3 m)
2 x 9-cylinder Sulzer diesel engines via twin screw.
Sank on 26 November 1939 after being torpedoed by a German U-boat at the mouth of the Humber river, UK, with the loss of eight lives. Ex-Polish Navy.
Built by Cantieri Riuniti del'Adriatico, Monfalcone, for the Gdynia-America Line under a barter arrangement whereby the PILSUDSKI and the BATORY would be constructed for six shipments of coal for the Italian State Railways, in lieu of cash.

PINE TREE MARINER (1952) See HENG LI (1993)

PINE TREE STATE (1921) See PRESIDENT GRANT (1946)

PING AN (1965)
9824 grt
476' x 64' x 40'5" depth (144.2 x 19.4 x 12.3 m)
Parsons turbine engines via single screw.
Broken up where she lay, off the Hook of Holland, after she grounded on 24 November 1965.
Built by Lithgows Ltd, Port Glasgow, for the Canadian Pacific Railway Co as the BEAVERGLEN (1945). Renamed BERMUDA HIBISCUS (1963 – Hibiscus Ltd).

PINKNEY, USS (APH-2) (1942) See PRIVATE ELDEN H. JOHNSON (1946)

PIRANGY (1928)
3810 grt; 732 psrs
361' x 45' x 25'8" (110 x 13.7 x 7.8 m)
Blohm & Voss 3-cylinder triple expansion engine via single screw.
Broken up for scrap in 1960. Ex-Cia Commercio e Navegacao, Brazil.
Built by Blohm & Voss, Hamburg, for the Hamburg South American Line as the ANTONINA (1898). Renamed HAIMON (1922 – Roland-Linie AG) and ANCONA (1927 – North German Lloyd).

PISA (1897) See ASCUTNEY (1917)

PISTHEVAIA INDUSTRIA (1935)
10078 grt; 580 psrs

516' x 59' x 27'4" (157.4 x 18 x 8.3 m)
Richardsons, Westgarth 4-cylinder quadruple expansion engine via single screw.
Owned by the Russian government, she was broken up for scrap at a price of US$120 per light displacement ton at Kaohsiung in 1979.
Built by Sir Raylton Dixon & Co, Middlesbrough, for the Lamport & Holt Line as the VASARI (1909). Renamed ARCTIC QUEEN (1928 – Hellyer Bros Ltd, Hull) after her conversion into a fishery depot ship, off Iceland.

PITTSBURGH (1913) See PENNLAND (1926)

PITTSBURGH (1922) See PENNLAND (1926)

PITTSBURGH (1968) See St LOUIS (1969)

PLAINFIELD (1918) See NORTH SEA (1935)

PLANTER (1946)
6618 grt; 81 psrs
415' x 56' x 25'7" (125.8 x 17 x 7.8 m)
Wallsend Slipway 4-cylinder quadruple expansion engines via single screw.
Broken up for scrap at Ghent in 1958. Ex-Harrison Line.
Built by Swan Hunter & Wigham Richardson Ltd, Newcastle, for the Harrison-Rennie Line as the passenger-cargo liner INKOSI (1937). Renamed EMPIRE CHIVALRY (1941 – British Ministry of War Transport), which was sunk at her berth in London by German bombers on 7 September 1940 and raised to be rebuilt as the PLANTER.

PLASSY (1901)
7400 grt; 171 psrs
450' x 54' x 31'6" depth (136.4 x 16.4 x 9.6 m)
Caird & Co 6-cylinder triple expansion engines via twin screw.
Broken up for scrap in 1924.
Built by Caird & Co, Greenock, for the P&O Line.

PLATTSBURGH (1919) See NEW YORK (1921)

PLAYA DE FORMENTOR (1955) See CIUDAD DE BARCELONA (1956)

PLAYA DE PALMANOVA (1956) See CIUDAD DE BURGOS (1956)

PLEIAS (1964)
4626 grt; 436 psrs
377' x 52' x 20' (114.2 x 15.8 x 6.1 m)
2 x 8-cylinder MAN diesel engines via twin screw.
Owned by Kavounides Shipping Co Ltd, Piraeus.
Built by Chantiers et Ateliers de Provence, Port de Bouc, for the French government as the banana carrier CHARLES PLUMIER (1938). Renamed LARGS, HMS (1940) after the British Royal Navy seized her during World War Two. Renamed again as the CHARLES PLUMIER (1948) when the French Line purchased her.

PLUS ULTRA (1928)
4180 grt
324' x 48' x 20' (98.2 x 14.5 x 6.1 m)
Euskalduna de Construcion 3-cylinder triple expansion engines via twin screw.
Passenger ferry owned and operated by Trasmediterranea.
Built by Union Naval de Levante, Valencia.

POBEDA (1946)
9828 grt; 404 psrs
480' x 61' x 29' (145.5 x 18.5 x 8.8 m)
2 x 8-cylinder Schichau-Sulzer diesel engines via twin screw.
Cruise ship operating in the Black Sea.
Built by Schichau Shipyards, Danzig, for the Hamburg-America Line as the MAGDELENA (1928). Renamed IBERIA (1934 – Hamburg-America Line).

POBYEDA (1946) See POBEDA (1946)

POCAHONTAS (1917) See KARLSRUHE (1928)

POELAU BRAS (1929)
9278 grt; 56 psrs
495' x 63' x 33' (157.6 x 18.6 x 11 m)
8-cylinder Sulzer diesel engines via single screw.
Sank on 7 March 1942 after being bombed by Japanese aircraft south of Sumatra.
Built by Nederlandsche Scheepsbouw & Dok Maatschappij (NDSM) 'De Schelde', Vlissingen, for the Nederland Line as a passenger-cargo ship.

POELAU LAUT (1929)
9272 grt; 58 psrs
494' x 61' x 33' (157.6 x 18.6 x 11 m)
8-cylinder Sulzer diesel engine via single screw.
Broken up for scrap by Dah Chong Hong in Hong Kong in 1959.
Built by Nederlandsche Scheepsbouw & Dok Maatschappij (NDSM), Vlissingen, for the Nederland Line as a passenger-cargo ship.

POELAU ROEBIAH (1928)
9250 grt; 58 psrs
495' x 61' x 33' (157.6 x 18.6 x 11 m)
8-cylinder Sulzer diesel engine via single screw.
Sank after being torpedoed by the German U-75 south of Jamaica on 6 July 1943.
Built by Rotterdamsche Droogdok Maatschappij (RDM), Rotterdam, for the Nederland Line as a passenger-cargo ship.

POELAU TELLO (1929)
9272 grt; 56 psrs
495' x 61' x 33' (157.6 x 18.6 x 11 m)
8-cylinder Sulzer diesel engine via single screw.
Sank on 27 January 1942 after being attacked by Japanese bombers at Emmahaven, Padang.
Built by Koninklijke Maatschappij 'De Schelde', Flushing, for the Nederland Line as a passenger-cargo ship.

POET (1979)
19645 grt; 2000 psrs
523' x 71' x 33' (159.3 x 21.7 x 10 m)
Geared turbine engine via single screw.
Owned by the Hawaiian Eugenia Corporation, she sank in October 1980 without trace in the mid-Atlantic.
Built by the Kaiser Corporation, Richmond, California, for the US Maritime Commission as the Class C4-S-A1 troop transport GENERAL OMAR BUNDY (AP-152) (1944), which acted as a migrant ship after World War Two. Laid up for the period 1949–63. Renamed as a cargo ship PORTMAR (1964 – Calmar Steamship Co) and PORT (1976 – Adbury Steamship Co).

POLAND (1920) See NATALE (1925)

POLAR CHIEF (1929) See POLAR CHIEF (1946)

POLAR CHIEF (1946)
5478 grt
445' x 53' x 28' (134.8 x 16.1 x 8.5 m)
Palmer 3-cylinder triple expansion engine via single screw.
Broken up for scrap in 1952 by WH Arnott Young & Co Ltd, Dalmuir. Ex-South Georgia Co Ltd.
Built by Palmers Shipbuilding Ltd, Jarrow, for the Beaver Line as the MONTCALM (1897). Renamed CRENELLA (1916 – Anglo-Saxon Petroleum Co), as a whaling depot ship REY ALFONSO (1923 – C Nielsen & Co, Norway), ANGLO-NORSE (1927 – Anglo Whaling Co), POLAR CHIEF (1929 – Falkland Whaling Co) and EMPIRE CHIEF (1941 – British Ministry of War Transport).

POLARIS (1975) See SCANDINAVIA (1984)

POLARIS (1992)
20326 grt; 540 psrs
583' x 81' x 20'6" (176.6 x 24.4 x 6.2 m)
2 x 18-cylinder B+W diesel engines via twin screw.
Owned by Enfold Shipping Co Ltd, Cyprus, and operated by Nordo-Link.
Built by Helsingor Shipyards, Helsingor, for DFDS as the passenger-freight ferry DANA FUTURA (1975). Renamed DAMMAM EXPRESS (1976 –

Atlanta Shipping Corporation), DROSSELFELS (1976 – DDG-Hansa, Bremen) and SKANE LINK (1989 – Nordo-Link).

POLARLYS (1996)
11341 grt; 737 psrs
51 cars
403' x 67' x 13' (122.1 x 20.3 x 4.7 m)
4 x 9-cylinder Bergen-Normo diesel engines via twin screw.
Passenger-car-cargo cruise ship owned and operated by Troms Fylkes DS on the Norwegian coastal service.
Built by Ulstein Vaerft, Ulsteinvik.

POLAR PRINCESS (1989) See ALANDIA (1992)

POLERIC (1912)
7682 grt; 850 psrs
462' x 52' x 25'8" (140 x 15.8 x 7.8 m)
T Richardson & Sons 6-cylinder triple expansion engines via twin screw.
Broken up for scrap in 1929. Ex-Bank Line.
Built by Swan Hunter Shipyards for the Wilson Line as the cattle transport CONSUELO (1900). Renamed CAIRNRONA (1908 – Thompson Line) and ALBANIA (1911 – Cunard Steamship Co Ltd).

POLLUX (1994) See THEOFILOS (1995)

POLONIA (1913) See BATAVIA (1919)

POLONIA (1921)
7890 grt; 800 psrs
450' x 56' x 31' (136.4 x 17 x 9.4 m)
8-cylinder quadruple expansion engines via twin screw.
Broken up for scrap in Italy in 1939. Ex-Gydnia American Line.
Built by Barclay, Curle & Co, Glasgow, for the Russian American Line as the KURSK (1910).

POLONIA (1995)
29875 grt; 920 psrs
172 cars + 55 railway coaches
561' x 92' x 20' (169.9 x 28 x 6.2 m)
4 x 6-cylinder Wartsila diesel engines via twin screw.

Passenger-car-train ferry owned by Euroafrica and operated by the Unity Line, Szczecw, Poland.
Built by Langsten Shipyards, Tomrefjord, at a cost of US$70,000,000.

POLYNESIE (1955) See GOLDEN GLORY (1976)

POLYXENA (1914)
5211 grt; 968 psrs
409' x 51' x 25'4" (124.7 x 15.4 x 7.7 m)
3-cylinder triple expansion engine via single screw.

After the British government seized the ship in 1914, she sank on 11 November 1917 after being torpedoed by a German U-boat 57 miles (95 km) west of Fastnet.
Built by JL Thompson & Sons, Sunderland, for North German Lloyd as the MARIA RICKMERS (1896). Renamed HELGOLAND (1900 – North German Lloyd).

POMERANIA (1978)
12087 grt; 984 psrs
275 cars + 26 trailers
420' x 64' x 18' (127.4 x 19.5 x 5.4 m)
4 x 6-cylinder Sulzer diesel engines via twin screw.

Passenger-car-cargo ferry owned by Polish Baltic Shipping Co and operated by Pol Ferries.
Built by Stocznia Szczecinska, Szczecin.

POMPEI (1900)
3410 grt; 1300 psrs
351' x 41' x 23' (106.8 x 12.4 x 6.7 m)
A & J Inglis 2-cylinder compound engine via single screw.
Broken up for scrap at La Spezia in 1905. Ex-Italian Line.
Launched by A & J Inglis, Glasgow, for the Ulster Steamship Co as the BENGORE HEAD (1881). Renamed BOHEMIA (1881 – Hamburg-America Line) and POMPEJI (1898 – Sloman Shipping Co).

POMPEJI (1898) See POMPEI (1900)

PONCE (1899) See TAI ER CHUANG (1955)

POOLE ANTELOPE (1973) See CALEDONIA (1997)

PORT (1976) See POET (1979)

PORT ADELAIDE (1916)
8144 grt; 812 psrs
491' x 61' x 32'4" depth (148.8 x 18.5 x 9.8 m)
Wallsend Slipway 6-cylinder triple expansion engines via twin screw.
Passenger ship owned by the Commonwealth & Dominion Line, she sank on 3 February 1917 after being torpedoed by the German submarine U-81 180 miles (300 km) south-west of Fastnet.
Built by Swan Hunter & Wigham Richardson, Newcastle, for the Indra Line as the INDRAPURA (1911), which was regularly employed as a migrant ship.

PORT ANTONIO (1901) See RESI PASA (1929)

PORTARITISSA (1955)
7469 grt; 1294 psrs
457' x 57' x 29' (138.5 x 17.3 x 8.8 m)
2 x Westinghouse DRG turbine engines via single screw.
Broken up for scrap at Osaka in 1958. Ex-Marinos & Frangos, UK.
Built by the Merchant Shipbuilding Corporation, Chester, Pennsylvania, for the Shawmut Steamship Co Inc, New York, as the MOUNT CARROLL (1921). Renamed MAUNIWILI (1925 – Matson Line), SOCRATES (1946 – Transatlantica Financiera Industrial, Panama) and SOUTHERN ALBATROSS (1955 – Transatlantica Financiera Industrial, Panama).

PORT DE St NAZAIRE (1921) See KOUANG (1929)

PORTELET (1987) See BARONESS M (1990)

PORTELET (1988) See BARONESS M (1990)

PORT HENDERSON (1905) See PORTO SAID (1913)

PORT HOBART (1946)
11877 grt; 128 psrs
541' x 71' x 29'8" (163.9 x 21.5 x 9 m)
2 x 8-cylinder Harland & Wolff diesel engines via twin screw.
Broken up for scrap at Shanghai in 1970.
Launched by Harland & Wolff Ltd, Belfast, as the passenger-cargo ship EMPIRE WESSEX (1946) and completed for the Port Line as the PORT HOBART.

PORTHOS (1915)
12633 grt; 298 psrs
511' x 62' x 42'1" depth (154.8 x 18.8 x 12.8 m)
Schneider & Co 6-cylinder triple expansion engines via twin screw.
Broken up for scrap in 1945 after being heavily bombed and heeling over in shallow water on 8 November 1942 during an Allied landing at Casablanca.
Built by Chantiers et Ateliers de la Gironde, Bordeaux, for Messageries Maritimes.

PORT JACKSON (1904) See WAIPARA (1904)

PORT KINGSTON (1904) See TAHITI (1911)

PORTLAND (1968)
11389 grt; 2000 psrs
523' x 72' x 30'7" depth (158.5 x 21.8 x 9.3 m)
2 x Westinghouse DRG turbine engines via single screw.
Owned and operated by Containership Chartering Services, New York.
Built by the Kaiser Corporation, Richmond, California, for the US Navy as a Class A4-S-A1 troop transport GENERAL D. E. AULTMAN (AP-156) (1945).

PORTMAR (1964) See POET (1979)

PORT MELBOURNE (1955) See PRINCESS DANAE (1997)

PORT NAPIER (1916) See MAR BIANCO (1938)

PORT NICHOLSON (1914)
10624 grt; 750 psrs
490' x 61' x 32'9" depth (148.5 x 18.6 x 10 m)
Workman, Clark 6-cylinder triple expansion engines via twin screw.
Passenger-cargo ship owned by the Commonwealth & Dominion Line, she sank on 15 January 1917 after hitting a mine laid by the German U-1 15 miles (25 km) west of Dunkirk.
Built by Workman, Clark & Co Ltd, Belfast, for the Tyser Line, London, as the MAKARINI (1912) which was regularly employed as a migrant vessel.

PORTO (1915)
6263 grt
455' x 51' x 29'8" depth (137.9 x 15.5 x 9 m)
F Schichau 6-cylinder triple expansion engines via twin screw.
Built by F Schichau, Gdansk, for North German Lloyd as the PRINZ HEINRICH (1894).

PORTO LEONE (1988) See WANG FU (1993)

PORTO RICO (1920)
4760 grt
371' x 45' x 25'2" (112.4 x 13.6 x 7.6 m)
Flensburger 4-cylinder quadruple expansion engines via single screw.
Broken up for scrap at Mobile, Alabama, in 1933 after running aground at the entrance to San Juan harbour, Puerto Rico, on 9 March 1933. Ex-New York & Porto Rico Steamship Co Line.
Built by Flensburger Schiffsbau, Flensburg, as the PRINZ JOACHIM (1903). Renamed MOCCASIN (1917).

PORTO SAID (1913)
5026 grt; 147 psrs
440' x 46' x 29' (134 x 14.1 x 8.8 m)
William Denny 4-cylinder triple expansion engine via single screw.
Passenger-cargo ship owned by Elder Dempster, she sank in December 1915 after being torpedoed by the German U-39 off Cyrenaica in the Mediterranean.

Launched by William Denny & Brothers, Dumbarton, for Shaw Savill Albion as the COLON (1885) and completed as the ARAWA (1898). Renamed LAKE MEGANTIC (1900 – Beaver Line), PORT HENDERSON (1905 – Imperial Direct Line) and ARRAPO (1912 – Italian Line).

PORT PIRIE (1947)

10561 grt; 50 psrs
529' x 68' X 23' (160.3 x 20.6 x 6.7 m)
Doxford diesel engines via twin screw.
Broken up for scrap at Castellon by V Davalillo in 1972.
Built by Swan Hunter & Wigham Richardson Ltd, Newcastle, for the Port Line as a passenger-cargo ship.

PORT ROYAL (1901) See MIDHAT PACHA (1911)

PORT SYDNEY (1955) See SWITZERLAND (1996)

PORTUGAL (1929) See QANZA (1929)

PORTUGAL (1946)

5270 grt; 438 psrs
392' x 48' x 19'7" (118.8 x 14.5 x 6 m)
New York Shipbuilding Co 3-cylinder triple expansion engines via single screw.
Broken up for scrap at La Spezia in 1952. Ex-Empresa de Navegacio Mercante SARL.
Built by the New York Shipbuilding Co, Camden, New Jersey, as the PRESIDENT (1906). Renamed DOROTHY ALEXANDER (1916 – Pacific Steamship Lines Ltd) and COLUMBIA (1938 – Alaska Steamship Co Inc).

POSEIDON (1966)

10172 grt; 1528 psrs
40 cars
484' x 63' x 21'6" (146.7 x 19.1 x 6.5 m)
6 x Parsons DRG turbine engines via twin screw.
Broken up for scrap at La Spezia in 1969. Ex-Typaldos Lines.
Built by Pennhoet, St Nazaire, for CGT, Marseilles, as the passenger-car ferry VILLE DALGER (1935).

POSEIDON (1994)

15237 grt; 622 psrs
525' x 82' x 20' (159.1 x 24.8 x 6 m)
2 x 18-cylinder Pielstick diesel engines via twin screw.
Passenger ferry owned by P Shipping Ltd and operated by Med Link Lines.
Launched by Koyo Dockyard Co Ltd, Mihara, for Shin Nihonkai Ferry KK, Otaru, as the FERRY RAIRAKKU(1970) and completed as the SUZURAN MARU (1970). Renamed FERRY IZU (1970), FERRY LILAC (1970) and UTOPIA (1980 – Nishinihon Shosen).

POSEIDON EXPRESS (1989)

7824 grt; 2450 psrs
470' x 68' x 19' (142.3 x 20.7 x 5.8 m)
2 x 16-cylinder Pielstick engines via twin screw.
Passenger ferry operated by Arkadia Lines, Greece. On 20 April 1996 she sank in Paros harbour in 100' (30 m) of water and salvage attempts were considered. She had entered the harbour in gale conditions and then had to take sudden evasive action as another ferry, the 4555 grt NAIAS II (Agapitos Line) snapped her moorings and swung straight into the side of the POSEIDON EXPRESS. Her captain finally managed to berth the ship and disembark the 256 passengers and all vehicles. The damage report confirmed that the vessel had suffered a 33 (10 m) gash in her aft hull and the loss of a propeller; water poured into her engine room, all power was lost and she heeled over to settle on her port side, effectively blocking two of the three berths.
Built by Cantieri Navale di Pietra Ligure, Pietra, for SNCM as the PROVENCE (1974).

POSEIDON EXPRESS 2 (1996) See EXPRESS POSEIDON (1999)

POSEIDONIA (1969)

3706 grt; 989 psrs
342' x 50' x 14'6" (103.6 x 15.3 x 4.4 m)
2 x 12-cylinder Sulzer diesel engines via twin screw.

Broken up for scrap by Fercomit SpA at Brindisi in 1985. Ex-Mediterranean Lines.
Built by William Denny & Brothers, Dumbarton, for Coast Lines Group as the INNISFALLEN (1948). Renamed INNISFALLEN I (1969 – British & Irish Steam Packet Co Ltd).

POSEIDONIA (1988) See LA PATRIA (2000)

P&OSL AQUITAINE (1999)

28833 grt; 1350 psrs
710 cars or 120 trailers
539' x 91' x 21' (163.3 x 27.7 x 6.4 m)
4 x 8-cylinder Sulzer diesel engines via twin screw.

Passenger-car ferry owned and operated by P&O Stena Line.
Laid down by Boelwerf Temse Yards, Antwerp, for RMT, Belgium, as the KONING BOUDEWIJN (1990) and completed as PRINS FILIP (1992 – RMT, at a cost of US$50,000,000) and STENA ROYAL (1998 – Stena Line).

P&OSL BURGUNDY (1999)

28138 grt; 1800 psrs
600 cars or 120 trailers
593' x 92' x 21' (179.7 x 27.8 x 6.3 m)
4 x 8-cylinder Sulzer diesel engines via twin screw.

Passenger-car-cargo ferry owned and operated for P&O Stena Line Ltd.
Built by Schichau Seebeckwerft, Bremerhaven, for the P&O Group as the PRIDE OF BURGUNDY (1993) at a cost of US$130,000,000 after first having been laid down as a pure freight ferry.

P&OSL CALAIS (1999)

26433 grt; 2290 psrs
650 cars or 104 trailers
560' x 93' x 20' (169.6 x 28.4 x 6.1 m)
3 x 14-cylinder Sulzer DRG diesel engines via triple screw.

Passenger-car-cargo ferry owned and operated by P&O Stena Line Ltd.
Built by Schichau Seebeckwerft, Bremerhaven, for P&O Steam Navigation Co as the PRIDE OF CALAIS (1987 – P&O Group).

P&OSL CANTERBURY (1999)

25243 grt; 1800 psrs
723 cars or 107 trailers
540' x 91' x 21' (163.5 x 27.6 x 6.5 m)
2 x 7-cylinder Sulzer diesel engines via twin screw.

Ice-strengthened passenger-car-cargo ferry owned and operated by P&O Stena Line Ltd.
Laid down by Kockums Varv AB, Malmo, for Rederi AB Nordo as the RoRo ferry SCANDINAVIA (1979) and completed as the RoRo ferry TZAREVETZ (1982 – Bulgarian State Shipping Co). Renamed FIESTA (1988 – Sea Containers), FANTASIA (1990 – Sealink British Ferries) and STENA FANTASIA (1990 – Stena Line/Sealink Stena Line, 1994/Stena Line, UK, 1997).

P&OSL DOVER (1998)

26433 grt; 2290 psrs
650 cars or 104 trailers
560' x 93' x 20' (169.6 x 28.3 x 6.1 m)
3 x 14-cylinder Sulzer SRG diesel engines via triple screw.

Passenger-car-cargo ferry owned and operated by P&O Stena Line Ltd.
Built by Schichau Seebeckwerft, Bremerhaven, for the Stanhope Steamship Co Ltd, London, as the PRIDE OF DOVER (1987 – P&O European Ferries).

P&OSL KENT (1998)

20446 grt; 1825 psrs
460 cars or 64 trailers
436' x 77' x 19' (163.5 x 23.2 x 5.7 m)
3 x 12-cylinder Sulzer diesel engines via triple screw.

Passenger-car-cargo RoRo ferry owned and operated by P&O Stena Line Ltd.
Built by Schichau Seebeckwerft, Bremerhaven, for Townsend Car Ferries Ltd as the SPIRIT OF FREE ENTERPRISE (1980). Renamed PRIDE OF KENT (1987 – P&O European Ferries).

P&OSL PICARDY (1999)

13601 grt; 1326 psrs
350 cars or 60 trailers

435' x 77' x 19' (131.9 x 23.2 x 5.7 m)
3 x 12-cylinder Sulzer diesel engines via triple screw.

Passenger-car-cargo ferry owned and operated by P&O Stena Line Ltd, but laid up in Dunkirk during 2000 and listed for sale at US$10,000,000.
Built by Schiechau Seebeckwerft, Bremerhaven, for Townsend Car Ferries Ltd as the PRIDE OF FREE ENTERPRISE (1980). Renamed PRIDE OF BRUGES (1988 – P&O European Ferries).

P&OSL PROVENCE (1998)

28559 grt; 2214 psrs
550 cars or 82 trailers or 85 rail coaches
502' x 92' x 21' (152.2 x 28 x 6.5 m)
4 x 12-cylinder Sulzer diesel engines via twin screw.

Passenger-car-cargo-train ferry owned and operated by P&O Stena Line Ltd.
Built by Chantiers du Nord et de la Mediterranee, Dunkirk, for Stena Line as the STENA JUTLANDICA (1983). Renamed STENA EMPEREUR (1996 – Stena Line).

POTENGY (1938)

3204 grt; 820 psrs
340' x 42' x 25' (103.6 x 12.8 x 7.6 m)
D & W Henderson 3-cylinder triple expansion engine via single screw.
Believed lost during the war in the Atlantic. Ex-Cia Commercio e Navegacao, Brazil.
Built by D & W Henderson Ltd, Glasgow, for the Allan Line as the BRAZILIAN (1890). Renamed CORCOVADO (1910 – Cia Commercio e Navagacao, Brazil).

POTOMAC (1921)

9709 grt; 1880 psrs
499' x 58' x 37'4" depth (151.2 x 17.6 x 11.3 m)
JC Tecklenborg 8-cylinder quadruple expansion engines via twin screw.
Broken up for scrap in Holland in 1928. Ex-United States Lines.
Built by JC Tecklenborg, Geestemunde, for North German Lloyd as the NECKAR (1901). Renamed ANTIGONE, USS (1917 – US Navy).

POTSDAM (1900) See SONDERBURG (1941)

POTSDAM (1935) See SAFINA-E-HUJJAJ (1961)

POVL ANKER (1978)

12131 grt; 1500 psrs
300 cars
400' x 73' x 17' (121.2 x 22 x 5.2 m)
4 x 16-cylinder Alpha diesel engines via twin screw.
Passenger-car ferry owned and operated by Bornholmstrafikken on the Denmark–Sweden service.
Built by Aalborg Vaerft AS, Aalborg.

POWHATAN (1917) See PRESIDENT FILLMORE (1922)

PRAGUE (1930)
4218 grt; 548 psrs
366' x 50' x 15' (110.9 x 15.2 x 4.5 m)
4 x Brown-Curtis SRG turbine engines via twin screw.
Broken up for scrap by Thomas W Ward Ltd at Barrow-in-Furness in 1947 after catching fire on 14 March 1947 and sinking alongside her refitting dock.
Built by John Brown & Co Ltd, Clydebank, for the London & Northeastern Railway.

PRESIDENT (1906) See PORTUGAL (1946)

PRESIDENT (1969) See SHAHEED SALAHUDDIN (1981)

PRESIDENT (1984) See FENJA (1999)

PRESIDENT (1985) See PHILIPPINES (1999)

PRESIDENT ADAMS (1922) See PRESIDENT GRANT (1940)

PRESIDENT ADAMS (1941) See PRESIDENT ADAMS, USS (AP-19) (1943)

PRESIDENT ADAMS, USS (AP-19) (1943)
9255 grt; 96 psrs
492' x 70' x 27' (149 x 21.2 x 8.2 m)
Geared turbine engines via single screw.
Broken up for scrap in San Pedro, California, in 1973.
Built as the C-3 Class PRESIDENT ADAMS, USS (AP-38) (1941) by Newport News Shipyards & Drydock Corporation, Newport News, Virginia, for the US Navy.

PRESIDENT ADAMS (1950) See BAY STATE (1980)

PRESIDENT AGUIRRE (1966) See KOBENHAVN (1966)

PRESIDENT ARTHUR (1922) See CITY OF HONOLULU (1924)

PRESIDENT ARTHUR (1924) See CITY OF HONOLULU (1927)

PRESIDENT BUCHANAN (1924) See REPUBLIC, USS (AP-33) (1941)

PRESIDENT BUCHANAN (1938) See PRESIDENT BUCHANAN (1945)

PRESIDENT BUCHANAN (1945)
10533 grt; 78 psrs
502' x 62' x 28'3" depth (152.1 x 18.8 x 8.6 m)
2 x New York Shipbuilding Co 4-cylinder triple expansion engines via twin screw.
Broken up for scrap at Oakland, California, in 1956. Ex-US Army.
Built by New York Shipbuilding Company, Camden, New Jersey, for the US Shipping Board as the PANHANDLE STATE (1920). Renamed PRESIDENT MONROE (1922 – Dollar Line), PRESIDENT BUCHANAN (1938 – American President Lines) and EMILY H. M. WEDER (1943 – US Army).

PRESIDENT CLEVELAND (1922) See TASKER H. BLISS, USS (AP-42) (1942)

PRESIDENT CLEVELAND (1947) See ORIENTAL PRESIDENT (1973)

PRESIDENT COOLIDGE (1931)
21936 grt; 990 psrs
654' x 81' x 32' (198.2 x 24.5 x 9.7 m)
Westinghouse turbo-electric engines via twin screw.
Sank on 26 October 1942 in deep water, with the loss of two lives out of 5,000 on board, when she entered a complex US-laid minefield at the entrance to Espiritu Santo harbour, New Hebrides, and struck several mines. As a beaching attempt on to a reef commenced, she rolled over on her side as she hit the bottom and slipped off into deeper water.
Built by Newport News Shipbuilding & Drydock Co, Newport News, Virginia, for the Dollar Steamship. Line.

PRESIDENT DE CAZALET (1948) See ARCADI (1971)

PRESIDENT DOUMER (1933)
11898 grt; 903 psrs
469' x 64' x 37'8" depth (142.1 x 19.4 x 11.5 m)
B+W 16-cylinder diesel engines via twin screw.
Sank on 30 October 1942, with the loss of 260 lives, after being torpedoed by the German U-604 north-east of Madiera.
Built by Constructions Navales, La Ciotat, for Messageries Maritimes.

PRESIDENTE PERON (1948) See ARGENTINA (1956)

PRESIDENTE WILSON (1920) See MARCO POLO (1936)

PRESIDENTE YEIWENE (1992) See CALEDONIA (1997)

PRESIDENTE YEIWENE (1993) See CALEDONIA (1997)

PRESIDENT FILLMORE (1922)
10532 grt; 2170 psrs
502' x 62' x 28'3" depth (152.1 x 18.8 x 8.6 m)
New York Shipbuilding Co 8-cylinder quadruple expansion engines via twin screw.
Broken up for scrap at Baltimore in 1928. Ex-Dollar Line.
Laid down by Vulcan Shipyards, Stettin, for the Hamburg-America Line as the BATAVIA (1898) and completed as the HAMBURG (1900). Renamed RED CROSS (1914 – International Red Cross), HAMBURG (1914 – Hamburg-America Line), POWHATAN (1917 – US Navy), NEW ROCHELLE (1920 – Baltic Steamship Corporation of America) and HUDSON (1921 – United States Mail).

PRESIDENT FILLMORE (1929) See PANAMANIAN (1940)

PRESIDENT FILLMORE (1940) See PRESIDENT FILLMORE (1946)

PRESIDENT FILLMORE (1946)
10533 grt; 78 psrs
523' x 62' x 32' (158.5 x 18.8 x 9.7 m)
2 x 4-cylinder triple expansion engines via twin screw.
Broken up for scrap at Oakland, California, in 1948. Ex-US Army.
Built by the New York Shipbuilding Co, Camden, New Jersey, for the US Shipping Board as the OLD NORTH STATE (1920). Renamed PRESIDENT VAN BUREN (1922 – United States Lines), PRESIDENT FILLMORE (1940 – American President Lines) and MARIGOLD (1944 – US Army).

PRESIDENT GARFIELD (1922) See PRESIDENT MADISON (1946)

PRESIDENT GARFIELD (1941) See THOMAS JEFFERSON, USS (AP-60) (1942)

PRESIDENT GRANT (1907) See REPUBLIC, USS (AP-33) (1941)

PRESIDENT GRANT (1922) See PRESIDENT GRANT (1946)

PRESIDENT GRANT (1940)
10516 grt; 78 psrs
523' x 62' x 28' (158.5 x 18.8 x 8.5 m)
2 x 4-cylinder triple expansion engines via twin screw.
Acquired from American President Lines by the US Shipping Board as an army transport, she was abandoned as a total constructive loss on 26 February

1944 after becoming wrecked on the Ulna Reef in Milne Bay on 17 November 1943. Her crew had toiled for three and a half months to repair her after she first struck, only to see a freak giant wave split her in two.
Built by the New York Shipbuilding Co, Camden, New Jersey, for United States Mail Lines as the CENTENNIAL STATE (1921). Renamed PRESIDENT ADAMS (1922 – United States Lines).

PRESIDENT GRANT (1946)

14187 grt; 550 psrs
535' x 72' x 41' depth (162.1 x 21.8 x 12.4 m)
4 x Bethlehem Shipbuilding Corporation geared turbine engines via twin screw.
Broken up for scrap at Wilmington, Delaware, in 1948. Ex-US Maritime Commission.
Built by the Bethlehem Shipbuilding Corporation, Sparrow's Point, Maryland, for the Admiral Line as the PINE TREE STATE (1920). Renamed PRESIDENT GRANT (1922), HARRIS, USS (AP-8) (1940 – US Navy) and HARRIS, USS (A-PA-2) (1943).

PRESIDENT HARDING (1922) See VILLE DE BRUGES (1940)

PRESIDENT HARRISON (1923) See KACHIDOKI MARU (1942)

PRESIDENT HAYES (1924) See PRESIDENT TYLER (1945)

PRESIDENT HAYES (1941) See PRESIDENT HAYES, USS (A-AP-20) (1943)

PRESIDENT HAYES, USS (A-AP-20) (1943)

9255 grt; 96 psrs
492' x 70' x 27' (149.1 x 21.2 x 8.2 m)
Geared turbine engine via single screw.
Owned by US Army.
Built as the C-3P Class PRESIDENT HAYES (1941) by Newport News Shipbuilding & Drydock Co, Newport News, Virginia, for American President Lines.

PRESIDENT HAYES (1951) See STATE OF MAINE (1973)

PRESIDENT HOOVER (1931)

21936 grt; 490 psrs
654' x 81' x 32' (198.2 x 24,5 x 9.7 m)
General Electric turbo-electric engines via twin screw.
Broken up by a Japanese shipbreaker where she lay in 1938 after running aground on rocks at 1.00 am on 11 December 1937 near the Japanese-owned Hoishito Island, off the north coast of Taiwan.
Built by Newport News Shipbuilding & Drydock Co, Newport News, Virginia, for the Dollar Steamship Line Inc.

PRESIDENT HOOVER (1957) See REGINA PRIMA (1973)

PRESIDENT JACKSON (1922) See PRESIDENT JACKSON (1946)

PRESIDENT JACKSON (1940) See PRESIDENT JACKSON, USS (T-PA-18) (1943)

PRESIDENT JACKSON (AP-37) (1942) See PRESIDENT JACKSON, USS (T-PA-18) (1943)

PRESIDENT JACKSON, USS (T-PA-18) (1943)

9255 grt; 96 psrs
465' x 70' x 33'5" depth (140.9 x 21.2 x 10.2 m)
2 x Newport News Shipbuilding DRG turbine engines via single screw.
Broken up for scrap at Kaohsiung in 1973. Ex-US Army.
Built by Newport News Shipbuilding & Drydock Company, Newport News, Virginia, for the US Shipping Board as the C-3P class PRESIDENT JACKSON (1940). Reclassified as the PRESIDENT JACKSON (AP-37) (1942).

PRESIDENT JACKSON (1946)

14124 grt; 550 psrs

535' x 72' x 50' depth (162.1 x 21.8 x 15.2 m)
4 x Newport News Shipbuilding geared turbine engines via twin screw.
Broken up for scrap by American Shipbreakers Inc at Wilmington, Delaware, in 1948. Ex-US Maritime Commission.
Built by Newport News Shipbuilding & Drydock Company, Newport News, Virginia, for the Admiral Line as the passenger-cargo ship SILVER STATE (1921). Renamed PRESIDENT JACKSON (1922) and ZEILIN, USS (AP-9) (1942 – US Navy). Reclassified as the ZEILIN, USS (APA-3) (1942).

PRESIDENT JACKSON (1950) See STATE (1990)

PRESIDENT JEFFERSON (1922) See PRESIDENT JEFFERSON (1946)

PRESIDENT JEFFERSON (1946)

14174 grt; 550 psrs
535' x 72' x 28' (162.1 x 21.8 x 8.5 m)
Turbine engines via twin screw.
Broken up for scrap at San Pedro, California, in 1948. Ex-US Navy.
Laid down by the New York Shipbuilding Co, Camden, New Jersey, for the Admiral Line as the C. M. SCHWAB (1918) and completed as the WENATCHEE (1921). Renamed PRESIDENT JEFFERSON (1922 – Admiral Line), HENRY T. ALLEN (1940 – US Army), HENRY T. ALLEN, USS (APA-15) (1942) and HENRY T. ALLEN, USS (AG-90) (1945 – US Navy).

PRESIDENT JOHNSON (1929) See TAGUS (1949)

PRESIDENT LINCOLN (1907) See PRESIDENT LINCOLN, USS (1914)

PRESIDENT LINCOLN, USS (1914)

18168 grt; 3828 psrs
length 616' x beam 68' (186.7 x 20.6 m)
8-cylinder quadruple expansion engine via twin screw.
Sank on 31 May 1918, with 26 lives lost, after being torpedoed by the German U-90 in mid-Atlantic.
Laid down by Harland & Wolff Ltd, Belfast, for the Leyland Line as the SCOTIAN (1903), launched as the SCOTIAN (1904) and completed as the PRESIDENT LINCOLN (1907 – Leyland Line) after the SCOTIAN was laid up incomplete for three years.

PRESIDENT LINCOLN (1922) See CABO DE BUENA ESPERENZA (1940)

PRESIDENT McKINLEY (1922) See J. FRANKLIN BELL, USS (APA-16) (1942)

PRESIDENT MADISON (1922) See PRESIDENT QUEZON (1939)

PRESIDENT MADISON (1940) See PRESIDENT MADISON (1946)

PRESIDENT MADISON (1946)

10496 grt; 78 psrs
523' x 62' x 32' (158.5 x 18.8 x 9.7 m)
2 x 4-cylinder triple expansion engines via twin screw.
Broken up for scrap by Consolidated Builders Inc in Vancouver, Washington, in 1948. Ex-US Maritime Commission.
Built by the New York Shipbuilding & Drydock Co, Camden, New Jersey, for the US Shipping Board as the BLUE HEN STATE (1921). Renamed PRESIDENT GARFIELD (1922 – United States Lines), PRESIDENT MADISON (1940 – American President Lines), KENMORE, USS (AP-62) (1942 – US Navy) and REFUGE, USS (AH-11) (1944 – US Navy).

PRESIDENT MONROE (1922) See PRESIDENT BUCHANAN (1945)

PRESIDENT MONROE (1940) See MARIANNA V (1965)

PRESIDENT MONROE, USS (AP-104) (1943) See MARIANNA V (1965)

PRESIDENT MONROE (1946) See MARIANNA V (1965)

PRESIDENT PIERCE (1922) See HUGH L. SCOTT, USS (AP-43) (1942)

PRESIDENT P MONTT (1908) See JANUA (1928)

PRESIDENT POLK (1922) See PRESIDENT TAYLOR (1940)

PRESIDENT POLK (1941) See MINOTAUROS (1966)

PRESIDENT POLK, USS (AP-104) (1943) See MINOTAUROS (1966)

PRESIDENT QUEZON (1939)
14124 grt; 560 psrs
535' x 72' x 27'8" depth (162.1 x 21.8 x 8.4 m)
4 x Fore River Shipbuilding Co geared turbine engines via twin screw.
Owned by Philippine Mail Line, she was abandoned after being wrecked on 16 January 1940 on Tanega Shima in the Tiukiu Islands, off the Japanese coast, during her delivery voyage to new owners in the Philippines.
Built by the New York Shipbuilding & Drydock Co, Camden, New Jersey, for the Admiral Line as the BAY STATE (1920). Renamed PRESIDENT MADISON (1922 – Philippine Mail Line) which capsized and sank at her Seattle berth on 24 March 1933. She was raised and refurbished over an eight month period.

PRESIDENT ROOSEVELT (1922) See JOSEPH T. DICKMAN, USS (AP-13) (1943)

PRESIDENT ROOSEVELT (1961) See OCEAN EXPLORER I (1998)

PRESIDENT TAFT (1922) See VILLE DE BRUGES (1940)

PRESIDENT TAFT (1922) See WILLARD A. HOLBROOK (1944)

PRESIDENT TAYLOR (1940)
10533 grt; 78 psrs
502' x 62' x 28'3" depth (152.1 x 18.8 x 8.6 m)
2 x New York Shipbuilding Co 4-cylinder triple expansion engines via twin screw.
Operated by the US War Shipping Administration, she was abandoned after striking rocks off Canton Island on 14 February 1942, then being attacked weeks later by Japanese aircraft which totally destroyed her.
Built by the New York Shipbuilding & Drydock Co, Camden, New Jersey, for the US Shipping Board as the GRANITE STATE (1921). Renamed PRESIDENT POLK (1922 – United States Lines).

PRESIDENT TYLER (1940) See PRESIDENT TYLER (1945)

PRESIDENT TYLER (1945)
10533 grt; 78 psrs
502' x 62' x 28'3" depth (152.1 x 18.8 x 8.6 m)
New York Shipbuilding Co 8-cylinder triple expansion engines via twin screw.
Broken up for scrap at Philadelphia, USA, in 1957 after being laid up in the Hudson river, New York, since 1947. Ex-US Army.
Built by the New York Shipbuilding & Drydock Co, Camden, New Jersey, for the US Shipping Board as the CREOLE STATE (1920). Renamed PRESIDENT HAYES (1924 – Pacific Mail Steamship Co), PRESIDENT TYLER (1940 – American President Lines), HOWARD A. McCURDY (1945 – US Army) and laid up for the period 1947–57.

PRESIDENT VAN BUREN (1922) See PRESIDENT FILLMORE (1946)

PRESIDENT VAN BUREN (1941) See THOMAS R. STONE, USS (APA-30) (1942)

PRESIDENT WILSON (1922) See CABO DE HORNOS (1940)

PRESIDENT WILSON (1948) See ORIENTAL EMPRESS (1973)

PRESVIA (1963)
10155 grt; 60 psrs
491' x 65' x 30'10" (148.8 x 19.7 x 9.1 m)
2 x 6-cylinder Sulzer diesel engines via twin screw.
Broken up for scrap in Japan in 1963. Ex-Belvientos Cia Navigation, Panama.
Built by Wilton Fijenoord, Schiedam, for the Holland America Line as the DAMSTERDIJK (1930). Renamed DALERDYK (1949 – Holland America Line).

PRETORIA (1878) See SAIDIEH (1907)

PRETORIA (1936) See KRI TANJUNG PANDAN (1946)

PRETORIA CASTLE (1938) See WARWICK CASTLE (1947)

PRETORIA CASTLE (1948) See S. A. ORANJE (1966)

PRETORIAN (1901)
7650 grt; 550 psrs
437' x 53' x 29'7" (133.2 x 16.2 x 9 m)
Richardson, Westgarth 3-cylinder triple expansion engine via single screw.
Broken up for scrap at Garston, Liverpool, in 1926 after being laid up since 1922.
Built by Furness, Withy & Co Ltd, West Hartlepool, for the Allan Line.

PREVELI (1995) See PREVELIS (2000)

PREVELIS (2000)
15254 grt; 1600 psrs
470' x 78' x 17' (142.5 x 23.5 x 5.2 m)
2 x 12-cylinder Pielstick diesel engines via twin screw.
Passenger ferry built by Imabari Zosen, Imabari, for Shikoku Kaihatsu Ferry KK, Toyo, as the FERRY ORANGE No.2 (1980) and renamed PREVELI (1995 – ANEK).

PRIAMURIE (1957)
5261 grt; 333 psrs
403' x 53' x 17'6" (122.2 x 16.1 x 5.3 m)
2 x 6-cylinder MAN diesel engines via twin screw.
Owned by the Far East Shipping Co, Vladivostok.
Built by Mathias-Thesen, Wismar, for the Black Sea Shipping Co, Odessa, as the VLADIVOSTOK (1960).

PRIAMURYE (1957)
4871 grt
length 390' x draft 22' (118.2 x 6.7 m)
Diesel-electric engines via twin screw.
Owned by the Russian government, she erupted in fire while in a Japanese port and, after blazing fiercely for 18 hours and being totally gutted on 18 May 1988, it was found that eleven passengers had died. Because the ship had been chartered to a Communist Youth League, some believed that the Russians delayed calling the Japanese fire brigade to attend at ship's side in an attempt to make political use out of the incident.
Built for the Russian government.

PRIDE OF AILSA (1992) See PRIDE OF AL SALAM 95 (1996)

PRIDE OF AL SALAM 95 (1996)
12503 grt; 2500 psrs
370 cars or 60 trailers
460' x 74' x 17'6" (139.4 x 22.4 x 5.3 m)
3 x 8-cylinder Stork-Werkspoor diesel engines via triple screw.
Passenger-car-cargo ferry owned by Gold Star Navigation Co SA and operated by El Salam Shipping & Trading Establishment.
Built by IHC Gusto NV, Schiedam, for Townsend Car Ferries Ltd as the FREE ENTERPRISE VI (1972). Renamed PRIDE OF SANDWICH (1987 – P&O Ferries) and PRIDE OF AILSA (1992 – P&O North Sea Ferries Ltd).

PRIDE OF BILBAO (1993)
37583 grt; 2500 psrs
580 cars or 62 trailers
584' x 96' x 21' (177 x 29 x 6.5 m)
4 x 12-cylinder Wartsila-SEMT-Pielstick diesel engines via twin screw.

Ice-strengthened passenger-car-cargo ferry owned by Irish Continental Group/Irish Ferries (which paid Irish Pds 57,000,000 for her) and chartered to P&O European Ferries (Portsmouth) Ltd until 2001, with an option to extend the charter until 2006.
Built by Wartsila-Turku for the Viking Line as the OLYMPIA (1986).

PRIDE OF BRUGES (1988) See P&OSL PICARDY (1999)

PRIDE OF BURGUNDY (1993) See P&OSL BURGUNDY (1999)

PRIDE OF CALAIS (1987) See P&OSL CALAIS (1999)

PRIDE OF CANTERBURY (1987) See ROMILDA (1993)

PRIDE OF CHERBOURG (1989) See BARLOVENTO (2000)

PRIDE OF CHERBOURG (1994)
14760 grt; 1316 psrs
380 cars
474' x 77' x 17'6" (143.7 x 23.4 x 5.4 m)
3 x 8-cylinder Stork-Werkspoor diesel engines via triple screw.
Ferry owned by P&O Steam Navigation Co Ltd and operated by P&O European Ferries (Portsmouth) Ltd.
Built by Aalborg Vaerft AS, Aalborg, for Thoresen Car Ferries as the VIKING VALIANT (1975). Renamed PRIDE OF LE HAVRE (1989 – P&O Group).

PRIDE OF CHERBOURG II (1994) See BARLOVENTO (2000)

PRIDE OF DOVER (1987) See P&OSL DOVER (1999)

PRIDE OF FLANDERS (1992)
16776 grt; 688 psrs
220 cars or 40 trailers
498' x 78' x 24' (151 x 23.6 x 7.3 m)
2 x 12-cylinder NYK-Pielstick diesel engines via twin screw.

Reverted to pure freight operations in 1995 for P&O European Ferries.
Built by Hyundai Heavy Industries Co Ltd, Ulsan, for Stena Container Line Ltd, London, as the passenger-cargo RoRo ferry MERZARIO ESPANIA (1978). Renamed MERZARIO HISPANIA (1979 – Stena Container Line Ltd) and NORDIC FERRY (1979 – Townsend-Thoresen Ferries).

PRIDE OF FREE ENTERPRISE (1980) See P&OSL PICARDY (1999)

PRIDE OF GALVESTON (1991) See COPA CASINO (1993)

PRIDE OF HAMPSHIRE (1989)
14760 grt; 1316 psrs
380 cars
474' x 77' x 17'6" (143.7 x 23.4 x 5.4 m)
3 x 8-cylinder Stork-Werkspoor diesel engines via triple screw.
Passenger-car ferry owned by P&O Steam Navigation and operated by P&O European Ferries (Portsmouth) Ltd.

Built by Aalborg Vaerft AS, Aalborg, for Townsend Car Ferries Ltd as the VIKING VENTURER (1975).

PRIDE OF HYTHE (1988) See LABURNAM (1993)

PRIDE OF KENT (1987) See POSL KENT (1998)

PRIDE OF LE HAVRE (1986) See BARLOVENTO (2000)

PRIDE OF LE HAVRE (1994)
33336 grt; 1720 psrs
575 cars
531' x 96' x 21'6" (161 x 29 x 6.5 m)
4 x 8-cylinder Zgoda-Sulzer diesel engines via twin screw.

Passenger-car ferry operated by P&O European Ferries Ltd.
Built by Schichau Seebeckwerft, Bremerhaven, for the Olau Line as the OLAU HOLLANDIA (1989) at a cost of £63,000,000.

PRIDE OF MISSISSIPPI (1988) See CAPO CASINO (1993)

PRIDE OF PORTSMOUTH (1994)
33336 grt; 1720 psrs
550 cars or 120 trailers
531' x 96' x 21' (161 x 29 x 6.5 m)
4 x 8-cylinder Zgoda-Sulzer diesel engines via twin screw.

Passenger-car-cargo ferry operated by P&O European Ferries Ltd.
Built by Schichau Seebeckwerft, Bremerhaven, for the Olau Line as the OLAU BRITANNIA (1990) at a cost of £63,000,000.

PRIDE OF RATHLIN (1992)
12503 grt; 630 psrs
340 cars or 60 trailers
460' x 74' x 17'6" (139.4 x 22.4 x 5.3 m)
3 x 8-cylinder Stork-Werkspoor DRG diesel engines via triple screw.
Passenger-car-cargo ferry owned by Howill Shipping Ltd, London, and operated by P&O European Ferries Ltd, but has been on the sale lists since late 1999.
Built by IHC Gusto BV, Schiedam, for Townsend Car Ferries Ltd as the FREE ENTERPRISE VII (1973). Renamed PRIDE OF WALMER (1988 – P&O European Ferries).

PRIDE OF SAN DIEGO (1991) See ENCHANTED SUN (1999)

PRIDE OF SANDWICH (1987) See PRIDE OF AL SALAM 95 (1996)

PRIDE OF SUFFOLK (1992)
16776 grt; 688 psrs
220 cars or 40 trailers
498' x 72' x 24' (151 x 21.7 x 7.3 m)
2 x 12-cylinder Pielstick diesel engines via twin screw.

Passenger-car-cargo ferry which reverted to pure freight operations only for P&O European Ferries Ltd.
Built by Hyundai Heavy Industries Co Ltd, Ulsan, for Stena Container Line Ltd, London, as the STENA TRANSPORTER (1978). Renamed FINNROSE (1979 – OT Redlerierna, Sweden), STENA TRANSPORTER (1980 – Stena Container Line) and BALTIC FERRY (1980 – European Ferries Ltd).

PRIDE OF TORQUAY (1947) See HELLENIC PRINCE (1948)

PRIDE OF WALMER (1988) See PRIDE OF RATHLIN (1992)

PRIDE OF WINCHESTER (1994) See VITSENTZOS KARNAROS (1994)

PRIMERO DE JUNIO (1974)
6813 grt; 100 psrs
429' x 59' x 22'6" (130 x 17.9 x 6.8 m)
Sulzer 10-cylinder diesel engine via single screw.
Passenger-cargo ship owned by the government of Mexico and used now as a training ship.
Built by Soc Espanola Construccion Naval, Bilbao, for Aznar as the passenger-cargo ship MONTE ANAGA (1959).

PRIMORJE (1945)
3161 grt
300' x 44' x 16' (90.9 x 13.3 x 4.8 m)
Neptun Werft 6-cylinder triple expansion and turbine engines via twin screw.
Built by Neptunwerft, Rostock, for Turkish Maritime Lines as the SALON (1939) but delivery was blocked by the Germans, only to lose the ship to the Russians after World War Two as a war prize.

PRIMROSE (1999)
6276 grt; 1400 psrs
290 cars or 36 trailers
391' x 68' x 15' (118.4 x 20.7 x 4.5 m)
2 x 18-cylinder Atlantique-Pielstick diesel engines via twin screw.
Passenger-car-cargo ferry owned by Dianthus Maritime Co Ltd, Cyprus, and operated by Denval Shipping Co, UK.
Built by John Cockerill Shipyards, Hoboken, for P&O European Ferries Ltd as the PRINCESSE MARIE CHRISTINE (1975).

PRINCE (1991) See MOBY LALLI (2000)

PRINCE (1995) See MINOAN PRINCE (1995)

PRINCE (1996)
21545 grt; 1704 psrs
385 cars or 70 trailers
590' x 78' x 21' (182.4 x 23.7 x 6.5 m)
4 x 12-cylinder Lindholmen-Pielstick geared diesel engines via twin screw.

Ferry owned by DFDS Scandinavian Seaways and on charter to Cotunav, Tunisia.
Built by Lubecker Flender, Lubeck, for Tor Line AB as the TOR BRITANNIA (1975). Renamed SCANDINAVIAN STAR (1981 – Scandinavian World Cruises), TOR BRITANNIA (1982 – DFDS Scandinavian Seaways) and PRINCE OF SCANDINAVIA (1991 – DFDS Scandinavian Seaways).

PRINCE BAUDOUIN (1934)
3050 grt

375' x 46' x 21'4" (108 x 13 x 6.5 m)
2 x 24-cylinder J Cockerill, Seraing oil engines.
Built by Soc Anon John Cockerill, Hoboken, Belgium, for the Belgian government.

PRINCE DAVID (1930) See CHARLTON MONARCH (1948)

PRINCE DE BRETAGNE (1975) See VEGA (1990)

PRINCE GEORGE (1948)
5812 grt; 260 psrs
350' x 52' x 18' (106.1 x 15.8 x 5.5 m)
Triple expansion engines via twin screw.
Declared a total constructive loss when she was gutted by fire on 15 October 1995 at Britannia Beach, near Squamish, British Columbia. She had been laid up there since 1989, after serving as an accommodation ship in British Columbia.
Built by Yarrows Ltd, Esquimalt, BC, for the Canadian National Railways.

PRINCE HENRY (1930) See EMPIRE PARKESTON (1947)

PRINCE HENRY, HMCS (1940) See EMPIRE PARKESTON (1947)

PRINCE LAURENT (1974) See SUPERFERRY II (1993)

PRINCE LUDWIG (1903) See ORCADES (1921)

PRINCE OF BRITTANY (1978) See BEAUPORT (1991).

PRINCE OF FUNDY (1970) See BEAUPORT (1991).

PRINCE OF SCANDINAVIA (1991) See PRINCE (1996).

PRINCE PHILIPPE (1948) See STROMMA REX (1973).

PRINCE PHILIPPE (1973) See EXPRES ATHINA (1998).

PRINCE ROBERT (1930) See LUCANIA (1951).

PRINCESA AMOROSA (1989)
5026 grt; 327 psrs
342' x 52' x 15' (103.6 x 15.8 x 4.5 m)
2 x Harland & Wolff 10-cylinder diesel engines via twin screw.

Owned by Princesa Amorosa Co Ltd and cruising for Louis Cruise Lines.
Built by Harland & Wolff Ltd, Belfast, for Coast Lines Ltd as the SCOTTISH COAST (1957). Renamed GALAXIAS (1969 – Hellenic Lines SA).

PRINCESA CYPRIA (1990)

9984 grt; 917 psrs
413' x 64' x 17' (125 x 19.3 x 5.2 m)
2 x 12-cylinder B+W diesel engines via twin screw.
Owned by Princesa Cypria Co Ltd and operated as a cruise ship by Louis
Cruise Lines.
Built by Cantieri Navale de Tirrenio e Riuniti SpA, Riva Tregoso, for DFDS
as the passenger RoRo ferry PRINSESSE MARGRETHE (1968). Renamed
LU JIANG (1984 – Fujian Provence Shipping Co, Xiamen Kina) and ASIA
ANGEL (1988 – Interorient Navigation Co Ltd).

PRINCESA ISABEL (1962) See ODYSSEUS (1988)

PRINCESA LEOPOLDINA (1962) See CORAL PRINCESS
(1993)

PRINCESA MARISSA (1986)
10487 grt; 853 psrs
9 cars
444' x 66' x 18' (134.4 x 19.9 x 5.5 m)
2 x 8-cylinder Sulzer diesel engines via twin screw.

Passenger cruise-ferry owned by Princesa Marissa Co Ltd and operated by
Louis Cruise Lines.
Built by Wartsila, Helsinki, for Finnlines as the FINNHANSA (1966).
Renamed PRINSESSAN (1977 – Birka Line).

PRINCESA OCEANICA (1995) See SAPPHIRE (1996)

PRINCESA OLGA (1935) See SERPA PINTO (1940)

PRINCESA VICTORIA (1993)
14583 grt; 550 psrs
577' x 71' x 28' (169.7 x 21.5 x 8.5 m)
2 x 7-cylinder Fiat diesel engines via twin screw.

Cruise ship for Louis Cruise Lines, Cyprus, but placed on the sale lists in late
1999 while acting as a floating hotel in the Middle East.
Built by Harland & Wolff Ltd, Belfast, for the Union Castle Line as the
DUNNOTTAR CASTLE (1936) and DUNNOTTAR CASTLE, HMS (1939 –
British Royal Navy). Renamed VICTORIA (1958 – Incres Steamship Co) and
THE VICTORIA (1977 – Chandris Group).

PRINCE SOYA (1995)
3217 grt; 650 psrs
316' x 50' x 13' (95.7 x 15 x 4 m)
2 x 8-cylinder Daihatsu diesel engines via twin screw.
Owned and operated by Higashi Nipponkai Ferry Zosen, Setoda.
Built by Naikai, Japan.

PRINCESS (1921) See MADISON (1923)

PRINCESS (1980)
3008 grt; 245 psrs
311' x 41' x 14' (94.2 x 12.4 x 4.2 m)
4 x Fairbank-Morse diesel engines via twin screw.
Cruise ship built by Lake Washington Shipyards for the US Navy as the US
Navy seaplane carrier KYPROS (1944). Renamed MYCONOS (1964 –
Typaldos, Greece), ARTEMIS (1973) and ARTEMIS K (1973).

PRINCESS (1996) See JABAL ALI I (1999)

PRINCESS ABETO (1970) See MALAYSIA BARU (1971)

PRINCESS ADELAIDE (1911) See ANGELIKA (1949)

PRINCESS ALICE (1911) See AEGAEON (1949)

PRINCESS ANNE-MARIE (1960)
4200 grt; 1200 psrs
140 cars
345' x 58' (104.6 x 17.7 m)
Owned and operated by Harms, Germany.
Built by Aalborg Shipyards, Aalborg.

PRINCESS ASTRID (1968) See EXPRESS HERMES (1999)

PRINCESS CHARLOTTE (1908) See MEDITERRANEAN
(1950)

PRINCESS CHRISTINE (1998)
4030 grt; 1777 psrs
40 cars + 30 rail wagons
424' x 58' x 14' (128.5 x 17.7 x 4.3 m)
2 x 6-cylinder B+W diesel engines via twin screw.
Owned and operated by Audrey Ventures Ltd, Wilmington, Delaware.
Built by Cantieri Navale de Terrenio e RiunitiSpA, Riva Tregoso, for the
Italian State Railways as the SAN FRANCESCO DI PAOLA (1964).

PRINCESS DANAE (1997)
9783 grt; 657 psrs
533' x 70' x 25' (162.4 x 21.4 x 7.6 m)
2 x 6-cylinder B+W diesel engines via twin screw.
Cruise ship owned by Arcalia Shipping and chartered until December 2001 to
Nouvelle Frontieres.
Built by Harland & Wolff Ltd, Belfast, for the Port Line as the cargo ship (12
passengers) PORT MELBOURNE (1955). Renamed THERISOS EXPRESS
(1972 – Delian Cruise Lines), DANAE (1974 – Delian Athena Cruises),
ANAR (1992 – Prestige Cruises), STARLIGHT PRINCESS (1992 – Prestige
Cruises) and BALTICA (1994 – Ellice Marine Co Ltds, Sunshine Cruise
Lines).

PRINCESSE ASTRID (1968) See BARI EXPRESS (1985)

PRINCESSE BENEDIKTE (1954)
4100 grt; 1200 psrs
100 cars
length 375' x draft 15' (113.6 x 4.5 m)
Diesel engines via twin screw.
Ferry operated by the Danish State Railways.
Built by Helsingor Shipyards, Helsingor.

PRINCESS ELISABETH (1964)
5200 grt; 1200 psrs
140 cars
length 345' x beam 58' (104.6 x 17.7 m)
Owned and operated by Harms, Germany.
Built by Aalborg Shipyards, Aalborg.

PRINCESS ELIZABETH (1930) See HIGHLAND QUEEN
(1973)

PRINCESSE MARIE CHRISTINE (1975) See PRIMROSE
(1999)

PRINCESS HELENE (1930) See CARINA II (1967)

PRINCESS IRENE (1913)
5934 grt; 1500 psrs
395' x 54' x 28' (119.7 x 16.4 x 8.5 m)
4 x turbine engines via twin screw.
Commandeered by the British Admiralty as a minelayer in 1914, she was totally destroyed on 27 May 1915 when her wartime cargo of mines was detonated by fire within Sheerness harbour. One life was lost.
Built by William Denny & Bros, Dumbarton, for the Canadian Pacific Steamship Co.

PRINCESS ITALIA (1969) See SAPPHIRE (1996)

PRINCESS JOAN (1930) See HERMES (1961)

PRINCESS KATHLEEN (1924)
5875 grt; 1000 psrs
368' x 60' x 18' (111.5 x 18.2 x 5.5 m)
4 x Brown-Curtis turbine engines via twin screw.
Sank in a gale at the highest tide of the season on 7 September 1952 after she had run aground on Lena Point, in the Lynn Canal, 31 miles (52 km) north of Juneau at low tide. She was then completely swamped by the sudden incoming tide, which happened to be the highest tide of the season, and broke her back.
Built by John Brown Ltd, Clydebank, for the Canadian Pacific Railways, Montreal.

PRINCESS LOUISE (1921)
4032 grt; 1261 psrs
327' x 48' x 34' (99.1 x 14.5 x 10.3 m)
4-cylinder triple expansion engine via single screw.
Sank in four fathoms of water at Long Beach, Los Angeles, harbour on the evening of 30 October 1989. She had been moved from her permanent berth where she had operated since 1970 for Princess Louise Corporation as a restaurant, to allow a dinner-cruise boat alongside. As she moved from her berth she capsized, sank and was refloated to be towed to Catalina Island for intended scuttling.
Built by the Wallace Shipbuilding & Drydock Co, North Vancouver, BC, for the Canadian Pacific Steamship Co as a passenger-cargo ship.

PRINCESS M (1985) See JABAL ALI I (1999)

PRINCESS MAHSURI (1982) See BERLIN (1985)

PRINCESS MARGARET (1914)
5934 grt; 1500 psrs
395' x 54' x 28' (119.7 x 16.4 x 8.5 m)
4 x turbine engines via twin screw.
Broken up for scrap by Hughes Bolckow at Blyth in 1929.
Built by William Denny & Bros, Dumbarton, for the Canadian Pacific Steamship Co as a passenger ship. At the outbreak of World War One she was commandeered by the British Admiralty for service as a minelayer, but returned to her Canadian owners at the conclusion of hostilities.

PRINCESS MARGARET (1931) See MACAU (1964)

PRINCESS MARGUERITE (1925)
5875 grt; 1500 psrs
30 cars
368' x 60' x 18' (111.5 x 18.2 x 5.5 m)
4 x Brown-Curtis SRG turbine engines via twin screw.
Sank as a troop transport at 3.07 pm on 17 August 1942, with the loss of 49 lives, after being torpedoed by the German U-83 in the Mediterranean between Port Said and Cyprus.
Built by John Brown Ltd, Clydebank, for the Canadian Pacific Railway Co, Montreal.

PRINCESS MARGUERITE (1949)
5911 grt; 1800 psrs
50 cars
374' x 56' x 16' (113.3 x 17.1 x 4.8 m)
2 x BTH Co Ltd (Rugby) turbine-electric engines via twin screw.
Broken up for scrap at Alang in 1996. Ex-restaurant ship.

Built by Fairfield Shipbuilding & Engineering Co Ltd, Glasgow, for the Canadian Pacific Railway Co, Montreal. The ship was laid up in 1991 and then leased to Vessel Holdings Ltd, Nassau, to be operated by Seaco as an accommodation ship on their construction sites during the period 1991–95. She was then sold to Malaysian hotel interests in 1995.

PRINCESS MARGUERITE III (1994)
4903 grt; 987 psrs
429' x 79' x 13' (130 x 28.9 x 4 m)
2 x 16-cylinder Mirrlees diesel engines via twin screw.
Owned and operated by the Victoria Line.
Built by Victoria Machinery Co, Victoria, BC, for the British Columbia Ferry Corporation as the QUEEN OF BURNABY (1965). Renamed ROYAL VICTORIAN (1994 – Victoria Line Ltd).

PRINCESS MATOIKA, USS (1917) See CITY OF HONOLULU (1927)

PRINCESS MAUD (1934) See VENUS (1965)

PRINCESS OF ACADIA (1951)
6800 grt; 750 psrs
130 cars
358' x 62' x 14'6" (108.5 x 18.8 x 4.4 m)
SRG turbine engines via twin screw.
Passenger-car ferry owned and operated by the Canadian Pacific Railway Co, Montreal.
Built by Fairfield Shipbuilding & Engineering Co Ltd, Glasgow.

PRINCESS OF ACADIA (1963) See HENRY OSBORNE (1972)

PRINCESS OF ACADIA (1971)
10051 grt; 650 psrs
159 cars + 33 trailers
480' x 67' x 15' (146.3 x 20.5 x 4.6 m)
4 x 16-cylinder General Electric geared diesel engines via twin screw.
Passenger-car-cargo ferry owned and operated by Bay Ferries since their 1997 acquisition of Marine Atlantic in Canada.
Launched by St John Shipbuilding & Drydock Co for the Canadian Pacific Steamship Co as PRINCESS OF NOVA (1971) and completed as PRINCESS OF ACADIA (1971).

PRINCESS OF NAINAMO (1951) See HENRY OSBORNE (1972)

PRINCESS OF NAINAMO (1971) See HENRY OSBORNE (1972)

PRINCESS OF NEGROS (1994)
4494 grt; 1050 psrs
392' x 66' x 15' (118.9 x 20.1 x 4.6 m)
4 x 8-cylinder Fuji diesel engines via twin screw.
Passenger ferry owned and operated by Negros Navigation Inc.
Built by Kochi Jyuko, Kochi, for Ehime Hanshin Ferry KK, Matsuyama, as the OKUDOGO 2 (1973). Renamed HAPPY PRINCESS (1987 – Tai Peng Steamship Co Ltd).

PRINCESS OF NEW UNITY (1997)
12572 grt; 1079 psrs
99 cars + 111 trailers
611' x 79' x 21' (185 x 24 x 6.4 m)
4 x 12-cylinder Kawasaki-MAN diesel engines via twin screw.
Passenger-car-cargo ferry owned and operated by Sulpicio Ferries, Manila.
Built by Kurushima Dock Co Ltd, Imbari, for Nippon Kosoku Ferry Co Ltd, Tokyo, as the SUN FLOWER 8 (1973). Renamed SUN FLOWER TOSA (1991 – Blue Highway Line Co Ltd).

PRINCESS OF NOVA (1971) See PRINCESS OF ACADIA (1971)

PRINCESS OF PARADISE (1994)
9466 grt; 1697 psrs
97 cars + 27 trailers
550' x 73' x 20'6" (166.7 x 22 x 6.2 m)
2 x 16-cylinder Mitsubishi-MAN diesel engines via twin screw.

Passenger-car-cargo ferry owned and operated by Sulpicio, Manila.
Built by Mitsubishi Heavy Industries Ltd, Shimonoseki, for Arimura Sangyo KK, Naha, as the HIRYU (1974). Renamed JIAN ZHEN (1985 – China-Japan International Ferry Co Ltd).

PRINCESS OF SCANDINAVIA (1991)

22528 grt; 1704 psrs
440 cars
590' x 78' x 21' (182.4 x 23.7 x 6.3 m)
4 x 12-cylinder Lindholmen-Pielstick PC3- geared diesel engines via twin screw.

Passenger-car ferry owned by DFDS and operated by Scandinavian Seaways.
Built by Flender Werft, Lubeck, for Tor Line AB, Gothenburg, as the TOR SCANDINAVIA (1976). Renamed HOLLAND EXPO (1979 – World Wide Expo, Holland), TOR SCANDINAVIA (1979 – Scandinavian Seaways), WORLD WIDE EXPO (1982 – World Wide Expo, Holland) and TOR SCANDINAVIA (1983 – DFDS).

PRINCESS OF TASMANIA (1959) See TEBAH 2000 (1999)

PRINCESS OF THE CARIBBEAN (1997)

3553 grt; 1041 psrs
365' x 50' x 16' (110.5 x 15.2 x 4.8 m)
2 x 8-cylinder Mitsubishi diesel engines via twin screw.
Passenger ferry owned and operated by Sulpicio Ferries, Manila.
Built by Mitsubishi Heavy Industries Ltd, Shimonoseki, for Ogasawara Kaiun KK, Tokyo, as the OGASAWARA MARU (1979).

PRINCESS OF THE ORIENT (1991)

13575 grt; 3900 psrs
140 cars
640' x 79' x 21' (195 x 24 x 6.5 m)
2 x 18-cylinder Pielstick diesel engines via twin screw.
Passenger-car ferry owned and operated by Sulpicio Ferries, Manila, she capsized and sank within one hour on 19 September 1998 in heavy seas running in the mouth of Manila Bay. One hundred and twenty lives were lost.
Built by Kurushima Dock Co, Imabari, for Nippon Kosoku Ferry Co Ltd, Tokyo, as the SUN FLOWER 11 (1974). Renamed SUN FLOWER SATSUMA (1991 – Blue Highway Line).

PRINCESS OF THE PACIFIC (1993)

5538 grt; 653 psrs
50 cars + 33 trailers
544' x 67' x 23' (137.5 x 20.2 x 7 m)
2 x 12-cylinder NYK-Pielstick diesel engines via twin screw.
Passenger-car-cargo ferry owned and operated by Sulpicio Ferries, Manila.
Built by Yamanishi Ishinomaki for Terukiki Yusen, Japan, as the NEW QUEEN CORAL (1982).

PRINCESS OF THE UNIVERSE (1996)

11919 grt; 711 psrs
133 cars + 136 trailers
571' x 88' x 20'6" (173 x 26.8 x 6.2 m)
2 x 12-cylinder MAN diesel engines via twin screw.
Passenger-car-cargo ferry owned and operated by Sulpicio, Manila.
Built by Kanda Zosensho KK, Kawajiri, for Hankyu Ferry Co Ltd as the NEW YAMOTO (1983).

PRINCESS OF THE WORLD (1996)

9627 grt; 887 psrs
100 cars + 95 trailers

548' x 79' x 22' (166 x 24 x 6.6 m)
2 x 12-cylinder MAN diesel engines via twin screw.
Passenger-car-cargo ferry owned and operated by Sulpicio Lines, Manila.
Built by Naikai Shipbuilding & Engineering Co, Setoda, for Kinkai Yusen Kaisha as the MARIMO (1972).

PRINCESS OF VANCOUVER (1955) See NAN HAI MING ZHU (1993)

PRINCESS OF WALES (1899) See MIDNIGHT SUN (1901)

PRINCESS OKINAWA (1978)

4931 grt; 500 psrs
430' x 66' x 26' (130.3 x 20 x 7.8 m)
2 x 12-cylinder MAN diesel engines via twin screw.
Passenger ferry owned and operated by Ryukyu Kaiun KK, Naha.
Built by Onomichi Zosen, Onomichi.

PRINCESS PATRICIA (1949)

6062 grt; 1800 psrs
50 cars
374' x 58' x 16' (113.3 x 17.7 x 4.8 m)
2 x turbo-electric engines via twin screw.
Broken up for scrap at Kaohsiung in 1989.
Built by Fairfield Shipbuilding & Engineering Co, Glasgow, for the Canadian Pacific Railway Co, Montreal, as a passenger-car ferry.

PRINCETOWN (1916) See ALESIA (1917)

PRINCE VALDEMAR (1902) See INDIEN (1907)

PRINCIPE ALFONSO (1930) See CIUDAD DE PALMA (1930)

PRINCIPE DE ASTURIAS (1914)

8371 grt; 2044 psrs
length 460' x beam 58' (193.4 x 17.6 m)
Quadruple expansion engines via twin screw.
Sank in ten minutes, with the loss of 415 lives, when she struck rocks in a dense fog at 4.15 am on 3 March 1916 off Sebastiao Point, Brazil. She then suffered a massive explosion which tore the bottom out of the ship and broke her in two.
Built by Russell & Co, Glasgow, for Pinillos, Izquierdu y Cia, Cadiz.

PRINCIPE DE VIANA (1920)

5550 grt
410' x 50' x 23'3" (124.2 x 15.2 x 7.1 m)
R Napier 3-cylinder triple expansion engine via single screw.
Built by Napier & Miller, Glasgow, for Royal Mail Lines as the TAGUS (1899).

PRINCIPE DI PIEMONTE (1907) See FOLIA (1916)

PRINCIPE DI UDINE (1908)

7785 grt; 1273 psrs
451' x 55' x 25'1" (137.4 x 16.8 x 7.6 m)
Barclay Curle 8-cylinder quadruple expansion engines via twin screw.
Broken up for scrap in 1930.
Built by Barclay, Curle & Co, Glasgow, for Lloyd Sabaudo.

PRINCIPELLO (1914) See MARIANNA IX (1982)

PRINCIPE PERFEITO (1961) See MARIANNA 9 (1984)

PRINCIPESA JOLANDA (1907)

9200 grt
length 486' (147.3 m)
Broken up for scrap after capsizing during her launching on 21 September 1907.
Launched for Lloyd Sabaudo.

PRINCIPESSA GIOVANNA (1923) See SAN GIORGIO (1947)

PRINCIPESSA MAFALDA (1909)

9210 grt; 1700 psrs
485' x 56' x 32'6" depth (147 x 17 x 9.9 m)

Soc Esercizio Bacini 8-cylinder quadruple expansion engines via twin screw. Sank in four and a half hours on 25 October 1927 near Abrolhos Island, off Brazil. Her propeller shaft had snapped and tore a gaping hole in her port side through which the sea poured into the engine room, causing the boilers to explode – she capsized and went to the bottom, taking 303 lives with her. Built by Societa Esercizio Bacini, Riva Tregoso, for Navigazione Generale Italiana.

PRINCIPESSA MARIA (1923)
8539 grt; 400 psrs
461' x 59' x 29'2" depth (139.7 x 17.9 x 8.8 m)
4 x Soc Anon Franco Tosi DRG turbine engines via twin screw.
Owned and operated by the government of Argentina.
Built by Cantieri Navale Franco Tosi, Taranto, for Lloyd Sabaudo.

PRINS ALBERT (1937)
3200 grt; 1700 psrs
length 372' x draft 12'6" (112.7 x 3.8 m)
Diesel engines via twin screw.
Scrapped in 1969.
Built by John Cockerill Shipyards, Hoboken, for RMT, Belgium, as a passenger ferry.

PRINS ALBERT (1967)
8120 grt; 1800 psrs
300 cars or 156 cars + 26 trailers
441' x 65' x 17' (133.6 x 19.7 x 3.8 m)
Passenger-car-cargo ferry built by Wartsila, Turku, for the Lion Steamship Co.

PRINS ALBERT (1978) See EUROVOYAGER (1998)

PRINS ALEX ANDER (1881) See AURELIA (1901)

PRINS BERTIL (1960) See SHOROK I (1998)

PRINS BERTL (1964) See TIAN KUN (1991)

PRINS DER NEDERLANDEN (1914) See AQUILEJA (1935)

PRINS DER NEDERLANDEN (1957) See VIETNAM HEROICO (1973)

PRINSEN (1977) See SKROTADES (1987)

PRINSENDAM (1936) See NIEUW AMSTERDAM (1938)

PRINSENDAM (1973)
9150 grt; 375 psrs
427' x 75' x 20' (130.1 x 22.7 x 6.1 m)
4 x 8-cylinder Stork-Werkspoor diesel engines via twin screw.
Sank on 11 October 1980 79 miles (131 km) west of Sitka, in the Gulf of Alaska. A fire had erupted in her main engine room at 12.30 am on 4 October and a valiant effort was made to tow her to Portland, Oregon, three days later but was frustrated by the ship taking a 35 degree list, while the fires burning deep in her bowels were buckling plates and letting in water. She suddenly pushed her bow down and went under, while the crew quickly severed the towline. This was her second fire, the first occurring shortly after her completion, on 24 April 1979, totally destroying her superstructure just a few days before she was due to be handed over to her owners, the Holland-America Line.
Built by De Merwede Shipyards, Hardinxveld, for the Holland America Line.

PRINSES AMALIA (1874) See AMALIA (1906)

PRINSES BEATRIX (1939)
4353 grt; 1800 psrs
380' x 42' x 13'6" (115.2 x 14.2 x 4.1 m)
2 x 10-cylinder Sulzer diesel engines via twin screw.
Broken up for scrap by Jos de Smedt at Antwerp, Belgium, in 1969.
Built by De Schelde for Zeeland Line.

PRINSES BEATRIX (1958)
4668 grt; 1500 psrs
120 cars
337' x 60' x 16' (102.2 x 18.1 x 4.8 m)
4 x 9-cylinder MAN diesel engines via twin screw.
Owned by Provinciale Stoombootdiensten, Zeeland.
Built by J & K Smit, Kinderdijk.

PRINSES BEATRIX (1978) See DUC DE NORMANDIE (1986)

PRINSES CHRISTINA (1968) See PRINSES-CHRISTINA (1968)

PRINSES-CHRISTINA (1968)
6831 grt; 1000 psrs
106 cars + 79 trailers
375' x 61' x 15' (113.6 x 18.6 x 4.6 m)
5 x 8-cylinder MAN diesel engines via twin screw.
Passenger-car-cargo ferry owned and operated by Provinciale Stoomboot Diensten (PSD), Flushing.
Built by De Merwede BV, Hardinxveld.

PRINSES IRENE (1960) See KRI TANJUNG OISINA (1978)

PRINSES JULIANA (1910) See COSTA RICA (1910)

PRINSES JULIANA (1986)
8166 grt; 1000 psrs
234 cars or 106 cars + 79 trailers
375' x 63' x 15'6" (113.6 x 19.2 x 4.7 m)
6 x 6-cylinder Stork-Werkspoor diesel engines via twin screw.
Passenger-car-cargo ferry operated by Provinciale Stoomboot Diensten (PSD), Flushing.
Built by De Merwede BV, Hardinxveld.

PRINSES MARGRIET (1961) See ENNA G (1970)

PRINSES MARIE-ESMERALDA (1975) See BENI ANSAR (2000)

PRINSES PAOLA (1966) See TROPIC SEA (2000)

PRINSESSAN (1968) See SKROTADES (1987)

PRINSESSAN (1968) See PRINCESA MARISSA (1986)

PRINSESSAN BIRGITTA (1974) See KING OF SCANDINAVIA (1995)

PRINSESSAN BIRGITTA (1982) See NORMANDY (1997)

PRINSESSAN CHRISTINA (1969) See COMMODORE (1999)

PRINSESSAN DESIREE (1965) See ARTEMIS I (1996)

PRINSESSAN DESIREE (1971) See BOHUS (1994)

PRINSESSE ANNE-MARIE (1960) See JOCHEN STEFFEN (1999)

PRINSESSE BENEDIKTE (1959) See SALEM FLOWER (1998)

PRINSESSE ELISABETH (1964) See HINRICH-WILHELM KOPF (1998)

PRINSESSE MARGRETHE (1957) See SKROTADES (1987)

PRINSESSE MARGRETHE (1968) See PRINCESA CYPRIA (1990)

PRINSESSEN (1968) See SKROTADES (1987)

PRINSESSE RAGNHILD (1966) See JI MEI (1983)

PRINSESSE RAGNHILD (1976)
16332 grt; 896 psrs
600 cars
563' x 79' x 19' (170.5 x 24 x 5.8 m)
2 x 20-cylinder Stork-Werkspoor diesel engines via twin screw.
Passenger-car ferry owned by Jahre Line, Oslo.
Built by HWD, Kiel.

PRINSESSE RAGNHILD (1981)
35438 grt; 1875 psrs
770 cars
668' x 81' x 19' (202.4 x 24.5 x 5.8 m)
2 x 20-cylinder Werkspoor diesel engines via twin screw.

Ice-strengthened passenger-car ferry owned by the Skagerat Line and operated by the Color Line, Norway.
Built by Howaldtswerke AG, Kiel, for the Jahre Line and insured currently for US$66,000,000.

PRINSES SOPHIE (1890) See DJEYHUN (1914)

PRINS FILIP (1992) See P&OSL AQUITAINE (1999)

PRINS HAMLET (1966) See THESSALONIKI (1997)

PRINS HAMLET (1987) See NIEBOROW (1989)

PRINS HENRIF AF DANMARK (1969) See ODESSA I (1999)

PRINS HENRIK (1974) See GIOVENTU (1999)

PRINS JOACHIM (1980)
16071 grt; 2000 psrs
200 cars
499' x 75' x 18'6" (151.2 x 22.7 x 5.6 m)
6 x 16-cylinder B+W diesel engines via twin screw.

Ice-strengthened passenger-car ferry owned by the Danish government and operated by Scandlines.
Built by AS Nakskov Skibsvaerft, Nakskov.

PRINS JOHAN FRISO (1997)
7865 grt; 1000 psrs
200 cars
375' x 63' x 16' (113.6 x 19.2 x 4.8 m)
4 x 9-cylinder Stork-Wartsila diesel engines via twin screw.
Built by Koninklijke Scheldegroep BV, Vlissingen, for Provinciale Zeeland, Vlissingen.

PRINS OBERON (1970) See AMBASSADOR (1993)

PRINS PHILIPPE (1973) See EXPRES ATHINA (1998)

PRINS VAN ORANJE (1871) See MARIA (1900)

PRINS WILLEM ALEXANDER (1970)
3472 grt; 1000 psrs
374' x 61' x 20' (113.6 x 18.6 x 6.1 m)
Passenger ferry operated by Provinciale Stoomboot Diensten (PSD), Flushing.
Built by De Merwede, Hardinxveld.

PRINS WILLEM VAN ORANJE (1953) See AUGUST 8th (1976)

PRINZ ADALBERT (1904) See ALESIA (1917)

PRINZ EITEL FRIEDRICH (1904) See MOUNT CLAY (1920)

PRINZESS ALICE (1903) See CITY OF HONOLULU (1927)

PRINZESSIN VICTORIA LUISE (1900)
4419 grt; 192 psrs
408' x 47' x 27' (124.2 x 14.4 x 8.2 m)
8-cylinder quadruple expansion engines via twin screw.
Owned by the Hamburg-America Line, she broke up after striking rocks on 16 December 1906 under the lighthouse off Port Royal, Jamaica. The captain had plotted the incorrect course during the absence of a pilot and subsequently shot himself in his cabin shortly after the ship grounded.
Built by Blohm & Voss, Hamburg.

PRINZESS IRENE (1900) See KARLSRUHE (1928)

PRINZ FRIEDRICH WILHELM (1908) See MONTNAIRN (1925)

PRINZ HAMLET (1970) See THESSALONIKI (1997)

PRINZ HAMLET (1973) See NIEBOROW (1989)

PRINZ HAMLET II (1973) See GOLFINHO AZUL (1999)

PRINZ HEINRICH (1894) See PORTO (1915)

PRINZ HENRIK AF DANMARK (1969) See ODESSA (1975)

PRINZ JOACHIM (1903) See PORTO RICO (1920)

PRINZ LUDWIG (1903) See ORCADES (1921)

PRINZ OBERON (1978) See AMBASSADOR (1993)

PRINZ OSKAR (1902) See ORION (1917)

PRINZ REGENT LUITPOLD (1894) See PIETRO CALVI (1915)

PRINZ SIGISMUND (1902) See MIKHAIL LOMONOSOV (1945)

PRINZ SIGISMUND (1903) See BAMBRA (1916)

PRIVATE ELDEN H. JOHNSON (1946)
7486 grt; 95 psrs
430' x 62' x 37'5" depth (130.3 x 18.8 x 11.4 m)
3 x General Electric DRG turbine engines via single screw.
Broken up for scrap at Kaohsiung in 1971.
Built by Moore Drydock Co, Oakland, California, for Alcoa Steamship Corporation Inc as the passenger-cargo ship ALCOA CORSAIR (1941).
Renamed PINKNEY, USS (APH-2) (1942 – US Navy).

PRIVATE WILLIAM H. THOMAS (T-AP-184) (1943) See PRIVATE WILLIAM H. THOMAS (T-AP-185) (1946)

PRIVATE WILLIAM H. THOMAS (T-AP-185) (1946)
7486 grt; 95 psrs
430' x 62' x 37'5" depth (130.3 x 18.8 x 11.4 m)
5 x General Electric DRG turbine engines via single screw.

Broken up for scrap by Tung Ho Enterprise Corporation, Taiwan, at Kaohsiung in 1971. Ex-MARAD.

Built by Moore Drydock Co, Oakland, California, for the Alcoa Steamship Corporation Inc as the passenger-cargo ship ALCOA CRUISER (1941). Renamed RIXEY, USS (AP-3) (1942 – US Navy). Reclassified as the PRIVATE WILLIAM H. THOMAS (T-AP-184) (1943).

PROCTER (1901)
4189 grt; 168 psrs
400' x 43' x 33' (121.2 x 13 x 10 m)
4-cylinder compound inverted H+W engine via single screw.
Broken up for scrap at Mumbai in 1901 for tender of £10,706.
Built by Harland & Wolff Ltd, Belfast, for P&O Lines as the SHANNON (1881) at a cost of £129,435.

PROCYON (1980) See RASLAN (1983)

PROFESSOR GRUVEL (1922)
3192 grt
Blair & Co 3-cylinder triple expansion engine via single screw.
Built by C Mitchell & Co, Newcastle, for Nelson Donkin & Co as the BOMBAY (1882).

PROFESSOR GUL (1995)
11450 grt; 202 psrs
509' x 60' x 27' (154.3 x 18.3 x 8.3 m)
2 x 6-cylinder B+W diesel engines via twin screw.
Passenger ferry operated by the Caspian Shipping Co, Baki.
Built by Uljanik, Pula, as the SOVIETSKAYA BYELORUSSIJA (1986) and BELORUS (1994 – Caspian Shipping Co).

PROFESSOR WOERMANN (1904) See ARAFURA MARU (1930)

PROME (1894) See LOCKSLEY HALL (1901)

PROME (1937)
7043 grt; 76 psrs
462' x 59' x 27' (140 x 17.9 x 8.2 m)
3 x turbine engines via single screw.
Broken up for scrap at Bruges in 1962.
Built by William Denny & Bros, Dumbarton, for the Henderson Line.

PROOT (1914) See PRUT (1914)

PROTEA (1920) See AROSA KULM (1952)

PROTEA (1976)
11434 grt; 446 psrs
523' x 68' x 25' (159.3 x 20.8 x 7.6 m)
2 x 10-cylinder Adriatico-Sulzer diesel engines via twin screw.
Broken up for scrap at Kaohsiung in 1980. Ex-Lloyd Triestino.
Built by Cantieri Riuniti dell'Adriatico, Monfalcone, for Lloyd Triestino as the AFRICA (1952).

PROVENCE (1951) See AEGEAN SPIRIT (2000)

PROVENCE (1966) See NAIAS II (1983)

PROVENCE (1974) See POSEIDON EXPRESS (1989)

PROVENCE (1999) See P&OSL PROVENCE (1999)

PROVENCE II (1914)
13753 grt; 1382 psrs
627' x 65' x 38'3" depth (191 x 19.8 x 11.6 m)
2 x Chantiers et Ateliers de la Loire 4-cylinder triple expansion engines via twin screw.
Owned by the French Navy as an armed merchant cruiser when she sank on 26 February 1916, with the loss of 830 lives, after being torpedoed by the German U-35 south of Cape Matapan, in the Aegean Sea.
Built by Pennhoet, St Nazaire, for the French Line as the passenger liner LA PROVENCE (1906).

PROVIDENCE (1920)
11996 grt; 798 psrs
512' x 60' x 43'5" depth (155.2 x 18.2 x 13.2 m)
Forges et Chantiers de la Mediterranee 6-cylinder triple expansion engines via twin screw.
Broken up for scrap at La Spezia in 1952.
Laid down in 1914 by Forges et Chantiers de la Mediterranee, La Seyne, for the Fabre Line but not completed until 1920.

PRUT (1914)
3500 grt; 380 psrs
360' x 43' x 31' depth (109.1 x 13 x 9.4 m)
Compound single engine via single screw.
As a minesweeper, she was scuttled by her crew in October 1914 when the German battle cruiser GOEBEN was bearing down upon her to claim a capture, off Sebastopol.
Built by Elder Shipyard for the Castle Line as KINFAUNS CASTLE (1880). Renamed MOSKWA (1883 – Russian Volunteer Fleet Association).

PRYGONA (1921)
7550 grt; 680 psrs
446' x 52' x 31' (135.9 x 15.9 x 9.4 m)
6-cylinder triple expansion engine via twin screw.
Broken up for scrap by Petersen & Albeck at Copenhagen in 1925. Ex-Fabre Line.
Built by Barclay, Curle & Co, Glasgow, for Elder Dempster's Beaver Line as the LAKE ERIE (1899). Renamed TYROLIA (1913 – Canadian Pacific Steamship Co). In 1914 she was made up as a dummy replica of the expedition cruise ship HMS CENTURION for Navimag. Renamed the naval oiler SAXOL (1916 – British Royal Navy) and ASPENLEAF (1916 – Lane & McAndrew).

PUEBLA (1941) See JUAN DE GARAY (1947)

PUERTO MONTT (1966) See KOBENHAVN (1966)

PUERTO RICO (1938) See ADANA (1948)

PUERTO RICO (1949) See LA JENELLE (1969)

PUERTO VALLARTA (1974)
7005 grt; 96 psrs
359' x 58' x 15' (108.9 x 17.6 x 4.6 m)
2 x 12-cylinder Deutz diesel engines via twin screw.
Passenger ferry owned by the government of Mexico and operated by Transbordadores.
Built by Jos L Meyer, Papenburg.

PULASKI (1930) See EMPIRE PENRYN (1946)

PUNTA EUROPA (1980)
3717 grt; 1237 psrs
120 cars + 18 trailers
328' x 56' x 19' (99.5 x 17 x 5.8 m)
2 x 12-cylinder Deutz diesel engines via twin screw.
Passenger-car-cargo ferry owned and operated by Euroferrys, but for sale at US$2,500,000.
Built by Barreras, Vigo, for Islena di Navigacion SA, Algeciras.

PUTRI BINTANG (1997) See AMUSEMENT WORLD (1998)

PYOTR PERVYY (1989) See PETR PERVYY (1990)

PYTHEAS (1922) See KOUANG (1929)

PYTHIA (1909) See READY (1931)

QE 2 (1967) See QUEEN ELIZABETH 2 (1967)

QORMI (1976) See CALEDONIA (1997)

QUANZA (1929)
6403 grt; 532 psrs
438' x 53' x 25' (132.7 x 16.1 x 7.6 m)
2 x 3-cylinder Blohm+Voss triple expansion engines via twin screw.
Broken up for scrap in 1968.
Built by Blohm & Voss, Hamburg, for Cia Nacional de Navegacao, Lisbon, as the passenger-cargo vessel PORTUGAL (1929).

QUEBEC (1903)
3342 grt; 800 psrs
346' x 44' x 24'6" (105.4 x 13.4 x 7.5 m)
R Napier 3-cylinder triple expansion engine via single screw.
Owned by the French Line, she sank on 24 January 1917 at the mouth of the River Gironde after hitting a mine laid by the German U-21.
Laid down by Napier & Sons, Glasgow, for the Royal Mail Line as the EBRO (1896) and completed as the QUEBEC.

QUEBEC (1928) See PASSENGER No. 1 (1966)

QUEEN ANNA MARIA (1964) See THE TOPAZ (1998)

QUEEN CONSTANTINA (2000) See JOYWAVE (2000)

QUEEN CORAL (1972) See HANAA (1992)

QUEEN CORAL 2 (1975) See QUEEN FLOWER 2 (1983)

QUEEN CORAL (1993)
4924 grt; 500 psrs
66 cars
462' x 68' x 20' (140 x 20.5 x 6.2 m)
2 x 9-cylinder Pielstick diesel engines via twin screw.
Operated by the Marix Line, Japan.
Built by Hayashikane Shosen KK, Shimonoseki.

QUEEN DIAMOND (1986)
9022 grt; 965 psrs
50 cars + 105 trailers
498' x 83' x 17' (150.9 x 25 x 5.5 m)
2 x 8-cylinder Mitsubishi-MAN diesel engines via twin screw.
Ferry operated by Diamond Ferry, Japan.
Built by Kurushima Dock Co, Onishi.

QUEEN ELENI (1995) See JOYWAVE (2000)

QUEEN ELIZABETH (1940) See SEAWISE UNIVERSITY (1970)

QUEEN ELIZABETH 2 (1967)

70327 grt; 1850 psrs
963' x 105' x 32' (293.5 x 32 x 9.7 m)
9 x MAN-B+W 9-cylinder diesel-electric engines via twin screw.
Cruise ship operated by Cunard Lines.
Built by John Brown & Co Ltd, Clydebank, at a cost of US$84,000,000.

QUEEN EMMA (1940) See KONINGIN EMMA (1948)

QUEEN FLOWER 2 (1983)
6814 grt; 1080 psrs
424' x 57' x 17' (128.6 x 17.4 x 5.2 m)
2 x 18-cylinder Pielstick diesel engines via twin screw.
Passenger ferry operated by Kurushima Dockyard, Imabari.
Built by Hayashokane Zosen, Nagasaki, for Terukuni Yusen KK, Kagoshima, as the QUEEN CORAL (1975).

QUEEN FREDERICA (1954)
21239 grt; 1178 psrs
582' x 83' x 29' (177.3 x 25.3 x 8.8 m)
8 x SRG turbine engines via twin screw.
Broken up for scrap at Piraeus at the end of 1978 after she had been gutted by fire on 1 February 1978, following her sale to the breakers yard.
Built by William Cramp & Sons Ship & Engine Building Company, Philadelphia, Pennsylvania, for the Matson Line as the MALOLO (1927) at a cost of US$6,000,000. Renamed MATSONIA (1938 – Matson Line), ATLANTIC (1949 – Home Lines) and VASSILISSA FREIDERIKI (1954 – National Hellenic American Line). Only her stern bore this name while the bow carried the name QUEEN FREDERICA, although the ship's formal registration documents were in the name of the VASSILISSA FREIDERIKI.

QUEEN M (1986) See CARLO R (1990)

QUEEN MARY (1936)
81237 grt; 2139 psrs
1018' x 118' x 39' (300.5 x 35.8 x 11.8 m)
4 x John Brown Ltd SRG turbines via quadruple screw.
At a permanent berth as a museum and hotel at Long Beach, Los Angeles, California, following a US$70,000,000 refurbishment by the City of Los Angeles in 1967. She was purchased from Cunard Lines, UK, for US$3,450,000.
Built by John Brown & Co, Clydebank for Cunard-White Star Lines.

QUEEN ODYSSEY (1994) See SEABOURN LEGEND (1996)

QUEEN OF ALBERNI (1976)
5863 grt; 1415 psrs
295 cars or 150 cars + 28 trailers
457' x 89' x 18' (139.3 x 27.1 x 5.5 m)
2 x 12-cylinder MaK diesel engines via twin screw.

Passenger-car-cargo ferry owned by Central Trust, Canada, and operated by BC Ferries Corporation, Victoria, BC.
Built by Vancouver Shipyards, North Vancouver, BC.

QUEEN OF BERMUDA (1933)
22552 grt; 733 psrs
590' x 76' x 27' (178.8 x 23.3 x 8.2 m)
Turbo-electric engines via quadruple screw.
Broken up for scrap at Faslane, Scotland, in 1967 for a tender figure of US$450,000 from Shipbreaking Industries Ltd.
Built by the Vickers-Armstrong Co, Barrow-in-Furness, for the Furness-Bermuda Line.

QUEEN OF BERMUDA (1988) See UNIVERSE EXPLORER (1996)

QUEEN OF BURNABY (1965) See PRINCESS MARGUERITE III (1994)

QUEEN OF COQUITLAM (1976)
6551 grt; 1466 psrs
264 cars + 14 trailers
460' x 89' x 17'6" (139.4 x 23.9 x 5.3 m)
2 x 12-cylinder MaK diesel engines via twin screw.

Passenger-car-cargo ferry owned by Royal Trust, Canada, and operated by BC Ferries Corporation, Victoria, BC.
Built by Burrard Drydock Co Ltd, North Vancouver, BC.

QUEEN OF COWICHAN (1976)
6551 grt; 1966 psrs
362 cars or 264 cars + 14 trailers
429' x 89' x 17'6" (130 x 23.9 x 5.3 m)
4 x 10-cylinder Fairbanks-Morse geared diesel engines via twin screw.
Passenger-car-cargo ferry owned by Canadian Trustco and operated by BC Ferries Corporation, Victoria, BC.
Built by Victoria Machinery Depot Co, Victoria, BC.

QUEEN OF ESQUIMALT (1965)
9309 grt; 1394 psrs
376 cars or 240 cars + 12 trailers
429' x 89' x 17'6" (130 x 23.9 x 5.3 m)
4 x 10-cylinder Fairbanks-Morse geared diesel engines via twin screw.
Passenger-car-cargo ferry operated by BC Ferries Corporation, Victoria, BC.
Built by Victoria Machinery Depot Co, Victoria, BC.

QUEEN OF JIN JIANG (1993) See HENG LI (1993)

QUEEN OF NANAIMO (1965)
4939 grt; 1187 psrs
192 cars
429' x 89' x 17'6" (130 x 23.9 x 5.3 m)
2 x 16-cylinder Mirrlees diesel engines via twin screw.
Passenger-car ferry operated by BC Ferries Corporation, Victoria, BC.
Built by Victoria Machinery Depot Co, Victoria, BC.

QUEEN OF NASSAU (1954) See ELIZABETH A (1967)

QUEEN OF NEW WESTMINSTER (1964)
8785 grt; 1390 psrs
286 cars or 144 cars + 30 trailers
429' x 89' x 17'6" (130 x 23.9 x 5.3 m)
2 x 16-cylinder Mirrlees diesel engines via twin screw.
Passenger-car-cargo ferry operated by BC Ferries Corporation, Victoria, BC.
Built by Victoria Machinery Depot Co, Victoria, BC.

QUEEN OF OAK BAY (1981)
6969 grt; 1465 psrs
362 cars or 264 cars + 14 trailers
457' x 91' x 18' (139 x 27.6 x 5.5 m)
2 x 12-cylinder Krupp-MaK diesel engines via twin screw.
Passenger-car-cargo ferry owned by Xerox Finance Inc, Canada, and operated by BC Ferries Corporation, Victoria, BC.
Built by Burrard Yarrows Shipyard, Victoria, BC.

QUEEN OF PRINCE RUPERT (1966) See QUEEN OF PRINCE RUPERT (1980)

QUEEN OF PRINCE RUPERT (1980)
5864 grt; 458 psrs
80 cars or 40 cars + 8 trailers
334' x 62' x 15' (101.1 x 18.7 x 4.6 m)
4 x 8-cylinder Mirrlees diesel engines via twin screw.

Passenger-car-cargo ferry operated by BC Ferries Corporation, Victoria, BC. Built by Victoria Machinery Depot Co, Victoria, BC for BC Ferry Systems as the QUEEN OF PRINCE RUPERT (1966). Renamed VICTORIA PRINCESS (1980 – Victoria Line Ltd).

QUEEN OF SAANICH (1963)
9302 grt; 1394 psrs
338 cars or 226 cars + 12 trailers
429' x 89' x 17'6" (130 x 23.9 x 5.3 m)
4 x 10-cylinder Fairbanks-Morse geared diesel engines via twin screw.
Passenger-car-cargo ferry operated by BC Ferries Corporation, Victoria, BC.
Built by Victoria Machinery Depot, Victoria, BC.

QUEEN OF SCANDINAVIA (1990)
33745 grt; 1867 psrs
480 cars
548' x 94' x 22' (166.1 x 28.4 x 6.8 m)
4 x 12-cylinder Pielstick diesel engines via twin screw.

Passenger-car ferry owned by DFDS and operated by Scandinavian Seaways. Laid down by the Wartsila, Turku, shipyards as the SKANDIA (1979), christened SILVIA REGINA (1980) for the Silja Line, but completed as the FINLANDIA (1981) for the Finland Steamship Company.

QUEEN OF SIDNEY (1963)
3128 grt; 989 psrs
138 cars or 82 cars + 8 trailers
338' x 75' x 12'6" (102.4 x 22.6 x 3.8 m)
2 x 16-cylinder Mirrlees diesel engines via twin screw.
Passenger-car-cargo ferry operated by BC Ferries Corporation, Victoria, BC.
Built by Victoria Machinery Depot Co, Victoria, BC for the BC Toll Authority as the SIDNEY (1960).

QUEEN OF SURREY (1974) See QUEEN OF THE NORTH (1980)

QUEEN OF SURREY (1981)
6969 grt; 1465 psrs
362 cars or 264 cars + 14 trailers
457' x 91' x 18' (139 x 27.6 x 5.5 m)
2 x 12-cylinder Krupp-MaK diesel engines via twin screw.

Passenger-car-cargo ferry owned by Xerox Finance Inc, Canada, and operated by BC Ferries Corporation, Victoria, BC.
Built by Burrard Yarrows Shipyard, North Vancouver, BC.

QUEEN OF THE NORTH (1980)
8889 grt; 750 psrs
250 cars
413' x 65' x 16' (125 x 19.7 x 4.9 m)
2 x 16-cylinder MAN diesel engines via twin screw.

Passenger-car ferry operated by BC Ferries Corporation, Victoria, BC.
Built by AG Weser, Bremerhaven, for the Stena Line as the STENA DANICA (1969). Renamed QUEEN OF SURREY (1974 – British Columbia Ferries).

QUEEN OF TSAWWASSEN (1962)
3127 grt; 989 psrs
138 cars
338' x 75' x 12'6" (102.4 x 22.6 x 3.8 m)
2 x 16-cylinder Mirrlees diesel engines via twin screw.

Ferry operated by BC Ferries Corporation, Victoria, BC.
Built by Burrard Drydock Co Ltd, North Vancouver, BC, for the BC Toll Authority as the TSAWWASSEN (1960).

QUEEN OF VANCOUVER (1963)
9257 grt; 1360 psrs
286 cars or 225 cars + 12 trailers
428' x 75' x 12'6" (130 x 24 x 3.8 m)
2 x 9-cylinder MaK diesel engines via twin screw.
Passenger-car-cargo ferry operated by BC Ferries Corporation, Victoria, BC.
Built by Burrard Drydock Co Ltd, North Vancouver, BC, for British Columbia Ferries as the CITY OF VANCOUVER (1962).

QUEEN OF VICTORIA (1963)
9357 grt; 1360 psrs

286 cars or 225 cars + 12 trailers
428' x 75' x 12'6" (130 x 24 x 3.8 m)
2 x 9-cylinder MaK diesel engines via twin screw.

Passenger-car-cargo ferry operated by BC Ferries Corporation, Victoria, BC, but sold on 20 December 2000 to a Dominican Republic ferry operator for US$326,000. She will be renamed QUEEN OF OCOA in 2001.
Built by Victoria Machinery Depot Co Ltd, Victoria, BC, for British Columbia Ferries as the CITY OF VICTORIA (1962).

QUEENS, USS (APA-103) (1944) See TEXAS CLIPPER (1998)

QUEEN VERGINA (1989) See ALAMIRA (1997)

QUEEN VERGINA (1990)
11286 grt; 525 psrs
150 cars + 19 trailers
396' x 71' x 21' (120 x 21.5 x 6.3 m)
5 x 16-cylinder Pielstick diesel engines via twin screw.
Ice-strengthened passenger-car-cargo ferry owned by Paradise Island Maritime Co Ltd, Piraeus, and operated by Vergina Ferries Hellas Ltd, Piraeus.
Built by Marine Industries Ltd, Sorel, for CN Marine, Halifax, as the AMBROSE SHEA (1967). Renamed AMBROSE (1990 – CN Marine).

QUIBERON (1982)
8314 grt; 1140 psrs
250 cars + 30 trailers
426' x 69' x 16' (128 x 21 x 4.9 m)
4 x 6-cylinder Stork-Werkspoor diesel engines via twin screw.

Passenger-car-cargo ferry owned and operated by Brittany Ferries.
Built by Werft Nobiskrug, Rendsburg, for Svenska Lastbil AB as the NILS DACKE (1975).

QUINNEBAUG, USS (1918) See JEFFERSON (1920)

QUIRIGUA (1932) See SAMALA (1958)

QUIRIGUA (1946) See SAMALA (1958)

RADISSON DIAMOND (1992)
20295 grt; 354 psrs
423' x 105' x 26'6" (128.2 x 31.8 x 8.1 m)
4 x 8-cylinder Wartsila diesel engines via twin screw.

Cruise ship for Radisson Seven Seas Cruises, Finland.
Built by Rauma-Repola Yard, Finland, for Diamond Cruise Ltd at a cost of
£125,000,000.

RADNIK (1947)
6509 grt; 51 psrs
437' x 53' x 25'6" (133.3 x 16.1 x 7.8 m)
Newport News 3-cylinder triple expansion engine via single screw.
Broken up for scrap by Brodospas at Split in 1952. Ex-the Yugoslav Line.
Built by Newport News Shipbuilding & Drydock Co, Newport News,
Virginia, for the Matson Line as the passenger-cargo ship LURLINE (1908).
Renamed CHIRIKOF (1928 – Alaska Packers' Association).

RAED B (1980) See SATURNUS (1991)

RAETORIA (1920)
6438 grt; 1000 psrs
486' x 53' x 34' depth (147.3 x 16.1 x 10.3 m)
Hawthorne Leslie 6-cylinder triple expansion engines via twin screw.
Broken up for scrap in 1924. Ex-London Steamship & Trading Corporation
Ltd.
Built by R & W Hawthorn, Leslie & Co, Hebburn-on-Tyne, for the Russian
Volunteer Fleet as the KHERSON (1896). Renamed LENA (1903 – Russian
Navy) and KHERSON 1906 – Russian Volunteer Fleet).

RAFAELLO (1990) See ATHINA I (1999)

RAFFAELLO (1965)
45933 grt; 1775 psrs
904' x 99' x 34' (275.5 x 30.2 x 10.3 m)
4 x Ansaldo DRG steam turbine engines via twin screw.
Broken up for scrap at Gadani Beach, Karachi, in 1991 after she had suffered
severe war damage in February 1983 from Iraqi missiles during the Iran–Iraq
conflict. She had served since 1976 at Bandar-E-Bushehur as a dormitory ship
for the Iranian Navy, for which the Iranian government paid the ship's owners
US$9,000,000.
Built by Cantieri Riuniti dell'Adriatico, Trieste, for the Italian Line.

RAGA QUEEN (1986) See HOLGER (1999)

RAGLAN CASTLE (1897) See READY (1931)

RAGLAN CASTLE (1908) See READY (1931)

RAINBOW (1992) See THE EMERALD (1996)

RAINBOW BELL (1996)
13597 grt; 350 psrs
77 cars + 154 trailers
647' x 89' x 22' 11" (196 x 27 x 6.7 m)
2 x 14-cylinder Nippon-Pielstick diesel engines via twin screw.
Passenger-car-cargo ferry owned and operated by Kyuetse Ferry, Higashi-ku.
Built by Mitsubishi Heavy Industries, Shimonoseki.

RAINBOW LOVE (1997)
13621 grt; 350 psrs
77 cars + 154 trailers
647' x 89' x 22' 11" (196 x 27 x 6.7 m)
2 x 14-cylinder Nippon-Pielstick diesel engines via twin screw.
Passenger-car-cargo ferry owned and operated by Kyuetse Ferry, Higashi-ku.
Built by Mitsubishi Heavy Industries, Shimonoseki.

RAJPUTANA (1926)
16644 grt; 600 psrs
568' x 71' x 43' (172.1 x 21.5 x 13 m)
2 x quadruple expansion engines via twin screw.
Sank on 13 April 1941, with the loss of 41 lives, after being torpedoed at dawn
by the German U-108, south of Iceland.
Built by Harland & Wolff Ltd, Greenock, for the P&O Line.

RAJULA (1926) See RANGAT (1973)

RAKAIA (1946)
8213 grt; 50 psrs
457' x 63' x 37'8" depth (138.5 x 19.1 x 11.5 m)
Harland & Wolff 8-cylinder diesel engines via single screw.
Broken up for scrap by the Lee Sing Co, Hong Kong. Ex-New Zealand
Shipping Co Ltd.
Built by Harland & Wolff Ltd, Belfast, for the British Ministry of War
Shipping as the EMPIRE ABERCORN (1945).

RAKUYO MARU (1921)
9419 grt
460' x 60' x 30'7" (139.4 x 18.2 x 9.3 m)
4 x Mitsubishi DRG turbine engines via twin screw.
Sank on 12 September 1944 after being torpedoed by the USS SEALION II
in the Tonkin Gulf. Of 1,318 Allied prisoners of war on board, only 295 were
saved.
Built by Mitsubishi Dockyard for Toyo Kisen Kaisho.

RAMADA AL-SALAM (1990)
15371 grt; 300 psrs
584' x 84' x 27' (177.9 x 25.6 x 8.2 m)
General Electric DRG turbine engines via twin screw.
Hotel ship in Kuwait and registered as the RAMADA AL-SALAM
HOTEL SHIP. She was badly damaged during the Iraqi invasion in 1991
and then cannibalised for parts to repair her sister ship SANTA ROSA
which is now the EMERALD (1997). She has now been completely broken
up for scrap.
Built by Newport News Shipbuilding & Dockyard Co, Newport News,
Virginia, for the Grace Line as the SANTA PAULA (1958). Renamed
STELLA POLARIS (1972 – Oceanic Sun Line Special Shipping Co Inc,
Piraeus, a Marriott Hotel subsidiary) and KUWAIT MARRIOTT HOTEL
(1976 – Marriott Hotel Group).

RANCHI (1925)
16974 grt; 590 psrs
570' x 71' x 28' (173.7 x 21.6 x 8.5 m)
2 x quadruple expansion engines via twin screw.
Broken up for scrap by British Iron & Steel Corporation at Newport, Wales,
in 1953 for a tender figure of US$400,000.
Built by Hawthorne, Leslie & Co Ltd, Newcastle, for the P&O Line.

RANDFONTEIN (1958) See HERBERT (1996)

RANEEM I (1994) See SHOROK I (1998)

RANG (1962)
16969 grt; 411 psrs
552' x 70' x 34' (168.2 x 21.3 x 10.4 m)
2 x 5-cylinder Sulzer diesel engines via twin screw.
Broken up for scrap at Split in 1962 by Brodospas.

Built by John Brown & Co Ltd, Clydebank, for the New Zealand Shipping Co Ltd as the RANGITATA (1929).

RANGAT (1973)
8496 grt; 1770 psrs
477' x 62' x 26' (144.5 x 18.8 x 7.9 m)
2 x triple expansion engines via twin screw.
Broken up for scrap by Mahara Shotra Rolling Industries Co Ltd at Mumbai, India, in 1975. Ex-Shipping Corporation of India.
Built by Barclay, Curle & Company, Glasgow, for British India Line as the RAJULA (1926).

RANGATIRA (1910)
10118 grt; 1000 psrs
478' x 61' x 31'3" depth (144.8 x 18.5 x 9.5 m)
Workman, Clark 6-cylinder triple expansion engines via twin screw.
Abandoned as a total loss after running aground on 31 March 1916 on Robben Island in Table Bay, following heavy usage of her as a migrant ship.
Built by Workman, Clark & Co Ltd, Belfast, for Shaw Savill & Albion.

RANGATIRA (1931)
6152 grt; 794 psrs
956' x 58' x 17' (127.7 x 17.6 x 5.2 m)
2 x British Thompson Houston turbo-electric engines via twin screw.

Broken up for scrap by Fortune & Co at Hong Kong in 1968. She had actually been purchased from the Union Steamship Co of New Zealand by Manners Navigation Co, Hong Kong, to break up for scrap, but she was sold on the same day, 4 September 1967, to the Fortune Co.
Built by Vickers-Armstrong Ltd, Barrow-in-Furness, for the Union Steamship Co of New Zealand.

RANGATIRA (1972) See CARLO R (1990)

RANGITANE (1929)
16712 grt; 411 psrs
552' x 70' x 34' (168.2 x 21.3 x 10.4 m)
Sulzer 10-cylinder diesel engines via twin screw.
Scuttled on 27 November 1940 after her capture by the German raiders ORION and KOMET 300 miles (500 km) east of East Cape, New Zealand, during the course of which 16 lives were lost.
Built by Swan Hunter Shipbuilders Ltd, Newcastle, for the New Zealand Shipping Co Ltd.

RANGITANE (1949) See ORIENTAL ESMERALDA (1969)

RANGITATA (1929) See RANG (1962)

RANGITIKI (1929)
16985 grt; 404 psrs
552' x 70' x 34' (168.2 x 21.3 x 10.4 m)
2 x 6-cylinder Doxford (replacing the original 2 x 5-cylinder Sulzers) diesel engines via twin screw.
Broken up for scrap at Santander in 1962.
Built by John Brown & Co Ltd, Clydebank, for the New Zealand Shipping Co Ltd.

RANGITOTO (1949) See ORIENTAL CARNAVAL (1969)

RANGOL (1914) See BRITISH MAPLE (1920)

RANPURA (1925) See RANPURA, HMS (1944)

RANPURA, HMS (1944)
16585 grt; 590 psrs
570' x 71' x 43' (172.7 x 21.5 x 13 m)
2 x quadruple expansion engines via twin screw.
Broken up for scrap at La Spezia in 1961. Ex-British Admiralty.
Built by Hawthorne, Leslie & Co Ltd, Newcastle, for the P&O Line as the RANPURA (1925) at a cost of £200,000.

RAPIDO (1898) See TEREK (1904)

RASA SAYANG (1973) See RASA SAYANG (1980)

RASA SAYANG (1980)
18739 grt; 877 psrs
578' x 72' x 27' (176.2 x 22 x 8.2 m)
2 x 8-cylinder Stork-Werkspoor diesel engines via twin screw.
Broken up on the spot where she sank, on 27 August 1980, in shallow water at Kynosoura, Greece. She had been towed here after her engine room caught fire in her refitting dock at Piraeus. Three years earlier, on 2 June 1977, two lives were lost when she caught fire in the Malacca Straits.
Built by Swan Hunter & Wigham Richardson Ltd, Newcastle, for the Norwegian America Line as the BERGENSFJORD (1956). Renamed DE GRASSE (1971 – French Line), CORAL RIVIERA (1973 – Coral Riviera Ltd), RASA SAYANG (1973 – Thoresen & Co Ltd) and GOLDEN MOON (1978 – Sunlit Cruises Ltd, Cyprus).

RASHID (1927)
3444 grt; 129 psrs
320' x 44' x 27' (97 x 13.3 x 8.2 m)
Triple expansion engines via twin screw.
Broken up for scrap at Savona in 1934. Ex-Khedivial Mail Steamship Co.
Built by DJ Dunlop & Company, Port Glasgow, for the Union Steamship Co of New Zealand as the ATUA (1906).

RASLAN (1983)
14155 grt; 806 psrs
489' x 71' x 19' (148.1 x 21.5 x 5.8 m)
4 x 12-cylinder Stork-Werkspoor diesel engines via twin screw.
Owned by Qatar Transport & Marine Services Co, she was broken up for scrap as a sheep carrier at Kaohsiung in 1984 after being gutted by fire at sea on 11 July 1988. She had previously caught fire at 7.15 am on 12 September 1974 south-west of Key West, Florida, while cruising for the Cunard Line when a ruptured fuel tank ignited and the ship was totally engulfed in flames. Firefighters reboarded her 24 hours later and she was declared safe to tow to Key West. She was declared a total loss.
Built by P Smit Jr, Rotterdam, for the Cunard Line as the cruise ship CUNARD AMBASSADOR (1972). Renamed as the livestock carrier LINDA CLAUSEN (1975 – C Clausen, Copenhagen) and PROCYON (1980 – Qatar Transport & Marine Services Co).

RATA HILLS (1976) See BALBEK (2000)

RAVELLO (1941)
8806 grt; 480 psrs
473' x 63' x 28' (145.5 x 19.4 x 8.5 m)
8-cylinder Fiat diesel engine via single screw.
Broken up for scrap as a cargo ship at La Spezia in 1971.
Built by Cantieri Navigation Riuniti, Genoa, for Flotta Lauro.

RAWALPINDI (1925)
16697 grt; 595 psrs
568' x 71' x 47' (172.1 x 21.5 x 14.2 m)
2 x quadruple expansion engines via twin screw.
Sank as an armed merchantman on 23 November 1939, with the loss of 266 lives, after the German battleships SCHARNHORST and GNEISNAU opened fire on her simultaneously, 266 miles (443 km) south-east of Iceland. Their combined massive firepower broke the ship in two.
Built by Harland & Wolff Ltd, Greenock, for the P&O Line.

RAZMAK (1925) See MONOWAI (1930)

READY (1931)
4401 grt; 205 psrs
384' x 46' x 24'8" (116.4 x 13.9 x 7.5 m)
Barclay Curle 3-cylinder triple expansion engines via single screw.
Broken up for scrap in 1937 as an oil refinery ship at Rosyth. Ex-Hvalfanger AS.
Laid down by Barclay Curle & Co Ltd, Glasgow, for the Union-Castle Mail Steamship Co Ltd as the DUNLUCE CASTLE (1897) and completed as the RAGLAN CASTLE (1897 – Union-Castle Mail Steamship Co Ltd). Renamed HANNA (1905 – Russian government), SAINT DOMINGO (1905 – Akties Det Ostasiatiske Kompagai), RAGLAN CASTLE (1908 – Union-Castle Mail Steamship Co Ltd) and PYTHIA (1909 – Pythia Steamship Co Ltd).

RECHERCHE (1930) See MADALI (1948)

RECHID PACHA (1911) See RESI PASA (1928)

RED CROSS (1914) See PRESIDENT FILLMORE (1922)

RE D'ITALIA (1907)
6237 grt; 2020 psrs
length 430' x beam 53' (131.1 x 16.2 m)
6-cylinder triple expansion engines via twin screw.
Broken up for scrap at Genoa in 1929.
Built by Sir James Laing, Sunderland, for Lloyd Sabaudo.

REEF ENDEAVOUR (1996)
3125 grt; 138 psrs
241' x 59' x 11'6" (73 x 18 x 3.5 m)
2 x 6-cylinder Yanmar diesel engines via twin screw.

Cruise ship operated by Captain Cook Cruises, Sydney, New South Wales.
Built by Fiji Marine Shipyard.

REFUGE, USS (AH-11) (1944) See PRESIDENT MADISON (1946)

REGAL EMPRESS (1993)
21909 grt; 1068 psrs
612' x 79' x 28' (186.5 x 24.1 x 8.5 m)
2 x Klockner-Humboldt-Deutz diesel engines (replacing in 1983 the original machinery of 4 x Pametrada DRG turbine engines) via twin screw.
Cruise ship owned by Regal Cruises and operated by International Shipping Partners.
Built on a keel originally laid down for an aircraft carrier by Alexander Stephen & Sons Ltd, Glasgow, for the Greek Line as the OLYMPIA (1953). Laid up from 1974 to 1982. Renamed CARIBE (1982 – Sally Line via their subsidiary Commodore Cruises) and CARIBE I (1983 – Sally Line, with installation of diesel engines).

REGAL PRINCESS (1991)

70285 grt; 1596 psrs
804' x 105' x 25'6" (243.6 x 31.8 x 7.8 m)
4 x 8-cylinder MAN-B+W diesel-electric engines via twin screw.
Cruise ship owned and operated by P&O Princess Cruises.
Built by Fincantieri, Monfalcone, for the P&O Group at a cost of US$277,000,000.

REGAL VOYAGER (1994)
12547 grt; 460 psrs
250 cars or 100 trailers
465' x 72' x 18'6" (141.8 x 22 x 5.6 m)
2 x 16-cylinder LAtlantique-Pielstick diesel engines via twin screw.

Cruise ship operated by St Thomas Cruises Ltd after conversion from a passenger-car-cargo RoRo ferry.
Built by Dubigeon-Normandie SA, Nantes, for Nouvelle Cie de Paquebots (Chargeurs Reunis) as the MASSALIA (1971). Renamed STENA BALTICA (1984 – Stena Cargo Line Ltd, Nassau), ISLAND FIESTA (1984- Stena Cargo Line Ltd, Nassau), SCANDINAVIAN STAR (1985 – SeaEscape) and CANDI (1990 – Vognmandsruten KS, Nassau).

REGENCY (1982)
4811 grt; 185 psrs
340' x 52' x 15' (103 x 15.8 x 4.5 m)
2 x 10-cylinder diesel engines via twin screw.
Owned by the Triton Holding Corporation, she was declared a total loss after grounding during a typhoon at Batangas, Philippines, on 11 October 1989.
Built by Harland & Wolff Ltd, Belfast, for Coast Lines Ltd as the IRISH COAST (1953). Renamed ORPHEUS (1968 – Epirotiki Cruise Lines), SEMIRAMIS II (1969 – Epirotiki Cruise Lines), ACHILLEUS (1969 – Epirotiki Cruise Lines) and APOLLON II (1969 – Epirotiki Cruise Lines).

REGENT ISLE (1995) See CHINA SEA DISCOVERY (2000)

REGENT JEWEL (1993) See CALYPSO (1994)

REGENT MOON (1986) See COSTA ALLEGRA (1990)

REGENT RAINBOW (1993) See THE EMERALD (1996)

REGENT SEA (1985) See SEA (1996)

REGENT SKY (1993)
26000 grt; 1600 psrs
754' x 94' x 23' (228.6 x 28.5 x 6.9 m)
4 x 12-cylinder Wartsila diesel engines via twin screw.
Still being converted from a planned RoRo ferry into a cruise ship in the Avlis Shipyard, Chalkis. The incomplete hull of the intended Stena Line vessel STENA POLONICA was towed from the Stocznia im Komuny Paryskiej Shipyards, Gdynia, to Chalkis in 1990, following a cancelled contract from Stena and a protracted period on the stocks, from 1979 to 1986. Ultimately, Regency Cruises acquired the hull and commissioned Avlis Shipyards to complete the ship. However, Regency collapsed, with the company's ship assets and brand name eventually being bought by Avlis, with a scheduled completion date fixed for 2001 at a cost of US$170,000,000.
Built by Wartsila-Abo for Rederi AB Nordstjernan as the RoRo container ship ferry MARGARET JOHNSON (1969).

REGENT SPIRIT (1993) See SALAMIS GLORY (1996)

REGENT STAR (1986) See SEA HARMONY (1996)

REGENT SUN (1986) See COSTA MARINA (1990)

REGENT SUN (1988) See SUN (1998)

REGGIO (1960)
3713 grt; 1800 psrs
25 cars + 50 trailers or 13 rail coaches
416' x 58' x 14' (126.1 x 17.7 x 4.2 m)
2 x 6-cylinder B+W diesel engines via twin screw.
Passenger-car-cargo-train ferry operated by Italian State Railways.
Built by Cantieri Riuniti, Genoa,.

REGINA (1904)
4280 grt; 400 psrs
393' x 48' x 31'4" depth (119 x 14.5 x 9.5 m)
T Richardson & Sons 3-cylinder triple expansion engine via single screw.
Owned by M Jebsen, Germany, she was broken up for scrap at Genoa in 1908 after being towed from Mozambique via Durban following her running aground, then being refloated.
Laid down by Barclay, Curle & Co, Glasgow, for the Castle Line as the ARMADALE CASTLE (1882) and completed as the ROSLIN CASTLE (1883 – Castle Line).

REGINA (1918) See WESTERNLAND (1930)

REGINA (1964) See REGINA PRIMA (1973)

REGINA (1978) See EL-TOR (1998)

REGINA BALTICA (1996)
18345 grt; 1500 psrs
510 cars + 54 trailers
479' x 83' x 18' (145 x 25.2 x 5.5 m)
4 x 12-cylinder Pielstick diesel engines via twin screw.

Ice-strengthened passenger-car-cargo RoRo ferry owned and operated by Estline.
Built by Wartsila-Turku for Sally Line as the VIKING SONG (1980) at a cost of US$33,000,000. Renamed BRAEMAR (1985 – Fred Olsen Line), BALTIKA (1991 – Baltic Shipping Co), ANNA KARENINA (1991 – Baltic Shipping Co) and ANNA K (1996 – Baltic Shipping Co).

REGINA D'ITALIA (1907)
6560 grt; 2020 psrs
430' x 53' x 25' (131.1 x 16.2 x 7.6 m)
G Clark Ltd 6-cylinder triple expansion engine via twin screw.
Broken up for scrap in 1928 in Italy.
Laid down by Sir James Laing, Sunderland, for the Prince Line, UK, as the SERBIAN PRINCE (1906) and completed as the REGINA DITALIA for Lloyd Sabaudo.

REGINA MAGNA (1972) See FILIPINAS SAUDI I (1980)

REGINA MARIS (1966) See ALEX ANDER (1983)

REGINA MARIS (1980) See ALEX ANDER (1983)

REGINA MARIS (1996)
4012 grt; 166 psrs
314' x 46' x 16' (95 x 14 x 4.8 m)
2 x 8-cylinder Krupp diesel engines via twin screw.
Cruise ship for Memnon Cruises, Cairo.
Built by Krupp Shipyards, Kiel, for a US multi-millionaire as his private

schooner-rigger motor yacht ORION (1929). Renamed VIXEN, USS (PG-53) (1942 – US Navy), ORION (1950 – Pacific Cruise Lines) and ARGONAUT (1964 – Epirotiki Cruise Lines, which also registered the ship under the name ARGONAFTIS).

REGINA PRIMA (1973)
10972 grt; 650 psrs
493' x 64' x 26' (149.4 x 19.4 x 7.9 m)
DRG turbine engines via twin screw.
Broken up for scrap at Izmir in 1985. Ex-Chandris Lines.
Built by Bethlehem Steel Company, Quincy, Massachusetts, for the President of the Panama Railroad Steamship Co as his private yacht PANAMA (1939) at a cost of US$4,000,000. Renamed JAMES L. PARKER (1941 – US government), PANAMA (1946 – American President Lines), PRESIDENT HOOVER (1957 – American President Lines) and REGINA (1964 – Chandris Lines).

REGINA RENAISSANCE (1992) See RENAISSANCE SEVEN (1998)

REGISTAN (1921) See ARAUCO (1935)

REGULA (1997)
3774 grt; 580 psrs
105 cars
235' x 54' x 13'9" (71.2 x 16.3 x 4.2 m)
4 x 8-cylinder Deutz diesel engines via twin screw.
Passenger-car ferry owned and operated by Saaremaa Shipping Co Ltd, Saaremaa.
Built by Meyer Werft, Papenburg.

REINA (1961) See MELINA (1964)

REINA DEL MAR (1956)
21501 grt; 1047 psrs
601' x 78' x 27' (183.2 x 23.8 x 8.2 m)
Parsons geared turbine engines via twin screw.
Broken up for scrap by Tung Cheng Steel Manufacturing Company at Kaohsiung in 1975.
Built by Harland & Wolff Ltd, Belfast, for the Pacific Steam Navigation Co Ltd.

REINA DEL MAR (1981)
13581 grt; 414 psrs
516' x 72' x 24' (157.3 x 22 x 7.3 m)
4 x DRG turbine engines via twin screw.
Operated by World Cruise Lines, she sank almost exactly where the RASA SAYANG settled to the bottom in similar circumstances nine months earlier. REINA DEL MAR was gutted by fire on 28 May 1981 and rolled over and sank three days later.
Built by Vickers-Armstrong Walker Naval Yard, Newcastle, for Furness, Withy & Company as the OCEAN MONARCH (1951). Renamed VARNA (1967 – Balkanturist Co) and VENUS (1979 – World Cruise Lines). She had also been given a temporary name of RIVIERA in 1979.

REINA DEL PACIFICO (1931)
17872 grt; 888 psrs
574' x 76' x 31' (173.9 x 23 x 9.4 m)
B+W 12-cylinder diesel engines via twin screw.
Broken up for scrap by John Cashmore Ltd at Newport, Wales, in 1958.
Built by Harland & Wolff Ltd, Belfast, for the Pacific Steam Navigation Company.

REINA VICTORIA EUGENIA (1913) See ARGENTINA (1931)

REINE ASTRID (1956)
3800 grt; 1700 psrs
374' x 50' x 13' (113.3 x 15.2 x 3.9 m)
2 x 12-cylinder Sulzer diesel engines via twin screw.
Partially broken up for scrap, but the centre section of the hull and superstructure was converted by Belgian RMT engineers into a floating jetfoil terminal at Dover for the Boeing craft. It served this purpose until 1997 when it was also broken up for scrap.
Built by John Cockerill, Hoboken, for RMT, Belgium.

REINE ASTRID (1983) See AL MANSOUR (1997)

REINE MATHILDE (1989) See BEAUPORT (1991)

RELIANCE (1926)
19821 grt; 819 psrs
590' x 81' x 39'7" depth (178.8 x 24.5 x 12 m)
2 x JC Tecklenborg 4-cylinder combination triple expansion turbine engines via triple screw.
Owned by United American Lines, she was broken up for scrap by Krupp, Bremerhaven, in 1940 after being gutted by a mysterious fire on 7 August 1938 at Hamburg.
Launched by JC Tecklenborg Shipyards, Geestemunde, for the Hamburg-America Line as the JOHANN HEINRICH BURCHARD (1914). Renamed LIMBURGIA (1920 – Royal Holland Lloyd).

RELIEF (1898) See LANAO (1937)

RELIEF, USS (1902) See LANAO (1937)

REMBRANDT (1906)
5876 grt; 165 psrs
421' x 48' x 34'6" (132.3 x 14.6 x 9.1 m)
4-cylinder Nederlandsche Fabriek van Werktuigen quadruple expansion engines via single screw.
Broken up for scrap by Frank Rijsdisk, Hendrik Ido Ambacht.
Built by Nederlandsche Scheepsbouw Maatschappij, Amsterdam, for the Nederland Steamship Co.

REMBRANDT (1997) See THE BIG RED BOAT IV (2000)

REMO (1927) See SAN SERGIO (1952)

REMUERA (1911)
11276 grt; 530 psrs
502' x 62' x 30' (153 x 18.9 x 9.1 m)
Triple expansion engines via twin screw.
Sank on 26 August 1940 after being hit by a torpedo launched from a German aircraft off Rattray Head, north-east of Scotland and south of the Moray Firth.
Built by William Denny & Bros, Dumbarton, for the New Zealand Shipping Co.

REMUERA (1962) See ARAMAC (1964)

RENAISSANCE (1966) See WORLD RENAISSANCE (1998)

RENAISSANCE 1 (1989) See THE MERCURY (1998)

RENAISSANCE 2 (1990) See THE NEPTUNE (1998)

RENAISSANCE 3 (1990) See GALAPAGOS EXPLORER II (1998)

RENAISSANCE 4 (1990) See CLELIA II (1997)

RENAISSANCE 5 (1990) See MEGASTAR SAGITTARIUS (2000)

RENAISSANCE 6 (1991) See MEGASTAR CAPRICORN (2000)

RENAISSANCE 7 (1991) See RENAISSANCE SEVEN (1998)

RENAISSANCE 8 (1992)
4280 grt; 114 psrs
297' x 50' x 12' (90 x 15 x 3.6 m)
2 x 8-cylinder MAN-B+W-Alpha diesel engines via twin screw.
Cruise ship operated by Renaissance Cruises.
Built by Nuovi Cantieri Apuania Shipyard.

RENAISSANCE SEVEN (1998)
4280 grt; 114 psrs
300' x 50' x 12' (91 x 15 x 3.7 m)
2 x 8-cylinder MAN-B+W-Alpha diesel engines via twin screw.
Ice-strengthened passenger ruise ship owned by Luxury Lines and operated by Renaissance Cruises Inc.

Built by Nuovi Cantieri Apuania Shipyard for Renaissance Cruises Inc as the RENAISSANCE SEVEN (1991). Renamed REGINA RENAISSANCE (1992).

RENETTA (1972) See NISSOS RODOS (1977)

REPOSE, USS (1918) See LANAO (1937)

REPUBBLICA DI AMALFI (1989)
42567 grt; 57 psrs
1226 TEUs
710' x 99' x 31' (215.2 x 30 x 9.4 m)
Sulzer 8-cylinder diesel engines via single screw.
Passenger-cargo ship operated by Grimaldi Lines until recently when she became a freight ship.
Built by Fincantieri Shipyards, Castellammare di Stabia.

REPUBBLICA DI GENOVA (1988)
42567 grt; 57 psrs
3500 cars + 1350 TEUs
719' x 99' x 31' (217.9 x 30 x 9.4 m)
Sulzer 8-cylinder diesel engines via single screw.
Passenger-cargo ship operated by Grimaldi Lines until recently when she became a freight ship.
Built by Fincantieri Shipyards, Castellammare di Stabia.

REPUBBLICA DI PISA (1987)
48622 grt; 54 psrs
1226 TEUs
700' x 99' x 30' (212.1 x 30 x 9.1 m)
Sulzer 8-cylinder diesel engine via single screw.
Passenger-cargo ship owned by Grand Traghetti, Italy, and operated by Grimaldi Lines until recently when she became a freight ship.
Built by Fincantieri Shipyards, Castellammare di Stabia.

REPUBBLICA DI VENEZIA (1987)
48622 grt; 56 psrs
1226 TEUs
700' x 99' x 31' (212.1 x 30 x 9.4 m)
Sulzer diesel engine via single screw.
Passenger-cargo ship owned by Grand Traghetti, Italy, and operated by Grimaldi Lines until recently when she became a freight ship.
Built by Fincantieri Shipyards, Breda, Venice.

REPUBLIC (1871) See CITTA DI NAPOLI (1902)

REPUBLIC (1903)
15378 grt; 2200 psrs
585' x 68' x 31' (178.3 x 20.7 x 9.4 m)
8-cylinder quadruple expansion engines via twin screw.
Owned by White Star Line, she sank in 34 fathoms on 24 January 1909, taking four lives with her, after a head-on collision with the 5000 grt Lloyd Italiano steamer FLORIDA the day before, 175 miles (292 km) east of the Ambrose Lightship. The FLORIDA had torn a massive hole in the REPUBLIC, destroying several bulkheads and allowing the sea to pour in. There may have been a greater loss of life except for the fact that she was equipped with wireless and sent the first transmitted SOS, which resulted in the rescue of 2,000 people.
Built by Harland & Wolff Ltd, Belfast, for the Dominion Line as the COLUMBUS (1903).

REPUBLIC (1924) See REPUBLIC, USS (AP-33) (1941)

REPUBLIC, USS (AP-33) (1941)
18078 grt; 1951 psrs
616' x 68' x 48'3" depth (187.8 x 20.7 x 14.6 m)
2 x Harland & Wolff 4-cylinder quadruple expansion engines via twin screw.
Broken up for scrap at Baltimore in 1952. Ex-US Army hospital ship.
Laid down by Harland & Wolff Ltd, Belfast, for the Leyland Line as the SERVIAN (1903). She was left incomplete for two years and then completed as PRESIDENT GRANT (1907 – Hamburg-America Line). Renamed PRESIDENT BUCHANAN (1924 – US government) and REPUBLIC (1924 – United States Lines).

RESCUE, USS (AH-18) (1945)
6185 grt; 444 psrs
403' x 61' x 29'9" depth (122.1 x 18.5 x 9.1 m)
Newport News SRG turbine engines via twin screw.
Broken up for scrap at Ballard, Washington, in 1959.
Built by Newport News Shipbilding, Newport News, Virginia, for Eastern Steamship Lines as the SAINT JOHN (1932). Renamed ANTAEUS, USS (AS-21) (1941 – US Navy)

RESI PASA (1929)
4450 grt; 150 psrs
370' x 46' x 22' (112.1 x 13.9 x 6.7 m)
Triple expansion engine via single screw.
Broken up for scrap. Ex-government of Turkey.
Built by Sir Raylton Dixon & Co Ltd, Middlesbrough, for the Imperial Direct Line as the PORT ANTONIO (1901). The name change in 1929 was meant to reflect the modern outlook of the new operator, Turkiye Seyrisefain Idaresi.

RESOLUTE (1922) See LOMBARDIA (1935)

RESURGENT (RFA) (1953)
9403 grt; 180 psrs
477' x 62' x 25' (145.3 x 18.9 x 7.6 m)
Scotts 6-cylinder diesel engine via single screw.
Broken up for scrap as a Royal Fleet Auxiliary vessel in both Avilez (where the superstructure was removed) and Gijon, Spain, in 1982 by Asturamerican Shipping Co Ltd, Panama.
Built by Scotts Shipbuilding & Engineering Company, Greenock, for the China Navigation Company as the CHANGCHOW (1951).

RETAINER (A329) (1953)
9393 grt; 180 psrs
477' x 62' x 25' (145.3 x 18.9 x 7.6 m)
Scotts 6-cylinder diesel engine via single screw.
Broken up for scrap at Barcelona in 1980 as a Royal Fleet Auxiliary (UK).
Built by Scotts Shipbuilding & Engineering Company, Greenock, for the China Navigation Company as the CHUNGKING (1950).

RETHIMNON (1972)
7291 grt; 1344 psrs
450 cars
428' x 75' x 18' (129.8 x 22.6 x 5.5 m)
2 x 14-cylinder MAN diesel engines via twin screw.
Passenger-car ferry owned by Cretan Maritime and operated by ANEK.
Built by Sumitomo Shipbuilding & Machinery Co Ltd, Yokosuka, for Central Ferry Co Ltd, Kobe, as the ferry CENTRAL No.5 (1971).

REWA (1906) See HOSPITAL SHIP. No. 5 (1914)

REX (1932)
51062 grt; 2258 psrs
880' x 96' x 33' (266.7 x 29.1 x 10 m)
12 x Parsons SRG turbine engines via quadruple screw.
Broken up for scrap at Trieste in 1947 after raising her from the seabed just south of Trieste. She had been sunk there on 9 September 1944 by British bombers.
Built by Ansaldo Shipyards, Genoa, for the Italian Line.

REY ALFONSO (1923) See POLAR CHIEF (1946)

REYNA FILIPINA (1978)
5486 grt; 450 psrs
397' x 53' x 18' (120.4 x 16 x 5.5 m)
4 x 7-cylinder Fiat geared diesel engines via twin screw.
Built by Soc Italiani per Construzione Navali Meccaniche for Tirrenia as the CARALIS (1957). Renamed SWEET HOME (1973 – Sweet Lines Inc) and SAMPAGUITA (1978).

REYNELLA (1940) See SAN SERGIO (1952)

REYNIERSZ (1948) See KENINGAU (1960)

R FOUR (1999)
30277 grt; 684 psrs

594' x 84' x 19'6" (180 x 25.5 x 5.9 m)
4 x 12-cylinder Wartsila diesel engines via twin screw.
Cruise ship owned and operated by Renaissance Cruises.
Built by Chantiers de l'Atlantique, St Nazaire, at a cost of US$ 180,000,000.

R FIVE (2000)
30277 grt; 684 psrs
594' x 84' x 19'6" (180 x 25.5 x 5.9 m)
4 x 12-cylinder Wartsila diesel engines via twin screw.
Cruise ship owned and operated by Renaissance Cruises.
Built by Chantiers de l'Atlantique, St Nazaire, for Renaissance Cruises at a cost of $180,000,000.

RHAETIA (1883) See SUMNER (1900)

RHAETIA (1905) See BLACK ARROW, USS (1919)

RHAMANI (1928)
5291 grt
410' x 54' x 25'11" (124.2 x 16.4 x 7.6 m)
Rankin & Blackmore 3-cylinder triple expansion engines via single screw.
Built by Lithgows Ltd, Port Glasgow, for the Bombay & Persia Steamship Co Ltd.

RHAPSODY (1982) See SEA HARMONY (1996)

RHAPSODY (1995)
17495 grt; 750 psrs
535' x 75' x 19' (163 x 22.8 x 5.8 m)
4 x 7-cylinder B+W geared diesel engines via twin screw.

Cruise ship owned by Mediterranean Shipping Cruises and chartered to Star Lauro Cruises, Italy.
Laid down by Burmeister & Wain, Copenhagen, for the Cunard Line as the CUNARD CONQUEST (1975) and completed as the CUNARD PRINCESS (1976) by Industrie Navale Meccaniche Affina Shipyard, La Spezia.

RHAPSODY OF THE SEAS (1997)
78491 grt; 2477 psrs
920' x 106' x 25' (278.9 x 32.2 x 7.6 m)
4 x 12-cylinder Wartsila diesel-electric engines via twin screw.
Cruise ship operated by Royal Caribbean International.

Built by Chantiers de l'Atlantique, St Nazaire, at a cost of US$275,000,000.

RHEIN (1899) See SUSQUEHANNA (1917)

RHENANIA (1909) See FELTRE (1915)

RHODESIA (1918) See GALWAY CASTLE (1911)

RHODESIA CASTLE (1951)
17041 grt; 552 psrs
576' x 74' x 28' (175.5 x 22.6 x 8.5 m)
Geared turbine engines via twin screw.
Broken up for scrap by Chin Ho Fa Steel & Iron Co at Kaohsiung in 1967.
Built by Harland & Wolff Ltd, Belfast, for the Union Castle Line.

RHODOS (1989) See RODOS (1989)

RHYNA (1906)
3689 grt; 500 psrs
403' x 40' x 30'6" depth (122.8 x 12.3 x 9.3 m)
Barrows Shipbuilding Co Ltd 2-cylinder compound engine via single screw.
Broken up for scrap in Italy in 1906.
Built by Barrow Shipbuilding Co Ltd, Barrow-in-Furness, for the Red Star Line as the RHYNELAND (1879).

RHYNLAND (1879) See RHYNA (1906)

RICHARD WITH (1993)
11205 grt; 691 psrs
50 cars
402' x 63' x 16' (121.8 x 19.2 x 4.9 m)
2 x 6-cylinder Krupp-MaK diesel engines via twin screw.
Passenger-car ferry operated by Ofotens Og Vesteraalen, Narvik.
Built by Volkswerft GmbH Shipyard, Strasland, at a cost of US$63,000,000.

RICHELIEU (1913) See PASSENGER No. 3 (1966)

RIETFONTEIN (1939) See DEVON (1967)

RIF (1988) See HANAA (1992)

RIGA (1905) See TRANSBALT (1920)

RIJNDAM (1901) See RYNDAM (1901)

RIMUTAKA (1901)
7765 grt; 340 psrs
457' x 58' x 26' (139.3 x 17.7 x 7.9 m)
Triple expansion engines via twin screw.
Broken up for scrap at Pembroke, Wales, in 1930.
Built by William Denny & Bros, Dumbarton, for the New Zealand Shipping Co.

RIMUTAKA (1938) See ACAPULCO (1961)

RINA (1902)
3232 grt
380' x 38' x 28'5" depth (115.2 x 11.5 x 8.6 m)
J Howden 3-cylinder triple expansion engine via single screw.
Broken up for scrap at Genoa in 1903.
Built by R Duncan & Co, Port Glasgow, for Duke of Argylle Steamship Co Ltd as the DUKE OF ARGYLL (1873).

RINJANI (1984)
13860 grt; 1737 psrs
472' x 77' x 19'6" (143 x 23.3 x 5.9 m)
2 x 6-cylinder MaK diesel engines via twin screw.
Passenger ferry owned by the government of Indonesia and operated by PT Pelni.
Built by Meyer Werft, Papenburg.

RIO BRAVO (1924) See MERKUR (1934)

RIO DE JANIERO MARU (1930)
9627 grt
473' x 62' x 26' (143.3 x 18.8 x 7.9 m)
Mitsubishi 12-cylinder diesel engines via twin screw.

Sank on 17 February 1944 after being attacked by US aircraft.
Built by Mitsubishi Dockyard for Mitsui OSK.

RIO DE LA PLATA (1941) See FAIRSEA (1949)

RIO DE LA PLATA (1950)
11317 grt; 116 psrs
550' x 66' x 26' (166.7 x 20 x 7.9 m)
Fiat diesel engines via twin screw.
Broken up for scrap at Buenos Aires in 1968, four years after she burnt out during a refit at the Demarchi Shipyard, Buenos Aires, on 19 November 1964.
Built by Ansaldo Shipyards, Genoa, for the Argentine State Line.

RIO GALLEGOS (1942) See ROLAND VON BREMEN (1966)

RIO JACHAL (1943) See IRPINIA (1955)

RIO JACHAL (1950)
11317 grt; 116 psrs
550' x 66' x 26' (166.7 x 20 x 7.9 m)
Broken up for scrap at Buenos Aires in 1970 following a series of catastrophes: catching fire in New York on 28 September 1962 and being towed to Buenos Aires and repaired in April 1964, then catching fire again in Buenos Aires on 17 April 1968, which finally destroyed her.
Built by Ansaldo Shipyards, Genoa, for the Argentine State Line.

RIOJANO (1897) See YUTE (1916)

RION (1904) See RION (1913)

RION (1913)
7270 grt; 1586 psrs
486' x 58' x 26' (147.3 x 17.6 x 7.9 m)
Hawthorne Leslie 12-cylinder triple expansion engines via twin screw.
Broken up for scrap in Italy in 1922. Ex-Russian Navy.
Built by R & W Hawthorn, Leslie & Co, Hebburn-on-Tyne, for the Russian Volunteer Fleet as the SMOLENSK (1901). Renamed RION (1904 – Russian Navy) and SMOLENSK (1906 – Russian Volunteer Fleet).

RIO PANUCO (1924) See NEPTUNA (1935)

RIO TUNUYAN (1949) See RIO TUNUYAN (1952)

RIO TUNUYAN (1952)
11317 grt; 116 psrs
550' x 66' x 26' (166.7 x 20 x 7.9 m)
2 x 10-cylinder Fiat diesel engines via twin screw.
Broken up for scrap at San Pedro, Argentina in 1977. Ex-E.L.M.A..Built by Ansaldo Shipyards, Genoa, for the Argentine State Line as the passenger-cargo ship RIO TUNUYAN (1949). Renamed EVITA (1952 – government of Argentina)

RIOUW (1914)
7624 grt; 197 psrs
451' x 56' x 27'6" (142.7 x 17 x 9.2 m)
D Rowan & Co 3-cylinder triple expansion steam engines via single screw.
Broken up for scrap in Osaka in 1933 after Metallici, Turin, won the tender but then resold the vessel.
Built by A McMillan & Son Ltd, Dumbarton, for the Nederlandsche Steamship Co, with only ten passengers accommodated. The passenger capacity was increased to 197 in 1920, but reverted in 1924 to the original ten.

RIPA (1997)
23180 grt; 1300 psrs
610' x 78' x 27' (186 x 23.8 x 8.2 m)
4 x Parsons DRG turbine engines via twin screw.
Broken up for scrap at Gadani Beach, Karachi, in 1997. Ex-P&O Holidays, Sydney.
Built by Fairfield Shipbuilding & Engineering Co, Glasgow, for the Bibby Line as the OXFORDSHIRE (1957). Renamed FAIRSTAR (1963 – Sitmar Line).

RITA MARIA (1953)
3749 grt; 70 psrs

369' x 45' x 19' (111.8 x 13.6 x 5.8 m)
2 x 7-cylinder Atlas diesel engine via single screw.
Built by Cia Uniao Fabril, Lisbon, for Soc Geral de Comercio Industria e Transportes, Lisbon, as a passenger-cargo ship.

RITSURIN (1990)
3577 grt; 475 psrs
382' x 66' x 15' (115.9 x 20 x 4.6 m)
2 x 8-cylinder NYK-Pielstick diesel engines via twin screw.
Passenger ferry operated by Kato Kisen, Japan.
Built by Hayashikane Dockyard, Nagasaki.

RIVERA (1917)
6506 grt; 1830 psrs
421' x 56' x 27'8" (129.2 x 17.2 x 8.4 m)
4-cylinder quadruple expansion engine via single screw.
Broken up for scrap in Danzig in 1938. Ex-Uruguay.
Built by Flensburger Schiffbau, Flensburg, for the Hamburg-America Line as the SILVIA (1903).

RIVERINA (1905)
4758 grt; 378 psrs
370' x 50' x 22'8" (112.1 x 15.2 x 6.9 m)
Richardson Westgarth 3-cylinder triple expansion engines via single screw.
Broken up where she lay after grounding on Ninety Mile Beach, Victoria, Australia, near Gabo Island during a storm and huge seas on 17 April 1927.
Built by J Laing & Sons, Sunderland, for Huddart Parker Ltd.

RIVIERA (1979) See REINA DEL MAR (1979)

RIVIERA II (2000)
16292 grt; 420 psrs
100 cars
429' x 63' x 17'6" (130 x 19.1 x 5.4 m)
2 x 7-cylinder B+W diesel engines via twin screw.
Passenger ship owned and operated by Royal Hispania Cruises, Panama.
Built by Union Naval de Levante SA, Valencia, for Trasmediterranea as the passenger-car ferry LAS PALMAS DE GRAN CANARIA (1967). Renamed as the cruise ship CROWN DEL MAR (1987 – owned by Maritima Albatros, Spain, and chartered to Crown Cruise Line). Laid up from 1990 to 1994 awaiting sale at US$8,000,000. Renamed DON JUAN (1995 – Hamlet Cruises, Elsinore) and D JUAN (1998 – Royal Hispania Cruises, Panama).

RIVIERA PRIMA (1961) See VIKING PRINCESS (1965)

RIVIERA STAR (1996) See OCEAN EXPLORER I (1998)

RIXEY, USS (AP-3) (1942) See PRIVATE WILLIAM H. THOMAS (1946)

ROADA (1984) See SREDETZ (1986)

ROANOKE (1901) See KOMMIYUT (1948)

ROBERT BORNHOFEN (1939) See SPERBRECHER (1939)

ROBERT E. LEE (1924)
5184 grt; 670 psrs
390' x 54' x 30' depth (118.2 x 16.4 x 9.1 m)
Newport News SRG turbine engines via single screw.
Sank on 30 July 1942 after being torpedoed in the Gulf of Mexico.
Built by Newport News Shipbuilding, Newport News, Virginia, for the Dominion Steamship Co.

ROBERT E. LEE (1969) See ROBERT TOOMBS (1973)

ROBERT LEY (1938)
27288 grt; 1774 psrs
length 669' x beam 79' (202.7 x 23.9 m)
6 x 6-cylinder MAN diesel engines via twin screw.
Broken up for scrap by TW Ward Ltd at Inverkeithing in 1947. She had been towed from Hamburg where she had burned out and settled on the harbour bottom following an Allied air raid on 24 March 1945.

Built by Howaldtswerke AG, Hamburg, for the German Workers' Front and operated and managed on their behalf by the Hamburg-America Line.

ROBERT TOOMBS (1973)
13100 grt; 900 psrs
523' x 72' x 26'6" (159.3 x 21.8 x 8 m)
2 x Westinghouse DRG turbine engines via single screw.
Broken up for scrap at Kaohsiung in 1980. Ex-Waterman Group, New York.
Built by the Kaiser Corporation, Richmond, California, for the US Maritime Commission as the Class C4-S-A1 troop transport GENERAL LEROY ELTINGE, USS (AP-154) (1945). Renamed ROBERT E. LEE (1969 – Waterman Carriers, New York). Reclassified as the GENERAL LEROY ELTINGE, USNS (T-AP-154) (1950 – US Navy).

ROBIN HOOD (1977) See TIAN E (1985)

ROBIN HOOD (1978) See TIAN E (1985)

ROBIN HOOD (1979) See TIAN E (1985)

ROBIN HOOD (1986) See FEDRA (1987)

ROBIN HOOD (1989) See NILS HOLGERSSON (1993)

ROBIN HOOD (1993)
39750 grt; 1044 psrs
500 cars
585' x 92' x 19' (177.2 x 28 x 5.7 m)
4 x MAN-B+W diesel engines via twin screw.
Passenger-car ferry operated by TT-Line.
Built by Kvaerner Masa-Yards, Turku, for the TT-Line as the NILS HOLGERSSON (1989).

ROBIN HOOD (1995)
26800 grt; 317 psrs
155 cars
593' x 91' x 20' (179.6 x 27.9 x 6 m)
4 x 6-cylinder Krupp-MaK diesel-electric engines via twin screw.

Passenger-car RoRo ferry operated by TT Line GmbH, Hamburg.
Built by Finnyards Oy, Rauma, at a cost of Finmarks 500,000,000.

ROCHAMBEAU (1911)
12678 grt; 1876 psrs
598' x 63' x 27' (182.2 x 19.3 x 8.2 m)
2 x 4-cylinder triple expansion engines via quadruple screw.
Broken up for scrap by Gosselin & Dumouries at Dunkirk in 1934.
Built by Penhoet, St Nazaire, for the French Line.

ROCHAMBEAU (1942) See MARECHAL JOFFRE (1945)

ROCK HILL VICTORY (1945) See ENTRE RIOS (1947)

RODANTHI (1995)
13457 grt; 2200 psrs
311 cars
451' x 74' x 19'6" (136.6 x 22.4 x 5.9 m)
2 x 16-cylinder Pielstick diesel engines via twin screw.
Passenger-car ferry owned by Ikaria Shipping and operated by GA Ferries.
Built by Naikai Zosen, Setoda, for Higashi Nippon Ferry KK, Tomakomai, as the VIRGO (1974).

ROD-EL-FARAG (1938)
6369 grt; 106 psrs
446' x 55' x 28'6" (135.2 x 16.7 x 8.7 m)
Triple expansion engine via single screw.
Owned by Soc Misr de Navigation Maritime, Alexandria, she was leased to the British Ministry of War Transport during World War Two and became one of 12 ships which were totally destroyed in Mumbai Harbour when an ammunition vessel exploded, on 14 April 1944.
Built by William Denny & Bros, Dumbarton, for the Henderson Line as the CHINDWIN (1910) at a cost of £86,292.

RODOS (1989)
7948 grt; 1443 psrs
400 cars + 60 trailers
437' x 75' x 18' (132.3 x 22.7 x 5.5 m)
2 x 16-cylinder Pielstick diesel engines via twin screw.
Passenger-car-cargo ferry owned by the DANE Sea Line, Greece.
Built by Nipponkai Heavy Industries, Toyama, for Taiheiyo Enkai Ferry KK, Nagoya, as the passenger-car-cargo ferry ARGO (1973). Renamed FERRY KOGANE MARU (1980 – Sado Kisen KK) and PEGASUS (1984).

ROGALIN (1978) See ROGALIN (1992)

ROGALIN (1983) See ROGALIN (1992)

ROGALIN (1989) See ROGALIN (1992)

ROGALIN (1992)
10241 grt; 984 psrs
170 cars or 17 trailers
418' x 64' x 17' (126.8 x 19.5 x 5.2 m)
2 x 16-cylinder Pielstick diesel engines via twin screw.

Ice-strengthened passenger-car-cargo ferry owned by Abacus Co Ltd and operated by the Polish Baltic Shipping Co.
Built by Dubigeon-Normandie, Nantes, for the Finnish Steamship Co as the AALLOTAR (1972). Renamed ROGALIN (1978 – Pol Ferries), EDDA (1983 – Farship HF, Reykjavik), ROGALIN (1983 – Pol Ferries), CELTIC PRIDE (1987 – Swansea-Cork Ferries), ROGALIN (1989 – Pol Ferries) and CELTIC PRIDE (1991 – Swansea Cork Ferries).

ROHILLA (1880) See ROHILLA MARU (1900)

ROHILLA (1906) See HOSPITAL SHIP. No. 5 (1914)

ROHILLA MARU (1900)
3869 grt; 134 psrs
386' x 40' x 27' (117 x 12.1 x 8.2 m)
2-cylinder inverted engine via single screw.
Owned by Toyo Kisen KK, she was abandoned as a total constructive loss after becoming wrecked and breaking her back on Manaita Rock, at Ujina, in the China Inland Sea in July 1905.
Built by Caird & Company, Greenock, for the P&O Line as the ROHILLA (1880) at a cost of £86,937. She was sold to Toyo Kisen KK for £10,792.

ROHNA (1926)
8602 grt; 60 psrs
479' x 62' x 26'5" (145.2 x 18.8 x 8 m)
Hawthorne Leslie 8-cylinder quadruple expansion engines via twin screw.
Sank in 30 minutes on 26 November 1943, with 1,170 lives lost, off the North African coast after becoming the first merchantman sunk in World War Two. She was the victim of a HS293 radio-controlled missile released by a German

Heinkel 177 bomber.
Built by Hawthorne Leslie & Co Ltd, Newcastle, for the British India Steam Navigation Co Ltd.

ROI BAUDOUIN (1965) See GEORGIOS EXPRESS (1983)

ROI LEOPOLD III (1956) See NAJD (1978)

ROLAND (1893) See BAHRIAHMER (1911)

ROLAND VON BREMEN (1966)
4400 grt; 1900 psrs
376' x 52' x 19'6" (114 x 15.8 x 5.9 m)
2 x 6-cylinder B+W diesel engines via twin screw.
Cruise ship owned by Bremen Seebaderdienst.
Built by Helsingor Shipyards, Helsingor, for J Laurtizen as the fruit ship INDIAN REEFER (1939). Renamed RIO GALLEGOS (1942 – government of Argentina) and INDIAN REEFER (1946 – J Lauritzen).

ROLLO (1920)
3658 grt; 317 psrs
345' x 44' x 25'6" (104.5 x 13.3 x 7.7 m)
Barclay Curle 3-cylinder triple expansion engine via single screw.
Broken up for scrap by Petersen & Albeck at Copenhagen in 1932. Ex-Ellerman's Wilson Line.
Built by Barclay, Curle & Co, Glasgow, for Elder Dempster & Co as the FANTEE (1899). Renamed ITALIAN (1915 – Ellerman & Papayanni)

ROMA (1902)
5665 grt; 1454 psrs
411' x 46' x 28'6" depth (125.3 x 14 x 8.7 m)
Forges et Chantiers de la Mediterranee 3-cylinder triple expansion engine via single screw.
Broken up for scrap at La Seyne in 1928.
Built by Forges et Chantiers de la Mediterranee, La Seyne, for the Fabre Line.

ROMA (1926) See AQUILA (1941)

ROMA (1948) See DOULOS (1978)

ROMA (1950)
14976 grt; 1145 psrs
492' x 69' x 29' (150 x 21 x 18.8 m)
2 x Allis-Chalmers SRG turbine engines via single screw.
Broken up for scrap at Savona in 1967. Ex-Flotta Lauro.
Laid down by the Seattle-Tacoma Shipbuilding Corporation, Tacoma, Washington, for the US government as the Class C-3 cargo ship GLACIER (1942) and launched as the auxiliary aircraft carrier GLACIER, USS (1943 – US Navy). Renamed ATHELING, HMS (1943 – British Royal Navy).

ROMA (1967) See CARIBIA 2 (1973)

ROMANIA (1924)
4996 grt; 1625 psrs
394' x 48' x 25'7" (120 x 14.7 x 7.8 m)
Esercizio Bacini 6-cylinder triple expansion engines via twin screw.
Broken up for scrap in 1928. Ex-Sitmar Line.
Built by Soc Esercizio Baccini, Riva Trigoso, for Lloyd Italiano as the INDIANA (1905).

ROMANIC (1903) See SCANDINAVIAN (1912)

ROMANTICA (1960)
3743 grt; 221 psrs
328' x 45' x 25' (99.5 x 13.6 x 7.6 m)
D Rowan & Co 3-cylinder triple expansion engine via single screw.
Broken up for scrap in Keratzini, Greece, in 1979 after being laid up for over two years. Ex-Armadores Romantica SA, Piraeus.
Built by the Blythswood Shipbuilding Co Ltd, Glasgow, for Furness, Withy & Co Ltd as the FORT TOWNSHEND (1935). Renamed EL AMIR SAUD (1952 – King Saud, as private motor yacht) and MANSOUR (1956 – Haji Abdullah Alireza & Co, Jeddah).

ROMANTICA (1991)

9511 grt; 570 psrs
488' x 60' x 21' (148.7 x 18.3 x 6.4 m)
2 x 8-cylinder + 1 x 6-cylinder MAN-type diesel-electric engines via single screw.
Broken up for scrap at Alexandria in 1999 (ex-New Paradise Cruises) after being declared a total constructive loss following a fire which ignited on 4 October 1997, 100 miles (168 km) south of Limassol. She made port and disembarked all passengers while listing badly in excess of 20 degrees, then was towed into shallow water outside the harbour where she quietly settled. The cruise ship PRINCESA VICTORIA stood by to make rescues while an RAF helicopter pulled people up out of the sea.
Built by Blohm & Voss, Hamburg, for the Hamburg-America Line as the passenger-cargo ship HUASCARAN (1938). Renamed BEAVERBRAE (1948 – Canadian Pacific Steamship Co), passenger ship AURELIA (1954 – Cogedar Line), cruise ship ROMANZA (1970 – Chandris Group) and then laid up in Eleusis Bay from 1984 to 1990.

ROMANZA (1970) See ROMANTICA (1991)

ROME (1881) See VECTIS (1904)

ROMEU (1918)

3070 grt; 86 psrs
322' x 40' x 22' (97.5 x 13.2 x 6.1 m)
Soc Espanola de Construccion Naval triple expansion engine via single screw.
Owned by Gobierno de la Republica de Guinea Equatorial.
Built by Soc Espanola de Construccion Naval SA, Cartagena.

ROMILDA (1992) See EXPRESS ARTEMIS (2000)

ROMILDA (1993)

4985 grt; 800 psrs
280 cars or 24 trailers
408' x 64' x 14'6" (123.6 x 19.5 x 4.4 m)
3 x 8-cylinder Stork-Werkspoor diesel engines via triple screw.

Passenger-car-cargo ferry operated by GA Ferries, Greece.
Built by Verolme Schweepswerf, Alblasserdam, for Townsend Car Ferries Ltd as the FREE ENTERPRISE VIII (1974). Renamed PRIDE OF CANTERBURY (1987 – P&O European Ferries).

ROMOLO (1926)

9780 grt; 420 psrs
507' x 62' x 26' (154.5 x 18.9 x 7.9 m)
Stablimento Tecnico 12-cylinder diesel engines via twin screw.
Deliberately sunk by seven rounds of gunfire from the Australian armed merchantman MANOORA, at 3.15 pm on 12 June 1940, following ROMOLO catching fire and listing heavily 220 miles (367 km) south-west of Nauru.
Built by Stabilimento Tecnico Triestina, Trieste, for Lloyd Triestino.

R ONE (1998)

30277 grt; 684 psrs
684' x 84' x 19'6" (180 x 25.5 x 5.9 m)
4 x 12-cylinder Wartsila diesel engines via twin screw.
Cruise ship owned and operated by Renaissance Cruises.
Built by Chantiers de l'Atlantique, St Nazaire, at a cost of $190,000,000.

ROON (1902) See CONSTANTINOUPOLIS (1920)

ROSA DE FONSECA (1962) See ATHIRAH (1992)

ROSALIA (1972)

5725 grt; 2000 psrs
100 cars + 43 rail wagons
467' x 62' x 18' (141.5 x 18.8 x 5.5 m)
4 x 6-cylinder Fiat diesel engines via twin screw.
Passenger-car-train ferry owned by Italian State Railways and operated by Ferrovie Stato on the Italy–Sicily service.
Built by Cantieri Navale del Tirreno e Riuniti, Ancona.

ROSCOMMON (1912)

7581 grt
451' x 55' x 30'6" (136.7 x 16.7 x 9.2 m)
Workman, Clark 6-cylinder triple expansion engines via twin screw.
Owned by the Union Steamship Company of New Zealand, she sank on 21 August 1917 after being torpedoed by a German U-boat off Tory Island.
Built by Workman, Clark, Belfast, for Houlder Bros Ltd (a Furness, Withy Group subsidiary) as the OSWESTRY GRANGE (1902).

ROSE CITY (1907) See ROSE ISLE (1930)

ROSE ISLE (1930)

3468 grt; 150 psrs
336' x 43' x 22'3" (101.8 x 13 x 6.8 m)
Delaware River Co 3-cylinder triple expansion engines via single screw.
Broken up for scrap at Long Beach, California, in 1935 after serving as a floating casino off Southern California.
Built by Delaware River Co, Chester, Pennsylvania, as the YUMURI (1889). Renamed BADGER, USS (1898 – US Navy), LAWTON (1900), LAWTON, USS (1902 – US Navy) and ROSE CITY (1907 –).

ROSELLA (1980)

16850 grt; 1700 psrs
535 cars or 145 cars + 43 trailers
449' x 80' x 18' (136 x 24.2 x 5.4 m)
4 x 12-cylinder Wartsila-Pielstick diesel engines via twin screw.

Ice-strengthened passenger-car-cargo ferry owned by the SF Line, Finland, and operated by the Viking Line.
Built by Wartsila, Turku.

ROSETTA (1880) See ROSETTA MARU (1900)

ROSETTA MARU (1900)

3502 grt; 184 psrs
391' x 40' x 26'8" (119.1 x 12.2 x 8.1 m)
2-cylinder compound inverted engine via single screw.
Broken up for scrap in Japan in 1907 by Toyo Kisen KK for a tender of £10,789.
Built by Harland & Wolff Ltd, Belfast, for the P&O Line at a cost of £81,325 as the ROSETTA (1880).

ROSLAGEN (1989)

6652 grt; 1200 psrs
220 cars + 26 trailers
359' x 57' x 15' (108.7 x 17.3 x 4.6 m)
2 x 12-cylinder Deutz diesel engines via twin screw.
Passenger-car-cargo ferry owned and operated by Eckerolinjen, Sweden, on the Sweden–Aland Islands service.

Built by Jos L Meyer, Papenburg, for the Sally Line as the VIKING 3 (1972). Renamed WASA EXPRESS (1976 – Vaasanlaivat, Sweden), VIKING 3 (1983 – Sally Line) and WASA EXPRESS (1984 – Vaa San Laivat, Sweden).

ROSLIN CASTLE (1883) See REGINA (1904)

ROSSIA (1946) See ANIVA (1985)

ROSSIJA (1917) See HUSO MARU (1938)

ROSSINI (1963)
13225 grt; 672 psrs
528' x 69' x 27' (161 x 21 x 8.2 m)
2 x 10-cylinder Sulzer diesel engines via twin screw.
Broken up for scrap at La Spezia in 1977. Ex-Italia.
Built by Cantieri Riuniti dell'Adriatico, Trieste, for Lloyd Triestino as the NEPTUNIA (1951).

ROSSIYA (1946) See ROSSIA (1946)

ROSTOCK (1976) See STAR WIND (1999)

ROSTOCK LINK (1992) See PENELOPE A (2000)

ROTNA (1971) See VIRGEM DE FATIMA (2000)

ROTORUA (1911)
11130 grt; 534 psrs
502' x 62' x 41' depth (153 x 19 x 12.4 m)
Triple expansion engines via triple screw.
Sank on 22 March 1917, with the loss of one life, after being torpedoed by the German U-17 24 miles (40 km) east of Start Point, Devon, in the English Channel.
Built by William Denny & Brothers, Dumbarton, for the New Zealand Shipping Co Ltd.

ROTORUA (1923)
12112 grt; 671 psrs
544' x 61' x 30' (165.8 x 18.5 x 9.1 m)
2 x John Brown Ltd quadruple expansion engines via twin screw.
Acquisitioned from the New Zealand Shipping Co by the British War Shipping Controller. The ship sank in 20 minutes on 11 December 1940, with the loss of 19 lives, after being torpedoed by the German U-96 110 miles (183 km) west of St Kilda, off northern Scotland.
Built by John Brown & Company, Glasgow, for the Federal Steam Navigation Co as the SHROPSHIRE (1911).

ROTTERDAM (1897) See DWINSK (1913)

ROTTERDAM (1908)
24149 grt; 3210 psrs
667' x 77' x 33' (202.1 x 23.3 x 10 m)
Harland & Wolff Ltd 2 x 4-cylinder quadruple expansion engines via twin screw.
Broken up for scrap by F Rijsdijk at Rotterdam in 1940.
Built by Harland & Wolff Ltd, Belfast, for the Holland America Line at a cost of US$5,000,000.

ROTTERDAM (1959) See REMBRANDT (1997)

ROTTERDAM (1997)
59652 grt; 1320 psrs
782' x 107' x 25'6" (237 x 32.3 x 7.8 m)

5 x 16-cylinder Sulzer diesel-electric engines via twin screw.
Cruise ship for the Holland America Line.
Built by Fincantieri, Breda, at a cost of US$300,000,000.

ROUSSILLON (1919)
8742 grt; 1460 psrs
482' x 58' x 35'8" depth (146.1 x 17.6 x 10.8 m)
AG Weser 8-cylinder quadruple expansion engines via twin screw.
Broken up for scrap at Pasajes, Spain, in 1931. Ex-French Line.
Built by AG Weser, Bremen, for North German Lloyd as the GOEBEN (1906), then claimed as a war prize by the French government.

ROUSSILLION (1970) See THESSALONIKI (1997)

ROYAL CLIPPER (1977)
3007 grt; 1100 psrs
298' x 47' x 16'6" (90.3 x 14.3 x 5 m)
Turbine engine via single screw.
Passenger ferry operating for Through Fun Corporation, Monrovia, she suffered an engine room explosion on 6 December 1977 and was declared a total constructive loss after having burnt out at her berth in Montreal. She was ultimately broken up for scrap in 1982 by McAllister Towing & Salvage Ltd, Montreal.
Built by Oskarhamns, Helsingor, for the Bore Line as the BORE III (1952). Renamed the LOWELL THOMAS EXPLORER (1976 – Midwest Cruises Panama SA).

ROYAL DREAM (1997) See SILVER STAR (1998)

ROYALE (1983) See SEABREEZE I (1989)

ROYAL EDWARD (1910)
11117 grt; 1000 psrs
545' x 60' x 26'8" (165.2 x 18.2 x 8.1 m)
3 x Fairfield turbine engines via triple screw.
Owned by Canadian Northern Steamships, Toronto, she sank on 14 August 1915, with the loss of 935 lives, after being torpedoed by the German U-14 in the Aegean Sea, while en route to Gallipoli. She was the first British troopship to be torpedoed in World War One.
Built by Fairfield Shipbuilding & Engineering Co Ltd, Glasgow, for the Egyptian Mail Steamship Co as the CAIRO (1908).

ROYAL GEORGE (1910)
11146 grt; 460 psrs
545' x 60' x 27' (166.1 x 18.2 x 8.2 m)
3 x turbine engines via triple screw.
Broken up for scrap at Wilhelmshaven in 1922. Ex-Cunard Steamship Co.
Built by Fairfield Shipbuilding & Engineering Co Ltd, Glasgow, for the Egyptian Mail Steamship Co as the HELIOPOLIS (1907).

ROYAL KAWANOE (1990) See DIONISIOS SOLOMOS (1999)

ROYAL MAJESTY (1992) See NORWEGIAN MAJESTY (1997)

ROYAL NIIHAMA (1990)
3982 grt; 600 psrs
72 trailers
381' x 69' x 15' (115.6 x 21 x 4.5 m)
2 x 8-cylinder Pielstick diesel engines via twin screw.
Passenger-cargo ferry owned and operated by the government of the PR of China.
Built by Sanoyas Corporation, Mitsushima.

ROYAL OCEANIC (1985) See THE BIG RED BOAT I (1997)

ROYAL ODYSSEY (1981) See SUN (1998)

ROYAL ODYSSEY (1991) See NORWEGIAN STAR (1997)

ROYAL PACIFIC (1992)
13176 grt; 700 psrs
445' x 71' x 20' (135.6 x 21.5 x 6.1 m)
2 x 10-cylinder MAN diesel engines via twin screw.
Owned by Anchor of the Seas Ltd, Bahamas, she sank quickly on 23 August

1992, with four lives lost and 535 saved, after being rammed amidships at night by the 350 feet (106 m) Taiwanese trawler TE FU No. 51, 12 miles (20 km) south of Port Dickson in the Malacca Straits.
Built by the Cockatoo Island Docks & Engineering Co Pty Ltd, Sydney, for the Australian National Line as the EMPRESS OF AUSTRALIA (1965) at a cost of £2,600,000. Renamed EMPRESS (1985 – Phineas Navigation Ltd, Cyprus).

ROYAL PRINCE (1980) See COPA CASINO (1998)

ROYAL PRINCESS (1984)
44348 grt; 1260 psrs
761' x 96' x 26' (230.6 x 29.1 x 8 m)
4 x 6-cylinder Pielstick DRG diesel engines via twin screw.

Cruise ship owned and operated by P&O Princess Cruises.
Built by Wartsila Shipyards, Helsinki, for the P&O Group at a cost of US$150,000,000.

ROYAL SCOTMAN (1936) See APOLLO (1969)

ROYAL SCOTSMAN (1967) See APOLLO (1969)

ROYAL SEAS (1996) See ISLAND ADVENTURE (1998)

ROYAL STAR (1991)
5067 grt; 294 psrs
367' x 51' x 17'6" (111.2 x 15.5 x 5.3 m)
2 x 7-cylinder Fiat diesel engines via twin screw.
Cruise ship based in Kenya for Starline, Switzerland, as the African Safari Club.
Built by Cantieri Riuniti dell'Adriatico, Trieste, for the Adriatica Line as the passenger-cargo ship SAN GIORGIO (1956). Renamed CITY OF ANDROS (1976 – Cycladic Cruises) and OCEAN ISLANDER (1985 – Ocean Cruise Lines).

ROYAL ULSTERMAN (1936) See SOUNION (1970)

ROYAL VICTORIAN (1994) See PRINCESSE MARGUERITE III (1994)

ROYAL VIKING QUEEN (1992) See SEABOURN LEGEND (1996)

ROYAL VIKING SEA (1973) See NORWEGIAN STAR (1997)

ROYAL VIKING SKY (1973) See HYUNDAI KUMGANG (1998)

ROYAL VIKING STAR (1972) See BLACK WATCH (1996)

ROYAL VIKING SUN (1988) See SEABOURN SUN (1999)

ROZEL (1989) See SCIROCCO (1993)

R SEVEN (2000)
30277 grt; 684 psrs
594' x 84' x 19'6" (180 x 25.5 x 5.9 m)
4 x 12-cylinder Wartsila diesel engines via twin screw.
Cruise ship built by Chantiers de l'Atlantique, St Nazaire, for Renaissance Cruises at a cost of US$180,000,000.

R SIX (2000)
30277 grt; 684 psrs
594' x 84' x 19'6" (180 x 25.5 x 5.9 m)
4 x 12-cylinder Wartsila diesel engines via twin screw.
Cruise ship owned and operated by Renaissance Cruises.
Built by Chantiers de l'Atlantique, St Nazaire, at a cost of US$175,000,000.

R THREE (1999)
30277 grt; 684 psrs
594' x 84' x 19'6" (180 x 25.5 x 5.9 m)
4 x 12-cylinder Wartsila diesel engines via twin screw.
Cruise ship owned and operated by Renaissance Cruises.
Built by Chantiers de l'Atlantique, St Nazaire, at a cost of US$180,000,000.

R TWO (1998)
30277 grt; 684 psrs
594' x 84' x 19'6" (180 x 25.5 x 5.9 m)
4 x 12-cylinder Wartsila diesel engines via twin screw.
Cruise ship owned and operated by Renaissance Cruises.
Built by Chantiers de l'Atlantique, St Nazaire, at a cost of US$180,000,000.

RUAHINE (1891) See ANTONIO LOPEZ (1900)

RUAHINE (1909) See AURIGA (1949)

RUAHINE (1951) See ORIENTAL RIO (1968)

RUAPEHU (1884) See GWALIOR (1900)

RUAPEHU (1901)
7705 grt; 340 psrs
457' x 58' x 26' (139.3 x 17.7 x 7.9 m)
3-cylinder triple expansion engine via single screw.
Broken up for scrap at Savona in 1931.
Built by William Denny & Bros, Dumbarton, for the New Zealand Shipping Co Ltd as the RUAPEHU (1901). Renamed AUSTRALASIAN (1901 – for a five-voyage charter to the Allan Line) and then reverted to RUAPEHU (1901 – New Zealand Shipping Co Ltd).

RUFFORD HALL (1888) See MOTOHIRA MARU No. 2 (1904)

RUGEN (1972)
12289 grt; 1468 psrs
220 cars + 42 trailers
502' x 62' x 18'6" (152.2 x 18.8 x 5.6 m)
4 x 9-cylinder MAN diesel engines via twin screw.

Ice-strengthened passenger-car-cargo ferry owned by DFO and operated by Scandlines Hansa.
Built by VEB Schiffswerft Neptun, Rostock.

RUGIA (1905)
6598 grt; 900 psrs
409' x 53' x 28' (124.8 x 16.1 x 8.5 m)
Bremer Vulkan 4-cylinder quadruple expansion engine via single screw.
Broken up for scrap in Hamburg in 1932.
Built by Bremer Vulkan, Vegesack, for the Hamburg-America Line.

RUNIC (1901) See NEW SEVILLA (1930)

RUS (1988)
12798 grt; 412 psrs
150 cars
462' x 69' x 18'6" (140 x 21 x 5.6 m)
4 x 6-cylinder Zgoda-Sulzer diesel engines via twin screw.

Cruise ship operated by the Far East Shipping Co, Vladivostok.
Built by A Warski, Gdansk, as the KONSTANTIN CHERNENKO (1987).

RUSJ (1904) See RUSS (1904)

RUSJ (1962) See RUSS (1952)

RUSJ (1988) See RUSS (1988)

RUSS (1904)
5099 grt; 1030 psrs
448' x 49' x 34'6" (136.7 x 14.9 x 10.5 m)
Fairfield & Co 5-cylinder triple expansion engine via single screw.
Broken up for scrap in 1927. Ex-Russian Navy.
Built by Fairfield Shipbuilding & Engineering Co Ltd, Glasgow, for North German Lloyd as the LAHN (1888).

RUSS (1917) See HUSO MARU (1938)

RUSS (1952)
12931 grt; 419 psrs
498' x 66' x 25' (150.1 x 20 x 7.6 m)
2 x 8-cylinder diesel engines via twin screw.
Broken up for scrap by Han Sung Salvage Co at Inchon in 1979. Ex-Russian Navy which had claimed her as war reparations, despite the fact that the vessel had been laying on the bed of the Swinemunde harbour since 1945.
Built by Blohm & Voss, Hamburg, for the Hamburg-America Line as the CORDILLERA (1933).

RUSS (1988) See RUS (1988)

RUSSIA (1908) See HUSO MARU (1938)

RUSSIAN (1914)
8825 grt; 60 psrs
513' x 59' x 28' (156.2 x 18 x 8.5 m)
3-cylinder triple expansion engine via single screw.
Owned by Leyland Lines and operated by the White Star Line, she sank on 14 December 1916 after being torpedoed by a German U-boat south of Malta.
Built by Harland & Wolff Ltd, Belfast, for the White Star Line as the VICTORIAN (1895).

RUTH ALEX ANDER (1922)
8135 grt; 525 psrs
439' x 56' x 26'2" (133 x 17 x 7.9 m)
Owned by Admiral Line, she sank on 31 December 1941 after a Japanese bomber attack off Balikpapan, Borneo, which involved the loss of one life.

Built by AG Vulcan, Stettin, for North German Lloyd as the SIERRA CORDOBA (1913). Renamed CALLAO (1917).

RUTHENIA (1913) See CHORAN MARU (1942)

RUYS (1937)
14304 grt; 663 psrs
559' x 72' x 30' (169.4 x 21.8 x 9.1 m)
3 x 8-cylinder Sulzer diesel engines via triple screw.
Broken up for scrap at Kaohsiung in 1968 for a tender figure of US$500,000.
Built by Blohm & Voss, Hamburg, for Royal Interocean Lines.

RUZZUTAK (1928) See MARIA ULYANOVA (1937)

RYE (1963)
8481 grt; 95 psrs
439' x 62' x 34'5" (133 x 18.8 x 10.5 m)
Turbine engine via single screw.
Broken up for scrap in Kobe in 1963 after a successful tender and name change. As the ALCOA CORSAIR, she had been refloated following a collision with the Italian freighter LORENZO MARCCELLO in the Mississippi river, an episode that cost 10 lives. The stricken ship was beached on the river banks near Empire, Louisiana, on 22 October 1960.
Laid down by the Oregon Shipbuilding Corporation for the US Navy as the HARNETT, USS (APA-240) (1945). Renamed ALCOA CORSAIR (1946 – Alcoa Steamship Co).

RYNDAM (1901)
12535 grt; 1998 psrs
length 575' x beam 62' (175.3 x 19 m)
2 x 3-cylinder triple expansion engines via twin screw.
Broken up for scrap at Rotterdam in 1929.
Built by Harland & Wolff Ltd, Belfast, for the Holland America Line. The builder misspelt the ship's name, but Holland America decided to retain the error and did so in all future RYNDAMs.

RYNDAM (1951) See COPA CASINO (1993)

RYNDAM (1968) See COPA CASINO (1993)

RYNDAM (1994)
55451 grt; 1266 psrs
720' x 90' x 25' (218.2 x 27.3 x 7.5 m)
5 x 12-cylinder Sulzer diesel-electric engines via twin screw.

Cruise ship owned by Holland-America, Netherlands, and operated by the Holland-America Line.
Built by Fincantieri, Monfalcone, for the Holland America Line at a cost of US$225,000,000.

SAALE (1886) See MADISON (1923)

SAARBRUCKEN (1923) See TOSCANA (1948)

SABARMATI (1949)
3750 grt; 1250 psrs
342' x 53' x 22' (103.6 x 16.1 x 6.7 m)
3 x Harland & Wolff Ltd SRG turbine engines via single screw.
Built by Harland & Wolff Ltd, Belfast, for the Shipping Corporation of India
as a passenger liner.

SABAUDIA (1941)
29307 grt; 1350 psrs
675' x 83' x 35'4" (204.5 x 25.2 x 10.7 m)
Sulzer 30-cylinder diesel engines via triple screw.
Owned by the Italian Line, she was broken up for scrap at Trieste in 1949. She
had been a troopship and was sunk in Trieste harbour by Allied bombers on 6
July 1944.
Built by Cantieri Riuniti dell'Adriatico, Monfalcone, for the Swedish
American Line as the STOCKHOLM (1940).

SABIJA (1949) See ARMELLE (1968)

SABINE (1898) See UMZINTO (1921)

SABINE (1900)
3329 grt; 160 psrs
314' x 46' x 20'3" (95.2 x 13.9 x 6.2 m)
Delaware River Co 3-cylinder triple expansion engines via single screw.
Broken up for scrap at Philadelphia, Pennsylvania, in 1923. Ex-CH Mallory &
Co.
Built by Delaware River Co, Chester, Pennsylvania, for CH Mallory & Co as
the LEONA (1889).

SABOR (1906) See CHALEUR (1913)

SABRINA (1990)
12521 grt; 694 psrs
616' x 82' x 23' (186.5 x 24.8 x 6.9 m)
2 x 9-cylinder Pielstick diesel engines via single screw.
Passenger ferry operated by Kinkai Yusen Kaisha, Tokyo.
Built by Kanada Karajiri.

SACHEM (1917) See CUBA (1920)

SACRAMENTO (1914) See KOUANG (1929)

SAFARI (1994) See LOBO MARINHO (1996)

SAFE CHRISTINA (1981) See COMMODORE (1999)

SAFINA-E-ABID (1971)
5578 grt; 166 psrs
418' x 57' x 22'6" (127.4 x 17.3 x 6.8 m)
4-cylinder Doxford diesel engine via single screw.
Broken up for scrap as a pilgrim ship at Gadani Beach, Karachi, in 1992. Ex-
Pakistan Shipping Corporation.
Built by Taikoo Dockyard, Hong Kong, for the China Navigation Company as
the ANSHUN (1951).

SAFINA-E-ARAB (1951)
9600 grt; 210 psrs
450' x 57' x 23' (137.1 x 17.4 x 7 m)
Triple expansion engines via twin screw.
Broken up for scrap at Gadani Beach, Karachi, in 1958. Ex-Pan-Islamic
Steamship Co, Karachi.
Built by Harland & Wolff Ltd, Belfast, for the Bibby Line as the
OXFORDSHIRE (1920).

SAFINA-E-ARAB (1962)
8477 grt; 1294 psrs
461' x 60' x 23' (139.7 x 18.3 x 7 m)
5-cylinder Sulzer diesel engine via single screw.
Broken up for scrap as a pilgrim ship in 1996.
Built by Soc Espanola de Construccion Naval SA, Cadiz, for the Pan-Islamic
Steamship Co.

SAFINA-E-ARAFAT (1969) See SAFINA-E-SIAHAT (1970)

SAFINA-E-HUJJAJ (1961)
17528 grt; 393 psrs
634' x 74' x 27'6" (193.2 x 22.6 x 8.4 m)
DRG turbine engines via twin screw.
Broken up for scrap by Chemicec Impex at Gadani Beach, Karachi, in 1976
as a 2,600 passenger pilgrim ship. Ex-Pan-Islamic Steamship Co.
Built by Blohm & Voss, Hamburg, for the Hamburg-America Line as the
POTSDAM (1935). Renamed EMPIRE JEWEL (1945 – British Ministry of
Transport) and EMPIRE FOWEY (1946 – British Ministry of Transport).

SAFINA-E-MURAD (1951)
7474 grt; 248 psrs
442' x 55' x 24'4" (134.7 x 16.7 x 7.4 m)
2 x 4-cylinder quadruple expansion engines via twin screw.
Broken up for scrap in Karachi in 1953. Ex-Pan-Islamic Steamship Co.
Passenger ship laid down for the Woermann Line as the MARIE
WOERMANN (1914) by Reigerstieg Schiffswerft, Hamburg, but work ceased
upon the outbreak of World War One. After the war she was passed to
Rotterdamsche-Lloyd, Holland, and completed as the TJERIMAI (1921).
Renamed EL NIL (1933 – Societe Mise de Navigation Maritime, Egypt), she
acted as HOSPITAL SHIP No 53 (1943 – British Ministry of War and
managed by Furness-Withy).

SAFINA-E-NUSRAT (1953)
7821 grt; 120 psrs
484' x 58' x 30'6" depth (147.6 x 17.6 x 9.3 m)
William Denny & Brothers 3-cylinder triple expansion engine via single
screw.
Broken up for scrap at Karachi in 1957. Ex-Pan-Islamic Steamship Co.
Built by William Denny & Bros, Dumbarton, for the British & Burmese
Steam Navigation Co Ltd as the BURMA (1914). Renamed FLORENTIA
(1949 – Cia de Navegacion Florencia).

SAFINA-E-SIAHAT (1970)
9440 grt; 631 psrs
479' x 62' x 23' (145.2 x 18.8 x 7 m)
2 x 8-cylinder Schneider diesel engines via twin screw.
Broken up for scrap as a pilgrim ship at Gadani Beach, Karachi, in 1971, after
she was gutted by fire. Ex-Pan Islamic Steamship Co Ltd, Karachi.
Built by Pennhoet, St Nazaire, for Nouvelle Cie de Paquetbots as the
GENERAL LECLERC (1951). Renamed GENERAL LECLERCQUE (1969
– Cie Nouvelle de Paquetbots) and SAFINA-E-ARAFAT (1969 – Pan Islamic
Steamship Co, Karachi).

SAGA (1940) See NESSEBAR (1964)

SAGA (1966) See CAPTAIN ZAMAN I (1998)

SAGA (1972) See CAPTAIN ZAMAN II (1998).

SAGAFJORD (1965) See SAGA ROSE (1997)

SAGA ROSE (1997)
25147 grt; 588 psrs
620' x 82' x 27' (189 x 25 x 8.2 m)
2 x 9-cylinder Sulzer diesel engines via twin screw.
Cruise ship for Saga Holidays International, UK.
Built by Societe des Forges et Chantiers de la Mediterranee, Toulon, for the
Norwegian America Line as the SAGAFJORD (1965) at a cost of
US$20,000,000. Renamed GRIPSHOLM (1996 – Transocean Tours,
Bremen).

SAGA STAR (1981) See SAGA STAR (1993)

SAGA STAR (1993)
17672 grt; 181 psrs
100 trailers
482' x 79' x 21' (146 x 24 x 6.3 m)
4 x 8-cylinder Lindholmen-Pielstick diesel engines via twin screw.

Chartered to the TT-Line.
Built by Kalmar, Gotaverken, for Sweferry as the passenger-cargo ferry SAGA STAR (1981). Renamed GIROLATA (1989 – Cie Meridionale, Marseilles).

SAGA WIND (1984) See SEA WIND (1989)

SAGITTAIRE (1938) See OCEANIC RELIANCE (1956)

SAGUACHE (1919) See CANTUARIA (1940)

SAIDIEH (1907)
3200 grt; 170 psrs
350' x 40' x 23'4" (106.1 x 12.1 x 7.1 m)
J & J Thompson 3-cylinder triple expansion engines via single screw.
Owned by the Quebec Steamship Co, she sank on 1 June 1915 after being torpedoed by a German U-boat six miles (10 km) north-east of Elbow Bay.
Built by William Denny & Bros, Dumbarton, for the Union Line as the PRETORIA (1878).

SAINT:
For all ships commencing with the abbreviated form 'ST' or the complete spelling of 'SAINT' refer under SAINT.

ST. ALBANS (1910)
4119 grt; 99 psrs
367' x 47' x 24' (111.2 x 14.2 x 7.3 m)
Workman, Clark 3-cylinder triple expansion engine via single screw.
Broken up for scrap at Yokohama in 1931. Ex-Australasian United Steam Navigation Co Ltd.
Built by Workman, Clark & Co Ltd, Belfast, for the Eastern & Australian Steamship Co.

ST. ANSELM (1980) See ISLA DE BOTAFOC (1999)

SAINT AUGUSTIN (1929) See CAPO LENA (1935)

ST. BRENDAN (1985) See MOBY VINCENT (1990)

ST. CHRISTOPHER (1981) See IBN BATOUTA (1998)

ST. CLAIR (1960) See AL KHAIRAT (1977)

ST. CLAIR (1977) See NUSA PERJUANG (1992)

ST. CLAIR (1982) See AL SALAM 89 (1992)

ST. CLAIR (1991)
8696 grt; 1000 psrs
160 cars

389' x 61' x 17' (118 x 18.5 x 5.1 m)
2 x 12-cylinder MAN diesel engines via twin screw.
Passenger-car ferry owned and operated by P&O Scottish Ferries following short-term charter Truckline/Brittany Ferries in 1991–92.
Built by Schichau Seebeckwerft Shipyards, Bremerhaven, for GT Ferries, Gedser, as the TRAVEMUNDE (1971). Renamed NJEGOS (1980 – Prekookeanska Plovidba, Jugoslavia), TREGASTEL (1985 – Sally Line) and TREG (1991 – P&O Scottish Ferries Ltd).

ST. CLAIR II (1977) See AL KHAIRAT (1977)

ST. CLAIR II (1992) See NUSA PEJUANG (1992)

SAINT COLUM I (1982) See EXPRESS POSEIDON (1999)

SAINT COLUMB (1982) See EXPRESS POSEIDON (1999)

ST. COLUMBA (1977) See EXPRESS AFRODITE (1997)

ST. DAVID (1947) See HOLYHEAD (1970)

ST. DAVID (1980) See STENA CALEDONIA (1990)

ST. DOMINGO (1904) See SUSANNA II (1919)

ST. DOMINGO (1905)
4324 grt; 205 psrs
384' x 36' x 20' (92.1 x 10.9 x 6.1 m)
Barclay Curl 3-cylinder triple expansion engines via single screw.
Broken up for scrap in 1937.
Built by Barclay Curle & Co Ltd, Glasgow, for Castle Mail Packets Co Ltd as the RAGLAN CASTLE (1897), although publicised under the name DUNLUCE CASTLE (1897).

ST. EDMUND (1974) See SCIROCCO (1993)

SAINT ELOI (1929) See ARAUCO (1935)

SAINT ELOI (1975) See MOBY LOVE II (1998)

ST. EZEKIEL MORENO (1996)
7057 grt; 670 psrs
45 cars + 104 trailers
465' x 74' x 18' (140.9 x 22.4 x 5.5 m)
2 x 18-cylinder Mitsubishi-MAN diesel engines via twin screw.
Passenger-car-cargo ferry owned and operated by Negros Navigation, Iloilo, following acquisition for US$12,000,000.
Built by Hayashikane Shipbuilding, Shimonoseki, for Fuji Ferry KK, Tokyo, as the ISE MARU (1973). Renamed MIYASAKI (1978 – Nippon Car Ferry KK, Tokyo).

ST. GEORGE (1968) See TEXAS TREASURE (2000)

SAINT GERMAIN (1951)
3094 grt; 1000 psrs
25 cars + 36 rail coaches
380' x 61' x 13'6" (115.2 x 18.5 x 4.1 m)
2 x 9-cylinder B+W diesel engines via twin screw.
Passenger-car-train ferry operated by French State Rail (SNCF).
Built by Elsinore Shipyards, Elsinore.

ST. HELENA (1977) See INDOCEANIQUE (1994)

ST. HELENA (1990)
6767 grt; 132 psrs
56 TEUs
347' x 63' x 20' (105 x 19 x 6 m)
2 x 6-cylinder Mirrlees diesel engines via twin screw.
Passenger-cargo ship operated by Curnow Shipping Ltd, UK.
Built by A & P Appledore Ltd, Aberdeen, at a cost of £19,000,000.

ST. HELENA ISLAND (1990) See INDOCEANIQUE (1994)

SAINT HUGO (1912) See BEPPE (1932)

SAINT JOHN (1932) See RESCUE, USS (AH-18) (1945)

ST. JOSEPH THE WORKER (1995)
6090 grt; 500 psrs
500' x 75' x 17' (151.5 x 22.8 x 5.1 m)
2 x 18-cylinder MAN diesel engines via twin screw.
Passenger ferry owned and operated by Negros Navigation Co Inc.
Built by Kanda Zosensho KK for Hankyu Ferry, Tokyo, as the HANKYU No. 24 (1976).

ST. JULIEN (1989) See NURA NOVA (1999)

SAINT KILLIAN (1978) See MEDINA STAR (1999)

SAINT KILLIAN II (1982) See MEDINA STAR (1999)

SAINT-LAURENT (1905)
5607 grt; 712 psrs
392' x 51' x 28'8" depth (119.5 x 15.4 x 8.7 m)
Chantiers et Ateliers de St Nazaire 3-cylinder triple expansion engine via single screw.
Purposely sunk by torpedo in Malta harbour on 5 February 1917 when she caught fire with her holds crammed with explosives.
Built by Chantiers de Normandie, Grand Quevilly, for the French Line.

ST. LAWRENCE (1927) See PASSENGER No. 2 (1966)

SAINT LAWRENCE VICTORY (1945) See ARMELLE (1968)

ST. LOUIS (1895) See ST. LOUIS (1920)

ST. LOUIS (1895) See NASHVILLE (1917)

ST. LOUIS (1920)
11629 grt; 1340 psrs
554' x 63' x 29'5" (168.8 x 19.2 x 8.9 m)
William Cramp & Sons 12-cylinder quadruple expansion engines via twin screw.
Broken up for scrap at Genoa in 1924 after refloating her in Hoboken, New Jersey, where she had caught fire and been scuttled on 4 April 1920. Ex-US government.
Built by William Cramp & Sons, Philadelphia, Pennsylvania, for the American Line as the ST. LOUIS (1895). Renamed LOUISVILLE, USS (1917 – US Navy).

ST. LOUIS (1928)
16732 grt; 973 psrs
544' x 72' x 42'1" depth (164.8 x 21.8 x 12.8 m)
2 x 12-cylinder MAN diesel engines via twin screw.
Broken up for scrap at Bremerhaven in 1952 after a conversion to a floating restaurant in Hamburg in 1947.
Built by Bremer Vulcan, Bremen, for the Hamburg-America Line.

ST. LOUIS (1969)
18362 grt; 2000 psrs
685' x 78' x 30'1" (207.6 x 23.6 x 9.1 m)
2 x Kaiser Corporation DRG turbine engines via single screw.
Broken up as a container ship for scrap at Kaohsiung in 1987. Ex-Sea Land Service.
Built by the Kaiser Corporation, Richmond, California, for the US Maritime Commission as the Class C4-S-A1 troop transport GENERAL M. L. HERSEY, USS (AP-148) (1944). Reclassified as the GENERAL M. L. HERSEY, USAT (1946 – US Army) and as the GENERAL M. L. HERSEY, USNS (T-AP-148) (1950 – US Navy). Renamed as the container ship PITTSBURGH (1968).

SAINT LUC (1929) See BELLA (1956)

ST. LUCIE (1991) See TROPIC SEA (2000)

ST. MELONS (1937) See TOZAN MARU (1937)

SAINT NICHOLAS (1918)
4997 grt; 98 psrs

400' x 48' x 22' (121.9 x 14.6 x 6.7 m)
Triple expansion engines via twin screw.
Broken up for scrap at Brest after towing her from nearby Benodet where, as a French Navy auxiliary vessel, she had stranded herself during the initial tow from Rochefort to Brest.
Built x Alexander Stephen & Sons, Glasgow, for the P&O Line at a cost of £51,377 as the MAZAGON (1894). Renamed TEIKOKU MARU (1913 – K Yamashita).

ST. NICHOLAS (1983) See NORMANDY (1997)

ST. PATRICK (1948) See AGAPITOS I (1973)

SAINT PATRICK (1973) See EXPRESS POSEIDON (1999)

SAINT PATRICK II (1982) See VILLE DE SETE (2000)

ST. PAUL (1895) See ST. PAUL (1919)

ST. PAUL (1919)
11629 grt; 1370 psrs
554' x 63' x 29'5" (168.8 x 19.2 x 8.9 m)
William Cramp & Sons 12-cylinder quadruple expansion engines via twin screw.
Broken up for scrap at Wilhelmshaven in 1923. Ex-American Line passenger liner.
Built by William Cramp & Sons, Philadelphia, Pennsylvania, for the American Line as the ST. PAUL (1895). Renamed KNOXVILLE, USS (1914 – US Navy).

ST. PAULIA (1971)
5956 grt; 1010 psrs
389' x 68' x 19' (118 x 20.5 x 5.7 m)
2 x 12-cylinder Pielstick via twin screw.
Passenger ferry operated by Nippon Car Ferry KK., Tokyo.
Built by Nippon Kokan KK., Shimitzu.

ST. PETERSBURG (1892) See SOVIETSKAYA ROSSIJA (1921)

ST. PETER THE APOSTLE (1993)
6951 grt; 950 psrs
500' x 74' x 17' (151.5 x 22.8 x 5.1 m)
2 x 18-cylinder MAN-Pielstick diesel engines via twin screw.
Passenger ferry owned and operated by Negros Navigation Co Inc.
Built by Kanda Zosensho KK, for Hankyu Ferry Co, Tokyo, as the HANKYU No. 32 (1976).

SAINT RENE (1921) See CAPO LENA (1935)

SAINT ROCH (1929) See MADALI (1948)

ST. SUNNIVA (1987)
6350 grt; 407 psrs
200 cars
343' x 62' x 15' (104 x 18.9 x 4.6 m)
2 x 12-cylinder Stork-Werkspoor diesel engines via twin screw.

Passenger-car ferry owned and operated by P&O Scottish Ferries, UK
Built by Helsingor Shipbuilding, Helsingor, for Fred Olsen Lines as the DJURSLAND (1972). Renamed LASSE II (1974 – Jydsk Faergefart AS) and nf PANTHER (1979 – Townsend Thoresen, European Ferries Group).

SAINT SUNNIVA (1988) See BENCHIJIGUA (1994)

SAKHALIN (1930) See KRASNOYARSK (1939)

SAKHALIN No. 1 (1973)
9305 grt; 72 psrs
26 railway wagons + trailers
419' x 67' x 22' (127 x 20.3 x 6.6 m)
6 x 10-cylinder Fairbanks-Morse diesel engines via twin screw.
Ice-strengthened passenger-car train ferry operated on the Japan–Sakhalin Island service, since 26 April 1995, by a consortium of Japanese shipping companies with the support of both the Russian and Japanese governments. Built by Yantar Yard, Kaliningrad, for the Sakhalin Shipping Co, Kholmsk.

SAKHALIN No. 2 (1974)
9305 grt; 72 psrs
26 railway wagons + trailers
419' x 67' x 22' (127 x 20.3 x 6.6 m)
6 x 10-cylinder Fairbanks-Morse diesel engines via twin screw.
Ice-strengthened passenger-car train ferry operated on the Japan–Sakhalin Island service, since 26 April 1995, by a consortium of Japanese shipping companies with the support of both the Russian and Japanese governments. Built by Yantar Yard, Kaliningrad, for the Sakhalin Shipping Co, Kholmsk.

SAKHALIN No. 3 (1974)
9305 grt; 72 psrs
26 railway wagons + trailers
419' x 67' x 22' (127 x 20.3 x 6.6 m)
6 x 10-cylinder Fairbanks-Morse diesel engines via twin screw.
Ice-strengthened passenger-car train ferry operated on the Japan–Sakhalin Island service, since 26 April 1995, by a consortium of Japanese shipping companies with the support of both the Russian and Japanese governments. Built by Yantar Yard, Kaliningrad, for the Sakhalin Shipping Co, Kholmsk.

SAKHALIN No. 4 (1975)
9305 grt; 72 psrs
26 railway wagons + trailers
419' x 67' x 22' (127 x 20.3 x 6.6 m)
6 x 10-cylinder Fairbanks-Morse diesel engines via twin screw.
Ice-strengthened passenger-car train ferry operated on the Japan–Sakhalin Island service, since 26 April 1995, by a consortium of Japanese shipping companies with the support of both the Russian and Japanese governments. Built by Yantar Yard, Kaliningrad, for the Sakhalin Shipping Co, Kholmsk.

SAKHALIN No. 5 (1976)
9305 grt; 72 psrs
26 railway wagons + trailers
419' x 67' x 22' (127 x 20.3 x 6.6 m)
6 x 10-cylinder Fairbanks-Morse diesel engines via twin screw.
Ice-strengthened passenger-car train ferry operated on the Japan–Sakhalin Island service, since 26 April 1995, by a consortium of Japanese shipping companies with the support of both the Russian and Japanese governments. Built by Yantar Yard, Kaliningrad, for the Sakhalin Shipping Co, Kholmsk.

SAKHALIN No. 6 (1982)
9305 grt; 72 psrs
26 railway wagons + trailers
419' x 67' x 22' (127 x 20.3 x 6.6 m)
6 x 10-cylinder Fairbanks-Morse diesel engines via twin screw.
Ice-strengthened passenger-car train ferry operated on the Japan–Sakhalin Island service, since 26 April 1995, by a consortium of Japanese shipping companies with the support of both the Russian and Japanese governments. Built by Yantar Yard, Kaliningrad, for the Sakhalin Shipping Co, Kholmsk.

SAKHALIN No. 7 (1982)
9305 grt; 72 psrs
26 railway wagons + trailers
419' x 67' x 22' (127 x 20.3 x 6.6 m)
6 x 10-cylinder Fairbanks-Morse diesel engines via twin screw.
Ice-strengthened passenger-car train ferry operated on the Japan–Sakhalin Island service, since 26 April 1995, by a consortium of Japanese shipping companies with the support of both the Russian and Japanese governments. Built by Yantar Yard, Kaliningrad, for the Sakhalin Shipping Co, Kholmsk.

SAKHALIN No. 8 (1985)
9305 grt; 72 psrs
26 railway wagons + trailers
419' x 67' x 22' (127 x 20.3 x 6.6 m)
6 x 10-cylinder Fairbanks-Morse diesel engines via twin screw.
Ice-strengthened passenger-car train ferry operated on the Japan–Sakhalin Island service, since 26 April 1995, by a consortium of Japanese shipping companies with the support of both the Russian and Japanese governments. Built by Yantar Yard, Kaliningrad, for the Sakhalin Shipping Co, Kholmsk.

SAKHALIN No. 9 (1986)
9305 grt; 72 psrs
26 railway wagons + trailers
419' x 67' x 22' (127 x 20.3 x 6.6 m)
6 x 10-cylinder Fairbanks-Morse diesel engines via twin screw.
Ice-strengthened passenger-car train ferry operated on the Japan–Sakhalin Island service, since 26 April 1995, by a consortium of Japanese shipping companies with the support of both the Russian and Japanese governments. Built by Yantar Yard, Kaliningrad, for the Sakhalin Shipping Co, Gdansk.

SAKURA (1971) See ZHI LOU LIN (1982)

SAKURA MARU (1962) See ZHI LOU LIN (1982)

SALAH-EL-DIN (1960) See MERCANTILE VICTORY (1963)

SALAM (1999)
11110 grt; 1500 psrs
212 cars + 28 rail wagons
475' x 58' x 19'6" (144 x 17.6 x 5.9 m)
8 x 12-cylinder MTU diesel engines via twin screw.

Broken up for scrap in 1999. Ex-Alcyon Shipping Co Ltd, Athens.
Built by Werft Nobiskrug, Rendsburg, for Deutsche Fahrrgesselschaft Ostee, Puttgarden, as the DEUTSCHLAND (1972). Renamed EL SALAM 97 (1998 – El Salam Shipping & Trading Establishment).

SALAMIS (1899) See KAMARIMA (1919)

SALAMIS GLORY (1996)
10440 grt; 413 psrs
492' x 62' x 18'6" (150 x 19 x 5.6 m)
2 x 7-cylinder Krupp-B+W diesel engines via twin screw.
Owned and operated as a cruise ship by Salamis Lines, Cyprus, following its purchase from the collapsed Regency Cruises for US$3,500,000.
Built by Brodogradiliste Uljanik, Pula, for Cia Nacional de Navegacao Costeira Autarquia Federal, Rio de Janeiro, as the ANNA NERY (1962). Renamed DANAOS (1978 – Kavounides Shipping Co), CONSTELLATION (1978 – Kavounides Shipping Co), MORNING STAR (1992 – A Lelakis) and REGENT SPIRIT (1993 – Regency Cruises).

SALAMIS STAR (2000)
14105 grt; 1185 psrs
495' x 76' x 16'6" (150 x 22.9 x 5 m)
2 x 16- cylinder MAN diesel engines via twin screw.
Passenger ferry owned and operated by Salamis Lines, Cyprus.
Built by Kanda Zosensho KK, Kobe, for Hankyu Ferry KK, Shimonoseki, as the FERRY AKASHI (1972). Renamed DAME M (1994 – Marlines).

SALAVERRY (1917) See CHLOE (1924)

SALEM EXPRESS (1989)
4771 grt; 1200 psrs

170 cars

377' x 59' x 15'6" (114.2 x 17.8 x 4.7 m)

4 x 8-cylinder Pielstick diesel engines via twin screw.

Passenger-car ferry owned and operated by Samatour, Alexandria, she sank on 15 December 1991, with the loss of 464 lives, after striking coral reefs in the Red Sea off the Egyptian port of Safaga, 360 miles (600 kilometres) south of Suez.

Built by Forges et Chantiers de la Mediterranee, La Seyne, for Cie Generale Transatlantique as the FRED SCAMARONI (1965). Renamed NUITS ST. GEORGE (1980 – Dunkerque Ramsgate Ferries Ltd, Marseilles), LORD SINAI (1982 – Lord Maritime Enterprise) and AL TAHRA (1988 – Lord Maritime Enterprise).

SALEM FLOWER (1993) See AL SALAM TABA I (1998)

SALEM FLOWER (1997)

6145 grt; 1500 psrs

120 cars

366' x 57' x 14'6" (111 x 17.2 x 4.4 m)

2 x 7-cylinder diesel engines via twin screw.

Passenger-car ferry operated by Samatour Shipping Co, Alexandria.

Built by Helsingor Vaerft, Helsingor, for the Danish State Railways as the passenger-train ferry PRINSESSE BENEDIKTE (1959). Renamed VICTORY I (1988 – Navsimar), AL NASR I (1993 – International Maritime Centre), CARLA (1995), PHOENICIAN SEA (1995), SALEM MOON (1995 – owned by Salem Moon SA and operated by Samatour Shipping Co, Alexandria).

SALEM MOON (1995) See SALEM FLOWER (1998)

SALLY ALBATROSS (1986) See SUPERSTAR TAURUS (2000)

SALLY ALBATROSS (1992) See SUPERSTAR TAURUS (2000)

SALLY CARAVELLE (1990) See COLUMBUS CARAVELLE (1994)

SALLY CLIPPER (1990) See WORLD DISCOVERER II (2000)

SALLY EXPRESS (1983) See BOUGHAZ (1988)

SALLY SKY (1988) See LARKSPUR (1999)

SALLY STAR (1987) See PENELOPE A (2000)

SALON (1939) See PRIMORJE (1945)

SALOPIAN, HMS (1939)

10549 grt; 276 psrs

502' x 60' x 29'1" (152.1 x 18.2 x 8.8 m)

Sulzer 16-cylinder diesel engines via twin screw.

Operated by the British Royal Navy, she sank on 13 May 1941 after being hit by five torpedoes from the German U-98 400 miles south-east of Cape Farewell, Greenland.

Built by Fairfield Shipbuilding & Engineering Co Ltd, Glasgow, for the Bibby Line as the SHROPSHIRE (1926).

SALSETTE (1908)

5842 grt; 220 psrs

440' x 53' x 20' (134.1 x 16.2 x 6.1 m)

2 x quadruple expansion engines via twin screw.

Sank within 50 minutes, with 15 lives lost, on 20 July 1917 after being torpedoed by the German U-40 in the English Channel, south-west of Portland Bill.

Built by Caird & Co, Greenock, for the P&O Line at a cost of £210,689.

SALTA (1949)

12053 grt; 1379 psrs

492' x 70' x 29'5" (149.1 x 21.2 x 8.9 m)

2 x Allis-Chalmers DRG turbine engines via single screw.

Broken up for scrap as a passenger liner at Buenos Aires in 1966. Ex-Dodero Line.

Built by the Seattle-Tacoma Shipbuilding Corporation for the US Navy as the auxiliary aircraft carrier JAMAICA, USS (1942). Renamed SHAH, HMS (1943 – British Royal Navy).

SALVIA MARU (1972) See TELAGA FITMA (2000)

SALVIA MARU (1992) See TELAGA FITMA (2000)

SALVIA MARU No. 2 (1992) See SALVIA MARU (1992)

SALWEEN (1938)

7063 grt; 74 psrs

462' x 59' x 27' (140 x 17.9 x 8.2 m)

Turbine engine via single screw.

Broken up for scrap at Hong Kong in 1962.

Built by William Denny & Bros, Dumbarton, for the Henderson Line as a passenger-cargo ship.

SAMA 1 (2000)

3783 grt; 750 psrs

80 cars

361' x 50' x 15' (109.4 x 15.2 x 4.5 m)

2 x 12-cylinder Pielstick diesel engines via twin screw.

Broken up for scrap at Aliaga in 2000 after being acquired by Samos Icaria, Piraeus, for DM16,000,000, and operated by Arkadia Lines as a passenger-car cargo ferry.

Built by Hanseatische Werft GmbH, Hamburg, for the TT-Line as the NILS HOLGERSSON (1962). Renamed GOSTA BERLING (1967 – TT-Line), ESCAPADE (1967 – Svenska Lloyd), GOSTA BERLING (1975 – TT-Line), MARY POPPINS (1975 – TT-Line & Shoham Cyprus Ltd) and SAMAINA (1976).

SAMAINA (1976) See SAMA 1 (2000)

SAMALA (1958)

6982 grt; 100 psrs

416' x 60' x 24'1" (126 x 18.2 x 7.3 m)

2 x General Electric turbo-electric engines via twin screw.

Broken up for scrap at Kaohsiung in 1964. Ex-Elders & Fyffes.

Built by the Bethlehem Steel Corporation, Quincy, Massachusetts, for the United Fruit Steamship Co as the QUIRIGUA (1932). Renamed MIZAR, USS (AF-12) (1941 – US Navy) and QUIRIGUA (1946 – United Fruit Steamship Co).

SAMANTHA (1983) See SEA (1996)

SAMARA (1912)

6000 grt; 100 psrs

446' x 49' x 29'9" (135.2 x 14.8 x 9 m)

Triple expansion engines via twin screw.

Built by Harland & Wolff Ltd, Belfast, for the Bibby Line as the passenger-cargo liner STAFFORDSHIRE (1894).

SAMARIA (1921)

19848 grt; 2200 psrs

624' x 74' x 32'8" (189.1 x 22.4 x 9.9 m)

6 x Cammell Laird DRG turbine engines via twin screw.

Broken up for scrap at Inverkeithing in 1956 for a tender figure of £317,500.

Built by Cammell Laird & Co Ltd, Birkenhead, for the Cunard Line as a passenger ship.

SAMLAND (1906) See SAMLAND (1913)

SAMLAND (1913)

9748 grt; 1900 psrs

510' x 58' x 28'11" (155.4 x 17.6 x 8.5 m)
New York Shipbuilding Co 6-cylinder triple expansion engines via twin screw.
Broken up as a cargo ship for scrap in 1931. Ex-Red Star Line.
Built by the New York Shipbuilding Co, Camden, New Jersey, for the White Star Line as the passenger liner MISSISSIPPI (1902). Renamed SAMLAND (1906 – Red Star Line) and BELGIC (1911 – White Star Line).

SAMOS SKY (1976) See THE EMERALD (1996)

SAMPAGUITA (1978) See REYNA FILIPINA (1978)

SAMPIERO CORSO (1936) See FORTUNE MARINER (1968)

SAMPO (1960)
3540 grt; 150 psrs
250' x 58' x 20'6" (75 x 17.4 x 6.2 m)
4 x 5-cylinder Wartsila-Sulzer diesel engines via twin screw.
Cruising ice-breaker vessel owned and operated by Yaanmurtaja Kemi Icebreaker Ltd, Kemi.
Built by Sandvikens, Helsinki.

SAMSUN (1951)
6543 grt; 426 psrs
433' x 57' x 19' (131.2 x 17.4 x 5.8 m)
4 x DRG turbine engines via twin screw.
Broken up for scrap in Aliaga in 1983.
Built by Ansaldo, Genoa, for Turkish Maritime Lines.

SAMSUN (1985)
10583 grt; 598 psrs
418' x 64' x 17'6" (126.7 x 19.4 x 5.3 m)
4 x 6-cylinder Zgoda-Sulzer diesel engines via twin screw.
Passenger-cargo ship operated by Turkish Maritime Lines, but for sale as of 31 December 2000.
Built by Stocznia Szczecinska, Szczecin.

SAMUEL CHASE, USS (AP-56) (1942) See SAMUEL CHASE, USS (APA-26) (1942)

SAMUEL CHASE, USS (APA-26) (1942)
7997 grt; 100 psrs
465' x 70' x 27'4" depth (140.9 x 21.2 x 8.3 m)
2 x General Electric DRG turbine engines via single screw.
Broken up for scrap at Brownsville, Texas, in 1973. Ex-MARAD.
Built by Ingalls Shipbuilding Corporation, Pascagoula, for American South African Line Inc as the AFRICAN METEOR (1941). Renamed SAMUEL CHASE, USS (AP-56) (1942 – US Navy).

SAN ANDRES (1966) See ELIZABETH A (1967)

SANDEFJORD (1992)
5678 grt; 1135 psrs
65 cars
328' x 60' x 14'6" (99.5 x 18.3 x 4.4 m)
2 x 12-cylinder Pielstick diesel engines via twin screw.

Passenger-car ferry owned and operated by Color Line.
Laid down by Orenstein Koppel & Luebecker, Lubeck, for the Swedish Kalmar Line as the TERJE VIGEN (1965). Launched as the VIKING III (1965 – Townsend Thoresen Ltd), SCANDINAVIA (1986 – Da-No Linjen, Oslo) and FENNO STAR (1990 – Jakob Line).

SAN FERNANDO (1896) See FELTRIA (1916)

SAN FRANCESCO DI PAOLA (1964) See PRINCESS CHRISTINE (1998)

SAN FRANCISCO (1948) See DJAKARTA RAYA (1952)

SAN GENNARO (1917) See COLOMBO (1921)

SAN GEORGIO (1965)
4755 grt; 800 psrs
367' x 51' x 17'6" (111.2 x 15.5 x 5.3 m)
2 x 7-cylinder Fiat diesel engines via twin screw.
Built by Cantieri Riuniti dell'Adriatico for Adriatica Lines.

SANG FAJAR (1975)
3155 grt; 400 psrs
323' x 47' x 18' (97.9 x 14.2 x 5.5 m)
3-cylinder Doxford diesel engine via twin screw.
Owned by Malaysian Shipping Corporation, Penang.
Built by A & J Inglis Ltd, Glasgow, for the China Navigation Co Ltd as the SOOCHOW (1947). Renamed KOTO RATU (1975 – Pacific International Lines (Pte) Ltd, Singapore).

SAN GIORGIO (1907) See NAPOLI (1921)

SAN GIORGIO (1947)
8955 grt; 640 psrs
460' x 59' x 25' (140.2 x 18 x 7.6 m)
Geared turbine engines via twin screw.
Broken up for scrap as a passenger-cargo liner at Savona in 1953. Ex-Lloyd Triestino.
Built by Cantieri Navigation Franco Tosi, Taranto, for Lloyd Sabaudo as the cargo vessel PRINCIPESSA GIOVANNA (1923).

SAN GIORGIO (1956) See ROYAL STAR (1991)

SAN GIOVANNI (1907) See PALERMO (1921)

SAN GIOVANNI BATTISTA (1937)
5686 grt; 92 psrs
400' x 52' x 28'5" (121.2 x 15.8 x 8.6 m)
D & W Henderson 3-cylinder triple expansion engine via single screw.
Owned by Cia Ligure di Navigazione, she sank on 19 January 1943 after being scuttled by the Italians at Tripoli.
Built by D & W Henderson, Glasgow, for the Harrison-Rennie Line as the passenger-cargo ship INGOMA (1913).

SAN GIOVANNINO (1949)
10048 grt; 180 psrs
509' x 60' x 29'6" (155.1 x 18.1 x 8.9 m)
Workman, Clark 6-cylinder triple expansion engines via twin screw.
Owned by Cia de Navigazione Florencia SA, Panama, she was broken up for scrap at La Spezia in 1953.
Built by Workman, Clark & Co Ltd, Belfast, for the Blue Funnel Line as the passenger-cargo liner ASCANIUS (1910).

SAN GIUSTO (1918)
8474 grt; 1292 psrs
503' x 58' (152.4 x 17.6 m)
6-cylinder triple expansion engines via triple screw.
Broken up for scrap as a passenger liner at Trieste in 1924. Ex-Cosulich Line.
Laid down by AG Vulcan, Stettin, for the Hamburg-America Line as the VENETIA (1890), but completed as the FURST BISMARCK (1891). Renamed DON (1904 – Russian government), MOSKVA (1906 – Russian Volunteer Fleet Association) and GAEA (1913 – Austrian Navy).

SANGOLA (1947)
8647 grt; 1415 psrs
479' x 63' x 26' (145.2 x 19.1 x 7.9 m)
Doxford 8-cylinder diesel engines via twin screw.
Broken up for scrap in Japan in 1963.
Built by Barclay, Curle & Company, Glasgow, for the British India Line.

SAN GUGLIELMO (1911)
8344 grt; 2425 psrs

490' x 56' x 33'5" depth (148.5 x 17 x 10.2 m)
2 x D & W Henderson 6-cylinder triple expansion engines via twin screw.
Sank on 8 January 1918 after being attacked by the deck gun of the German U-63 and then a torpedo, near Loano in the Gulf of Genoa.
Built by D & W Henderson & Co, Glasgow, for Soc Italia di Navigazione, Genoa, as a passenger liner.

SAN JACINTO (1904)
6069 grt; 131 psrs
380' x 53' x 24'7" (115.2 x 16 x 7.5 m)
Delaware River Co 6-cylinder triple expansion engines via twin screw.
Sank on 22 April 1942 after being torpedoed 300 miles (500 km) south-west of Bermuda.
Built by the Delaware River Co, Chester, Pennsylvania, for the Mallory Steamship Co.

SAN JORGE (1938)
10006 grt; 60 psrs
542' x 62' x 35' depth (164.2 x 18.8 x 10.6 m)
Guttehoffnungshutte 3-cylinder quadruple expansion engine via single screw.
Broken up for scrap at Gadani Beach in 1981. Ex-Argentinian government as a tanker.
Built by Blohm & Voss, Hamburg, for Yacimientos Petroliferos Fiscales, Buenos Aires, as a tanker-passenger vessel.

SAN JUAN (1975)
18455 grt; 2000 psrs
695' x 79' x 30'4" (211.8 x 23.9 x 9.2 m)
2 x Westinghouse DRG turbine engines via single screw.
Broken up in 1989. Ex-Puerto Rico Maritime Shipping Authority.
Built by the Kaiser Corporation, Richmond, California, for the US Maritime Commission as the Class C4-S-A1 troop carrier GENERAL C. H. MUIR (AP-142) (1945). Renamed as the container ship CHICAGO (1968 – Sea Land Services).

SAN LORENZO (1920)
6576 grt; 2373 psrs
417' x 54' x 21'3" (126.4 x 16.4 x 6.5 m)
Newport News 8-cylinder quadruple expansion engines via twin screw.
Broken up for scrap at Trieste in 1934.
Built by Newport News Shipbuilding, Newport News, Virginia, for the Texas Steamship Co as the BRAZOS (1907).

SAN LORENZO (1951)
11674 grt; 60 psrs
558' x 68' x 37' depth (170 x 20.7 x 11.2 m)
2 x 5-cylinder B+W diesel engines via single screw.
Operating as an oil tanker-passenger ship for Yacimientos Petroliferos Fiscales, Buenos Aires.
Built by P Smit Jr, Rotterdam, for YPF, Buenos Aires.

SAN LORENZO RUIZ (1996)
6826 grt; 2000 psrs
96 cars
436' x 75' x 18' (132.1 x 22.7 x 5.5 m)
2 x 16-cylinder Pielstick diesel engines via twin screw.
Passenger-car ferry purchased for US$12,000,000 by Negros Navigation Co Inc.
Built by Nipponkai Heavy Industries Co Ltd, Toyama, for Taiheiyo Enkai Ferry KK, Nagoya, as the AL NASL (1973). Renamed EBINO (1976 – Sea.Com.Car, Japan).

SAN MARCO (1956) See CITY OF MYKONOS (1977)

SAN MARCO (1965)
4755 grt; 800 psrs
367' x 51' x 17'6" (111.2 x 15.5 x 5.3 m)
2 x 7-cylinder Fiat diesel engines via twin screw.
Built by Cantieri Riuniti dell'Adriatico, Trieste, for Adriatica Lines.

SAN MARINO (1962) See ORIENTAL FALCON (1963)

SANNIO (1906) See NAPOLI (1913)

SAN PAULO (1913) See UMBRIA (1914)

SAN PEDRO (1970)
18420 grt; 380 psrs
684' x 78' x 30'1" (207.3 x 23.6 x 9.1 m)
2 x Joshua Hendy Ironworks DRG turbine engines via single screw.
Broken up for scrap at Kaohsiung in 1988. Ex-Sea Land Services.
Built by the Kaiser Corporation Inc, Vancouver, Washington, for the US Maritime Commission as a Class C4-S-A3 troopship MARINE CARDINAL (1945). Renamed as the container ship BALTIMORE (1967 – Sea Land Services).

SAN ROSSORE (1916) See JANUA (1928)

SAN SERGIO (1952)
9780 grt; 420 psrs
507' x 62' x 26'3" (153.6 x 18.8 x 8 m)
Stablimento Tecnico 12-cylinder diesel engines via twin screw.
Built by Stablimento Tecnico, Trieste, for Lloyd Triestino as the REMO (1927). Renamed REYNELLA (1940 – Commonwealth of Australia).

SANSOVINO (1989)
10977 grt; 1088 psrs
272 cars
403' x 64' x 17'6" (122 x 19.4 x 5.3 m)
2 x 6-cylinder GMT diesel engines via twin screw.
Passenger-car ferry operated by Adriatica di Navigazione.
Built by Fincantieri, Ancona.

SANTA ANA (1917) See JOHN L. CLEM (1941)

SANTA ANA (1931) See MOUNT McKINLEY (1936)

SANTA ANA (1973)
6131 grt; 1126 psrs
389' x 68' x 19' (118 x 20.5 x 5.7 m)
2 x 6-cylinder Kawasaki-MAN diesel engines via twin screw.
Passenger ferry operated by Negros Navigation Co Inc, Philippines.
Built by Hashiyama Zosen, Imabari, for Kansai Kisen KK as the NICHINAN MARU (1972). Renamed FERRY MUROTO (1973 – Kansai Kisen KK).

SANTA BARBARA (1928) See McCAWLEY, USS (APA-4) (1943)

SANTA BARBARA (1946) See SANTA MONICA (1966)

SANTA CATHERINE (1994)
11050 grt; 1000 psrs
433' x 66' x 18'6" (131.1 x 20 x 5.6 m)
2 x 9-cylinder Fiat diesel engines via twin screw.
Passenger ferry owned by El Salam Maritime Transport Co SA and operated by El Salam Shipping & Trading Establishment, Cairo.
Built by Italcantieri SpA, Castellammare di Stabia, for Tirrenia as the LEOPARDI (1971).

SANTA CECILIA (1921) See LYNGENFJORD (1933)

SANTA CECILIA (1931) See JOHN L. CLEM (1941)

SANTA CECILIA (1946) See JULIA (1968)

SANTA CLARA (1930) See SUSAN B. ANTHONY, USS (AP-72) (1942)

SANTA CLARA (1946)
8357 grt; 52 psrs
459' x 63' x 25'10" (139.1 x 19.1 x 7.6 m)
2 x General Electric DRG turbine engines via single screw.
Broken up for scrap at Castellon in 1970 following been laid up for 11 years. Ex-US government.
Built by the Federal Shipbuilding & Drydock Co, Kearny, New Jersey, for the Grace Line as a passenger-cargo liner.

SANTA CRISTINA (1967) See SOFIA (1968)

SANTA CRUZ (1947) See TAGUS (1949)

SANTA CRUZ DE TENERIFE (1966) See SOL OLYMPIA II (1985)

SANTA CRUZ DE TENERIFE (1994)
10473 grt; 1120 psrs
280 cars
385' x 68' x 17' (130.8 x 20.7 x 5.2 m)
2 x 7-cylinder MAN-B+W diesel engines via twin screw.
Built by Union Naval de Levante, Bilbao, for Trasmediterranea as a passenger-cargo ship at a cost of US$75,000,000.

SANTA ELENA (1933)
9135 grt; 290 psrs
484' x 72' x 25'8" (146.7 x 21.8 x 7.8 m)
2 x General Electric DRG turbine engines via twin screw.
Sank on 6 November 1943 after being torpedoed while under tow off Philippeville, Algeria.
Built by the Federal Shipbuilding & Drydock Co, Kearny, New Jersey, for the Grace Line as a passenger-cargo liner.

SANTA ELENA (1962) See SUN (1969)

SANTA ELISA (1919) See BARANOF (1936)

SANTA FE (1947)
7383 grt
439' x 62' x 28'7" (133 x 18.8 x 8.7 m)
2 x Westinghouse DRG turbine engines via single screw.
Broken up for scrap as a cargo ship at Campana in 1974. Ex-Dodero Line.
Built by Bethlehem-Fairfield Shipyard Inc, Baltimore, Maryland, for the US War Shipping Administration as the GUSTAVAS VICTORY (1945). She operated as a migrant ship after World War Two.

SANTA FLORENTINA (1983)
4343 grt; 1050 psrs
353' x 68' x 15' (107 x 20.6 x 4.6 m)
4 x 8-cylinder Fuji diesel engines via twin screw.
Passenger ferry operated by the Negros Navigation Co Inc.
Built by Kochi Jyuko KK., Kochi, for Ehime Ferry KK., Matsuyama, as the passenger ship OKUDOGO 2 (1972).

SANTA INEZ (1928) See BOWDITCH, USS (AGS-4) (1940)

SANTA ISABEL (1931)
5641 grt; 189 psrs
380' x 49' x 24'10' (115.2 x 14.8 x 7.3 m)
Nederlandsche Scheepsbouw Maats 3-cylinder triple expansion engine via single screw.
Broken up for scrap at Baltimore in 1939. Ex-Grace Line.
Built by Nederlandsche Scheepsbouw Maats, Amsterdam, for the Panama Line as the passenger-cargo liner VENEZUELA (1915).

SANTA ISABEL (1946) See SOFIA (1968)

SANTA LUCIA (1911) See CANADA (1912)

SANTA LUCIA (1933) See LEEDSTOWN, USS (AP-73) (1942)

SANTA LUISA (1918) See MOUNT McKINLEY (1936)

SANTA LUISA (1946) See LUISA (1968)

SANTA MAGDALENA (1963)
11219 grt; 121 psrs
547' x 79' x 29' (166.7 x 24.1 x 8.9 m)
2 x General Electric DRG turbine engines via single screw.
Broken up for scrap at Kaohsiung in 1988.
Built by the Bethlehem Shipbuilding Corporation, Sparrow's Point, for the Grace Line as a passenger-cargo ship.

SANTA MARGARITA (1946)
8357 grt; 52 psrs

459' x 63' x 28' (139.1 x 19.1 x 8.5 m)
Turbine engine via single screw.
Broken up for scrap at Bilbao in 1969. Built by the North Carolina Shipbuilding Corporation, Wilmington, for the Grace Line as a passenger-cargo ship.

SANTA MARIA (1928) See SURRIENTO (1948)

SANTA MARIA (1946) See SUN (1969)

SANTA MARIA (1953)
20906 grt; 1078 psrs
609' x 76' x 27' (185.9 x 23.2 x 8.2 m)
6 x Parsons DRG turbine engines via twin screw.
Broken up for scrap at Kaohsiung in 1973.
Built by John Cockerill Shipyards, Hoboken, Belgium, for Cia Colonial de Navegacao, Lisbon, as a passenger liner.

SANTA MARIA (1963)
11888 grt; 121 psrs
547' x 79' x 27' (166.7 x 24.1 x 8.3 m)
2 x General Electric DRG turbine engines via single screw.
Broken up for scrap at Kaohsiung in 1988.
Built by the Bethlehem Shipbuilding Corporation, Sparrow's Point, Maryland, for the Grace Line as a passenger-cargo ship.

SANTA MARIANA (1963)
11181 grt; 125 psrs
547' x 79' x 29' (166.7 x 24.1 x 8.9 m)
2 x General Electric DRG turbine engines via single screw.
Broken up for scrap at Kaohsiung in 1988.
Built by the Bethlehem Shipbuilding Corporation, Sparrow's Point, Maryland, for the Grace Line as a passenger-cargo container ship.

SANTA MARTA (1906)
4937 grt; 103 psrs
379' x 50' x 25' (114.8 x 15.2 x 7.6 m)
Triple expansion engine via single screw.
Broken up for scrap at Baltimore, USA, in 1948.
Built by Workman, Clark & Co, Belfast, for the United Fruit Steamship Co as a passenger-cargo ship.

SANTA MERCEDES (1964) See PATRIOT STATE (1984)

SANTA MONICA (1946) See COSMOS TRADER (1966)

SANTA MONICA (1964) See COSMOS TRADER (1966)

SANTA MONICA (1966)
8357 grt; 52 psrs
459' x 63' x 28' (139.1 x 19.1 x 8.5 m)
DRG turbine engine via single screw.
Broken up for scrap at Bilbao in 1969. Ex-Grace Line.
Built by the North Carolina Shipbuilding Corporation, Wilmington, for the Grace Line as the SANTA BARBARA (1946).

SANT ANDREA (1979) See AVRASYA I (1996)

SANT' ANNA (1910)
9350 grt; 2070 psrs
470' x 57' x 42'7" (143.3 x 17.3 x 12.9 m)
Forges et Chantiers de la Mediterranee 6-cylinder triple expansion engines via twin screw.
Sank on 11 May 1918 after being torpedoed 26 miles (42 km) east of Cape Bon, Tunis.
Built by Forges et Chantiers de la Mediterranee, La Seyne, for the Fabre Line as a passenger liner.

SANTA OLIVIA (1931) See NEGBAH (1948)

SANTA OLIVIA (1947) See ATHENAI (1960)

SANTA PAULA (1952) See ACROPOLIS (1961)

SANTA PAULA (1958) See RAMADA AL-SALAM HOTEL SHIP.
(1990)

SANTAREM (1909) See SANTAREM (1917)

SANTAREM (1917)
6757 grt; 950 psrs
420' x 55' x 27'8" (127.9 x 16.6 x 8.4 m)
Bremer Vulkan 4-cylinder quadruple expansion engine via single screw.
Broken up for scrap in 1962. Ex-French Line.
Launched by Bremer Vulkan, Vegesack, for North German Lloyd as the passenger liner EISENACH (1908), completed as the SANTAREM (1909) and then seized by the Brazilian government in 1917.

SANTA RITA (1929) See WILLIAM WARD BURROWS, USS (AP-6)
(1940)

SANTA ROSA (1932) See ATHINAI (1961)

SANTA ROSA (1948) See CAPO MANARA (1948)

SANTA ROSA (1958) See THE EMERALD (1996)

SANTA SOFIA (1946) See COSMOS MARINER (1966)

SANTA SOFIA (1966) See SUN (1969)

SANTA SOFIA (1964) See COSMOS MARINER (1966)

SANTA TERESA (1918) See ERNEST HINDS (1942)

SANTA URSULA (1951) See ALEXI H (1979)

SANTHIA (1950) See STATE OF HARYANA (1967)

SANTIAGO (1896) See JEHANGIR (1914)

SANTIAGO (1908) See ARMONIA (1909)

SANTIAGO (1916)
3909 grt; 142 psrs
371' x 45' x 25'3" (112.4 x 13.6 x 7.7 m)
A Stephen & Sons 3-cylinder triple expansion engine via single screw.
Broken up for scrap in Italy in 1933. Ex-Soc Anon Comercial Braun & Blanchard, Chile.
Built by Alex Stephen & Sons, Glasgow, for the Furness Line as the passenger-cargo ship LOYALIST (1901). Renamed BYRON (1902 – Lamport & Holt).

SANTIAGO DE CUBA (1994) See THE EMPRESS (1994)

SANTOS MARU (1952) See HUI HSING (1974)

SANUKI MARU (1974) See SANUKI MARU (1997)

SANUKI MARU (1997)
3611 grt; 2350 psrs
293' x 52' x 12'6" (88.9 x 15.8 x 3.8 m)
4 x 6-cylinder Daihatsu diesel engines via twin screw.
Passenger train ferry owned and operated by PT Dharma Lautan Utama, Surabaya.
Built by Naikai Zosen, Setoda, for Japan National Railways as the SANUKI MARU (1974). Renamed GOOD SAVIOUR I (1997 – Rowys Shipping SA).

SAO JORGE (1916) See AMBOIM (1925)

SAO LUIZ (1906)
3551 grt; 834 psrs
378' x 40' x 28'6" (115.3 x 12.3 x 8.7 m)
2-cylinder compound engine via single screw.
She was wrecked on the Rio Grande do Norte, Brazil, on 11 January 1911 while operating for Commercio e Navagacao, Rio de Janeiro.
Built by D & W Henderson & Co, Glasgow, for the Anchor Line as the passenger liner NUBIA (1882).

S. A. ORANJE (1966)
28629 grt; 645 psrs
747' x 84' x 32' (226.4 x 25.5 x 10 m)
2 x Parsons DRG turbine engines via twin screw.
Broken up for scrap by Chin Tai Steel Enterprises at Kaohsiung in 1975. Ex-Safmarine.
Built by Harland & Wolff Ltd, Belfast, for the Union Castle Line as the passenger-cargo liner PRETORIA CASTLE (1948) at a cost of £3,000,000.

SAO VINCENTE (1916) See LOANDA (1925)

SAPFO (1973) See SAPPHO (1973)

SAPPHIRE (1996)
12263 grt; 650 psrs
492' x 68' x 22' (150 x 20.8 x 6.7 m)
2 x 9-cylinder Sulzer diesel engines via twin screw.

Owned by Louis Cruises, Cyprus, and chartered for a short term to France Croisieres.
Built by Cantieri Navale Felszegi, Muggia, for Costa Lines as the ITALIA (1967). Renamed PRINCESS ITALIA (1969 – P&O Princess Cruises), OCEAN PRINCESS (1983 – Ocean Cruise Lines), SEA PRINCE (1993 – Sunshine Cruise Line) and PRINCESA OCEANICA (1995 – Louis Cruises).

SAPPHIRE SEAS (1993) See OCEAN EXPLORER I (1998)

SAPPHO (1973)
6916 grt; 1200 psrs
124 cars + 100 containers
463' x 69' x 17'6" (140.3 x 20.8 x 5.3 m)
4 x 6-cylinder Mirrlees diesel engines via twin screw, but had new Wartsila diesel engines installed in 1993.

Passenger-car-cargo RoRo ferry operated by Maritime Co of Lesvos SA, Mytilene.
Built by Cammell Laird &Co, Birkenhead, for Ellerman Lines as the SPERO (1966). Renamed SAPFO (1973 – Maritime Co of Lesvos SA, Mytilene).

SAPPORO MARU (1974) See BLUE SKY (2000)

SARA I (1990) See GURGEN-2 (1996)

SARANAC, USS (1919) See HAMILTON (1922)

SARASVATI (1949)
3750 grt; 1250 psrs
342' x 53' x 22' (103.6 x 16.1 x 6.7 m)
3 x Harland & Wolff Ltd SRG turbine engines via single screw.
Built by Harland & Wolff Ltd, Belfast, for the Shipping Corporation of India as a passenger liner.

SARATOGA (1907) See MERCY, USS (AH-4) (1917)

SARAY STAR (1994)
9000 grt; 716 psrs
100 cars
429' x 64' x 16' (130 x 19.3 x 4.8 m)
2 x 7-cylinder B+W diesel engines via twin screw.
Owned by Libton Shipping Ltd, Malta, and operated by European Seaways, she sank on 13 June 1994 after a galley fire had erupted three days earlier and engulfed the ship 28 miles (46 km) north of Cephalonia, without loss of life.
Built by Union Naval de Levante SA, Bilbao, for Trasmediterranea, Bilbao, as the passenger-car ferry CIUDAD DE COMPOSTELA (1967). Renamed EUROPEAN STAR (1992 – European Seaways Inc).

SARDEGNA (1901) See SARDEGNA (1912)

SARDEGNA (1912)
5255 grt; 1449 psrs
418' x 47' x 27'6" (127.5 x 14.4 x 8.4 m)
N Odero & Co 3-cylinder triple expansion engine via single screw.
Broken up for scrap in 1928. Ex-Sitmar Line.
Built by Soc Esercizio Baccini, Riva Trigoso, for Navigazione Generale Italia as the SARDEGNA (1901).

SARDEGNA (1935)
11452 grt; 1279 psrs
512' x 66' x 34'3" (155.2 x 20 x 10.4 m)
2 x Bremer Vulkan 3-cylinder triple expansion engines via twin screw.
Owned by the Italian Line, she sank on 29 December 1940 after being torpedoed by the Greek submarine PROTEUS in the Mediterranean near Saseno, Albania.
Built by Bremer Vulkan, Vegesack, for North German Lloyd as the passenger liner SIERRA VENTANA (1923).

SARDEGNA (1952)
5208 grt; 560 psrs
385' x 53' x 18' (116.6 x 16 x 5.5 m)
4 x 6-cylinder Fiat diesel engines via twin screw.
Passenger-cargo RoRo ferry in Italy operated by Tirrenia.
Built by Construzioni Navali Meccaniche, Naples.

SARDEGNA BELLA (1993)
6942 grt; 1170 psrs
215 cars
363' x 59' x 16' (110 x 18 x 4.8 m)
2 x 16-cylinder MAN diesel engines via twin screw.

Ice-strengthened passenger-car ferry owned and operated by Sardegna Lines SA, but for sale as at 31 December 2000.
Built by AS Langesund & Frammas Mekaniske Verkstad, Sandefjord, for the Stena Line as the STENA BRITANNICA (1967). Renamed WICKERSHAM (1968 – Alaska Marine Highway System Inc), VIKING 6 (1974 – Sally Line),

GOELO (1980 – Brittany Ferries), VIKING 6 (1982 – Sally Line), SOL OLYMPIA (1982 – Sol Line), SUN EXPRESS (1985 – Sally Line), VIKING 6 (1985 – Sally Line) and MOBY DREAM (1986 – NavArMa, Italy).

SARDINIA (1898) See AMBOIM (1925)

SARDINIA (1902)
6574 grt; 160 psrs
450' x 52' x 30' (137.2 x 15.9 x 9.2 m)
2 x triple expansion engines via twin screw.
Broken up for scrap by Kishimoto KKK at Osaka in 1925 for a tender figure of £15,000.
Built by Barclay, Curle & Co, Glasgow, for the P&O Line at a cost of £130,917.

SARDINIA NOVA (1989)
7322 grt; 930 psrs
300 cars
453' x 71' x 18' (137.3 x 21.6 x 5.5 m)
4 x 12-cylinder Pielstick diesel engines via twin screw.

Ice-strengthened passenger-car ferry owned by Nuovo Tras-Tirreno and operated by Dano Linsten on the Denmark–Norway service.
Built by Lubecker Flender Werke, Lubeck, for the Tor Line as the TOR ANGLIA (1966). Renamed ESPRESSO OLBIA (1976 – Trans Tirreno Express SpA).

SARDINIA REGINA (1996)
13004 grt; 1800 psrs
460 cars
409' x 69' x 16'6" (123.9 x 20.9 x 5 m)
6 x 16-cylinder Nohab-Polar diesel engines via twin screw.

Owned and operated by Tourship Italia SpA, La Spezia.
Built by Jozo Lozovina-Mosor, Trogir, for the Gotland Line as the VISBY (1972). Renamed DROTTEN (1980 – Gotland Line), CORSICA VIVA II (1985 – Corsica Ferries) and CORSICA REGINA (1989 – Corsica Ferries).

SARDINIA VERA (1987)
5443 grt; 1129 psrs
500 cars
399' x 64' x 19'6" (120.8 x 19.5 x 6 m)
2 x 12-cylinder MaK diesel engines via twin screw.

Passenger-car ferry owned by Corsica Ferries and operated by Sardinia Ferry.

Built by Rickmers Werft, Bremerhaven, for Stena Line as the STENA ATLANTICA (1975). Renamed MARINE ATLANTICA (1975 – Marine Atlantic) and CORSICA VERA (1986 – Tourship Co SA, Panama).

SARDINIA VIVA (1992) See HAPPY DOLPHIN (1999)

SARNIA (1961) See SAUDI GOLDEN STAR (1979)

SAROMA (1975) See CAMELLIA (1990)

SAROMA MARU (1975) See CAMELLIA (1990)

SARPEDON (1923)
11321 grt; 155 psrs
530' x 62' x 34'9" depth (161.6 x 19 x 10.6 m)
4 x Cammell Laird SRG turbine engines via twin screw.
Broken up for scrap by John Cashmore Ltd at Newport, Wales, in 1953. Ex-Ocean Steamship Co Ltd (Blue Funnel Line).
Built by Cammell Laird &Co, Birkenhead, for the Blue Funnel Line as a passenger-cargo liner.

SARVISTAN (1919)
7431 grt; 1997 psrs
430' x 54' x 39'6" depth (131.2 x 16.6 x 12 m)
JC Tecklenborg 6-cylinder triple expansion engines via twin screw.
Broken up for scrap.
Built by JC Tecklenborg, Geestemunde, for North German Lloyd as the passenger liner FRANKFURT (1900) which was seized by the UK in 1919.

SASSARI (1960)
4013 grt; 596 psrs
341' x 47' x 18' (105.2 x 14.2 x 5.5 m)
Triple expansion engines via twin screw.
Broken up for scrap at La Spezia in 1962.
Built by William Cramp & Sons, Philadelphia, Pennsylvania, for the Peninsular & Occidental Steamship Company as the passenger liner CUBA (1921). Renamed PACE (1947 – Ignazio Messina & Co, Genoa).

SASSNITZ (1959) See MEGI (2000)

SASSNITZ (1989)
21154 grt; 800 psrs
220 cars
566' x 78' x 19' (171.5 x 23.6 x 5.8 m)
4 x 12-cylinder MAN-B+W diesel engines via twin screw.

Passenger-car ferry owned and operated by Scandlines Hansa on the Germany–Sweden service.
Built by Danyard AS, Aalborg, for Deutsche Reichsbahn.

SATRUSTEGUI (1952) See ISLA DE CABRERA (1974)

SATURNIA (1910)
8611 grt; 300 psrs
456' x 55' x 27'5" depth (137.9 x 16.7 x 8.3 m)
Dunsmuir & Jackson 6-cylinder triple expansion engines via twin screw.
Broken up for scrap in Italy in 1929.
Built by C Connell, Glasgow, for the Donaldson Line as a passenger-cargo ship.

SATURNIA (1927) See SATURNIA (1946)

SATURNIA (1946)
24346 grt; 1370 psrs
632' x 79' x 29' (191.5 x 23.9 x 8.8 m)
2 x 8-cylinder Sulzer diesel engines via twin screw.
Broken up for scrap at La Spezia in 1965. Ex-Italian Line.
Built by Cantieri Navale Triestino, Monfalcone, for the Cosulich Line as the passenger liner SATURNIA (1927).
Renamed FRANCES Y. SLANGER USS (1944 – US Navy).

SATURNUS (1991)
8739 grt; 464 psrs
250 cars
429' x 58' x 16' (130 x 17.5 x 4.9 m)
4 x 12-cylinder Nohab-Polar diesel engines via twin screw.

Ice-strengthened passenger-car ferry owned by Shiphall Marine, Piraeus, and operated by Ventouris Enterprises, Piraeus.
Built by Trondheims, Trondheim, for RA Nordo as the SCANDINAVIA (1974). Renamed RAED B (1980 – Alwalid Cia Naviera SA, Panama), ATLAS III (1983 – Corinthian Navigation Co, Limassol) and EUROPA II (1987 – Puma Lines Ltd, Limassol).

SAUDI (1956)
5973 grt; 999 psrs
426' x 57' x 25' (129 x 17.3 x 7.6 m)
Triple expansion & Bauer Wach turbine via single screw.
As a pilgrim ship, she sank on 26 June 1973, with 41 lives lost, after capsizing in heavy seas lashed by monsoonal rains and winds off Cape Guardafui near Socotra Island.
Built by Lithgows Ltd, Glasgow, for the Mogul Line as a passenger ship.

SAUDI FILIPINAS I (1980) See FILIPINAS SAUDI I (1980)

SAUDI GOLDEN STAR (1979)
3992 grt; 1400 psrs
322' x 53' x 14' (97.6 x 16 x 4.2 m)
2 x Pametrada DRG turbine engines via twin screw.
Broken up for scrap at Gadani Beach, Karachi, in 1987. Ex-Hitta Establishment, Saudi Arabia.
Built by J Samuel White & Co Ltd, Cowes (Isle of Wight, UK) for British Rail as the SARNIA (1961) at a cost of £1,500,000. Renamed AQUAMART (1978 – Supasave Supermarkets (Midlands) Ltd, Guernsey, and Channel Cruises Ltd) and GOLDEN STAR (1979 – Grecian Fertility).

SAUDI MOON (1964) See MIR (1998)

SAUDI MOON (1976) See OURANOS (1999)

SAUDI MOON I (1978) See THE EMPRESS (1994)

SAUDI PHIL I (1977) See FILIPINAS SAUDI I (1980)

S. A. VAAL (1966) See THE BIG RED BOAT III (2000)

SAVANNAH (1962)
22000 grt; 60 psrs
595' x 78' x 29'6" (181.5 x 23.8 x 8.9 m)
Babcock + Wilcox De Laval nuclear reactor & geared steam turbines via single screw.
Laid up in the James river, Virginia, from August 1995 after funds expired to maintain her static display as the world's first nuclear-powered merchant vessel at the Patriot's Point Maritime Museum in South Carolina. Her atomic

reactor has been removed.
Built by the New York Shipbuilding Corporation, Camden, New Jersey for States Maine Lines Inc as a passenger-cargo ship at a cost of US$47,000,000.

SAVAS (1939) See DARESSALAM (1939)

SAVOIE (1940)
10196 grt; 365 psrs
532' x 61' x 27'2" (162.1 x 18.5 x 8.2 m)
Quadruple expansion engines via twin screw.
Owned by the French government, she sank on 8 November 1942 off Casablanca during the Allied landings in North Africa in World War Two.
Built by Workman, Clark & Co Ltd, Belfast, for Royal Mail Lines as the passenger-cargo liner ARAGUAYA (1906). Renamed KRALJICA MARIJA (1930 – Jugoslavenski Lloyd, Dubrovnik).

SAXOL (1916) See PRYGONA (1921)

SAXON (1900)
12970 grt; 799 psrs
571' x 64' x 38'6" depth (173 x 19.5 x 11.7 m)
Harland & Wolff 8-cylinder quadruple expansion engines via twin screw.
Broken up for scrap by Hughes Bolckow & Co at Blyth in 1935.
Built by Harland & Wolff Ltd, Belfast, for the Union Castle Line as a passenger liner.

SAXONIA (1900)
14197 grt; 1463 psrs
580' x 64' x 41'6" depth (176.8 x 19.5 x 12.6 m)
2 x John Brown Ltd 4-cylinder quadruple expansion engines via twin screw.
Broken up for scrap at Rotterdam in 1925 for a tender figure of £47,000.
Built by John Brown & Co Ltd, Clydebank, for the Cunard Steamship Co as a passenger liner.

SAXONIA (1954) See LEONID SOBINOV (1973)

SAXONSTAR (1920) See SAXON STAR (1929)

SAXON STAR (1929)
5464 grt; 60 psrs
420' x 54' x 28'6" (127.3 x 16.4 x 8.7 m)
Hawthorne Leslie 3-cylinder triple expansion engine via single screw.
Broken up for scrap at Savona by Soc Anon Recuperi Mealalica in 1934. Ex-Blue Star Line.
Built by Hawthorn, Leslie Co Ltd, Hebburn, for the Federal Steam Navigation Co Ltd as the KENT (1899). Renamed BRODLEA (1915 – Brodlea Steamship Co Ltd) and SAXONSTAR (1920 – Union Cold Storage Co Ltd).

SCANDINAVIA (1969)
5209 grt; 165 psrs
416' x 51' x 18' (126.8 x 15.5 x 5.5 m)
Gotaverken-B+W diesel engines via twin screw.
Converted from a cruise ship into a floating club and restaurant at Mitohama Beach near Osezaki, Japan, for Prince Hotels and still bearing her original name of STELLA POLARIS on the bow.
Built by AB Gotaverken, Gothenburg, for the Bergen Line as the passenger ship STELLA POLARIS (1929).,

SCANDINAVIA (1974) See SATURNUS (1991)

SCANDINAVIA (1979) See P&OSL CANTERBURY (1999)

SCANDINAVIA (1982) See VIKING SERENADE (1990)

SCANDINAVIA (1986) See SANDEFJORD (1992)

SCANDINAVIAN (1912)
11394 grt; 1200 psrs
566' x 59' x 35'9" depth (172.5 x 18 x 10.9 m)
Harland & Wolff 8-cylinder triple expansion engine via twin screw.
Broken up for scrap at Emden by Klasmann und Lentze of Hamburg in 1923.
Ex-Canadian Pacific Steamship Co.
Built by Harland & Wolff Ltd, Belfast, for the Dominion Line as the passenger liner NEW ENGLAND (1898). Renamed ROMANIC (1903 – White Star Line).

SCANDINAVIAN DAWN (1990) See TEXAS TREASURE (2000)

SCANDINAVIAN SAGA (1988) See ENCHANTED SUN (1999)

SCANDINAVIAN SEA (1982) See DISCOVERY I (1986)

SCANDINAVIAN SKY (1985) See EL-TOR (1998)

SCANDINAVIAN SKY II (1986) See TEXAS TREASURE (2000)

SCANDINAVIAN SONG (1990) See THE EMPRESS (1994)

SCANDINAVIAN STAR (1981) See PRINCE (1996)

SCANDINAVIAN STAR (1984) See REGAL VOYAGER (1994)

SCANDINAVIAN SUN (1982) See DISCOVERY SUN (1995)

SCANDINAVICA (1978) See SEMINOLE EXPRESS (1997)

SCANDINAVICA (1987) See KING OF SCANDINAVIA (1995)

SCANDINAVICA (1989) See KING OF SCANDINAVIA (1995)

SCANDOLA (1999)
4508 grt; 850 psrs
800 cars
496' x 77' x 20' (150.4 x 23.4 x 6 m)
2 x 8-cylinder Sulzer diesel engines via twin screw.

Passenger-car ferry owned by Cie Meridonale de Navigation, France, after purchase for US$38,000,000.
Built by Van der Geissen de Noord, Krimpen, for Strintzis Lines as the passenger-cargo ferry VIA LIGURE (1992 – Tirrenia). Renamed IONIAN STAR (1994 – Strintzis Lines Shipping SA).

SCANIA (1972)
3474 grt; 800 psrs
100 cars
245' x 54' x 12'6" (74.2 x 16.5 x 3.8 m)
2 x 12-cylinder Nohab-Polar diesel engines via twin screw.

Passenger-car ferry owned and operated by Saaremaa Shipping Co Ltd, Estonia.
Built by Aalborg Vaerft, Aalborg, for Sweferry.

SCANMAIL (1932) See CAYRU (1940)

SCANPENN (1932) See BUARQUE (1940)

SCANSTATES (1932) See CANTUARIA (1940)

SCANYORK (1932) See MAUA (1939)

SCENT OF SEA (1997) See NORTIA (1999)

SCHAM (1912)
3662 grt; 705 psrs
362' x 44' x 21'3" (109.7 x 13.3 x 6.5 m)
R Napier & Sons 3-cylinder triple expansion engine via single screw.
Owned by Administration de Nav A Vapore Ottoman, she was broken up for scrap at Savona, Italy, in 1955 after serving 37 years as a coal hulk. This followed her refloating in 1918 from the Sea of Marmora, near Istanbul, where she was sunk by a torpedo from the British submarine E-11.
Built by Napier & Miller Ltd, Glasgow, for the Aberdeen Line as the passenger liner AUSTRALASIAN (1884).

SCHARNHORST (1908) See LA BOURDONNAIS (1921)

SCHARNHORST (1935) See SHINYO MARU (1943)

SCHENECTADY (1919) See MAUA (1939)

SCHIFF 14 (1942) See TOPEKA (1976)

SCHLESWIG (1902)
6955 grt; 220 psrs
449' x 52' x 30'4" depth (136 x 15.8 x 9.2 m)
AG Vulcan 6-cylinder triple expansion engines via twin screw.
Owned and operated by the Hamburg-America Line.
Built by AG Vulcan, Stettin.

SCHULPENGAT (1990)
8311 grt; 1320 psrs
245 cars or 156 cars + 25 trailers
364' x 62' x 12'6" (110.4 x 18.7 x 3.8 m)
3 x 6-cylinder Caterpillar diesel engines via twin screw.
Owned and operated by Texels Eigen Stoomboot Onderneming (TESO), Den Hoorn, Island of Texel, Holland.
Built by Verolme, Heusden.

SCHWABENSTEIN (1954) See ORIENTAL RULER (1967)

SCILLA (1985)
5619 grt; 1500 psrs
170 cars + 45 rail wagons
479' x 62' x 19'6" (145 x 18.8 x 5.9 m)
4 x 6-cylinder GMT diesel engines via twin screw.
Passenger-cargo-train ferry owned by Italian State Railways and operated by Ferrovie Stato.
Built by Fincantieri, Castellammare di Stabia.

SCINDIA (1890) See HUA TONG (1930)

SCINDIA (1900)
5178 grt; 64 psrs
401' x 49' x 27'8" (122.1 x 15 x 8.4 m)
D & W Henderson 3-cylinder triple expansion engine via single screw.
Broken up for scrap in 1927.
Built by D & W Henderson Ltd, Glasgow, for the Anchor Line as a passenger-cargo liner.

SCIROCCO (1974) See SCIROCCO (1993)

SCIROCCO (1986) See SCIROCCO (1993)

SCIROCCO (1993)
11177 grt; 951 psrs
296 cars or 33 trailers
430' x 74' x 17' (130.3 x 22.4 x 7.6 m)
4 x 8-cylinder Stork-Werkspoor diesel engines via twin screw.
Passenger-car-cargo ferry operated by Ferrimaroc for the Cenargo Group.
Built by Cammell Laird & Co, Birkenhead, at a cost of £7,500,000 for British

Rail as the ST. EDMUND (1974). Renamed SCIROCCO (1974 – Cenargo Ferry Co), KEREN (1985 – Cenargo Ferry Company but managed by the Ministry of Defence), SCIROCCO (1986 – Cenargo Ferry Co) and ROZEL (1989 – Cenargo Navigation Ltd).

SCORPIO (1999)
11347 grt; 1800 psrs
460 cars or 150 cars + 30 trailers
480' x 73' x 15' (145.6 x 22 x 4 m)
Gas turbine engines plus 4 x MTU diesel engines via quadruple screw.
Passenger-car-cargo ferry owned and operated by Tirrenia, Italy.
Built by Fincantieri, Riva Trigoso.

SCOT (1891) See VASCO NUNEZ DE BALBOA (1923)

SCOTIA (1921)
3441 grt; 1505 psrs
383' x 45' x 26'2" (116 x 13.6 x 7.9 m)
SRG turbine engines via twin screw.
Sank on 1 June 1940 during troop evacuations off Dunkirk beach after German dive bombers scored two direct hits on her, causing massive internal explosions and resulting in 300 deaths.
Built by William Denny & Brothers Ltd, Dumbarton, for the London and North Western Railway at a cost of £400,000.

SCOTIAN (1904) See PRESIDENT LINCOLN (1907)

SCOTIAN (1911) See MARGLEN (1922)

SCOTIA PRINCE (1982)
12087 grt; 1500 psrs
250 cars or 26 trailers
413' x 64' x 16'6" (125 x 19.5 x 5 m)
2 x 18-cylinder Pielstick diesel engines via twin screw.

Passenger-car-cargo RoRo ferry owned by the Transworld Steamship Co, Panama, and operated by Prince of Fundy Cruises on the USA–Canada east coast service.
Built by Brodogradiliste, Kraljevica, for Stena Line as the STENA OLYMPICA (1972).

SCOTLAND (1958) See HANSEATIC (1968)

SCOTSTOUN, HMS (1939)
17046 grt; 1404 psrs
552' x 70' x 29' (167.3 x 21.2 x 8.8 m)
DRG turbine engines via twin screw.
Acquired by the British Admiralty, she sank as an armed merchant cruiser on 13 June 1940, with the loss of six lives, after being torpedoed six times by the German U-25 80 miles (133 km) west of Barra Island, in the Outer Hebrides.
Built by Alexander Stephen & Sons, Glasgow, for the Anchor Line as the passenger liner CALEDONIA (1925).

SCOTTISH COAST (1957) See PRINCESA AMOROSA (1989)

SCYTHIA (1921)
19930 grt; 2200 psrs
674' x 73' x 30' (189.1 x 22.1 x 9.1 m)
6 x Brown-Curtis DRG turbine engines via twin screw.
Broken up for scrap at Inverkeithing in 1958.
Built by Vickers-Armstrong Ltd, Barrow-in-Furness, for the Cunard Line as a passenger liner.

SEA (1996)
23191 grt; 842 psrs
631' x 82' x 27' (192.3 x 24.9 x 8.2 m)
2 x 9-cylinder Gotaverken diesel engines via twin screw.
Laid up in Tampa, Florida, at the time of publication, following the bankruptcy of Regency Cruises and the ship's arrest in March 1997 at Freeport and several subsequent auctions.
Built by Ansaldo Shipyards, Genoa, for the Swedish American Line as the passenger liner GRIPSHOLM (1957). Renamed NAVARINO (1975 – Karageorgios Cruises), SAMANTHA (1983 – Multiship Italia), NAVARINO (1983 – Karageorgios Cruises) and REGENT SEA (1985 – Regency Cruises).

SEABOURN GODDESS I (1999)
4253 grt; 118 psrs
347' x 50' x 13'6" (105 x 15 x 4.1 m)
2 x 12-cylinder Wartsila-Vasa diesel engines via twin screw.
Cruise ship owned and operated by Cunard Line.
Built by Wartsila-Helsinki for Norske Cruise as the cruise ship SEA GODDESS I (1984).

SEABOURN GODDESS II (1999)
4260 grt; 117 psrs
347' x 50' x 13'6" (105 x 15 x 4.1 m)
2 x 12-cylinder Wartsila-Vasa diesel engines via twin screw.

Cruise ship owned and operated by Cunard Line.
Built by Wartsila-Helsinki for Norske Cruise as the cruise ship SEA GODDESS (1985).

SEABOURN LEGEND (1991) See SEABOURN LEGEND (1996)

SEABOURN LEGEND (1996)
9975 grt; 212 psrs
446' x 63' x 16'6" (135 x 19 x 5 m)
4 x 12-cylinder BergenNormo diesel engines via twin screw.
Owned and operated by Seabourn Cruise Line.
Laid down by Schichau Seebeckwerfte, Bremerhaven, for the Seabourn Cruise Line as the SEABOURN LEGEND (1991) at a cost of US$85,000,000 and completed as the ROYAL VIKING QUEEN (1992) for the Royal Viking Line. Renamed QUEEN ODYSSEY (1994 – Royal Cruise Line).

SEABOURN PRIDE (1988)
9975 grt; 212 psrs
439' x 63' x 16'6" (133 x 19 x 5 m)
4 x 12-cylinder Bergen-Normo diesel engines via twin screw.
Cruise ship owned and operated by Seabourn Cruise Lines.
Built by Schichau Seebeckwerfte, Bremerhaven.

SEABOURN SPIRIT (1989)
9975 grt; 212 psrs
439' x 63' x 16'6" (133 x 19 x 5 m)

4 x 12-cylinder Bergen-Normo diesel engines via twin screw.

Cruise ship for Seabourn Cruise Lines.
Built by Schichau Seebeckwerfte.

SEABOURN SUN (1999)
37485 grt; 756 psrs
670' x 95' x 24' (203 x 28.8 x 7.3 m)
4 x 8-cylinder rubber-dampened Sulzer diesel engines via twin screw.

Cruise ship owned and operated by Seabourn Cruise Lines.
Built by Wartsila-Turku for the Royal Viking Line as the ROYAL VIKING SUN (1988) at a cost of US$125,000,000.

SEABREEZE I (1989)
21010 grt; 840 psrs
606' x 79' x 27' (184.7 x 24 x 8.2 m)
Ansaldo DRG turbine engines via twin screw.
Owned by merchant bankers DLJ and operated by International Partners, she sank 200 miles (340 km) east of Cape Charles, West Virginia, on 17 December 2000. Her engine room was flooded while manned by 34 crew and officers en route from Boston to Charleston for repairs. All on board were rescued by two US Coastguard HH-60 helicopters after being alerted by two C-130 Hercules.
Built by Ansaldo Shipyards, Genoa, for the Costa Line as the FEDERICO C (1958). Renamed ROYALE (1983 – Greyhound Bus Co) and STARSHIP ROYALE (1983 – Premier Cruise Line).

SEA CLUB (1981) See A. REGINA (1979)

SEA DANCER (1994) See GALAPAGOS DISCOVERY (1998)

SEAFRANCE CEZANNE (1996)
25122 grt; 1800 psrs

630 cars
540' x 89' x 26' (163.5 x 27 x 7.9 m)
2 x 7-cylinder Sulzer diesel engines via twin screw.
Passenger-car-cargo ferry owned and operated by Sea France.
Laid down by Kockums Varv, Malmo, for Nordo as the ARIADNE (1980), built as the SOCA (1980), but completed as the TRAPEZITZA (1980) for the Bulgarian State Shipping Co. Renamed CHANNEL SEAWAY (1989 – Sealink British Ferries) and FIESTA (1990 – Stena Line).

SEAFRANCE MANET (1997)
15093 grt; 1800 psrs
300 cars
426' x 74' x 16'6" (129.1 x 22.4 x 5 m)
2 x 16-cylinder Pielstick diesel engines via twin screw.

Passenger-car ferry operated by SeaFrance.
Built by Dubigeon-Normandie, Nantes, for SNCF as the CHAMPS ELYSEE (1984). Renamed STENA PARISIEN (1992 – Stena Line).

SEAFRANCE MONET (1995) See VOLCAN DE TACANDE (2000)

SEAFRANCE NORD PAS-DE-CALAIS (1996)
13727 grt; 80 psrs
85 cars or 40 rail wagons
528' x 74' x 19'6" (160.1 x 22.4 x 5.9 m)
2 x 16-cylinder Sulzer diesel engines via twin screw.

Passenger-car train ferry (converted from the original dedicated train ferry) owned and operated by SeaFrance.
Built by Chantiers du Nord et de la Mediterranee, Dunkirk, for SNCF as the train ferry NORD PAS-DE-CALAIS (1987) at a cost of French francs 224,000,000.

SEAFRANCE RENOIR (1996)

15612 grt; 1400 psrs
330 cars
429' x 76' x 16'6" (130 x 23 x 5 m)
2 x 18-cylinder Pielstick diesel engines via twin screw.
Passenger-car ferry owned and operated by SeaFrance on the France–UK service.
Built by Nouvelle des Ateliers et Chantiers du Havre for SNCF Sealink as the COTE DAZUR (1981).

SEA GIRT (1919) See WHARTON, USS (AP-7) (1939)

SEA GODDESS I (1984) See SEABOURN GODDESS I (1999)

SEA GODDESS II (1985) See SEABOURN GODDESS II (1999)

SEA HARMONY (1992) See SEA HARMONY II (1993)

SEA HARMONY (1996)
24414 grt; 950 psrs
642' x 81' x 26' (195.8 x 24.7 x 7.9 m)
4 x 16-cylinder Wartsila-Pielstick diesel engines via twin screw.
Laid up since 1995, the cruise ship is now being operated by Perosea Shipping Co SA, Piraeus.
Laid down by Harland & Wolff Ltd Belfast for the Holland America Line as the STATENDAM (1957) and completed by Wilton-Fijenoord, at a cost of £16,000,000, after the hull had been towed to Holland. Renamed RHAPSODY (1982 – Pacquet Cruises) and REGENT STAR (1986 – Regency Cruises).

SEA HARMONY II (1993)
4129 grt; 1500 psrs
250 cars
477' x 61' x 17' (144.6 x 18.4 x 5.1 m)
8 x 6-cylinder Daihatsu diesel engines via twin screw.
Passenger-car ferry built by Hitachi Zosen, Mukaishima, for Japan Railways as the ISHIKARI MARU (1977). Renamed LADY TERRY (1989 – Poseidon Lines Shipping Co), LASITHI (1990 – Poseidon Lines Shipping Co) and SEA HARMONY (1992 – Delrem Shipping Co Ltd).

SEA LUCK I (1976) See INDEPENDENCE (1982)

SEAMAR (1964) See CARONI (1975)

SEANG BEE (1909) See SEANG BEE MARU (1931)

SEANG BEE MARU (1931)
5849 grt; 100 psrs
446' x 49' x 29'6" (135.2 x 14.8 x 8.9 m)
Triple expansion engines via twin screw.
Broken up for scrap at Osaka in 1931. Ex-China & Southern Trading Co (Lim Chin Tsong, Yangon).
Built by Harland & Wolff Ltd, Belfast, for the Bibby Line as the passenger-cargo liner SHROPSHIRE (1882). Renamed SEANG BEE (1909 – Lim Chin Tsong, Yangon)

SEANG CHOON (1911)
5807 grt; 100 psrs
446' x 49' x 29'6" (135.2 x 14.8 x 8.9 m)
Triple expansion engines via twin screw.
Owned by Lim Chin Tsong, Yangon, she sank on 10 July 1917 after being torpedoed.
Built by Harland & Wolff Ltd, Belfast, for the Bibby Line as the passenger-cargo ship CHESHIRE (1889).

SEA PALACE (1991) See TROPIC SEA (2000)

SEA PRINCE (1993) See SAPPHIRE (1996)

SEA PRINCE V (1995) See SAPPHIRE (1996)

SEA PRINCESS (1979) See VICTORIA (1995)

SEA PRINCESS (1999)
77441 grt; 2185 psrs
856' x 106' x 26' (259.4 x 32.1 x 7.9 m)

4 x 16-cylinder Sulzer diesel engines via twin screw.
Cruise ship owned by CP Shipping and operated by P&O Princess Cruises.
Built by Fincantieri, Monfalcone, at a cost of US$295,000,000.

SEA SERENADE (1992)
8552 grt; 1200 psrs
250 cars or 34 trailers
477' x 63' x 16'6" (144.6 x 19 x 5.1 m)
8 x 6-cylinder Daihatsu diesel engines via twin screw.

Passenger-car-cargo ferry owned by Transcargo Shipping Co and operated by Poseidon Lines Shipping Co, Piraeus.
Built by Hakodate Shipyard for the Department of Railways, government of Japan, as the SORACHI MARU (1976). Renamed LADY TERRY (1990 – Poseidon Shipping Co, Athens).

SEASPEED CHALLENGER (1974) See HORNBEAM (1992)

SEASPEED MASTER (1976) See TAMBU EXPRESS (1980)

SEATRAILER (1998)
13271 grt; 641 psrs
465' x 74' x 18' (140.9 x 22.5 x 5.5 m)
2 x 18-cylinder MAN diesel engines via twin screw.
Passenger ferry owned by Valentine Marine Ltd and operated by Agapitos Express Ferries.
Built by Hayashikane Zosen, Shimonoseki, for Fuji Ferry KK, Tokyo, as the SHIMA MARU (1973). Renamed FERRY KUROSHIO (1978 – Osaka Shosen Mitsu Senpaku KK).

SEATTLE MARU (1909)
5853 grt
420' x 50' x 30' (127.3 x 15.2 x 9 m)
Triple expansion engines via twin screw.
Sank on 16 July 1944 after being torpedoed by the USS PIRANHA in the Sulu Sea.
Built by Kawasaki Dockyard, Kobe, for OSK.

SEA VENTURE (1971) See PACIFIC PRINCESS (1975)

SEA VENTURE (1991) See OCEAN HOME (1999)

SEAWARD (1970) See FLAMENCO (1997)

SEAWARD (1988) See NORWEGIAN SEA (1997)

SEA WAVE (1990) See KARDEN (1995)

SEAWAY (1993) See TAXIARCHIS (1999)

SEAWAY HOBART (1984) See TAXIARCHIS (1999)

SEAWIND (1989)
15887 grt; 300 psrs
60 cars
512' x 73' x 17' (155 x 22 x 5.2 m)
4 x 9-cylinder Ruston diesel engines via twin screw.
Passenger-car ferry owned by Silja Line and operated by Seawind Lines.
Built by Danyard for the TT-Saga Line as the SVEALAND (1971). Renamed SAGA WIND (1984 – TT-Line).

SEAWIND CROWN (1990)
24568 grt; 660 psrs
641' x 80' x 27' (195.5 x 24.2 x 8.2 m)
4 x Westinghouse DRG turbine engines via twin screw.
Cruise ship operated by Premier Cruise Lines.
Built by Cockerill-Ougree Shipyards, Hoboken, for Cia Colonial de Navegacao, Lisbon, as the passenger ship INFANTE DOM HENRIQUE (1961). Renamed VASCO DA GAMA (1988 – Arcalia Shipping Co, Lisbon).

SEAWIND ROYALE (1991) See NOAHS ARK (1999)

SEAWING (1994)
16710 grt; 918 psrs
539' x 75' x 21' (163.4 x 23 x 6.5 m)
4 x 10-cylinder Fiat diesel engines via twin screw.

Cruise ship operating for Airtours, UK, after purchase from the Norwegian Cruise Line at US$24,000,000 and back on the sales lists mid-1999.
Built by Cantieri Navali del Tirreno e Riuniti SpA, Genoa, for the Norwegian Cruise Line as the SOUTHWARD (1971).

SEAWISE UNIVERSITY (1970)
83673 grt; 2348 psrs
1031' x 118' x 39' (312.4 x 38.8 x 11.8 m)
4 x SRG turbine engines via quadruple screw.
Owned by the CY Tung Group, she sank on 10 January 1972 in 13 m (43 feet) of water in Hong Kong harbour after being gutted by fire and capsizing during an extensive and expensive refit following the ship's purchase for US$2,600,000. She has been gradually broken up since 1974, with the hulk now incorporated into a land reclamation project.
Built by John Brown & Co Ltd, Clydebank, for the Cunard Line as the QUEEN ELIZABETH (1940). Renamed ELIZABETH (1969 – The Queen Ltd).

SEA WORLD (1984) See HAI SHANG SHI JIE (1998)

SEBASTIANO CABOTO (1947)
8967 grt; 835 psrs
485' x 62' x 26' (149.2 x 19 x 7.9 m)
Fiat 9-cylinder diesel engine via single screw.
Broken up for scrap as a cargo ship at Kaohsiung in 1979. Ex-Lloyd Triestino.
Laid down by Ansaldo Shipyards, Genoa, for the Italian Line as the passenger liner MARIO VISENTINI (1947).

SECHELT QUEEN (1963) See MUSKEGON CLIPPER (1989)

SEDGWICK (1898) See NEAPOLETANO (1905)

SEGOVIA (1931) See BLUMENTHAL (1957)

SEGURA (1906) See CHIGNECTO (1913)

SEIKAN MARU No. 7 (1973)
3499 grt; 700 psrs
363' x 55' x 16' (110 x 16.8 x 4.8 m)
2 x 14-cylinder Nippon Kokan diesel engines via single screw.
Passenger ferry operated by Higashi Nihon, Japan.
Built by Naikai Zosen, Setoda.

SEIKAN MARU No. 12 (1946)
3161 grt
390' x 52' x 15'6" (118.1 x 15.9 x 4.7 m)
Passenger-train ferry owned and operated by Seikan Railway Ferries until her sale on 10 September 1965.
Built by Sumitomo Heavy Industries, Yokosuka.

SEMIEN (1936) See LUGANO (1942)

SEMINOLE (1925)
5896 grt; 446 psrs
388' x 54' x 20' (117.6 x 16.4 x 6 m)
2 x Newport news SRG turbine engines via single screw.
Broken up for scrap at Baltimore, USA, in 1952.
Built by Newport News Shipbuilding, Newport News, Virginia, for the Clyde Mallory Steamship Co.

SEMINOLE EXPRESS (1997) See MAGIC 1 (1999)

SEMIRAMIS II (1969) See REGENCY (1982)

SEMO EXPRESS FERRY 2 (1998) See COZY ISLAND (1999)

SENG KONG No. 1 (1964)
3964 grt; 84 psrs
336' x 51' x 20' (102.4 x 15.5 x 6.1 m)
B+W 6-cylinder diesel engine via single screw.
Owned by Chan Kai Kit, she was broken up for scrap at Singapore in 1965 after being arrested in Singapore and laying idle for a year before a court case was convened.
Built by Caledon Shipbuilding & Engineering Co Ltd, Dundee, for the Blue Funnel Line as the passenger-cargo liner CHARON (1936).

SENLAC (1973) See EXPRESS APOLLON (1997)

SENSATION (1993)
70367 grt; 2040 psrs
860' x 102' x 26' (260.6 x 30.9 x 7.8 m)
6 x 12-cylinder Sulzer diesel-electric engines via twin screw.

Cruise ship owned and operated by Carnival Cruise Lines.
Built by the Kvaerner Masa-Yard, Helsinki, for the Carnival Cruise Line at a cost of US$400,000,000. This price represented a 40% increase over the US$287,000,000 original contract accepted by Wartsila, prior to its collapse and takeover by Kvaerner.

SEQUANA (1912)
5450 grt; 96 psrs
430' x 50' x 28'5" (130.3 x 15.2 x 8.6 m)
Workman, Clark 3-cylinder triple expansion engine via single screw.
Built by Workman, Clark & Co Ltd, Belfast, for City Line & Ellerman Lines as the passenger-cargo liner CITY OF CORINTH (1898).

SERBIAN PRINCE (1906) See REGINA DITALIA (1907)

SERDICA (1988) See ASK (1991)

SERENADE (1999)
13804 grt; 757 psrs
531' x 65' x 23' (161.8 x 19.8 x 7 m)
2 x 7-cylinder Pennhoet-B+W diesel engines via twin screw.

Owned and operated by Louis Cruise Lines.
Built by Ateliers et Chantiers de l'Atlantique, St Nazaire, for the Fabre Line as the passenger ship JEAN MERMOZ (1957). Renamed MERMOZ (1970 – Paquet Cruises).

SERGEANT CHARLES E. MOWER (1946) See SGT. CHARLES E. MOWER (1946)

SERPA PINTO (1940)
8480 grt; 498 psrs
450' x 57' x 25'6" (136.4 x 17.3 x 7.7 m)
Quadruple expansion engines via twin screw.
Broken up for scrap in Belgium in 1955 for a tender figure of US$230,000.
Ex-Cie Colonial de Navegacao, Lisbon.
Built by Workman, Clark & Co, Belfast, for the Royal Mail Steam Packet Co as the passenger-cargo ship EBRO (1914). Renamed PRINCESA OLGA (1935 – Yugoslav Lloyd, Split).

SERVIA (1924) See CARINTHIA (1925)

SERVIAN (1903) See REPUBLIC, USS (AP-33) (1941)

SESTRIERE (1943)
8652 grt
476' x 61' x 25'11" (144.2 x 18.5 x 7.6 m)
Fiat 8-cylinder diesel engine via single screw.
Broken up as a migrant-cargo ship at Vado in 1970. Ex-Costa Line.
Built by Cantieri Navale Franco Tosi, Taranto, for Italnavi.

SETIABUDHI (1961)
7338 grt; 1112 psrs
503' x 64' x 27' (152.5 x 19.5 x 8.3 m)
8-cylinder Fiat diesel engine via single screw.
Passenger-cargo ship owned by Jakarta Lloyd-PT Perusahaan Pelayaran Samudra, Jakarta.
Built by Mitsubishi Zosen KK, Hiroshima.

SEVEN SEAS (1954)
12575 grt; 1007 psrs
492' x 69' x 22' (150 x 21.2 x 6.7 m)
7-cylinder Busch-Sulzer diesel engine via single screw.
Broken up for scrap by Van Heyghen Freres at Ghent in 1977 after serving as a student hostel for the University of Rotterdam since 1966. Prior to this she had been a passenger liner.

Launched by Sun Shipbuilding & Drydock Co, Chester, Pennsylvania, for Moore McCormack Lines as the Class C3 cargo ship MORMACMAIL (1940) and completed for the US Navy as the auxiliary aircraft carrier LONG ISLAND, USS (CVE-1) (1941). Renamed NELLY (1949 – Caribbean Land & Shipping Corporation).

SEVEN SEAS (1975) See ATHIRAH (1992)

SEVEN SEAS NAVIGATOR (1999)
25000 grt; 490 psrs
560' x 81' x 21' (170.6 x 24.8 x 6.6 m)
4 x 8-cylinder Wartsila diesel engines via twin screw.

Built by Mariotti Shipyards, Genoa, for the Vaslov Group, Monte Carlo. She was marketed by Radisson Seven Seas Cruises after Vaslov purchased the unfinished hull of the ice-strengthened research vessel AKADEMIK NICOLAY PILYU (1999), being constructed in Ukraine for the Russian Academy of Sciences, and then completing the construction at a total cost of US$200,000,000.

17 DE OCTUBRE (1950) See LIBERTAD (1955)

SEYDLITZ (1903)
8859 grt; 1906 psrs
450' x 55' x 35'9" (136.4 x 16.7 x 10.9 m)
F Schichau 6-cylinder triple expansion engines via twin screw.
Broken up for scrap at Bremerhaven in 1933.
Built by F Schichau, Danzig, for North German Lloyd as a passenger liner.

S. F. PANTHER (1973) See NUSA PERJUANG (1992)

SGT. CHARLES E. MOWER (1946)
7486 grt
Broken up for scrap at Portland, Oregon, in 1969.
Built as the ALCOA COURIER (1941). Renamed TRYON, USS (APH-1) (1942 – US Navy).

SHAH, HMS (1943) See SALTA (1949)

SHAHD FAYEZ (1991) See TEBAH 2000 (1999)

SHAHEED SALAHUDDIN (1981)
12457 grt; 919 psrs
531' x 65' x 23' (161.8 x 19.8 x 7 m)
2 x 9-cylinder B+W diesel engines via twin screw.
Broken up for scrap by Karafuli Metal Works, Chittagong, in 1985. Ex-Bangladeshi Navy.
Built by Penhoet, St Nazaire, for Cie de Navigation Fraissinet et Cyprien Fabre, Marseilles, as the GENERAL MANGIN (1953). Renamed PRESIDENT (1969 – Philippine President Line), EASTERN QUEEN (1972 – Cia de Navegacion Abeto SA), HIZBUHL-BAHR (1977 – Bangladesh Shipping Corporation, for whom she was a pilgrim ship until requisitioned by the Navy).

SHAH NAJAF (1906)
4636 grt; 153 psrs
400' x 45' x 28'9" (122 x 13.8 x 8.8 m)
2-cylinder compound inverted engine via single screw.
Broken up for scrap at Mumbai in 1908. Ex-Shah Steam Navigation Co, Mumbai.

Built by Caird & Co, Greenock, for the P&O Line as the passenger-cargo liner CHUSAN (1884) at a cost of £120,000.

SHAH NAJAM (1905)
4397 grt; 153 psrs
400' x 45' x 28'9" (122 x 13.8 x 8.8 m)
2-cylinder compound inverted engine via single screw.
Broken up for scrap at Mumbai in 1908. Ex-Shah Steam Navigation Co, Mumbai.
Built by Caird & Co, Greenock, for the P&O Line as the passenger-cargo liner BENGAL (1884) at a cost of £120,000.

SHAH NASIR (1906) See FAKHRI (1909)

SHAH NAWAZ (1906) See NAJMI (1909)

SHAH NOOR (1901)
4189 grt; 195 psrs
390' x 42' x 32'6" (118.9 x 12.8 x 9.9 m)
Compound inverted engine via single screw.
Broken up for scrap at Mumbai in 1905. Ex-Shah Steam Navigation Co, Mumbai.
Built by William Denny & Bros, Dumbarton, for the P&O Line as the passenger-cargo liner CLYDE (1881).

SHAH NOOR (1905)
4136 grt; 171 psrs
400' x 42' x 24' (122 x 12.7 x 7.3 m)
Triple expansion engine via single screw.
Broken up as a pilgrim ship for scrap by Mazagon Powder Works at Mumbai in 1908. Ex-Shah Steam Navigation Co, Mumbai.
Built William Denny & Bros, Dumbarton, for the P&O Line at a cost of £125,937 as the COROMANDEL (1884).

SHAHRAZAD (1985)
6921 grt; 940 psrs
429' x 60' x 17'6" (130 x 18.2 x 5.3 m)
2 x 6-cylinder Sulzer diesel engines via twin screw.
Owned by Marinvest Funds SA, Panama. She sank on 21 September 1985 in the Red Sea.
Built by Forges et Chantiers de la Mediterranee, La Seyne, for Cie de Navigation Paquet, Marseilles, as the passenger liner AVENIR (1967). Renamed ESPRESSO CORINTO (1976 – Trans Tirreno Express SpA, Cagliari).

SHALOM (1964) See SUN (1998)

SHAMROCK (1943)
6678 grt; 280 psrs
415' x 50' x 30' depth (125.8 x 15.2 x 9.1 m)
W Cramp & Sons 6-cylinder triple expansion engines via twin screw.
Broken up for scrap at Oakland, California, in 1948.
Built by William Cramp & Sons, Philadelphia, Pennsylvania, for the New York & Cuba Mail Steamship Co as the HAVANA (1906). Renamed COMFORT, USS (AH-3) (1917 – US Navy), HAVANA (1927 – New York & Cuba Mail Steamship Co), YUCATAN (1935 – New York & Cuba Mail Steamship Co) and AGWILEON (1940 – Atlantic Gulf & West Indies Steamship Lines).

SHAMS (1961)
8929 grt; 200 psrs
470' x 66' x 22' (142.4 x 20 x 6.7 m)
2 x 9-cylinder B+W diesel engines via twin screw.
Broken up for scrap at Gadani Beach in 1994 after use as a pilgrim ship. Ex-Pakistan Shipping Corporation, Karachi.
Built by Hitachi, Osaka, for Crescent Shipping Lines Ltd, Karachi.

SHANGHAI (1978)
13809 grt; 240 psrs
558' x 70' x 28' (170.1 x 21.3 x 8.5 m)
2 x Parsons DRG turbine engines via single screw.
Broken up for scrap at Shanghai in 1996. Ex-China Merchants Steam Navigation Co Ltd.
Built by John Cockerill Shipyards, Hoboken, Belgium, for Cie Maritime Belge as the passenger-cargo ship BAUDOUINVILLE (1957). Renamed

CATHAY (1961 – P&O Group) and KENGHSHIN (1976 – China Merchants Steam Navigation Co Ltd).

SHANGHAI MARU (1923)
5259 grt; 344 psrs
395' x 54' x 20' (119.7 x 16.4 x 6.1 m)
4 x William Denny SRG turbine engines via twin screw.
Built by William Denny & Brothers Co Ltd, Dumbarton, for NYK.

SHANG No. 7 (1935) See KIZAN MARU (1938)

SHANGRI-LA WORLD (1991) See LEISURE WORLD (1994)

SHANNON (1881) See PROCTER (1901)

SHARM EL-SHEIKH (1987) See DAHAB (1994)

SHAULA (1943) See OLIMPIA (1947)

SHAWMUT (1902) See CONTINENTAL (1948)

SHAWMUT, USS (CM-4) (1917) See OGLALA, USS (1928)

SHAWNEE (1927) See PARTIZANKA (1947)

SHELBY, USS (APA-105) (1945) See ORIENTAL PEARL (1965)

SHENG SHENG (1998)
8075 grt; 700 psrs
180 cars
386' x 63' x 14' (117 x 19.1 x 4.2 m)
2 x 12-cylinder Pielstick diesel engines via twin screw.

Owned and operated by Weihai Ferry Co, Weihai.
Built by Soc Nouvelle des Ateliers et Chantiers du Havre, Le Havre, for JS Hagen, Oslo, to ge operated by Da No Line as the TERGE VIGEN (1972). Renamed ARMORIQUE (1976 – Brittany Ferries) and MIN NAN (1993 – China Ocean Shipping Co, Shanghai).

SHERMAN (1898) See CALAWAII (1923)

SHIDZUOKA MARU (1912)
6469 grt
409' x 49' x 27'6" (123.9 x 14.8 x 8.4 m)
Triple Kawasaki Dockyard 6-cylinder triple expansion engines via twin screw.
Abandoned as a total constructive loss after running aground on 14 May 1933.
Built by Kawasaki Dockyard, Kobe, for NYK.

SHIMA MARU (1973) See FERRY KUROSHIO (1978)

SHIMPO MARU (1910) See WALTER HOLKEN (1919)

SHINANO MARU (1900)
6388 grt; 238 psrs
447' x 50' x 33'6" (135.6 x 15 x 10.2 m)
2 x triple expansion engines via twin screw.
Broken up for scrap in Japan in 1951.
Built by D & W Henderson, Glasgow, for NYK as a passenger-cargo ship.

SHINKAI MARU (1911)
3525 grt
336' x 43' x 22'3" (101.8 x 13 x 6.8 m)
Delaware River Co 3-cylinder triple expansion engine via single screw.
Broken up for scrap at Osaka in 1930. Ex-Ogifyu Sotaro.
Built by Delaware River Shipbuilding Works, Chester, Pennsylvania, for the

New York & Cuba Mail Steamship Co as the YUCATAN (1890).

SHINKOKO MARU (1914) See ANDRE CHENIER (1921)

SHINKO MARU (1970) See TACLOBAN PRINCESS (1990)

SHINKO MARU (1989)
3611 grt; 495 psrs
379' x 68' x 16'6" (114.7 x 20.6 x 5 m)
2 x 9-cylinder Niigata-Pielstick diesel engines via twin screw.
Owned and operated by King Fung Marine Co Ltd, Hau Lien.
Built by Fukuoka Shipyard, Fukuoka.

SHIN SAKURA MARU (1972)
17389 grt; 552 psrs
577' x 80' x 26' (175.8 x 24.6 x 7.9 m)
8-cylinder Mitsubishi diesel engine via single screw.
Broken up for scrap in 1999 as a cruise ship. She had operated for her first nine years as a worldwide floating trade exhibition ship, and then for 18 years as a student education ship. Sold to Pan Yu Shipbreakers by Mitsui-OSK Lines for US$1,000,000.
Built by Mitsubishi Heavy Industries, Kobe, for Mitsui-OSK.

SHINYO MARU (1911)
13384 grt; 1021 psrs
558' x 62' x 31'9" (169 x 18.8 x 9.7 m)
3 x Mitsubishi turbine engines via triple screw.
Broken up for scrap in Japan in 1936.
Built by Mitsubishi Dockyard for Toto Kisen Kaisha as a passenger liner.

SHINYO MARU (1943)
18184 grt; 293 psrs
652' x 74' x 29' (197.6 x 22.4 x 8.8 m)
Turbo-electric engines via twin screw.
As an aircraft carrier for the Japanese Navy during World War Two, she sank on 17 November 1944 after being torpedoed by the USS BARB 140 miles (233 km) north-east of Shanghai. Of 769 people on board, 688 lost their lives while 81 were picked up by another US submarine, the USS NORWHAL.
Built by AG Weser, Bremen, for North German Lloyd as the passenger-cargo liner SCHARNHORST (1934). Renamed JINYO (1942 – government of Japan).

SHINZAN MARU (1925) See TRETI KRABOLOV (1929)

SHIRETOKO MARU (1972) See N. KAZANTZAKIS (1990)

SHIRLEY (1963)
12019 grt; 1310 psrs
511' x 62' x 30' (154.8 x 18.8 x 9.1 m)
6-cylinder triple expansion engines via twin screw.
Broken up for scrap in Vladivostok in 1970. Ex-Eddie Steamship Co, Vladivostok.
Built by Bremer Vulkan, Vegesack, for North German Lloyd as the passenger liner SIERRA MORENA (1924). Renamed DER DEUTSCHE (1934 – Deutsche Arbietsfront GmbH) and ASIA (1946 – government of the USSR).

SHIZUOKA MARU (1912)
6568 grt
409' x 49' x 27'6" (123.9 x 14.8 x 8.4 m)
2 x Kawasaki Dockyard 6-cylinder triple expansion engines via twin screw.
Abandoned in May 1933 as a total constructive loss after running aground on 23 April.
Built by Kawasaki Dockyard, Kobe, for NYK.

SHOHO MARU (1923)
3460 grt; 895 psrs
25 railway wagons
362' x 52' x 14' (109.7 x 15.9 x 4.3 m)
Passenger-train ferry sunk by US bombers outside Aomori harbour on 14 July 1945.
Built by Sumitomo Heavy Industries, Yokosuka, for the Seikan Railway Ferries Co.

SHOROK I (1998)
3526 grt; 1020 psrs
80 cars
297' x 50' x 15' (90 x 15.3 x 4.6 m)
2 x 6-cylinder Nohab diesel engines via twin screw.

Passenger-car-cargo ship owned and operated by William Marine Transporter, Egypt.
Built by Aarhus Flydedok, Aarhus, for Lion Ferry as the PRINS BERTL (1960). Renamed CALMAR NYCKEL (1964 – Rederi AB Nordo), HOLMIA (1965 – Silja Line), FLAMINIA NUOVA (1971 – Navagazione Toscana SpA, Livorno), CAPO BIANCO (1974 – Toscana Regionale Marittima SpA, Livorno), DANIA MARINE (1992 – Saudi Navigation Co), RANEEM I (1994 – Raneem Navigation Co, Jeddah) and SHOUROK (1997 – El Salam Shipping & Trading Establishment).

SHOROUK (1995) See AL QAMAR (1999)

SHOTA RUSTAVELI (1968)
21725 grt; 750 psrs
578' x 77' x 26' (176.2 x 23.5 x 7.9 m)
2 x 7-cylinder Sulzer diesel engines via twin screw.
Ice-strengthened cruise ship owned by the Black Sea Shipping Co subsidiary Redwood Shipping Co, Odessa, and laid up in Iliychevsk, Ukraine, since 1998 for legal reasons.
Built by Mathias-Thesen Werft, Wismar.

SHOUROK (1997) See SHOROK I (1998)

SHROPSHIRE (1882) See SEANG BEE MARU (1931)

SHROPSHIRE (1911) See ROTORUA (1923)

SHROPSHIRE (1926) See SALOPIAN, HMS (1939)

SIBAJAK (1927)
12342 grt; 527 psrs
530' x 62' x 28' (160.6 x 18.9 x 8.5 m)
2 x 8-cylinder Sulzer diesel engines via twin screw.
Broken up for scrap at Hong Kong in 1959.
Built by De Schelde NV, Vissingen, for Royal Rotterdam Lloyd.

SIBARI (1970)
5768 grt; 2000 psrs
467' x 42' x 14'6" (141.5 x 12.7 x 4.4 m)
4 x 6-cylinder Fiat diesel engines via twin screw.
Passenger-cargo RoRo ferry owned by Italian State Railways and operated by Ferrovie Stato on the Italy–Sicily service.
Built by Italcantieri SpA, Castellammare di Stabia.

SIBERIA (1902) See SIBERIA MARU (1916)

SIBERIA MARU (1916)
11785 grt; 1560 psrs
552' x 63' x 21'8" (167.3 x 19.1 x 6.6 m)
Newport News 8-cylinder quadruple expansion engines via twin screw.
Broken up for scrap at Kobe in 1935. Ex-NYK, Japan.
Built by Newport News Shipbuilding & Drydock Company, Newport News, Virginia, for Pacific Fast Mail as the SIBERIA (1902).

SIBIR (1929)
3767 grt; 292 psrs
333' x 48' x 25'6" (100 x 14.5 x 7.8 m)
Russian Diesel Works 6-cylinder diesel engine via single screw.

Believed lost in World War Two.
Built by Severney Shipbuilding Yard, St Petersburg, for the Russian government.

SIBIR (1946)
8791 grt; 284 psrs
439' x 56' x 24' (133 x 17 x 7.3 m)
Triple expansion engines via twin screw.
Owned and operated by the USSR after being awarded the ship as a war prize after World War Two.
Built by Bremer Vulkan, Vegesack, for North German Lloyd as the SIERRA SALVADA (1912). Renamed OCEANA (1927 – Hamburg-America Line), AVARE (1945), PEER GYNT (1945 – Viktor Schuppe), NEPTUNIA (1945) and EMPIRE TARNE (1945).

SIBONEY (1918) See CHARLES A. STAFFORD (1944)

SICAMOUS (1912) See NIAGARA (1913)

SICILIA (1900) See SICILIA (1912)

SICILIA (1901)
6696 grt; 160 psrs
450' x 52' x 30' (137.3 x 15.9 x 9.2 m)
2 x Barclay Curle 6-cylinder triple expansion engines via twin screw.
Broken up for scrap by Kishimoto KKK at Osaka in 1926.
Built by Barclay, Curle & Co, Glasgow, for the P&O Line as a passenger-cargo liner at a cost of £152,088.

SICILIA (1912)
5229 grt; 1412 psrs
418' x 47' x 27'6" (127.5 x 14.4 x 8.4 m)
N Odero 3-cylinder triple expansion engine via single screw.
Broken up for scrap in 1929. Ex-Sitmar Line.
Built by Soc Esercizio Baccini, Riva Trigoso, for Navigazione Generale Italiana, Genoa, as the passenger liner SICILIA (1900).

SICILIA (1952)
5230 grt; 560 psrs
348' x 53' x 17' (115.5 x 16 x 5.2 m)
4 x 6-cylinder Fiat diesel engines via twin screw.
Passenger-cargo RoRo ferry owned and operated by Tirrenia.
Built by Cantieri Riuniti, Palermo.

SICILIAN (1899) See BRUTON (1923)

SICILIAN (1917) See BRUTON (1923)

SIDI BEL ABBES (1948) See APOLLONIA (1963)

SIDI OKBA (1947) See ELECTRA (1964)

SIDNEY (1960) See QUEEN OF SIDNEY (1963)

SIERRA (1900) See SIERRA (1923)

SIERRA (1923)
6135 grt; 460 psrs
417' x 50' x 18' (127.1 x 15.2 x 5.5 m)
Triple expansion engines via twin screw.
Broken up for scrap at Osaka in 1935. Ex-Oceanic Steamship Co.
Built by William Cramp & Sons, Philadelphia, Pennsylvania, for the Oceanic Steamship Co as the passenger liner SIERRA (1900). Renamed GDANSK (1921 – Polish American Navigation Corporation).

SIERRA CORDOBA (1913) See RUTH ALEX ANDER (1922)

SIERRA CORDOBA (1924)
11492 grt; 1310 psrs
491' x 66' x 34'3" depth (148.8 x 20 x 10.4 m)
Bremer Vulkan 6-cylinder triple expansion engines via twin screw.
Sank on 18 January 1948, off Esbjerg, when the towing cable snapped while en route to the UK from Hamburg where the ship had been gutted by fire.
Built by Bremer Vulkan, Vegesack, for North German Lloyd as a passenger liner.

SIERRA MORENA (1924) See SHIRLEY (1963)

SIERRA NEVADA (1922) See MADRID (1935)

SIERRA NEVADA (1932) See EMPIRE HALLADALE (1946)

SIERRA SALVADA (1912) See SIBIR (1946)

SIERRA SALVADA (1932) See EMPIRE TROOPER (1940)

SIERRA VENTANA (1913) See AMERIQUE (1926)

SIERRA VENTANA (1923) See SARDEGNA (1935)

SIFNOS (1987) See ORESTES (1999)

SIFNOS EXPRESS (1990) See ORESTES (1999)

SILESIA (1979)
10553 grt; 984 psrs
277 cars or 26 trailers
421' x 64' x 18' (127.6 x 19.5 x 5.4 m)
4 x 6-cylinder Zgoda-Sulzer diesel engines via twin screw.

Passenger-car-cargo ferry owned by Polska Zegwea Morsk and operated by
Pol Ferries.
Built by Stocznia Szczecinska, Szczecin

SILJA EUROPA (1993)
59914 grt; 3013 psrs
341 cars
666' x 106' x 22' (201.8 x 32 x 6.8 m)
4 x 6-cylinder MAN-B+W diesel engines via twin screw.

Ice-strengthened passenger-car ferry acquired by Sea Containers Ltd, UK, in
1999.
Laid down by Jos L Meyer Shipyards, Papenburg, for Rederi AB Slite to be
operated by Viking Line as the EUROPA (1991), but completed for the Silja
Line at a cost of US$280,000,000 as the SILJA EUROPA.

SILJA FESTIVAL (1990)
34414 grt; 2000 psrs
360 cars + 60 trailers

554' x 104' x 21'6" (168 x 31.6 x 6.5 m)
4 x 12-cylinder Pielstick diesel engines via twin screw.
Passenger-car-cargo ferry owned and operated by Silja Line Oy, Helsinki.
Built by Wartsila-Helsinki for Silja Line Oy as the WELLAMO (1986).

SILJA KARNEVAL (1992) See COLOR FESTIVAL (1994)

SILJA SCANDINAVIA (1992) See GABRIELLA (1997)

SILJA SERENADE (1990)
58376 grt; 2614 spsrs
450 cars or 60 trailers
670' x 104' x 23' (203 x 31.5 x 7 m)
4 x 9-cylinder Wartsila-Vasa diesel engines via twin screw.

Ice-strengthened passenger-car ferry acquired by Sea Containers Ltd, UK, in
1999.
Built by Kvaerner-Masa Yards, Turku, for Effjohn International to be operated
by the Silja Line.

SILJA STAR (1979) See STENA SAGA (1994)

SILJA STAR (1980) See WASA QUEEN (1992)

SILJA STAR (1990) See ESTONIA (1993)

SILJA SYMPHONY (1991)
58377 grt; 2670 psrs
450 cars or 60 trailers
670' x 104' x 23' (203 x 31.5 x 7 m)
4 x 9-cylinder Wartsila-Vasa diesel engines via twin screw.

Ice-strengthened passenger-car ferry acquired by Sea Containers Ltd, UK, in
1999.
Built by the Kvaerner-Masa Yard for Effjohn International for operation by the
Silja Line.

SILVER CLOUD (1994)
16927 grt; 296 psrs
514' x 70' x 17'6" (155.8 x 21.2 x 5.3 m)
2 x 6-cylinder Wartsila diesel engines via twin screw.
Cruise ship owned by V-Ships, Monaco, and cruising for Silversea Cruises
Ltd.
Laid down by Francesco Visentine, Viareggio, and completed by J Mariotti
Shipyards, Genoa, at a cost of US$125,000,00.

SILVER PALOMA (1986) See MEGI (2000)

SILVER QUEEN (1973) See SILVER QUEEN (1998)

SILVER QUEEN (1998)
4043 grt; 800 psrs
360' x 57' x 16'6" (109 x 17.4 x 5 m)
2 x 8-cylinder Niigata diesel engines via twin screw.
Owned by PT Dharma Lauton Utama and operated by Hayashi Marine Co Ltd, Nagasaki.
Built by Narasaki Shipyard, Muroran as the SILVER QUEEN (1973). Renamed DONG YANG EXPRESS FERRY No. 5 (1984 – Dong Yang Express Ferry Co Ltd).

SILVER QUEEN (1998)
6190 grt; 600 psrs
92 trailers
442' x 69' x 19' (134 x 21 x 5.7 m)
2 x 16-cylinder Pielstick diesel engines via twin screw.
Passenger-cargo ferry owned and operated by Kawasaki Kinkai Kisen.
Built by Mitsubishi Heavy Industries, Shimonoseki.

SILVER QUEEN 2 (1982)
4821 grt; 439 psrs
68 cars + 52 trailers
398' x 68' x 17' (120.6 x 20.5 x 5.2 m)
2 x 8-cylinder Pielstick diesel engines via twin screw.
Passenger-car-cargo ferry owned and operated by Silver Ferry, Japan.
Built by Niigata Engineering, Niigata.

SILVER SHADOW (2000)
25000 grt; 390 psrs
601' x 82' x 19'6" (182.1 x 24.8 x 5.9 m)
4 x 6-cylinder Wartsila diesel engines via twin screw.
Owned and operated by Silversea Cruises.
Built by Francesco Visentini Shipyard, Donada, with fit-out at the J Mariotti Shipyards, Genoa, at a total cost of US$150,000,000.

SILVER STAR (1998)
5261 grt; 314 psrs
403' x 53' x 17' (12 x 16 x 5.2 m)
2 x 6-cylinder MAN diesel engines via twin screw.
Ice-strengthened cruise ship owned by Silverstar Shipping Co Ltd, Haifa, and operated by Mano Maritime Ltd, Haifa.
Built by Mathias-Thesen, Wismar, for the Black Sea Shipping Co, Odessa, as the BASHKIRIYA (1964). Renamed ODESSA SONG (1992 – Black Sea Shipping Co, Odessa) and ROYAL DREAM (1997 – Transorient Overseas SA). The ship was arrested in Haifa for unpaid debts which were eventually settled to the court's satisfaction and the ship passed into the hands of Silversea Shipping.

SILVER STATE (1921) See PRESIDENT JACKSON (1946)

SILVER WIND (1995)
16927 grt; 296 psrs
514' x 70' x 17'6" (155.8 x 21.2 x 5.3 m)
2 x 6-cylinder Wartsila diesel engines via twin screw.
Cruise ship owned by V-Ships, Monaco, and cruising for Silversea Cruises Ltd.
Laid down by Francesco Visentine, Viareggio, and completed by J Mariotti Shipyards, Genoa, at a cost of US$125,000,000.

SILVIA (1900) See RIVERA (1917)

SILVIA REGINA (1981) See STENA SAGA (1994)

SIMON BOLIVAR (1927)
8309 grt; 60 psrs
420' x 59' x 27'7" (127.3 x 17.9 x 8.4 m)
Roterdam Droogd Maats quadruple expansion engine via single screw.
Sank in shallow water on 18 November 1939 after striking a mine at 12.30 pm 25 miles (42 km) from Harwich and approaching Longsand Head. A total of 130 lives were lost.
Built for Royal Nederlands Steamship Co by Roterdam Droogd Maats, Rotterdam.

SINABUNG (1997)
14716 grt; 1906 psrs
483' x 77' x 19'6" (146.5 x 23.4 x 5.9 m)
2 x 8-cylinder MaK diesel engines via twin screw.
Passenger container ship operated by the Indonesian government.
Built by Meyer Werft, Papenburg.

SINAI (1948)
3899 grt
352' x 45' x 26' (106.7 x 13.6 x 7.9 m)
Richardson, Westgarth 3-cylinder triple expansion engines via single screw.
Built by Furness, Withy & Co Ltd, West Hartlepool, for the Hamburg-America Line as the SPREEWALD (1907). Renamed LUCIA, HMS (1914 – British War Ministry).

SINAIA (1922)
8567 grt; 654 psrs
459' x 56' x 34'3" depth (139.1 x 17 x 10.4 m)
Barclay Curle 6-cylinder triple expansion engines via twin screw.
Broken up for scrap in 1947 after she was raised from the Marseilles harbour seabed. She had sank when scuttled by the retreating Germans in August 1944.
Built by Barclay, Curle & Co, Glasgow, for the Fabre Line as a passenger liner.

SINALOA (1958)
7513 grt; 100 psrs
448' x 60' x 25'3" (135.8 x 18.2 x 7.7 m)
2 x General Electric turbo-electric engines via twin screw.
Broken up for scrap at Bruges in 1964. Ex-Elders & Fyffes.
Built by the Bethlehem Steel Corporation, Quincy, Massachusetts, for the United Fruit Steamship Co as the passenger-cargo ship VERAGUA (1932). Renamed MERAK, USS (AF-21) (1942 – US Navy) and VERAGUA (1946 – United Fruit Steamship Co).

SINBAD (1977) See SINBAD I (1978)

SINDBAD I (1978)
28582 grt; 670 psrs
763' x 83' x 32' (232.5 x 25.3 x 9.7 m)
Parsons DRG turbine engines via twin screw.
Owned by Kinvara Bay Shipping Co, she was broken up for scrap at Kaohsiung in 1980 after being laid up in Hong Kong since 1976.
Built by Harland & Wolff Ltd, Belfast, for the Union Castle Line as the passenger-cargo liner PENDENNIS CASTLE (1959). Renamed OCEAN QUEEN (1976 – Ocean Queen Navigation Corporation) and SINBAD (1977 – Kinvara Bay Shipping Corporation).

SINDIBAD I (1982)
5298 grt; 954 psrs
70 cars + 24 trailers
415' x 63' x 17' (125.8 x 19.2 x 5.2 m)
2 x 7-cylinder Fiat diesel engines via twin screw.
Passenger-car-cargo ferry operated by El-Salam Shipping Co, Jeddah.
Built by Construzioni Navale Meccaniche for Traghetti Delle Isol as the CANGURO ROSSO (1965). Renamed ESPRESSO ROSSO (1978 – Trasporti Marittimi Combinati SpA, Palermo).

SINDORO (1900) See PEDRO GOMES (1922)

SIR CARADO (1983) See HUA LU (1994)

SIRDHANA (1947)
8608 grt; 1301 psrs
479' x 63' x 26' (145.2 x 19.1 x 7.9 m)
2 x 4-cylinder Doxford diesel engines via twin screw.
Broken up for scrap by Nan Feng Steel Enterprise Co Ltd at Kaohsiung in 1972.
Built by Swan Hunter Shipbuilders Ltd, Newcastle, for the British India Line as a passenger liner.

SIRIMAU (1990)
6041 grt; 969 psrs
330' x 60' x 14' (100 x 18.3 x 4.2 m)
2 x 6-cylinder Krupp-MaK diesel engines via twin screw.
Passenger ferry operated by P T Pelni, Indonesia.
Built by Jos L Meyer GmbH, Papenburg, for the Indonesian government.

SIRIUS (191)

8917 grt; 300 psrs
100 cars + 80 trailers or coaches
498' x 60' x 27'6" (150.1 x 18.2 x 8.4 m)
1 x Fairfield DRG turbine engine via single screw.
Broken up for scrap as a passenger-car-cargo RoRo ferry at Skaramanga in 1980. Ex-Hellenic Cruises.
Built by Fairfield Shipbuilding & Engineering Co Ltd, Glasgow, for the Bibby Line as the passenger liner WARWICKSHIRE (1948). Renamed HANIA (1965 – Typaldos Lines, who registered the name HANIA but publicised her as the incorrectly spelt CHANEA).

SIR ROBERT BOND (1975)

11197 grt; 260 psrs
75 cars + 26 trailers
444' x 71' x 16' (134.5 x 21.5 x 4.9 m)
4 x 12-cylinder Ruston Paxman diesel engines via twin screw.
Passenger-car ferry owned by the Minister of Works, Services & Administration, Canadian government, and operated by Marine Atlantic.
Built by Port Weller Drydocks Ltd, St Catherines, Ontario, for CN Marine, Halifax, as a passenger-car-train ferry.

SISES (1948)

9177 grt
475' x 61' x 28'3" (143.9 x 18.5 x 8.6 m)
Fiat 7-cylinder diesel engine via single screw.
Broken up for scrap as a migrant-cargo ship at La Spezia in 1978. Ex-Costa Line.
Built by Cantieri Navale di Taranto for Italnavi.

SITERRANEAN SKY (1987)

16533 grt; 850 psrs
350 cars
541' x 71' x 28'6" (164.8 x 21.6 x 8.7 m)
2 x 6-cylinder Hawthorn Leslie-Doxford diesel engines via twin screw.
Laid up since 1998 in Eleusis Bay awaiting sale at US$1,600,000 as a passenger-car ferry. She had been operated in Argentina by Padiestra Oceanica Navigation Panama Golden Cruises.
Built by Vickers-Armstrong Ltd, Newcastle, for Ellerman Lines as the passenger liner CITY OF YORK (1953). Renamed MEDITERRANEAN SKY (1971 – Karageorgios Lines).

SITIA (1967) See NEW YORK FORTUNE I (1997)

SITMAR FAIRWIND (1988) See ALBATROSS (1993)

SIX AOLA (1911)

4937 grt; 103 psrs
379' x 50' x 25' (114.8 x 15.2 x 7.6 m)
Triple expansion engine via single screw.
Sank on 12 June 1942 after being torpedoed off Bocas Del-Toro, Panama.
Built by Workman, Clark & Co, Belfast, for the United Fruit Steamship Co as a passenger-cargo ship.

SJAELLAND (1979)

3046 grt; 1500 psrs
110 cars
364' x 58' x 13' (110.4 x 17.7 x 4 m)
2 x 6-cylinder B+W diesel engines via twin screw.
Now a music centre and restaurant.
Built by Helsingor Shipyard, Helsingor, for the Danish government as the passenger-car ferry DRONNING INGRID (1951).

SKAGEN (1990)

12333 grt; 1325 psrs
430 cars
428' x 63' x 16'6" (129.8 x 19.1 x 5 m)
4 x 6-cylinder Stork-Werkspoor diesel engines via twin screw.
Passenger-car ferry owned by Skagerak Line and operated by Color Line, Norway, on the Norway–Denmark service.
Built by Aalborg Vaerft, Aalborg, for AS Kristiansands DS (Fred Olsen Line) as the BORGEN (1975).

SKANDIA (1961) See ISLA DE CUBAGUA (1975)

SKANDIA (1979) See QUEEN OF SCANDINAVIA (1990)

SKANDIA (1980) See BALTIC KRISTINA (1997)

SKANDYNAWIA (1970) See TIAN HU (1981)

SKANE (1966) See MOBY KING (1990)

SKANE (1998)

42705 grt; 600 psrs
500 cars + 110 trailers
657' x 96' x 21'6" (199 x 29 x 6.5 m)
4 x 6-cylinder MAN-B+W diesel engines via twin screw.

Ice-strengthened passenger-car-cargo RoRo train ferry owned and operated by Stena Line.
Built by Astilleros Espanoles Puerta Real, Cadiz, for Scandlines AB, Helsingborg

SKANE LINK (1989) See POLARIS (1992)

SKAUBRYN (1951)

9786 grt; 1221 psrs
440' x 57' x 21'6" (133.3 x 17.3 x 6.5 m)
9-cylinder Gotaverken diesel engine via single screw.
Sank on 6 April 1958 while under tow by the Dutch tug CYCLOOP from a position 300 miles (500 km) south-east of Socotra Island, in the Indian Ocean. She had caught fire in the engine room one week earlier, on 31 March. Only one life was lost, while 1,300 souls were rescued by the freighter CITY OF SYDNEY.
Laid down by Oresundsvarvet AB, Landskrona, as a freighter, but completed for DS AS Eikland & AS Salamis, Oslo, as a migrant ship by Howaldtswerke AG, Kiel.

SKAUGUM (1948) See OCEAN BUILDER (1964)

SKIPPER CLEMENT (1965) See EUROPA I (1998)

SKROTADES (1987)

4317 grt; 1200 psrs
40 cars
397' x 53' x 17' (120.3 x 16.2 x 5.2 m)
2 x 8-cylinder B+W diesel engines via twin screw.
Broken up for scrap at Gadani Beach in 1987. Ex-Fayez Trading & Shipping Establishment, Jeddah.
Built by Helsingor Shipyards, Helsingor, for DFDS, Mariehamn, as the passenger-car ferry PRINCESSE MARGRETHE (1957). Renamed PRINSESSAN (1968 – Sessan Line), PRINSESSEN (1971 – Rederi AB, Mariehamn), PRINSEN (1977 – Birka Line) and WID (1978 – Fayez Trading & Shipping Establishment, Jeddah).

SKUDENES (1987) See NINDAWAYMA (1993)

SKY PRINCESS (1988) See PACIFIC SKY (2000)

SKYTTEREN (1928)
12686 grt; 226 psrs
565' x 63' x 33' (172.2 x 19.3 x 10 m)
Quadruple expansion engines via twin screw.
Owned by H Vistendahl, Tondsberg, as a whaling factory ship, she sank on 1 April 1942 after her Norwegian crew scuttled her off Maseskjaer, Sweden, to prevent the Germans capturing her.
Built by Harland & Wolff Ltd, Belfast, for the White Star Line as the passenger liner SUEVIC (1901).

SKYWARD (1969) See LEISURE WORLD (1994)

SLAMAT (1924)
11636 grt; 400 psrs
510' x 62' x 35'2" (154.5 x 18.8 x 10.7 m)
Kon Maats de Schelde turbine engines via twin screw.
Sank on 27 April 1941 after a single German Luftwaffe bomber (JG-77) attack off Nauplia, Greece, with the loss of 200 lives and the rescue of 700 by the British destroyers DIAMOND and WRYNECK. Later on that same day, both destroyers were sunk and another 650 of the SLAMAT's original survivors died.
Built by De Schelde, Flushing, for Rotterdam Lloyd as a passenger-cargo liner.

SLAPY (1960) See GUANGHUA (1960)

SLAVIJA (1976) See EUROPA (1998)

SLAVONIA (1904)
10606 grt; 2099 psrs
526' x 60' x 33' (160.3 x 18.3 x 10 m)
2 x 3-cylinder Wallsend Slipway triple expansion engines via twin screw.
Owned by the Cunard Steamship Co, she was abandoned as a total constructive loss after she struck rocks during a dense fog, on 10 June 1909, two miles (3 km) south-west of Flores Island in the Azores.
Launched by Sir James Laing Shipyard, Sunderland, for the British India Line as the passenger liner YAMUNA (1902).

SMITH VICTORY (1945) See FAIRWIND (1963)

SMOLENSK (1901) See RION (1913)

SMOLENSK (1906) See RION (1913)

SMOLNI (1929) See SMOLNYY (1929)

SMOLNYY (1929)
3767 grt; 292 psrs
341' x 48' x 19' (103.3 x 14.5 x 5.8 m)
6-cylinder Russki diesel engine via single screw.
Passenger-cargo ship in Russian waters.
Built by Severney Shipbuilding Yard, St Petersburg, for the Russian government.

SMYRIL (1975)
3430 grt; 800 psrs
120 cars
306' x 55' x 14' (92.7 x 16.7 x 4.2 m)

4 x 14-cylinder B+W diesel engines via twin screw.
Passenger-car-cargo RoRo ferry owned and operated by the Faroese government.
Built by Aalborg Vaerft, Aalborg, for the Mols Line as the MORTEN MOLS (1969).

SOBIESKI (1939) See GRUZIA (1950)

SOBRAL (1918) See GENERAL METZINGER (1924)

SOBRAON (1900)
7382 grt; 171 psrs
450' x 54' x 31'6" (136.4 x 16.4 x 9.6 m)
2 x triple expansion engines via twin screw.
Abandoned as a total constructive loss on 24 April 1901 when she ran ashore in dense fog on Tung Yung Island, north-east of Fuzhou.
Built by Caird & Co, Greenock, for the P&O Line as a passenger-cargo ship at a cost of £160,515.

SOCA (1980) See SEAFRANCE CEZANNE (1996)

SOCIETY ADVENTURER (1991) See HANSEATIC (1993)

SOCRATES (1938) See MOOR B (1967)

SOCRATES (1946) See PORTARITISSA (1955)

SOFIA (1919)
5491 grt; 1630 psrs
360' x 48' x 26'10" (109.7 x 14.6 x 7.9 m)
Lloyds Austriaco 3-cylinder triple expansion engine via single screw.
Broken up for scrap in 1929. Ex-Cosulich Lines.
Built by Lloyd Austriaco, Trieste, for Unione Austriaca as the passenger liner SOFIA HOHENBERG (1905).

SOFIA (1968)
8357 grt; 52 psrs
length 459' x beam 63' (139.1 x 19.1 m)
Turbine engine via single screw.
Broken up for scrap at Kaohsiung in 1970. Ex-Anchor Shipping Corporation.
Built by North Carolina Shipbuilding Corporation, Wilmington, for the Grace Line as the passenger-cargo ship SANTA ISABEL (1946). Renamed SANTA CRISTINA (1967 – Grace Line).

SOFIA (1998) See ENCHANTED SUN (1999)

SOFIA HOHENBERG (1905) See SOFIA (1919)

SOFOKLIS VENIZELOS (1999) See SOPHOCLES V (1999)

SOJUS (1980)
23009 grt; 1551 psrs
646' x 72' x 28' (195.8 x 21.8 x 8.5 m)
8 x SRG turbine engines via twin screw.
Broken up for scrap in 1981. Ex-Russian government.
Built by Blohm & Voss, Hamburg, for the Hamburg-America Line as the ice-strengthened passenger liner ALBERT BALLIN (1923). Renamed HANSA (1935 – Hamburg-America Line) and then SOVETSKY SOJUS (1950 – Russian government). The Russians salvaged the hull in 1949 from where it sank, while under tow, off Warnemund on 6 March 1945 when the HANSA struck a mine. The ship was completely rebuilt as a passenger-cargo ship, but in 1954 SOVETSKY SOJUS was swept by fire and rebuilt once again.

SOLACE (1944) See ANKARA (1948)

SOL CHRISTIANA (1985) See OCEAN MAJESTY (1991)

SOL EXPRESS (1982) See TUXEDO ROYALE (1988)

SOLGLIMT (1928) See SONDERBURG (1941)

SOL OLYMPIA (1982) See SARDEGNA BELLA (1993)

SOL OLYMPIA II (1985)
9000 grt; 750 psrs
100 cars
429' x 63' x 16' (130 x 19.1 x 4.8 m)
2 x 7-cylinder B+W diesel engines via twin screw.
Cruise ship acquired by Sun Med Lines, Limassol, in 1985 for US$1,600,000. She was gutted by fire on 6 June 1986 while laid up at a berth in Eleusis Bay and her remaining hull was sold to Nigdeliler Hurdacilik AS, Aliaga, for breaking up into scrap in 1987.
Built by Union Naval de Levante SA, Espanola, for Trasmediterranea as the passenger-cargo ship SANTA CRUZ DE TENERIFE (1966).

SOL PHRYNE (1977)
5855 grt; 630 psrs
389' x 52' x 22'3" (117.9 x 15.8 x 6.8 m)
4 x Mitsubishi DRG turbine engines via twin screw.
Sank on 6 December 1991 while in service as an army transport during the civil war in the Balkans. Chartered from Sol Lines by the Yugoslavian Navy and stationed in Bijela.
Built by Mitsubishi Shipbuilding & Engineering Co, Kobe, for the government of Japan (Department of Railways) as the train ferry TAISETSU MARU (1948). Renamed AEOLIS (1967 – Efthymiadis, Piraeus).

SOMALI (1901)
6708 grt; 160 psrs
450' x 52' x 30' (137.2 x 15.9 x 9.2 m)
2 x Caird & Co triple expansion engines via twin screw.
Broken up for scrap by Petersen & Albeck at Copenhagen in 1924.
Built by Caird & Co, Greenock, for the P&O Line at a cost of £153,242 as a passenger-cargo ship.

SOMERSET (1903)
7010 grt; 204 psrs
461' x 58' x 31' depth (139.7 x 17.6 x 9.4 m)
2 x John Brown 3-cylinder triple expansion engines via twin screw.
Sank on 26 July 1917 after being torpedoed 230 miles (383 km) west of Cape Finistere, near Ushant.
Built by John Brown & Co, Clydebank, for the Federal Steam Navigation Co Ltd as a passenger-cargo ship.

SOMERSET (1911) See CITY OF ATHENS (1917)

SOMERSET (1928)
3648 grt; 170 psrs
309' x 46' x 19'3" (93.6 x 13.9 x 5.8 m)
Engines via single screw.
Broken up for scrap at Baltimore in 1938. Ex-Merchants & Miners Line.
Built by the New York Shipbuilding Co for Merchants & Miners Line as the passenger-cargo liner SUWANEE (1911). Renamed CITY OF ROME (1917 – Savannah Line).

SOMERSETSHIRE (1921)
9648 grt; 550 psrs
450' x 57' x 23' (137.1 x 17.4 x 7 m)
2 x 6-cylinder B+W diesel engines via twin screw.
Broken up for scrap by TW Ward Ltd at Barrow-in-Furness in 1954.
Built by Harland & Wolff Ltd, Belfast, for the Bibby Line as a passenger liner.

SOMME (1920) See VILLE DE GAND (1940)

SONDERBURG (1941)
12606 grt; 2292 psrs
571' x 62' x 34'6" depth (174 x 18.8 x 10.5 m)
2 x 3-cylinder Blohm & Voss triple expansion engines via twin screw.
Owned by the German government, she was broken up for scrap in the UK, in 1947, after raising her at Cherbourg where she had been scuttled by the Germans on 15 June 1944.
Built by Blohm & Voss, Hamburg, for the Holland America Line as the passenger liner POTSDAM (1900). Renamed STOCKHOLM (1915 – Swedish American Line) and a whaling fleet mother ship SOLGLIMT (1928 – C Nielson & Co, Larvik).

SONG HOI (1921) See TAI WAY FOONG (1923)

SONG OF AMERICA (1982) See SUNBIRD (1999)

SONG OF FLOWER (1989)
8282 grt; 172 psrs
409' x 53' x 16' (124 x 16 x 4.9 m)
2 x 10-cylinder Wichmann diesel engines via twin screw.

Cruise ship operated by Radisson Seven Seas Cruises Ltd.
Built by Kristiansands Mek Verksteds AS Fearley & Eger as the RoRo cargo ship FERNHILL (1974). Renamed BEGONIA (1975 – Abrasco Navigation Co) and EXPLORER STARSHIP (1986 – Exploration Cruise Lines) after a conversion to a cruise ship at a cost of US$34,800,000.

SONG OF NORWAY (1970) See SUNDREAM (1997)

SONOMA (1900)
6279 grt; 460 psrs
417' x 50' x 18' (127.1 x 15.2 x 5.5 m)
W Cramp & Sons 6-cylinder triple expansion engines via twin screw.
Broken up for scrap at Osaka in 1934.
Built by William Cramp & Sons, Philadelphia, Pennsylvania, for the Oceanic Steamship Co as a passenger liner.

SONTAY (1907)
7236 grt; 239 psrs
467' x 53' x 32'7" depth (141.4 x 16.1 x 9.9 m)
Messageries Maritimes 6-cylinder triple expansion engine via twin screw.
Sank on 16 April 1917 after being torpedoed by the German U-33, with 49 lives lost.
Built by Messageries Maritimes, La Ciotat, for Messageries Maritimes as a passenger-cargo ship.

SONTAY (1936) See SUNLOCK (1955)

SOOCHOW (1947) See SANG FAJAR (1975)

SOPHIA (1966)
8945 grt; 1000 psrs
499' x 63' x 15' (151.3 x 19 x 4.6 m)
6-cylinder MAN diesel engine via single screw.
Broken up for scrap in 1977 at Eleusis as a passenger-cargo-RoRo ferry, after being beached at Keratsini where she heeled over on her port side and had to be declared a total constructive loss. Ex-Constantine S Efthymiadis, Piraeus.
Built by Kockums MV AB, Malmo, for the Wallenius Group, Sweden, as the oil tanker SOYA BIRGITTA (1953).

SOPHOCLES (1900)
4753 grt; 70 psrs
440' x 44' x 28'9" depth (133.3 x 13.3 x 8.8 m)
Harland & Wolff Ltd 4-cylinder quadruple expansion engines via twin screw.
Broken up for scrap at Morecambe, Lancashire, in 1908. Ex-Aberdeen Line.
Built by Harland & Wolff Ltd, Belfast, for the White Star Line as the passenger-cargo ship IONIC (1883).

SOPHOCLES (1922) See TAMAROA (1926)

SOPHOCLES V (1999)
13384 grt; 700 psrs
154 cars or 77 trailers
634' x 89' x 22' (192 x 27 x 6.7 m)

2 x 12-cylinder Pielstick diesel engines via twin screw.
Passenger-car-trailer ferry owned and operated by ANEK Lines after acquiring the vessel for US$ 35,000,000.
Built by Mitsubishi Heavy Industries, Shimonoseki, for Higashi Nippon Ferry KK as the HERMES (1990). Renamed SOFOKLIS VENIZELOS (1999 – ANEK Lines)

SORACHI MARU (1955)
3428 grt
43 rail coaches
393' x 57' x 15'6" (119.1 x 17.3 x 4.7 m)
Sulzer diesel engines via twin screw.
Passenger-train ferry owned by the Japanese government (Department of Railways). Reported sold on 28 August 1976.
Built by the Uraga Dockyard Co.

SORACHI MARU (1976) See SEA SERENADE (1992)

SOUDAN (1901)
6680 grt; 160 psrs
450' x 52' x 30' (137.2 x 15.9 x 9.2 m)
2 x triple expansion engines via twin screw.
Broken up for scrap by Kishimoto KKK at Osaka in 1926.
Built by Caird & Co, Greenock, for the P&O Line as a passenger-cargo ship at a cost of £152,270.

SOUNION (1970)
3290 grt; 1200 psrs
340' x 48' x 14' (103 x 14.5 x 4.2 m)
2 x 8-cylinder B+W diesel engines via twin screw.
Broken up for scrap at Perama after refloating her from a position where she sank in the shallows at Beirut on 3 March 1973.
Built by Harland & Wolff Ltd, Belfast, for Burns Laird Lines Ltd as the ROYAL ULSTERMAN (1936). Renamed CAMMELL LAIRD (1968 – Burns Laird Lines).

SOUTH BEND (1919) See DJAKARTA RAYA (1952)

SOUTHERN ALBATROSS (1955) See PORTARITISSA (1955)

SOUTHERN CROSS (1920) See WHARTON, USS (AP-7) (1939)

SOUTHERN CROSS (1955) See IMPERIAL MAJESTY (1999)

SOUTHERN CROSS (1955)
4302 grt; 137 psrs
336' x 51' x 22' (101.8 x 15.5 x 6.7 m)
2 x Newport News DRG turbine engines via twin screw.
Broken up for scrap at Antwerp in 1959. Ex-White Steamship Co.
Built by Newport News Shipbuilding, Newport News, Virginia, for Red I D Lines as the passenger-cargo ship CARACAS (1927). Renamed DENALI (1938 – Alaska Steamship Co) and CUBA (1955 – Peninsula & Occidental Steamship Co).

SOUTHERN CROSS (1995) See FLAMENCO (1997)

SOUTHERN KINGDOM (1993) See WANG FU (1993)

SOUTHERN PRINCE (1929) See ANNA C (1947)

SOUTHERN QUEEN (1996)
3990 grt; 1367 psrs
295' x 48' x 14' (89.3 x 14.6 x 4.2 m)
2 x 12-cylinder Sulzer diesel engines via twin screw.
Owned and operated by Chijin Shipping SA.
Built by Hashihama Zosen, Imabari, for Kansai Kisen KK, Osaka, as the passenger-cargo ship MAYA MARU (1996).

SOUTHLAND (1915)
12018 grt; 1162 psrs
580' x 60' x 38'2" depth (176.8 x 18.2 x 11.6 m)
John Brown 8-cylinder quadruple expansion engines via twin screw.
Owned by the White Star Line, she sank on 4 September 1917, with four lives lost, after being hit by two torpedoes from the German U-70 140 miles (233 km) north-west of Tory Island, off the Irish coast. She had survived a torpedo attack by the U-14 in the Mediterranean two years before, on 2 September 1915.
Built by John Brown & Co Ltd, Clydebank, for the Red Star Line as the passenger liner VADERLAND (1900).

SOUTHWARD (1971) See SEAWING (1994)

SOVEREIGN OF THE SEAS (1988)
73192 grt; 2282 psrs
874' x 106' x 25' (264.8 x 32.1 x 7.6 m)
4 x 9-cylinder Pielstick diesel engines via twin screw.

Cruise ship owned by Wilhelmsen and operated by Royal Caribbean Cruise Lines Inc, USA.
Built by Chantiers de l'Atlantique, St Nazaire, at a cost of US$183,500,000.

SOVETSKY
Ships names prefixed as such are listed under SOVIETSKAYA.

SOVIET
Ships names prefixed as such are listed under SOVIETSKAYA.

SOVIETSKAYA ARMENIYA (1985) See AZERBAIJAN (1985)

SOVIETSKAYA AZERBAIDZHAN (1963)
8840 grt; 290 psrs
30 rail coaches
440' x 60' x 15' (133.7 x 18.3 x 4.4 m)
4 x 10-cylinder Fairbanks-Morse diesel-electric engines via triple screw.
Passenger-train ferry operated by the Caspian Shipping Co.
Built by Krasnoye Sormovo, Gorkiy, for the Russian government.

SOVIETSKAYA BYELORUSSIYA (1986) See PROFESSOR GUL (1995)

SOVIETSKAYA DAGESTAN (1984) See DAGISTAN (1984)

SOVIETSKAYA GRUZIYA (1986) See MERCURY-1 (1995)

SOVIETSKAYA KALMYKIYA (1985) See AKADEMIK M. TOPCHUBASHOV (1995)

SOVIETSKAYA KAZAKHSTAN (1968)
8840 grt; 290 psrs
30 rail coaches
440' x 60' x 15' (133.3 x 18.2 x 4.5 m)
4 x 10-cylinder diesel engines via triple screw.
Passenger-train ferry operated by the Caspian Shipping Co.
Built by Krasnoye Sormovo, Gorky, for the Russian government.

SOVIETSKAYA KIRGIZIYA (1986) See AKADEMIK HESEN ALIYEV (199)

SOVIETSKAYA ROSSIJA (1921)
3133 grt; 858 psrs
length 350' x beam 40' (106 x 12 m)
Engines via single screw.
Broken up for scrap in 1925.
Built by Caird & Co, Greenock, for the Hamburg-America Line as the passenger liner THURINGIA (1870). Renamed PETERSBURG (1878 – Russian Volunteer Fleet), ST. PETERSBURG (1892 – Russian Volunteer Fleet) and BEREZAN (1893 – Imperial Russian Navy).

SOVIETSKAYA SOJUS (1950) See SOJUS (1980)

SOVIETSKAYA SOJUS (1990)
23460 grt; 96 psrs
length 500' x beam 51' (151.5 x 15.5 m)
Nuclear engines via twin screw.

Owned by the Murmansk Shipping Co, Murmansk.

SOVIETSKAYA TADZHIKSTYA (1984)
11450 grt; 202 psrs
510' x 60' x 18' (154.6 x 18.3 x 5.5 m)
2 x 6-cylinder B+W diesel engines via twin screw.
Passenger ferry operated by the Caspian Shipping Co.
Built by Brodogradiliste Uljanik, Pula, for the USSR government.

SOVIETSKAYA TURKMENIA (1963) See SOVIETSKAYA
TURKMENISTAN (1963)

SOVIETSKAYA TURKMENISTAN (1963)
8840 grt; 290 psrs
30 rail coaches
440' x 60' x 15' (133.3 x 18.2 x 4.5 m)
4 x 10 cylinder Fairbanks-Morse diesel-electric engines via triple screw.
Passenger-train ferry operated by the Caspian Shipping Co.
Built by Krasnoye Sormovo, Gorkiy for the Russian government.

SOVIETSKAYA UZBEKISTAN (1967)
8840 grt; 290 psrs
30 rail coaches
440' x 60' x 15' (133.3 x 18.2 x 4.5 m)
4 x 10-cylinder Fairbanks-Morse diesel-electric engines via triple screw.
Passenger-train ferry operated by the Caspian Shipping Co.
Built by Krasnoye Sormovo, Gorkiy, for the Russian government.

SOVIETSKI
Ships names prefixed as such are listed under SOVIETSKAYA.

SOVIETSKIY
Ships names prefixed as such are listed under SOVIETSKAYA.

SOYA BIRGITTA (1953) See SOPHIA (1966)

SOYA-MARGARETA (1952) See MINOS (1964)

SPAARNDAM (1922)
8857 grt; 978 psrs
466' x 58' x 30' (141.2 x 17.6 x 9.1 m)
Turbine engine via single screw.
Sank on 27 November 1939, with five lives lost, after she hit a magnetic mine laid in the Thames estuary, three miles (5 km) east-nor-east of the Tongue Lightship.
Built by Nieuwe Waterweg, Schiedam, for the Holland America Line as a passenger liner.

SPARTAN (1882) See FIUME (1900)

SPARTAN (1952)
4244 grt; 620 psrs

180 cars
411' x 60' x 18'6" (125.1 x 18.1 x 5.7 m)
2 x 4-cylinder Skinner Unaflow engines via twin screw.
Laid up since 1979 in Luddington, Michigan, by the owners Lake Michigan Carferry Inc.
Built by Christy Corporation, Sturgeon Bay, Wisconsin, for the Chesapeake & Ohio Railroad as passenger-car ferry at a cost of US$5,000,000.

SPARVIERO (1943)
30418 grt; 2700 psrs
711' x 83' x 30'2" (215.5 x 25.2 x 9.2 m)
4 x 6-cylinder MAN diesel engines via quadruple screw.
Owned by the Italian Navy, she was broken up for scrap at Genoa in 1947 after refloating her from Genoa harbour. She had been scuttled by the Germans on 25 September 1944.
Built by Ansaldo Shipyards, Genoa, for Navigazione Generale Italiana as the AUGUSTUS (1928).

SPERBRECHER (1939)
6723 grt
412' x 66' x 34'4" depth (124.8 x 20 x 10.4 m)
W Doxford 3-cylinder triple expansion engines via single screw.
Sank on 12 September 1942 after hitting a mine laid in the Porsangen Fjord off Honnigsvad, Norway.
Built by W Doxford & Sons Ltd, Sunderland, for the British Shipping Controller as the WAR BERYL (1918). Renamed BOTHWELL (1920 – Canadian Pacific Railway Co), TOWER CROWN (1934 – Tower Steamship Co Ltd), MOUNT OSSA (1937 – Atlanticos Steamship Co Ltd & Kulukudidis Shipping Co SA) and ROBERT BORNHOFEN (1939 – R Bornhofen).

SPERO (1966) See SAPPHO (1973)

SPHINX (1914) See SUBIACO (1940)

SPIRIT OF BRITISH COLUMBIA (1993)
18747 grt; 2100 psrs
470 cars
553' x 88' x 17' (167.5 x 26.6 x 5 m)
4 x 6-cylinder MAN-B+W diesel engines via twin screw.

Passenger-car ferry operated by the British Columbia Ferry Corporation, Victoria, BC.
Built by Yarrows Shipyards, Vancouver Island, for the British Columbia Ferry Corporation at a cost of C$139,000,000.

SPIRIT OF FREE ENTERPRISE (1980) See P&OSL KENT (1998)

SPIRIT OF INDEPENDENCE (1995) See HAPPY DOLPHIN (1999)

SPIRIT OF LONDON (1972) See SOUTHERN CROSS (1994)

SPIRIT OF TASMANIA (1993)
31356 grt; 1800 psrs
520 cars or 45 trailers
531' x 91' x 20' (161 x 27.6 x 6.2 m)
4 x 8-cylinder Krupp-MaK diesel engines via twin screw.
Passenger-car ferry operated by TT (Transport Tasmania)-Line across Bass Strait from Melbourne, Victoria, to Devonport, Tasmania.
Built by Werft Nobiskrug, Rendsburg, for the TT-Line, Lubeck (Trelleborg-

Travemunde Line) as the PETER PAN (1986).

SPIRIT OF VANCOUVER ISLAND (1994)
18747 grt; 2100 psrs
470 cars
553' x 88' x 17' (167.5 x 26.6 x 5 m)
4 x 6-cylinder MAN-B+W diesel engines via twin screw.
Passenger-car ferry operating for the British Columbia Ferry Corporation.
Built by Yarrows Shipyards, Vancouver Island, for the Corporation at a cost of C$130,000,000.

SPLENDID (1994)
39109 grt; 1870 psrs
1010 cars
706' x 91' x 22' (214 x 27.6 x 6.7 m)
4 x 8-cylinder Sulzer diesel engines via twin screw.
Passenger-car ferry operated by the Grandi Navi Veloci Grimaldi subsidiary of the Grimaldi Group.
Built by Nuovi Cantieri Apuania Shipyards for Grimaldi Group.

SPLENDOUR OF THE SEAS (1997)
69490 grt; 2060 psrs
868' x 106' x 24'6" (263 x 32 x 7.5 m)
5 x 12-cylinder Wartsila-Vasa diesel-electric engines via twin screw.

Built by Chantiers de l'Atlantique, St Nazaire, for the Royal Caribbean Cruise Line as a cruise ship at a cost of US$300,000,000.

SPLIT 1700 (1997)
4020 grt; 750 psrs
175 cars
364' x 59' x 14'6" (110.2 x 18 x 4.4 m)
4 x 9-cylinder MAN diesel engines via twin screw.

Ice-strengthened passenger-car ferry owned by SEM Maritime Inc, Panama.
Built by Werft Nobiskrug, Rendsburg, for the Lion Steamship Co as the

KRONPRINS CARL GUSTAF (1966). Renamed WILANOW (1975 – Pol Ferries).

SPREE (1890) See URAL (1904)

SPREEWALD (1907) See SINAI (1948)

SPROGO (1962)
6590 grt; 1500 psrs
200 cars or 10 rail coaches + 20 wagons
358' x 57' x 15' (108.5 x 17.2 x 4.5 m)
2 x 7-cylinder B+W diesel engines via twin screw.
Passenger-car-cargo train ferry owned by Danish government and laid up in Svendborg since 1998.
Built by Helsingor Shipyard, Helsingor.

SPURN POINT, HMS (1945) See LAKEMBA (1947)

SREDETZ (1986)
8342 grt; 422 psrs
380' x 62' x 17' (115.1 x 18.8 x 5.1 m)
2 x 9-cylinder Stork-Werkspoor diesel engines via twin screw.
Passenger-cargo ferry owned by the government of Bulgaria and operated by Navibulgar following her purchase for US$1,800,000.
Built by Cantieri Navale Cassaro, Messina, as the LAURO RUSSOTTI (1975). Renamed SEASPEED MASTER (1976 – Seaspeed Ferries Corporation, Piraeus), TAMBU EXPRESS (1980 – Nosira Shipping Ltd), ADELAIDE (1984) and ROADA (1984 – Roada Rederi AB).

ST./SAINT
For all ships commencing with the abbreviated form of ST., or spelt out in full, refer under 'SAINT'.

STAFFETTA ADRIATICA (1973) See CONCORD (1992)

STAFFETTA JONICA (1980) See ARBOREA (1987)

STAFFETTA LIGURE (1979) See FUDI (2000)

STAFFETTA MEDITERRANEA (1979) See TORRES (1988)

STAFFETTA TIRRENICA (1973) See AL SALAM 91 (1993)

STAFFORD (1967) See NEW YORK FORTUNE I (1997)

STAFFORD MARU (1959)
10701 grt; 109 psrs
502' x 62' x 29'7" (152.1 x 18.8 x 9 m)
Sulzer 16-cylinder diesel engine via twin screw.
Broken up for scrap at Osaka in 1959.
Built by Fairfield Shipbuilding & Engineering Co Ltd, Glasgow, for the Bibby Line as the passenger-cargo ship STAFFORDSHIRE (1928).

STAFFORDSHIRE (1894) See SAMARA (1912)

STAFFORDSHIRE (1928) See STAFFORD MARU (1959)

STALWART, HMAS (A-215) (1966) See TARA II (1997)

STALWART, HMAS (D-215) (1969) See TARA II (1997)

STAMPALIA (1912)
8999 grt; 2650 psrs
477' x 56' x 29' (145.2 x 17 x 8.8 m)
Wallsend Slipway 6-cylinder triple expansion engines via twin screw.
Sank on 17 August 1916 after being torpedoed by the German U-47 in the Aegean Sea.
Built by Cantieri Navale Riuniti, La Spezia, for Navigazione General Italia as the passenger liner OCEANIA (1909).

STAMVEIEN (1988) See HUA LU (1994)

STANLEYVILLE (1926)
6750 grt; 90 psrs

405' x 54' x 25'6" (122.7 x 16.4 x 7.8 m)
3 x John Brown Ltd DRG turbine engines via single screw.
Ex-Cie Belge Maritime.
Built by John Brown Ltd, Clydebank, for Elder Dempster Lines as the
passenger-cargo ship EKARI (1920).

STAR AQUARIUS (1993)
44012 grt; 1378 psrs
584' x 98' x 20' (176.9 x 29.6 x 6 m)
4 x 9-cylinder Wartsila-Sulzer diesel engines via twin screw.

Cruise ship for Star Cruises, Singapore, after acquisition at US$85,000,000.
Built by Wartsila, Turku, for the Viking Line as the passenger-car ferry
ATHENA (1989). Renamed LANGKAPURI STAR AQUARIUS (1993 – Star
Cruises, Singapore) during conversion to a cruise ship for initial registration
of the name. She was sold to DFDS at the end of 2000 for delivery in February
2001.

STARDANCER (1985) See VIKING SERENADE (1990)

STARKE (1931)
3092 grt; 230 psrs
26 rail coaches
367' x 52' x 18' (111.2 x 15.8 x 5.5 m)
2 x 3-cylinder Lindholmens Angmaskiner diesel engines via twin screw.

Broken up for scrap by Personer AD, Ystad, in 1972. Ex-Swedish State Rail.
Built by Deutsche Werke, Kiel, as an ice-strengthened passenger-train ferry.

STARLIGHT PRINCESS (1992) See PRINCESS DANAE (1997)

STAR ODYSSEY (1994) See BLACK WATCH (1996)

STAR OF TEXAS (1993) See APOLLO (1998)

STAR OF VENICE (1992)
6269 grt; 484 psrs
65 cars
437' x 57' x 20' (132.4 x 17.3 x 6.1 m)
4 x Wallsend Slipway-Parsons DRG turbine engines via twin screw.
Owned by Valgas Trading Co Ltd, Vanuatu, and operated by Star of Venice
Navigation SA, Panama.
Built by Swan Hunter Shipbuilders Ltd, Newcastle, for the Bergen Line as the
passenger ship LEDA (1953). She retained the name on charter to Stord Vaerft
for shipyard worker accommodation (1977). Renamed NAJLA (1979 –
Kuwait Livestock Trading & Transport Co), ALBATROS (1981 – Dolphin
Hellas Shipping SA, Piraeus), ALEGRO (1984 – Dolphin Hellas Shipping
SA, Piraeus), ALBATROSS (1985 – Dolphin Hellas Shipping Co, Piraeus),
and AMALFI (1989 – Star Lauro charter). She has been under arrest in San
Giorgio since late 1999.

STAR PISCES (1994)
40053 grt; 2192 psrs
584' x 96' x 20' (177 x 29 x 6.1 m)
4 x 9-cylinder Wartsila-Sulzer diesel engines via twin screw.

Cruise ship owned and operated by Star Cruises, Singapore, who converted
her from a passenger-car ferry.
Built by Wartsila for Rederi Slite AB as the passenger-car ferry KALYPSO
(1990 – Viking Line).

STAR PRINCESS (1989) See ARCADIA (1997)

STARSHIP ATLANTIC (1988) See MELODY (1997)

STARSHIP MAJESTIC (1989) See FLAMENCO (1997)

STARSHIP OCEANIC (1988) See THE BIG RED BOAT I (1997)

STARSHIP ROYALE (1983) See SEABREEZE I (1989)

STARTRAILER (1998)
6138 grt; 770 psrs
447' x 73' x 17' (135.5 x 22 x 5.2 m)
2 x 16-cylinder Ishikawajima diesel engines via twin screw.
Owned and operated by Cameron Marine Ltd, Piraeus.
Built by Kanda Zosensho KK, Kure, for Nishinihon Ferry KK, Kobe, as the
TSUKUSHI (1972). Renamed HANKYU No. 16 (1976 – Hankyu Ferry KK,
Tokyo) and FERRY PUKWAN (1983 – Pukwan Ferry Co Ltd).

STARWARD (1968) See BOLERO (1995)

STAR WIND (1999)
13788 grt; 400 psrs
96072 cubic feet of cargo space
522' x 75' x 21'6" (158.3 x 22.7 x 6.5 m)
4 x MAN diesel engines via twin screw.

Ferry owned by the Silja Line and operated by the Seawind Line.
Built by Bergen Shipyards, Bergen, for Scandline Hansa as the ROSTOCK
(1977).

STATE (1990)
12660 grt; 392 psrs
531' x 73' x 27' (160.9 x 22.1 x 8.2 m)
General Electric geared turbine engines via single screw.
Retired to the reserve fleet at Fort Eustis, James river, Virginia, in 1974 by the
New York Military Academy.
Laid down by the New York Shipbuilding Co, Camden, New Jersey, for
American President Lines as the PRESIDENT JACKSON (1950) and
completed as BARRETT,USS (T-AP-196) (1951 – US Navy). Renamed
EMPIRE STATE (1973 – New York State Maritime College).

STATENDAM (1898) See MARGLEN (1922)

STATENDAM (1914) See JUSTICIA (1917)

STATENDAM (1929)
28291 grt; 1654 psrs
697' x 81' x 49'4" depth (211.2 x 24.5 x 15 m)
4 x Harland & Wolff Ltd SRG turbine engines via twin screw.
Broken up for scrap at Rotterdam, Holland, in 1940 after her total destruction by fire during a German artillery barrage and aerial bombardment of Rotterdam on 14 May 1940.
Laid down by Harland & Wolff Ltd, Belfast, for the Holland America Line in 1921, launched in 1924 and completed as a passenger liner by Wilton's Machinefabriek & Scheepswerft, Schiedam, after being towed there in 1929.

STATENDAM (1957) See SEA HARMONY (1996)

STATENDAM (1993)
55451 grt; 1629 psrs
720' x 101' x 35' (218.2 x 30.1 x 10.6 m)
5 x 12-cylinder Sulzer diesel-electric engines via twin screw.

Cruise ship owned and operated by the Holland-America Line.
Built by Wilton-Fijenoord Machinefabriek & Scheepswerf, Schiedam.

STATE OF ANDAMAN (1957) See ANDAMANS (1958)

STATE OF BOMBAY (1954)
8521 grt; 900 psrs
456' x 62' x 26' (138.2 x 18.8 x 7.9 m)
JG Kincaid 8-cylinder triple expansion engines via twin screw.
In service in India.
Built by William Hamilton & Co, Glasgow, for the Shipping Corporation of India as the passenger liner EL HIND (1948). Renamed JAL AZAD (1954 – Scindia Steam Navigation Co Ltd).

STATE OF CALIFORNIA (1891) See COAMO (1901)

STATE OF HARYANA (1967)
8908 grt; 1193 psrs
479' x 63' x 26' (145.2 x 19.1 x 7.9 m)
2 x 4-cylinder Doxford diesel engines via twin screw.
Broken up for scrap at Mumbai in 1977. Ex-Shipping Corporation of India.
Built by Barclay, Curle & Co, Glasgow, for the British India Line as the passenger liner SANTHIA (1950).

STATE OF MADRAS (1954)
8580 grt; 900 psrs
456' x 62' x 26' (138.2 x 18.8 x 7.9 m)
Wallsend Slipway-Kincaid 8-cylinder triple expansion engines via twin screw.
Operating for the Shipping Corporation of India.
Built by William Hamilton & Co, Glasgow, for the Scindia Steam Navigation Co as the passenger liner JALJAWAHAR (1948).

STATE OF MAINE (1962)
9978 grt; 202 psrs
493' x 64' x 26' (149.4 x 19.4 x 7.9 m)
Turbine engines via twin screw.
Broken up for scrap at Wilmington, Delaware, in 1973 after serving as a training ship for the Maine Maritime Academy.
Built by the Bethlehem Steel Co, Quincy, Massachusetts, for the Panama Line as the passenger-cargo ship ANCON (1939) at a cost of US$4,000,000.

Renamed ANCON, USS (AP-66) (1942 – US government), ANCON, USS (AGC-4) (1943 – US government) and ANCON (1946 – Panama Line).

STATE OF MAINE (1973)
13319 grt; 392 psrs
533' x 73' x 27' (161.5 x 22.1 x 8.2 m)
General Electric geared turbine engines via single screw.
Retired in 1995 as a training ship operated by the Maine Maritime Academy.
Built by the New York Shipbuilding Co, Camden, for American President Lines as the PRESIDENT HAYES (1951). Renamed as the Class P2-S1-DN1 troop transport UPSHUR, USS (T-AP-198) (1952 – US Navy).

STAVANGERFJORD (1918)
14015 grt; 675 psrs
553' x 64' x 26' (167.6 x 19.4 x 7.9 m)
2 x 4-cylinder quadruple expansion engines via twin screw.
Broken up for scrap at the Shun Fung Ironworks in Hong Kong in 1964 for a tender figure of US$420,000.
Built by Cammell Laird & Co, Birkenhead, for the Norwegian America Line as a passenger liner.

STEADFAST (1919) See HAYWOOD, USS (APA-6) (1941)

STEEL ARTISAN (1942) See PHILIPPINE TOURIST I (1978)

STEFAN (1988)
15024 grt; 779 psrs
503' x 69' x 29' (153.3 x 21 x 8.8 m)
2 x General Electric DRG turbine engines via twin screw.
Broken up for scrap in 2000 at Aliaga. She had been laid up north of the Avlis Shipyard from September 1991 to December 1996, after serving as a refugee accommodation hotel in Gothenburg. She was then purchased by Courage Maritime SA, Piraeus, only to be ultimately sent to the breakers. Ex-Tony Travel Agency Ltd, Piraeus.
Laid down by Wilton Fijenoord Shipyards, Schiedam, for the Holland America Line as the passenger-cargo ship DIEMERDYK (1950) and completed as the passenger liner MAASDAM (1952). Renamed STEFAN BATORY (1968 – Polish Ocean Lines).

STEFAN BATORY (1968) See STEFAN (1988)

STEIGERWALD (1912) See LA PEROUSE (1928)

STELLA D'ITALIA (1926)
5550 grt; 315 psrs
425' x 50' x 25'4" (128.8 x 15.2 x 7.7 m)
G Clark Ltd 6-cylinder triple expansion engines via twin screw.
Ex-Cosulich Line.
Built by Sir James Laing, Sunderland, for the Quebec Steamship Co as the passenger liner BERMUDIAN (1905). Renamed FORT HAMILTON (1919 – Furness Lines).

STELLA V (1969) See STELLA SOLARIS (1970)

STELLA MARINA (1954) See TOPEKA (1976)

STELLA MARIS II (1966) See VIKING BORDEAUX (1998)

STELLA OCEANIS (1967)
5500 grt; 369 psrs
347' x 56' x 15' (105 x 17 x 4.6 m)
2 x 7-cylinder Sulzer diesel engines via twin screw.
Cruise ship chartered to Royal Olympic Cruises Ltd, Piraeus.
Built by Cantieri Riuniti dell'Adriatico, Monfalcone, for Kavounides Shipping Co Ltd as the car ferry APHRODITE (1965).

STELLA POLARIS (1927) See SCANDINAVIA (1969)

STELLA POLARIS (1972) See RAMADA AL-SALAM HOTEL (1990)

STELLA SCARLETT (1974) See GELTING SYD (1982)

STELLA SOLARIS (1970)
17490 grt; 620 psrs
532' x 72' x 26' (162 x 22 x 7.9 m)
6 x Parsons DRG turbine engines via twin screw.

Cruise ship for Royal Olympic Cruises, Piraeus.
Built by Ateliers et Chantiers de France, Dunkirk, for Messageries Maritimes as the passenger-cargo ship CAMBODGE (1953). Renamed STELLA V (1969 – Sun Line, Greece).

STELVIO (1959)
4408 grt; 79 psrs
385' x 54' x 19' (116.7 x 16.4 x 5.8 m)
2 x 5-cylinder Sulzer diesel engines via twin screw.
Broken up for scrap at Perama Bay in 1987.
Built by Ansaldo Shipyards, Leghorn, for Adriatica Lines as a passenger-cargo vessel.

STENA (1974) See CORSICA MARINA II (1986)

STENA ADVENTURER (1996) See EXPRESS AFRODITE (1997)

STENA ANTRIM (1991) See IBN BATOUTA (1998)

STENA ARCADIA (1995) See ENCHANTED SUN (1999)

STENA ATLANTICA (1971) See CAPTAIN ZAMAN II (1998)

STENA ATLANTICA (1975) See SARDINIA VERA (1987)

STENA BALTICA (1978) See IALYSSOS (1982)

STENA BALTICA (1983) See BALTIC KRISTINA (1997)

STENA BALTICA (1984) See REGAL VOYAGER (1994)

STENA BALTICA (1988) See NIEBOROW (1989)

STENA BRITANNICA (1967) See SARDEGNA BELLA (1993)

STENA BRITANNICA (1991) See STENA SAGA (1994)

STENA BRITANNICA (2000)
33769 grt; 453 psrs
160 trailers
621' x 95' x 19'8" (188.3 x 28.7 x 6 m)
4 x 8-cylinder Sulzer diesel engines via twin screw.
Ro-pax owned and operated by Stena Line.
Built by Espanolas Puerto Real, Cadiz.

STENA CALEDONIA (1990)

12619 grt; 1000 psrs
309 cars
429' x 73' x 16'6" (130 x 22 x 5 m)
2 x 16-cylinder Crossley-Pielstick diesel engines via twin screw.
Passenger-car ferry owned and operated by Stena Line Ltd, Ashford.
Built by Harland & Wolff Ltd, Belfast, for Sealink UK as the ST. DAVID (1980) at a cost of £16,000,000.

STENA CAMBRIA (1999) See ISLA DE BOTAFOC (1999)

STENA CARRIER (1970) See HOLGER (1999)

STENA CHALLENGER (1991)
18523 grt; 500 psrs
480 cars or 120 trailers
508' x 79' x 18' (154 x 24 x 5.5 m)
2 x 8-cylinder Wartsila-Sulzer diesel engines via twin screw.

Passenger-car-cargo RoRo ferry owned by Canadian Marine Atlantic after acquiring the vessel for US$40,000,000, and then leasing her back to Stena AB.
Built by Fosen Mek Verksteder, Rissa, for Stena Line at a cost of £35,000,000.

STENA DANICA (1965) See LADY CARIBE I (1998)

STENA DANICA (1969) See QUEEN OF THE NORTH (1980)

STENA DANICA (1974) See VOLCAN DE TACANDE (2000)

STENA DANICA (1983)
28727 grt; 2274 psrs
555 cars or 36 cars + 76 trailers
502' x 92' x 21' (152.2 x 28 x 6.3 m)
4 x 12-cylinder Sulzer diesel engines via twin screw.

Passenger-car-cargo ferry owned by KB Stena Danica and operated by Stena Line.
Built by Chantiers du Nord et de la Mediterranee, Dunkirk, for the Stena Line.

STENA DRIVER (1984) See ASK (1991)

STENA EMPEREUR (1996) See P&OSL PROVENCE (1998)

STENA EUROPE (1994) See STENA EUROPE (1998)

STENA EUROPE (1998)
24828 grt; 2076 psrs
530 cars or 70 trailers
492' x 86' x 20' (149 x 26 x 6.1 m)
4 x 12-cylinder Nohab-Wartsila-Vasa diesel engines via twin screw.
Passenger-car-cargo ferry owned and operated by Stena Line.

Built by Gotaverken, Gothenburg, for the Sessan Line as the KRONPRINSESSAN VICTORIA (1981). Renamed STENA SAGA (1988 – Stena Line), STENA EUROPE (1994 – Stena Line) and LION EUROPE (1997 – Lion Ferry).

STENA FANTASIA (1990) See P&OSL CANTERBURY (1999)

STENA FELICITY (1990) See VISBY (1997)

STENA GALLOWAY (1990)
12175 grt; 1200 psrs
309 cars or 30 cars + 62 trailers
425' x 71' x 15'6" (128.8 x 21.5 x 4.7 m)
2 x 16-cylinder Crossley-Pielstick diesel engines via twin screw.

Passenger-car-cargo ferry owned and operated by Stena Line.
Built by Harland & Wolff Ltd, Belfast, for Sealink UK as the GALLOWAY PRINCESS (1980).

STENA GERMANICA (1967) See A. REGINA (1979)

STENA GERMANICA (1988)
39178 grt; 2500 psrs
550 cars or 55 cars + 80 trailers
578' x 94' x 22' (175 x 28.5 x 6.6 m)
4 x 16-cylinder Zgoda-Sulzer diesel engines via twin screw.

Passenger-car-cargo ferry owned and operated by Stena Line.
Built by Stocznia Im Komuny Paryskiey, Gdynia, for Stena Line as the STENA SCANDINAVICA (1988).

STENA HENGIST (1991) See EMPRESS ARTEMIS (2000)

STENA HIBERNIA (1991) See EXPRESS AFRODITE (1997)

STENA HORSA (1991) See EXPRESS PENELOPE (2000)

STENA INVICTA (1991) See COLOR VIKING (2000)

STENA JUTLANDICA (1973) See EUROFERRYS ATLANTICA (1999)

STENA JUTLANDICA (1983) See P&OSL PROVENCE (1998)

STENA JUTLANDICA (1996)
29691 grt; 1500 psrs
476 cars or 122 trailers
609' x 94' x 19'6" (184.4 x 28.4 x 6 m)
4 x 9-cylinder MAN-B+W diesel engines via twin screw.
Ice-strengthened passenger-car-cargo ferry owned and operated by Stena Line.
Laid down by Van der Giessen-de-Noord Yard, Krimpen, for Rederi AB, Goteborg, as the STENA JUTLANDICA III (1996), but completed as the STENA JUTLANDICA at a cost of £66,000,000.

STENA JUTLANDICA III (1996) See STENA JUTLANDICA (1996)

STENA LONDONER (1992) See VOLCAN DE TACANDE (2000)

STENA NAUTICA (1974) See CORSICA MARINE SECONDA (1999)

STENA NAUTICA (1981) See AL MANSOUR (1997)

STENA NAUTICA (1983) See VOLCAN DE TACANDE (2000)

STENA NAUTICA (1991) See STENA NAUTICA (1996)

STENA NAUTICA (1996)
19763 grt; 2000 psrs
410 cars
442' x 81' x 18' (134 x 24.4 x 5.5 m)
2 x 8-cylinder MAN-B+W diesel engines via twin screw.

Passenger-car ferry on charter from Stena Line to Trasmediterranea from 1996.
Built by Nakskov Skibsvaerft AS, Nakskov, for Danish State Railways as the NILS KLIM (1986). Renamed STENA NAUTICA (1991 – Stena Line), ISLE OF INNISFREE (1992 – British & Irish), LION KING (1995 – Lion Ferries) and LION KING II (1996 – Stena Line).

STENA NORDICA (1974) See VOLCAN DE TACANDE (2000)

STENA NORDICA (1975) See AL MANSOUR (1997)

STENA NORDICA (1979) See AL MANSOUR (1997)

STENA NORDICA (1980) See AL MANSOUR (1997)

STENA NORDICA (1981) See VOLCAN DE TACANDE (2000)

STENA NORDICA (1983) See COMMODORE (1999)

STENA NORDICA (1986) See MARKO POLO (1988)

STENA NORDICA (1988) See FANTAASIA (1998)

STENA NORMANDICA (1974) See MOBY VINCENT (1990)

STENA NORMANDY (1991) See NORMANDY (1997)

STENA OCEANICA (1978) See AMUSEMENT WORLD (1998)

STENA OLYMPICA (1972) See SCOTIA PRINCE (1982)

STENA PARISIEN (1992) See SEAFRANCE MANET (1996)

STENA POLONICA (1987) See EL EFTHERIOS (1997)

STENA PRINCE (1997) See COMMODORE (1999)

STENA ROYAL (1998) See POSL AQUITAINE (1999)

STENA SAGA (1978) See AMUSEMENT WORLD (1998)

STENA SAGA (1988) See STENA EUROPE (1998)

STENA SAGA (1994)
33750 grt; 2000 psrs
450 cars
548' x 94' x 22' (166.1 x 28.4 x 6.7 m)
4 x 12-cylinder Pielstick diesel engines via twin screw.

Ice-strengthened passenger-car ferry operating for the Stena Line.
Laid down by Wartsila-Turku for the Silja Line as the SILJA STAR (1979) and completed as the SILVIA REGINA (1981 – Stena Line). Renamed STENA BRITANNICA (1991 – Stena Line BV, Hook of Holland).

STENA SCANDINAVICA (1973) See MEDINA STAR (1999)

STENA SCANDINAVICA (1982) See KING OF SCANDINAVICA (1995)

STENA SCANDINAVICA (1988) See STENA GERMANICA (1988)

STENA SEAPACER 1 (1999) See FINNCLIPPER (1999)

STENA SEAPACER 2 (1999) See FINNEAGLE (1999)

STENA SHIPPER (1977) See CHONG MING DAO (1998)

STENA SHIPPER (1980) See CHONG MING DAO (1998)

STENA SHIPPER (1986) See CHONG MING DAO (1998)

STENA TOPPER (1977) See NEPTUNIA (1997)

STENA TRANSPORTER (1978) See PRIDE OF SUFFOLK (1992)

STENA TRANSPORTER (1980) See PRIDE OF SUFFOLK (1992)

STENA TRAVELLER (1992) See TT TRAVELLER (1997)

STENA TRAVELLER (1995) See TT TRAVELLER (1997)

STEN BALTICA (1984) See REGAL VOYAGER (1994)

STEN STURE (1959) See ANDAMAN PRINCESS (1989)

STEPHEN (1910)
4435 grt; 146 psrs
376' x 50' x 23'6" (113.9 x 15.2 x 7.2 m)
Northeast Maritime Engineering 3-cylinder triple expansion engine via single screw.
Built by Hawthorne, Leslie & Co Ltd, Newcastle, for the Booth Line as a passenger-cargo liner.

STEUBEN (1938)
14690 grt; 484 psrs
551' x 65' x 43'7" depth (167 x 19.7 x 13.2 m)
Vulkan Werke 8-cylinder triple expansion engines via twin screw.
Owned by North German Lloyd, she sank in ten minutes on 10 February 1945, with the loss of 3,000 lives, after being torpedoed twice by the Russian submarine S-13 in the Baltic Sea, off Stolpmunde, Germany.
Built by AG Vulkan, Stettin, for the Hamburg-America Line as the MUNCHEN (1923). Renamed GENERAL VON STEUBEN (1931 – Hamburg-America Line) after raising, refloating and rebuilding her when she sank following a fire in her cargo holds on 11 February 1930.

STEVENS (1967)
9644 grt; 125 psrs
473' x 66' x 27' (143.3 x 20 x 8.2 m)
Turbine engine via single screw.
Broken up for scrap at Kearny, New Jersey, in 1979 after serving as a floating dormitory for the Stevens Institute of Technology, Hoboken, New Jersey.
Built by the Bethlehem Shipbuilding Corporation, Sparrow's Point, Maryland, for the US Navy as the DAUPHIN, USS (1944). Renamed as the passenger-cargo ship EXOCHORDA (1947 – American Export Isbrandtsen Line).

STIRLING CASTLE (1936)
25554 grt; 783 psrs
725' x 82' x 32' (219.7 x 24.8 x 9.7 m)
2 x 10-cylinder B+W diesel engines via twin screw.
Broken up for scrap at Mihara in 1966 for a tender figure of £360,000.
Built by Harland & Wolff Ltd, Belfast, for the Union Castle Line as a passenger liner.

STOCKHOLM (1915) See SONDERBURG (1941)

STOCKHOLM (1938)
28000 grt; 1350 psrs
675' x 83' x 38'8" (204.5 x 25.2 x 11.8 m)
Sulzer 30-cylinder diesel engines via triple screw.
Broken up for scrap at Trieste in December 1938. This followed a fire which destroyed her overnight, on 20 December 1938, during her fitting out, seven months after being launched on 29 May 1938.
Launched by Cantieri Riuniti dell'Adriatico, Monfalcone, for the Swedish American Line.

STOCKHOLM (1940) See SABAUDIA (1941)

STOCKHOLM (1948) See VALTUR PRIMA (1999)

STONEWALL JACKSON (1970) See ALEX STEPHENS (1973)

STRAAT BANKA (1952) See UNITED VANTAGE (1978)

STRAAT MAKASTAR (1951) See MERCURY BAY (1978)

STRAITS MARU (1956)
3502 grt; 475 psrs
361' x 40' x 34'3" (109.9 x 12.3 x 10.4 m)
J Elder & Co 3-cylinder triple expansion engine via single screw.
Broken up for scrap at Osaka in 1956. Ex-Straits Towing Co, Vancouver.
Built by William Denny & Bros, Dumbarton, for the British & North American Royal Mail Steam Packet Co as the passenger liner PARTHIA (1870). Renamed VICTORIA (1892 – Northern Pacific Lines) and as a log barge named STRAITS No. 27 (1955 – Straits Towing Co, Vancouver).

STRAITS No. 27 (1955) See STRAITS MARU (1956)

STRASSBURG (1941)
16981 grt; 634 psrs
573' x 70' x 28' (173.6 x 21.2 x 8.5 m)
Sulzer 20-cylinder diesel engines via twin screw.
Sunk as a German hospital ship on 20 September 1943 by British torpedo boats. She had struck a mine north of Ijmuiden, Holland, 19 days earlier and

wallowed as she attempted beaching.
Built by Wilton Fijenoord Shipyards, Schiedam, for Rotterdam Lloyd as the passenger liner BALOERAN (1930).

STRATHAIRD (1931)
22568 grt; 1069 psrs
664' x 80' x 29' (201.2 x 24.4 x 8.8 m)
2 x turbo-electric engines via twin screw.

Broken up for scrap by Shun Fing Ironworks Co at Hong Kong in 1962 for a tender figure of £382,500.
Built by Vickers-Armstrong Ltd, Barrow-in-Furness, for the P&O Line as a passenger liner.

STRATHALLAN (1938)
23722 grt; 1011 psrs
664' x 84' x 30' (202.3 x 25.6 x 9.1 m)
6 x SRG turbine engines via twin screw.
Sank on 22 December 1942, with the loss of four lives out of a total of 5,122 troops and nurses. She had been under tow from a position where she had suffered massive internal damage, on 21 December 1942, from a torpedo fired by the German U-562 40 miles (67 km) north of Ouahran, Algeria.
Built by Vickers-Armstrong Ltd, Barrow-in-Furness, for the P&O Line as a passenger liner.

STRATHEDEN (1937) See MARIANNA LATSIS (1966)

STRATHMORE (1935) See HENRIETTA LATSIS (1966)

STRATHNAVER (1931)
22270 grt; 1252 psrs
664' x 80' x 29' (201.2 x 24.4 x 8.8 m)
2 x turbo-electric engines via twin screw.
Broken up for scrap by Shun Fing Ironworks Co at Hong Kong in 1962 for a tender figure of £325,000.
Built by Vickers-Armstrong Ltd, Barrow-in-Furness, for the P&O Line as a passenger liner.

STROMMA REX (1973)
3701 grt; 1638 psrs
373' x   x 12'6" (113 x   x 3.8 m)
2 x 12-cylinder Cockerill-Sulzer diesel engines via twin screw.

Broken up for scrap in 1973 by Personer AB, Ystad.
Built by John Cockerill SA, Hoboken, for RMT, Belgium, as the passenger ferry PRINCE PHILIPPE (1948).

STUBBENKAMMER (1971) See PETRONILA MATA (1998)

STUTTGART (1924)
13387 grt; 990 psrs

551' x 65' x 34' (167 x 19.7 x 10.3 m)
6-cylinder triple expansion engines via twin screw.
Passenger liner owned by Deutsche Arbeitsfront, she was purposely sunk, with all dead on board, outside Gotenhafen (now Gdynia) harbour after she had completely burnt out on 9 October 1943 following a bombing attack by Allied aircraft.
Built by AG Vulkan, Stettin, for North German Lloyd.

STUYVESANT (1930) See AEOLIA (1950)

SUBIACO (1940)
11375 grt; 384 psrs
498' x 61' x 40'6" depth (151 x 18.5 x 12.3 m)
Ateliers et Chantiers de la Loire 6-cylinder triple expansion engines via twin screw.
Broken up for scrap at Genoa, Italy, in 1946, after raising her from the harbour bed where she sank on 5 January 1944 following an American air raid.
Built by Ateliers et Chantiers de la Loire, St Nazaire, for Messageries Maritimes as the SPHINX (1914).

SUBIC ADVENTURE (1994) See PETRONILA MATA (1998)

SUECIA (1929) See ISTHMIA (1966)

SUEH (1914) See MOUZINHO (1930)

SUEVIC (1901) See SKYTTEREN (1928)

SUFFOLK (1902)
7573 grt; 224 psrs
460' x 58' x 31'2" depth (139.4 x 17.6 x 9.5 m)
2 x John Brown Ltd 3-cylinder triple expansion engines via twin screw.
Broken up for scrap in England in 1927. Ex-P&O Line.
Built by John Brown & Co Ltd, Clydebank, for the Federal Steam Navigation Co as a passenger-cargo ship.

SUFFREN (1920) See VENEZUELA (1956)

SUFFREN (1923)
12334 grt; 2102 psrs
550' x 62' x 35'6" (167.5 x 18.9 x 10.8 m)
Blohm & Voss 8-cylinder quadruple expansion engines via twin screw.
Broken up for scrap at Genoa in 1929. Ex-French Line.
Built by Blohm & Voss, Hamburg, for the Hamburg-America Line as the passenger liner BLUCHER (1901). Seized by the Brazilian government and renamed LEOPOLDINA (1917).

SUGBU (1989) See SUPERFERRY 8 (1996)

SUISEN (1996)
17329 grt; 507 psrs
80 cars + 122 trailers
658' x 83' x 23' (199.5 x 25.2 x 7 m)
2 x 18-cylinder Pielstick diesel engines via twin screw.
Passenger-car-cargo ferry operated by Shin-Nihonkai Ferry Co Ltd.
Built by Ishikawajima Harima Heavy Industries Ltd, Tokyo.

SULACO (1958)
6963 grt; 100 psrs
447' x 60' x 25'3" (135.5 x 18.2 x 7.7 m)
2 x General Electric turbo-electric engines via twin screw.
Broken up for scrap at Bruges, Belgium, in 1964. Ex-Elders & Fyffes.
Built by Newport News Shipbuilding & Drydock Co, Newport News, Virginia, for the Unifruit Steamship Co as the TALAMANCA (1931).
Renamed TALAMANCA, USS (AF-15) (1942 – US Navy).

SULTAN KL (1968)
4250 grt; 69 psrs
370' x 50' x 22' (112.8 x 15.2 x 6.7 m)
2 x 6-cylinder Armstrong-Sulzer diesel engines via twin screw.
Broken up for scrap at Kaohsiung in 1970 after stranding in Manila Bay, Philippines.
Built by R & W Hawthorn, Leslie & Co Ltd, Hebburn-on-Tyne, for the Union Steamship Co of New Zealand as the passenger-cargo ship MATUA (1937).

SUMATRA (1895) See MOSSAMEDES (1916)

SUMMER STAR (1985) See AVRASYA I (1996)

SUMNER (1900)
3739 grt; 1300 psrs
350' x 43' x 29'1" depth (106.7 x 13 x 8.8 m)
Reiherstieg 2-cylinder compound engine via single screw.
Owned by the US Army as a troop transport, she was wrecked on 11 December 1916 on the Barnegat Shoals, New Jersey.
Built by Reiherstieg, Hamburg, for the Hamburg-America Line as the passenger liner RHAETIA (1883). Renamed CASSIUS (1898 – US Navy).

SUN (1969)
8357 grt; 52 psrs
459' x 63' x 28' (139.1 x 19.1 x 8.5 m)
Turbine engines via twin screw.
Broken up for scrap at Kaohsiung in 1969. Ex-Anchor Shipping Corporation.
Built by the North Carolina Shipbuilding Corporation, Wilmington, for the Grace Line as the passenger-cargo ship SANTA MARIA (1946). Renamed SANTA ELENA (1962 – Grace Line) and SANTA SOFIA (1966 – Grace Line).

SUN (1998)
25320 grt; 836 psrs
629' x 81' x 26' (191.7 x 24.8 x 7.9 m)
4 x Parsons DRG turbines via twin screw.
Cruise ship currently laid up in Freeport and with the previous nameplate of SUN VENTURE having the second word painted out to leave SUN. Ex-Regency Cruises.
Built by Chantiers de l'Atlantique, St Nazaire, for Zim Lines as the passenger ship SHALOM (1964). Renamed HANSEATIC (1967 – German Atlantic Line), DORIC (1973 – Home Lines), ROYAL ODYSSEY (1981 – Royal Cruise Lines), REGENT SUN (1988 – Regency Cruises), SUN VENTURE (1996 – Royal Venture Cruise Line) and TOPAZ (1997 – Thomson Cruises).

SUN AMBASSADOR (1990) See THE FIESTA (1991)

SUN BEACH (1996) See APOLLON HELLAS (1999)

SUNBIRD (1999)
37584 grt; 1412 psrs
703' x 93' x 22' (213 x 28.2 x 6.7 m)
4 x 8-cylinder Wartsila-Sulzer diesel engines via twin screw.

Cruise ship owned by Airtours, UK, who purchased her for US$95,000,000.
Built by Wartsila-Helsinki for Royal Caribbean International as the SONG OF AMERICA (1989) at a cost of US$140,000,000.

SUN BOAT (1983) See MEDIA II (1993)

SUNBOAT (1985) See ATHINA I (1999)

SUNDA (1895) See HOKOKU MARU (1914)

SUNDANCER (1983) See IONIAN EXPRESS (1994)

SUNDREAM (1997)
22945 grt; 1150 psrs
637' x 79' x 22' (193 x 23.8 x 6.7 m)
4 x 9-cylinder Wartsila-Sulzer diesel engines via twin screw.

Cruise ship owned and operated by Airtours, UK, after their purchase and renaming of this vessel for US$40,000,000.
Built by Wartsila-Helsinki for the Royal Caribbean Cruise Line as the SONG OF NORWAY (1970).

SUN EXPRESS (1985) See SARDEGNA BELLA (1993)

SUN FIESTA (1990) See CALYPSO (1995)

SUN FIESTA (1992) See OCEAN EXPLORER I (1998)

SUN FIESTA (1993) See AMUSEMENT WORLD (1998)

SUN FLOWER (1972)
12130 grt; 1124 psrs
208 cars or 84 trailers
607' x 79' x 21' (185 x 24 x 6.4 m)
4 x 12-cylinder Kawasaki-MAN geared diesel engines via twin screw.
Passenger-car-cargo ferry owned by the Kurushima Dockyard and operated by Kansai Kisen, Japan.
Built by Kawasaki Dockyard, Kobe, for Taiyo Ferry KK, Kanda.

SUN FLOWER 2 (1972)
12111 grt; 1124 psrs
208 cars or 84 trailers
607' x 79' x 21' (185 x 24 x 6.4 m)
4 x 12-cylinder Kawasaki-MAN geared diesel engines via twin screw.
Passenger-car-cargo ferry owned by the Kurushima Dockyard and operated by Kansai Kisen, Japan.
Launched by Kawasaki Dockyard, Kobe, for Taiyo Ferry KK, Kanda, as the SUNRISE (1972).

SUN FLOWER 5 (1973) See SUPERFERRY 10 (1993)

SUN FLOWER 7 (1979) See MINOAN PRINCE (1995)

SUN FLOWER 8 (1973) See PRINCES OF NEW UNITY (1997)

SUN FLOWER 11 (1974) See PRINCESS OF THE ORIENT (1991)

SUN FLOWER ERIMO (1991)
11272 grt; 634 psrs
587' x 88' x 21'6" (178 x 26.7 x 6.5 m)
2 x 9-cylinder Pielstick diesel engines via twin screw.
Passenger ferry operated by Nippon Enkai, Japan.
Built by Ishikawajima, Tokyo, for the Blue Highway Line as the ERIMO MARU (1989).

SUN FLOWER KIRISHIMA (1993)
12418 grt; 711 psrs
140 cars
614' x 84' x 22' (186 x 25.5 x 6.6 m)
2 x 12-cylinder Pielstick diesel engines via twin screw.
Passenger ferry owned by Mitsui OSK and chartered to the Blue Highway Line.
Built by Mitsubishi Heavy Industries Ltd, Shimonoseki.

SUN FLOWER MITO (1993)
11782 grt; 514 psrs
140 cars
614' x 84' x 22' (186 x 25.5 x 6.6 m)
2 x 12-cylinder Pielstick diesel engines via twin screw.
Passenger-car ferry owned by Mitsui OSK and chartered to the Blue Highway Line.
Built by Mitsubishi Heavy Industries Ltd, Shimonoseki.

SUN FLOWER OARAI (1991)
15139 grt; 656 psrs
105 cars + 70 trailers
587' x 82' x 21'6" (178 x 24.8 x 6.5 m)
2 x 8-cylinder Mitsubishi-MAN diesel engines via twin screw.
Passenger-car-cargo ferry owned and operated by Nippon Enkai, Japan.
Built by Hayashikane Shipbuilding, Shimonoseki, for the Blue Highway Line as the OARAI MARU (1987).

SUN FLOWER OSAKA (1991) See SUPERFERRY 10 (1993)

SUN FLOWER SAPPORO (1991) See BLUE SKY (2000)

SUN FLOWER SATSUMA (1991) See PRINCESS OF THE ORIENT (1991)

SUN FLOWER TOSA (1991) See PRINCESS OF NEW UNITY (1997)

SUNLOCK (1955)
8917 grt; 766 psrs
487' x 58' x 24'10" (147.6 x 17.8 x 7.3 m)
Bremer Vulkan 3-cylinder triple expansion engine via single screw.
Broken up for scrap in Japan in 1959. Ex-Wheelock Marden & Co, Panama.
Built by Bremer Vulkan, Vegesack, for the Hamburg-America Line as the BAYERN (1921). Renamed SONTAY (1936 – Messageries Maritimes).

SUNNY BOAT (1986) See MEDIA II (1993)

SUN PRINCESS (1974) See FLAMENCO (1997)

SUN PRINCESS (1995)
77441 grt; 1950 psrs
855' x 105' x 26' (259.1 x 31.8 x 7.9 m)
4 x 16-cylinder Sulzer diesel-electric engines via twin screw.

Cruise ship owned by Corot Shipping and operated by P&O Princess Cruises.
Built by Fincantieri Navale Italiani, Monfalcone, for the P&O Group at a cost of US$295,000,000.

SUNRISE (1972) See SUN FLOWER 2 (1972)

SUNRISE IV (1979) See PEGANCIA (1980)

SUNSHINE COAST QUEEN (1967)
5010 grt; 340 psrs
150 cars
360' x 77' x 18' (109 x 23.4 x 5.4 m)
4 x 8-cylinder Nordberg diesel engines via twin screw.
Icebreaker class hulled passenger-cargo RoRo ferry owned by the Canadian government and operated by the Ministry of Transport for the province of British Columbia.
Built by the Great Lakes Engineering Works, River Rouge, Michigan, for Marine Atlantic as the VACATIONLAND (1952). Renamed JACK DALTON (1960 – Cie de Navigation Nord-Sud) and PERE NOUVEL (1962 – Cie de Navigation Nord-Sud).

SUNSHINE FUJI (1984) See MABUHAY SUNSHINE (1996)

SUN VENTURE (1996) See SUN (1998)

SUN VIKING (1973) See HYUNDAI PONGNAE (1998)

SUN VISTA (1997)
30440 grt; 1106 psrs
702' x 94' x 28' (214 x 28.6 x 8.5 m)
2 x De Laval DRG turbine engines via twin screw.
Cruise ship owned by Metro Holdings, Singapore, following her acquisition for US$62,500,000, and operated by Sun Cruises, Singapore. She sank stern-first at 1.15 am on 21 May 1999 following an engine room fire which erupted four hours earlier in the Andaman Sea, 60 miles (100 km) off Penang in the Malacca Strait. She was declared a navigation hazard, but legal dispute as to which party was responsible for the removal of the hulk was still ongoing at the end of 2000.
Built by Cantieri Riuniti dell'Adriatico, Monfalcone, for Lloyd Triestino as the GALILEO GALILEI (1963). Renamed GALILEO (1984 – Chandris Group) and MERIDIAN (1990 – Celebrity Cruises).

SUN VIVA (1998) See MEGASTAR SAGITTARIUS (2000)

SUN VIVA 2 (1998) See MEGASTAR CAPRICORN (2000)

SUNWARD (1966) See THE EMPRESS (1994)

SUNWARD (1991) See HYUNDAI KUMGANG (1998)

SUNWARD (1992) See HYUNDAI KUMGANG (1998)

SUNWARD II (1977) See TRITON (1991)

SUPERFAST I (1995)
23663 grt; 1397 psrs
98 cars
573' x 79' x 21' (173.7 x 24 x 6.3 m)
4 x 12-cylinder Zgoda-Sulzer diesel engines via twin screw.
Passenger-car ferry owned by Attika Enterprises, Patras, and operated by Superfast Ferries, Greece.
Built by Schichau Seebeckwerft AG, Bremerhaven for Attika Enterprises.

SUPERFAST II (1995)
23663 grt; 1397 psrs
98 cars
573' x 79' x 21' (173.7 x 24 x 6.3 m)
4 x 12-cylinder Zgoda-Sulzer diesel engines via twin screw.

Passenger-car ferry owned by Attika Enterprises, Patras, and operated by Superfast Ferries, Greece.
Built by Schichau Seebeckwerft AG, Bremerhaven, for Attika Enterprises.

SUPERFAST III (1998)

29067 grt; 1400 psrs
1000 cars or 140 cars + 122 trailers
640' x 83' x 21'6" (194 x 25 x 6.5 m)
4 x 16-cylinder Sulzer diesel engines via twin screw.
Passenger-car-cargo RoRo ferry operated by a joint venture between Superfast Ferries and Attika Enterprises.
Built by the Kvaerner-Masa Yards, Turku, at a cost of US$100,000,000.

SUPERFAST IV (1998)

29067 grt; 1400 psrs
1000 cars or 140 cars + 122 trailers
640' x 83' x 21'6" (194 x 25 x 6.5 m)
4 x 16-cylinder Wartsila diesel engines via twin screw.
Passenger-car-cargo RoRo ferry operated by a joint venture between Superfast Ferries and Attika Enterprises.
Built by the Kvaerner-Masa Yards, Turku, at a cost of US$100,000,000.

SUPERFAST V (2000)

31500 grt; 1606 psrs
1000 cars
673' x 83' x 21'6" (203.9 x 25 x 6.5 m)
4 x 16-cylinder Sulzer diesel engines via twin screw.
Passenger-car-cargo RoRo ferry operating for a joint venture between Superfast Ferries and Attika Enterprises.
Built by HDW, Kiel, at a cost of US$200,000,000.

SUPERFAST VI (2000)

31500 grt; 1606 psrs
1000 cars
673' x 83' x 21'6" (203.9 x 25 x 6.5 m)
4 x 16-cylinder Sulzer diesel engines via twin screw.
Passenger-car-cargo RoRo ferry operating for a joint venture between Superfast Ferries and Attika Enterprises.
Built by HDW, Kiel, at a cost of US$200,000,000.

SUPERFERRY (1991)

7454 grt; 2700 psrs
500 cars + 90 TEUs
455' x 77' x 18'6" (137.9 x 23.4 x 5.6 m)
2 x 18-cylinder Pielstick diesel engines via twin screw.
Passenger-car ferry operated by Strintzis Line.
Built by Hashiyama Zosen, Imabari, for Ocean Ferry KK, Tokushima, as the CASSIOPEIA (1972). Renamed IZU MARU No.3 (1976 – Ocean Tokyo Ferry KK, Kitakyushu) and IONIAN STAR (1991 – Strintzis Line).

SUPERFERRY I (1992)

9184 grt; 302 psrs
90 TEUs
437' x 68' x 19' (132.4 x 20 x 5.8 m)
4 x 8-cylinder Wartsila diesel engines via twin screw.
Passenger ferry owned and operated by WG & A Jebsens Ship Management Inc, Manila.
Built by Shikoku Dockyard, Takamatsu, as the VENUS (1975). Renamed ABOITIZ SUPERFERRY I (1989 – Aboitiz Shipping Corporation).

SUPERFERRY II (1993)

8798 grt; 2000 psrs
389' x 65' x 16' (118 x 19.8 x 4.8 m)
2 x 18-cylinder Pielstick diesel engines via twin screw.
Passenger ferry operating for the Strintzis Line, Greece.
Built by NV Boelwerf SA, Tamise, for RMT, Belgium, as the PRINCE LAURENT (1974). Renamed IONIAN EXPRESS (1992 – Strintzis Line).

SUPERFERRY 2 (1996)

11405 grt; 900 psrs
100 TEUs
457' x 73' x 19'5" (138.6 x 22.2 x 5.9 m)
2 x 14-cylinder MAN diesel engines via twin screw.
Passenger-cargo ferry owned and operated by WG & A Jebsens Shipmanagement Inc, Philippines.
Built by Onomichi Zosen, Onomichi, for Meimon Taiyo Ferry as the FERRY SUMIYOSHI (1973). Renamed ABOITIZ SUPERFERRY II (1995 – WG & A Jebsens Shipmanagement Inc) and ABOITIZ SUPERFERRY 2 (1996 – WG & A Jebsens Shipmanagement Inc).

SUPERFERRY 3 (1993)

9847 grt; 980 psrs
389' x 68' x 19' (118 x 20.5 x 5.7 m)
2 x 10-cylinder Pielstick diesel engines via twin screw.
Passenger ferry owned and operated by WG & A Jebsens Ship Management Inc, Manila.
Built by Hayashikane Zosen, Shimonoseki, for Nippon Car Ferry KK, Hyuga, as the HAMAYU (1971). Renamed ABOITIZ SUPERFERRY III (1993).

SUPERFERRY 5 (1996)

4967 grt; 444 psrs
418' x 68' x 18' (126.6 x 20.7 x 5.5 m)
2 x 9-cylinder Pielstick diesel engines via twin screw.
Passenger ferry owned and operated by WG & A Jebsens Ship Management Inc, Manila.
Built by Naikai Setoda, Setoda, for Silver Higashi Nippon as the FERRY HAKOZAKI (1973). Renamed FERRY COSMO (1992) and ABOITIZ SUPERFERRY V (1994).

SUPERFERRY 6 (1993)

9757 grt; 832 psrs
535' x 72' x 21' (162 x 21.7 x 6.3 m)
2 x 18-cylinder Ishikawajima diesel engines via twin screw.
Passenger ferry owned and operated by WG & A Jebsens Ship Management Inc, Manila.
Built by Koyo Dockyard Co Ltd, Mihara, for Tokyo Ferry KK, Kitakyushu, as the FERRY TONE (1973). Renamed FERRY SHIRAYURI (1976), HERA (1988) and DAN NOH (1989 – Osaka Kokusai).

SUPERFERRY 7 (1994)

4996 grt; 2015 psrs
110 TEUs
464' x 71' x 17'6" 140.5 x 21.5 x 5.4 m)
Broken up for scrap after catching fire in the North Harbour of Manila on 26 March 1997 and being declared a total constructive loss. Ex-WG & A Jebsens Ship Management Inc, Manila.
Built by Towa Shipbuilding, Shimonoseki, for Oshima Unyu KK as the passenger-cargo ferry NAMINOUE MARU (1980).

SUPERFERRY 8 (1996)

7878 grt; 280 psrs
100 TEUs
518' x 67' x 17' (157.1 x 20.2 x 5.6 m)
2 x 12-cylinder Pielstick diesel engines via twin screw.
Passenger ferry owned and operated by WG & A Jebsens Ship Management Inc, Manila.
Built by Usuki Tekkosho, Saiki, for Oshima Unyu KK, Naze, as the AKEBONO MARU (1977). Renamed SUGBU (1989 – William Lines, Manila) and WILLINES MABUHAY 3 (1995 – WG & A Jebsens Shipmanagement Inc, Manila).

SUPERFERRY 10 (1993)

13321 grt; 1079 psrs
79 cars + 100 trailers
607' x 79' x 21' (185 x 24 x 6.4 m)
4 x 12-cylinder Kawasaki-MAN diesel engines via twin screw.
Passenger ferry owned and operated by WG & A Jebsens Ship Management Inc, Manila.
Built by Kurushima Dockyard Co, Imabari, for Nippon Kosoku Ferry Co, Tokyo, as the SUN FLOWER 5 (1973). Renamed SUN FLOWER OSAKA (1991 – Nippon Kosoku Ferry Co, Tokyo).

SUPERFERRY 11 (1996) See OUR LADY OF BANNEUX (1999)

SUPERFERRY 12 (1996)

11914 grt; 711 psrs
133 cars + 136 trailers + 202 TEUs
568' x 88' x 20' (172.1 x 26.7 x 6.2 m)
2 x 12-cylinder MAN diesel engines via twin screw.
Passenger ferry owned and operated by WG & A Jebsens Ship Management Inc, Manila.
Built by Kanda Zosensho KK, Kawajiri, for Hankyu Ferry KK, Shimonoseki, as the NEW MIYAKO (1984).

SUPERFERRY 14 (2000)
10181 grt; 1050 psrs
510' x 77' x 19' (154.5 x 23.3 x 5.8 m)
2 x 18-cylinder Pielstick diesel engines via twin screw.
Passenger ferry owned and operated by WG & A Jebsens Shipmanagement Inc.
Buily by Hayashikani Shipbuilding & Engineering Co Ltd, Shimonoseki, for Sanpo Kaiun KK, Imabari, as the WHITE SANPO 2 (1981).

SUPERFERRY ATLANTIC (2000)
29000 grt; 1600 psrs
100 cars
566' x 85' x 21'6" (171.4 x 25.7 x 6.5 m)
4 x 8-cylinder MAN-B+W diesel engines via twin screw.
Passenger-car ferry owned and operated by Strintzis Lines.
Built by Van der Giessen-de-Noord, Krimpen.

SUPERFERRY HELLAS (1998) See BLUE HORIZON (2000)

SUPERFERRY ITHAKI (2000) See BLUE SKY ITHAKI (2000)

SUPERFERRY PACIFIC (2000)
29000 grt; 1600 psrs
100 cars + 125 trailers
564' x 85' x 21'6" (171 x 25.7 x 6.5 m)
4 x 8-cylinder MAN-B+W diesel engines via twin screw.
Owned and operated by Strintzis Lines Shipping SA, Piraeus.
Built by Van der Giessen-du-Noord, Krimpen.

SUPERFLEX ALFA (1987) See DIFKO NYBORG (1990)

SUPERFLEX BRAVO (1987) See MERCANDIA VIII (1993)

SUPERFLEX DELTA (1989) See GITTE 3 (1999)

SUPERFLEX ECHO (1989) See DIFKO FYN (1995)

SUPERFLEX FOXTROT (1989) See PANTOKRATOR (1994)

SUPERFLEX GOLF (1989) See ANTONIO MACHADO (1994)

SUPERFLEX HOTEL (1989) See MIGUEL HERNANDEZ (1995)

SUPERFLEX INDIA (1988) See DVD No. IV (1995)

SUPERFLEX JULIET (1988) See DVD No. 1 (1995)

SUPERFLEX KILO (1989) See ANJA II (1998)

SUPERFLEX LIMA (1989) See BAIA DE TOGOS DOS SANTOS (1995)

SUPERFLEX MIKE (1989) See DVD No. III (1995)

SUPERFLEX NOVEMBER (1989) See MERCANDIA IV (1989)

SUPERFLEX WHISKEY (1988) See DVD No. II (1999)

SUPER NAIAS (1996) See EXPRESS ARIS (1999)

SUPERSTAR ARIES (1999)
37012 grt; 758 psrs

655' x 92' x 27' (198.5 x 27.9 x 8.2 m)
2 x 7-cylinder MAN diesel engines via twin screw.
Ice-strengthened cruise ship owned and operated by Star Cruises, Singapore, after acquisition of the ship for US$75,000,000.
Built by Bremer-Vulkan Shipyards, Vegesack, for HAPAG-Lloyd as the EUROPA (1981) at a cost of US$120,000,000. Renamed SUPERSTAR EUROPE (1999 – Star Cruises).

SUPERSTAR CAPRICORN (1997) See HYUNDAI KUMGANG (1998)

SUPERSTAR EUROPE (1999) See SUPERSTAR ARIES (1999)

SUPERSTAR GEMINI (1995)
19093 grt; 916 psrs
541' x 76' x 16'6" (164 x 23 x 5 m)
4 x 8-cylinder Wartsila diesel engines via twin screw.

Cruise ship owned by Star Cruises, Singapore, and chartered out to Thomson Cruises, UK.
Built by Union Naval de Levante SA, Valencia, for the Cunard Line as the CROWN JEWEL (1992).

SUPERSTAR LEO (1998)
75338 grt; 1960 psrs
886' x 105' x 26' (268.6 x 31.8 x 7.9 m)
4 x 14-cylinder MAN-B+W diesel-electric engines via twin screw.

Cruise ship owned and operated by Star Cruises, Singapore.
Built by Meyer-Werft, Papenburg, at a cost of US$350,000,000.

SUPERSTAR SAGITTARIUS (1998) See HYUNDAI PONGNAE (1998)

SUPERSTAR TAURUS (2000)
25611 grt; 950 psrs
462 cars
524' x 83' x 18' (158.8 x 25.2 x 5.5 m)

4 x 12-cylinder Pielstick diesel engines via twin screw.
Ice-strengthened cruise ship owned by Neptune Orient and chartered to Star Cruises, Singapore, until 2003.
Built by Wartsila, Turku, for the Viking Sally Line as the passenger-car ferry VIKING SAGA (1980). Renamed as the SALLY ALBATROSS (1986 – Sally Line) and LEEWARD (1995 – Norwegian Cruise Line).

SUPERSTAR VIRGO (1999)
75338 grt; 2800 psrs
879' x 105' x 26' (266.4 x 31.8 x 7.9 m)
4 x 14-cylinder MAN-B+W diesel-electric engines via twin screw.

Cruise ship owned and operated by Star Cruises, Singapore.
Built by Meyer-Werft, Papenburg, at a cost of US$350,000,000.

SURAT (1912)
4444 grt; 60 psrs
360' x 47' x 27'7" (109.1 x 14.2 x 8.4 m)
Hawthorne Leslie 3-cylinder triple expansion engine via single screw.
Broken up for scrap by Sui Dah, Shanghai.
Built by Armstrong Mitchell & Co, Newcastle, for the Ellerman Line as the passenger-cargo ship JOHANNESBURG (1895).

SURREY (1899) See BRODFIELD (1915)

SURRIENTO (1948)
10699 grt; 1080 psrs
498' x 64' x 25' (151.8 x 19.5 x 7.6 m)
2 x 8-cylinder Sulzer diesel engines via twin screw.
Broken up for scrap at La Spezia in 1966. Ex-Achille Lauro.
Built by Furness Shipbuilding Co Ltd, Haverton Hill-on-Tees, for the Grace Steamship Company, New York, as the passenger liner SANTA MARIA (1928). Renamed BARNETT, USS (APA-11) (1940 – US Navy). Reclassified as the BARNETT, USS (APA-5) (1943).

SURRIENTO (1989) See VALTUR PRIMA (1999)

SUSAN B. ANTHONY, USS (AP-72) (1942)
8183 grt; 170 psrs
483' x 64' x 25' (146.4 x 19.4 x 7.6 m)
2 x General Electric turbine engines via twin screw.
Sank on 7 June 1944 when it struck a mine laid off a Normandy beachhead during World War Two.
Built by the New York Shipbuilding Co, Camden, for the Grace Line as the passenger-cargo liner SANTA CLARA (1930).

SUSANNA II (1919)
4046 grt; 152 psrs
396' x 43' x 28'5" depth (120 x 13 x 8.6 m)
Barclay Curle 3-cylinder triple expansion engine via single screw.
Broken up for scrap in 1936. Ex-Madrical and Co, Manila.
Built by Barclay Curle & Co Ltd, Glasgow, for the Castle Line as the passenger-cargo ship DOUNE CASTLE (1890). Renamed SAINT DOMINGO (1904), CURONIA (1904 – Russian East Asiatic Co) and KAIJO MARU (1913 – Goshi Kaisha Kishimoto Shokai, Darien).

SUSQUEHANNA, USS (1917)
10058 grt; 3451 psrs
520' x 58' x 36'7" (158.5 x 17.6 x 11.1 m)
2 x Blohm & Voss 4-cylinder quadruple expansion engines via twin screw.
Broken up for scrap at Yokohama in 1928. Ex-United States Lines.

Built by Blohm & Voss, Hamburg, for North German Lloyd as the passenger liner RHEIN (1899).

SUSSEX (1899) See MONGOLIA (1925)

SUSSEX (1900)
5474 grt; 64 psrs
420' x 54' x 28'7" (127.3 x 16.4 x 8.7 m)
Hawthorne Leslie 3-cylinder triple expansion engine via single screw.
Broken up for scrap in Japan in 1931.
Built by R & W Hawthorn, Leslie & Co Ltd, Newcastle, for the Federal Steam Navigation Co Ltd as a passenger-cargo ship.

SUWA MARU (1912)
11758 grt; 372 psrs
516' x 63' x 29' (156.4 x 19.1 x 8.8 m)
2 x triple expansion engines via twin screw.
Destroyed by the USS FINBACK and USS SEADRAGON on 5 April 1943, following the ship running aground near Wake Island a week after she was torpedoed by the USS TUNNY.
Built by Mitsubishi Shipbuilding & Engineering Works, Nagasaki, for NYK, Japan.

SUWANEE (1911) See SOMERSET (1928)

SUZURAN (1996)
17345 grt; 507 psrs
80 cars + 122 trailers
658' x 83' x 23'6" (199.5 x 25 x 7.1 m)
2 x 18-cylinder Pielstick diesel engines via twin screw.
Passenger-car-cargo ferry operated by Shin-Nihonkai KK Ferry Co Ltd.
Built by Ishikawajima-Harima Heavy Industries Ltd, Tokyo.

SUZURAN MARU (1970) See POSEIDON (1994)

SVALBARD (1946) See TOPEKA (1976)

SVANETIA (1960) See SVANETIYA (1960)

SVANETIYA (1960) See TALLIN (1965)

SVANHOLM (1962) See MELINA (1964)

SVEA (1966) See CAPTAIN ZAMAN II (1998)

SVEA (1984) See COLOR FESTIVAL (1994)

SVEABORG (1905) See EKATERINOSLAV (1906)

SVEABORG (1968) See IALYSSOS (1982)

SVEA CORONA (1975) See IONIAN EXPRESS (1994)

SVEA CORONA (1984) See JUPITER (1998)

SVEA DROTT (1966) See MOBY BABY (1990)

SVEA JARL (1962) See ANDAMAN PRINCESS (1989)

SVEALAND (1971) See SEA WIND (1989)

SVEA REGINA (1972) See EL-TOR (1998)

SVEA SCARLETT (1993) See MERCANDIA VIII (1993)

SVEA STAR (1974) See DISCOVERY SUN (1995)

SVENO MARINA (1984) See JABAL ALI (1999)

SVETI STEFAN (2000)
6918 grt; 550 psrs
205 cars or 40 trailers
363' x 54' x 17'2" (110 x 16.5 x 5.2 m)
2 x 16-cylinder Pielstick diesel engines via twin screw.

Passenger-car ferry owned by Fortune Overseas Navigation Ltd Inc and operated by Prekookeanska Plovidba, Croatia, after beig laid up for four years. Built by Bergens Mek Verksteder, Bergen, for Brittany Ferries as the CORNOUAILLES (1977). Renamed HAVELET (1989 – Condor Ferries Ltd).

SVIR (1935) See ALEX ANDR MOZHAJSKI (1954)

SWAKOPMUND (1907) See ARAFURA MARU (1930)

SWEET FAITH (1970)
3277 grt; 1200 psrs
341' x 49' x 16' (103.3 x 14.8 x 4.8 m)
2 x 9-cylinder B+W diesel engines via twin screw..
Broken up for scrap in 1980 by Mario R Cruel & Julito Macapagal, Quezon City. Ex-Sweet Lines Inc, Manila.
Built by Helsingor Vaerft, Helsingor, for the United Steamship Co, Copenhagen, as the H. P PRIOR (1950).

SWEET GLORY (1988)
4634 grt; 818 psrs
399' x 68' x 17' (120.8 x 20.5 x 5.1 m)
4 x 6-cylinder Niigata diesel engines via twin screw.
Passenger ferry operated in Japan by Sweet Lines Inc, Manila.
Built by Koyo Dockyard Co Ltd, Mihara, for Osaka Kochi Tokkyu Ferry KK, Osaka, as the FERRY KATSURA (1971). Renamed SWEET RORO 2 (1983 – Sweet Lines Inc).

SWEET HOME (1973) See REYNA FILIPINA (1978)

SWEET RORO 2 (1983) See SWEET GLORY (1988)

SWITZERLAND (1996)
16310 grt; 420 psrs
533' x 70' x 26'6" (162.4 x 21.4 x 8.1 m)
2 x 6-cylinder Doxford diesel engines via twin screw.
Cruise ship leased back to Leisure Cruises, Switzerland, until 2002 after purchasing the DAPHNE from Costa Cruises for US$11,000,000.
Built by Harland & Wolff Ltd, Belfast, for the Port Line as the cargo ship PORT SYDNEY (1955). Renamed AKROTIRI EXPRESS (1972 – Chion Shipping Co of JC Carras, Greece) and DAPHNE (1975 – Costa Cruises).

SYDNEY (1950) See CARIBIA 2 (1973)

SYLVANIA (1956) See ALBATROS (1993)

SYMPHONY (1995) See AEGEAN SPIRIT (1999)

SYRIA (1901) See GIOVANNA (1924)

SYRIA (1962)
4423 grt; 538 psrs
356' x 55' x 14'6" (108 x 16.6 x 4.4 m)
9-cylinder MAN diesel engine via single screw.
Operating as a pilgrim ship for the Mubarak Shipping Co, Alexandria, she sustained massive damage when she grounded on the north-east coast of Crete on 20 August 1981. She was refloated one week later, towed to harbour and withdrawn from service. She has been laid up for over 19 years.
Built by Deutsche Werft AG., Hamburg, for the United Arab Maritime Co, Alexandria.

TABA I (1997) See AL SALAM TABA I (1998)

TABINTA (1930)
8156 grt
469' x 62' x 28'11" (142 x 18.8 x 8.5 m)
Werkspoor 8-cylinder diesel engine via single screw.
Broken up for scrap at Hong Kong in 1961.
Built by Nederlandsche Scheepsbouw, Amsterdam, for the Nederland Line.

TABORA (1912)
8106 grt; 375 psrs
468' x 55' x 27' (141.8 x 16.7 x 8.2 m)
Quadruple expansion engines via twin screw.
Sank in 1916 at Dar-es-Salaam after a gunfire bombardment from HMS HYACINTH.
Built by Blohm & Voss, Hamburg, for the German East Africa Line.

TACK TAI (1973)
5299 grt; 73 psrs
391' x 55' x 22' (119.2 x 16.7 x 6.7 m)
2 x 7-cylinder Denny-Sulzer diesel engines via twin screw.
Broken up for scrap at Shanghai in 1975. Ex-Khymer Shipping Co, Panama.
Built by William Denny & Brothers, Dumbarton, for the Union Steamship Company of New Zealand as the TOFUA (1951).

TACLOBAN PRINCESS (1990)
3079 grt; 662 psrs
72 cars or 63 trailers
364' x 64' x 16' (110.3 x 19.3 x 4.8 m)
4 x 6-cylinder Niigata diesel engines via twin screw.
Passenger ferry operated by Sulpicio Lines, Philippines.
Built by Fukuoka Zosen, Fukuoka, for Nihon Kaiun KK, Tokyo, as the SHINKO MARU (1970).

TACOMA MARU (1909)
5772 grt
420' x 50' x 25'7" (127.3 x 15.2 x 7.8 m)
Kawasaki Dockyard 6-cylinder triple expansion engines via twin screw.
Sank on 1 February 1944 after being torpedoed by the USS HAKE off Halmahera Island, Indonesia.
Built by Kawasaki Dockyard, Kobe, for Osaka Shosen Kaisha, Japan.

TADJIKISTAN (1961) See TADZHIKISTAN (1961)

TADLA (1919) See TARI (1934)

TADOUSSAC (1928) See PASSENGER No. 1 (1966)

TADZHIKISTAN (1961) See WANG FU (1993)

TAG EL SALAM (1998)
5493 grt; 1124 psrs
210 cars or 21 trailers
388' x 64' x 14' (117.5 x 19.4 x 4.3 m)
3 x 12-cylinder MAN diesel engines via triple screw.

Pilgrim ship owned by Felfela Inc, SA, Egypt, and operated by El Salam Shipping & Trading Establishment.
Built by NV Scheepswerf Gusto, Schiedam, for Townsend Car Ferries Ltd as the FREE ENTERPRISE IV (1969). Renamed FALSTER LINK (1988 – GT-Link).

TAGUS (1898) See PRINCIPE DE VIANA (1920)

TAGUS (1949)
15543 grt; 1050 psrs
616' x 65' x 31' (187.8 x 19.7 x 9.4 m)
8-cylinder quadruple expansion engines via twin screw.
Broken up for scrap at Savona in 1952. Ex-Tagus Navigation Co, Portugal.
Laid down by the New York Shipbuilding Corporation, Camden, New Jersey, for the Atlantic Transport Line as the MINNEKAHDA (1904) and completed as the MANCHURIA (1904 – Pacific Fast Mail). Renamed PRESIDENT JOHNSON (1929 – Dollar Line) and SANTA CRUZ (1947 – Tagus Navigation Co, Portugal).

TAHITI (1911)
7585 grt; 515 psrs
480' x 55' x 27' (146.3 x 16.7 x 8.2 m)
Triple expansion engines via twin screw.
Owned by the Union Steamship Co of New Zealand, she sank stern first on 17 August 1930 in 3,000 fathoms of water. Her starboard propellor shaft had snapped and pierced its hull two days earlier, 460 miles (766 km) south of Rarotonga. All survived.
Built by Alexander Stephen & Sons, Glasgow, for the Imperial Direct West Mail Co (a subsidiary of Elder Dempster) as the PORT KINGSTON (1904).

TAHITIEN (1953) See ATALANTE (1972)

TAI ER CHUANG (1955)
3503 grt; 96 psrs
317' x 42' x 20'1" (96 x 12.7 x 6.1 m)
Harlan & Hollingsworth 3-cylinder triple expansion engine via single screw.
Broken up for scrap at Hong Kong in 1956 .
Built by Harlan & Hollingsworth Co, Wilmington, Delaware, for the New York & Porto Rico Steamship Co as the PONCE (1899). Renamed KING HSING (1946 – Chung Hsing Steamship Co Ltd) and VEST BAY (1950 – Far Eastern & Panama Transport Corporation).

TAIHOKU MARU (1934)
7548 grt; 60 psrs
485' x 57' x 32'9" depth (147 x 17.3 x 10 m)
A Stephen & Sons 3-cylinder triple expansion engines via single screw.
Sank in 1944 after a US submarine attack.
Built by A Stephen & Sons Ltd, Glasgow, for the Hamburg-America Line as the BETHANIA (1899). Renamed PARISIAN (1916 – F Leyland & Co Ltd), ESTHER DOLLAR (1918 – Dollar Steamship Lines) and CHIEF SHIDEGATE (1930).

TAINUI (1908) See EMPIRE TRADER (1940)

TAIPING (1926)
4324 grt; 191 psrs
368' x 48' x 24' (112.1 x 14.6 x 7.3 m)
3-cylinder triple expansion engine via single screw.
Broken up for scrap at Hong Kong in 1961.
Built by the Hong Kong & Whampoa Dockyard Co for the Australian-Oriental Line Ltd.

TAIPOOLOY (1958)
3547 grt; 71 psrs
328' x 48' x 18'6" (99.4 x 14.5 x 5.6 m)
Triple expansion engine via single screw.
Owned by the Shun Cheong Steam Navigation Co, Hong Kong.
Built by the Hong Kong & Whampoa Dock Co for the Taiping Steamship Navigation Co Ltd as the WING SANG (1938). Renamed WEST INDIAN (1954).

TAIPOOSEK (1962)
3099 grt; 1064 psrs
365' x 52' x 25' (110.5 x 15.9 x 7.6 m)

7-cylinder B+W diesel engine via single screw.
Owned by the Shun Cheong Steam Navigation Co.
Built by Moss Vaerft & Dokk AS, Moss.

TAIPOOSHAN (1969)
11651 grt; 283 psrs
471' x 66' x 25'6" (142.7 x 20 x 7.8 m)
2 x 4-cylinder Doxford diesel engines via twin screw.
Broken up for scrap by Fu Chiang Steel & Iron Co at Kaohsiung in 1975 following a five-year period laid up in the River Fal from 1965 to 1969. Ex-Shun Cheong Steam Navigation Co.
Built by Vickers-Armstrong Ltd, Newcastle, for Elder Dempster Lines as the APAPA (1948).

TAIREA (1924)
7933 grt; 136 psrs
465' x 60' x 26'11" (140.9 x 18.2 x 7.9 m)
Barclay Curle 8-cylinder triple expansion engines via twin screw.
Broken up for scrap at Blyth in 1952 by the British Iron & Steel Co.
Built by Barclay, Curle & Co, Glasgow, for the British India Line.

TAISEIYO MARU (1932)
19782 grt; 1440 psrs
678' x 72' x 33'3" (206.6 x 22 x 10.1 m)
2 x John Brown Ltd 4-cylinder quadruple expansion engines via twin screw.
Broken up for scrap at Osaka in 1933 for a tender figure of £39,000 after having been sold on by scrap merchant Hughes Bolckow, Blyth. The latter had secured the vessel for breaking up with a tender figure of £20,000.
Built by John Brown & Co Ltd, Clydebank, for the Cunard Steamship Co as the CARONIA (1905).

TAISETSU MARU (1948) See SOL PHRYNE (1977)

TAISETSU MARU (1965)
5375 grt; 1330 psrs
436' x 60' x 17' (132 x 18.2 x 5.2 m)
8 x 12-cylinder B+W diesel engines via twin screw.
Owned and operated since 1988 by Hayashi Marine as a floating hotel in Nagasaki.
Built by Mitsubishi Heavy Industries Ltd, Yokohama, for the government of Japan (Department of Railways).

TAIWAN (1969) See NAN HU (1983)

TAI WAY FOONG (1923)
4971 grt; 266 psrs
410' x 48' x 26' (124.2 x 14.5 x 7.9 m)
Triple expansion via single screw.
Broken up for scrap in Japan in 1924 after serving as an accomodation ship for bank staff in the wake of the Yokohama earthquake on 1 September 1923.
Built by Caird & Company, Greenock, for the P&O Line at a cost of £133,078 as the ORIENTAL (1889). Renamed HONG KHENG (1904) and SONG HOI (1921).

TAI WHA (1989)
8134 grt; 1204 psrs
Passenger ferry operated by the Taiwan Navigation Co on the Taiwan–Japan service.

TAIYO (1941)
17127 grt; 285 psrs
562' x 74' x 29' (170.3 x 22.4 x 8.8 m)
2 x Zoelly-geared turbine engines via twin screw.
Sank as an aircraft carrier on 18 August 1944 after being torpedoed by the USS RASHER 22 miles (37 km) south-west of Cape Bojeador, Luzon.
Launched on 19 September 1940 by Mitsubishi Heavy Industries, Nagasaki, as the passenger-cargo liner KASAGU MARU for NYK, Japan, but completed as an aircraft carrier.

TAIYO MARU (1920)
14457 grt; 1389 psrs
580' x 65' x 31'2" depth (175.8 x 19.7 x 9.5 m)
Blohm & Voss 8-cylinder quadruple expansion engines via twin screw.

Owned by Toyo Kisen KK, Tokyo, she sank on 8 May 1942 after being torpedoed by the USS GRENADIER in the South China Sea, south-west of Kyushu.
Built by Blohm & Voss, Hamburg, as the CAP FINISTERRE (1911) for the Hamburg-South American Line.

TAIYUAN
12103 grt
532' x 68' x 28'9" (161.2 x 20.6 x 8.8 m)
Harland & Wolff Ltd 6-cylinder diesel engines via twin screw.
Broken up for scrap at Kaohsiung in 1978.
Built by Harland & Wolff Ltd, Glasgow, for British Phosphate Commissioners as the TRIASTER (1955).

TAIYU MARU (1923)
5995 grt
440' x 52' x 21'4" (133.3 x 15.8 x 6.5 m)
Doxford 3-cylinder diesel engines via twin screw.
Broken up for scrap in 1930.
Built by W Doxford & Sons Ltd, Sunderland, for P&O Steam Navigation Ltd as the BANCA (1900).

TAJ MAHAL (1928) See VICEROY OF INDIA (1929)

TAKACHIHO MARU (1975) See MILLENNIUM EXPRESS (2000)

TAKLIWA (1924)
7936 grt; 136 psrs
465' x 60' x 26'11" (140.9 x 18.2 x 7.9 m)
Barclay Curle 8-cylinder triple expansion engines via twin screw.
Operating for the British Royal Navy, she was abandoned after stranding and burning out in the South Nicobar Islands on 15 October 1945.
Built by Barclay, Curle & Co, Glasgow, for the British India Line.

TALAMANCA (1931) See SULACO (1958)

TALAMANCA, USS (AF-15) (1942) See SULACO (1958)

TALAMBA (1924)
8018 grt; 4224 psrs
466' x 60' x 27' (141.2 x 18.2 x 8.2 m)
Hawthorne Leslie 8-cylinder triple expansion engines via twin screw.
Operating for the British Admiralty, she sank on 11 July 1943 as a hospital ship, with the loss of five lives, after being bombed by German aircraft the day before at 10.00 pm, three miles (5 km) off Avola Anchorage, Sicily.
Built by Hawthorn, Leslie & Co, Newcastle, for the British India Line.

TALLIN (1965)
3290 grt; 250 psrs
335' x 48' x 13' (101.5 x 14.6 x 3.8 m)
2 x 8-cylinder Russki diesel engines via twin screw.
Ice-strengthened vessel in service for the Russian government.
Built by the A Zhdanov Shipbuilding Yard, St Petersburg, for the Russian government as the SVANETIYA (1960).

TALLINK (1990) See EL-TOR (1989)

TALMA (1923)
10004 grt; 135 psrs
471' x 59' x 27'1" (143.6 x 18.1 x 8.2 m)
Hawthorne Leslie 4-cylinder quadruple expansion engine via single screw.
Broken up for scrap by Thomas W Ward at Inverkeithing in 1949.
Built by Hawthorne, Leslie & Co Ltd, Newcastle, for the British India Line.

TALOS (1995) See IERAPETRA (1999)

TALTHYBIUS (1911) See EMPIRE EVENLODE (1947)

TAMAROA (1926)
12375 grt; 159 psrs
519' x 63' x 33' (158.2 x 19.2 x 10 m)
4 x Harland & Wolff Ltd DRG turbine engines via twin screw.

Broken up for scrap by Hughes Bolckhou at Blyth in 1957. Ex-Shaw Savill & Albion.

Built by Harland & Wolff Ltd, Belfast, for the Aberdeen Line as the SOPHOCLES (1922).

TAMBU EXPRESS (1980) See SREDETZ (1986)

TAMELE (1945) See GOLDEN CITY (1967)

TAMIRA (1984) See AL FAHAD (1986)

TAMPOMAS (1956)
7150 grt; 1142 psrs
422' x 62' x 21' (127.9 x 18.7 x 6.4 m)
8-cylinder MAN diesel engine via single screw.
Sank on 25 January 1981, with the loss of 374 lives, in the Java Sea 500 miles (834 km) north-east of Djakarta, after being engulfed by fire which started in the car deck.
Built by De Schelde, Vlissingen, for the government of Indonesia as a passenger-cargo ferry.

TAMPOMAS II (1980)
6139 grt; 718 psrs
250 cars
424' x 75' x 18' (128.6 x 22.7 x 5.6 m)
2 x 9-cylinder Mitsubishi diesel engines via twin screw.
Passenger-car-cargo RoRo ferry owned by the National Fleet Development Corporation, Djakarta.
Built by Misubishi Heavy Industries Ltd, Shimonoseki, for the Central Ferry Co, Kobe, as the CENTRAL No.6 (1971). Renamed EMERALD (1980 – Arimura Sangyo KK, Naha) and GREAT EMERALD (1980).

TANDA (1914) See TANDA (1919)

TANDA (1919)
6956 grt; 100 psrs
431' x 58' x 28'6" (130.6 x 17.6 x 8.7 m)
Triple expansion engines via twin screw.
Owned by the E & A Line, she sank on 15 July 1944 after being torpedoed off Mangalore.
Built by A Stephen & Sons, Glasgow, for the British India Line as the TANDA (1914). Renamed as the hospital ship MADRAS (1914 – Indian government).

TANGANJIKA (1922)
8540 grt; 315 psrs
449' x 58' x 26'8" depth (136 x 17.6 x 8.1 m)
4 x Blohm & Voss SRG turbine engines via single screw.
Broken up for scrap in 1947 at Dover. She had been raised from the bed of Wilhelmshaven harbour where she had sank as a depot ship on 4 November 1943 after being bombed.
Built by Blohm & Voss, Hamburg, for the Hamburg-America Line.

TANGANYIKA (1922) See TANGANJIKA (1922)

TANGER (1972) See AL RASHEED II (1992)

TANGO MARU (1905)
6893 grt; 234 psrs
456' x 50' x 30'4" depth (138.2 x 15.2 x 9.2 m)
Mitsubishi 3-cylinder triple expansion engines via twin screw.
Sank on 13 November 1943 after a US aircraft attack in the East China Sea.
Built by the Mitsubishi Dockyard for NYK, Japan.

TANGPAKORN (1984) See MANAR (2000)

TANNENBURG (1934)
5504 grt; 1000 psrs
398' x 51' x 27'3" depth (120 x 15.5 x 8.3 m)
2 x F Schichau turbine engines via twin screw.
Sank on 7 July 1941 as a minelayer after hitting a mine near Oland.
Built by Stettiner Oderweke, Stettin, for the German government and operated by the Hamburg-America Line.

TAORMINA (1908)
8921 grt; 2560 psrs
482' x 58' x 34'2" (146.9 x 17.8 x 10.4 m)
D & W Henderson 6-cylinder triple expansion engines via twin screw.
Broken up for scrap at Savona in 1929.
Built by D & W Henderson Ltd, Glasgow, for Italia.

TAOS VICTORY (1945) See NEON (1966)

TARA II (1997)
12068 grt
518' x 68' x 20' (157 x 20.6 x 6.1 m)
2 x 16-cylinder Sulzer diesel engines via twin screw.
Passenger ferry owned and operated by Lumen Maritime SA.
Built by Cockatoo Dockyard & Engineering Pty Ltd for the Royal Australian Navy as the destroyer tender and escort maintenance ship STALWART, HMAS (A-215) (1966) and as the destroyer escort ship STALWART, HMS (D-215) (1968). Renamed HER MAJESTY M (1990 – owned by Sea Royal Ferries and operated by Marlines).

TARAK L (1989) See KING OF SCANDINAVIA (1995)

TARAS SHEVCHENKO (1967)
21100 grt; 750 psrs
578' x 78' x 26' (176.2 x 23.5 x 7.9 m)
2 x 7-cylinder Sulzer diesel engines via twin screw.
Ice-strengthened cruise liner owned by the Black Sea Shipping Co, Odessa, via its subsidiary Cable Navigation Co and currently laid up in Iliychevsk, Ukraine, for legal reasons.
Built by Mathias-Thesen Werft, Wismar.

TARAZED, USS (AF-13) (1941) See BLEXEN (1957)

TAREK B (1980) See VEGA (1990)

TARI (1934)
4026 grt; 174 psrs
368' x 45' x 24'6" (111.5 x 13.6 x 4 m)
Richardson, Westgarth 3-cylinder triple expansion engine via single screw.
Operated by Denizyollari Idaresi, Turkey.
Built by Furness, Withy & Co Ltd, Hartlepool, for the Hamburg-America Line as the FRANKENWALD (1908). Renamed TADLA (1919 – Cie de Navigation Paquet).

TARIQ IBN ZIYAD (1995)
21659 ger; 1312 psrs
446 cars
506' x 83' x 20' (153.3 x 25.2 x 6 m)
2 x 12-cylinder Wartsila diesels via twin screw.
Ferry operated by Algerie Ferries (ENTMV).
Built by Union Naval de Levante SA.

TARKWA (1944) See GOLDEN LION (1967)

TAROONA (1935) See DORIC FERRY (1982)

TARQUAH (1902)
3850 grt; 80 psrs
360' x 44' x 14'3" (109.1 x 13.3 x 4.3 m)
A Stephen & Sons 3-cylinder triple expansion engine via single screw.
Sank on 7 July 1917 after being torpedoed ten miles (17 km) from Bull Rock.
Built by A Stephen & Sons Ltd, Glasgow, for Elder Dempster Lines.

TARSUS (1946)
9451 grt; 465 psrs
475' x 62' x 27' (143.9 x 18.8 x 8.2 m)
Turbine engine via single screw.
Owned by Turkish Maritime Lines, she was abandoned as a total loss on 14 December 1960 after being gutted by fire following a series of maritime mishaps. These commenced with the Yugoslav tanker PETER ZORANIC colliding with the tanker WORLD HARMONY in the Bosphorus Sea; then the PETER ZORANIC caught fire and continued under uncontrolled power to collide with the TARSUS which was about to enter a dry dock.

Built by the New York Shipbuilding Company, Camden, New Jersey, for American Export Lines as the EXOCHORDA (1931). Renamed HARRY LEE, USS (AP-17) (1940 – US Navy). Reclassified as the HARRY LEE, USS (AP-10) (1943 – US Navy).

TARUYASU MARU (1942) See EMPIRE EVENLODE (1947)

TASIKMALAJA (1951)
3679 grt; 434 psrs
345' x 46' x 27' (104.5 x 13.9 x 8.2 m)
Sun Shipbuilding Co 4-cylinder triple expansion engine via single screw.
Broken up for scrap at Hong Kong in 1955. Ex-Juan Ysmael, Panama.
Built by Sun Shipbuilding & Drydock Co, Chester, Pennsylvania, for the Inter-Island Steam Navigation Co as the HALEAKALA (1923). Renamed CHRISTOBAL (1949 – Far Eastern Panamanian Navigation Co, Shanghai).

TASKER H. BLISS, USS (AP-42) (1942)
14124 grt; 560 psrs
535' x 72' x 36'8" depth (162.1 x 21.8 x 11.2 m)
4 x Newport News turbine engines via twin screw.
Owned by the US Navy, she sank on 12 November 1942 after being torpedoed by the German U-130 during troop landings at Fedala, Morocco.
Built by the Newport News Shipbuilding & Drydock Company, Newport News, Virginia, for the US Shipping Board as the type "535" transport GOLDEN STATE (1921). Renamed PRESIDENT CLEVELAND (1922 – Pacific Mail Steamship Co) and GENERAL TASKER H. BLISS (1941 – US Army, before her assignment to the US Navy).

TASMAN (1921)
5172 grt
492' x 39' x 26' (118.8 x 11.8 x 7.9 m)
Earle's Co Ltd 3-cylinder triple expansion engines via single screw.
Off Lloyds Register as at 1958.
Built by Earle's Co Ltd for Koninklijke Java-China Packetv Lijnen, NV.

TASMANIA (1955) See UNION RELIANCE (1961)

TASSILI (1973)
12268 grt; 475 psrs
200 cars or 130 trailers
421' x 72' x 18'6" (128.3 x 22 x 5.6 m)
2 x 9-cylinder Mitsubishi diesel engines via twin screw.
Passenger-car-cargo ferry owned and operated by ENTMV. Broken up for scrap in 2000.
Built by Mitsubishi Heavy Industries, Shimonoseki, for the Central Ferry Co, Kobe, as the CENTRAL No.1 (1971).

TATAMAILAU (1990)
6041 grt; 969 psrs
329' x 60' x 14' (99.8 x 18.3 x 4.2 m)
2 x 6-cylinder Krupp-MaK diesel engines via twin screw.
Passenger ferry owned by the government of Indonesia and operated by P T Pelni, Indonesia .
Built by Mcycr Werfte, Papenburg.

TATARIYA (1961)
3219 grt; 250 psrs
333' x 48' x 13' (100.9 x 14.5 x 3.9 m)
2 x 8-cylinder Russian diesel engines via single screw.
In service for the Russian government.
Built by the A Jdanov Shipyard, St Petersburg.

TATSUTA MARU (1930) See TATUTA MARU (1938)

TATUTA MARU (1938)
16955 grt; 839 psrs
584' x 71' x 28'6" (178 x 21.5 x 8.7 m)
4 x 8-8-cylinder Mitsubishi-Sulzer diesel engines via quadruple screw.
Owned by NYK, Japan, she sank on 8 February 1943, with all 148 lives lost, after being torpedoed by the USS TARPON 42 miles (70 km) east of Izu Mikura-Jima, Japan.
Built by Mitsubishi Shipbuilding & Engineering Company, Nagasaki, as the passenger ship TATSUTA MARU (1930) at a cost of Yen 11,215,000.

TAURIC (1891) See WELSHMAN (1904)

TAURUS (1998)
11347 grt; 1800 psrs
460 cars or 150 cars + 30 trailers
480' x 73' x 13' (145.6 x 22 x 4 m)
2 x GE Marine gas turbine engines plus 4 x 5-cylinder MTU diesel engines via quadruple screw.
Passenger-car-cargo ferry owned and operated by Tirrenia.
Built by Fincantieri, Riva Trigoso.

TAXIARCHIS (1999)
10749 grt; 700 psrs
448' x 88' x 20'6" (135.8 x 26.7 x 6.2 m)
2 x 12-cylinder Pielstick diesel engines via twin screw.
Passenger ferry owned and operated by Maritime Co, SA, Lesvos.
Built by Framnaes MV, Sandefjord, for the Union Steamship Co of New Zealand as the UNION HOBART (1976). Renamed SEAWAY HOBART (1984 – Union Steamship Co of New Zealand), SEAWAY I (1993 – Sontak Shipping Co Ltd, & AK Ventouris, Limassol), AGIA METHODIA (1994 – Ventouris Lines) and EUROMANTIQUE (Icemare Shipping Co, SA).

TAYGETOS (1980) See OCEAN HOME (1999)

TEBAH 2000 (1999)
6262 grt; 750 psrs
130 cars
372' x 58' x 16' (113.4 x 17.6 x 4.8 m)
2 x 9-cylinder Stork-Werkspoor diesel engines via twin screw.
Pilgrim ship.
Built by the New South Wales State Dockyard, Newcastle, for the Australian National Line as the passenger-car-cargo ferry PRINCESS OF TASMANIA (1959). Renamed MARINE CRUISER (1975 – Canadian National Railways), MAJORCA ROSE (1984), NOMI (1984), NOMI (1984), EQUATOR (1984 – Equator Shipping Co Ltd), ADRIATIC STAR (1984), LAMPEDUSA (1988), SHAHD FAYEZ (1991 – Fayez Trading, Shipping & Connecting Co Ltd) and AL MAHROUSA (1991 – Al Mahar Marine Agents Co, Saudi Arabia).

TEGELBERG (1938)
14281 grt; 663 psrs
559' x 72' x 30' (169.4 x 21.8 x 9.1 m)
3 x 8-cylinder Sulzer diesel engines via triple screw.
Broken up for scrap at Kaohsiung in 1968.
Built by the Netherlands Shipbuilding Company, Amsterdam, for Royal Interocean Lines.

TEIA MARU (1942)
17537 grt; 386 psrs
566' x 70' x 33'6" depth (171.5 x 21.2 x 10.2 m)
Sulzer 20-cylinder diesel engines via twin screw.
Captured by the Japanese in 1942 as the ARAMIS (1931) and renamed, she sank on 18 August 1944 when torpedoed by the USS RASHER, 150 miles (259 km) west of Negra Point, Luzon.
Built by Forge et Chantiers de la Mediterranee, La Seyne, for Messageries Maritimes as the ARAMIS (1931).

TEIBI MARU (1942)
10268 grt; 299 psrs
476' x 61' x 41' depth (144.2 x 18.5 x 12.4 m)
2 x JC Tecklenborg DRG turbine engines via twin screw.
Captured by the Japanese in 1942, she sank on 10 October 1943 after being torpedoed by the USS BONEFISH off Annam, Vietnam.
Built by JC Tecklenborg, Geestemunde, for Messageries Maritimes as the BERNARDIN DE SAINT PIERRE (1926).

TEIDE (1925)
3829 grt; 1045 psrs
356' x 44' x 25'5" depth (108.4 x 13.3 x 7.7 m)
AG Vulcan 3-cylinder triple expansion engines via twin screw.
Under the ownership of Cia Trasatlantica, she was declared a total loss when wrecked at Bata, Spanish Guinea, on 10 June 1932.
Built by AG Vulcan, Stettin, for North German Lloyd as the CREFELD (1895). Renamed ESPANA N0.4 (1918 – Cia Trasatlantica).

TEIKOKU MARU (1913) See SAINT NICHOLAS (1918)

TEIKO MARU (1942)
15105 grt; 420 psrs
565' x 65' x 41'4" depth (171.2 x 19.7 x 12.5 m)
Chantiers et Ateliers de la Gironde 6-cylinder triple expansion engines via twin screw.
Sank on 22 February 1944 after being torpedoed by the USS PUFFER off the Natauna Islands, Indonesia. She had already been gutted by fire in October 1941 in Shanghai and was rebuilt.
Built by Chantiers et Ateliers de la Gironde, Bordeaux, for Mesageries Maritimes as the D'ARTAGNAN (1924).

TEIRITU MARU (1944) See LE CONTE DE LISLE (1950)

TEISTIN (1980) See MOBY ALE (1997)

TEKIRDAG (1977)
3213 grt; 1185 psrs
300' x 54' x 14' (91.3 x 16.5 x 4.2 m)
2 x 6-cylinder Werkspoor diesel engines via twin screw.
Passenger ferry operated by Turkish Maritime on the Turkey–Greece service.
Built by Denizcilik Camialti, Istanbul.

TELA (1927)
4083 grt; 58 psrs
342' x 48' x 28'2" depth (103.6 x 14.5 x 8.5 m)
Workman, Clark 4-cylinder triple expansion engines via single screw.
Built by Workman, Clark & Co, Glasgow, for the Ellis Steamship Corporation.

TELAGA FITMA (2000)
3079 grt; 350 psrs
307' x 36' x 13' (93 x 14 x 4 m)
2 x 8-cylinder Niigata diesel engines via twin screw.
Owned and operated by Telaga Citra Aradi, Indonesia.
Built by Nakai Zosen Taguma for Tokai Kisen KK, Tokyo, as the passenger ship SALVIA MARU (1972).

TEL AVIV (1928)
8145 grt; 2190 psrs
length 460' x beam 56' (140.2 x 17.1 m)
6-cylinder Rankin & Blackmore triple expansion engines via twin screw.
Broken up for scrap at Trieste in 1934. Ex-Lloyd Triestino.
Built by Russell & Co, Port Glasgow, for Unione Austriaca as the MARTHA WASHINGTON (1908).

TENADORES (1912)
7782 grt; 143 psrs
470' x 55' x 29' (142.4 x 16.7 x 8.8 m)
2 x quadruple expansion engines via twin screw.
Owned by Deutsche Levante, this ship was wrecked beyond salvage on 28 December 1918 on Ile d'Yeu in the Bay of Biscay.
Built by Workman, Clark & Co, Glasgow, for the United Fruit Steamship Co.

TENEDOS (1903)
3564 grt; 1461 psrs
345' x 44' x 29'2" (105 x 13.3 x 8.8 m)
Wallsend Slipway 3-cylinder triple expansion engine via single screw.
Transferred from the Deutsche Levant to the Turkish Navy in 1904, she sank after being torpedoed by the British submarine E-19 near Akbash.
Built by Armstrong, Mitchell & Co, Walker-on-Tyne, for the Hamburg-America Line as the ITALIA (1889). Renamed MILANO (1900- Sloman Line).

TENNYSON (1902) See VALPARAISO (1917)

TENYO MARU (1908)
13402 grt; 759 psrs
575' x 63' x 29' (174.2 x 19.1 x 8.9 m)
3 x turbine engines via triple screw.
Broken up for scrap in Japan in 1933. Ex-NYK.
Built by the Mitsubishi Dockyard for Toyo Kisen Kaisha as a passenger ship.

TEREK (1904)
7363 grt; 1100 psrs
length 463' x beam 56' (140.3 x 17 m)
6-cylinder triple expansion engines via twin screw.
Broken up for scrap as an auxilliary cruiser in 1907. Ex-Russian Volunteer Fleet.
Built by Laird Bros, Birkenhead, for the Hamburg-America Line as the COLUMBIA (1889). Renamed RAPIDO (1898 – Spanish government) and COLUMBIA (1899 – Hamburg-America Line).

TERJE VIGEN (1972) See MIN NAN (1993)

TERJE VIGEN (1975) See NUSA PEJUANG (1992)

TERRA (1987)
18400 grt; 720 psrs
594' x 76' x 29' (181 x 23.1 x 8.8 m)
2 x 8-cylinder B+W diesel engines via twin screw.
Broken up for scrap at Gadani Beach in 1987. Ex-Karageorgios Lines.
Built by Harland & Wolff Ltd, Belfast, for the Union Castle Line as the passenger-cargo ship BLOEMFONTEIN CASTLE (1950). Renamed as the passenger-car ferry PATRIS (1959 – Chandris Group), MEDITERRANEAN ISLAND (1979 – Karageorgios Lines) and MEDITERRANEAN STAR (1982 – Karageorgios Lines).

TERRIFICA (1992) See OCEAN EXPLORER I (1998)

TERTIUM MILLENNIUM (2000) See PASCOLI 96 (2000)

TERUKUNI MARU (1924)
3586 grt
352' x 42' x 19'8" (106.7 x 12.7 x 6 m)
R Napier 3-cylinder triple expansion engines via single screw.
Broken up for scrap. Ex-Harada Kisen KK, Japan.
Built by Napier & Miller Ltd, Glasgow, for the Eastern & Australian Line as the EASTERN (1899).

TERUKUNI MARU (1929)
11931 grt; 249 psrs
511' x 64' x 29' (154.8 x 19.5 x 8.8 m)
2 x 10-cylinder Mitsubishi-Sulzer diesel engines via twin screw.
Sank in 45 minutes on 21 November 1939 after hitting a mine laid in the Thames Estuary off Harwich.
Built by Mitsubishi Heavy Industries, Nagasaki, for NYK as a passenger-cargo ship.

TEUTONIA (1899) See CITY OF HONOLULU (1927)

TEXAS CLIPPER (1965) See TEXAS CLIPPER (1998)

TEXAS CLIPPER (1998)
9644 grt; 147 psrs
473' x 66' x 27' (143.3 x 20 x 8.2 m)
Bethlehem Steel Corporation DRG turbine engine via single screw.
Owned and operated by the government of the USA (Department of Transportation).
Built by Bethlehem Steel Corporation, Sparrow's Point, Maryland, for the US Navy as the attack transport QUEENS, USS (APA-103) (1944). Rebuilt by Bethlehem Steel Corporation for American Export Isbrandtsen Lines as the passenger-cargo ship EXCAMBION (1948) and then laid up in 1959 by the US government. Renamed as the training ship TEXAS CLIPPER (1965 – Texas Aviation & Maritime University) and then laid up at Beaumont (1994 – State of Texas) prior to being laid up in the Reserve Fleet. Renamed TEXAS CLIPPER 2 (1997).

TEXAS CLIPPER 2 (1997) See TEXAS CLIPPER (1998)

TEXAS TREASURE (2000)
9337 grt 1170 psrs
420' x 68' x 16'6" (127.3 x 20.6 x 5 m)
4 x 9-cylinder Ruston diesel engines via twin screw.
Cruise ship owned by MSJ Shipping Ltd and operated by SeaEscape Cruises Ltd.

Built by Swan, Hunter Shipbuilding, Wallsend, for Sealink UK Ltd, as the passenger ferry ST. GEORGE (1968). Renamed PATRA EXPRESS (1984 – Sealink UK), SCANDINAVIAN SKY II (1986 – SeaEscape), SCANDINAVIAN DAWN (1990 – SeaEscape), DISCOVERY DAWN (1996 – Discovery Cruise Line) and ISLAND DAWN (1998 – International Shipping Partners Inc).

THE AZUR (1987)

14717 grt; 665 psrs
200 cars
465' x 74' x 18' (141.8 x 22.6 x 5.5 m)
2 x 12-cylinder L'Atlantique-Pielstick diesel engines via twin screw.

Cruise ship operated by Festival Cruises.
Built by Dubigeon-Normandie SA, Nantes, for Southern Ferries Ltd (a P&O Group subsidiary) as the EAGLE (1971). Renamed AZUR (1975 – Paquet Cruises, Marseille).

THE BIG RED BOAT I (1997)

38772 grt; 1562 psrs
782' x 96' x 28' (237 x 29 x 8.5 m)
4 x De Laval turbine engines via twin screw.
Cruise ship owned by Club Vacaciones and operated by PullmanTours, Spain, following purchase for US$20,000,000 in December 2000.
Built by Cantieri Riuniti dell'Adriatico, Monfalcone, for Home Lines as the OCEANIC (1965). Renamed ROYALE OCEANIC (1985 – Greyhound Bus Co), STARSHIP OCEANIC (1988 – Premier Cruises) and OCEANIC (1997 – Premier Cruises).

THE BIG RED BOAT II (2000)

32753 grt; 1158 psrs
716' x 96' x 28' (217 x 29 x 8.5 m)
4 x De Laval turbine engines via twin screw.
Cruise ship purchased by Cammell Laird & Co Ltd, Hebburn-on-Tyne, from the Receivers appointed to the previous owners, Lowline Cruises (PSV) Ltd, London, in 1999, and chartered to Premier Cruises, Miami.
Built by Cantieri Riuniti dell'Adriatico, Monfalcone, for the Costa Line as the EUGENIO C (1966). Renamed EUGENIO COSTA (1987 – Costa Line), AMERICAN PIONEER (1994 – American Family Cruises) and EDINBURGH CASTLE (1997 – Lowline Cruises, London).

THE BIG RED BOAT III (2000)

31793 grt; 1432 psrs
760' x 90' x 32' (231.7 x 27.5 x 9.7 m)
4 x DRG turbine engines via twin screw.
Cruise ship sold by Premier Cruise's receiver for US$16,000,000 in December 2000.
Built by John Brown & Co Ltd, Clydebank, for the Union-Castle Line as the TRANSVAAL CASTLE (1861). Renamed S.A. VAAL (1966 – South African Marine Lines), FESTIVALE (1978 – Carnival Cruise Lines) and ISLAND BREEZE (1996 – chartered to Dolphin Cruises).

THE BIG RED BOAT IV (2000)

39674 grt; 1050 psrs
748' x 94' x 19' (227.9 x 28.7 x 8.8 m)
6 x DRG turbine engines via twin screw.
Cruise ship sold by Premier Cruise's receiver for US$26,500,000 in December 2000.
Built by the Rotterdam Drydock Co for Holland America Lines as the ROTTERDAM (1959). Renamed REMBRANDT (1997 – International Shipping Partners (UK) Ltd).

THE EMERALD (1996)

26431 grt; 1188 psrs
584' x 84' x 27' (177.9 x 25.6 x 8.2 m)
4 x General Electric DRG turbine engines via twin screw.

Cruise ship owned by Louis Cruises and chartered to Thompson Holidays, UK.
Built by Newport News Shipbuilding, Newport News, Virginia, for the Grace Line as the passenger-cargo ship SANTA ROSA (1958) at a cost of US$25,000,000. Renamed SAMOS SKY (1976 – Vintero Sales Corporation, New York), DIAMOND ISLAND (1990 – Coral Cruise Line), PACIFIC SUN (1991 – Coral Cruise Line), RAINBOW (1992 – Coral Cruise Line), REGENT RAINBOW (1992 – Regency Cruises) and EMERALD (1996 – Louis Cruise Lines).

THE EMPRESS (1994)

10558 grt; 380 psrs
458' x 68' x 18' (138.8 x 20.6 x 5.5 m)
2 x 12-cylinder B+W diesel engines via twin screw.
Cruise ship operated by Empress Cruise Lines, Kuala Lumpur, after exercising an option to purchase in 2000 at a cost of US$15,000,000 over 76 months.
Built by the AS Bergen Shipyard, Bergen, for the Norwegian Caribbean Line as the SUNWARD (1966). Renamed ILE DE BEAUTE (1973 – CGT), GRAND FLOTEL (1977 – static floating hotel in Saudi Arabia), SAUDI MOON I (1978 – Al Sabah Maritime Services Co Ltd, Jeddah), OCEAN SPIRIT (1988 – Ocean Quest International), SCANDINAVIAN SONG (1990 – SeaEscape), SANTIAGO DE CUBA (1994 – Tschudi & Eitzen Shipmanagement (Singapore) Pte Ltd) and EMPRESS (1994).

THE FIESTA (1991)

10596 grt; 570 psrs
487' x 64' x 21'6" (147.6 x 19.4 x 6.5 m)
4 x AEG DRG turbine engines via twin screw.
Sank in October 1991 after catching fire at her refitting berth, at Drapetzona near Piraeus, where she was undergoing a US$20,000,000 refurbishment for Festival Shipping & Tourist Enterprises, Liberia.
Built by Howaldtswerft-Deutsche Werft AG, Hamburg, for Zim Lines under the World War Two Repatriation Payment Scheme to the Jewish nation as the THEODORE HERZL (1957). Renamed CARNIVALE (1969 – New Horizons Shipping Ltd, London), FREEPORT (1976 – Bahama Cruise Lines), VERA CRUZ I (1977 – New Horizons Shipping Ltd, London), VERACRUZ PRIMERO (1977 – Freeport Cruise Lines), VERA CRUZ (1977) and SUN AMBASSADOR (1990).

THE MERCURY (1998)

4077 grt; 111 psrs
290' x 53' x 12' (88 x 16 x 3.6 m)
2 x 12-cylinder MAN-B+W-Alpha diesel engines via twin screw.
Cruise casino ship owned and operated by Universal Cruises, Singapore.
Built by Cantiers Navale Ferrari Shipyards, La Spezia, for Renaissance Cruises as the RENAISSANCE 1 (1989) at a cost of US$28,000,000.

THEMISTOCLES (1908)

6045 grt; 1600 psrs
400' x 50' x 26'11" (121.9 x 15.2 x 7.9 m)
G Clark Ltd 6-cylinder triple expansion engines via twin screw.
Broken up for scrap at Piraeus in 1933. Ex-Greek National Line.
Built by J Priestman & Co Ltd, Sunderland, for the Hellenic Transatlantic Line

as the MORAITIS (1907) which was the first Greek-owned passenger liner on the North Atlantic.

THEMISTOCLES (1911)
11231 grt; 359 psrs
517' x 63' x 29'6" (157.6 x 19.2 x 8.9 m)
Harland & Wolff Ltd 8-cylinder quadruple expansion engines via twin screw.
Broken up for scrap by Arnott Young & Company at Dalmuir in 1947.
Built by Harland & Wolff Ltd, Belfast, for the Aberdeen Line.

THE NEPTUNE (1998)
4077 grt; 111 psrs
290' x 53' x 12' (88 x 16 x 3.6 m)
2 x 12-cylinder MAN-B+W-Alpha diesel engines via twin screw.
Cruise casino ship owned and operated by Universal Cruises, Singapore.
Built by Cantiers Navale Ferrari, La Spezia, as the RENAISSANCE 2 (1990) at a cost of US$28,000,000.

THENIA (1988) See MOBY RIDER (1998)

THEODORE (1997)
5583 grt; 1500 psrs
100 cars + 30 rail wagons or 13 rail coaches
446' x 58' x 16' (135.2 x 17.7 x 4.8 m)
8 x 12-cylinder Maybach diesel-electric engines via twin screw.

Broken up for scrap in India in 1997. Ex-Deutsche Bundesbahn.
Built by Howaldswerft Deutsche Werft AG., Kiel, as the passenger-car-train ferry THEODOR HEUSS (1957).

THEODORE HERZL (1957) See THE FIESTA (1991)

THEODOR HEUSS (1957) See THEODORE (1997)

THEOFILOS (1995)
19212 grt; 917 psrs
470 cars or 45 trailers
490' x 79' x 18' (149.4 x 24 x 5.5 m)
2 x 16-cylinder Pielstick geared diesel engines via twin screw.

Owned and operated by Maritime Company of Lesvos SA.
Built by Werft Nobiskrug, Rendsburg, for the TT-Line, Lubeck, as the NILS HOLGERSSON (1975). Renamed ABEL TASMAN (1985 – TT Line, Tasmania) and POLLUX (1994 – Ventouris Group, after her purchase for US$19,250,000) .

THEOPHILE GAUTIER (1926)
8194 grt; 278 psrs
441' x 56' x 34'9" depth (133.5 x 17 x 10.6 m)
Cie de Construction Mec 12-cylinder diesel engines via twin screw.
Sank after being torpedoed on 4 October 1941 by the British submarine TALISMAN off the island of Eubaeo in the Aegean Sea, with 19 lives lost.
Built by Chantiers et Ateliers de France, Dunkirk, for Messageries Maritimes as a passenger-cargo ship.

THEOSKEPASTI (1986)
3749 grt; 1140 psrs
175 cars
321' x 61' x 15' (97.3 x 18.6 x 4.5 m)
2 x 9-cylinder Sulzer diesel engines via twin screw.

Ice-strengthened passenger-car ferry operated by Theoskepasti Shipping, Piraeus.
Built by Wartsila, Helsinki, for the Silja Line as the NORDIA (1962). Renamed ISLE DE COCHE (1974 – Cia Consolidado De Ferrys, Pampatar, Venezuela).

THE PHILIPPINE TOURIST I (1978)
4776 grt; 286 psrs
40 cars
374' x 53' x 18' (113.3 x 16.1 x 5.5 m)
8-cylinder B+W diesel engine via single screw.
Owned by Dashwood Finance Co Ltd, Manila, who have her laid up in Cebu City.
Hull constructed by Thornycroft, Southampton, and ship completed by Akers MV, Oslo, for Fred Olsen Lines as the cruise ship BRAEMAR (1953). Renamed THE PHILIPPINE TOURIST (1975 – Dashwood Finance Co Ltd, Manila).

THERISOS EXPRESS (1972) See PRINCESS DANAE (1997)

THERMOPYLAE (1972) See AGAPITOS I (1973)

THESEUS (1968) See ORPHEUS (1969)

THESEUS (1992)
6653 grt; 454 psrs
470 cars or 70 TEUs
393' x 54' x 15'2" (119 x 16.5 x 4.6 m)
4 x 12-cylinder British-Polar diesel engines via single screw.
Passenger-car-cargo ferry owned by Olympia II Shipping and operated by Miras D, Greece.
Built by Verolme, Cork, for British and Irish Ferries as the DUNDALK (1975). Renamed STENA SILOR (1980 – Stena Sealink) and WINDCYBI (1991 – Stena Line Ltd). Laid up since 1987 in Keratsini.

THESSALONIKI (1914)
4682 grt; 2000 psrs
421' x 47' x 18'6" (128.4 x 14.2 x 5.6 m)
3-cylinder triple expansion engine via single screw.
Owned by the Greek National Line, she sank on 5 January 1916 in mid-Atlantic during a raging storm 350 miles (583 km) east of Sandy Hook, New Jersey. She had previously been shaken by a series of explosions in the engine room which had somehow become flooded on 22 December 1915. After ensuring that all passengers and crew had been rescued by the ships PATRIS and FLORIZEL, the captain ordered the seacocks to be opened to hasten the ship's end.
Built by Workman, Clark, Belfast, for the City Line as the CITY OF VIENNA (1889).

THESSALONIKI (1997)
10499 grt; 1290 psrs
300 cars or 156 cars + 26 trailers
443' x 66' x 19' (134 x 20 x 5.7 m)
2 x 8-cylinder Sulzer diesel engines via twin screw.
Passenger-car-cargo ferry owned and operated by Thessaloniki Shipping Ltd.
Built by Wartsila-Turku for the Lion Steamship Co as the PRINS HAMLET (1966). Renamed PRINZ HAMLET (1969 – Lion Ferry & HADAG joint venture), ROUSSILLION (1970 – French Line) and KAMIROS (1980 – Dodekankisiaki Shipping Co SA, Rodos).

THE TOPAZ (1998)
32327 grt; 1050 psrs
644' x 86' x 29' (195 x 26 x 8.8 m)
2 x Pametrada geared turbine engines via twin screw.
Cruise ship owned by Topaz International Shipping Inc, Piraeus.
Built by Fairfield & Co, Govan, for Canadian Pacific Steamships as the EMPRESS OF BRITAIN (1956). Renamed QUEEN ANNA MARIA (1964 – Greek Line), CARNIVALE (1975 – Carnival Cruise Lines), FIESTAMARINA (1993 – Turquoise Sea Shipping Inc) and OLYMPIC (1994 – Royal Olympic Cruises).

THE VICTORIA (1977) See PRINCESA VICTORIA (1993)

THE VIKING (1908)
4644 grt; 364 psrs
421' x 46' x 29'3" depth (127.6 x 13.9 x 8.9 m)
T Richardson & Sons 3-cylinder triple expansion engine via single screw.
Broken up for scrap at Zwijndrecht, Holland, in 1913. Ex-Polytechnic Cruising Association.
Built by J & G Thompson, Glasgow, for the Union Line as the MOOR (1881). Renamed LA PLATA (1901 – Royal Mail Line).

THE VIKING (1913) See VIKNOR, HMS (1914)

THE VIKING (1981) See BOUGHAZ (1988)

THE VIKING (1983) See MOBY LALLI (2000)

THE VIKING (1988) See WASA PRINCE (1992)

33 ORIENTALES (1966) See JOYWAVE (2000)

THISTLE (1944)
6484 grt; 278 psrs
414' x 58' x 22'8" (125.5 x 17.6 x 6.9 m)
2 x New York Shipbuilding Co turbine engines via single screw.
Broken up for scrap at San Francisco, California, in 1957. Ex-US Department of Commerce.
Built by the New York Shipbuilding Corporation for the Matson Line as the MUNARGO (1921). Renamed MUNARGO, USS (AP20) (1941 – US Navy).

THJELVAR (1973) See DELFINI (1996)

THJELVAR (1997) See PENELOPE A (2000)

THOMAS II (1995) See OLYMPIA I (1997)

THOMAS HAVILAND (1971) See VACATIONLAND (1971)

THOMAS H. BARRY (1941)
11520 grt; 530 psrs
508' x 71' x 19'5" (153.9 x 21.5 x 5.9 m)
General Electric turbo-electric engines via twin screw.
Broken up for scrap at Baltimore in 1957. Ex-US Department of Commerce.
Built by Newport News Shipbuilding & Drydock Co, Newport News, for the Ward Line, New York, as the ORIENTE (1930).

THOMAS JEFFERSON, USS (AP-30) (1943)
9260 grt; 96 psrs
492' x 70' x 27' (149.1 x 21.2 x 8.2 m)
Geared turbine engines via single screw.
Broken up for scrap by Zidell Exploration Inc at Portland, Oregon, in 1973. Ex-US Navy.
Laid down by Newport News Shipbuilding & Engineering Company, Newport News, Virginia, for American President Lines as the PRESIDENT GARFIELD (1940). Completed as the THOMAS JEFFERSON, USS (AP-60) (1942 – US Navy).

THOMAS MANN (1993) See CROWN OF SCANDINAVIA (1994)

THOMAS R. STONE, USS (AP-59) (1942) See THOMAS R. STONE, USS (APA-29) (1943)

THOMAS R. STONE, USS (APA-29) (1943)
9260 grt; 96 psrs
492' x 70' x 27' (149.1 x 21.2 x 8.2 m)
Turbine engines via twin screw.
Owned by the US Navy when she was broken up in 1944 on the beach where she was driven after her towline had snapped, en route to Algeria for salvage by Le Material Economique, Algiers. She had been torpedoed on 7 November 1942 in shallow water.
Built by Newport News Shipbuilding & Engineering Company, Newport News, Virginia, for American President Lines as the PRESIDENT VAN BUREN (1941).

THONG NHAT (1978) See MEDOUSA (1997)

THOR HEYERDAHL (1993) See VANA TALLINN (1994)

THURINGIA (1870) See SOVIETSKAYA ROSSIJA (1921)

THURINGIA (1923) See EMPIRE DEBEN (1945)

THYSVILLE (1957) See AUSTRALASIA (1965)

TIAN 2 (1985)
4053 grt
347' x 50' x 17' (105 x 15.2 x 5.2 m)
Shanghai Diesel Engine Works turbine engine via single screw.
Owned and operated by the Dalian Steam Shipping Co, Dalian.
Built by Xingang, Tianjin, as the GONG NONG BING (1966).

TIAN E (1985)
7988 grt; 691 psrs
150 cars
412' x 64' x 17' (124.9 x 19.3 x 5.2 m)
2 x B+W diesel engines via twin screw.

Passenger-car ferry owned by Citex and operated by Dalian Steamships on the Hong Kong–Korea service after purchase for US$7,250,000 in 1985.
Built by Cantieri Navale de Tirrenio e Riuniti SpA, Riva Trigoso, for DFDS as the AALBORGHUS (1969). Renamed DANA SIRENA (1971 – DFDS), OLAU DANA (1975 – Olau Line), ROBIN HOOD (1977 – TT Line), DANA SIRENA (1977 – DFDS), ROBIN HOOD (1978 – TT Line), DANA SIRENA (1978 – DFDS), ROBIN HOOD (1979 – TT Line) and DANA CORONA (1979 – DFDS).

TIAN HU (1981)
5492 grt; 948 psrs
396' x 56' x 19' (120 x 17 x 5.8 m)
2 x 6-cylinder Shanghai Diesel Works-Sulzer diesel engines via single screw.
Ice-strengthened passenger-cargo ferry owned and operated by Guangdong Province, Hong Kong, & Macau Navigation Co, Guangzhou.
Built by NV Zaanlandsche Scheepsbouw Maatschappij.

TIAN HU (1981)
3899 grt; 760 psrs
291' x 54' x 17'8" (88.2 x 16.4 x 5.4 m)
2 x 12-cylinder Deutz diesel engines via twin screw.

Passenger ferry owned and operated by Cosco.
Built by Zaanlandsche for Rederi AB Gotland as the VISBY (1964). Renamed SKANDYNAWIA (1970).

TIAN HUAI (1999)
5002 grt; 948 psrs
396' x 56' x 19' (120 x 17 x 5.8 m)
2 x 6-cylinder Sulzer diesel engines via twin screw.
Passenger ferry owned and operated by China Shipping Passenger Liner Co Ltd, Dalian.
Built by Xingang Shipyard, Tianjin.

TIAN IN 2 (1995) See DONG CHUN (2000)

TIAN JIANG (1984)
5492 grt; 948 psrs
422' x 56' x 19' (128 x 17 x 5.8 m)
2 x 6-cylinder Shanghai Diesel Works-Sulzer diesel engines via twin screw.
Passenger ferry owned and operated by Dalian Steamshipping Co, Dalian.
Built by Xingang Shipyard, Tianjin.

TIAN KUN (1991)
6066 grt; 900 psrs
162 cars + 24 trailers
379' x 59' x 15'6" (114.9 x 17.8 x 4.7 m)
4 x 16-cylinder MAN diesel engines via twin screw.

Passenger-car-cargo ferry owned by the China Ocean Shipping Co and operated by the Dalian Steamship Co, Dalian.
Built by Werft Nobiskrug, Rendsburg, for Lion Ferry as the PRINS BERTIL (1964). Renamed LEIF ERIKSSON (1966 – Canadian National Railway), IONIAN STAR (1976 – Strintzis Lines) and ORIENT STAR (1990 – Antarctica Shipping Ltd, Valetta).

TIAN PENG (1991)
6760 grt; 1000 psrs
220 cars

364' x 60' x 14'6" (110.2 x 18.1 x 4.4 m)
4 x 18-cylinder MAN diesel engines via twin screw.
Passenger-car ferry operated by the Dalian Steamship Co, China.
Built by Werft Nobiskrug, Rendsburg, for the British & Irish Steam Packet Co at a cost of £2,000,000 as the MUNSTER (1969). Renamed FARAH I (1983 – Jordan NSL).

TIAN YUN (1984)
5500 grt; 948 psrs
396' x 56' x 19' (120 x 17 x 5.8 m)
2 x 6-cylinder Shanghai Diesel Works-Sulzer diesel engines via twin screw.
Passenger ferry owned and operated by the government of China (Bureau of Maritime Transport Administration).
Built by Xingang Shipyard, Tianjin.

TIDAR (1988)
13853 grt; 1737 psrs
472' x 77' x 19'6" (143 x 23.3 x 5.9 m)
2 x 6-cylinder MaK geared diesel engines via twin screw.
Passenger ferry operated by PT Pelni, Indonesia.
Built by Meyer Werft, Papenburg, for the Indonesian government.

TIDEWATER (1946) See CONTINENTAL (1948)

TIEN HU (1981) See TIAN HU (1981)

TIEN IN (1991) See ORIENTAL PEARL (1998)

TIENTSIN (1898) See FAKHRI (1909)

TIEPOLO (1983) See AL SALAM TABA I (1998)

TIERRA DEL FUEGO (1987) See CARLA E (1991)

TIGER, HMS (1914)
11621 grt; 1850 psrs
550' x 59' x 27'2" (167.6 x 18 x 8.2 m)
John Brown & Co 6-cylinder triple expansion engines via twin screw.
Passenger ship owned by the British Admiralty and converted to a replica of the capital ship TIGER, she sank on 30 May 1915 after being torpedoed by the German U-8 off Mudros, in the Aegean Sea.
Built by John Brown & Co Ltd, Clydebank, for the American Line as the MERION (1902).

TIGER nf (1978) See ALANDSFARJAN (1987)

TIGER (1985) See ALANDSFARJAN (1987)

TILAWA (1924)
10004 grt; 115 psrs
length 471' x beam 59' (143.6 x 18.1 m)
Quadruple expansion engine via single screw.
Sank on 23 November 1942, with the loss of 280 lives, after being torpedoed twice by the Japanese submarine I-29 in the Indian Ocean. The British cruiser HMS BIRMINGHAM rescued 678 people.
Built by Hawthorne, Leslie & Company, Newcastle, for the British India Line.

TILONGKABILA (1995)
6041 grt; 969 psrs
329' x 60' x 14' (99.8 x 18.3 x 4.2 m)
2 x 6-cylinder Krupp-MaK diesel engines via twin screw.
Passenger ship owned by the government of Indonesia and operated by PT Pelnia.
Built by Meyer Werft, Papenburg.

TILTHORN (1954) See TOPEKA (1976)

TIMOR (1951) See KIM ANN (1974)

TINTAGEL CASTLE (1896) See LIGER (1912)

TINTORETTO (1983) See GURGEN-2 (1996)

TIONESTA (1903)
4272 grt
363' x 45' x 12'6" (110 x 13.6 x 3.8 m)
Quadruple expansion engines via single screw.
Broken up for scrap at Hamilton, Ontario, in 1940 after having served as a cruise ship on the Great Lakes system.
Built by the American Shipbuilding Co, Cleveland, for the Anchor Line (Erie & Western Transportation Co).

TIPASA (1971)
9598 grt; 1100 psrs
TEUs
389' x 69' x 20' (118 x 20.8 x 6 m)
2 x 12-cylinder Pielstick diesel engines via twin screw.
Passenger-cargo ferry owned and operated by ENTMV, Algiers.
Built by Mitsubishi Heavy Industries Ltd, Kobe, for ENTMV as the PHENIX (1971).

TIPTON (1918) See ADMIRAL BENSON (1927)

TIRHAN (1938)
3088 grt; 700 psrs
325' x 44' x 19' (98.5 x 13.3 x 5.8 m)
Neptun Werk 6-cylinder triple expansion engines and turbines via twin screw.
Operated by Turkish Maritime Lines.
Built by Neptun, Rostock.

TIRIMUJGHIAN (1906)
4579 grt; 1817 psrs
391' x 47' x 31'2" (119 x 14.2 x 9.5 m)
Fairfield 3-cylinder triple expansion engine via single screw.
Owned by the Turkish government, she sank in 1914 in the Black Sea after an attack by the Russians.
Built by the Fairfield Shipbuilding & Engineering Co, Glasgow, for North German Lloyd as the passenger ship DRESDEN (1888). Renamed HELIUS (1903 – Union-Castle Line).

TIRPITZ (1914) See EMPRESS OF AUSTRALIA (1922)

TITANIC (1912)
46329 grt; 2603 psrs
882' x 92' x 34' (267.3 x 27.9 x 10.3 m)
Harland & Wolff triple expansion engines via triple screw.
Sank on 14 April 1912 on her maiden voyage when she struck an iceberg 370 miles (617 km) east of Cape Race, Newfoundland, and slid into deep water, taking 1,593 lives with her.
Built by Harland & Wolff Ltd, Belfast, for the White Star Line.

TITIAN NUSANTARA (2000)
5532 grt; 850 psrs
335' x 64' x 16'5" (101.6 x 19.3 x 5 m)
4 x 6-cylinder Niigata diesel engines via twin screw.
Passenger-cargo ship owned and operated by Prima Vista, Indonesia.
Built by Fukuoka Zosen KK, Fukuoka.

TITIBY MARU (1938) See KAMAKURA MARU (1939)

TIVIVES (1911)
5017 grt; 103 psrs
394' x 50' x 25' (119.4 x 15.2 x 7.6 m)
2 x Workman, Clark triple expansion engines via single screw.
Sank on 21 October 1943 after being attacked by enemy aircraft in the Mediterranean.
Laid down by Workman, Clark & Co, Belfast, for the United Fruit Steamship Co as the PERALTA (1911).

TIZIANO (1970) See IVAN ZAJC (1992)

TJALDUR (1967)
3190 grt; 340 psrs
313' x 44' x 19' (94.8 x 13.3 x 5.8 m)
7-cylinder Krupp diesel engine via single screw.
Broken up for scrap by HP Heuvelman at Krimpen on the Nieuwe Waterweg, Holland, in 1969. Ex-PF Skipafelagid Foroyar, Thorshavn.
Built by AB Chrichton-Vulkan, Turku, for the Bergen Line as the ASTREA (1941).

TJERIMAI (1921) See SAFINA-E-MURAD (1951)

TJILUWAH (1951) See KOTA SINGAPURE (1972)

TJISADANE (1931)
9600 grt; 162 psrs
440' x 62' x 29' (133.3 x 18.8 x 8.8 m)
Workspoor 8-cylinder diesel engine via single screw.
Built by Nederlandsche Scheepsbouw Maatschappij, Amsterdam, for Royal Interocean Lines.

TJITJALENGKA (1939)
10972 grt; 1229 psrs
476' x 65' x 28' (144.2 x 19.7 x 8.5 m)
Stork-Werkspoor 6-cylinder diesel engine via single screw.
Broken up for scrap at Hong Kong in 1968 by Ming Hing & Co.
Built by the Netherlands Shipbuilding Co, Amsterdam, for Royal Interocean Lines.

TJIWANGI (1950) See KOTA BALI (1971)

TJUT NJAK DHIEN (1965) See KRI TANJUNG OISINA (1978)

TOBOLSK (1952)
3498 grt; 346 psrs
334' x 47' x 18' (101.2 x 14.2 x 5.5 m)
2 x 6-cylinder Fiat diesel engines via twin screw.
Cruise ship for the Russian government.
Built by Cantieri del Mediterraneo.

TOFUA (1908)
4345 grt; 145 psrs
350' x 48' x 21' (106.1 x 14.5 x 6.4 m)
2 x William Denny & Brothers triple expansion engines via twin screw.
Broken up for scrap at Kobe in 1934.
Built by William Denny & Bros, Dumbarton, for the Union Steamship Company of New Zealand.

TOFUA (1951) See TACK TAI (1973)

TOGO (1938) See TOPEKA (1976)

TOGO (1943) See TOPEKA (1976)

TOGO (1956) See TOPEKA (1976)

TOKACHI MARU (1948)
3048 grt
387' x 52' x 16'6" (117.3 x 15.8 x 5 m)
4 x Mitsubishi DRG turbine engines via twin screw.
Owned by the Japanese government (Department of Railways).
Built by Mitsubishi Shipbuilding & Engineering Co.

TOKACHI MARU (1970)
7400 grt
474' x 61' x 23'8" (143.6 x 18.5 x 7.2 m)
4 x Mitsubishi DRG turbine engines via twin screw.
Built by Hitachi Zosen, Mukalshima, for the government of Japan (Department of Railways).

TOKYO MARU (1969) See DIPOLOG PRINCESS (1989)

TOLEDO (1922)
8106 grt; 656 psrs
468' x 55' x 27' (141.8 x 16.7 x 8.2 m)
8-cylinder quadruple expansion engines via twin screw.
Broken up for scrap in Italy in 1934 after being laid up in Hamburg for three years.
Built by the Reihersteig Co, Hamburg, for the German East Africa Line as the KIGOMA (1914). Renamed ALGERIA (1921 – Anchor Line).

TOLEMAIDE (1913)
3000 grt; 60 psrs
330' x 41' x 18'6" (100 x 12. x 5.6 m)
Hall, Russell 3-cylinder triple expansion engine via single screw.
Owned by Sicilia Soc Di Navegazione, Palermo.
Built by Hall, Russell & Co, Aberdeen, for the Rennie Line as the INSIZWA (1899).

TOLETELA (1977)
13868 grt; 1014 psrs
300 cars
497' x 68' x 22' (151.5 x 20.8 x 6.6 m)
2 x 16-cylinder Bazan-MAN geared diesel engines via twin screw.
Passenger-cargo RoRo ferry operated by General National Transport Maritime (a government department), Libya.
Built by Union Naval de Levante, Valencia, for Naviera Aznar, Bilbao, as the MONTE TOLEDO (1974).

TOLOA (1917)
7191 grt; 131 psrs
425' x 54' x 29' (128.8 x 16.4 x 8.8 m)
2 x triple expansion engines via twin screw.
Broken up for scrap at Oakland, California, in 1947. Ex-US Navy.
Built by Workman, Clark & Co, Belfast, for the United Fruit Steamship Co.

TOMASO DI SAVOIE (1908)
7914 grt; 1273 psrs
451' x 55' x 25'1" (137.4 x 16.8 x 7.6 m)
Barclay Curle 8-cylinder quadruple expansion engines via twin screw.
Broken up for scrap in Italy in 1928.
Built by Barclay, Curle & Co, Glasgow, for Lloyd Sabaudo.

TONG AN (1983)
7225 grt; 144 psrs
440' x 59' x 25' (133.2 x 17.9 x 7.6 m)
6-cylinder B+W diesel engine via single screw.
Owned by the government of China and operated by Fujian Shipping Co, Fuzhou.
Built by Union Levante, Valencia, for Trasmediterranea as the VILLA DE BALBAO (1962). Renamed NEW PHOENIX (1981 – Sin Chiao Shipping (Pte) Ltd, Singapore).

TONGARIRO (1901)
7661 grt; 340 psrs
457' x 58' x 30'5" (139.3 x 17.6 x 9.2 m)
Hawthorne Leslie 6-cylinder triple expansion engines via twin screw.
Abandoned as a total loss in January 1917. She had broken her back exactly five months earlier, on 30 August 1916, after running aground on Bull Rocks off Portland Island, in Hawkes Bay, New Zealand.
Built by Hawthorn, Leslie & Co, Newcastle, for the New Zealand Shipping Co.

TONG HAN (1960) See HYSAN (1971)

TONG HOO (1961) See LYDIA (1966)

TONG HU (1992)
6476 grt; 576 psrs
428' x 56' x 14' (129.7 x 17 x 4.2 m)
2 x 10-cylinder B+W diesel engines via twin screw.
Passenger-cargo ship owned and operated by Guangdong Shantou Navigation Co.
Built by Espanola de Construccion Navigation, Cadiz, for Fluvial, Argentina, as the CIUDAD DE BUENOS AIRES (1964). Renamed MING YI (1979 – Guangdong Province, Hong Kong & Macau Navigation Co) and GU LANG YU (1979 – China Ocean Shipping Co, Tsingtau).

TONKIN (1898) See LOTUS (1912)

TOPAZ (1997) See SUN (1998)

TOPAZ (1998) See THE TOPAZ (1998)

TOPEKA (1976)
6789 grt; 900 psrs
438' x 58' x 24' (133.8 x 18 x 7.3 m)
Bremer Vulkan 8-cylinder diesel engine via single screw.
Owned by Lineas Agromar, Colombia, she was abandoned as a total loss on 24 November 1984 when she dragged her anchors and ran aground off Coatzacoalcos, Mexico.
Built by Bremer Vulkan, Vegesack, for the Woermann Line as the TOGO (1938). Renamed as the merchant raider SCHIFF 14 (1942 – German government), CORONEL (1942 – German government, who painted this name on the bow and stern sections, but her official identity remained as SCHIFF), TOGO (1943 – German government), SVALBARD (1946 – Norwegian government), the cargo ship TILTHORN (1954 – AS Tilthorn, Norway), STELLA MARINA (1954 – AS Tilthorn), TOGO (1956 – German Africa Line) and LACASIELLE (1968 – Taboga Enterprises Inc, Panama).

TOR ANGLIA (1966) See SARDINIA NOVA (1989)

TOR BRITANNIA (1975) See PRINCE (1996)

TOR BRITANNIA (1982) See PRINCE (1991)

TOR HOLLANDIA (1967) See OURANOS (1999)

TORRE DEL GRECO (1982) See CAPO SANDALO (1988)

TORRES (1957)
4208 grt; 388 psrs
379' x 50' x 17' (114.8 x 15.2 x 5.2 m)
4 x 7-cylinder Fiat diesel engines via twin screw.
Passenger ferry owned and operated by Tirrenia, Naples.
Built by Riuniti, Ancona.

TORRES (1988)
18702 grt; 1314 psrs
400 cars
488' x 75' x 21' (148 x 22.7 x 6.3 m)
2 x 12-cylinder GMT diesel engines via single screw.
Passenger-cargo RoRo ferry operating for Tirrenia, Naples.
Built by Cantieri Navale Riuniti SpA, Ancona, for Adriatica SpA di Navagazione, Cagliari, as the STAFFETTA MEDITERRANEA (1979).

TOR SCANDINAVIA (1976) See PRINCESS OF SCANDINAVIA (1991)

TOR SCANDINAVIA (1979) See PRINCESS OF SCANDINAVIA (1991)

TOR SCANDINAVIA (1983) See PRINCESS OF SCANDINAVIA (1991)

TORTONA (1909) See AUSONIA (1911)

TORTUGA (1957)
6982 grt; 100 psrs
length 415' x beam 60' (125.8 x 18.2 m)
Turbo-electric engines via twin screw.
Broken up for scrap at Bruges in 1964. Ex-Salen Rederierna AB, Sweden.
Built by the Bethlehem Shipbuilding Corporation, Quincy, New Jersey, for the Unifruit Steamship Co as the passenger-cargo ship ANTIGUA (1931).

TOSA (1971) See OUR LADY OF MANAOAG (1992)

TOSA MARU (1965)
5059 grt; 1800 psrs
27 rail coaches
310' x 52' x 12' (97.7 x 15.9 x 3.6 m)
2 x 14-cylinder B+W diesel engines via twin screw.
Passenger-train ferry operated by Kambara Kisen KK, Tokyo, for the Japanese State Railways.
Built by Mitsubishi Heavy Industries Ltd, Shimonoseki.

TOSCANA (1900)
4113 grt; 1362 psrs
363' x 44' x 19'2" (110 x 13.3 x 5.8 m)
N Odero & Co 3-cylinder triple expansion engines via single screw.
Owned by Transoceanica, she sank on 5 February 1918 after colliding with the French ship MOLIERE near Gibraltar.
Built by N Odero & Co, Genoa, for Italia Societa di Navigazione a Vapore, Genoa.

TOSCANA (1948)
9442 grt; 826 psrs
459' x 58' x 28' (139.9 x 17.7 x 8.5 m)
Triple expansion engines via twin screw.
Broken up for scrap at Genoa in 1962. Ex-Lloyd Triestino.
Built by AG Weser, Bremen, for North German Lloyd as the SAARBRUCKEN (1923).

TOSCANA (1994)
13885 grt; 600 psrs
560 cars
548' x 73' x 19' (166.2 x 22.1 x 5.8 m)
Sulzer 16-cylinder diesel engine via single screw.
Owned and operated by Tirrenia Navigazioni, Naples.
Built by Visentini, Donada.

TOTOMI MARU (1905)
3412 grt
333' x 46' x 20' (100.9 x 14 x 6.1 m)
G Clark Ltd 3-cylinder triple reduction engines via single screw.
Broken up for scrap in 1933.
Built by SP Austin & Sons, UK, for NYK as the passenger-cargo ship GRAFTON (1901).

TOURANE (1904) See KARNAK (1912)

TOURS (1920) See VILLE DE MONS (1940)

TOUYA MARU (1947)
3898 grt
392' x 52' x 15'6" (118.7 x 15.9 x 4.7m)
Passenger-train ferry engulfed by a typhoon (designated No 15) and sank on 26 September 1954 outside Hakodate harbour with the loss of 1155 lives.
Built by Mitsubishi Heavy Industries, Kobe for the government of Japan (Department of Railways).

TOWADA MARU (1957)
6148 grt; 1500 psrs
7 rail coaches & 18 wagons
394' x 59' x 15'6" (119.4 x 17.9 x 4.7 m)
2 x Mitsubishi-Sulzer diesel engines via twin screw.
Passenger-train ferry owned by the Japanese government (Department of Railways), but reported sold on 21 July 1977.
Built by Mitsubishi Heavy Industries Ltd.

TOWADA MARU (1966) See DELTA FILIPINE DREAM (1992)

TOWER CROWN (1934) See SPERBRECHER (1939)

TOZAN MARU (1937)
4782 grt
389' x 54' x 25'3" (117.9 x 16.4 x 7.7 m)
J Dickinson & Sons Ltd 3-cylinder triple expansion engine via single screw.
Abandoned after becoming wrecked on Goto Island on 6 March 1938.
Built by JL Thompson & Sons Ltd, Sunderland, for Century Shipping Co Ltd as the BATSFORD (1914). Renamed HAMDALE (1927 – Turnbull Coal & Shipping Co Ltd) and ST. MELONS (1937 – Barry Shipping Co Ltd).

TRABZON (1949) See ERKIN 2 (1967)

TRACKER, HMS (1943) See CORRIENTES (1949)

TRADEWIND (1954)
6361 grt 261 psrs

Broken up for scrap at Ghent in 1956. Ex-Caribbean Atlantic Steamship Co. Built for the New York & Cuba Mail Line as the passenger-cargo ship MEXICO (1906). Renamed ALEUTIAN (1929 – Alaska Steamship Co).

TRAFFORD HALL (1905)
5321 grt; 94 psrs
397' x 50' x 29' depth (120.3 x 15.2 x 8.8 m)
Barclay Curle 3-cylinder triple expansion engine via single screw.
Broken up for scrap in Italy in 1934 for a tender of £7,000.
Built by Barclay Curle & Co Ltd, Glasgow, for the City Line.

TRANS ASIA (1993)
3797 grt; 964 psrs
92 cars
310' x 58' x 14'6" (94 x 17.7 x 4.4 m)
4 x 8-cylinder Niigata diesel engines via twin screw.
Owned and operated by Trans-Asia Shipping Lines Inc.
Built by Kanda Zosensho KK, Kure, for Sado Kisen KK as the passenger-car ferry KOGANE MARU (1972).

TRANSBALT (1920)
11397 grt; 2700 psrs
515' x 62' x 34'5" depth (157.3 x 18.9 x 10.5 m)
8-cylinder quadruple expansion engines via twin screw.
Owned by Sovtorgflot, Russia, she sank on 13 June 1945 when the captain of the USS SWORDFISH incorrectly identified her as a Japanese vessel and attacked her in the La Perouse Channel.
Built by Blohm & Voss, Hamburg, for the Hamburg-America Line as the BELGRAVIA (1899). Renamed RIGA (1905 – Russian Navy).

TRANSCOLORADO (1967)
12420 grt; 3800 psrs
523' x 72' x 32'5" (158.5 x 21.8 x 9.8 m)
2 x Westinghouse DRG turbine engines via single screw.
Owned by Hudson Waterways Corporation, New York, as a car carrier.
Built by the Kaiser Corporation, Richmond, California, for the US Maritime Commission as the Class C4-S-A3 troop transport MARINE ADDER (1945).
Engaged after World War Two in some immigrant sailings.

TRANSCOLUMBIA (1967)
12420 grt; 900 psrs
520' x 72' x 32'5" (157.6 x 21.8 x 9.8 m)
2 x Joshua Hendry Ironworks DRG turbine engines via single screw.
Broken up at Kaohsiung as a car transporter in 1988. Ex-Hudson Waterways Corporation Inc, New York.
Built by the Kaiser Corporation, Richmond, California, for the US Maritime Commission as the Class C4-S-A3 troop carrier MARINE LYNX (1945).
After World War Two she was converted into a passenger ship and chartered to the Matson Line.

TRANSCONTAINER I (1969) See NIOBE I (1993)

TRANSEUROPA (1995)
32354 grt; 114 psrs
293 TEUs
604' x 95' x 24'6" (183 x 28.7 x 7.4 m)
4 x 8-cylinder Zgoda-Sulzer diesel engines via twin screw.
Ice-strengthened passenger-car-cargo RoRo ferry owned and operated by Poseidon Schiffahrt AG, Lubeck.
Built by Stocznia Gdanska SA, Gdansk, at a cost of Finnmarks 330,000,000.

TRANSHAWAII (1968) See AMOCO VOYAGER (1982)

TRANSIDAHO (1969) See CAROLINA (1975)

TRANSILVANIA (1927)
8262 grt; 50 psrs
496' x 55' x 35'9" depth (150.3 x 16.7 x 10.9 m)
Harland & Wolff Ltd 6-cylinder triple expansion engines via twin screw.
Broken up for scrap at Genoa in 1933. Ex-Ditta L Pittaluga.
Built by Harland & Wolff Ltd, Belfast, as the EUROPEAN (1896). Renamed TROPIC (1923 – White Star Line) and ARTICO (1924 – Soc Anon Ligure di Navigazioni a Vapores).

TRANSILVANIA (1938)

6672 grt; 250 psrs
432' x 58' x 16' (130.9 x 17.6 x 4.8 m)
2 x 12-cylinder B+W diesel engines via twin screw.
Capsized at Constanta, Roumania, in 1987.
Built by Burmeister & Wain Shipyards, Copenhagen, for the Roumanian government to operate an express passenger service from Constanta to Alexandria.

TRANSINDIANA (1969)

13489 grt; 2000 psrs
633' x 72' x 26'6" (191.8 x 21.8 x 8 m)
2 x Westinghouse DRG turbine engines via single screw.
Broken up for scrap at Brownsville, Texas, in 1983. Ex-Hudson Waterways Corporation Inc, New York.
Built by the Kaiser Corporation, Richmond, California, for the US Maritime Commission as the Class C4-S-A1 troop carrier GENERAL W. C. LANGFITT, USS (AP-151) (1945). Reclassified as the GENERAL W. C. LANGFITT, USAT (1946 – US Army), GENERAL W. C. LANGFITT, USNS (T-AP-151) (1950 – US Navy). She operated as a migrant ship after World War Two until she was laid up in the James river, Virginia, for the period 1958–68.

TRANSLUBECA (1990)

24727 grt; 84 psrs
220 trailers
520' x 83' x 29' (157.6 x 25.2 x 8.8 m)
2 x 12-cylinder Wartsila diesel engines via twin screw.
Owned by Poseidon Schiffahrt and operated by Finncarriers.
Built by Stocznia Gdanska, Gdansk.

TRANSOREGON (1968) See AMOCO TRADER (1982)

TRANSPORT 57 (1899) See BRUTON (1923)

TRANSVAAL CASTLE (1961) See THE BIG RED BOAT III (2000)

TRANSYLVANIA (1914)

14315 grt; 2383 psrs
567' x 67' x 27'6" (171.8 x 20.3 x 8.4 m)
Scotts SRG turbine engines via twin screw.
Sank on 4 May 1917, with the loss of 413 lives, after being torpedoed by the German U-63 only two and a half miles (4 km) south of Cape Vado in the Gulf of Genoa.
Built by Scotts Shipbuilding & Engineering Co Ltd, Greenock, for the Cunard Steamship Co Ltd.

TRANSYLVANIA (1925)

16923 grt; 1423 psrs
578' x 70' x 31'3" depth (175.2 x 21.2 x 9.5 m)
6 x Fairfield SRG turbine engines via twin screw.
Sank as an armed merchant cruiser while under tow on 10 August 1940, with the loss of 48 lives, after being torpedoed by the German U-56 35 miles (58 km) west of Inishtrahull, Northern Ireland.
Built by Fairfield Shipbuilding & Engineering Company, Glasgow, for the Anchor Line.

TRAPEZITZA (1980) See SEAFRANCE CEZANNE (1996)

TRAS-OS-MONTES (1916) See NYASSA (1924)

TRAVELLER (1981)

20362 grt; 449 psrs
584' x 87' x 29' (178 x 26.3 x 8.7 m)
2 x 6-cylinder Harland & Wolff-B+W diesel engines via twin screw.
Broken up as a car transporter at Kaohsiung in 1982. Ex-Ace Navigation Co Ltd.
Built by Harland & Wolff Ltd, Belfast, for the Royal Mail Line as the ARAGON (1960). Renamed ARANDA (1968 – Shaw Savill Line), HOEGH TRAVELLER (1971 – Leif Hoegh & Co, Norway) and HUAL TRAVELLER (1978 – Ace Navigation Co Ltd).

TRAVEMUNDE (1964) See APOLLONIA II (1990)

TRAVEMUNDE (1971) See ST. CLAIR (1991)

TRAVEMUNDE (1981) See PENELOPE A (2000)

TRAVEMUNDE LINK (1981) See PENELOPE A (2000)

TREASURE ISLAND (1998) See HYUNDAI SEOLBONG (2000)

TREG (1991) See ST. CLAIR (1991)

TREGASTEL (1985) See ST. CLAIR (1991)

TREGOR (1980) See MAGIC I (1999)

TRELLEBORG (1958) See NISSOS KYPROS (1993)

TRELLEBORG (1982)

20028 grt; 800 psrs
200 cars + 35 rail rolling stock
562' x 79' x 19' (170.2 x 23.8 x 5.8 m)
4 x 8-cylinder MAN diesel engines via twin screw.

Passenger-train ferry owned and operated by Scandlines Hansa on the Sweden–Germany service.
Built by Oresundvarvet AB, Landskrona, for the Swedish government.

TREMONT (1902) See ESMERALDA (1950)

TRENT (1899) See TRENT, HMS (1915)

TRENT, HMS (1915)

5525 grt; 480 psrs
410' x 50' x 23'3" (124.2 x 15.2 x 7.1 m)
R Napier & Sons 3-cylinder triple expansion engine via single screw.
Broken up for scrap in 1922.
Built by Napier & Miller, Glasgow, for Royal Mail Lines as the passenger ship TRENT (1899).

TRENTHAM HALL (1875) See MEXICO (1900)

TRENTON (1966) See BORINQUEN (1975)

TRETI KRABOLOV (1929)

4078 grt
375' x 48' x 25'7" depth (113.6 x 14.5 x 7.8 m)
Furness, Westgarth 3-cylinder triple expansion engine via single screw.
Built by Sir Raylton Dixon & Co, Middlesbrough, for the Elder Dempster Line as the MONMOUTH (1903). Renamed SHINZAN MARU (1925 – Kishimoto KK).

TRIADIC (1948)

7459 grt; 60 psrs
440' x 57' x 27' (133.3 x 17.3 x 8.2 m)
Allis-Chalmers, Canada, 3-cylinder triple expansion engine via single screw.
Broken up for scrap at Shanghai in 1977. Ex-British Phosphate Commission.
Built by West Coast Shipbuilders, Vancouver, BC, for the British Royal Navy as the supply ship DUNGENESS, HMS (1945). Renamed LEVUKA (1947 – Pacific Shipowners).

TRIASTER (1955) See TAIYUAN

TRIER (1923) See ERKIN (1936)

TRITON (1986)
16907 grt; 1226 psrs
539' x 71' x 25' (164.4 x 21.7 x 7.6 m)
6 x SRG turbine engines via twin screw.
Owned by Taiwanese shipbreakers, she was broken up for scrap at Kaohsiung in 1986 for a tender price of US$63 per displacement ton (12214). The ship had been swamped by cyclone 'Wayne' in mountainous seas and then rolled on her side in shallow water in Kaohsiung.
Built by Barclay, Curle & Company, Glasgow, for the British India Line as the UGANDA (1952).

TRITON (1991)
14151 grt; 706 psrs
484' x 71' x 19' (147.5 x 22 x 5.8 m)
4 x 12-cylinder Stork-Werkspoor geared diesel engines via twin screw.

Cruise ship owned and operated by Royal Olympic Cruises, Greece, after purchase from the Norwegian Caribbean Cruise Line for US$36,000,000.
Built by Rotterdamsche Drydock Mij, Rotterdam, for the Cunard Line as the CUNARD ADVENTURER (1971). Renamed SUNWARD II(1977 – Norwegian Caribbean Cruise Line).

TROJAN (1880) See ISLAM (1902)

TROMP (1984) See MOBY PRINCE (1985)

TROPIC (1923) See TRANSILVANIA (1927)

TROPICALE (1981)
36674 grt; 1022 psrs
670' x 87' x 23' (203 x 26.4 x 7 m)
2 x 7-cylinder Sulzer diesel engines via twin screw.
Cruise ship owned by Tropicale Cruises and operated by Carnival Cruises Lines.
Built by Aalborg Vaerft, Aalborg, for Carnival Cruise Lines.

TROPICANA (1988) See TROPIC SEA (2000)

TROPIC SEA (2000)
4772 grt; 801 psrs
386' x 52' x 12'5" (117.1 x 15.9 x 3.8 m)
2 x 12-cylinder Sulzer diesel engines via twin screw.
Passenger ship owned and operated by South Carolina Maritime Services.
Built by John Cockerill Shipyards, Hoboken, for RMT, Belgium, as the train ferry PRINSES PAOLA (1966). Renamed TROPICANA (1988 – Sea Lane Maritime & SeaEscape), SEA PALACE (1990 – owned by Guiness Mahon & Co Ltd and operated by Options Inc), the offshore casino cruise ship ST. LUCIE (1991 – Winstone Cruise Lines Ltd) and TROPICANA (1994 – owned by Jubilee of Bahamas Inc and operated by Ship Management & Catering, USA).

TROPIC STAR (1991) See NEW YORK FORTUNE I (1997)

TROPIC STAR II (1992) See ENCHANTED SUN (1999)

TROTTER (1981)
20362 grt; 449 psrs
584' x 87' x 29' (178 x 26.3 x 8.8 m)

2 x 6-cylinder Harland & Wolff-B+W diesel engines via twin screw.
Broken up for scrap as a car transporter at Kaohsiung in 1982. Ex-Ace Navigation Co Ltd.
Built by Harland & Wolff Ltd, Belfast, for the Royal Mail Line as the ARLANZA (1960). Renamed ARAWA (1968 – Shaw Savill Line), HOEGH TRANSIT (1971 – Hoegh & Co), HOEGH TROTTER (1972 – Hoeg & Co, as a car carrier) and HUAL TROTTER (1978 – Ace Navigation Co Ltd).

TROUBRIDGE (1961) See KARDEN (1995)

TROUNCER, HMS (1945) See EMPIRE GULL (1958)

TROY, USS (1919) See MINNESOTA (1919)

TRUVA (1966)
4332 grt; 584 psrs
100 cars
300' x 54' x 14' (90.9 x 16.4 x 4.2 m)
4 x 8-cylinder Motorenwerk Mannheim Diesel engines via twin screw.
Passenger-car ferry operated by Turkish Maritime Lines on the Istanbul–Izmir service.
Built by Dubigeon-Normandie, Nantes.

TRYON, USS (APH-1) (1942) See SGT. CHARLES E. MOWER (1946)

TSAWWASSEN (1960) See QUEEN OF TSAWWASSEN (1962)

TSUGARU MARU (1924)
3460 grt; 895 psrs
25 railway wagons
362' x 52' x 14' (109.7 x 15.9 x 4.3 m)
Passenger-train ferry sunk by US bombers in the west Tsugaru Kaikyo Strait on 14 July 1945.
Built by Sumitomo Heavy Industries, Yokosuka, for Seikan Railway Ferries.

TSUGARU MARU (1965) See AL JAWAHER (1988)

TT TRAVELLER (1992) See TT TRAVELLER (1997)

TT TRAVELLER (1997)
18332 grt; 500 psrs
480 cars
508' x 79' x 18' (154 x 24 x 5.5 m)
2 x 8-cylinder Wartsila-Sulzer diesel engines via twin screw.

Passenger-car ferry operated by TT-Line, Travemunde.
Built by Bruce Shipyards, Landskrona, for the Stena Line as the STENA TRAVELLER (1992). Renamed TT TRAVELLER (1992 – TT-Line) and STENA TRAVELLER (1995 – Stena Line).

TUBANTIA (1913)
13911 grt; 1520 psrs
540' x 66' x 27'6" depth (163.6 x 20 x 8.4 m)
A Stephen & Sons 8-cylinder quadruple expansion engines via twin screw.
Sank in four and a half hours on 16 March 1916 after being torpedoed by the German U-13 close to the Noordhinder lightship.
Built by A Stephen & Sons Ltd, Glasgow, for Koninkl Hollansche Lloyd as a passenger ship.

TUCUMAN (1947) See BUCEPHALOS (1966)

TUHOBIC (1965) See ABU RASHID (1984)

TUNG LONG (1966)

10942 grt; 50 psrs
520' x 65' x 31' (160.3 x 19.7 x 9.4 m)
2 x 8-cylinder MAN diesel engines via twin screw.
Passenger-cargo ship owned by Chung Lien Navigation Co SA, Monrovia, she was broken up for scrap at Kaohsiung in 1966.
Built by Wilton Fijenoord, Schiedam, for the Holland America Line as the DELFTDIJK (1929). Renamed DONGEDYK (1952 – Holland America Line).

TUNGUE (1916)

8066 grt; 1460 psrs
449' x 55' x 35'8" depth (136.9 x 16.9 x 10.8 m)
F Schichau 6-cylinder triple expansion engines via twin screw.
Seized by Portugal, but sank in the Mediterranean on 17 November 1917 after being torpedoed by a German U-boat.
Built by F Schichau, Danzig, for North German Lloyd as the ZIETEN (1902).

TUNISIAN (1900) See MARBURN (1922)

TURAKINA (1902)

8073 grt; 360 psrs
473' x 60' x 31' depth (144.1 x 18.2 x 9.4 m)
Hawthorne Leslie 6-cylinder triple expansion engines via twin screw.
Sank on 13 August 1917 after being torpedoed by a German U-boat 120 miles (200 km) west of the Scilly Isles, UK.
Built by Hawthorne, Leslie & Co, Newcastle, for the New Zealand Shipping Co.

TURELLA (1979) See FANTAASIA (1998)

TURKMENIA (1961) See TURKMENYA (1961)

TURKMENYA (1961)

5127 grt; 250 psrs
401' x 52' x 17' (122.2 x 15.8 x 5.2 m)
2 x 6-cylinder MAN diesel engines via twin screw.
This ice-strengthened ship has been laid up since 1991 by the Far Eastern Shipping Company, Vladivostok. She had been gutted by fire and sank on 9 November 1986, with two deaths involved, and was subsequently refloated.
Built by Mathias-Thesen, Wismar, for the Far Eastern Shipping Company, Vladivostok.

TURRIALBA (1906)

4937 grt; 103 psrs
379' x 50' x 25' (114.8 x 15.2 x 7.6 m)
Triple expansion engine via single screw.
Broken up for scrap at Baltimore, USA, in 1949.
Built by Workman, Clark, Belfast, for the United Fruit Steamship Co.

TUSCANIA (1915)

14348 grt; 2420 psrs
549' x 67' x 41'7" depth (167.4 x 20.3 x 12.6 m)
4 x Stephen & Sons SRG turbine engines via twin screw.
Sank on 5 February 1918, with 166 lives lost, after being torpedoed by the German U-77 seven miles (12 km) north of the Rathlin Light, Northern Ireland.
Built by Alex Stephen & Sons, Glasgow, for the Cunard Steamship Co Ltd.

TUSCANIA (1922) See NEW YORK (1955)

TUSCANSTAR (1920) See LUGANO (1942)

TUTKU (1996) See ALICE (1997)

TUXEDO PRINCESS (1983)

4042 grt; 1400 psrs
103 cars
353' x 57' x 12' (107 x 17.3 x 3.6 m)
2 x Pametrada DRG turbine engines via twin screw.
Floating hotel/restaurant owned by Michael Quadirini and registered to Riverzest Ltd, berthed in the River Tyne at Gateshead, UK.
Built as the passenger-car ferry CALEDONIAN PRINCESS (1961) by William Denny & Bros, Dumbarton, for British Railways.

TUXEDO ROYALE (1988)

3644 grt; 864 psrs
205 cars
364' x 57' x 13' (111.8 x 17.3 x 3.9 m)
2 x Pametrada DRG turbine engines via twin screw.
Floating hotel/restaurant, owned by Michael Quadirini and registered to Riverzest Ltd, berthed in the River Wear at Sunderland, UK.
Built by Swan Hunter & Wigham Richardson Ltd, Newcastle, for British Railways as the passenger-car ferry DOVER (1965). Renamed EARL SIWARD (1977 – Sealink UK) and SOL EXPRESS (1982 – Sol Ferries, Limassol).

TYNDAREUS (1916)

11347 grt; 2000 psrs
507' x 63' x 41'6" depth (153.6 x 19.1 x 12.6 m)
Scotts 6-cylinder triple expansion engines via twin screw.
Broken up for scrap as a pilgrim ship at Hong Kong in 1960. Ex-Ocean Steamship Co Ltd (Blue Funnel Line).
Built by Scotts Shipbuilding & Engineering Co, Greenock, for the Blue Funnel Line as a US Pacific coast log carrier; then converted into a troop transport during World War Two; with a further conversion, in 1950, into a pilgrim ship at a cost of US$250,000.

TYNWALD (1986) See LAURO EXPRESS (1990)

TYROLIA (1913) See PRYGONA (1921)

TYRONE (1912)

6684 grt
451' x 55' x 30'6" depth (137 x 16.7 x 9.3 m)
Workman, Clark 6-cylinder triple expansion engines via single screw.
Abandoned after becoming wrecked on 27 September 1913 near Otago Heads, New Zealand, during her delivery voyage to her new owners.
Built by Workman, Clark & Co Ltd, Belfast, for the Houlder Line Ltd as the DRAYTON GRANGE (1902).

TYRRHENIA (1922) See LANCASTRIA (1924)

TYRSUS (1961) See EL SALAM EL SAUDI (1995)

TYRSUS (1994) See EL SALAM EL SAUDI (1995)

TYSFJORD (1993)

3695 grt; 399 psrs
105 cars
277' x 50' x 14' (84 x 15 x 4.1 m)
2 x 6-cylinder Bergen-Normo diesel engines via twin screw.
Built by Fiskerstrand, Bergen, for Ofoten & Vesteraalen, Narvik, for the Bognes–Skarberget service at a cost of Norwegian Kronor 200,000,000.

TZAREVETZ (1982) See P&OSL CANTERBURY (1999)

UARDA (1902) See CHLOE (1924)

UBENA (1928) See EMPIRE KENT (1945)

UGANDA (1952) See TRITON (1986)

UGOLINO VIVALDI (1947)
8967 grt; 835 psrs
485' x 62' x 26' (149.2 x 19 x 7.9 m)
Fiat 6-cylinder diesel engine via single screw.
Broken up for scrap at Trieste, Italy, in 1978. Ex-Lloyd Triestino.
Laid down by SA Ansaldo Shipyards, Genoa, for the Italian Line as the FERRUCCIO BUONAPACE (1945).

UIGE (1954)
10001 grt; 571 psrs
477' x 63' x 26'6" (145.4 x 19.2 x 8.1 m)
Cockerill-B+W 8-cylinder diesel engine via single screw.
Broken up at Lisbon, Portugal, in 1980 after a four-year period laid up.
Built by John Cockerill Shipyards, Hoboken, Belgium, for Cia Colonial de Navegacao, Lisbon, as a passenger-cargo ship.

UKRAINA (1928)
4957 grt
354' x 51' x 25'2" (107.3 x 15.5 x 7.6 m)
Russian Diesel Works 12-cylinder diesel engines via twin screw.
Built by the Baltic Shipbuilding Yard, St Petersburg, for the Russian government.

UKRAINA (1938)
6406 grt; 410 psrs
436' x 58' x 18'6" (132 x 17.6 x 5.7 m)
B+W diesel engine via twin screw.
Built by Burmeister & Wain, Copenhagen, for the Black Sea Shipping Company, Odessa.

UKRAINA (1948)
6970 grt; 640 psrs
432' x 58' x 19' (120.9 x 17.6 x 5.7 m)
2 x 12-cylinder B+W diesel engines via twin screw.
Chartered to SeaEscape in 1996 by her Russian owners.
Built by Burmeister & Wain, Copenhagen, for the Romanian government as the BASARABIA (1938).

UKRAINA (1994) See ISLAND ADVENTURE (1998)

ULIMAROA (1908)
5828 grt; 414 psrs
400' x 52' x 25'4" (121.9 x 15.8 x 7.7 m)
Gourlay Brothers 6-cylinder triple expansion engines via twin screw.
Broken up for scrap at Osaka in 1934.
Built by Gourlay Brothers Ltd, Dundee, for Huddart Parker Ltd

ULSTER MONARCH (1929)
3851 grt; 510 psrs
359' x 46' x 15' (108.8 x 13.9 x 4.5 m)
2 x 10-cylinder Harland & Wolff-B+W diesel engines via twin screw.
Broken up for scrap at Ghent, Belgium, in 1966.
Built by Harland & Wolff Ltd, Belfast, for the Belfast Steamship Co..

ULSTER PRINCE (1930)
3735 grt; 510 psrs
346' x 46' x 15' (104.8 x 13.9 x 4.5 m)
2 x 10-cylinder Harland & Wolff-B+W diesel engines via twin screw.
Abandoned in April 1941 during troop evacuations from Greece, after running aground near Nauplia and then being attacked by enemy aircraft from which she caught fire and was gutted.
Built by Harland & Wolff Ltd, Belfast, for the Belfast Steamship Company as a passenger ferry.

ULSTER PRINCE (1946) See ODYSSEUS (1969)

ULSTER PRINCE (1967) See MANAR (2000)

ULSTER QUEEN (1930)
3735 grt; 510 psrs
346' x 46' x 15' (104.8 x 13.9 x 4.5 m)
2 x 10-cylinder Harland & Wolff-B+W diesel engines via twin screw.
Broken up for scrap in Belgium in 1949.
Built by Harland & Wolff Ltd, Belfast, for the Belfast Steamship Company as a passenger ferry.

ULSTER QUEEN (1967) See LA PATRIA (2000)

ULTONIA (1900)
10402 grt; 2220 psrs
500' x 57' x 33'9" depth (152.4 x 17.5 x 10.3 m)
Furness, Westgarth 6-cylinder triple expansion engine via twin screw.
Sank on 27 June 1917, with one life lost, after an attack by the German U-boat U-53 350 miles (582 km) south-west of Lands End, UK.
Laid down by CS Swan & Hunter, Wallsend, for the Cunard Steamship Company Ltd as the cattle transport YAMUNA (1898).

ULUA (1917) See OCTANS, USS (AF-26) (1943)

ULYSSES (1913)
14499 grt; 250 psrs
580' x 68' x 40'2" depth (176.8 x 20.6 x 12.2 m)
Workman, Clark 6-cylinder triple expansion engines via twin screw.
Sank on 11 April 1942 after being torpedoed by the German U-160 off Palm Beach, Florida, near Cape Hatteras.
Built by Workman, Clark & Co Ltd, Belfast, for the Blue Funnel Line at a cost of £250,000.

UMBRIA (1902) See UMBRIA (1914)

UMBRIA (1914)
5020 grt; 1103 psrs
401' x 47' x 19'5" (122.3 x 14.2 x 5.9 m)
Orlando 4-cylinder quadruple expansion engine via single screw.
Broken up for scrap in 1932. Ex-Sitmar Line.
Built by Fratelli Orlando, Leghorn, for Navigazione Generale Italia, Genoa, as the UMBRIA (1902). Renamed SAO PAULO (1913 – Italia).

UME MARU (1910)
4093 grt; 96 psrs
385' x 45' x 28' (116.7 x 13.6 x 8.5 m)
Triple expansion engine via single screw.
Broken up for scrap in 1926.
Built by Caird & Co, Greenock, for the P&O Line as the JAVA (1892) at a cost of £72,104. She was sold in 1910 to Mr Hasada, Yokohama, for £7,383.

UMGENI (1938) See WINNEBA (1957)

UMHLALI (1905)
3388 grt; 100 psrs
348' x 43' x 17'2" (105.5 x 13 x 5.2 m)
G Clark 3-cylinder triple expansion engine via single screw.
Abandoned as a total constructive loss after running aground on 15 September 1909 in fog near Cape Point, on the south-west African coast.
Built by Sir James Laing & Son Ltd, Sunderland, for Bullard, King & Co (Natal Line).

UMKUZI (1924)
5147 grt; 168 psrs
419' x 50' x 28' (127 x 15.2 x 8.5 m)
Triple expansion engines via twin screw.
Broken up for scrap in 1938. Ex-Bullard, King & Co.
Built by Barclay, Curle & Co, Glasgow, for the Union Castle Line as the CLUNY CASTLE (1903).

UMSINI (1985)
13853 grt; 1737 psrs

475' x 77' x 19' (144 x 23.4 x 5.9 m)
2 x 6-cylinder MaK geared diesels via twin screw.
Ferry operated by PT Pelni.
Built by the Jos L Meyer Shipyard, Papenburg, for the Directorate-General of
Sea Communication, government of Indonesia.

UMTALI (1936) See CALABAR (1957)

UMTATA (1935)
8141 grt; 106 psrs
451' x 61' x 25'6" (136.7 x 18.5 x 7.8 m)
Swan Hunter 6-cylinder triple expansion engines via twin screw.
Sank on 9 March 1942 following a torpedo attack by the German U-161 off
Miami, Florida, to where she was being towed after already suffering a
crippling torpedo assault while in Castries Harbour, St Lucia, a few days
earlier.
Built by Swan Hunter, Newcastle, for the Ellerman and Bucknall Lines.

UMVOTI (1924)
5167 grt; 168 psrs
419' x 50' x 28'3" depth (127 x 15.2 x 8.6 m)
Barclay Curle 6-cylinder triple expansion engine via single screw.
Scuttled to form a block ship in Folkestone harbour entrance in 1940 by the
British Admiralty, after their acquisition of the vessel.
Built by Swan Hunter, Newcastle, for Bucknall Lines as the COMRIE
CASTLE (1903).

UMZINTO (1921)
3805 grt
371' x 43' x 27'5" depth (112.4 x 13 x 8.3 m)
Muir & Houston 3-cylinder triple expansion engine via single screw.
Built by Harland & Wolff Ltd, Belfast, as the MARINO (1894). Renamed
SABINE (1898 – Union-Castle Mail Steamship Co Ltd).

UNION HOBART (1976) See TAXIARCHIS (1999)

UNION RELIANCE (1961)
7638 grt; 600 psrs
492' x 70' x 22'3" (149.1 x 21.2 x 6.8 m)
4 x Busch-Sulzer 7-cylinder diesel engines via single screw.
Broken up in New Orleans in 1962 after a collision with the Norwegian tanker
BERAN on 7 November 1961, after which fire raged throughout both vessels.
Ex-China Union Lines, Taiwan.
Laid down by the Sun Shipbuilding & Drydock Co, Chester, Pennsylvania, for
the Moore McCormack Line as the C3-type cargo ship MORMACLAND
(1939) and completed for the US Navy. She was then commissioned as the
auxiliary aircraft carrier ARCHER, HMS (1941 – British Royal Navy).
Renamed the cargo ship ARCHER (1945 – British Ministry of War
Transport), EMPIRE LAGAN (1946 – British Ministry of War Transport),
converted to the passenger ship ANNA SALEN (1946 – Salen Group) and
TASMANIA (1955 – Hellenic Mediterranean Line).

UNITED CHALLENGER (1976) See KHALEEJ EXPRESS (1976)

UNITED STATES (1903)
10095 grt; 1513 psrs
520' x 58' x 29'4" depth (158.5 x 17.7 x 8.9 m)
A Stephen & Sons 6-cylinder triple expansion engines via twin screw.
Broken up for scrap at Leghorn, Italy, in 1935 after being gutted by fire at her
Copenhagen berth on 2 September 1935.
Built by Alexander Stephen & Sons, Glasgow, for the Scandinavian-American
Line.

UNITED STATES (1952)
53329 grt; 1928 psrs
990' x 101' x 31' (301.8 x 31 x 9.4 m)
4 x Westinghouse DRG turbines via quadruple screw.
Owned by Marmara Marine Inc, USA, following her purchase for
US$2,600,000 and berthed at Pier 82 in the Philadelphia naval shipyard while
her future is being carefully mapped out.
Built by Newport News Shipbuilding & Drydock Co, Newport News,
Virginia, for the United States Line at a cost of US$78,000,000, of which
US$55,000,000 was subsidised by the US Navy. On 3 June 1999 she was
elevated to a place on the US National Register of Historic Places.

UNITED VANTAGE (1978)
50 psrs
Broken up for scrap in 1988.
Built in Rotterdam as the passenger-cargo ship STRAAT BANKA (1951) and
renamed MERCURY LAKE (1977).

UNITED VICTORY (1943) See ALCOA CAVALIER (1947)

UNITED VICTORY (1944) See CLEOPATRA (1956)

UNIVERSAL HONOLULU (1974) See AUGUST 8th (1976)

UNIVERSE (1976)
18100 grt; 554 psrs
564' x 76' x 28' (171.9 x 23.2 x 8.5 m)
General Electric SRG turbines via single screw.
Broken up for scrap at Alang in 1996. Ex-Seawise Foundation, Hong Kong.
Built by the Sun Shipbuilding & Drydock Co, Chester, Pennsylvania, for the
US Maritime Commission as the C4-type cargo ship BADGER MARINER
(1953). Renamed ATLANTIC (1959 – American Export Lines) and
UNIVERSE CAMPUS (1971 – Seawise Foundation, Hong Kong).

UNIVERSE CAMPUS (1971) See UNIVERSE (1976)

UNIVERSE EXPLORER (1996)
22162 grt; 736 psrs
617' x 86' x 27' (188.2 x 26.2 x 8.2 m)
2 x GE DRG turbines via twin screw.
Owned by V-Ships Marine and chartered out to World Explorer Cruises.
Built by the Ingalls Shipbuilding Corporation Inc, Pascagoula, for Moore
McCormack Lines as the BRASIL (1958). Renamed VOLENDAM (1972 –
Holland America Line), MONARCH SUN (1975 – Monarch Cruise Line),
VOLENDAM (1978 – Holland America Line), ISLAND SUN (1984 – CY
Tung Group, as an accommodation ship), LIBERTE (1985 – American Hawaii
Cruises), CANADA STAR (1986 – Bermuda Star Line), QUEEN OF
BERMUDA (1988 – Bermuda Star Line), ENCHANTED ODYSSEY (1990 –
Commodore Cruise Line) and ENCHANTED SEAS (1990 – Commodore
Cruise Line).

UNYO (1942)
17128 grt; 285 psrs
562' x 73' x 29' (170.3 x 22.5 x 8.8 m)
2 x geared turbines via twin screw.
Owned by the Japanese government who converted the vessel into an aircraft
carrier. She sank on 17 September 1944 after being struck by a torpedo the
previous day from the USS BARB, 200 miles south-east of Tongsha Island in
the South China Sea.
Built by the Mitsubishi Shipbuilding & Engineering Co, Nagasaki, for NYK
as the passenger-cargo ship YAWATA MARU (1940).

UPSHUR (1952) See STATE OF MAINE (1973)

UPSHUR, USNS (T-AP-198) (1952) See STATE OF MAINE (1973)

URAL (1904)
7840 grt; 906 psrs
528' x 52' x 36'9" depth (160 x 15.8 x 11.2 m)
AG Vulcan 8-cylinder triple expansion engines via twin screw.
Owned by the Russian government as an auxiliary cruiser which sank on 27
May 1904 during the battle of Tsushima in the Russo–Japanese conflict. A 12"
(.04 m) shell pierced her engine room with a resultant explosion that nearly
split her in half.
Built by AG Vulcan, Stettin, for North German Lloyd as the SPREE (1890).
Renamed KAISERIN MARIA THERESIA (1899 – North German Lloyd).

URANIA (1926) See CARIBIA (1965)

URANIA II (1950)
6175 grt; 102 psrs
441' x 53' x 29'8" depth (134.3 x 16.2 x 9 m)
Barclay Curle 3-cylinder triple expansion engine via single screw.
Broken up for scrap at La Spezia, Italy, in 1954. Ex-Fratelli Grimaldi.

Built by Barclay, Curle & Co, Glasgow, for the Anchor Line as the CASTALIA (1906). Renamed MARENGO (1949 – Soc Cooperativa di Navigazione Grimaldi).

URANIUM (1908) See FELTRIA (1916)

URD (1991)
11030 grt; 610 psrs
291 cars
498' x 68'6" x 19'6" (150.8 x 20.8 x 5.9 m)
4 x 12-cylinder Wartsila diesel engines via twin screw.

Pasenger-car ferry owned and operated by Scandlines.
Built by Nouvi Cantieri Apuania SpA, Carrara, for the Castello Hellas Shipping Co, Piraeus, as the EASY RIDER (1981 – Seafreight Highway). Renamed BOYANA (1989 – So Mejduneroden Automobile Transport, Bourgas) and AKTIV MARINE (1990 – KS Arka Marine II, Arhus).

URUGUAY (1931)
10348 grt; 425 psrs
482' x 61' x 32'7" depth (146.1 x 18.5 x 9.9 m)
2 x William Denny & Sons 3-cylinder triple expansion engines via triple screw.
Owned by the Spanish Line and broken up for scrap in 1942. She had been refloated from the bottom of Valencia harbour where she was sunk on 1 January 1939 during an air attack.
Built by William Denny & Bros, Dumbarton, for the Spanish Line as the INFANTA ISABEL DE BORBON (1913).

URUGUAY (1938)
20237 grt; 747 psrs
601' x 80' x 20'6" (182.1 x 24.2 x 6.2 m)
2 x General Electric turbo-electric engines via twin screw.
Broken up for scrap by the North American Smelting Co for a tender of US$200,000 at Bordertown, New Jersey, in 1964, following a nine-year period

laid up. Ex-Moore McCormack Lines.
Built by Newport News Shipbuilding & Drydock Co, Newport News, Virginia, for the Panama Pacific Line as the CALIFORNIA (1928).

URUGUAY (1956)
12627 grt; 96 psrs
530' x 71' x 27'6" (160.6 x 21.5 x 8.4 m)
Geared turbines via twin screw.
Broken up for scrap in Argentina in 1973. Ex-Elma Lines.
Built by Vickers-Armstrong Ltd, Newcastle, for Elma Lines as the EVA PERON (1950).

URUGUAY STAR (1948)
10722 grt; 73 psrs
503' x 68' x 31' (152.4 x 20.6 x 9.4 m)
Parsons geared turbines via single screw.
Broken up for scrap by Nan Feng Steel Enterprise Company at Kaohsiung in 1972.
Built by Cammell Laird, Birkenhead, for the Blue Star Line.

URUNGAL (1927)
5400 grt
390' x 55' x 27'9" depth (118.2 x 16.7 x 8.5 m)
A Stephen & Sons turbine engines via single screw.
Broken up where she lay after running aground at Barwon Heads, Port Philip Bay, Australia, in November 1940.
Built by A Stephen & Sons Ltd, Glasgow, for Khedivial Mail Steamship & Graving Dock Co Ltd as the FEZARA (1922).

UTOPIA (1980) See POSEIDON (1994)

UTOPIA 3 (1995)
15771 grt; 646 psrs
535' x 72' x 21' (162 x 21.7 x 6.3 m)
2 x 14-cylinder MAN diesel engines via twin screw.
Passenger ferry owned by Utopia Line SA and operated by Nishinippon Kisen.
Built by Koyo Dockyard Co Ltd, Mihara, for Tokyu Ferry KK, Kitakyushu, as the FERRY TENRYU (1973). Renamed FERRY SUZURAN (1995 – Tokyu Ferry KK, Kitakyushu).

UZBEKISTAN (1962) See OMEGA (2000)

VACATIONLAND (1952) See SUNSHINE COAST QUEEN (1967)

VACATIONLAND (1971)
3038 grt; 487 psrs
155 cars + 16 trailers
323' x 69' x 16'6" (97.9 x 20.8 x 5 m)
2 x English Electric diesel-electric engines via twin screw.
Ferry owned by the Canadian government and operated by Marine Atlantic.
Built by Port Weller Drydock Ltd, St Catherines, Ontario, for CN Marine Inc, Charlottetown PE I as the THOMAS HAVILAND (1971).

VADERLAND (1900) See SOUTHLAND (1915)

VALBANERA (1906)
5099 grt; 1000 psrs
400' x 48' x 25'2" (121.2 x 14.5 x 7.6 m)
Dunsmuir & Jackson 3-cylinder triple expansion engine via single screw.
Disappeared on 12 September 1919, with 400 passengers and 88 crewmen, in the Caribbean, north of Havana during a hurricane. She had made radio contact with both Havana and Key West at 1.15 pm that same day and one week later a US submarine chaser located the ship in 40 feet (12 m) of clear water near the Rebecca Shoals light beacon, 46 miles (77 km) west of Key West. The ship was reported to be in perfect condition.
Built by C Connell & Co, Glasgow, for Pinolus Izquierdo y Cia, Cadiz.

VAL DE LOIRE (1993)
31395 grt; 1800 psrs
550 cars or 120 trailers
531' x 91' x 20'6" (161 x 27.6 x 6.2 m)
4 x 8-cylinder MaK diesel engines via twin screw.

Owned by Wallenius Line and bareboat-chartered for 20 years to Swedcarrier. Built by Seebeckwerft AG, Bremerhaven, for the TT Line as the NILS HOLGERSSON (1987) at a cost of £70,000,000.

VALETTA (1883) See ALAVIA (1903)

VALON (1980)
5142 grt; 1200 psrs
210 cars
404' x 57' x 16' (122.4 x 17.3 x 4.8 m)
2 x Pametrada DRG turbine engines via twin screw.
Broken up for scrap by HH Steel Ltd at Gadani Beach, Karachi, in 1981. Ex-Seafaith Navigation Co, Cyprus.
Built by A Stephen & Sons Ltd, Glasgow, for the British Railways Board as the AVALON (1963) at a cost of £2,000,000.

VALPARAISO (1908)
4930 grt; 1988 psrs
430' x 48' x 21' (130.3 x 14.6 x 6.4 m)
Fairfield 3-cylinder triple expansion engine via single screw.
Under the ownership of Lloyd del Pacifico, she sank after being torpedoed by a German U-boat off the Libyan coastline on 14 October 1917.
Built by Fairfield Shipbuilding & Engineering Co, Glasgow, for North German Lloyd as the GERA (1890).

VALPARAISO (1917)
3901 grt; 142 psrs
372' x 45' x 18'8" (112.7 x 13.6 x 5.7 m)
A Stephen & Sons 3-cylinder engine via single screw.
Owned by a Chilean company.
Built by A Stephen & Sons Ltd, Glasgow, for the Donaldson Line as the EVANGELINE (1900). Renamed TENNYSON (1902 – Lamport & Holt).

VALTUR PRIMA (1999)
16144 grt; 520 psrs
525' x 69' x 24' (159.1 x 20.9 x 7.3 m)
2 x 8-cylinder Wartsila diesel engines via twin screw.
Ice-strengthened cruise ship owned by the Nina Cruise Line SpA, Genoa, and operated by Club Valtur, Rome.
Built by Gotaverken in Gothenburg for the Swedish-American Line as the liner STOCKHOLM (1948). Renamed VOLKERFREUNDSCHAFT (1960 – Deutsche Seereederei), VOLKER (1985 – Deutsche Seereederei), FRIDTJOF NANSEN (1986 – Deutsche Seereederei), SURRIENTO (1989 – Star Lauro) and ITALIA PRIMA (1993 – Cie di Navigazione NINA, Naples).

VAN (1927)
7530 grt; 224 psrs
460' x 58' x 28'2" (139.4 x 17.6 x 8.5 m)
2 x John Brown 3-cylinder triple expansion engines via twin screw.
Broken up for scrap in 1933. Ex-M Gumuchdjian, Belgium.
Built by John Brown Ltd, Clydebank, for the Federal Steam Navigation Co Ltd as the ESSEX (1902).

VANA TALLINN (1994)
11966 grt; 878 psrs
350 cars or 100 trailers
500' x 75' x 18'6" (152.5 x 22.7 x 5.6 m)
4 x 8-cylinder B+W geared diesel engines via twin screw.

Passenger-car-cargo ferry owned by Hansatee, Estonia, and operated by Tallink Ferries on the Tallinn–Stockholm service.
Laid down as LADY CLEMENTINE (1974) and completed by the Aalborg Shipyard, Aalborg, for Det Forenede DS, Copenhagen as the DANA REGINA (1974). Renamed NORD ESTONIA (1990 – Est Line) and THOR HEYERDAHL (1993 – Larvik Line).

VANCOUVER ISLAND PRINCESS (1987) See NAN HAI MING ZHU (1993)

VANDYCK (1911)
10328 grt; 610 psrs
511' x 61' x 26'6" (155.6 x 18.6 x 8 m)
Quadruple expansion engines via twin screw.
Sunk on 27 October 1914 by explosive charges attached to her hull by the crew of the German cruiser KARLSRUHE. The ship had been captured the day before, following warning gunfire 700 miles (1167 km) west of St Paul's Rocks, Atlantic Ocean. All passengers and crew were transferred from the VANDYCK to another captured passenger vessel, the ASCUNCION, prior to the scuttling taking place.
Built by Workman, Clarke & Co, Belfast, for the Lamport & Holt Line, Liverpool.

VANDYCK (1922)
13233 grt; 680 psrs
526' x 64' x 39'3" depth (159.4 x 19.4 x 11.9 m)
4 x Workman, Clark DRG turbine engines via twin screw.
Sank with the loss of seven lives on 11 June 1940 after a German aircraft attack north of Harstad, Norway.

Built by Workman, Clarke & Company, Belfast, for the Lamport & Holt Line, Liverpool.

VAN GOGH (1999)
15402 grt; 650 psrs
256 cars + 23 trailers
515' x 72' x 20' (157 x 21.8 x 6.2 m)
2 x 18-cylinder Wartsila-Pielstick diesel engines via twin screw.
Cruise ship owned by Eltek Europe, Holland, and chartered to Nouvelle Frontieres until 2002 with an option to purchase.
Built by Wartsilo-Abo for the Black Sea Shipping Co, Odessa, as the GRUZIYA (1975). Renamed ODESSA SKY (1995 – Black Sea Shipping Co). She was laid up at Wilhelmshaven during 1996–98, prior to becoming CLUB I (1998 – Eltek Europe BV, Holland) and CLUB CRUISE I (1999 – Club Cruise Enterprise & Travelling Service).

VANIA (1984)
5110 grt; 520 psrs
22 cars + 77 trailers
416' x 56' x 18' (126 x 20 x 5.5 m)
2 x 12-cylinder Pielstick diesel engines via twin screw.
Passenger-car-cargo ferry owned and operated by Higashi Nippon Ferry Co Ltd, Hakodate.
Built by Naikai Setoday.

VANKOWA (1967) See VANMINT (1968)

VANLENE (1967)
8354 grt; 536 psrs
473' x 62' x 29' (143.3 x 18.8 x 8.8 m)
Sulzer 8-cylinder diesel engine via single screw.
Owned by Marlene Shipping, she was abandoned as a total loss after running aground on 14 March 1972 at the entrance to Barkley Sound, Vancouver Island.
Built by Mitsubishi Heavy Industries, Kobe, for OSK as the cargo vessel AFRICA MARU (1951).

VANMINT (1968)
8343 grt; 534 psrs
473' x 62' x 29' (143.3 x 18.8 x 8.8 m)
Sulzer 8-cylinder diesel engine via single screw.
Broken up for scrap at Kaohsiung in 1976. Ex-State Shipping Co.
Built by Central Japan Heavy Industries, Kobe, for OSK as the AMERICA MARU (1950). Renamed VANKOWA (1967 – State Shipping Co).

VAN RENSSELAER (1920)
4241 grt; 128 psrs
342' x 48' x 24'3" (104.2 x 14.5 x 7.4 m)
Nederlandsche FB v. Werkspoor 3-cylinder triple expansion engine via single screw.
Destroyed by German aircraft following her crippling by a magnetic mine and beaching herself near Ijmuiden on 10 June 1940.
Built by Nederlandsche Scheepsbouw Mij, Amsterdam, for Koninklijke Nederlandsche Stoomboot Maatschappij.

VAN RIEBEECK (1948)
4962 grt; 238 psrs
374' x 53' x 20' (113.3 x 16.1 x 6.1 m)
Hawthorn Leslie-Werkspoor 8-cylinder diesel engine via single screw.
Built by Van der Giessen-de Noord, Krimpen, for Koninklijke Java-China Pakketvaart Linjen NV.

VAN RIEMSDIJK (1948) See HERO (1972)

VARNA (1967) See REINA DEL MAR (1981)

VARUNA (1987) See BLUE HORIZON (2000)

VARUNA (1998)
13654 grt; 630 psrs
77 cars + 154 trailers
634' x 89' x 23' (192 x 27 x 6.7 m)
2 x 12-cylinder Nippon-Pielstick diesel engines via twin screw.
Owned and operated by Higashi Nippon Ferry.
Built by Mitsubishi Heavy Industries, Shimonseki.

VASARI (1909) See PISCHEVAYA INDUSTRIYA (1935)

VASCO DA GAMA (1988) See SEAWIND CROWN (1990)

VASCO NUNEZ DE BALBOA (1923)
8063 grt; 408 psrs
531' x 55' x 27'3" (151.5 x 16.7 x 8.3 m)
William Denny 6-cylinder triple expansion engines via twin screw.
Broken up for scrap in Italy in 1927. Ex-Cia Trasatlantica.
Built by William Denny & Bros, Dumbarton, for the Union Line as the SCOT (1891). Renamed OCEANIA (1906 – Hamburg-America Line) and ALFONSO XIII (1916 – Cia Trasatlantica).

VASILEFS CONSTANTINOS (1914) See BYRON (1924)

VASILISSA FREIDERIKI (1954) See QUEEN FREDERICA (1954)

VASILIY SOLOVYEV SEDOY (1982) See PETR PERVYY (1990)

VASNA (1917) See NAVAL HOSPITAL SHIP. No. 4 (1939)

VASSAR VICTORY (1945) See BEGONA (1957)

VASSILISSA SOPHIA (1917) See LEASOWE CASTLE (1917)

VATAN (2000) See MANAR (2000)

VATERLAND (1914) See LEVIATHAN (1919)

VATERLAND (1940)
54282 grt; 1312 psrs
length 824' x beam 98' (249.7 x 29.7 m)
Turbo-electric engines via twin screw.
Broken up for scrap at Hamburg in 1948 after Allied bombing on 25 July 1943 had destroyed the ship before her completion.
Launched on 28 April 1940 by Blohm & Voss, Hamburg, for the Hamburg-America Line.

VATSLAV VOROVSKIY (1959) See VAZLAV BOROVSKY (1959)

VAUBAN (1912) See VAUBAN (1913)

VAUBAN (1913)
10660 grt; 610 psrs
511' x 61' x 26'6" (155.6 x 18.6 x 8 m)
8-cylinder quadruple expansion engines via twin screw.
Broken up for scrap by TW Ward & Co at Inverkeithing in 1932 for a tender figure of £8,500. Ex-Lamport & Holt.
Built by Workman, Clark & Company, Belfast, for the Lamport & Holt Line as the VAUBAN (1912). Renamed ALCALA (1913 – Royal Mail Lines).

VAZLAV BOROVSKIJ (1959) See VAZLAV BOROVSKY (1959)

VAZLAV BOROVSKY (1959)
4722 grt; 333 psrs
401' x 52' x 17' (121.5 x 15.8 x 5.2 m)
2 x 6-cylinder MAN diesel engines via single screw.
Built by Mathias-Thesen, Wismar, for the Black Sea Shipping Co, Odessa.

VECTIS (1904)
5545 grt; 333 psrs
449' x 44' x 33'6" (136.1 x 13.5 x 10.2 m)
Triple expansion engine via single screw.
Broken up for scrap in Italy in 1913. Ex-P&O Line.
Built as the ROME (1881) by Caird & Company, Greenock, for the P&O Line.

VEDA (1986) See ORIENTAL PEARL II (2000)

VEDIC (1917)
9332 grt; 1250 psrs
480' x 58' x 31'6" (145.5 x 17.6 x 9.5 m)
4 x Harland & Wolff SRG turbine engines via twin screw.

Broken up for scrap at Rosyth in 1934 for a tender figure of £10,400.
Built by Harland & Wolff Ltd, Belfast, for the White Star Line as a cargo ship, but converted into a migrant ship in 1925.

VEENDAM (1923)
15652 grt; 586 psrs
576' x 67' x 22'5" (174.5 x 20.3 x 6.8 m)
4 x Harland & Wolff Ltd SRG turbine engines via twin screw.
Broken up for scrap at Baltimore, USA, in 1953.
Built by Harland & Wolff Ltd, Govan, for the Holland America Line.

VEENDAM (1972) See ENCHANTED ISLE (1994)

VEENDAM (1975) See ENCHANTED ISLE (1994)

VEENDAM (1978) See ENCHANTED ISLE (1994)

VEENDAM (1996)
55451 grt; 1266 psrs
723' x 102' x 25' (219.1 x 30.9 x 7.6 m)
5 x 12-cylinder Sulzer diesel-electric engines via twin screw.

Cruise ship operated by Holland America Westours Inc.
Built by Fincantieri Breda, Venice, at a cost of US$225,000,000.

VEGA (1900) See YAHIKO MARU (1904)

VEGA (1938)
7287 grt; 365 psrs
425' x 58' x 20' (128.8 x 17.6 x 20 m)
2 x 10-cylinder CRDA-Sulzer diesel engines via twin screw.
Sank on 4 May 1945 after a Russian bomber attack on the port of Eckernforde, Germany.
Built by Cantieri Riuniti dell'Adriatico, Trieste, for the Bergen Line.

VEGA (1973) See MYTILENE (1990)

VEGA (1990)
8881 grt; 500 psrs
430' x 62' x 14' (130.3 x 18.9 x 4.3 m)
4 x 12-cylinder Nohab-Polar diesel engines via twin screw.

Passenger ferry owned by the Hobart Shipping Co, Piraeus, and operated by Ventouris Group Enterprises SA, Piraeus.
Built by Trondheims, Trondheim, as the FALSTER (1975). Renamed PRINCE DE BRETAGNE (1975), FALSTER (1975), TAREK B (1980 – Alwalid Compania Navier SA, Panama), ATLAS IV (1983) and EUROPA (1986).

VEGA (1990)
13384 grt; 600 psrs
20 cars + 67 trailers
444' x 69' x 14' (134.6 x 21 x 5.7 m)
2 x 14-cylinder Nippon-Pielstick diesel engines via twin screw.
Passenger-car-cargo ferry owned and operated by Higashi Nippon Ferry Co Ltd, Hakodate.
Built by Mitsubishi Heavy Industries, Shimonoseki.

VELA (1979)
3664 grt; 500 psrs
398' x 59' x 17'6" (120.6 x 17.8 x 5.3 m)
2 x 14-cylinder Pielstick diesel engines via twin screw.
Passenger ferry owned and operated by Higashi Nippon Ferry Co Ltd, Hakodate.
Built by Naikai Zosen, Setoda.

VELASQUEZ (1905)
7542 grt
466' x 59' x 29'9" depth (141.2 x 17.9 x 9.1 m)
Richardson, Westgarth 3-cylinder triple expansion engine via single screw.
Abandoned as a total loss after becoming stranded in dense fog on Sebastion Island near Santos, Brazil, on 16 October 1908.
Built by Sir Raylton Dixon & Co, Middlesbrough, for Lamport & Holt.

VENERE (1905)
3692 grt; 500 psrs
403' x 40' x 30'6" depth (122.8 x 12.3 x 9.3 m)
2-cylinder compound engine via single screw.
Broken up for scrap in Italy in 1906.
Built by Barrow Shipbuilding Co, Barrow-in-Furness, for the Red Star Line as the BELGENLAND (1879).

VENETIA (1890) See SAN GIUSTO (1918)

VENEZIA (1907)
6827 grt; 1940 psrs
457' x 51' x 30'9" depth (139.3 x 15.6 x 9.4 m)
Swan Hunter 6-cylinder triple expansion engines via twin screw.
Destroyed by fire on 19 October 1919 in the North Atlantic while chartered to CGT.
Built by Swan Hunter & Wigham Richardson, Wallsend, for the Fabre Line.

VENEZUELA (1912)
5206 grt; 1108 psrs
394' x 48' x 27' (120.2 x 14.6 x 8.2 m)
N Odero 6-cylinder triple expansion engines via twin screw.
Broke her back and sank on 5 October 1920 after she dragged her anchor in the Casablanca Roads and ran aground on 7 March 1920.
Built by Cantieri Ligure-Anconetani, Ancona, for La Veloce as the BRASILE (1912).

VENEZUELA (1915) See SANTA ISABEL (1931)

VENEZUELA (1923)
6847 grt; 1630 psrs
420' x 52' x 27'7" depth (128 x 15.8 x 8.4 m)
Wallsend Slipway 6-cylinder triple expansion via twin screw.
Broken up for scrap in 1928. Ex-La Veloce.
Launched by Sir WG Armstrong, Whitworth & Co, Newcastle, for Bucknall Lines as the MARITZBURG (1904) and completed as the MENDOZA (1905-Lloyd Italiano). Renamed CASERTA (1914 – Italian Line).

VENEZUELA (1956)
18769 grt; 785 psrs
618' x 71' x 29' (187.3 x 21.5 x 8.8 m)
Parsons geared turbine engines via twin screw.
Broken up for scrap at La Spezia in 1962. She had been refloated, on 16 April 1962, from the position where she was beached immediately following her striking rocks near the Iles de Lerins, ten miles (17 km) off Cannes four weeks earlier (17 March 1962). The manner of the ship's grounding led to beliefs that her radar had been deliberately jammed as part of a plot for persons unknown to steal her cargo of bullion. In 1940 she had been deliberately sunk by the

Germans to form an obstacle in the River Gironde, near Bordeaux, during their retreat. Ex-Grimaldi-Siosa Line Group.
Laid down by Cammell Laird & Co Ltd, Birkenhead, for the French Line as the SUFFREN (1920) and completed as the DE GRASSE (1924). Renamed EMPRESS OF AUSTRALIA (1953 – Canadian Pacific Steamships Co).

VENICE (1967) See HERO (1972)

VENILIA (1988) See DA-IN (1995)

VENILIA (1999)
6118 grt; 450 psrs
14 cars + 67 trailers
444' x 69' x 18'8" (134.6 x 21 x 5.7 m)
2 x 12-cylinder Nippon-Pielstick diesel engines via twin screw.
Owned and operated by Higashi Nippon Ferry.
Built by Mitsubishi Heavy Industries, Shimonoseki.

VENTURA (1900)
6253 grt; 460 psrs
417' x 50' x 18' (127.1 x 15.2 x 5.5 m)
Triple expansion engines via twin screw.
Broken up for scrap at Osaka in 1934.
Built by William Cramp & Sons, Philadelphia, Pennsylvania, for the Oceanic Steamship Company.

VENUS (1931)
6269 grt; 413 psrs
420' x 54' x 20' (127.3 x 16.4 x 6.1 m)
2 x 10-cylinder B+W diesel engines via twin screw.
Broken up for scrap by Shipbreaking Industries Ltd at Faslane in 1968. She had been sunk during World War Two in Hamburg harbour, but was raised in 1945 for a refit and then returned to service in 1948.
Built by the Elsinore Shipyard, Elsinore, for the Bergen Line.

VENUS (1965)
3022 grt; 1200 psrs
100 cars
330' x 51' x 11'6" (100 x 15.5 x 3.5 m)
Geared turbine engines via twin screw.
Broken up for scrap in 1973 following four years service as a workers' floating hotel in Copenhagen. Ex-Cyprus Sea Cruises (Limassol) Ltd.
Built by William Denny & Bros, Dumbarton, for the London, Midland and Scottish Railway as the passenger ferry PRINCESS MAUD (1934).

VENUS (1966)
11209 grt; 527 psrs
462' x 68' x 21' (141.6 x 20.6 x 6.4 m)
2 x 18-cylinder Pielstick diesel engines via twin screw.
Passenger ferry operated on the UK–Norway service in the summertime and then reverting to the name BLACK PRINCE to cruise for Fred Olsen Lines, Oslo, during the winter season until the agreement ceased in 1986.
Built by Lubecker Flenderwerft, Lubeck.

VENUS (1975) See KEFALONIA (1995)

VENUS (1975) See SUPERFERRY I (1992)

VENUS (1979) See REINA DEL MAR (1981)

VENUS (1989)
14549 grt; 878 psrs
475' x 81' x 18' (144 x 24.4 x 5.5 m)
2 x 18-cylinder B+W diesel engines via twin screw.
Passenger ferry owned by Delbe Maritime and chartered to Swansea-Cork Ferries until 2003.
Built by Helsingor Werft, Helsingor, for DFDS as the RoRo cargo ferry DANA GLORIA (1975). Renamed DRACHENFELS (1976 – DDG Hansa charter), DANA HAFNIA (1977 – DFDS), GEDSERLINK (1986 – GT Ruten) and GEDSER (1986 – GT Ruten).

VENUS (1990) See KING OF SCANDINAVIA (1995)

VENUS (1995)
7198 grt; 600 psrs
20 cars + 87 trailers
457' x 57' x 18' (136.6 x 17.4 x 5.4 m)
2 x 18-cylinder Pielstick diesel engines via twin screw.
Passenger-car-cargo ferry operated by Higashi Nippon Ferry, Hakodate.
Built by Mitsubishi Heavy Industries, Shimonoseki, for the Higashi Nippon Ferry.

VENUS VENTURER (1984) See DISCOVERY I (1986)

VERA (1980) See MARIANNA IX (1982)

VERA CRUZ (1952)
21765 grt; 1296 psrs
610' x 76' x 28' (185.9 x 23 x 8.5 m)
6 x Parsons DRG turbine engines via twin screw.
Broken up for scrap at Kaohsiung in 1973.
Built by John Cockerill Shipyards, Hoboken, Belgium, for Cia Colonial de Navegacao, Lisbon, as a passenger ship.

VERA CRUZ (1977) See THE FIESTA (1991)

VERA CRUZ I (1977) See THE FIESTA (1991)

VERACRUZ PRIMERO (1977) See THE FIESTA (1991)

VERAGUA (1932) See SINALOA (1958)

VERAGUA (1946) See SINALOA (1958)

VERBANIA (1935) See EMPIRE TAMAR (1940)

VERDI (1963)
13226 grt; 672 psrs
529' x 69' x 27' (161 x 21 x 8.2 m)
2 x 18-cylinder Sulzer diesel engines via twin screw.
Broken up for scrap at La Spezia in 1977. Ex-Italian Line.
Built by Cantieri Riuniti dell'Adriatico, Monfalcone, for Lloyd Triestino as the OCEANIA (1951).

VERGA (1978) See DIMITROULA (1997)

VERGINA (1979) See MIR (1998)

VERGINA CITY (1991) See VERGINA SKY (1993)

VERGINA CITY (1992)
3155 grt; 1280 psrs
295' x 43' x 13' (89.4 x 13.4 x 3.9 m)
2 x 8-cylinder Mitsubishi diesel engines via twin screw.
Broken up for scrap in 1995 following her being gutted by fire, in July of that year, while being operated by Ayios Efthimios Navigation Co Ltd, Piraeus.
Built by Uraga Heavy Industries Ltd, Uraga, for Kansai Kyuko Ferry Co Ltd, Beppu, as the IVORY MARU (1967).

VERGINA SKY (1993)
4668 grt; 318 psrs
295' x 48' x 14' (89.4 x 14.5 x 4.2 m)
2 x 10-cylinder Pielstick diesel engines via twin screw.
Owned and operated by Vergina Ferries Hellas Ltd, but for sale at US$2,900,000 as at time of publication.
Built by Hashihama, Imabari, for Stability Line Inc as the YUFU (1971). Renamed VERGINA CITY (1991 – Ayios Efthymios Navigation Co Ltd, Piraeus) and CRETA SKY (1992 – Open Season Shipping Inc, Piraeus).

VERITAS (1967)
8072 grt
471' x 61' x 26'2" (142.7 x 18.5 x 7.9 m)
Fiat 6-cylinder diesel engine via single screw.
Broken up for scrap at Kaohsiung in 1971.
Built by Cantieri Riuniti dell'Adriatico, Monfalcone, for Soc Italiana di Armamento as the ANDREA GRITTI (1943).

VERONA (1908)

8240 grt; 2680 psrs
482' x 58' x 26'2" (147 x 17.8 x 7.9 m)
Workman, Clark 6-cylinder triple expansion engine via twin screw.
Sank on 11 May 1918 after being torpedoed by the German U-52 off Cape Pellaro, Italy.
Launched by Workman, Clark, Belfast, for Navigazione General Italia.

VERONESE (1905)

7063 grt
465' x 59' x 29'9" depth (140.9 x 17.9 x 9.1 m)
Workman, Clark 8-cylinder diesel engines via single screw.
Abandoned after running on to the Boa Nova Rocks, off Leixoes, in mountainous seas on 16 January 1913, with the loss of 43 lives.
Built by Workman, Clark, Belfast for Lamport & Holt.

VERONIQUE (1904) See AMAZONAS (1923)

VERSAILLES (1987) See VOLCAN DE TACANDE (2000)

VERYR (1964)

6993 grt; 54 psrs
453' x 93' x 25' (137.3 x 19.1 x 7.6 m)
B+W 6-cylinder diesel engine via single screw.
Broken up for scrap at Onimichi in 1964.
Built by Nakskov Skibsvaerft, Nakskov, for the East Asiatic Company, Copenhagen, as the FALSTRIA (1941).

VESTA (1979)

3664 grt; 500 psrs
398' x 59' x 17' (120.6 x 17.8 x 5.2 m)
2 x 14-cylinder Pielstick diesel engines via twin screw.
Passenger ferry operating in Japan by Higashi Nippon Ferry KK, Hakodate.
Built by Naikai Zosen, Setoda.

VEST BAY (1950) See TAI ER CHUANG (1955)

VESTERALEN (1983)

6262 grt; 550 psrs
40 cars
358' x 54' x 15' (108.6 x 16.5 x 4.5 m)
2 x 16-cylinder Normo diesel engines via twin screw.
Passenger-car-cargo ferry operating for OVDS, Narvik.
Built by Kaarbos, Harstad.

VESTRIS (1912)

10494 grt; 610 psrs
511' x 61' x 26'6" (155.6 x 18.6 x 8 m)
8-cylinder quadruple expansion engines via twin screw.
Owned by the Royal Mail Steam Packet Co, she sank two days out of New York, with the loss of 112 lives, after capsizing on 12 November 1928. Her coal bunkers and cargo had shifted, bringing about an uncontrollable list 300 miles (500 km) from the Hampton Roads, off the coast of Virginia. A total of 325 persons were rescued by the tanker MYRIAM, AMERICAN SHIPPER (American Merchant Lines), BERLIN (North German Lloyd) and the USS WYOMING.
Built by Workman, Clark & Company, Belfast, for the Lamport & Holt Line.

VETERAN MORYU (1994)

3908 grt; 149 psrs
338' x 48' x 20' (102.4 x 14.4 x 6 m)
Neptun Shipworks turbine engine via single screw.

Converted for academic use as a marine research vessel for the Marine Hydrophysical Institute of Ukraine.
Built by the Neptun Shipworks, Rostock, for the Russian government as the passenger ship LOMONOSOV (1957).

VIA ADRIATICO (1992)

14398 grt; 74 psrs
496' x 77' x 19'6" (150.3 x 25.7 x 6.5 m)
2 x 8-cylinder Zgoda-Sulzer diesel engines via twin screw.
Passenger-cargo ship owned and operated by Tirrenia Navigazioni, Naples.
Built by Tille (Frisian) Harlingen.

VIACHESLAV MOLOTOV (1940) See BALTIKA (1957)

VIA LIGURE (1992) See SCANDOLA (1999)

VIA MEDITERRANEO (1968) See EXPRESSO CATANIA (1993)

VIASILAV SOLOVYEN SEDOV (1982) See MIKHAIL SUSLOV (1982)

VIA TIRRENO (1992)

14398 grt; 74 psrs
496' x 77' x 19'6" (150.3 x 25.7 x 6.5 m)
2 x 8-cylinder Zgoda-Sulzer diesel engines via twin screw.
Passenger-cargo ship owned and operated by Tirrenia Navigazioni, Naples.
Built by Van der Giessen-du-Noord, Krimpen.

VICENTE (1916) See LOANDA (1925)

VICENTE PUCHOL (1969) See ARCADIA (1991)

VICEROY OF INDIA (1929)

19648 grt; 673 psrs
612' x 76' x 41'5" depth (185.5 x 23 x 12.6 m)
2 x British Thompson-Houston turbo-electric engines via twin screw.
Sank on 11 November 1942, with the loss of four lives, after being torpedoed by the German U-407 34 miles (57 km) off Oran.
Laid down as the TAJ MAHAL (1928) by Alexander Stephen & Sons Ltd, Glasgow, for the P&O Line, but completed as the VICEROY OF INDIA.

VICTORIA (1892) See STRAITS MARU (1956)

VICTORIA (1898) See NATALE (1925)

VICTORIA (1902)

5967 grt; 605 psrs
401' x 52' x 26'2" (121.5 x 15.8 x 7.9 m)
Fairfield 6-cylinder triple expansion engines via twin screw.
Broken up for scrap in Holland in 1923.
Built by Fairfield & Co Ltd, Glasgow, for the Pacific Steam Navigation Co.

VICTORIA (1931)

13098 grt; 666 psrs
540' x 70' x 23'10" (163.6 x 21.2 x 7 m)
Sulzer 32-cylinder diesel engines via quadruple screw.
Sank on 24 January 1942 after being attacked by a British torpedo aircraft in the Gulf of Sidra, Libya.
Built by Cantieri Riuniti dell'Adriatico, Trieste, for Lloyd Triestino as a passenger ship.

VICTORIA (1952)

3310 grt; 810 psrs
340' x 53' x 17' (103 x 16 x 5.2 m)
2 x 7-cylinder B+W diesel engines via twin screw.
Passenger ferry in Spain.
Launched by Union Naval de Levante, Valencia, for Cia Trasmediterranea as the 5 DE AGUSTO (1952) and completed as VICTORIA.

VICTORIA (1953) See ANASTASIS (1978)

VICTORIA (1958) See PRINCESA VICTORIA (1993)

VICTORIA (1977) See THE VICTORIA (1977)

VICTORIA (1995)
28891 grt; 714 psrs
660' x 86' x 26' (201.2 x 26.2 x 7.9 m)
2 x 9-cylinder Gotaverken diesel engines via twin screw.
Cruising for P&O Cruises.
Built by John Brown & Co Ltd, Clydebank, for the Swedish-American Line as the KUNGSHOLM (1965) at a cost of US$20,000,000. Renamed SEA PRINCESS (1979 – P&O Princess Cruises).

VICTORIA LUISE (1911) See HANSA (1921)

VICTORIAN (1895) See RUSSIAN (1914)

VICTORIAN (1905) See MARLOCH (1922)

VICTORIA PRINCESS (1980) See QUEEN OF PRINCE RUPERT (1980)

VICTORIOUS (1919) See GEORGE F. ELLIOTT, USS (AP-13) (1941)

VICTORY (1989)
17113 grt; 950 psrs
51 cars + 147 trailers
617' x 73' x 22'4" (187.1 x 22 x 6.8 m)
2 x 8-cylinder Mitsubishi diesel engines via single screw.
Passenger-car ferry purchased for US$28,500,000 in 1998 by the Grimaldi Group and operated by their subsidiary, Grandi Navi Veloce.
Built by Mitsubishi Heavy Industries Ltd, Kobe, for Higashi Nippon Ferry Co Ltd & Eiyu Shoji KK, Muroran.

VICTORY (2000) See CARNIVAL VICTORY (2000)

VICTORY I (1989) See SALEM FLOWER (1997)

VIENNA (1898) See YAHIKO MARU (1904)

VIENNA (1929)
4227 grt; 548 psrs
366' x 50' x 15' (110.9 x 15.2 x 4.5 m)
4 x Brown-Curtis SRG turbine engines via twin screw.
Broken up for scrap by Van Heyghen Freres yard at Ghent, Belgium, in 1960.
Built by John Brown & Co Ltd, Clydebank, for London & North Eastern Railways.

VIET-NAM (1952) See MALAYSIA BARU (1971)

VIETNAM HEROICO (1973)
7221 grt; 182 psrs
432' x 57' x 23' (130.9 x 17.3 x 7 m)
Stork-Werkspoor 6-cylinder diesel engine via single screw.
Military training and troopship in the service of the Cuban government.
Built by NV Scheepsbouwerf Gebroedes Pot, Bolnes, for the Royal Netherlands Steamship Co as the PRINS DER NEDERLANDEN (1957).

VIEW OF NAGASAKI (1989) See DAEDALUS (1989)

VIGNESSWARA (1990) See IONIS (1998)

VIKING (1908) See THE VIKING (1908)

VIKING (1913) See THE VIKING (1913)

VIKING (1964) See MEDIA II (1993)

VIKING (1981) See THE VIKING (1981)

VIKING (1983) See THE VIKING (1983)

VIKING (1988) See THE VIKING (1988)

VIKING I (1964) See MEDIA II (1993)

VIKING I (1970) See FAGR (1998)

VIKING I (1984) See FAGR (1998)

VIKING II (1964) See CESME STERN (1997)

VIKING III (1967) See SANDEFJORD (1992)

VIKING 2 (1982) See BOHUS (1994)

VIKING 2 (1986) See LARKSPUR (1999)

VIKING 3 (1972) See ROSLAGEN (1989)

VIKING 3 (1983) See ROSLAGEN (1989)

VIKING 4 (1973) See EXPRESS OLYMPIA (1990)

VIKING 5 (1974) See BOUGHAZ (1988)

VIKING 6 (1974) See SAREDGNA BELLA (1994)

VIKING 6 (1982) See SARDEGNA BELLA (1994)

VIKING 6 (1985) See SARDEGNA BELLA (1994)

VIKING BORDEAUX (1998)
3008 grt; 180 psrs
290' x 46' x 14'6" (88 x 14 x 4 m)
2 x 8-cylinder Deutz diesel engines via twin screw.
Owned by Royal Olympic Cruises and chartered to Viking Bordeaux SA, Luxembourg.
Built by Adler Werft, Bremen, for Bremer-Helgoland-Dienst Argo-Reederei as the cruise ship BREMERHAVEN (1960). Renamed STELLA MARIS II (1965 – Royal Olympic Cruises).

VIKINGFJORD (1969) See GOLFINHO AZUL (1999)

VIKING OF THE SEAS (2001) New name for VIKING SERENADE scheduled for the change in 2001.

VIKING PRINCESS (1965)
12812 grt; 324 psrs
537' x 64' x 22' (162.7 x 19.4 x 7.6 m)
Sulzer 16-cylinder diesel engines via twin screw.
Owned by Viking Cruise Lines, she was broken up for scrap at Bilbao in 1966 following a tow from Port Royal, Jamaica. She had experienced an engine room explosion, killing two persons, and raging fire 60 miles (100 km) southeast of Guantanamo Bay, Cuba, on 8 April 1966. The Liberian NAVIGATOR had towed her to Port Royal for a survey, but she was declared beyond repair. Built by Ateliers et Chantiers de la Loire, St Nazaire, for Messageries Maritimes as the LAVOISIER (1950). Renamed RIVIERA PRIMA (1961 – Commerciale Maritime Petroli SpA, Palermo).

VIKING PRINCESS (1984) See PALM BEACH PRINCESS (1997)

VIKING SAGA (1980) See SUPERSTAR TAURUS (2000)

VIKING SALLY (1980) See ESTONIA (1993)

VIKING SERENADE (1990)
40132 grt; 2104 psrs
530 cars
610' x 90' x 22'6" (184.8 x 27.3 x 6.8 m)
2 x 9-cylinder B+W diesel engines via twin screw.

Cruise ship for Sunshine Cruises (a joint venture formed by First Choice Holidays and Royal Caribbean International) following the ship's purchase for US$95,000,000 in 1999. She is scheduled to be renamed VIKING OF THE SEAS (2001).
Built by Dubigeon-Normandie, Nantes, for DFDS and Scandinavian World Cruises as the SCANDINAVIA (1982). Renamed STARDANCER (1985 – Sundance Cruises).

VIKING SONG (1980) See REGINA BALTICA (1996)

VIKING VALIANT (1975) See PRIDE OF CHERBOURG II (1994)

VIKING VENTURER (1975) See PRIDE OF HAMPSHIRE (1986)

VIKING VICTORY (1976) See MEDIA II (1993)

VIKING VISCOUNT (1976) See VITSENTZOS KARNAROS (1994)

VIKING VOYAGER (1976) See BARLOVENTO (2000)

VIKNOR, HMS (1914)
5361 grt; 280 psrs
421' x 50' x 25' (127.6 x 15.2 x 7.6 m)
R Napier 3-cylinder triple expansion engine via single screw.
Armed merchant cruiser for the British Royal Navy with the 10th Cruiser Squadron, she disappeared, with all 284 hands, off the north coast of Ireland after making radio contact with the Malin Head signal station on 12 January 1915.
Built by R Napier & Company, Glasgow, for the Royal Mail Steam Packet Company as the ATRATO (1889). Renamed THE VIKING I (1913 – Viking Cruising Company).

VILLA (1985)
5619 grt; 1500 psrs
479' x 61' x 14'6" (145 x 18.4 x 5.9 m)
4 x 6-cylinder GMT diesel engines via twin screw.
Passenger ferry owned by Italian State Railways and operated by Ferrovie Stato.
Built by Fincantieri, Palermo.

VILLA DE AGAETE (1975)
4274 grt; 1042 psrs
180 cars
335' x 62' x 16'6" (101.6 x 18.8 x 5 m)
8 x 8-cylinder Wartsila-Vasa diesel engines via twin screw.

Passenger-car ferry operated by Trasmediterranea.
Built by Wartsila, Helsinki, for the Silja Line as the FLORIA (1970).

VILLA DE BILBAO (1962) See TONG AN (1983)

VILLA DE MADRID (1931)
6942 grt; 369 psrs
419' x 56' x 20' (127 x 17 x 6.1 m)
Krupp 18-cylinder diesel engines via twin screw.
Built by Krupp, Hamburg, for Cia Trasmediterranea, Spain, as a passenger ferry.

VILLANDRY (1964) See DELOS (1986)

VILLE D'ALGER (1935) See POSEIDON (1966)

VILLE D'AMIENS (1924)
7143 grt; 90 psrs
441' x 54' x 35'8" depth (133.6 x 16.4 x 10.8 m)
Kincaid 3-cylinder triple expansion engine via single screw.
Broken up for scrap at La Seyne in 1953.
Built by the North of Ireland Shipbuilding Co, Londonderry, for Cie Havraise Peninsulaire as a passenger-cargo ship.

VILLE D'ANVERS (1940) See AROSA KULM (1952)

VILLE D'ARLON (1940)
3462 grt; 120 psrs
381' x 45' x 17'2" (115.5 x 13.6 x 5.2 m)
4 x William Denny turbine engines via twin screw.
Owned by Soc Maritime Anversoise, Belgium, she sank on 2 December 1940 after being torpedoed in mid-Atlantic.
Built by William Denny & Bros, Dumbarton, for the London Midland & Scottish Railway Co as the CAMBRIA (1921). Renamed AMERICAN TRAVELER (1924 – American Merchant Lines).

VILLE DE BORDEAUX (1956) See NESSEBAR (1964)

VILLE DE BRUGES (1940)
13869 grt; 436 psrs
535' x 72' x 31' (162.1 x 21.8 x 9.4 m)
4 x SRG turbine engines via twin screw.
Owned by Soc Maritime Anversoise, Belgium, she was beached on 14 May 1940 after a massive German bombing attack in the River Scheldt, Belgium, and was later broken up for scrap.
Laid down by the New York Shipbuilding Company, Camden, New Jersey, for the United States Line as the LONE STAR STATE (1922), launched as the PRESIDENT TAFT (1922) and completed as the PRESIDENT HARDING (1922).

VILLE DE GAND (1940)
7590 grt; 120 psrs
448' x 58' x 26'4" (135.8 x 17.6 x 8 m)
2 x General Electric DRG turbine engines via single screw.
Owned by Soc Maritime Anversoise, Belgium, she sank on 18 August 1940 after being torpedoed by the German U-48 west of Ireland.
Built by the American International Shipbuilding Corporation, Hog Island, Pennsylvania, for the US Shipping Board as the SOMME (1920). Renamed AMERICAN IMPORTER (1924 – American Merchant Lines).

VILLE DE HASSELT (1940)
7430 grt; 74 psrs
448' x 58' x 35'9" depth (135.8 x 17.6 x 10.9 m)
2 x General Electric DRG turbine engines via single screw.
Owned by Soc Maritime Anversoise, Belgium, she sank on 31 August 1940 after being torpedoed west of the Hebrides.
Built by the American International Shipbuilding Corporation, Hog Island, Pennsylvania, for the US Shipping Board as the MARNE (1920). Renamed AMERICAN TRADER (1924 – American Merchant Lines).

VILLE DE LIEGE (1940)
7430 grt; 74 psrs
448' x 58' x 35'9" depth (135.8 x 17.6 x 10.9 m)
2 x General Electric DRG turbine engines via single screw.
Owned by Soc Maritime Anversoise, Belgium, she sank on 13 April 1941 after being torpedoed 700 miles (1170 km) east of Cape Farewell, Greenland.
Built by the American International Shipbuilding Corporation, Hog Island, Pennsylvania, for the US Shipping Board as the OURCQ (1920). Renamed AMERICAN FARMER (1924 – American Merchant Lines).

VILLE DE MARSEILLE (1951) See VILLE DE MARSEILLE (1956)

VILLE DE MARSEILLE (1956)
9576 grt; 653 psrs
466' x 64' x 20v (141.2 x 19.4 x 6.1 m)

SRG turbine engines via twin screw.
Built by Forges et Chantiers de la Mediterranee, La Seyne, for Cie Generale Transatlantique as the VILLE DE MARSEILLE (1951). Renamed MAROC (1956 – Cie Generale Transatlantique).

VILLE DE MONS (1940)
7430 grt; 74 psrs
448' x 58' x 35'9" depth (135.8 x 17.6 x 10.9 m)
2 x General Electric DRG turbine engines via single screw.
Owned by Soc Maritime Anversoise, Belgium, she sank on 2 September 1940 after being torpedoed by the German U-47 north-west of Ireland.
Built by the American International Shipbuilding Corporation, Hog Island, Pennsylvania, for the US Shipping Board as the TOURS (1920). Renamed AMERICAN SHIPPER (1924 – American Merchant Lines).

VILLE DE NAMUR (1940)
7430 grt; 120 psrs
448' x 58' x 31' (135.8 x 17.6 x 9.4 m)
2 x GE turbine engines via single screw.
Owned by Soc Maritime Anversoise, Belgium, she sank on 19 June 1940 after being torpedoed in the Bay of Biscay, with 25 lives lost.
Built by the American International Shipbuilding Corporation, Hog Island, Pennsylvania, for the US Shipping Board as the cargo ship AISNE (1920). Renamed AMERICAN MERCHANT (1924 – American Merchant Lines).

VILLE DE SETE (2000)
11481 grt; 1000 psrs
300 cars + 35 trailers
449' x 80' x 18' (136.1 x 24.2 x 5.4 m)
4 x 12-cylinder Pielstick diesel engines via twin screw.

Ice-strengthened passenger-car-cargo ferry owned and operated by Balearic Express.
Built by JJ Seitas, Hamburg, for the SF Line, Mariehamn, as the AURELLA (1972). Renamed ST. PATRICK II (1982 – Irish Ferries) and EGNATIA II (1998 – Hellenic Mediterranean Lines, under a two-year lease-purchase plan from Irish Ferries).

VILLE DE STRASBOURG (1920)
7138 grt; 90 psrs
425' x 54' x 28'3" depth (129.5 x 16.4 x 8.6 m)
Kincaid 3-cylinder triple expansion engine via single screw.
Broken up for scrap at Faslane in 1952.
Built by the North of Ireland Shipbuilding Company, Londonderry, for Cie Havraise Peninsulaire.

VILLE DE TUNIS (1952) See MEGALONISSOS KRITI (1967)

VILLE DE VERDUN (1920)
7007 grt; 90 psrs
425' x 54" x 28'3" (129.5 x 16.4 x 8.6 m)
Kincaid 3-cylinder triple expansion engine via single screw.
Sank on 17 October 1942 after being torpedoed off Taiwan.
Built by the North of Ireland Shipbuilding Company, Londonderry, for Cie Havraise Peninsulaire.

VILLE D'ORAN (1936) See MT. OLYMPUS (1965)

VIMINALE (1925)
8658 grt; 360 psrs
450' x 57' x 27' (137.2 x 17.4 x 8.2 m)
Stablimento Tecnico 12-cylinder diesel engines via twin screw.
Sank on 27 May 27 1943 by British patrol boats and aircraft off Cape Vaticano, Italy.
Built by Cantieri San Rocco SA, Trieste, for Lloyd Triestino.

VINCENT (1912) See GUJARAT (1913)

VINETA (1913) See CAP POLONIO (1914)

VINLAND STAR (1995) See CITY OF MYKONOS (1977)
Sale to Vinland Cruise Line aborted, but VINLAND STAR had been fully registered.

VIRGEM DE FATIMA (2000)
3931 grt; 1200 psrs
291' x 53' x 13' (99.3 x 16.2 x 4 m)
4 x 9-cylinder MAN diesel engines via twin screw.
Passenger-car ferry owned and operated by Sao Tome Trading following purchase for US$350,000.
Built by Adler Werft, Bremen, as the KALLE (1962). Renamed ROTNA (1971) and GHAWDEX (1979 – Gozo Channel, Malta).

VIRGEN DE AFRICA (1953) See AFRICA (1986)

VIRGILIO (1928)
11718 grt; 640 psrs
506' x 62' x 27'2" (153.3 x 18.8 x 8.2 m)
2 x 8-cylinder B+W diesel engines via twin screw.
Broken up for scrap in 1945 following her refloating from Toulon harbour. She had sank here after being scuttled by the Germans in June 1944.
Built by Cantieri ed Officini Meridionali, Baia, for the Italian Line.

VIRGIN DE CHURRUCA (1952) See ISLA DE FORMENTERA (1973)

VIRGINIA (1906) See GARIBALDI (1911)

VIRGINIA (1914)
4510 grt; 1126 psrs
375' x 46' x 26'5" depth (114.3 x 14.1 x 8 m)
D & W Henderson 3-cylinder triple expansion engine via single screw.
Broken up for scrap in Italy in 1923. Ex-Soc Italiana di Navigazioni Mediterraneo.
Built by D & W Henderson, Glasgow, for the Anchor Line as the ALGERIA (1891). Renamed CYRILL (1912 – Jebsen & Diederichsen, Germany).

VIRGINIA (1928) See BRAZIL (1938)

VIRGINIAN (1905) See HOMELAND (1951)

VIRGINIE (1907)
5330 grt; 350 psrs
358' x 49' x 26'8" depth (109.2 x 15 x 8 m)
Forges et Chantiers de la Mediterranee 3-cylinder triple expansion engine via single screw.
Broken up for scrap in Holland in 1934.
Launched by Forges et Chantiers de la Mediterranee, La Seyne, for the French Line as the MALOU (1903) and completed as the VIRGINIE.

VIRGIN MARY (1999)
5591 grt; 280 psrs
70 cars + 50 rail wagons
419' x 62' x 16' (127.7 x 18.7 x 4.9 m)
2 x 12-cylinder Pielstick diesel engines via twin screw.

Passenger-car cargo train ferry owned and operated by MBRS Lines, Quezon City.
Built by Dubigeon-Normandie, Nantes, as the freight ferry ARATIKA (1974) at a cost of NZ$9,000,000 for Tranzrail, but further converted into a passenger-car-cargo-train ferry in Hong Kong in 1976 at a cost of NZ$5,000,000.

VIRGO (1974) See RODANTHI (1995)

VIRGO (1990)
6358 grt; 600 psrs
20 cars + 88 trailers
444' x 74' x 19' (134.6 x 22.4 x 5.7 m)
2 x 14-cylinder Pielstick diesel engines via twin screw.
Passenger-car-cargo ferry owned and operated by Higashi Nippon Ferry Co Ltd, Hakodate.
Built by Mitsubishi Heavy Industries Ltd, Shimonoseki.

VIRONIA (1994) See MELOODIA (1996)

VISBY (1964) See TIAN HU (1981)

VISBY (1972) See SARDINIA REGINA (1996)

VISBY (1980) See VISBY (1997)

VISBY (1997)
23842 grt; 1832 psrs
517 cars or 54 trailers
480' x 81' x 19' (145.6 x 24.5 x 5.7 m)
4 x 8-cylinder B+W diesel engines via twin screw.

Passenger-car-cargo ferry owned by Rederi AB Gotland, Visby, and operated by Destination Gotland.
Built by Oresundsvarvet AB, Landskrona, for Rederi AB Gotland as the VISBY (1980). Renamed FELICITY (1990 – Sealink British Ferries) and STENA FELICITY (1990 – Sealink Stena).

VISCOUNTESS M (1992) See MILLENNIUM EXPRESS II (2000)

VISEVICA (1964) See ABU-HOSNA (1984)

VISION OF THE SEAS (1998)
78340 grt; 2435 psrs
838' x 106' x 25' (254 x 32.1 x 7.6 m)
4 x 12-cylinder Wartsila diesel engines via twin screw.

Cruise ship built by Chantiers de l'Atlantique, St Nazaire, for Royal Caribbean International, Miami, at a cost of US$275,000,000.

VISTAFJORD (1973) See CARONIA (1999)

VISTAMAR (1989)
7478 grt; 354 psrs
386' x 56' x 15' (117 x 17 x 4.6 m)
2 x 12-cylinder Wartsila diesel engines via twin screw.
Cruise ship owned by Hoteles Marline Universal Shipping, Roquetas, Panama, and operated as a cruise ship by Marinos Hoteles SA, Roquetas.
Built by Union de Navale de Levante, Valencia.

VITSENTZOS KORNAROS (1994)
9735 grt; 1200 psrs
320 cars
474' x 77' x 18' (143.7 x 23.4 x 5.4 m)
3 x 8-cylinder Stork-Werkspoor diesel engines via triple screw.
Passenger-car ferry operated by LANE Lines, Piraeus.
Built by Aalborg Vaerft, Aalborg, for the Stanhope Steamship Co Ltd, London, as the VIKING VISCOUNT (1976). Renamed PRIDE OF WINCHESTER (1989 – P&O European Ferries (Portsmouth) Ltd).

VITTORE CARPACCIO (1992)
4706 grt; 1350 psrs
60 cars + 16 trailers
347' x 57' x 13'5" (105 x 17.3 x 4.1 m)
4 x 12-cylinder Bergens-Normo diesel engines via twin screw.
Passenger-car-cargo ferry owned and operated by Sicilia Regionale Mariitima SpA.
Built by Bergens Shipyard for Misr Edco Shipping Co Ltd as the EL ARISH (1980). Renamed DANIA MARINE (1991 – Caromar AS).

VITTORIA (1902) See CITTA DI NAPOLI (1902)

VITTORIO MOCCAGATTA (1942) See ANTONIOTTO USODIMARE (1948)

VIXEN, USS (1942) See REGINA MARIS (1996)

VLADIVOSTOK (1960) See PRIAMURIE (1968)

VOLANS (1983)
5011 grt; 520 psrs
416' x 66' x 18' (126.2 x 20 x 5.5 m)
2 x 12-cylinder Pielstick diesel engines via twin screw.
Passenger ferry owned and operated by the government of China.
Built by Naikai, Setoda, for Higashi Nippon Ferry Co Ltd, Hakodate.

VOLCAN DE TACANDE (2000)
12962 grt; 1800 psrs
425 cars
412' x 77' x 16'6" (124.9 x 23.4 x 5.3 m)
2 x 18-cylinder Pielstick diesel engines via twin screw.

Passenger-car ferry owned and operated by Naviera Armas SA, Canary Islands.
Launched by Brodogradiliste, Trogir, for Stena Line as the STENA NORDICA (1974) and completed as the STENA DANICA (1974). Renamed STENA NORDICA (1981 – Stena Line), STENA NAUTICA (1983 – Stena Line), VERSAILLES (1987 – Sealink UK), STENA LONDONER (1992 – Stena Sealink Line) and SEAFRANCE MONET (1996 – SeaFrance SA).

VOLCAN DE TAMASITE (1996)
11668 grt; 1750 psrs
318' x 68' x 16' (115.4 x 20.6 x 4.9 m)
4 x 6-cylinder B+W diesel engines via twin screw.

Ice-strengthened passenger ferry owned by Naviera Armas SA.
Built by Helsingor Vaerft AS, Helsingor, for Mols Linien, Denmark, as the
MAREN MOLS (1975). Renamed MAREN MO (1996 – Mols Linien).

VOLCAN DE TAUCE (1995)
9807 grt; 256 psrs
62 trailers
396' x 66' x 17'6" (120 x 20 x 5.3 m)
2 x 6-cylinder MWM diesel engines via twin screw.
Passenger-cargo ferry owned and operated by Naviera Armas SA, Las Palmas.
Built by the HJ Barreras Shipyard, Vigo, at a cost of US$22,000,000.

VOLCANO DE TENAGUA (1999)
4291 grt; 1042 psrs
200 cars
335' x 62' x 16' (107.6 x 18.7 x 4.9 m)
8 x 8-cylinder Wartsila-Vasa diesel engines via twin screw.

Passenger-car ferry owned by Naviera Armas SA, Curbelo, and operated by
Trasmediterranea.
Built by Wartsila-Helsinki for the Silja Line as the BOTNIA (1967). Renamed
CIUDAD DE LA LAGUNA (1975).

VOLENDAM (1922)
15434 grt; 1175 psrs
572' x 67' x 33' (173.3 x 20.4 x 10 m)
4 x SRG turbine engines via twin screw
Broken up for scrap by Hendrik Ido Ambacht at Rotterdam in 1952.
Built by Harland & Wolff Ltd, Govan, for the Holland America Line.

VOLENDAM (1972) See UNIVERSE EXPLORER (1996)

VOLENDAM (1978) See UNIVERSE EXPLORER (1996)

VOLENDAM (1999)

60906 grt; 1440 psrs
780' x 107' x 26'6" (238 x 32.4 x 8 m)
5 x 12-cylinder Sulzer diesel-electric engines via twin screw.
Built by Fincantieri, Marghera, for the Holland America Line at a cost of
US$300,000,000.

VOLGA (1939)
9965 grt; 903 psrs
467' x 56' x 24'3" (141.5 x 17 x 7.4 m)
Soc Espanola de Construccion Naval SRG turbine engines via twin screw.
Owned by Russian Navy.
Built by Soc Espanola de Construccion Naval, Bilbao, for Cia Trasatlantica as
the JUAN SEBASTIAN ELCANO (1928).

VOLKER (1985) See VALTUR PRIMA (1999)

VOLKERFREUNDSCHAFT (1960) See VALTUR PRIMA (1999)

VOLTAIR (1907)
8618 grt; 60 psrs
485' x 58' x 34'1" depth (147 x 17.6 x 10.3 m)
D & W Henderson 3-cylinder triple expansion engine via single screw.
Sank on 2 December 1916 after being attacked by the German raider
MOEWE 650 miles (1048 km) west of Fastnet.
Built by D & W Henderson & Co Ltd, Glasgow, for the Lamport & Holt Line.

VOLTAIRE (1923)
13248 grt; 680 psrs
526' x 64' x 39'3" depth (155.6 x 18.6 x 11.9 m)
Workman, Clark 8-cylinder quadruple expansion engines via twin screw.
Sank with the loss of 75 lives in one and a half hours on 4 April 1941 after she
was attacked at dawn by the German raider THOR, 300 miles (500 km) west
of the Cape Verde Islands.
Built by Workman, Clarke & Co Ltd, Belfast, for the Lamport & Holt Line.

VOLTURNO (1908)
3581 grt; 1024 psrs
340' x 43' x 20'7" (103 x 13 x 6.3 m)
Fairfield 6-cylinder triple expansion engines via twin screw.
Sank on 10 October 1913 in mid-Atlantic, with 136 lives lost, after catching
fire the day before and then being rocked by an explosion in the forward hold.
Launched as a job number in 1906 by Fairfield Shipbuilding & Engineering
Co, Glasgow, for Navigazione Italo-Americano and completed as the
VOLTURNO for the Volturno Steamship Co.

VOLUBILIS (1919)
4496 grt; 120 psrs
386' x 47' x 27'7" depth (117 x 14.2 x 8.4 m)
William Beardmore 3-cylinder triple expansion engine via single screw.
Broken up for scrap in 1931. Ex-Cie Generale Transatlantique.
Built by William Beardmore & Co, Dalmuir, for the Eastern & Australian Line
as the EMPIRE (1902).

VONDEL (1907)
5866 grt; 164 psrs
422' x 48' x 30' (132.3 x 14.6 x 9.1 m)
4-cylinder Nederlandsche Fabriek quadruple expansion engine via single
screw.
Broken up in 1930 by Frank Rijsdijk, Hendrik Ido Ambacht.
Built by Nederlandsche Scheepsbouw Maatschappij, Rotterdam, for
Nederlands Steamship Co.

VON STEUBEN (1919)
14908 grt; 1651 psrs
664' x 66' x 29' (202.2 x 20 x 6.1 m)
2 x 8-cylinder quadruple expansion engines via twin screw.
Broken up for scrap by the Boston Iron & Steel Company at Baltimore, USA,
in 1923. Ex-US Shipping Board.
Built by the Vulkan Shipyard, Stettin, for North German Lloyd as the
KRONPRINZ WILHELM (1901). She was seized and renamed by the US
government which transferred her to the US Navy in 1915 as a troopship.

VON STEUBEN, USS (1915) See VON STEUBEN (1919)

VORTIGERN (1969) See MILOS EXPRESS (2000)

VOYAGER (1985) See NEW YORK FORTUNE I (1997)

VOYAGER OF THE SEAS (1999)
137300 grt; 3114 psrs
1021' x 127' x 29' (309.4 x 38.5 x 8.8 m)

6 x 12-cylinder Wartsila-Vasa diesel-electric engines via triple screw, including 2 Azipods.
Built by Kvaerner-Masa Yards Inc, Helsinki, for Royal Caribbean International at a cost of US$500,000,000.

VULCAIN (1921)
7155 grt; 2060 psrs
length 460' x beam 52' (140.2 x 15.9 m)
6-cylinder triple expansion engines via twin screw.
Broken up for scrap in 1937. Ex-French Navy.
Built by Blohm & Voss, Hamburg, for the Hamburg-America Line as the PHOENICIA (1895). Renamed KRONSTADT (1904 – Russian Navy), FLEISS (1918 – German government) and KRONSTADT (1919 – Russian Navy).

VULCANIA (1928) See CARIBIA (1965)

VYACHESLAV MOLOTOV (1940) See BALTIKA (1957)

WACHTFELS (1913) See ANTINOUS (1923)

WADAI (1922) See GOGOL (1946)

WADI ALNEEL (1993)
5123 grt; 1100 psrs
225 cars or 80 cars + 20 trailers
378' x 56' x 15' (114.6 x 17 x 4.5 m)
2 x 10-cylinder Wichmann diesel engines via twin screw.
Passenger-car-cargo ship owned and operated by the National Navigation Co, Egypt, after acquisition of the vessel for US$17,000,000. The company has now returned the ship to the international sales lists.
Built by Hasund MV, Ulsteinvik, for Askoy Bergen as the KYSTVEIEN (1988).

WAHEHE (1914) See CORSICA (1951)

WAHINE (1913)
4436 grt; 300 psrs
374' x 52' x 25'6" (114 x 15.8 x 7.8 m)
3 x turbine engines via triple screw.
Abandoned as a total loss after she ran on to the Masella Reef in the Arafura Sea, north of Darwin, on 15 August 1951.
Built by William Denny & Bros, Ltd, Dumbarton, for the Union Steamship Co of New Zealand.

WAHINE (1966)
8948 grt; 928 psrs
200 cars
489' x 73' x 25'6" (149 x 22 x 7.8 m)
3 x turbo-electric engines via twin screw.
Broken up on site in 1969 after lying on her starboard side for nearly a year. This followed desperate efforts to make Wellington harbour in New Zealand. In the worst-recorded storm in the history of Cook Strait, which separates the North and South Islands of the dominion, winds reached 123 mph (205 kph) and visibility was down to zero. The ship, sailing from Lyttleton northwards to Wellington, was driven on to the notorious Barrett's Reef outside the harbour at 6.41 am on 11 April 1968 and lost her starboard propeller. She freed herself, but was uncontrollable and ran aground at the entrance to Chafer's Passage leading into the deep water harbour. She was holed below the waterline, rolled over in 12 metres (40 feet) of water and settled on her starboard side. Fifty-one lives were lost from the ship's complement of 735 passengers and crew, and many of their families brought actions against the ship's owners, the Union Steamship Company.
Built by Fairfield Shipbuilding & Engineering Co at Govan for the Union Steamship Co of New Zealand.

WAIALEALE (1928) See MOLENO (1947)

WAIMANA (1911) See WAIMANA (1946)

WAIMANA (1932) See WAIMANA (1946)

WAIMANA (1946)
10389 grt; 1006 psrs
494' x 63' x 29' (150.6 x 19 x 8.8 m)
Triple expansion engines via twin screw.
Broken up for scrap at Milford Haven, UK, in 1952.
Built by Workman, Clark & Co, Belfast, for the White Star Line as the WAIMANA (1911). Renamed HERMINIUS (1926 – Aberdeen Line), WAIMANA (1932 – Shaw Savill & Albion) and EMPIRE WAIMANA (1941 – British Ministry of War Transport).

WAIPARA (1904)
5505 grt; 338 psrs
421' x 54' x 28'6" depth (127.6 x 16.4 x 8.7 m)
Northeast Marine Engineering 3-cylinder triple expansion engine via single screw.
Broken up in 1938 for a price of £12,500.

Laid down by Northeast Marine, Newcastle, for the Port Line as the passenger-cargo ship PORT JACKSON (1904), but completed as the WAIPARA.

WAITOMO (1916) See ENGLESTAN (1927)

WAKASHIO MARU (1973) See MINOAN PRINCE (1995)

WAKEFIELD, USS (AP-21) (1941)
29627 grt; 1200 psrs
705' x 86' x 30'9" (213.6 x 26.1 x 9.4 m)
6 x SRG turbine engines via twin screw.
Broken up for scrap by Union Metals & Alloy Inc, Kearny, New Jersey, in 1965 as a transport ship after an 18-year period laid up in the Hudson river, New York, by the US Navy.
Built by the New York Shipbuilding Corporation, Camden, New Jersey, for United States Lines as the MANHATTAN (1932).

WAKOOL (1898) See LE MYRE DE VILLERS (1917)

WAKOOL (1913) See ANDRE CHENIER (1921)

WALMER CASTLE (1902)
12546 grt; 754 psrs
576' x 64' x 38'6" depth (175.6 x 19.5 x 11.7 m)
Harland & Wolff Ltd 8-cylinder quadruple expansion engines via twin screw.
Broken up for scrap at Blyth in 1932.
Laid down as the CELT (1900) by Harland & Wolff Ltd, Belfast, for the Union Castle Line and completed as the WALMER CASTLE.

WALRUS (1996)
15343 grt; 556 psrs
494' x 65' x 17'2" (149.7 x 19.7 x 5.2 m)
4 x 9-cylinder Bergen-Normo diesel engines via twin screw.
Cruise ship owned and operated by Crown Cruise Lines SA, San Diego, California, as a casino ship out of Hong Kong. She was marketed as the NEPTUNE but not registered as such.
Built by Union Naval de Levante, Valencia, for Crown Cruise Lines as the CROWN MONARCH (1990). Renamed NAUTICAN (1994 – Chinese International Holdings & Singapore Cruises).

WALTER HOLKEN (1919)
4319 grt; 96 psrs
397' x 45' x 28' (121.1 x 13.7 x 8.5 m)
Caird & Co 3-cylinder triple expansion engine via single screw.
Broken up for scrap in 1924. Ex-Schroder Holker & Fischer.
Built by Caird & Co, Greenock, for P&O Lines as the JAPAN (1893) at a cost of £70,022. Renamed SHIMPO MARU (1910) after her sale to Mr Kishimoto, Osaka, for £8,497.

WANAKA (1970) See BALBEK (2000)

WANDILLA (1912) See ARNO (1938)

WANGANELLA (1931)
9876 grt; 408 psrs
474' x 64' x 25' (144.5 x 19.5 x 7.6 m)
2 x 8-cylinder Harland & Wolff-B+W diesel engines via twin screw.
Broken up for scrap at Kaohsiung in 1970 after 8 years ownership. Ex-Hang Fung Shipping & Trading Company Ltd, Hong Kong.
Launched by Harland & Wolff Ltd, Belfast, for the British & African Steam Navigation Company as the ACHIMOTA (1931) at a cost to that stage of £520,000. She was completed as the WANGANELLA for Huddart Parker & Company Ltd at a renegotiated cost of £346,376.

WANG FU (1993)
3787 grt; 250 psrs
333' x 48' x 13' (100 x 14.5 x 3.6 m)
2 x 8-cylinder Skoda diesel engines via twin screw.
Owned by Mainkey Holdings Ltd, Hong Kong, and operated by Great Sino Shipping Co Ltd, Hong Kong.
Built by A Jdanov Shipyard, St Petersburg, for the Black Sea Shipping Company, Odessa, as the passenger-cargo ship TADZHIKISTAN (1961). Renamed KISTAN (1988 – Precious Inc), PORTO LEONE (1988),

OLYMPIC FLAME (1988), CHANG SHENG (1989 – Chang Sheng Navigation SA, Panama), ALICE PRINCESS (1992 – Chang Sheng Navigation SA, Panama) and SOUTHERN KINGDOM (1993 – Great Sino Shipping Co).

WANGONI (1920) See CHUKOTKA (1946)

WAPPEN (1964) See HELGOLAND (1985)

WAPPEN VON HAMBURG (1962) See HELGOLAND (1985)

WAPPEN VON HAMBURG (1965) See WAPPEN VON HAMBURG (1984)

WAPPEN VON HAMBURG (1984)
4192 grt; 1800 psrs
360' x 50' x 14' (109.1 x 15.2 x 4.2 m)
2 x 12-cylinder MAN diesel engines via twin screw.
Ice-strengthened ferry owned by Nordic Schiffahrtsgesell Schaft GmbH and operated by Seetouristik GmbH & Co KG..
Built by HWD, Hamburg, for the Hamburg Harbor Company as the WAPPEN VON HAMBURG (1965). Renamed JATTEN FINN (1965 – Skagen Line) and LUCAYA (1965).

WAR ARGUS (1918) See DJATINEGARA (1952)

WARATAH (1908)
9339 grt; 850 psrs
465' x 59' x 27' (141.7 x 18.1 x 8.2 m)
2 x quadruple expansion engines via twin screw.
Vanished without trace, taking 211 lives with her, between Durban and Capetown about 28 July 1909. She was discovered 90 years later, in 1999, to be lying on the seabed at 370 (112 m) seven miles (11.5 km) off the Transkei coast, north of East London.
Built by Barclay, Curle & Co, Glasgow, for the Blue Anchor Line.

WAR BERYL (1918) See SPERBRECHER (1939)

WARILDA (1912)
7712 grt; 423 psrs
429' x 57' x 34'1" depth (130 x 17.3 x 10.3 m)
Beardmore 8-cylinder quadruple expansion engines via twin screw.
Sank on 3 August 1918 as a hospital ship after being torpedoed in the English Channel off Le Havre, with 123 lives lost.
Built by William Beardmore & Co Ltd, Dalmuir, for the Adelaide Steamship Co.

WAR LINNET (1918) See MONCALIERI (1920)

WARNEMUNDE (1963) See ADMIRAL (1996)

WAROONGA (1939)
9365 grt
511' x 64' x 32' (154.8 x 19.4 x 9.7 m)
William Denny 4-cylinder triple expansion engines via twin screw.
Sank on 5 April 1943 after being torpedoed in the North Atlantic.
Built by William Denny & Brothers Ltd, Dumbarton, for the New Zealand Shipping Co Ltd as the HORORATA (1914).

WAR PERIDOT (1918) See BOSWORTH (1920)

WAR PIDGEON (1918) See CARIGNANO (1920)

WARRIGAL (1893) See LATONA (1906)

WARRNAMBOOL (1892) See KUT (1919)

WAR SURF (1919) See WILLIAM P. BIDDLE (1946)

WARSZAWA (1920) See MADISON (1926)

WARWICK CASTLE (1877) See KERASOUNDE (1911)

WARWICK CASTLE (1931)
20107 grt; 699 psrs

677' x 76' x 37'4" depth (205.2 x 23 x 11.3 m)
2 x 8-cylinder B+W diesel engines via twin screw.
Sank on 12 November 1942, with the loss of 63 lives, after being torpedoed by the German U-413 200 miles off the coast of Portugal.
Built by Harland & Wolff Ltd, Belfast, for the Union Castle Line.

WARWICK CASTLE (1947)
17387 grt; 539 psrs
594' x 76' x 29' (180 x 23 x 8.8 m)
Harland & Wolff Ltd16-cylinder diesel engines via twin screw.
Broken up for scrap at Barcelona in 1962. Sold to the British Admiralty during World War Two and resold to the Union Castle Line after the war.
Built by Harland & Wolff Ltd, Belfast, for the Union Castle Line as the PRETORIA CASTLE (1938).

WARWICKSHIRE (1902)
7950 grt; 100 psrs
470' x 58' x 27'5" depth (142.4 x 17.6 x 8.3 m)
Harland & Wolff Ltd 8-cylinder quadruple expansion engines via twin screw.
Broken up for scrap in 1932.
Built by Harland & Wolff Ltd, Belfast, for the Bibby Line.

WARWICKSHIRE (1948) See SIRIUS (1971)

WASA EXPRESS (1976) See ROSLAGEN (1989)

WASA EXPRESS (1983) See FAGR (1998)

WASA EXPRESS (1984) See ROSLAGEN (1989)

WASA EXPRESS (1997) See PENELOPE A (2000)

WASA JUBILEE (1998) See COLOR VIKING (2000)

WASA KING (1990) See ESTONIA (1993)

WASA PRINCE (1988) See PEDER OLSEN (1992)

WASA QUEEN (1992)
16545 grt; 1400 psrs
290 cars
499' x 73' x 19' (153.1 x 22.3 x 5.8 m)
4 x 12-cylinder L'Atlantique-Pielstick SRG diesel engines via twin screw.

Ice-strengthened passenger-cargo RoRo ferry owned and operated by Silja Lines.
Built by Dubigeon-Normandie, Nantes, for Bore Angfartygs, Abo, as the BORE STAR (1975). Renamed SILJA STAR (1980 – Silja Line), ORIENT EXPRESS (1986 – Europe Cruise Lines), CLUB SEA (1987 – Club Sea Incorporated), ORIENT EXPRESS (1987 – Sea Containers, on short charter), EUROSUN (1989 – Europe Cruise Line, on short charter by Effjohn), ORIENT EXPRESS (1990 – Sea Containers, on short charter), EUROSUN (1990 – Europe Cruise Line, on short charter to Effjohn) and ORIENT SUN (1992 – Orient Line, Singapore).

WASA STAR (1981) See PETER WESSEL (1984)

WASHINGTON (1923) See GREAT CANTON (1923)

WASHINGTON (1929) See OCEANIC RELIANCE (1956)

WASHINGTON (1933) See WASHINGTON (1946)

WASHINGTON (1946)

29627 grt; 1106 psrs
705' x 86' x 33'3" depth (213.6 x 26.1 x 10.1 m)
6 x Parsons SRG turbine engines via twin screw.
Broken up for scrap in 1964 by Lipsett Inc and Union Metals & Minerals & Alloys Corporation for a tender of US$238,126. Ex-US Maritime Commission.
Built by the New York Shipbuilding Co, Camden, New Jersey, for the United States Lines as the WASHINGTON (1933). Renamed MOUNT VERNON, USS (AP-22) (1941 – US Navy).

WASSAU (1901) See ISLAM (1902)

WATERMAN (1947) See MARGARITA (1963)

WATERMAN (1968) See COPA CASINO (1993)

WAWEL (1973) See EUROFAST (2000)

WAYLAND, HMS (1942)

13867 grt; 1647 psrs
540' x 65' x 30'11" depth (163.6 x 19.7 x 9.1 m)
4 x Vickers-Armstrong DRG turbine engines via twin screw.
Broken up as a British Royal Navy heavy repair ship for scrap at Troon, Scotland, in 1948.
Built by Vickers-Armstrong Ltd, Barrow-in-Furness, for the Cunard Line as the ANTONIA (1922).

WAZLAV WOROVSKY (1959) See VAZLAV VOROVSKY (1959)

W. C. LANGFITT, USAT (1946) See TRANSINDIANA (1969)

WEI DONG (1990) See GOLDEN BRIDGE (1990)

WEIMAR (1891) See ARMONIA (1909)

WELLAMO (1975) See JUPITER (1998)

WELLAMO (1986) See SILJA FESTIVAL (1990)

WELSHMAN (1904)

5728 grt
461' x 49' x 23'2" (140.4 x 15 x 7 m)
Harland & Wolff Ltd 6-cylinder triple expansion engines via twin screw.
Broken up for scrap at Barrow-in-Furness in 1929. Ex-Leyland Line.
Built by Harland & Wolff Ltd, Belfast, for the White Star Line as the TAURIC (1891).

WENATCHEE (1921) See PRESIDENT JEFFERSON (1946)

WEST BAY (1957)

7105 grt; 1025 psrs
452' x 56' x 23'1" (137.8 x 17 x 7 m)
Bremer Vulkan 7-cylinder diesel engine via single screw.
Broken up for scrap by Eisen und Metal AG at Hamburg, Germany, in 1962. Ex-Duff, Herbert & Mitchell.
Built by Bremer Vulkan, Vegesack, for North German Lloyd as the cargo ship NURNBERG (1936). Renamed DUNDALK BAY (1948 – HP Lenaghan's Bay Line) which transported migrants after World War Two.

WESTERDAM (1946)

12149 grt; 134 psrs
518' x 66' x 31' (157 x 20 x 9.4 m)
MAN 10-cylinder diesel engines via twin screw.
Broken up for scrap at Alicante in 1965. She had sunk on 27 August 1940 as a result of Allied bombing, been raised, only to be sunk again by the Dutch resistance in September 1944 and raised again in 1945.
Laid down by Wilton Fijenoord Shipyard, Schiedam, for Holland-America Lines in September 1939 and completed in 1946.

WESTERDAM (1988)

53872 grt; 1773 psrs
798' x 95' x 24' (243.2 x 29.7 x 7.3 m)

2 x 10-cylinder MAN-B+W diesel engines via twin screw.
Cruise ship operated by Holland-America Lines.
Built by Meyer Weft Shipyard, Papenburg, for Home Lines as the HOMERIC (1986) at a cost of US$145,000,000.

WESTERNLAND (1930)

16313 grt; 550 psrs
601' x 68' x 41'2" depth (182.1 x 20.6 x 12.5 m)
Harland & Wolff Ltd combination 4-cylinder triple expansion and turbine engines via triple screw.
Broken up for scrap at Blyth in 1947. Ex-Red Star Line.
Laid down in 1913 as an un-named cargo vessel and completed as the passenger ship REGINA (1918) by Harland & Wolff Ltd, Glasgow, for the Dominion Line.

WESTERN OCEAN (1930)

4828 grt; 212 psrs
400' x 48' x 27'5" depth (123 x 14.5 x 10.3 m)
Newport News 3-cylinder triple expansion engine via single screw.
Abandoned at sea in 1934.
Built by Newport News Shipbuilding, Newport News, Virginia, for the Cromwell Steamship Co as the COMUS (1900).

WESTERN PRINCE (1929)

10926 grt; 102 psrs
516' x 65' x 26'6" (156.4 x 19.7 x 8.1 m)
Kincaid-B+W 16-cylinder diesel engines via quadruple screw.
Sank with the loss of 16 lives, on 14 December 1940, after being torpedoed twice by the German U-96 500 miles (840 km) west of the Orkney Islands.
Built by Napier & Miller Ltd, Glasgow, for Furness, Withy & Co, London.

WESTERN WORLD (1922) See LEONARD WOOD, US (APA-12) (1941)

WESTERWALD (1908) See LIMA (1916)

WEST INDIAN (1954) See TAIPOOLOY (1958)

WESTMEATH (1912) See NORDICO (1926)

WESTMINSTER (1903)

3726 grt; 170 psrs
400' x 40' x 28'7" depth (121.9 x 12.3 x 8.7 m)
William Denny 4-cylinder quadruple expansion engines via single screw.
Broken up for scrap at Genoa in 1903.
Built by the Barrow Shipbuilding Company, Barrow, for the Ducal Line as the DUKE OF WESTMINSTER (1882).

WESTMOUNT (1902) See C. LOPEZ Y LOPEZ (1905)

WESTPHALIA (1923) See GENERAL ARTIGAS (1930)

WEST POINT, USS (AP-23) (1942) See AMERICAN STAR (1993)

WESTRALIA (1929) See WOOLAMBI (1961)

WEST STAR (1970) See XING HU (1979)

WESTWARD (1990) See BLACK WATCH (1996)

WHAKATANE (1900) See MONCENISIO (1924)

WHARTON, USS (AP-7) (1939)
13788 grt; 430 psrs
535' x 72' x 27'8" depth (156.4 x 21.8 x 8.4 m)
4 x Westinghouse DRG turbine engines via twin screw.
Broken up for scrap by Boston Metals in Baltimore, Maryland, in 1952. Ex-US Maritime Commission following decommissioning from the US Navy in 1947.
Laid down by the New York Shipbuilding Corporation for the Matson Line as the MANMASCO (1919) and completed as the SEA GIRT (1919). Renamed SOUTHERN CROSS (1920 – Munson Line).

WHITE PALACE (1924) See CITY OF HONOLULU (1927)

WHITE SANPO 2 (1981) See SUPERFERRY 14 (2000)

WICKERSHAM (1968) See SARDEGNA BELLA (1994)

WICKLOW (1970)
8644 grt; 550 psrs
468' x 63' x 26'6" (142.6 x 19.2 x 8.1 m)
Geared turbine via single screw.
Broken up as a cargo ship for scrap at Whampoa in 1974. Ex-Wicklow Shipping Co, Gibraltar.
Built by William Denny & Bros Ltd, Dumbarton, for the Indo-China Steam Navigation Company the EASTERN QUEEN (1950).

WID (1978) See SKROTADES (1987)

WILANOW (1975) See SPLIT 1700 (1997)

WILBO (1924)
4588 grt; 1350 psrs
415' x 46' x 27'9" depth (144.8 x 13.9 x 8.5 m)
Fairfield 3-cylinder triple expansion engine via single screw.
Broken up for scrap in Italy in 1924. Ex-German Line.
Built by Fairfield Shipbuilding & Engineering Co, Glasgow, for the Castle Line as the ARUNDEL CASTLE (1895). Renamed BIRMA (1905 – East Asiatic Line), MITAU (1909 – Russian American Line), BIRMA (1918 – East Asiatic Line) and JOSEF PILSUDSKI (1921 – Polish American Line).

WILCANNIA (1899) See ANDRE CHENIER (1921)

WILHELM GUSTLOFF (1937)
25484 grt; 1465 psrs
684' x 77' x 26'5" depth (207.3 x 23.3 x 8 m)
4 x 8-cylinder MAN diesel engines via twin screw.
Capsized and sank in 18 fathoms, with the loss of 5,196 lives, on 30 January 1945 after being torpedoed three times by the Soviet submarine S-13 in the Baltic Sea, near Stolpmunde. This is the worst recorded loss of life at sea to date.
Built by Blohm & Voss, Hamburg, for the German Workers' Front.

WILHELMINA (1909)
6975 grt; 146 psrs
451' x 54' x 33'6" depth (136.7 x 16.4 x 10.2 m)
Newport News 4-cylinder triple expansion engines via twin screw.
Sank on 2 December 1940 after being torpedoed west of the Hebrides.
Built by Newport News Shipbuilding & Drydock Co, Newport News, Virginia, for Matson Lines.

WILLARD A. HOLBROOK (1944)
14124 grt; 560 psrs
535' x 72' x 28' (162.1 x 21.8 x 8.5 m)
4 x turbines via twin screw.
Broken up for scrap at Baltimore, USA, in 1957 after an eight-year period laid up in the James river, Virginia. Ex-US Navy.
Laid down by the Bethlehem Shipbuilding Co, Sparrow's Point, for the US Shipping Board as the BERTICE (1920) and completed as the Type '535' transport BUCKEYE STATE (1921). Renamed PRESIDENT TAFT (1922 – Pacific Mail Line), GENERAL WILLARD A. HOLBROOK (1941 – US Army) and ARMIN W. LEUSCHNER (1943 – US Army).

Built by the Bethlehem Shipbuilding Co, Sparrow's Point, Maryland, for the US Shipping Board.

WILLEHAD (1894) See WYANDOTE (1917)

WILLEM RUYS (1947) See ACHILLE LAURO (1965)

WILLEMSTAD (1950) See MOOR B (1967)

WILLIAM (1992) See CESME STERN (1997)

WILLIAM AND MARY VICTORY (1945) See MENDOZA (1947)

WILLIAM CARSON (1958)
8273 grt; 262 psrs
58 cars + 6 trailers
351' x 70' x 19' (106.4 x 21.2 x 5.8 m)
6 x 12-cylinder Fairbanks-Morse diesel-electric engines via triple screw.
Sank bow first on 3 June 1977 off the coast of Labrador after striking Arctic icefloes.
Built by Canadian Vickers for Canadian National Railways as an ice-strengthened passenger-car ferry at a cost of US$11,200,000. The official delivery year of 1955 was formally registered prior to the discovery that the ship had been assigned to a specific route which could not be serviced without major and expensive reconstruction work. This was carried out at Channel-Port aux Basques, Newfoundland, and the maiden voyage was hence delayed until 1958.

WILLIAM O. DERBY, USAT (1946) See GENERAL WILLIAM O. DERBY, USNS (T-AP-127) (1950)

WILLIAM O'SWALD (1914) See LOMBARDIA (1935)

WILLIAM P. BIDDLE (1946)
8378 grt; 80 psrs
495' x 56' x 35'2" depth (150 x 17 x 10.7 m)
De Laval DRG turbine engine via single screw.
Broken up for scrap at Baltimore USA, in 1957. Ex-National Defence Reserve Fleet, James River, Virginia.
Laid down as the WAR SURF (1919) by the Bethlehem Shipbuilding Corporation, Alameda, California, for the British government, but completed as the freight ship ECLIPSE (1920) for the US government, to be operated by the Baltimore Mail Steamship Co, Baltimore, Maryland. Renamed CITY OF HAMBURG (1931 – Baltimore Mail Line) and CITY OF SAN FRANCISCO (1938 – Panama Pacific Line), prior to acquisition by the US Navy as the WILLIAM P. BIDDLE (AP-15) (1940).

WILLIAM POPE (1971) See HOLIDAY ISLAND (1971)

WILLIAM WARD BURROWS, USS (AP-6) (1940)
4577 grt; 117 psrs
371' x 53' x 21'11" (112.4 x 16.1 x 6.4 m)
B+W diesel engines via twin screw.
Broken up for scrap at Long Beach, California, in 1957. Ex-US Navy.
Built by Burmeister & Wain, Copenhagen, for the Grace Line as the SANTA RITA (1929).

WILLINES MABUHAY 2 (1994) See SUPERFERRY 7 (1994)

WILLINES MABUHAY 3 (1995) See SUPERFERRY 8 (1996)

WILLINES MABUHAY 5 (1986) See SUPERFERRY 9 (1995)

WILLINES MABUHAY 6 (1995) See OUR LADY OF GOOD VOYAGE (1999)

WILLOCHRA (1913) See FORT VICTORIA (1920)

WILTSHIRE (1912)
10390 grt; 131 psrs
544' x 61' x 33' (165.8 x 18.5 x 10 m)
Quadruple expansion engines via twin screw.
Abandoned as a total loss after she ran aground in a violent storm, on 30 May

1922, and broke in two the next day on the rocks of Rosalie Bay, Great Barrier Island, New Zealand.
Built by John Brown & Co Ltd, Clydebank, for the Federal Steam Navigation Co.

WIMMERA (1904)
3022 grt; 260 psrs
335' x 43' x 20'6" (102.1 x 13.1 x 6.2 m)
Triple expansion engine via single screw.
Sank on 16 August 1918 in 30 minutes, with the loss of 27 lives, after striking a mine laid by the German raider WOLFF.
Built by Caird & Co, Greenock, for Huddart Parker & Co Ltd.

WINCHESTER CASTLE (1930)
20001 grt; 587 psrs
657' x 75' x 32' (199.1 x 22.7 x 9.7 m)
2 x 10-cylinder B+W diesel engines via twin screw.
Broken up for scrap at Mihara in 1960.
Built by Harland & Wolff Ltd, Belfast, for the Union Castle Line.

WINDHUK (1937) See LEJEUNE, USS (AP-74) (1944)

WIND SONG (1988)
5703 grt; 148 psrs
442' x 53' x 14' (134 x 16 x 4.2 m)
3 x 6-cylinder Wartsila diesel-electric engines via single screw.

Motor-sailer cruise ship owned by Carnival Cruise Lines and operated by their subsidiary Windstar Cruises, Nassau.
Built by Ateliers et Chantiers du Havre.

WINDSOR CASTLE (1922)
18967 grt; 604 psrs
686' x 72' x 32' (207.9 x 21.8 x 9.7 m)
Parsons SRG oil-fired turbine engines via twin screw.
Sank on 23 March 1943, with the loss of one life, after being attacked by a German torpedo bomber 110 miles north-west of Cape Tenes, Algeria.
Built by John Brown & Co Ltd, Clydebank, for the Union Castle Line.

WINDSOR CASTLE (1960) See MARGARITA L (1977)

WIND SPIRIT (1998)
14983 grt; 386 psrs
617' x 66' x 16'6" (187 x 20 x 5 m)
4 x 6-cylinder Wartsila diesel engines via twin screw.
Motor-sailer cruise ship owned by Carnival Cruise Lines and operated by Windstar Cruises, Bahamas.
Built by Societe Nouvelle des Ateliers et Chantiers du Havre for Club Med, Marseilles, as the CLUB MED II (1992) at a French-government subsidised cost of US$100,000,000.

WIND STAR (1986)
5307 grt; 148 psrs
442' x 53' x 14' (134 x 16 x 4.2 x 4.2 m)
3 x 6-cylinder Wartsila diesel-electric engines via twin screw.

Motor/sailer cruise ship owned by Carnival Cruise Lines and operated by their subsidiary Windstar Cruises, Nassau.
Built by Societe Nouvelle des Ateliers et Chantiers du Havre.

WIND SURF (1997)
14745 grt; 312 psrs
617' x 66' x 16'6" (187 x 20 x 5 m)
4 x 8-cylinder Wartsila diesel- electric engines via twin screw.

Owned by Carnival Cruise Lines which purchased the ship for US$45,000,000 and operates it through their subsidiary Windstar Cruises, Nassau.
Laid down by Societe Nouvelle des Ateliers et Chantiers de Havre for Club Med as the LA FAYETTE 1988) at a cost of US$100,000,000. Renamed CLUB MED (1989 – Club Med) and CLUB MED 1 (1990 – Club Med).

WINDWARD (1993) See NORWEGIAN WIND (1998)

WINDWARD PRIDE (1997) See BALTIC KRISTINA (1997)

WING SANG (1938) See TAIPOOLOY (1958)

WING SHING (1921)
5206 grt; 1080 psrs
411' x 48' x 30'5" depth (125.1 x 14.7 x 9.2 m)
4-cylinder quadruple expansion engine via single screw.
Wrecked in Hong Kong on 18 August 1923. Ex-Lau Wei Chun.
Built by William Denny & Bros, Dumbarton, for British India Line as the JELUNGA (1890). Renamed SANTIAGO (1895 – Cia Trasatlantica), JELUNGA (1896 – British India Line) and JEHANGIR (1914 – Lau Wei Chun).

WINNEBA (1957)
8355 grt; 105 psrs
468' x 61' x 25' (141.8 x 18.5 x 7.6 m)
Triple expansion engine via twin screw.
Broken up for scrap at Antwerp, Belgium, in 1963. Ex-Elder Dempster Lines.
Built by Swan Hunter, Newcastle, for the Natal Line as the UMGENI (1938).

WINONA (1972) See HUI HSING (1974)

WINRICH VON KNIPRODE (1940) See KERGUELEN (1945)

WINSTON CHURCHILL (1967) See MAYAN EMPRESS (1996)

WIRAKEL (1953) See CITY OF TARANTO (1989)

WISCONSIN (1929) See KASZUBY (1957)

WISMAR II (1994) See NORRONA (1996)

WISTERIA (1995) See BENI ANSAR (2000)

WISTERIA (1998) See BENI ANSAR (2000)

WITTEKIND (1894) See FREEDOM (1919)

WOLFE, HMS (1939)
16418 grt; 1810 psrs
575' x 70' x 27'6" (174.2 x 21.1 x 8.4 m)
DRG turbine engines via twin screw.
Broken up for scrap as an armed merchant cruiser at Faslane in 1952. Ex-British Ministry of Transport.
Built by John Brown & Co Ltd, Clydebank, for Canadian Pacific Steamships as the MONTCALM (1921).

WOLVERINE STATE (1921) See KACHIDOKI MARU (1942)

WOOLAMBI (1961)
8108 grt; 344 psrs
448' x 60' x 33'6" (136.5 x 18.2 x 10.2 m)
2 x 8-cylinder Harland & Wolff diesel-type engines via twin screw.
Broken up for scrap in Japan in 1962. Ex-Asian & Pacific Shipping Co Ltd, Suva.
Built by Harland & Wolff Ltd, Belfast, for Huddart Parker & Co Ltd as the WESTRALIA (1929). Renamed DELFINO (1959 – Asian & Pacific Shipping Co, Suva).

WOOLOOMOOLOO (1891) See KHARTUM (1919)

WOOSTER VICTORY (1945) See MONTSERRAT (1957)

WORCESTERSHIRE (1931) See KANNON MARU (1961)

WORKENDAM (1889) See HARBIN (1900)

WORLD DISCOVERER (1976)
3724 grt; 139 psrs
280' x 50' x 15' (85.3 x 15.2 x 4.5 m)
2 x 8-cylinder Atlas-MaK diesel engines via twin screw.

Declared a total constructive loss after she was virtually stripped bare of her fittings and structural items by the local militia who were in rebellious mood following political upheaval in the Solomon Islands Group. This followed this ice-strengthened cruise ship being ripped open by a topical coral reef at 4.00 pm on 30 April 2000 and beached on Ngella Island by her captain, after ferrying all passengers and some crew members to shore. Her owners, tradco

Cruises Inc, were unable to place a salvage team on board..
Launched by Unterweser AG, Hamburg, for Bewa Cruises as the BEWA DISCOVERER (1973) and completed as the DISCOVERER (1974). She was chartered out for two years by the shipyard following the collapse of Bewa Cruises during construction.

WORLD DISCOVERER II (2000)
6057grt; 299 psrs
354' x 50' x 14'6" (107.3 x 15.2 x 4.4 m)
2 x 6-cylinder Wartsila-Vasa diesel engines via twin screw.

Ice-strengthened cruise ship owned by SK Shipping Co Ltd, South Korea, and operated by Society Expeditions, USA.
Built by Rauma-Repola for Delfin Cruises (and phoenix Maritime Shipping Inc, Panama) as the DELFIN CLIPPER (1989). Renamed SALLY CLIPPER (1990 – Delfin Cruises), DELFIN STAR (1995 – Delfin Cruises) and DREAM 21 (1997 – SK Shipping Co Ltd, South Korea).

WORLD OF RESIDENSEA (2001) See THE WORLD OF RESIDENSEA (2001)

WORLD RENAISSANCE (1978) See WORLD RENAISSANCE (1998)

WORLD RENAISSANCE (1998)
11724 grt; 550 psrs
492' x 69' x 20' (149.1 x 20.1 x 6.1 m)
4 x 7-cylinder B+W-type diesel engines via twin screw.

Owned and operated by Royal Olympic Cruises, Greece, after her purchase from the PT Modesi Group's subsidiary Klub Awani, Indonesia, but again for sale in 1999 for US$16,000,000.
Built by Pennhoet, St Nazaire, for Cie Francaise de Navigation as the RENAISSANCE (1966). Renamed HOMERIC (1977 – Epirotiki Cruises), WORLD RENAISSANCE (1978 – Epirotiki Cruises) and AWANI DREAM (1996 – Klub Awani, Indonesia).

WORLD WIDE EXPO (1982) See PRINCESS OF SCANDINAVIA (1991)

WOUDRICHEM (1915) See IRIS (1924)

WURTEMBERG (1921) See JAN WELLEM (1935)

WURZBURG (1900) See LOANDA (1925)

WYANDOTTE (1917)
4761 grt; 1301 psrs

383' x 46' x 27'2" (116.9 x 14 x 8.2 m)
Blohm & Voss 6-cylinder triple expansion engine via twin screw.
Broken up for scrap at Baltimore in 1924. Ex-US government.
Built by Blohm & Voss, Hamburg, for North German Lloyd as the WILLEHAD (1894).

WYANDRA (1902)
4058 grt; 350 psrs

341' x 46' x 25'4" (103.3 x 14 x 7.7 m)
Triple expansion engine via single screw.
Broken up for scrap in Nagoya in 1926 for a tender figure of US$17,000.
Built by A Stephen & Sons, Glasgow, for the Australasian United Steam Navigation Co Ltd.

WYREEMA (1908) See DOM PEDRO I (1926)

XIANG XUE LAN (1996)
12304 grt; 348 psrs
293 TEUs
497' x 79' x 24' (150.5 x 24 x 7.2 m)
2 x 6-cylinder Krupp-MaK diesel engines via single screw.
Passenger-container ship owned and operated by Hinterland Chartering SA, Hong Kong.
Built by MTW Schiffswerft, Wismar.

XI DING XIANG (1996) See ARAFURA LILY (1996)

XING HU (1979)
4438 grt; 268 psrs
346' x 52' x 14' (104.9 x 15.8 x 4.3 m)
2 x 9-cylinder B+W diesel engines via twin screw.
Passenger ship owned and operated on the Chinese coastal service by the government of China, but currently laid up in the Pearl river at Guangzhou

awaiting sale at an estimated US$1,000,000.
Built by Soc Espanola de Construccion de Naval SA, Cadiz, for Cruceros Lines as the CABO IZZARA (1967). Renamed WEST STAR (1970 – West Line) and DONA MONTSERRAT (1975 – Negros Navigation Inc, Manila).

XIN JIAN ZHEN (1994)
14543 grt; 355 psrs
218 TEUs
517' x 48' x 20' (156.7 x 14.8 x 6.2 m)
2 x 14-cylinder Pielstick diesel engines via twin screw.
Passenger-container ship owned and operated by the China-Japan International Ferry Company on the Kobe–Osaka–Yokohama–Shanghai service.
Built by the Onomichi Dockyard Co, Kobe.

XX ANIVERSARIO (1973)
7215 grt; 182 psrs
432' x 57' x 23' (130.9 x 17.3 x 7 m)
9-cylinder Stork-Werkspoor diesel engine via single screw.
Military training and troopship in the service of the Cuban government.
Built by NV Scheppesbouwerfe Gebroeders Pot, Bolnes, for the Royal Netherlands Steamship Co as the passenger ship ORANJE NASSAU (1957).

YAHIKO MARU (1904)
3172 grt; 300 psrs
330' x 42' x 23'4" (100 x 12.9 x 7.1 m)
3-cylinder Blair & Company triple expansion engine via single screw.
Owned by Itaya Shosen Kabishiki Kaisha, she was wrecked and abandoned on 2 May 1920 in the Tsugaru Strait, Japan.
Built by Raylton Dixon & Company, Middlesbrough, for North German Lloyd as the passenger ship GULF OF MEXICO (1893). Renamed VIENNA (1898 – Austro-Americana Steamship Company) and VEGA (1900 – J White, Genoa).

YALE, USS (1898) See PHILADELPHIA (1920)

YALE (1907) See GREYHOUND, USS (IX-106) (1943)

YAMAL (1992)
20646 grt; 100 psrs
495' x 69' x 36' (150 x 20.9 x 10.9 m)
2 x nuclear reactors via triple screw.
Icebreaker cruising Antarctic for the Murmansk Shipping Company, Murmansk.
Built by Baltyyskiy Sudost, St Petersburg.

YAMUNA (1898) See ULTONIA (1900)

YAMUNA (1902) See SLAVONIA (1904)

YAN JING (1990)
9960 grt; 442 psrs
446' x 68' x 20'6" (135 x 20.6 x 6.3 m)
Pielstick 18-cylinder engine via single screw.
Passenger ferry owned and operated by the Tianjin Jinshen Ferry Co Ltd, Tianjin.
Built by Onomichi Shipbuilding, Onomichi.

YAO HUA (1967) See ORIENT PRINCESS (1987)

YAPEYU (1951) See IRAN CREMONA (1980)

YARA (1974)
4129 grt; 989 psrs
324' x 50' x 18' (98.7 x 15.2 x 5.5 m)
2 x 7-cylinder British Polar diesel engines via single screw.
Operating on the service between Saudi Arabia and the Sudan since 1990 for Fayez Trading & Shipping Establishment, Jeddah.
Built by Evans Deakin Ltd, Brisbane, for the State Shipping Co, Perth, as the passenger ship KANGAROO (1962). Renamed HONG KONG FIR (1973 – Cia de Navigation Abeto, Hong Kong).

YARMOUTH (1926) See ELIZABETH A (1967)

YARMOUTH (1958) See ELIZABETH A (1967)

YARMOUTH CASTLE (1954) See ELIZABETH A (1967)

YARMOUTH CASTLE (1957) See ELIZABETH A (1967)

YARMOUTH CASTLE (1964)
5043 grt; 306 psrs
379' x 56' x 20' (114.8 x 17 x 6.1 m)
Turbine engines via single screw.
In the ownership of Yarmouth Cruise Lines, she sank in five hours at 6.15 am on 13 November 1965, with the loss of 94 lives, in the North West Providence Channel, Bahamas. Fire had swept through every deck from a storage area in Cabin 610.
Built by William Cramp & Sons Shipbuilding & Engine Building Co, Philadelphia, Pennsylvania, for Eastern Steamship Lines as the passenger ship EVANGELINE (1927).

YARRAWONGA (1891) See HERMIONE (1903)

YASAKA MARU (1914)
10932 grt; 512 psrs
505' x 64' x 33'4" depth (153 x 19.4 x 10.1 m)
Kawasaki Dockyard 6-cylinder triple expansion engines via twin screw.
Sank on 21 December 1915 after being torpedoed by the German U-38 60 miles (100 km) from Port Said, Egypt. No lives were lost as the French destroyer LABORIEUX rescued 268 passengers and crew.
Built by Kawasaki Dockyard for NYK, Japan, as a passenger ship.

YASUKUNI MARU (1930)
11930 grt; 315 psrs
527' x 64' x 28'9" (160 x 19.4 x 8.8 m)
Sulzer 20-cylinder diesel engines via twin screw.
Sank on 31 January 1944 after being torpedoed north-west of the Truk Islands by USS TRIGGER.
Built by Mitsubishi, Nagasaki, for NYK, Japan, as a passenger ship.

YAWATA MARU (1940) See UNYO (1942)

YELLOWSTONE (1965)
11034 grt; 550 psrs
523' x 72' x 24' (158.5 x 21.8 x 7.3 m)
Geared turbine engine via single screw.
Owned and operated by Rio Grande Transport Inc as a bulk carrier, she sank on 13 June 1978 after a collision with the Algerian ship IBN BATOUTA 77 miles south-east of Gibraltar.
Built by the Kaiser Corporation, Vancouver, Washington, for the US Shipping Administration as the C4-S-A3 troop transport MARINE PERCH (1945) which operated as a migrant ship after World War Two.

YERMAK (1973)
14058 grt; 85 psrs
443' x 86' x 36' (135 x 26.1 x 11 m)
9 x 12-cylinder Sulzer diesel-electric engines via triple screw.
Expedition icebreaker-cruise vessel owned by the Russian government and operated by the Far East Shipping Company, Vladivostok.
Built by Wartsila, Helsinki.

YESILADA (1971)
3100 grt; 890 psrs
288' x 52' x 14' (87.2 x 15.7 x 4.2 m)
4 x 12-cylinder B+W diesel engines via twin screw.
Passenger-ferry operated by Turkish Maritime Lines, Istanbul.
Built by Aalborg Vaerft AS, Aalborg, for AS Larvik Frederikshavn Ferjen, Larvik, as the PETER WESSEL (1968).

YEYE (1991) See CALEDONIA (1997)

YOFU MARU (1971) See VERGINA SKY (1992)

YOKOHAMA MARU (1912)
6143 grt
406' x 49' x 27'6" (123 x 14.8 x 8.4 m)
Mitsubishi 6-cylinder triple expansion engines via twin screw.
Sank on 10 March 1942 after a US aircraft attack.
Built by Mitsubishi Dockyard for NYK.

YONGALA (1903)
3664 grt; 240 psrs
350' x 45' x 27'2" depth (106.1 x 13.7 x 8.2 m)
Wallsend Slipway 3-cylinder triple expansion engine via single screw.
Sank on 23 March 1911 during a cyclone between Mackay and Townsville, Queensland, but the actual position was unknown until the ship was discovered in 1958, off Cape Bowling Green near Townsville. There was evidence that she had capsized.
Built by Armstrong Whitworth & Co, Newcastle, for the Adelaide Steamship Company as a passenger ship.

YONG LIAN (1995) See DVD No. 1 (1999)

YONG LIAN (1997) See DVD No. 1 (1999)

YONG QIANG (1997) See DVD II (1999)

YORCK (1906)
8976 grt; 1460 psrs
481' x 57' x 35'5" depth (145.8 x 17.3 x 10.8 m)
F Schichau 8-cylinder quadruple expansion engines via twin screw.
Broken up for scrap in Elbing, Danzig, in 1932.
Built by F Schichau, Danzig, for North German Lloyd as a passenger ship.

YORK (1963) See FANTASIA (1964)

YORK (1964) See YORK MARU (1974)

YORK MAR (1964) See YORKMARU (1974)

YORK MARU (1974)
11421 grt; 3000 psrs
523' x 72' x 32'10" (158.5 x 21.8 x 9.7 m)
2 x Westinghouse geared turbine engine via single screw.
Broken up for scrap in Spain in 1974. Ex-Hou Yung Steamship Company.
Built by the Kaiser Corporation, Richmond, California, for the US Navy as the Class C4-S-A1 troop transport GENERAL H. L. SCOTT (AP-136) (1944). Renamed YORKMAR (1964 – Bethlehem Steel Corporation Shipping Division).

YORKSHIRE (1889) See ESTONIA (1907)

YORKSHIRE (1920)
10184 grt; 305 psrs
504' x 58' x 32' (152.7 x 17.6 x 9.7 m)
2 x DRG turbine engines via twin screw.
Sank on 17 October 1939, with the loss of 58 lives, after being torpedoed by the German U-37 250 miles north-west of Cape Finisterre.
Built by Harland & Wolff Ltd, Belfast, for the Bibby Line.

YOSHINO MARU (1921)
8950 grt; 322 psrs
480' x 58' x 29' (145.5 x 17.6 x 8.8 m)
8-cylinder quadruple expansion engines via twin screw.
Broken up for scrap in Japan in 1938. Ex-NYK, which was given the ship by the government of Japan as part of World War One reparations.
Built by the Schichau Company, Danzig, for North German Lloyd as the passenger ship KLEIST (1906).

YOTEI MARU (1948)
3896 grt; 1126 psrs
18 railway wagons
392' x 52' x 15'6" (118.7 x 15.9 x 4.7 m)
Passenger-train ferry housed in the Museum of Maritime Science, Tokyo, since 1965.
Built by Mitsubishi Heavy Industries, Kobe, for the government of Japan (Department of Railways).

YOTEI MARU (1965)
8311 grt; 1200 psrs
48 rail coaches
392' x 52' x 17'2" (118.7 x 15.9 x 5.2 m)
8 x 12-cylinder B+W diesel engines via twin screw.
Passenger-train ferry now housed in the Museum of Maritime Sciences, Tokyo.
Built by Hitachi Shipbuilding & Engineering Co, Sakurajima, for the government of Japan (Department of Railways).

YPIRANGA (1911) See BISCO 9 (1950)

YUCATAN (1890) See SHINKAI MARU (1911)

YUCATAN (1935) See SHAMROCK (1943)

YUFU (1971) See VERGINA SKY (1993)

YU HUA (1974) See HERBERT (1996)

YU JIN XIANG (1995)
12304 grt; 348 psrs
489' x 75' x 20' (148.2 x 22.7 x 6.1 m)
2 x 9-cylinder Zgoda-Sulzer diesel engines via twin screw.
Owned and operated by China Shipping Container Lines, Shanghai.
Built by Merwede, Hardinxveld.

YUKON (1923)
5747 grt; 199 psrs
360' x 50' x 32'2" depth (109.1 x 15.2 x 9.8 m)
William Cramp & Sons 6-cylinder triple expansion engines via twin screw.
Abandoned as a total loss when she was wrecked on 4 February 1946 in Johnstone Bay, Prince William Sound.
Built by William Cramp & Sons Co, Philadelphia, Pennsylvania, for the New York & Cuba Mail Steamship Co as the passenger ship MEXICO (1899). Renamed COLON (1905 – Isthmian Canal Commission, Panama).

YUM (1982) See LEROS (1997)

YU MEI (1991)
5703 grt; 180 psrs
403' x 56' x 24' (122.2 x 17 x 7.4 m)
Sulzer 5-cylinder diesel engine via single screw.
Broken up in China in 1998 as an ice-strengthened training ship operated by Xiamen Cheng Yi Shipping, which ceased carrying passengers from the first year of ownership, 1991. Ex-government of China.
Built by Stocznia Szczecinska, Szczecin, for the government of Poland as the passenger-cargo ship ANTONI GARNUSZEWSKI (1974).

YUMURI (1889) See ROSE ISLE (1930)

YURI DOLGORUKY (1950)
25377 grt; 950 psrs
681' x 72' x 42'1" depth (206.4 x 21.8 x 12.8 m)
8 x Blohm & Voss SRG turbine engines via twin screw.
Broken up for scrap as a Russian government whaling fleet mother ship in 1977.
Launched as the passenger ship HAMBURG (1926) but not completed until 1936 by Blohm & Voss, Hamburg, for the Hamburg-America Line. During World War Two she was sunk as a German navy accommodation ship by a mine near Sassnitz, Germany, on 7 March 1945. She was refloated in 1950 and rebuilt by the Russians on the island of Rugen.

YURI DOLGORUKY (1950) See YURI DOLGORUKI (1950)

YUTE (1916)
4740 grt
400' x 44' x 27' (121.9 x 13.5 x 8.2 m)
2 x D Rollo & Sons quadruple expansion engines via single screw.
Owned by Cia Navigation Gui, Puzcuana, she disappeared without trace about 17 November 1920 after being in distress 240 miles (400 km) south of Cape May, Delaware.
Built by Barrow Shipbuilding Company, Barrow-in-Furness, for George Warren & Company as the BORDERER (1884). Renamed RIOJANO (1897 – MM de Arrotagui).

Z

ZAANDAM (1939)
10909 grt; 140 psrs
502' x 64' x 33'3" (152.1 x 19.4 x 10.1 m)
2 x 6-cylinder MAN diesel engines via twin screw.
Sank on 2 November 1942, with the loss of 130 lives, after being torpedoed twice by the German U-174 400 miles (666 km) off Cape Recife, Brazil.
Built by Wilton-Fijenoord, Schiedam, for the Holland America Line as a passenger ship.

ZAANDAM (2000)
63000 grt; 1440 psrs
780' x 106' x 26'6" (238 x 32.2 x 8 m)
5 x 12-cylinder Sulzer diesel engines via twin screw.

Cruise ship operated by Holland-America.
Built by Fincantieri, Marghera, at a cost of US$300,000,000.

ZACAPA (1909)
4937 grt; 103 psrs
379' x 50' x 25' (114.8 x 15.2 x 7.6 m)
Triple expansion engine via single screw.
Broken up for scrap at Bordertown, New Jersey, in 1949.
Built by Workman, Clark & Company, Belfast, for the Tropical Fruit Steamship Company.

ZAGREB (1947) See ARMELLE (1968)

ZAHRET MISR (1993) See AL SALAM TABA I (1998)

ZAKROS (1971)
9957 grt
518' x 65' x 30' (157 x 19.6 x 9 m)
8-cylinder Gotaverken diesel engines via single screw.
Passenger-cargo ferry owned by a joint venture of ANEK and Minoan Lines, Piracus.
Built by AS Framnaes MV, Sandefjord, for Willy Oppens Rederi AS as the oil tanker EMERALD (1953). Renamed MORGEDAL (1962 – F Tenvig & Co, Oslo), FERMITA (1964 – Ugland Shipping Co AS) and EFTHYCOSTA II (1969 – Constantine S Efthymiadis).

ZAMBOANGA (1989)
5747 grt; 896 psrs
386' x 63' x 18' (117 x 19 x 5.4 m)
2 x 14-cylinder Pielstick diesel engines via twin screw.
Passenger ferry operated by William, Gothong & Aboitiz in the Philippines.
Built by Niigata Engineering Co, Niigata, for WG & A, Manila, as the EMERALD AMAMI (1975). Renamed FERRY AMAMI (1987 – Oshima Unyu KK, Naze).

ZAMZAM (1933)
8059 grt; 235 psrs
467' x 54' x 28' (141.5 x 16.4 x 8.5 m)
Quadruple expansion engines via twin screw.

Under the ownership of the Misr Line, she sank on 17 April 1941, with the loss of 331 lives, when the German raider TAMESIS opened fire on this neutral vessel in the South Atlantic, four days out from Capetown.
Built by Harland & Wolff Ltd, Belfast, for the Bibby Line as the LEICESTERSHIRE (1909). Renamed BRITISH EXHIBITOR (1931 – British National Exhibition Ship Ltd).

ZAM ZAM (1975)
5173 grt; 268 psrs
383' x 54' x 19' (116.1 x 16.4 x 5.8 m)
2 x 8-cylinder Fiat diesel engines via twin screw.
Operating as a pilgrim ship for Orri Navigation Lines, Jeddah.
Built by Cantiere Navale Di Taranto for Adriatica Lines as the passenger ship ENOTRIA (1951).

ZAYATTHIA (1899) See GWALIOR (1900)

ZEALANDIA (1910)
7995 grt; 1116 psrs
443' x 56' x 27' (134.1 x 17 x 8.2 m)
A Stephen & Sons 6-cylinder triple expansion engines via twin screw.
Broken up in Holland in 1935.
Built by Alexander Stephen & Sons, Glasgow, for Royal Holland Lloyd as a passenger ship.

ZEALANDIA (1910)
6683 grt; 446 psrs
410' x 55' x 23' (124.2 x 16.7 x 7 m)
John Brown 8-cylinder quadruple expansion engines via twin screw.
Broken up by Japanese salvage merchants in 1957 where she lay. She had been sunk during a Japanese bomber attack on Darwin harbour, Australia, on 19 February 1942. Three lives had been lost in the incident.
Built by John Brown & Co Ltd, Clydebank, for Huddart Parker Ltd.

ZEALANDIC (1911) See MAMARI (1932)

ZEELAND (1901) See MINNESOTA (1927)

ZEELAND (1920) See MINNESOTA (1927)

ZEELAND (1984) See MARKO POLO (1988)

ZEILIN (1940) See PRESIDENT JACKSON (1946)

ZEILIN, USS (AP-9) (1942) See PRESIDENT JACKSON (1946)

ZEILIN, USS (APA-3) (1942) See PRESIDENT JACKSON (1946)

ZENIT (1961)
4404 grt; 154 psrs
347' x 48' x 20'6" (105 x 14.4 x 6.2 m)
2 x 8-cylinder Gorlitzer diesel engines via single screw.
Operating for the Russian government as a student education ship.
Built by Neptun-Werft, Rostock.

ZENITH (1992)
47255 grt; 1374 psrs
682' x 95' x 24' (206.7 x 28.8 x 7.3 m)
2 x 9-cylinder & 2 x 6-cylinder MAN-B+W diesel engines via twin screw.

Cruise ship operated by Celebrity Cruise Lines.
Built by Jos L Meyer Shipyards, Papenburg, for the Chandris Group at a cost of US$210,000,000.

ZENITH (1995)
4943 grt; 1100 psrs
110 cars
376' x 57' x 15' (113.9 x 17.3 x 4.5 m)
2 x Pametrada DRG turbine engines via twin screw.
The vessel caught fire in the engine room, with the blaze quickly spreading upwards and then the ship listing 17 degrees and beaching on Arm Chair Island, in Hong Kong harbour. She had been on a delivery voyage to her new Chinese owners, Galaxy Shipholding SA, Hong Kong, in 1995. She was declared a total constructive loss and broken up for scrap at Hong Kong in 1996.
Built by Harland & Wolff Ltd, Belfast, for the British Transport Commission as the passenger-car ferry DUKE OF ARGYLL (1956). Renamed NEPTUNIA (1975 – Libra Maritime Company, Piraeus), CORINTHIA (1987 – Scanmed)), FAITH POWER (1993 – Power Sea Transportation SA) and FAIRY PRINCESS (1994).

ZENOBIA (1980)
10528 grt; 140 psrs
175 trailers
545' x 76' x 25' (165.2 x 23 x 7.7 m)
2 x 7-cylinder Sulzer diesel engines via twin screw.
Sank in five minutes in 1980 off Cyprus.
Built by Kockums Varv AB, Malmo, for the GSEL Line as a passenger-cargo ferry.

ZEPHIROS (1972) See NEPTUNE (1972)

ZEPPELIN (1915) See DRESDEN (1927)

ZERALDA (1976)
9747 grt; 1167 psrs
389' x 69' x 20' (118 x 20.8 x 6.1 m)
2 x 12-cylinder Pielstick diesel engines via twin screw.
Passenger ferry owned and operated by ENTMV.
Built by Nippon Kokan KK, Shimizu, for Japan Car Ferry KK, Tokyo, as the BOUGAINVILLEA (1971).

ZEUS (1971) See JUPITER (1971)

ZHE YING (1989) See YU MEI (1991)

ZHI LUO LAN (1982)
12470 grt; 952 psrs
515' x 69' x 22'8" (157 x 21 x 7.6 m)
7-cylinder Mitsubishi-Sulzer diesel engine via single screw.
Owned by the government of China and operated by Guangzhou Maritime

Transport (Group) Co, Guangzhou, the ship has been laid up pending a sale.
Built by Mitsubishi Industries Ltd, Kobe, for Nihon Sangyo Junko Mihonichi as the SAKURA MARU (1962). Renamed SAKURA (1971 – (Oshima Unyu KK., Naze).

ZI DING JIANG (1996) See ARAFURA LILY (1996)

ZIETEN (1903) See TUNGUE (1916)

ZION (1956) See DOLPHIN IV (1987)

ZI YU LAN (1996)
16071 grt
497' x 79' x 22'6" (150.5 x 24 x 6.9 m)
2 x 6-cylinder Krupp-MaK diesel engines via single screw.
Passenger-container ship owned and operated by the China Shipping Passenger Liner Co Ltd, Dalian.
Built by MTW Schiffswerft, Wismar, for the Hoi Wah Shipping Co.

ZUIDERDAM (1942)
12150 grt; 134 psrs
length 518' x beam 66' (157 x 20 m)
MAN diesel engines via twin screw.
Broken up for scrap in Ghent by Van Heyghen Freres in 1948 after being raised from the Nieuwe Waterweg, Rotterdam. She had been purposely sunk by the Germans to form a harbour blockade on 22 September 1944. She had also been sunk in an uncompleted state after being bombed on 28 August 1941, but was raised in 1942 and rebuilt.
Launched by Wilton-Fijenoord, Schiedam, for Holland America Lines in 1941 as a passenger ship.

ZUIDERKRUIS (1947) See ZUIDERKRUIS (A-853) (1963)

ZUIDERKRUIS (A-853) (1963)
9178 grt; 800 psrs
455' x 62' x 28' (138.7 x 18.9 x 8.5 m)
2 x General Electric DRG turbine engines via single screw.
Broken up for scrap in 1969 at Bilbao after serving as an accommodation and store ship for Den Helder Naval Base staff since 1963.
Built by the Oregon Shipbuilding Corporation, Portland, for the US Maritime Commission as the passenger-cargo ship CRANSTON VICTORY (1944). Renamed ZUIDERKRUIS (1947 – Royal Rotterdam Lloyd).

ZUNGERU (1904) See LEGAZPI (1911)

ZUNGERU (1908) See LEGAZPI (1911)

ZUR (1966) See ABU YUSSUF (1984)

ZVIR (1966) See ABU YUSSUF (1984)

Footnote
Every reference to a passenger vessel falling within the strict criteria of this book has been meticulously cross-referenced with all other publications. Now and again, there would be conflicting data. When this has occurred, I have sought out other information sources (ie shipyards, ship brokers, shipping companies, etc) and adopted a majority rules determination. That is, until the final arbiter comes into play: *Lloyds Register of Shipping*.

Epilogue

The old seafarers say that when a ship changes its name, it changes its luck!

In some instances, this has been so. But the number of alterations to ships' names, and the almost perpetual 'moving feast' of ferries swapping owners, routes, charterers and names, has done the majority of them little harm. Perhaps then we may look at the overall findings in preparing this Directory in that light.

Like human beings, who are split between those who lead a frenetic life or go from womb-to-tomb without any exciting events taking place, so does this seem to be true of the shipping industry, wherein ships can either go from the slipway to the scrapyard without any instance of note, or be confronted with all manner of 'happenings' on the way.

And the 'doomsdayers' of the mid-1960s, who claimed that aircraft and speedier communications, leading to speedier travel requirements, would spell death to passenger shipping, have seen a resurgence in shipbuilding and in tonnages that have been totally unforeseen. On a definite note of optimism for my beloved ships, the following pages of shipyard schedules featuring new buildings support the view that passenger vessels are here to stay and are gaining in technological advances which make them grander, safer and faster (if indeed sea travel should ever want to be fast).

During research for this book, it was evident that there were many more orders being contemplated by the industry. It was interesting to note the sudden downturn in interest in any significant new building within the ferry sector at this time, although the Greek ferry tragedy involving the sinking of the *Express Samina* on 27 September 2000, and the subsequent suspension of all Greek ferries pending an investigation, may accelerate new vessel order placements. And the Greek government's declaration that all Greek-registered ships would now have to be retired at 30 years of age (previously 35 years of age) will have repercussions benefiting the shipyards, which no doubt will see more new vessel orders being placed and contracts for conversions on those ships which have at least ten years' operational life in SOLAS terms left in them.

The intrusion of HSS and catamaran ferry designs, in combination with the English Channel tunnel operation and the withdrawal of duty-free shopping concessions to ferry passengers travelling between European ports, has had an impact on the immediate future plans of the ferry owners and operators. In the Scandinavian countries, massive arched bridges are being constructed over sounds and between islands to the delight of the everyday motorist, but alas the poor ferry operators! Even so, the limitations of catamaran ferries ('fair weather ferries') in generally not being able to handle bad weather elements in the Channel, North Sea, Baltic Sea, etc, will act as a deterrent for ferry companies considering changing from the traditional ferry designs. The high-speed ships will forge a niche in many fleets and do not present the problems showing up in the catamaran area. There is still a place for the 'new guard', but owners must take into account that their fleets cannot include vessels that may only operate for virtually half a year. And then the owners or operators have to attempt to place the vessel on charter in calmer waters somewhere else in the world.

Striking a positive note in this epilogue, the future still looks rewarding for the traditionalists. And this writer, for one, feels very comfortable after the turbulent upheaval within the passenger shipping trade in the 1960s. Apart from highly encouraging data releases from time-to-time by the various agencies monitoring the travel sector, I am supported by the sheer weight of evidence from public relation data sheets and bulletins issued by shipyards and shipping companies involved in creating brand new ships, as listed below. In round figures (as of the publication date of this book), there are 157 ships on order between 2001 and 2005, with a collective berth availability of 247,000 (an average of 1,575 per ship), a total gross tonnage of 7,774,000,000 (an average of 49,516 grt per ship), and a gross cost of US$41,500,000,000 (an average of US$264,000,000 per ship).

This list of new buildings represents firmly contracted ships, due for delivery in the specified year. Options taken out at the time of the firm contract signings, between the owner and the shipyard, could possibly double in future years if taken up. Data is included as known at the time of this book's publication.

So into the 'twenty-fast' century, with these initial ships and many more!

2001

ADVENTURE OF THE SEAS
142000 grt; 3144 psrs
1026' x 129' x 29'6" (310.9 x 39.1 x 10 m)
6 x 12-cylinder Wartsila diesel engines via triple screw.
In build by Kvaerner-Masa Yard, Turku, for the Royal Caribbean International Cruise Line at a cost of US$500,000,000.

BITHIA
35000 grt; 2781 psrs
700 cars + 70 trailers
708' x 87' x 21'8" (214.6 x 26.4 x 6.6 m)
4 x 12-cylinder Wartsila diesel engines via twin screw.
Passenger-car-trailer ferry for Tirrenia Navigazioni Lines.
Being built by Fincantieri, Castellammare di Stabia.

BLUE STAR CHIOS
10193 grt; 1800 psrs
420 cars or 135 cars + 60 trailers
409' x 62' x 16'8" (123.8 x 18.9 x 5.1 m)
4 x 9-cylinder Wartsila diesel engines via twin screw.
Passenger-car ferry for Strintzis Lines.
Being built by Hellenic Shipyards, Perama.

BLUE STAR MYKONOS
10193 grt; 1800 psrs
420 cars or 135 cars + 60 trailers
409' x 62' x 16'8" (123.8 x 18.9 x 5.1 m)
4 x 9-cylinder Wartsila diesel engines via twin screw.
Passenger-car ferry for Strintzis Lines.
Being built by Hellenic Shipyards, Perama.

CARNIVAL PRIDE
85700 grt; 2680 psrs
957' x 106' x 26' (290 x 32.2 x 7.8 m)
6 x 9-cylinder Wartsila 'smokeless' diesel engines via Azipod twin screw.
Cruise ship for Carnival Cruise Lines, Miami.
Being built by Kvaerner-Masa Yard, Helsinki, at a cost of US$375,000,000.

CARNIVAL SPIRIT
85619 grt; 2680 psrs
957' x 106' x 26' (290 x 32.2 x 7.8 m)
6 x 9-cylinder Wartsila 'smokeless' diesel engines via Azipod twin screw.
Cruise ship for Carnival Cruise Lines, Miami.
Being built by Kvaerner-Masa Yard, Helsinki, at a cost of US$375,000,000.

CONSTELLATION
91000 grt; 1950 psrs
length 925' x beam 105' (280.3 x 31.8 m)
Gas-electric turbine engines via twin screw.
Cruise ship for Celebrity Cruises.
Being built by Chantiers de l'Atlantique, St Nazaire.

DORO LONDO
14800grt; 2170 psrs
483' x 77' x 19'5" (146.5 x 23.4 x 5.9 m)

2 x 8-cylinder MAK diesel engines via twin screw.
Passenger ferry owned and operated by the government of Indonesia.
Being built by Meyer Werft, Papenburg.

EUROPEAN AMBASSADOR

24500grt; 405 psrs
375 cars + 123 trailers
561' x 79' x 19'8" (170 x 24 x 6 m)
4 x 18-cylinder Wartsila diesel engines via twin azimuthing screw.
Passenger-cargo ship for P&O Management Irish Sea.
Being built by Mitsubishi Heavy Industries, Shimonoseki.

EUROPEAN VISION

58600 grt; 1250 psrs
828' x 95' x 29' (251 x 28.8 x 8.8 m)
2 x GE Marine gas turbine engines via twin azimuthing screw.
Cruise ship for Festival/First European Cruises.
Being built by Chantiers de l'Atlantique, St Nazaire, at a cost of
Euro333,000,000.

FESTOS PALACE

30000 grt; 2200 psrs
1000 cars or 270 cars + 130 trailers
693' x 85' x 24' (210 x 25.8 x 7.3 m)
4 x 16-cylinder Wartsila diesel engines via twin screw.
Ferry for Minoan Shipping Lines.
Being built by Sestri Cantieri Navale, Genoa, at a cost of US$130,000,000.

GOLFO DEI CORALLI

17150 grt; 308 psrs
500 cars
649' x 77' x 20'8" (196.6 x 23.4 x 6.3 m)
2 x 9-cylinder Wartsila diesel engines via twin screw.
Ro Pax ferry for Sarda di Navigazione.
Being built by Stocznia Szczekinska Porta.

GOLDEN PRINCESS

108865 grt; 2600 psrs
951' x 118' x 26' (289.9 x 36 x 8 m)
6 x 16-cylinder Sulzer diesel engines via twin screw.
Cruise ship for P&O Princess Cruises
Being built by Fincantieri Navali Italiani, Monfalcone, at a cost of
US$450,000,000.

HELLENIC SPIRIT

32694 grt; 1850 psrs
654 cars or 106 cars + 107 trailers
4 x 12-cylinder Wartsila diesel engines via twin screw.
Passenger-car ferry owned and operated by ANEK, Greece.
Being built by Bruces Shipyard, Landskronar, and FOSEN Mek Verksteder,
Fevaagat, a cost of US$90,000,000.

INFINITY

90280grt; 2449 psrs
965' x 106' x 26' (292.4 x 32 x 7.9 m)
2 x GE Marine gas-electric turbine engines via twin Azipod screw.
Cruise ship for Celebrity Cruises.
Being built by Chantiers de l'Atlantique, St Nazaire, at a cost of
US$350,000,000.

KRITI IV

31500 grt; 1850 psrs
120 cars + 130 trailers
673' x 85' x 22'4" (204 x 25.8 x 6.8 m)
4 x 12-cylinder Wartsila diesel engines via twin screw.
Passenger-car trailer ferry for ANEK.
Hull being built by Bruces Shipyard, Landskronor, and to be completed by
Fosen Mek Versteder, Rissa.

KRITI V

31500 grt; 1850 psrs
120 cars + 130 trailers
673' x 85' x 22'4" (204 x 25.8 x 6.8 m)
4 x 12-cylinder Wartsila diesel engines via twin screw.

Passenger-car trailer ferry for ANEK.
Hull being built by Bruces Shipyard, Landskronor, and to be completed by
Fosen Mek Versteder, Rissa.
While on the slips, she was contracted to another party for delivery in 2002 as
the LEFKA ORI (2002).

MEGA EXPRESS 2

23700 grt; 1880 psrs
550 cars
570' x 82' x 21'8" (172.7 x 24 x 6.6 m)
4 x 12-cylinder Wartsila diesel engines via twin screw.
Cruise ferry for the Tourship Group, Italy.
Being built by Cantieri Navale Fratellia Orlandi, Italy, at a cost of
US$85,000,000.

MILLENNIUM II

87000 grt; 2524 psrs
965' x 106' x 26' (292.4 x 32 x 7.9 m)
2 x General Electric gas turbine engines via twin Azipod screw.
Cruise ship for Celebrity Cruises.
Being built by Chantiers de l'Atlantique, St Nazaire, at a cost of
US$350,000,000.

MOBY FREEDOM

Did not proceed with keel laying. Same data as MOBY WONDER.

MOBY WONDER

33500 grt; 1880 psrs
665 cars
578' x 92' x 23' (175 x 27.6 x 7 m)
4 x 12-cylinder Wartsila diesel engines via twin screw.
Ice-strengthened passenger-car ferry for Moby Lines (Nav Ar Ma), Italy.
Being built by Daewoo Heavy Industries, South Korea, at a cost of
US$155,000,000.

NEW RAINBOW BELL

23000 grt; 150 psrs
62 cars + 161 trailers
Length 598' x Beam 87' (181.3 x 26.4 m)
Cruise ferry being built for Kyuetsu Ferry, Japan, by Mitsubishi Heavy
Industries, Shimonoseki.

NILS HOLGERSSON

34500 grt; 744 psrs
627' x 97' x 20'6" (190 x 29.5 x 6.2 m)
5 x 8-cylinder Caterpillar-MaK diesel engines via twin azimuthing screw.
Passenger-cargo ferry for TT-Line GmbH, Hamburg.
Being built by SSW Fahr und Special Schiffbau GmbH, Bremerhaven.

NORWEGIAN STAR

91000 grt; 2244 psrs
851' x 106' x 26' (258 x 32 x 8 m)
4 x 14-cylinder MAN-B+W diesel-electric engines via twin Azipod screw.
Cruise ship for Norwegian Cruise Line.
Hull fabricated by Bremer Vulkan, Vegesack, with completion of the vessel by
Meyer Werft, Papenburg, at a total cost of $325,000,000.
Construction commenced as the SUPERSTAR LEO for Star Cruises, but
taken over by NCL following a policy shift by the two companies.

NORWEGIAN SUN

77104 grt; 2450 psrs
851' x 106' x 26'4" (258 x 32 x 8 m)
6 x 7-cylinder MAN-B + W diesel-electric engines via twin azimuthing screw.
'Sky Class' Cruise ship for Norwegian Cruise Line.
Having her hull fabricated by Mathias-Thesen Werft, Wismar, with
completion of the vessel being undertaken by Meyer-Werft, Papenburg, at a
total cost of US$325,000,000.

OCEANOS See OKEANOS below

OKEANOS

26995 grt; 1300 psrs
100 cars + 116 trailers
700' x 83' x 21'8" (212 x 25 x 6.6 m)

4 x 12-cylinder Wartsila diesel engines via twin screw.
Passenger-car-cargo ferry for Minoan Line Shipping SA.
Being built by Samsung Heavy Industries, Koje, at a cost of US$78,000,000.

PETER PAN
34500 grt; 744 psrs
627' x 97' x 20'6" (190 x 29.5 x 6.2 m)
5 x 7-cylinder Caterpillar- diesel engines via twin azimuthing screw.
Passenger-cargo ferry for TT-Line, Hamburg.
Being built by SSW Fahr und Special Schiffbau GmbH, Bremerhaven.

PRIDE OF HULL
59580 grt; 1360 psrs
250 cars + 400 trailers
710' x 104' x 20' (215 x 31.5 x 6 m)
4 x 9-cylinder MAN diesel engines via twin azimuthing screw
Cruise ferry for P&O North Sea Ferries Ltd.
Being built by Fincantieri, Marghera, at a cost of US$126,000,000.

PRIDE OF ROTTERDAM
59925 grt; 1360 psrs
250 cars + 400 trailers
710' x 104' x 20' (215 x 31.5 x 6 m)
4 x 9-cylinder MAN diesel engines via twin azimuthing screw
Cruise ferry for P&O North Sea Ferries Ltd.
Being built by Fincantieri, Marghera, at a cost of US$126,000,000.

PROMETHEUS
26995 grt; 1000 psrs
600 cars or 150 cars + 120 trailers
700' x 83' x 25' (212 x 25 x 6.6 m)
4 x 12-cylinder Wartsila diesel engines via twin screw.
Being built by Samsung Heavy Industries Co. Ltd., Koje, for Minoan Lines.

RADIANCE OF THE SEAS
90090 grt; 2500 psrs
970' x 106' x 28' (294 x 32.2 x 8.5 m)
2 x GE Marine diesel engines via twin Azipod screw.
'Vantage Class' cruise ship for Royal Caribbean International.
Being built by Meyer Werft, Papenburg, at a cost of US$350,000,000.

REGENT SKY
50000 grt; 1600 psrs
754' x 94' x 22' (228.6 x 28.5 x 6.7 m)
4 x 6-cylinder Wartsila diesel engines via twin azimuthing screw.
For sale after the collapse of Regent Cruises.
Being built by Gdanska, Poland.

R EIGHT
30277 grt; 684 psrs
594' x 84' x 19'6" (180 x 25.5 x 5.9 m)
4 x 12-cylinder Wartsila diesel engines via twin screw.
'R One class' cruise ship for Renaissance Cruises.
Being built by Chantiers de l'Atlantique, St Nazaire, at a cost of US$175,000,000.

SEA CHARIOT
12000 grt
498' x 66' x 14'9" (151 x 20 x 4.5 m)
2 x Wartsila diesel engines via twin screw.
Cruise ship for Omnium Enterprises, Panama.
Being built by MEKAP, Perama.

SEAFRANCE RODIN
34000 grt; 1900 psrs
700 cars or 120 trailers
611' x 92' x 21'5" (185 x 28 x 6.5 m)
4 x Wartsila diesel engines via twin screw.
Ro Pax ferry for SeaFrance.
Being built by Aker Finn Shipyards, Rauna, at a cost of US$125,000,000.

SEVEN SEAS MARINER
46500 grt; 769 psrs
713' x 95' x 21'5" (216 x 28.8 x 6.5 m)
2 x diesel engines via twin Azipod screw.

'New Class' cruise ship for V-Ships and Radisson Seven Seas Cruises.
Being built by Chantiers de l'Atlantique, St Nazaire, at a cost of US$300,000,000.

SILVER WHISPER
28258 grt; 388 psrs
601' x 82' x 19'8" (182 x 24.8 x 6 m)
4 x Wartsila diesel engines via twin azimuthing screw.
Cruise ship for Silversea Cruises.
Being built by T Mariotti Yard, Visentini, at a cost of US$150,000,000.

SOROLLA
28275 grt; 1000 psrs
166 cars + 99 trailers
568' x 86' x 20' (172 x 26.2 x 6.2 m)
4 x Wartsila diesel engines via twin azimuthing screw.
Passenger-car-cargo ferry for Transmediterranea.
Being built by Hijos de Barrera SA, Vigo, at a cost of US$75,000,000.

SUMMIT
87000 grt; 2449 psrs
970' x 106' x 26'4" (294 x 32.2 x 8 m)
2 x GE Marine diesel engines via twin azimuthing screw.
Cruise ship for Celebrity Cruises.
Being built by Chantiers de l'Atlantique, St Nazaire, at a cost of US$350,000,000.

SUN BAY
3000 grt; 96 psrs
length 292' (88.5 m)
Cruise ship owned by Sun Cruises, Nassau, and operated by Columbus Seereisen.
Built by Cassens-Werft, Germany.

SUPERFAST VII
29800 grt; 610 psrs
1000 cars
673' x 83' x 21'6" (203.9 x 25 x 6.5 m)
4 x 16-cylinder Sulzer diesel engines via twin screw.
Ice-strengthened passenger-car-cargo ferry for joint venture between Superfast Ferries and Attika Enterprises.
Being built by HDW, Kiel, at a cost of US$200,000,000.

SUPERFAST VIII
29800 grt; 610 psrs
1000 cars
673' x 83' x 21'6" (203.9 x 25 x 6.5 m)
4 x 16-cylinder Sulzer diesel engines via twin screw.
Ice-strengthened passenger-car-cargo ferry for joint venture between Superfast Ferries and Attika Enterprises.
Being built by HDW, Kiel, at a cost of US$200,000,000.

SUPERFAST IX
29800 grt; 604 psrs
100 cars + 125 trailers
673' x 84' x 21' (203.9 x 25.4 x 6.4 m)
4 x 16-cylinder Sulzer diesel engines via twin azimuthing screw.
Ice-strengthened passenger-car-cargo ferry for joint venture between Superfast Ferries and Attika Enterprises.
Being built by HDW, Kiel.

SUPERFAST X

29800 grt; 604 psrs
100 cars + 125 trailers
673' x 84' x 21' (203.9 x 25.4 x 6.4 m)
4 x 16-cylinder Sulzer diesel engines via twin azimuthing screw.
Ice-strengthened passenger-car-cargo ferry for joint venture between Superfast Ferries and Attika Enterprises.
Being built by HDW, Kiel.

SUPERFAST LEVANTE

17391 grt; 2000 psrs
100 cars + 125 trailers
521' x 83' x 21'5" (158 x 25.2 x 6.5 m)
4 x 6-cylinder Wartsila diesel engines via twin azimuthing screw.
Passenger-car ferry for Transmediterranea.
Being built by Union Levante, Valencia.

SUPERFERRY CHIOS

2100 psrs
350 cars
Passenger-car ferry for Strintzis Lines.
Being built by Hellenic Shipyards, Skaramangas.

SUPERFERRY EUROPE

1600 passengers
106 cars + 130 trailers
568' x 85' x 21' (172 x 25.7 x 6.3 m)
Passenger-car-cargo ferry for Strintzis Lines.
Being built by Van der Giessen-de-Noord, Krimpen.

SUPERFERRY MYCONOS

18000 grt; 2100 psrs
350 cars
451' x 51' x 17' (136.7 x 21 x 5.2 m)
Equipped with 4 x 12-cylinder Wartsila diesel engines via twin screw.
Passenger-car ferry for Strintzis Lines.
Being built by Van der Giessen-de-Noord, Krimpen.

SUPERFERRY STRINTZIS

1600 passengers
106 cars + 130 trailers
568' x 85' x 21' (172 x 25.7 x 6.3 m)
Passenger-car-cargo ferry for Strintzis Lines.
Being built by Van der Giessen-de-Noord, Krimpen.

SUPERSTAR LEO See NORWEGIAN STAR (2001)

SUPERSTAR LIBRA I

91000 grt; 2300 psrs
970' x 106' x 26' (294 x 32.2 x 8 m)
4 x 14-cylinder MAN-B+W diesel engines via twin Azipod screw.
Cruise ship for Star Cruises.
Being built by Meyer Werft, Papenburg, at a cost of US$380,000,000.

ULYSSES

52000 grt; 1800 psrs
1300 cars + 260 trailers and/or coaches
682' x 102' x 21' (208 x 31.2 x 6.4 m)
4 x 9-cylinder MaK diesel engines via twin screw.
Cruise-ferry for Irish Ferries.
Being built by Aker Finnyards Oy, Rauma, at a cost of Euro 98,000,000.

WORLD OF RESIDENSEA

44000 grt; 430 owner/guest/passenger capacity
644' x 98' x 22' (195.2 x 29.7 x 6.7 m)
Bruce's Shipyard diesel engines via twin screw.
Cruise ship catering to penthouses, suites and 88 apartments purchased outright, with owners pooling upkeep and costs into a ship fund controlled by Residensea Ltd.
Being built by Fosen Mek Verksteder AS, Fevaag, at a cost of US$262,000,000.

2002

ADVENTURE OF THE SEAS

142000 grt; 3840 psrs
1026' x 129' x 29'6" (310.9 x 39.1 x 10 m)
6 x 12-cylinder Wartsila diesel engines via triple Azipod screw (1 fixed and 2 azimuthing).
'Voyager Class' cruise ship for Royal Caribbean International.
To be built by Kvaerner-Masa Yard Inc, Turku, at a cost of US$500,000,000.

ARANUI III

10000 grt; 200 psrs
Passenger-cargo ship being built for Cie Polynesienne de Transport Maritime, Papeele, by Santiernul Naval Constantza.

BLUE STAR NAXOS

10193 grt; 1500 psrs
210 cars or 104 cars + 35 trailers
4 x 9-cylinder Wartsila diesel engines via twin screw.
Passenger-car ferry being built for Strintzis Lines SA by Daewoo Shipbuilding Yards, Seoul.

BLUE STAR PAROS

10193 grt; 1500 psrs
210 cars or 104 cars + 35 trailers
4 x 9-cylinder Wartsila diesel engines via twin screw.
Passenger-car ferry being built for Strintzis Lines SA by Daewoo Shipbuilding Yards, Seoul.

BRILLIANCE OF THE SEAS

85000 grt; 2100 psrs
970' x 106' x 28' (294 x 32.2 x 8.5 m)
2 x General Electric gas-turbine engines via twin Azipod screw.
'Vantage Class' cruise ship for Royal Caribbean International.
To be built by Meyer Werft, Papenburg, at a cost of US$350,000,000.

CARNIVAL CONQUEST

101509 grt; 2758 psrs
893' x 118' x 27' (270.1 x 35.8 x 8.2 m)
6 x 16-cylinder Sulzer diesel engines via twin screw.
Cruise ship for Carnival Cruise Lines.
Being built by Fincantieri, Monfalcone, at a cost of US$450,000,000.

CARNIVAL LEGEND

84000 grt; 2112 psrs
960' x 106' x 25'7" (291 x 33.2 x 7.8 m)
6 x 9-cylinder Wartsila diesel engines via twin Azipod screw.
Cruise ship for Carnival Cruise Lines.
Being built by Kvaerner-Masa Yards., Helsinki, at a cost of US$375,000,000.

CENTURION

91000 grt; 950 psrs
length 925' x beam 105' (280.3 x 31.8 m)
Gas-electric turbine engines via twin screw.
Cruise ship for Celebrity Cruises.
Being built by Chantiers de l'Atlantique, St Nazaire.

CORAL PRINCESS

88000 grt; 1950 psrs
length 970' x beam 106' (294 x 32.2 m)
3 x GE Marine combined diesel and gas turbine engines.
Cruise ship for Princess Cruises.
Being built by Chantiers de l'Atlantique, St Nazaire, at a cost of $450,000,000.

EUROPA PALACE

37500 grt; 2200 psrs
650 cars + 120 trailers
706' x 87' x 23' (214 x 26.4 x 7 m)
4 x 16-cylinder Wartsila diesel engines via twin screw.
Passenger-car-trailer ferry for Minoan Lines.
Being built by Fincantieri subsidiary Sestri Cantieri Navali, Genoa, at a cost of $130,000,000.

EUROPEAN DREAM
49000 grt; 1250 psrs
length 713' x beam 95' (216 x 28.8 m)
2 x GE Marine gas turbine engines via twin azimuthing screw.
Cruise ship for Festival/First European Cruises.
Being built by Chantiers de l'Atlantique, St Nazaire, at a cost of Euro333,000,000.

EUROPEAN HIGHLANDER
Passenger-car ferry being built for P&OSL by Mitsubishi Heavy industries.

FINNMARKEN
15000 grt; 634 psrs
length 457' x beam 71' (138.5 x 21.5 m)
Passenger ferry for OVDS (Hurtigruten Group).
Being built by Kleven Shipyard, Ulsteinvik.

HAMNAVOE
12000 grt; 600 psrs
68 cars or 30 trailers/coaches
length 363' x beam 61' (110 x 18.5 m)
Passenger-car ferry being built for Northlink Orkney and Shetland Ferries Ltd (a consortium owned by the Royal Bank of Scotland and Caledonian MacBrayne) and operated by Northlink Ferries.
Built by Aker Finnyards, Rauma, at a cost of £30,000,000.

HJALTLAND
12000 grt; 600 psrs
68 cars or 30 trailers/coaches
length 413' x beam 64' (125 x 19.5 m)
Passenger-car ferry being built for Northlink Orkney and Shetland Ferries Ltd (a consortium owned by the Royal Bank of Scotland and Caledonian MacBrayne) and operated by Northlink Ferries.
Built by Aker Finnyards, Rauma at a cost of £35,000,000.

HROSSEY
12000 grt; 600 psrs
68 cars or 30 trailers/coaches
length 413' x beam 64' (125 x 19.5 m)
Passenger-car ferry being built for Northlink Orkney and Shetland Ferries Ltd (a consortium owned by the Royal Bank of Scotland and Caledonian MacBrayne) and operated by Northlink Ferries.
Built by Aker Finnyards, Rauma at a cost of £35,000,000.

JANAS
35000 grt; 2781 psrs
700 cars + 70 trailers
708' x 87' x 21'8" (214.6 x 26.4 x 6.6 m)
4 x 12-cylinder Wartsila diesel engines via twin screw.
Passenger-car-trailer ferry for Tirrenia Navigazioni Lines.
Being built by Fincantieri, Castellammare di Stabia.

KENDERIS EXPRESS
1800 psrs
450 cars or 200 cars + trailers/coaches
A 'Corsair 1400' passenger-car ferry for NEL.
Being built by Alstrom St Navaire.

LA SUPERBA
50000 grt; 3000 psrs
1000 cars
length 696' x beam 100' (211 x 30.4 m)
Passenger-car ferry for Grand Naval Velocci.
Being built by Nuova Cantieri Apauania Marina di Carrara.

LEFKA ORI See KRITI V (2001)

LILAC
40000 grt; 888 psrs
58 cars + 146 trailers
length 660' x beam 87' (200 x 26.5 m)
Passenger-car ferry for Shin Nihonkai Ferry
Being built by Ishikawajima Heavy Industries, Yokohama.

MEDITERRANEE
44500 grt; 2600 psrs
700 cars + 146 trailers
611' x 92' x 21'8" (185 x 28.6 x 6.6 m)
3 x 9-cylinder Wartsila diesel engines via twin screw.
Passenger-car ferry for SNCM, Paris.
Being built by Fincantieri, Ancona, at a cost of $114,000,000.

NEW RAINBOW LOVE
23000 grt; 150 psrs
62 cars + 161 trailers
length 598' x beam 89' (181.3 x 26.4 m)
Cruise ferry for Kyuetsa Ferry, Japan.
Built by Mitsubishi Heavy Industries, Shimonoseki.

NGGAPULU
14800 grt; 2170 psrs
483' x 77' x 19'5" (146.5 x 23.4 x 4.9 m)
2 x 8-cylinder MaK diesel engines via twin screw.
Passenger ship for the Indonesian government.
Being built by Meyer Werft, Papenburg, for operation by PT Pelni.

NORRONA
Passenger ship for the Smyril Line.
Being built by Flensburger Werft.

NORWEGIAN DAWN
91000 grt; 2300 psrs
970' x 106' x 26' (294 x 32.3 x 8 m)
4 x 14-cylinder MAN-B + W diesel engines via twin Azipod screw.
Cruise ship for Norwegian Caribbean Line.
Being built by Meyer Werft, Papenburg, at a cost of $380,000,000.
Commenced construction as the SUPERSTAR SCORPIO for Star Cruises, but taken over by NCL following a policy switch by both companies.

OLYMPIC EXPLORER
24500 grt; 850 psrs
590' x 84' x 24' (178.8 x 25.5 x 7.3 m)
4 x 9-cylinder Wartsila diesel engines via twin screw.
Cruise ship for Royal Olympic Cruises, Greece.
Being built by Blohm & Voss, Hamburg, at a cost of US$177,000,000.

OLYMPIC PALACE
37500 grt; 2200 psrs
650 cars + 120 trailers
706' x 87' x 23' (214 x 26.4 x 7 m)
4 x 16-cylinder Wartsila diesel engines via twin screw.
Passenger-car-trailer ferry for Minoan Lines.
Being built by Fincantieri subsidiary Sestri Cantieri Navali, Genoa, at a cost of $130,000,000.

PARTENOPE
25000 grt; 860 psrs
75 cars + 156 trailers
length 614' x beam 89' (186 x 26.6 m)
Passenger-car ferry for Tomasos Costantino Maritimi
Being built by Visentini at a cost of US$ 80,000,000.

ROMANTIKA
40000 grt; 2500 psrs
800 cars
length 657' x beam 96' (198.8 x 29 m)
4 x diesel engines via twin screw.
Cruise ferry for Tallink
Being built by Aker Finnyards, Rauma, at a cost of US$221,000,000.

STAR PRINCESS
109000 grt; 2600 psrs
941' x 119' x 26'4" (285 x 36 x 8 m)
6 x 16-cylinder Sulzer diesel engines via twin azimuthing screw.
Cruise ship for P&O Princess Cruises.
Being built by Fincantieri at a cost of US$425,000,000.

STENA BALTICA
31189 grt; 1800 psrs
500 cars
length 535' x beam 86' (162 x 26 m)
Ro-Pax ferry being built for the Stena Line.

SUPERFAST XI
30000 grt; 1550 psrs
600 cars or 100 cars + 130 trailers
660' x 83' x 21' (200 x 25 x 6.4 m)
4 x 12-cylinder Wartsila diesel engines via twin screw.
Passenger-car ferry for Superfast Ferries (Attica Enterprises SA, Greece).
To be built by Flender Werft AG, Lubeck.

SUPERFAST XII
30000 grt; 1550 psrs
600 cars or 100 cars + 130 trailers
660' x 83' x 21' (200 x 25 x 6.4 m)
4 x 12-cylinder Wartsila diesel engines via twin screw.
Passenger-car ferry for Superfast Ferries (Attica Enterprises SA, Greece).
To be built by Flender Werft AG, Lubeck.

SUPERSTAR LIBRA II
85000 grt; 2300 psrs
970' x 106' x 26' (294 x 32.2 x 8 m)
4 x 14-cylinder MAN-B+W diesel engines via twin Azipod screw.
Cruise ship for Norwegian Cruise Line.
Being built by Meyer Werft, Papenburg, at a cost of US$380,000,000.

SUPERSTAR SCORPIO See NORWEGIAN DAWN (2002)

TROLLFJORD
16000 grt; 982 psrs
50 cars
439' x 71' x 16'2" (133 x 21.5 x 4.9 m)
2 x diesel engines via twin screw.
Passenger-car ferry for Troms Fylkes.
Being built by Bruces Shipyard, Landskrona.

YUKARI
36600 grt; 888 psrs
58 cars + 146 trailers
length 660' x beam 87' (200 x 26.5 m)
Cruise ferry for Shin Nihonkai Ferry
Being built by Ishikawajima Heavy Industries, Yokohama.

ZUIDERDAM
91000 grt; 2300 psrs
957' x 107' x 25'7" (290 x 32.3 x 7.8 m)
7 x Sulzer gas turbine and diesel electric engines via twin Azipod screw.
Cruise ship for Holland America Line.
Being built by Fincantieri, Marghera, at a cost of US$400,000,000.

2003

BRETAGNE II
2250 psrs
700 cars
Being built for Brittany Ferries by Chantiers de l'Atlantique, St Nazair, at a cost of Euro 160,000,000.

CARNIVAL GLORY
101672 grt; 2758 psrs
893' x 117' x 27' (272 x 35.5 x 8.2 m)
6 x 16-cylinder Sulzer diesel engines via twin screw.
Cruise ship for Carnival Cruise Lines.
To be built by Fincantieri, Monfalcone, at a cost of US$450,000,000.

COSTA FORTUNA
105000 grt; 2720 psrs
To be built by Fincantieri Navali SpA, Sestre Ponente, at a cost of US$400,000,000.

COSTA MEDITERRANEA
86000 grt; 2154 psrs
963' x 106' x 25'6" (291.7 x 32.2 x 7.8 m)
6 x 9-cylinder Wartsila diesel engines via twin Azipod screw.
Cruise ship being built by Kvaerner-Masa Yards, Helsinki for Costa Cruises at a cost of US$350,000,000.

CRYSTAL SERENITY
68000 grt; 1080 psrs
length 825' x beam 106'3" (250 x 32.2 m)
Diesel engines via azimuthing pod screw.
Being built for Crystal Cruises, Japan, by Chantiers de l'Atlantique, St Nazaire.

DIAMOND PRINCESS
113000 grt; 2600 psrs
957' x 124' x 27'7" (290 x 37.5 x 8.1 m)
5 x Wartsila-GE Marine diesel engines via twin screw.
Cruise ship for Princess Cruises.
To be built by Mitsubishi Heavy Industries, Nagasaki.

ISLAND PRINCESS
88000 grt; 1950 psrs
970' x 106' x 26'4" (294 x 32.2 x 8 m)
3 x Wartsila-GE Marine diesel-electric engines via twin screw.
Cruise ship for Princess Cruises.
To be built by Chantiers de l'Atlantique, St Nazaire, at a cost of US$330,000,000.

LA SUPREMA
48500 grt; 2800 psrs
1000 cars
696' x 100' (211 x 30.4 m)
Passenger-car ferry for Grand Naval Velocci.
Being built by Nuovi Cantieri Apuania, Marina di Carrera.

MEGA EXPRESS III
23700 grt
Being built for Lota Maritime, Corsica, by Cantieri Navale Fratelli, Orlando, at a cost of Euro 80,000,000.

MOBY FREEDOM
2000 psrs
700 cars or 120 trailers
Passenger-car ferry for Moby Lines
Being built by Daewoo Shipbuilding & Engineering Industries, Kyungam, at a cost of US$68,000,000.

MOBY WONDER
2000 psrs
700 cars or 120 trailers
Passenger-car ferry for Moby Lines
Being built by Daewoo Shipbuilding & Engineering Industries, Kyungam, at a cost of US$68,000,000.

MONT ST. MICHEL
36000 grt; 2200 psrs
600 cars + 175 trailers
length 578' x beam 92' (250 x 32.2 m)
Ro-Pax ferry for Brittany Ferries
Being built by Van der Giessen, Krimpen, at a cost of US$130,000,000.

NAVIGATOR OF THE SEAS
137276 grt; 3840 psrs
1027' x 127' x 28'4" (311.1 x 38.6 x 8.6 m)
6 x 12-cylinder Wartsila diesel engines via triple screw.
'Voyager' class cruise ship for Royal Caribbean International.
Being built by Kvaener-Masa Yards Inc, Helsinki.

NORRONA
40000 grt; 1482 psrs
800 cars or 400 cars + 130 trailers
538' x 99' x 20' (163.3 x 30 x 6 m)

4 x 6-cylinder MaK diesel engines via twin screw.
RoRo passenger-car ferry for the Smyril Line.
Being built by Flensburg SG Shipyard, Ludbeck.

OOSTERDAM

84000 grt; 1848 psrs
951' x 107' x 25'7" (290 x 32.3 x 7.8 m)
7 x 16-cylinder Sulzer gas turbine and diesel-electric engines via twin Azipod screw.
Cruise ship for Holland America Line.
Being built by Fincantieri Navali SpA.

QUEEN MARY 2

150000 grt; 2620 psrs
1131' x 131' x 32'10" (342.7 x 39.4 x 9.7 m)
6 x General Electric gas turbine diesel-electric engines via quadruple Mermaid azimuthing screw (2 x fixed forward and 2 x azimuthing aft).
Cruise ship for Carnival Cruise Lines' Cunard subsidiary.
To be built at Chantiers de l'Atlantique, St Nazaire, at a cost of US$780,000,000.

SERENADE OF THE SEAS

88000 grt; 2100 psrs
'Vantage' class cruise ship for Royal Caribbean International.
Being built by Meyer Werft, Papenburg.

SEVEN SEAS VOYAGER

45000 grt; 769 psrs
708' x 101' x 21'6" (216 x 28.8 x 6.5 m)
4 x 6-cylinder Wartsila diesel engines via twin azimuthing screw.
Cruise ship for Radisson Seven Seas Cruises.
To be built by Mariotti as part-owner with V-Ships at a cost of US$300,000,000.

2004

CARNIVAL MIRACLE

84000 grt; 2112 psrs
957' x 106' x 25'7" (290 x 32.2 x 7.8 m)
6 x 9-cylinder Wartsila diesel engines via twin screw.
Cruise ship in the 'Spirit Class' for Carnival Cruise Lines.
To be built by the Kvaerner-Masa Yard, Helsinki, at a cost of US$375,000,000.

CARNIVAL VALOR

110000 grt; 2974 psrs
Cruise ship for Carnival Cruise Lines.
To be built by Fincantieri, Monfalcone, at a cost of US$500,000,000.

COSTA MAGICA

105000 grt; 2720 psrs
To be built by Fincantieri Navali SpA, Sestre Ponente, at a cost of US$400,000,000.

JEWEL OF THE SEAS

88000 grt; 2100 psrs
'Vantage' class cruise ship for Royal Caribbean International.
Being built by Meyer Werft, Papenburg.

MARINER OF THE SEAS

137276 grt; 3840 psrs
1027' x 127' x 28'4" (311.1 x 38.6 x 8.6 m)
6 x 12-cylinder Wartsila diesel engines via triple screw.
'Voyager' class cruise ship for royal Caribbean international.
Being built by Kvaerner-Masa Yards Inc, Helsinki.

SAPPHIRE PRINCESS

110000 grt; 2600 psrs
957' x 124' x 26'4" (290 x 37.5 x 8 m)
6 x Wartsila-GE Marine diesel engines via twin screw.
Cruise ship for Princess Cruises.
To be built by Mitsubishi Heavy Industries, Nagasaki, at a cost of US$500,000,000.

2005

QUEEN VICTORIA

100000 grt; 1968 psrs
Diesel-electric engines via twin Azipod screw
Cruise ship for Cunard Line.
Being built by Fincantieri at a cost of US$400,000,000.

New Build (names not yet announced)

As this book goes into production, the European shipbuilding fraternity is being swamped by orders for new vessels to the extent that they are revising an old 'coopcrative' strategy whereby one yard constructs the hull, then another yard completes the building – with the owners' consent, of course. This ploy has been used to preserve the monopoly that European shipyards have enjoyed for about one century. But the Asian yards are emerging as threats; even the United States is slowly getting into the act by enacting legislation compelling cruise ships solely intended for US territorial sailing (eg Hawaii, US mainland coastal regions, etc) to be constructed in US yards.

Is the cruise ship industry and attendant shipbuilding industry gaining strength? The answer would appear to be 'Yes' from the summary earlier in this epilogue. The injection of 247,000 new berths into the marketplace will serve to benefit the cruising public by way of lower berth pricing, or deals to fill berths for some lines, and a larger stock of berths for sale by individual companies, among which are several that sail to capacity practically every voyage.

But is there a hidden danger lurking?

Well, not really, but common sense would seem to be pointing out that the aged 'liners of the past' which were hurriedly converted into cruise ships, refurbished, sometimes rebuilt, but always needing constant attention, are gradually opening up a void as they depart the scene for scrapyards. The ever-tightening rules and standards under SOLAS 2010 could sound the death-knell for the remaining old brigade of passenger vessels. It is doubtful that even the substitution of diesel power for the outmoded steam turbines would save the 'ladies' of yesteryear. Of the 'old brigade', either still sailing in service or 'resting' laid up, there remain between 12 and 20 vessels with turbine engine machinery sitting deep within their hulls. So quiet, so smooth and such downright erratic machinery, now in its twilight years.

Could it be that the shipyards are producing new metal to replace old, with the only real advance being the greater passenger capacity and more efficient propulsion technologies?

An imminent change will be the introduction of the 'black box', a concept used in commercial aircraft and to be adopted by the shipping industry and installed in all new buildings at a date yet to be determined. The box will be mandatory equipment in all merchant marine vessels, regardless of their type or classification.

The twenty-first century will be full of interest, commencing with the following firm contracts and option take-ups for ships for which no ship name announcements were available as at the date of this book going to press. They are listed in order of the year of delivery specification:

2001

Attica Enterprises SA
Passenger-car ferry (1500 psrs; 1000 cars) being built by HWD, Kiel, at a cost of US$112,000,000.

Celebrity Cruise Line
Cruise ship (85000 grt; 2000 psrs) being built at a cost of US$350,000,000.

Corsica Ferries/Sardinia Ferries
2 x cruise ferries (300 cabin capacity) to be built by Cantieri Orlando.

GA Ferries
Passenger-car ferry (length 495' x beam 83' (150 x 25 m) 4 x diesel engines).

Kyjetsi Ferry, Hygashi-Ku
2 x RoPax ferries (11500 grt) being built by Mitsubishi Heavy Industries, Shimonoseki, as job numbers 1079 and 1080.

Irish Continental Group
Cruise ferry (50000 grt; 2000 psrs; 1300 cars or 260 trailers; 4 x engines) being built by Aker Finnyards, Rauma, at a cost of Euro 100,000,000.

Minoan Lines
'Samsung 1281' is the yard identification of this passenger-car-cargo ferry (28500 grt; 1250 psrs; 100 cars + 150 trailers; 700' x 83' x 21'8" (212 x 25 x 6.6 m); 4 x 12-cylinder Wartsila diesel engines via twin screw) being built by Samsung Heavy Industries, Koje, at a cost of US$78,000,000.

Moby Lines
2 x cruise ferries (600 psrs) to be built by Daewoo Shipbuilding & Heavy Industries, Kyungnam.

P&O European Ferries
'Euro Class' Ro-pax ferry (24500 grt; 405 psrs; 400 cars or 130 trailers) being built by Mitsubishi Heavy Industries, Shimonoseki, at a cost of US$85,000,000.

Royal Olympic Cruises
Cruise ship to be built (25000 grt; 800 psrs).

Tirrenia
Passenger-car ferry (35000 grt; 2781 psrs; 700 cars + 72 trailers; 708' x 87' x 21'8" [214.6 x 26.4 x 6.6 m]; 4 x 12-cylinder Wartsila diesel engines via twin screw) to be built by Fincantieri, Castellemare di Stabia at a cost of US$95,000,000.

2002

Attica Enterprises SA
Passenger-car ferry (1500 psrs; 1000 cars) to be built by HWD, Kiel, at a cost of US$112,000,000.

Brittany Ferries
Passenger-car-cargo ferry (36000 grt; 2000 psrs; 600 cars + 175 trailers; length 578' x beam 92' [175 x 28 m]) to be built by Van der Giessen, Krimpen at a cost of US$130,000,000.

Celebrity Cruises
'Millennium Class' cruise ship (85000 grt; 1950 psrs) to be built by Chantiers de l'Atlantique, St Nazaire, at a cost of US$350,000,000.

Estonian Shipping Co
Passenger-cargo ferry (52000 grt; 2050 psrs; 4100 m vehicle lanes) to be built by Aker Finnyards at a cost of US$108,000,000. Possibly two vessels to be built, but this is not yet confirmed.

Grand Navi Veloce
Cruise ferry (50000 grt; 3000 psrs; length 636' x beam 91' [212 x 30.4 m]) to be built by Nuovi Cantieri Apuania.

Indonesian government
Passenger ferry of 14600 grt being built by Meyer Werft, Papenburg.

Lakshadweep Territory Administration, India
Cruise ship (700 psrs) being built by the Hindustan Shipyard for the operator, the Shipping Corporation of India.

Luxus Cruises Ltd
2 x cruise ships (28000 grt; 400 psrs) to be built, subject to UK subsidies being passed, by Cammell Laird Ltd at a cost of US$430,000,000 each.

Ministry of Defence, UK
2 x RoRo ferries to be built by Harland & Wolff Ltd, Belfast, at a cost of US$100,000,000 each.
4 x RoRo ferries to be built in Germany at a cost of US$100,000,000 each.

Norwegian Cruise Line
2 x 'Norwegian Sky Class' cruise ships (80000 grt; 2000 psrs) to be built by Meyer-Werft, Papenburg, at a cost of US$351,000,000 each.

P&O/Aida Cruise Line
'New class' of cruise ship (41200 grt; 1573 psrs) to be built by Aker MTW-Werft.

P&O Princess Cruise Line
'New Class' cruise ship (88000 grt; 1950 psrs) to be built by Chantiers de l'Atlantique, St Nazaire.

Radisson Seven Seas Cruises
Cruise ship (45000 grt; 769 psrs) to be built by Visentini and Mariotti Yards at a cost of US$190,000,000.

ResidenSea Ltd
A second penthouse/apartment luxury ship residence (50000 grt) is to be built by Fosen at a cost of US$280,000,000.

Royal Caribbean International
'Voyager Class' cruise ship (137276 grt; 3840 psrs; 1027' x 127' x 28'4" [311.1 x 38.6 x 8.6 m]; 6 x 12-cylinder Wartsila diesel engines via triple screw) to be built by Kvaerner-Masa Yards Inc, Helsinki.

Star Cruises
'Superstar Libra Class' cruise ship (2300 psrs) to be built by Meyer-Werft, Papenburg.

Stena RoRo Line
2 x Stena 4-Runner Mark II class ferries being built in Dalian, China.

Stena RoRo Line
Stena Seamaster class passenger-car/trailer ferry being built by Hyundai Heavy Industries, South Korea.

Tirrenia
Passenger-car ferry (35000 grt; 2781 psrs; 700 cars + 72 trailers; 708' x 87' x 21'8" [214.6 x 26.4 x 6.6 m]; 4 x 12-cylinder Wartsila diesel engines via twin screw) to be built by Fincantieri, Castellemare di Stabia at a cost of US$95,000,000.

Tomasos Costantino Trasporti Maritime
25000 grt; 860 psrs
75 cars + 156 trailers
length 614' x beam 88' (186 x 26.6 m)
Passenger-car ferry being built by Visentini at a cost of US$80,000,000.

Trasmediterranea
Passenger-car-cargo ferry (22000 grt; 600 psrs; 89 cars + 142 trailers; 597' x 80' x 21'6" [180 x 24.3 x 6.5 m]; 4 x 9-cylinder Wartsila diesel engines via twin screw) to be built by Astilleros Espanoles SS, Seville.

Turkish Maritime Lines
2 x passenger-car ferries to be built by Akers Finnyards, Rauma.

2003

American Hawaii Cruises
Cruise ship.
Attica Enterprises SA
Passenger-car ferry (1500 psrs; 1000 cars) to be built by HWD, Kiel, at a cost of US$112,000,000.

Carnival Cruise Lines
Cruise ship (101000 grt; 3350 psrs) to be built at a cost of US$450,000,000.

Celebrity Cruises
Cruise ship (85000 grt; 1900 psrs).

Costa Crociere
84000 grt; 2112 psrs
963' x 106' x 25'6" (291.7 x 32.2 x 7.8 m)
6 x 9-cylinder Wartsila diesel engines via twin Azipod screw.
Cruise ship for Costa Cruises
Being built by Kvnerner-Masa Yards at a cost of US$375,000,000.

ENTMV
1300 psrs
300 cars or 42 trailers
479' x 79' x 20' (145 x 24 x 6 m)
2 x engines.
Being built by IZAR Shipyards, Seville.

ENTMV
1300 psrs
300 cars or 42 trailers
479' x 79' x 20' (145 x 24 x 6 m)
2 x engines.
Ro-Pax ferry being built by HJ Barreras, Vigo.

Festival/First European Cruises
Cruise ship (80000 grt; 1800 psrs) to be built by Chantiers de l'Atlantique, St Nazaire.

Grand Navi Veloce
Cruise ferry (50000 grt; 3000 psrs; length 636' x 91' [212 x 30.4 m]) to be built by Nuovi Cantieri Apuania; .

Holland America Line
'New Class' cruise ship (84000 grt; 1800 psrs; Azipod screw) to be built by Fincantieri, Marghera, at a cost of US$400,000,000.

Mediterranean Shipping Company
60000 grt; 2200 psrs
Equipped with twin Azipod screw.
Being built by Chantiers de l'Atlantique, St Nazaire, at a cost of US$250,000,000.

NYK
See Crystal Cruises.

P&O/Aida Cruises
'New Class' cruise ship (41200 grt; 1573 psrs) to be built by Aker MTW-Werft.

P&O Princess Cruise Line
Cruise ship (88000 grt; 1950 psrs) to be built by Chantiers de l'Atlantique.
'New Class' cruise ship (113000 grt; 2600 psrs) to be built by Mitsubishi Heavy Industries, Japan.

Porto Santo Line, Madeira
Passenger-car ferry being built in two stages: the hull in St Petersburg and completion at the Portuguese shipyard of Viana do Castelo.

Royal Caribbean International
'Vantage Class' cruise ship (88000 grt; 2100 psrs) to be built by Meyer Werft, Papenburg.
'Voyager Class' cruise ship (137276 grt; 3840 psrs; 1027' x 127' x 28'4" [311.1 x 38.6 x 8.6 m]; 6 x 12-cylinder Wartsila diesel engines via triple screw) to be built by Kvaerner-Masa Yards Inc, Turku.

Smyril Line
1480 psrs
length 543' x beam 99' (164.6 x 30 m)
RoRo ferry being built by Flender Werft AG, Lubeck.

SNCM
Passenger-car-cargo ferry (550 psrs; 130 cars + 160 trailers; 578' x 99' [175 x 30 m]) to be built by Van der Giessen-de Noord.

Star Cruises
'Sagittarius' Class cruise ship (100000 grt; 1500 psrs) to be built at a cost of US$500,000,000.

Stena RoRo Line
Passenger-car/trailer ferry of the Stena 'Seamaster' class being built by Hyundai Heavy Industries, South Korea.

TFDS (Hurtigruten Cruises)
Cruise ferry (15000 grt; 675 psrs) to be built by Fosen MekVerksteder.

Tomasos Costantino Trasporti Maritime
25000 grt; 860 psrs
75 cars + 156 trailers
length 614' x beam 88' (186 x 26.6 m)
Passenger-car ferry being built by Visentini at a cost of US$80,000,000.

United States Lines
Cruise ship referred to as 'Project America 1' (72000 grt; 1900 psrs) to be built by Ingalls Shipbuilding Yards, Pascagoula, Mississippi, USA.

2004

American Hawaii Cruises
Cruise ship.

Festival/First European Cruises
2 x cruise ships (55000 grt; 2400 psrs) to be built by Chantiers de l'Atlantique, St Nazaire.

Holland America Line
2 x 'Vista Class' cruise ships (84000 grt; 1848 psrs; Azipod screw) to be built by Fincantieri, Marghera, at a cost of US$400,000,000 each.

Mediterranean Shipping Company
60000 grt; 1600 psrs
Twin Mermaid azimuthing screw.
Cruise ship being built by Chantiers de l'Atlantique, St Nazaire, at a cost of US$250,000,000.

Mediterranean Shipping Company
60000 grt; 2200 psrs
Equipped with twin Azipod screw
Being built by Chantiers l'Atlantique, St Nazaire, at a cost of US$250,000,000.

OVDS (Hurtigruten Cruises)
Cruise ferry (15000 grt; 675 psrs) to be built by Kleven Verst.

P&O Cruises Ltd
'Grand Class' cruise ship (110000 grt; 2600 psrs) to be built by Fincantieri.

Princess Cruise Line
Cruise ship (109000 grt; 2600 psrs) to be built by Mitsubishi Heavy Industries, Japan.

Royal Caribbean International
'Vantage Class' cruise ship (88000 grt; 2100 psrs) to be built by Meyer Werft, Papenburg.

SeaAmerica Cruise Line
Cruise ship (72000 grt; 1900 psrs; 840' x 106' x 26'3" [254.5 x 32 x 8 m]; 4 x Wartsila diesel engines via twin Azipod screw) to be built by Litton-Ingalls Shipbuilding Corporation, Pascagoula, Mississippi, USA, at a cost of US$400,000,000.

United States Lines
Cruise ship referred to as 'Project America 2' (72000 grt; 1900 psrs) to be built by Ingalls Shipbuilding Yards, Pascagoula, Mississippi, USA.

2005

Holland America Line
'Vista Class' cruise ship (84000 grt; 1800 psrs; length 951' [288.2 m]; equipped with diesel-electric plus gas turbine engines via twin Azipod screw) to be built by Fincantieri, Marghera, at a cost of US$400,000,000.

OVDS (Hurtigruten Cruises)
Cruise ferry (15000 grt; 675 psrs) to be built by Kleven Verst.

Star Cruises
'Sagittarius Class' cruise ship (100000 grt; 1500 psrs) to be built at a cost of US$500,000,000.

Late Breaking News

While the presses were completing their publication of this book, the many maritime contacts of the author have been party to a last-minute 'ring-around' for the latest events within this fascinating industry.

The following reported events have been researched and, in most instances, been confirmed:

ALTAS (2001) See LANGELAND IV below

AMERIKANIS (1967)
After being laid up in Eleusis Bay since 1997, and Tampa Bay Florida for one year, she has been sold for scrap to Indian shipbreakers, ex-Piraeus, in 2001 for US$2,000,000 (US$148 per deadweight ton).

ARKONA (1985)
At the conclusion of its 10-year bareboat charter in 2001, she will be transferred to P&O's German company and renamed ASTORIA.

ARTEMIS I (1996)
Being renamed GABRIELLE in 2001.

ASTORIA (2001)
See ARKONA above

BEAUPORT (1991)
Being placed on the international sale lists in June 2001 at a figure of US$8,500,000.

BELOFIN I (1998)
Sank while under tow 50 miles (84 kms) west of Capetown on 21 October 2000. The Russian tug IRSIS was used for the tow to Gadani Beach.

BLUE GALAXY (2000)
To be chartered by Turkish Marmara Line from Strintzis Lines and renamed CESME 2 (2001).

BLUE ISLAND (2000)
To be chartered by Turkish Marmara Line from Strintzis Lines and renamed CESME 1 (2001).

BRAEMAR (2001) See CROWN DYNASTY below

BSP III (2001) See PRIDE OF RATHLIN (1992) below

CAPO CARBONARA (1988)
To be placed on the international sales list with her sister ship CAPO SPARTIVENTO (1988) in 2001 at US$5,700,000.

CAPO SPARTIVENTO (1988)
To be placed on the international sales list with her sister ship CAPO CARBONARA (1988) in 2001 at US$6,300,000.

CESME 1 (2001) See BLUE ISLAND (2000) above

CESME 2 (2001) See BLUE GALAXY (2000) above

CHINA SEA DISCOVERY (2001) See FAIR PRINCESS (1997) below

CHINA SEAS DISCOVERY (2000) See FAIR PRINCESS (1997) below

CITY OF CORK (2001) See VILLE DE SETE below

COSTA EUROPA (2001) See WESTERDAM below

COSTA TROPICALE (2001) See TROPICALE below

CROWN DYNASTY (2000)
With Commodore Cruises filing for Chapter 11 bankruptcy on 20 December 2000, this vessel was sold to Fred Olsen Lines for US$74,500,000 (including refit/refurbishment costs) in the same month. It is planned to rename her BRAEMAR in 2001.

CROWN PRINCESS (1990)
Following the complete acquisition by P&O of Aida Cruises, Germany, towards the latter part of 2000, this ship has been nominated by P&O to become part of the exclusive operation conducted by Aida Cruises with their existing ships AIDA and ARKONA. The repositioning of CROWN PRINCESS is expected to be early in 2002 and would make her the largest passenger ship in the German domestic market.

ELEFTHERIOS VENIZELOS (1997)
ANEK were reported to be keen to make an entry into the cruise ship market with this passenger-car-cargo ferry, and have reportedly set about a rebuild of the vessel for an October 2001 inaugural Mediterranean cruise.

EMERALD FORTUNE (2001) See FAIR PRINCESS below

ENCHANTED CAPRI (1998)
With Commodore Cruises filing for Chapter 11 bankruptcy on 20 December 2000, this vessel was reported have been laid up in New Orleans pending an outcome of various negotiations.

ENCHANTED ISLE (1994)
With Commodore Cruises filing for Chapter 11 bankruptcy on 20 December 2000, this vessel was reported have been laid up in New Orleans pending an outcome of various negotiations.

ENCHANTED SUN (1999)
To be renamed THE TALISMAN in 2001, and operated as a casino ship.

EUROPA (1988)
Scheduled for breaking up for scrap early in 2001.

EUROPE (1988)
Reported sunk while en route to the breakers in India for scrapping in early April, 2001.

FAIR PRINCESS (1997)
To be renamed LANZHUANSHI (2001) by its new owners, the Hainan government, in a joint venture with the China Shipping Company and managed by V Ships Leisure Group and V Ships Asia Pacific, with effect from 18 January 2001. Between the 1997 and 2001 names, this ship was also renamed CHINA SEAS DISCOVERY in December 2000, but this was an incorrect spelling of the name which was confirmed in February 2001 as CHINA SEA DISCOVERY (2001), although marketed as the casino ship EMERALD FORTUNE. The LANZHUANSHI will be the first dedicated cruise ship owned and operated by Tropical Island International Travel Agency, Haikou.

FANTASIA (2001) See MEDINA STAR below

FEDRA (1987)
Will be acquired by a Central American company and renamed YUCATAN EXPLORER (2001).

GABRIELLE (2001) See ARTEMIS I above

HYUNDAI KUMGANG (1998)
Withdrawn following the announcement by Hyundai Merchant Marine that it was withdrawing from the cruising industry at the conclusion of its existing charter from Star Cruises, Singapore.

HYUNDAI PONGNAE (1998)
Withdrawn following the announcement by Hyundai Merchant Marine that it was withdrawing from the cruising industry at the conclusion of its existing charter from Star Cruises, Singapore.

HYUNDAI PUNGAK (1999)
Withdrawn following the announcement by Hyundai Merchant Marine that it was withdrawing from the cruising industry at the conclusion of its existing charter from Star Cruises, Singapore.

KRITI III (2000)
To be renamed OLYMPIC CHAMPION in 2001.

LANGELAND IV (1999)
Is being sold to IMTC, Morocco, and renamed ALTAS in 2001.

LANZHUANSHI (2001) See FAIR PRINCESS (1997) above

LEIF ERICSON (2001) See STENA CHALLENGER below

LINDOS (2001) See NEW TOSA below

MARIANNA VI (1974)
Scheduled for breaking up for scrap in 2001.

MARIANNA 9 (1984)
Scheduled to be broken up for scrap in 2001.

MEDINA STAR (1999)
Reported sold for US$3,900,000, and to be renamed FANTASIA (2001).

MEGA STAR CAPRICORN (2000)
This compact cruise ship has been sold to Hebridean Princess Cruises, Skipton, North Yorkshire, UK, for delivery early in 2001 from Star Cruises, Singapore, as the HEBRIDEAN SPIRIT.

MEGA STAR SAGITTARIUS (2000)
Another compact cruise ship from Star Cruises, sold to Cruise West, USA, for early 2001 delivery and a name change to SPIRIT OF OCEANUS.

MOBY BLU (1982)
Still being advertised for sale into 2001 at US$1,500,000.

MONT SAINT MICHAEL
This will be the name of Brittany Ferries 2001 new build.

NEW TOSA (1990)
Passenger-car-ferry sold by Osaka Kocho, Tokyo, in 2000 to DANE Sealines, Greece, for delivery in 2001 as the LINDOS.

N. KAZANTZAKIS (1989)
To be purchased in May 2001 by Pacific Cruises (Hainan) Limited, Hong Kong, for US$12,000,000, and renamed MING FAI PRINCESS (2001).

NORWEGIAN LEO (2001) See SUPERSTAR LEO below

OCEAN (2002) See OCEAN PRINCESS below

OCEAN BREEZE (1992)
Sold for US$12,000,000 following the collapse of Premier Cruise Lines

OCEAN PRINCESS (2000)
An announcement has been made that this new cruise ship will be transferred from Princess Cruises to P&O Cruises in November 2002, and renamed OCEANA.

OCEAN VOYAGER (2001) See SUPERSTAR ARIES below

OLYMPIC CHAMPION (2001) See KRITI III below

PACIFIC PRINCESS (1975)
P&O intend to withdraw this ship from service in 2002.

PEARL OF SCANDINAVIA (2001) See STAR AQUARIUS (1993) below

P&OSL PICARDY (1999)
After being laid up in 2001 and widely advertised as being for sale at US$10,000,000, she was sold for US$4,900,000 to the Transeuropa Line via Seabourne Navigational Co Ltd.

PRIDE OF RATHLIN (1992)
Will be sold to PT Samudera, Indonesia, in 2001 and renamed BSP III.

PRINSENDAM (2002) See SEABOURN SUN (1999)

RAINBOW BELL (1996)
Being sold to ANEK Lines by Kyuetsu Ferry, Higashi-Ku, early in 2001.

ROYAL STAR (1991)
Listed for sale at US$15,000,000.

SANDEFJORD (1992)
Reported as sold to a Uruguayan shipping line and laid up at Drammen.

SEA (1996)
Sold for US$1,080,000 by Commodities Shipping Inc, USA, on 16 January 2001, for breaking up for scrap in India. The Dutch ocean-going tug SOLANO is scheduled to pick her up ex-Tampa Bay, Florida, about April 2001. The SEA has been laid up in Tampa Bay for over four years.

SEABOURN SUN (1999)
To be transferred at the end of April 2002 to the Holland-America Line and renamed PRINSENDAM.

SEAFRANCE RODIN (2001)
This to be the name of SeaFrance's latest new building in 2001.

SEAWING (1994)
Being sold to Louis Cruise Lines in 2001.

SPIRIT OF OCEANOS (2001) See MEGA STAR SAGITTARIUS above

SPIRIT OF OCEANUS (2001) See SUN VIVA below

STAR AQUARIUS (1993)

Sold for $100,000,000 by Star Cruises, Singapore, to DFDS in 2000 and scheduled for delivery in April 2001 as the AQUARIUS. This will follow internal conversions to the car deck area by the Aalborg Shipyard, then a new livery by Blohm & Voss, Hamburg, prior to final renaming mid-2001 as the PEARL [or QUEEN] OF SCANDINAVIA. The quoted acquisition price was for the ship, refurbishment and rebuilding.

STENA CHALLENGER (1991)

Will be changing its name to LEIF ERICSON in 2001.

SUN (1998)

Due to be broken up for scrap early 2001. Interior stripping has already commenced at her mooring in Freeport.

SUN VISTA (1997)

A report from the Bahamas Maritime Authority, dated December 2000, regarding the loss of this cruise ship in May 1999 indicates that the ship suffered severe deficiencies in safety equipment (in the area of fire detectors and dampers and electrical equipment). The report also highlighted serious faults with the main and auxiliary machinery which were critical factors in the ship's demise.

SUN VIVA (1997)

In March 2001, this cruise ship will be returning from charter to Sun Cruises and renamed SPIRIT OF OCEANUS by Star Cruises.

SUPERFAST VI (2000)

HDW was unable to honour the original delivery date of July 2000 due to mechanical breakdown within the ship's gearing system when undergoing sea trials. She is now scheduled for handover to her owners early in 2001. Additionally, her specified draft of 21'6 (6.5 m) has been exceeded by 8" (.2 m), as was the case with her sister ship SUPERFAST V (2000), and a higher fuel consumption may bring about a renegotiated delivery price for both vessels.

SUPERFERRY 3 (1993)

As this book was being published, this ferry was sold for US$800,000 to Chinese shipbreakers for scrap following a disastrous during routine dry dock maintenance in the Keppel Marine Shipyard, Cebu.

SUPERSTAR ARIES (1999)

To be owned and operated by Orient Lines in 2002, and renamed OCEAN VOYAGER.

SUPERSTAR LEO (1998)

Rumoured to be changing her name to NORWEGIAN LEO in 2001 following an inter-company transfer and repositioning to the Hawaiian Islands cruise circuit.

THE BIG RED BOAT I (1997)

Following the collapse of Premier Cruise Line, and its ceasing trading on 14 September 2000, this vessel and her three sisters were immediately suspended from service by the incoming administrators. It has been indicated by the liquidators that three ships are capable of being sold, while uncertainty remains as to the eventual fate of another one which has suffered continual mechanical problems for some time past.

THE BIG RED BOAT II (2000)

Following the collapse of Premier Cruise Line, and its ceasing trading on 14 September 2000, this vessel and her three sisters were immediately suspended from service by the incoming administrators. However, this vessel was quickly chartered on a short-term basis to Imperial Majesty Cruises, formerly laid up in Freeport. It has been indicated by the liquidators that three ships are capable of being sold, while uncertainty remains as to the eventual fate of another one which has suffered continual mechanical problems for some time past.

THE BIG RED BOAT III (2000)

Following the collapse of Premier Cruise Line, and its ceasing trading on 14 September 2000, this vessel and her three sisters were immediately suspended from service by the incoming administrators. It has been indicated by the liquidators that three ships are capable of being sold, while uncertainty remains as to the eventual fate of another one which has suffered continual mechanical problems for some time past.

THE BIG RED BOAT IV (2000)

Following the collapse of Premier Cruise Line, and its ceasing trading on 14 September 2000, this vessel and her three sisters were immediately suspended from service by the incoming administrators. It has been indicated by the liquidators that three ships are capable of being sold, while uncertainty remains as to the eventual fate of another one which has suffered continual mechanical problems for some time past.

TROPICALE (1981)

To be transferred in February 2001 from Carnival Cruises to Costa Cruises and renamed COSTA TROPICALE.

VICTORIA (1995)

To be sold by P&O Cruises in 2002.

VILLE DE SETE (2000)

Will be bareboat-chartered to Swansea-Cork Ferries in 2001 and renamed CITY OF CORK.

WESTERDAM (1988)

To be renamed COSTA EUROPA in April 2002 at the end of the 2001 cruising season, when the WESTERDAM is purchased by Costa Cruises pending a US Coastguard inspection clearance. Holland-America holds a Letter of Intent from Costa to this effect.

YUCATAN EXPLORER (2001) See FEDRA (1987).

Bibliography

I exhausted my own maritime library and the five four-drawer filing cabinets of clippings, notes and gatherings in the first six months of research for this book. Then I descended upon the State Library of New South Wales, Sydney; the suburban Strathfield transport specialist library; and, finally, the Vaughan Evans Library attached to the Australian National Maritime Museum to check on my work from the following excellent publications (including one of the most extensive collections of *Lloyds Register of Shipping*):

Registers and Directories
Fairplay World Shipping Directory, 1990–1997
Lloyds Maritime Directory, 1990–1997
Lloyds Register of Shipping, 1890–1999

Periodicals
Drydock
Fairplay Shipping Weekly
Marine News
Sea Breezes
Ships Monthly
The Naval Architect

Books
Anderson, Roy, *White Star*, T Stephenson & Sons, 1964
Andrews, Graeme, *A Log of Great Australian Ships*, Reed Publications, 1980
Andrews, Malcolm, *The Fabulous Fairstar*, Harper Collins, 1996
Ballard, Robert D, *The Lost Liners*, Allen & Unwin/Hodder & Stoughton, 1997
Baty, Scott, *Ships That Passed*, Reed Publishing, 1984
Brock, Bruno, and Klaus, *Soviet Bloc Merchant Ships*, Janes Publishing Co, 1981
Bonsor, NRP, *North Atlantic Seaway Volume 1*, David & Charles, 1975
— *North Atlantic Seaway Volume 2*, David & Charles, 1975
— *North Atlantic Seaway Volume 3*, David & Charles, 1975
— *North Atlantic Seaway Volume 4*, David & Charles, 1975
— *North Atlantic Seaway Volume 5*, David & Charles, 1975
— *South Atlantic Seaway*, Patrick Stephens, 1984
Braynard, Frank O, *Lives of the Liners*, Cornell Maritime Publications, 1947
Bremner, Stuart, *Home and Back*, Dreamweaver, 1984
Brennan, Frank, *The Australian Commonwealth Line*, Roebuck, 1978
Brewer, NH, *A Century of Style*, Reed, 1982
Cairis, Nicholas T, *Cruise Ships of the World*, Pegasus Books, 1988
— *North American Liners Since 1900*, Ian Allan Publishing, 1972
—- *Passenger Liners of the World Since 1893*, Bonanza Books, 1979
Cary, Alan L, *Mail Liners of the World*, Sampson Low, Marston & Co Ltd, 1936
Churchouse, Jack, *Glamour Ships of the Union Steamship Company of New Zealand*, Millwood Press, 1989
Cooke, Anthony, *Emigrant Ships*, Crmania Press, 1997
— *Liners and Cruise Ships*, Carmania Press, 1996
Cox, GW, *Bass Strait Crossing*, Melanie Publications, 1986
Dawson, Philip S, *British Superliners of the Sixties*, Conway Maritime, 1990
Dunn, Laurence, *Famous Liners of the Past – Belfast*, Adlard Coles, 1964
— *Merchant Ships: 1910–1929*, Blandford Press, 1973
— *Passenger Liners*, Adlard Coles, 1961 and 1965
— *Ships of the Union-Castle Line*, Adlard Coles, George Harrap and John de Graf, 1954
Emmons, G, *American Passenger Ships 1873–1983*, University of Delaware Press/Associated University Press
— *The Atlantic Liners: 1925–1970*, David & Charles, 1972
— *The Pacific Liners: 1927–1972*, Arco Publishing, 1970
Fildes, Robert D, *Ocean Liners 1984*, Searail Productions, 1984
— *The Ships That Serve Australia & New Zealand Volume 1*, Searail Productions, 1980
— *The Ships That Serve Australia & New Zealand Volume 2*, Searail Productions, 1980
Fitchett, TK, *The Great Liners*, Rigby, 1977
— *The Long Haul: Ships on the England–Australia Run*, Rigby, 1980
— *The Vanished Fleet: Australian Coastal Passenger Ships (1910–1960)*, Rigby, 1970
Gibbs, Charles RV, *British Passenger Ships of the Five Oceans*, Putnam, 1963
Gordon, K, *From Chusan To Sea Princess*, Allen & Unwin, 1985

Graham, C and Gillett, R, *Warships of Australia*, Rigby, 1977
Greenway, Ambrose, *A Century of North Sea Passenger Steamers*, Ian Allan Publishing, 1981
— *Soviet Merchant Ships*, Mason Publications, 1990
Harding, Stephen, *Great Liners at War*, Motorbooks International, 1997
Haws, Duncan, *Merchant Fleets Volume 2*, Patrick Stephens, 1979
— *Merchant Fleets Volume 4*, Patrick Stephens, 1980
— *Merchant Fleets Volume 5*, TCL Publications, 1982
— *Merchant Fleets Volume 6*, TCL Publications, 1984
— *Merchant Fleets Volume 7*, TCL Publications, 1980
— *Merchant Fleets Volume 8*, TCL Publications, 1980
— *Merchant Fleets Volume 9*, TCL Publications, 1986
— *Merchant Fleets Volume 10*, TCL Publications, 1987
— *Merchant Fleets Volume 11*, TCL Publications, 1987
— *Merchant Fleets Volume 12*, TCL Publications, 1987
— *Merchant Fleets Volume 13*, TCL Publications, 1988
— *Merchant Fleets Volume 14*, TCL Publications, 1988
— *Merchant Fleets Volume 15*, TCL Publications, 1988
— *Merchant Fleets Volume 16*, TCL Publications, 1989
— *Merchant Fleets Volume 17*, TCL Publications, 1989
— *Merchant Fleets Volume 18*, TCL Publications, 1990
— *Merchant Fleets Volume 19*, TCL Publications, 1990
— *Merchant Fleets Volume 20*, TCL Publications, 1990
— *Merchant Fleets Volume 21*, TCL Publications, 1990
— *Merchant Fleets Volume 27*, TCL Publications, 1994
— *Merchant Fleets Volume 28*, TCL Publications, 1995
— *Merchant Fleets Volume 29*, TCL Publications, 1995
— *Merchant Fleets Volume 30*, TCL Publications, 1996
— *Merchant Fleets Volume 31*, TCL Publications, 1996
— *Merchant Fleets Volume 32*, TCL Publications, 1997
— *Merchant Fleets Volume 33*, TCL Publications, 1997
— *Merchant Fleets Volume 36*, self-published, 1999
Hayami, Ikuzo, *Beautiful Ocean Liners*, Froebel-kan Co Ltd, 1970
Hornsby, David, *Ocean Ships*, Ian Allan Ltd, 2000
Ingram, CWN, *New Zealand Shipwrecks: 1795–1970*, Reed Publishing, 1972
Kirk, A, *Express Steamers of Cook Strait*, Reed Publishing, 1968
Kludas, Arnold, *Great Passenger Ships of the World Volume 1: 1858–1912*, Patrick Stephens, 1976
— *Great Passenger Ships of the World Volume 2: 1913–1923*, Patrick Stephens, 1976
— *Great Passenger Ships of the World Volume 3: 1924–1935*, Patrick Stephens, 1976
— *Great Passenger Ships of the World Volume 4: 1936–1950*, Patrick Stephens, 1976
— *Great Passenger Ships of the World Volume 5: 1951–1976*, Patrick Stephens, 1977
— *Great Passenger Ships of the World Volume 6: 1977–1986*, Patrick Stephens, 1986
Kohn, Roger, *Palm Line – The Coming of Age 1949–1970*, Palm Line Ltd, 1970
Lawson, Will, *Pacific Steamers*, Brown, Son and Ferguson, 1927
Le Fleming, HM, *Ships of the Blue Funnel Line*, Adlard Coles, 1961
Loney, Jack, *An Atlas of Australian Shipwrecks*, Reed Publishing, 1981
— *Australian Shipwrecks Volume 4 (1901–1986)*, Marine History Publications, 1987
— *Australian Shipwrecks Volume 5 (1986–1991)*, Marine History Publications, 1991
McAuley, Rob, *The Liners*, Boxtree (Macmillan), 1997
McCart, Neil, *Atlantic Liners of the Cunard Line: 1844–1990*, Patrick Stephens, 1987
— *Passenger Ships of the Orient Line*, Patrick Stephens, 1987
— *P&O's Canberra and Sea Princess*, Fan Publications, 1993
— *Twentieth Century Passenger Ships of the P&O*, Patrick Stephens, 1985
McNeill, DB, *Irish Passenger Steamship Services*, David & Charles, 1960
Maber, John M, *Channel Packets and Ocean Liners: 1850–1970*, HMSO, 1980
— *North Star To Southern Cross*, T Stephenson & Sons, 1967
Maxtone-Graham, John, *Liners to the Sun*, Macmillan Publishing, 1985 and 2000
Miller, William H, *British Ocean Liners*, Patrick Stephens, 1986
— *The Chandris Liners*, Carmania Press, 1993

— *Cruise Ships of the World*, Conway Maritime, 1988
— *Famous Ocean Liners*, Patrick Stephens, 1987
— *Fifty Famous Liners Volume 1*, Norton, 1985
— *Fifty Famous Liners Volume 2*, Norton, 1985
— *Fifty Famous Liners Volume 3*, Patrick Stephens, 1987
— *German Ocean Liners of the 20th Century*, Patrick Stephens, 1989
— *Great Cruise Ships and Ocean Liners*, Dover Publications, 1988
— *Last Atlantic Liners*, Conway Maritime, 1985
— *The Last Blue Water Liners*, Conway Maritime, 1986
— *Liner*, Patrick Stephens, 1986
— *Ocean Liners*, Mallard Press, 1990
— *Pictorial Encyclopedia of Ocean Liners: 1960–1994*, Dover Publications, 1995
— *Picture History of the Cunard Line: 1840–1990*, Dover Publications, 1991
— *Transatlantic Liners: 1945–1980*, David & Charles, 1981
— *Transatlantic Liners at War: The Story of the Queens*, David & Charles, 1985
Mitchell, WH, *Cunard Line – Post War History*, Marinart, 1975
Musk, George, *Canadian Pacific*, David & Charles, 1981
Parsons, Ronald, *Australian Coastal Passenger Ships*, Magill Publications, 1981
— *Australian Shipowners and Their Fleets*, Magill Publications, 1972
— *Steamers in the South*, Rigby, 1979
Pemberton, Barry, *Australian Coastal Shipping*, Melbourne University Press, 1979
Plowman, Peter, *Emigrant Ships to Luxury Liners*, University of New South Wales, 1994
— *Passenger Ships of Australia and New Zealand Volume 1 (1876–1912)*, Doubleday, 1981
— *Passenger Ships of Australia and New Zealand Volume 2 (1913–1980)*, Doubleday, 1981
Ransome-Wallis, P, *Merchant Ship Panorama*, Ian Allan Ltd, 1980
Robins, Nick, *Turbine Steamers of the British Isles*, Colourpoint Books, 1999
Sawyer, LA and Mitchell, W, *Liberty Ships*, Lloyds of London Press, 1985
— *From America to United States Volume 1*, World Ship Society, 1987
— *From America to United States Volume 2*, World Ship Society, 1987
— *From America to United States Volume 3*, World Ship Society, 1987
— *From America to United States Volume 4*, World Ship Society, 1987
— *Victory Ships and Tankers*, David & Charles, 1974

Smith, Eugene W, *Trans-Atlantic Passenger Ships*, George H Dean, 1947
— *Trans-Pacific Passenger Ships*, George H Dean, 1953
Stewart, IG, *Liberty Ships In Peacetime*, AN Stewart Marine Publications, 1992
— *The Ships that Serve New Zealand*, Reed, 1964
Talbot-Booth, EC, *Talbot-Booth's Merchant Ships in Profile Volume 1*, Marinart, 1978
— *Talbot-Booth's Merchant Ships in Profile Volume 2*, Marinart, 1978
— *Talbot-Booth's Merchant Ships in Profile Volume 3*, Marinart, 1978
Taylor, James, *Ellermans*, Wilton House Gentry Ltd, 1976
Tute, Warren, *Atlantic Conquest*, Cassell Publishing, 1962
Wall, Robert, *Ocean Liners*, Collins, 1978
Warwick, Ronald, *QE2*, WW Norton & Co, 1988
Waters, Sydney D, *Shaw Savill Line*, Whitcombe & Tombs Ltd, 1961
Watson, Milton H, *Disasters At Sea*, Patrick Stephens
— *U.S. Passenger Liners Since 1945*, Patrick Stephens
Wilkinson, W and Wilson, B, *The Main Line Fleet of Burns Philp*, Nautical Association of Australia, 1981
Williams, David, *Marine Disasters at Sea During World War One and World War Two*, Patrick Stephens, 1997
Williams, V and Kerbrech, W, *Damned By Destiny*, Kingfisher Publications, 1982
Wilson, EA, *Soviet Passenger Ships: 1917-1977*, World Ship Society, 1978
Yamado, Michio and Ikeda, Yoshiho, *Passenger Ships of the World*, Dr Yoshiho Ikeda, 1986

Company Publications

There are some beautiful publications produced in-house by major shipping companies. The following are those which most impressed me:

NYK (Nippon Yusen Kaisha), *Voyage of a Century*
P&O Cruises, *Oriana*
P&O Cruises, *The Story of*
Star Lauro Cruise Line, *M/N Achille Lauro*
Union Steamship Company of New Zealand, *The Union Steamship Company of New Zealand: 1875–1925*, 1925